STREET[illegible]
Buckinghamshire
and Milton Keynes
Amersham, Aylesbury, High Wycombe

www.philips-maps.co.uk
First published in 1990 by
Philip's, a division of
Octopus Publishing Group Ltd
www.octopusbooks.co.uk
Carmelite House
50 Victoria Embankment
London EC4Y 0DZ
An Hachette UK Company
www.hachette.co.uk

Fourth edition 2010
Third impression 2016
BUCDB

ISBN 978-1-84907-333-2 (spiral)

Speed camera data provided by
PocketGPSWorld.com Ltd

*All streets named in the source Ordnance Survey dataset at the time of publication are included in this Philip's Street Atlas.

Printed in China

Contents

III **Key to map symbols**

IV **Key to map pages**

VI **Route planning**

VIII Major administrative and Postcode boundaries

1 **Street maps** at 3½ inches to 1 mile

214 **Index** of towns, villages, streets, hospitals, industrial estates, railway stations, schools, shopping centres, universities and places of interest

Key to map symbols

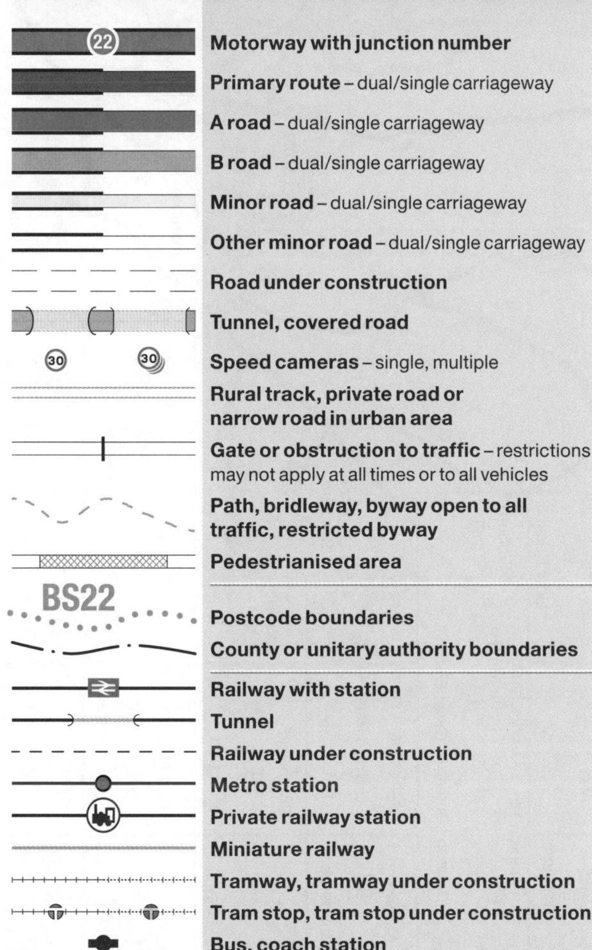

Motorway with junction number
Primary route – dual/single carriageway
A road – dual/single carriageway
B road – dual/single carriageway
Minor road – dual/single carriageway
Other minor road – dual/single carriageway
Road under construction
Tunnel, covered road
Speed cameras – single, multiple
Rural track, private road or narrow road in urban area
Gate or obstruction to traffic – restrictions may not apply at all times or to all vehicles
Path, bridleway, byway open to all traffic, restricted byway
Pedestrianised area

Postcode boundaries
County or unitary authority boundaries

Railway with station
Tunnel
Railway under construction
Metro station
Private railway station
Miniature railway
Tramway, tramway under construction
Tram stop, tram stop under construction
Bus, coach station

Ambulance station
Coastguard station
Fire station
Police station

Accident and Emergency entrance to hospital
Hospital

Place of worship
Information centre – open all year
Shopping centre, parking
Park and Ride, Post Office
Camping site, caravan site
Golf course, picnic site
Church ROMAN FORT Non-Roman antiquity, Roman antiquity

Univ Important buildings, schools, colleges, universities and hospitals
Woods, built-up area

River Medway Water name
River, weir
Stream
Canal, lock, tunnel
Water
Tidal water

58 87 246 Adjoining page indicators and overlap bands – the colour of the arrow and band indicates the scale of the adjoining or overlapping page (see scale below)

The dark grey border on the inside edge of some pages indicates that the mapping does not continue onto the adjacent page

The small numbers around the edges of the maps identify the 1-kilometre National Grid lines

Abbreviations

Abbreviation	Meaning	Abbreviation	Meaning
Acad	**Academy**	Meml	**Memorial**
Allot Gdns	**Allotments**	Mon	**Monument**
Cemy	**Cemetery**	Mus	**Museum**
C Ctr	**Civic centre**	Obsy	**Observatory**
CH	**Club house**	Pal	**Royal palace**
Coll	**College**	PH	**Public house**
Crem	**Crematorium**	Recn Gd	**Recreation ground**
Ent	**Enterprise**	Resr	**Reservoir**
Ex H	**Exhibition hall**	Ret Pk	**Retail park**
Ind Est	**Industrial Estate**	Sch	**School**
IRB Sta	**Inshore rescue boat station**	Sh Ctr	**Shopping centre**
Inst	**Institute**	TH	**Town hall / house**
Ct	**Law court**	Trad Est	**Trading estate**
L Ctr	**Leisure centre**	Univ	**University**
LC	**Level crossing**	W Twr	**Water tower**
Liby	**Library**	Wks	**Works**
Mkt	**Market**	YH	**Youth hostel**

The map scale on the pages numbered in blue is 3½ inches to 1 mile
5.52 cm to 1 km • 1: 18 103

0 ¼ mile ½ mile ¾ mile **1 mile**

0 250m 500m 750m **1km**

Key to map pages

113 Map pages at 3½ inches to 1 mile

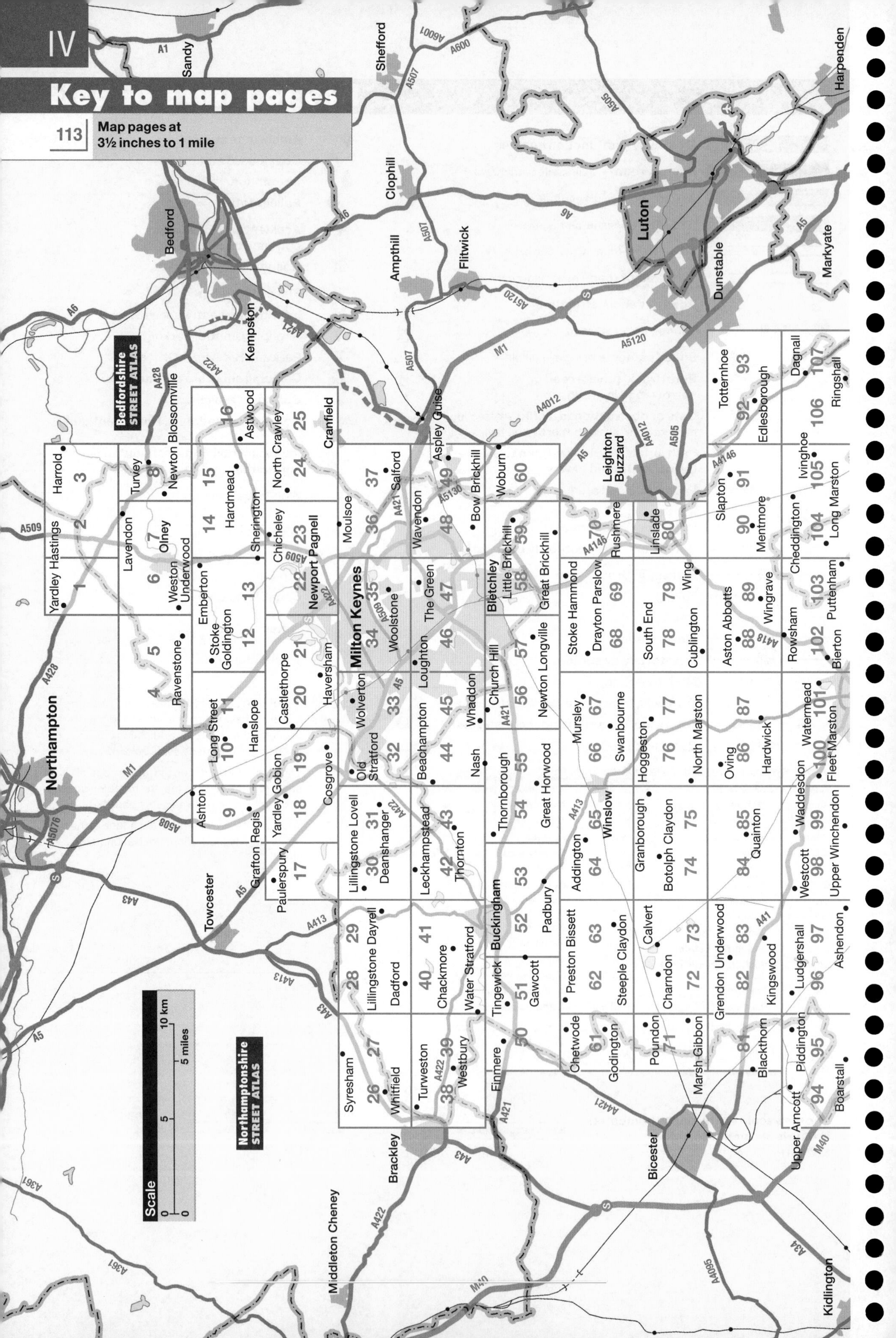

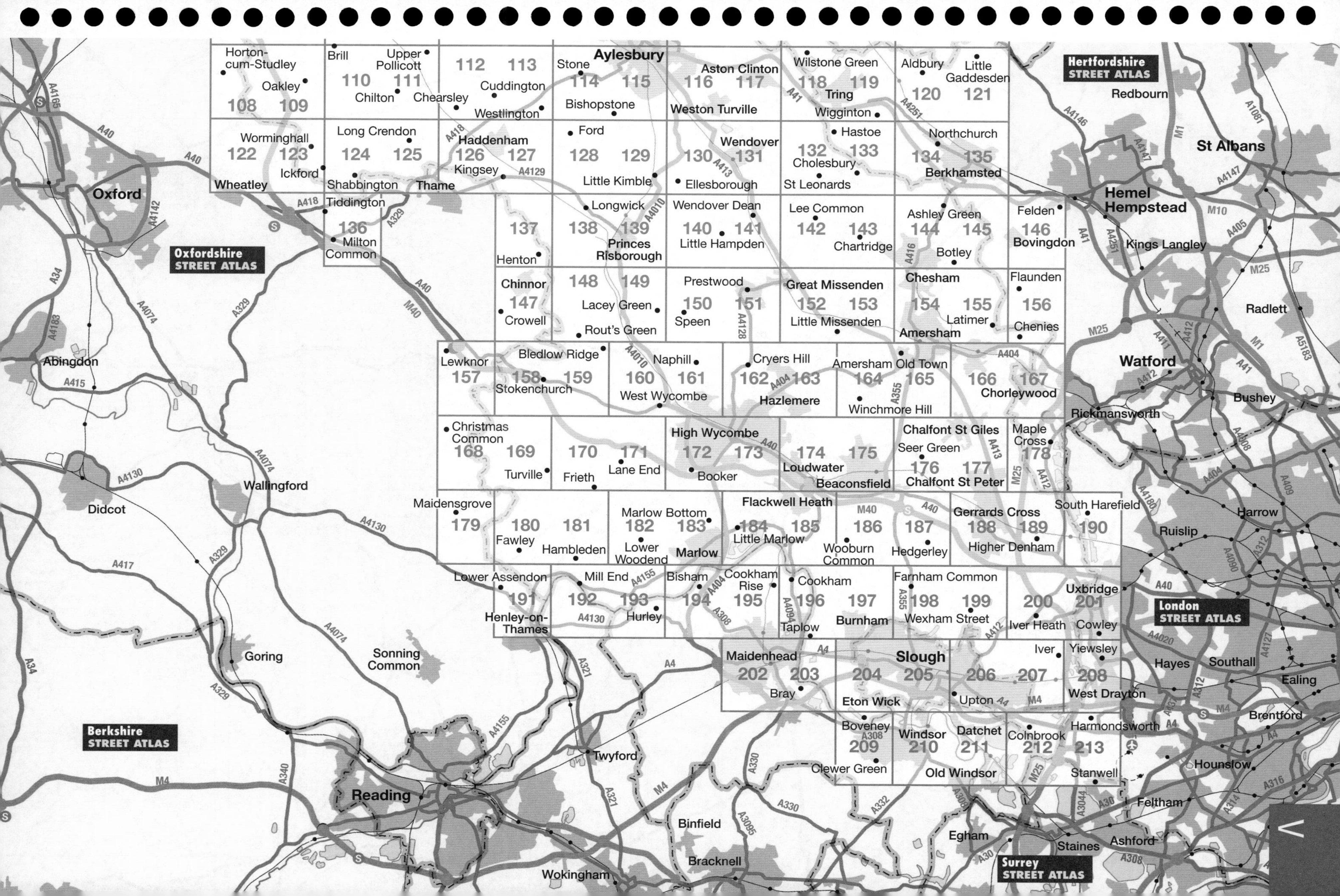
Hertfordshire STREET ATLAS
London STREET ATLAS
Surrey STREET ATLAS
Oxfordshire STREET ATLAS
Berkshire STREET ATLAS
St Albans
Redbourn
Radlett
Hemel Hempstead
Kings Langley
Watford
Bushey
Harrow
Ealing
Brentford
Southall
Hayes
Ruislip
Hounslow
Feltham
Ashford
Staines
Egham
Rickmansworth
South Harefield
Uxbridge
Cowley
Yiewsley
West Drayton
Harmondsworth
Stanwell
Colnbrook
Iver
Iver Heath
Datchet
Old Windsor
Windsor
Slough
Eton Wick
Boveney
Clewer Green
Upton
Maple Cross
Chorleywood
Chenies
Flaunden
Felden
Bovingdon
Little Gaddesden
Aldbury
Northchurch
Berkhamsted
Wilstone Green
Tring
Wigginton
Hastoe
Cholesbury
St Leonards
Lee Common
Chartridge
Ashley Green
Botley
Chesham
Latimer
Amersham
Amersham Old Town
Winchmore Hill
Great Missenden
Little Missenden
Chalfont St Giles
Seer Green
Chalfont St Peter
Gerrards Cross
Higher Denham
Hedgerley
Farnham Common
Wexham Street
Beaconsfield
Loudwater
Wooburn Common
Burnham
Cookham
Taplow
Maidenhead
Bray
Flackwell Heath
Little Marlow
Cookham Rise
Marlow
Bisham
Marlow Bottom
Lower Woodend
Mill End
Hurley
Hambleden
Fawley
Lower Assendon
Henley-on-Thames
Maidensgrove
Christmas Common
Turville
Frieth
Lane End
Booker
High Wycombe
West Wycombe
Naphill
Hazlemere
Cryers Hill
Prestwood
Speen
Wendover Dean
Little Hampden
Wendover
Ellesborough
Aston Clinton
Weston Turville
Aylesbury
Stone
Bishopstone
Ford
Little Kimble
Longwick
Princes Risborough
Lacey Green
Rout's Green
Bledlow Ridge
Stokenchurch
Lewknor
Chinnor
Crowell
Henton
Cuddington
Westlington
Haddenham
Kingsey
Chearsley
Upper Pollicott
Chilton
Long Crendon
Thame
Shabbington
Tiddington
Milton Common
Brill
Horton-cum-Studley
Oakley
Worminghall
Ickford
Wheatley
Oxford
Abingdon
Didcot
Wallingford
Goring
Sonning Common
Reading
Twyford
Wokingham
Binfield
Bracknell
108 109 110 111 112 113 114 115 116 117 118 119 120 121
122 123 124 125 126 127 128 129 130 131 132 133 134 135
136 137 138 139 140 141 142 143 144 145 146
147 148 149 150 151 152 153 154 155 156
157 158 159 160 161 162 163 164 165 166 167
168 169 170 171 172 173 174 175 176 177 178
179 180 181 182 183 184 185 186 187 188 189 190
191 192 193 194 195 196 197 198 199 200 201
202 203 204 205 206 207 208 209 210 211 212 213

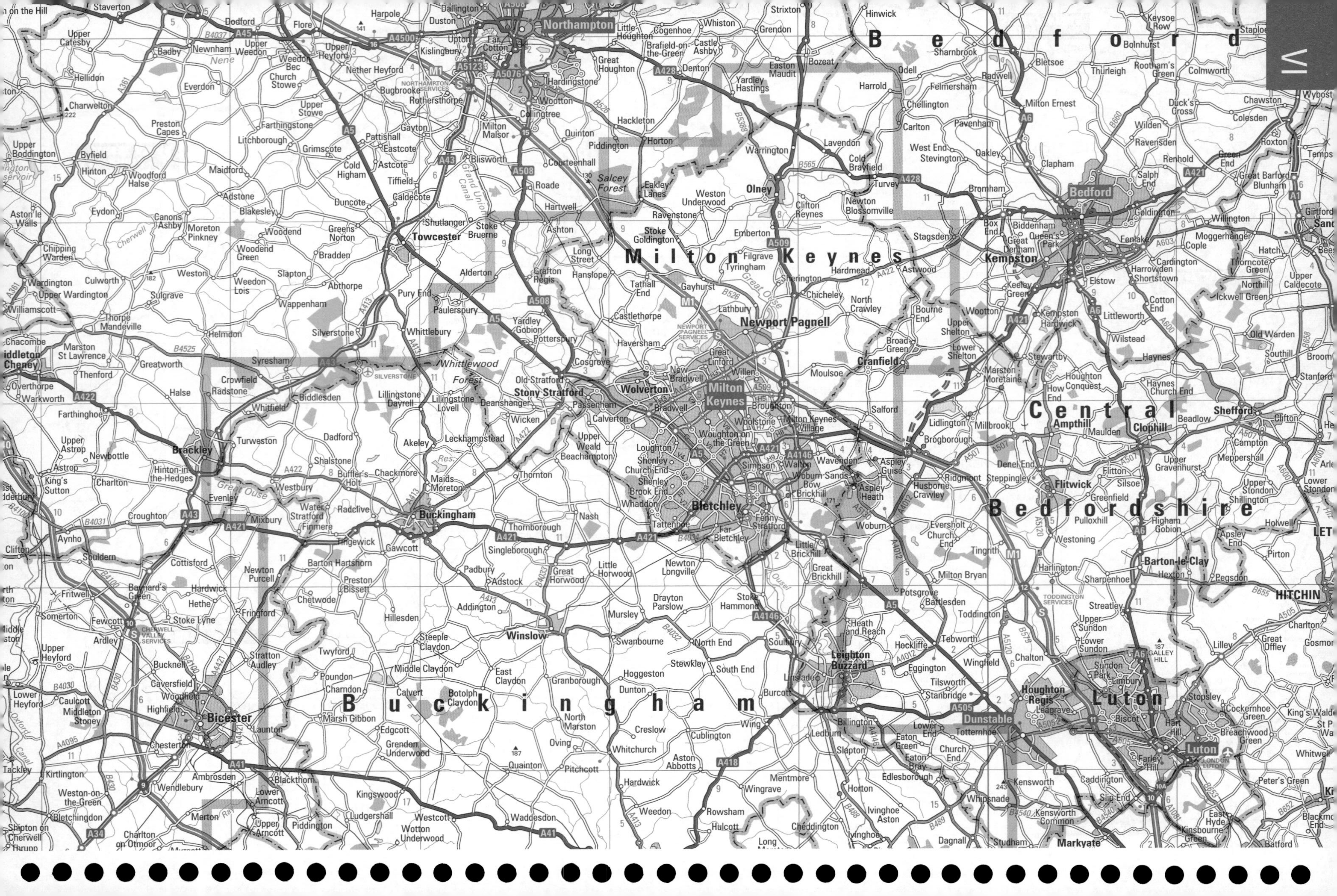

VI
Bedford
Milton Keynes
Central Bedfordshire
Buckingham
Luton
Northampton
Bedford
Kempston
Olney
Newport Pagnell
Towcester
Wolverton
Milton Keynes
Stony Stratford
Bletchley
Buckingham
Brackley
Bicester
Winslow
Leighton Buzzard
Dunstable
Houghton Regis
Luton
Ampthill
Flitwick
Clophill
Shefford
Barton-le-Clay
HITCHIN
Cranfield
Markyate

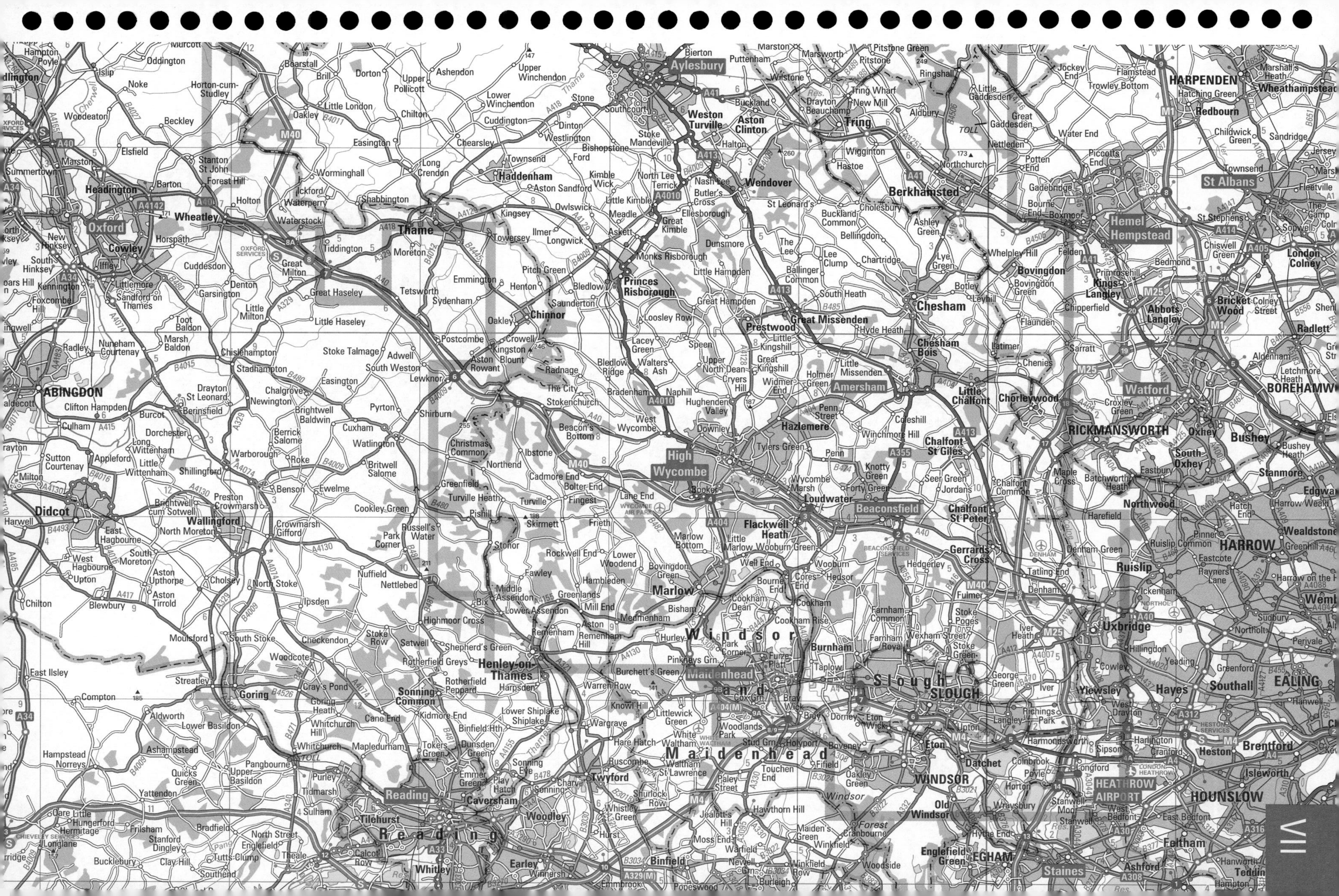
HARPENDEN
St Albans
Hemel Hempstead
Watford
BOREHAMWOOD
RICKMANSWORTH
HARROW
EALING
Southall
Hayes
Uxbridge
Ruislip
Northwood
HOUNSLOW
Brentford
Staines
EGHAM
WINDSOR
SLOUGH
Chesham
Amersham
Beaconsfield
Berkhamsted
Tring
Wendover
Aylesbury
Great Missenden
Prestwood
Princes Risborough
High Wycombe
Marlow
Maidenhead
Henley-on-Thames
Thame
Chinnor
Wheatley
Oxford
Cowley
Headington
ABINGDON
Didcot
Wallingford
Goring
Reading
Caversham
Woodley
Twyford
HEATHROW AIRPORT
M25
M40
M4
M1
A40
A41
A413
A404
A4010
A34

Major administrative and Postcode boundaries

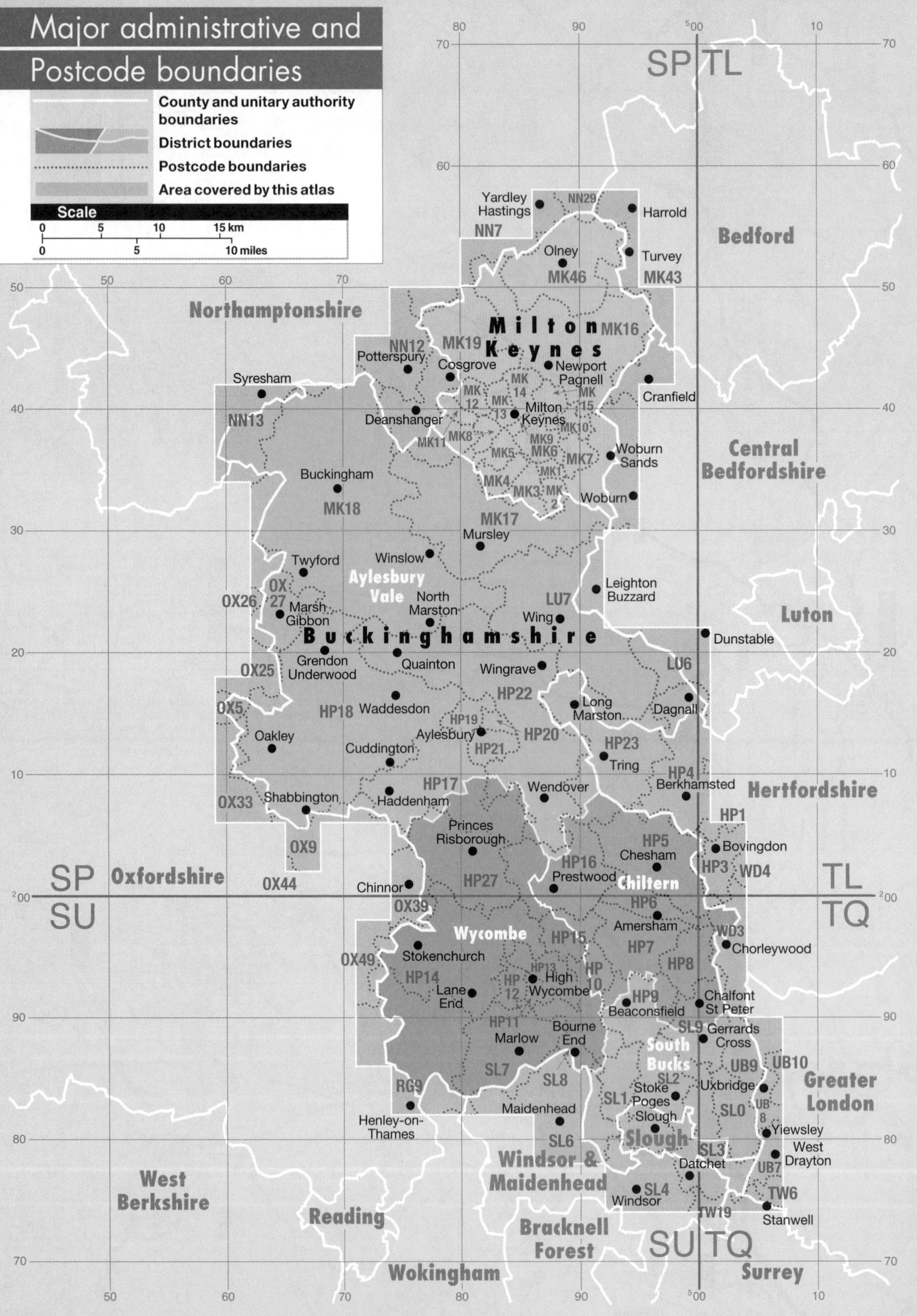

2

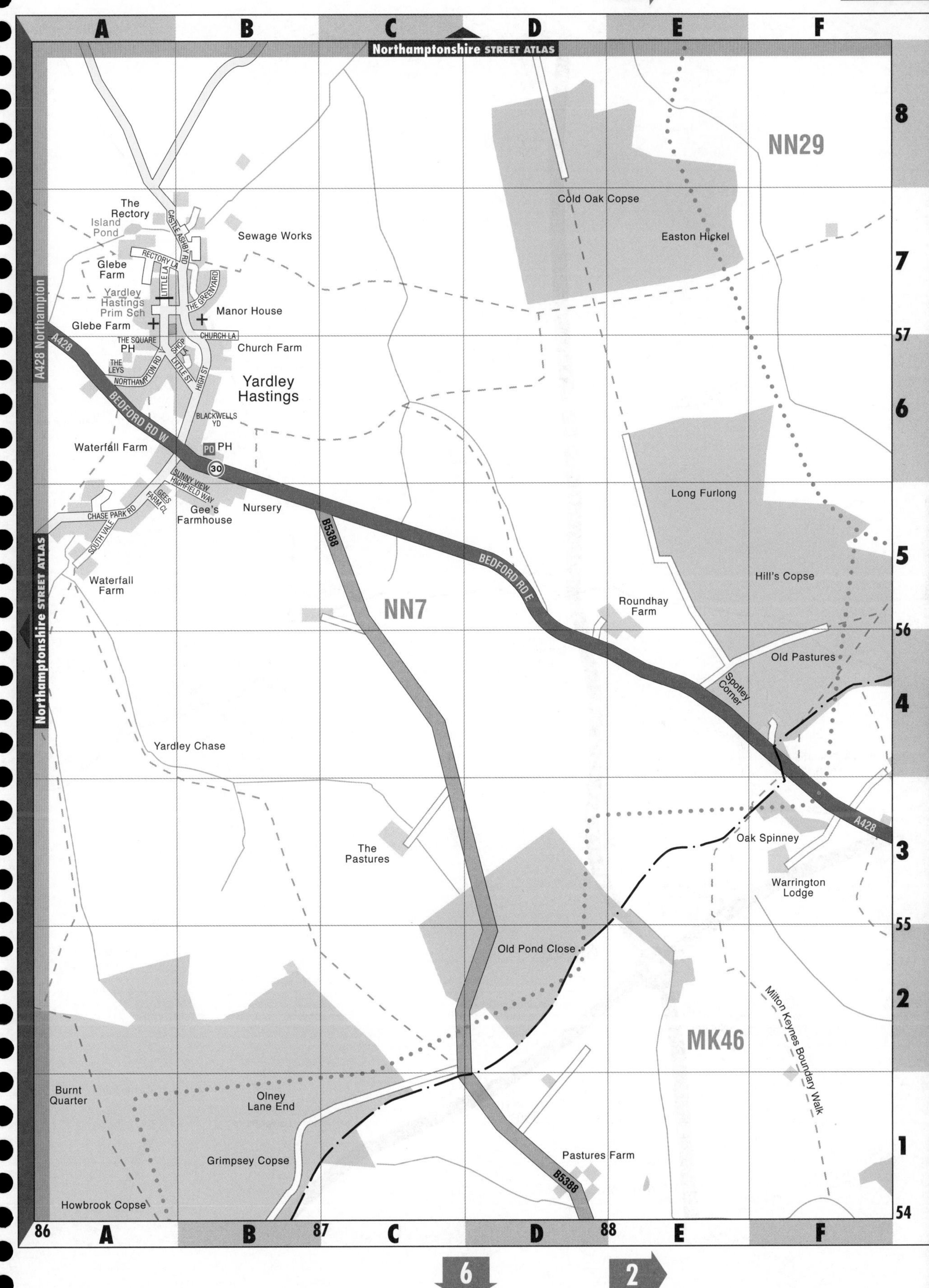

A
B
C
D
E
F
Northamptonshire STREET ATLAS
8
7
57
6
5
56
4
3
55
2
1
54
86
87
88
NN29
Cold Oak Copse
Easton Hickel
The Rectory
Island Pond
Sewage Works
Glebe Farm
Yardley Hastings Prim Sch
Manor House
Glebe Farm
CHURCH LA
Church Farm
THE SQUARE
PH
THE LEYS
NORTHAMPTON RD
LITTLE ST
HIGH ST
Yardley Hastings
A428 Northampton
A428
BEDFORD RD W
BLACKWELLS YD
PO
PH
Waterfall Farm
30
SUNNY VIEW
HIGHFIELD WAY
CHASE PARK RD
GEES FARM CL
SOUTH VALE
Gee's Farmhouse
Nursery
B5388
Long Furlong
BEDFORD RD E
Hill's Copse
Waterfall Farm
NN7
Roundhay Farm
Old Pastures
Spotley Corner
Yardley Chase
The Pastures
Oak Spinney
Warrington Lodge
Old Pond Close
Milton Keynes Boundary Walk
MK46
Burnt Quarter
Olney Lane End
Grimpsey Copse
Pastures Farm
Howbrook Copse
RECTORY LA
LITTLE LA
CASTLE ASHBY RD
THE GREENYARD

6

2

1

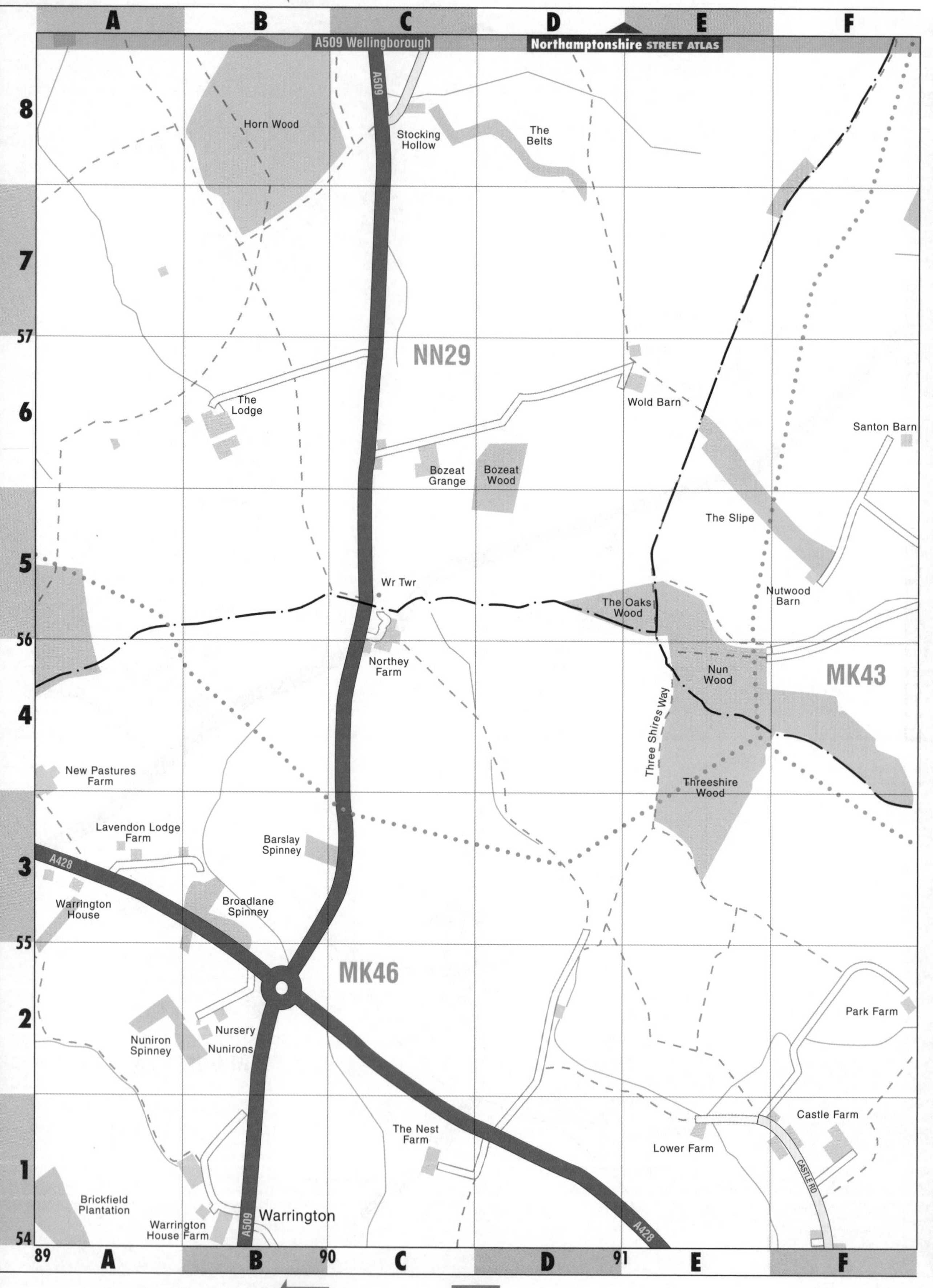
A
B
C
D
E
F
A509 Wellingborough
Northamptonshire STREET ATLAS
8
7
57
6
5
56
4
3
55
2
1
54
89
90
91
A509
Horn Wood
Stocking Hollow
The Belts
NN29
The Lodge
Wold Barn
Santon Barn
Bozeat Grange
Bozeat Wood
The Slipe
Wr Twr
Nutwood Barn
The Oaks Wood
Northey Farm
Nun Wood
MK43
Three Shires Way
New Pastures Farm
Threeshire Wood
Lavendon Lodge Farm
Barslay Spinney
A428
Warrington House
Broadlane Spinney
MK46
Park Farm
Nursery
Nuniron Spinney
Nunirons
Castle Farm
The Nest Farm
Lower Farm
CASTLE RD
Brickfield Plantation
Warrington
Warrington House Farm

1
7

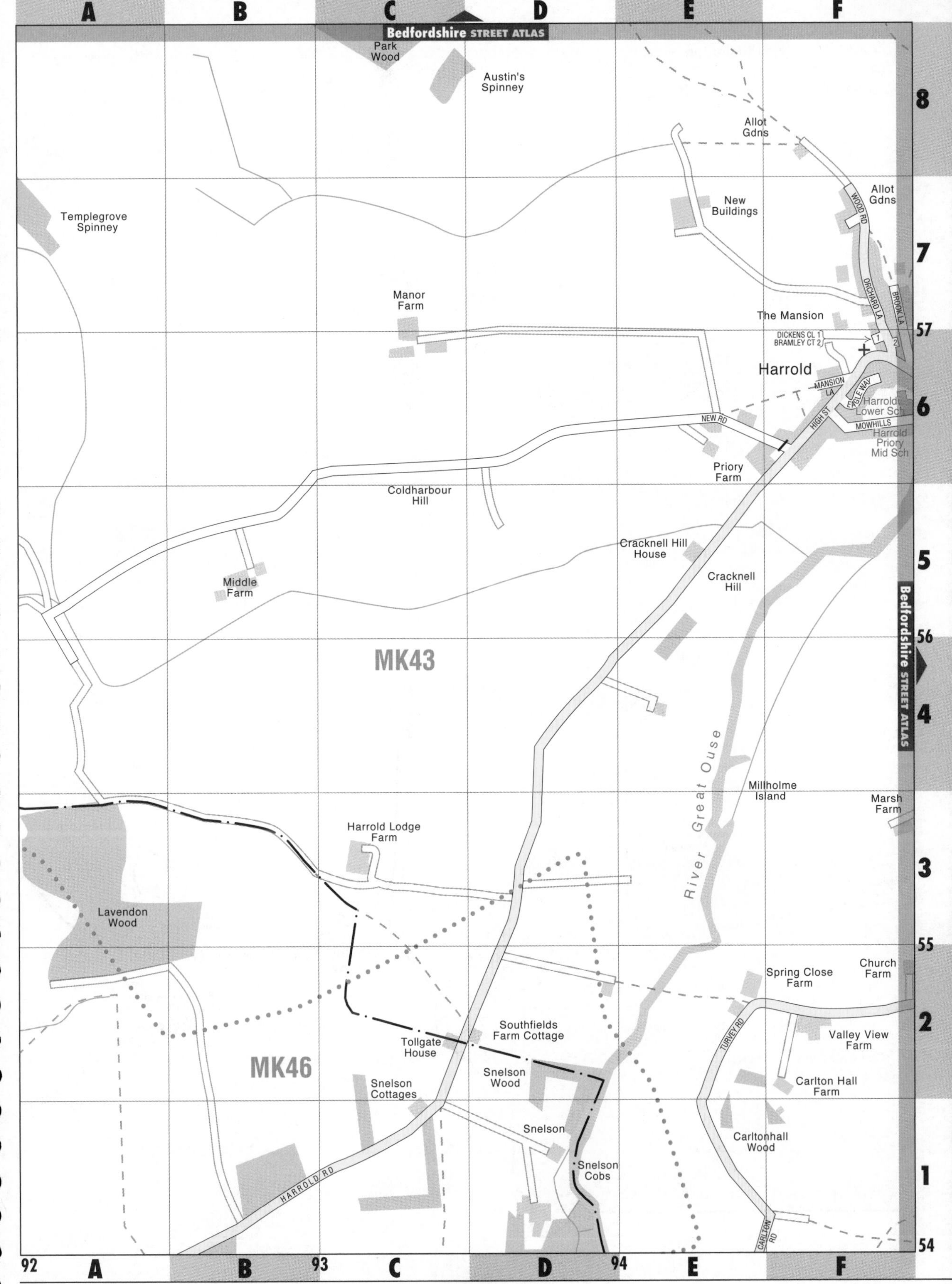
A
B
C
D
E
F
Bedfordshire STREET ATLAS
Park Wood
Austin's Spinney
8
Allot Gdns
Allot Gdns
New Buildings
WOOD RD
Templegrove Spinney
7
ORCHARD LA
BROOK LA
Manor Farm
The Mansion
57
DICKENS CL 1
BRAMLEY CT 2
Harrold
MANSION LA
EAGLE WAY
Harrold Lower Sch
6
NEW RD
HIGH ST
MOWHILLS
Harrold Priory Mid Sch
Priory Farm
Coldharbour Hill
Cracknell Hill House
5
Cracknell Hill
Middle Farm
56
MK43
4
River Great Ouse
Millholme Island
Marsh Farm
Harrold Lodge Farm
3
Lavendon Wood
55
Spring Close Farm
Church Farm
2
TURVEY RD
Valley View Farm
Southfields Farm Cottage
Tollgate House
MK46
Snelson Wood
Carlton Hall Farm
Snelson Cottages
Snelson
Carltonhall Wood
1
Snelson Cobs
HARROLD RD
CARLTON RD
54
92
93
94

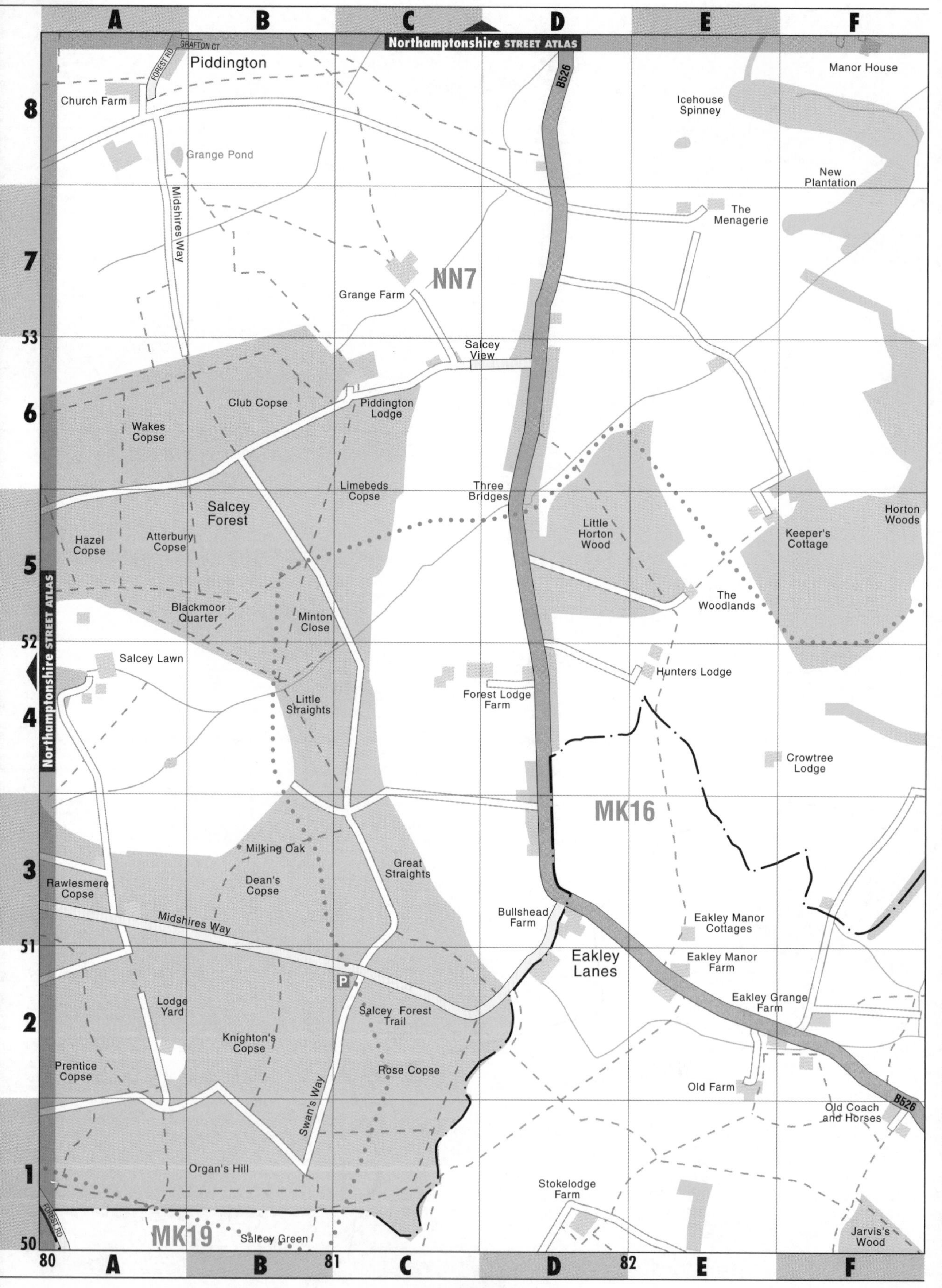

A B C D E F
Northamptonshire STREET ATLAS
Piddington
GRAFTON CT
FOREST RD
Church Farm
Manor House
Icehouse Spinney
B526
Grange Pond
New Plantation
Midshires Way
The Menagerie
NN7
Grange Farm
Salcey View
Club Copse
Piddington Lodge
Wakes Copse
Limebeds Copse
Three Bridges
Salcey Forest
Hazel Copse
Atterbury Copse
Little Horton Wood
Horton Woods
Keeper's Cottage
Blackmoor Quarter
Minton Close
The Woodlands
Salcey Lawn
Hunters Lodge
Little Straights
Forest Lodge Farm
Crowtree Lodge
MK16
Milking Oak
Rawlesmere Copse
Dean's Copse
Great Straights
Bullshead Farm
Midshires Way
Eakley Manor Cottages
Eakley Lanes
Eakley Manor Farm
P
Lodge Yard
Salcey Forest Trail
Eakley Grange Farm
Knighton's Copse
Prentice Copse
Rose Copse
Old Farm
Swan's Way
Old Coach and Horses
B526
Organ's Hill
Stokelodge Farm
MK19
Salcey Green
Jarvis's Wood
FOREST RD
8 7 53 6 5 52 4 3 51 2 1 50
80 81 82

11

6

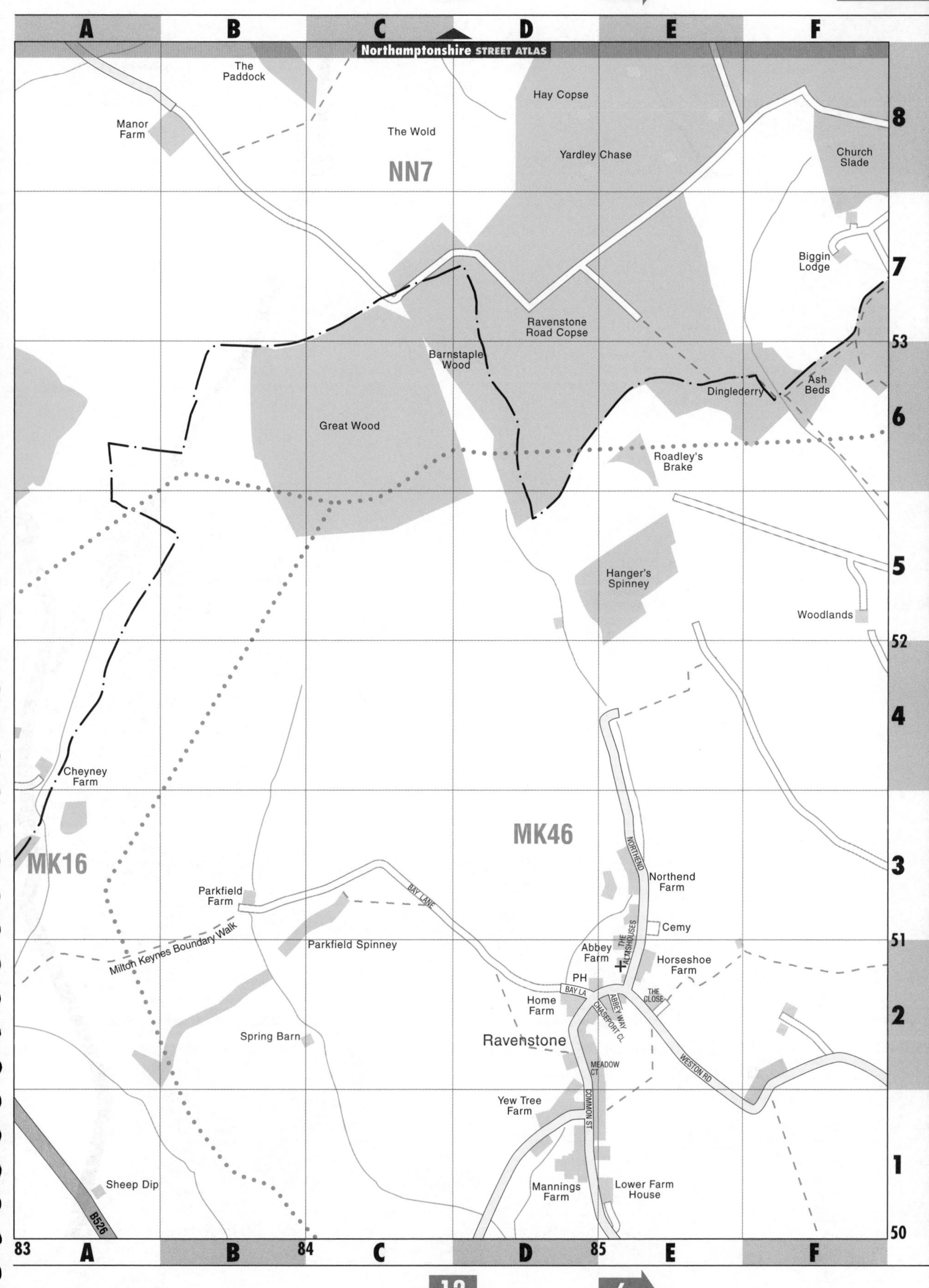

Northamptonshire STREET ATLAS
A
B
C
D
E
F
The Paddock
Manor Farm
The Wold
Hay Copse
Yardley Chase
Church Slade
NN7
Biggin Lodge
Ravenstone Road Copse
Barnstaple Wood
Dinglederry
Ash Beds
Great Wood
Roadley's Brake
Hanger's Spinney
Woodlands
Cheyney Farm
MK46
MK16
Northend Farm
NORTHEND
Parkfield Farm
BAY LANE
Cemy
THE ALMSHOUSES
Abbey Farm
Horseshoe Farm
Parkfield Spinney
Milton Keynes Boundary Walk
PH
BAY LA
THE CLOSE
Home Farm
ABBEY WAY
CHASEPORT CL
Spring Barn
Ravenstone
MEADOW CT
WESTON RD
Yew Tree Farm
COMMON ST
Sheep Dip
Mannings Farm
Lower Farm House
B526
8
7
53
6
5
52
4
3
51
2
1
50
83
84
85

12

6

5
1

5
13

F3
1 FOUNTAIN CT
2 BERRELL'S CT
3 ROSE CT
4 MARKET PL
5 OSBORN'S CT
6 CHURCH ST
7 PEMBROKE HO
8 CHANTRY RI
9 CLAY PIT LA
10 PEBODY PL
11 STONEMASONS CL
12 WAGSTAFF WY

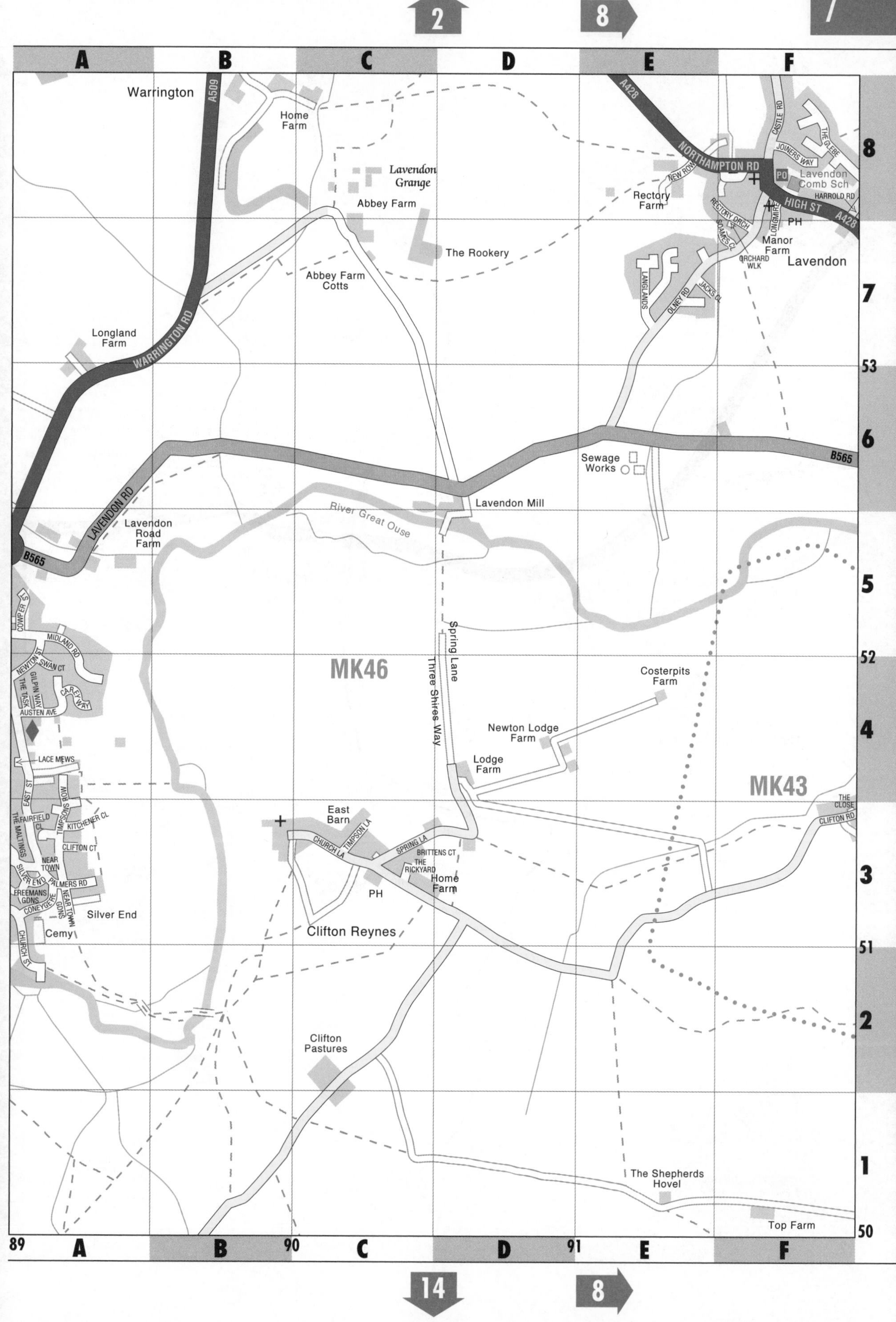

2
8
A B C D E F
Warrington
A509
Home Farm
Lavendon Grange
Abbey Farm
The Rookery
Abbey Farm Cotts
A428
NORTHAMPTON RD
NEW ROW
CASTLE RD
THE GLEBE
JOINERS WAY
PO
Lavendon Comb Sch
HARROLD RD
HIGH ST
Rectory Farm
RECTORY ORCH
SOAMES CL
LONGMIRE
PH
Manor Farm
ORCHARD WLK
Lavendon
LANGLANDS
OLNEY RD
JACKS CL
Longland Farm
WARRINGTON RD
B565
Sewage Works
Lavendon Mill
LAVENDON RD
Lavendon Road Farm
River Great Ouse
COWPER
MIDLAND RD
NEWTON ST
SWAN CT
GILPIN WAY
THE TASK
CAREY WAY
AUSTEN AVE
MK46
Spring Lane
Three Shires Way
Costerpits Farm
Newton Lodge Farm
Lodge Farm
LACE MEWS
MK43
THE CLOSE
CLIFTON RD
EAST ST
TIMPSONS ROW
FAIRFIELD CL
THE MALTINGS
KITCHENER CL
East Barn
TIMPSON LA
CHURCH LA
SPRING LA
BRITTENS CT
THE RICKYARD
Home Farm
CLIFTON CT
NEAR TOWN
SILVER END
PALMERS RD
FREEMANS GDNS
CONEYGERE
NEAR TOWN GDNS
PH
Silver End
Clifton Reynes
Cemy
CHURCH ST
Clifton Pastures
The Shepherds Hovel
Top Farm
8 7 53 6 5 52 4 3 51 2 1 50
89 90 91
14
8

7
3

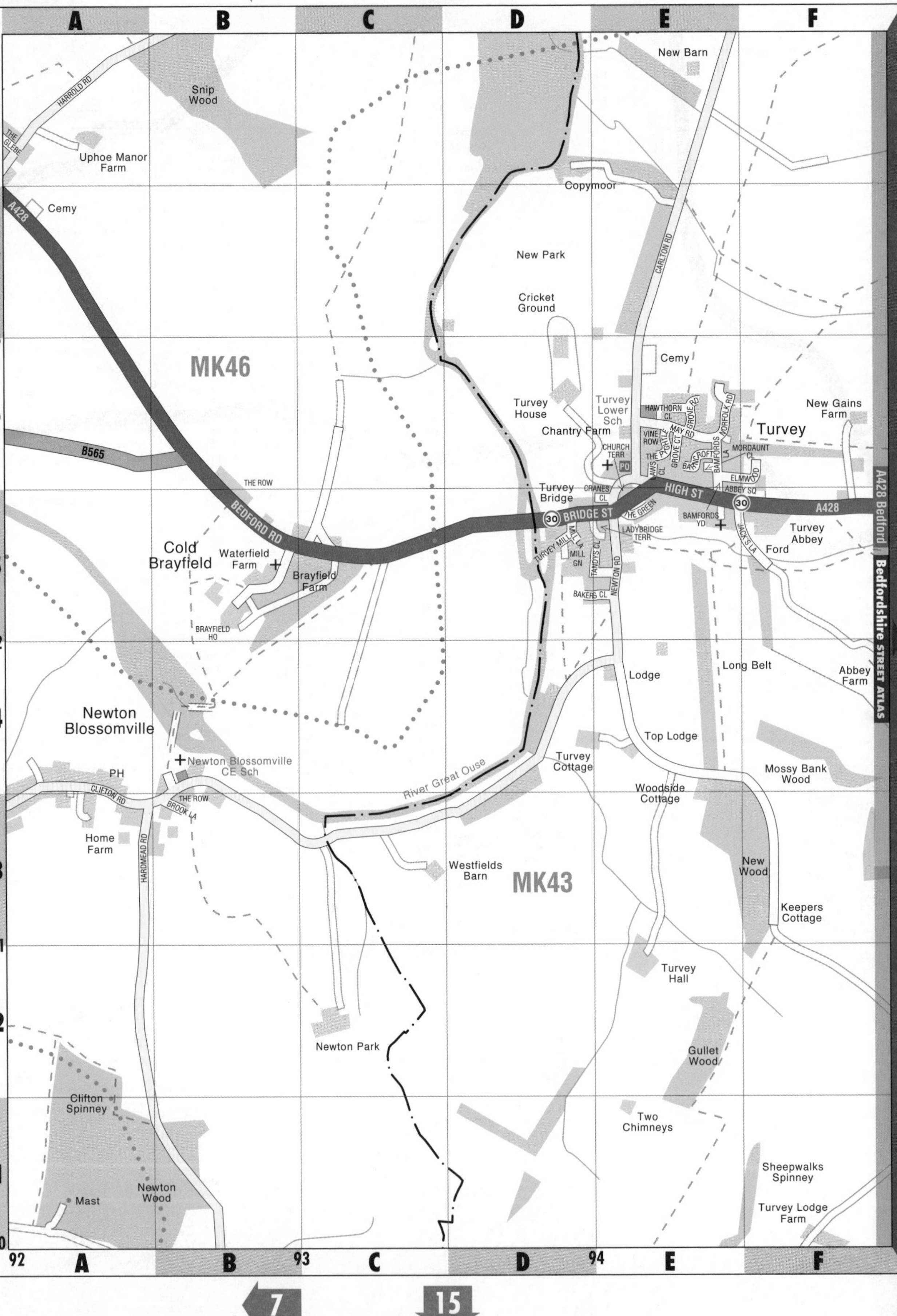

A B C D E F

New Barn
Snip Wood
HARROLD RD
THE GLEBE
Uphoe Manor Farm
Copymoor
Cemy
A428
New Park
CARLTON RD
Cricket Ground
MK46
Cemy
Turvey House
Turvey Lower Sch
Chantry Farm
HAWTHORN CL
GROVE RD
NORFOLK RD
New Gains Farm
Turvey
B565
VINE ROW
MAY RD
THE PIGHTLE
GROVE CT
BANCROFT
BAMFORDS LA
MORDAUNT CL
CHURCH TERR
PO
LAWS CL
ELMWOOD
THE ROW
Turvey Bridge
CRANES CL
HIGH ST
ABBEY SQ
A428 Bedford
BEDFORD RD
BRIDGE ST
THE GREEN
30
BAMFORDS YD
A428
TURVEY MILL
MILL LA
LADYBRIDGE TERR
JACK'S LA
Turvey Abbey
Cold Brayfield
Waterfield Farm
Brayfield Farm
MILL GN
TANDYS CL
NEWTON RD
Ford
BAKERS CL
BRAYFIELD HO
Lodge
Long Belt
Abbey Farm
Newton Blossomville
Top Lodge
Newton Blossomville CE Sch
Turvey Cottage
Mossy Bank Wood
PH
CLIFTON RD
River Great Ouse
Woodside Cottage
THE ROW
BROOK LA
Home Farm
HARDMEAD RD
Westfields Barn
MK43
New Wood
Keepers Cottage
Turvey Hall
Newton Park
Gullet Wood
Clifton Spinney
Two Chimneys
Sheepwalks Spinney
Mast
Newton Wood
Turvey Lodge Farm

8
7
53
6
5
52
4
3
51
2
1
50

92 A B 93 C D 94 E F

Bedfordshire STREET ATLAS

7
15

10

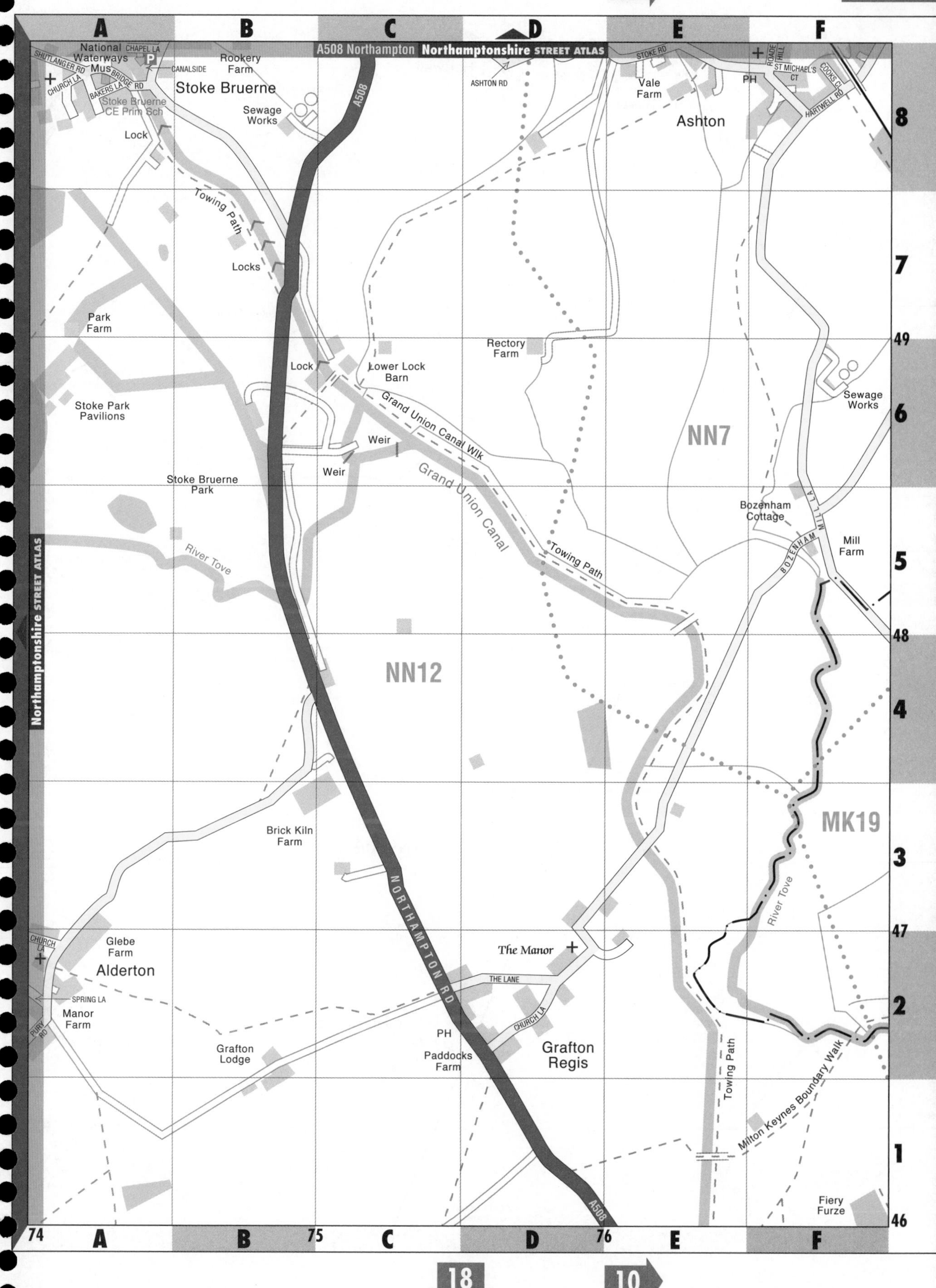

A508 Northampton
Northamptonshire STREET ATLAS
National Waterways Mus
CHAPEL LA
SHUTLANGER RD
CHURCH LA
BAKERS LA
BRIDGE RD
CANALSIDE
Rookery Farm
Stoke Bruerne
Stoke Bruerne CE Prim Sch
Sewage Works
Lock
Towing Path
Locks
Park Farm
Stoke Park Pavilions
Stoke Bruerne Park
River Tove
Lock
Lower Lock Barn
Weir
Weir
Grand Union Canal Wlk
Grand Union Canal
Towing Path
Rectory Farm
ASHTON RD
STOKE RD
Vale Farm
Ashton
PH
ROADE HILL
ST MICHAEL'S CT
COOKS CL
HARTWELL RD
Sewage Works
NN7
Bozenham Cottage
BOZENHAM MILL LA
Mill Farm
NN12
MK19
River Tove
Brick Kiln Farm
NORTHAMPTON RD
The Manor
THE LANE
CHURCH LA
Glebe Farm
Alderton
SPRING LA
Manor Farm
PURY RD
Grafton Lodge
PH
Paddocks Farm
Grafton Regis
Towing Path
Milton Keynes Boundary Walk
Fiery Furze
A508
A B C D E F
8 7 49 6 5 48 4 3 47 2 1 46
74 75 76

18

10

9

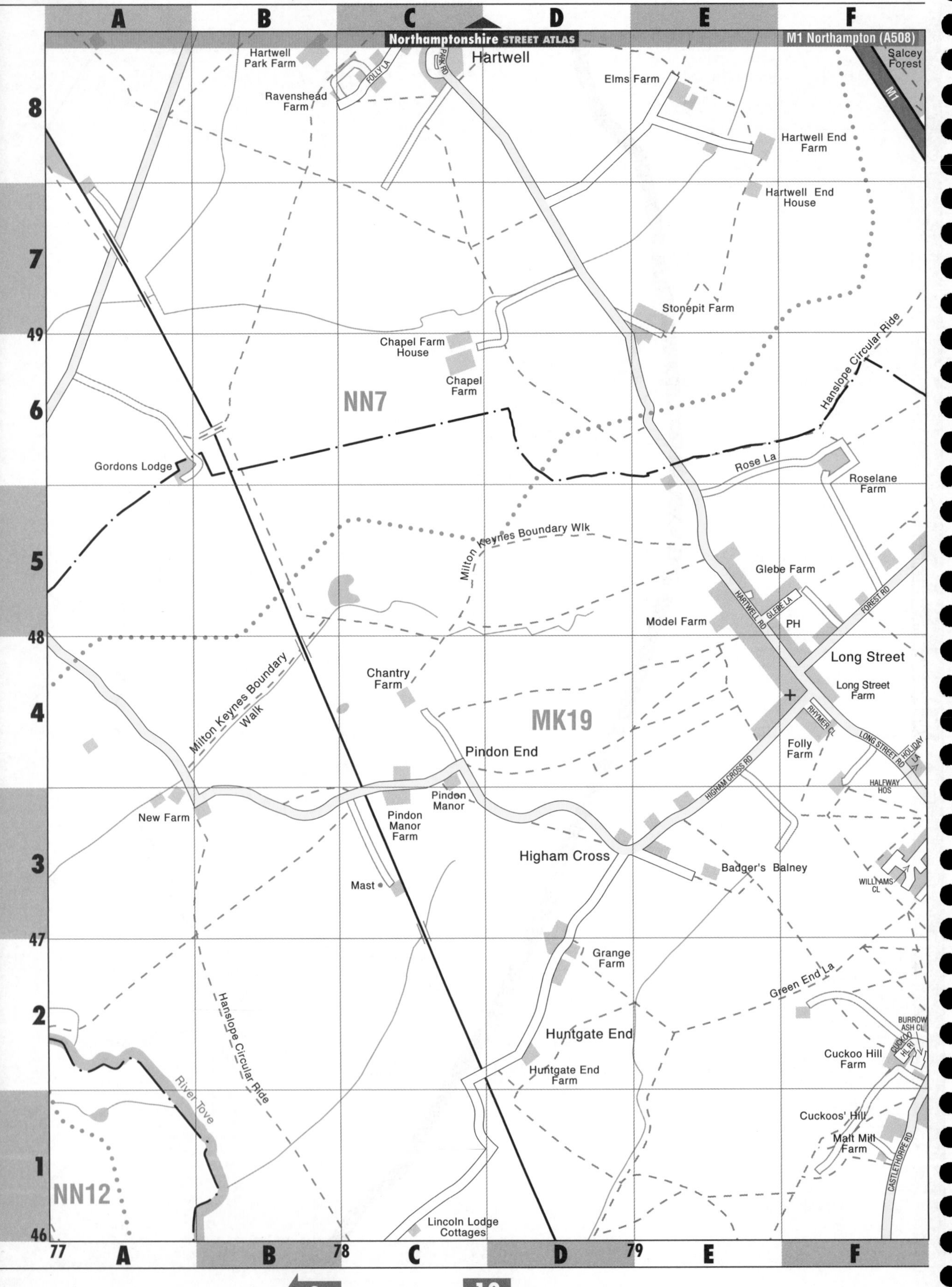

A
B
C
D
E
F
Northamptonshire STREET ATLAS
M1 Northampton (A508)
Salcey Forest
M1
Hartwell Park Farm
Ravenshead Farm
FOLLY LA
PARK RD
Hartwell
Elms Farm
Hartwell End Farm
Hartwell End House
8
7
49
6
5
48
4
3
47
2
1
46
Stonepit Farm
Chapel Farm House
Chapel Farm
NN7
Hanslope Circular Ride
Gordons Lodge
Rose La
Roselane Farm
Milton Keynes Boundary Wlk
Glebe Farm
HARTWELL RD
GLEBE LA
FOREST RD
Model Farm
PH
Long Street
Long Street Farm
Milton Keynes Boundary Walk
Chantry Farm
MK19
RHYMER CL
LONG STREET RD
HOLIDAY LA
Folly Farm
Pindon End
HIGHAM CROSS RD
HALFWAY HOS
New Farm
Pindon Manor
Pindon Manor Farm
Higham Cross
Badger's Balney
WILLIAMS CL
Mast
Grange Farm
Green End La
Hanslope Circular Ride
Huntgate End
BURROW ASH CL
CUCKOO HL RI
Cuckoo Hill Farm
Huntgate End Farm
River Tove
Cuckoos' Hill
Malt Mill Farm
CASTLETHORPE RD
NN12
Lincoln Lodge Cottages
77
A
B
78
C
D
79
E
F

9
19

4
12

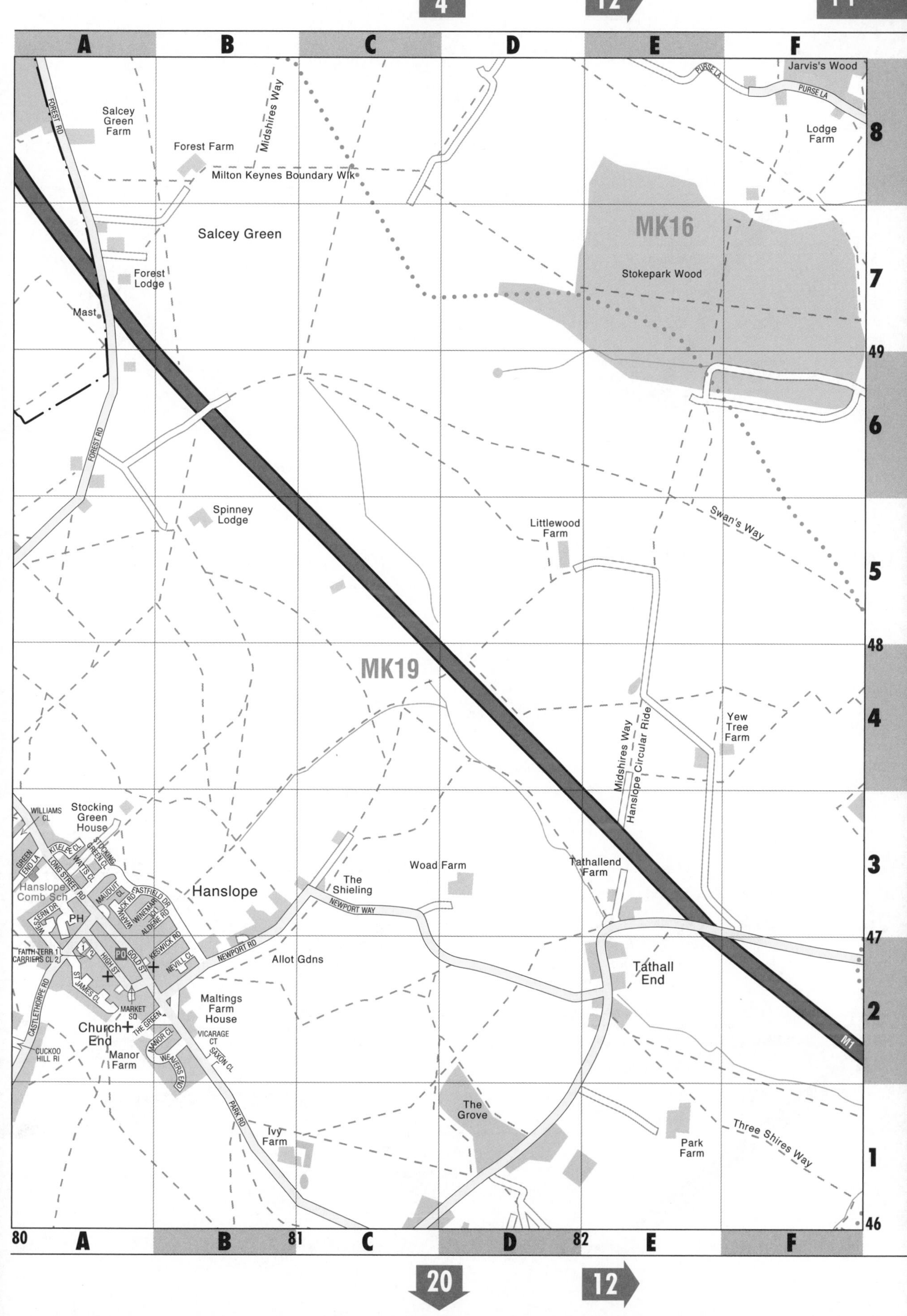
A
B
C
D
E
F
Jarvis's Wood
PURSE LA
Lodge Farm
FOREST RD
Salcey Green Farm
Forest Farm
Midshires Way
Milton Keynes Boundary Wlk
Salcey Green
MK16
Stokepark Wood
Forest Lodge
Mast
FOREST RD
Spinney Lodge
Littlewood Farm
Swan's Way
MK19
Yew Tree Farm
Midshires Way
Hanslope Circular Ride
WILLIAMS CL
Stocking Green House
Hanslope Comb Sch
Hanslope
The Shieling
NEWPORT WAY
Woad Farm
Tathallend Farm
PH
PO
NEWPORT RD
Allot Gdns
Tathall End
Maltings Farm House
MARKET SQ
Church End
VICARAGE CT
SAXON CL
CUCKOO HILL RI
Manor Farm
M1
The Grove
PARK RD
Ivy Farm
Park Farm
Three Shires Way
8
7
49
6
5
48
4
3
47
2
1
46
80
81
82

20
12

11
5

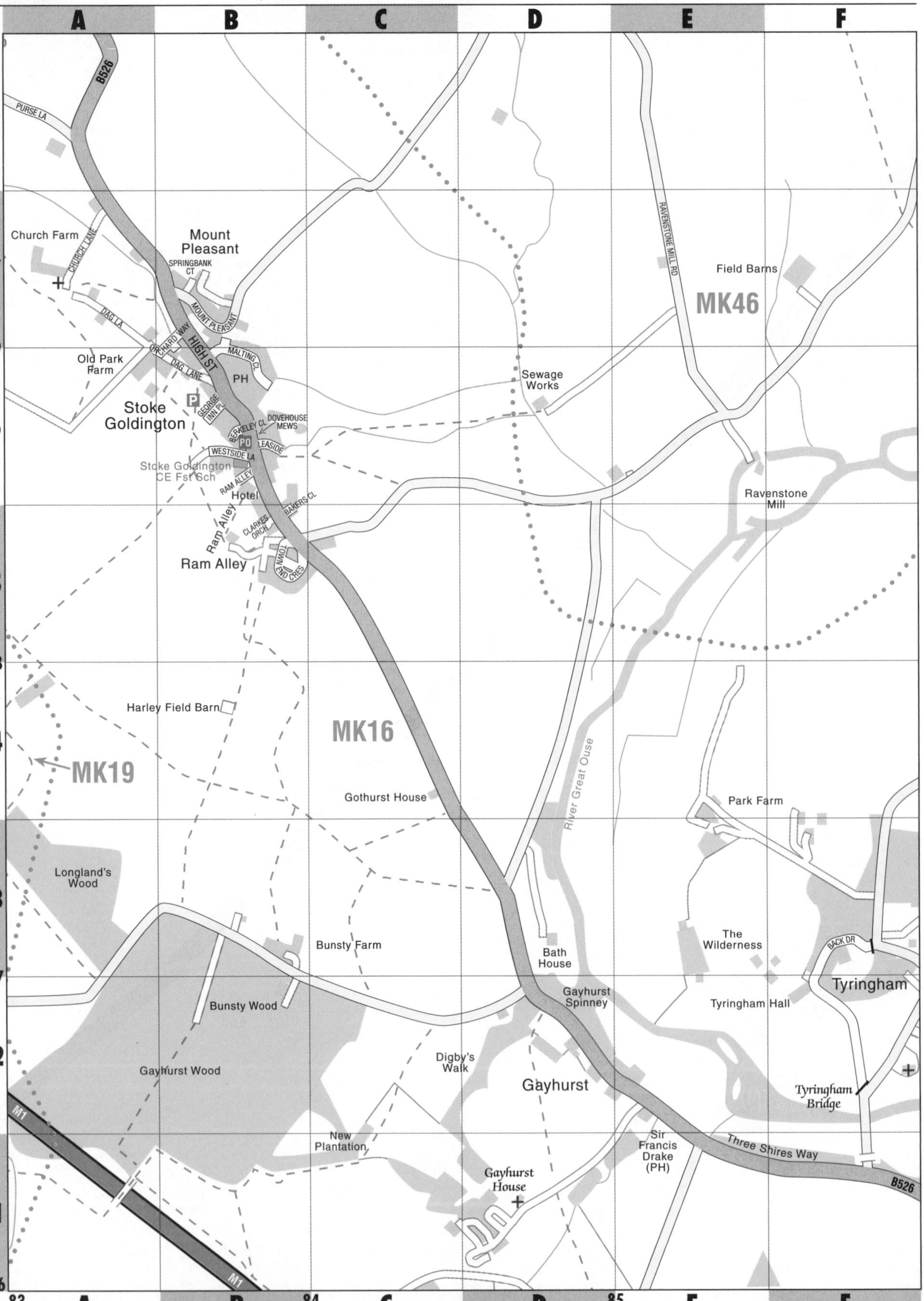

A B C D E F

8
7
49
6
5
48
4
3
47
2
1
46

B526
PURSE LA
Church Farm
CHURCH LANE
Mount Pleasant
SPRINGBANK CT
MOUNT PLEASANT
DAG LA
ORCHARD WAY
HIGH ST
MALTING CL
DAG LANE
Old Park Farm
PH
P
GEORGE INN PL
Stoke Goldington
DOVEHOUSE MEWS
BERKELEY CL
PO
LEASIDE
WESTSIDE LA
Stoke Goldington CE Fst Sch
RAM ALLEY
Hotel
BAKERS CL
CLARKES ORCH
Ram Alley
TOWN END CRES
Ram Alley
RAVENSTONE MILL RD
Field Barns
MK46
Sewage Works
Ravenstone Mill
Harley Field Barn
MK16
MK19
River Great Ouse
Gothurst House
Park Farm
Longland's Wood
Bunsty Farm
Bath House
The Wilderness
BACK DR
Tyringham
Bunsty Wood
Gayhurst Spinney
Tyringham Hall
Gayhurst Wood
Digby's Walk
Gayhurst
Tyringham Bridge
M1
New Plantation
Sir Francis Drake (PH)
Three Shires Way
Gayhurst House
B526
M1

83 A B 84 C D 85 E F

11
21

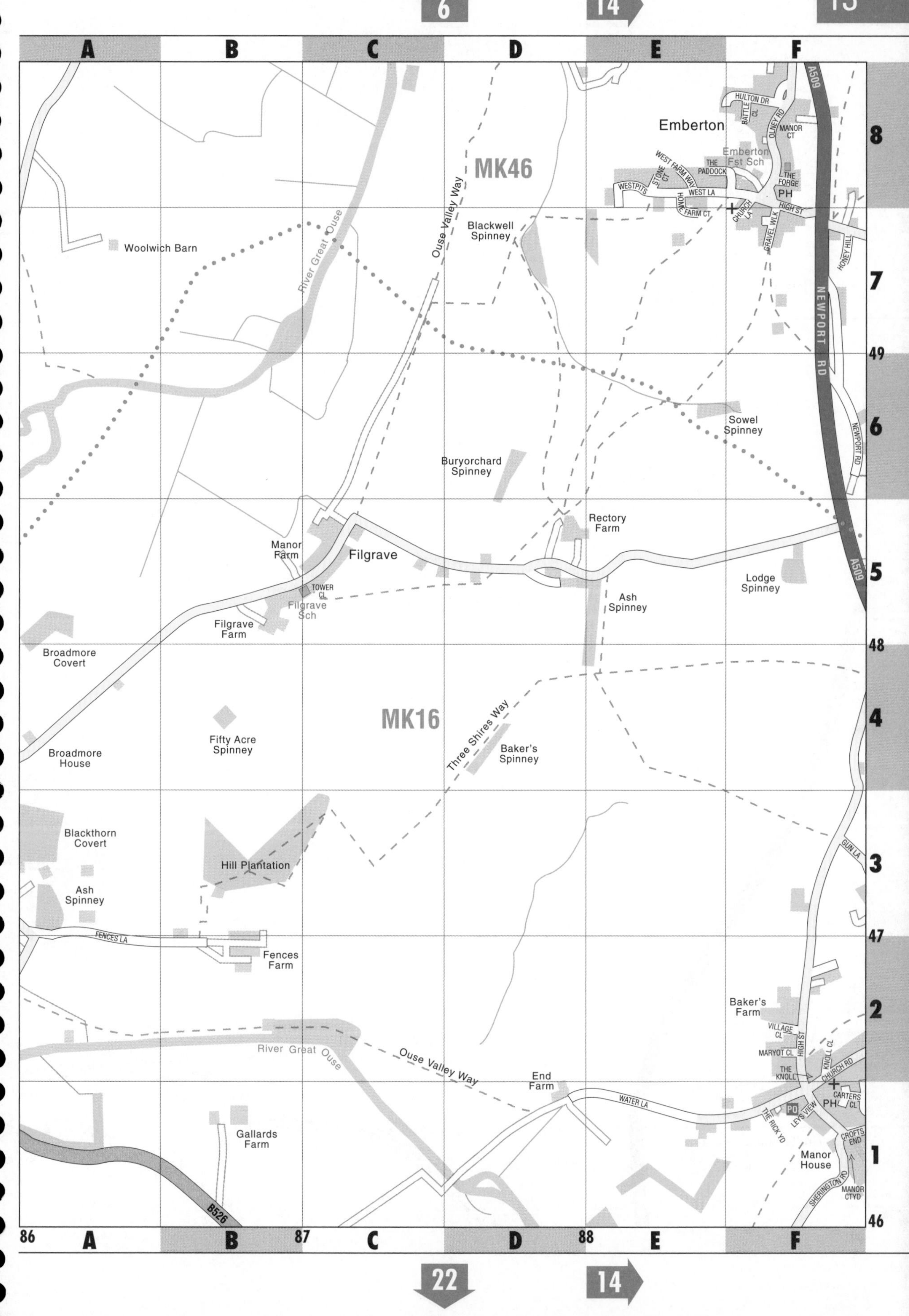

6
14
A
B
C
D
E
F
Emberton
HULTON DR
BATTLE CL
OLNEY RD
MANOR CT
Emberton Fst Sch
THE PADDOCK
WEST FARM WAY
STONE CT
WESTPITS
WEST LA
HOME FARM CT
CHURCH LA
THE FORGE
PH
HIGH ST
GRAVEL WLK
HONEY HILL
A509
NEWPORT RD
MK46
Ouse Valley Way
Blackwell Spinney
Woolwich Barn
River Great Ouse
Sowel Spinney
Buryorchard Spinney
Rectory Farm
Manor Farm
Filgrave
TOWER CL
Filgrave Sch
Filgrave Farm
Ash Spinney
Lodge Spinney
Broadmore Covert
MK16
Three Shires Way
Fifty Acre Spinney
Baker's Spinney
Broadmore House
Blackthorn Covert
Hill Plantation
Ash Spinney
GUN LA
FENCES LA
Fences Farm
Baker's Farm
VILLAGE CL
MARYOT CL
HIGH ST
KNOLL CL
CHURCH RD
THE KNOLL
River Great Ouse
Ouse Valley Way
End Farm
WATER LA
PO
PH
CARTERS CL
THE RICK YD
LEYS VIEW
CROFTS END
Manor House
SHERINGTON RD
MANOR CTYD
Gallards Farm
B526
8
7
49
6
5
48
4
3
47
2
1
46
86
87
88
22
14

13
7

A B C D E F

8
Three Shires Way
Rectory Farm
Petsoe Manor Farm
7
Petsoe End
Hill Farm
Clay Farm
Grange Farm
Petsoe Manor
49
MK46
6
Hollington Wood
Wood Farm
Mulducks
5
Parrages Wood
Seven Acre Covert
Short Wood
A509
48
4
3
MK16
Gowle's Farm
Thickthorn Wood
47
GUN LA
FIELD CL
CHURCH END
PH
PARK RD
2
Sherington
Sherington CE Fst Sch
CHURCH RD
GRIGGS ORCH
SCHOOL LA
PERRY LA
Grange Farm
Brickyard Cottage
CARTERS CL
CROFTS END
PERRY LANE
HILLVIEW
NEWPORT RD
Chicheley Brook
A422
Brandon's Wood
1
Crofts End
BEDFORD RD
Bedlam
BEDLAM WLK
BEDLAM LA
A509
Bedlam Spinney
A422
46

89 A B 90 C D 91 E F

13
23

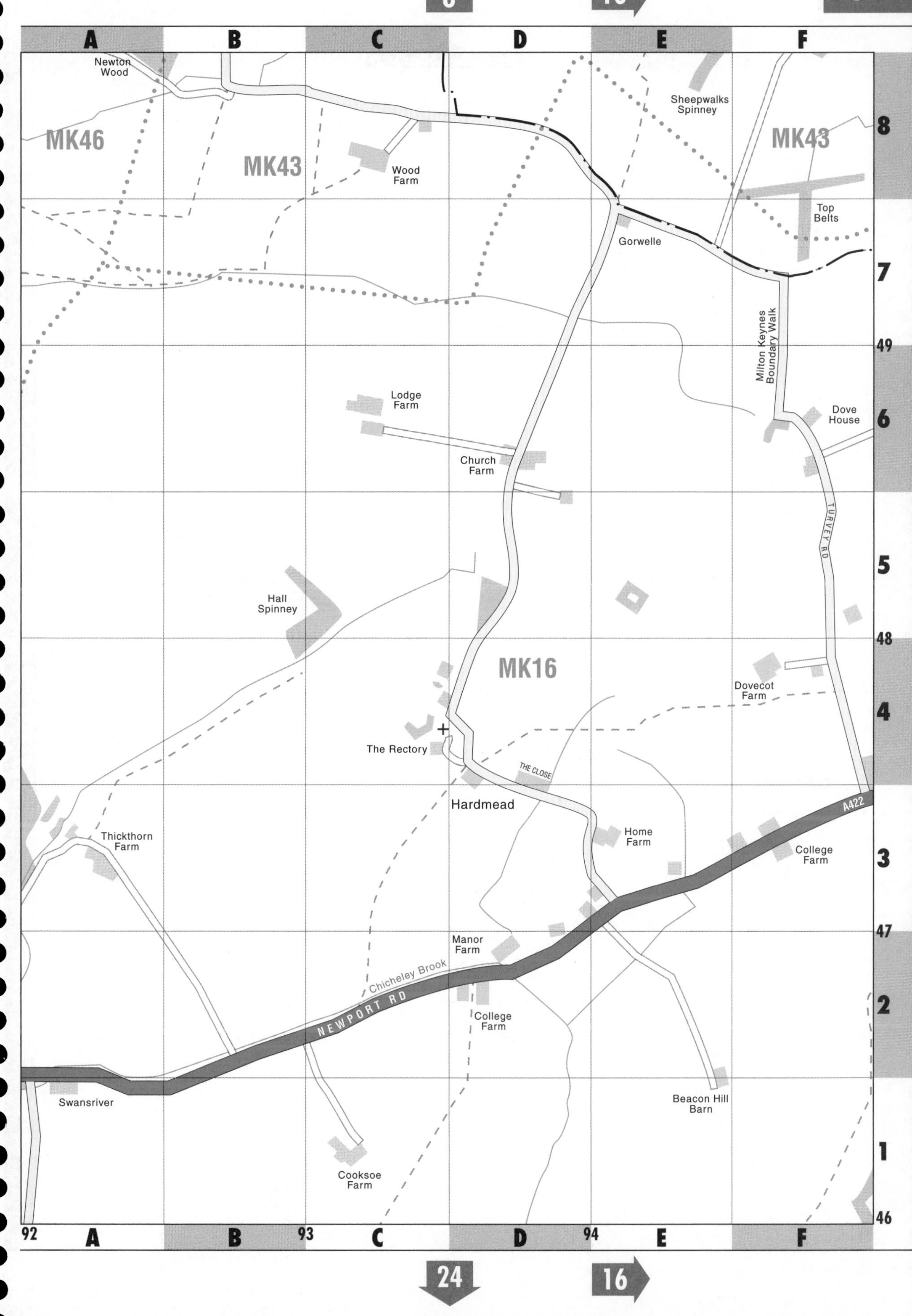
8
16
A
B
C
D
E
F
Newton Wood
MK46
MK43
Wood Farm
Sheepwalks Spinney
MK43
Top Belts
Gorwelle
Milton Keynes Boundary Walk
Lodge Farm
Dove House
Church Farm
TURVEY RD
Hall Spinney
MK16
Dovecot Farm
The Rectory
THE CLOSE
Hardmead
A422
Thickthorn Farm
Home Farm
College Farm
Manor Farm
Chicheley Brook
NEWPORT RD
College Farm
Swansriver
Beacon Hill Barn
Cooksoe Farm
8
7
49
6
5
48
4
3
47
2
1
46
92
93
94
24
16

15

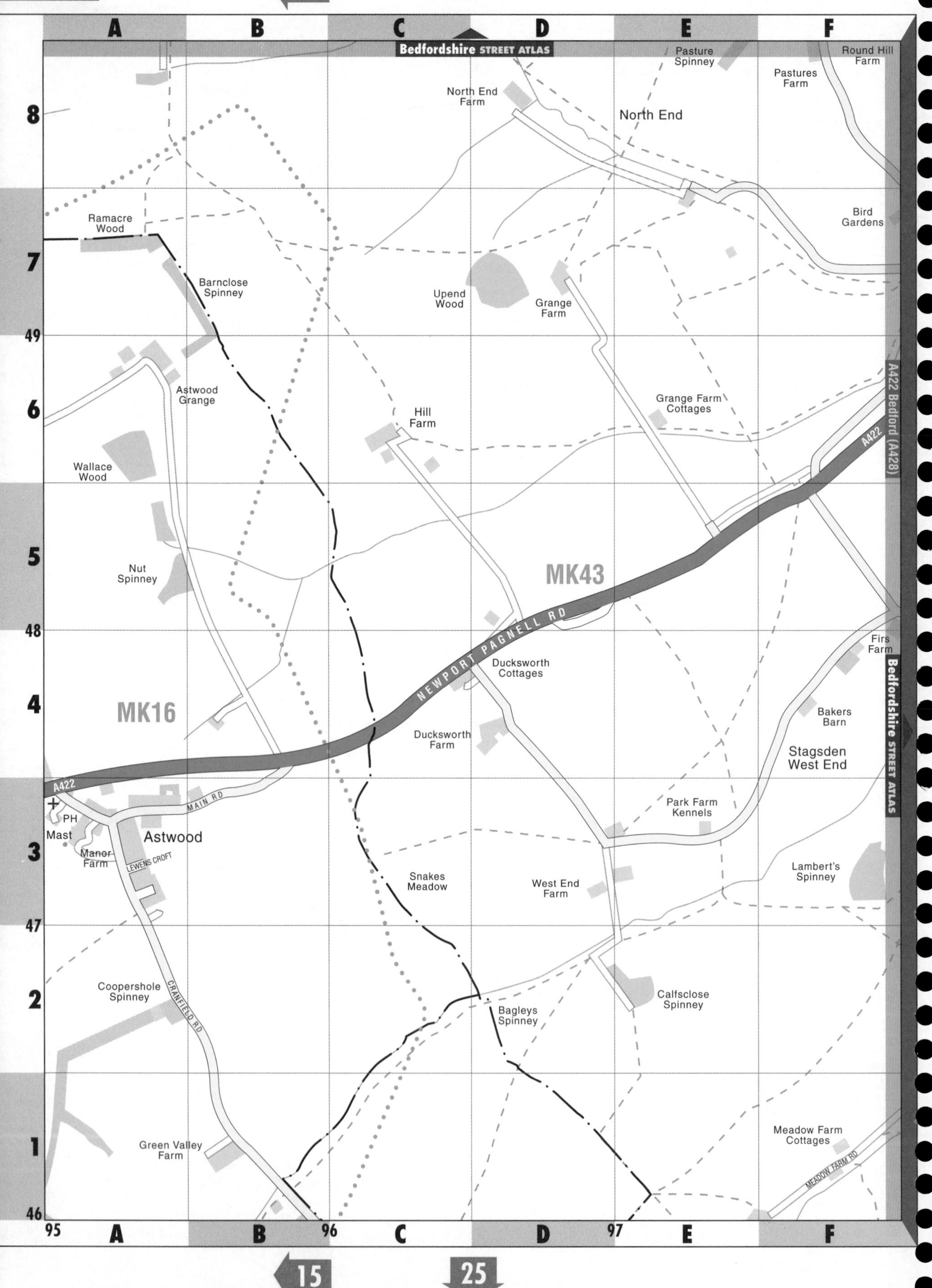
A
B
C
D
E
F
Bedfordshire STREET ATLAS
Pasture Spinney
Round Hill Farm
Pastures Farm
North End Farm
North End
Ramacre Wood
Bird Gardens
Barnclose Spinney
Upend Wood
Grange Farm
Astwood Grange
Grange Farm Cottages
Hill Farm
A422 Bedford (A428)
A422
Wallace Wood
Nut Spinney
MK43
NEWPORT PAGNELL RD
Firs Farm
Ducksworth Cottages
Bedfordshire STREET ATLAS
MK16
Bakers Barn
Ducksworth Farm
Stagsden West End
A422
MAIN RD
Park Farm Kennels
PH
Mast
Astwood
Manor Farm
LEWENS CROFT
Snakes Meadow
West End Farm
Lambert's Spinney
Coopershole Spinney
CRANFIELD RD
Calfsclose Spinney
Bagleys Spinney
Green Valley Farm
Meadow Farm Cottages
MEADOW FARM RD
8
7
49
6
5
48
4
3
47
2
1
46
95
96
97

15

25

18

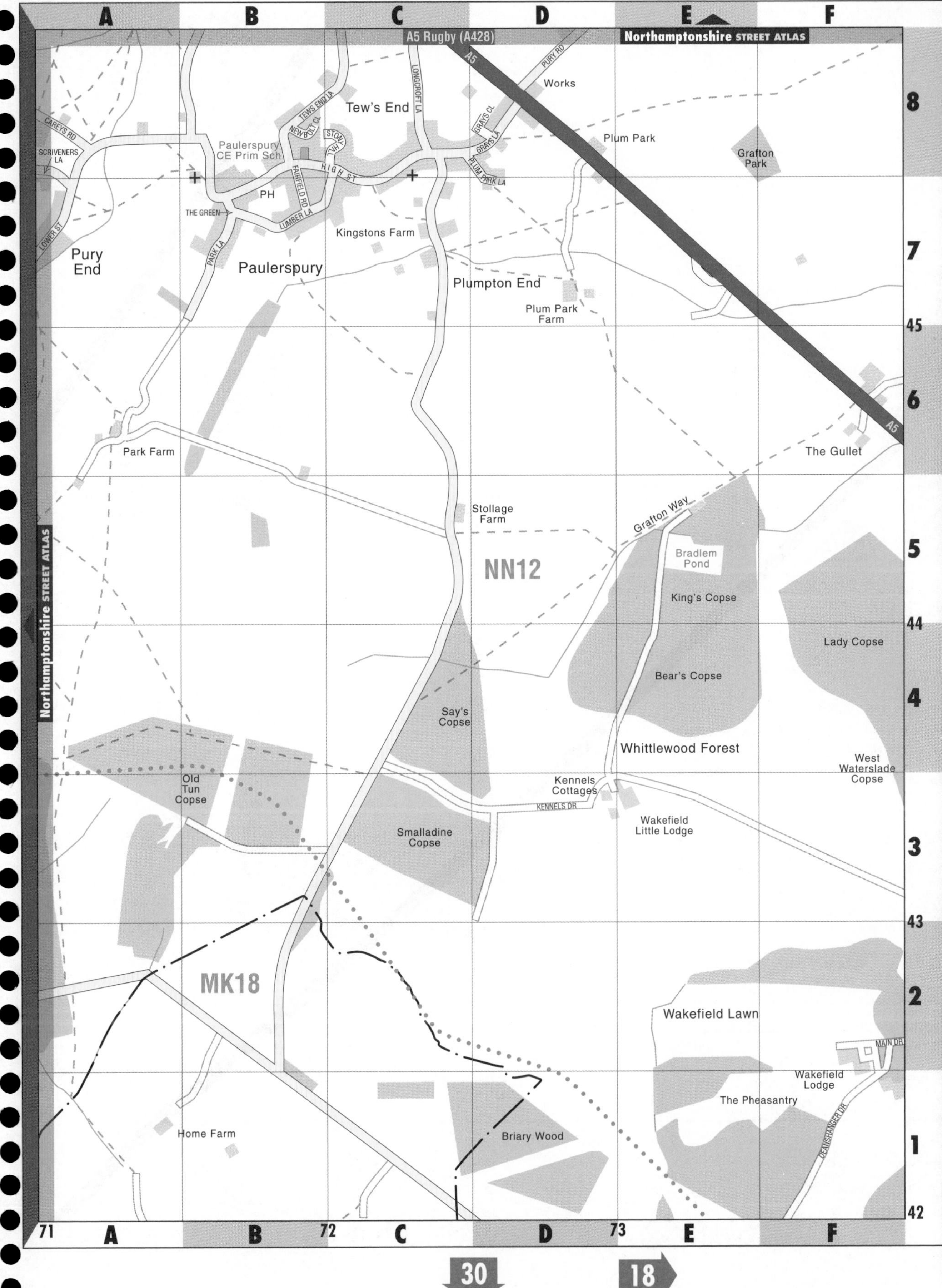
A
B
C
D
E
F
A5 Rugby (A428)
Northamptonshire STREET ATLAS
A5
PURY RD
Works
8
Tew's End
TEWS END LA
LONGCROFT LA
NEWBOTT CL
STONY HILL
GRAYS CL
GRAYS LA
CAREYS RD
SCRIVENERS LA
Paulerspury CE Prim Sch
Plum Park
Grafton Park
HIGH ST
PLUM PARK LA
FAIRFIELD RD
PH
THE GREEN
LUMBER LA
Kingstons Farm
LOWER ST
Pury End
PARK LA
Paulerspury
7
Plumpton End
Plum Park Farm
45
6
Park Farm
The Gullet
Stollage Farm
Grafton Way
Bradlem Pond
5
NN12
King's Copse
Northamptonshire STREET ATLAS
44
Lady Copse
Bear's Copse
4
Say's Copse
Whittlewood Forest
West Waterslade Copse
Old Tun Copse
Kennels Cottages
KENNELS DR
Smalladine Copse
Wakefield Little Lodge
3
43
MK18
2
Wakefield Lawn
MAIN DR
Wakefield Lodge
The Pheasantry
DEANSHANGER DR
Home Farm
Briary Wood
1
42
71
72
73

30
18

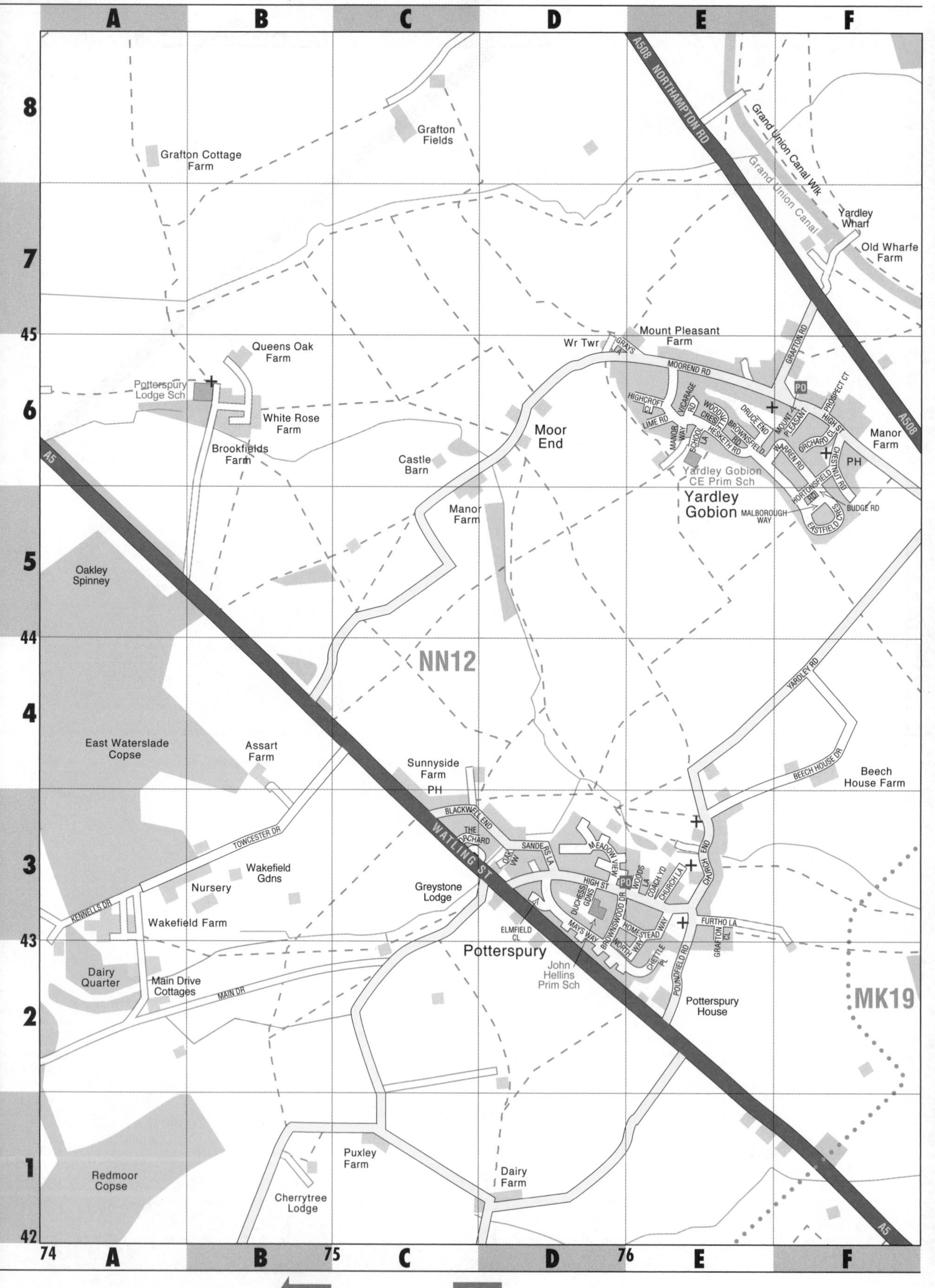
A
B
C
D
E
F
8
7
45
6
5
44
4
3
43
2
1
42
74
75
76
Grafton Fields
Grafton Cottage Farm
A508 NORTHAMPTON RD
Grand Union Canal Wlk
Grand Union Canal
Yardley Wharf
Old Wharfe Farm
Mount Pleasant Farm
Wr Twr
GRAYS
MOOREND RD
GRAFTON RD
PO
PROSPECT CT
HIGHCROFT CL
VICARAGE RD
LIME RD
MANOR WAY
SCHOOL LA
HESKETH RD
BROWNSFIELD RD
DRUCE END
MOUNT PLEASANT
HIGH ST
ORCHARD CL
WARREN RD
CHESTNUT RD
HORTONSFIELD RD
BUDGE RD
EASTFIELD CRES
MALBOROUGH WAY
Manor Farm
PH
A508
Queens Oak Farm
Potterspury Lodge Sch
White Rose Farm
Brookfields Farm
Moor End
Castle Barn
Manor Farm
Yardley Gobion CE Prim Sch
Yardley Gobion
A5
Oakley Spinney
NN12
YARDLEY RD
East Waterslade Copse
Assart Farm
Sunnyside Farm
PH
BEECH HOUSE DR
Beech House Farm
BLACKWELL END
THE ORCHARD
WATLING ST
TOWCESTER DR
SANDERS LA
MEADOW VIEW
OAK VW
WOODS LA
COACH YD
CHURCH LA
CHURCH END
HIGH ST
PO
Wakefield Gdns
Nursery
Greystone Lodge
KENNELLS DR
Wakefield Farm
DUCHESS GDNS
BROWNSWOOD DR
HOMESTEAD WAY
NORTH WAY
MAYS WAY
FURTHO LA
GRAFTON CL
ELMFIELD CL
CHETTLE PL
POUNDFIELD RD
Potterspury
John Hellins Prim Sch
Dairy Quarter
Main Drive Cottages
MAIN DR
Potterspury House
MK19
Puxley Farm
Dairy Farm
Redmoor Copse
Cherrytree Lodge
A5

10
20

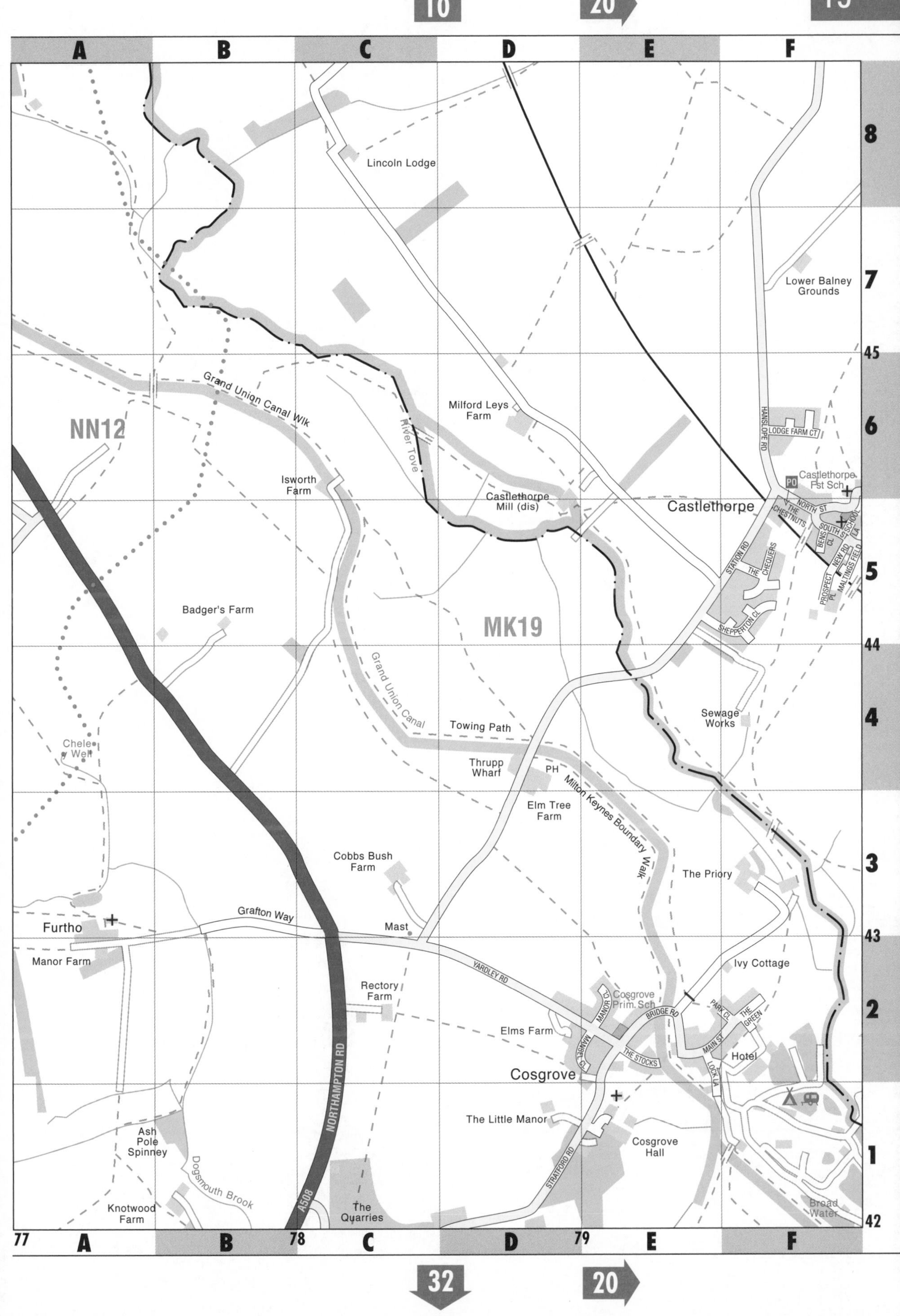
A
B
C
D
E
F
8
7
45
6
5
44
4
3
43
2
1
42
77
78
79
Lincoln Lodge
Lower Balney Grounds
NN12
Grand Union Canal Wlk
Milford Leys Farm
River Tove
HANSLOPE RD
LODGE FARM CT
Castlethorpe Fst Sch
PO
Isworth Farm
Castlethorpe Mill (dis)
Castlethorpe
NORTH ST
THE CHESTNUTS
SOUTH ST
SCHOOL LA
BENS CL
STATION RD
THE CHEQUERS
NEW RD
MALTINGS FIELD
PROSPECT PL
Badger's Farm
MK19
SHEPPERTON CL
Grand Union Canal
Towing Path
Sewage Works
Chele Well
Thrupp Wharf
PH
Milton Keynes Boundary Walk
Elm Tree Farm
Cobbs Bush Farm
The Priory
Grafton Way
Furtho
Mast
Manor Farm
YARDLEY RD
Ivy Cottage
Rectory Farm
Cosgrove Prim. Sch
MANOR CL
BRIDGE RD
PARK CL
THE GREEN
Elms Farm
MANSEL CL
THE STOCKS
MAIN ST
Hotel
LOCK LA
Cosgrove
NORTHAMPTON RD
The Little Manor
Ash Pole Spinney
STRATFORD RD
Cosgrove Hall
Dogsmouth Brook
Knotwood Farm
A508
The Quarries
Broad Water

32
20

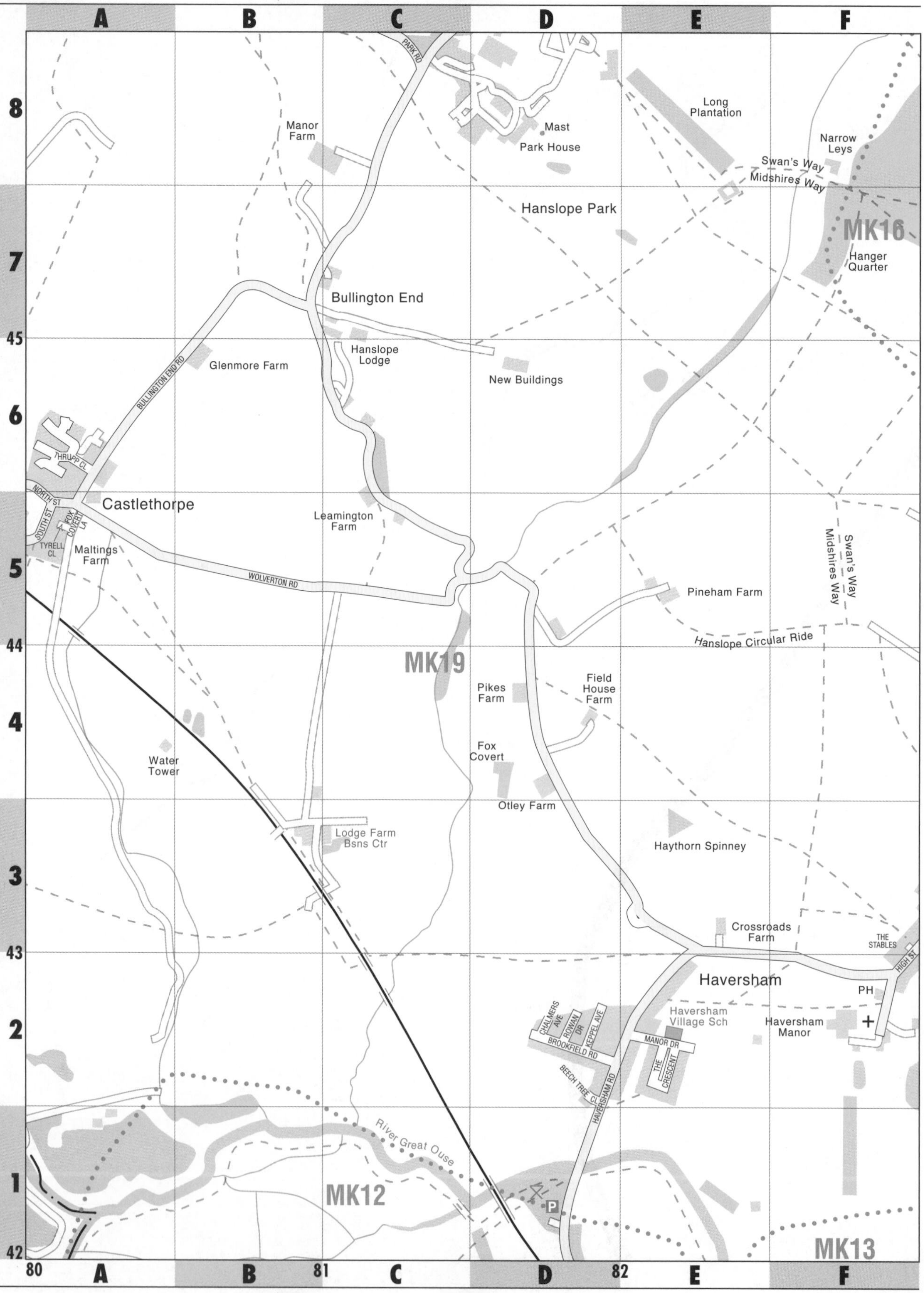

A B C D E F
8
7
45
6
5
44
4
3
43
2
1
42
80 81 82
PARK RD
Manor Farm
Mast
Park House
Long Plantation
Narrow Leys
Swan's Way
Midshires Way
Hanslope Park
MK16
Hanger Quarter
Bullington End
Hanslope Lodge
Glenmore Farm
New Buildings
BULLINGTON END RD
THRUPP CL
NORTH ST
Castlethorpe
SOUTH ST
FOX COVERT LA
TYRELL CL
Maltings Farm
Leamington Farm
WOLVERTON RD
Pineham Farm
Swan's Way
Midshires Way
Hanslope Circular Ride
MK19
Pikes Farm
Field House Farm
Water Tower
Fox Covert
Otley Farm
Lodge Farm Bsns Ctr
Haythorn Spinney
Crossroads Farm
THE STABLES
HIGH ST
Haversham
PH
CHALMERS AVE
ROWAN DR
KEPPEL AVE
BROOKFIELD RD
Haversham Village Sch
Haversham Manor
MANOR DR
THE CRESCENT
BEECH TREE CL
HAVERSHAM RD
River Great Ouse
MK12
P
MK13

12
22

Little Linford Wood Wildlife Reserve
Dairy Farm
Three Shires Way
Brownleys Spinney
Quarryhall
MK16
Mill Farm
Hoo Wood
Linford Wood
Swan's Way
Midshires Way
Wood Farm
Burnt Covert
FLORA THOMPSON DR
The Spinney
Little Linford
Hall Farm
Lakelane Spinney
The Serpentine
The Wilderness
Little Linford Park
MK19
LITTLE LINFORD LA
Hill Farm
Motel
Broadacre
Newport Pagnell Service Area
The Walnuts
Works
GIFFARD PARK RDBT
River Great Ouse
Great Linford Lakes
Giffard Park
Hanson Environmental Study Centre
MK14
PH
Sand and Gravel Pit
Grand Union Canal
WOLVERTON RD
Grand Union Canal Wlk
Stantonbury Wharf
The Manor House
Courtyard Arts Ctr
MILTON KEYNES
Stantonbury Park Farm
MK13
Great Linford
BEKONSCOT CT
ALMHOUSES

34
22

21 13

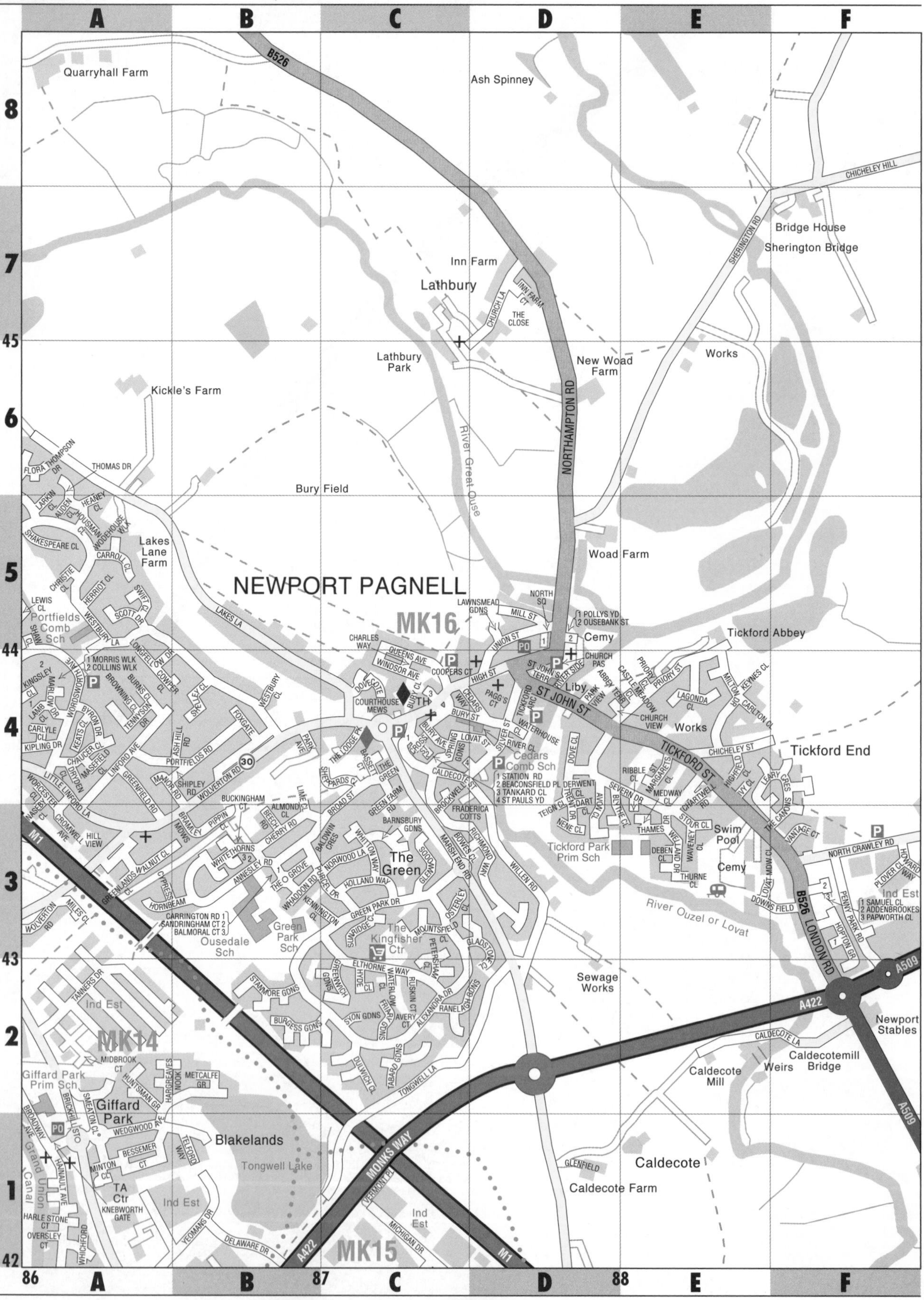

A B C D E F

8 7 45 6 5 44 4 3 43 2 1 42

B526
Quarryhall Farm
Ash Spinney
CHICHELEY HILL
Bridge House
Sherington Bridge
SHERINGTON RD
Inn Farm
Lathbury
INN FARM CT
CHURCH LA
THE CLOSE
Lathbury Park
New Woad Farm
Works
Kickle's Farm
NORTHAMPTON RD
River Great Ouse
FLORA THOMPSON DR
THOMAS DR
Bury Field
LARKIN CL
AUDEN CL
HEANEY CL
HOUSMAN CL
WORDSWORTH WLK
SHAKESPEARE CL
Lakes Lane Farm
CARROLL CL
Woad Farm
CHRISTIE CL
HERRIOT CL
SWIFT CL
NEWPORT PAGNELL
NORTH SQ
LEWIS CL
Portfields Comb Sch
SHAW CL
WESTBURY LA
SCOTT DR
LAKES LA
LAWNSMEAD GDNS
MILL ST
1 POLLYS YD
2 OUSEBANK ST
MK16
Cemy
Tickford Abbey
CHARLES WAY
UNION ST
PO
QUEENS AVE
WINDSOR AVE
COOPERS CT
HIGH ST
1 MORRIS WLK
2 COLLINS WLK
KINGSLEY CL
MARLOW DR
WORDSWORTH AVE
BROWNING CL
BURNS CL
LONGFELLOW DR
COWPER CL
SHELLEY CL
WESTBURY CL
DOVECOTE
COURTHOUSE MEWS
BURY CL
TH
CEDARS WAY
PAGG'S CT
ST JOHN'S TERR
RIVER SIDE
CHURCH PAS
ABBEY TERR
CASTLE MEADOW CL
PRIORY CL
PRIORY ST
MILTON DR
KEYNES CL
LAGONDA CL
CARLTON CL
Liby
ST JOHN ST
LAMB CL
BYRON DR
TENNYSON DR
FOXGATE
TICKFORD ARC
PARK VIEW
CHURCH VIEW
Works
CARLYLE CL
KEATS CL
ASH HILL RD
PARK AVE
BURY ST
TICKFORD ST
Tickford End
KIPLING DR
CHAUCER CL
PORTFIELDS RD
THE LODGE PK
BURY AVE
SPRING GDNS
LOVAT ST
SILVER ST
WATERHOUSE
DOVE CL
CHICHELEY ST
WORCESTER CL
DRYDEN CL
MASEFIELD CL
LINFORD AVE
MANOR RD
30
BASSETT CT
THE GREEN
CROSS CT
RIVER CL
Cedars Comb Sch
HIGHFIELD CL
IVY CL
LEARY CRES
LITTLE LINFORD LA
GREENFIELD RD
SHIPLEY RD
WOLVERTON RD
SHEPPARDS CL
CALDECOTE ST
1 STATION RD
2 BEACONSFIELD PL
3 TANKARD CL
4 ST PAULS YD
RIBBLE CL
ST MARGARETS CL
DERWENT CL
TRENT DR
SEVERN DR
MEDWAY CL
HARTWELL RD
NASEBY CT
BUCKINGHAM CT
ALMOND CL
LIME CL
BROAD ST
GREEN FARM RD
BROCKWELL
FREDERICA COTTS
DART CL
AVON CL
BLYTHE CL
THE CAMPIONS
TEIGN CL
NENE CL
THAMES
WELLAND DR
STOUR CL
Swim Pool
VANTAGE CT
M1
CROMWELL AVE
HILL VIEW
BRAMLEY MEWS
PIPPIN CL
BEECH RD
CHERRY RD
BARNSBURY GDNS
BALDWIN CRES
WHITTON WAY
MARSH END RD
BOWES CL
RICHMOND WAY
WILLEN RD
Tickford Park Prim Sch
DEBEN CL
WAVENEY CL
NORTH CRAWLEY RD
HOWARD WAY
PLOVER CL
WHITETHORNS
ANNESLEY RD
NORWOOD LA
The Green
GLENISTER
GREENLANDS
WALNUT CL
CYPRESS
HOLLAND WAY
THURNE CL
Cemy
LOVAT MDW CL
B526 LONDON RD
PENNY PARK RD
HOPTON GR
Ind Est
1 SAMUEL CL
2 ADDENBROOKES
3 PAPWORTH CL
WOLVERTON RD
MILES CL
HORNBEAM
THE GROVE
WHADDON RD
PURCELL DR
KENNINGTON CL
GREEN PARK DR
OSTERLEY CL
River Ouzel or Lovat
DOWNS FIELD
CARRINGTON RD 1
SANDRINGHAM CT 2
BALMORAL CT 3
Green Park Sch
SUNRIDGE CL
The Kingfisher Ctr
MOUNTSFIELD CL
GLADSTONE CL
Ousedale Sch
PETERSHAM CL
ELTHORNE WAY
HYDE CL
Sewage Works
A509
TANNERS DR
STANMORE GDNS
GREENWICH GDNS
WATERLOW CL
RUSKIN CT
ALEXANDRA DR
RANELAGH GDNS
A422
Newport Stables
Ind Est
BURGESS GDNS
SYON GDNS
FRIARY GDNS
AVERY CT
CALDECOTE LA
MK14
Caldecote Mill
Weirs
Caldecotemill Bridge
MIDBROOK CT
Giffard Park Prim Sch
HUNTSMAN GR
HARGREAVES NOOK
METCALFE GR
DULWICH CL
TABARD GDNS
TONGWELL LA
Giffard Park
SMEATON CL
BROADWAY AVE
BRICKHILL ST
PO
WEDGWOOD AVE
Blakelands
TELFORD WAY
A509
BESSEMER CT
MONKS WAY
Grand Union Canal
HAINAULT AVE
MINTON CT
Tongwell Lake
GLENFIELD
Caldecote
Caldecote Farm
TA Ctr
KNEBWORTH GATE
Ind Est
VERMONT PL
HARLE STONE CT
OVERSLEY CT
WHICHFORD
YEOMANS DR
Ind Est
MICHIGAN DR
DELAWARE DR
A422
MK15
M1

86 A B 87 C D 88 E F

21 35

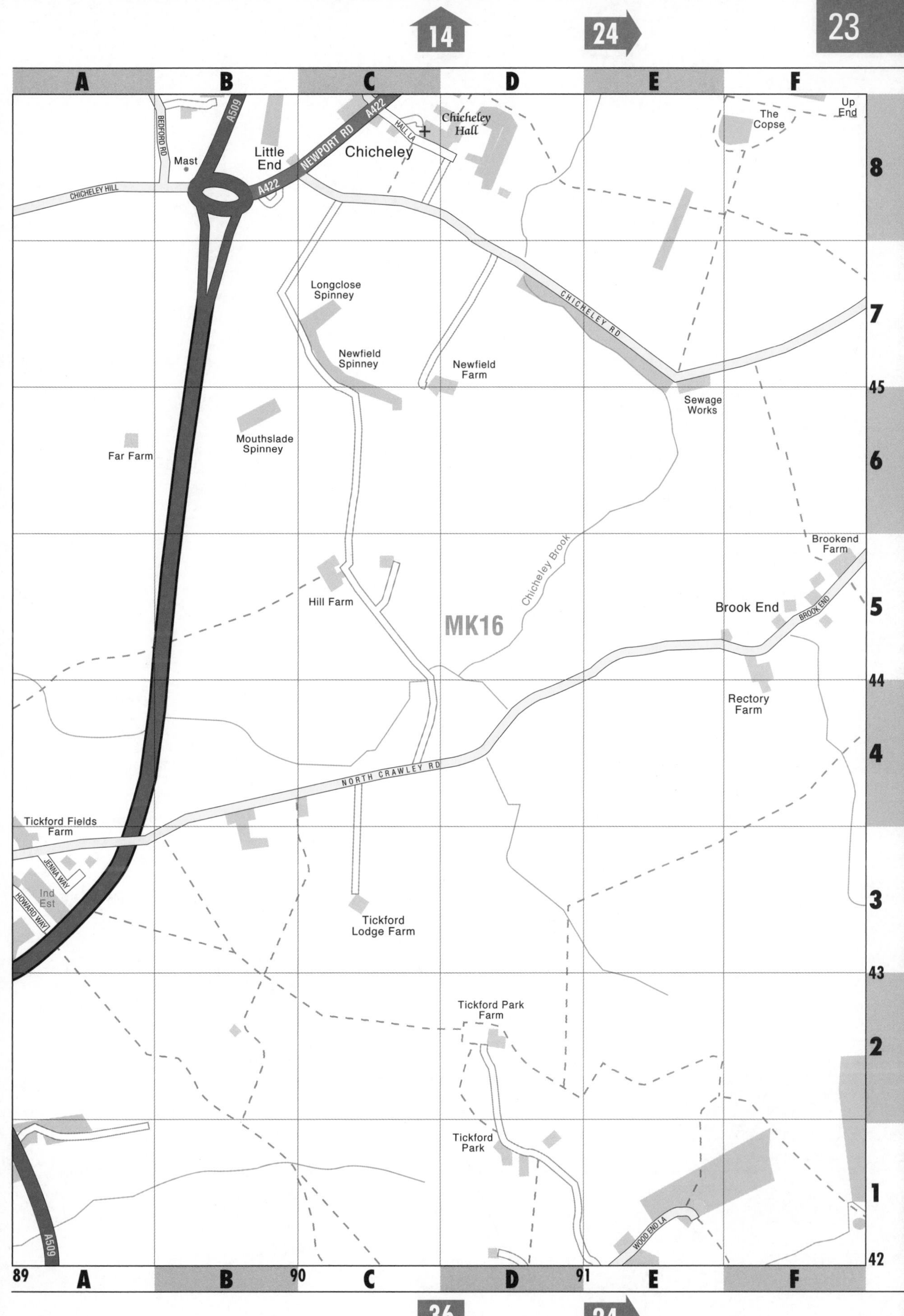
14
24
A
B
C
D
E
F
CHICHELEY HILL
BEDFORD RD
Mast
A509
Little
End
A422
NEWPORT RD
A422
Chicheley
HALL LA
Chicheley
Hall
The
Copse
Up
End
8
Longclose
Spinney
Newfield
Spinney
Newfield
Farm
CHICHELEY RD
7
45
Sewage
Works
Mouthslade
Spinney
Far Farm
6
Brookend
Farm
Hill Farm
Chicheley Brook
MK16
Brook End
BROOK END
5
44
Rectory
Farm
NORTH CRAWLEY RD
4
Tickford Fields
Farm
JENNA WAY
Ind
Est
HOWARD WAY
3
Tickford
Lodge Farm
43
Tickford Park
Farm
2
Tickford
Park
1
WOOD END LA
A509
42
89
90
91
36
24

23
15

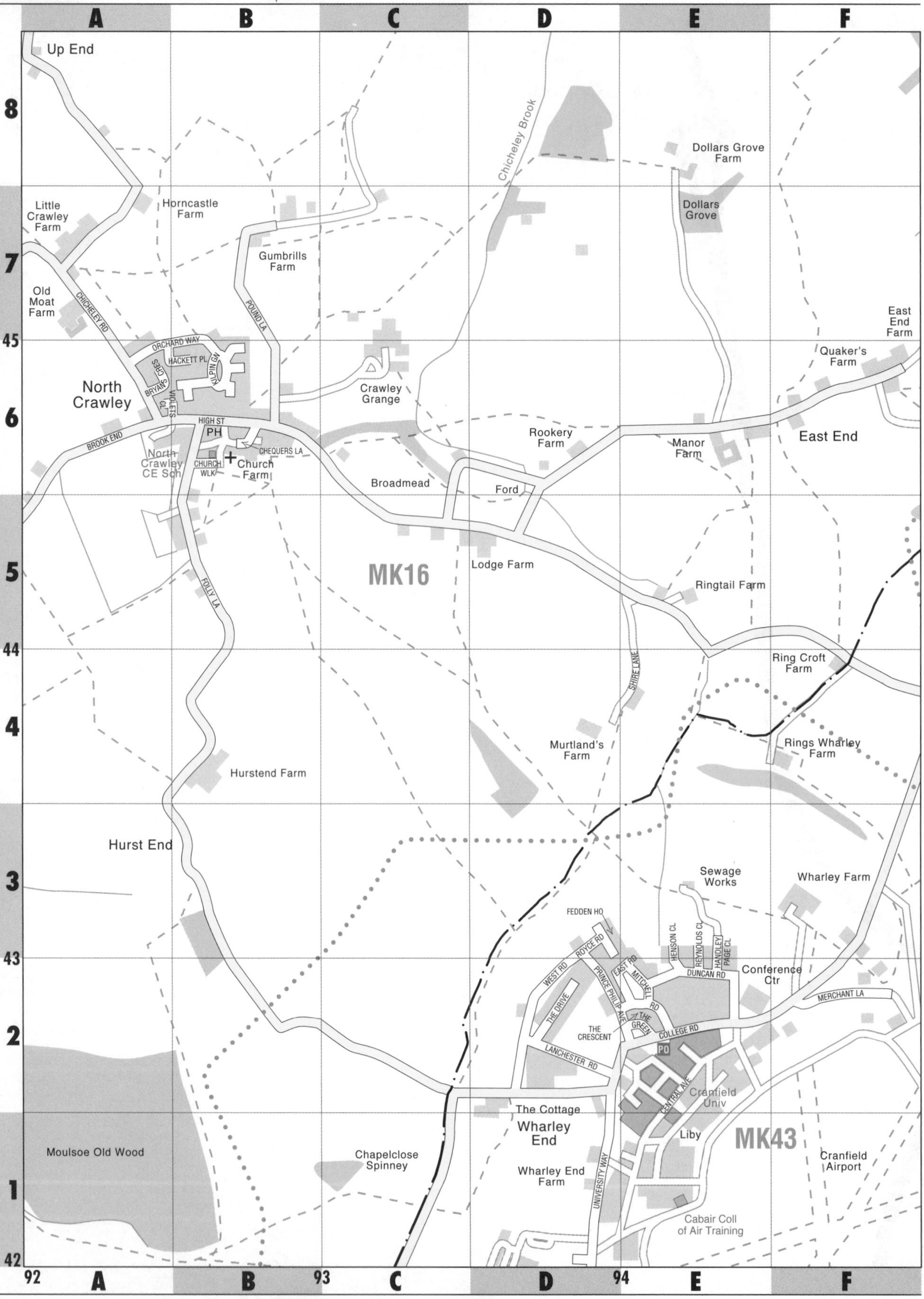

A B C D E F

8 7 45 6 5 44 4 3 43 2 1 42

Up End
Dollars Grove Farm
Chicheley Brook
Little Crawley Farm
Horncastle Farm
Dollars Grove
Gumbrills Farm
Old Moat Farm
CHICHELEY RD
POUND LA
East End Farm
ORCHARD WAY
HACKETT PL
KILPIN GN
BRYANS CRES
VIOLETS CL
North Crawley
Crawley Grange
Quaker's Farm
HIGH ST
PH
BROOK END
Rookery Farm
Manor Farm
East End
North Crawley CE Sch
CHEQUERS LA
CHURCH WLK
Church Farm
Broadmead
Ford
Lodge Farm
MK16
FOLLY LA
Ringtail Farm
Ring Croft Farm
SHIRE LANE
Murtland's Farm
Rings Wharley Farm
Hurstend Farm
Hurst End
Sewage Works
Wharley Farm
FEDDEN HO
HENSON CL
REYNOLDS CL
HANDLEY PAGE CL
ROYCE RD
WEST RD
EAST RD
PRINCE PHILIP AVE
MITCHELL RD
DUNCAN RD
Conference Ctr
THE DRIVE
MERCHANT LA
THE GREEN
THE CRESCENT
COLLEGE RD
PO
LANCHESTER RD
CENTRAL AVE
Cranfield Univ
The Cottage
Wharley End
Liby
MK43
Moulsoe Old Wood
Chapelclose Spinney
Wharley End Farm
UNIVERSITY WAY
Cranfield Airport
Cabair Coll of Air Training

92 A B 93 C D 94 E F

23
37

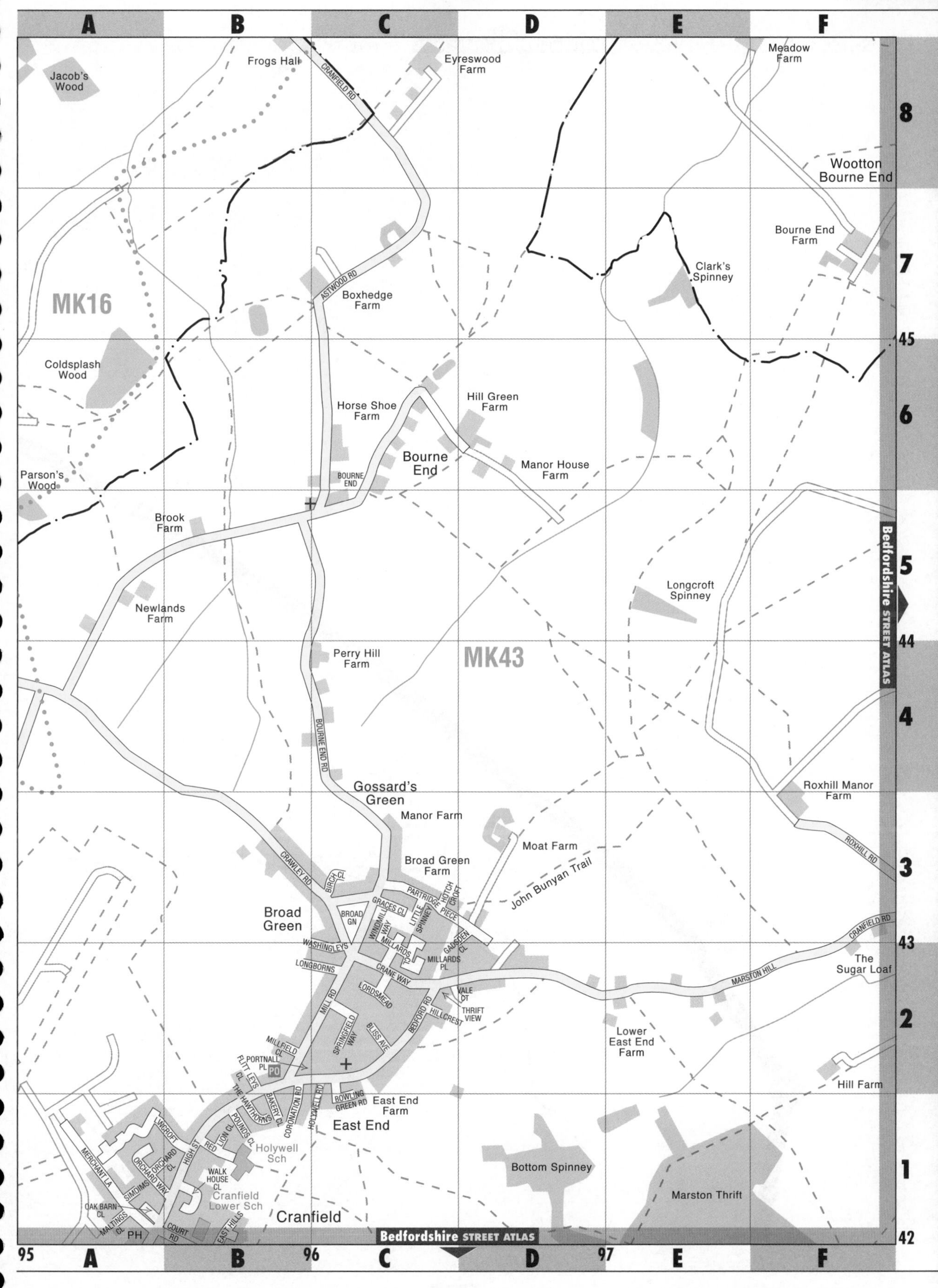
A
B
C
D
E
F
Frogs Hall
Eyreswood Farm
Meadow Farm
Jacob's Wood
CRANFIELD RD
8
Wootton Bourne End
Bourne End Farm
7
Clark's Spinney
ASTWOOD RD
Boxhedge Farm
MK16
45
Coldsplash Wood
Horse Shoe Farm
Hill Green Farm
6
Bourne End
Manor House Farm
BOURNE END
Parson's Wood
Brook Farm
5
Longcroft Spinney
Newlands Farm
44
Perry Hill Farm
MK43
4
BOURNE END RD
Gossard's Green
Roxhill Manor Farm
Manor Farm
Moat Farm
Broad Green Farm
John Bunyan Trail
ROXHILL RD
3
CRAWLEY RD
BIRCH CL
PARTRIDGE PIECE
HOTCH CROFT
GRACES CL
LITTLE SPINNEY
WINDMILL WAY
BROAD GN
Broad Green
WASHINGLEYS
MILLARDS
GADSDEN CL
43
CRANFIELD RD
LONGBORNS
MILLARDS PL
CRANE WAY
The Sugar Loaf
MARSTON HILL
VALE CT
LORDSMEAD
MILL RD
BEDFORD RD
THRIFT VIEW
HILLCREST
SPRINGFIELD WAY
BLISS AVE
2
Lower East End Farm
MILLFIELD CL
PORTNALL PL
PO
FLITT LEYS CL
Hill Farm
THE HAWTHORNS
BAKERY CL
CORONATION RD
HOLYWELL RD
BOWLING GREEN RD
East End Farm
East End
LINCROFT
POUNDS CL
LION CL
RED
Holywell Sch
MERCHANT LA
ORCHARD CL
HIGH ST
ORCHARD WAY
Bottom Spinney
1
SIMDIMS
WALK HOUSE CL
Cranfield Lower Sch
Marston Thrift
OAK BARN CL
MALTINGS CL
Cranfield
PH
COURT RD
EAST HILLS
42
95
96
97

A
B
C
D
E
F
Northamptonshire STREET ATLAS
Crowfield
B4525
Falcutt Hall Farm
Shortgrove Wood
Crowfield
Staplegate Farm
Whistley Wood
B4525
Pimlico
Kiln Farm
Radstone
Hoppersford Farm
Wrighton's Barn
A43
Coldharbour Farm
NN13
Northamptonshire STREET ATLAS
THE AVENUE
Whitfield House Farm
PH
TRENGOTHAL CT
CHESTNUT GN
FARRER CL
CHAPEL LA
Fox Covert
Whitfield
Manor Farm
Mill Bridge
River Great Ouse
MILL RD
Sewage Works
Ilett's Farm
Sundale
Bushy End Wood
Saw Mill
Versions Farm
Airstrip
NORTHAMPTON RD
TOP STATION RD
TURWESTON RD
A43
8
7
41
6
5
40
4
3
39
2
1
38
59
60
61
A
B
C
D
E
F

38

28

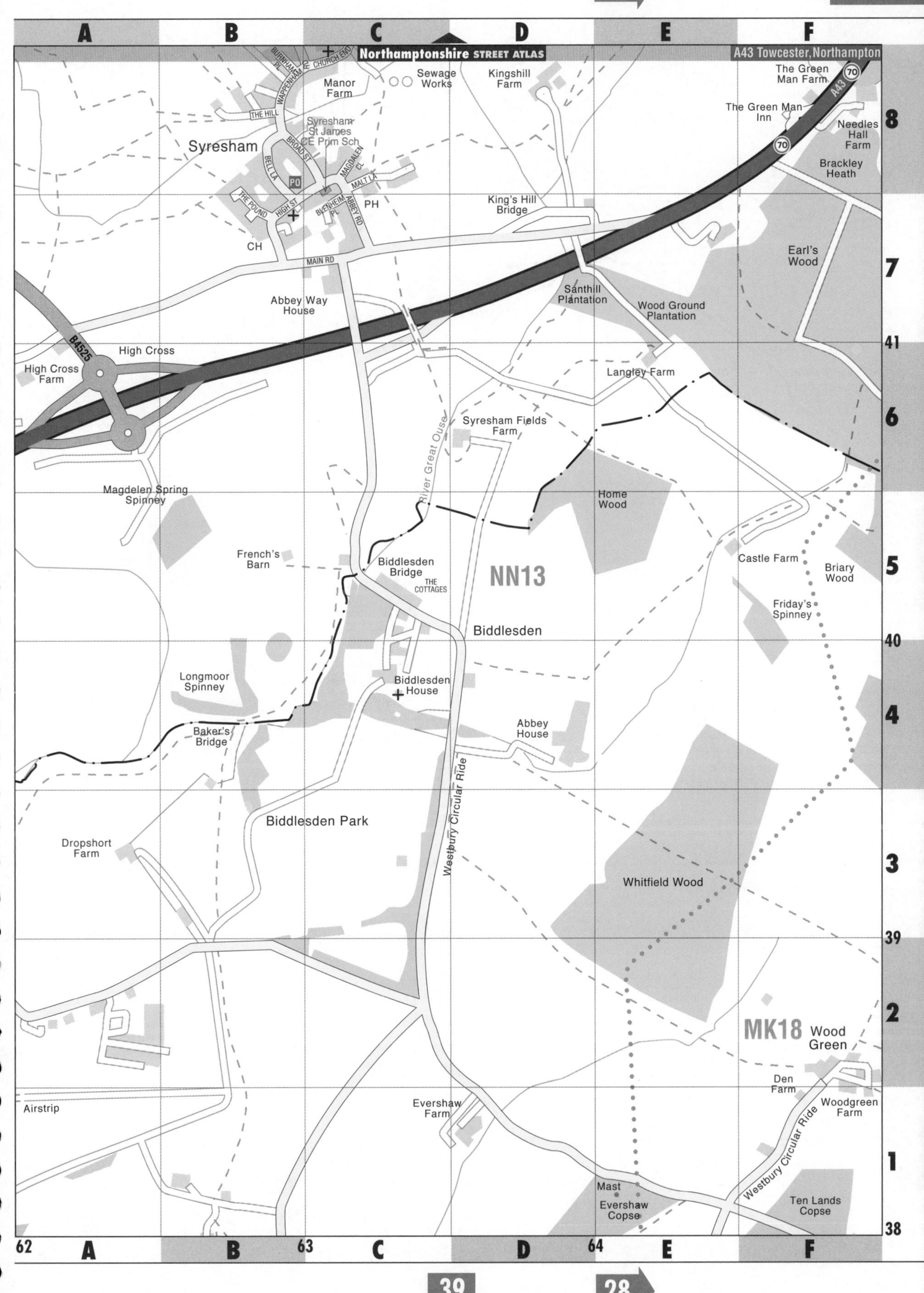
A
B
C
D
E
F
Northamptonshire STREET ATLAS
A43 Towcester, Northampton
Syresham
Manor Farm
Sewage Works
Kingshill Farm
The Green Man Farm
The Green Man Inn
Needles Hall Farm
Brackley Heath
Syresham St James CE Prim Sch
BURNHAM PL
WAPPENHAM RD
CHURCH END
THE HILL
BROAD ST
BELL LA
MAGDALEN CL
MALT LA
THE POUND
HIGH ST
BLENHEIM PL
ABBEY RD
PO
PH
CH
MAIN RD
King's Hill Bridge
Earl's Wood
Santhill Plantation
Wood Ground Plantation
Abbey Way House
High Cross
High Cross Farm
B4525
A43
70
Langley Farm
Syresham Fields Farm
River Great Ouse
Magdelen Spring Spinney
Home Wood
French's Barn
Biddlesden Bridge
THE COTTAGES
NN13
Castle Farm
Briary Wood
Friday's Spinney
Biddlesden
Longmoor Spinney
Biddlesden House
Abbey House
Baker's Bridge
Biddlesden Park
Westbury Circular Ride
Dropshort Farm
Whitfield Wood
MK18
Wood Green
Den Farm
Woodgreen Farm
Airstrip
Evershaw Farm
Mast
Evershaw Copse
Ten Lands Copse
8
7
41
6
5
40
4
3
39
2
1
38
62
63
64

39

28

27

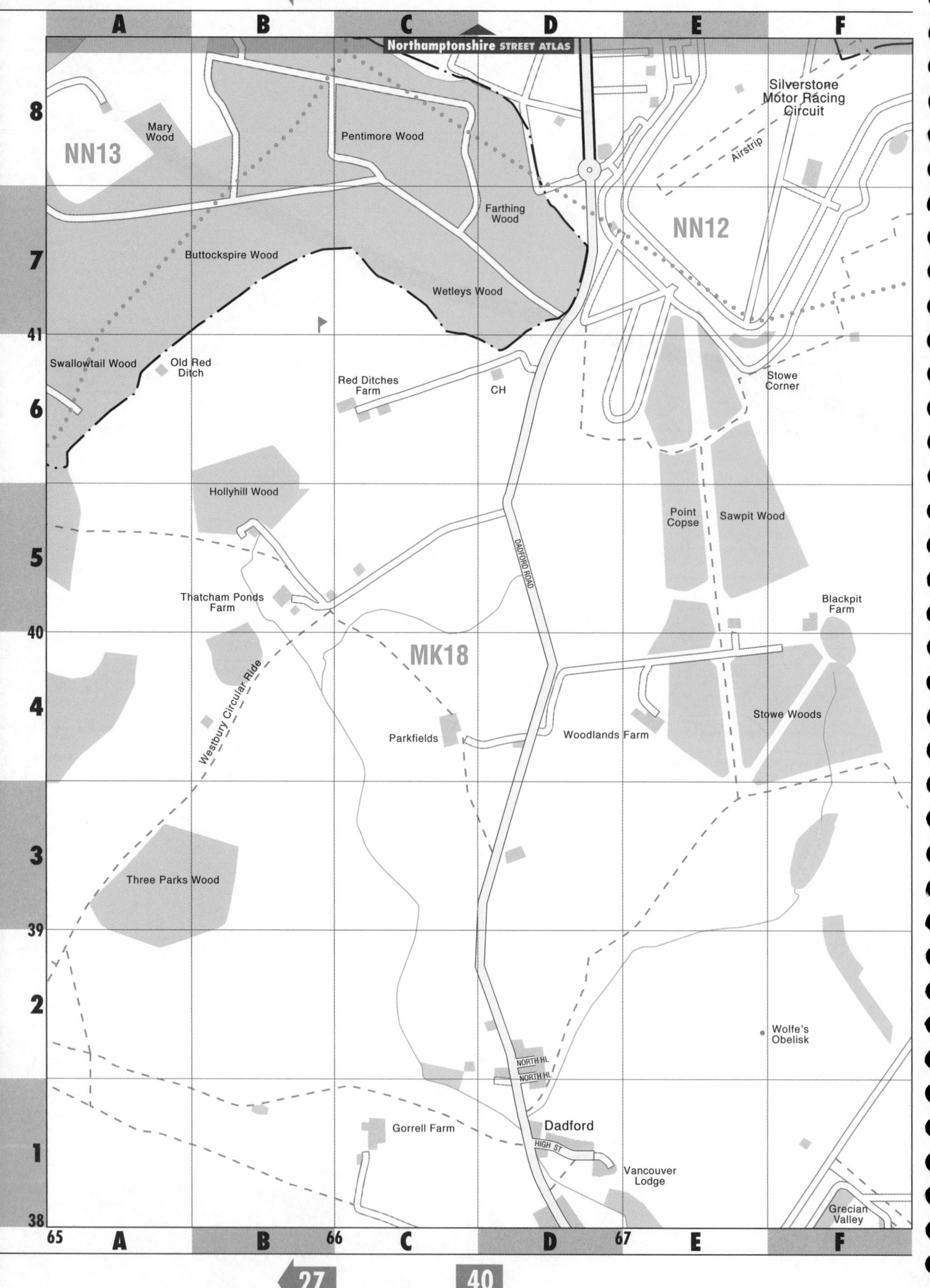
A
B
C
D
E
F
Northamptonshire STREET ATLAS
8
7
41
6
5
40
4
3
39
2
1
38
65
66
67
Mary Wood
NN13
Pentimore Wood
Silverstone Motor Racing Circuit
Airstrip
Farthing Wood
NN12
Buttockspire Wood
Wetleys Wood
Swallowtail Wood
Old Red Ditch
Red Ditches Farm
CH
Stowe Corner
Hollyhill Wood
Point Copse
Sawpit Wood
DADFORD ROAD
Thatcham Ponds Farm
Blackpit Farm
MK18
Westbury Circular Ride
Stowe Woods
Parkfields
Woodlands Farm
Three Parks Wood
Wolfe's Obelisk
NORTH HL
NORTH HL
Gorrell Farm
Dadford
HIGH ST
Vancouver Lodge
Grecian Valley

27
40

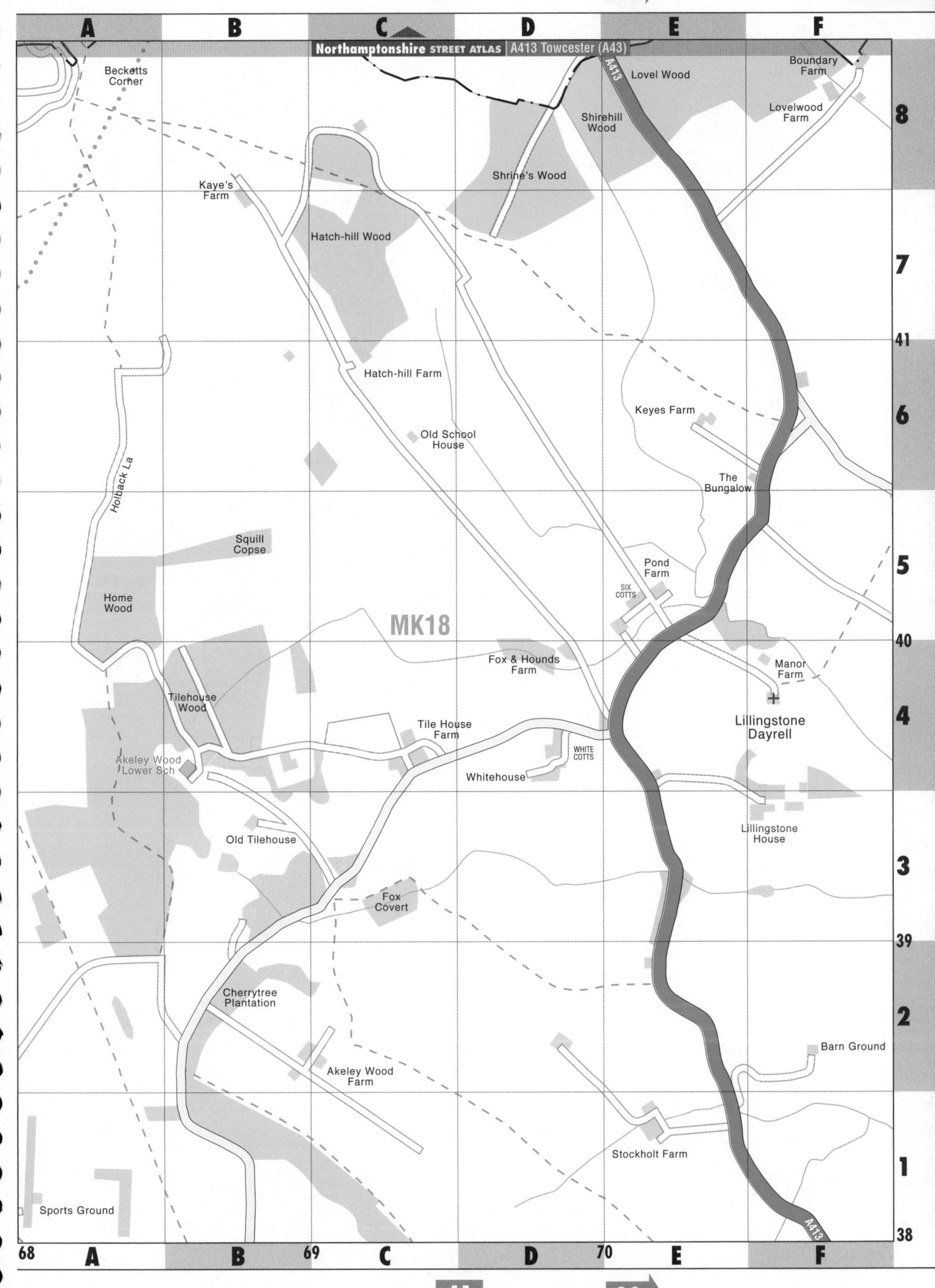
A
B
C
D
E
F
Northamptonshire STREET ATLAS
A413 Towcester (A43)
A413
Becketts Corner
Lovel Wood
Boundary Farm
Lovelwood Farm
Shirehill Wood
Shrine's Wood
Kaye's Farm
Hatch-hill Wood
Hatch-hill Farm
Keyes Farm
Old School House
The Bungalow
Holback La
Squill Copse
Pond Farm
SIX COTTS
Home Wood
MK18
Fox & Hounds Farm
Manor Farm
Tilehouse Wood
Tile House Farm
Lillingstone Dayrell
Akeley Wood Lower Sch
WHITE COTTS
Whitehouse
Old Tilehouse
Lillingstone House
Fox Covert
Cherrytree Plantation
Barn Ground
Akeley Wood Farm
Stockholt Farm
Sports Ground
A413
8
7
41
6
5
40
4
3
39
2
1
38
68
69
70

29
17

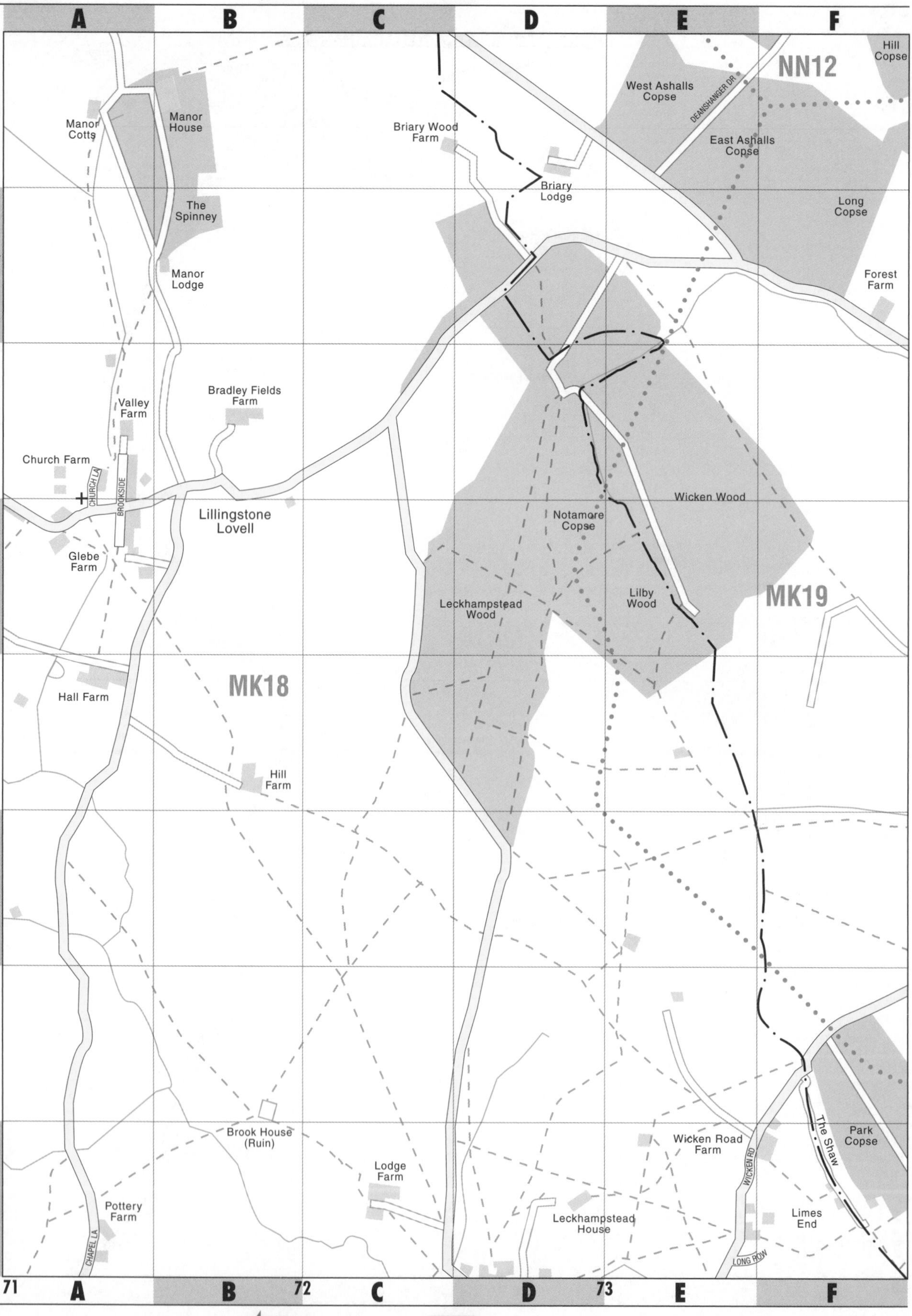

A B C D E F
8
7
41
6
5
40
4
3
39
2
1
38
71
72
73
Manor Cotts
Manor House
The Spinney
Manor Lodge
Valley Farm
Bradley Fields Farm
Church Farm
CHURCH LA
BROOKSIDE
Lillingstone Lovell
Glebe Farm
Hall Farm
MK18
Hill Farm
Pottery Farm
CHAPEL LA
Brook House (Ruin)
Lodge Farm
Briary Wood Farm
Briary Lodge
West Ashalls Copse
DEANSHANGER DR
NN12
East Ashalls Copse
Hill Copse
Long Copse
Forest Farm
Notamore Copse
Wicken Wood
Leckhampstead Wood
Lilby Wood
MK19
Wicken Road Farm
WICKEN RD
The Shaw
Park Copse
Limes End
LONG ROW
Leckhampstead House

29
42

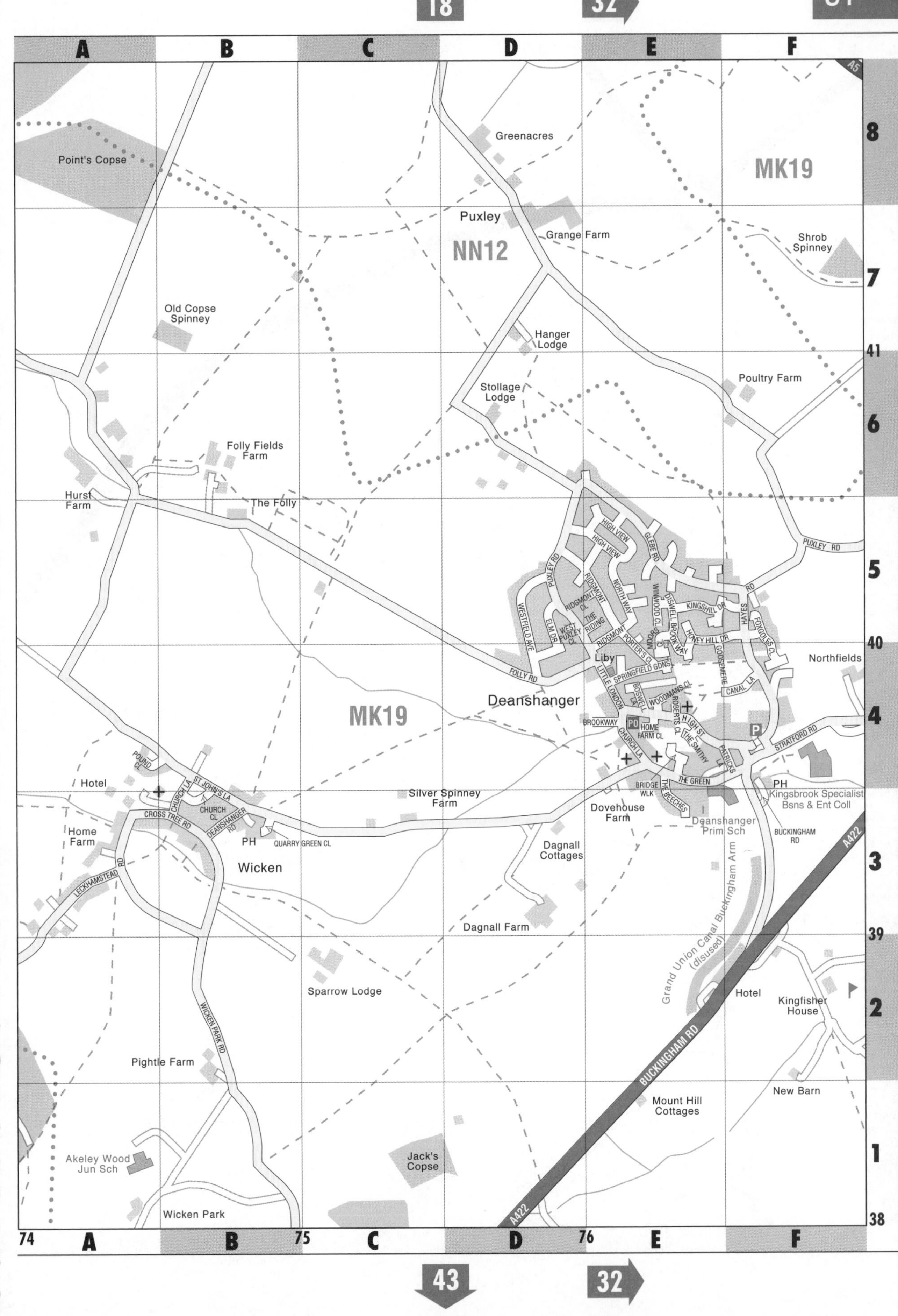
18
32
Point's Copse
Greenacres
MK19
Puxley
NN12
Grange Farm
Shrob Spinney
Old Copse Spinney
Hanger Lodge
Poultry Farm
Stollage Lodge
Folly Fields Farm
Hurst Farm
The Folly
Deanshanger
Northfields
MK19
Hotel
Silver Spinney Farm
Home Farm
Wicken
Dovehouse Farm
Dagnall Cottages
Deanshanger Prim Sch
Kingsbrook Specialist Bsns & Ent Coll
Dagnall Farm
Sparrow Lodge
Grand Union Canal Buckingham Arm (disused)
Hotel
Kingfisher House
Pightle Farm
New Barn
Mount Hill Cottages
Akeley Wood Jun Sch
Jack's Copse
Wicken Park
BUCKINGHAM RD
A422
A5
43
32

31
19

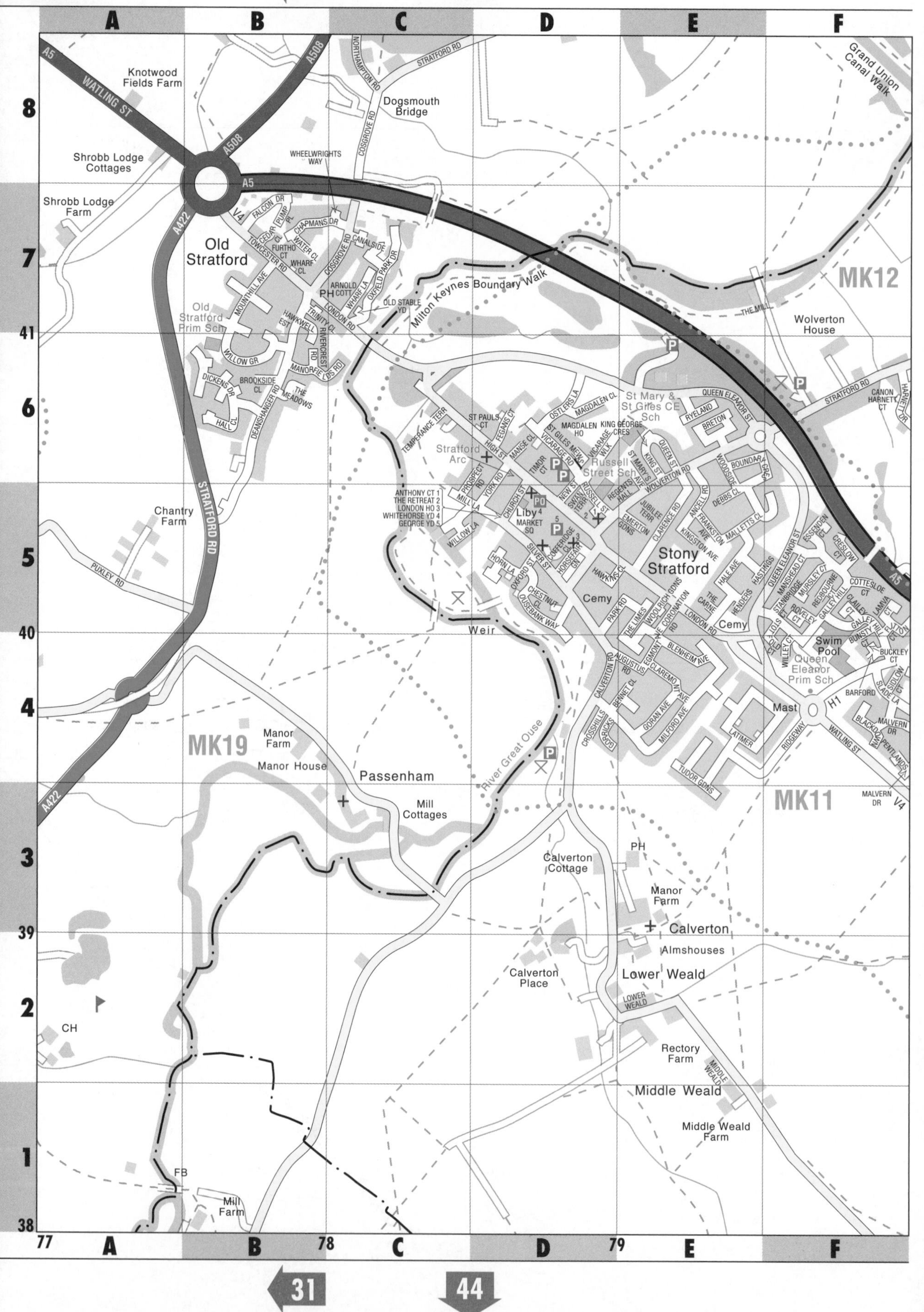
A
B
C
D
E
F
8
7
41
6
5
40
4
3
39
2
1
38
77
78
79
Knotwood Fields Farm
WATLING ST
A5
A508
Shrobb Lodge Cottages
Shrobb Lodge Farm
NORTHAMPTON RD
STRATFORD RD
Dogsmouth Bridge
COSGROVE RD
WHEELWRIGHTS WAY
Grand Union Canal Walk
A422
V4
Old Stratford
FALCON DR
CEDAR CL
PUMP PL
CHAPMANS DR
TOWCESTER RD
FURTHO CT
WATER CL
WHARF CL
CANALSIDE
OXFIELD PARK DR
WHARF LA
ARNOLD COTT
PH
MOUNTHILL AVE
Old Stratford Prim Sch
HAWKWELL EST
TRINITY CL
LONDON RD
OLD STABLE YD
Milton Keynes Boundary Walk
THE MILL
MK12
Wolverton House
WILLOW GR
RAVENCREST RD
MANORFIELDS RD
DICKENS DR
BROOKSIDE CL
THE MEADOWS
HALL CL
DEANSHANGER RD
OSTLERS LA
MAGDALEN CL
St Mary & St Giles CE Sch
QUEEN ELEANOR ST
STRATFORD RD
CANON HARNETT CT
HARNETT DR
RYELAND
BRETON
TEMPERANCE TERR
ST PAULS CT
FEGANS CT
MAGDALEN HO
KING GEORGE CRES
VICARAGE WLK
Stratford Arc
HIGH ST
MANSE CL
ST GILES MEWS
VICARAGE RD
Russell Street Sch
QUEEN ST
KING ST
ST MARY'S AVE
BOUNDARY CRES
WOODSIDE
PROSPECT RD
YORK RD
TIMOR CT
NEW ST
RUSSELL ST
REGENTS HALL
WOLVERTON RD
ANTHONY CT 1
THE RETREAT 2
LONDON HO 3
WHITEHORSE YD 4
GEORGE YD 5
MILL LA
CHURCH ST
PO
Liby
MARKET SQ
JUBILEE TERR
CLARENCE RD
ANCELL RD
DEBBS CL
FRANKSTON AVE
MALLETTS CL
ESSENDEN CT
CRESLOW CT
WILLOW LA
SILVER ST
COPPERIDGE CL
HORSEFAIR GN
EMERTON GDNS
KINGSTON AVE
Stony Stratford
HALE AVE
HASTINGS
QUEEN ELEANOR ST
MANSHEAD CT
MURSLEY CT
REDBOURNE CT
COTTESLOE CT
HORN LA
OXFORD ST
CHESTNUT CL
OUSEBANK WAY
HAWKINS CL
Cemy
PARK RD
THE LIMES
WOOLRICH GDNS
CORONATION RD
THE CARNE
LONDON RD
HENDERS
Cemy
STANBRIDGE CT
ROVELEY CT
GALLEY HILL
CLAILEY CT
LAMVA
Weir
Swim Pool
Queen Eleanor Prim Sch
BUNSTY
BUCKLEY CT
OLD CL
WILLEY CT
EGMONT AVE
BLENHEIM AVE
CALVERTON RD
AUGUSTUS RD
CLAREMONT AVE
BENNET CL
GORAN AVE
MILFORD AVE
Mast
H1
BARFORD
SLADE LA
MK19
Manor Farm
Manor House
CROSSHILLS
GORRICKS
River Great Ouse
LATIMER
RIDGEWAY
WATLING ST
BLACKDOWN
MALVERN DR
PENTLANDS
Passenham
TUDOR GDNS
MK11
MALVERN DR
V4
Mill Cottages
Calverton Cottage
PH
Manor Farm
Calverton
Almshouses
Calverton Place
Lower Weald
LOWER WEALD
CH
Rectory Farm
MIDDLE WEALD
Middle Weald
Middle Weald Farm
FB
Mill Farm

31
44

A6
1 MAIGNO WY
2 HAMON WY
3 ALVRIC WY
4 BRIDGE HOOK CL

20
34

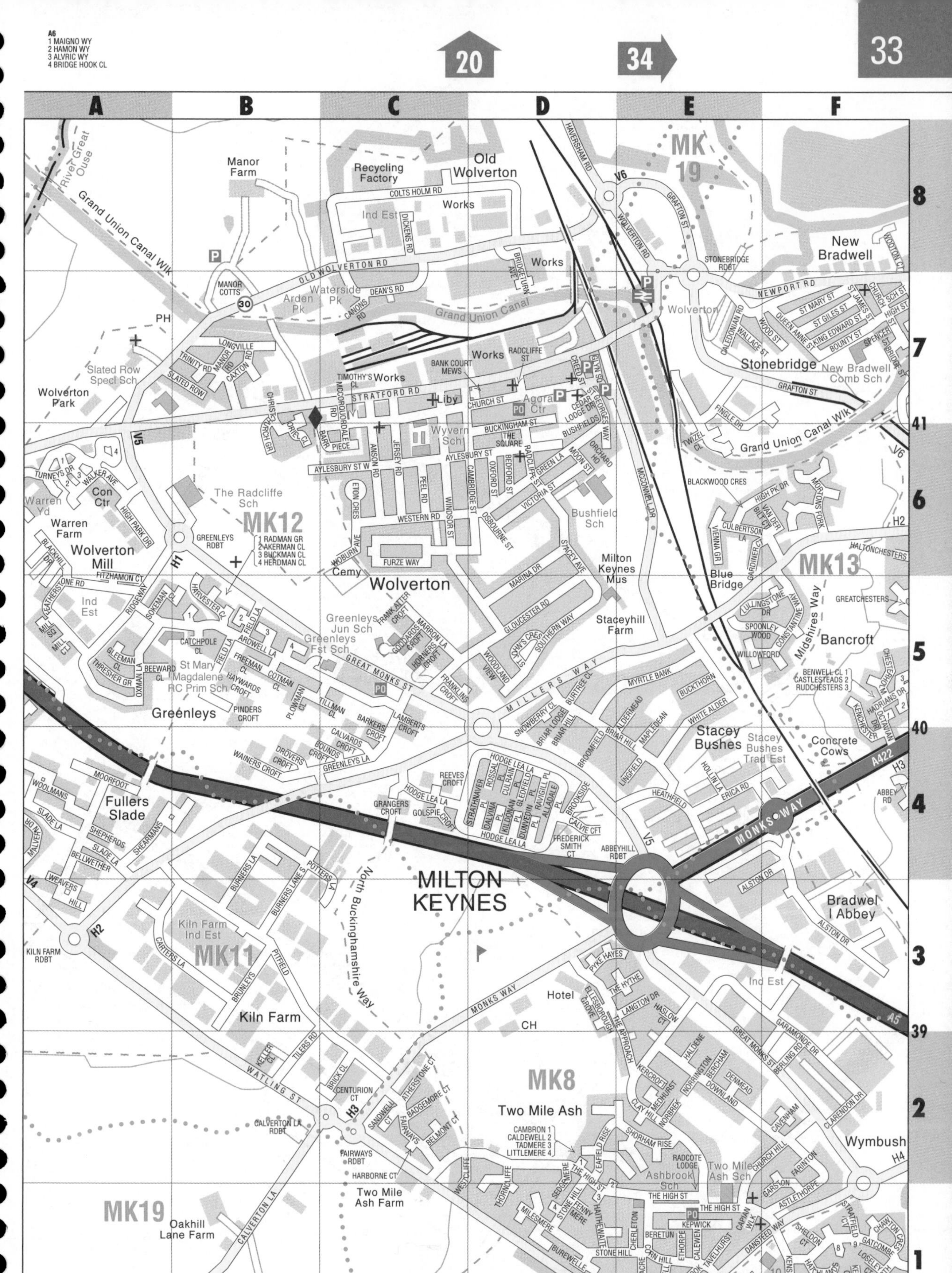

45
34

F1
1 PORTCHESTER CT
2 PETWORTH HO
3 ALBURY CT
4 CORSHAM CT
5 BOWOOD CT
6 ATTINGHAM HILL
7 LONGLEAT CT
8 PECKOVER CT
9 HOGARTHS CT

10 Holmwood Sch
11 KELMARSH COURT

33
21

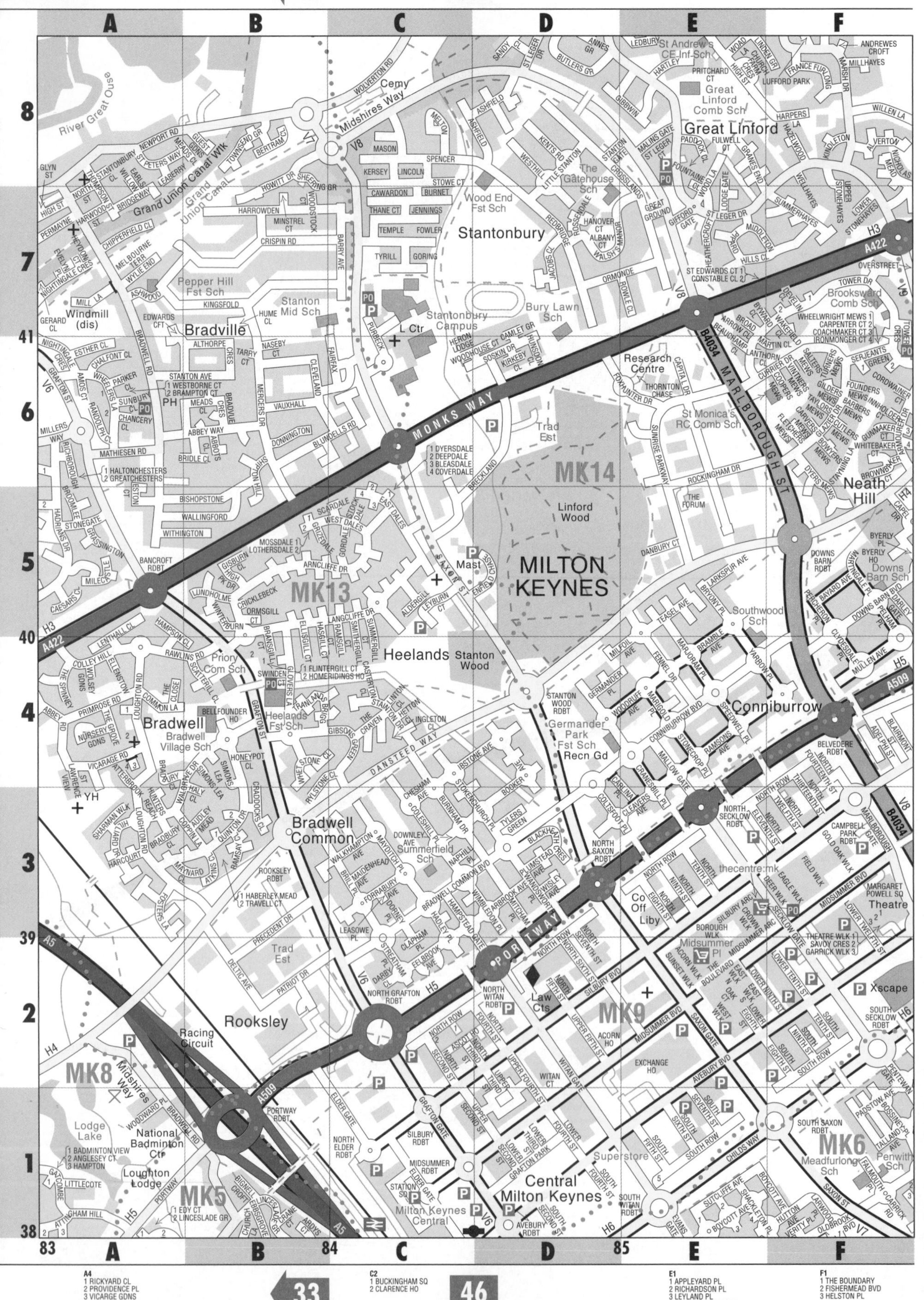

A4
1 RICKYARD CL
2 PROVIDENCE PL
3 VICARGE GDNS
4 ALEXANDRA CT

C2
1 BUCKINGHAM SQ
2 CLARENCE HO

E1
1 APPLEYARD PL
2 RICHARDSON PL
3 LEYLAND PL
4 BARRINGTON MEWS
5 PETERSFIELD GN

F1
1 THE BOUNDARY
2 FISHERMEAD BVD
3 HELSTON PL

33
46

22
36

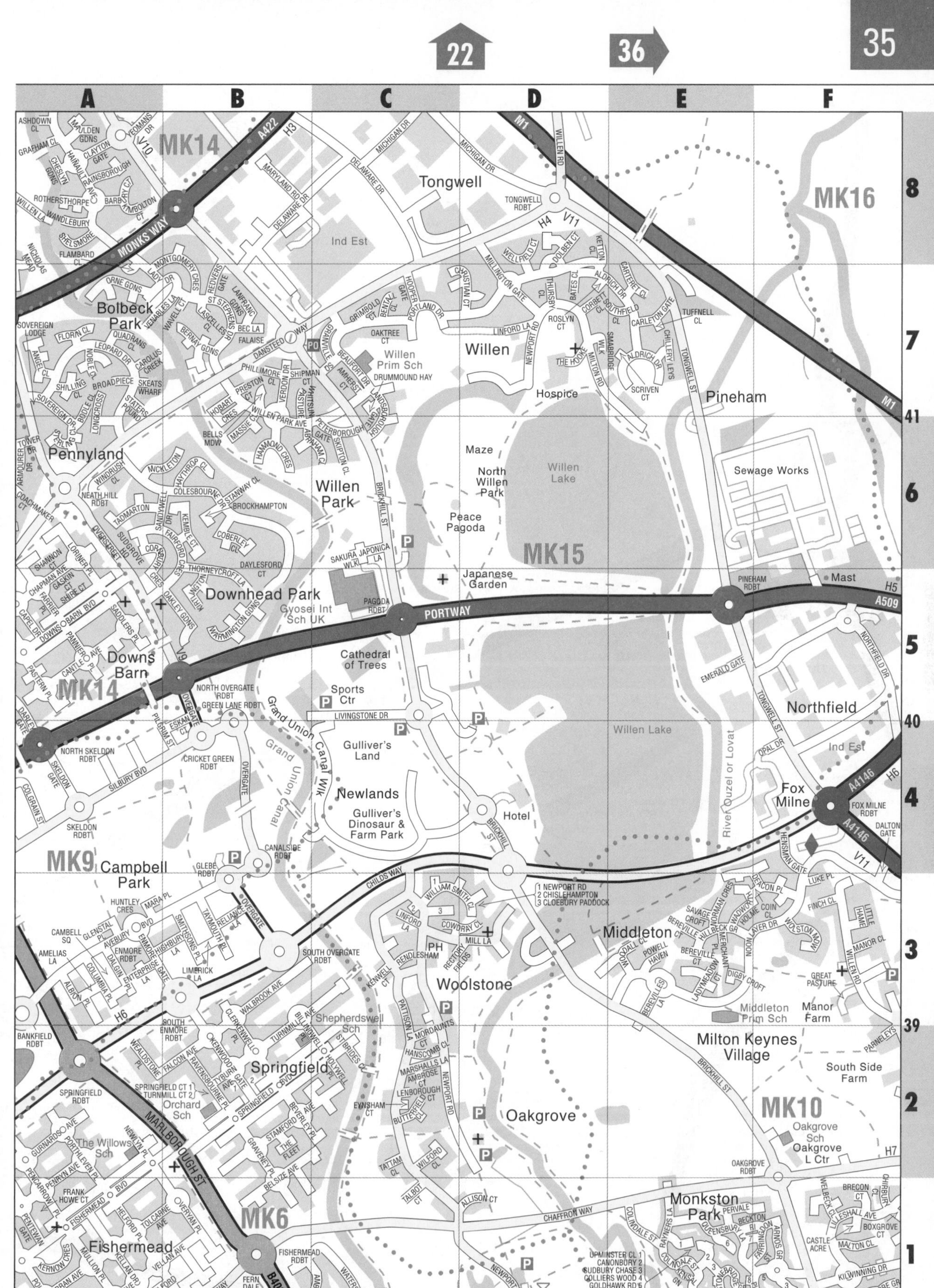

A1
1 POLMARTIN CT
2 PENGELLY CT
3 HELSTON PL

F1
1 TEWKESBURY LA
2 WOODSPRING CT
3 MAIDA VALE
4 PIMLICO CT
5 HENDON CT
6 ISLINGTON GR

47
36

35
23

A1
1 PERSHORE CROFT
2 STAVORDALE
3 TYNEMOUTH RISE
4 LEOMINSTER GATE

A3
1 FRESHFIELD AVE
2 PAIGNTON WAY

A4
1 WEYBOURNE RD
2 GOODDRINGTON PL
3 KELLING WAY

B1
1 LAUNDE
2 ST BOTOLPHS

B2
1 MAYPOOL WAY
2 BIGTON CHASE
3 KIDDERMINSTER WLK

35

B3
1 BLUE ANCHOR AVE
2 HAWORTH CFT
3 ROPLEY WAY
4 CLIPSTONE BROOK WAY
5 BUTTERFLY GATE
6 RAVENSGLASS CROFT
7 ARDLEY MEWS

48

24

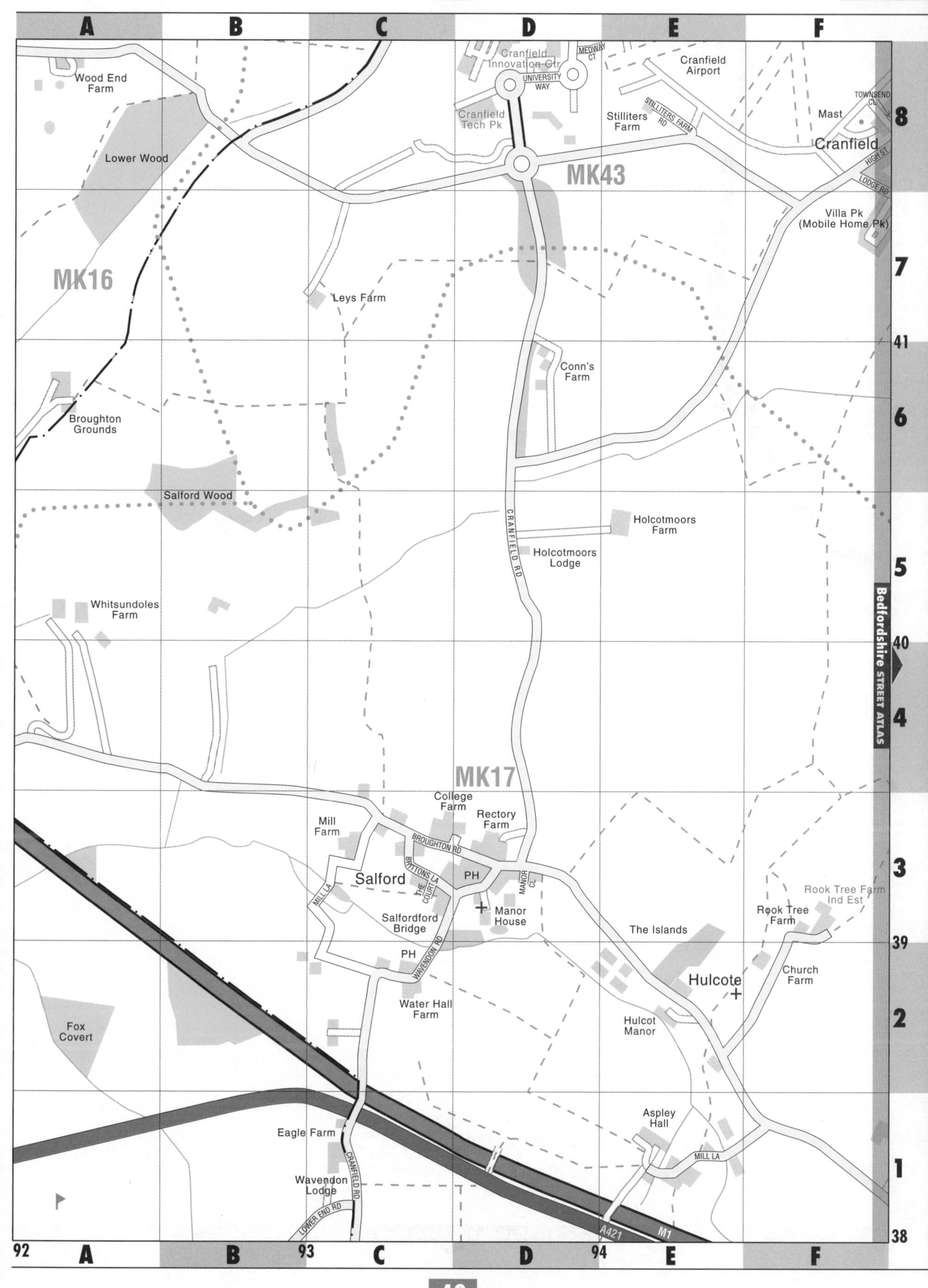

Wood End Farm
Lower Wood
Cranfield Innovation Ctr
MEDWAY CT
UNIVERSITY WAY
Cranfield Airport
Cranfield Tech Pk
Stilliters Farm
STILLITERS FARM RD
TOWNSEND CL
Mast
Cranfield
HIGH ST
LODGE RD
MK43
Villa Pk (Mobile Home Pk)
MK16
Leys Farm
Conn's Farm
Broughton Grounds
Salford Wood
Holcotmoors Farm
Holcotmoors Lodge
CRANFIELD RD
Whitsundoles Farm
Bedfordshire STREET ATLAS
MK17
College Farm
Rectory Farm
Mill Farm
BROUGHTON RD
BRITTONS LA
THE COURT
MANOR CL
Salford
PH
MILL LA
Manor House
Salfordford Bridge
The Islands
Rook Tree Farm Ind Est
Rook Tree Farm
Church Farm
Hulcote
WAVENDON RD
Water Hall Farm
Hulcot Manor
Fox Covert
Aspley Hall
Eagle Farm
MILL LA
Wavendon Lodge
LOWER END RD
A421
M1
A B C D E F
8 7 6 5 4 3 2 1
41 40 39 38
92 93 94

49

26

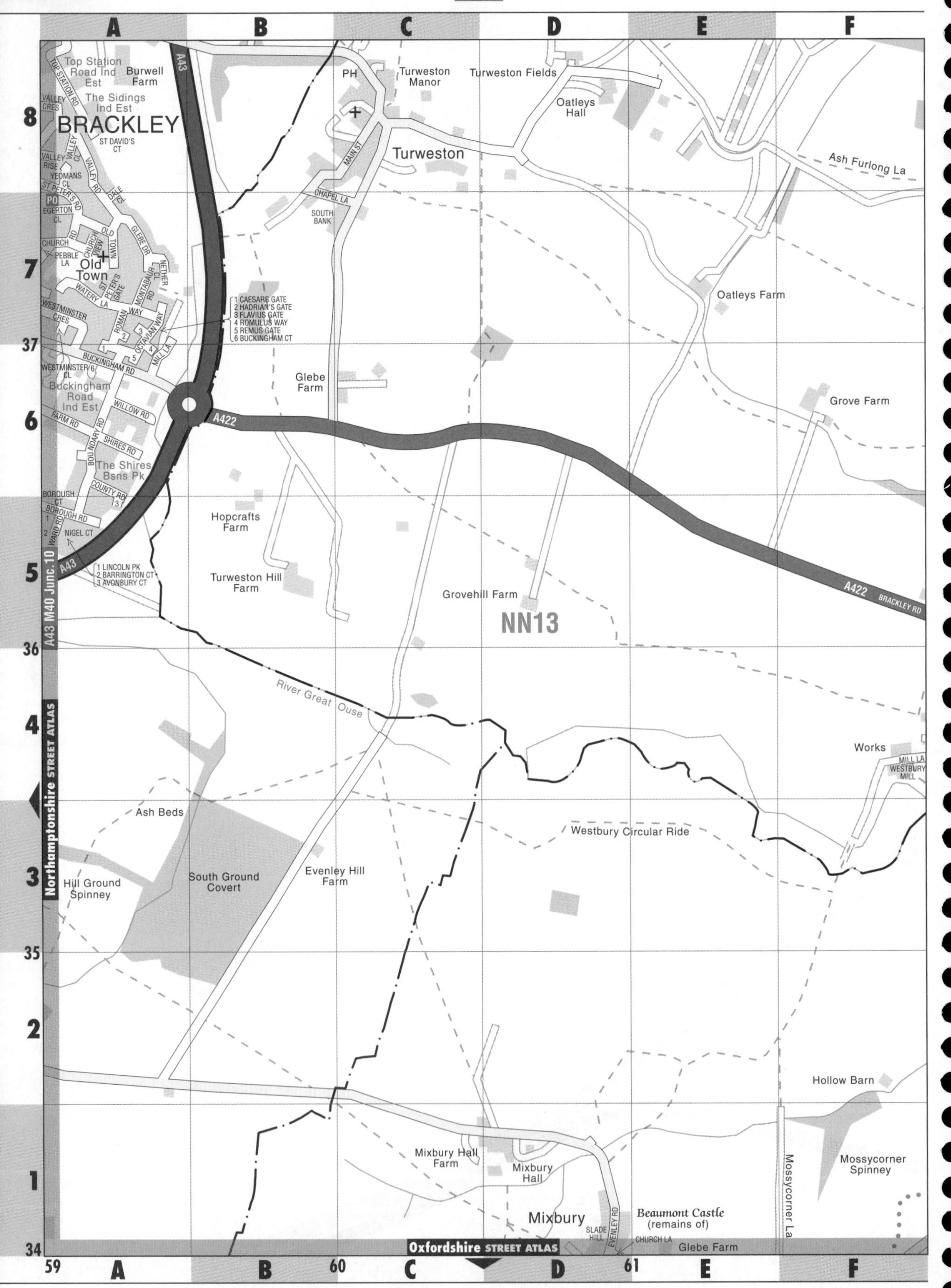

A B C D E F
BRACKLEY
Top Station Road Ind Est
Burwell Farm
The Sidings Ind Est
Old Town
Buckingham Road Ind Est
The Shires Bsns Pk
Turweston
Turweston Manor
Turweston Fields
Oatleys Hall
Ash Furlong La
Oatleys Farm
Glebe Farm
Grove Farm
Hopcrafts Farm
Turweston Hill Farm
Grovehill Farm
NN13
A43
A422
BRACKLEY RD
A43 M40 Junc.10
1 CAESARS GATE
2 HADRIAN'S GATE
3 FLAVIUS GATE
4 ROMULUS WAY
5 REMUS GATE
6 BUCKINGHAM CT
1 LINCOLN PK
2 BARRINGTON CT
3 AVONBURY CT
River Great Ouse
Works
MILL LA
WESTBURY MILL
Ash Beds
Westbury Circular Ride
Hill Ground Spinney
South Ground Covert
Evenley Hill Farm
Hollow Barn
Mossycorner Spinney
Mossycorner La
Mixbury Hall Farm
Mixbury Hall
Mixbury
Beaumont Castle (remains of)
Glebe Farm
SLADE HILL
EVENLEY RD
CHURCH LA
Northamptonshire STREET ATLAS
Oxfordshire STREET ATLAS
8 7 37 6 5 36 4 3 35 2 1 34
59 60 61

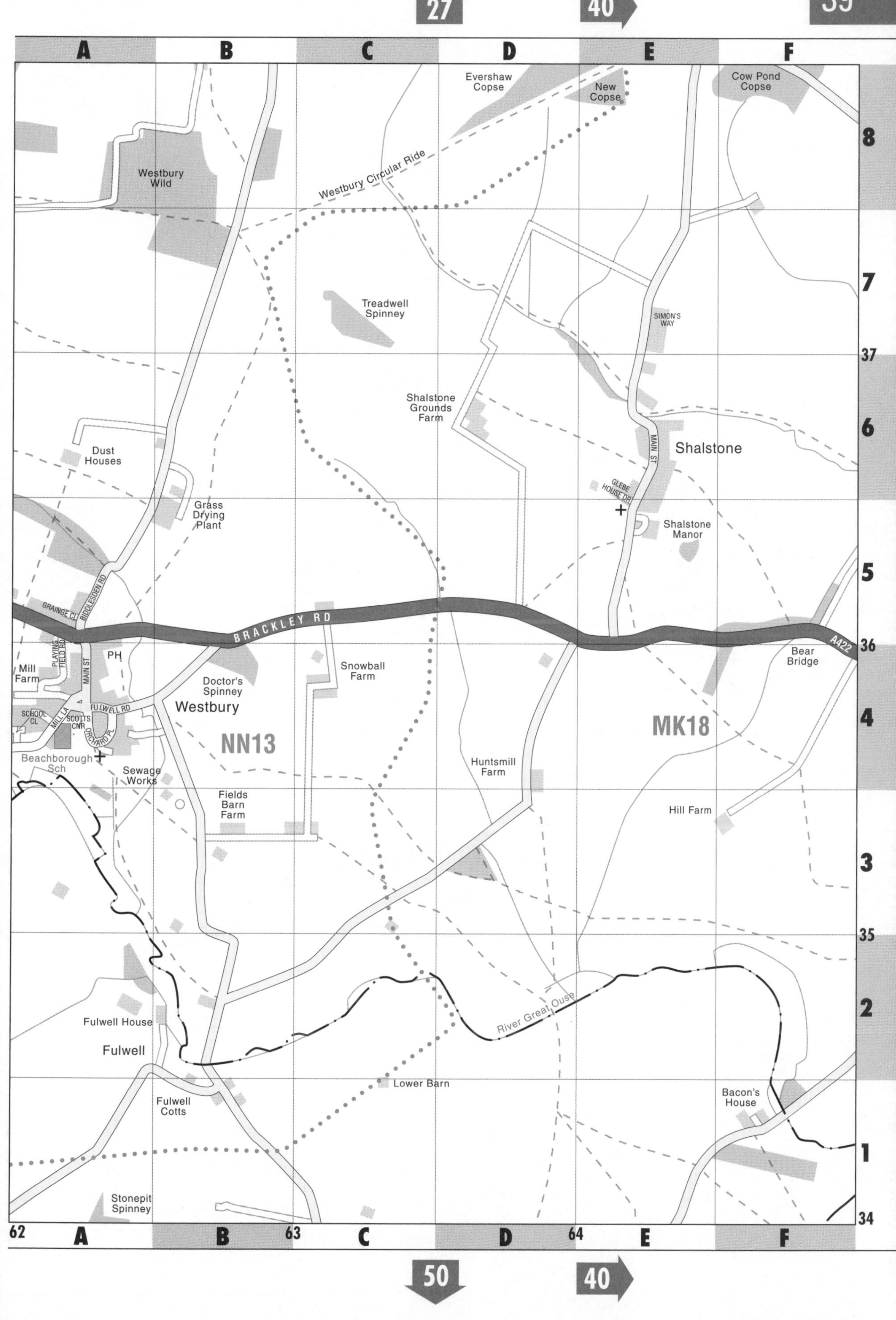
27
40
A
B
C
D
E
F
Evershaw Copse
New Copse
Cow Pond Copse
Westbury Wild
Westbury Circular Ride
Treadwell Spinney
SIMON'S WAY
Shalstone Grounds Farm
MAIN ST
Shalstone
GLEBE HOUSE DR
Shalstone Manor
Dust Houses
Grass Drying Plant
BIDDLESDEN RD
GRAINGE CL
BRACKLEY RD
A422
Bear Bridge
PLAYING FIELD RD
MAIN ST
PH
Mill Farm
Doctor's Spinney
Snowball Farm
Westbury
FULWELL RD
SCHOOL CL
MILL LA
SCOTTS CNR
ORCHARD PL
NN13
MK18
Beachborough Sch
Sewage Works
Huntsmill Farm
Fields Barn Farm
Hill Farm
Fulwell House
Fulwell
River Great Ouse
Lower Barn
Fulwell Cotts
Bacon's House
Stonepit Spinney
8
7
37
6
5
36
4
3
35
2
1
34
62
63
64
50
40

39
28

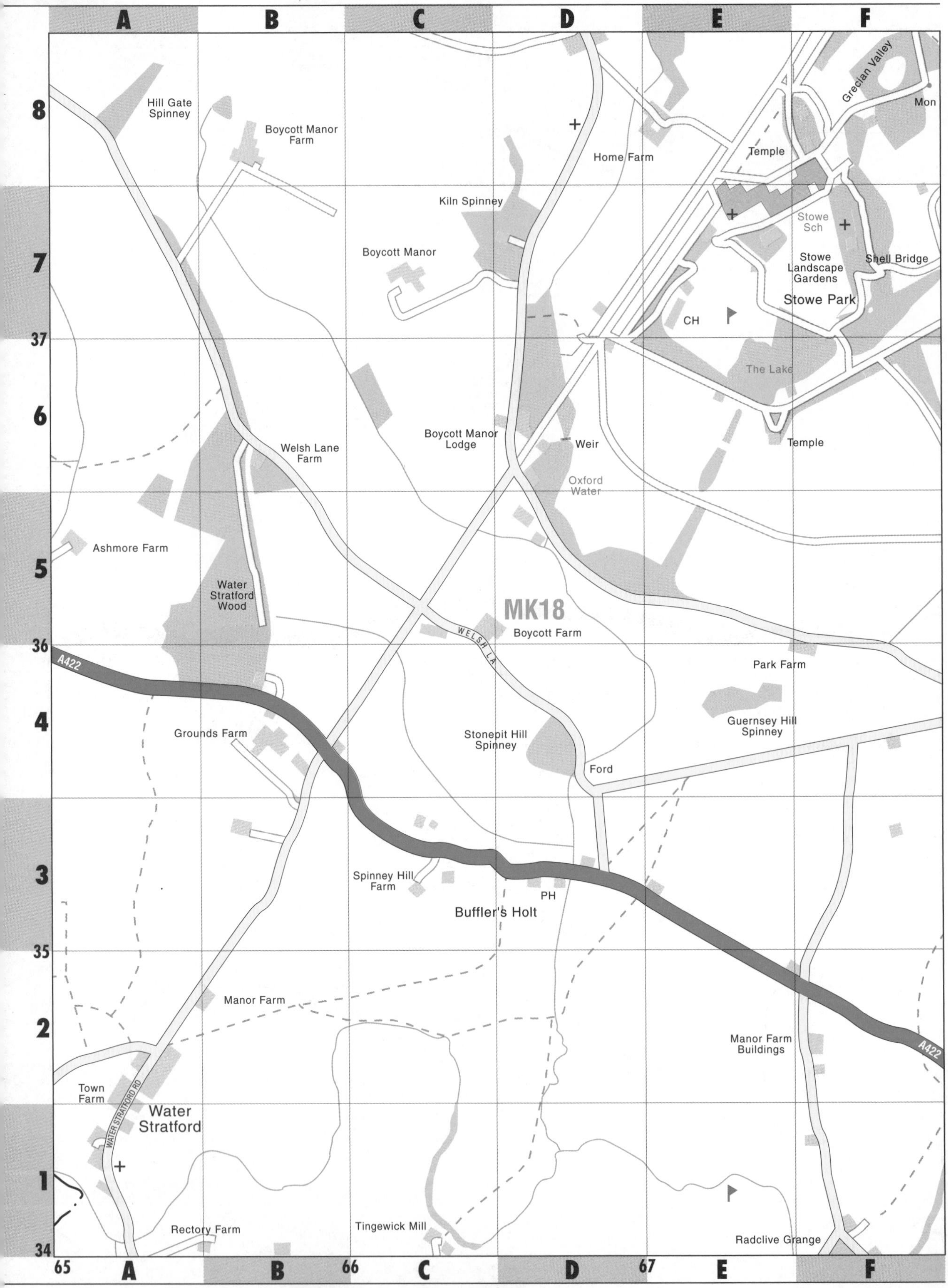

A B C D E F
8 7 37 6 5 36 4 3 35 2 1 34
Hill Gate Spinney
Boycott Manor Farm
Home Farm
Grecian Valley
Mon
Temple
Kiln Spinney
Stowe Sch
Boycott Manor
Stowe Landscape Gardens
Shell Bridge
Stowe Park
CH
The Lake
Boycott Manor Lodge
Weir
Temple
Welsh Lane Farm
Oxford Water
Ashmore Farm
Water Stratford Wood
MK18
Boycott Farm
WELSH LA
A422
Park Farm
Guernsey Hill Spinney
Grounds Farm
Stonepit Hill Spinney
Ford
Spinney Hill Farm
PH
Buffler's Holt
Manor Farm
Manor Farm Buildings
Town Farm
WATER STRATFORD RD
Water Stratford
Rectory Farm
Tingewick Mill
Radclive Grange
65 66 67

39
51

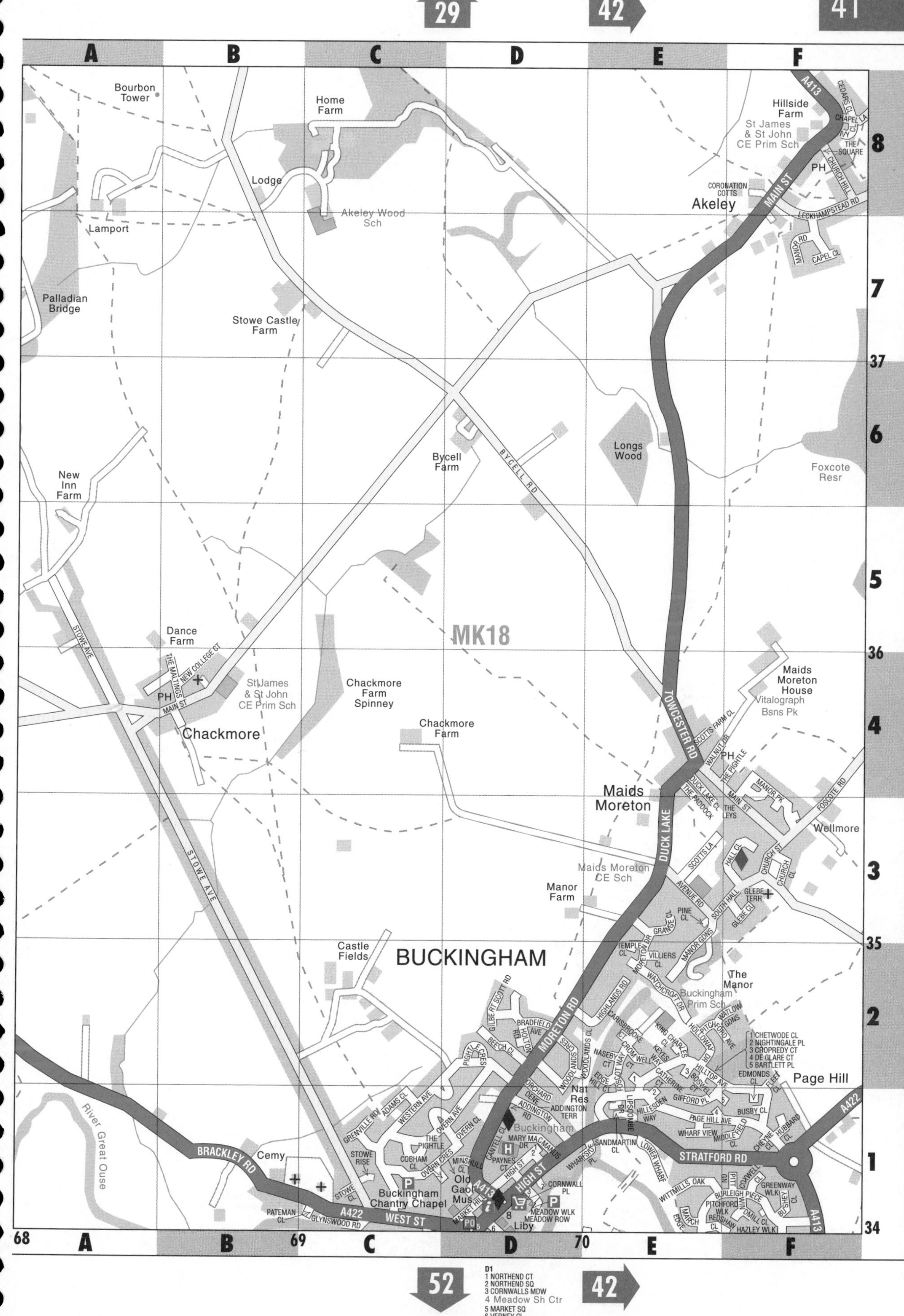
29
42
Bourbon Tower
Home Farm
Lodge
Akeley Wood Sch
Lamport
Palladian Bridge
Stowe Castle Farm
Hillside Farm
St James & St John CE Prim Sch
Akeley
CORONATION COTTS
MAIN ST
LECKHAMPSTEAD RD
MANOR RD
CAPEL CL
CEDARS CL
CHAPEL LA
IVY CL
THE SQUARE
CHURCH HILL
PH
A413
Longs Wood
Foxcote Resr
New Inn Farm
Bycell Farm
BYCELL RD
MK18
Dance Farm
THE MALTINGS
NEW COLLEGE CT
MAIN ST
PH
St James & St John CE Prim Sch
Chackmore
Chackmore Farm Spinney
Chackmore Farm
STOWE AVE
TOWCESTER RD
Maids Moreton House
Vitalograph Bsns Pk
SCOTTS FARM CL
WALNUT DR
THE PIGHTLE
MANOR PK
FOXCOTE RD
Maids Moreton
DUCK LAKE
DUCK LAKE CL
THE PADDOCK
THE LEYS
Wellmore
SCOTTS LA
HALL CL
CHURCH ST
CHURCH CL
Maids Moreton CE Sch
Manor Farm
AVENUE RD
SOUTH HALL
GLEBE TERR
GLEBE CL
PINE CL
TEMPLE CL
Castle Fields
BUCKINGHAM
MORETON DR
VILLIERS CL
MANOR GDNS
WATCHCROFT DR
The Manor
Buckingham Prim Sch
GILBERT SCOTT RD
BRADFIELD AVE
HOLTON RD
MORETON RD
HIGHLANDS RD
CARISBROOKE CT
KING CHARLES CL
HOLLOWAY DR
PITCHFORD AVE
WATLOW GDNS
1 CHETWODE CL
2 NIGHTINGALE PL
3 CROPREDY CT
4 DE CLARE CT
5 BARTLETT PL
EDMONDS CL
FLEET CL
Page Hill
PIGHTLE CRES
BEECH CL
WOODLANDS CRES
WOODLANDS CL
NASEBY CT
CROMWELL CT
KEYES WAY
CATHERINE CT
HILLTOP AVE
BOSWELL CT
EDGE HILL CT
FOSCOTT WAY
Nat Res
ORCHARD DENE
ADDINGTON RD
ADDINGTON TERR
HILLESDEN WAY
GIFFORD PL
PAGE HILL AVE
BUSBY CL
LIPSCOMBE DR
WHARF VIEW
MIDDLEFIELD CL
CHEYNE CL
HUBBARD CL
A422
ADAMS CL
WESTERN AVE
GRENVILLE RD
OVERN AVE
OVERN CL
THE PIGHTLE
Buckingham
CANTELL CL
MARY MACMANUS DR
PAYNES CT
SANDMARTIN CL
LOWER WHARF
STRATFORD RD
BRACKLEY RD
River Great Ouse
Cemy
STOWE RISE
COBHAM CL
OVERN CRES
MINSHULL CL
HIGH ST
HIGH ST
WHARFSIDE PL
CORNWALL PL
WITTMILLS OAK
GREENWAY WLK
COXWELL CL
PITT GN
BURLEIGH PIECE
BISHEY CL
STOWE CL
Buckingham Chantry Chapel
Old Gaol Mus
MARKET HILL
MEADOW WLK
MEADOW ROW
PITCHFORD WLK
REDSHAW CL
WINDMILL CL
MARCH EDGE
HAZLEY WLK
PATEMAN CL
GLYNSWOOD RD
A422
WEST ST
PO
Liby
A413
A B C D E F
8 7 37 6 5 36 4 3 35 2 1 34
68 69 70
52
42
D1
1 NORTHEND CT
2 NORTHEND SQ
3 CORNWALLS MDW
4 Meadow Sh Ctr
5 MARKET SQ
6 VERNEY CL
7 CECILS YARD
8 Buckingham Ctr

41 30

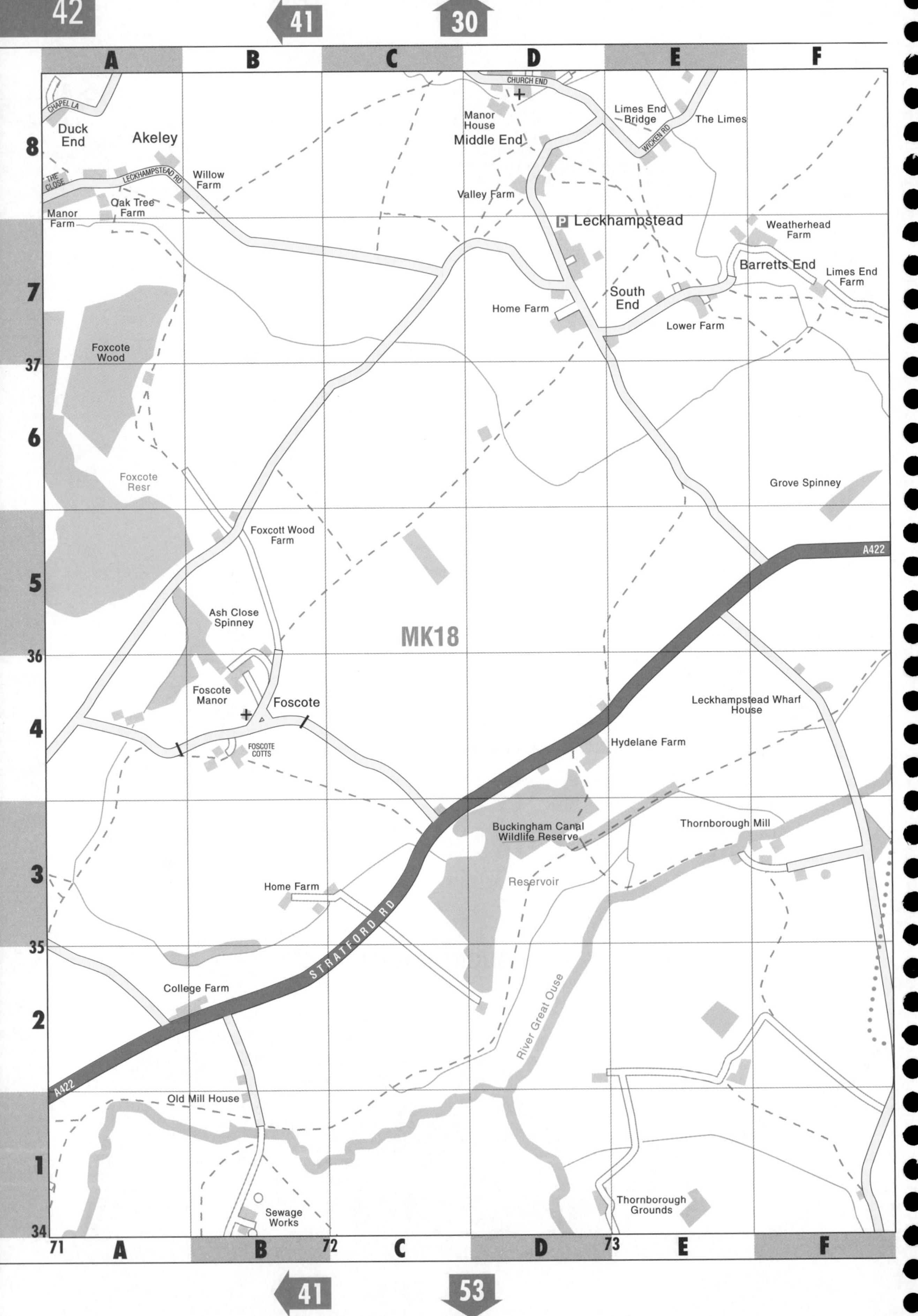

A B C D E F
8 7 37 6 5 36 4 3 35 2 1 34
71 72 73
CHURCH END
CHAPEL LA
Duck End
Akeley
Manor House
Middle End
Limes End Bridge
The Limes
WICKEN RD
THE CLOSE
LECKHAMPSTEAD RD
Willow Farm
Oak Tree Farm
Manor Farm
Valley Farm
Leckhampstead
Weatherhead Farm
Barretts End
Limes End Farm
South End
Home Farm
Lower Farm
Foxcote Wood
Foxcote Resr
Grove Spinney
Foxcott Wood Farm
A422
Ash Close Spinney
MK18
Foscote Manor
Foscote
FOSCOTE COTTS
Leckhampstead Wharf House
Hydelane Farm
Buckingham Canal Wildlife Reserve
Thornborough Mill
Reservoir
Home Farm
STRATFORD RD
River Great Ouse
College Farm
Old Mill House
Sewage Works
Thornborough Grounds

41 53

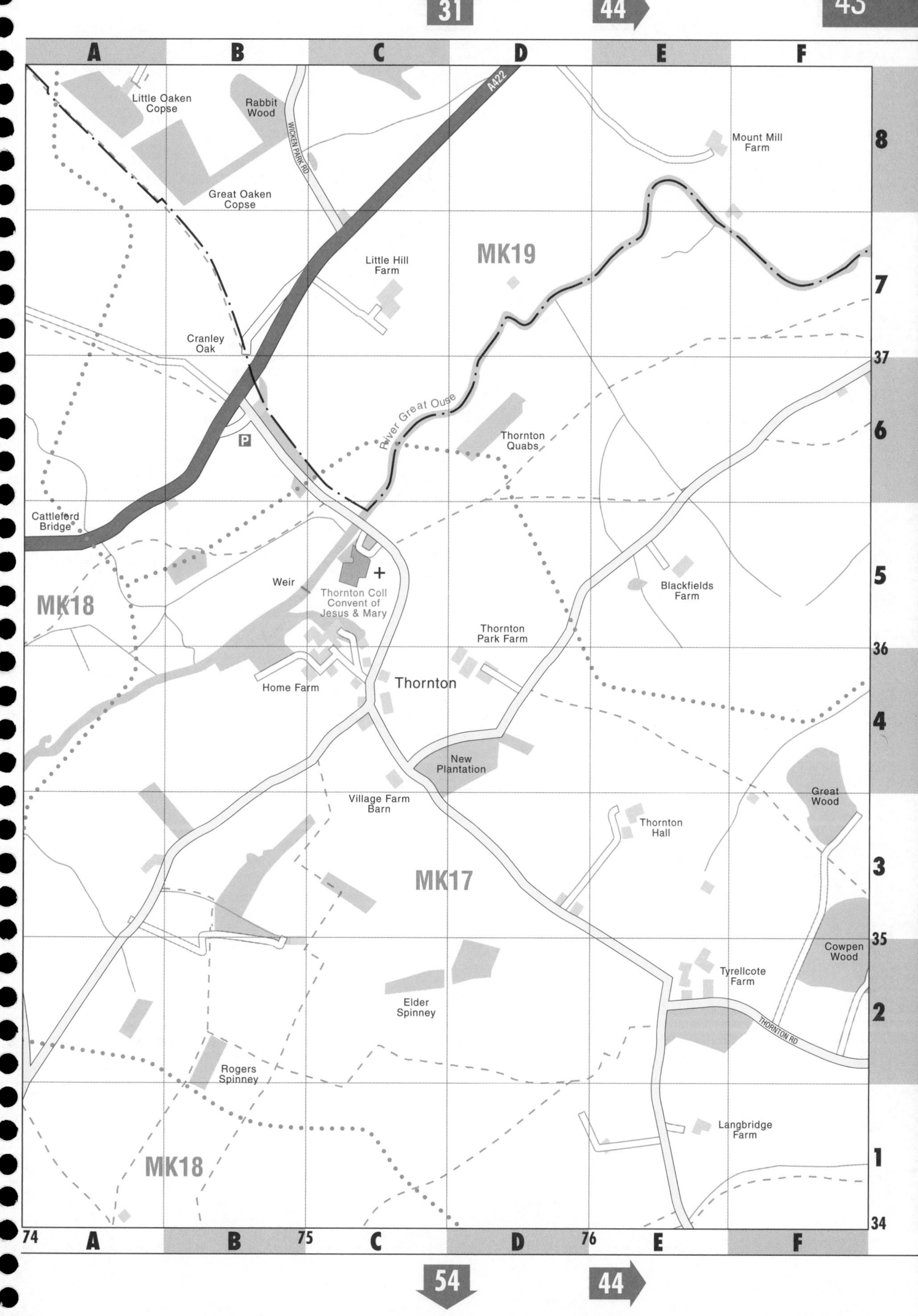
31
44
A
B
C
D
E
F
Little Oaken Copse
Rabbit Wood
WICKEN PARK RD
A422
Mount Mill Farm
8
Great Oaken Copse
Little Hill Farm
MK19
7
Cranley Oak
37
River Great Ouse
Thornton Quabs
6
Cattleford Bridge
Weir
Thornton Coll Convent of Jesus & Mary
Blackfields Farm
5
MK18
Thornton Park Farm
36
Home Farm
Thornton
4
New Plantation
Village Farm Barn
Great Wood
Thornton Hall
3
MK17
35
Cowpen Wood
Tyrellcote Farm
Elder Spinney
THORNTON RD
2
Rogers Spinney
Langbridge Farm
1
MK18
34
74
75
76
54
44

43
32

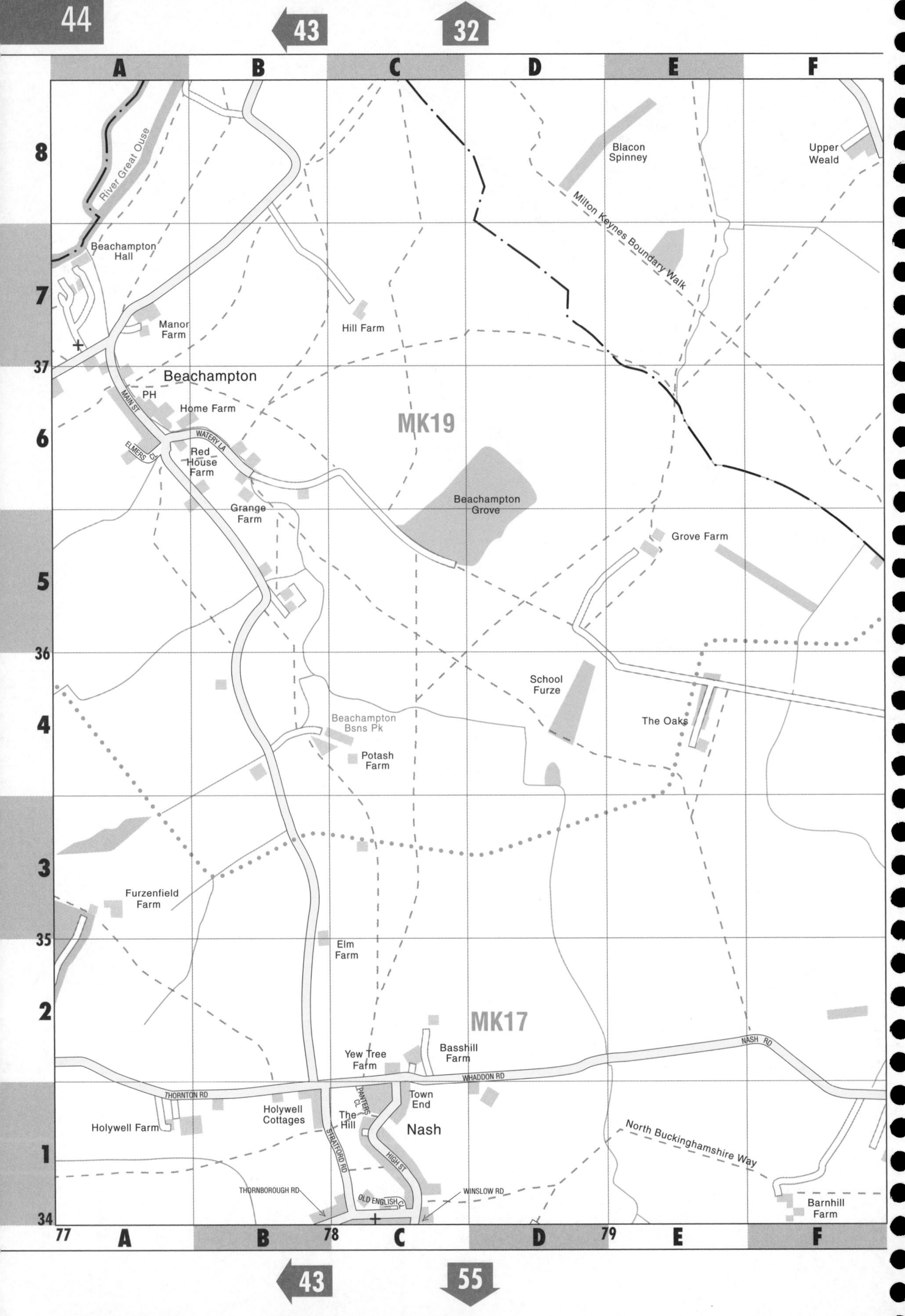
A
B
C
D
E
F
8
7
37
6
5
36
4
3
35
2
1
34
77
78
79
River Great Ouse
Beachampton Hall
Manor Farm
Hill Farm
Blacon Spinney
Upper Weald
Milton Keynes Boundary Walk
Beachampton
PH
Home Farm
MAIN ST
WATERY LA
ELMERS CL
Red House Farm
MK19
Grange Farm
Beachampton Grove
Grove Farm
School Furze
The Oaks
Beachampton Bsns Pk
Potash Farm
Furzenfield Farm
Elm Farm
MK17
Yew Tree Farm
Basshill Farm
NASH RD
WHADDON RD
THORNTON RD
PANTERS CL
Town End
Holywell Cottages
The Hill
Nash
Holywell Farm
STRATFORD RD
HIGH ST
North Buckinghamshire Way
THORNBOROUGH RD
WINSLOW RD
OLD ENGLISH CL
Barnhill Farm

43
55

F8
1 ALBURY CT
2 MENTMORE CT
3 SULGRAVE CT
4 HOUGHTON CT
5 RUSHTON CT
6 HUNTINGBROOKE
7 HAMPTON
8 WADDESDON CL
9 VYNE CRES

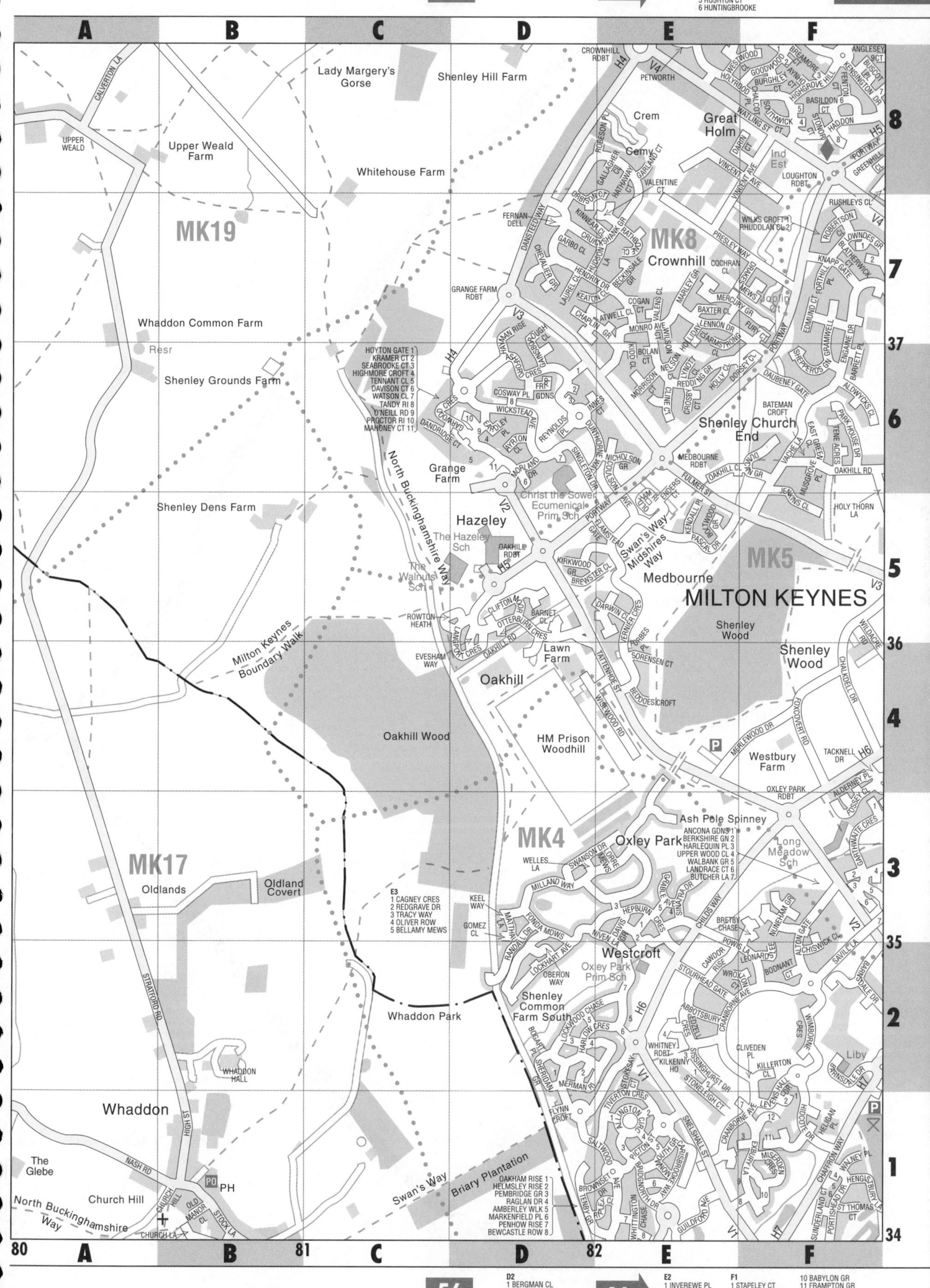

D2
1 BERGMAN CL
2 HAYWORTH PL
3 CRAWFORD WAY
4 STANWYCK LA
5 TIERNEY

E2
1 INVEREWE PL
2 BENMORE RI
3 DOCTON MILL
4 BERRINGTON GR
5 LEMMON WK
6 HARLOW CRES
7 CUSHING DR

F1
1 STAPELEY CT
2 DARTINGTON PL
3 MAPPERTON CL
4 NEWQUAY CL
5 HILBRE CT
6 CORSEWALL PL
7 BRANTWOOD CL
8 NYMANS GATE
9 GLENDURAGAN CT
10 BABYLON GR
11 FRAMPTON GR
12 RUSHFIELDS CL

45
34

A3
1 UPPERWOOD CL

B2
1 GROSMONT CL
2 GOATHLAND CROFT
3 LITTLE HABTON
4 LOWICK PL
5 STAGSHAW GR
6 TARNBROOK CL
7 HAZELHURST

B3
1 ALSTONEFIELD
2 GILLAMOOR CL
3 FADMOOR PL
4 APPLETON MEWS
5 HARTINGTON GR

45

C2
1 GREYSTONLEY
2 DENCHWORTH CT
3 MARSHAW PL
4 FERNBOROUGH HAVEN
5 SPARSHOLT CL

57

D1
1 HUNGERFORD HO
2 ASHBURNHAM CL
3 HOLLINWELL CL
4 DUNBAR CL
5 RIBBLE CRES

E1
1 SEVERN WAY
2 DERWENT DR

F1
1 DURHAM HO
2 PEMBROKE HO
3 RUTLAND HO
4 WALTHAM HO
5 SAWLEY HO
6 NORFOLK HO
7 FLINT HO

35
48

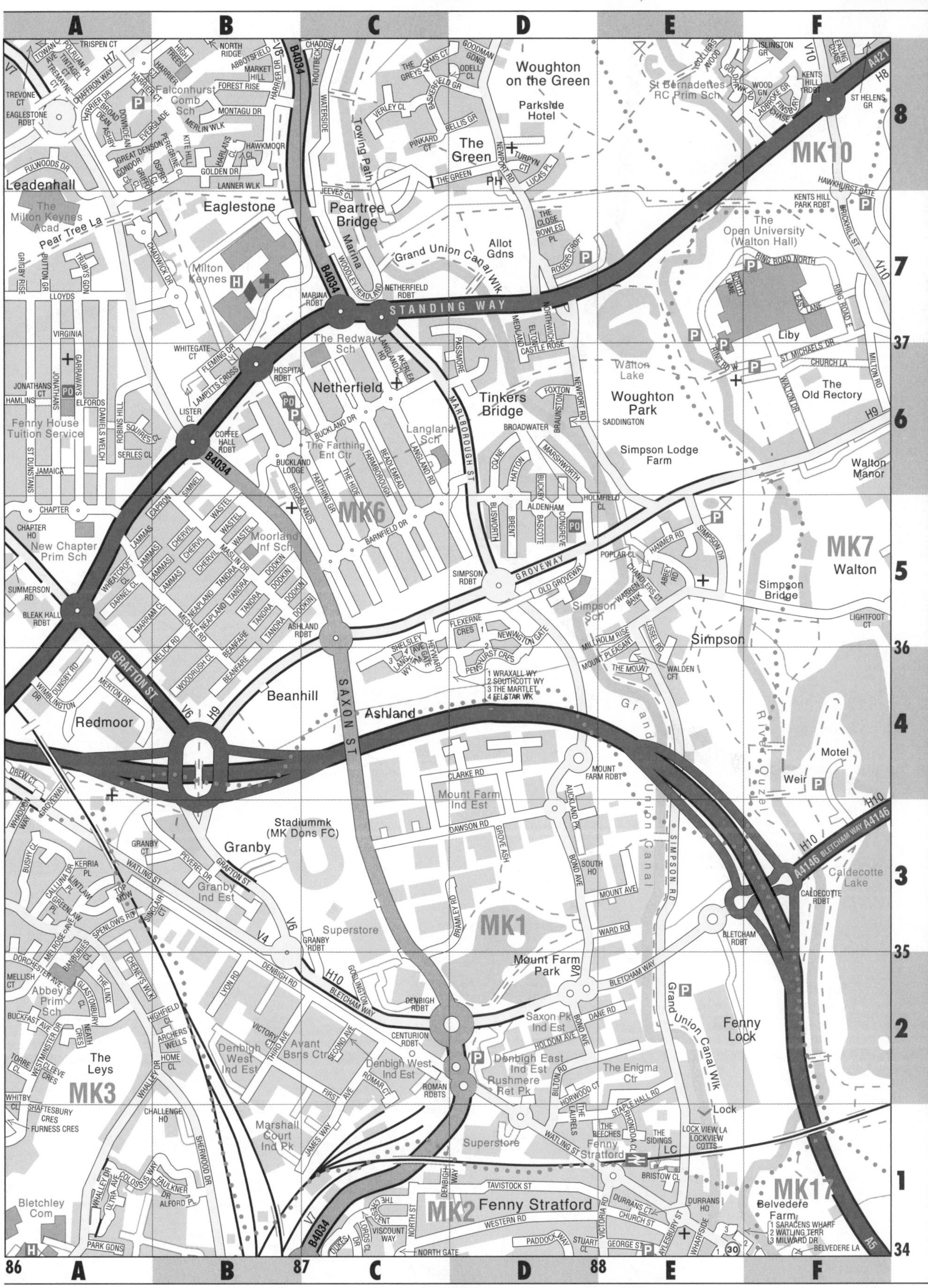
A
B
C
D
E
F
8
7
37
6
5
36
4
3
35
2
1
34
86
87
88
Leadenhall
The Milton Keynes Acad
Pear Tree La
Eaglestone
Falconhurst Comb Sch
Milton Keynes
Peartree Bridge
Marina
Towing Path
The Green
Woughton on the Green
Parkside Hotel
St Bernadettes RC Prim Sch
MK10
The Open University (Walton Hall)
Grand Union Canal Wlk
Allot Gdns
STANDING WAY
B4034
The Redway Sch
Netherfield
Langland Sch
The Farthing Ent Ctr
MK6
Tinkers Bridge
Walton Lake
Woughton Park
Simpson Lodge Farm
Liby
The Old Rectory
Walton Manor
MK7
Walton
Simpson Bridge
Simpson
Simpson Sch
GROVEWAY
Fenny House Tuition Service
New Chapter Prim Sch
Moorland Inf Sch
Beanhill
Ashland
Redmoor
GRAFTON ST
SAXON ST
Grand Union Canal
River Ouzel
Motel
Weir
Mount Farm Ind Est
Stadiummk (MK Dons FC)
Granby
Granby Ind Est
Superstore
MK1
Mount Farm Park
Caldecotte Lake
BLETCHAM WAY
A4146
A421
A5
Abbey's Prim Sch
The Leys
MK3
Denbigh West Ind Est
Avant Bsns Ctr
Denbigh East Ind Est
Saxon Pk Ind Est
Rushmere Ret Pk
The Enigma Ctr
Fenny Lock
Lock
Marshall Court Ind Pk
Fenny Stratford
MK2
MK17
Belvedere Farm
Bletchley Com
WATLING ST
1 SARACENS WHARF
2 WATLING TERR
3 MILWARD DR
1 WRAXALL WY
2 SOUTHCOTT WY
3 THE MARTLET
4 FELSTAR WK

58
48

A B C D E F
8 7 6 5 4 3 2 1
37 36 35 34
89 90 91
MILTON KEYNES
Kents Hill
Training Ctr
MK10
Ind Est
Brinklow
Glebe Farm
Wavendon Tower
The Old Rectory
Wavendon
Wavendon Manor
St Marys Wavendon Prim Sch
Church Farm
The Old Farm
Nursery
Wavendon Gate
Wavendon Gate Comb Sch
Walton Manor
Walnut Tree
MK7
Walton High Sch
Walton
Heronshaw Sch
Heronsgate Sch
Old Farm Park
Woodley's Farm
Browns Wood
Walton Park
Caldecotte Lake
Tilbrook
Tilbrook Ind Est
Wavendon Wood
Caldecotte
Bow Brickhill Crossing
Tilbrook Farm
Rectory Farm
Blind Pond Ind Est
Brown's Wood
MK17
Bow Brickhill Park
Bow Brickhill
Bow Brickhill Prim Sch
Weeks Covert
Bow Brickhill Heath
The Heath
Mast
CH
PH
Hotel
A421
A4146
A5130
V10
V11
H9
H10
NEWPORT RD
GROVEWAY
TONGWELL ST
BLETCHAM WAY
BRICKHILL ST
WOBURN SANDS RD
BOW BRICKHILL RD
STATION RD
CHURCH RD
WALTON RD
LC

37

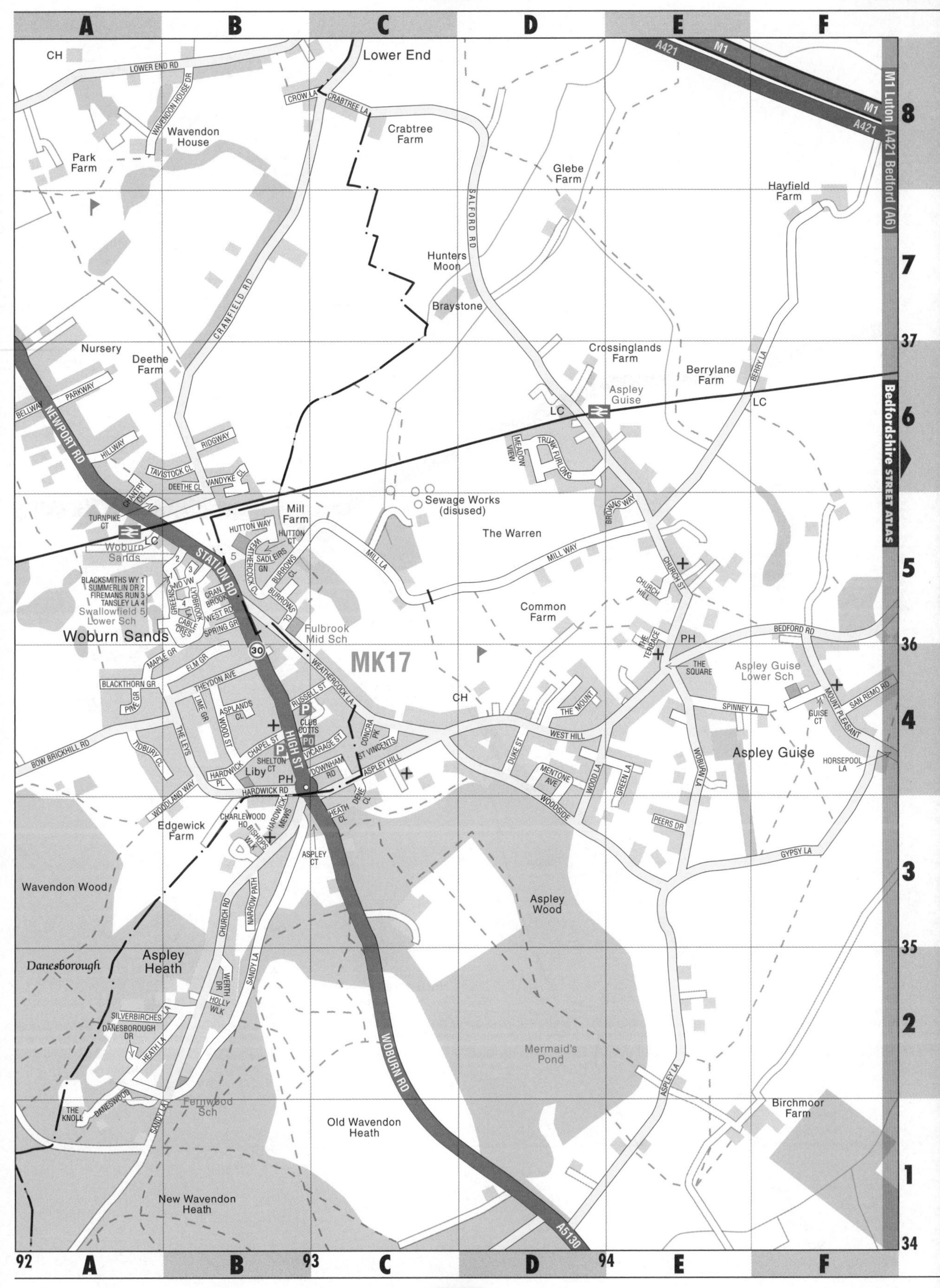
Lower End
Crabtree Farm
Wavendon House
Park Farm
Glebe Farm
Hayfield Farm
Hunters Moon
Braystone
Nursery
Deethe Farm
Crossinglands Farm
Berrylane Farm
Aspley Guise
Sewage Works (disused)
Mill Farm
The Warren
Woburn Sands
Common Farm
Fulbrook Mid Sch
Woburn Sands
MK17
Aspley Guise Lower Sch
Aspley Guise
Edgewick Farm
Wavendon Wood
Aspley Wood
Danesborough
Aspley Heath
Mermaid's Pond
Birchmoor Farm
Fernwood Sch
Old Wavendon Heath
New Wavendon Heath
M1 Luton A421 Bedford (A6)
Bedfordshire STREET ATLAS
STATION RD
HIGH ST
WOBURN RD
NEWPORT RD
SALFORD RD
CRANFIELD RD
MILL WAY
BEDFORD RD
WEST HILL
BOW BRICKHILL RD
HARDWICK RD
A5130
A421
M1

60

39

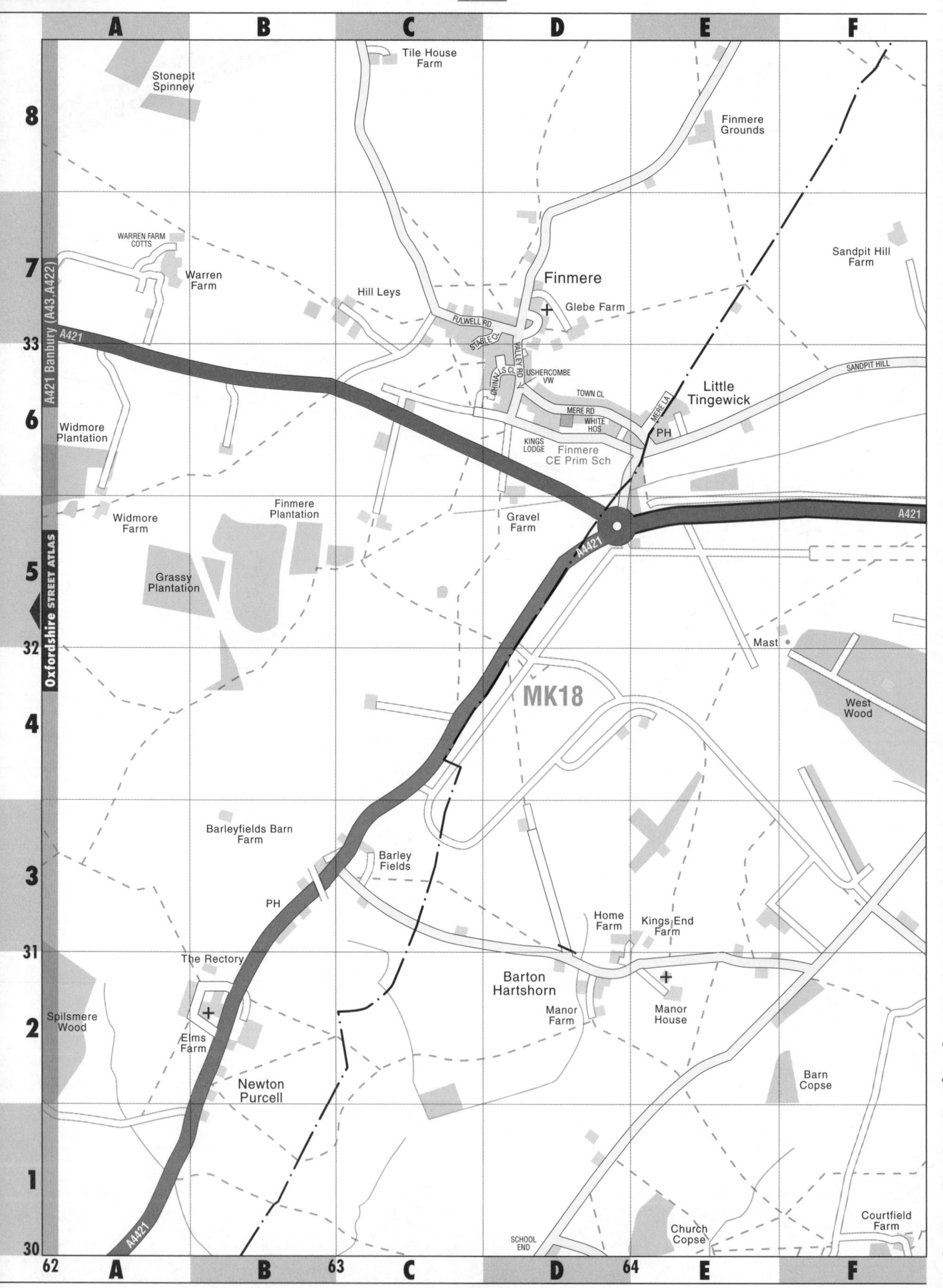
A
B
C
D
E
F
Tile House Farm
Stonepit Spinney
Finmere Grounds
WARREN FARM COTTS
Warren Farm
Sandpit Hill Farm
Finmere
Hill Leys
Glebe Farm
FULWELL RD
STABLE CL
VALLEY RD
CHINALLS CL
USHERCOMBE VW
TOWN CL
MERE RD
WHITE HOS
MERE LA
SANDPIT HILL
Little Tingewick
PH
KINGS LODGE
Finmere CE Prim Sch
Widmore Plantation
A421
A421 Banbury (A43,A422)
Oxfordshire STREET ATLAS
Finmere Plantation
Widmore Farm
Gravel Farm
A4421
Grassy Plantation
Mast
West Wood
MK18
Barleyfields Barn Farm
Barley Fields
PH
Home Farm
Kings End Farm
The Rectory
Barton Hartshorn
Manor Farm
Manor House
Spilsmere Wood
Elms Farm
Newton Purcell
Barn Copse
Church Copse
SCHOOL END
Courtfield Farm
8
7
33
6
5
32
4
3
31
2
1
30
62
63
64

61

40
52

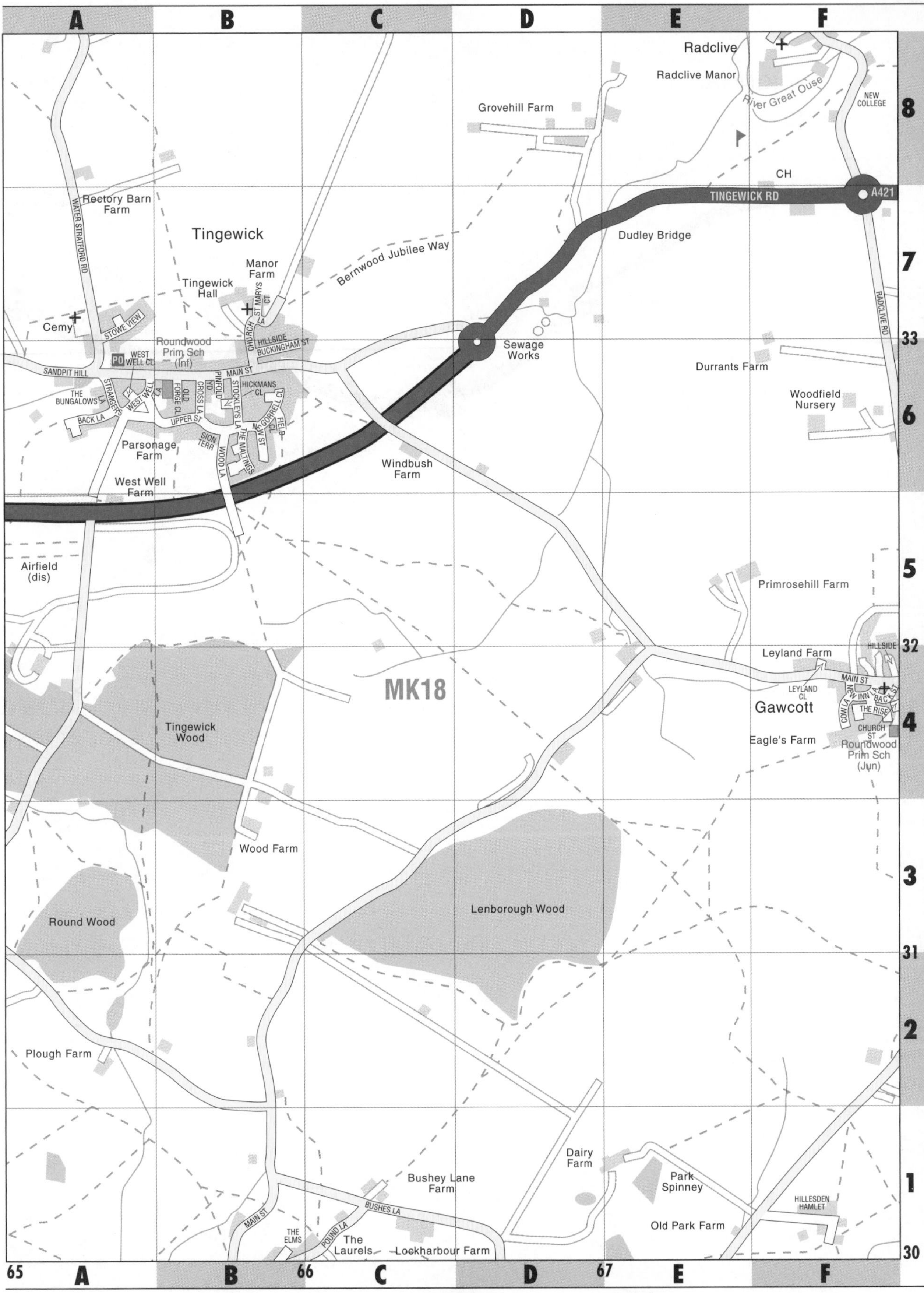

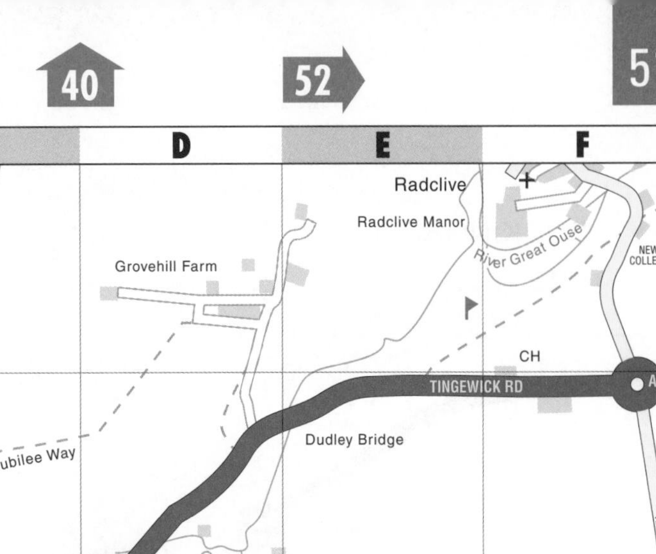
A
B
C
D
E
F
Radclive
Radclive Manor
River Great Ouse
NEW COLLEGE
Grovehill Farm
CH
TINGEWICK RD
A421
Rectory Barn Farm
WATER STRATFORD RD
Tingewick
Manor Farm
Tingewick Hall
Bernwood Jubilee Way
Dudley Bridge
RADCLIVE RD
Cemy
STOWE VIEW
ST MARYS CT
CHURCH LA
HILLSIDE
BUCKINGHAM ST
Roundwood Prim Sch (Inf)
PO
WEST WELL CL
SANDPIT HILL
Sewage Works
Durrants Farm
THE BUNGALOWS
STRANGERS LA
WEST WELL LA
OLD FORGE CL
CROSS LA
PINFOLD YD
MAIN ST
STOCKLEYS LA
HICKMANS CL
GORRELL CL
FIELD CL
NEW ST
BACK LA
UPPER ST
SION TERR
THE MALTINGS
WOOD LA
Woodfield Nursery
Parsonage Farm
Windbush Farm
West Well Farm
Airfield (dis)
Primrosehill Farm
HILLSIDE
Leyland Farm
MK18
MAIN ST
LEYLAND CL
NEW INN LA
BACK LA
COW LA
THE RISE
CHURCH ST
Gawcott
Tingewick Wood
Eagle's Farm
Roundwood Prim Sch (Jun)
Wood Farm
Lenborough Wood
Round Wood
Plough Farm
Dairy Farm
Bushey Lane Farm
Park Spinney
BUSHES LA
HILLESDEN HAMLET
MAIN ST
THE ELMS
POUND LA
The Laurels
Lockharbour Farm
Old Park Farm
8
7
33
6
5
32
4
3
31
2
1
30
65
66
67

62
52

51
41

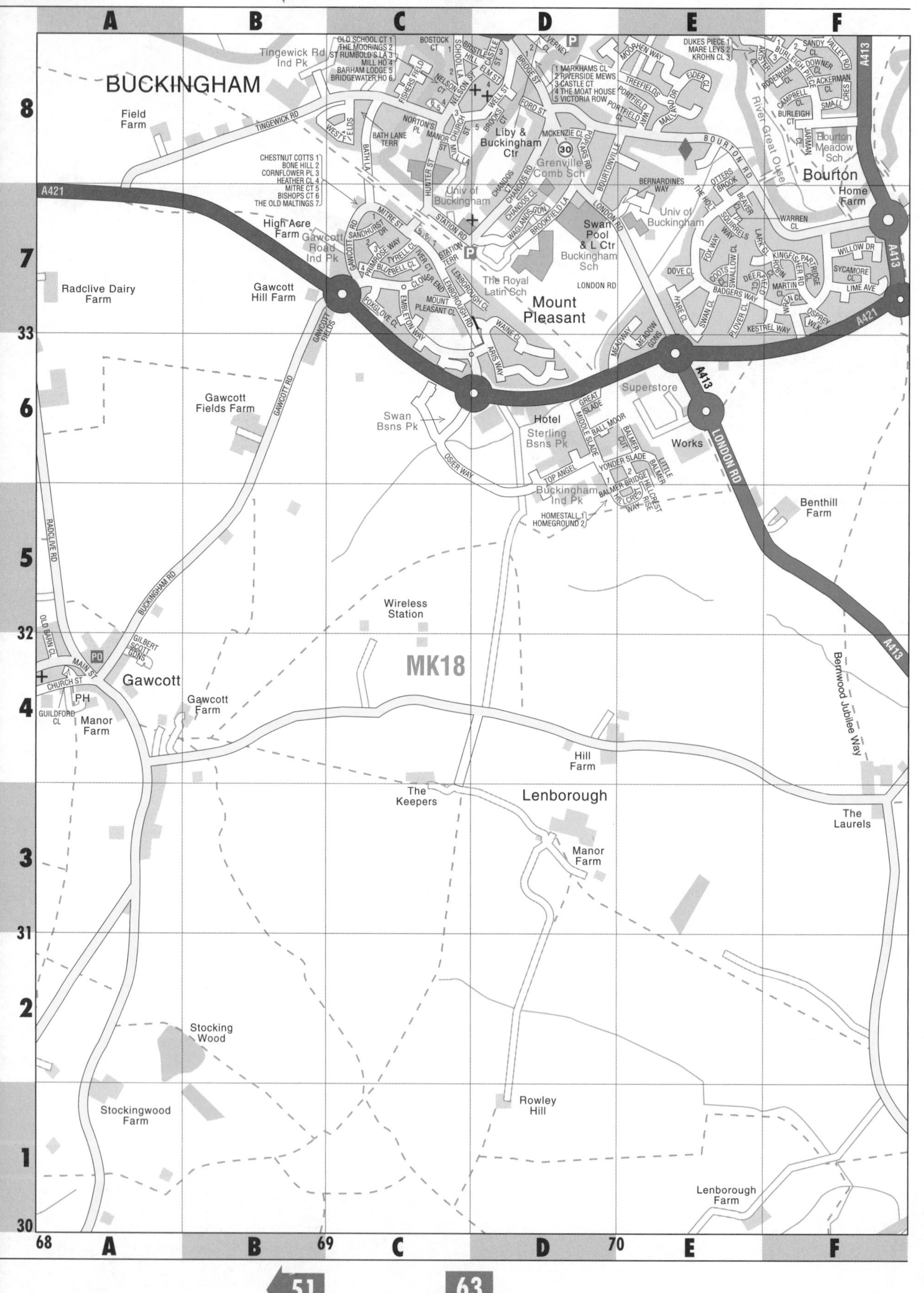
A
B
C
D
E
F
8
7
6
5
4
3
2
1
33
32
31
30
68
69
70
BUCKINGHAM
Tingewick Rd Ind Pk
Field Farm
TINGEWICK RD
A421
A413
OLD SCHOOL CT 1
THE MOORINGS 2
ST RUMBOLD'S LA 3
MILL HO 4
BARHAM LODGE 5
BRIDGEWATER HO 6
BOSTOCK CT
SCHOOL LA
NELSON ST
NELSON CT
FISHERS FIELD
WEST ST
ELM ST
CASTLE ST
BRIDGE ST
VERNEY CL
BRISTLE HILL
FORD ST
NORTON'S PL
MANOR ST
CHURCH ST
BROOKS CT
MILL LA
BATH LANE TERR
BATH LA
WEST FIELDS
HUNTER ST
Liby & Buckingham Ctr
1 MARKHAMS CL
2 RIVERSIDE MEWS
3 CASTLE CT
4 THE MOAT HOUSE
5 VICTORIA ROW
MOORHEN WAY
TREEFIELDS
PORTFIELD CL
PORTFIELD WAY
MALLARD DR
EIDER CL
MCKENZIE CL
POPLARS RD
Grenville Comb Sch
BOURTONVILLE
BOURTON RD
DUKES PIECE 1
MARE LEYS 2
KROHN CL 3
AKISTER CL
RODENHAM CL
BURLEIGH PIECE
SANDY CL
DOWNER CL
VALLEY RD
ACKERMAN CL
SMALL CRES
CAMPBELL CL
BURLEIGH CL
JARMAN CL
River Great Ouse
Bourton Meadow Sch
Bourton
Home Farm
CHESTNUT COTTS 1
BONE HILL 2
CORNFLOWER PL 3
HEATHER CL 4
MITRE CT 5
BISHOPS CT 6
THE OLD MALTINGS 7
Univ of Buckingham
STATION RD
CHANDOS RD
CHANDOS CL
WAGLANDS GDN
BROOKFIELD LA
BERNARDINES WAY
LONDON RD
THE HOLT
OTTERS BROOK
BEAVER CL
SQUIRRELS WAY
Univ of Buckingham
Swan Pool & L Ctr
Buckingham Sch
WARREN CL
WILLOW DR
High Acre Farm
Gawcott Road Ind Pk
MITRE ST
SANDHURST DR
PRIMROSE WAY
TYRELL CL
BLUEBELL CL
IVER CT
STATION TERR
GAWCOTT RD
CLOVER END
LENBOROUGH CL
LENBOROUGH RD
FOXGLOVE CL
EMBLETON WAY
MOUNT PLEASANT CL
The Royal Latin Sch
Mount Pleasant
LONDON RD
FOX WAY
DOVE CL
COOTS CL
SWALLOW CL
LARK CL
KINGFISHER RD
ROBIN CL
PARTRIDGE CL
DEERFIELD CL
MARTIN CL
WREN CL
BADGERS WAY
HARE CL
SWAN CL
PLOVER CL
KESTREL WAY
OSPREY WLK
SYCAMORE CL
LIME AVE
Radclive Dairy Farm
Gawcott Hill Farm
GAWCOTT FIELDS
WAINE CL
ARIS WAY
MEADWAY
MEADOW GDNS
Superstore
GAWCOTT RD
Gawcott Fields Farm
Swan Bsns Pk
Hotel
Sterling Bsns Pk
GREAT SLADE
BALL MOOR
MIDDLE SLADE
BALMER CUT
YONDER SLADE
LITTLE BALMER
Works
OSIER WAY
TOP ANGEL
Buckingham Ind Pk
BALMER BRIDGE
HILLCREST RISE
HILLCREST WAY
HOMESTALL 1
HOMEGROUND 2
Benthill Farm
RADCLIVE RD
BUCKINGHAM RD
Wireless Station
MK18
OLD BARN CL
MAIN ST
PO
GILBERT SCOTT GDNS
CHURCH ST
PH
GUILDFORD CL
Gawcott
Manor Farm
Gawcott Farm
Bernwood Jubilee Way
Hill Farm
The Keepers
Lenborough
The Laurels
Manor Farm
Stocking Wood
Stockingwood Farm
Rowley Hill
Lenborough Farm

51
63

42
54

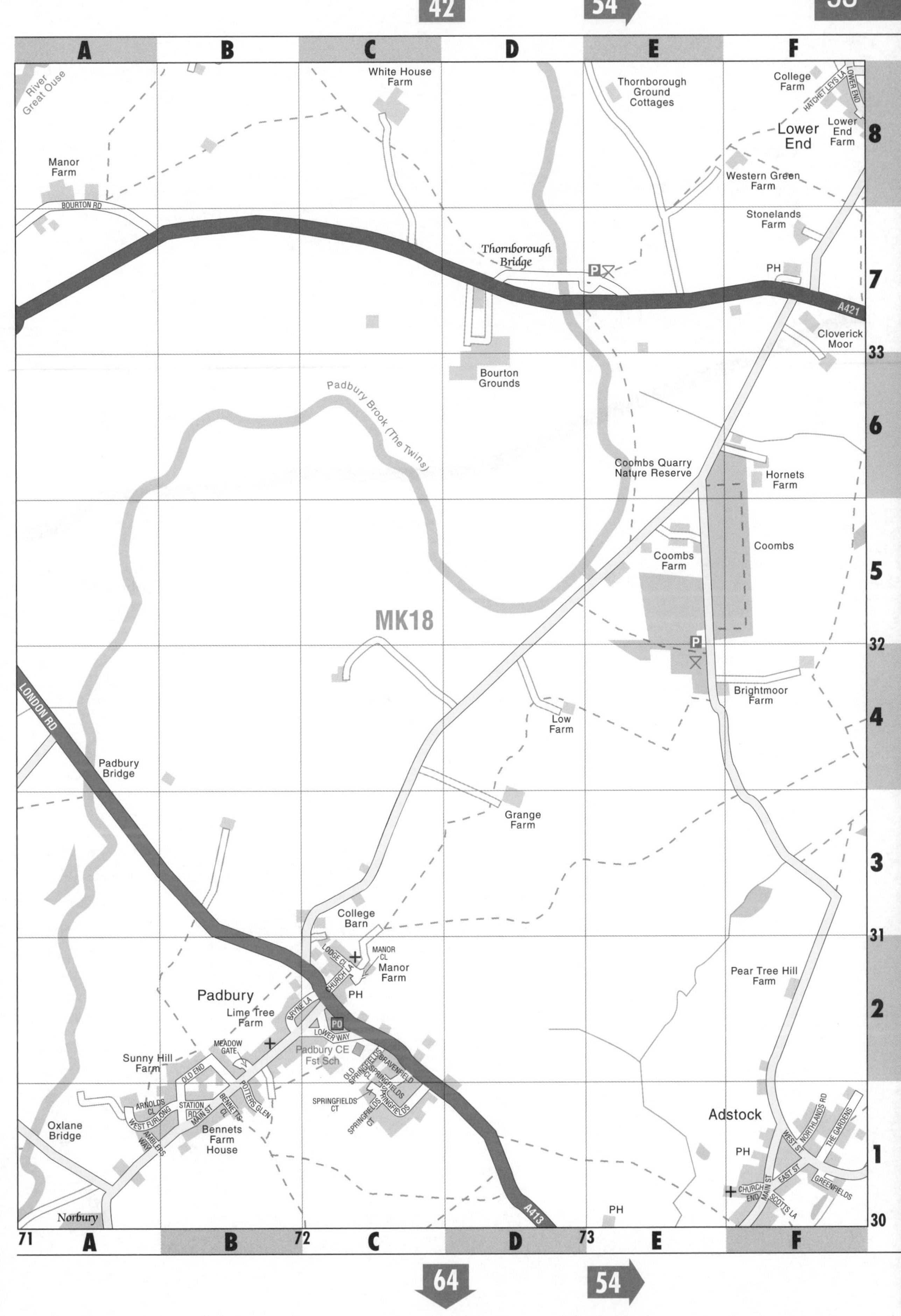
A
B
C
D
E
F
River Great Ouse
White House Farm
Thornborough Ground Cottages
College Farm
HATCHET LEYS LA
LOWER END
Lower End
Lower End Farm
Manor Farm
BOURTON RD
Western Green Farm
Stonelands Farm
Thornborough Bridge
PH
A421
Cloverick Moor
Bourton Grounds
Padbury Brook (The Twins)
Coombs Quarry Nature Reserve
Hornets Farm
Coombs
Coombs Farm
MK18
LONDON RD
Brightmoor Farm
Low Farm
Padbury Bridge
Grange Farm
College Barn
LODGE CL
CHURCH LA
MANOR CL
Manor Farm
PH
Pear Tree Hill Farm
Padbury
Lime Tree Farm
BRYNE LA
PO
LOWER WAY
MEADOW GATE
Padbury CE Fst Sch
Sunny Hill Farm
OLD END
ARNOLDS CL
WEST FURLONG
STATION RD
MAIN ST
BENNETTS CL
POTTERS GLEN
SPRINGFIELDS CT
BRAVENFIELD
Adstock
NORTHLANDS RD
THE GARDENS
WEST ST
Oxlane Bridge
AMBLERS WAY
Bennets Farm House
PH
EAST ST
GREENFIELDS
CHURCH END
MAIN ST
SCOTTS LA
Norbury
A413
PH
71
72
73
30
31
32
33
1
2
3
4
5
6
7
8

64
54

53
43

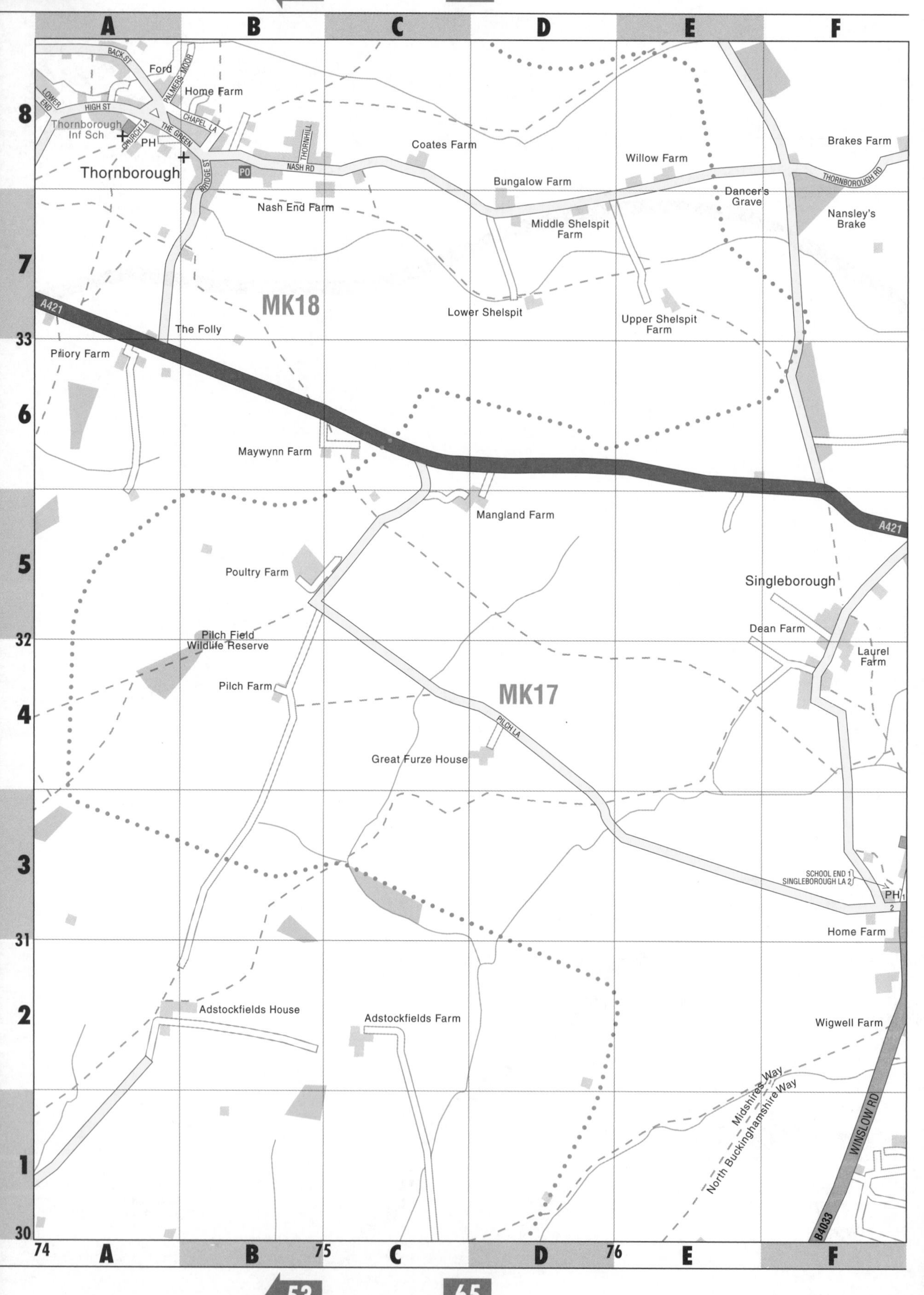
A
B
C
D
E
F
Ford
Home Farm
BACK ST
PALMERS MOOR
LOWER END
HIGH ST
CHAPEL LA
Thornborough Inf Sch
CHURCH LA
THE GREEN
PH
Thornborough
BRIDGE ST
PO
THORNHILL
NASH RD
Coates Farm
Willow Farm
Brakes Farm
THORNBOROUGH RD
Bungalow Farm
Dancer's Grave
Nash End Farm
Middle Shelspit Farm
Nansley's Brake
MK18
A421
Lower Shelspit
Upper Shelspit Farm
The Folly
Priory Farm
Maywynn Farm
Mangland Farm
A421
Poultry Farm
Singleborough
Dean Farm
Pilch Field Wildlife Reserve
Laurel Farm
Pilch Farm
MK17
PILCH LA
Great Furze House
SCHOOL END 1
SINGLEBOROUGH LA 2
PH
Home Farm
Adstockfields House
Adstockfields Farm
Wigwell Farm
Midshires Way
North Buckinghamshire Way
WINSLOW RD
B4033
8
7
33
6
5
32
4
3
31
2
1
30
74
75
76

53
65

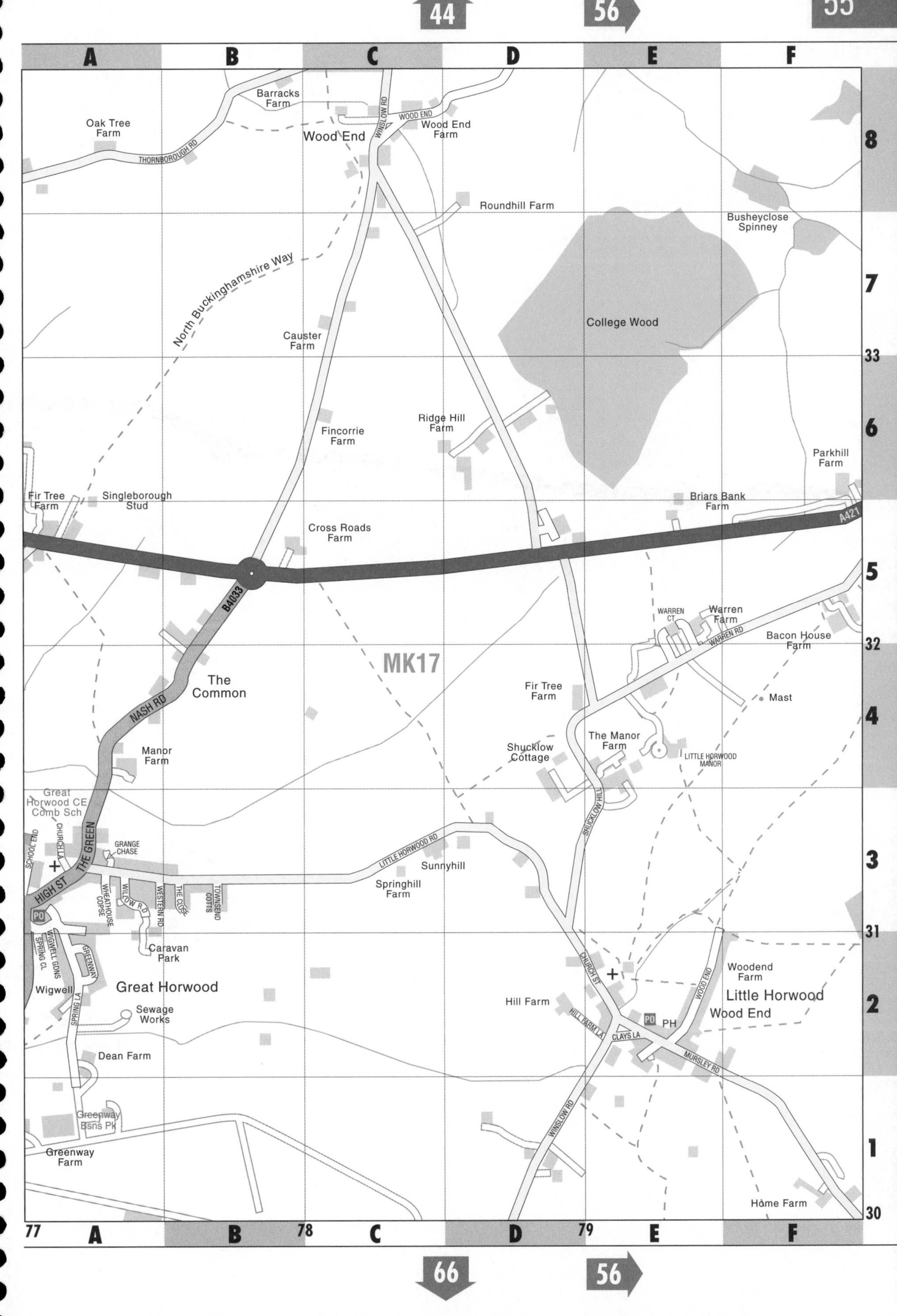

44
56
A
B
C
D
E
F
8
7
6
5
4
3
2
1
33
32
31
30
77
78
79
Oak Tree Farm
Barracks Farm
Wood End
Wood End Farm
THORNBOROUGH RD
WINSLOW RD
WOOD END
Roundhill Farm
Busheyclose Spinney
North Buckinghamshire Way
College Wood
Causter Farm
Fincorrie Farm
Ridge Hill Farm
Parkhill Farm
Fir Tree Farm
Singleborough Stud
Cross Roads Farm
Briars Bank Farm
A421
B4033
WARREN CT
Warren Farm
WARREN RD
Bacon House Farm
MK17
The Common
NASH RD
Fir Tree Farm
Mast
The Manor Farm
Shucklow Cottage
LITTLE HORWOOD MANOR
Manor Farm
Great Horwood CE Comb Sch
SCHOOL END
CHURCH LA
THE GREEN
GRANGE CHASE
HIGH ST
LITTLE HORWOOD RD
Sunnyhill
Springhill Farm
SHUCKLOW HILL
WHEATHOUSE COPSE
WILLOW RD
WESTERN RD
THE CLOSE
TOWNSEND COTTS
PO
Caravan Park
WIGWELL GDNS
SPRING CL
GREENWAY
Wigwell
Great Horwood
SPRING LA
Sewage Works
CHURCH ST
Woodend Farm
Little Horwood
Wood End
WOOD END
Hill Farm
HILL FARM LA
CLAYS LA
PH
MURSLEY RD
Dean Farm
WINSLOW RD
Greenway Bsns Pk
Greenway Farm
Home Farm
66
56

A
B
C
D
E
F
8
7
33
6
5
32
4
3
31
2
1
30
80
81
82
Church-hill Farm
Church Hill
Whaddon CE Sch
VICARAGE RD
STOCK LA
LADYMEAD CL
BRIARY VIEW
TENBY GR 1
CAISTER CT 2
SALTWOOD AVE 3
WHITTINGTON CHASE 4
GOODRICH GN 5
BYWELL CT 6
SHENLEY RD
KINGSMEAD RDBT
V1
H7
CHAFFRON WAY
ST ABBS CT
PORTISHEAD DR
LANDS END GR
GREAT ORMES
SNELSHALL ST
KELSEY CL
Bottlehouse Plantation
Bottlehouse Farm
BALCARY GR 1
THORPENESS CROFT 2
Tattenhoe Bare Farm
Priory Rise Sch
MK4
Tattenhoe Park
CODDIMOOR LA
Thickbare Wood
Coddimoor Farm
Coddimoor Farm
STEINBECK CRES
Whaddon Chase
Coddimoorhill Wood
STANDING WAY
A421
BOTTLE DUMP RDBT
Woodpond Farm
BUCKINGHAM RD
Hogpound Wood
A421
WARREN RD
Thrift Farm
Thrift Wood
Bottledump
FERNFIELD
Bletchley Leys Farm
Broadway Wood
Fernfield Farm
MK17
Chase Farm
CHASE FARM BARNS
Stearthill Farm
Midshires Way
Swan's Way
WHADDON RD
Lower Salden Farm
Weasels'
Norbury Coppice
Salden Crabtree Farm
Crabtree Farm
Salden Wood
(dis)
Middle Salden Wood
Springfield Farm
Aqueduct

F7
1 TENNYSON GR
2 KEATS WAY
3 HUGHES CROFT

46
58

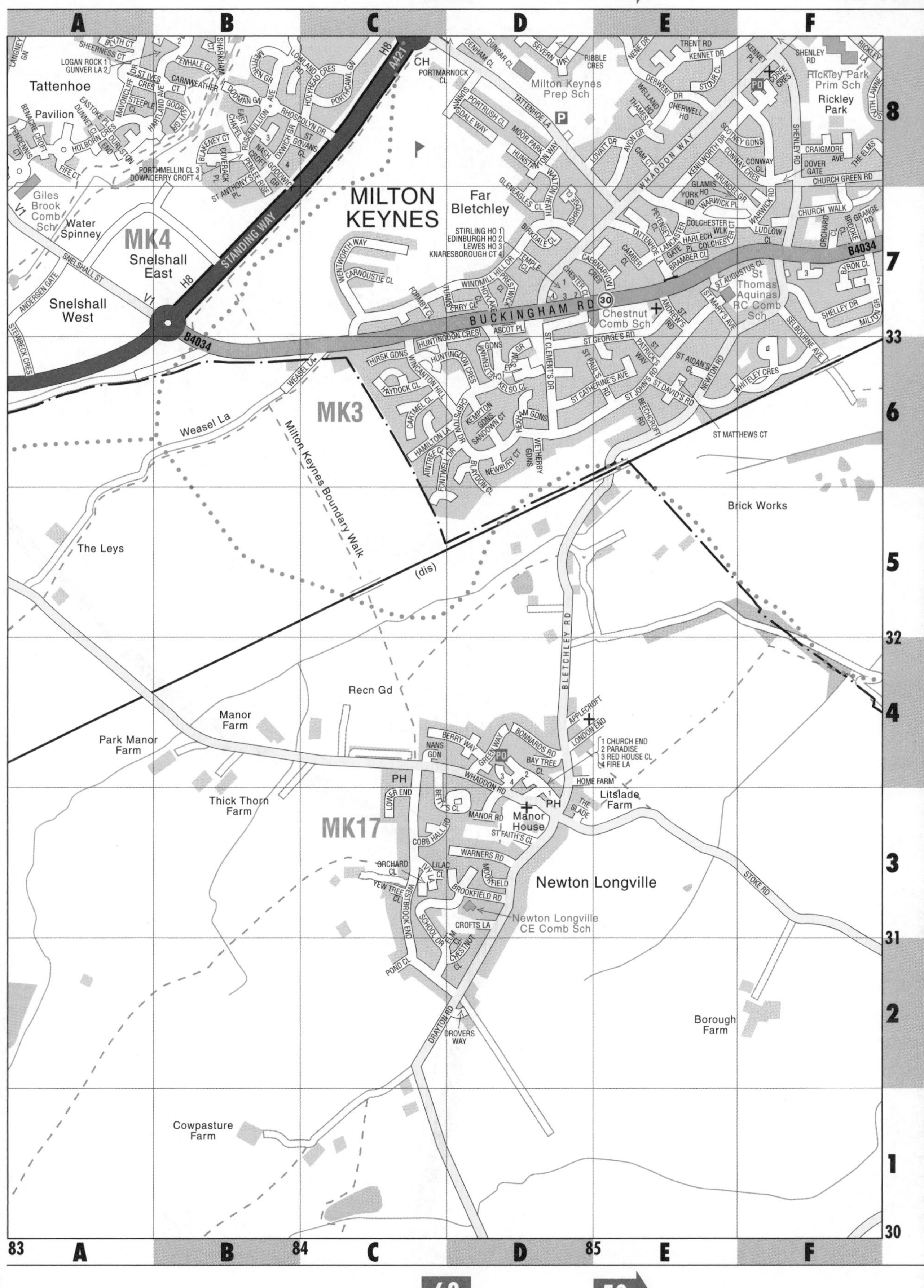

68
58

C8
1 ALEXANDER HO
2 LEE HO
3 CHRISTINE HO
4 WOODWARD HO
5 CAWKWELL WY
6 THE CONCOURSE
7 Agora Ctr

57

47

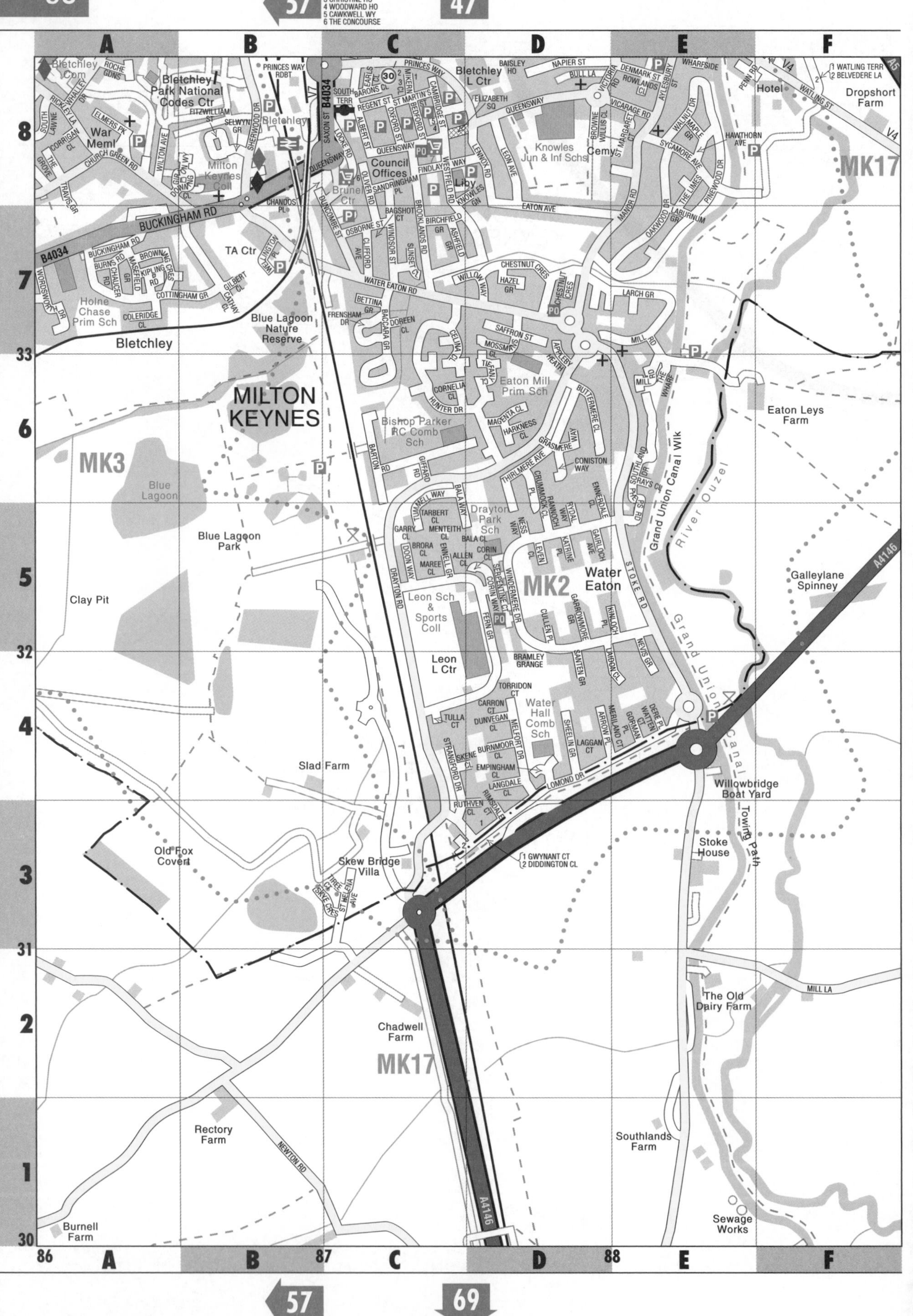

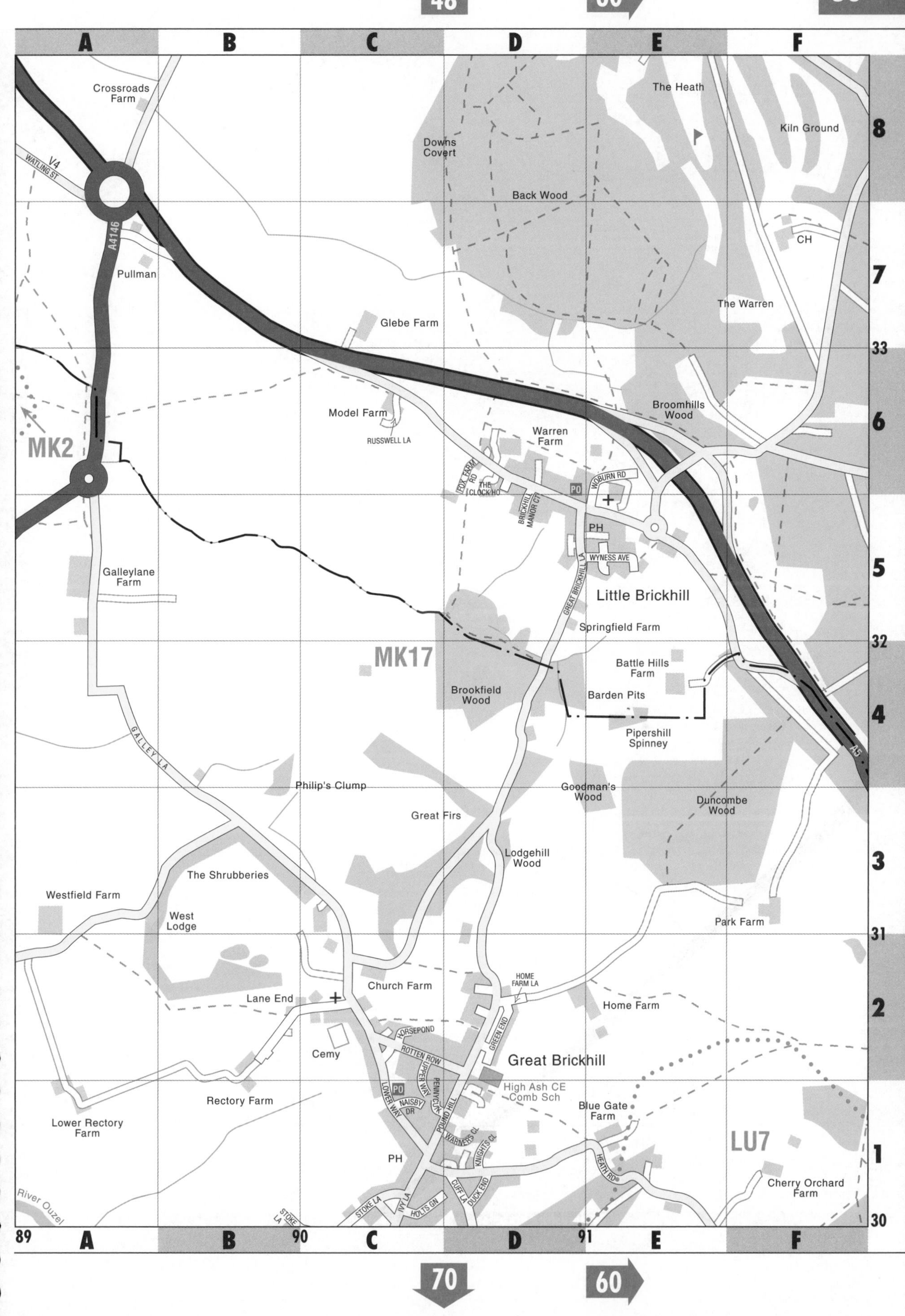
48
60
A B C D E F
Crossroads Farm
V4 WATLING ST
A4146
Pullman
Downs Covert
Back Wood
The Heath
Kiln Ground
CH
The Warren
Glebe Farm
Model Farm
RUSSWELL LA
Warren Farm
Broomhills Wood
MK2
FOX FARM RD
THE CLOCK HO
BRICKHILL MANOR CT
WOBURN RD
PO
PH
WYNESS AVE
GREAT BRICKHILL LA
Galleylane Farm
Little Brickhill
Springfield Farm
MK17
Battle Hills Farm
Brookfield Wood
Barden Pits
Pipershill Spinney
A5
GALLEY LA
Philip's Clump
Goodman's Wood
Duncombe Wood
Great Firs
Lodgehill Wood
The Shrubberies
Westfield Farm
West Lodge
Park Farm
Church Farm
HOME FARM LA
Lane End
Home Farm
HORSEPOND
ROTTEN ROW
GREEN END
Cemy
Great Brickhill
UPPER WAY
PENNYCUICK
High Ash CE Comb Sch
Rectory Farm
PO
LOWER WAY
NAISBY DR
POUND HILL
Blue Gate Farm
Lower Rectory Farm
WARNERS CL
KNIGHTS CL
LU7
PH
HEATH RD
CUFF LA
DUCK END
Cherry Orchard Farm
River Ouzel
STOKE LA
STOKE LA
IVY LA
HOLTS GN
8 7 33 6 5 32 4 3 31 2 1 30
89 90 91
70
60

59
49

A
B
C
D
E
F
8
7
33
6
5
32
4
3
31
2
1
30
92
93
94
New Wavendon Heath
Bells Copse
Tollhouse Grove
Hundreds Farm
Little Brickhill Copse
Charle Wood
Shire Oak
Lowe's Wood
Horsemoor Farm
Dolton's Farm
A5130 WOBURN RD
NEWPORT RD A5130
BIRCHMOOR GN
PH
CRAWLEY RD A4012
DRAKELOE CL
ELEANOR CL
ELEANOR WLK
BEDFORD ST
CASWELL LA
STAUNTON HO
MARQUIS CT
Woburn Lower Sch
PO
MARKET PL
TH
GEORGE ST
PARK ST
Woburn
TIMBER LA
HOWLAND PL
DUCK LA
LONDON END
LEIGHTON ST
BLOOMSBURY CL
A4012 Leighton Buzzard
Wayn Close
Pinfold Pond
Pinfoldpond
Crowholt Plantation
Job's Farm
Greensand Ridge Wlk
Utcoate Grange
Circuitt's Covert
Buttermilk Farm
Buttermilk Wood
MK17
Bedfordshire STREET ATLAS
A5
Nun Wood
Apesfield Farm
Sheeplane Belt
Milton Keynes Boundary Walk
Rammamere Farm
SHEEPLANE
PH
Sand Pit
Bushycommon Wood
Hill Farm
Arnold's Cottages
LU7
Rammamere Heath
Bragenham Wood
King's Wood National Nature Reserve
WOBURN RD
A5
LU7
Bedfordshire STREET ATLAS
A5 Dunstable

59

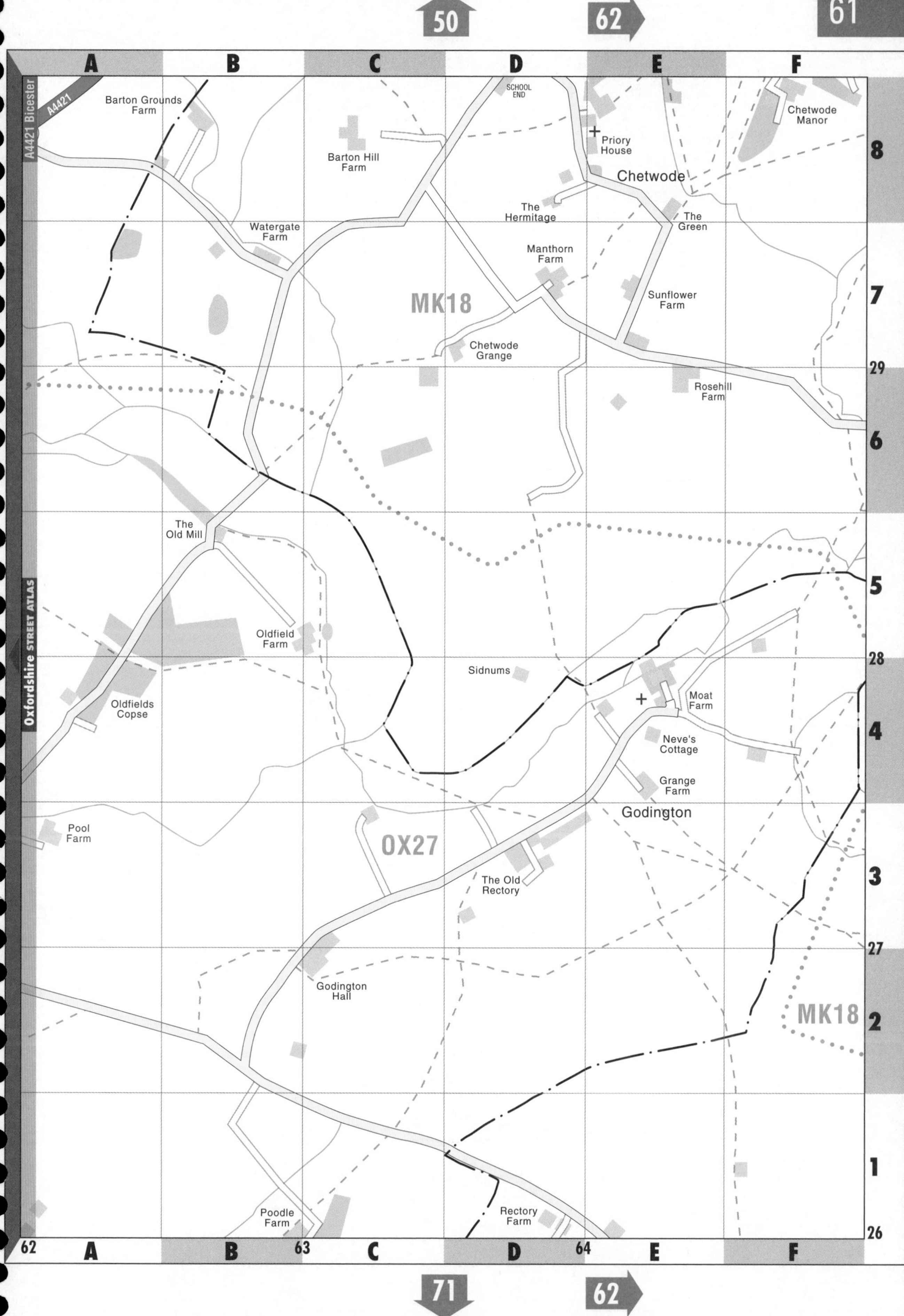
50
62
A
B
C
D
E
F
A4421 Bicester
A4421
Barton Grounds
Farm
SCHOOL
END
Priory
House
Chetwode
Manor
Barton Hill
Farm
Chetwode
The
Hermitage
The
Green
Watergate
Farm
Manthorn
Farm
MK18
Sunflower
Farm
Chetwode
Grange
Rosehill
Farm
The
Old Mill
Oldfield
Farm
Sidnums
Moat
Farm
Oldfields
Copse
Neve's
Cottage
Grange
Farm
Godington
Pool
Farm
OX27
The Old
Rectory
Godington
Hall
MK18
Poodle
Farm
Rectory
Farm
8
7
29
6
5
28
4
3
27
2
1
26
62
63
64
Oxfordshire STREET ATLAS
71
62

61
51

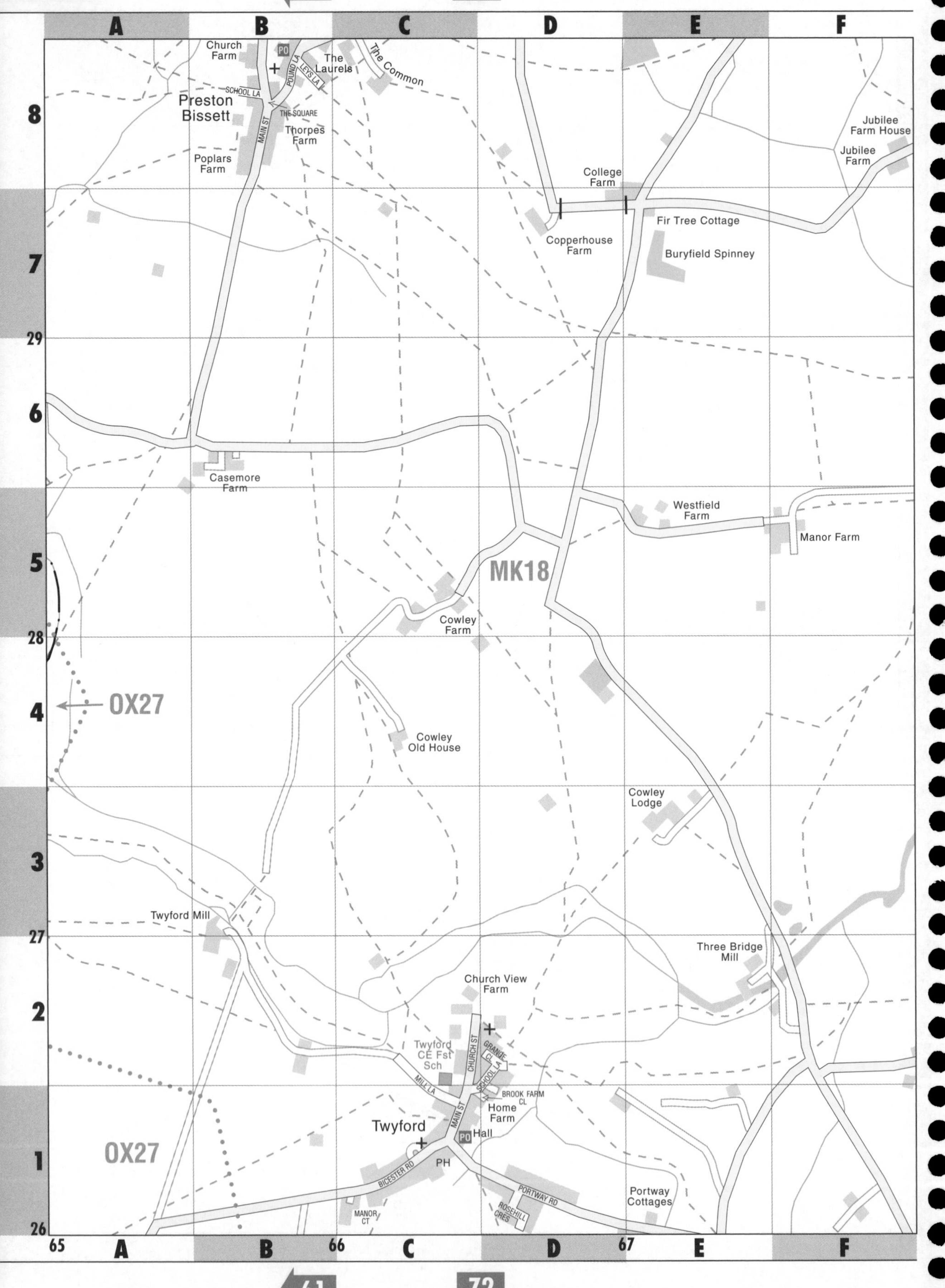
A
B
C
D
E
F
Church Farm
PO
The Laurels
The Common
POUND LA
LEYS LA
SCHOOL LA
Preston Bissett
THE SQUARE
MAIN ST
Thorpes Farm
Poplars Farm
8
Jubilee Farm House
Jubilee Farm
College Farm
Fir Tree Cottage
Copperhouse Farm
Buryfield Spinney
7
29
6
Casemore Farm
Westfield Farm
Manor Farm
5
MK18
Cowley Farm
28
4
OX27
Cowley Old House
Cowley Lodge
3
Twyford Mill
27
Three Bridge Mill
Church View Farm
2
Twyford CE Fst Sch
CHURCH ST
GRANGE CL
SCHOOL LA
MILL LA
BROOK FARM CL
Home Farm
MAIN ST
Twyford
PO
Hall
OX27
1
PH
BICESTER RD
PORTWAY RD
ROSEHILL CRES
MANOR CT
Portway Cottages
26
65
A
B
66
C
D
67
E
F

61
72

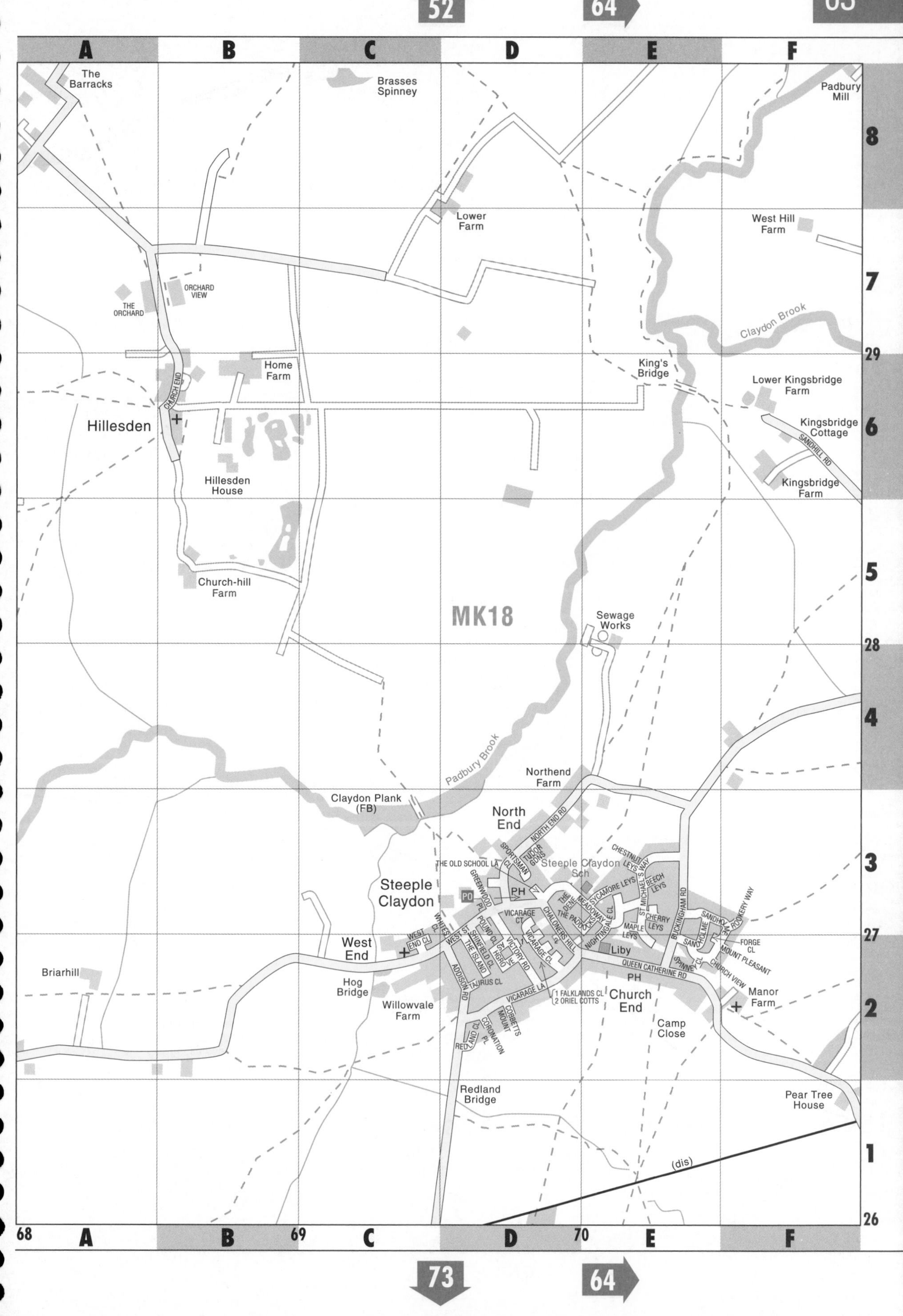
52
64
A
B
C
D
E
F
The Barracks
Brasses Spinney
Padbury Mill
8
Lower Farm
West Hill Farm
7
ORCHARD VIEW
THE ORCHARD
Claydon Brook
29
Home Farm
King's Bridge
Lower Kingsbridge Farm
CHURCH END
Hillesden
Kingsbridge Cottage
SANDHILL RD
6
Hillesden House
Kingsbridge Farm
5
Church-hill Farm
MK18
Sewage Works
28
4
Padbury Brook
Northend Farm
Claydon Plank (FB)
North End
NORTH END RD
CHESTNUT LEYS
3
SPORTSMAN CL
TUDOR GDNS
THE OLD SCHOOL LA
Steeple Claydon Sch
GREENWOOD PL
Steeple Claydon
PO
PH
SYCAMORE LEYS
BEECH LEYS
ST MICHAEL'S WAY
BUCKINGHAM RD
ROOKERY WAY
VICARAGE CT
THE PADDOCKS
CHERRY LEYS
MAPLE LEYS
NIGHTINGALE CL
SANDHOLME
WHITES CL
WEST END CL
West End
WEST ST
POUND CL
SHINFIELD CL
THE ISLAND
VICTORY RD
VICARAGE CL
CHALONERS HILL
Liby
FORGE CL
MOUNT PLEASANT
27
QUEEN CATHERINE RD
SPINNEY CL
CHURCH VIEW
Briarhill
Hog Bridge
ADDISON RD
TAURUS CL
PH
VICARAGE LA
1 FALKLANDS CL
2 ORIEL COTTS
Church End
Manor Farm
2
Willowvale Farm
COBBETTS MOUNT
CORONATION PL
REDLAND CL
Camp Close
Redland Bridge
Pear Tree House
1
(dis)
26
68
A
B
69
C
D
70
E
F

A B C D E F
8
7
29
6
5
28
4
3
27
2
1
26
A413
Folly Farm
MAIN ST
Adstock Manor Stud
A413
Wardens Farm
Padburyhill Farm
White Bridge
Hill Farm Cottages
Hill Farm
Claydon Brook
MK18
Herd's Hill Cottage
Claydon Hill Farm No 6
Claydon Hill Farm No 5
HERD'S HILL
Claydon Hill Farm
SANDHILL RD
Jubilee Bridge
Swan's Way
Windmillhill Farm
Verney Junction
PH
Littleworth Farm
Verney Junction Bsns Pk
Littleworth
JUBILEE COTTS
(dis)
Ashmore Farm House
Mount Pleasant Farm
Greenacres
Sandhill
Sandhill
Sandhill Farm
RAILWAY COTTS
LC
Rectory Farm
QUEEN CATHERINE RD
QUEEN CATHERINE RD
North Buckinghamshire Way
71 A B 72 C D 73 E F

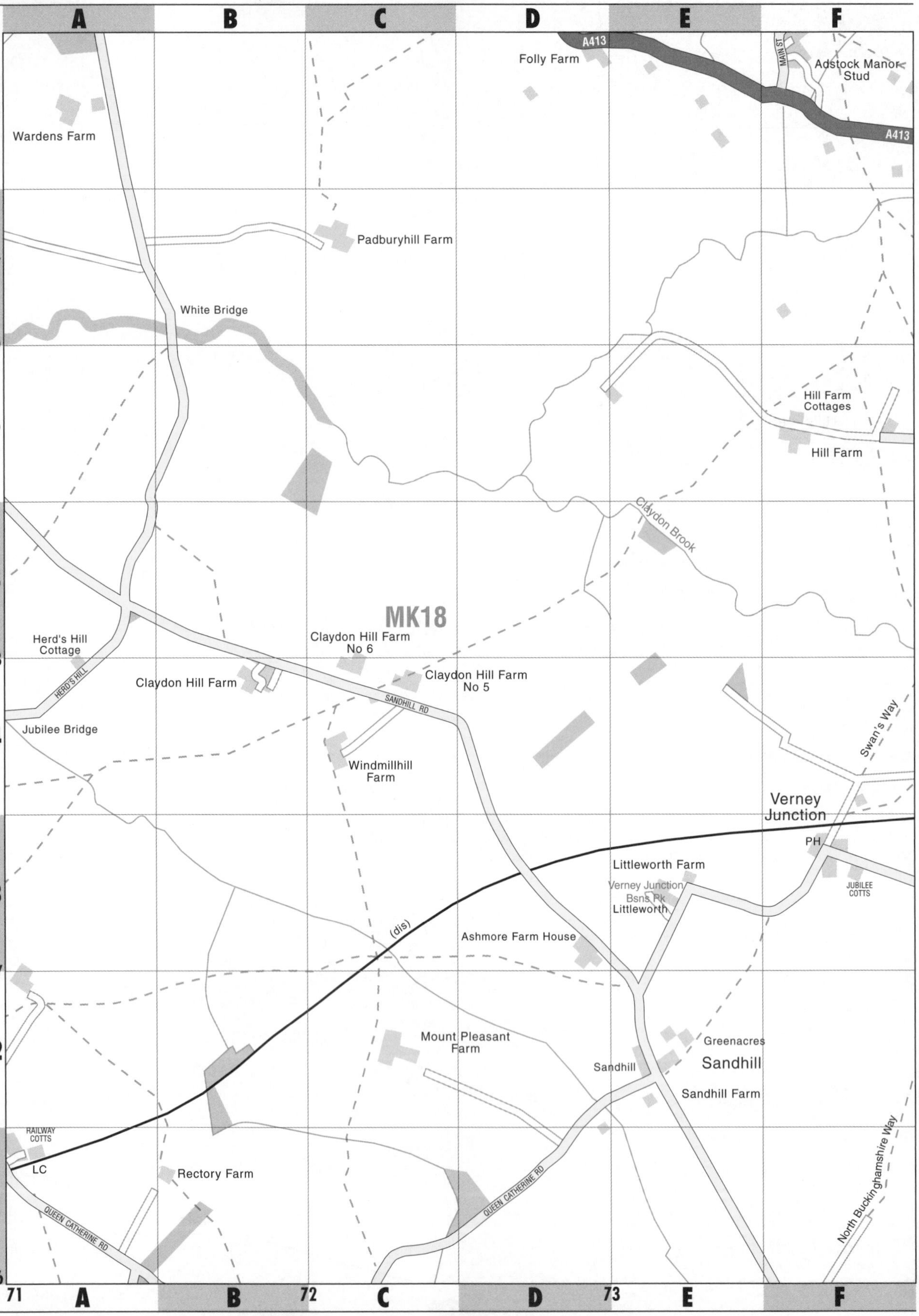

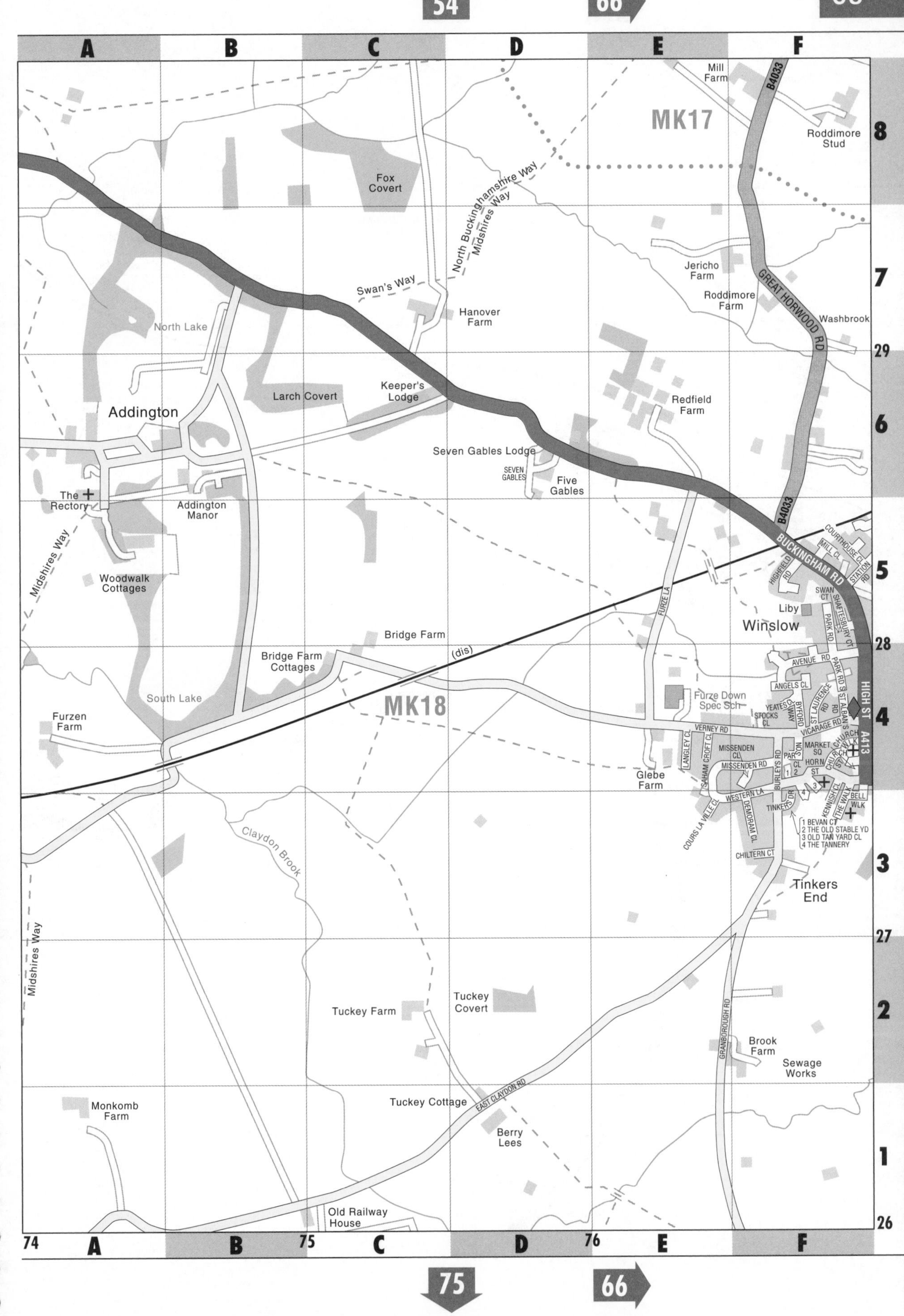
54
66
A B C D E F
MK17
Mill Farm
B4033
Roddimore Stud
Fox Covert
North Buckinghamshire Way
Midshires Way
Jericho Farm
Roddimore Farm
GREAT HORWOOD RD
Washbrook
Swan's Way
Hanover Farm
North Lake
Larch Covert
Keeper's Lodge
Redfield Farm
Addington
Seven Gables Lodge
SEVEN GABLES
Five Gables
The Rectory
Addington Manor
Midshires Way
Woodwalk Cottages
BUCKINGHAM RD
COURTHOUSE CL
MILL CL
STATION RD
HIGHFIELD RD
SWAN CT
SHAFTESBURY CT
PARK RD
FURZE LA
Liby
Winslow
Bridge Farm
Bridge Farm Cottages
(dis)
AVENUE RD
ANGELS CL
HIGH ST
A413
MK18
Furze Down Spec Sch
South Lake
Furzen Farm
VERNEY RD
MISSENDEN CL
MISSENDEN RD
MARKET SQ
HORN ST
CHURCH WLK
LANGLEY CL
SAHAM CROFT CL
BURLEYS RD
Glebe Farm
WESTERN LA
TINKERS DR
KENNISH CL
THE WALK
BELL WLK
COURS LA VILLE CL
DEMORAM CL
1 BEVAN CT
2 THE OLD STABLE YD
3 OLD TAN YARD CL
4 THE TANNERY
CHILTERN CT
Claydon Brook
Tinkers End
Midshires Way
Tuckey Farm
Tuckey Covert
GRANBOROUGH RD
Brook Farm
Sewage Works
Monkomb Farm
Tuckey Cottage
EAST CLAYDON RD
Berry Lees
Old Railway House
8 7 6 5 4 3 2 1
29 28 27 26
74 75 76
75
66

65
55

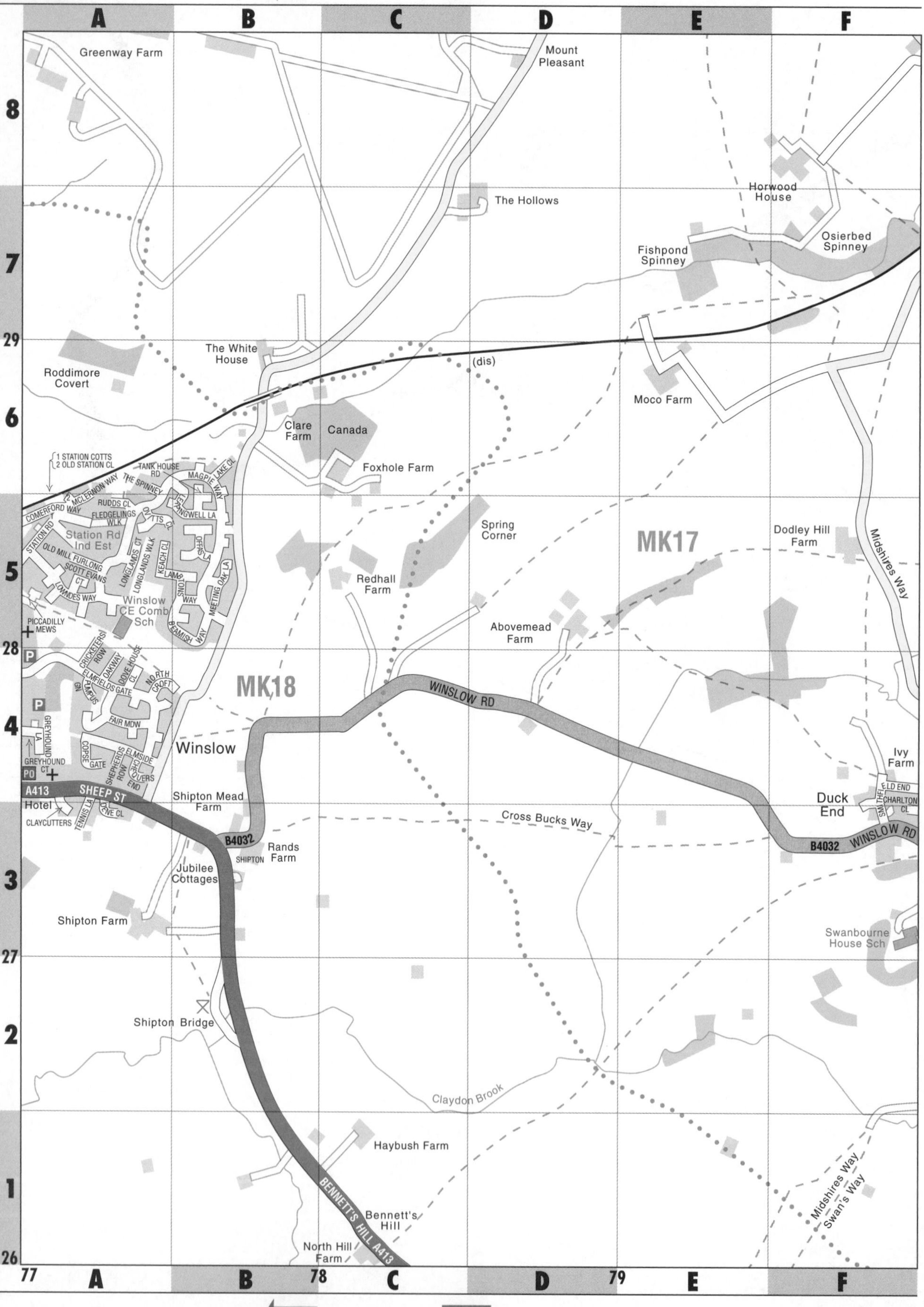

A B C D E F

8
7
29
6
5
28
4
3
27
2
1
26

Greenway Farm
Mount Pleasant
The Hollows
Horwood House
Osierbed Spinney
Fishpond Spinney
The White House
Roddimore Covert
(dis)
Moco Farm
Clare Farm
Canada
Foxhole Farm
1 STATION COTTS
2 OLD STATION CL
TANK HOUSE RD
MAGPIE WAY
LAKE CL
MCLERNON WAY
THE SPINNEY
RUDDS CL
COMERFORD WAY
FLEDGELINGS WLK
PINGWELL LA
STATION RD
Station Rd Ind Est
OLD MILL FURLONG
SCOTT EVANS CT
LONGLANDS CT
LONGLANDS WLK
KEACH CL
LAMPTONS WAY
MEETING OAK LA
LOWNDES WAY
Winslow CE Comb Sch
BEAMISH WAY
PICCADILLY MEWS
Spring Corner
MK17
Dodley Hill Farm
Midshires Way
Redhall Farm
Abovemead Farm
CRICKETERS ROW
OAKWAY
DOVE HOUSE CL
NORTH CROFT
ELMFIELDS GATE
FAIR MDW
MK18
WINSLOW RD
GREYHOUND LA
GREYHOUND CT
Winslow
COPSE GATE
SHEPHERDS ROW
ELMSIDE
CHEQUERS END
Ivy Farm
PO
A413
SHEEP ST
Hotel
CLAYCUTTERS
TENNIS LA
Shipton Mead Farm
Cross Bucks Way
Duck End
SMITHFIELD END
CHARLTON CL
B4032
WINSLOW RD
B4032
SHIPTON
Rands Farm
Jubilee Cottages
Shipton Farm
Swanbourne House Sch
Shipton Bridge
Claydon Brook
Haybush Farm
BENNETT'S HILL A413
Bennett's Hill
North Hill Farm
Midshires Way
Swan's Way

77 A B 78 C D 79 E F

65
76

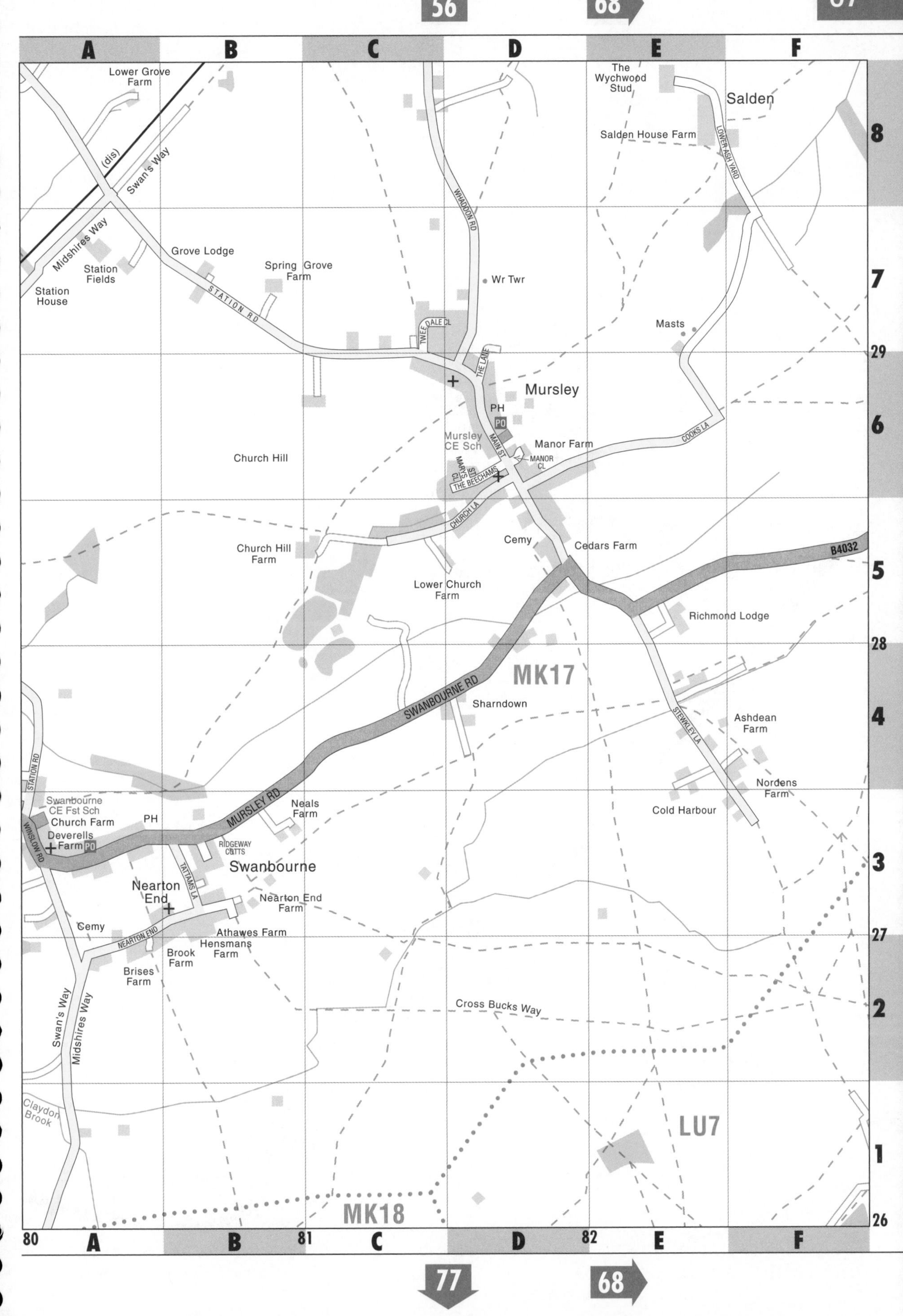
56
68
Lower Grove Farm
The Wychwood Stud
Salden
Salden House Farm
LOWER ASH YARD
(dis)
Swan's Way
Midshires Way
WHADDON RD
Grove Lodge
Station Fields
Station House
Spring Grove Farm
STATION RD
Wr Twr
TWEEDALE CL
Masts
THE LANE
Mursley
PH
PO
Mursley CE Sch
MAIN ST
Manor Farm
MANOR CL
COOKS LA
Church Hill
MARYS CL
STS
THE BEECHAMS
CHURCH LA
Church Hill Farm
Cemy
Cedars Farm
B4032
Lower Church Farm
Richmond Lodge
MK17
SWANBOURNE RD
Sharndown
Ashdean Farm
STEWKLEY LA
STATION RD
Nordens Farm
Swanbourne CE Fst Sch
Church Farm
PH
MURSLEY RD
Neals Farm
Cold Harbour
Deverells Farm
PO
WINSLOW RD
RIDGEWAY COTTS
Swanbourne
TATTAMS LA
Nearton End
Nearton End Farm
Cemy
NEARTON END
Athawes Farm
Hensmans Farm
Brook Farm
Brises Farm
Cross Bucks Way
Swan's Way
Midshires Way
Claydon Brook
LU7
MK18
77
68

67
57

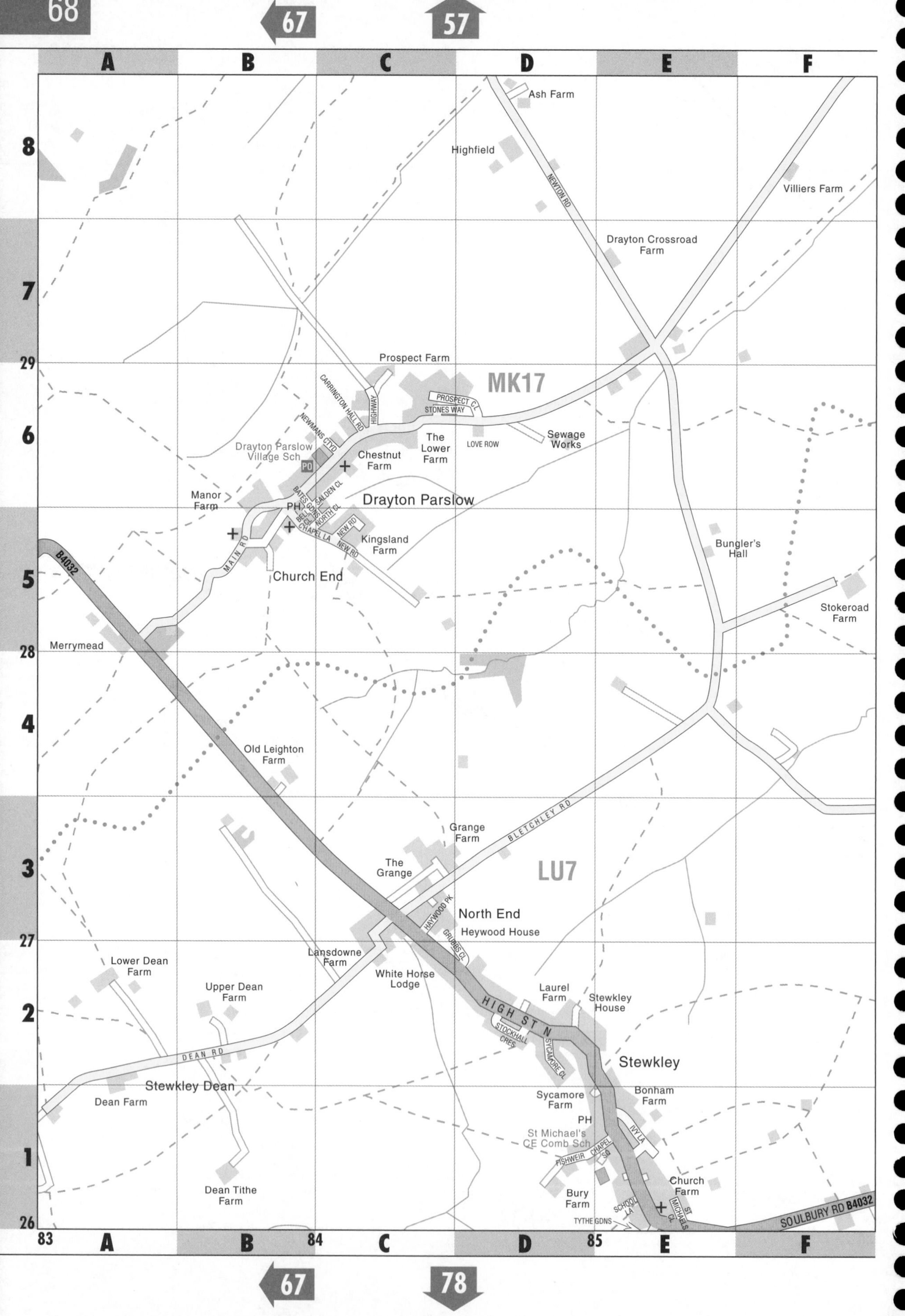
A
B
C
D
E
F
8
7
29
6
5
28
4
3
27
2
1
26
83
84
85
Ash Farm
Highfield
NEWTON RD
Villiers Farm
Drayton Crossroad
Farm
Prospect Farm
MK17
CARRINGTON HALL RD
HIGHWAY
PROSPECT CL
STONES WAY
NEWMANS CTYD
LOVE ROW
Sewage
Works
Drayton Parslow
Village Sch
PO
Chestnut
Farm
The
Lower
Farm
Manor
Farm
PH
SALDEN CL
BATES GDNS
NORTH CL
CHAPEL LA
NEW RD
Drayton Parslow
Kingsland
Farm
MAIN RD
B4032
Church End
Bungler's
Hall
Stokeroad
Farm
Merrymead
Old Leighton
Farm
BLETCHLEY RD
Grange
Farm
The
Grange
LU7
HAYWOOD PK
North End
Heywood House
GRUBBS CL
Lower Dean
Farm
Lansdowne
Farm
White Horse
Lodge
Upper Dean
Farm
Laurel
Farm
Stewkley
House
HIGH ST N
STOCKHALL CRES
SYCAMORE CL
DEAN RD
Stewkley
Stewkley Dean
Dean Farm
Sycamore
Farm
Bonham
Farm
PH
IVY LA
St Michael's
CE Comb Sch
FISHWEIR
CHAPEL SQ
Church
Farm
Dean Tithe
Farm
Bury
Farm
SCHOOL LA
ST MICHAELS CL
TYTHE GDNS
SOULBURY RD B4032

67
78

A
B
C
D
E
F
Stoke Hammond Lock
Grove Farm
Stoke Hammond
Swing Bridge
Fairfields
Tyrells Manor
Grand Union Canal
Oak Farm
Dorcas Farm
PH
MK17
Soulbury Ground Farm
Grand Union Canal Wlk
Longfield
Dean Farm
Kings Farm
DEAN FARM LA
A4146
Spring Farm
Rislip Farm
Upper Hollingdon Farm
Wellmead Farm
Hollingdon
Hollingdon Farm
Holly Bar Farm
Hollingdon Grange
Grove Farm
Soulbury
Cross Bucks Way
HOLLINGDON RD
Hollingdon Depot
LU7
PH
Manor Farm
STEWKLEY RD
HIGH RD
Larkshill Farm
LEIGHTON RD B4032
The Lodge
Vicarage Farm
Durrance Farm
Winscott Farm
SOULBURY RD
Soulbury Road Farm
The Plantation
Liscombe Park
8
7
29
6
5
28
4
3
27
2
1
26
86
87
88

69
59
A
B
C
D
E
F
8
7
29
6
5
28
4
3
27
2
1
26
89
90
91
Sewage
Works
Stockgrove
Farm
Ivy Lane
Farm
STOKE LA
IVY LA
River Ouzel
Stockgrove
Park Ho
MK17
Greensand Ridge Wlk
Paper
Mill
Visitor
Ctr
Partridge
Hill
Oak
Wood
Stockgrove
Country Park
Furze
Hill
Alders
Farm
Partridge
House
Upper Kiln
Farm
CH
Kiln
Farm
Shire
Oak
Red Bridge
Bragenham
Farm
Bragenham
Rushmere
Park
PH
BRAGENHAM LA
Stapleford
Mill
Stapleford
Farm
Ludley
Cottage
Bedfordshire STREET ATLAS
LINSLADE RD
A4146
Grand Union Canal
River Ouzel
LU7
Nares Gadley
Farm
Rushmere
Grand Union Canal Wlk
THE HEATH
HEATH CL
DUKES RIDE
CH
Chelmscote
Manor
Farm
Broad
Oak
Grange
Mill
OLD LINSLADE RD
SANDY LA
REDWOOD GLADE
PLANTATION RD
Cross Bucks Way
Greensand Ridge Wlk
TALL PINES
MANOR CT
Old Linslade
Manor
Old
Linslade
TAYLOR'S RIDE
OXENDON CT
ROBINSWOOD CL
WOODLAND AVE
DINGLE DELL
Corbettshill
Farm
Dollar
Farm
B4032
LEIGHTON RD
LEIGHTON
BUZZARD
STOKE RD
PH
GLOBE LA
Linslade
Wood
Sewage
Works
BOSSINGTON LA
THE MARTINS DR
Valley
Farm
69
80

61
72

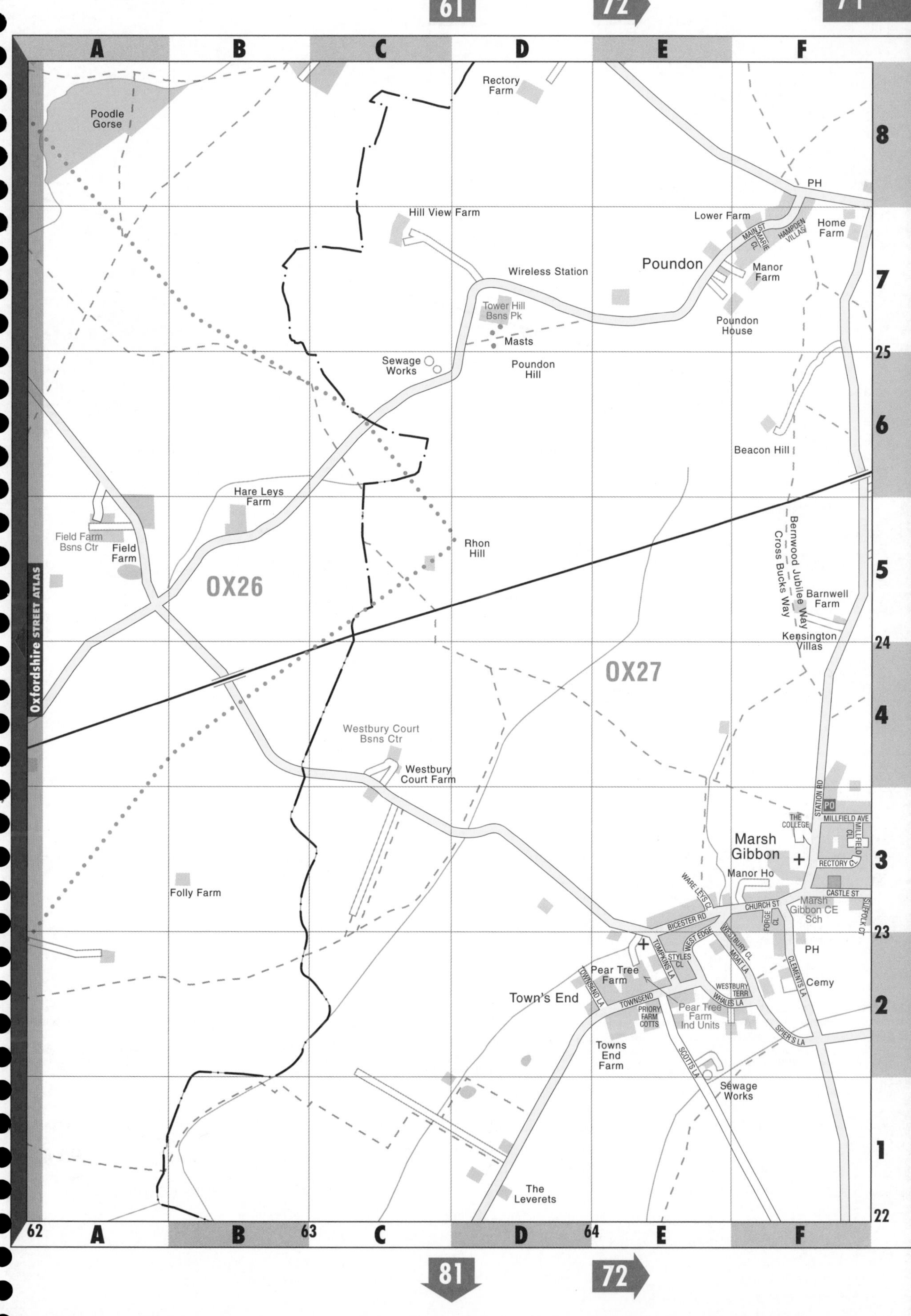
A
B
C
D
E
F
Rectory Farm
Poodle Gorse
8
PH
Hill View Farm
Lower Farm
Home Farm
MAIN ST
MARIE CL
HAMPDEN VILLAS
Poundon
Manor Farm
Wireless Station
7
Tower Hill Bsns Pk
Masts
Poundon House
25
Sewage Works
Poundon Hill
6
Beacon Hill
Hare Leys Farm
Bernwood Jubilee Way
Cross Bucks Way
Field Farm Bsns Ctr
Field Farm
Rhon Hill
OX26
5
Barnwell Farm
Oxfordshire STREET ATLAS
Kensington Villas
24
OX27
4
Westbury Court Bsns Ctr
Westbury Court Farm
STATION RD
PO
THE COLLEGE
MILLFIELD AVE
MILLFIELD CL
Marsh Gibbon
3
RECTORY CL
Manor Ho
CASTLE ST
WARE LEYS CL
Folly Farm
CHURCH ST
Marsh Gibbon CE Sch
BICESTER RD
FORGE CL
SUFFOLK CT
WEST EDGE
WESTBURY CL
23
TOMPKINS LA
STYLES CL
MOAT LA
PH
CLEMENTS LA
Pear Tree Farm
TOWNSEND LA
Cemy
WESTBURY TERR
Town's End
TOWNSEND
WHALES LA
2
PRIORY FARM COTTS
Pear Tree Farm Ind Units
SPIER'S LA
Towns End Farm
SCOTTS LA
Sewage Works
1
The Leverets
22
62
63
64

81
72

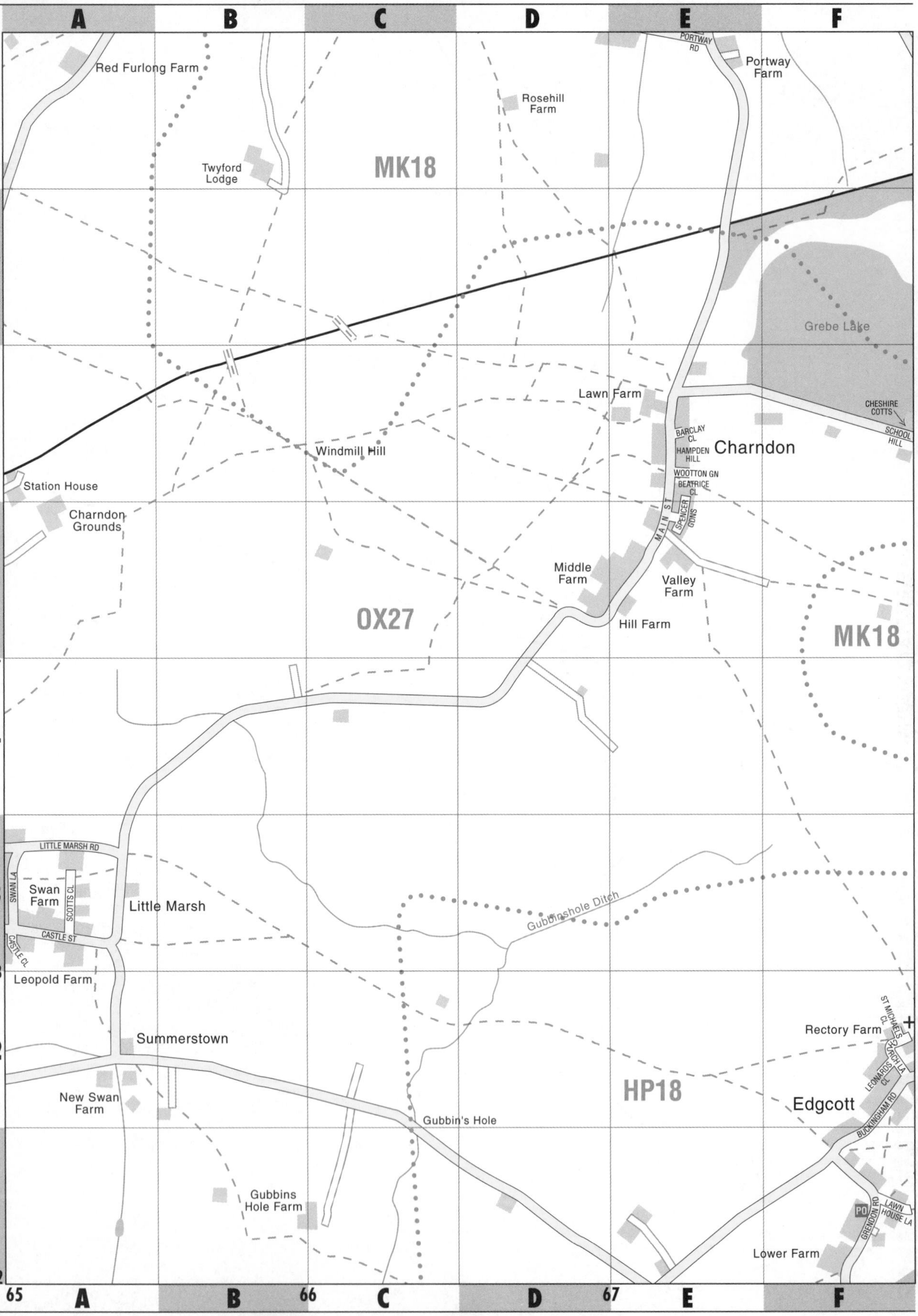

71
62

A B C D E F

8 7 25 6 5 24 4 3 23 2 1 22

Red Furlong Farm
Twyford Lodge
Rosehill Farm
MK18
PORTWAY RD
Portway Farm
Grebe Lake
Lawn Farm
CHESHIRE COTTS
SCHOOL HILL
BARCLAY CL
HAMPDEN HILL
Charndon
WOOTTON GN
BEATRICE CL
MAIN ST
SPENCER GDNS
Windmill Hill
Station House
Charndon Grounds
Middle Farm
Valley Farm
Hill Farm
OX27
MK18
LITTLE MARSH RD
SWAN LA
Swan Farm
SCOTTS CL
Little Marsh
CASTLE ST
CASTLE CL
Leopold Farm
Gubbinshole Ditch
Summerstown
New Swan Farm
Gubbin's Hole
HP18
Rectory Farm
ST MICHAELS CL
CHURCH LA
LEONARDS CL
Edgcott
BUCKINGHAM RD
Gubbins Hole Farm
PO
LAWN HOUSE LA
GRENDON RD
Lower Farm

65 A B 66 C D 67 E F

71
82

63
74

A
B
C
D
E
F
(dis)
Rose Hill Farm
Blackmoorhill
8
Shepherd's Furze Farm
Calvert Jubilee Wildlife Reserve
7
Blackmorehill Farm
CALVERT COTTS
25
Great Pond Farm
MK18
6
SCHOOL HILL
WERNER TERR
COTSWOLDS
BRACKLEY LA
WAY
Shrubs Wood
OX27
Calvert
TUSCANS CL
BRINDLES CL
BRICKHILL WAY
COTSWOLDS WAY
Knowl Hill
RUSTICS CL
SANDY RD
KILN CL
HEATHERS CL
5
SANDSTONE CL
Decoypond Wood
COTSWOLDS WAY
CLAY LA
COTSWOLDS WAY
TUDORS CL
24
THREE POINTS LA
Knowlhill Farm
4
Dunstyhill Farm
Dunsty Hill
OX27
Sheephouse Wood
Landfill Site
3
PERRY HILL
23
Lawn Hill Farm
Manor Farm
LAWN HILL
BUCKINGHAM RD
2
HP18
Moor Farm
Greatmoor
Rosall Farm
Prune Farm
1
HM Prison Springhill
HM Young Offender Inst Grendon
22
68
69
70

83
74

73
64

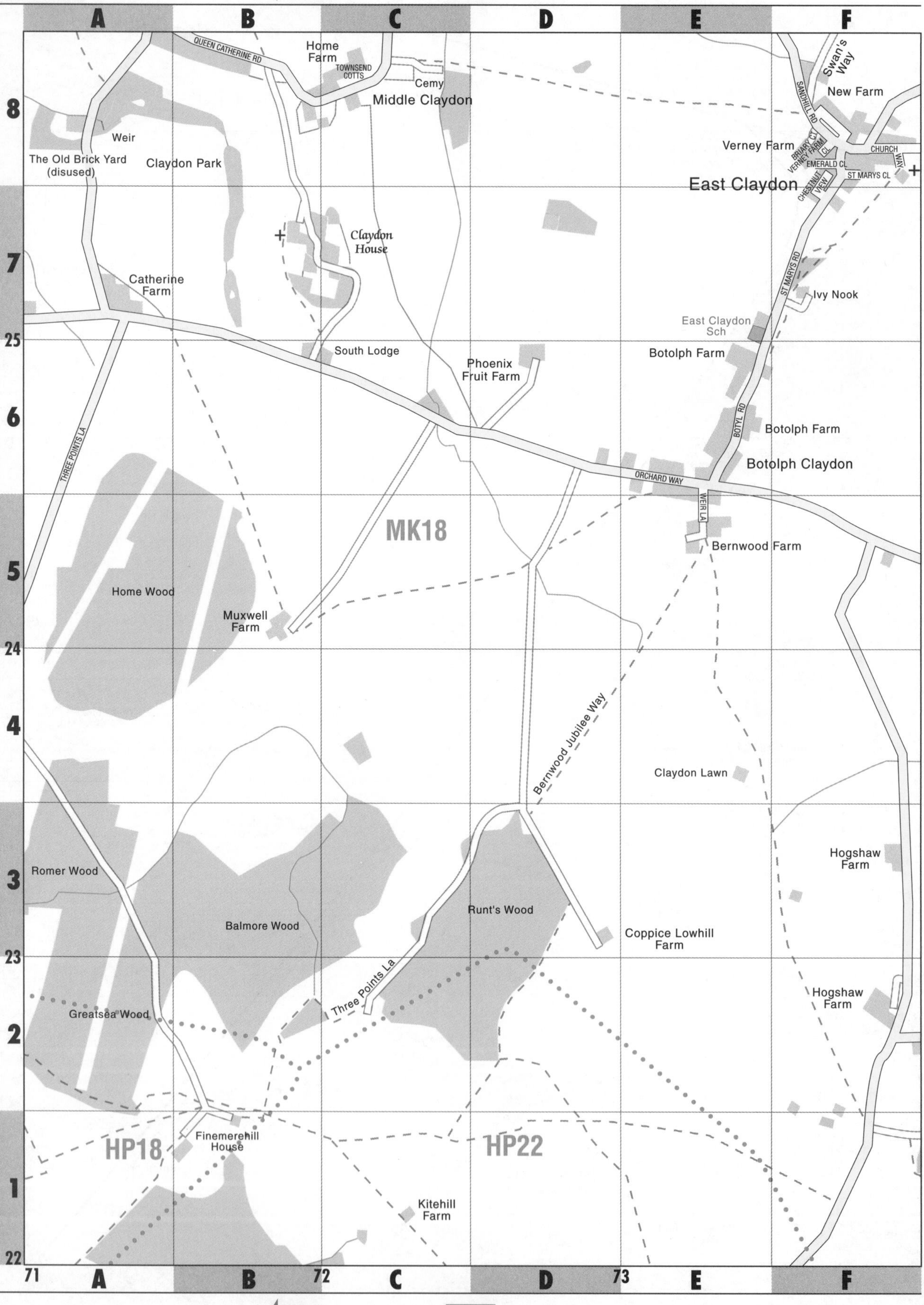

A B C D E F
8 7 6 5 4 3 2 1
25 24 23 22
QUEEN CATHERINE RD
Home Farm
TOWNSEND COTTS
Cemy
Middle Claydon
Weir
The Old Brick Yard (disused)
Claydon Park
Claydon House
Catherine Farm
South Lodge
Phoenix Fruit Farm
THREE POINTS LA
MK18
Home Wood
Muxwell Farm
Swan's Way
SANDHILL RD
New Farm
Verney Farm
BRIARY CL
VERNEY FARM CL
EMERALD CL
CHURCH WAY
ST MARYS CL
CHESTNUT VIEW
East Claydon
ST MARYS RD
Ivy Nook
East Claydon Sch
Botolph Farm
BOTYL RD
Botolph Farm
Botolph Claydon
ORCHARD WAY
WEIR LA
Bernwood Farm
Bernwood Jubilee Way
Claydon Lawn
Romer Wood
Balmore Wood
Runt's Wood
Coppice Lowhill Farm
Hogshaw Farm
Hogshaw Farm
Three Points La
Greatsea Wood
HP18
Finemerehill House
HP22
Kitehill Farm
71 72 73

73
84

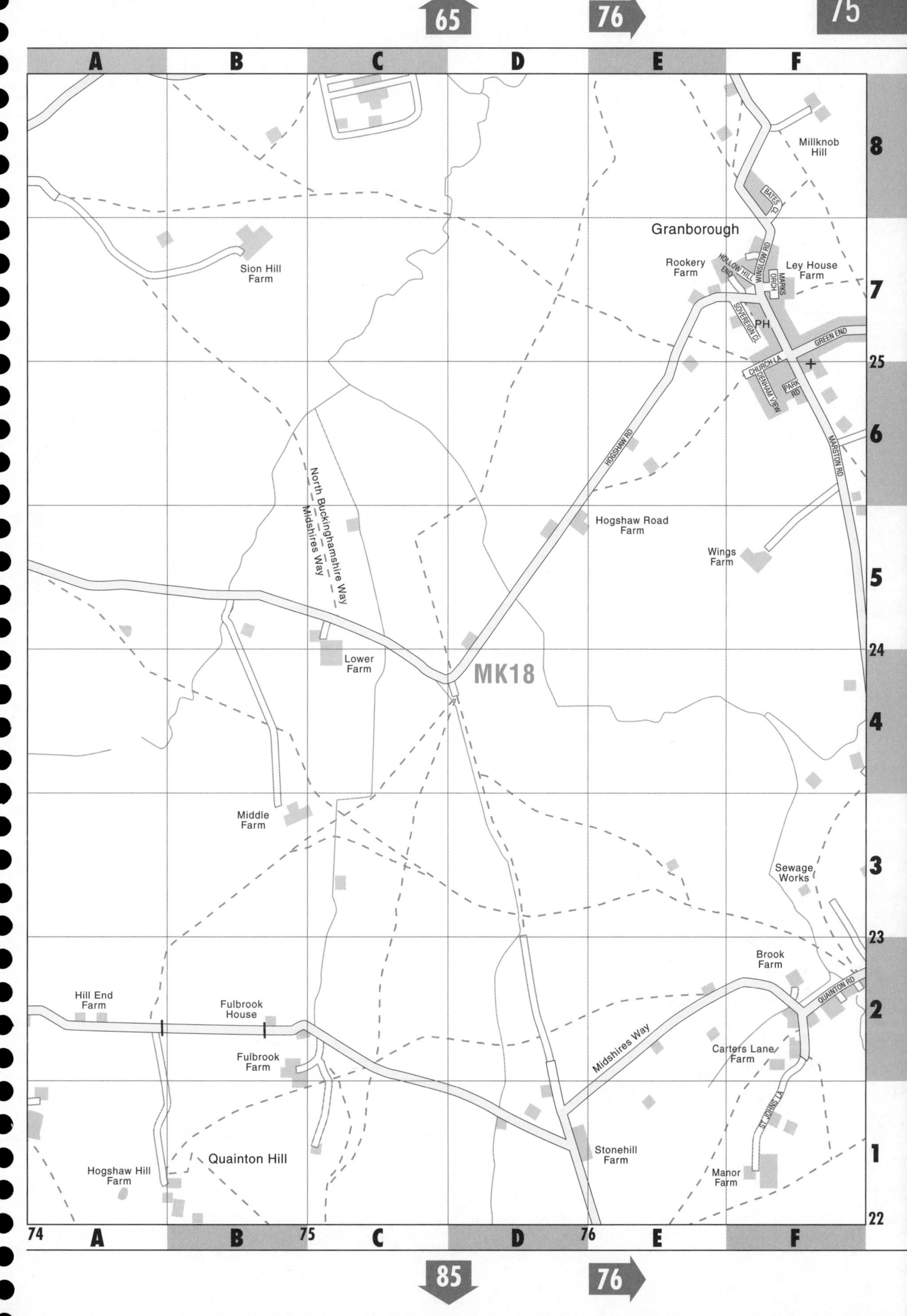
65
76
A
B
C
D
E
F
8
7
25
6
5
24
4
3
23
2
1
22
74
75
76
85
Millknob Hill
BATES CL
Granborough
Rookery Farm
HOLLOW HILL END
WINSLOW RD
ORCH
MARKS
Ley House Farm
SOVEREIGN CL
PH
GREEN END
CHURCH LA
DENHAM VIEW
PARK RD
MARSTON RD
Sion Hill Farm
HOGSHAW RD
North Buckinghamshire Way
Midshires Way
Hogshaw Road Farm
Wings Farm
Lower Farm
MK18
Middle Farm
Sewage Works
Brook Farm
QUAINTON RD
Hill End Farm
Fulbrook House
Fulbrook Farm
Midshires Way
Carters Lane Farm
ST JOHNS LA
Quainton Hill
Hogshaw Hill Farm
Stonehill Farm
Manor Farm

75
66

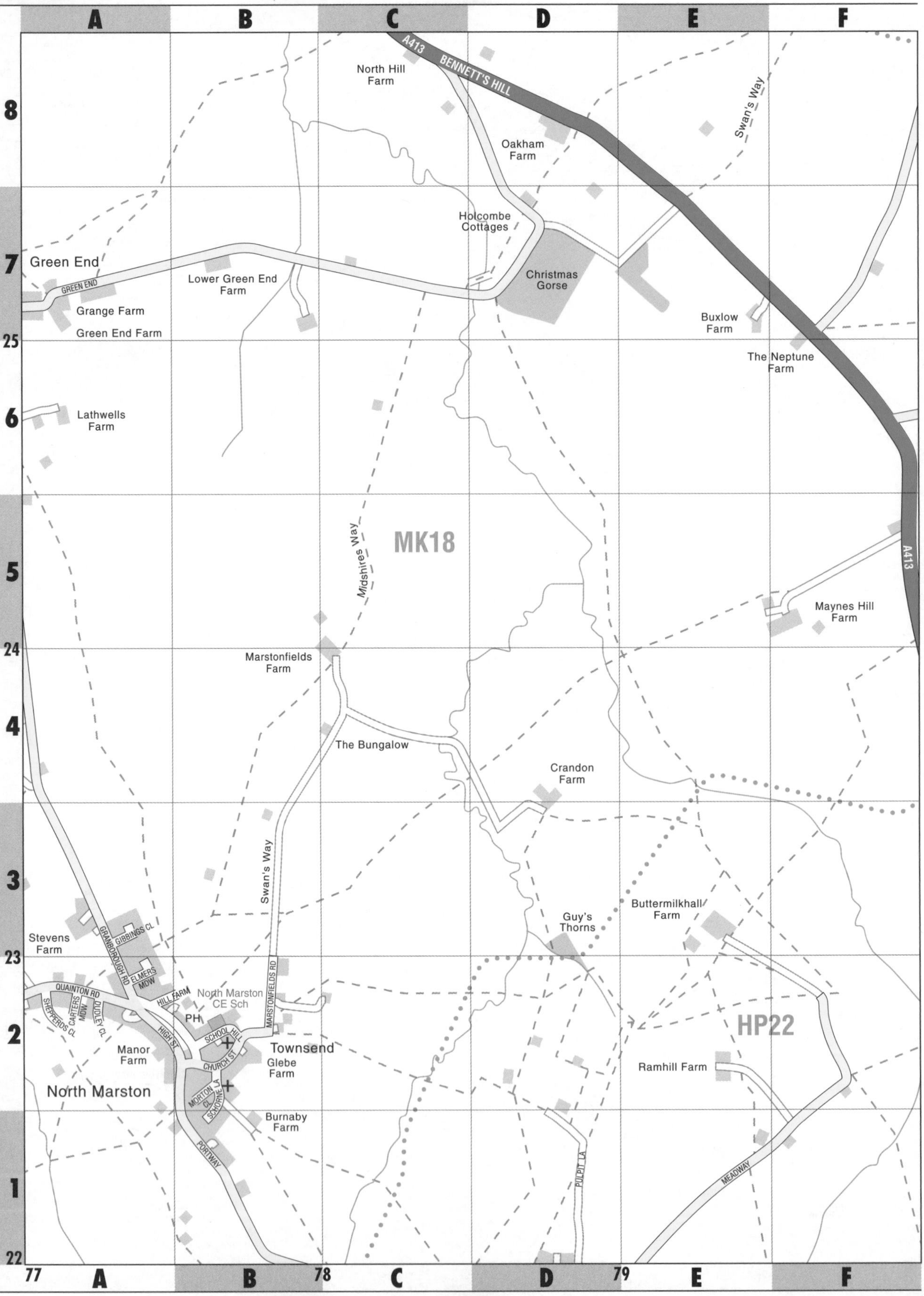

A B C D E F
8
7
25
6
5
24
4
3
23
2
1
22
77 78 79
North Hill Farm
A413 BENNETT'S HILL
Swan's Way
Oakham Farm
Holcombe Cottages
Green End
GREEN END
Lower Green End Farm
Christmas Gorse
Grange Farm
Green End Farm
Buxlow Farm
The Neptune Farm
Lathwells Farm
MK18
Midshires Way
A413
Maynes Hill Farm
Marstonfields Farm
The Bungalow
Crandon Farm
Swan's Way
Buttermilkhall Farm
Guy's Thorns
Stevens Farm
GRANBOROUGH RD
GIBBINGS CL
ELMERS MDW
QUAINTON RD
SHEPPERDS CL
CARTERS MDW
DUDLEY CL
HILL FARM
North Marston CE Sch
MARSTONFIELDS RD
PH
HIGH ST
SCHOOL HILL
Townsend
HP22
Manor Farm
CHURCH ST
Glebe Farm
Ramhill Farm
North Marston
MORTON CL
SCHORNE LA
Burnaby Farm
PORTWAY
PULPIT LA
MEADWAY

75
86

67
78

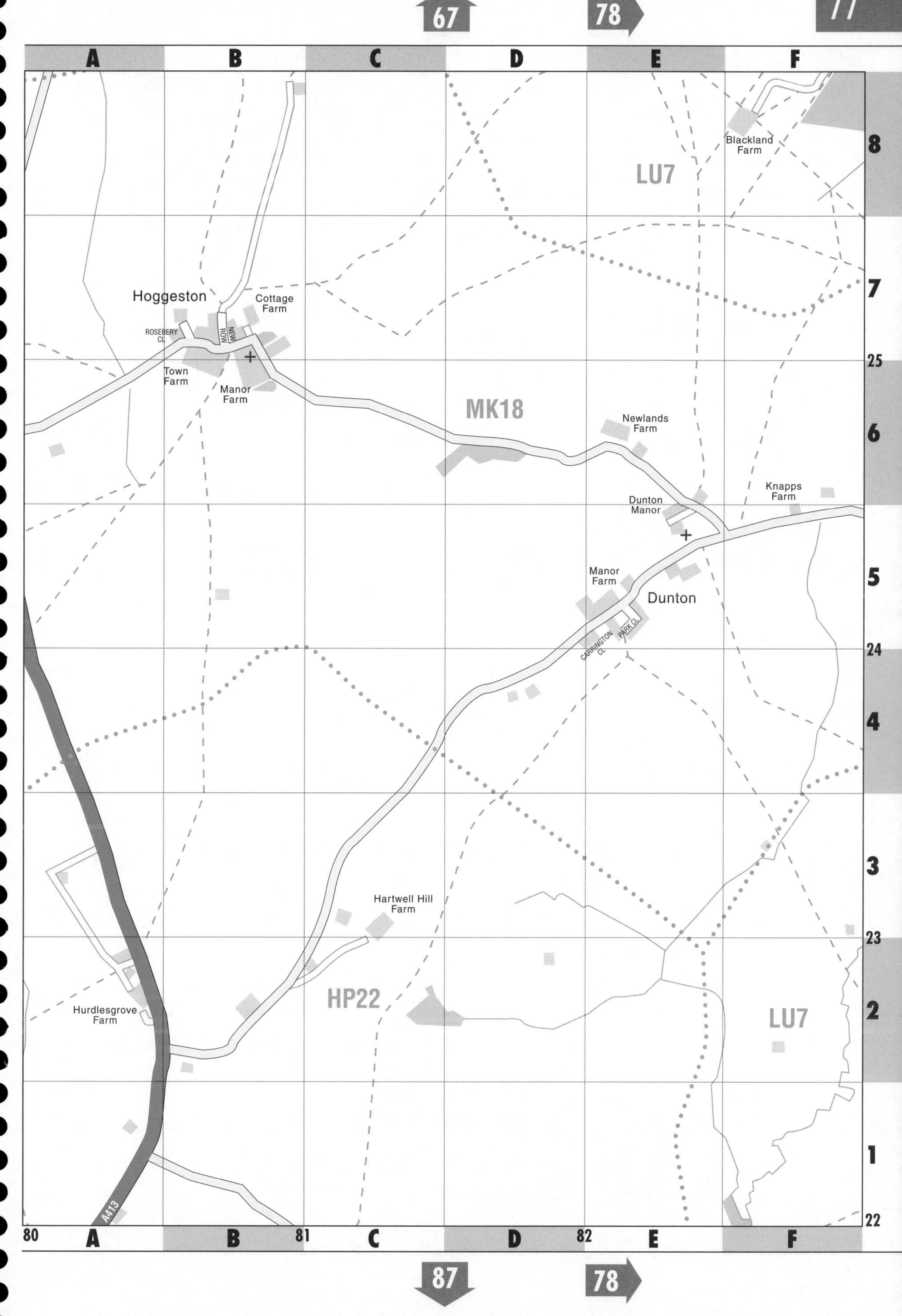
A
B
C
D
E
F
8
7
25
6
5
24
4
3
23
2
1
22
80
81
82
Hoggeston
Cottage Farm
ROSEBERY CL
NEW ROW
Town Farm
Manor Farm
MK18
LU7
Blackland Farm
Newlands Farm
Knapps Farm
Dunton Manor
Manor Farm
Dunton
CARRINGTON CL
PARK CL
Hartwell Hill Farm
HP22
Hurdlesgrove Farm
LU7
A413

87
78

77
68

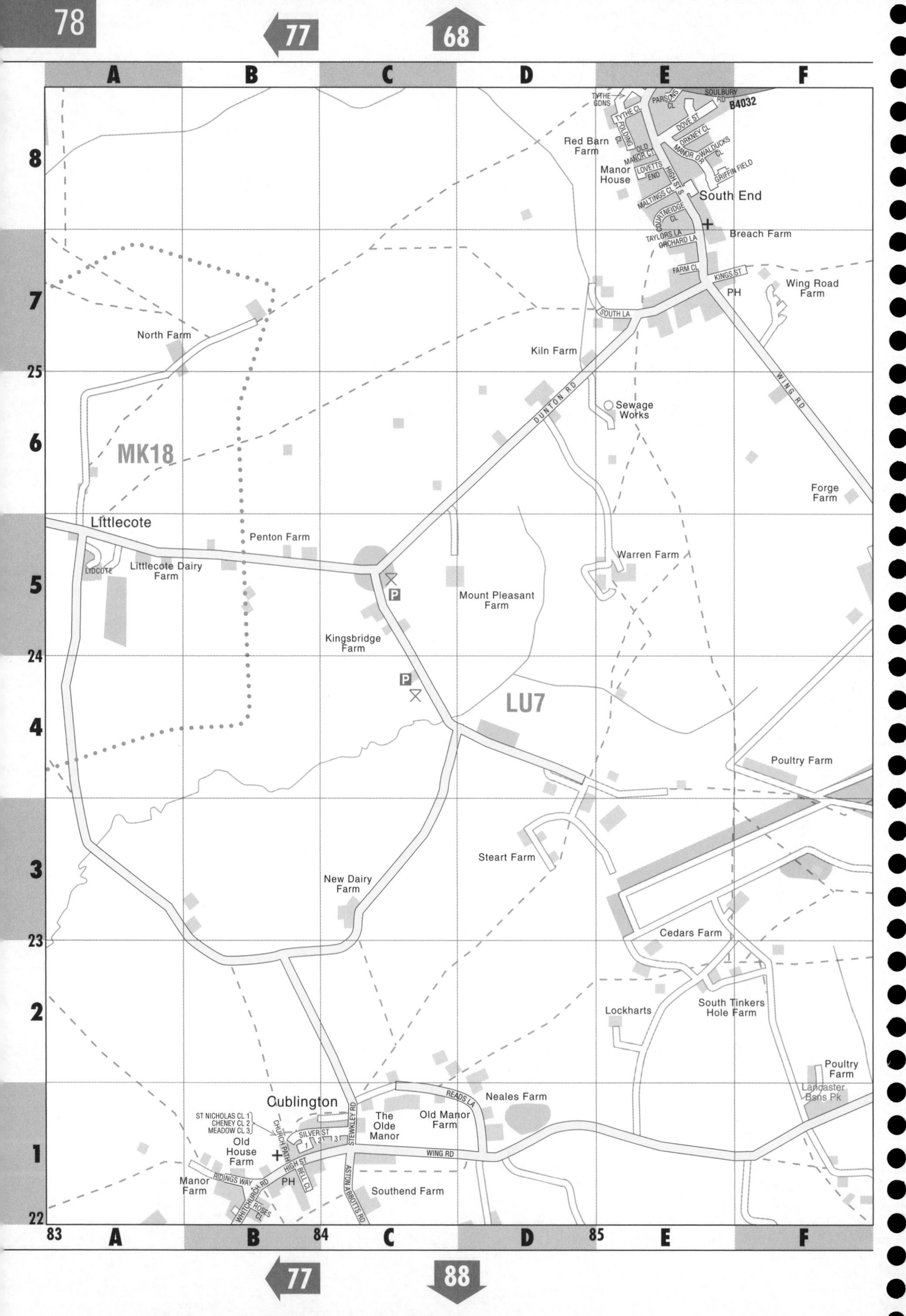
A
B
C
D
E
F
8
7
25
6
5
24
4
3
23
2
1
22
83
84
85
MK18
LU7
Littlecote
Littlecote Dairy Farm
LIDCOTE
North Farm
Penton Farm
Kingsbridge Farm
Mount Pleasant Farm
Red Barn Farm
Manor House
South End
Breach Farm
Wing Road Farm
PH
Kiln Farm
Sewage Works
Forge Farm
Warren Farm
DUNTON RD
WING RD
SOULBURY RD
B4032
TYTHE GDNS
TYTHE CL
PARSONS CL
DOVE ST
ORKNEY CL
WALDUCKS CL
GRIFFIN FIELD
MANOR DR
FOLDING CL
OLD MANOR CT
LOVETTS END
HIGH ST S
MALTINGS CL
COURTNEIDGE CL
TAYLORS LA
ORCHARD LA
FARM CL
KINGS ST
SOUTH LA
Poultry Farm
Steart Farm
New Dairy Farm
Cedars Farm
Lockharts
South Tinkers Hole Farm
Poultry Farm
Lancaster Bsns Pk
Cublington
Neales Farm
READS LA
The Olde Manor
Old Manor Farm
STEWKLEY RD
ST NICHOLAS CL 1
CHENEY CL 2
MEADOW CL 3
CHURCH PATH
SILVER ST
Old House Farm
HIGH ST
BELL CL
Manor Farm
RIDINGS WAY
WHITCHURCH RD
ROSES CL
ASTON ABBOTTS RD
Southend Farm

77
88

69
80

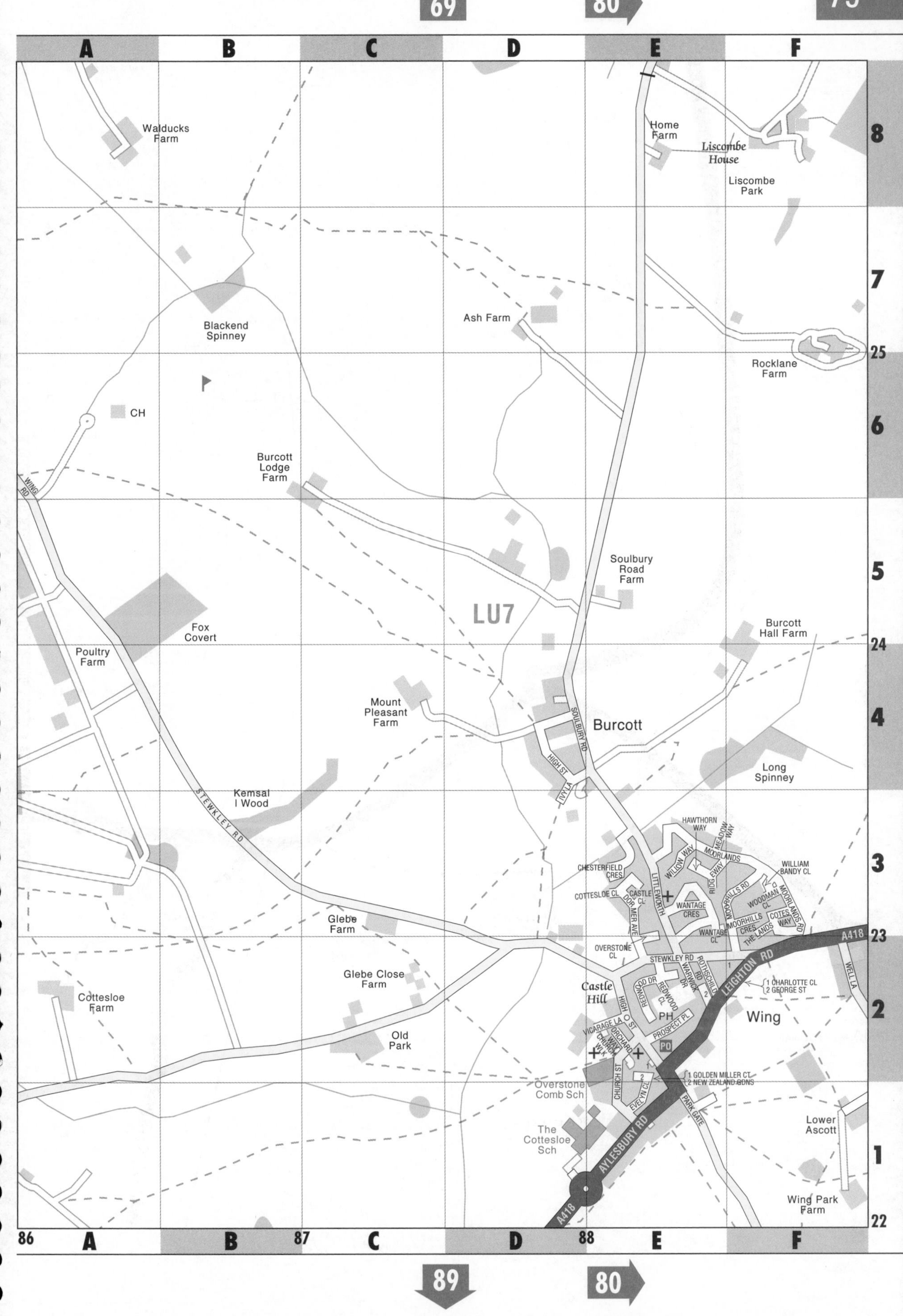
A
B
C
D
E
F
8
7
25
6
5
24
4
3
23
2
1
22
86
87
88
Waldducks Farm
Home Farm
Liscombe House
Liscombe Park
Blackend Spinney
Ash Farm
Rocklane Farm
CH
Burcott Lodge Farm
WING RD
Soulbury Road Farm
LU7
Fox Covert
Poultry Farm
Burcott Hall Farm
Mount Pleasant Farm
Burcott
SOULBURY RD
HIGH ST
IVY LA
Long Spinney
Kemsal I Wood
STEWKLEY RD
HAWTHORN WAY
MEADOW WAY
MOORLANDS
WILLOW WAY
CHESTERFIELD CRES
WILLIAM BANDY CL
COTTESLOE CL
CASTLE CL
LITTLEWORTH
RIDGEWAY
MOORHILLS RD
WANTAGE CRES
WOODMAN CL
MOORLANDS RD
COTES WAY
DORMER AVE
MOORHILLS CRES
THE LANDS
WANTAGE CL
Glebe Farm
OVERSTONE CL
STEWKLEY RD
A418
LEIGHTON RD
WELL LA
Glebe Close Farm
ROTHSCHILD RD
WARWICK DR
REDWOOD DR
REDWOOD CL
1 CHARLOTTE CL
2 GEORGE ST
Castle Hill
Cottesloe Farm
HIGH ST
PH
Wing
PROSPECT PL
VICARAGE LA
CHURCH WALK
ORCHARD WAY
PO
Old Park
CHURCH ST
1 GOLDEN MILLER CT
2 NEW ZEALAND GDNS
Overstone Comb Sch
EVELYN CL
PARK GATE
AYLESBURY RD
Lower Ascott
The Cottesloe Sch
Wing Park Farm
A418

89
80

79
70
E7
1 SPRINGFIELD CT
2 SPRINGSIDE
3 ROCKLEIGH CT
4 PARK VIEW CT
5 CASTLE HO
6 CHELSEA HO
F7
1 BASILDON CT
2 KILGOUR CT
3 YORK CT
4 ROSEBERY CT
5 TUDOR CT
6 ROPA CT
F8
1 ASHWELL ST
2 MILL RD
3 CROXLEY CT
Hop Gardens
Valley Farm
Linslade
Southcott Lower Sch
Greenleas Lower Sch
Linslade Lower Sch
Leighton Buzzard
LEIGHTON BUZZARD
Leighton Mid Sch
The Mary Bassett Lower Sch
Rock Lane
Southcourt Stud Farm
Tiddenfoot L Ctr
Cedars Upper Sch & Com Coll
Linslade Mid Sch
Tiddenfoot Waterside Park
Grovebury Road Ind Est
Grand Union Canal
Grand Union Canal Wlk
Two Ridges Link
River Ouzel
Greensand Ridge Walk
LU7
WING RD A418
LEIGHTON RD
A4146
A4012 GROVEBURY RD
B488
Waterloo Farm
Grimstone's Furze
Whitefields
Ascott Home Farm
Ascott
Chelsea Clump
Round Spinney
Ascott House
Grove Lock
Chucksell's Spinney
Grove House Stud
Well Lane Dairy
WELL LA
PH
Bedfordshire STREET ATLAS
A4012 Leighton Buzzard
A4146 Dunstable (A505 A5)
APPLE TREE CL 1
VILLAGE CT 2
EPSOM CL 3
1 COURTLANDS
2 IVESTER CT
3 ROCHESTER MEWS
89
90
91
22
23
24
25
1
2
3
4
5
6
7
8
79
90

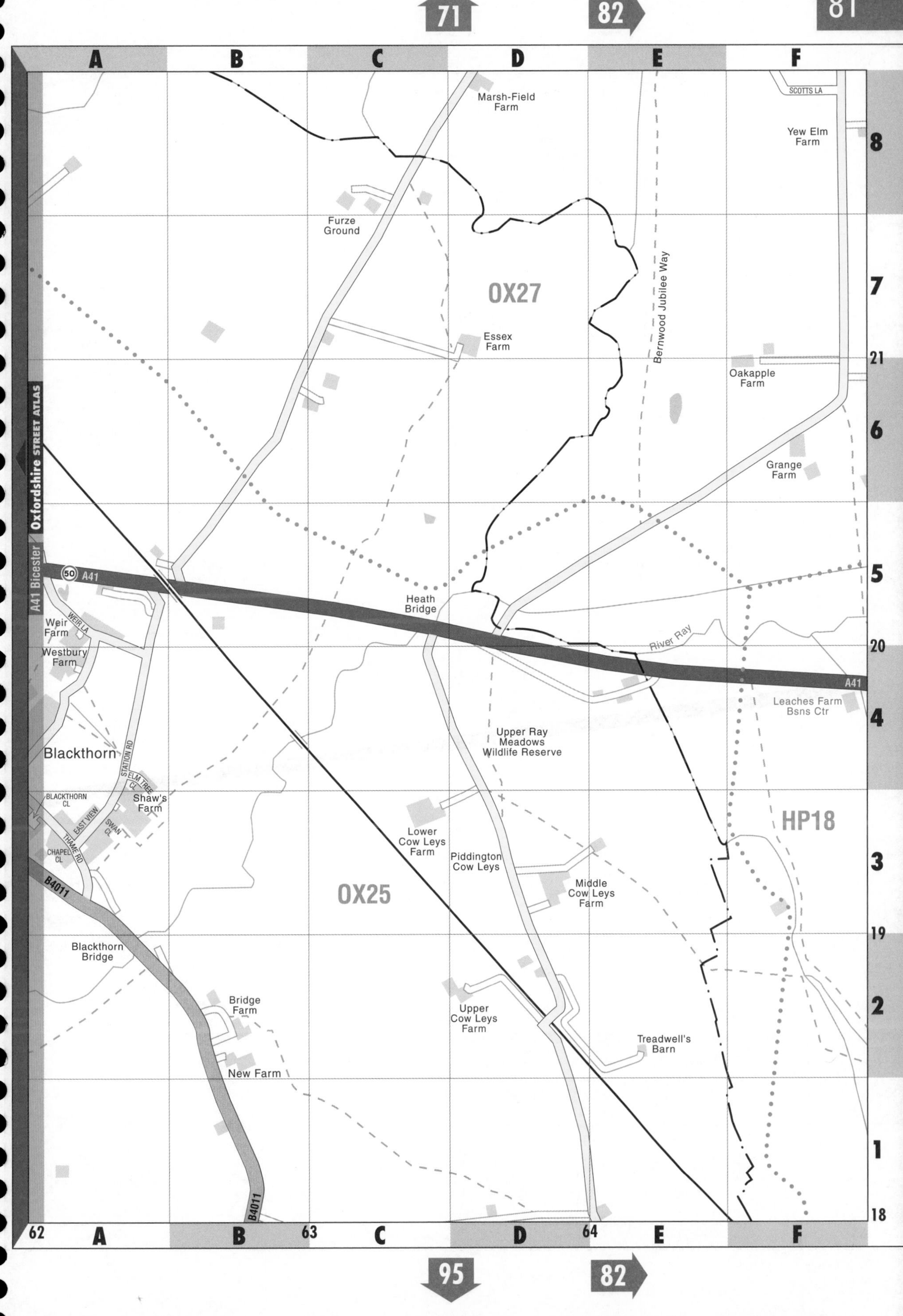

71
82
A
B
C
D
E
F
Marsh-Field Farm
SCOTTS LA
Yew Elm Farm
Furze Ground
OX27
Bernwood Jubilee Way
Essex Farm
Oakapple Farm
Grange Farm
Oxfordshire STREET ATLAS
A41 Bicester
50
A41
Heath Bridge
Weir Farm
WEIR LA
Westbury Farm
River Ray
A41
Leaches Farm Bsns Ctr
Upper Ray Meadows Wildlife Reserve
Blackthorn
STATION RD
ELM TREE CL
BLACKTHORN CL
Shaw's Farm
EAST VIEW
SWAN CL
THAME RD
CHAPEL CL
HP18
Lower Cow Leys Farm
Piddington Cow Leys
Middle Cow Leys Farm
B4011
OX25
Blackthorn Bridge
Bridge Farm
Upper Cow Leys Farm
Treadwell's Barn
New Farm
B4011
8
7
21
6
5
20
4
3
19
2
1
18
62
63
64
95
82

81
72

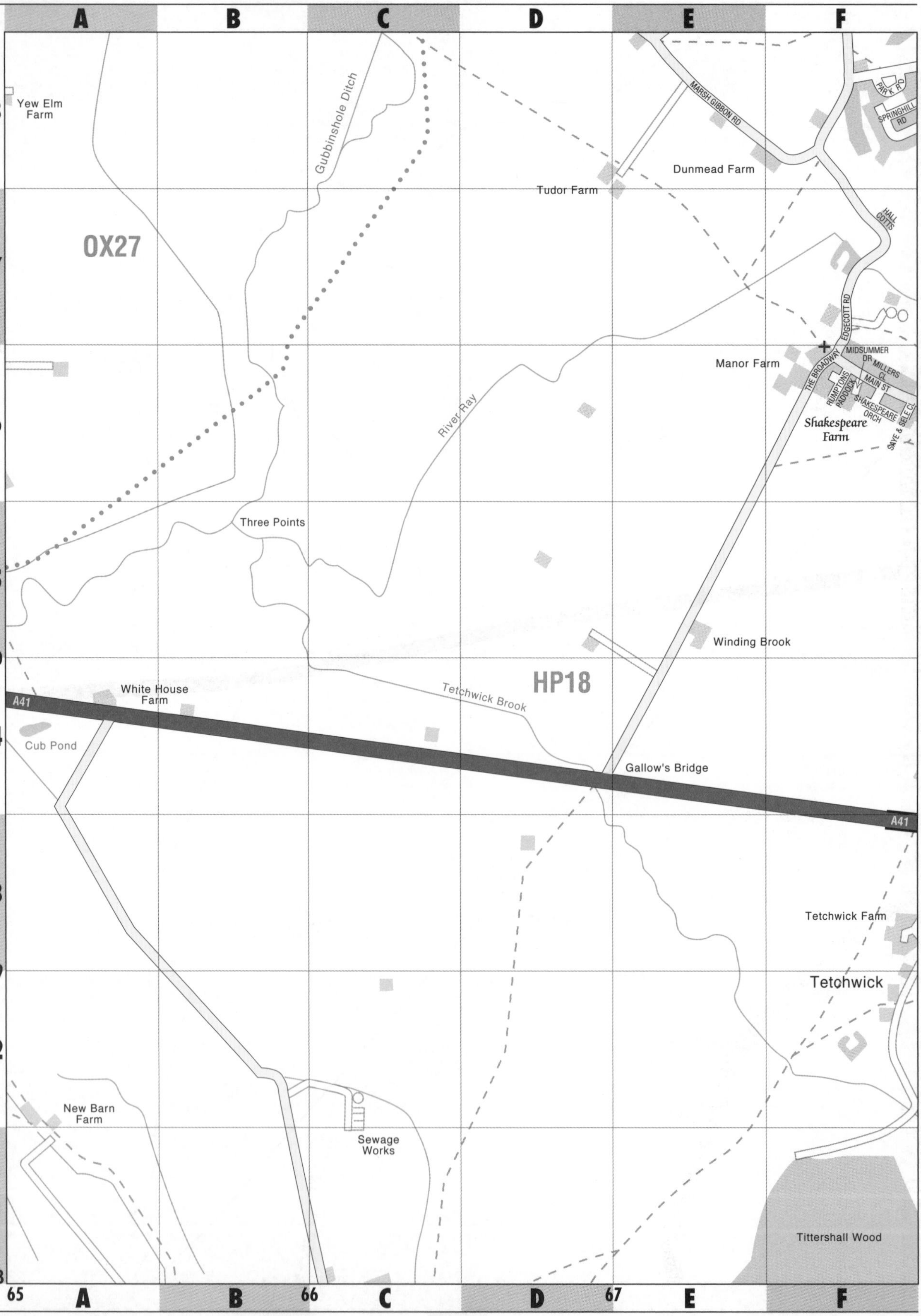

A B C D E F
8
7
21
6
5
20
4
3
19
2
1
18
Yew Elm Farm
OX27
Gubbinshole Ditch
MARSH GIBBON RD
PARK RD
SPRINGHILL RD
Dunmead Farm
Tudor Farm
HALL COTTS
EDGECOTT RD
MIDSUMMER DR
MILLERS CL
THE BROADWAY
MAIN ST
Manor Farm
RUMPTONS PADDOCK
SHAKESPEARE ORCH
SAYE & SELE CL
Shakespeare Farm
River Ray
Three Points
Winding Brook
HP18
White House Farm
A41
Tetchwick Brook
Cub Pond
Gallow's Bridge
A41
Tetchwick Farm
Tetchwick
New Barn Farm
Sewage Works
Tittershall Wood
65 A B 66 C D 67 E F

81
96

73
84

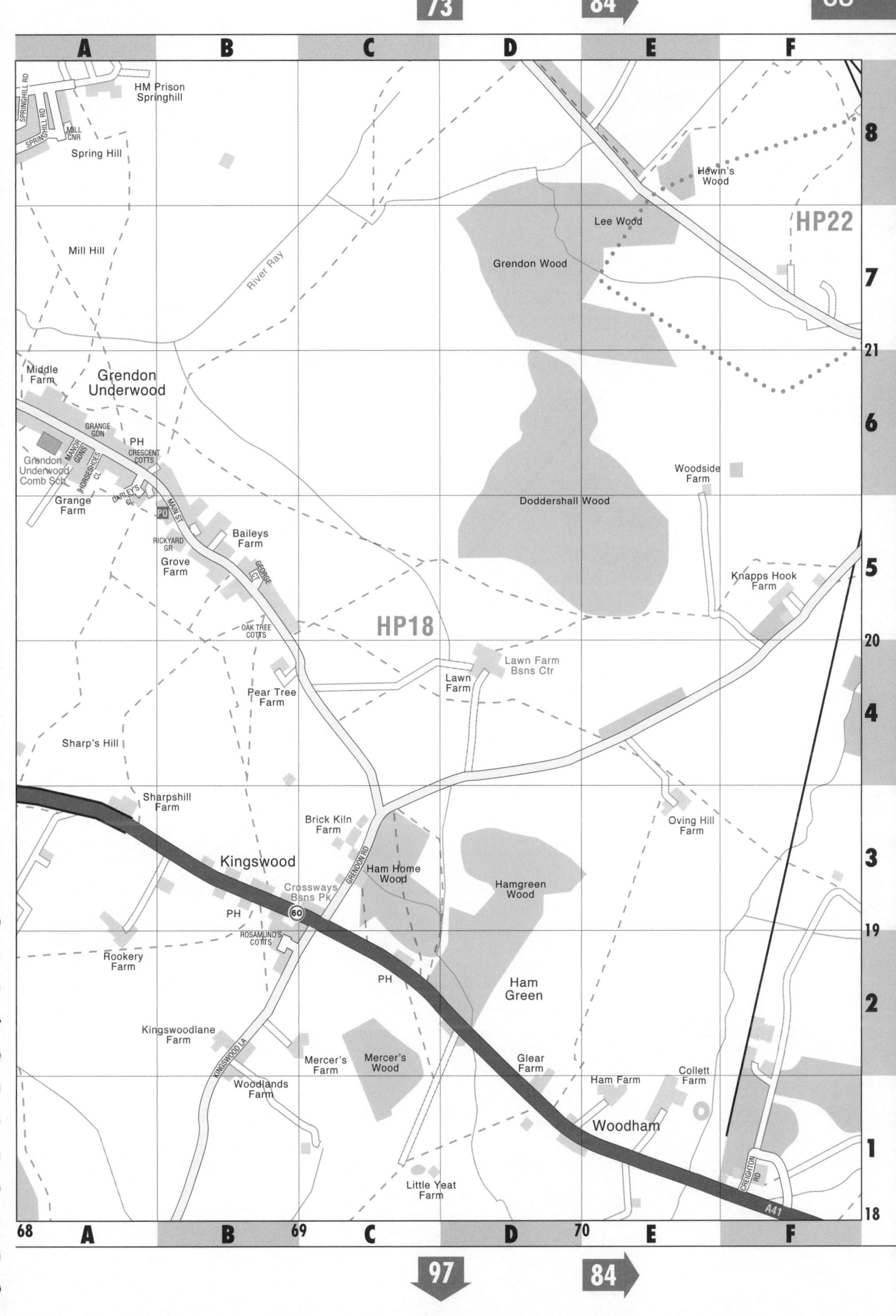
A
B
C
D
E
F
HM Prison
Springhill
Spring Hill
Mill Hill
River Ray
Grendon Wood
Lee Wood
Hewin's
Wood
HP22
Middle
Farm
Grendon
Underwood
GRANGE
GDN
PH
CRESCENT
COTTS
Grendon
Underwood
Comb Sch
Grange
Farm
Woodside
Farm
Doddershall Wood
Baileys
Farm
RICKYARD
GR
Grove
Farm
Knapps Hook
Farm
OAK TREE
COTTS
HP18
Lawn Farm
Bsns Ctr
Lawn
Farm
Pear Tree
Farm
Sharp's Hill
Sharpshill
Farm
Brick Kiln
Farm
Oving Hill
Farm
Kingswood
Ham Home
Wood
Hamgreen
Wood
Crossways
Bsns Pk
PH
ROSAMUND'S
COTTS
Rookery
Farm
PH
Ham
Green
Kingswoodlane
Farm
Mercer's
Farm
Mercer's
Wood
Glear
Farm
Ham Farm
Collett
Farm
Woodlands
Farm
Woodham
Little Yeat
Farm
A41
68
69
70
8
7
21
6
5
20
4
3
19
2
1
18

97
84

83
74

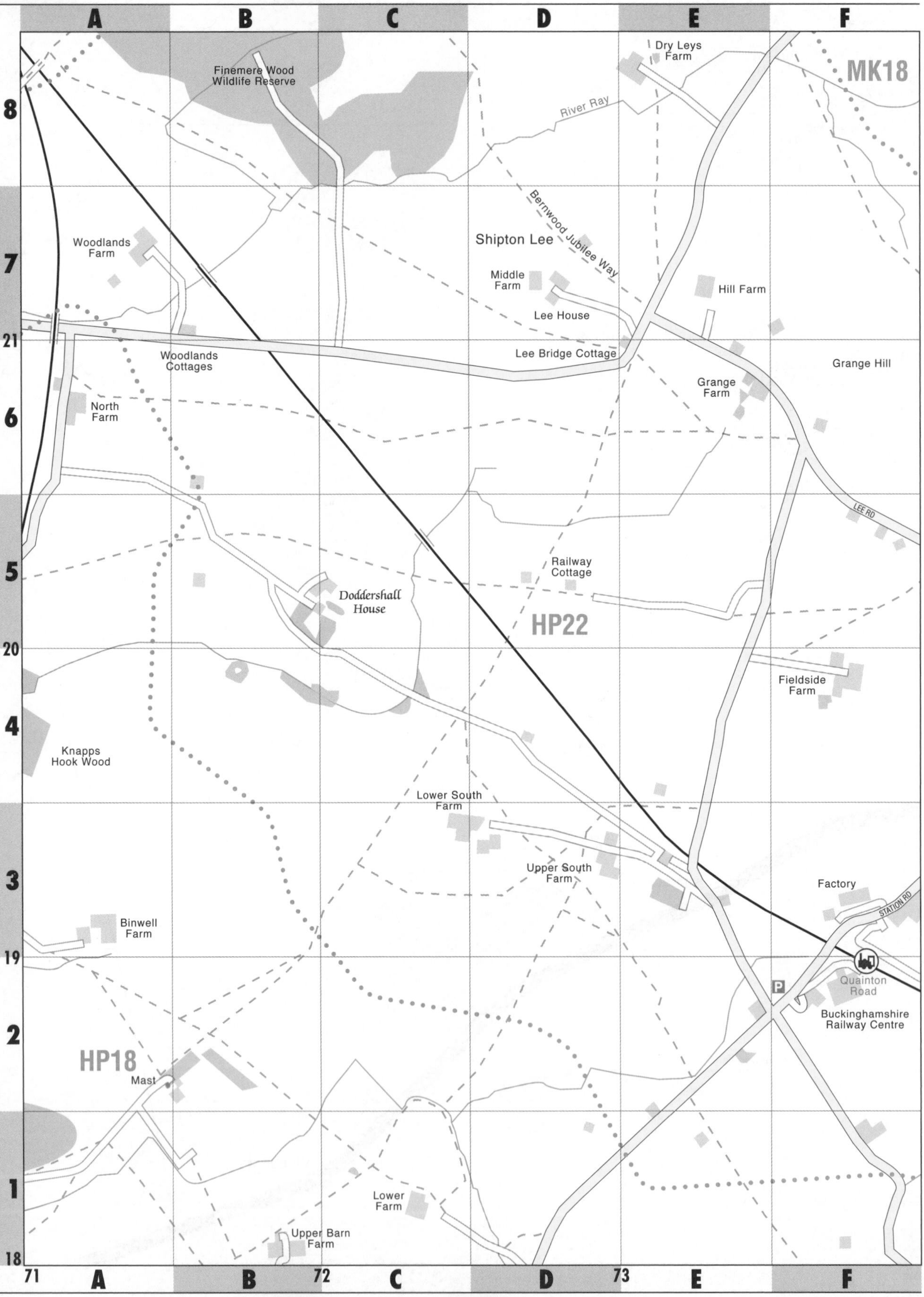

A
B
C
D
E
F
Dry Leys Farm
MK18
Finemere Wood Wildlife Reserve
River Ray
8
Bernwood Jubilee Way
Woodlands Farm
Shipton Lee
7
Middle Farm
Hill Farm
Lee House
21
Woodlands Cottages
Lee Bridge Cottage
Grange Hill
Grange Farm
North Farm
6
LEE RD
5
Railway Cottage
Doddershall House
HP22
20
Fieldside Farm
4
Knapps Hook Wood
Lower South Farm
Upper South Farm
3
Factory
STATION RD
Binwell Farm
19
Quainton Road
P
Buckinghamshire Railway Centre
2
HP18
Mast
1
Lower Farm
Upper Barn Farm
18
71
72
73

83
98

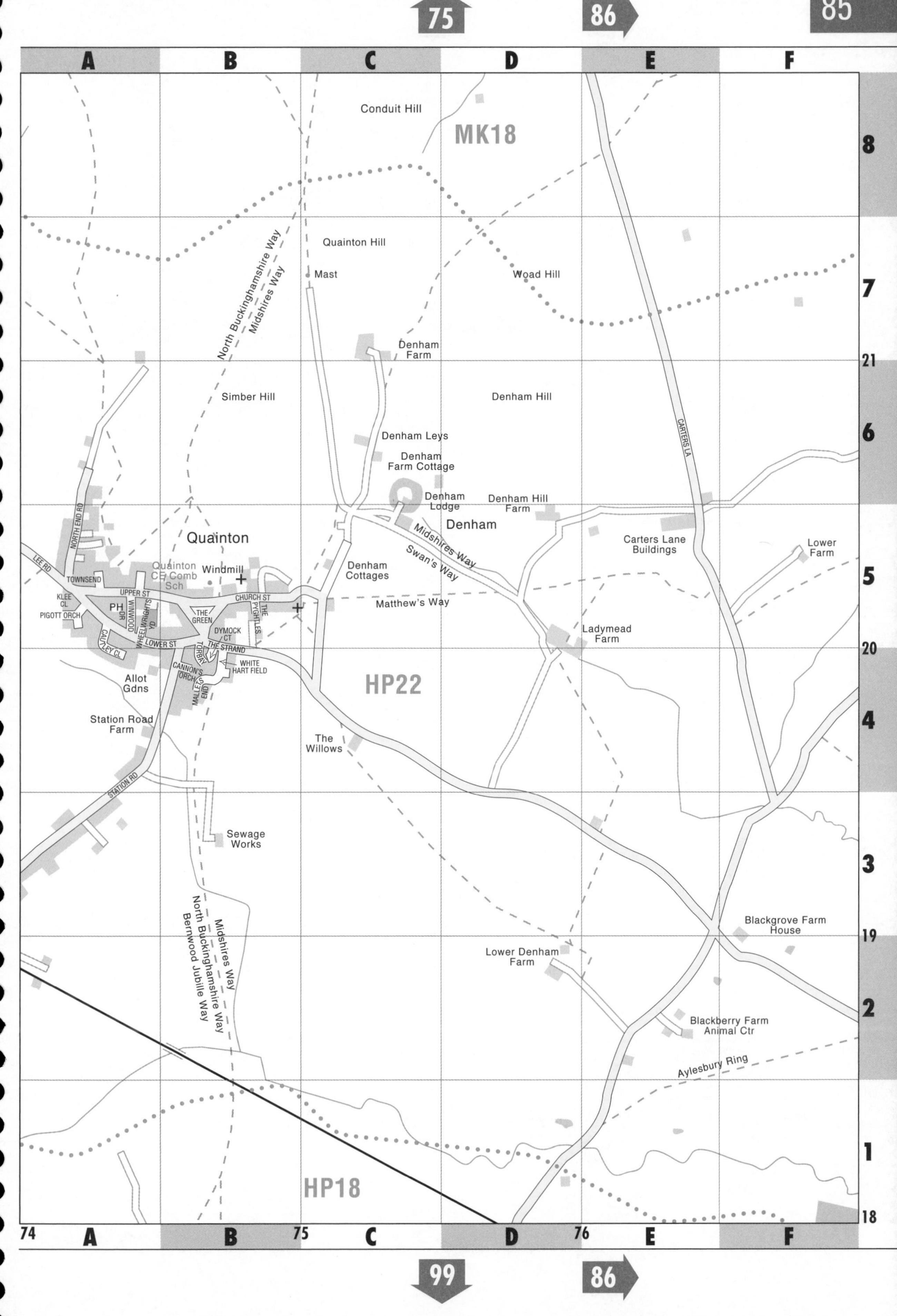
75
86
A
B
C
D
E
F
8
7
21
6
5
20
4
3
19
2
1
18
74
75
76
99
86
Conduit Hill
MK18
Quainton Hill
Mast
Woad Hill
North Buckinghamshire Way
Midshires Way
Denham Farm
Simber Hill
Denham Hill
Denham Leys
Denham Farm Cottage
Denham Lodge
Denham Hill Farm
Denham
CARTERS LA
NORTH END RD
Quainton
Carters Lane Buildings
Lower Farm
Quainton CE Comb Sch
Windmill
Midshires Way
Swan's Way
Denham Cottages
LEE RD
TOWNSEND
KLEE CL
UPPER ST
PH
PIGOTT ORCH
WINWOOD DR
WHEELWRIGHTS YD
THE GREEN
CHURCH ST
THE PYGHTLES
Matthew's Way
Ladymead Farm
CAULEY CL
LOWER ST
DYMOCK CT
THE STRAND
TORBAY
WHITE HART FIELD
CANNON'S ORCH
MALLETS END
Allot Gdns
HP22
Station Road Farm
The Willows
STATION RD
Sewage Works
Midshires Way
North Buckinghamshire Way
Bernwood Jubilee Way
Blackgrove Farm House
Lower Denham Farm
Blackberry Farm Animal Ctr
Aylesbury Ring
HP18

85
76

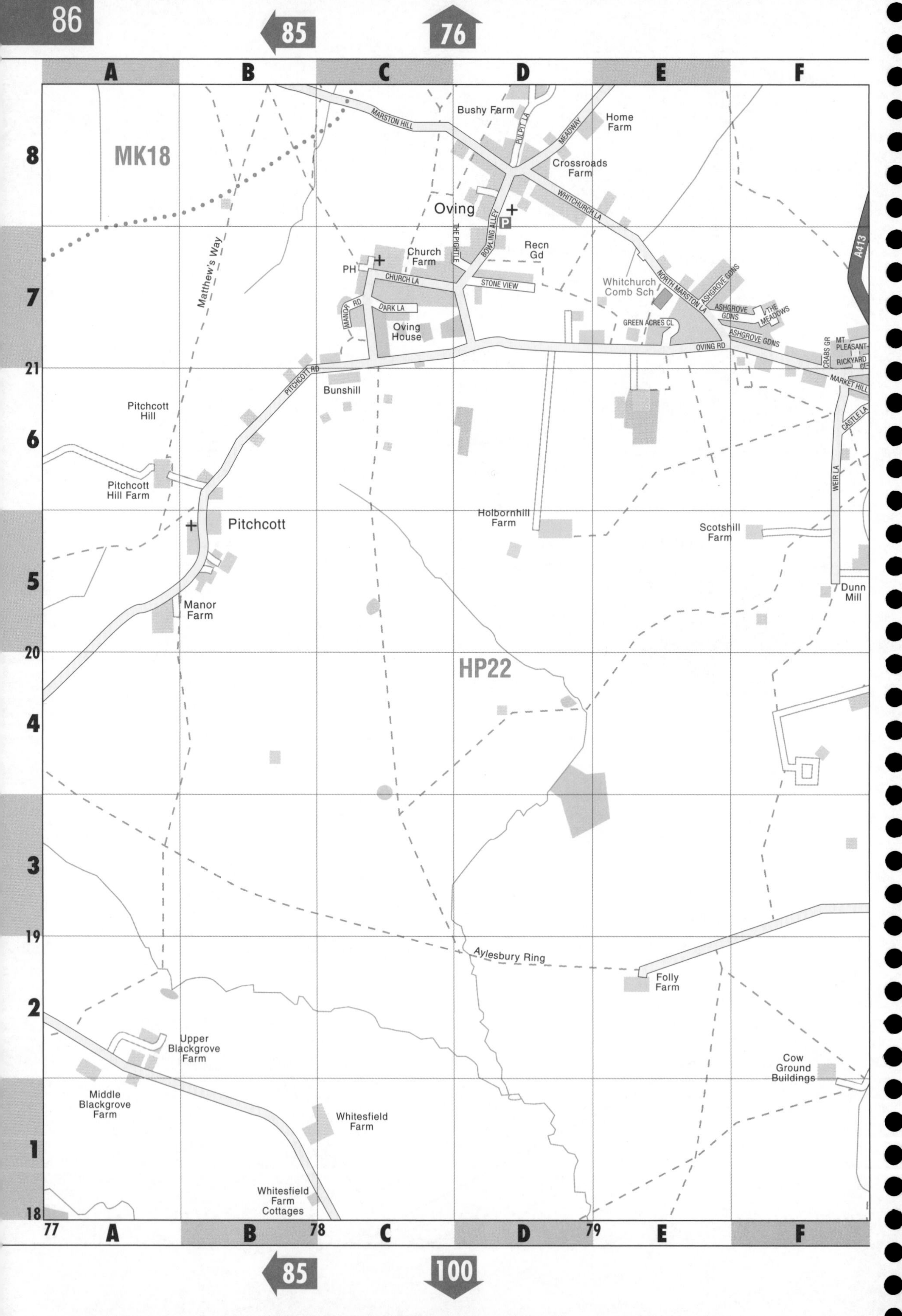
A
B
C
D
E
F
8
7
21
6
5
20
4
3
19
2
1
18
77
78
79
MK18
HP22
Marston Hill
Bushy Farm
Pulpit La
Meadway
Home Farm
Crossroads Farm
Oving
Whitchurch La
Matthew's Way
Church Farm
The Pightle
Bowling Alley
Recn Gd
PH
Church La
Stone View
Whitchurch Comb Sch
North Marston La
Ashgrove Gdns
Manor Rd
Dark La
Oving House
Green Acres Cl
The Meadows
Oving Rd
Crabs Gr
Mt Pleasant
Rickyard Cl
Market Hill
A413
Pitchcott Rd
Bunshill
Pitchcott Hill
Castle La
Pitchcott Hill Farm
Weir La
Pitchcott
Holbornhill Farm
Scotshill Farm
Manor Farm
Dunn Mill
Aylesbury Ring
Folly Farm
Upper Blackgrove Farm
Cow Ground Buildings
Middle Blackgrove Farm
Whitesfield Farm
Whitesfield Farm Cottages

85
100

77
88

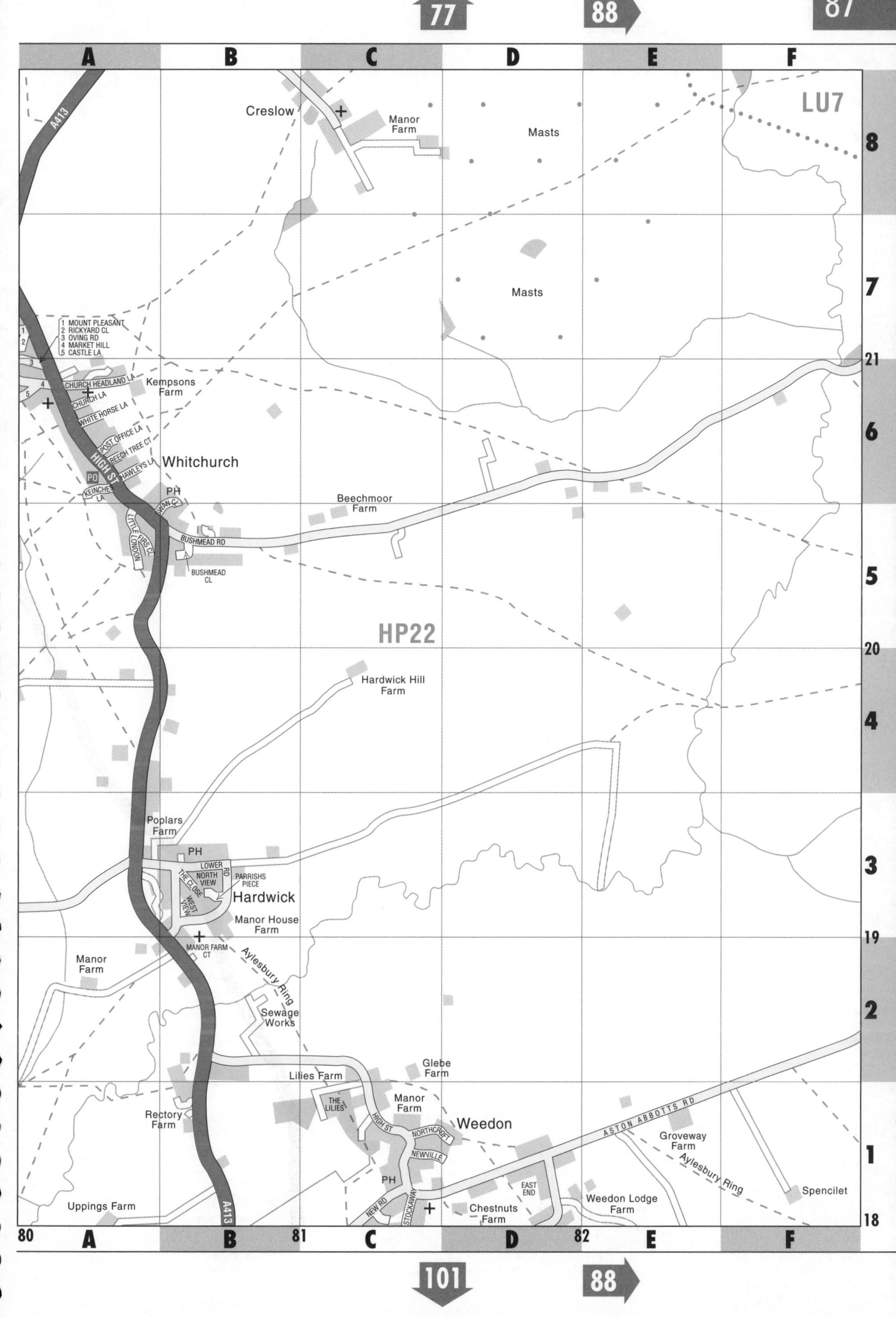
A
B
C
D
E
F
LU7
8
7
21
6
5
20
4
3
19
2
1
18
80
81
82
A413
Creslow
Manor
Farm
Masts
Masts
1 MOUNT PLEASANT
2 RICKYARD CL
3 OVING RD
4 MARKET HILL
5 CASTLE LA
CHURCH HEADLAND LA
CHURCH LA
WHITE HORSE LA
POST OFFICE LA
BEECH TREE CT
HAWLEYS LA
KEINCHES LA
HIGH ST
PO
Kempsons
Farm
Whitchurch
PH
LITTLE LONDON
FIRS CL
BUSHMEAD RD
BUSHMEAD
CL
Beechmoor
Farm
HP22
Hardwick Hill
Farm
Poplars
Farm
PH
LOWER RD
NORTH VIEW
THE CLOSE
WEST VIEW
PARRISHS
PIECE
Hardwick
Manor House
Farm
MANOR FARM
CT
Manor
Farm
Aylesbury Ring
Sewage
Works
Lilies Farm
Glebe
Farm
THE
LILIES
Manor
Farm
Rectory
Farm
HIGH ST
NORTHCROFT
NEWVILLE
Weedon
ASTON ABBOTTS RD
Groveway
Farm
Aylesbury Ring
Spencilet
PH
NEW RD
STOCKAWAY
EAST
END
Chestnuts
Farm
Weedon Lodge
Farm
Uppings Farm
A413

101
88

87
78

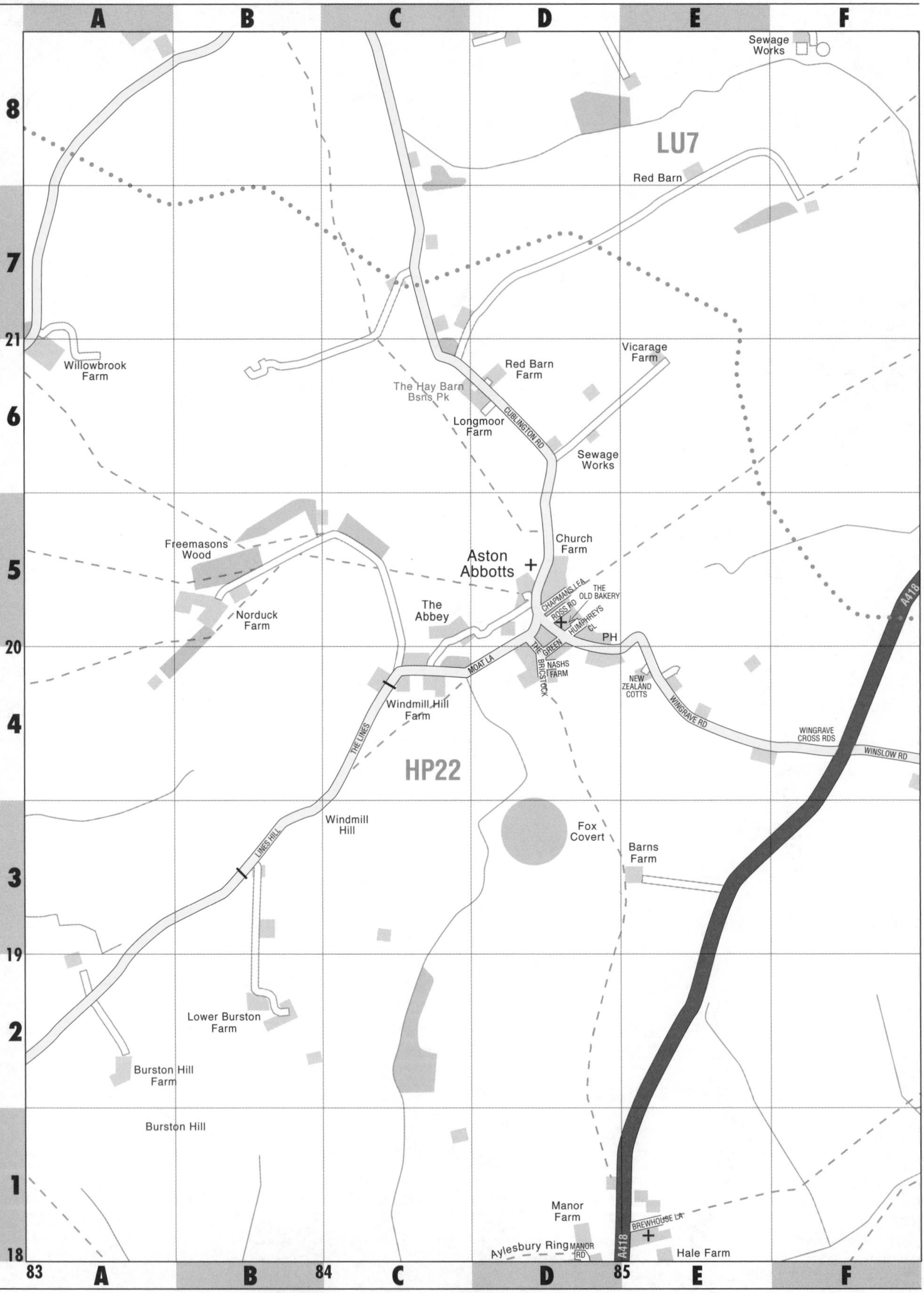

A B C D E F
8
7
21
6
5
20
4
3
19
2
1
18
LU7
Sewage Works
Red Barn
Willowbrook Farm
Vicarage Farm
Red Barn Farm
The Hay Barn Bsns Pk
Longmoor Farm
CUBLINGTON RD
Sewage Works
Freemasons Wood
Church Farm
Aston Abbotts
Norduck Farm
The Abbey
CHAPMANS LEA
THE OLD BAKERY
ROSS RD
HUMPHREYS CL
PH
THE GREEN
MOAT LA
THE BRICSTOCK
NASHS FARM
NEW ZEALAND COTTS
WINGRAVE RD
WINGRAVE CROSS RDS
WINSLOW RD
A418
Windmill Hill Farm
THE LINES
HP22
Windmill Hill
LINES HILL
Fox Covert
Barns Farm
Lower Burston Farm
Burston Hill Farm
Burston Hill
Manor Farm
BREWHOUSE LA
Aylesbury Ring
MANOR RD
A418
Hale Farm
83 A B 84 C D 85 E F

87
102

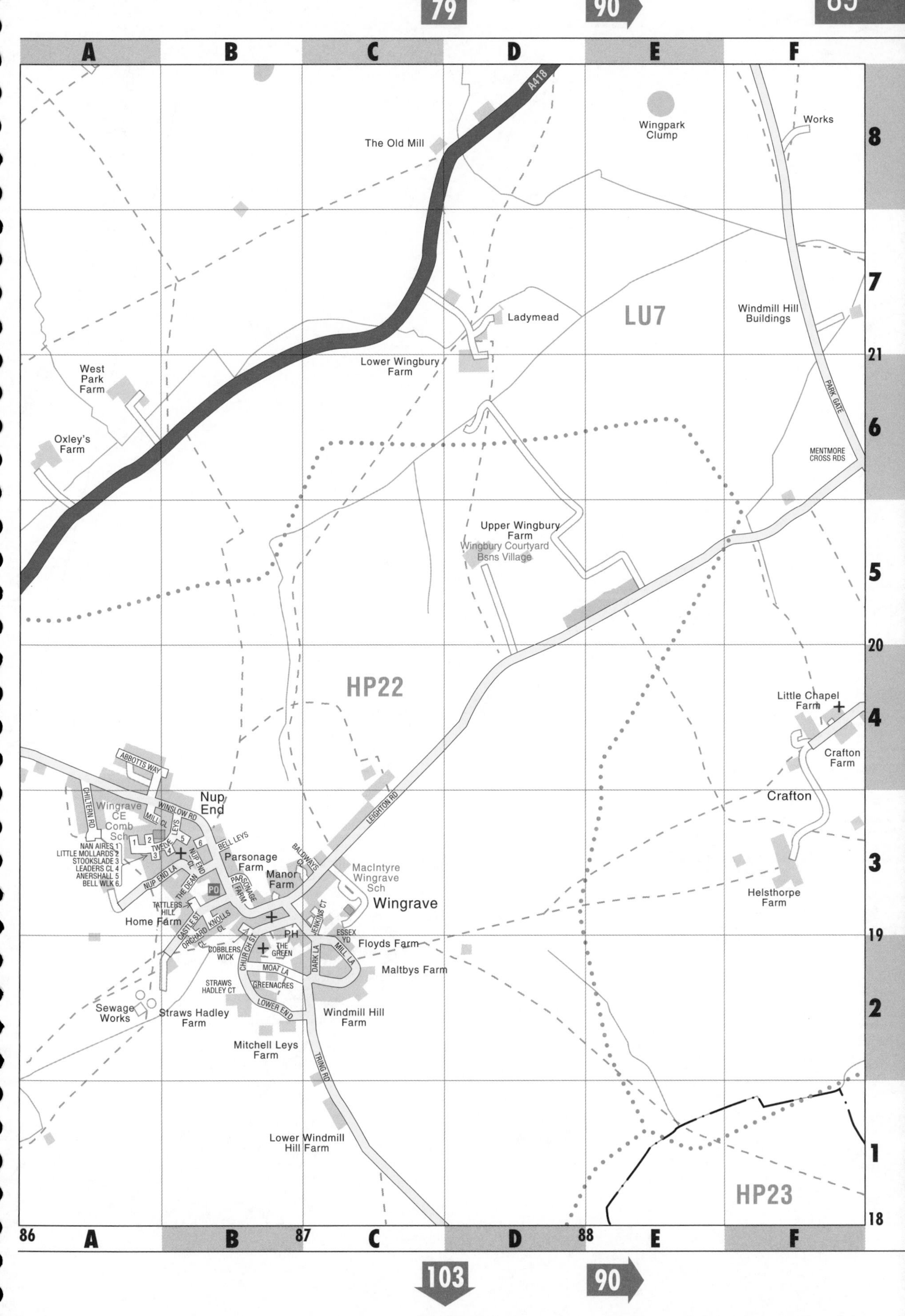
79
90
A
B
C
D
E
F
A418
The Old Mill
Wingpark
Clump
Works
8
Ladymead
LU7
Windmill Hill
Buildings
7
Lower Wingbury
Farm
21
West
Park
Farm
Oxley's
Farm
PARK GATE
6
MENTMORE
CROSS RDS
Upper Wingbury
Farm
Wingbury Courtyard
Bsns Village
5
20
HP22
Little Chapel
Farm
Crafton
Farm
4
Crafton
ABBOTTS WAY
Nup
End
CHILTERN RD
Wingrave
CE
Comb
Sch
WINSLOW RD
MILL CL
TWELVE LEYS
BELL LEYS
NUP END CL
LEIGHTON RD
BALDWAYS CL
NAN AIRES 1
LITTLE MOLLARDS 2
STOOKSLADE 3
LEADERS CL 4
ANERSHALL 5
BELL WLK 6
NUP END LA
THE DEAN
Parsonage
Farm
PARSONAGE FARM
Manor
Farm
MacIntyre
Wingrave
Sch
Wingrave
3
Helsthorpe
Farm
PO
TATTLERS HILL
Home Farm
CASTLE ST
ORCHARD CL
KNOLLS CL
PH
JENKINS CT
ESSEX YD
Floyds Farm
19
COBBLERS WICK
CHURCH ST
THE GREEN
DARK LA
MILL LA
MOAT LA
Maltbys Farm
STRAWS HADLEY CT
GREENACRES
LOWER END
Sewage
Works
Straws Hadley
Farm
Windmill Hill
Farm
2
Mitchell Leys
Farm
TRING RD
Lower Windmill
Hill Farm
1
HP23
18
86
87
88
103
90

89
80

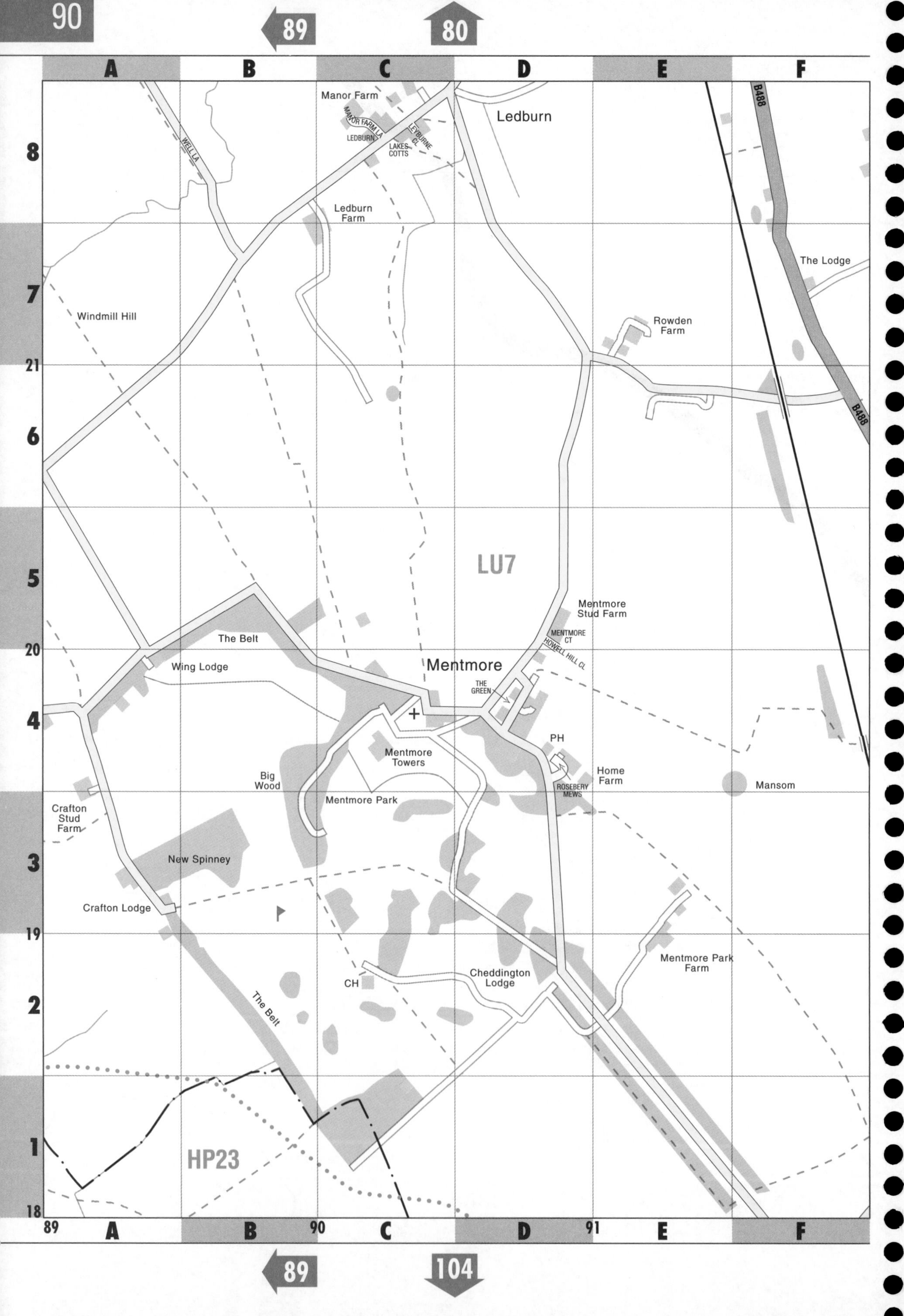
A
B
C
D
E
F
Manor Farm
Ledburn
MANOR FARM LA
LEDBURN
LEYBURNE CL
LAKES COTTS
WELL LA
B488
8
Ledburn Farm
The Lodge
7
Windmill Hill
Rowden Farm
21
6
LU7
5
Mentmore Stud Farm
MENTMORE CT
HOWELL HILL CL
The Belt
20
Wing Lodge
Mentmore
THE GREEN
4
PH
Mentmore Towers
Home Farm
Big Wood
ROSEBERY MEWS
Mansom
Crafton Stud Farm
Mentmore Park
3
New Spinney
Crafton Lodge
19
Mentmore Park Farm
Cheddington Lodge
CH
2
The Belt
1
HP23
18
89
90
91

89
104

92

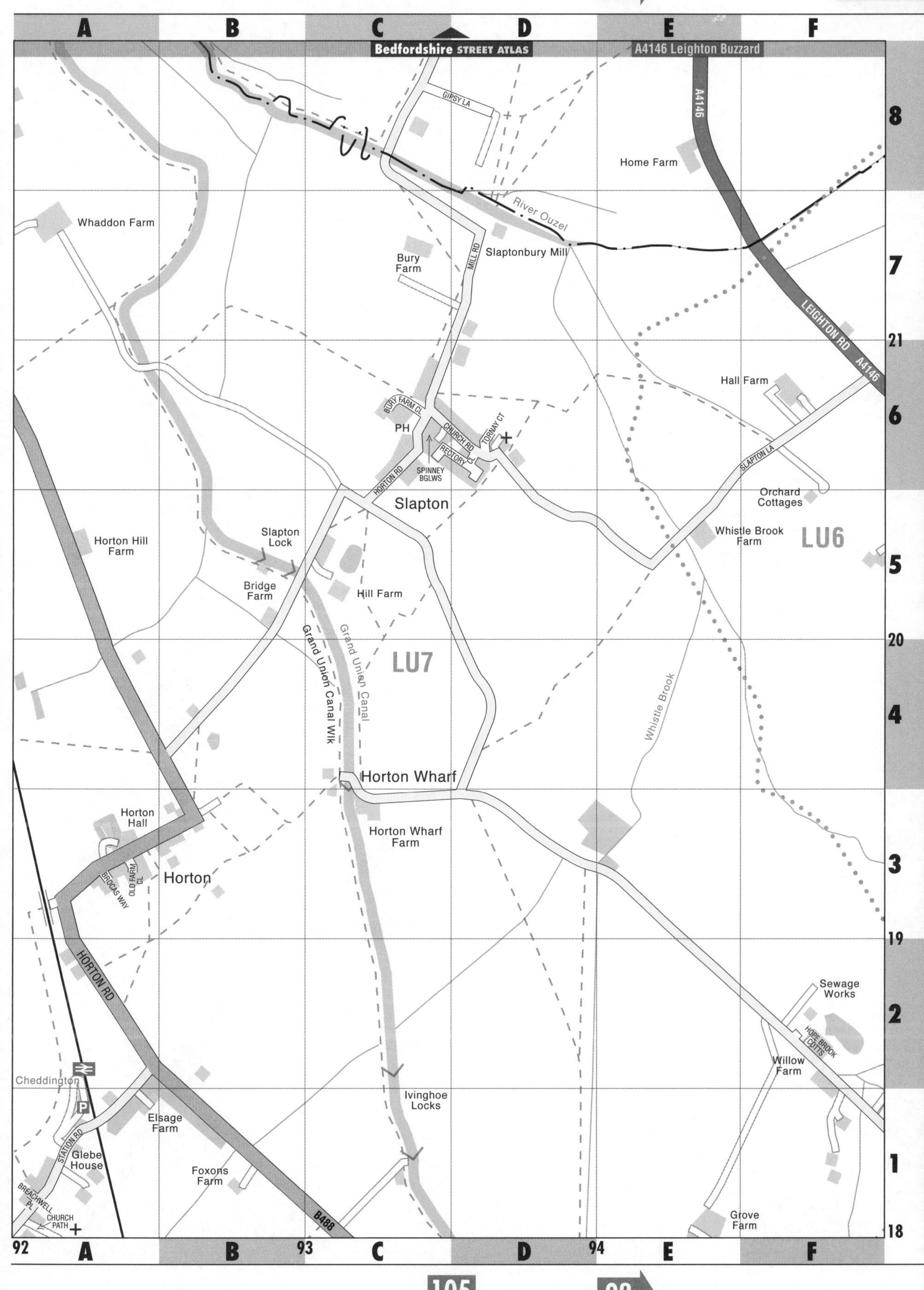
Bedfordshire STREET ATLAS
A4146 Leighton Buzzard
A B C D E F
8 7 21 6 5 20 4 3 19 2 1 18
92 93 94
GIPSY LA
A4146
Home Farm
River Ouzel
Whaddon Farm
Slaptonbury Mill
Bury Farm
MILL RD
LEIGHTON RD
Hall Farm
BURY FARM CL
PH
CHURCH RD
TORNAY CT
RECTORY CL
SPINNEY BGLWS
HORTON RD
SLAPTON LA
Orchard Cottages
Slapton
Slapton Lock
Whistle Brook Farm
LU6
Horton Hill Farm
Bridge Farm
Hill Farm
Grand Union Canal Wlk
Grand Union Canal
LU7
Whistle Brook
Horton Wharf
Horton Hall
Horton Wharf Farm
BROCAS WAY
OLD FARM CL
Horton
HORTON RD
Sewage Works
HOPE BROOK COTTS
Willow Farm
Cheddington
P
Ivinghoe Locks
Elsage Farm
STATION RD
Glebe House
Foxons Farm
BREACHWELL PL
CHURCH PATH
B488
Grove Farm

105

92

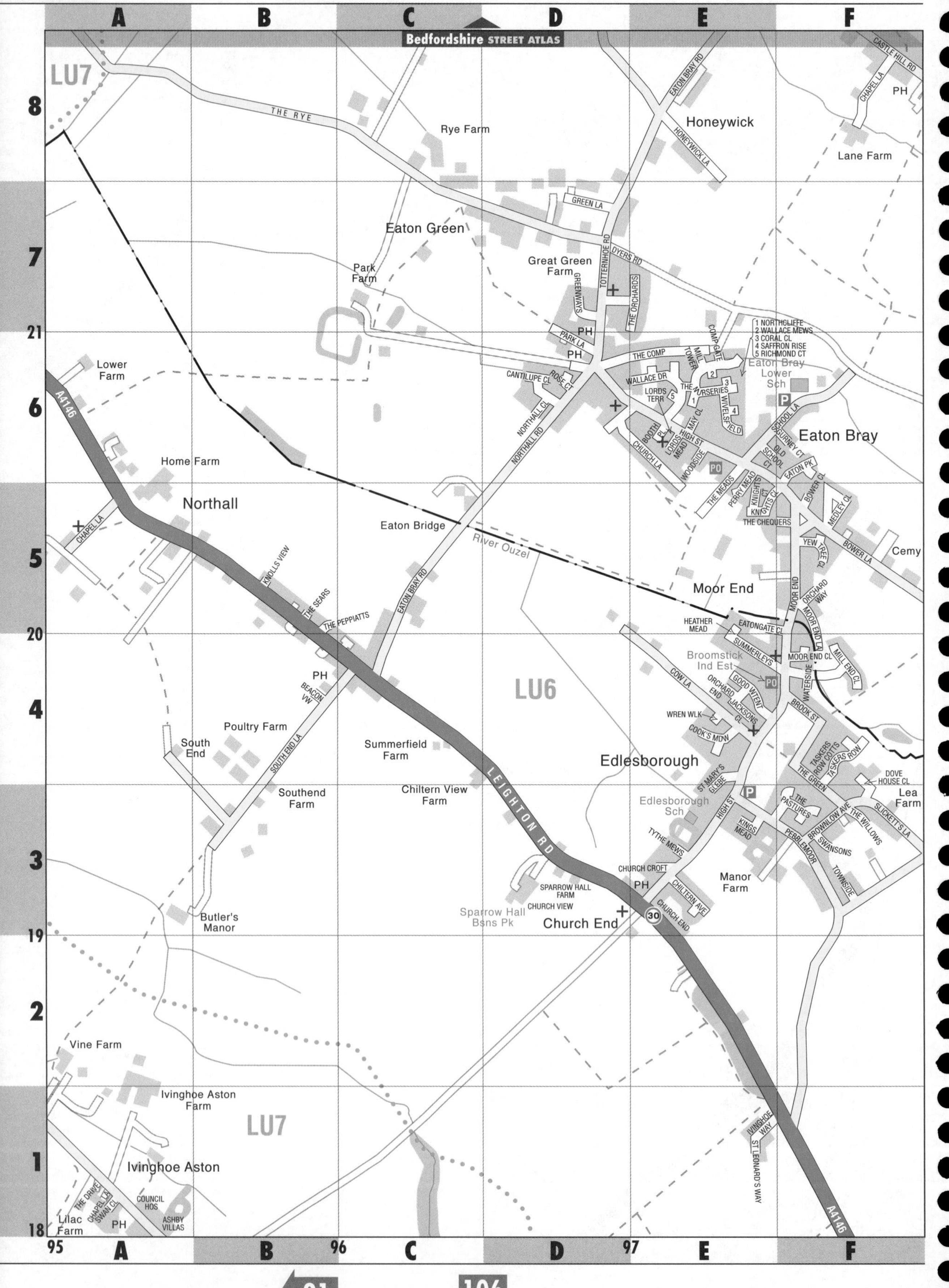
Bedfordshire STREET ATLAS
A
B
C
D
E
F
8
7
21
6
5
20
4
3
19
2
1
18
95
96
97
LU7
THE RYE
Rye Farm
Honeywick
EATON BRAY RD
HONEYWICK LA
CASTLE HILL RD
CHAPEL LA
PH
Lane Farm
GREEN LA
Eaton Green
Great Green Farm
GREENWAYS
TOTTERNHOE RD
DYERS RD
THE ORCHARDS
Park Farm
PH
PARK LA
PH
COMP GATE
1 NORTHCLIFFE
2 WALLACE MEWS
3 CORAL CL
4 SAFFRON RISE
5 RICHMOND CT
Eaton Bray Lower Sch
THE COMP
MILL TOWER
WALLACE DR
THE NURSERIES
CANTILUPE CL
ROSE CT
LORDS TERR
WIVELSFIELD
MAY CL
Lower Farm
A4146
NORTHALL CL
NORTHALL RD
BOOTH PL
LORDS MEAD
HIGH ST
CHURCH LA
WOODSIDE
SCHOOL LA
GURNEY CT
OLD SCHOOL CT
Eaton Bray
EATON PK
Home Farm
Northall
PO
THE MEADS
PERRY MEAD
KNIGHTS CT
BOWER CL
MEDLEY CL
THE CHEQUERS
CHAPEL LA
Eaton Bridge
River Ouzel
YEW TREE CL
BOWER LA
Cemy
KNOLLS VIEW
Moor End
MOOR END
ORCHARD WAY
THE SEARS
THE PEPPIATTS
EATON BRAY RD
HEATHER MEAD
EATONGATE CL
MOOR END LA
SUMMERLEYS
MOOR END CL
MILL END CL
Broomstick Ind Est
PH
BEACON VW
LU6
COW LA
ORCHARD END
GOOD WYENT
WATERSIDE
JACKSONS CL
BROOK ST
WREN WLK
COOK'S MDW
Poultry Farm
South End
SOUTH END LA
Summerfield Farm
Edlesborough
TASKERS ROW COTTS
TASKERS ROW
THE GREEN
DOVE HOUSE CL
Lea Farm
LEIGHTON RD
Southend Farm
Chiltern View Farm
ST MARY'S GLEBE
Edlesborough Sch
HIGH ST
THE PASTURES
BROWNLOW AVE
THE WILLOWS
SLICKETT'S LA
TYTHE MEWS
KINGS MEAD
PEBBLEMOOR
SWANSONS
TOWNSIDE
CHURCH CROFT
Manor Farm
PH
CHILTERN AVE
SPARROW HALL FARM
CHURCH VIEW
Butler's Manor
Sparrow Hall Bsns Pk
Church End
30
CHURCH END
Vine Farm
Ivinghoe Aston Farm
LU7
IVINGHOE WAY
ST LEONARD'S WAY
Ivinghoe Aston
THE DRIVE
CHAPEL LA
SWAN CL
COUNCIL HOS
ASHBY VILLAS
Lilac Farm
PH
A4146

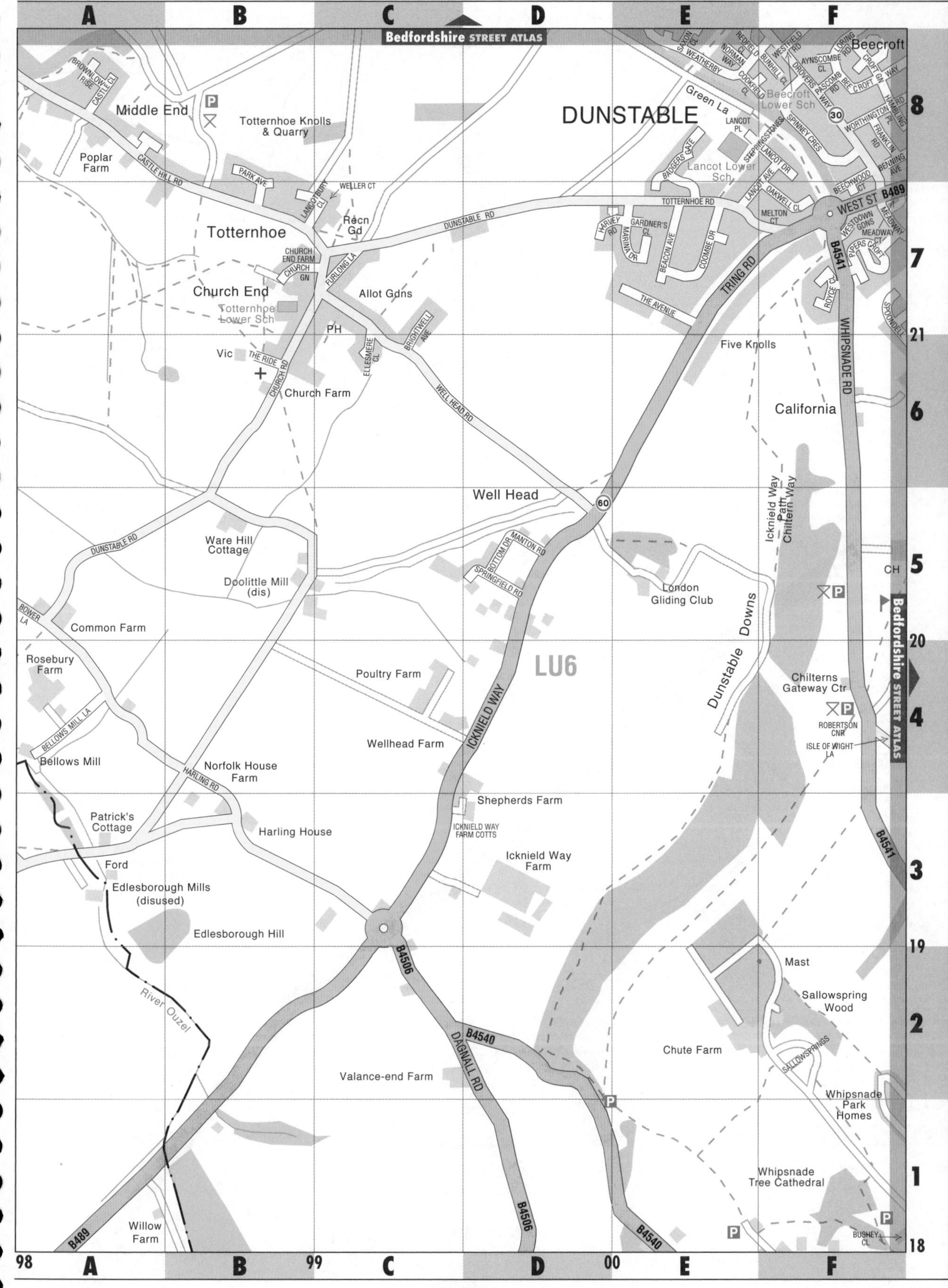
Bedfordshire STREET ATLAS
A
B
C
D
E
F
DUNSTABLE
Totternhoe
Middle End
Church End
Totternhoe Knolls & Quarry
Poplar Farm
Recn Gd
Allot Gdns
Totternhoe Lower Sch
PH
Vic
Church Farm
Beecroft
Beecroft Lower Sch
Lancot Lower Sch
Green La
DUNSTABLE RD
TOTTERNHOE RD
TRING RD
WEST ST
B489
B4541
WHIPSNADE RD
Five Knolls
California
Well Head
Icknield Way Path
Chiltern Way
Ware Hill Cottage
Doolittle Mill (dis)
London Gliding Club
Common Farm
Rosebury Farm
Poultry Farm
LU6
Dunstable Downs
Chilterns Gateway Ctr
CH
ROBERTSON CNR
ISLE OF WIGHT LA
Wellhead Farm
ICKNIELD WAY
Bellows Mill
Norfolk House Farm
HARLING RD
Shepherds Farm
ICKNIELD WAY FARM COTTS
Patrick's Cottage
Harling House
Icknield Way Farm
Ford
Edlesborough Mills (disused)
Edlesborough Hill
B4506
Mast
Sallowspring Wood
River Ouzel
B4540
DAGNALL RD
Valance-end Farm
Chute Farm
SALLOWSPRINGS
Whipsnade Park Homes
Whipsnade Tree Cathedral
Willow Farm
BUSHEY CL
8
7
21
6
5
20
4
3
19
2
1
18
98
99
00
60
30

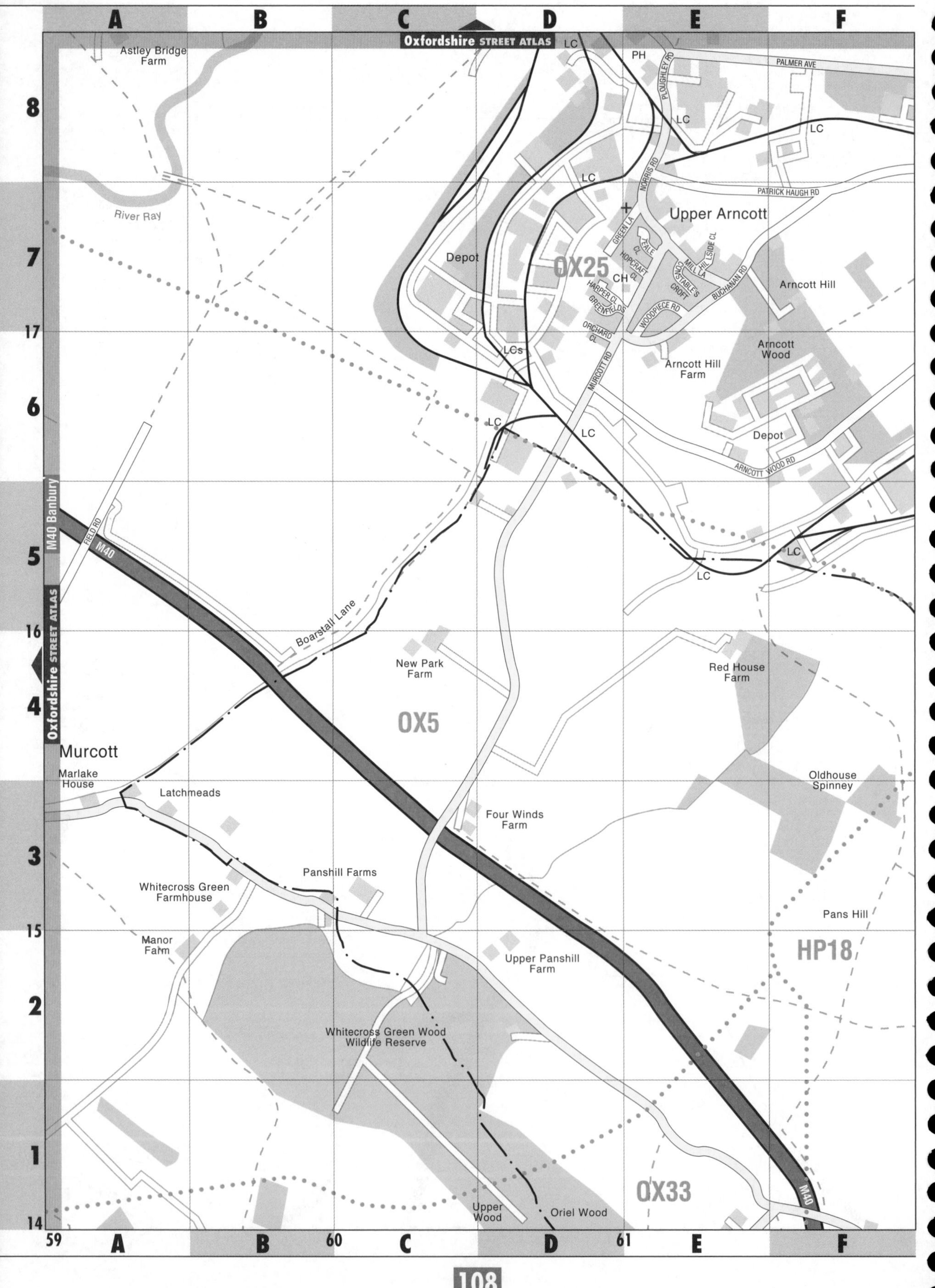

A
B
C
D
E
F
Oxfordshire STREET ATLAS
8
7
17
6
5
16
4
3
15
2
1
14
59
60
61
Astley Bridge Farm
River Ray
LC
PH
PLOUGHLEY RD
PALMER AVE
LC
LC
NORRIS RD
LC
PATRICK HAUGH RD
Upper Arncott
GREEN LA
TEALE CL
HILLSIDE CL
MILL LA
HOPCRAFT CL
CONSTABLE'S CROFT
BUCHANAN RD
Depot
OX25
CH
HARPER CL
GREENFIELDS
WOODPIECE RD
Arncott Hill
ORCHARD CL
LCs
Arncott Wood
Arncott Hill Farm
MURCOTT RD
LC
LC
Depot
ARNCOTT WOOD RD
M40 Banbury
FIELD RD
M40
LC
LC
Boarstall Lane
New Park Farm
Red House Farm
OX5
Murcott
Marlake House
Latchmeads
Oldhouse Spinney
Four Winds Farm
Panshill Farms
Whitecross Green Farmhouse
Pans Hill
Manor Farm
Upper Panshill Farm
HP18
Whitecross Green Wood Wildlife Reserve
OX33
M40
Upper Wood
Oriel Wood

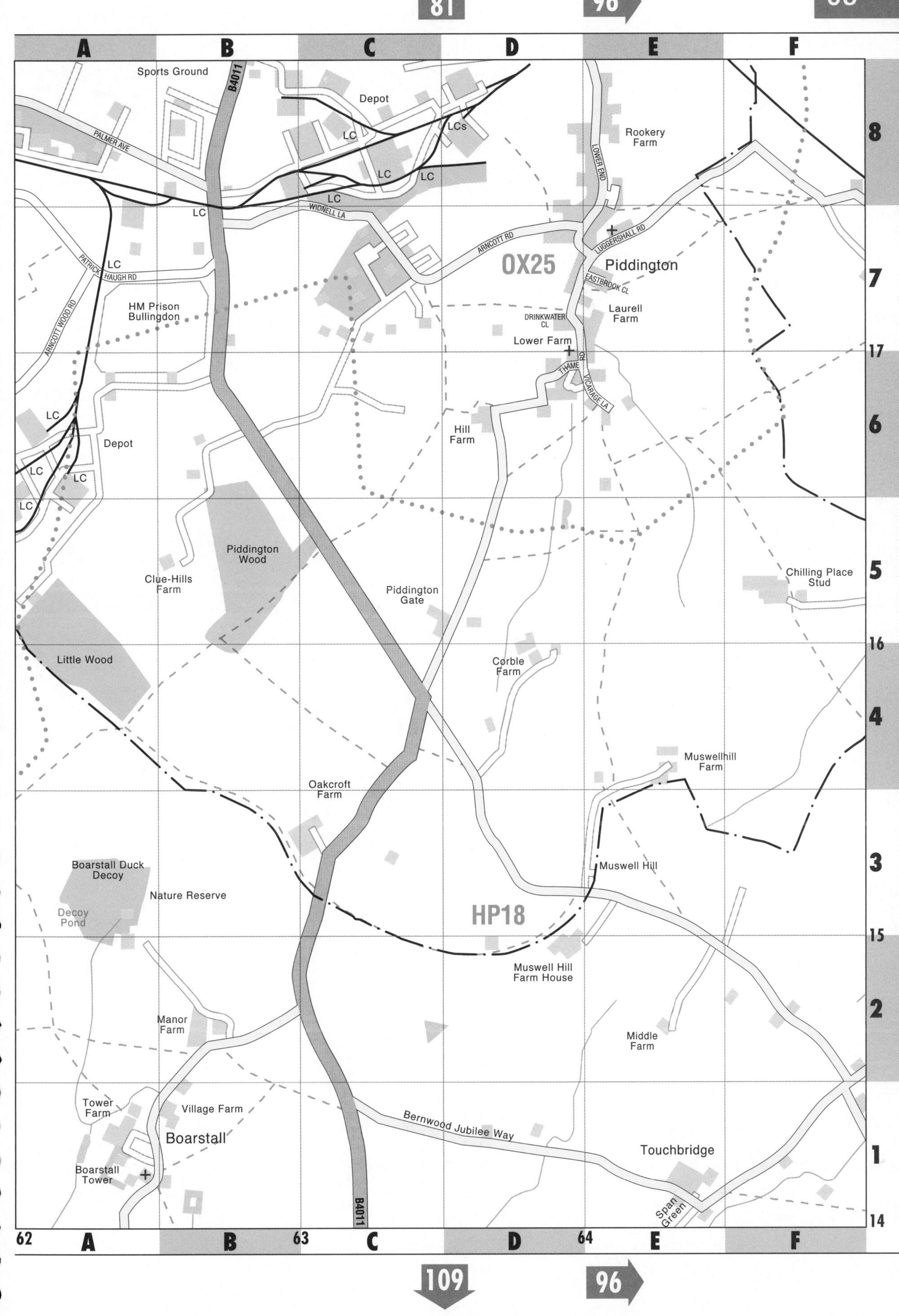
81
96
A
B
C
D
E
F
Sports Ground
B4011
Depot
LC
LCs
PALMER AVE
Rookery Farm
LOWER END
WIDNELL LA
ARNCOTT RD
LUGGERSHALL RD
OX25
Piddington
PATRICK HAUGH RD
EASTBROOK CL
HM Prison Bullingdon
ARNCOTT WOOD RD
Laurell Farm
DRINKWATER CL
Lower Farm
THAME RD
VICARAGE LA
Depot
Hill Farm
Piddington Wood
Clue-Hills Farm
Piddington Gate
Chilling Place Stud
Little Wood
Corble Farm
Muswellhill Farm
Oakcroft Farm
Boarstall Duck Decoy
Nature Reserve
Muswell Hill
Decoy Pond
HP18
Muswell Hill Farm House
Manor Farm
Middle Farm
Tower Farm
Village Farm
Boarstall
Bernwood Jubilee Way
Touchbridge
Boarstall Tower
Span Green
8
7
17
6
5
16
4
3
15
2
1
14
62
63
64
109
96

95
82

A
B
C
D
E
F
8
7
17
6
5
16
4
3
15
2
1
14
Nursery
Kings Farm
PIDDINGTON RD
D'Oyley's Farm
BICESTER RD
Rookery Farm
The Green
Tittershall Wood
Bridge Farm
DUCK LA
PH
Ludgershall
SALTERS CL
SALTERS LA
BROOK CL
Manor Farm
WHITE HART CL
HIGH ST
Glebe Farm
Eastfield Farm
CHURCH LA
Ludgershall Farm
WOTTON END
BRILL RD
KINGSWOOD LA
The Lake
Clearfields Farm
Long Wood
Poletrees Farm
Lapland Farm
HP18
The Warrells
Fivearch Wood
Fivearch Bridge
Rushbeds Wood Wildlife Reserve
Grenville's Wood
Lawn Farm
Tramway Farm
Rid's Hill
Brillbury Hall Farm
Coldharbour Farm
TRAM HILL
Dorton Park Farm
Brill Common
NORCOTTS KILN COTTS
Chinkwell Wood
Brill
Dorton
NORTH HILLS
THE LAWNS
TEMPLE ST
Windmill
WINDMILL ST
GODFREYS CL
Brill CE Comb Sch
Brook Farm
SOUTH HILLS
PH
HIGH LAND CL
Ct
BRAE HILL
65
66
67

95
110

83
98

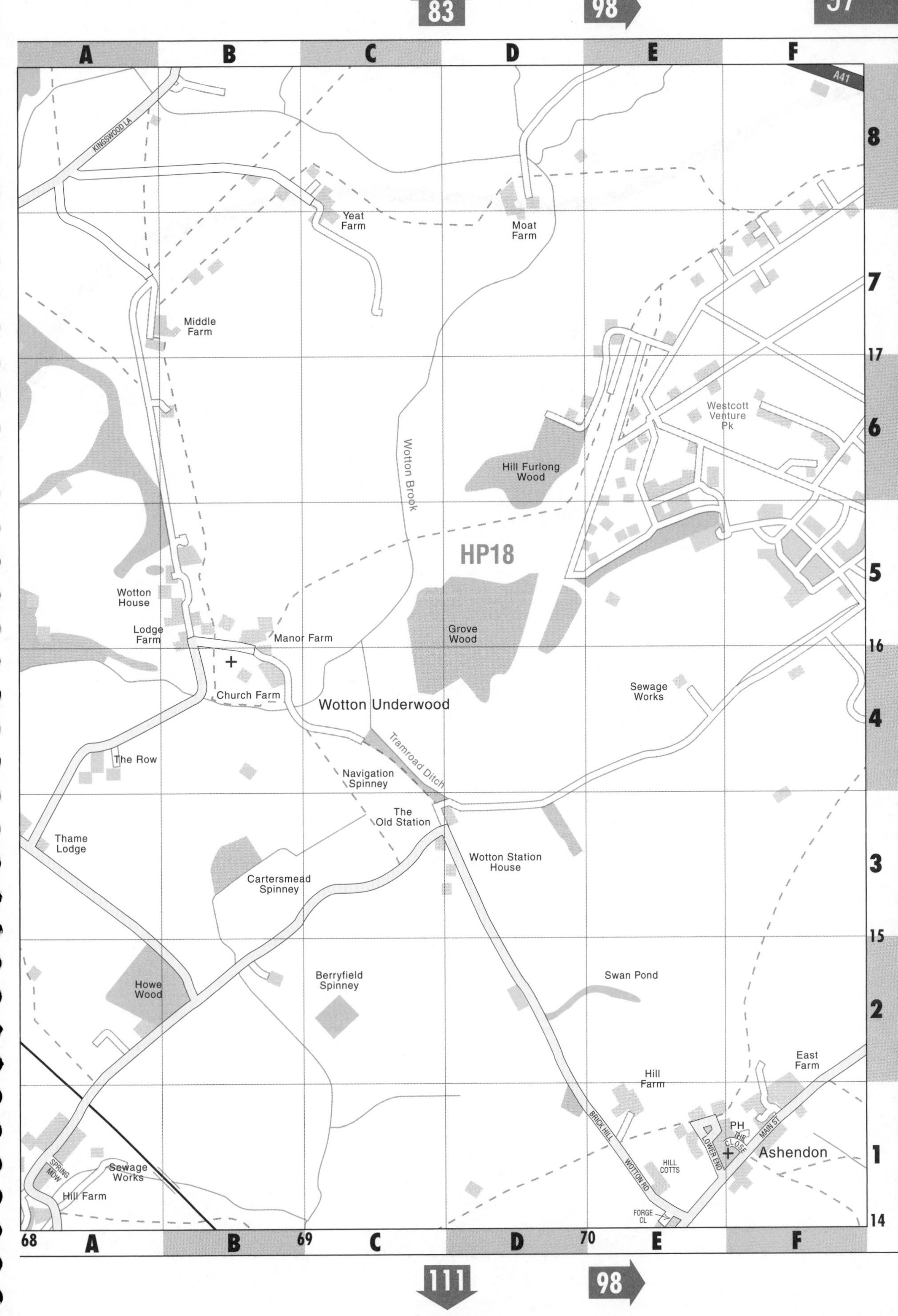
A
B
C
D
E
F
A41
KINGSWOOD LA
8
Yeat Farm
Moat Farm
7
Middle Farm
17
Westcott Venture Pk
6
Wotton Brook
Hill Furlong Wood
HP18
5
Wotton House
Lodge Farm
Manor Farm
Grove Wood
16
Church Farm
Wotton Underwood
Sewage Works
4
The Row
Tramroad Ditch
Navigation Spinney
The Old Station
Thame Lodge
Wotton Station House
3
Cartersmead Spinney
15
Howe Wood
Berryfield Spinney
Swan Pond
2
Hill Farm
East Farm
BRICK HILL
PH
THE CLOSE
MAIN ST
LOWER END
Ashendon
1
SPRING MDW
Sewage Works
Hill Farm
WOTTON RD
HILL COTTS
FORGE CL
14
68
69
70

111
98

97
84

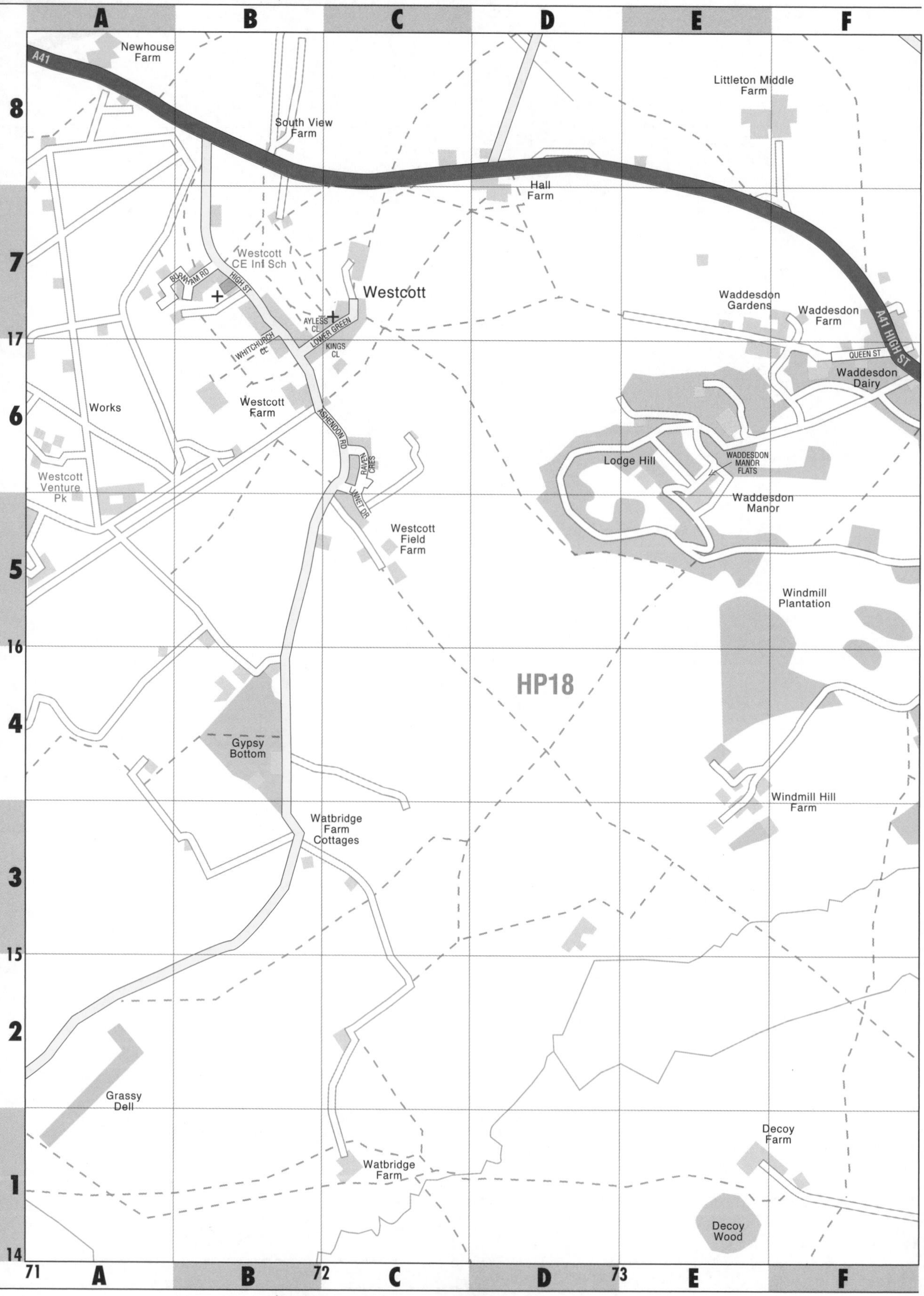

A
B
C
D
E
F
8
7
17
6
5
16
4
3
15
2
1
14
71
72
73
A41
A41 HIGH ST
Newhouse Farm
South View Farm
Littleton Middle Farm
Hall Farm
Westcott CE Inf Sch
BURNHAM RD
HIGH ST
Westcott
AYLESS CL
LOWER GREEN
KINGS CL
WHITCHURCH CL
Waddesdon Gardens
Waddesdon Farm
QUEEN ST
Waddesdon Dairy
Works
Westcott Farm
ASHENDON RD
RAVEN CRES
LINNET DR
Lodge Hill
WADDESDON MANOR FLATS
Waddesdon Manor
Westcott Venture Pk
Westcott Field Farm
Windmill Plantation
HP18
Gypsy Bottom
Windmill Hill Farm
Watbridge Farm Cottages
Grassy Dell
Decoy Farm
Watbridge Farm
Decoy Wood

97
112

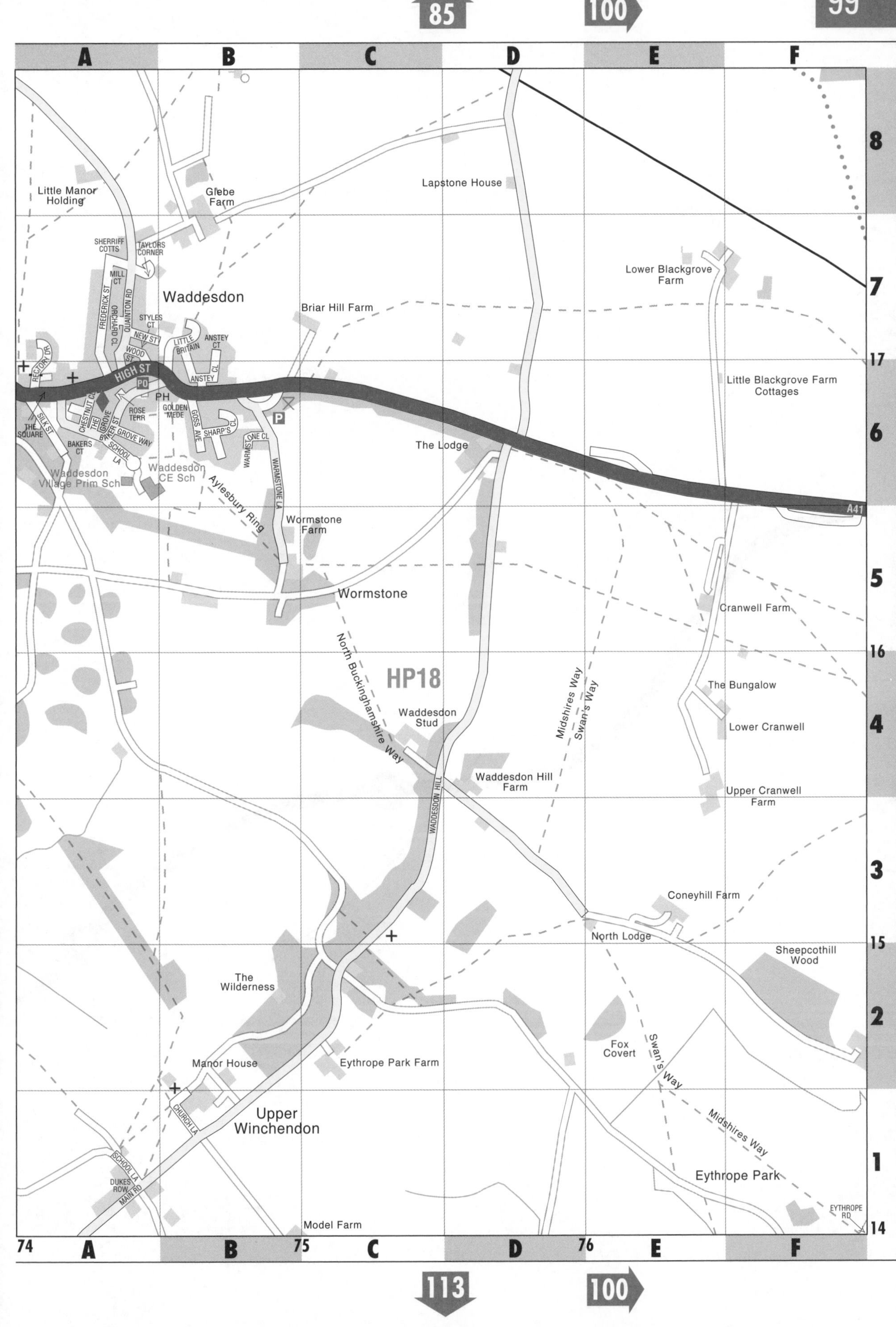
85
100
A
B
C
D
E
F
8
7
17
6
5
16
4
3
15
2
1
14
74
75
76
113
100
Little Manor Holding
Glebe Farm
Lapstone House
SHERRIFF COTTS
TAYLORS CORNER
MILL CT
Waddesdon
FREDERICK ST
ORCHARD CL
QUAINTON RD
STYLES CT
NEW ST
WOOD ST
LITTLE BRITAIN
ANSTEY CT
ANSTEY CL
RECTORY DR
HIGH ST
PO
PH
P
SILK ST
THE SQUARE
CHESTNUT CL
THE GROVE
BAKER ST
BAKERS CT
SCHOOL LA
GROVE WAY
ROSE TERR
GOLDEN MEDE
GOSS AVE
SHARP'S CL
WARMSTONE CL
WARMSTONE LA
Waddesdon Village Prim Sch
Waddesdon CE Sch
Aylesbury Ring
Briar Hill Farm
Lower Blackgrove Farm
Little Blackgrove Farm Cottages
The Lodge
A41
Wormstone Farm
Wormstone
Cranwell Farm
North Buckinghamshire Way
HP18
Waddesdon Stud
Midshires Way
Swan's Way
The Bungalow
Lower Cranwell
Waddesdon Hill Farm
WADDESDON HILL
Upper Cranwell Farm
Coneyhill Farm
North Lodge
Sheepcothill Wood
The Wilderness
Fox Covert
Manor House
Eythrope Park Farm
Upper Winchendon
CHURCH LA
SCHOOL LA
DUKES ROW
MAIN RD
Eythrope Park
EYTHROPE RD
Model Farm

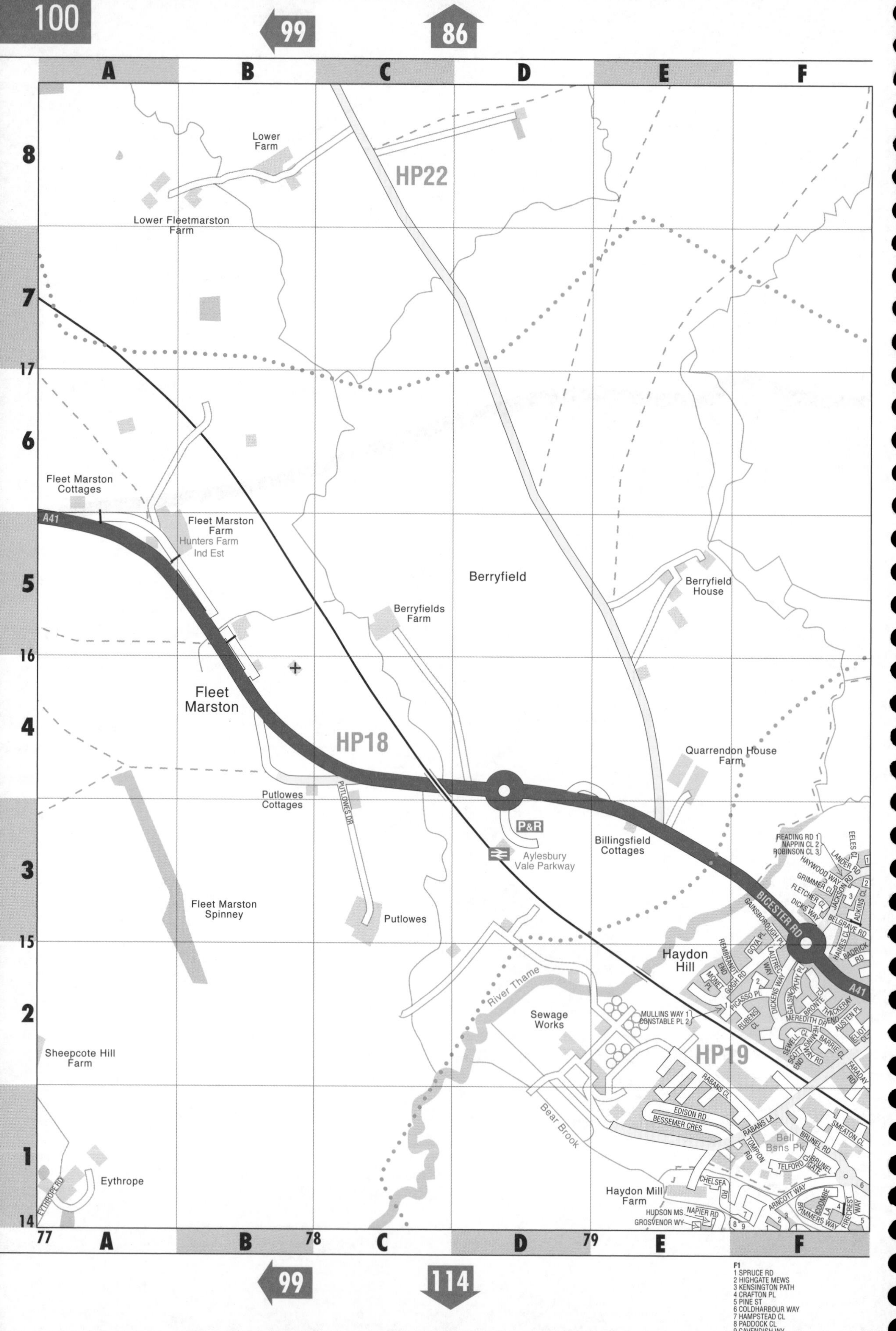
99
86
A
B
C
D
E
F
8
7
17
6
5
16
4
3
15
2
1
14
77
78
79
HP22
HP18
HP19
Lower Farm
Lower Fleetmarston Farm
Fleet Marston Cottages
A41
Fleet Marston Farm
Hunters Farm Ind Est
Berryfield
Berryfield House
Berryfields Farm
Fleet Marston
Quarrendon House Farm
Putlowes Cottages
PUTLOWES DR
P&R
Aylesbury Vale Parkway
Billingsfield Cottages
Fleet Marston Spinney
Putlowes
BICESTER RD
Haydon Hill
River Thame
Sewage Works
MULLINS WAY 1
CONSTABLE PL 2
Sheepcote Hill Farm
Bear Brook
RABANS CL
EDISON RD
BESSEMER CRES
RABANS LA
TOMPION RD
Bell Bsns Pk
BRUNEL RD
TELFORD CL
BRUNEL GATE
SMEATON CL
FARADAY RD
Eythrope
EYTHROPE RD
Haydon Mill Farm
CHELSEA RD
HUDSON MS
NAPIER RD
GROSVENOR WY
ARNCOTT WAY
COOMBE LA
BRAMMERS WAY
FIRECREST WAY
READING RD 1
NAPPIN CL 2
ROBINSON CL 3
EELES CL
LANDER RD
HAYWOOD WAY
GRIMMER CL
JACKSON RD
FLETCHER CL
DICKS WAY
ADKINS CL
BELGRAVE RD
HAINES CL
BADRICK RD
GAINSBOROUGH PL
GOYA PL
REMBRANDT END
LAUTREC WAY
MONET PL
GOGH RD
PICASSO PL
RUBENS CL
DICKENS WAY
GALSWORTHY PL
BRONTE CL
THACKERAY END
MEREDITH DR
AUSTEN PL
ELIOT CL
SEWELL CL
SCOTT END
BARRIE CL
A41
99
114
F1
1 SPRUCE RD
2 HIGHGATE MEWS
3 KENSINGTON PATH
4 CRAFTON PL
5 PINE ST
6 COLDHARBOUR WAY
7 HAMPSTEAD CL
8 PADDOCK CL
9 CAVENDISH WY

87

102

A B C D E F

8
7
17
6
5
16
4
3
15
2
1
14

Uppings Farm
A413
NEW RD
STOCKAWAY
Weedon Lodge Farm
Fields Farm
HP22
Evelyn's Patch
Grendon Hill Farm
HP18
Weedon Hill
Weedon Hill Farm
River Thame
St Peter's Church (remains of)
Watermead
AYLESBURY
HP19
Holman's Bridge
Hotel
Quarrendon
Elmhurst
Dunsham La
Aylesbury Vale Acad
Haydon Abbey Comb Sch
Alfred Rose Park
Manor Park
HM Young Offender Inst
Manor House
Park Sch
Stocklake Ind Est
HP20
Superstore
Trad Est
Broadfields Ret Pk
Aylesbury Bsns Ctr
Griffin Ind Mall
Clifton Bsns Pk
Griffin Lane Ind Est
Warren Ho
Bridgegate Bsns Pk
Aylesbury Ind Ctr
St Andrews Way Ind Est
The Courtyard
The Vale Ind Ctr
Altan Bsns Pk
Merlin Ctr
Royal Bucks
Mast
Thomas Hickman Sch
Elmhurst Sch

1 WELL MDW
2 HYTON SQ
3 PLUTO WAY

1 ANGUS RD
2 KERRY CL
3 GUERNSEY CL
4 HEREFORD WAY
5 DEVON RD
6 SUSSEX CL

KEMPSON CL 1
PRINTERS END 2

E3
1 HAWFINCH
2 MOORHEN CT
3 SHELDUCK CL
4 BITTERN WAY
E4
1 SANDPIPER
2 THE COMFREY
3 PLOVER WLK
4 THE PLOVER
5 WATERLILY
6 PIPIT WLK
7 PIPIT GDNS
F3
1 FULMAR PL
2 STORK CL
3 RAVEN CL
4 GULL WAY
5 OWL CL
6 THRUSH CL
7 PARTRIDGE WAY
8 BULLFINCH GDNS
9 CORNCRAKE
10 NUTHATCH
11 LANGSTONE CT
12 TURNER WLK
13 CLEVELAND PL
14 WHITE VIEW
15 ORCHARD CL

80 A B 81 C D 82 E F

A2
1 ALDERSON CL
2 WILLOW CT
3 HANOVER CL

B2
1 BERKELEY RISE
2 BROMPTON CL

D1
1 CAVERSHAM GN
2 WHARTON HO
3 WESTBURY HO
4 SILVERDALE CL
5 ESSEX HO
6 WHITEHALL ST
7 RIPON ST
8 BUCKINGHAM ST
9 Haydon Ind Sch

115

D2
1 DESBOROUGH GN
E1
1 THE MILLINERS
2 GLOVERS CT
3 RIDGEWAY CT
4 ST JOHN'S RD
5 CAMBRIDGE CL
6 Cambridge Close Ret Pk

102

F2
1 LISBURN PATH
2 CLARKE WLK
3 CHENEY WLK
4 DORMER CT
5 ROXWELL PATH
6 WESTWOOD WLK
7 HARRIS CT
8 BASE CL
9 OLDHAMS MDW
10 GURNEY CL
11 DEARING CL
12 MATTHEWS CL
13 VISCOUNT CL
14 LAWRENCE CL
15 St Louis RC Comb Sch

101
88

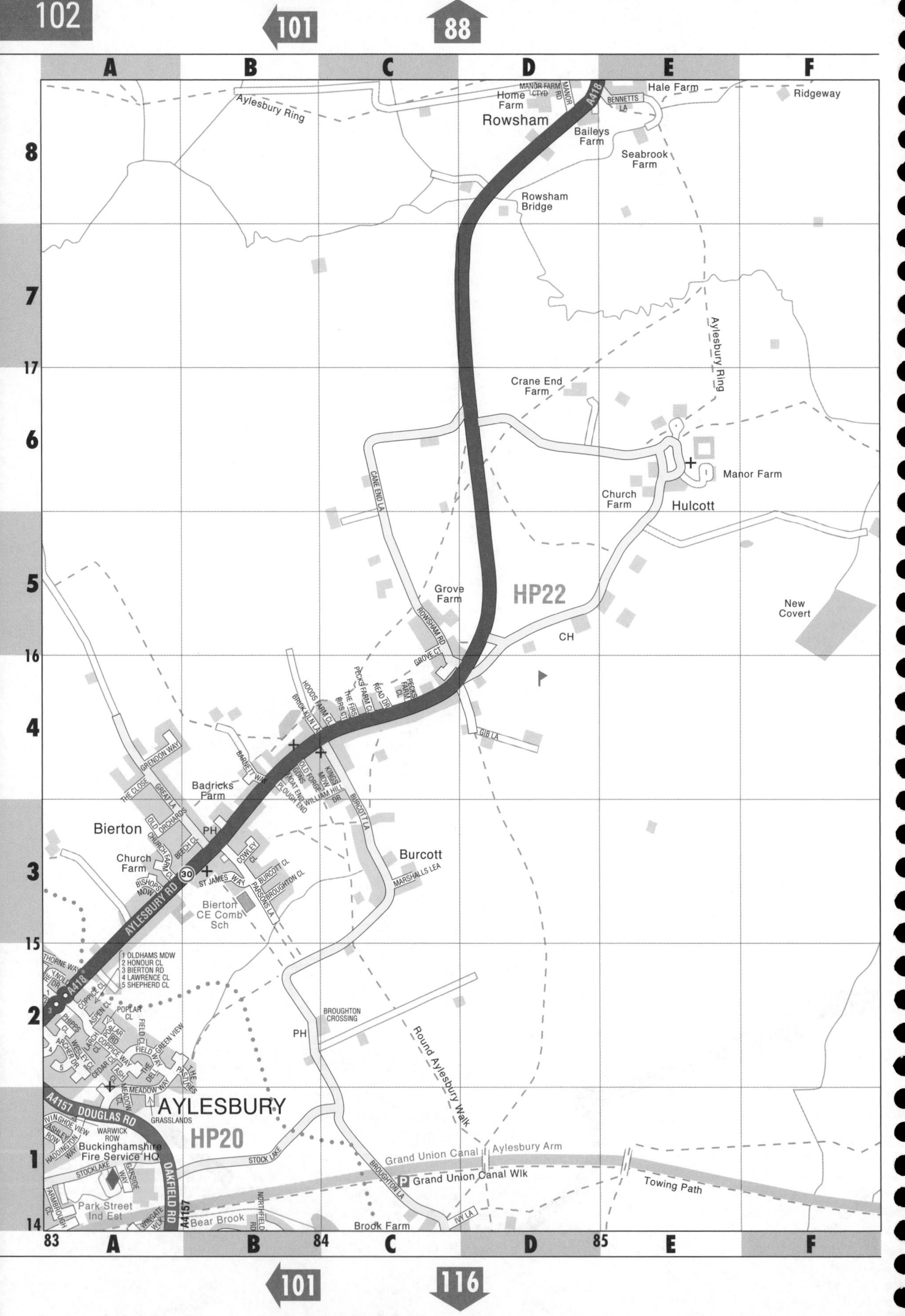

101
116

89
104

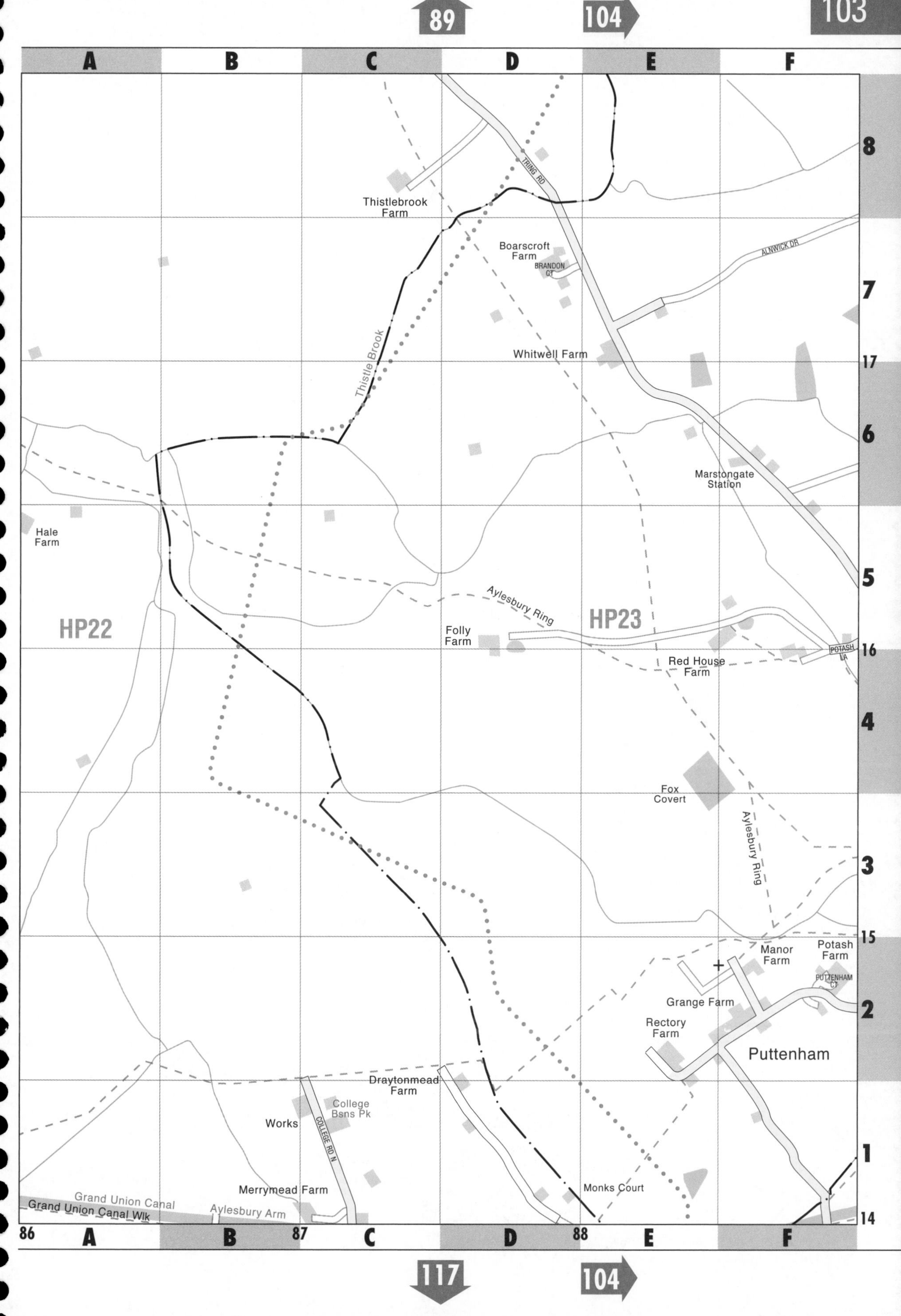

117
104

103
90

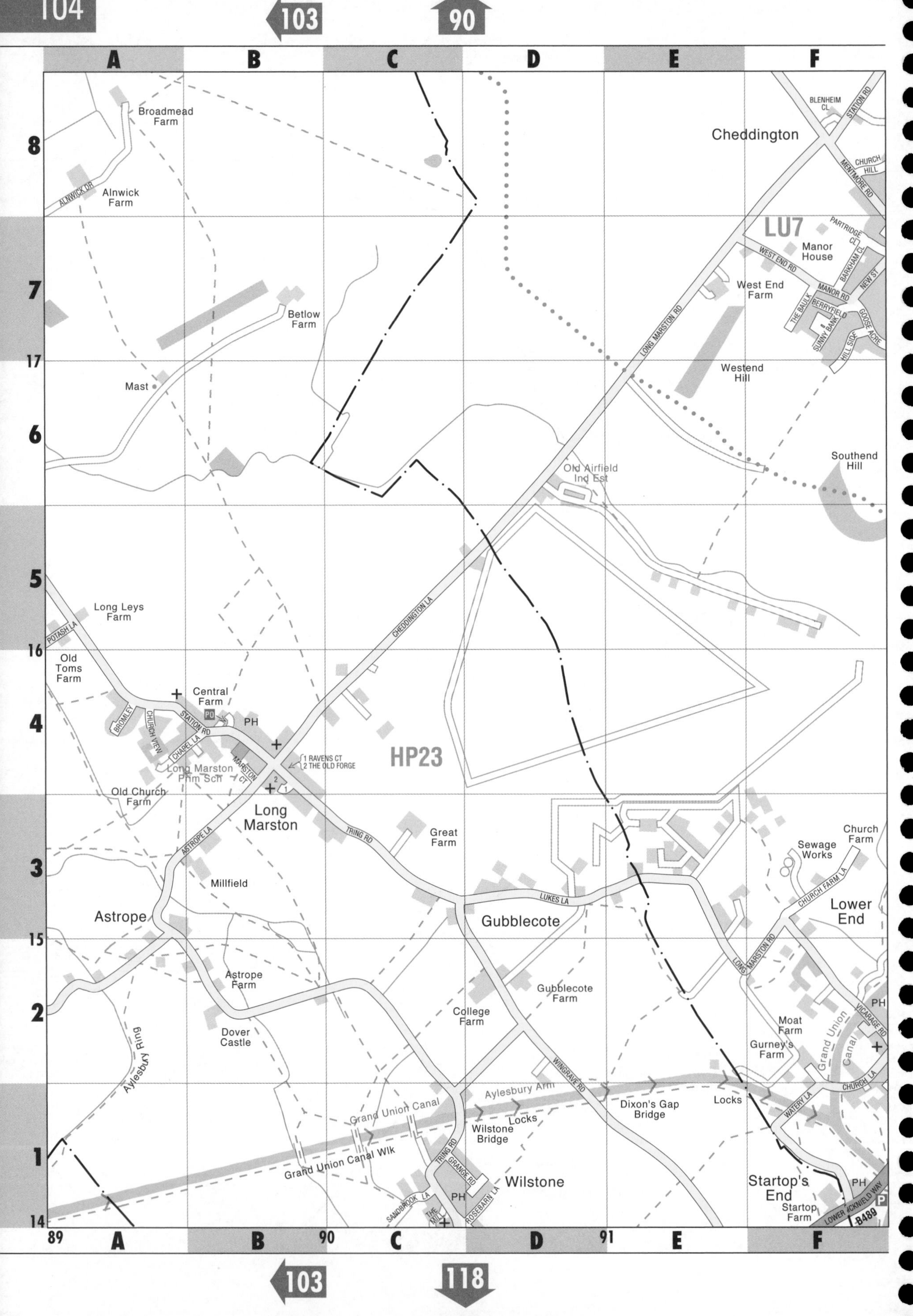

103
118

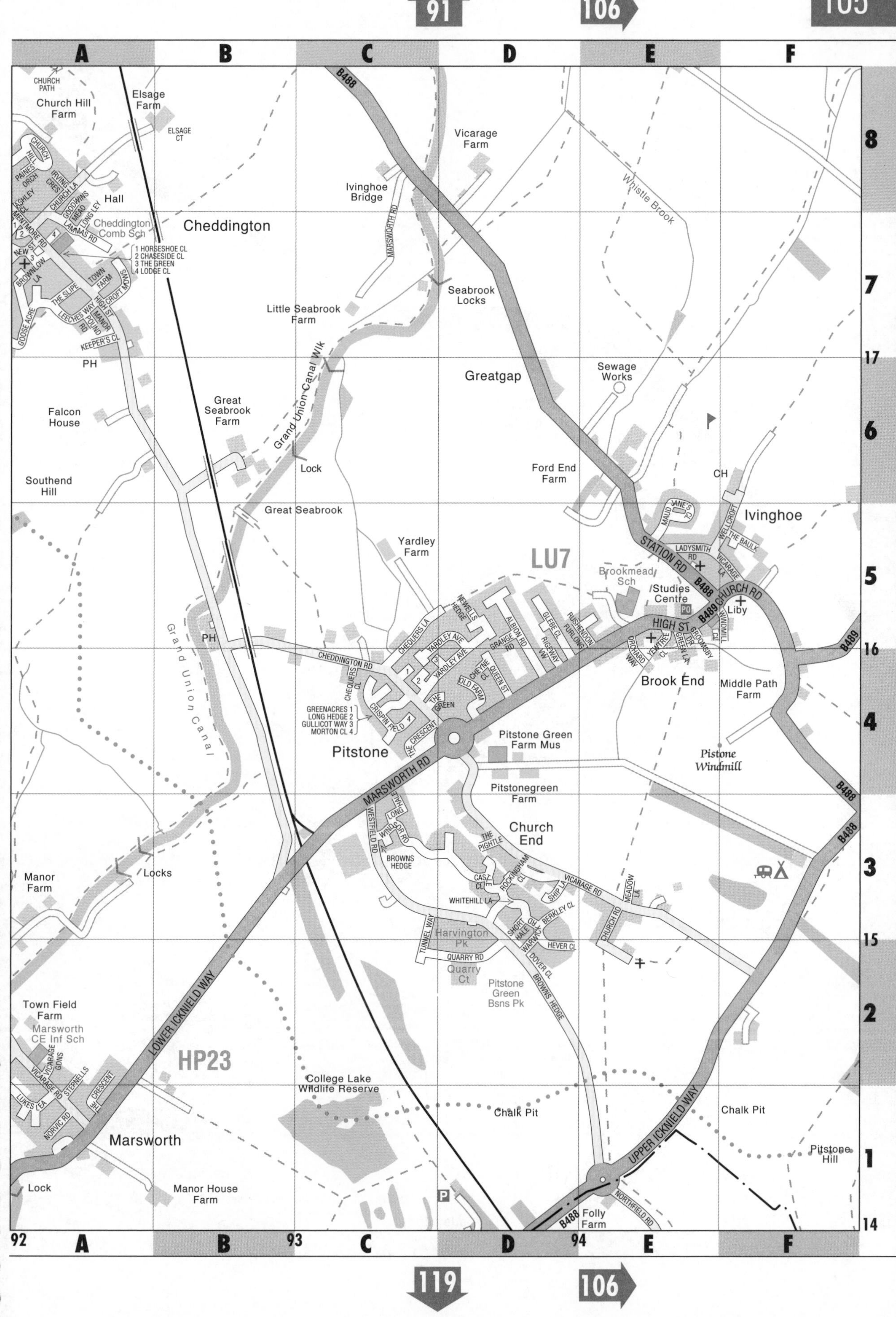
91
106
119
106
Church Hill Farm
Elsage Farm
Vicarage Farm
Ivinghoe Bridge
Cheddington
Cheddington Comb Sch
Hall
1 HORSESHOE CL
2 CHASESIDE CL
3 THE GREEN
4 LODGE CL
Seabrook Locks
Little Seabrook Farm
Whistle Brook
Greatgap
Sewage Works
Great Seabrook Farm
Grand Union Canal Wlk
Falcon House
Lock
Southend Hill
Great Seabrook
Ford End Farm
Ivinghoe
Yardley Farm
LU7
Brookmead Sch
Studies Centre
Liby
HIGH ST
STATION RD
CHURCH RD
CHEDDINGTON RD
Brook End
Middle Path Farm
GREENACRES 1
LONG HEDGE 2
GULLICOT WAY 3
MORTON CL 4
Pitstone
Pitstone Green Farm Mus
Pistone Windmill
MARSWORTH RD
Pitstonegreen Farm
Church End
Manor Farm
Locks
Harvington Pk
Quarry Ct
Pitstone Green Bsns Pk
Town Field Farm
Marsworth CE Inf Sch
LOWER ICKNIELD WAY
HP23
College Lake Wildlife Reserve
Chalk Pit
Chalk Pit
Marsworth
UPPER ICKNIELD WAY
Pitstone Hill
Lock
Manor House Farm
Folly Farm
Grand Union Canal
A B C D E F
92 93 94
14 15 16 17
1 2 3 4 5 6 7 8

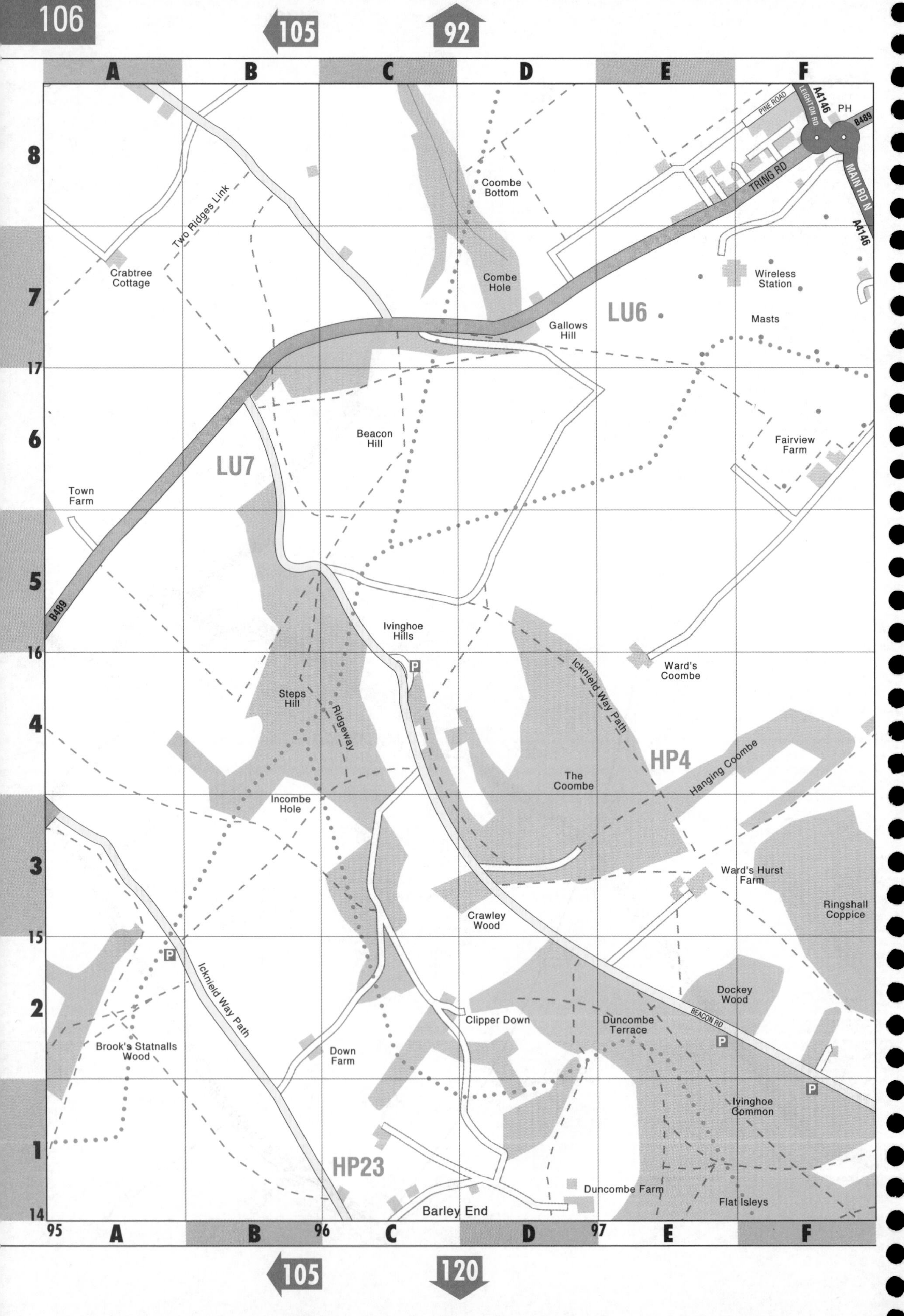
105
92
120
Crabtree Cottage
Two Ridges Link
Coombe Bottom
Combe Hole
Gallows Hill
LU6
Wireless Station
Masts
PH
PINE ROAD
LEIGHTON RD
A4146
B489
TRING RD
MAIN RD N
Beacon Hill
LU7
Town Farm
Fairview Farm
Ivinghoe Hills
Ward's Coombe
Icknield Way Path
Steps Hill
Ridgeway
HP4
Hanging Coombe
The Coombe
Incombe Hole
Ward's Hurst Farm
Ringshall Coppice
Crawley Wood
Dockey Wood
Clipper Down
Duncombe Terrace
BEACON RD
Brook's Statnalls Wood
Down Farm
Ivinghoe Common
HP23
Duncombe Farm
Flat Isleys
Barley End

93

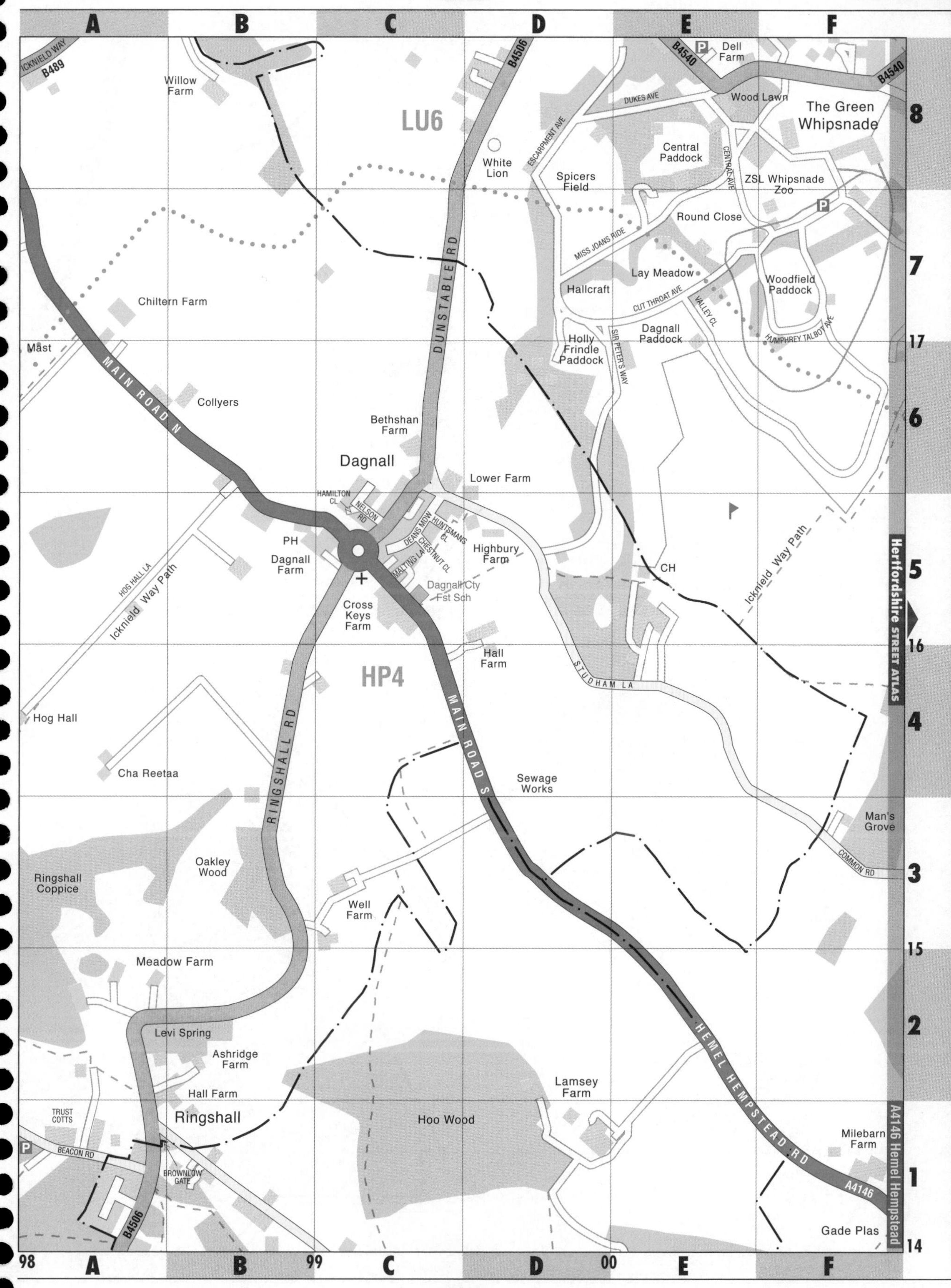

A
B
C
D
E
F
ICKNIELD WAY
B489
Willow Farm
B4506
LU6
B4540
Dell Farm
Wood Lawn
The Green
Whipsnade
DUKES AVE
Central Paddock
ESCARPMENT AVE
CENTRAL AVE
White Lion
Spicers Field
ZSL Whipsnade Zoo
Round Close
MISS JOANS RIDE
Lay Meadow
DUNSTABLE RD
Hallcraft
CUT THROAT AVE
VALLEY CL
Woodfield Paddock
Chiltern Farm
Dagnall Paddock
HUMPHREY TALBOT AVE
Holly Frindle Paddock
SIR PETER'S WAY
Mast
MAIN ROAD N
Collyers
Bethshan Farm
Dagnall
Lower Farm
HAMILTON CL
NELSON RD
DEANS MDW
HUNTSMANS CL
CHESTNUT CL
MALTING LA
PH
Dagnall Farm
Highbury Farm
CH
Icknield Way Path
HOG HALL LA
Icknield Way Path
Dagnall Cty Fst Sch
Cross Keys Farm
Hall Farm
HP4
STUDHAM LA
Hog Hall
RINGSHALL RD
MAIN ROAD S
Cha Reetaa
Sewage Works
Man's Grove
Oakley Wood
Ringshall Coppice
COMMON RD
Well Farm
Meadow Farm
Levi Spring
HEMEL HEMPSTEAD RD
Ashridge Farm
Lamsey Farm
Hall Farm
TRUST COTTS
Ringshall
Hoo Wood
Milebarn Farm
BEACON RD
BROWNLOW GATE
B4506
A4146
Gade Plas
A4146 Hemel Hempstead
Hertfordshire STREET ATLAS
8
7
17
6
5
16
4
3
15
2
1
14
98
99
00

121

94

A B C D E F
8
7
13
6
5
12
4
3
11
2
1
10
59 60 61
Old Arngrove
M40
New Arngrove Farm
Warren Farm
Gardner's Barn
Tippens Copse
Nursery
Sermin's Copse
RAGNALL'S LA
Studley Farm
BRILL RD
Pasture Farm
Horton-cum-Studley
MILL LA
CHURCH LA
VENTFIELD CL
THE GREEN
FORGE CL
Danes Brook
Manor Farm
New Farm
Studley Priory
PRIORY CL
STRAIGHT MILE RD
Moors Farm
OAKLEY RD
Hotel
Sewage Works
Oxfordshire STREET ATLAS
CH
OX33
HP18
P
Studley Wood
Oakley Wood
Corner Farm
Stanton Little Wood
The Moat
Bernwood Meadows Wildlife Reserve
York's Wood
Danesbrook Farm
Danes Brook
Moorbirge Brook
Oxfordshire Way
Hell Coppice
Menmarsh Guide Post
Moorbirge Bridge
MILL ST

122

95
110

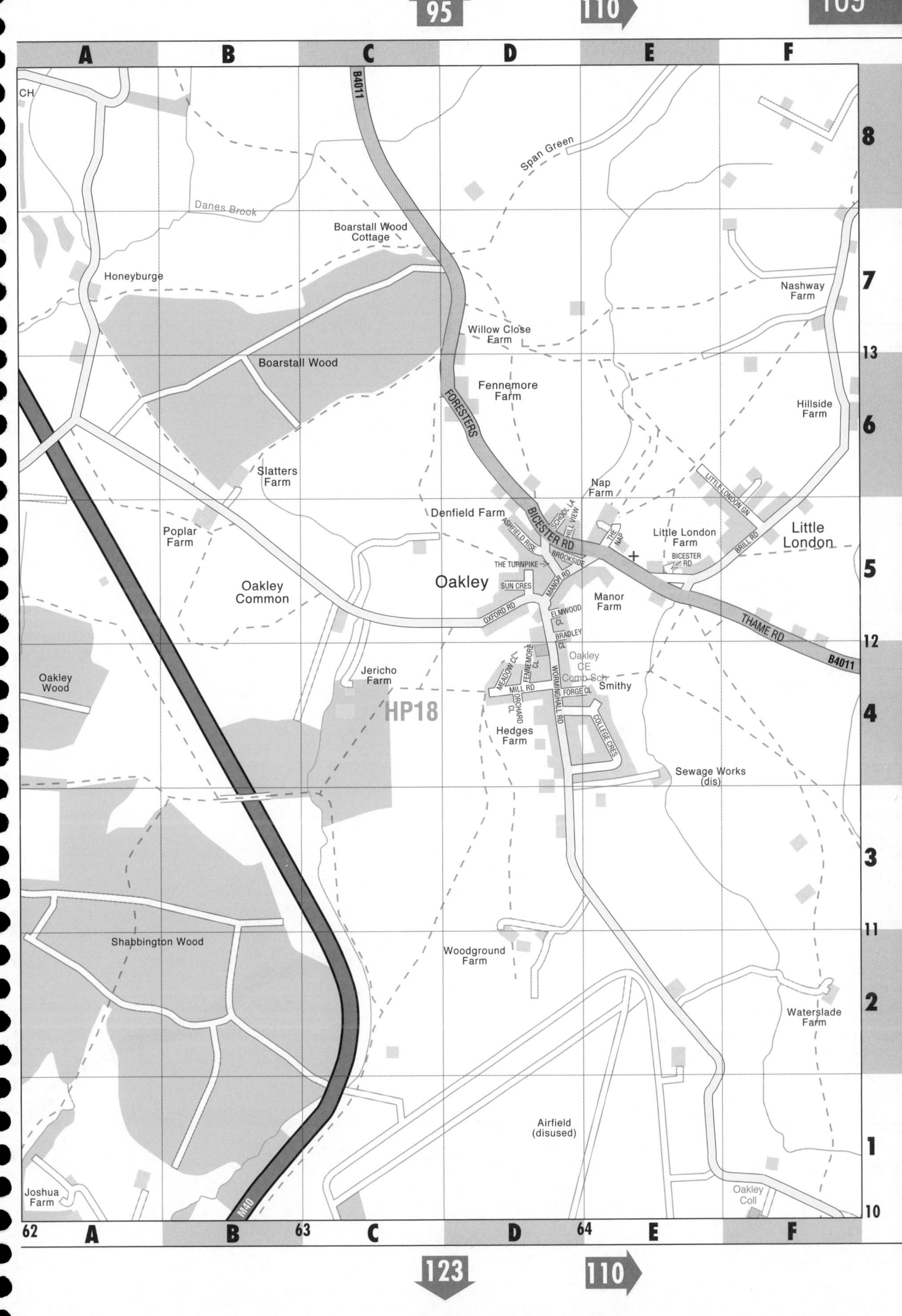

123
110

109
96

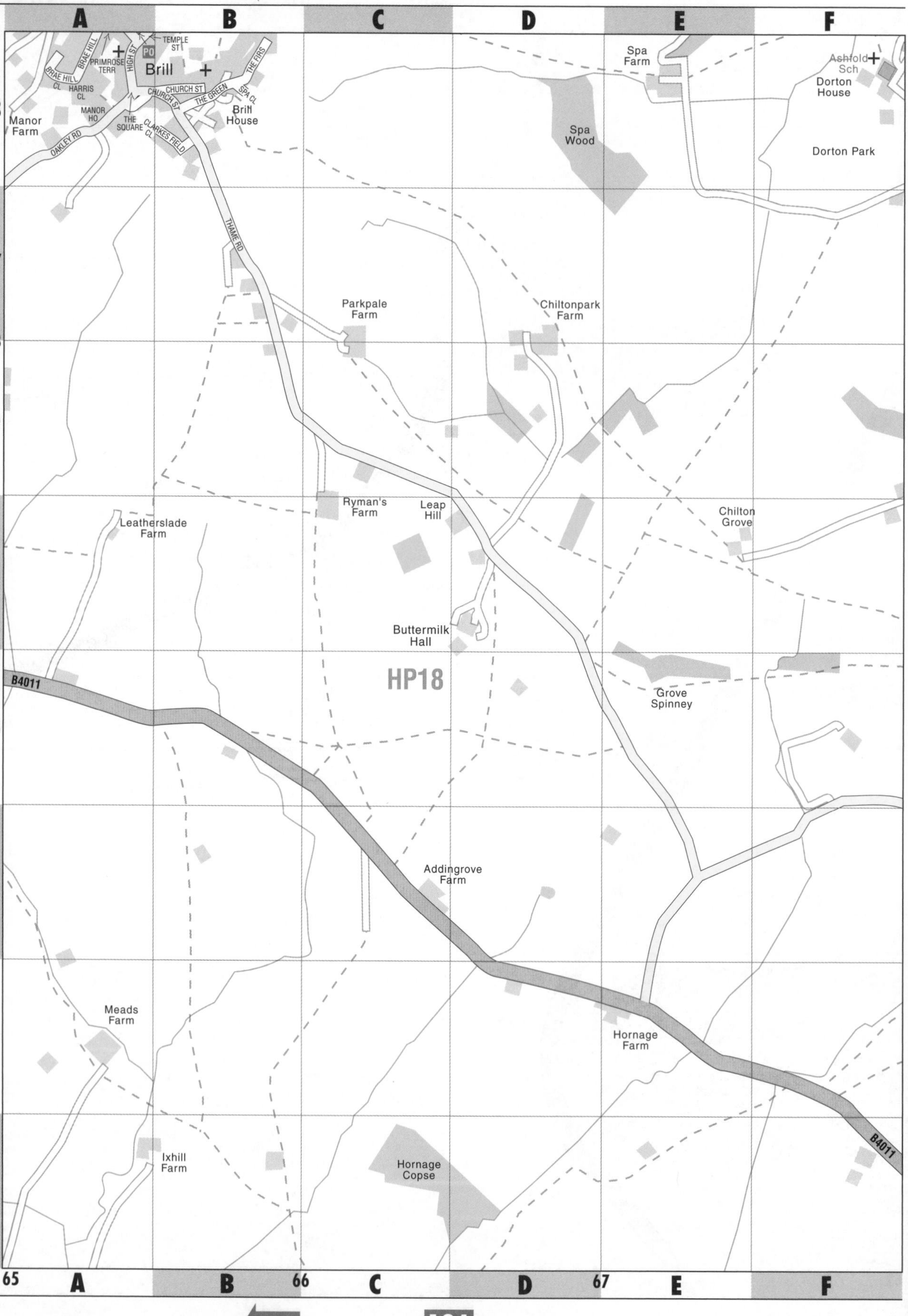

A B C D E F

8 7 13 6 5 12 4 3 11 2 1 10

Brill
Temple St
Brae Hill
Primrose Terr
High St
Brae Hill Cl
Harris Cl
Church St
The Green
Spa Cl
The Firs
Manor Ho
The Square
Clarkes Field
Clarkes Cl
Oakley Rd
Church St
Brill House
Manor Farm
Spa Farm
Spa Wood
Ashfold Sch
Dorton House
Dorton Park
Thame Rd
Parkpale Farm
Chiltonpark Farm
Ryman's Farm
Leap Hill
Leatherslade Farm
Chilton Grove
Buttermilk Hall
HP18
B4011
Grove Spinney
Addingrove Farm
Meads Farm
Hornage Farm
Ixhill Farm
Hornage Copse
B4011

65 A B 66 C D 67 E F

109
124

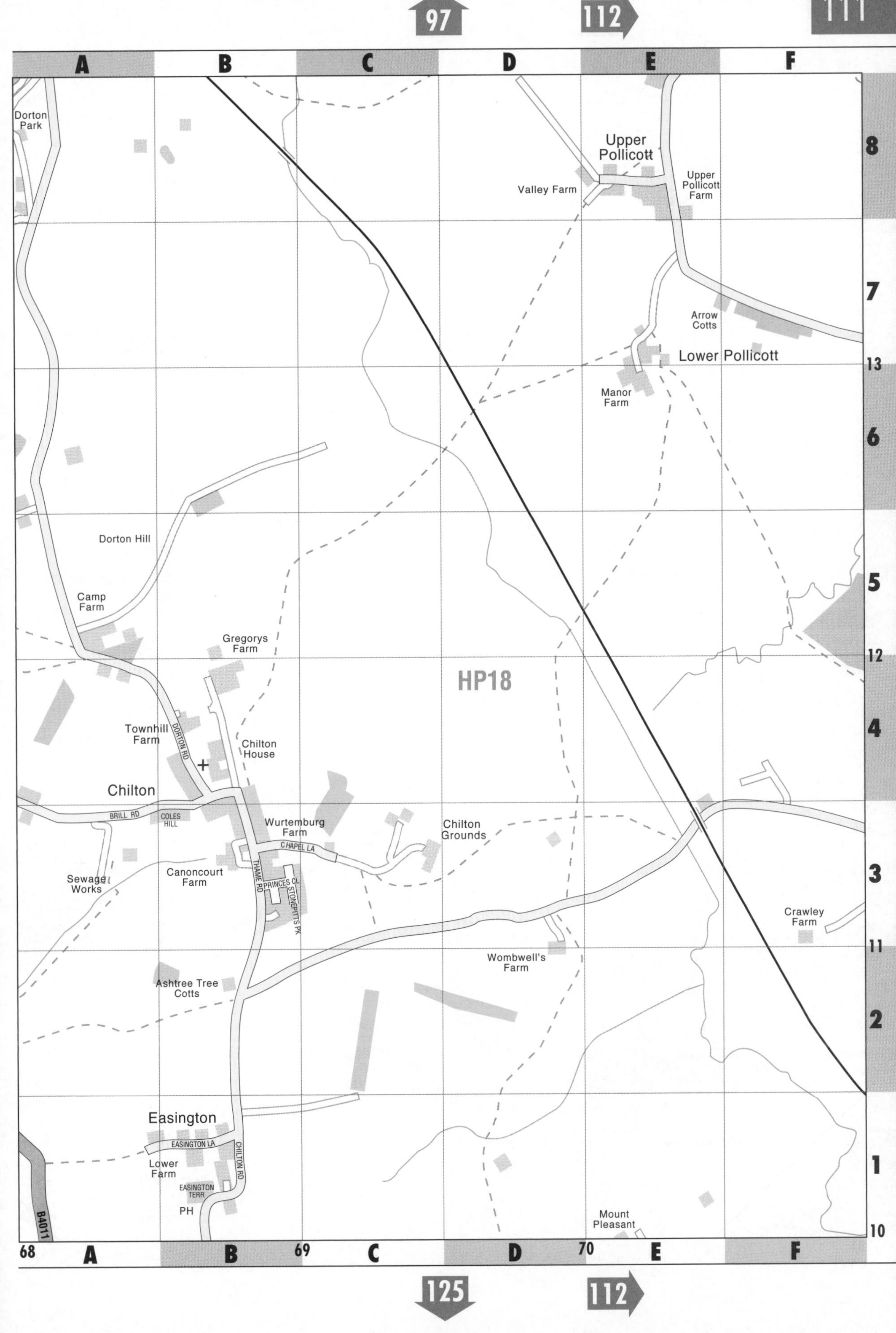
97
112
A
B
C
D
E
F
8
7
13
6
5
12
4
3
11
2
1
10
68
69
70
125
112
Dorton Park
Upper Pollicott
Valley Farm
Upper Pollicott Farm
Arrow Cotts
Lower Pollicott
Manor Farm
Dorton Hill
Camp Farm
Gregorys Farm
HP18
Townhill Farm
DORTON RD
Chilton House
Chilton
BRILL RD
COLES HILL
Wurtemburg Farm
Chilton Grounds
CHAPEL LA
Sewage Works
Canoncourt Farm
THAME RD
PRINCES CL
STONEPITTS PK
Crawley Farm
Wombwell's Farm
Ashtree Tree Cotts
Easington
EASINGTON LA
CHILTON RD
Lower Farm
EASINGTON TERR
PH
B4011
Mount Pleasant

111
98

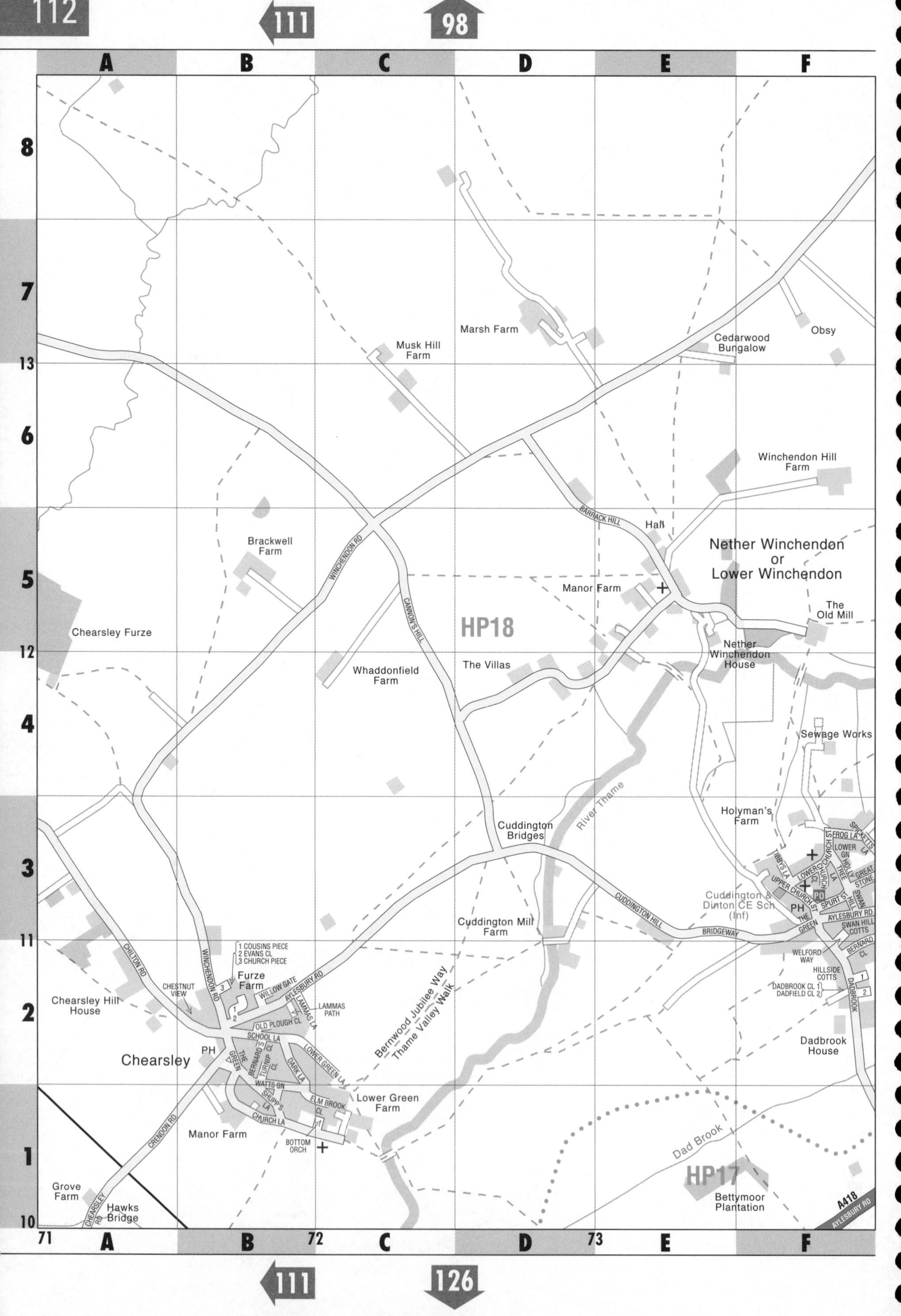

111
126

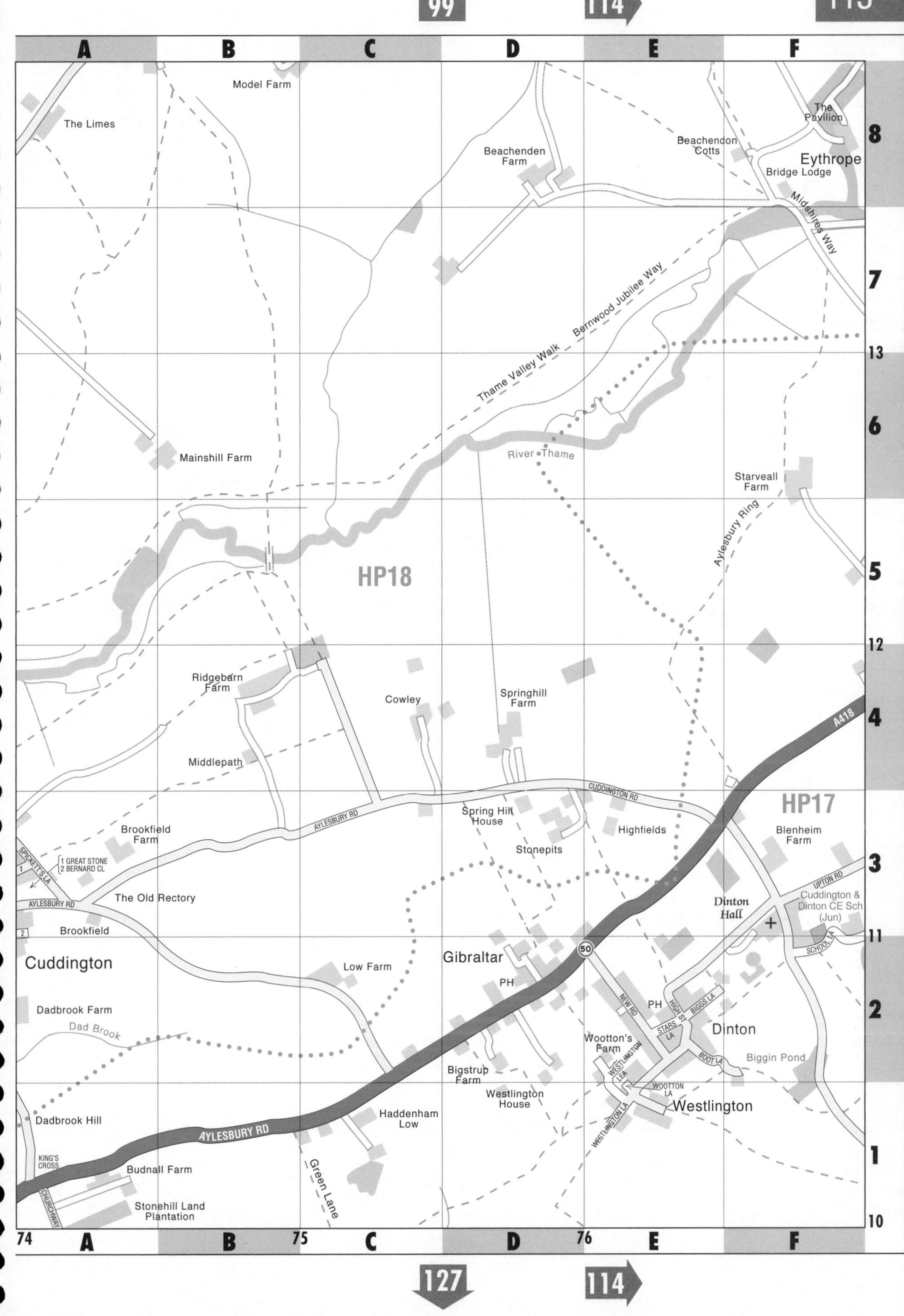
99
114
A
B
C
D
E
F
Model Farm
The Limes
Beachenden Farm
Beachendon Cotts
The Pavilion
Eythrope
Bridge Lodge
Midshires Way
Bernwood Jubilee Way
Thame Valley Walk
Mainshill Farm
River Thame
Starveall Farm
Aylesbury Ring
HP18
Ridgebarn Farm
Cowley
Springhill Farm
Middlepath
A418
HP17
Cuddington Rd
Aylesbury Rd
Spring Hill House
Highfields
Brookfield Farm
Stonepits
Blenheim Farm
Spickett's La
1 Great Stone
2 Bernard Cl
The Old Rectory
Upton Rd
Dinton Hall
Cuddington & Dinton CE Sch (Jun)
Brookfield
School La
Cuddington
Low Farm
Gibraltar
50
PH
New Rd
High St
Biggs La
Dadbrook Farm
Stars La
Dinton
Dad Brook
Wootton's Farm
Boot La
Biggin Pond
Westlington Lea
Bigstrup Farm
Wootton La
Westlington House
Westlington
Dadbrook Hill
Haddenham Low
Westlington La
Aylesbury Rd
King's Cross
Budnall Farm
Green Lane
Churchway
Stonehill Land Plantation
8
7
13
6
5
12
4
3
11
2
1
10
74
75
76
127
114

113
100

A B C D E F

8
7
13
6
5
12
4
3
11
2
1
10

Eythrope Park
HP18
River Thame
Weir Lodge
North Buckinghamshire Way
Littleworth Farm
Midshires Way
Arthur's Gorse
Burn Hill
Whaddon Hill Farm
HP19
NAPIER RD
GROSVENOR WAY
ARNCOTT WAY
NAPIER RD
PORTMAN MS
CUCKOO WAY
WARBLER CL
SPRUCE WAY
BRIMMERS WAY
SWALLOW LA
KINGSASH RD
CHALFORD WAY
GREAT MEADOW WAY
COOKS RD
VINEY LA
HICKMAN ST
TREBAH SQ 1
WREN PATH 2
LOOSE PATH 3
WATERPERRY MEWS 4
CROWELL MEWS 5
LONGDOWN MEWS 6
ROSEMOOR MEWS 7
LOWNES PATH 8
WIXON PATH 9
PAKENHAM CL 10
Lower Hartwell
Lower Hartwell Farm
The Nursery
Botts Furlong Farm
EYTHROPE RD
BELLE VUE
CHESTERFIELD CL
POPLARS CL
Cemy
Barnet's Close
UPPER HARTWELL
COTTAGE GROUNDS
CROMHAMSTONE
THE SPIERT
PO
GRIFFITHS ACRE
Park Hill
Hartwell House
A418
JEFFERIES RD
LONG FURLONG
FAITHFULL CL
DARVILL RD
OXFORD RD
THE GLEBE
BADGERS RISE
CHURCH WAY
STONE CROFT
MANOR FARM CL
CORN CL
PH
Stone CE Comb Sch
Beech Wlk
WARREN CL
HAGGAR ST
BEACON CL
CRESLOW WAY
ST JOHN'S
ST JOHNS RD
Stone
WHITECHURCH CL
ROUND HILL
LEE CRES
CHILTERN CL
CHILTERN AVE
BISHOPSTONE RD
MEADOWAY
MAYFLOWER CL
PH
WILLOWMEAD
Mast
A418
HP17
Stone House
Midshires Way
BITTENHAM CL
PORTWAY
SEDRUP LA
Calley Farm
Upton
TEMPLECROFT TERR
HOMESTEAD FARM
UPTON RD
UPTON TERR
Lower Farm
LOWER FARM GATE
Alwyn Lawn House
Sedrup
BISHOPSTONE
SCHOOL LA
Wallace Farm
Sewage Works
MEADOW COTTS
Pasture Farm
Chilboro Hill Farm
Aylesbury Ring

77 A B 78 C D 79 E F

113
128

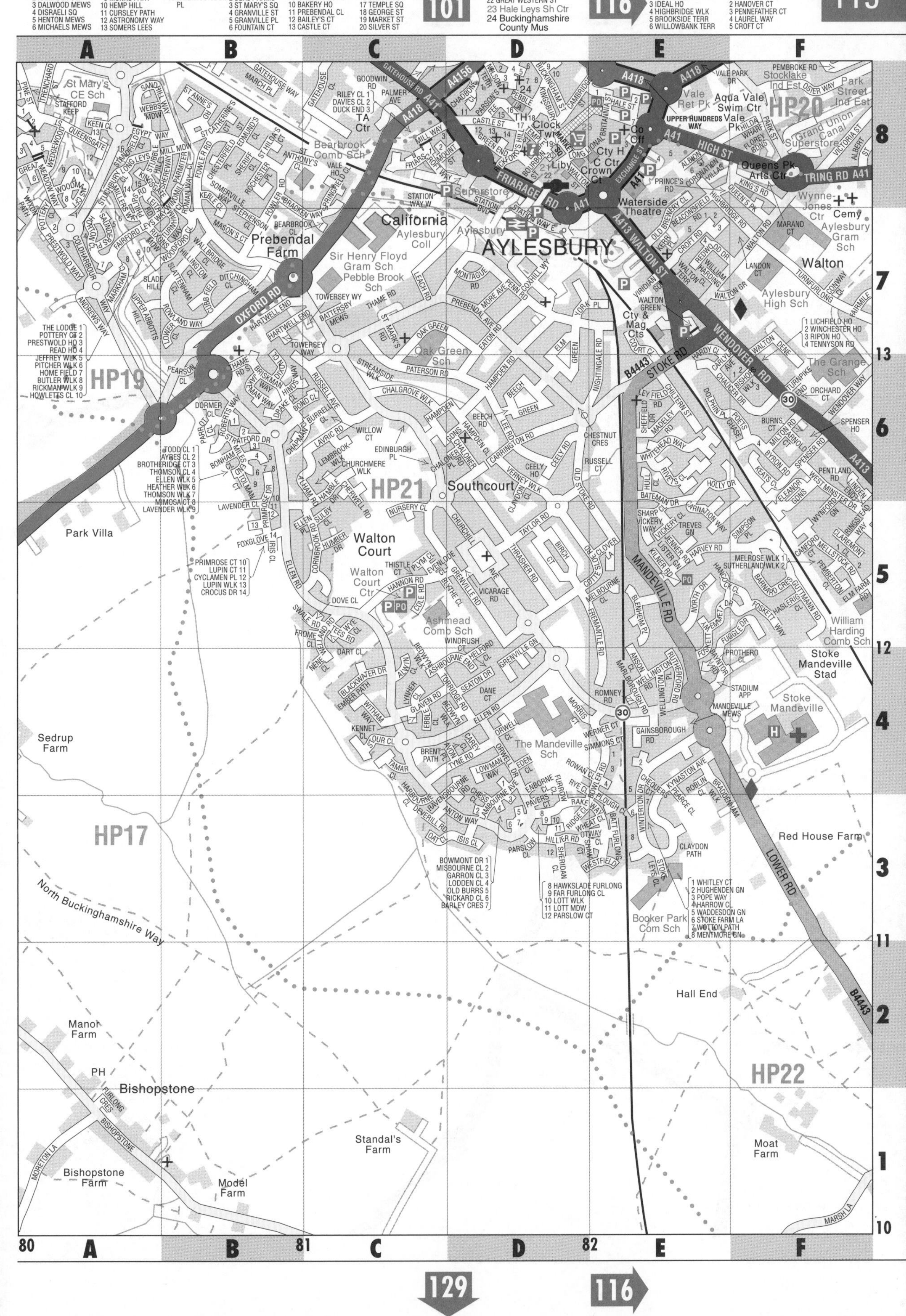

115
A8
1 CROMWELL MEWS
2 HAMPDEN SQ
3 DALWOOD MEWS
4 DISRAELI SQ
5 HENTON MEWS
6 MICHAELS MEWS
7 PHOENIX HO
8 SINGLETON WAY
9 MONKS PATH
10 HEMP HILL
11 CURSLEY PATH
12 ASTRONOMY WAY
13 SOMERS LEES
14 HOMESTEAD PL
15 ASHLEY CT
16 KNIGHTSBRIDGE PL
D8
1 PREBENDAL CT
2 DERBY ARMS
3 ST MARY'S SQ
4 GRANVILLE ST
5 GRANVILLE PL
6 FOUNTAIN CT
7 ST MARY'S ROW
8 VILLIERS BLDGS
9 CAMBRIDGE PL
10 BAKERY HO
11 PREBENDAL CL
12 BAILEY'S CT
13 CASTLE ST
14 ARCHWAYS
15 THE CHANTRY
16 CHURCH ST
17 TEMPLE SQ
18 GEORGE ST
19 MARKET ST
20 SILVER ST
101
D8
21 Red Friars Sq Sh Ctr
22 GREAT WESTERN ST
23 Hale Leys Sh Ctr
24 Buckinghamshire County Mus
116
E8
1 ANCHOR LA
2 RAILWAY ST
3 IDEAL HO
4 HIGHBRIDGE WLK
5 BROOKSIDE TERR
6 WILLOWBANK TERR
7 HIGH ST
E7
1 CHURCHILL CT
2 HANOVER CT
3 PENNEFATHER CT
4 LAUREL WAY
5 CROFT CT
A
B
C
D
E
F
St Mary's CE Sch
Bearbrook Comb Sch
TA Ctr
Clock Twr
Cty H
C Ctr
Crown Ct
Liby
Vale Ret Pk
Aqua Vale Swim Ctr
Vale Pk
Stocklake Ind Est
Park Street Ind Est
HP20
Grand Union Canal
Superstore
Queens Pk Arts Ctr
TRING RD A41
HIGH ST
Waterside Theatre
Wynne-Jones Ctr
Cemy
Aylesbury Gram Sch
Walton
Aylesbury High Sch
California
Aylesbury Coll
Prebendal Farm
Sir Henry Floyd Gram Sch
Pebble Brook Sch
AYLESBURY
OXFORD RD
Oak Green Sch
Cty & Mag Cts
The Grange Sch
HP19
HP21
Southcourt
Park Villa
Walton Court
Walton Court Ctr
Ashmead Comb Sch
The Mandeville Sch
William Harding Comb Sch
Stoke Mandeville Stad
Stoke Mandeville
MANDEVILLE RD
WENDOVER RD
STOKE RD
Sedrup Farm
HP17
North Buckinghamshire Way
Booker Park Com Sch
Red House Farm
LOWER RD
Hall End
HP22
Manor Farm
Bishopstone
Bishopstone Farm
Model Farm
Standal's Farm
Moat Farm
8
7
13
6
5
12
4
3
11
2
1
10
80
81
82
129
116

115
102

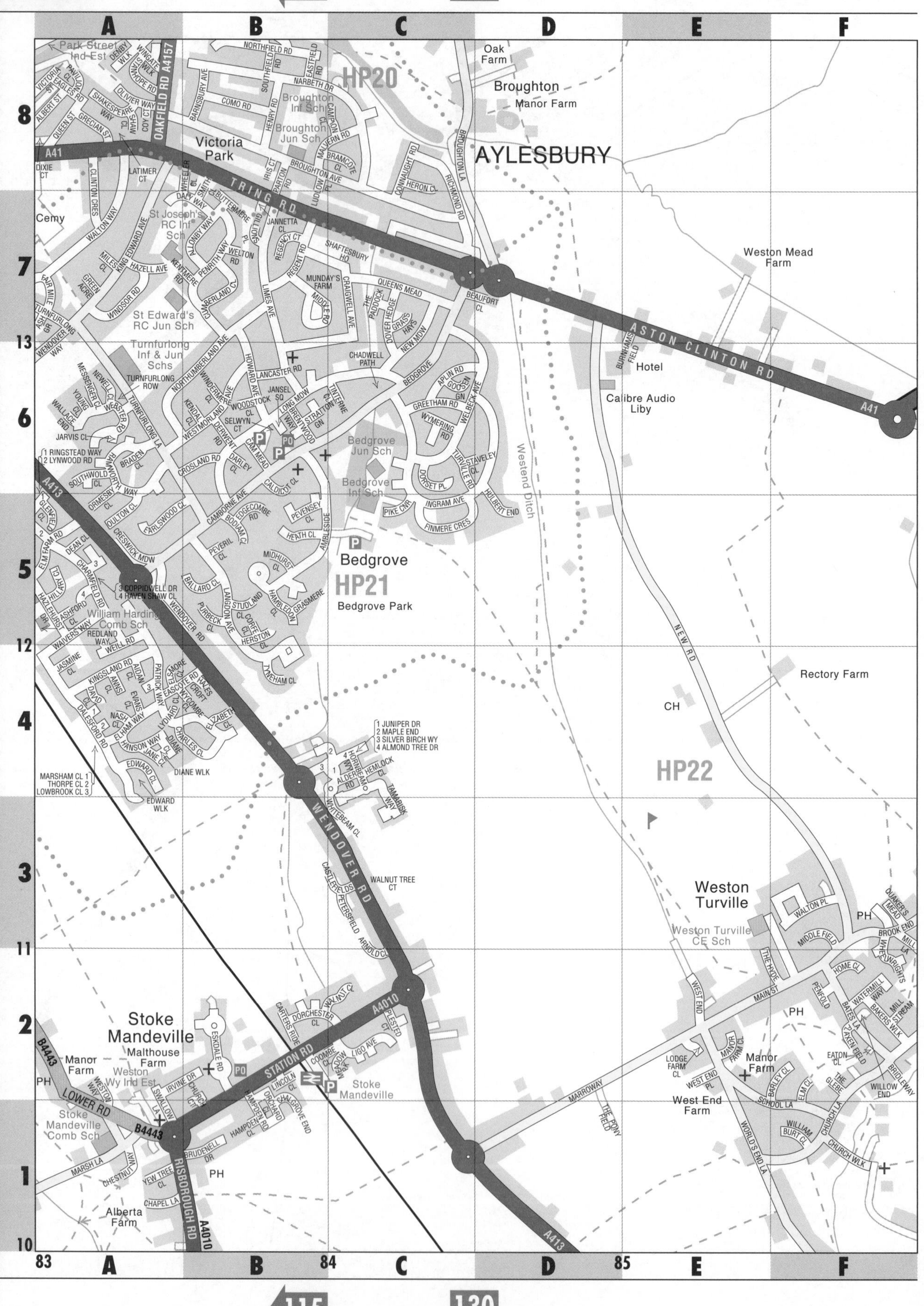

A B C D E F

115
130

103
118
A
B
C
D
E
F
Grand Union Canal Wlk
Grand Union Canal (Aylesbury Arm)
HP23
Aylesbury Ring
College Farm
COLLEGE RD N
Dropshort Farm
Works
Cherry Farm
A41
Lower Farm
ASTON CLINTON RD
Sunny Brook Farm
BALLARDS ROW
SUNNY BROOK CL
MODEL ROW
Buckland
NORMILL TERR
TURNER'S MDW
Aston Clinton
THE GREENWOOD 1
BROOK CL 2
BONHAM CT 3
GATES ORCH 4
Moat Farm
Church Farm
PEGGS LA
AYLESBURY RD
Brook Farm
LONG PLOUGH
ARCHIVE CL
CHAPEL DR
THE ORCHARD
NEW RD
PLEASAUNCE
Manor Farm
Nield's Farm
BROOK ST
GREEN END ST
GINGERS CL
GARLAND WAY
OVERSTRAND
ROTHSCHILD AVE
LONGCROFT
BEECHWOOD WAY
PUTNAMS DR
YORKE CL
WARWICK CL
TWITCHELL LA
TALBOT RD
CHESTNUT CL
ROSEBERY RD
BEECHWOOD HO
LOWER ICKNIELD WAY
Aston Clinton Sch
THE BURY
HAMS
PARSLEY CL
PH
WESTON CT
WESTON RD
STRATFORD CL
CHURCH CL
TURVEY CL
MILTON RD
BEACONSFIELD RD
Park Farm
CHURCH LA
LONDON RD
30
ORCHARD DR
PO
MOUNT CL
TOMPKINS CL
DEAN WAY
THE COURTYARDS
Aston Clinton Park
VIRAGE
Rookery Farm House
Old Rectory Farm
HP22
Splash Covert
P
Green Park
Wellonhead Bridge
STABLEBRIDGE RD
Bye Green
Airfield
BYE GN
BROOK END
ANSTEY BROOK
LOWER GN
Brook End
Brook Farm
MILL LA
Mill Farm
BROOKSIDE
Sewage Works
Grand Union Canal Wlk
B4009
CHILTERN WAY
Rosemead Covert
Aston Clinton Ragpits Wildlife Reserve
UPPER ICKNIELD WAY
Grand Union Canal Wendover Arm
Aylesbury Ring
HAREBRIDGE LA
CH
Marl Copse
Halton Camp
ROSEMEAD
Lower Farm
THE LEYS
OLD SCHOOL CL
Halton
Wendover Woods
BROOKSIDE
MCEWEN RIDE
Church Farm
CHESTNUT END
CHURCH VIEW
ST MICHAEL'S CL
Halton House
Aston Hill
MANSION HILL
8
7
13
6
5
12
4
3
11
2
1
10
86
87
88
131
118

117
104

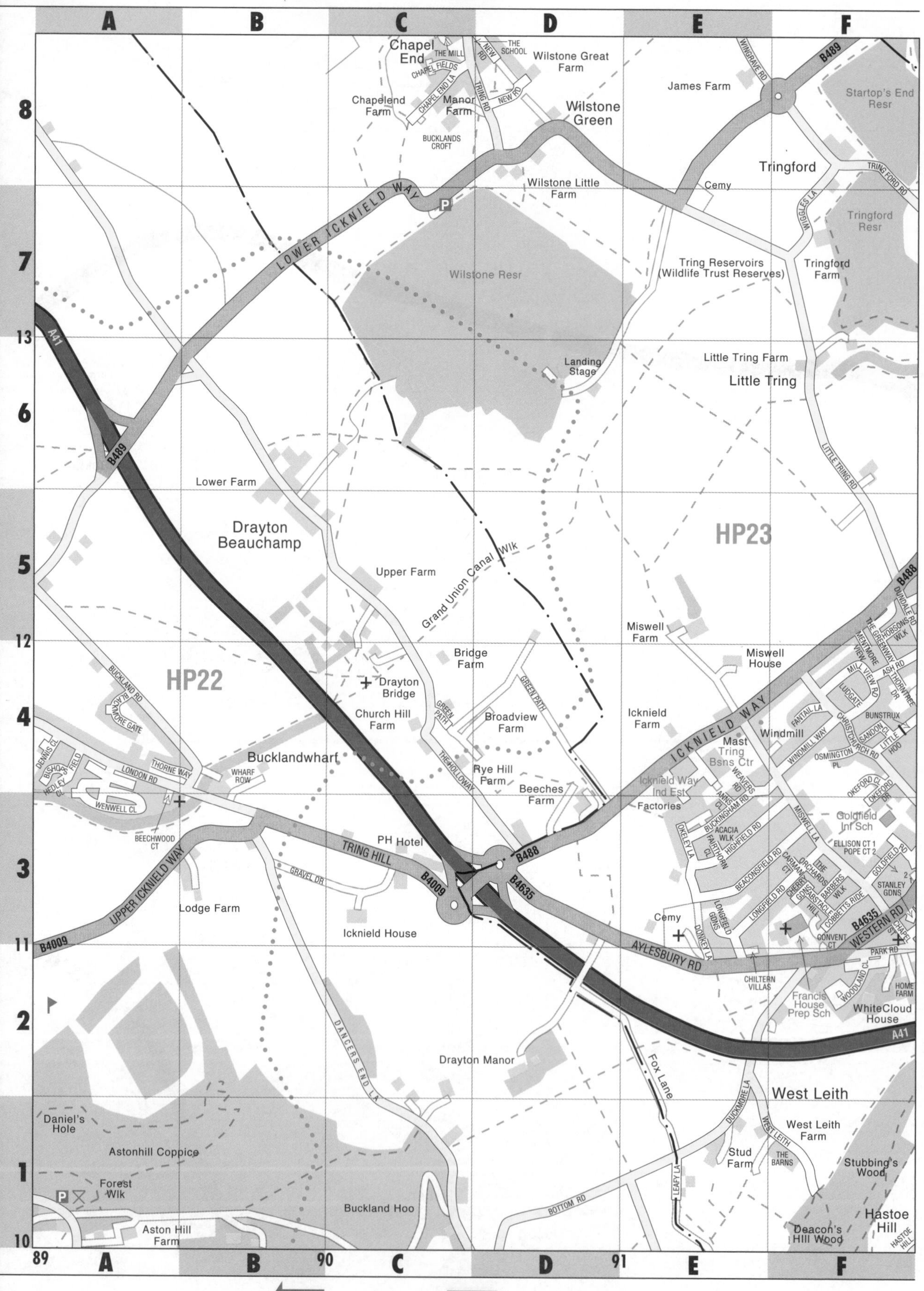
Chapel End
Wilstone Great Farm
James Farm
Chapelend Farm
Manor Farm
Wilstone Green
Startop's End Resr
Tringford
Wilstone Little Farm
Cemy
Tringford Resr
LOWER ICKNIELD WAY
Wilstone Resr
Tring Reservoirs (Wildlife Trust Reserves)
Tringford Farm
Landing Stage
Little Tring Farm
Little Tring
Lower Farm
Drayton Beauchamp
HP23
Upper Farm
Grand Union Canal Wlk
Miswell Farm
Miswell House
HP22
Bridge Farm
Drayton Bridge
Church Hill Farm
Broadview Farm
Icknield Farm
ICKNIELD WAY
Windmill
Mast
Tring Bsns Ctr
Bucklandwharf
Rye Hill Farm
Icknield Way Ind Est
Beeches Farm
Factories
Goldfield Inf Sch
PH Hotel
TRING HILL
UPPER ICKNIELD WAY
Lodge Farm
Icknield House
Cemy
AYLESBURY RD
CHILTERN VILLAS
Francis House Prep Sch
WhiteCloud House
Drayton Manor
Fox Lane
West Leith
West Leith Farm
Daniel's Hole
Astonhill Coppice
Stud Farm
Stubbing's Wood
Forest Wlk
Buckland Hoo
BOTTOM RD
Hastoe Hill
Deacon's Hill Wood
Aston Hill Farm
A B C D E F
8 7 13 6 5 12 4 3 11 2 1 10
89 90 91

105
120

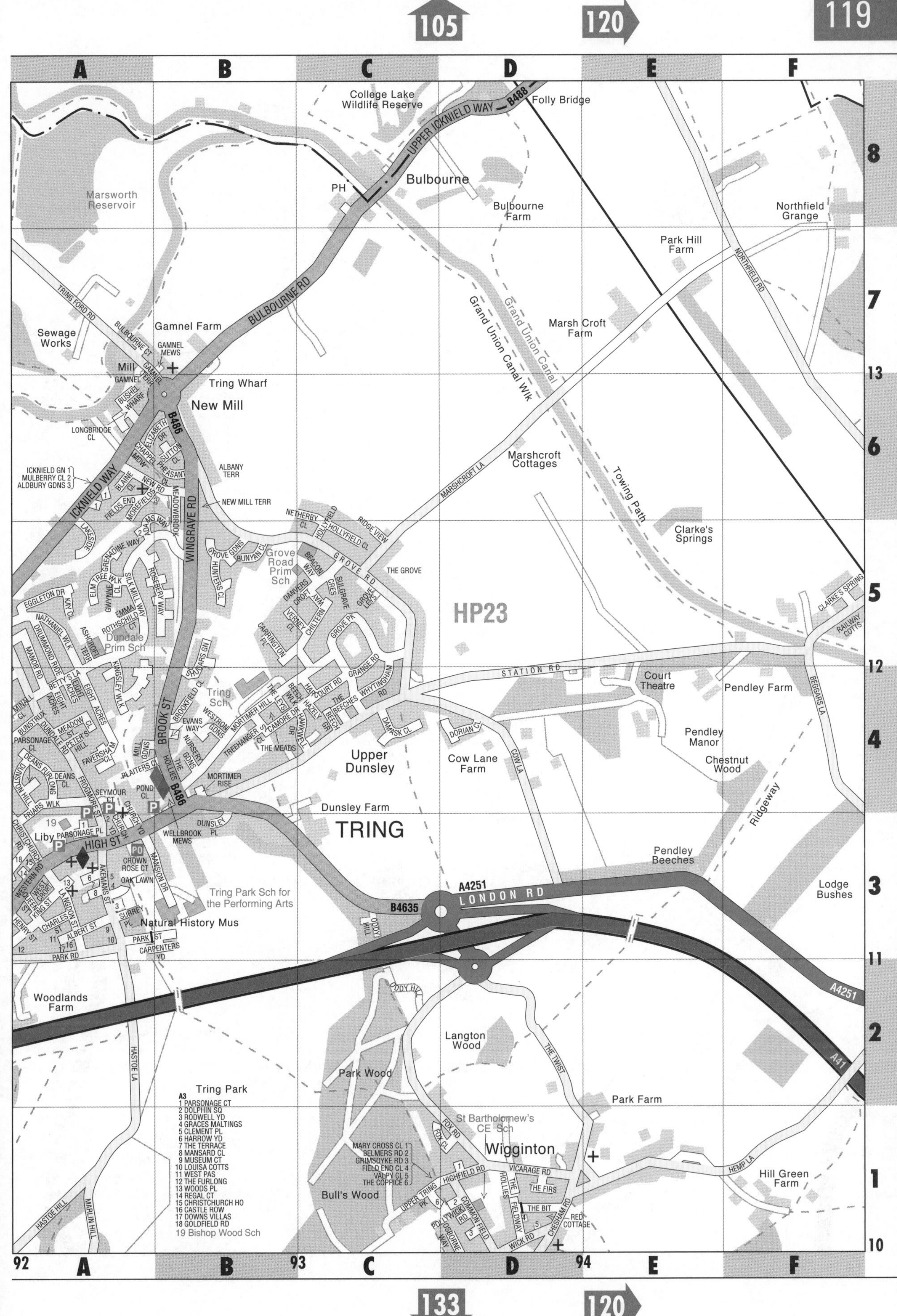

133
120

A B C D E F
8 7 13 6 5 12 4 3 11 2 1 10
95 96 97
Golding's Spring
Hanging Isley
Aldbury Nowers
Howlett's Wood
Walk Wood
Moneybury Hill
Sallow Copse
Tim's Spring
CH
Stocks House
STOCKS RD
Stock's Farm
Pitstone Common
Little Stocks
B4506
Bridgewater Monument
Ashridge Estate Visitors Ctr
Ridgeway
Aldbury Common
NORTHFIELD RD
Westland Farm
Aldbury Prim Sch
PH
Town Farm
Thunderdell Cottages
Church Farm
BEECHWOOD DR
Old Copse
HP4
POSTING HO
STATION RD
PO
Aldbury
TROOPER RD
TOMS HILL CL
TOMS HILL RD
Tring
ROYAL CT
FOG COTTS
HP23
STONEYCROFT
MALTING LA
Brightwood
Chiltern Way
Rail Copse
NEWGROUND RD
The Hangings
Tom's Hill
Tom's Hill House
Hertfordshire Way
BEGGARS LA
The Scrubs
Bottom Spring
Broomfield Spring
Grand Union Canal Wlk
Grand Union Canal
High Spring
A4251
New Ground Farm
HEMP LA
New Ground
TRING RD
Norcott Hill
Norcott Hall Farm
Northchurch Common
A41
BOTTOM HOUSE LA
Norcott Court Farm
Cow Roast Lock
Norcott Court
Cow Roast
Hill Farm
PH
WHARF LA

107

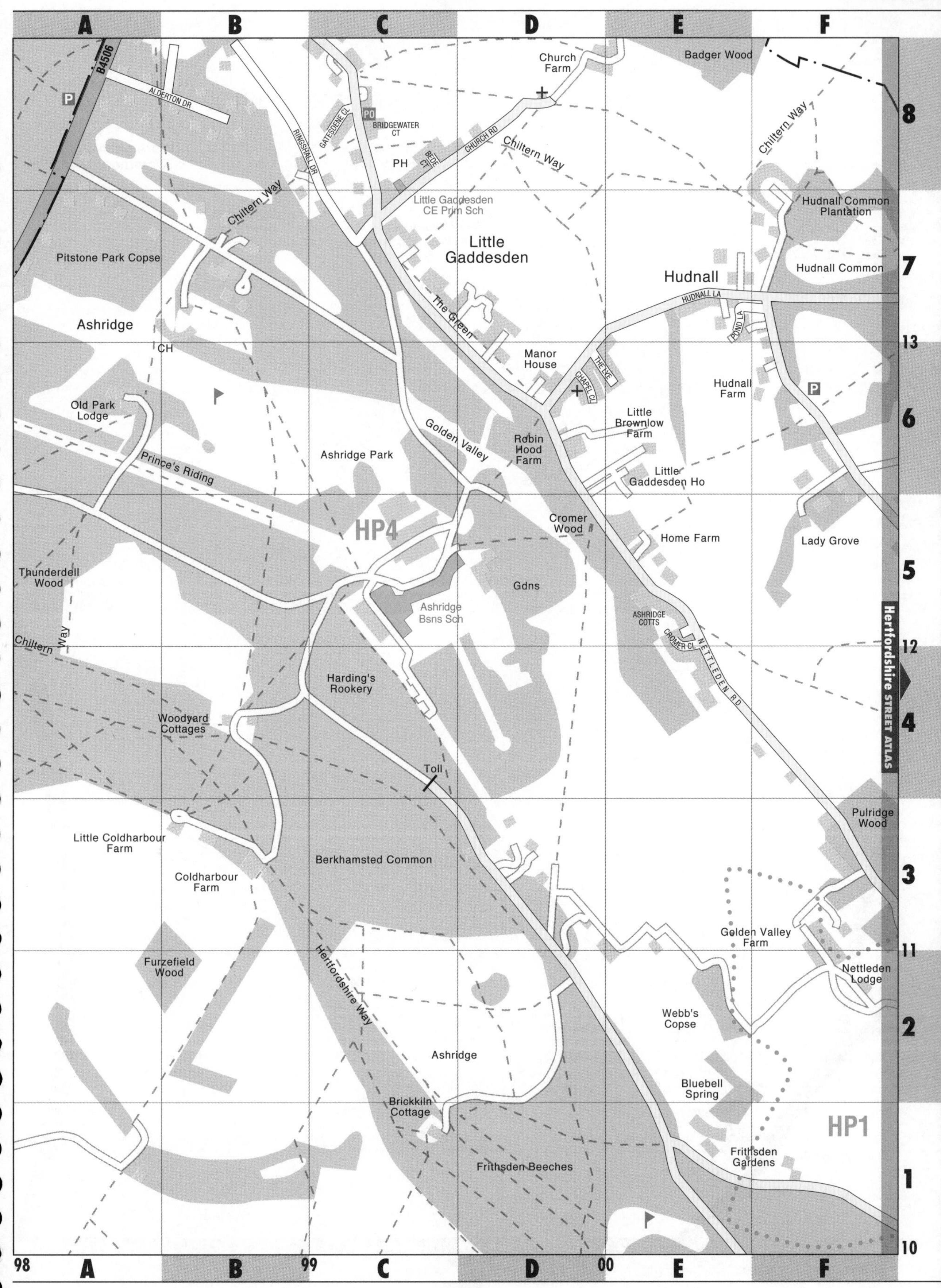

A
B
C
D
E
F
Church Farm
Badger Wood
B4506
P
ALDERTON DR
RINGSHALL DR
GATESDENE CL
PO
BRIDGEWATER CT
CHURCH RD
BEDE CT
PH
Chiltern Way
Little Gaddesden CE Prim Sch
Hudnall Common Plantation
Chiltern Way
Pitstone Park Copse
Little Gaddesden
Hudnall
Hudnall Common
HUDNALL LA
POND LA
The Green
Ashridge
CH
Manor House
THE LYE
CHAPEL CL
Hudnall Farm
P
Old Park Lodge
Little Brownlow Farm
Golden Valley
Robin Hood Farm
Prince's Riding
Ashridge Park
Little Gaddesden Ho
HP4
Cromer Wood
Home Farm
Lady Grove
Thunderdell Wood
Gdns
Ashridge Bsns Sch
ASHRIDGE COTTS
CROMER CL
NETTLEDEN RD
Chiltern Way
Harding's Rookery
Woodyard Cottages
Toll
Pulridge Wood
Little Coldharbour Farm
Berkhamsted Common
Coldharbour Farm
Golden Valley Farm
Furzefield Wood
Hertfordshire Way
Nettleden Lodge
Webb's Copse
Ashridge
Bluebell Spring
Brickkiln Cottage
HP1
Frithsden Gardens
Frithsden Beeches
8
7
13
6
5
12
4
3
11
2
1
10
98
99
00
Hertfordshire STREET ATLAS

135

108

A
B
C
D
E
F
8
7
09
6
5
08
4
3
07
2
1
06
59
60
61
MILL ST
Moorbirge Brook
Clearsale
Hursthill
HP18
Wood Farm
Waterperry Common
SMITHS LA
Commonleys Farm
Bernwood Forest
Waterperry Wood
Polecat End
Drunkard's Corner
Park Farm
Park Farm House
Oxfordshire Way
Parson's Farm
Polecat End Hollows
Marsh Copse
Ledall Cottage
M40
Holton Wood
OX33
Buryhook Barn
Holton Brook
B4027
Keeper's Cottage
Warren Farm
Pond Farm
Old Park Farm
Warren Wood
WHEATLEY RD
BURYHOOK CNR
Lyehill Quarries (dis)
Cottage Copse
A40 Oxford
Warwick Close Farm
A40
Wheatley Park Sch
Recn Gd
Holton
The Rectory
Holton Place
Liby
BARNS CL
Park Sports Ctr
John Watson Sch
Church Farm
Moat
Wheatley
Garden Copse
Brookes Univ (Wheatley Campus)
WESTFIELD RD
PARK HILL
LONDON RD
COLLEGE CL
Oxfordshire STREET ATLAS
A40 High Wycombe (M40)
M40 High Wycombe, London

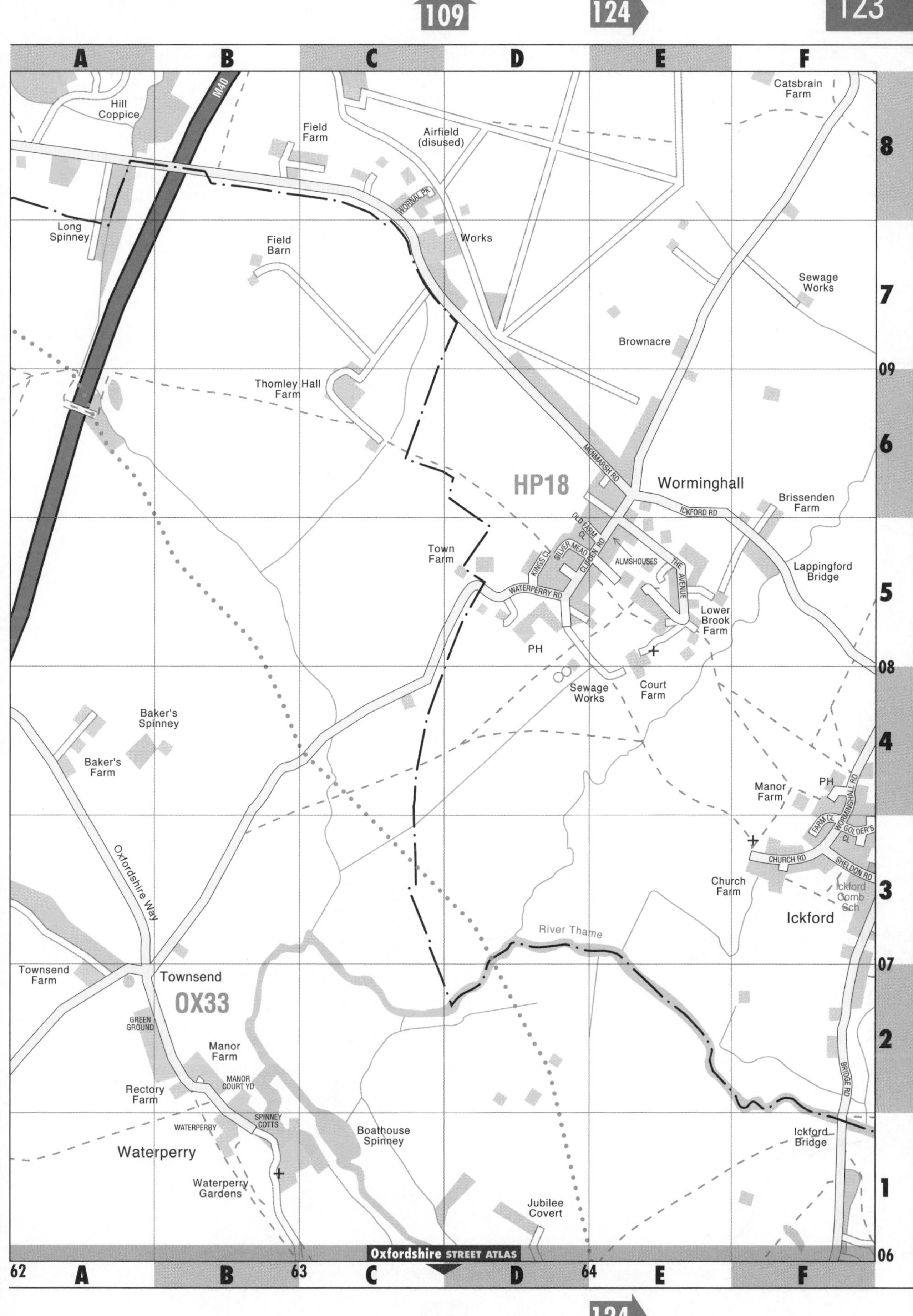
A
B
C
D
E
F
M40
Hill Coppice
Field Farm
Airfield (disused)
Catsbrain Farm
8
WORNAL PK
Long Spinney
Field Barn
Works
Sewage Works
7
Brownacre
09
Thomley Hall Farm
6
MENMARSH RD
HP18
Worminghall
ICKFORD RD
Brissenden Farm
OLD FARM CL
Town Farm
KINGS CL
SILVER MEAD
CLIFDEN RD
ALMSHOUSES
THE AVENUE
Lappingford Bridge
WATERPERRY RD
5
Lower Brook Farm
PH
08
Sewage Works
Court Farm
Baker's Spinney
Baker's Farm
4
Manor Farm
PH
WORMINGHALL RD
FARM CL
GOLDER'S CL
CHURCH RD
SHELDON RD
Oxfordshire Way
Church Farm
Ickford Comb Sch
3
Ickford
River Thame
Townsend Farm
Townsend
07
OX33
GREEN GROUND
Manor Farm
2
MANOR COURT YD
Rectory Farm
BRIDGE RD
WATERPERRY
SPINNEY COTTS
Boathouse Spinney
Ickford Bridge
Waterperry
Waterperry Gardens
1
Jubilee Covert
06
62
63
64

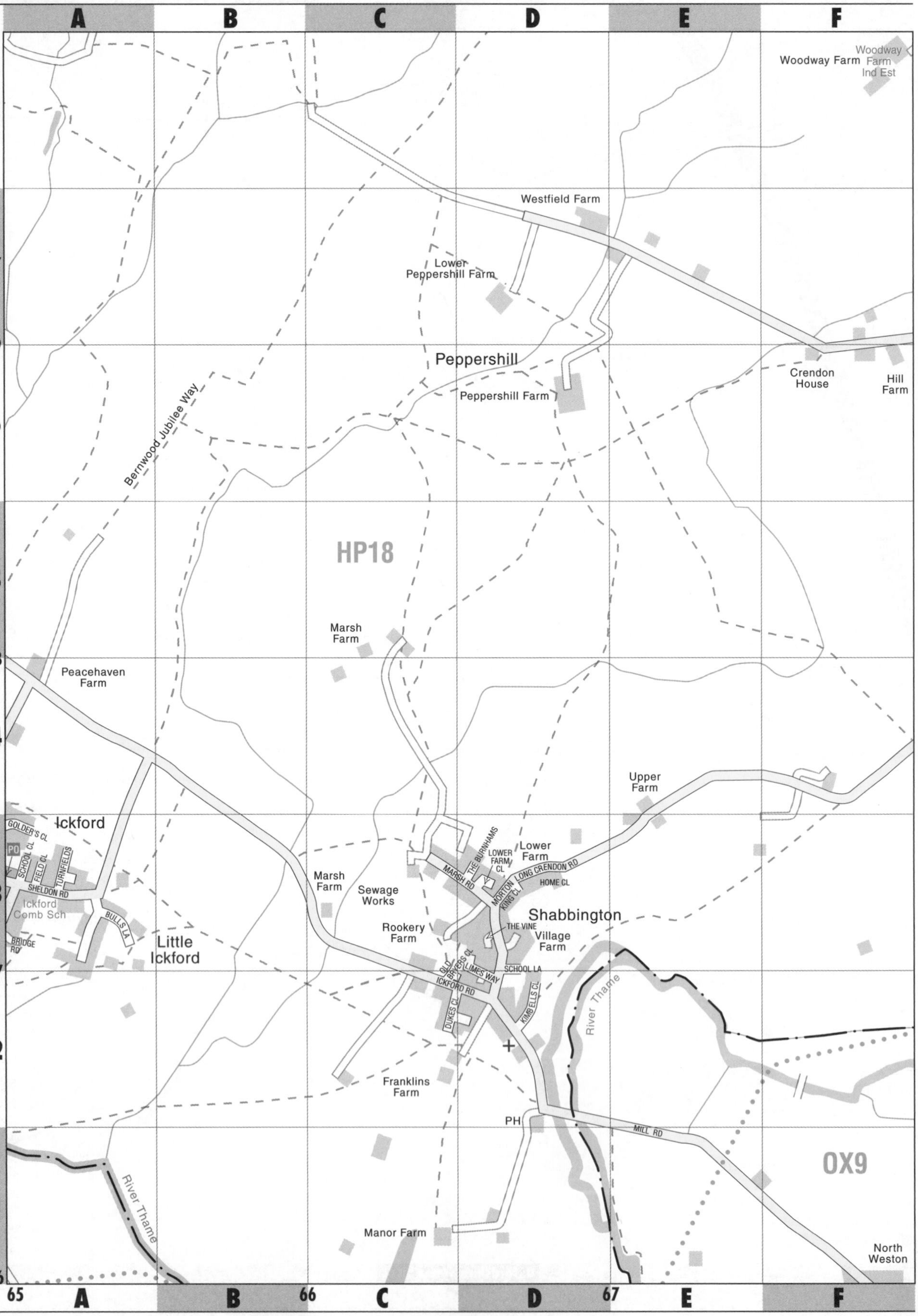

A B C D E F
8
7
09
6
5
08
4
3
07
2
1
06
65 66 67
Woodway Farm
Woodway Farm Ind Est
Westfield Farm
Lower Peppershill Farm
Peppershill
Peppershill Farm
Crendon House
Hill Farm
Bernwood Jubilee Way
HP18
Marsh Farm
Peacehaven Farm
Upper Farm
Ickford
GOLDER'S CL
PO
SCHOOL CL
FIELD CL
TURNFIELDS
SHELDON RD
Ickford Comb Sch
BULLS LA
BRIDGE RD
Little Ickford
Marsh Farm
Sewage Works
Rookery Farm
THE BURNHAMS
LOWER FARM CL
Lower Farm
MARSH RD
LONG CRENDON RD
HOME CL
MORTON KING CL
Shabbington
THE VINE
Village Farm
OLD BYRES CL
LIMES WAY
SCHOOL LA
ICKFORD RD
DUKES CL
KIMBELLS CL
River Thame
Franklins Farm
PH
MILL RD
OX9
River Thame
Manor Farm
North Weston

111
126

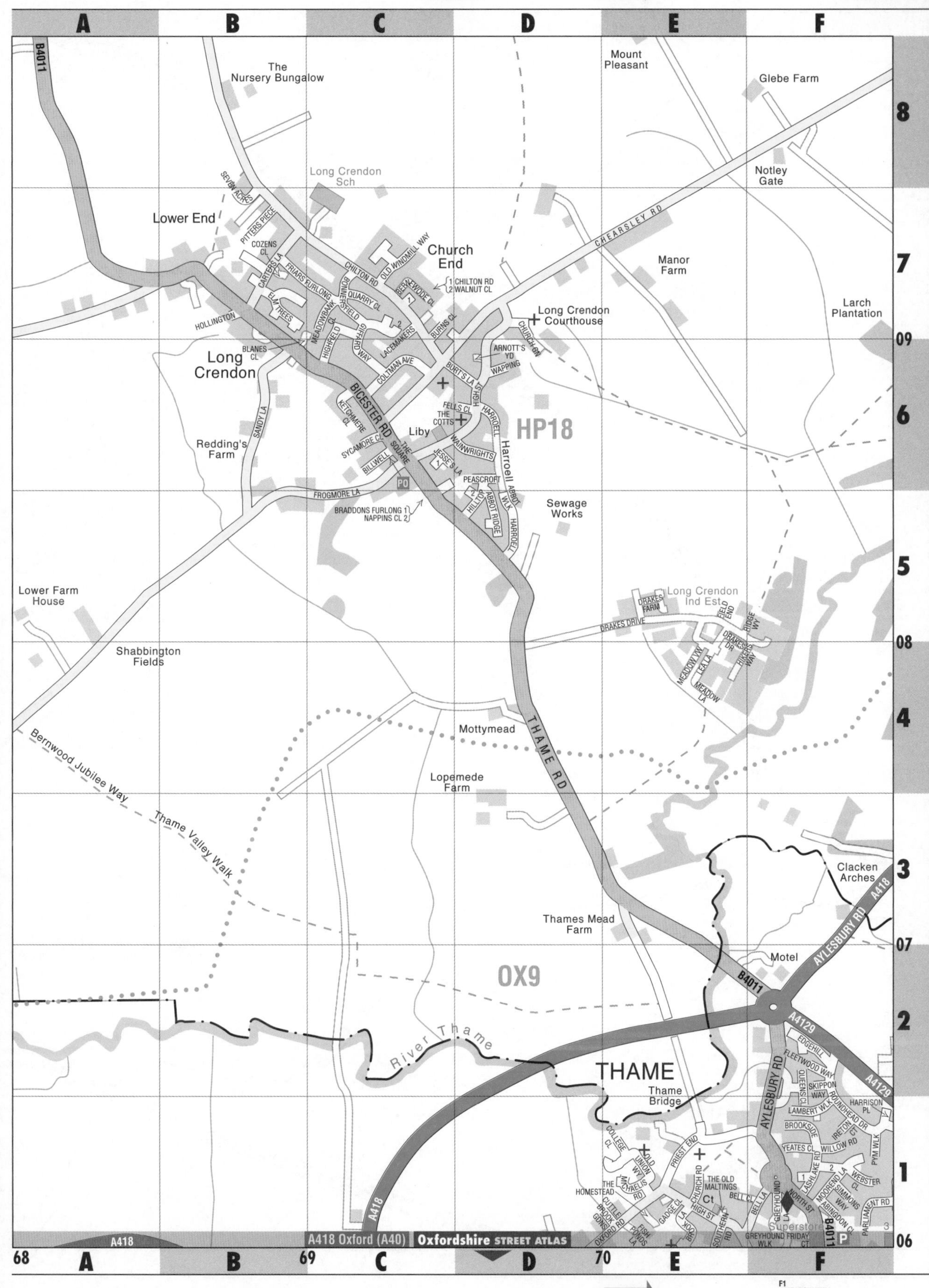

126

F1
1 MEADOW WAY
2 GREENWAY
3 Barley Hill Prim Sch

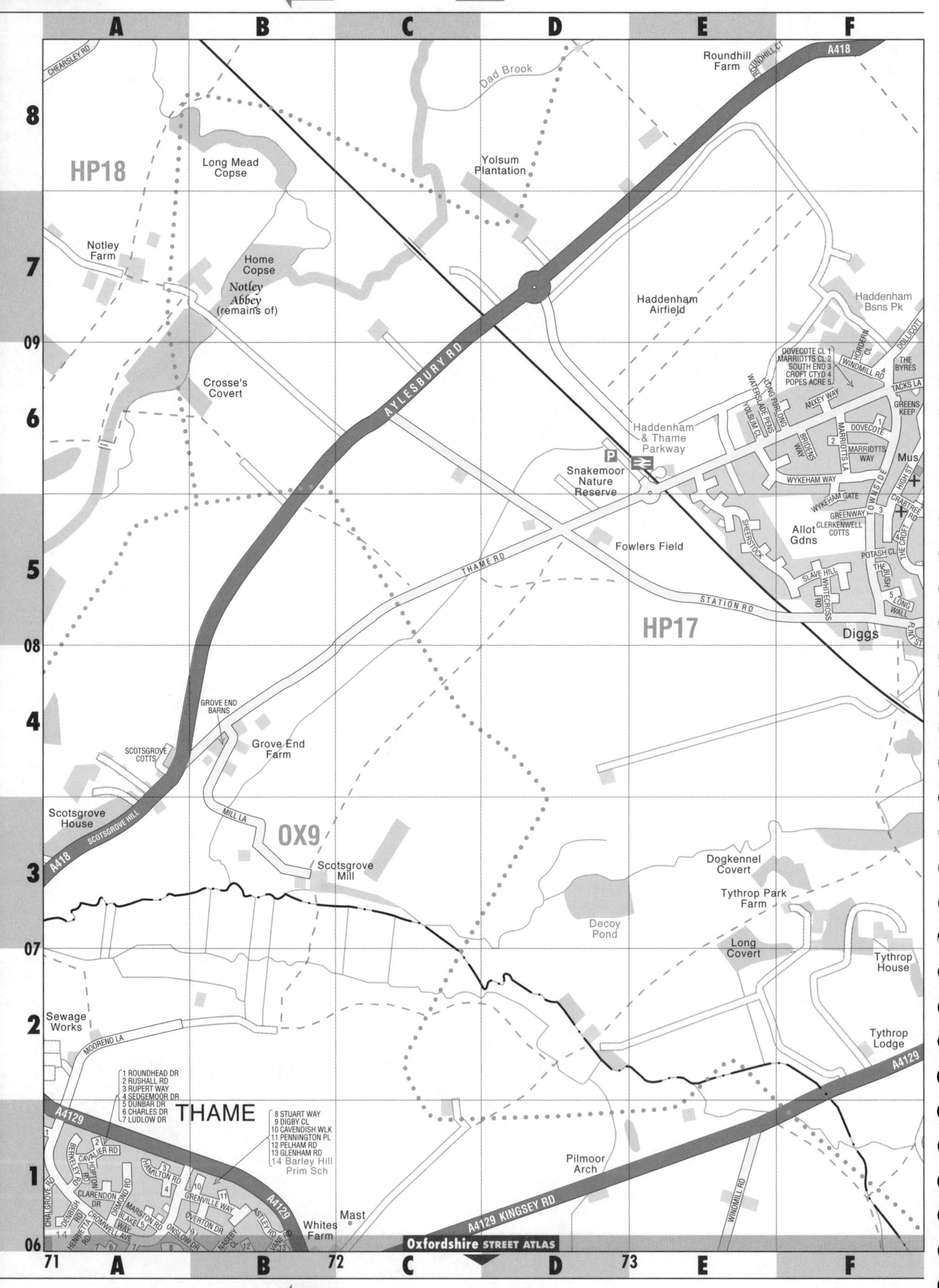
A
B
C
D
E
F
8
7
09
6
5
08
4
3
07
2
1
06
71
72
73
HP18
HP17
OX9
Long Mead Copse
Yolsum Plantation
Roundhill Farm
Dad Brook
A418
Notley Farm
Home Copse
Notley Abbey (remains of)
Haddenham Airfield
Haddenham Bsns Pk
Crosse's Covert
AYLESBURY RD
Haddenham & Thame Parkway
Snakemoor Nature Reserve
Fowlers Field
THAME RD
STATION RD
Allot Gdns
Diggs
Mus
GROVE END BARNS
Grove End Farm
SCOTSGROVE COTTS
Scotsgrove House
SCOTSGROVE HILL
MILL LA
Scotsgrove Mill
Dogkennel Covert
Tythrop Park Farm
Decoy Pond
Long Covert
Tythrop House
Tythrop Lodge
Sewage Works
MOOREND LA
THAME
A4129
Pilmoor Arch
A4129 KINGSEY RD
WINDMILL RD
Mast
Whites Farm
1 ROUNDHEAD DR
2 RUSHALL RD
3 RUPERT WAY
4 SEDGEMOOR DR
5 DUNBAR DR
6 CHARLES DR
7 LUDLOW DR
8 STUART WAY
9 DIGBY CL
10 CAVENDISH WLK
11 PENNINGTON PL
12 PELHAM RD
13 GLENHAM RD
14 Barley Hill Prim Sch
DOVECOTE CL 1
MARRIOTTS CL 2
SOUTH END 3
CROFT CTYD 4
POPES ACRE 5
Oxfordshire STREET ATLAS

113
128

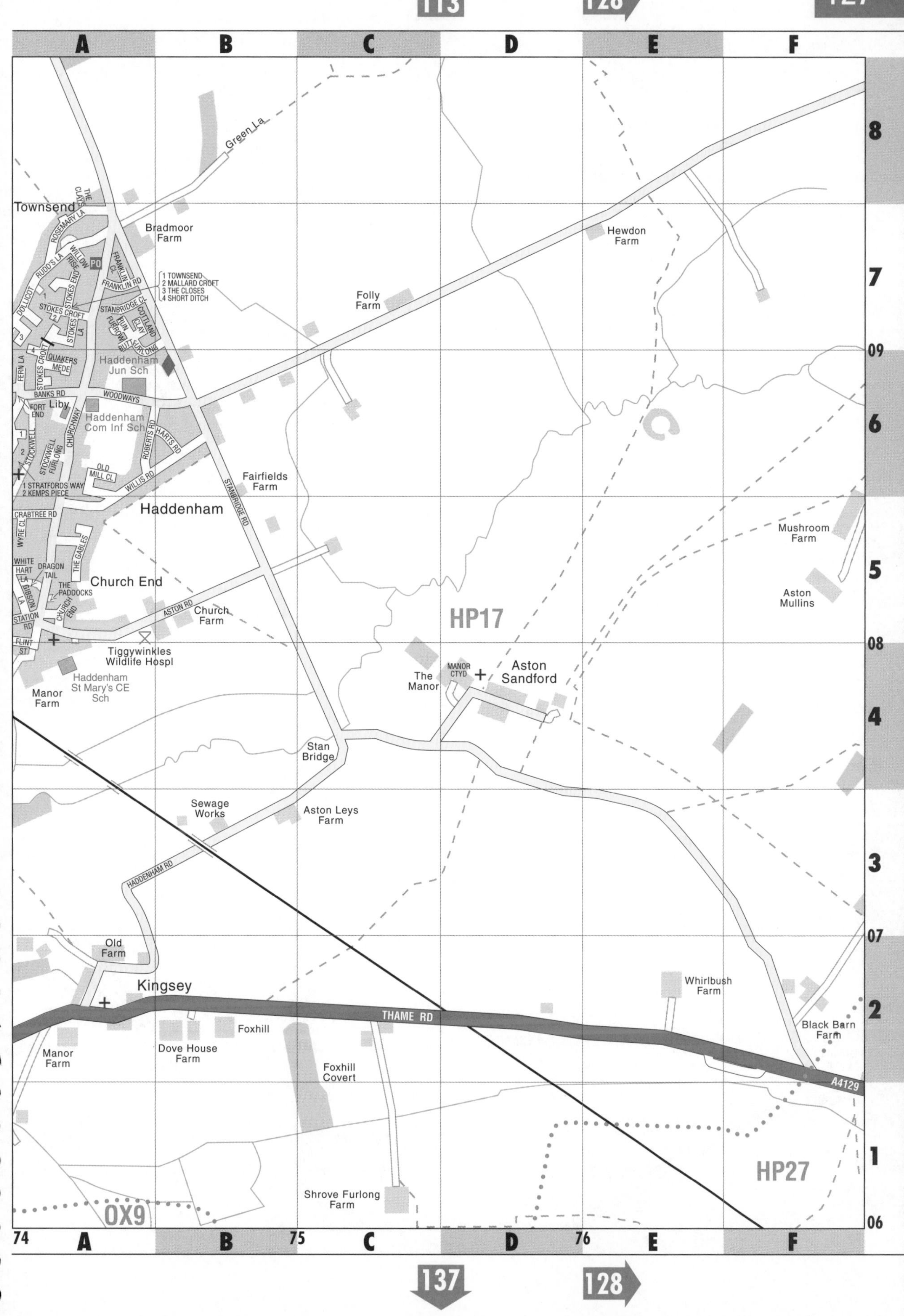

137
128

127
114

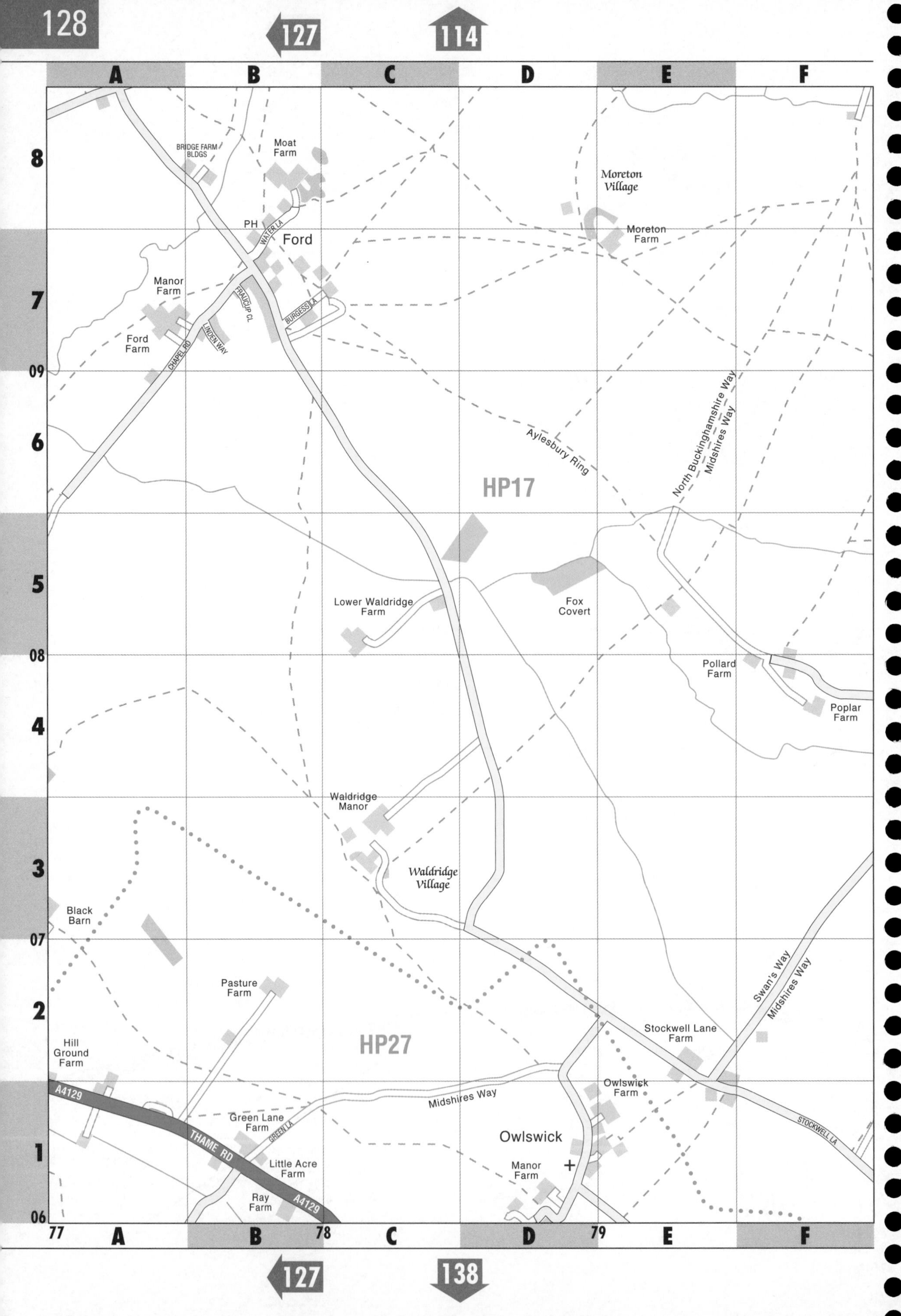

127
138

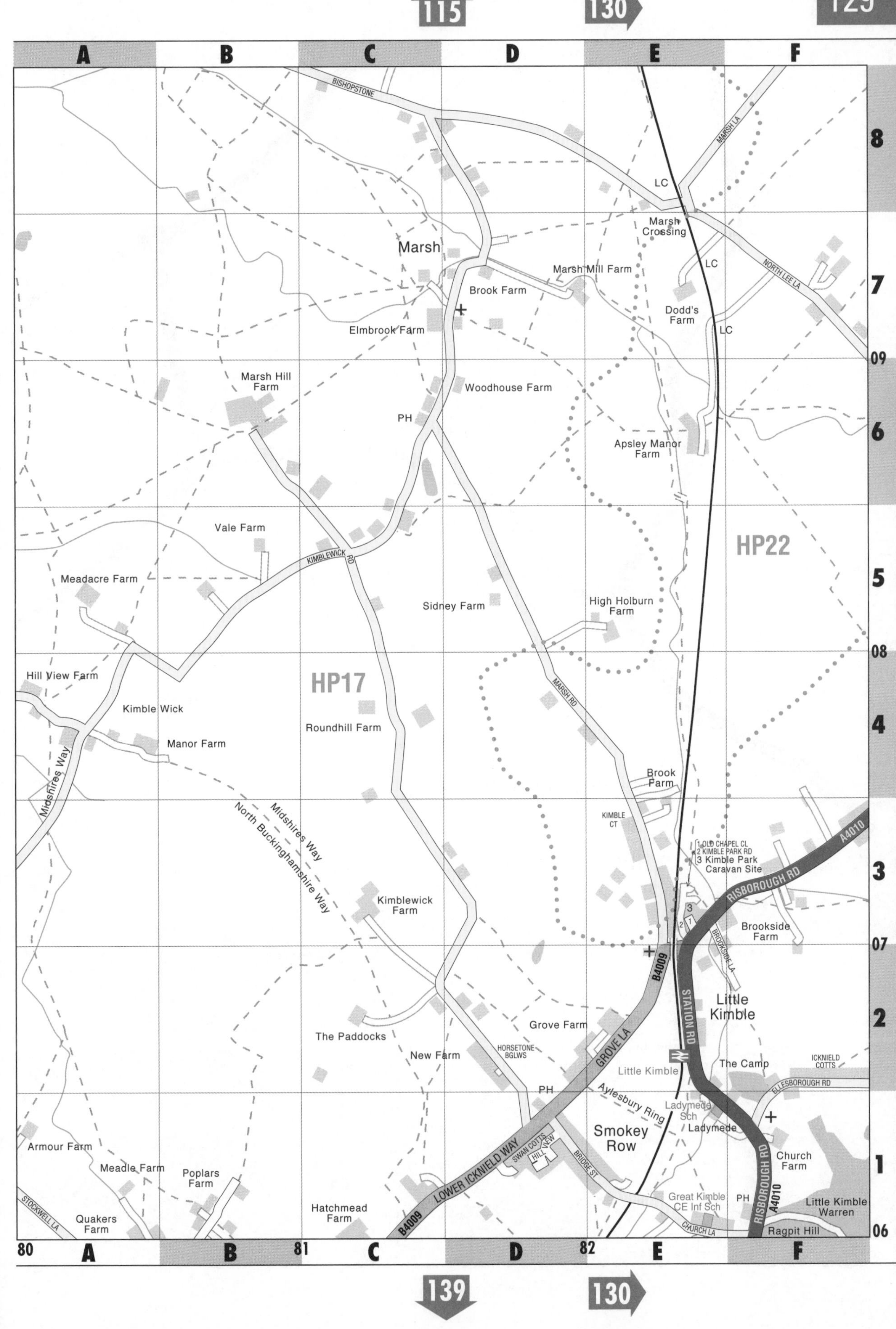
115
130
A
B
C
D
E
F
8
7
09
6
5
08
4
3
07
2
1
06
80
81
82
BISHOPSTONE
MARSH LA
LC
Marsh Crossing
Marsh
NORTH LEE LA
Marsh Mill Farm
Brook Farm
Dodd's Farm
Elmbrook Farm
Marsh Hill Farm
Woodhouse Farm
PH
Apsley Manor Farm
Vale Farm
HP22
KIMBLEWICK RD
Meadacre Farm
Sidney Farm
High Holburn Farm
Hill View Farm
HP17
Kimble Wick
MARSH RD
Roundhill Farm
Manor Farm
Midshires Way
Brook Farm
Midshires Way
North Buckinghamshire Way
KIMBLE CT
1 OLD CHAPEL CL
2 KIMBLE PARK RD
3 Kimble Park Caravan Site
A4010
RISBOROUGH RD
Kimblewick Farm
Brookside Farm
BROOKSIDE LA
B4009
STATION RD
Little Kimble
Grove Farm
GROVE LA
The Paddocks
New Farm
HORSETONE BGLWS
Little Kimble
The Camp
ICKNIELD COTTS
ELLESBOROUGH RD
PH
Aylesbury Ring
Ladymede Sch
Ladymede
Smokey Row
SWAN COTTS
HILL VIEW
BRIDGE ST
LOWER ICKNIELD WAY
Armour Farm
Church Farm
Meadle Farm
Poplars Farm
RISBOROUGH RD
A4010
Great Kimble CE Inf Sch
PH
Little Kimble Warren
STOCKWELL LA
Quakers Farm
Hatchmead Farm
B4009
CHURCH LA
Ragpit Hill
139
130

129 116

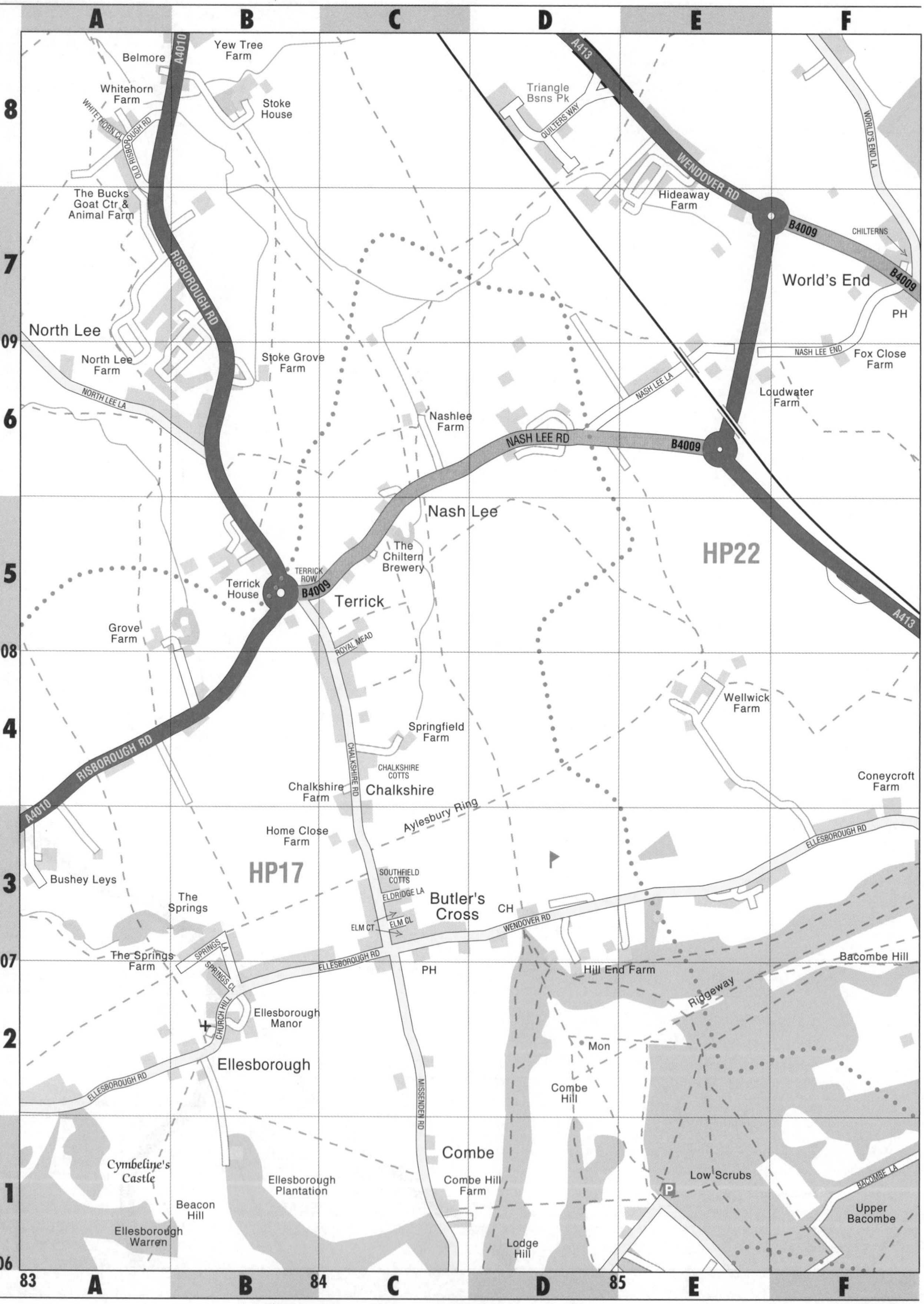

A B C D E F

8 7 09 6 5 08 4 3 07 2 1 06

Belmore
Yew Tree Farm
Whitehorn Farm
WHITEHORN CL
OLD RISBOROUGH RD
A4010
Stoke House
Triangle Bsns Pk
QUILTERS WAY
A413
WENDOVER RD
WORLD'S END LA
The Bucks Goat Ctr & Animal Farm
Hideaway Farm
B4009
CHILTERNS
RISBOROUGH RD
World's End
PH
North Lee
North Lee Farm
Stoke Grove Farm
NASH LEE END
Fox Close Farm
NORTH LEE LA
NASH LEE LA
Loudwater Farm
Nashlee Farm
NASH LEE RD
Nash Lee
The Chiltern Brewery
HP22
Terrick House
TERRICK ROW
Terrick
Grove Farm
ROYAL MEAD
Wellwick Farm
Springfield Farm
CHALKSHIRE RD
CHALKSHIRE COTTS
Chalkshire Farm
Chalkshire
Coneycroft Farm
Aylesbury Ring
Home Close Farm
ELLESBOROUGH RD
Bushey Leys
HP17
SOUTHFIELD COTTS
ELDRIDGE LA
Butler's Cross
CH
The Springs
ELM CT
ELM CL
WENDOVER RD
The Springs Farm
SPRINGS LA
SPRINGS CL
Bacombe Hill
PH
Hill End Farm
Ridgeway
CHURCH HILL
Ellesborough Manor
Mon
Ellesborough
Combe Hill
MISSENDEN RD
Combe
Cymbeline's Castle
Ellesborough Plantation
Combe Hill Farm
Low Scrubs
P
BACOMBE LA
Beacon Hill
Upper Bacombe
Ellesborough Warren
Lodge Hill

83 84 85

129 140

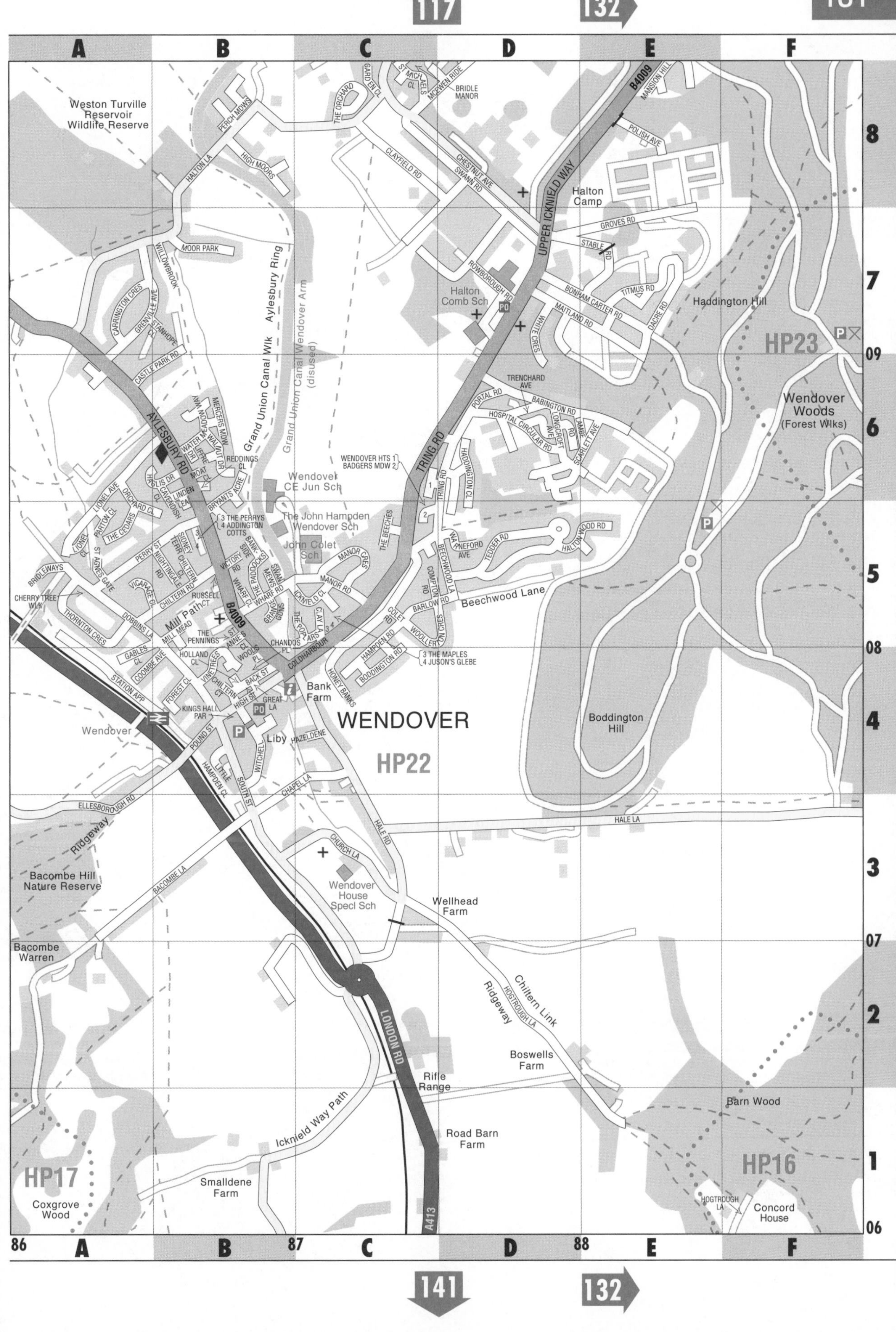
117
132
141
132
WENDOVER
HP22
HP23
HP17
HP16
Weston Turville Reservoir Wildlife Reserve
Halton Camp
Halton Comb Sch
Haddington Hill
Wendover Woods (Forest Wlks)
Wendover CE Jun Sch
The John Hampden Wendover Sch
John Colet Sch
Boddington Hill
Bank Farm
Liby
Wendover
Bacombe Hill Nature Reserve
Bacombe Warren
Wendover House Specl Sch
Wellhead Farm
Boswells Farm
Rifle Range
Barn Wood
Road Barn Farm
Smalldene Farm
Coxgrove Wood
Concord House
Grand Union Canal Wlk
Aylesbury Ring
Grand Union Canal Wendover Arm (disused)
Beechwood Lane
Icknield Way Path
Ridgeway
Chiltern Link
Mill Pathct
UPPER ICKNIELD WAY
TRING RD
AYLESBURY RD
LONDON RD
HALE LA
B4009
A413

131
118

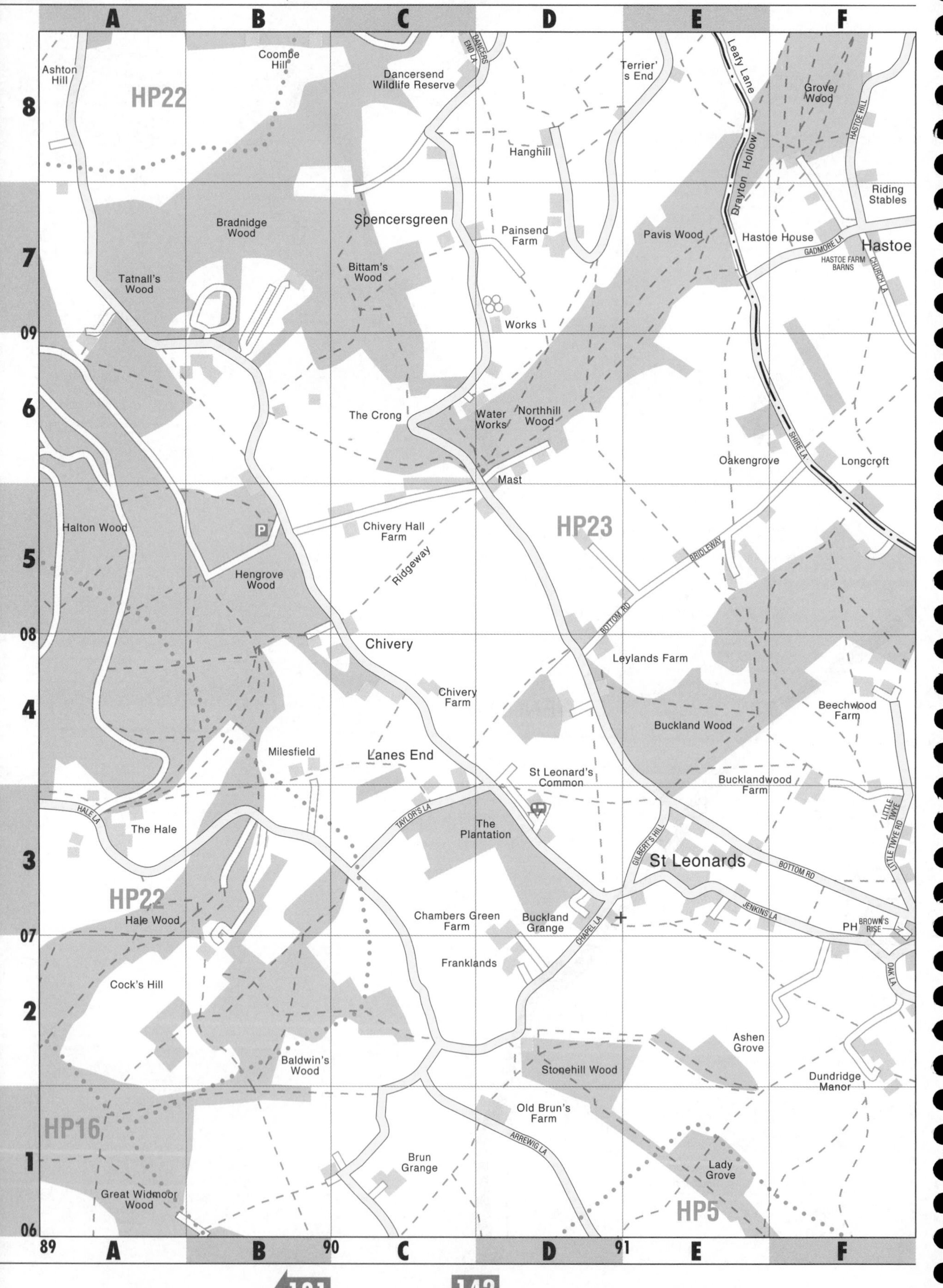

131
142

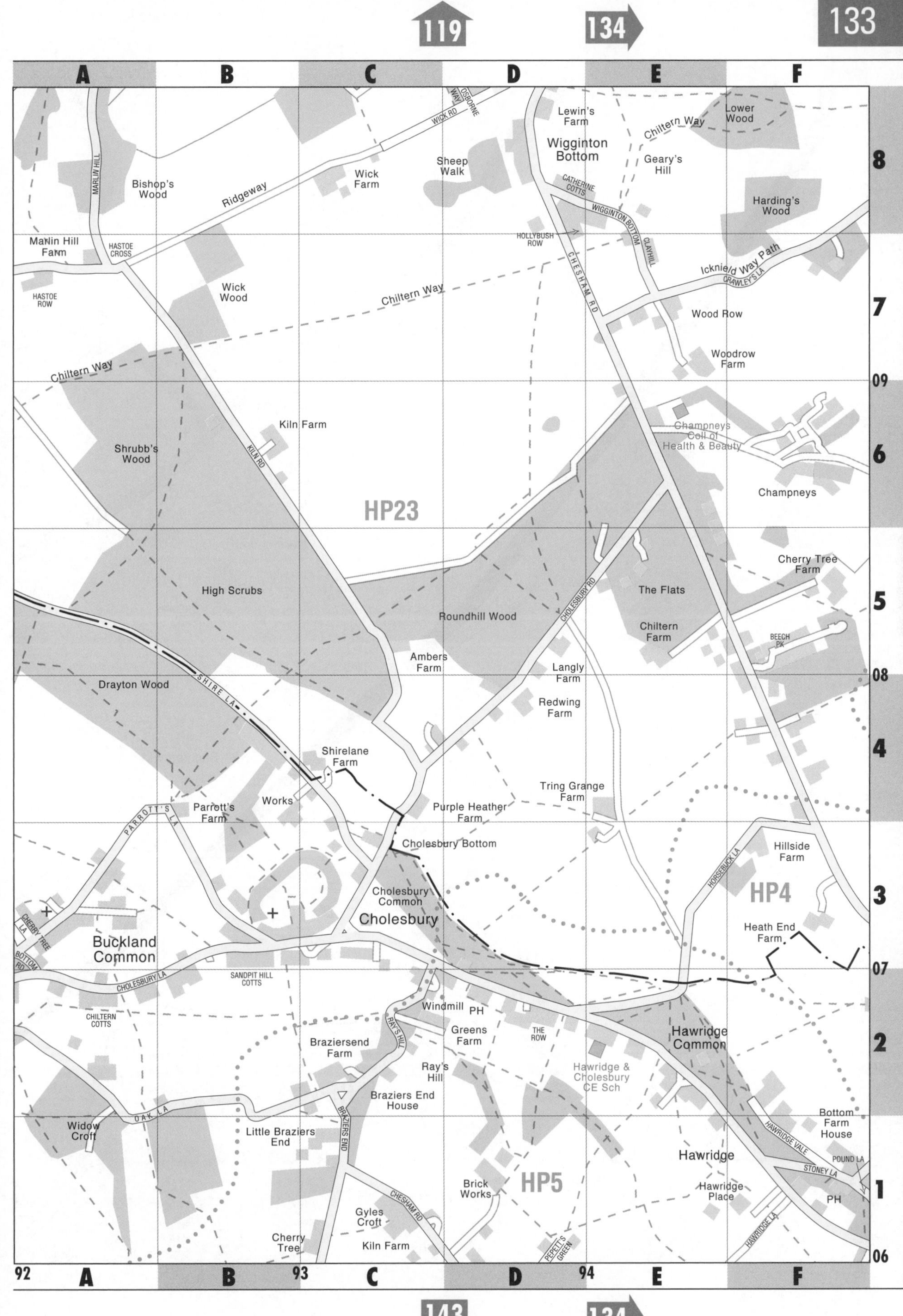
A B C D E F
8 7 09 6 5 08 4 3 07 2 1 06
92 93 94
Lewin's Farm
Lower Wood
Wigginton Bottom
Chiltern Way
Geary's Hill
Sheep Walk
Wick Farm
Bishop's Wood
Ridgeway
Harding's Wood
Marlin Hill Farm
HASTOE CROSS
HASTOE ROW
MARLIN HILL
WICK RD
OSBORNE WAY
CATHERINE COTTS
WIGGINTON BOTTOM
HOLLYBUSH ROW
CLAYHILL
CHESHAM RD
Icknield Way Path
CRAWLEY'S LA
Wick Wood
Wood Row
Woodrow Farm
Kiln Farm
KILN RD
Shrubb's Wood
Champneys Coll of Health & Beauty
Champneys
HP23
Cherry Tree Farm
High Scrubs
Roundhill Wood
CHOLESBURY RD
The Flats
Chiltern Farm
BEECH PK
Ambers Farm
Langly Farm
Drayton Wood
SHIRE LA
Redwing Farm
Shirelane Farm
Tring Grange Farm
Works
Parrott's Farm
PARROTT'S LA
Purple Heather Farm
Cholesbury Bottom
Hillside Farm
HORSEBUCK LA
HP4
Cholesbury Common
Cholesbury
Heath End Farm
Buckland Common
CHERRY TREE LA
BOTTOM RD
CHOLESBURY LA
SANDPIT HILL COTTS
CHILTERN COTTS
Windmill
PH
RAY'S HILL
Greens Farm
THE ROW
Braziersend Farm
Hawridge Common
Ray's Hill
Hawridge & Cholesbury CE Sch
Braziers End House
OAK LA
BRAZIERS END
Widow Croft
Little Braziers End
Hawridge
HAWRIDGE VALE
Bottom Farm House
POUND LA
STONEY LA
Brick Works
HP5
Hawridge Place
CHESHAM RD
Gyles Croft
HAWRIDGE LA
Cherry Tree
Kiln Farm
PEPETT'S GREEN

133 120

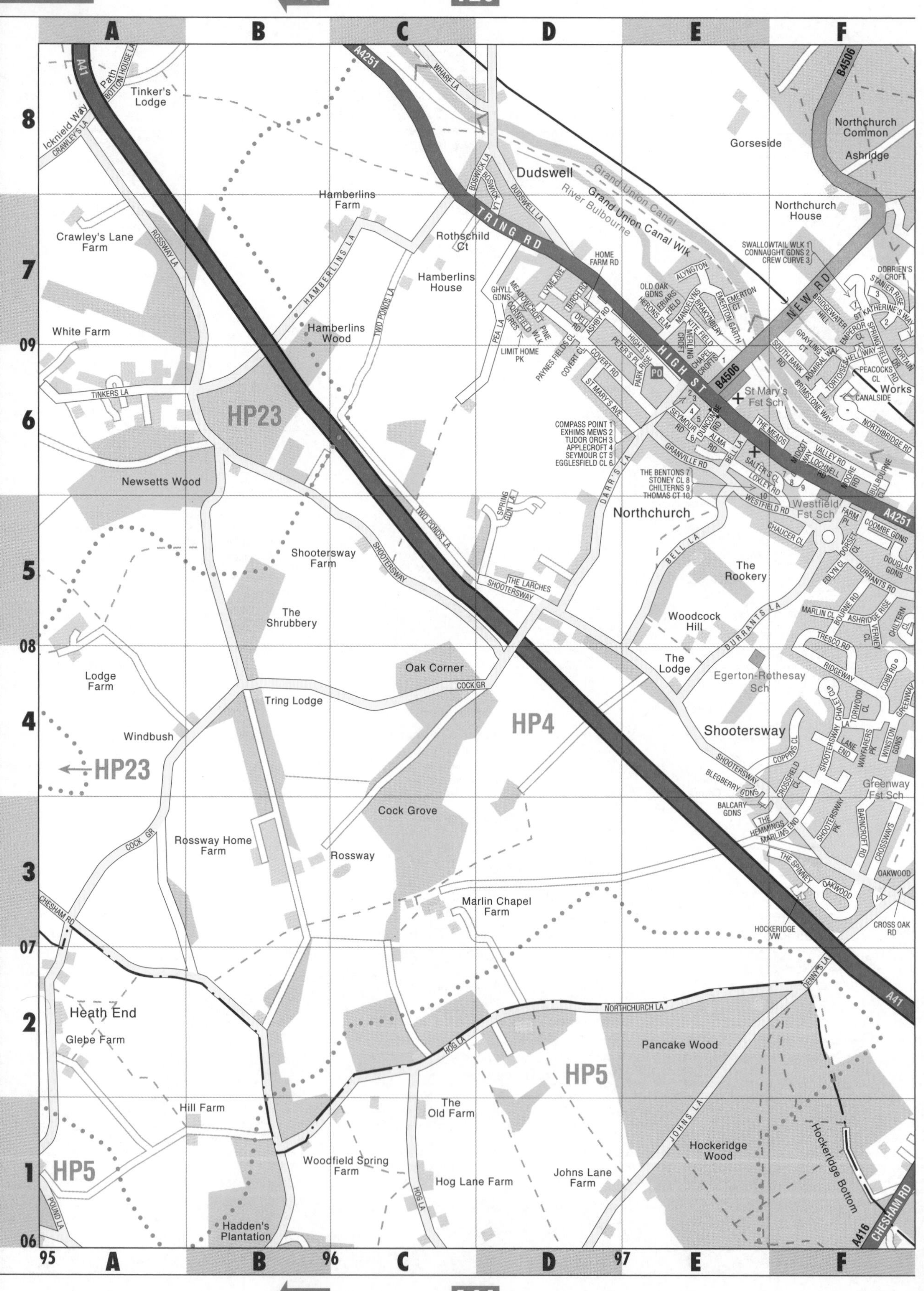
A B C D E F
8 7 09 6 5 08 4 3 07 2 1 06
95 96 97
Tinker's Lodge
Icknield Way
Crawley's La
Dudswell
Grand Union Canal
River Bulbourne
Grand Union Canal Wlk
Gorseside
Northchurch Common
Ashridge
Northchurch House
Hamberlins Farm
Crawley's Lane Farm
Rothschild Ct
Hamberlins House
Hamberlins Wood
White Farm
Tinkers La
HP23
Newsetts Wood
Tring Rd
High St
New Rd
St Mary's Fst Sch
Works
Northchurch
Westfield Fst Sch
Shootersway Farm
The Shrubbery
The Rookery
Woodcock Hill
The Lodge
Egerton-Rothesay Sch
Lodge Farm
Oak Corner
Tring Lodge
Windbush
HP4
Shootersway
Greenway Fst Sch
Cock Grove
Rossway Home Farm
Rossway
Marlin Chapel Farm
Heath End
Glebe Farm
Northchurch La
Pancake Wood
HP5
Hill Farm
The Old Farm
Hockeridge Wood
Hockeridge Bottom
Woodfield Spring Farm
Hog Lane Farm
Johns Lane Farm
Hadden's Plantation
A41
A4251
B4506
A416
Chesham Rd

121

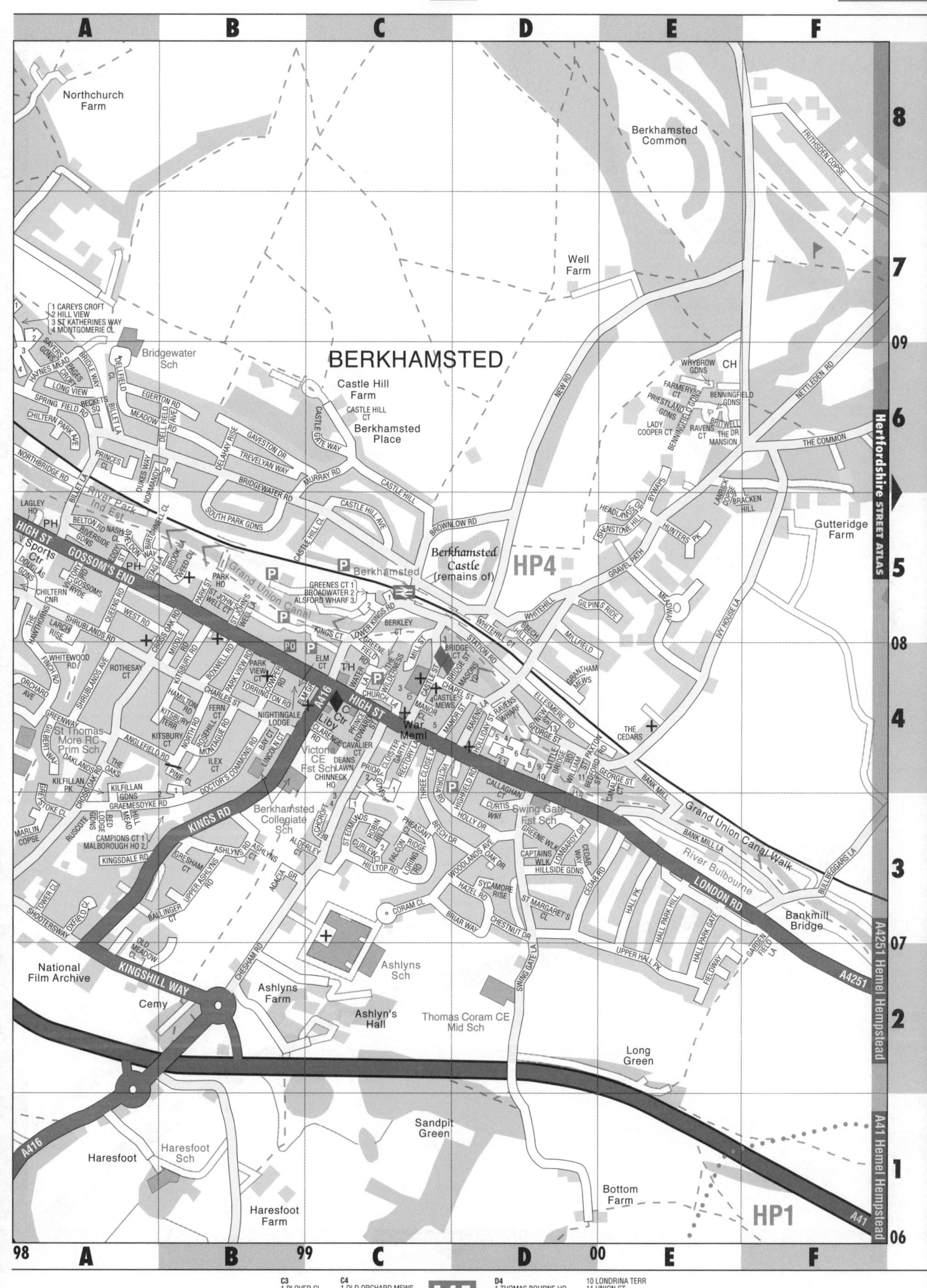

C3
1 PLOVER CL
2 KESTREL CL
3 DAVIS HO
4 FROST HO

C4
1 OLD ORCHARD MEWS
2 PRIORY CT
3 CHURCHGATES
4 WILLIAM FISKE HO
5 DOWER MEWS
6 Berkhamsted Sch

D4
1 THOMAS BOURNE HO
2 AUGUSTUS SMITH HO
3 COOPER WAY
4 GLASSMILL HO
5 NEW PROVIDENT PL
6 ROBERTSON RD
7 COSTINS WLK
8 MCDOUGALL RD
9 LONDRINA CT
10 LONDRINA TERR
11 UNION CT
12 OLD MILL GDNS
13 CAMBRIDGE TERR

145

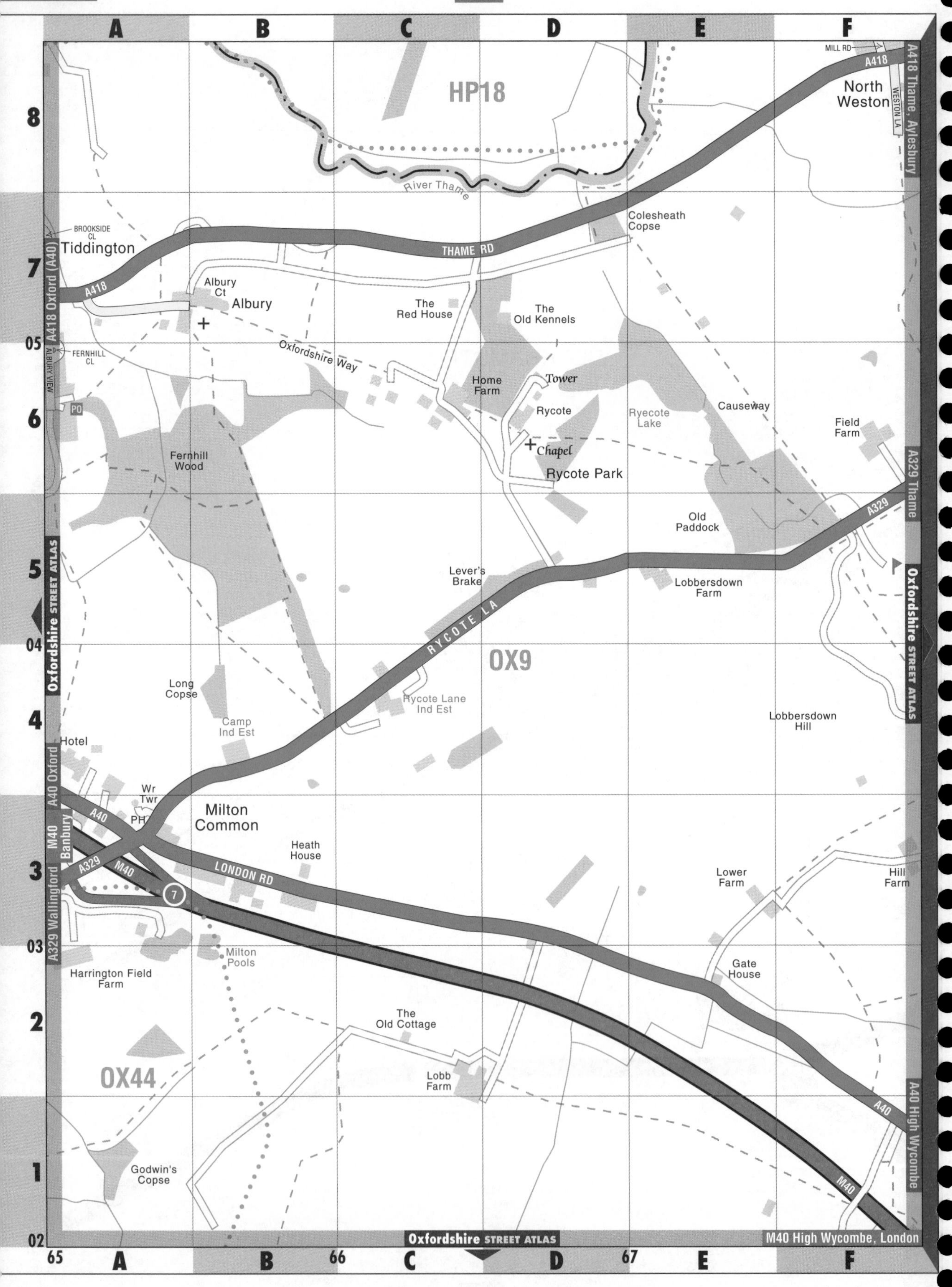
124
HP18
River Thame
North Weston
MILL RD
A418
WESTON LA
A418 Thame, Aylesbury
Tiddington
BROOKSIDE CL
THAME RD
Colesheath Copse
A418 Oxford (A40)
Albury Ct
Albury
The Red House
The Old Kennels
FERNHILL CL
ALBURY VIEW
Oxfordshire Way
Home Farm
Tower
Rycote
Ryecote Lake
Causeway
PO
Field Farm
Chapel
Rycote Park
Fernhill Wood
A329 Thame
A329
Old Paddock
Lever's Brake
Lobbersdown Farm
RYCOTE LA
OX9
Oxfordshire STREET ATLAS
Long Copse
Rycote Lane Ind Est
Camp Ind Est
Lobbersdown Hill
Hotel
Wr Twr
PH
Milton Common
A40 Oxford
A40
M40 Banbury
A329 Wallingford
M40
Heath House
LONDON RD
7
Lower Farm
Hill Farm
Milton Pools
Gate House
Harrington Field Farm
The Old Cottage
Lobb Farm
OX44
A40 High Wycombe
Godwin's Copse
M40 High Wycombe, London
A B C D E F
8 7 05 6 5 04 4 3 03 2 1 02
65 66 67

127
138

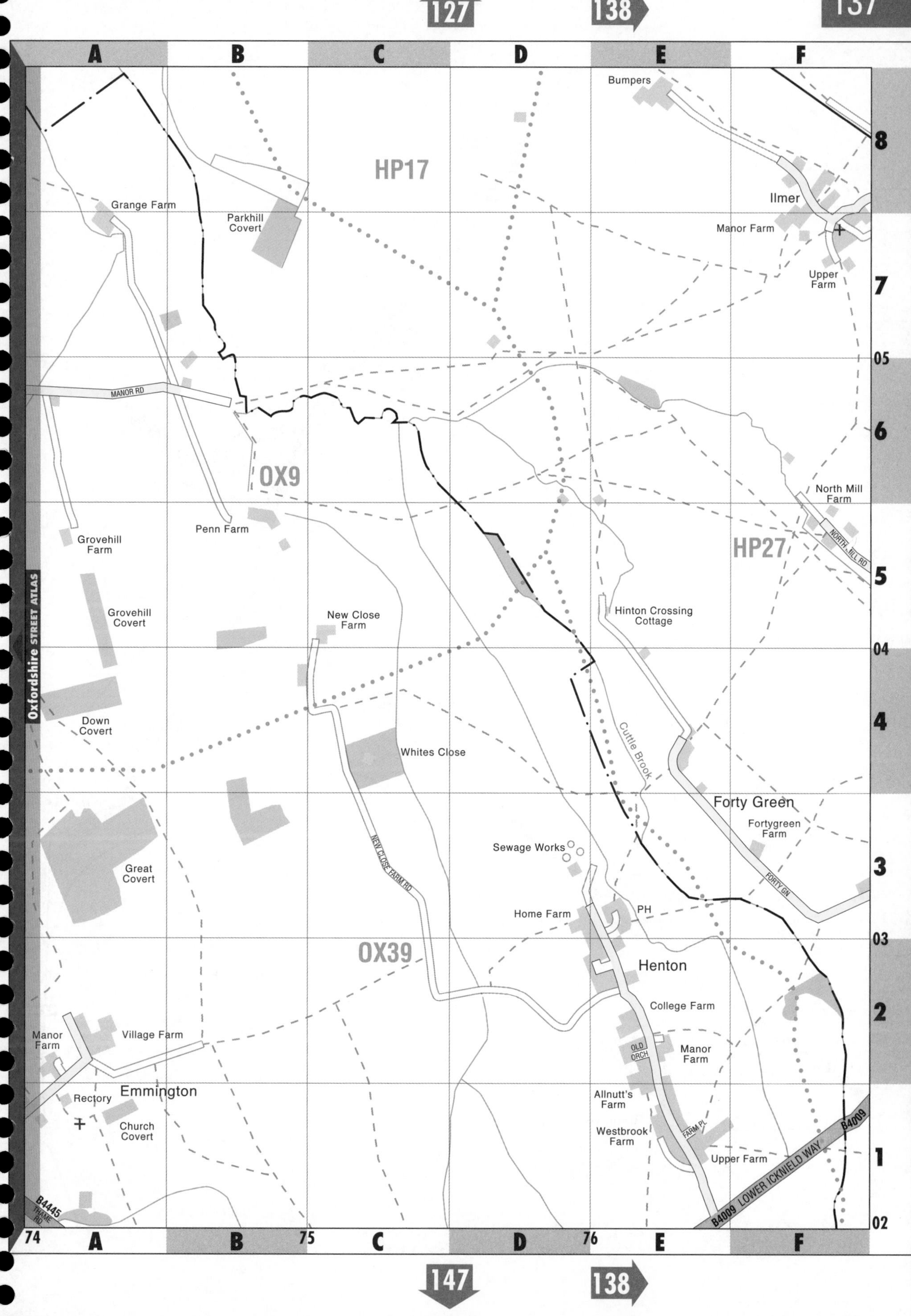

147
138

137
128

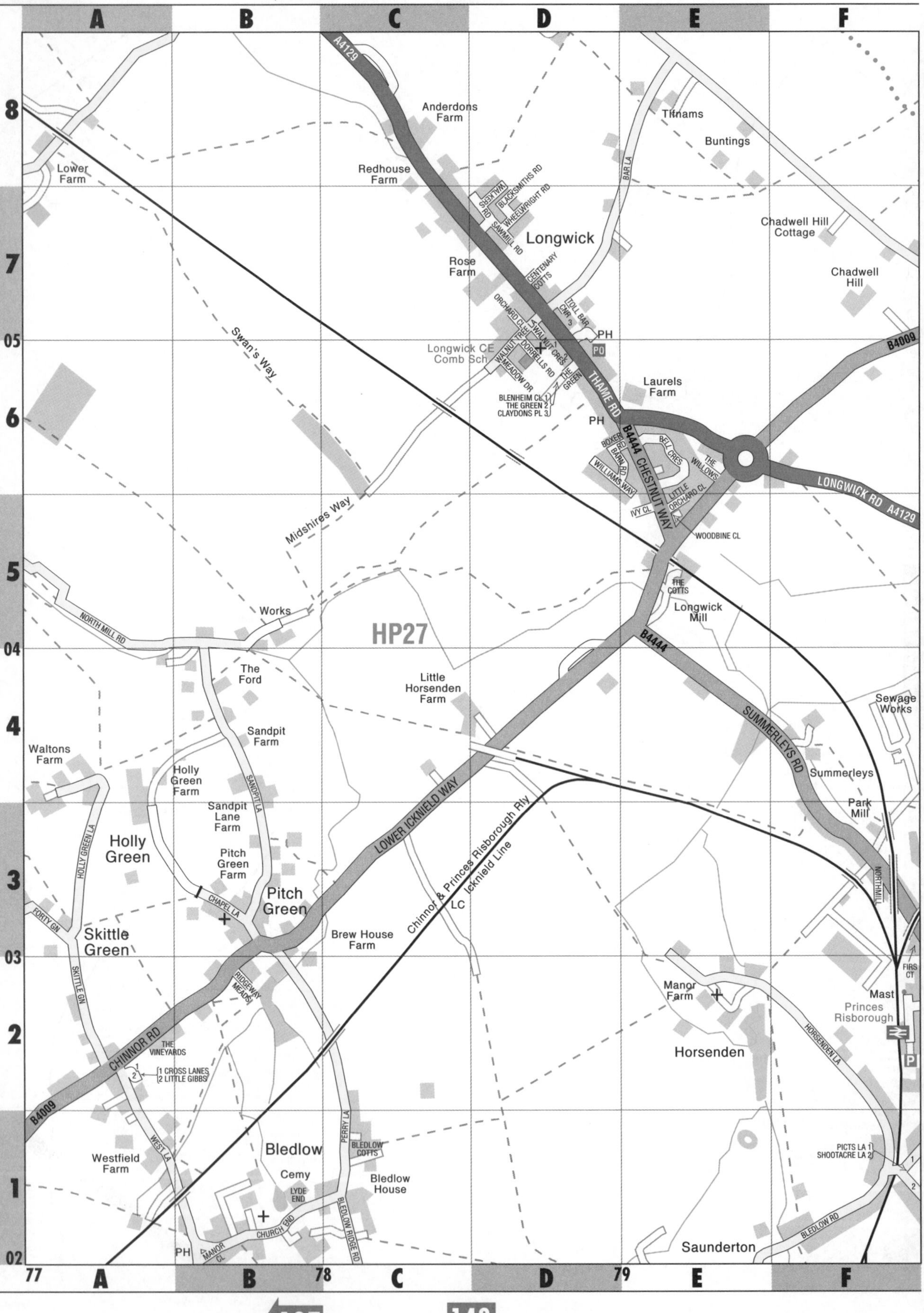

A B C D E F

8
Lower Farm
Anderdons Farm
Redhouse Farm
Tinams
Buntings
Longwick
Rose Farm
Chadwell Hill Cottage
Chadwell Hill
A4129
WALKERS RD
BLACKSMITHS RD
WHEELWRIGHT RD
SAWMILL RD
CENTENARY COTTS
BAR LA
TOLL BAR CNR 3
ORCHARD CL
WALNUT CRES
DORRELLS RD
WALNUT TREE
MEADOW DR
THE GREEN
PH
PO
Longwick CE Comb Sch
7
05
Swan's Way
Laurels Farm
THAME RD
B4009
BLENHEIM CL 1
THE GREEN 2
CLAYDONS PL 3
PH
6
B4444 CHESTNUT WAY
BOXER RD
BARN RD
BELL CRES
THE WILLOWS
WILLIAMS WAY
IVY CL
LITTLE ORCHARD CL
WOODBINE CL
LONGWICK RD A4129
Midshires Way
5
THE COTTS
Longwick Mill
Works
NORTH MILL RD
HP27
B4444
04
The Ford
Little Horsenden Farm
Sewage Works
4
Sandpit Farm
SUMMERLEYS RD
Waltons Farm
Holly Green Farm
Summerleys
SANDPIT LA
Sandpit Lane Farm
Park Mill
Holly Green
HOLLY GREEN LA
Pitch Green Farm
3
LOWER ICKNIELD WAY
Chinnor & Princes Risborough Rly
Icknield Line
NORTHMILL
CHAPEL LA
Pitch Green
LC
FORTY GN
Skittle Green
Brew House Farm
FIRS CT
03
SKITTLE GN
RIDGEWAY MEADS
Manor Farm
Mast
Princes Risborough
2
CHINNOR RD
THE VINEYARDS
HORSENDEN LA
Horsenden
1 CROSS LANES
2 LITTLE GIBBS
P
B4009
WEST LA
Bledlow
PERRY LA
BLEDLOW COTTS
PICTS LA 1
SHOOTACRE LA 2
Westfield Farm
Cemy
Bledlow House
1
LYDE END
CHURCH END
BLEDLOW RIDGE RD
BLEDLOW RD
PH
MANOR CL
Saunderton
02

77 A B 78 C D 79 E F

137
148

129
140

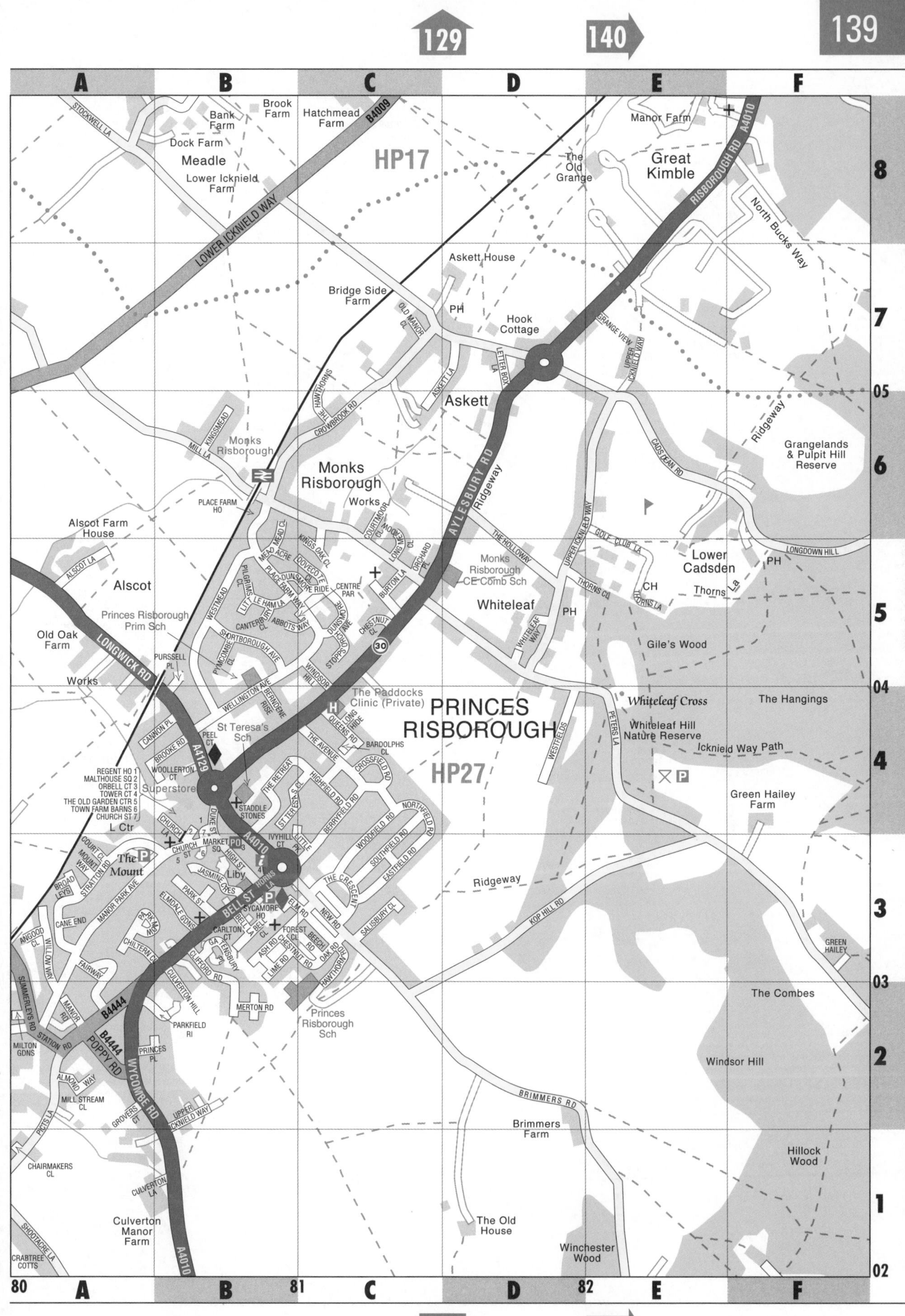
A
B
C
D
E
F
8
7
05
6
5
04
4
3
03
2
1
02
80
81
82
HP17
HP27
PRINCES RISBOROUGH
Monks Risborough
Askett
Great Kimble
Meadle
Alscot
Whiteleaf
Lower Cadsden
Brook Farm
Bank Farm
Hatchmead Farm
Dock Farm
Lower Icknield Farm
Manor Farm
The Old Grange
Askett House
Bridge Side Farm
Hook Cottage
Alscot Farm House
Old Oak Farm
Works
Princes Risborough Prim Sch
Monks Risborough CE Comb Sch
The Paddocks Clinic (Private)
St Teresa's Sch
Superstore
L Ctr
The Mount
Liby
Princes Risborough Sch
Grangelands & Pulpit Hill Reserve
Gile's Wood
Whiteleaf Cross
The Hangings
Whiteleaf Hill Nature Reserve
Icknield Way Path
Green Hailey Farm
The Combes
Windsor Hill
Hillock Wood
Brimmers Farm
The Old House
Winchester Wood
Culverton Manor Farm
North Bucks Way
Ridgeway
LOWER ICKNIELD WAY
RISBOROUGH RD
AYLESBURY RD
LONGWICK RD
WYCOMBE RD
B4009
A4010
A4129
B4444
REGENT HO 1
MALTHOUSE SQ 2
ORBELL CT 3
TOWER CT 4
THE OLD GARDEN CTR 5
TOWN FARM BARNS 6
CHURCH ST 7
BRIMMERS RD
KOP HILL RD
PETERS LA
LONGDOWN HILL
Thorns La
GOLF CLUB LA
UPPER ICKNIELD WAY
CADSDEAN RD
THE HOLLOWAY
BELL ST
HIGH ST
DUKE ST
STATION RD
POPPY RD
SUMMERLEYS RD
MANOR PARK AVE
WELLINGTON AVE
HIGHFIELD RD
NORTHFIELD RD
SOUTHFIELD RD
WOODFIELD RD
BERRYFIELD RD
CROSSFIELD RD
THE AVENUE
THE CRESCENT
NEW RD
SALISBURY CL
CROWBROOK RD
MILL LA
KINGSMEAD
STOCKWELL LA
ALSCOT LA
PH
CH

139
130

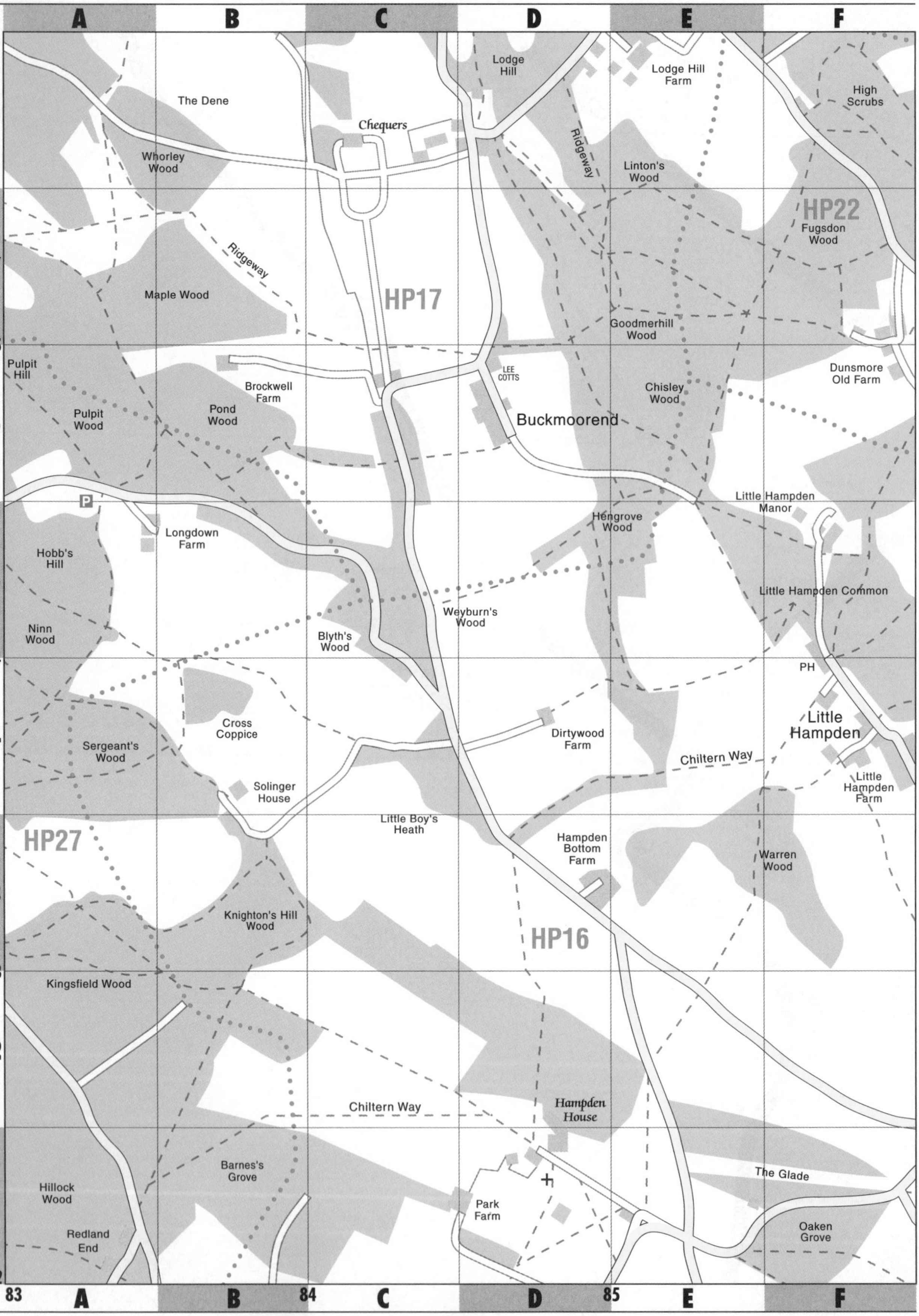

A B C D E F

8
7
05
6
5
04
4
3
03
2
1
02

The Dene
Whorley Wood
Chequers
Lodge Hill
Lodge Hill Farm
High Scrubs
Ridgeway
Linton's Wood
HP22
Fugsdon Wood
Ridgeway
Maple Wood
HP17
Goodmerhill Wood
Pulpit Hill
Brockwell Farm
LEE COTTS
Dunsmore Old Farm
Chisley Wood
Pulpit Wood
Pond Wood
Buckmoorend
Little Hampden Manor
P
Hengrove Wood
Longdown Farm
Hobb's Hill
Little Hampden Common
Weyburn's Wood
Ninn Wood
Blyth's Wood
PH
Cross Coppice
Dirtywood Farm
Little Hampden
Sergeant's Wood
Chiltern Way
Solinger House
Little Hampden Farm
Little Boy's Heath
HP27
Hampden Bottom Farm
Warren Wood
Knighton's Hill Wood
HP16
Kingsfield Wood
Chiltern Way
Hampden House
Barnes's Grove
The Glade
Hillock Wood
Park Farm
Oaken Grove
Redland End

83 A B 84 C D 85 E F

139
150

131
142

151
142

141 132

A B C D E F

HP23
Lordling Wood
TIMBERLEY LA
FURZE FIELD LA
SWAN LA
PH
Chiltern Way
Kingswood
ARREWIG LA
Erriwig Farm
HP5
PH
Lee Gate
Kingsgate Farm
Swan Bottom
Three Gates Farm
Bray's Wood
Gwenfa Farm
HP22
Chiltern Link
Lownde's Wood
Home Farm
Lee Clump
Lee Clump House
The Lee
Church Farm
BOWOOD LA
Church (restored)
PRINCES LA
PH
CROCKETTS LA
Lee Common CE Fst Sch
Hawthorn Farm
OXFORD ST
ST MARY'S CL
Bassibones Farm
PH
Rushmoor Wood
Lee Common
Lower Bassibones Farm
KING'S LA
MARTIN DELL COTTS
CHERRY TREE LA
HP16
Pipers
Hunt's Green
Hunt's Green Farm
Field End Grange
SLY CNR
Ballinger Bottom
Chiltern Link
CHILTERN RD
BLACKTHORNE LA
BALLINGER ROW
LEATHER LA
Hammonds Hall Farm
BLACKFIELD LA
Ballinger Common
Springfield Farm
Ballinger Farm
BALLINGER GRANGE
Ballinger Grove
Wr Twr
Havenfields
POTTER ROW
HERBERTS HOLE
Park Farm
Ballinger Bottom (South)
A413
BALLINGER RD
MEADOW LA
MARRIOTTS AVE
MARRIOTTS AVE
AYLESBURY RD
Bury Farm

8 7 05 6 5 04 4 3 03 2 1 02

89 A B 90 C D 91 E F

141 152

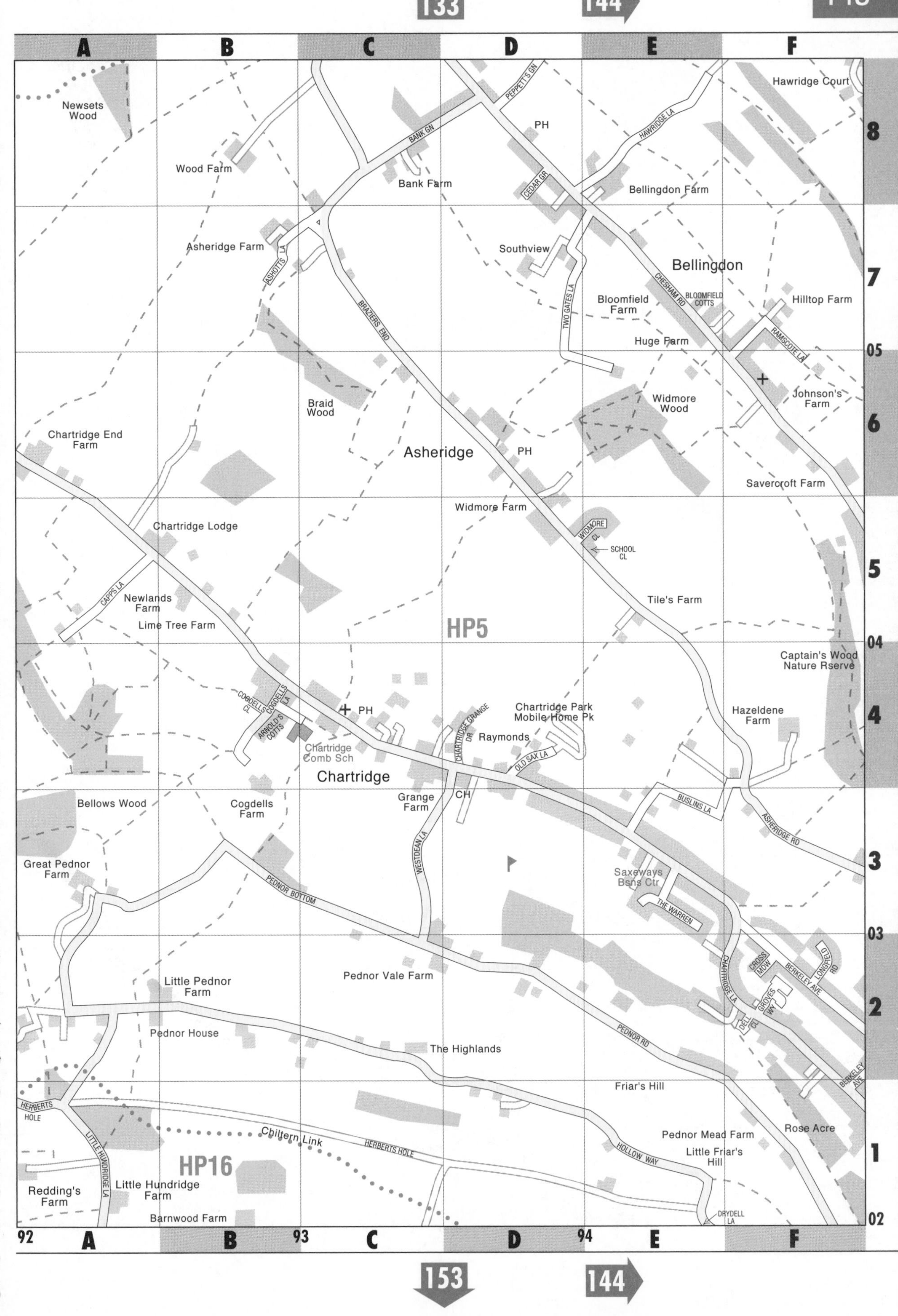
133
144
A
B
C
D
E
F
Newsets Wood
Wood Farm
Bank Farm
BANK GN
PEPPETT'S GN
PH
HAWRIDGE LA
Hawridge Court
CEDAR GR
Bellingdon Farm
Asheridge Farm
ASHOTTS LA
Southview
Bellingdon
BRAZIERS END
TWO GATES LA
Bloomfield Farm
CHESHAM RD
BLOOMFIELD COTTS
Hilltop Farm
RAMSCOTE LA
Huge Farm
Braid Wood
Widmore Wood
Johnson's Farm
Chartridge End Farm
Asheridge
PH
Savercroft Farm
Widmore Farm
Chartridge Lodge
WIDMORE CL
SCHOOL CL
CAPPS LA
Newlands Farm
Lime Tree Farm
Tile's Farm
HP5
Captain's Wood Nature Rserve
COGDELLS CL
COGDELLS LA
ARNOLD'S COTTS
PH
Chartridge Park Mobile Home Pk
Hazeldene Farm
CHARTRIDGE GRANGE DR
Raymonds
OLD SAX LA
Chartridge Comb Sch
Chartridge
Grange Farm
CH
BUSLINS LA
Bellows Wood
Cogdells Farm
ASHERIDGE RD
WESTDEAN LA
Great Pednor Farm
PEDNOR BOTTOM
Saxeways Bsns Ctr
THE WARREN
CROSS MDW
BERKELEY AVE
LONGFIELD RD
CHARTRIDGE LA
Little Pednor Farm
Pednor Vale Farm
GROVES WY
DELL CL
Pednor House
PEDNOR RD
The Highlands
BERKELEY AVE
Friar's Hill
HERBERTS HOLE
Chiltern Link
HERBERTS HOLE
LITTLE HUNDRIDGE LA
HOLLOW WAY
Pednor Mead Farm
Rose Acre
HP16
Little Friar's Hill
Redding's Farm
Little Hundridge Farm
Barnwood Farm
DRYDELL LA
8
7
05
6
5
04
4
3
03
2
1
02
92
93
94
153
144

143
134

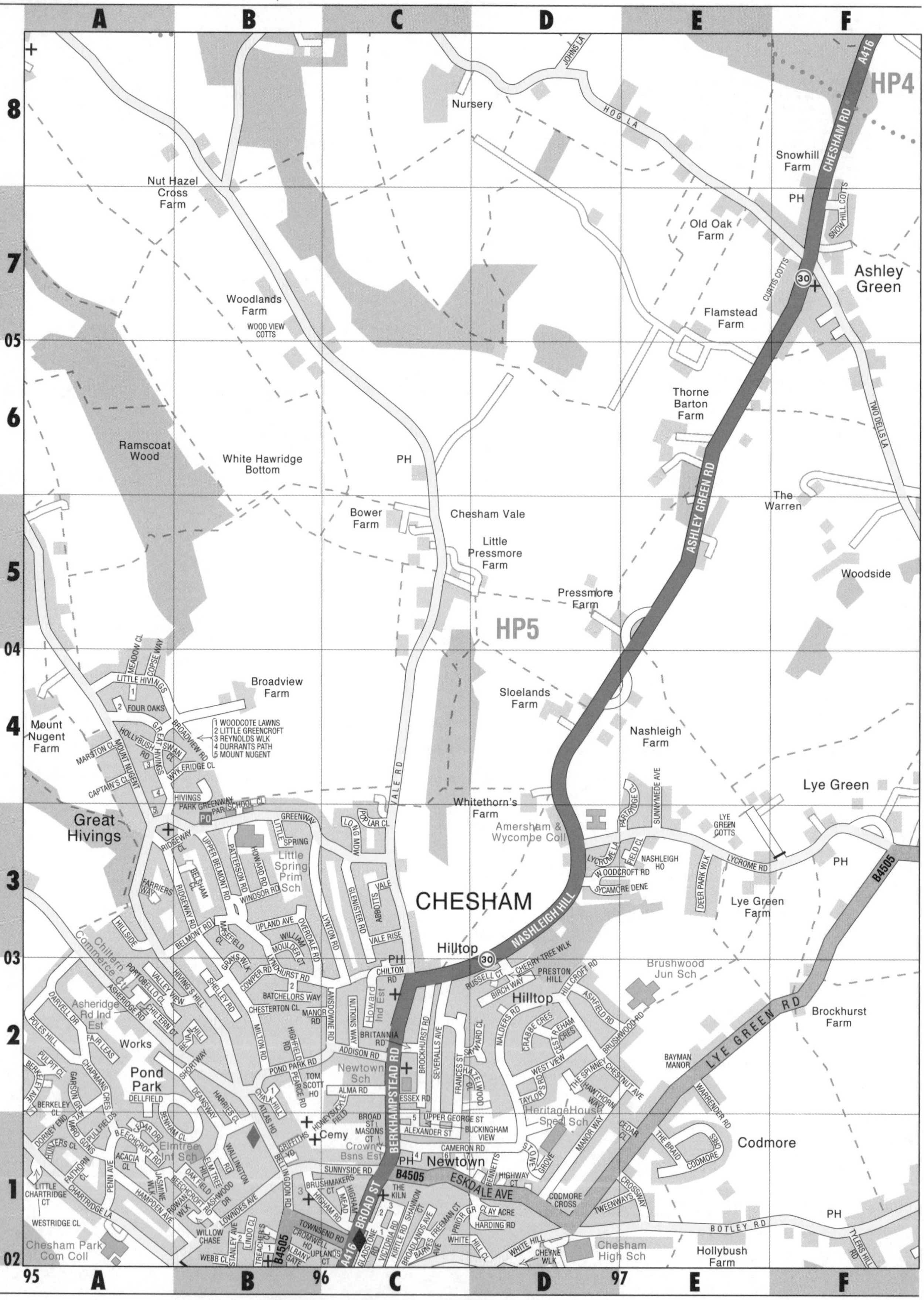

A B C D E F

8
7
05
6
5
04
4
3
03
2
1
02

95 96 97

HP4
HP5

Nursery
JOHNS LA
HOG LA
A416
CHESHAM RD
Snowhill Farm
PH
SNOWHILL COTTS
Nut Hazel Cross Farm
Old Oak Farm
CURTIS COTTS
Ashley Green
Woodlands Farm
WOOD VIEW COTTS
Flamstead Farm
Thorne Barton Farm
TWO DELLS LA
Ramscoat Wood
White Hawridge Bottom
PH
ASHLEY GREEN RD
The Warren
Bower Farm
Chesham Vale
Little Pressmore Farm
Woodside
Pressmore Farm
Broadview Farm
Sloelands Farm
MEADOW CL
COPSE WAY
LITTLE HIVINGS
FOUR OAKS
Mount Nugent Farm
1 WOODCOTE LAWNS
2 LITTLE GREENCROFT
3 REYNOLDS WLK
4 DURRANTS PATH
5 MOUNT NUGENT
Nashleigh Farm
MARSTON CL
HOLLYBUSH RD
MOUNT NUGENT
GREAT HIVINGS
SWAN CL
BROADVIEW RD
WYKERIDGE CL
CAPTAIN'S CL
HIVINGS
PARK GREENWAY
PARK SCHOOL CL
VALE RD
Whitethorn's Farm
SUNNYMEDE AVE
PARTRIDGE CL
Lye Green
Great Hivings
PO
GREENWAY
LITTLE SPRING
POPLAR CL
LONG MDW
Amersham & Wycombe Coll
LYE GREEN COTTS
RIDGEWAY CL
UPPER BELMONT RD
PATERSON RD
HOWARD RD
Little Spring Prim Sch
LYCROME LA
FIELD CL
NASHLEIGH HO
LYCROME RD
PH
B4505
FARRIERS WAY
BELSHAM CL
WINDSOR RD
ABBOTTS VALE
WOODCROFT RD
DEER PARK WLK
SYCAMORE DENE
CHESHAM
Lye Green Farm
HILLSIDE
RIDGEWAY RD
BELMONT RD
MASEFIELD CL
UPLAND AVE
OVERDALE RD
WILLIAM MOULDER CT
GLENISTER RD
LYNTON RD
VALE RISE
NASHLEIGH HILL
Hilltop
Chiltern Commerce Cl
PORTOBELLO CL
GRANS WLK
COWPER RD
LYNDHURST RD
PH
CHERRY TREE WLK
Brushwood Jun Sch
VALLEY VIEW
HIVINGS HILL
SHELLEY RD
BATCHELORS WAY
CHILTON RD
RUSSELL CT
BIRCH WAY
PRESTON HILL
HILLCROFT RD
ASHFIELD RD
DARVELL DR
Asheridge Rd Ind Est
ASHERIDGE RD
CHILTERN CT
CHESTERTON CL
MANOR RD
LANSDOWNE RD
NUTKINS WAY
Howard Ind Est
BROCKHURST RD
SEVERALLS AVE
SAYWARD CL
NALDERS RD
Hilltop
CRABBE CRES
CESTREHAM CRES
BRUSHWOOD RD
LYE GREEN RD
Brockhurst Farm
POLES HILL
FAIR LEAS
Works
BEVAN HILL
MILTON RD
HIGHFIELD RD
BRITANNIA RD
ADDISON RD
BERKHAMPSTEAD RD
FRANCES ST
HAZELWOOD
WEST VIEW
THE SPINNEY
CHESTNUT AVE
BAYMAN MANOR
PULPIT CL
CHAPMANS CRES
SHORTWAY
POND PARK RD
TOM SCOTT HO
Newtown Sch
ALMA RD
TAYLORS RD
HAWTHORN WAY
BERKLEY AVE
GARSON GR
Pond Park
DEANSWAY
HARRISS CL
PEARCE RD
ESSEX RD
Heritage House Spec Sch
WARRENDER RD
BERKELEY CL
WARD GDNS
DELLFIELD
BENHAM CL
CHALK HILL
ATLAS HO
HONEYSUCKLE FIELD
BROAD ST
UPPER GEORGE ST
MANOR WAY
CEDAR CL
THE BRAID
CODMORE CRES
Codmore
DORNEY END
BULLFIELDS
CEDAR DR
BEECHCROFT RD
Elmtree Inf Sch
GRIFFITHS YD
Cemy
MASONS CT
ALEXANDER ST
BUCKINGHAM VIEW
HUNTERS CL
ACACIA CL
Crown Bsns Est
CAMERON RD
STONEY GROVE
FAITHORN CL
PENN AVE
JASMINE WLK
ELM TREE HILL
WALLINGTON RD
BELLINGDON RD
PH
Newtown
BENNETTS
HIGHWAY CT
CROSSWAY
LITTLE CHARTRIDGE CT
CHARTRIDGE LA
HAMPDEN AVE
OAK FIELD
BEECHCROFT RD
DASHWOOD
SUNNYSIDE RD
B4505
ESKDALE AVE
TWEENWAYS
ROWAN WLK
LOWNDES AVE
BRUSHMAKERS CT
HIGHAM RD
THE KILN
SHANNON CT
CLAY ACRE
CODMORE CROSS
PH
WESTRIDGE CL
WILLOW CHASE
MEAD
BROAD ST
A416
PRIOR GR
HARDING RD
BOTLEY RD
TOWNSEND RD
GLADSTONE RD
VICTORIA RD
BROADLANDS AVE
FREEMAN CT
WHITE HILL
CHEYNE WLK
Chesham Park Com Coll
LINDO CL
STANLEY AVE
TREACHERS
B4505
CROMWELL HO
ALBANY GATE
UPLANDS CT
KIRTLE RD
BARNES AVE
WHITE HILL CL
Chesham High Sch
Hollybush Farm
TYLERS HILL RD
WEBB CL

B1
1 WESLEY HILL
2 UPPER MDW
3 Phoenix Bsns Ctr
B2
1 THE CHASE
2 NIGHTINGALE RD

C1
1 QUEENS RD
2 UPPER GLADSTONE RD
3 FRANCHISE ST
4 TURNERS WLK
5 GEORGE ST
6 CAMERON RD
7 GREATACRE

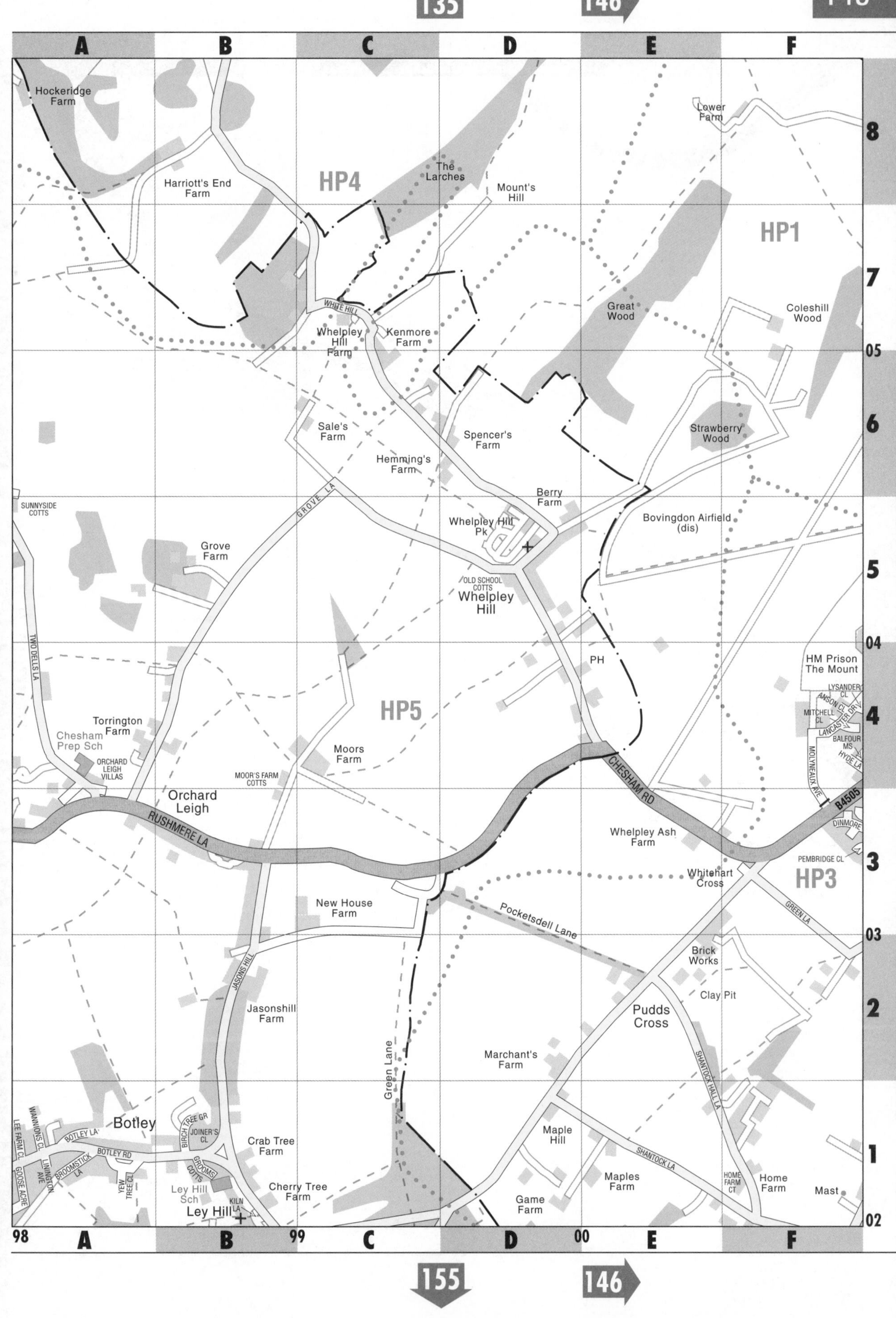
135
146
A
B
C
D
E
F
8
7
05
6
5
04
4
3
03
2
1
02
98
99
00
Hockeridge Farm
Harriott's End Farm
HP4
The Larches
Mount's Hill
Lower Farm
HP1
Great Wood
Coleshill Wood
WHITE HILL
Whelpley Hill Farm
Kenmore Farm
Sale's Farm
Hemming's Farm
Spencer's Farm
Strawberry Wood
Berry Farm
SUNNYSIDE COTTS
GROVE LA
Grove Farm
Whelpley Hill Pk
Bovingdon Airfield (dis)
OLD SCHOOL COTTS
Whelpley Hill
TWO DELLS LA
PH
HM Prison The Mount
LYSANDER CL
ANSON CL
MITCHELL CL
LANCASTER DR
HP5
Torrington Farm
Chesham Prep Sch
ORCHARD LEIGH VILLAS
Moors Farm
BALFOUR MS
HYDE LA
MOLYNEAUX AVE
MOOR'S FARM COTTS
Orchard Leigh
CHESHAM RD
B4505
DINMORE
RUSHMERE LA
Whelpley Ash Farm
PEMBRIDGE CL
Whitehart Cross
HP3
New House Farm
Pocketsdell Lane
GREEN LA
JASONS HILL
Brick Works
Clay Pit
Jasonshill Farm
Pudds Cross
Marchant's Farm
Green Lane
SHANTOCK HALL LA
Botley
WANNIONS CL
LEE FARM CL
BOTLEY LA
BOTLEY RD
BIRCH TREE GR
JOINER'S CL
Crab Tree Farm
Maple Hill
SHANTOCK LA
GOOSE ACRE
LININGTON AVE
BROOMSTICK LA
YEW TREE CL
GROOMS COTTS
Ley Hill Sch
Ley Hill
KILN LA
Cherry Tree Farm
Maples Farm
Game Farm
HOME FARM CT
Home Farm
Mast
155
146

145

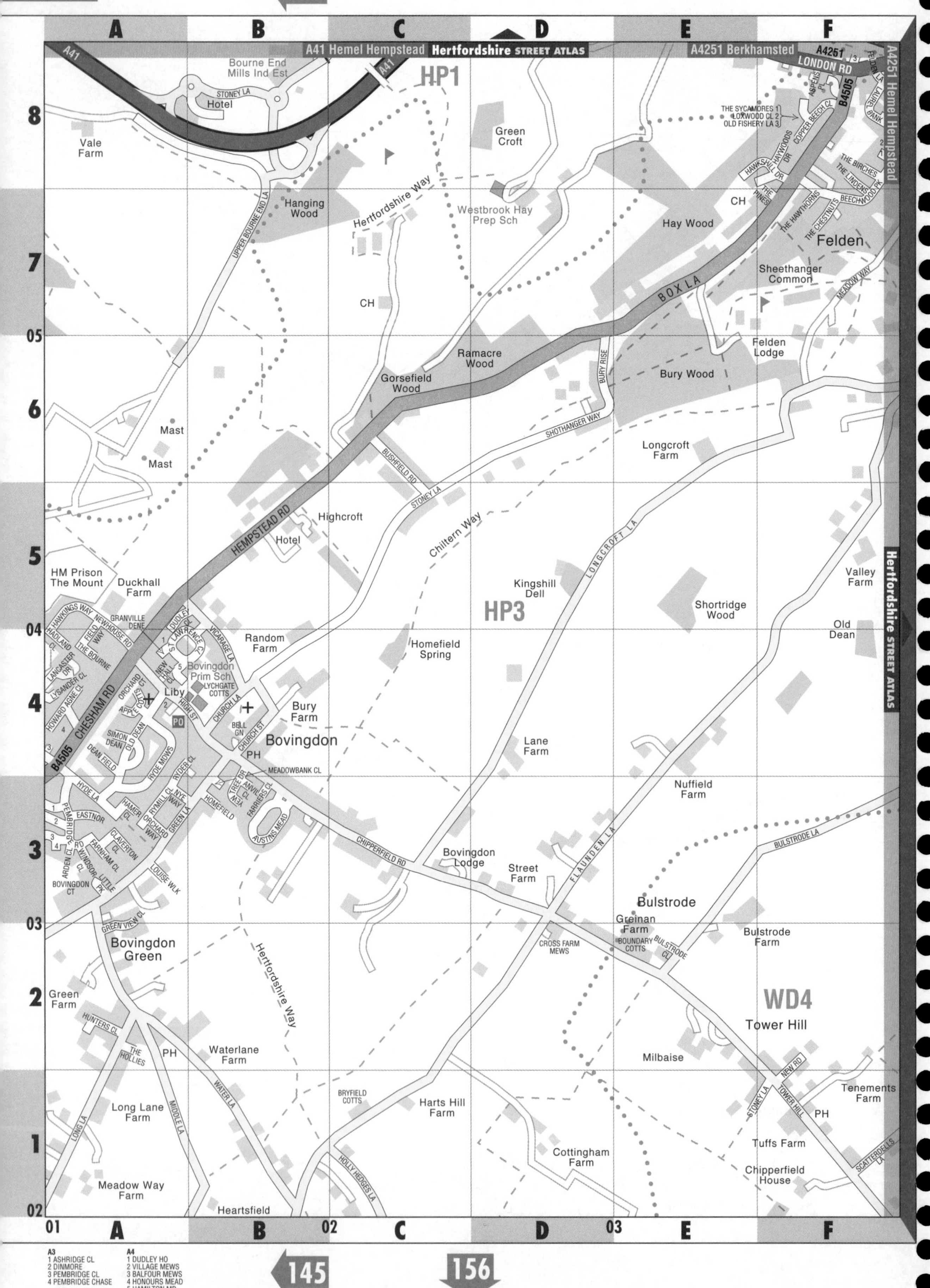

A3
1 ASHRIDGE CL
2 DINMORE
3 PEMBRIDGE CL
4 PEMBRIDGE CHASE

A4
1 DUDLEY HO
2 VILLAGE MEWS
3 BALFOUR MEWS
4 HONOURS MEAD
5 HAMILTON MD

145
156

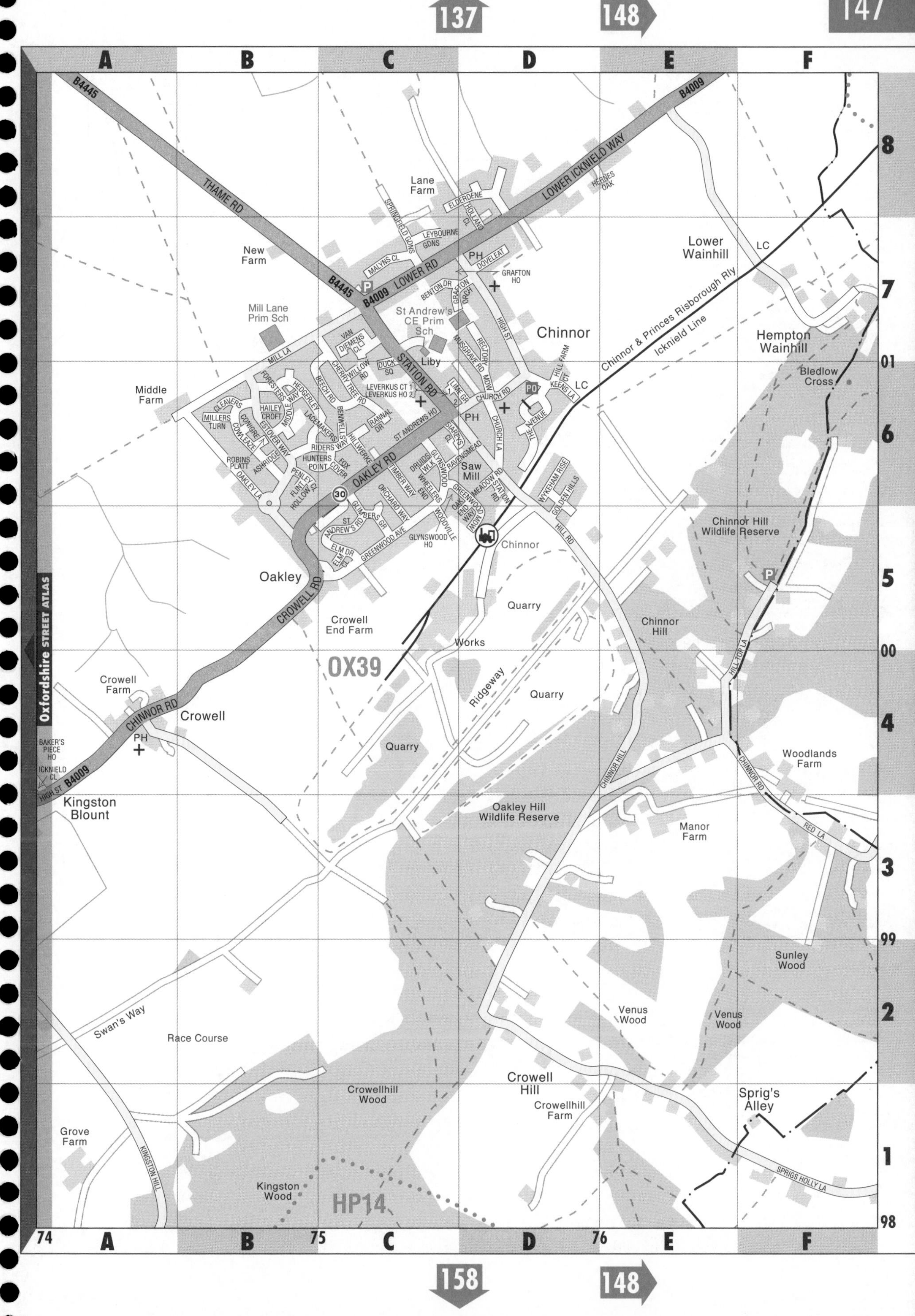

137
148
A
B
C
D
E
F
B4445
THAME RD
B4009
LOWER ICKNIELD WAY
HERNES OAK
Lane Farm
ELDERDENE
HOLLAND CL
SPRINGFIELD GDNS
LEYBOURNE GDNS
New Farm
MALYNS CL
PH
DOVELEAT
GRAFTON HO
LOWER RD
B4445
B4009
P
BENTON DR
GRAFTON ORCH
Mill Lane Prim Sch
St Andrew's CE Prim Sch
HIGH ST
Chinnor
Lower Wainhill
LC
Chinnor & Princes Risborough Rly
Icknield Line
Hempton Wainhill
Bledlow Cross
MILL LA
VAN DIEMENS CL
WILLOW RD
CHERRY TREE RD
DUCK SQ
STATION RD
Liby
MUSGRAVE RD
RECTORY MDW
HILL FARM CT
KEENS LA
LC
Middle Farm
FORESTERS
HEDGERLEY
BEECH RD
LEVERKUS CT
LEVERKUS HO
LIME GR
CHURCH RD
PO
THE AVENUE
CLEAVERS
HAILEY CROFT
MIDDLE WAY
LACEMAKERS
BENWELLS
RANNAL DR
MILLERS TURN
CONIGRE
COWLEAZE
ESTOVER WAY
RIDERS WAY
HILLWERKE
ST ANDREWS HO
PH
SHARPS CL
CHURCH LA
ROBINS PLATT
ASHRIDGE
HUNTERS POINT
FOX COVER
OAKLEY RD
DRUIDS WLK
GLYNSWOOD
RAVENSMEAD
Saw Mill
WYKEHAM RISE
GOLDEN HILLS
OAKLEY LA
PENLEY CL
FLINT HOLLOW
30
TIMBER WAY
WHEELERS END
ORCHARD WAY
MEADOW RD
STATION RD
GREENWOOD WAY
OAK END WAY
GLIMBERS GR
ST ANDREW'S RD
GREENWOOD AVE
GLYNSWOOD HO
WOODVILLE
HILL RD
ELM DR
ELM CL
Chinnor
Chinnor Hill Wildlife Reserve
Oakley
CROWELL RD
Quarry
Crowell End Farm
P
Chinnor Hill
Works
OX39
HILL TOP LA
Crowell Farm
Ridgeway
Quarry
CHINNOR RD
Crowell
PH
BAKER'S PIECE HO
ICKNIELD CL
HIGH ST
B4009
Quarry
CHINNOR HILL
Woodlands Farm
CHINNOR RD
Kingston Blount
Oakley Hill Wildlife Reserve
Manor Farm
RED LA
Sunley Wood
Swan's Way
Race Course
Venus Wood
Venus Wood
Crowell Hill
Crowellhill Wood
Crowellhill Farm
Sprig's Alley
Grove Farm
KINGSTON HILL
SPRIGS HOLLY LA
Kingston Wood
HP14
8
7
01
6
5
00
4
3
99
2
1
98
74
75
76
Oxfordshire STREET ATLAS
158
148

147
138

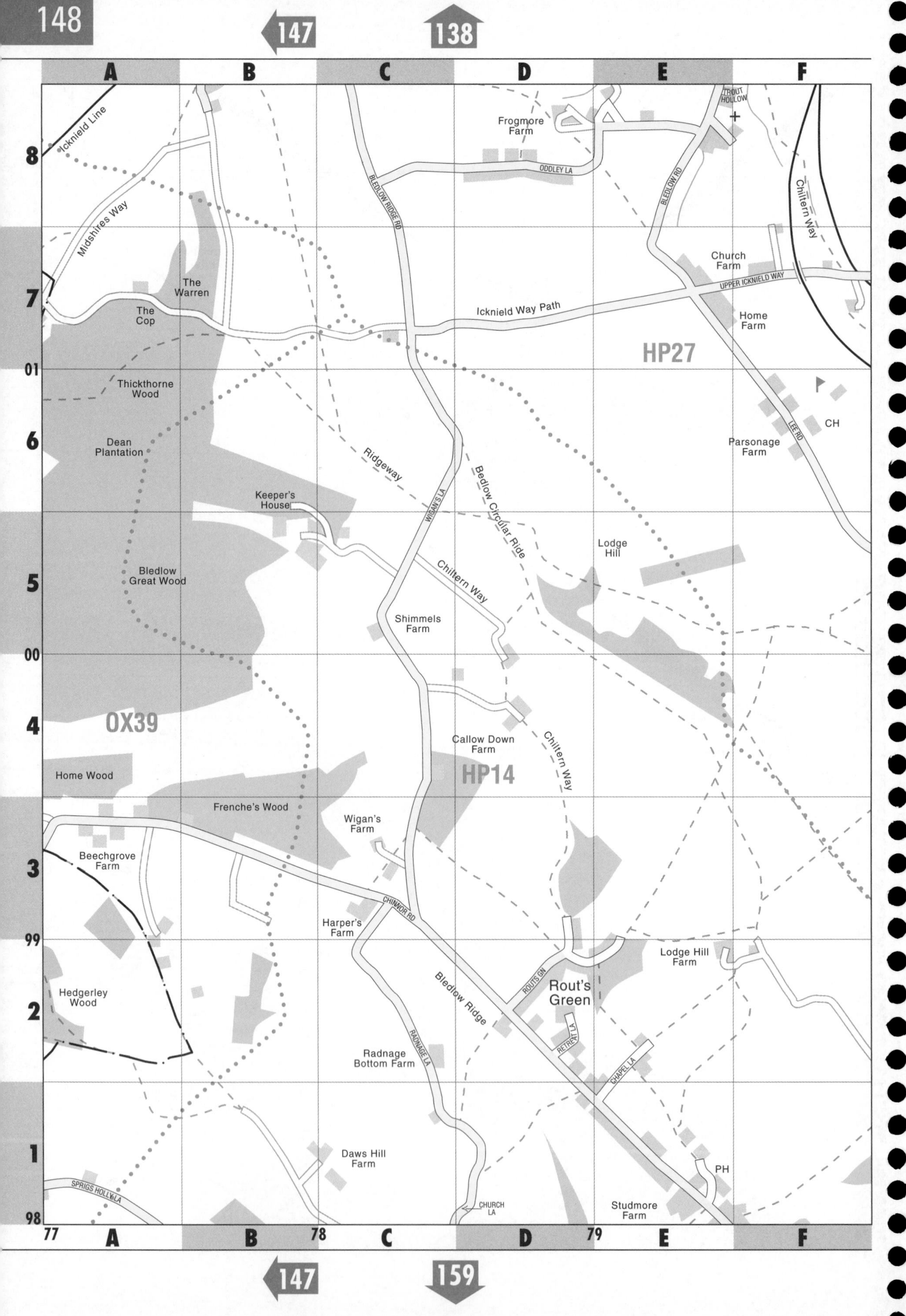

147
159

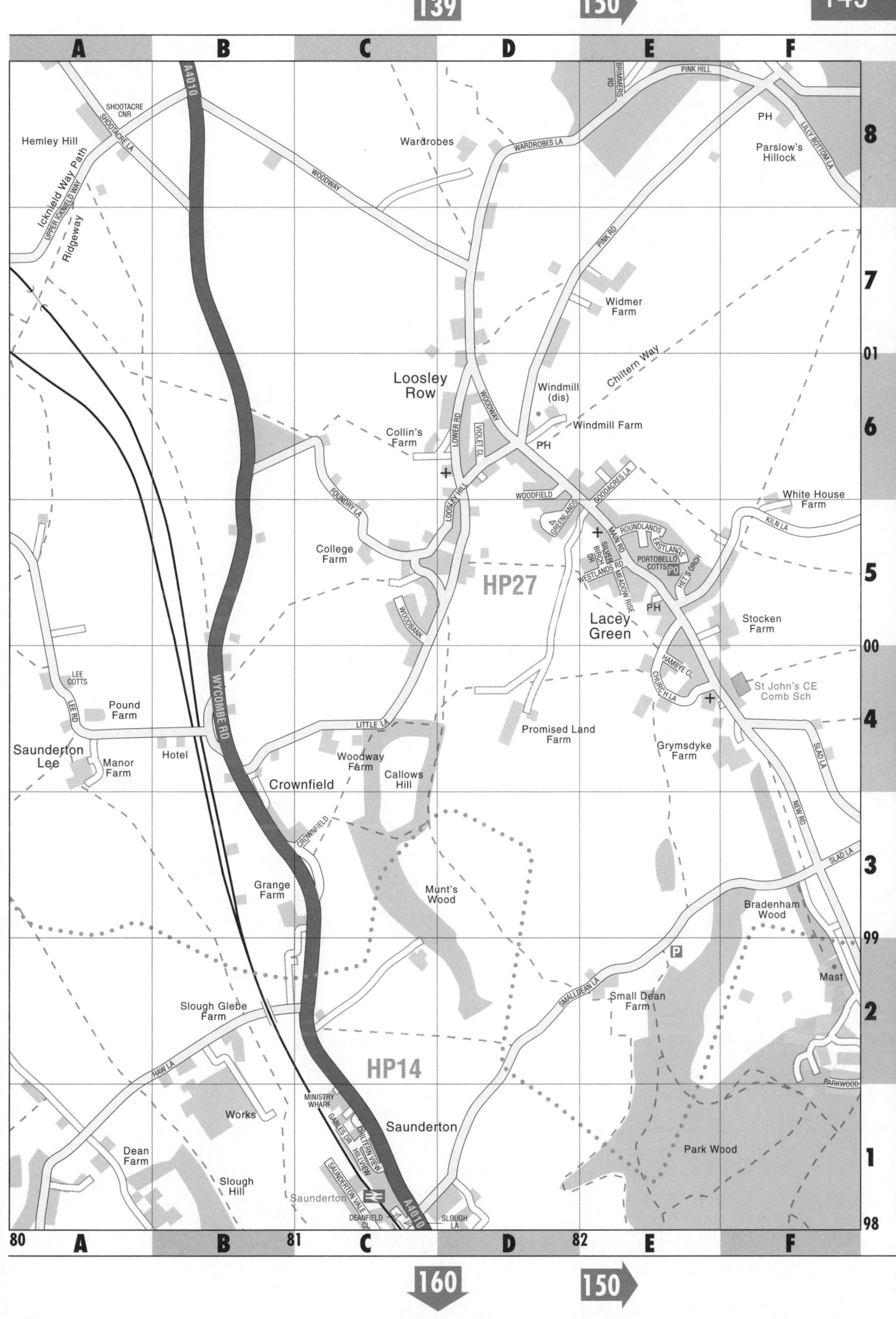
139
150
A
B
C
D
E
F
8
7
01
6
5
00
4
3
99
2
1
98
80
81
82
160
150
A4010
SHOOTACRE CNR
SHOOTACRE LA
Hemley Hill
Icknield Way Path
UPPER ICKNIELD WAY
Ridgeway
WOODWAY
Wardrobes
WARDROBES LA
BRIMMERS RD
PINK HILL
PH
LILLY BOTTOM LA
Parslow's Hillock
PINK RD
Widmer Farm
Chiltern Way
Loosley Row
Windmill (dis)
Windmill Farm
Collin's Farm
LOWER RD
VIOLET CL
WOODWAY
PH
FOUNDRY LA
LOOSLEY HILL
WOODFIELD
GREENLANDS
GOODACRES LA
ROUNDLANDS
EASTLANDS
MAIN RD
SILVER BIRCH DR
PORTOBELLO COTTS
PO
HET'S ORCH
WESTLANDS RD
MEADOW RISE
White House Farm
KILN LA
College Farm
HP27
WOODBANK
Lacey Green
PH
Stocken Farm
HAMBYE CL
CHURCH LA
St John's CE Comb Sch
LEE COTTS
LEE RD
Pound Farm
WYCOMBE RD
LITTLE LA
Promised Land Farm
Saunderton Lee
Manor Farm
Hotel
Woodway Farm
Callows Hill
Crownfield
Grymsdyke Farm
SLAD LA
NEW RD
CROWNFIELD
SLAD LA
Grange Farm
Munt's Wood
Bradenham Wood
P
Mast
SMALLDEAN LA
Small Dean Farm
Slough Glebe Farm
HAW LA
HP14
PARKWOOD
Works
MINISTRY WHARF
GABLES DR
CHILTERN VIEW
HILLVIEW
Saunderton
Dean Farm
Slough Hill
SAUNDERTON VALE
Saunderton
DEANFIELD CL
SLOUGH LA
A4010
Park Wood

149 140

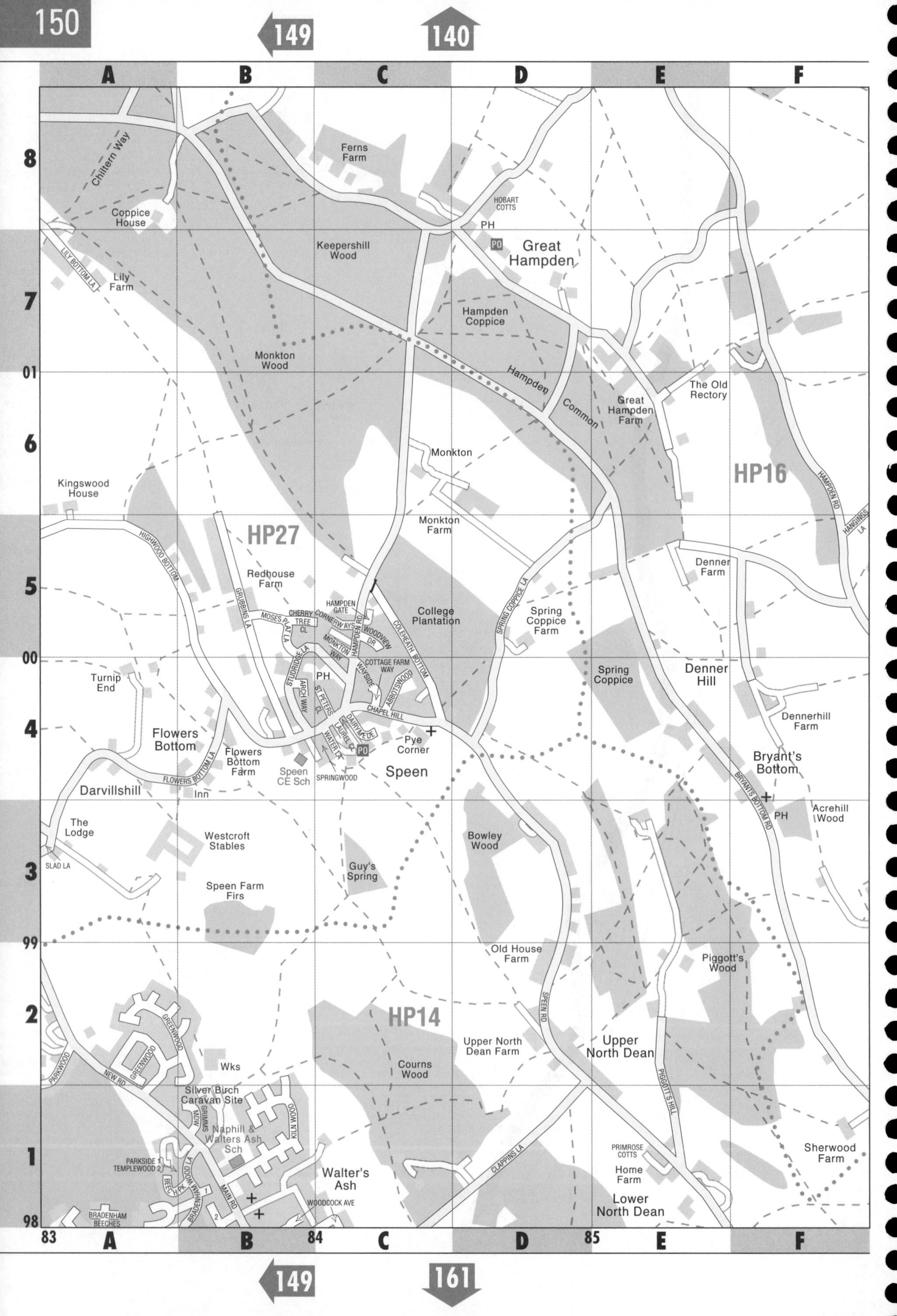

149 161

141
152

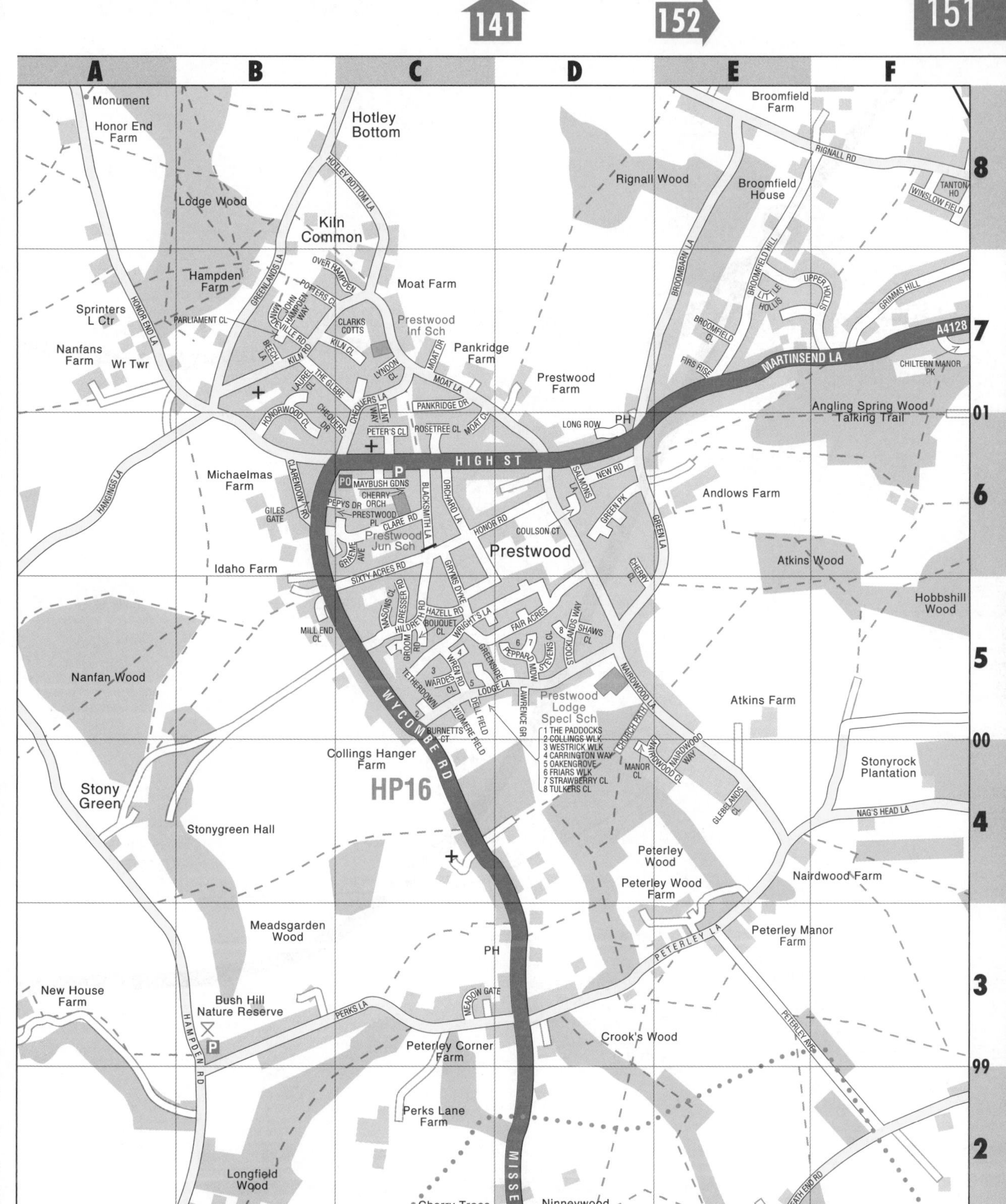

162
152

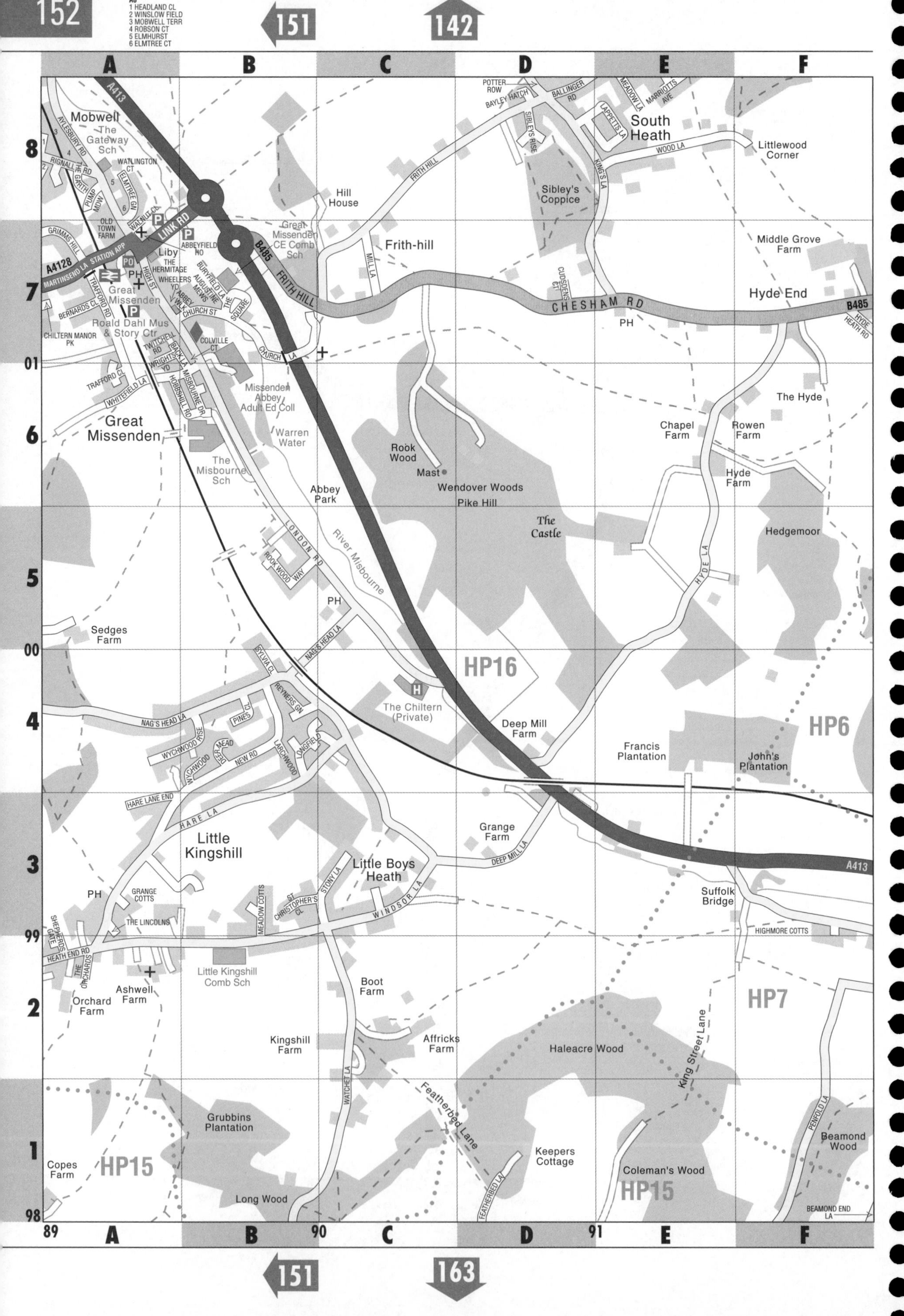
152
A8
1 HEADLAND CL
2 WINSLOW FIELD
3 MOBWELL TERR
4 ROBSON CT
5 ELMHURST
6 ELMTREE CT
151
142
A
B
C
D
E
F
8
7
01
6
5
00
4
3
99
2
1
98
89
90
91
A413
Mobwell
The Gateway Sch
AYLESBURY RD
RIGNALL RD
THE GARTH
PUMP MDW
ELMTREE GN
WATLINGTON CT
OLD TOWN FARM
WALNUT CL
LINK RD
GRIMMS HILL
A4128
MARTINSEND LA
STATION APP
ABBEYFIELD HO
Liby
THE HERMITAGE
WHEELERS YD
BURYFIELD LA
AUGUSTINE MEWS
THE SQUARE
HIGH ST
ABBEY WALK
CHURCH ST
PH
Great Missenden
TRAFFORD RD
BERNARDS CL
Roald Dahl Mus & Story Ctr
CHILTERN MANOR PK
TWITCHELL RD
WRIGHTS YD
BACK LA
COLVILLE CT
CHURCH LA
TRAFFORD CL
WHITEFIELD LA
HOBBSHILL RD
MISBOURNE DR
Missenden Abbey Adult Ed Coll
Great Missenden
Warren Water
The Misbourne Sch
Great Missenden CE Comb Sch
B485
FRITH HILL
Hill House
Frith-hill
MILL LA
FRITH HILL
POTTER ROW
BAYLEY HATCH
BALLINGER RD
SIBLEYS RISE
MEADOW LA
MARRIOTTS AVE
LAPPETTS LA
South Heath
WOOD LA
KING'S LA
Sibley's Coppice
Littlewood Corner
Middle Grove Farm
CUDSDENS CT
CHESHAM RD
PH
Hyde End
B485
HYDE HEATH RD
The Hyde
Chapel Farm
Rowen Farm
Hyde Farm
Rook Wood
Mast
Wendover Woods
Pike Hill
The Castle
Hedgemoor
Abbey Park
LONDON RD
River Misbourne
ROOK WOOD WAY
HYDE LA
PH
Sedges Farm
NAG'S HEAD LA
HP16
SYLVIA CL
REYNERS GN
The Chiltern (Private)
Deep Mill Farm
Francis Plantation
John's Plantation
HP6
NAG'S HEAD LA
PINES CL
WYCHWOOD RISE
DEER MEAD
NEW RD
LARCHWOOD
LONGFIELD
WYCHWOOD
HARE LANE END
HARE LA
Little Kingshill
Grange Farm
DEEP MILL LA
Little Boys Heath
STONY LA
A413
Suffolk Bridge
PH
GRANGE COTTS
MEADOW COTTS
ST CHRISTOPHER'S CL
WINDSOR LA
THE LINCOLNS
HIGHMORE COTTS
SHEPHERDS GATE
HEATH END RD
THE ORCHARDS
Little Kingshill Comb Sch
Ashwell Farm
Orchard Farm
Boot Farm
HP7
Kingshill Farm
Affricks Farm
Haleacre Wood
King Street Lane
WATCHET LA
Featherbed Lane
Grubbins Plantation
PENFOLD LA
Beamond Wood
Keepers Cottage
Coleman's Wood
Copes Farm
HP15
FEATHERBED LA
HP15
Long Wood
BEAMOND END LA
151
163

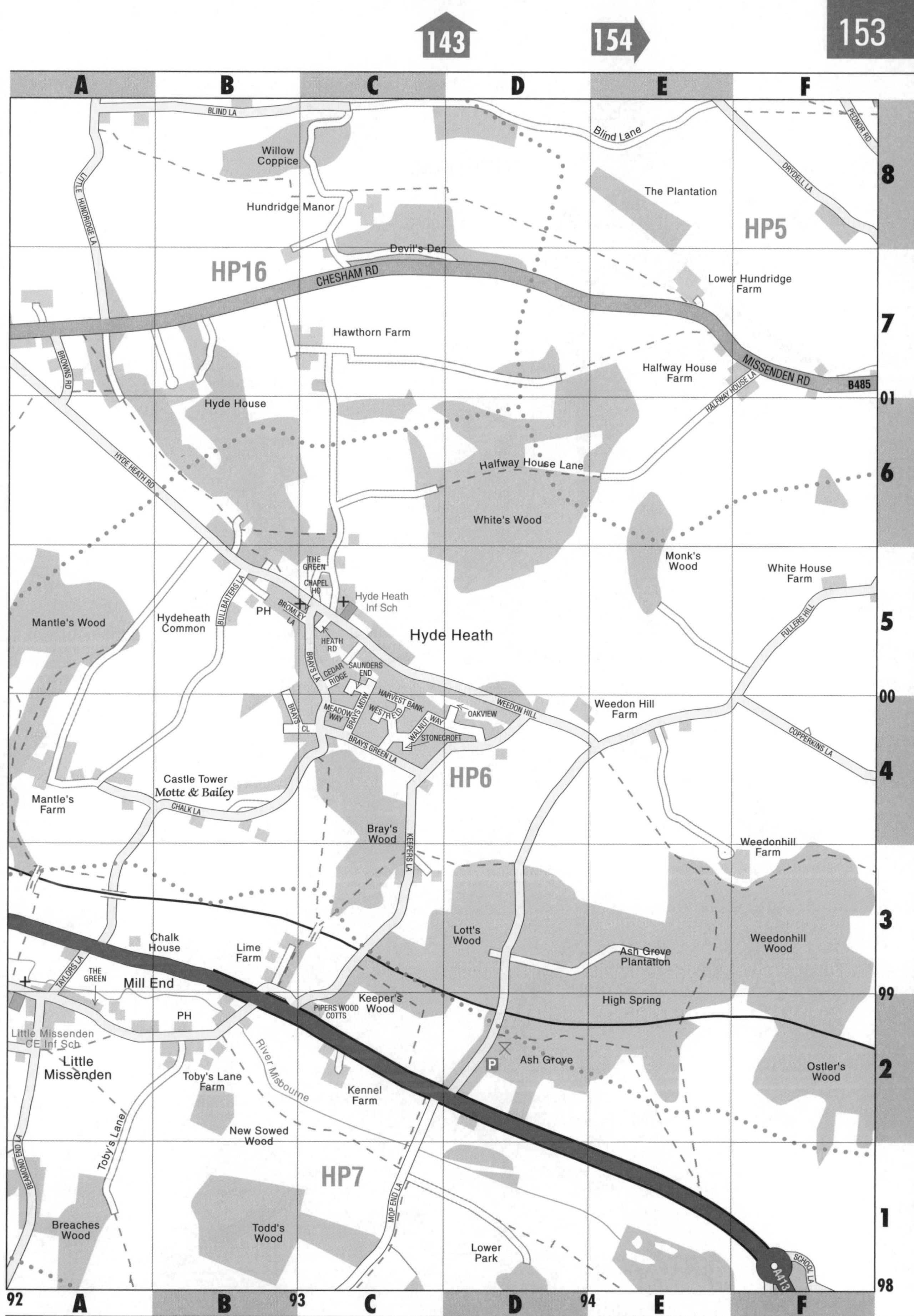
143
154
A
B
C
D
E
F
BLIND LA
Blind Lane
Willow Coppice
Hundridge Manor
The Plantation
HP5
LITTLE HUNDRIDGE LA
DRYDELL LA
PEDNOR RD
Devil's Den
HP16
CHESHAM RD
Lower Hundridge Farm
Hawthorn Farm
MISSENDEN RD
B485
Halfway House Farm
HALFWAY HOUSE LA
BROWNS RD
Hyde House
HYDE HEATH RD
Halfway House Lane
White's Wood
Monk's Wood
White House Farm
THE GREEN
CHAPEL HD
Hyde Heath Inf Sch
Mantle's Wood
Hydeheath Common
BULLBAITERS LA
PH
BROMLEY LA
Hyde Heath
FULLERS HILL
HEATH RD
BRAYS LA
CEDAR RIDGE
SAUNDERS END
HARVEST BANK
WEEDON HILL
Weedon Hill Farm
BRAYS CL
MEADOW WAY
BRAYS MDW
WESTFIELD
OAKVIEW
WALNUT WAY
STONECROFT
BRAYS GREEN LA
COPPERKINS LA
HP6
Castle Tower
Motte & Bailey
Mantle's Farm
CHALK LA
Bray's Wood
KEEPERS LA
Weedonhill Farm
Chalk House
Lime Farm
Lott's Wood
Weedonhill Wood
Ash Grove Plantation
TAYLORS LA
THE GREEN
Mill End
PIPERS WOOD COTTS
Keeper's Wood
High Spring
PH
Little Missenden CE Inf Sch
Little Missenden
River Misbourne
Ash Grove
P
Ostler's Wood
Toby's Lane Farm
Kennel Farm
New Sowed Wood
Toby's Lane
BEAMOND END LA
HP7
MOP END LA
Breaches Wood
Todd's Wood
Lower Park
SCHOOL LA
A413
8
7
01
6
5
00
4
3
99
2
1
98
92
93
94
164
154

153
144

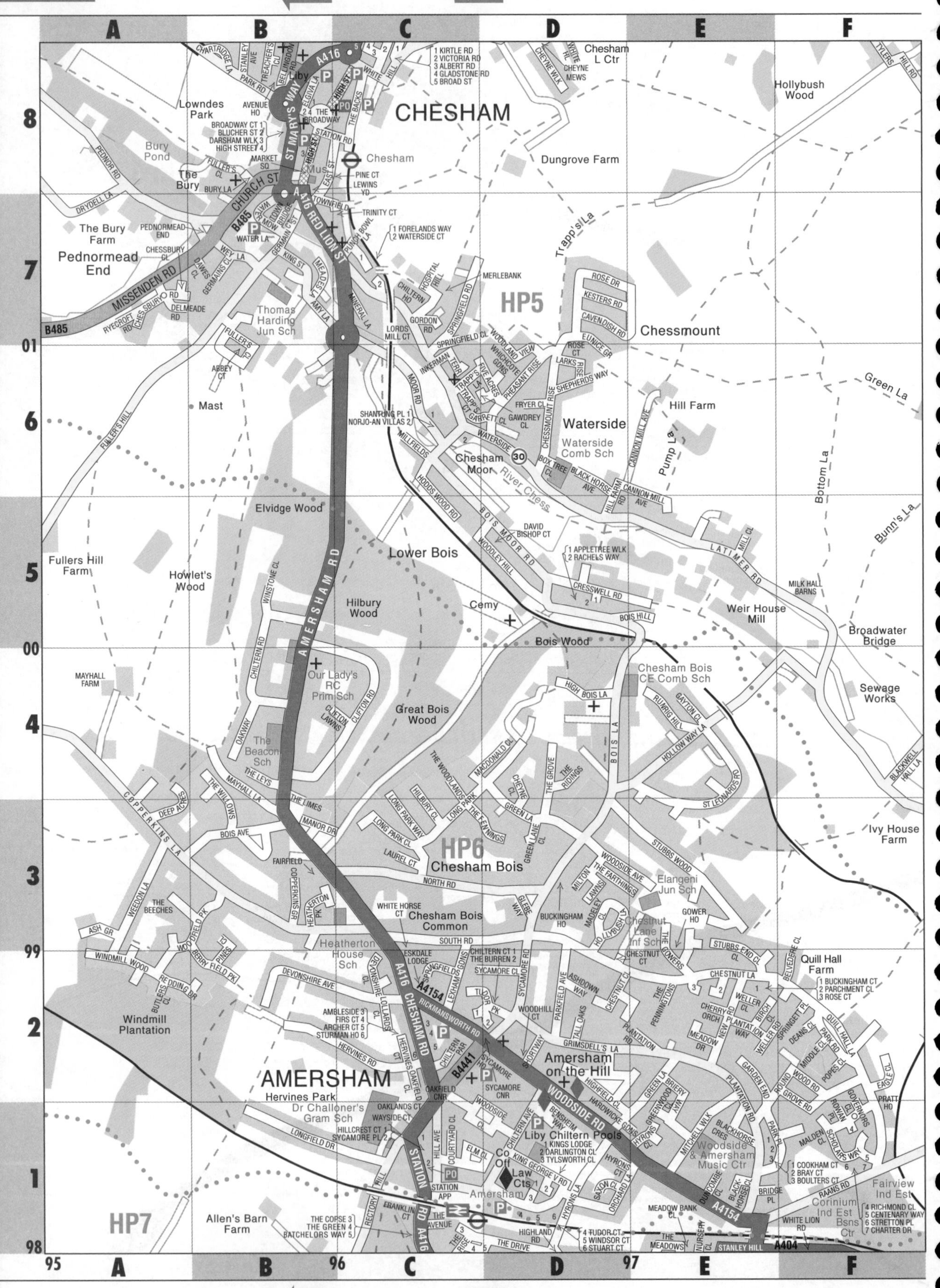

153
165

145
156

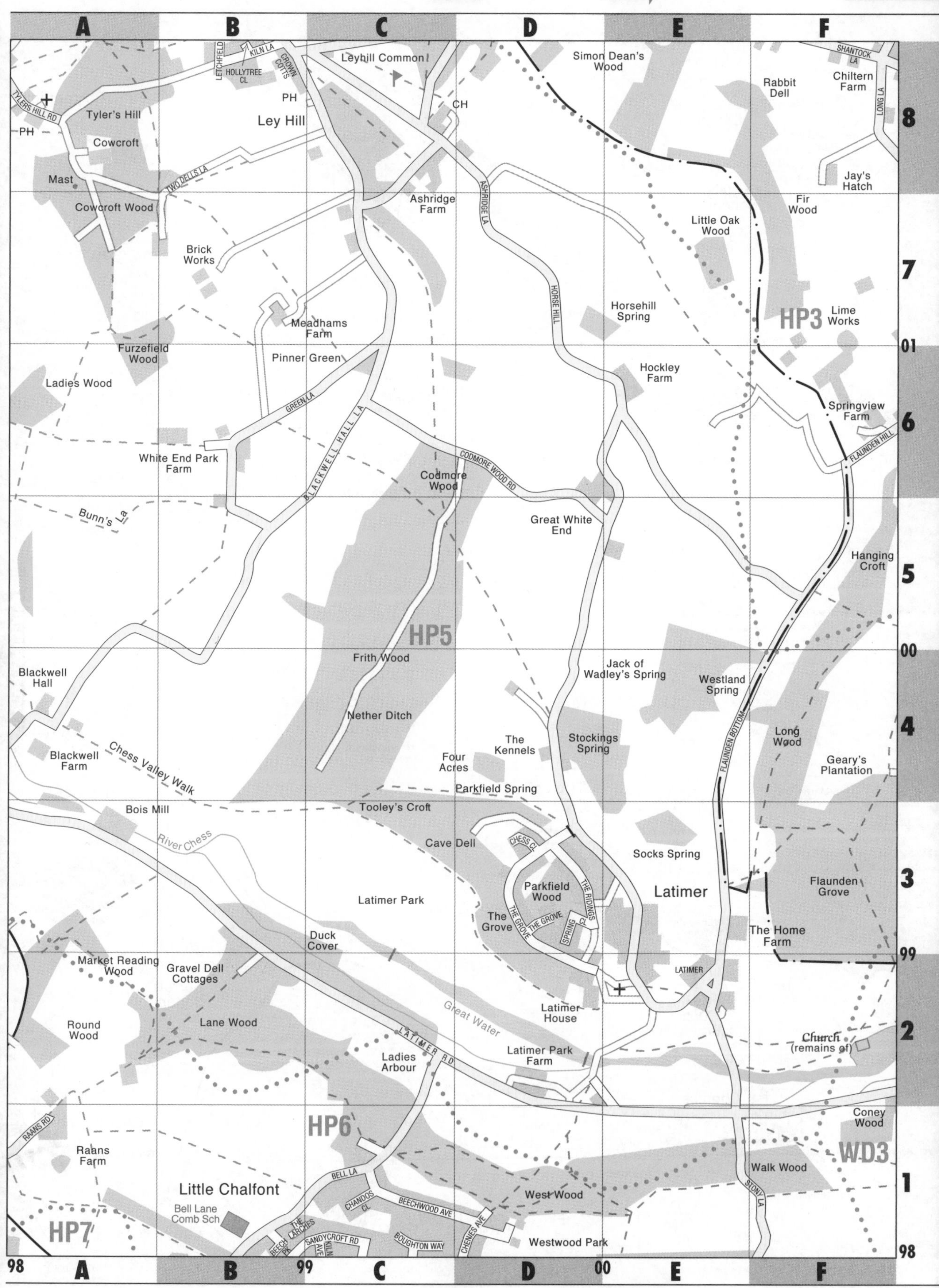

166
156

155 146

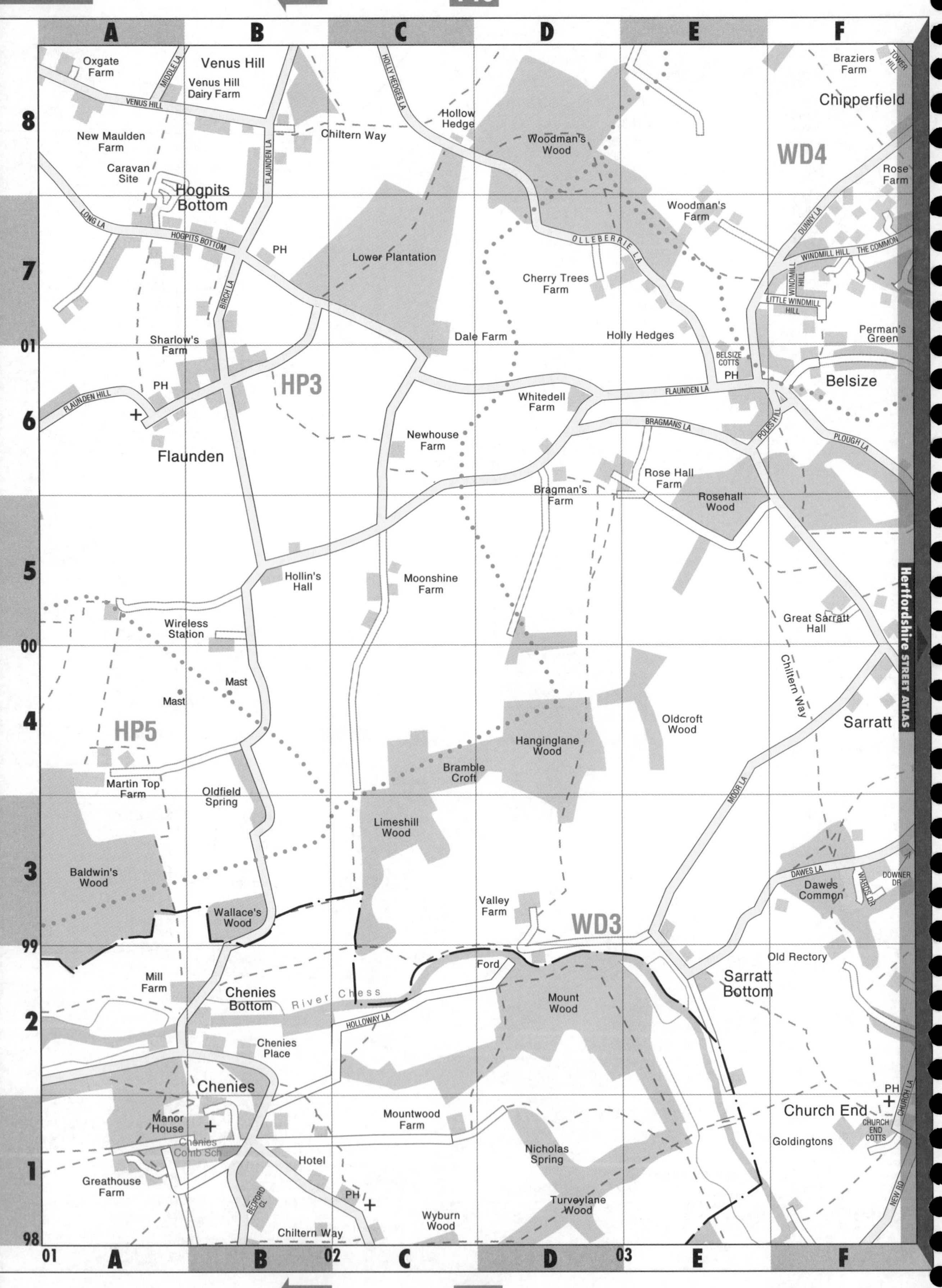

155 167

158

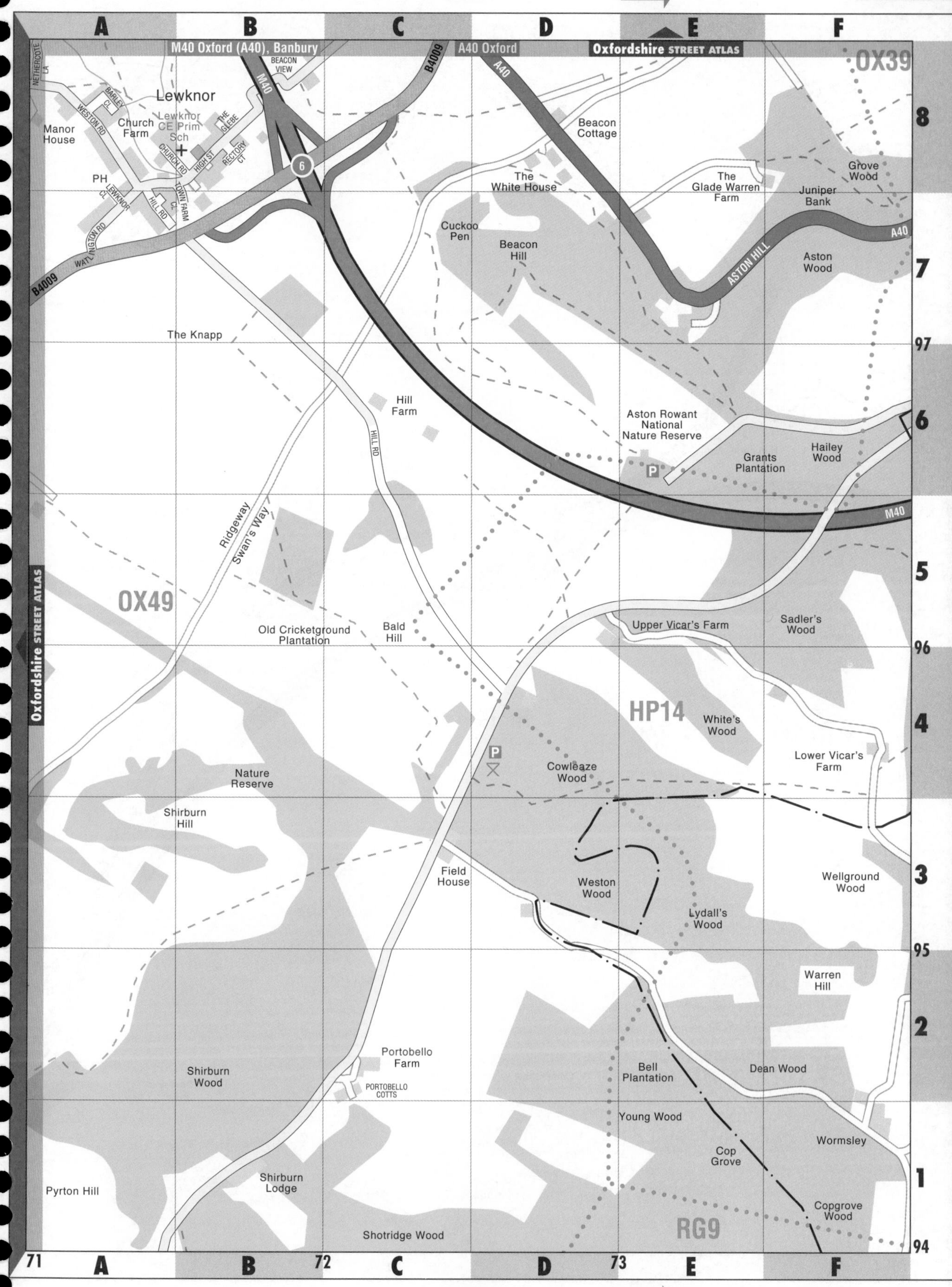

A
B
C
D
E
F
M40 Oxford (A40), Banbury
A40 Oxford
Oxfordshire STREET ATLAS
OX39
Lewknor
Manor House
Church Farm
Lewknor CE Prim Sch
PH
Beacon Cottage
The White House
The Glade Warren Farm
Grove Wood
Juniper Bank
Cuckoo Pen
Beacon Hill
ASTON HILL
Aston Wood
The Knapp
Hill Farm
HILL RD
Aston Rowant National Nature Reserve
Grants Plantation
Hailey Wood
M40
A40
B4009
Ridgeway
Swan's Way
OX49
Old Cricketground Plantation
Bald Hill
Upper Vicar's Farm
Sadler's Wood
HP14
White's Wood
Lower Vicar's Farm
Cowleaze Wood
Nature Reserve
Shirburn Hill
Field House
Weston Wood
Wellground Wood
Lydall's Wood
Warren Hill
Portobello Farm
PORTOBELLO COTTS
Shirburn Wood
Bell Plantation
Dean Wood
Young Wood
Wormsley
Cop Grove
Pyrton Hill
Shirburn Lodge
Copgrove Wood
Shotridge Wood
RG9
8
7
97
6
5
96
4
3
95
2
1
94
71
72
73

168

158

157
147

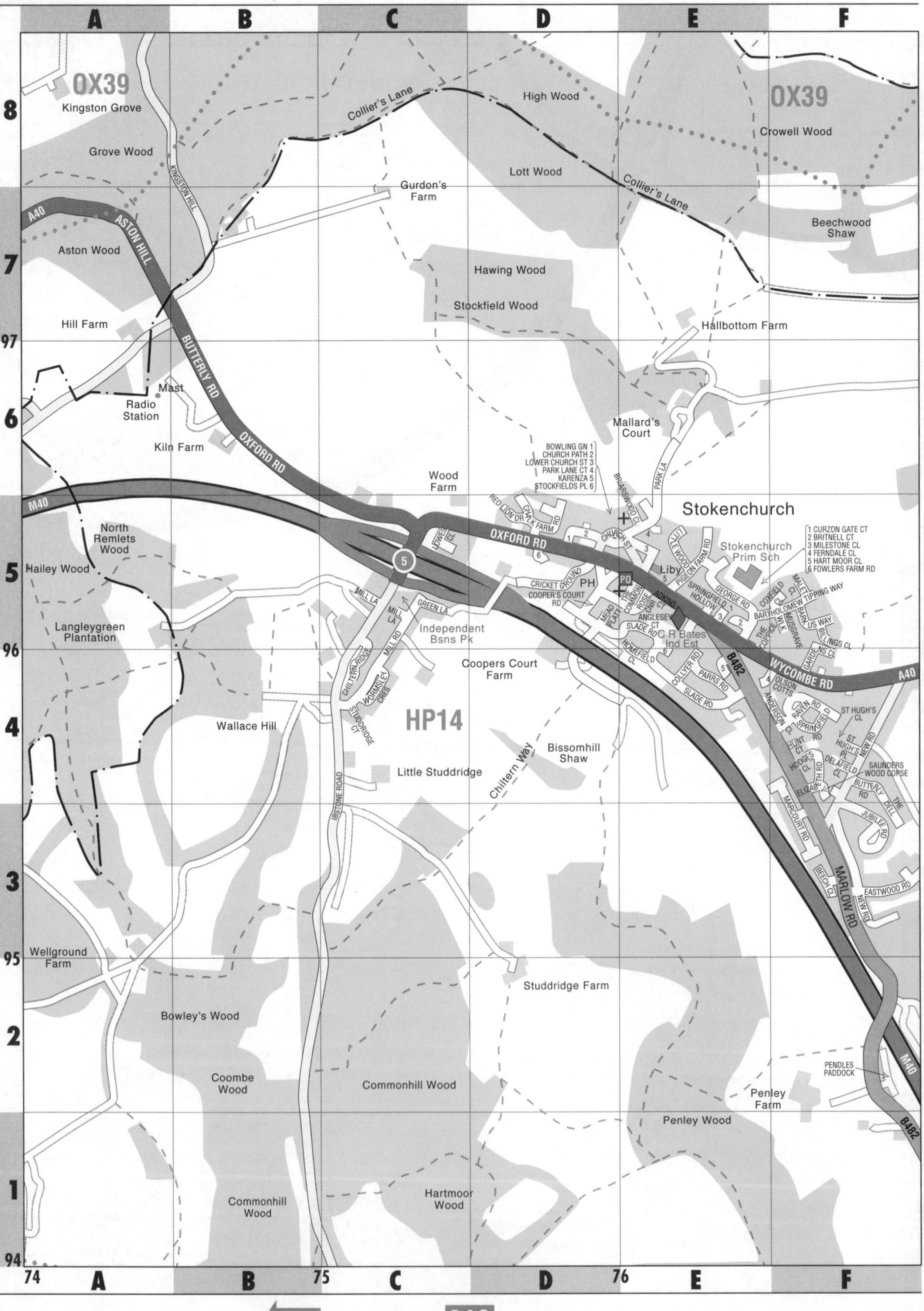
A
B
C
D
E
F
OX39
Kingston Grove
Grove Wood
Collier's Lane
High Wood
OX39
Crowell Wood
Lott Wood
Gurdon's Farm
KINGSTON HILL
Collier's Lane
A40
ASTON HILL
Beechwood Shaw
Aston Wood
Hawing Wood
Stockfield Wood
Hill Farm
Hallbottom Farm
BUTTERLY RD
Mast
Radio Station
Mallard's Court
Kiln Farm
OXFORD RD
BOWLING GN 1
CHURCH PATH 2
LOWER CHURCH ST 3
PARK LANE CT 4
KARENZA 5
STOCKFIELDS PL 6
Wood Farm
PARK LA
BRIARSWOOD CL
M40
Stokenchurch
North Remlets Wood
RED LION DR
CHALK FARM RD
LOWES CL
OXFORD RD
CHURCH ST
Stokenchurch Prim Sch
1 CURZON GATE CT
2 BRITNELL CT
3 MILESTONE CL
4 FERNDALE CL
5 HART MOOR CL
6 FOWLERS FARM RD
Hailey Wood
5
PIGEON FARM RD
Liby
PH
PO
CRICKET GROUND
COOPER'S COURT RD
MILL LA
GREEN LA
SPRINGFIELD HOLLOW
GEORGE RD
COXFIELD CL
MALLET CL
TIPPING WAY
BARTHOLOMEW CL
BARK US WAY
Langleygreen Plantation
Independent Bsns Pk
MILL RD
ADKINS
ANGLESEY CT
SLADE RD
C R Bates Ind Est
THE COPPICE
MUSGRAVE WLK
BILLINGS CL
HOMEFIELD CL
COLLYER RD
PARRS RD
B482
WYCOMBE RD
A40
Coopers Court Farm
CHILTERN RIDGE
WORMSLEY CRES
SLADE RD
OLSON COTTS
ANDERSON CL
RAVEN RD
ST HUGH'S CL
HP14
STUDDRIDGE CT
Wallace Hill
SPRINGFIELD RD
Bissomhill Shaw
HUNT CT
ST HUGH'S PL
NEW RD
Chiltern Way
HODGES CL
DELAFIELD CL
SAUNDERS WOOD COPSE
Little Studdridge
ELIZABETH RD
BUTTERLY RD
THE DELL
IBSTONE ROAD
MARCOURT RD
JUBILEE RD
BEECH CL
MARLOW RD
EASTWOOD RD
NEW RD
Wellground Farm
Studdridge Farm
Bowley's Wood
M40
PENDLES PADDOCK
Coombe Wood
Commonhill Wood
Penley Farm
Penley Wood
B482
Commonhill Wood
Hartmoor Wood
8
7
97
6
5
96
4
3
95
2
1
94
74
75
76

157
169

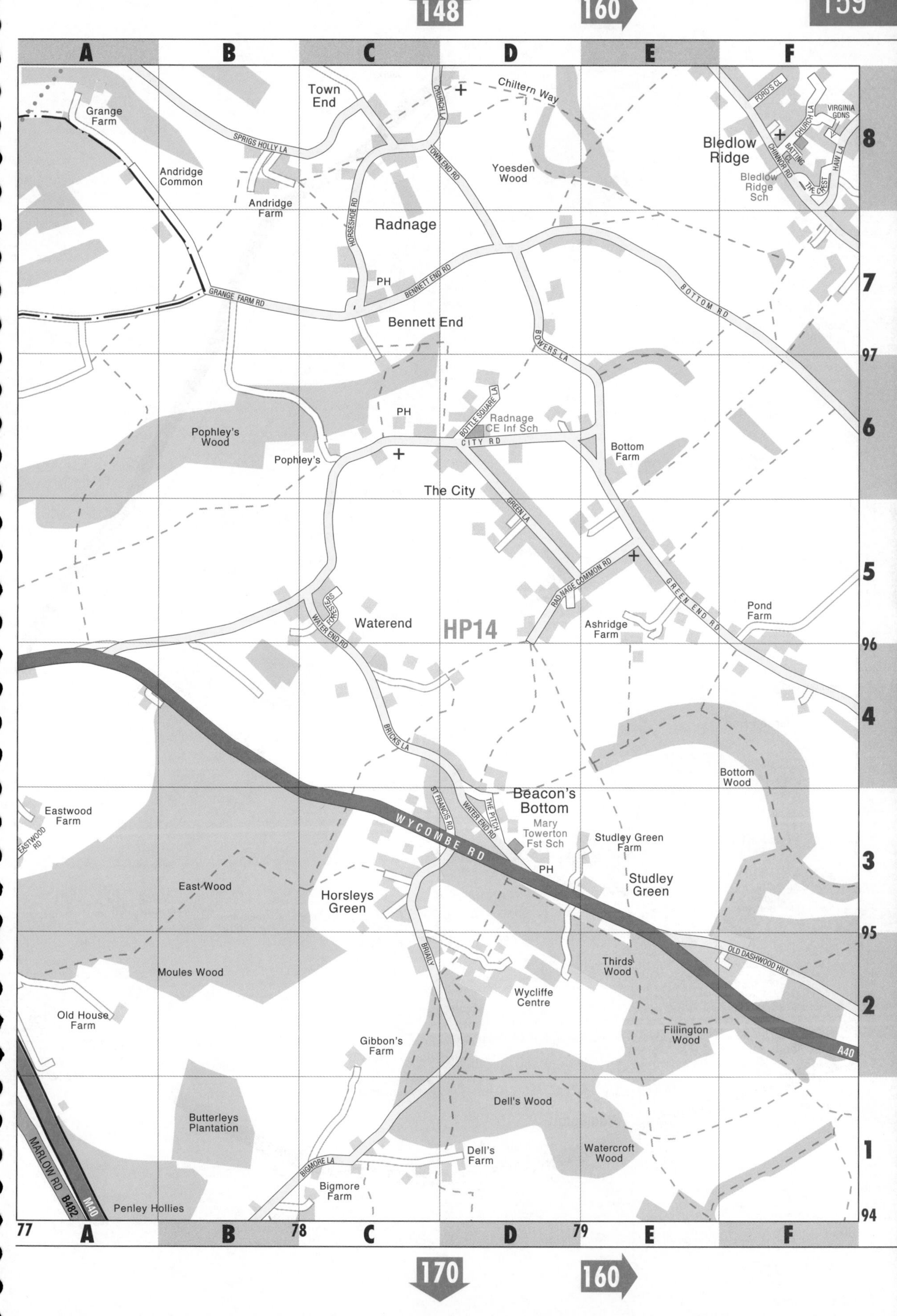
148
160
A
B
C
D
E
F
Town End
Chiltern Way
Grange Farm
Andridge Common
Andridge Farm
SPRIGS HOLLY LA
CHURCH LA
TOWN END RD
Yoesden Wood
Radnage
HORSESHOE RD
Bledlow Ridge
Bledlow Ridge Sch
FORD'S CL
CHURCH LA
VIRGINIA GDNS
BATTING CL
CHINNOR RD
HAW LA
THE CREST
8
GRANGE FARM RD
PH
BENNETT END RD
Bennett End
BOTTOM RD
7
BOWERS LA
97
PH
Pophley's Wood
Pophley's
BOTTLE SQUARE LA
Radnage CE Inf Sch
CITY RD
Bottom Farm
6
The City
GREEN LA
RADNAGE COMMON RD
5
FORESTERS
WATER END RD
Waterend
HP14
Ashridge Farm
GREEN END RD
Pond Farm
96
4
BRICKS LA
Bottom Wood
Eastwood Farm
EASTWOOD RD
ST FRANCIS RD
WATER END RD
THE PITCH
Beacon's Bottom
Mary Towerton Fst Sch
Studley Green Farm
WYCOMBE RD
PH
Studley Green
3
East Wood
Horsleys Green
95
BRIAILY
Thirds Wood
OLD DASHWOOD HILL
Moules Wood
Wycliffe Centre
2
Old House Farm
Fillington Wood
A40
Gibbon's Farm
Dell's Wood
Butterleys Plantation
MARLOW RD
B482
M40
BIGMORE LA
Dell's Farm
Watercroft Wood
1
Bigmore Farm
Penley Hollies
94
77
78
79
170
160

159
149

159
171

150
162

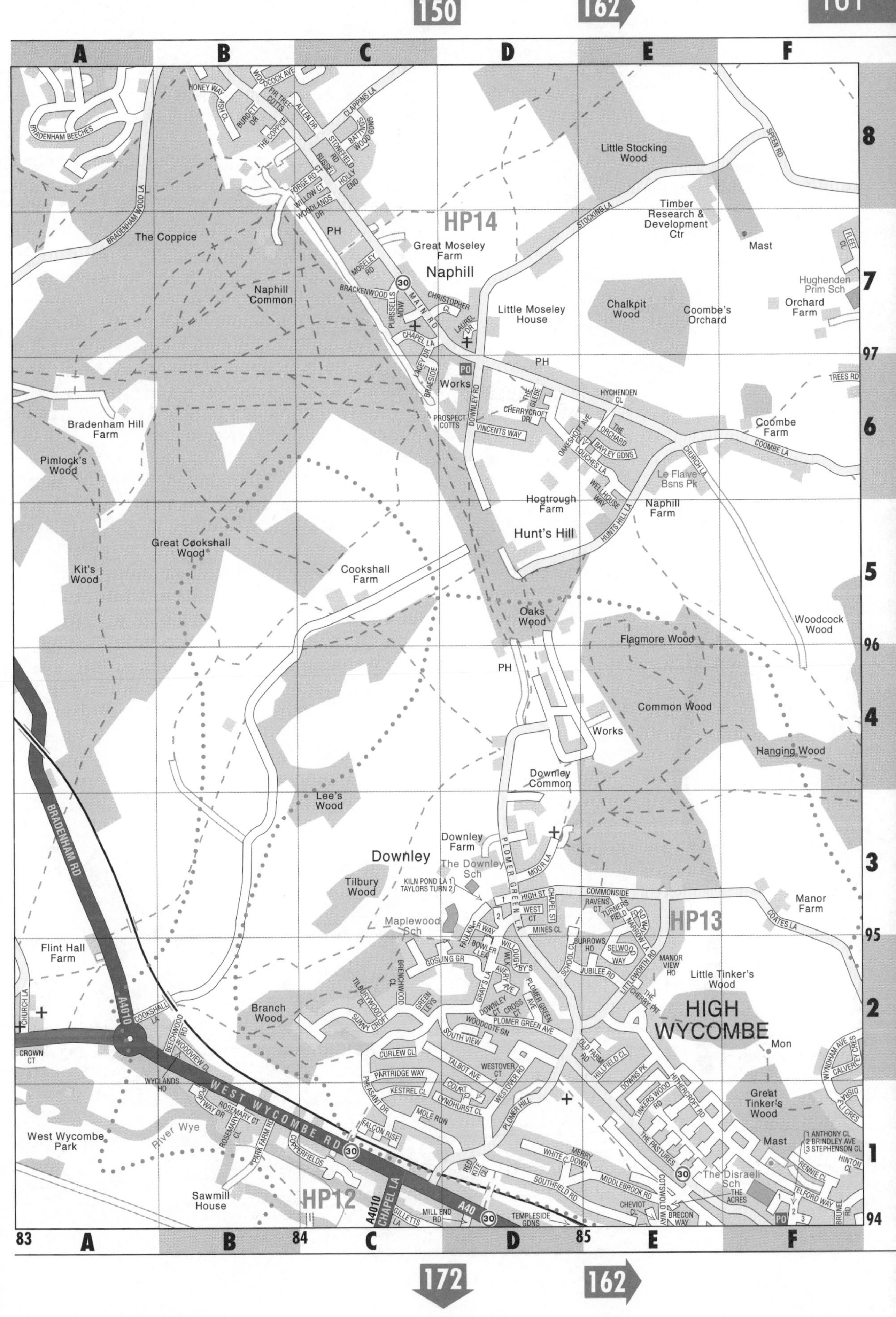

172
162

161
151

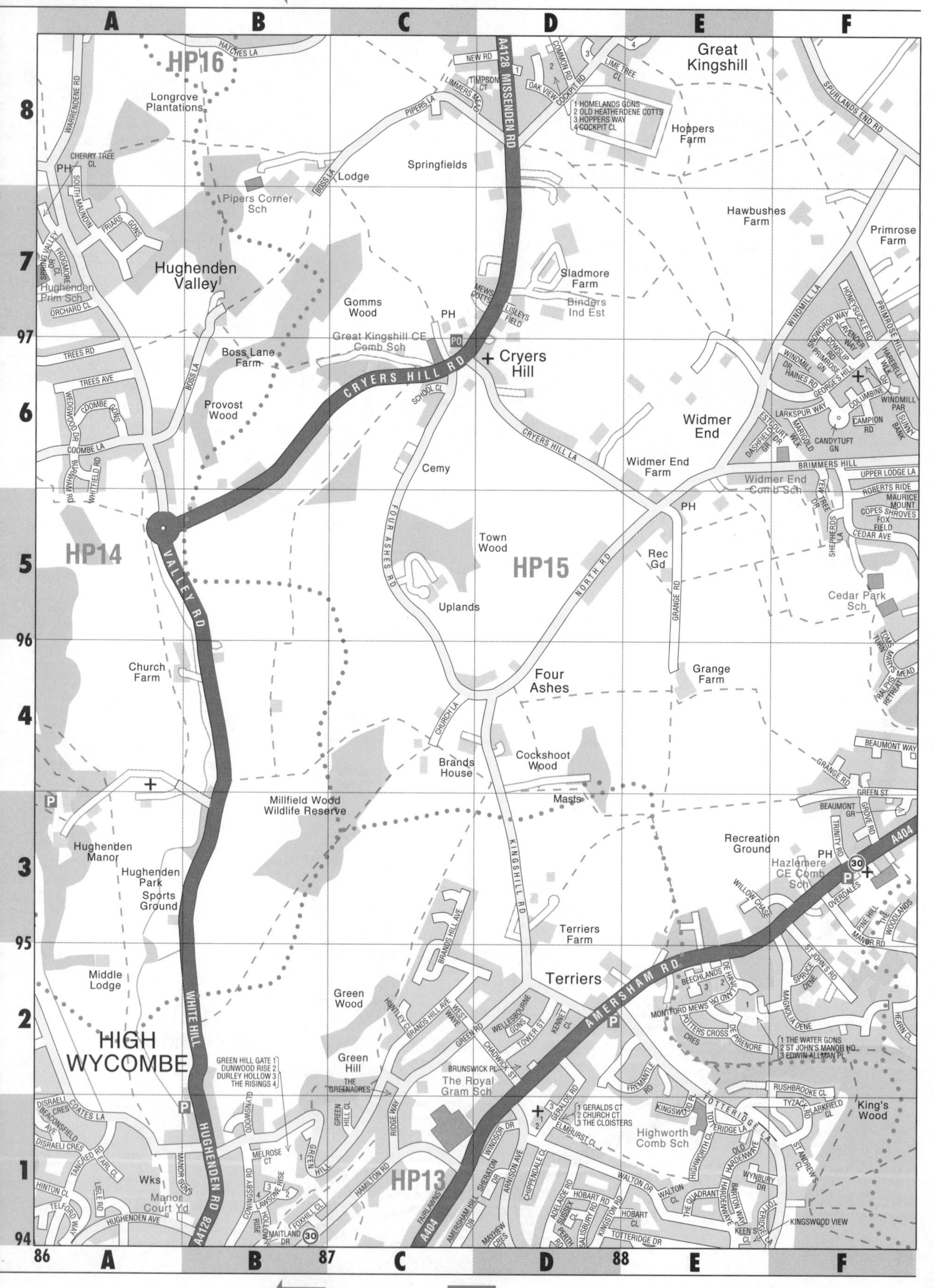

161
173

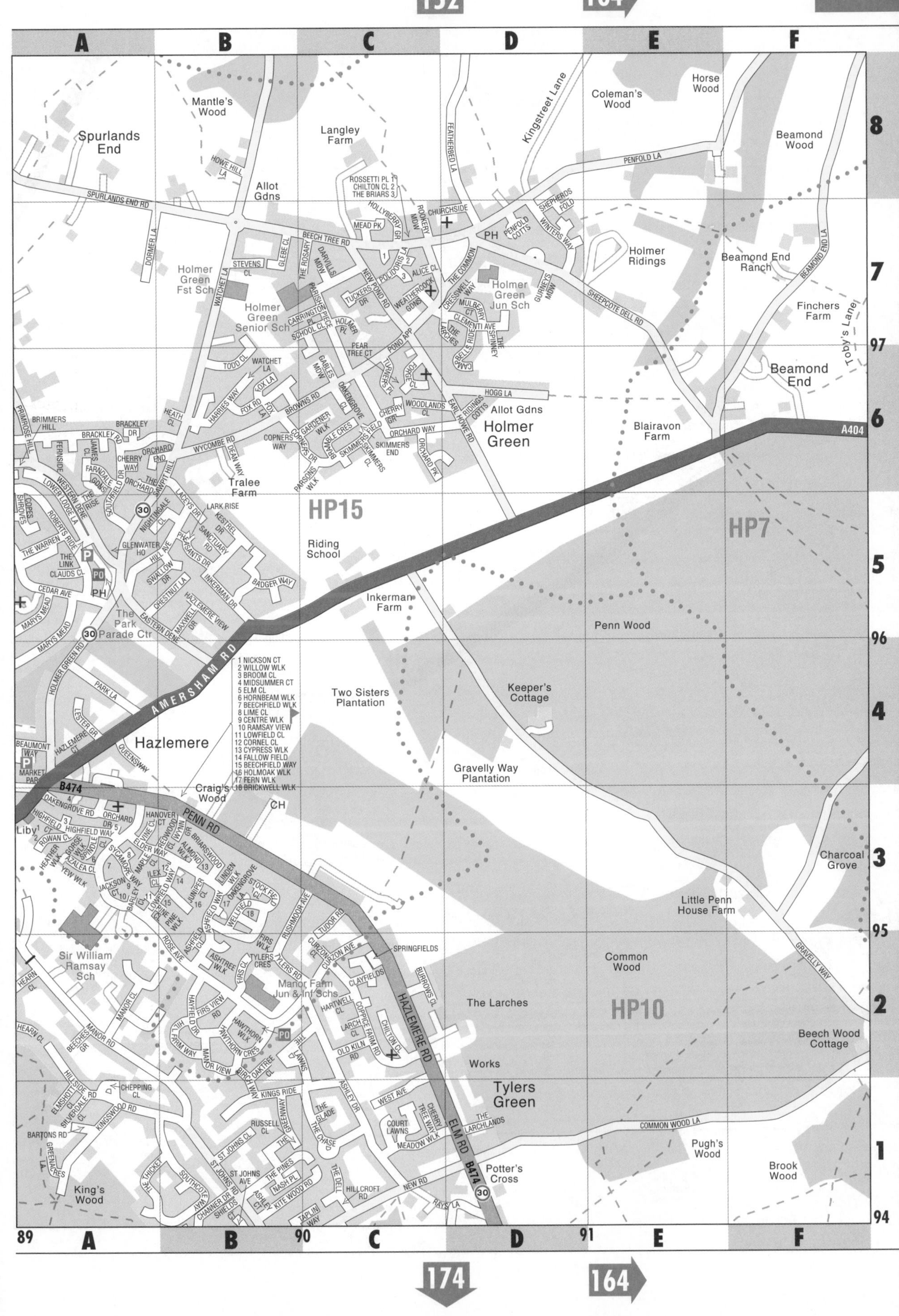
152
164
Mantle's Wood
Spurlands End
Langley Farm
Coleman's Wood
Horse Wood
Beamond Wood
Kingstreet Lane
Allot Gdns
Holmer Green Fst Sch
Holmer Green Senior Sch
Holmer Green Jun Sch
Holmer Ridings
Beamond End Ranch
Finchers Farm
Toby's Lane
Beamond End
Blairavon Farm
Holmer Green
Tralee Farm
HP15
HP7
Riding School
Inkerman Farm
Penn Wood
The Park Parade Ctr
Two Sisters Plantation
Keeper's Cottage
Hazlemere
Gravelly Way Plantation
Craig's Wood
Charcoal Grove
Little Penn House Farm
Sir William Ramsay Sch
Common Wood
Manor Farm Jun & Inf Schs
The Larches
HP10
Beech Wood Cottage
Works
Tylers Green
Pugh's Wood
Brook Wood
Potter's Cross
King's Wood
AMERSHAM RD
PENN RD
HAZLEMERE RD
ELM RD
A404
B474
1 NICKSON CT
2 WILLOW WLK
3 BROOM CL
4 MIDSUMMER CT
5 ELM CL
6 HORNBEAM WLK
7 BEECHFIELD WLK
8 LIME CL
9 CENTRE WLK
10 RAMSAY VIEW
11 LOWFIELD CL
12 CORNEL CL
13 CYPRESS WLK
14 FALLOW FIELD
15 BEECHFIELD WAY
16 HOLMOAK WLK
17 FERN WLK
18 BRICKWELL WLK
174
164

163
153

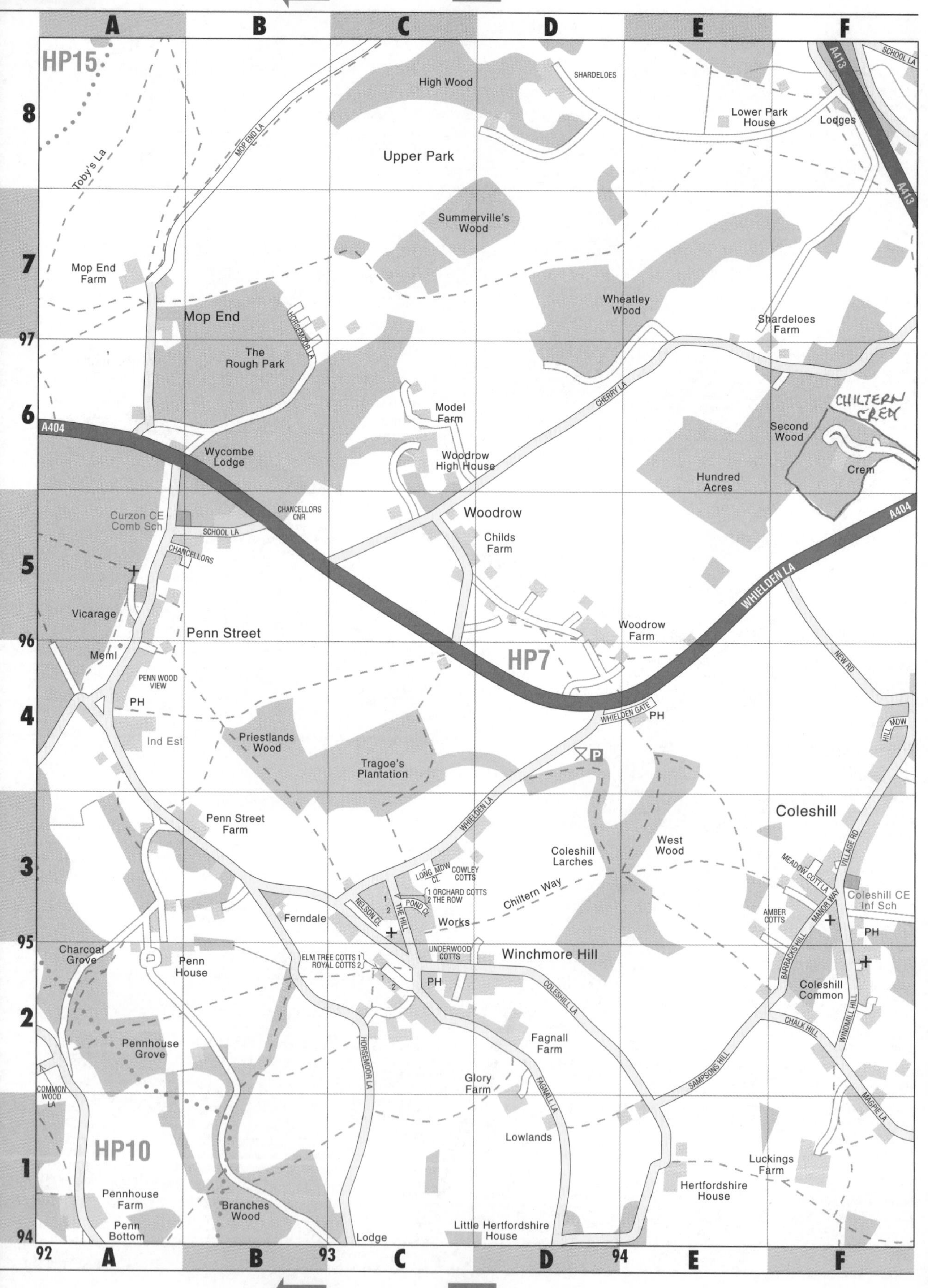

163
175

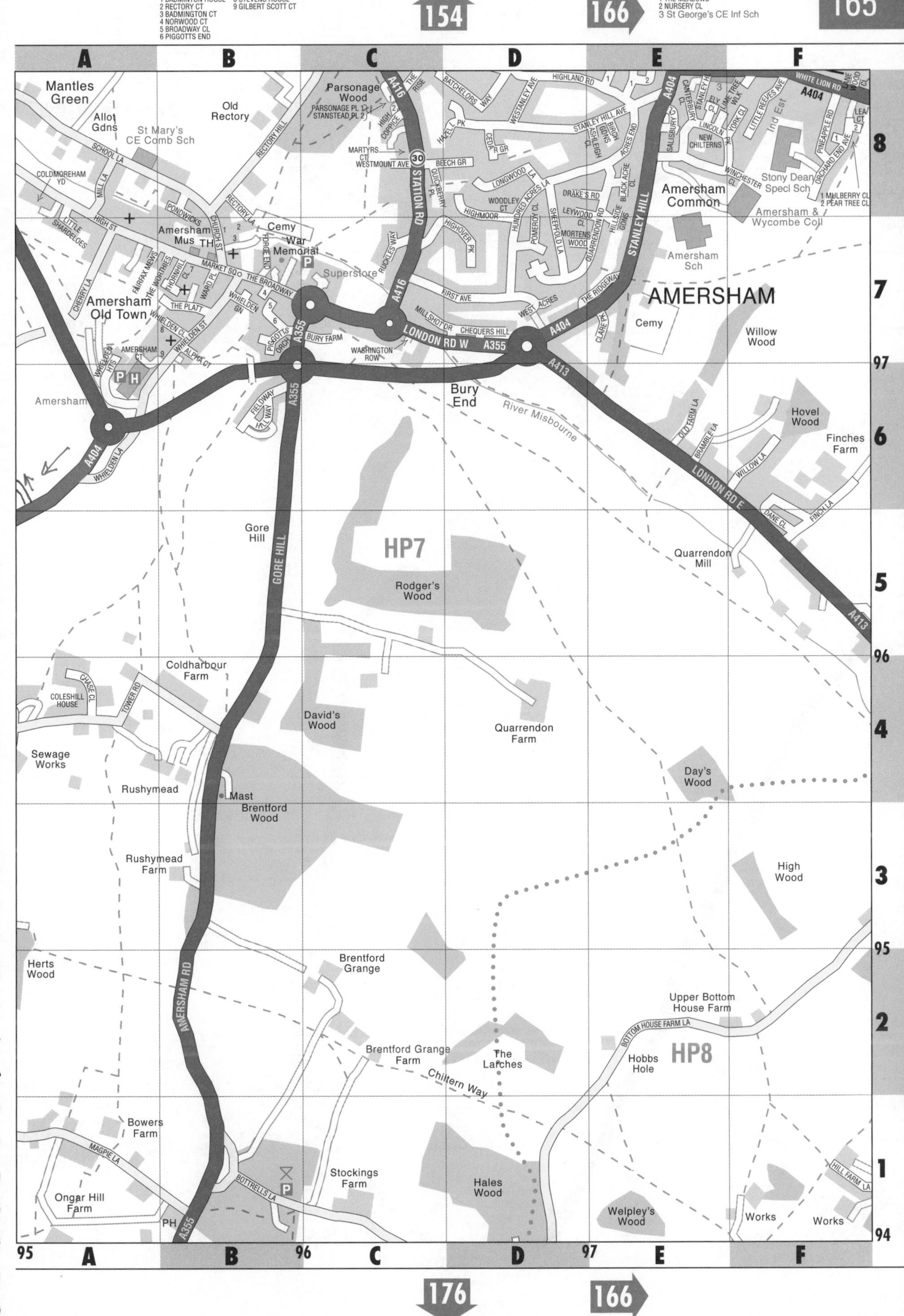
A
B
C
D
E
F
Mantles Green
Allot Gdns
Old Rectory
St Mary's CE Comb Sch
Parsonage Wood
PARSONAGE PL 1
STANSTEAD PL 2
SCHOOL LA
COLDMOREHAM YD
MILL LA
RECTORY HILL
THE RISE
HIGH COPPICE
MARTYRS CT
WESTMOUNT AVE
STATION RD
A416
BATCHELORS WAY
HIGHLAND RD
WESTANLEY AVE
STANLEY HILL AVE
HAZELL PK
CEDAR GR
BEECH GR
QUICKBERRY PL
LONGWOOD LA
WOODLEY CT
HUNDRED ACRES LA
HIGHMOOR
DRAKE'S RD
LEYWOOD CL
MORTENS WOOD
POMEROY CL
SHEEPFOLD LA
QUARRENDON RD
HILLSIDE GDNS
BLACK ACRE CL
ACRES END
BIRCH GDNS
ASHLEIGH CL
STANLEY HILL
A404
SALISBURY CL
CANTERBURY CL
STANLEY HL
ELY CL
LIME TREE WLK
LINCOLN PK
YORK CL
NEW CHILTERNS
LITTLE REEVES AVE
Ind Est
WHITE LION RD
LANE WOOD CL
PINEAPPLE RD
ORCHARD END AVE
LEA CT
WINCHESTER CL
Stony Dean Specl Sch
1 MULBERRY CL
2 PEAR TREE CL
Amersham Common
Amersham & Wycombe Coll
Amersham Sch
AMERSHAM
Cemy
Willow Wood
8
7
97
6
5
96
4
3
95
2
1
94
LITTLE SHARDELOES
HIGH ST
PONDWICKS
CHURCH ST
RECTORY LA
Amersham Mus
TH
Cemy
War Memorial
FORGE END
Superstore
RUCKLES WAY
HIGHOVER PK
MARKET SQ
THE BROADWAY
FAIRFAX MEWS
THE WORTHIES
THORNHILL CL
WARD PL
WHIELDEN GN
CHERRY LA
Amersham Old Town
THE PLATT
WHIELDEN CL
WHIELDEN ST
AMERSHAM CT
ALPHA CT
PIGGOTTS ORCH
BURY FARM
WASHINGTON ROW
A355
FIRST AVE
MILLSHOTT DR
CHEQUERS HILL
WEST ACRES
THE RIDGEWAY
CLARE PK
LONDON RD W
A413
WHIELDEN HTS
Amersham
FIELDWAY
HILL WAY
Bury End
River Misbourne
OLD FARM LA
BRAMBLE LA
Hovel Wood
Finches Farm
WILLOW LA
LONDON RD E
DANE CL
FINCH LA
WHIELDEN LA
Gore Hill
GORE HILL
HP7
Rodger's Wood
Quarrendon Mill
Coldharbour Farm
CHASE CL
COLESHILL HOUSE
TOWER RD
David's Wood
Quarrendon Farm
Sewage Works
Rushymead
Mast
Brentford Wood
Day's Wood
Rushymead Farm
High Wood
Herts Wood
Brentford Grange
AMERSHAM RD
Upper Bottom House Farm
BOTTOM HOUSE FARM LA
Brentford Grange Farm
The Larches
Hobbs Hole
HP8
Chiltern Way
Bowers Farm
MAGPIE LA
Stockings Farm
Hales Wood
HILL FARM LA
BOTTRELLS LA
Ongar Hill Farm
PH
Welpley's Wood
Works
Works
95
96
97

165
155

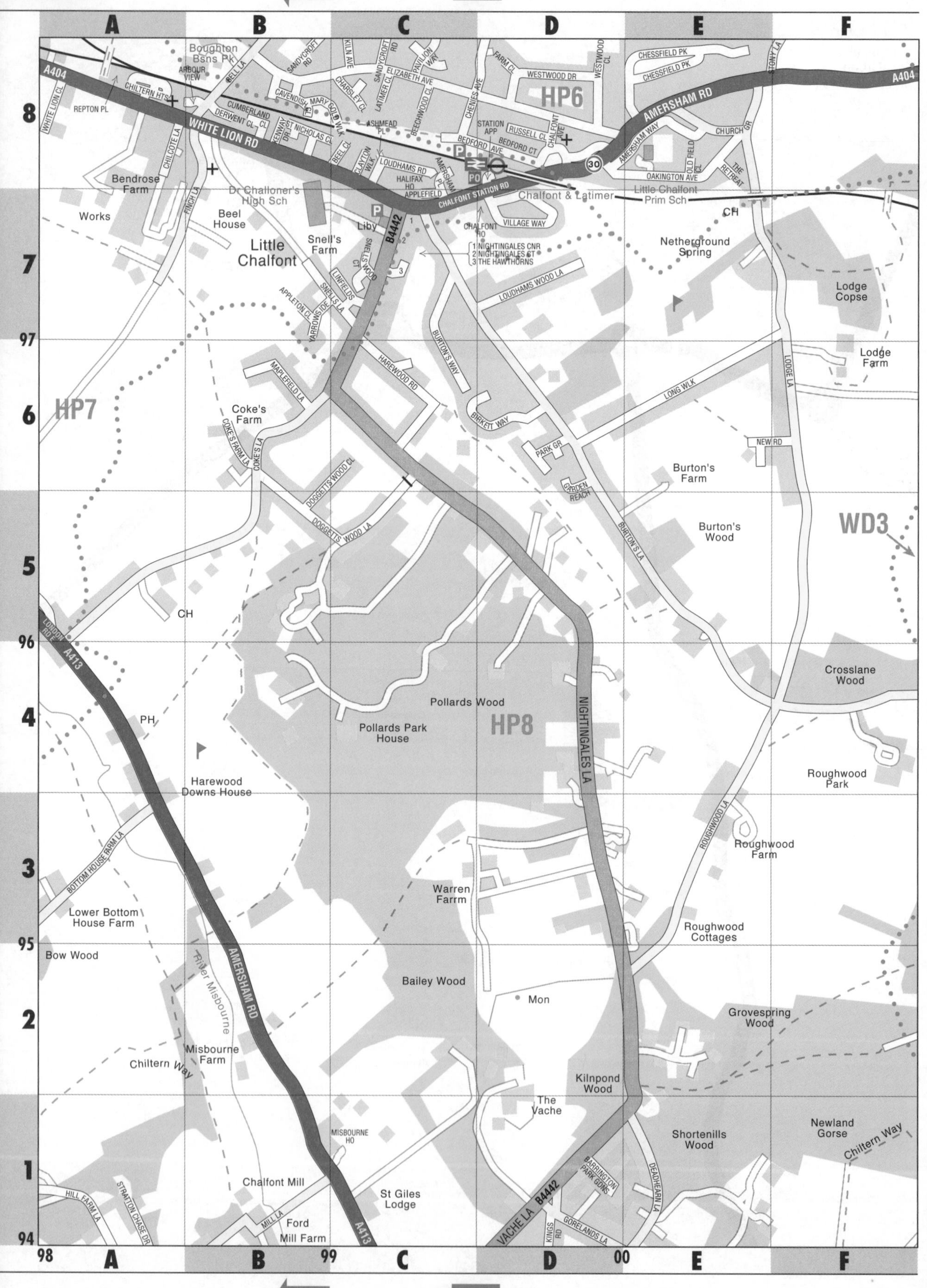

165
177

156

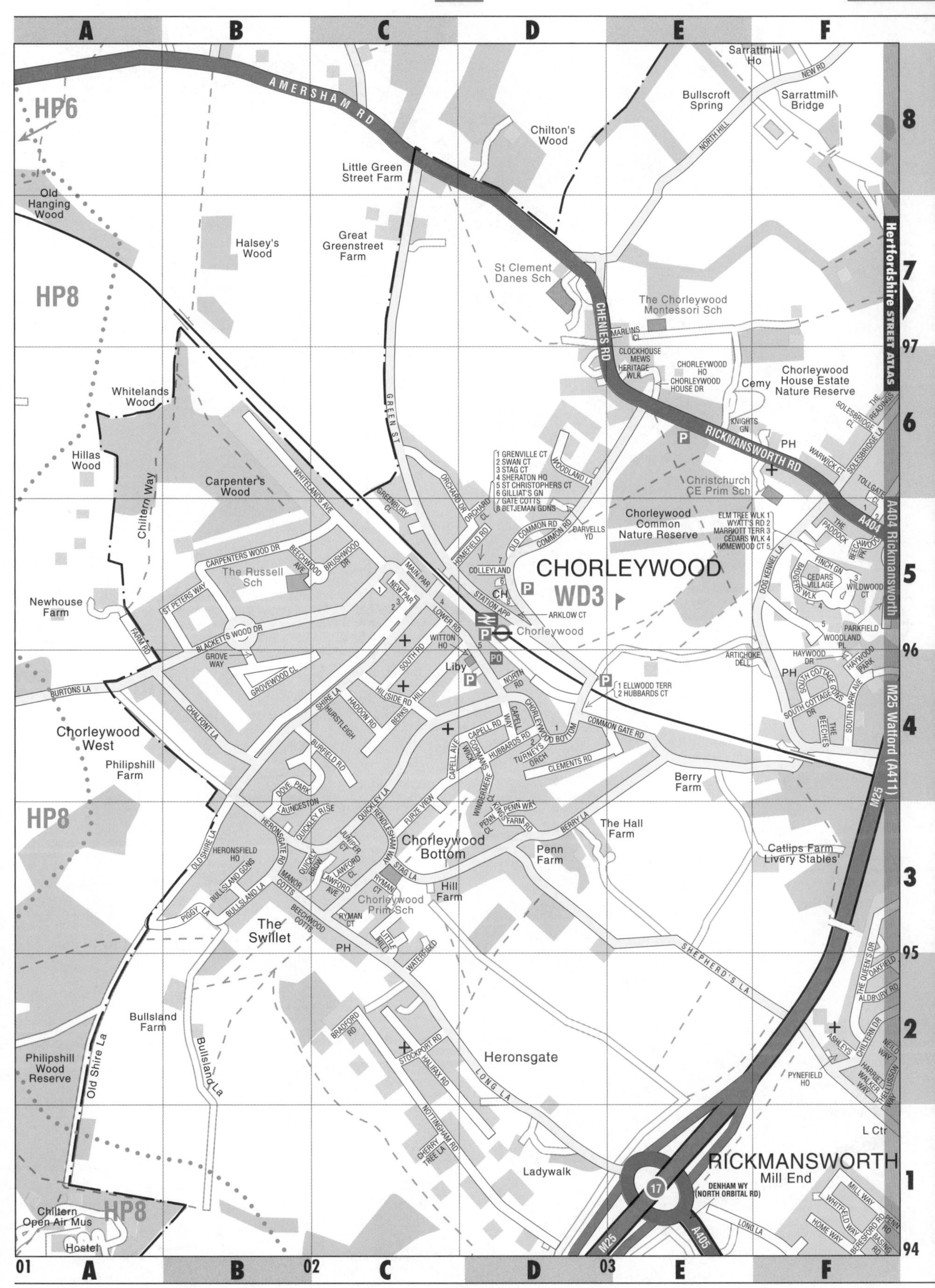
AMERSHAM RD
HP6
HP8
Old Hanging Wood
Halsey's Wood
Little Green Street Farm
Great Greenstreet Farm
Chilton's Wood
St Clement Danes Sch
Sarrattmill Ho
Bullscroft Spring
Sarrattmill Bridge
NORTH HILL
NEW RD
The Chorleywood Montessori Sch
CHENIES RD
MARLINS CL
CLOCKHOUSE MEWS
HERITAGE WLK
CHORLEYWOOD HO
CHORLEYWOOD HOUSE DR
Cemy
Chorleywood House Estate Nature Reserve
KNIGHTS GN
RICKMANSWORTH RD
Christchurch CE Prim Sch
Chorleywood Common Nature Reserve
CHORLEYWOOD
WD3
Chorleywood
Whitelands Wood
Hillas Wood
Carpenter's Wood
Chiltern Way
The Russell Sch
Newhouse Farm
Chorleywood West
Philipshill Farm
GREEN ST
1 GRENVILLE CT
2 SWAN CT
3 STAG CT
4 SHERATON HO
5 ST CHRISTOPHERS CT
6 GILLIAT'S GN
7 GATE COTTS
8 BETJEMAN GDNS
ELM TREE WLK 1
WYATT'S RD 2
MARRIOTT TERR 3
CEDARS WLK 4
HOMEWOOD CT 5
1 ELLWOOD TERR
2 HUBBARDS CT
ARKLOW CT
COMMON GATE RD
Berry Farm
The Hall Farm
Penn Farm
Catlips Farm Livery Stables
Chorleywood Bottom
Hill Farm
Chorleywood Prim Sch
The Swillet
Bullsland Farm
Bullsland La
Old Shire La
Philipshill Wood Reserve
Heronsgate
SHEPHERD'S LA
LONG LA
Ladywalk
Chiltern Open Air Mus
Hostel
RICKMANSWORTH
Mill End
DENHAM WY (NORTH ORBITAL RD)
A404
A405
M25
A404 Rickmansworth
M25 Watford (A411)
Hertfordshire STREET ATLAS
PYNEFIELD HO
L Ctr
A B C D E F
8 7 6 5 4 3 2 1
97 96 95 94
01 02 03

157

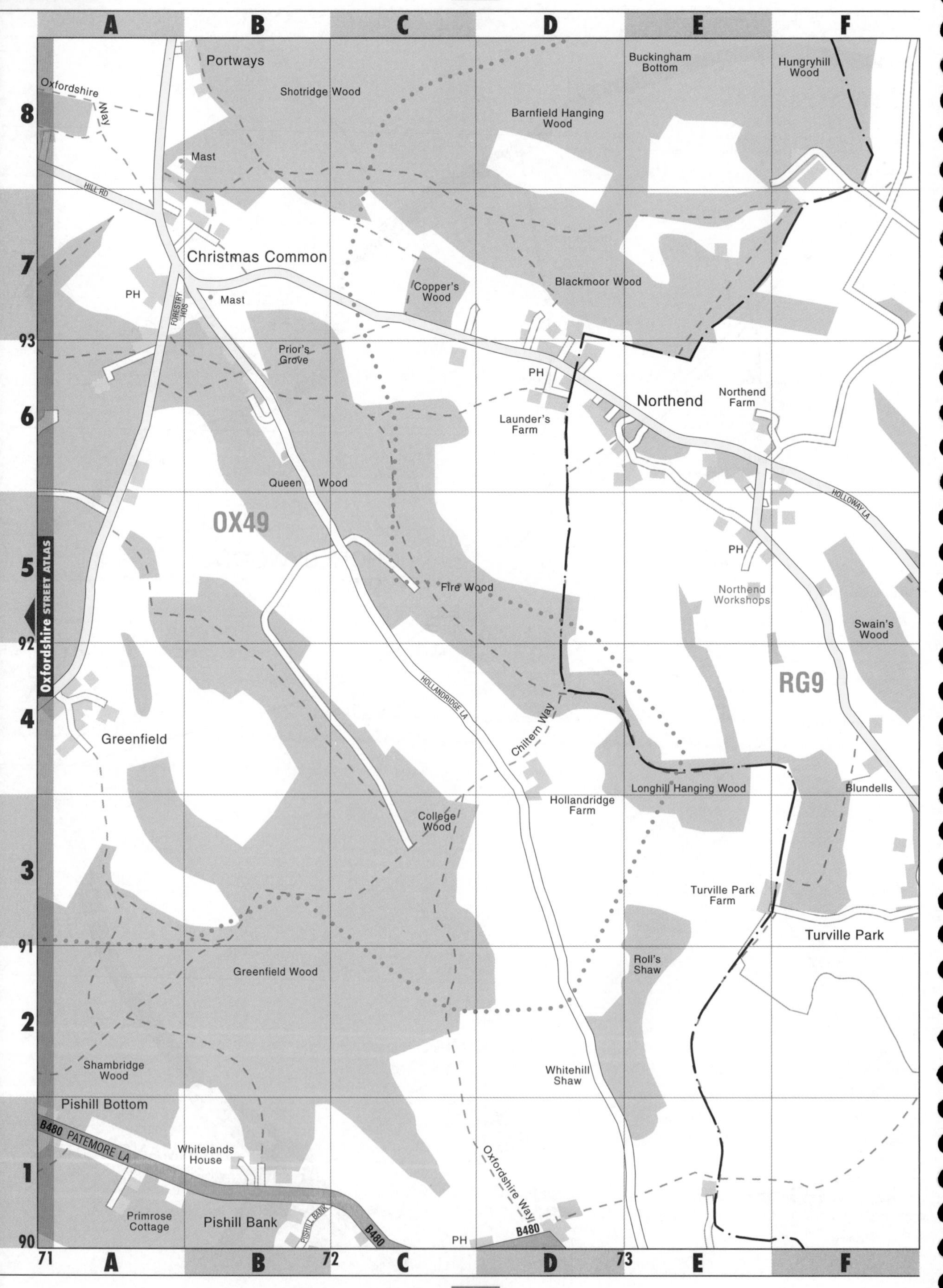

A B C D E F
8 7 93 6 5 92 4 3 91 2 1 90
71 72 73
Portways
Oxfordshire Way
Shotridge Wood
Buckingham Bottom
Hungryhill Wood
Barnfield Hanging Wood
Mast
HILL RD
Christmas Common
PH
Mast
FORESTRY HOS
Copper's Wood
Blackmoor Wood
Prior's Grove
PH
Northend
Northend Farm
Launder's Farm
HOLLOWAY LA
Queen Wood
OX49
PH
Fire Wood
Northend Workshops
Oxfordshire STREET ATLAS
Swain's Wood
HOLLANDRIDGE LA
RG9
Greenfield
Chiltern Way
Longhill Hanging Wood
Blundells
Hollandridge Farm
College Wood
Turville Park Farm
Turville Park
Greenfield Wood
Roll's Shaw
Shambridge Wood
Whitehill Shaw
Pishill Bottom
B480 PATEMORE LA
Whitelands House
Oxfordshire Way
Primrose Cottage
Pishill Bank
PISHILL BANK
B480
PH
B480

179

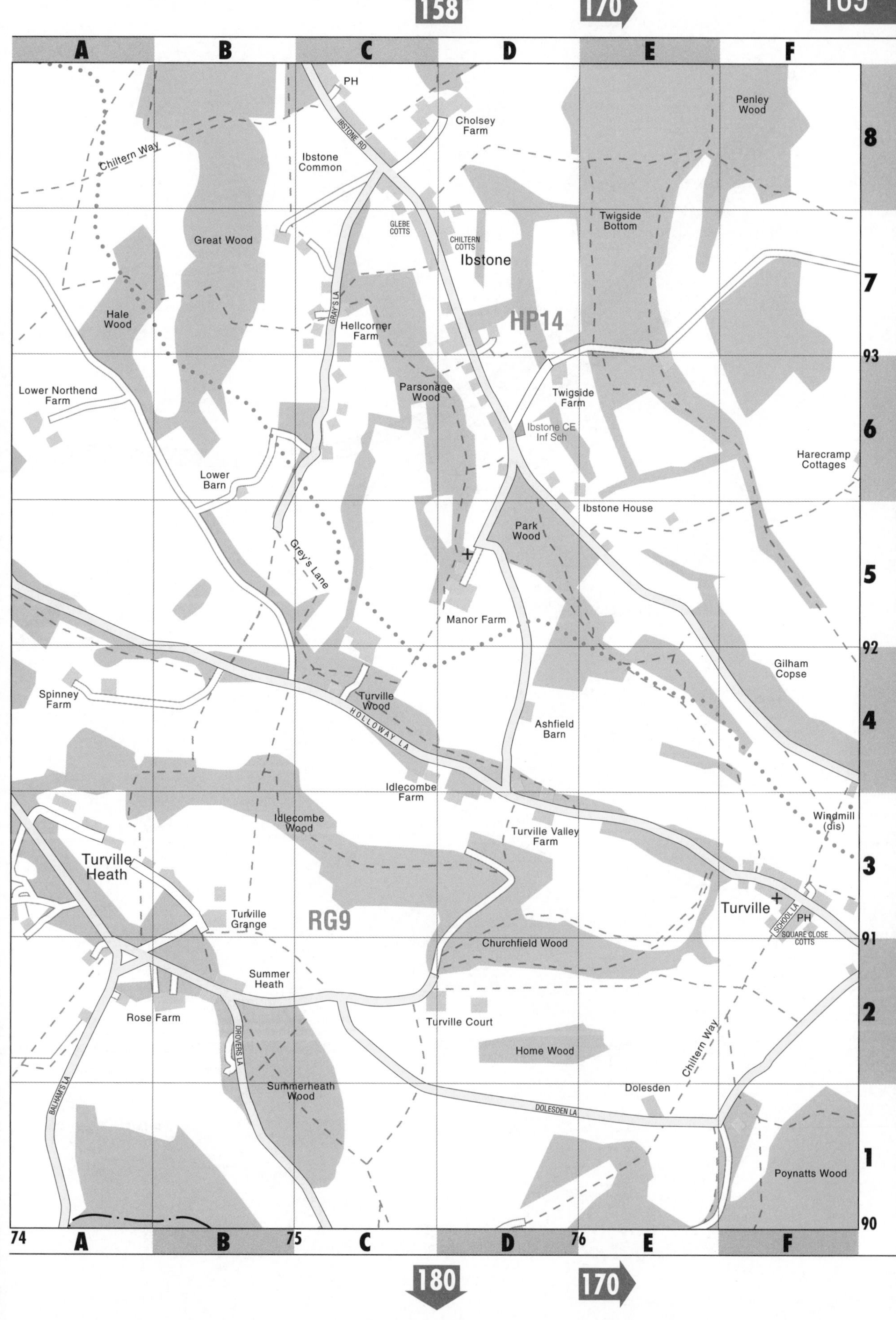
158
170
A
B
C
D
E
F
PH
Penley Wood
Cholsey Farm
Chiltern Way
Ibstone Common
IBSTONE RD
8
Twigside Bottom
Great Wood
GLEBE COTTS
CHILTERN COTTS
Ibstone
7
Hale Wood
GRAY'S LA
Hellcorner Farm
HP14
93
Lower Northend Farm
Parsonage Wood
Twigside Farm
Ibstone CE Inf Sch
6
Harecramp Cottages
Lower Barn
Ibstone House
Park Wood
Grey's Lane
5
Manor Farm
92
Gilham Copse
Spinney Farm
Turville Wood
HOLLOWAY LA
Ashfield Barn
4
Idlecombe Farm
Idlecombe Wood
Turville Valley Farm
Windmill (dis)
Turville Heath
3
Turville
SCHOOL LA
PH
Turville Grange
RG9
SQUARE CLOSE COTTS
Churchfield Wood
91
Summer Heath
Rose Farm
Turville Court
2
DROVERS LA
Home Wood
Chiltern Way
Summerheath Wood
Dolesden
BALHAM'S LA
DOLESDEN LA
1
Poynatts Wood
90
74
75
76
180
170

A B C D E F

8 7 93 6 5 92 4 3 91 2 1 90

Barn Wood
Leygrove's Wood
Chequers Manor Farm
Watercroft Farm
Pound Wood
HP14
Huckenden Farm
PH
MARLOW RD
M40
B482
BIGMORE LA
Kensham Farm
Pound Farm
Cadmore End CE Comb Sch
Cadmore End Common
Cadmore End
PH
NEW RD
Bolter End
BOLTER END LA
Hill Farm
Rackley's Farm
PH
Hanger Wood
CHEQUERS LA
FININGS RD B482
Priestley's Farm
Gravesend
Manor Farm
Mill Hanging Wood
FINGEST LA
Hanger Farm
Hanover Hill
Long Copse
Turville Hill
Fingest
RG9
PH
Fingest Wood
Mousells Wood
Dovers Farm
DOLESDEN LA
Murrage Farm
Chiltern Way
Maiden House
Spurgrove
PH
SPURGROVE LA
Goddard's Wood
Adam's Wood
Little Frieth
PERRIN SPRINGS LA
ELLERY RISE
Poynatts Farm
Bottom Wood
Frieth
PH
Colliers Farm
INNINGS GATE
PH
Maiden Farm
SHOGMOOR LA
Lower Goddards Farm
Stud Farm
Upper Goddards
PARMOOR LA
HAYLES FIELD
Frieth CE Comb Sch
SHOGMOOR LA
Skirmett

77 A B 78 C D 79 E F

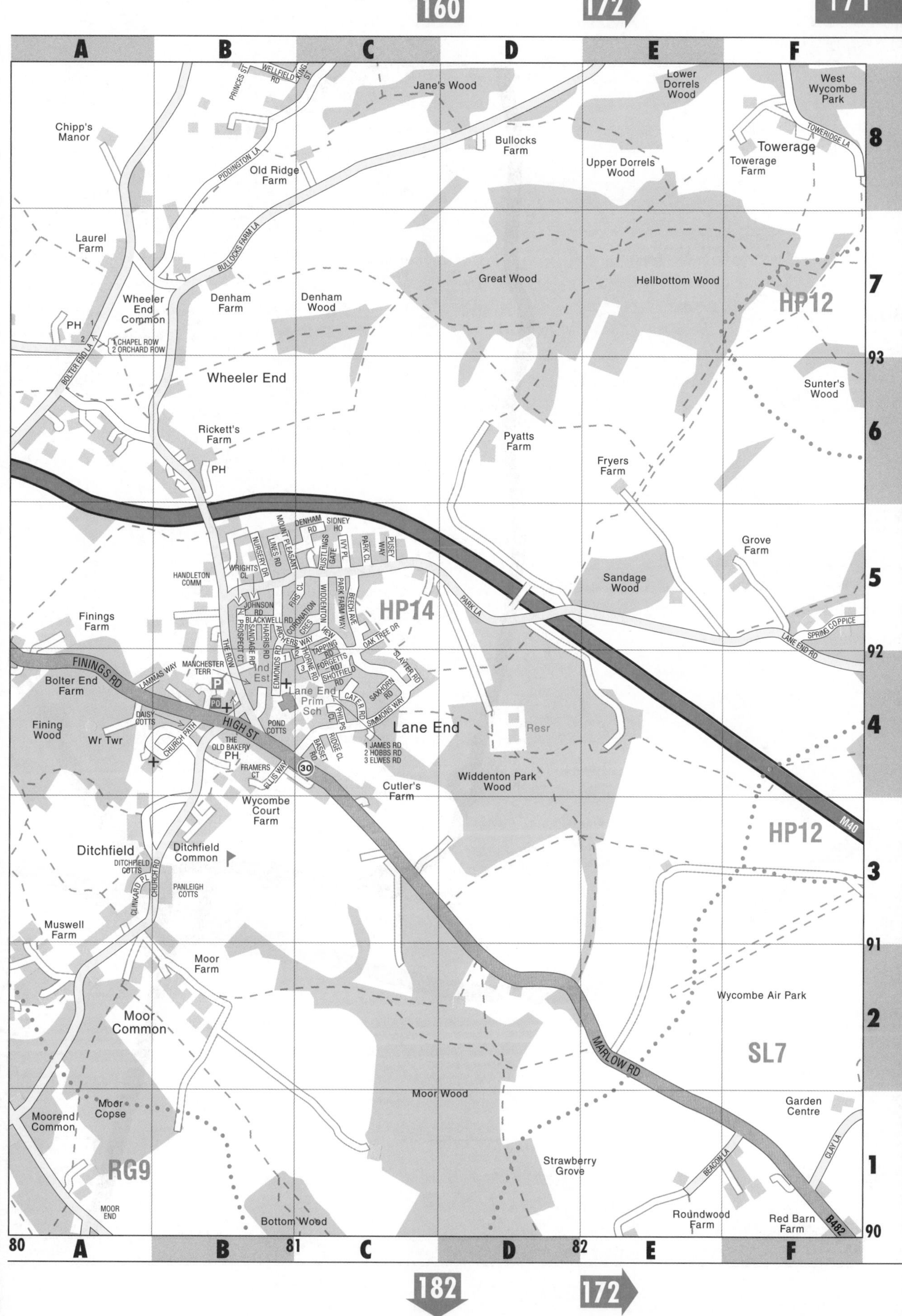
160
172
A
B
C
D
E
F
Jane's Wood
Lower Dorrels Wood
West Wycombe Park
Chipp's Manor
Bullocks Farm
Towerage
Towerage Farm
Old Ridge Farm
Upper Dorrels Wood
PIDDINGTON LA
BULLOCKS FARM LA
TOWERIDGE LA
Laurel Farm
Great Wood
Hellbottom Wood
HP12
Wheeler End Common
Denham Farm
Denham Wood
PH
1 CHAPEL ROW
2 ORCHARD ROW
BOLTER END LA
Wheeler End
Sunter's Wood
Rickett's Farm
Pyatts Farm
Fryers Farm
Grove Farm
Sandage Wood
HANDLETON COMM
Finings Farm
HP14
PARK LA
SPRING COPPICE
LANE END RD
FININGS RD
Bolter End Farm
LAMMAS WAY
MANCHESTER TERR
Ind Est
Lane End Prim Sch
Fining Wood
Wr Twr
DAISY COTTS
CHURCH PATH
HIGH ST
THE OLD BAKERY
POND COTTS
Lane End
Resr
1 JAMES RD
2 HOBBS RD
3 ELWES RD
FRAMERS CT
ELLIS WAY
Widdenton Park Wood
Cutler's Farm
Wycombe Court Farm
M40
HP12
Ditchfield
Ditchfield Common
DITCHFIELD COTTS
PANLEIGH COTTS
CLINKARD PL
CHURCH RD
Muswell Farm
Moor Farm
Wycombe Air Park
Moor Common
MARLOW RD
SL7
Moor Wood
Garden Centre
Moor Copse
Moorend Common
RG9
Strawberry Grove
BEACON LA
CLAY LA
MOOR END
Bottom Wood
Roundwood Farm
Red Barn Farm
B482
80
81
82
90
91
92
93
1
2
3
4
5
6
7
8
182
172

171
161

D8
1 BANNER CT
2 ST GEORGES CT
3 FRYERS CT
4 ABERCROMBY CT
5 MOONSTONE CT

E7
1 DILWYN CT
2 PENDRILL HO
3 BARCLAY CT
4 GILBERT HO
5 CHILTERN CT
6 CUTLER'S CT
7 LEE CT
8 SANDOWN CT
9 CARRINGTON CT
10 Brow Bsns Ctr

F7
1 CEDAR TERR
2 WEST RICHARDSON ST
3 HAYDEN HO
4 NEEDHAM CT
5 EAST RICHARDSON ST
6 WESTBOURNE ST
7 VERNON BLDG
8 Wye River Bsns Ctr

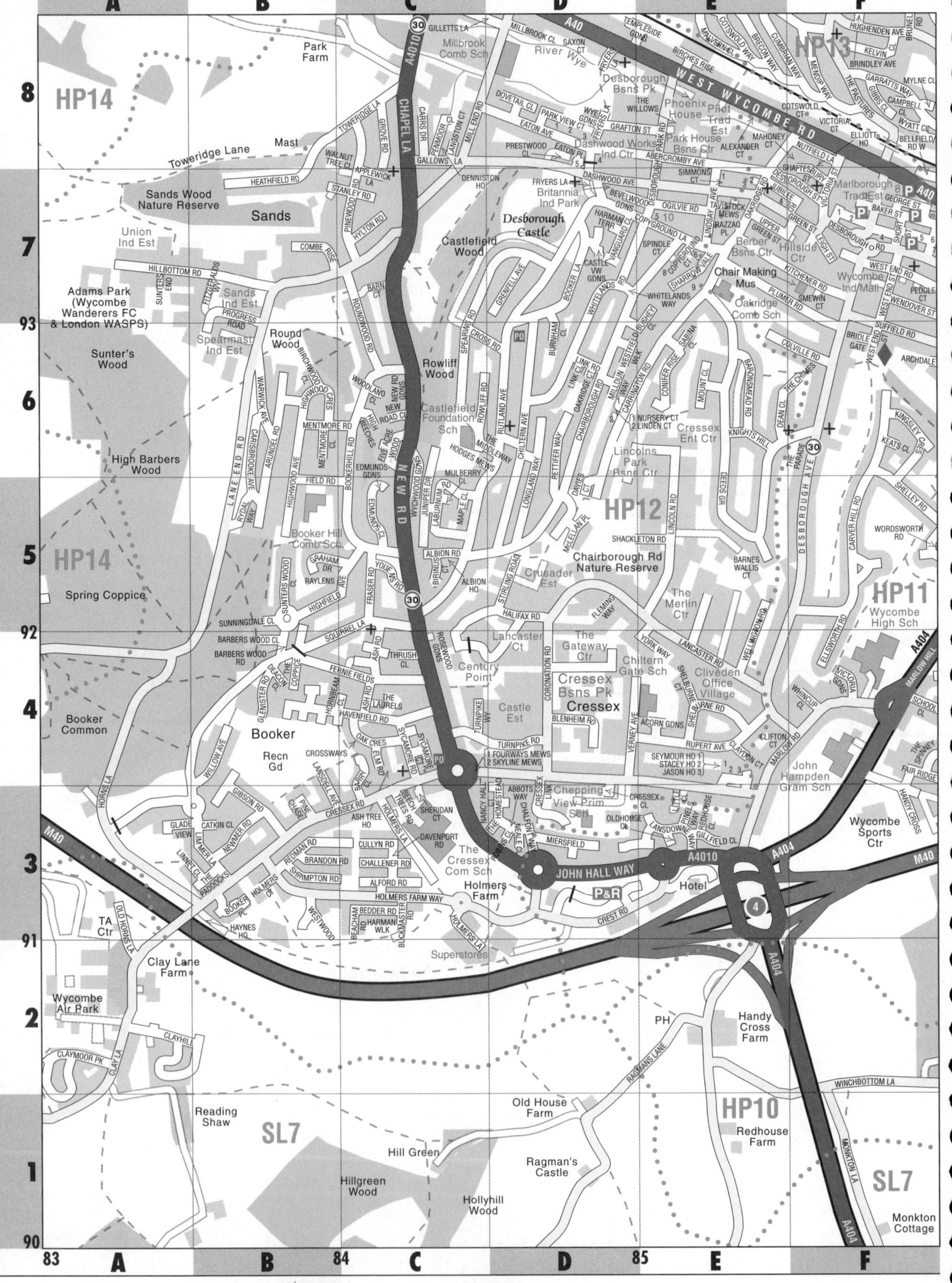

171
183

A7
1 BUCKINGHAM PL
2 COLLINS HO
3 DOVEHOUSE RD
4 THE GALLERIES
5 OXFORD ST
6 OCTAGON PAR
7 BULL LA
8 QUEEN SQ
9 WHITE HART ST
10 OCTAGON ARC
11 DOVECOT RD

B7
1 NIGHTINGALE CT
2 CHRISTIES CT
3 LIVERPOOL VICTORIA HO
4 WESLEY DENE
5 THAME HO
6 CASTLE PL
7 CHURCH SQ
8 SANDRINGHAM CT
9 CLARENCE CT
10 BENJAMIN HO
11 EDGECOTE HO
12 GREENWAY CT
13 BEECHWOOD PL
14 DESBOROUGH HO
15 CONEGRA CT
16 HAVENFIELD CT
17 Hamilton Prim Sch
18 Wycombe Mus & Gdn

162

C7
1 SOUTHBOURNE
2 PETERBOROUGH AVE
3 DONNYBROOK HO
4 ALBERT ST
5 TOWNFIELD RD
6 BOWSTRIDGE CT

174

F7
1 ARUNDEL HO
2 STIRLING HO
3 NOTTINGHAM HO
4 CARISBROOKE HO
5 HARLECH HO
6 BODIAM HO
7 WARWICK HO

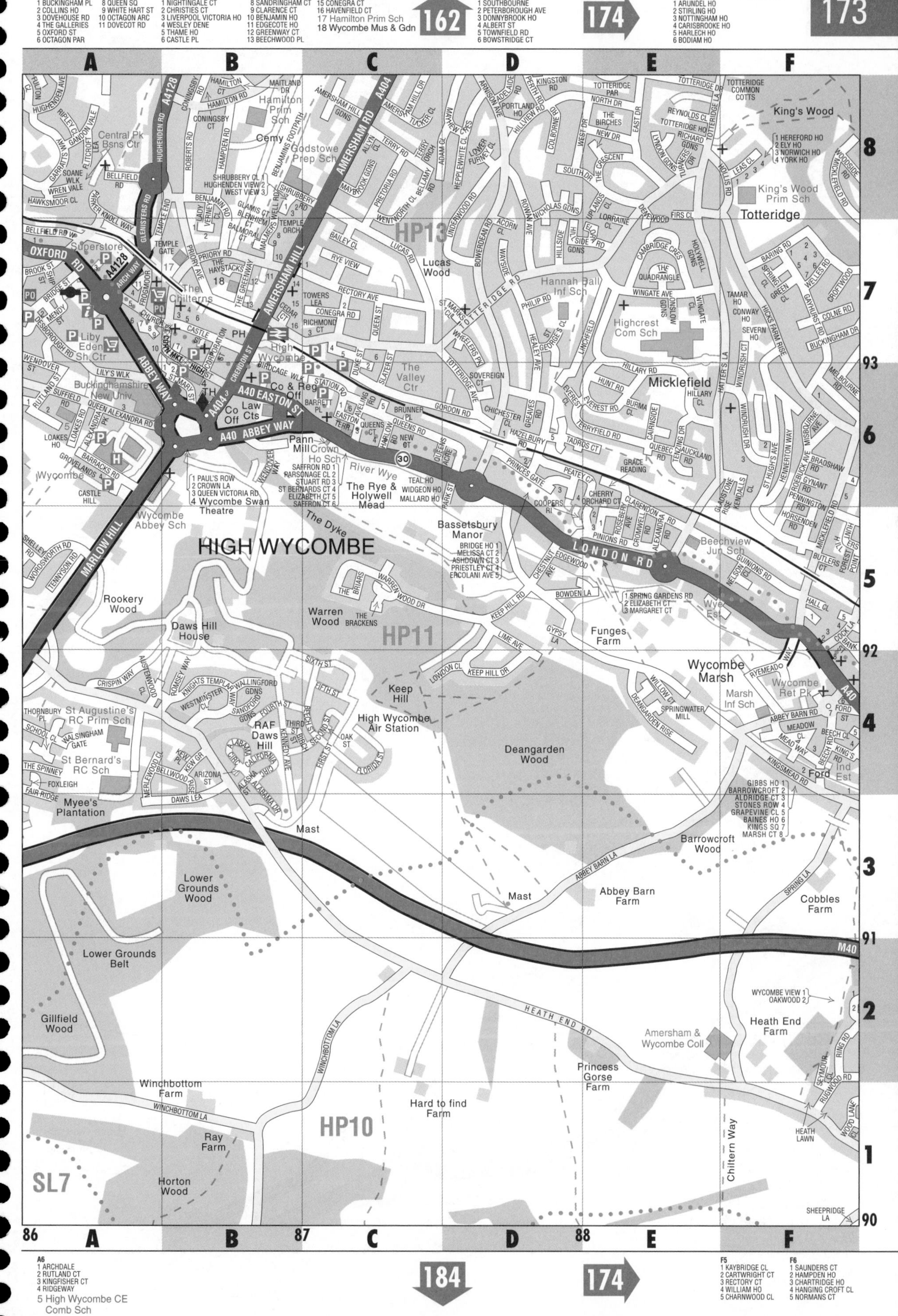

184

174

A6
1 ARCHDALE
2 RUTLAND CT
3 KINGFISHER CT
4 RIDGEWAY
5 High Wycombe CE Comb Sch

F5
1 KAYBRIDGE CL
2 CARTWRIGHT CT
3 RECTORY CT
4 WILLIAM HO
5 CHARNWOOD CL

F6
1 SAUNDERS CT
2 HAMPDEN HO
3 CHARTRIDGE HO
4 HANGING CROFT CL
5 NORMANS CT

173
163

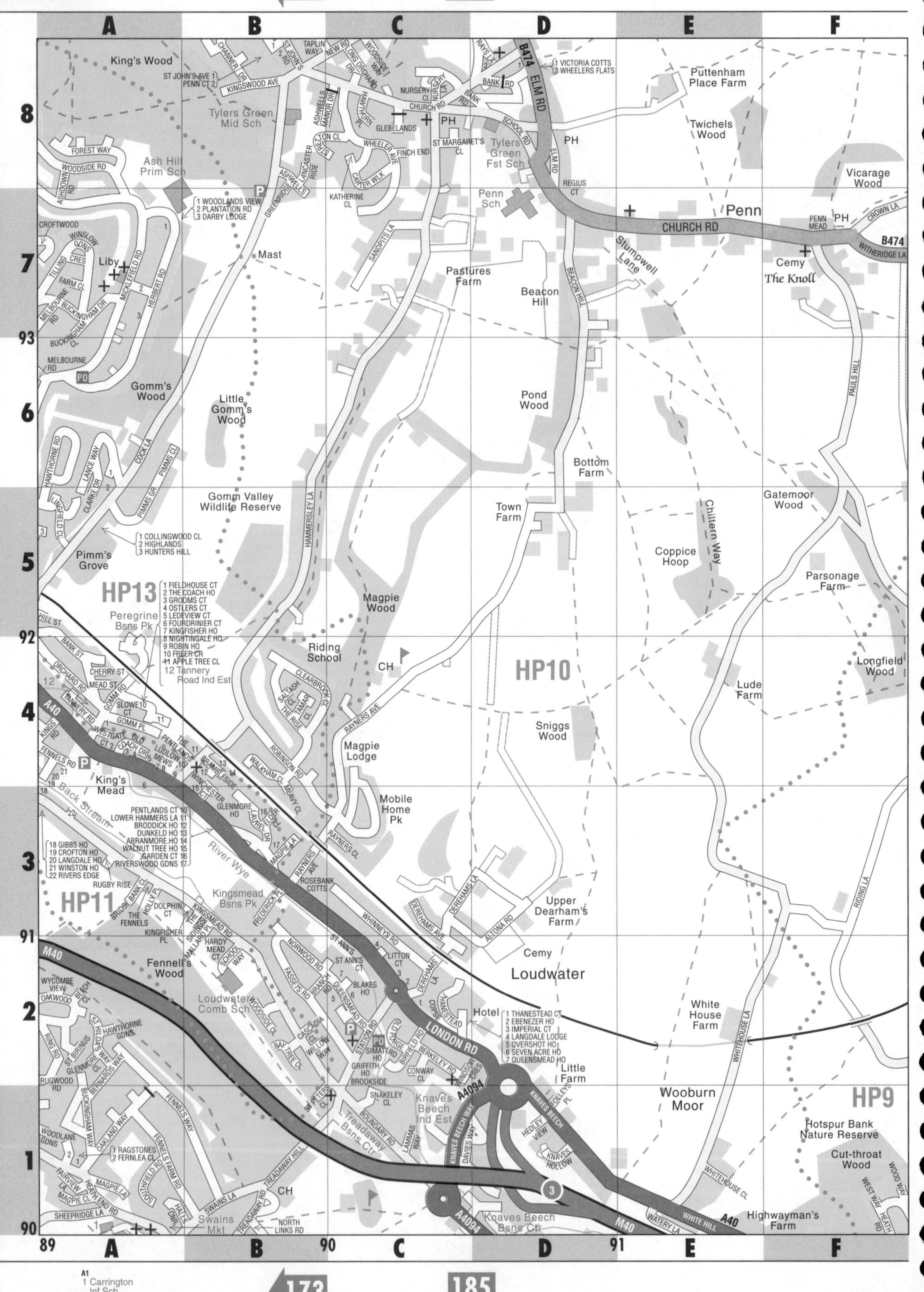

173
185

164
176

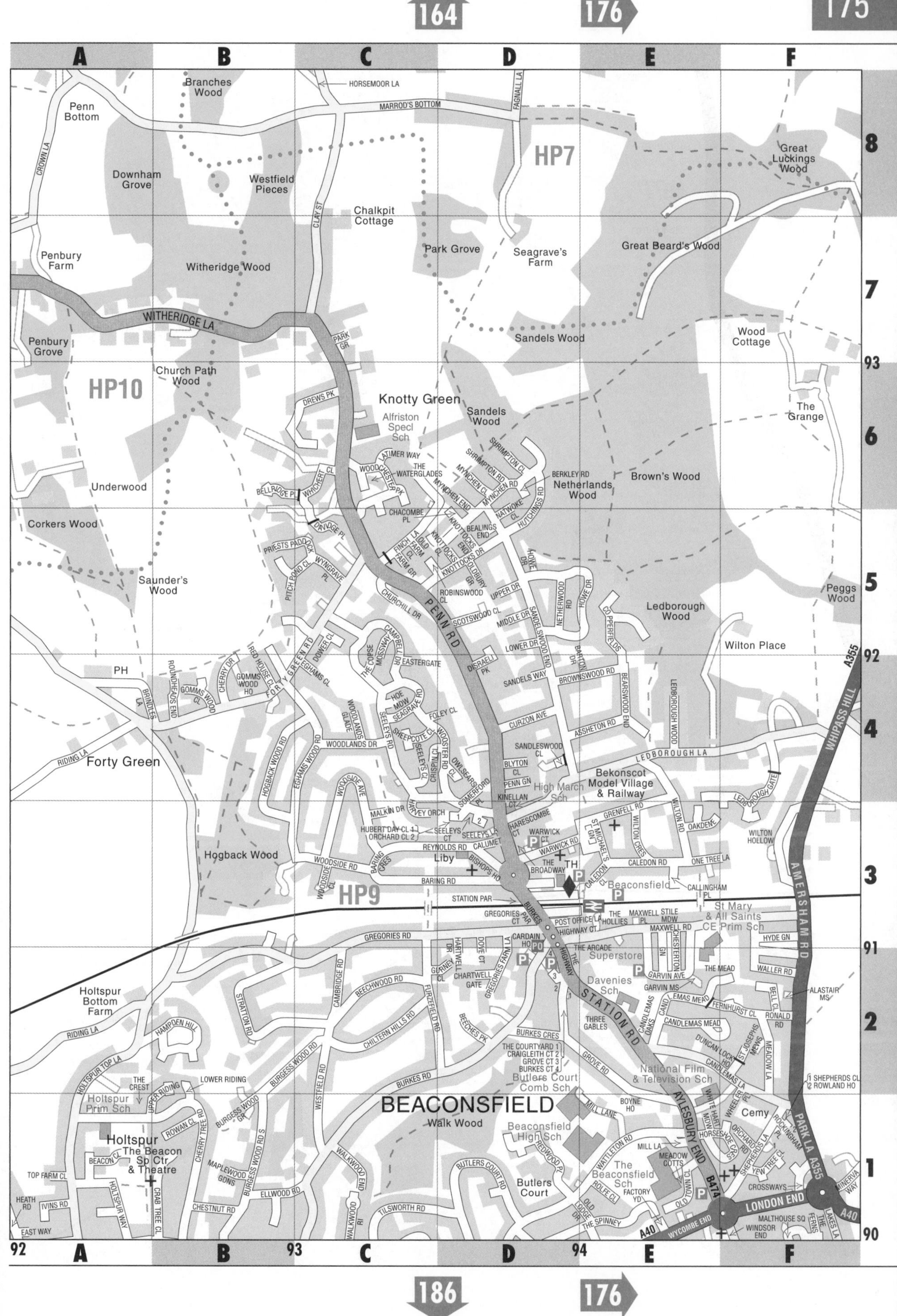

186
176

175
165

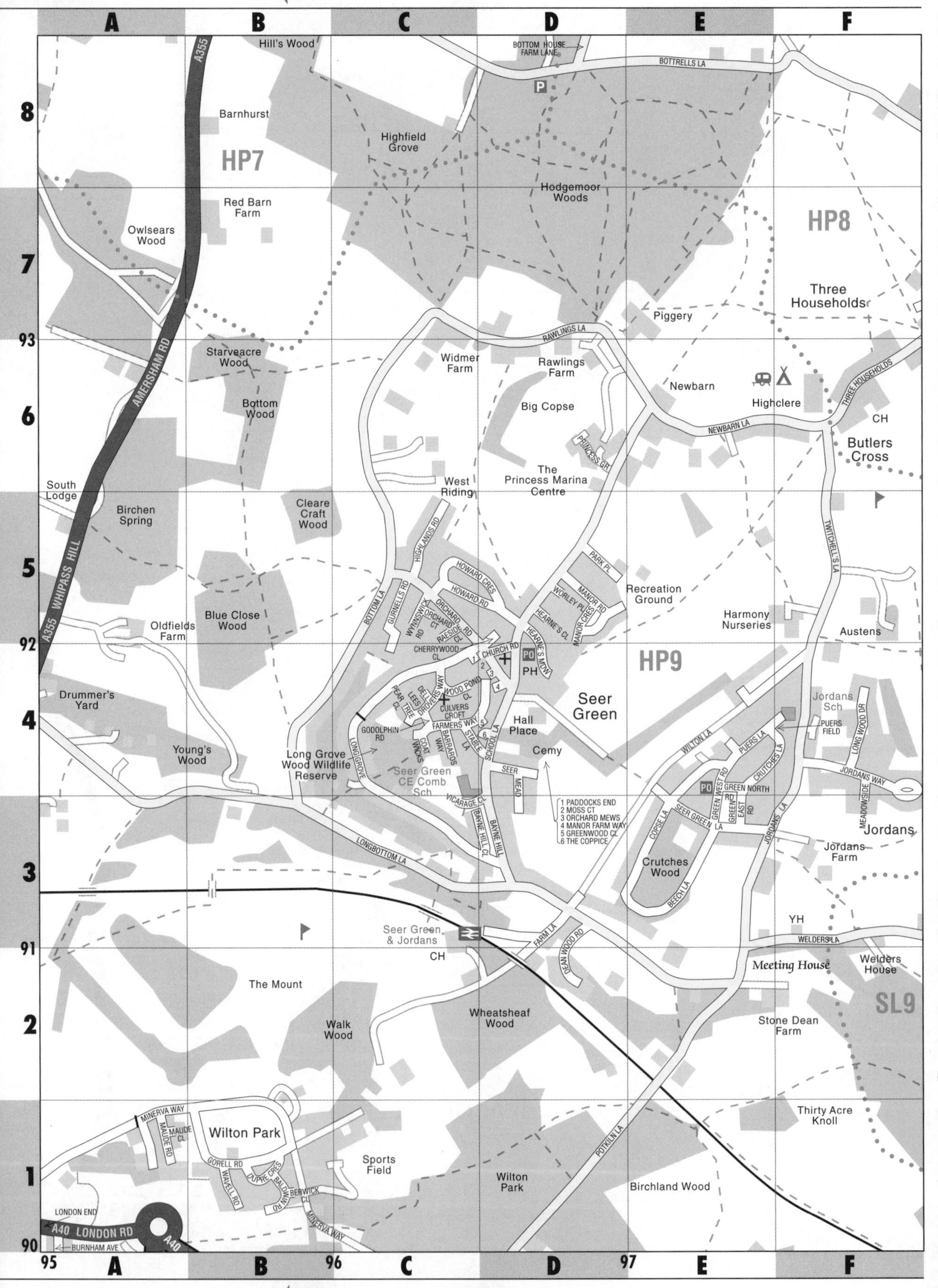

175
187

166

A B C D E F

Chalfont St Giles

HP8

HP9

SL9

Chalfont Common

Chalfont St Peter

Shrubs Wood

Chiltern Open Air Mus

Gorelands

Rowan Farm

Ashwell's Farm

Turners Wood

Chiltern Way

Milton's Cottage (Mus)

Chalfont St Giles Inf Sch

Chalfont St Giles Jun Sch

Allot Gdns

Top Farm

Cemy

Skipping's Farm

Chalfont Ctr for Epilepsy

Dibden Hill Farm

Narcot Farm

Bramleys Farm

Greyhound Training Track

Bowstridge

River Misbourne

Farm Wood

Grove Farm

Grove Lodge

Outfield Stables

Windmill Farm

Gravel Hill

Robertswood Comb Sch

Woodlands Farm

Pond Warren Wood

Chalfont Grove

Outfield Plantation

Grove Wood

Chalfont St Peter Inf Sch

The Chalfonts Com Coll

Chalfont L Ctr

Welder's Wood

Chalfonts & Gerrards Cross Com

Allot Gdns

Chalfont St Peter Jun Sch

Convent

The Ash Beds

Goldhill Common

Great Legs Wood

Layter's Green

Layter's Green Farm

Caravan Park

Malms Wood

Hogtrough Wood

1 MEADOW VIEW
2 HODGEMOOR VIEW
3 THREE HOUSEHOLDS
4 HOMEFARM CT

1 UP CNR
2 WILLIAM SHAKMAN HO
3 CHURCH FARM HO

BARTLETTS 1
EDITH BELL HO 2
HILL HOUSE CL 3

TUNMERS CT 1
TUNMERS HO 2

1 ELLWOOD HO
2 ST PETER'S CT
3 ACACIA HO

8 7 93 6 5 92 4 3 91 2 1 90

98 A B 99 C D 00 E F

188
178

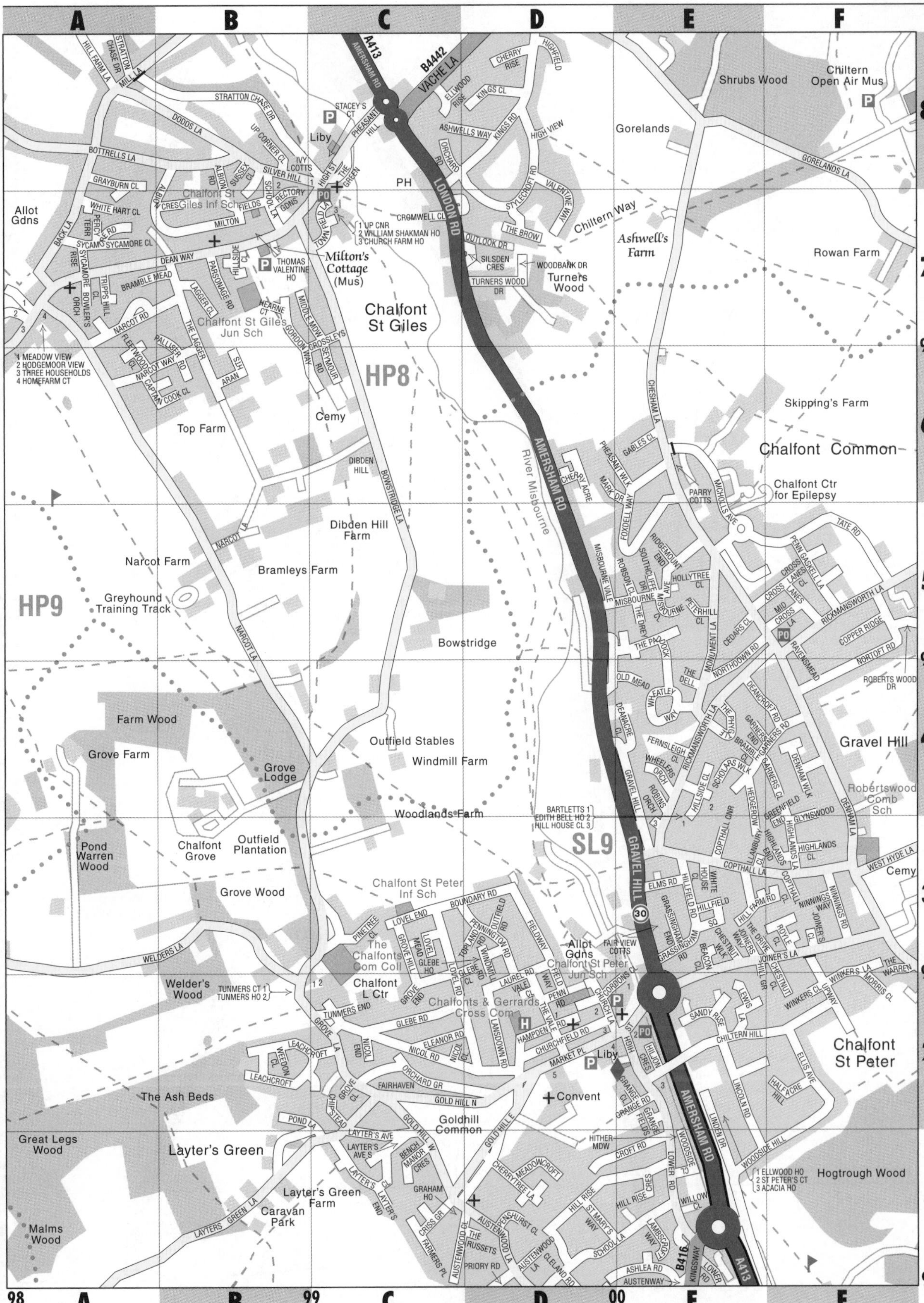

D2
1 STRINGERS COTTS
2 ADSTOCK MEWS
3 THE BROADWAY
4 BUCKINGHAM PAR
5 MARKET HO

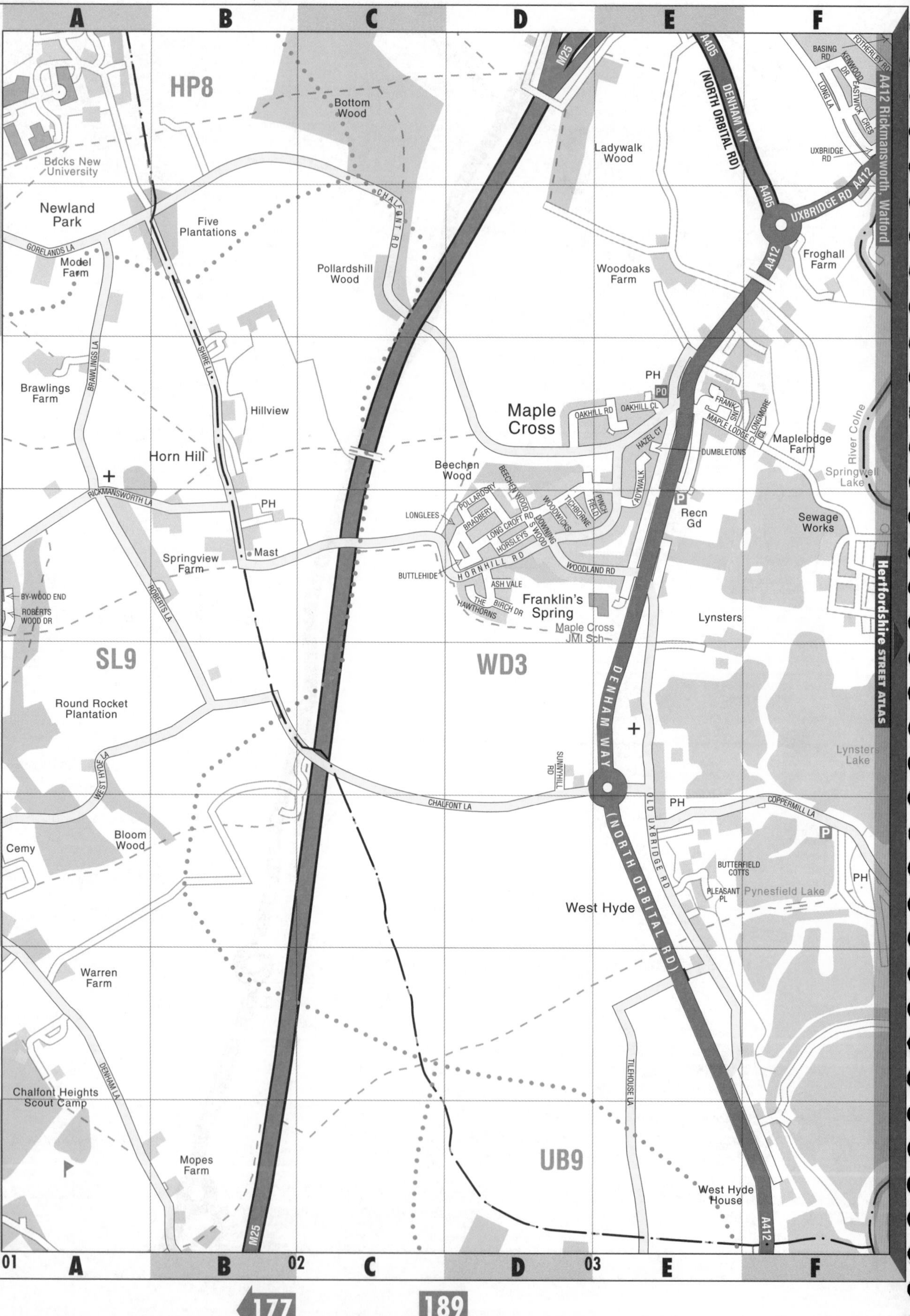
A
B
C
D
E
F
8
7
93
6
5
92
4
3
91
2
1
90
01
02
03
HP8
SL9
WD3
UB9
Bucks New University
Newland Park
GORELANDS LA
Model Farm
Five Plantations
Bottom Wood
CHALFONT RD
Pollardshill Wood
M25
Ladywalk Wood
A405
DENHAM WY
(NORTH ORBITAL RD)
UXBRIDGE RD
A412
BASING RD
KENWOOD DR
EASTWICK CRES
LONG LA
FOTHERLEY RD
UXBRIDGE RD
A412 Rickmansworth, Watford
Woodoaks Farm
Froghall Farm
Brawlings Farm
BRAWLINGS LA
SHIRE LA
Hillview
Horn Hill
PH
PO
Maple Cross
OAKHILL RD
OAKHILL CL
FRANK SN
LONGMORE CL
MAPLE LODGE CL
Maplelodge Farm
DUMBLETONS
HAZEL CT
River Colne
Springwell Lake
RICKMANSWORTH LA
Beechen Wood
BEECHEN WOOD
POLLARDSRY
BRADBERY
LONGLEES
LONG CROFT RD
WOODWICKS
DOWNING
TICHBORNE
PINCH FIELD
LADYWALK
HORSLEYS
S WOOD
Recn Gd
Sewage Works
Mast
Springview Farm
HORNHILL RD
WOODLAND RD
BUTTLEHIDE
ASH VALE
THE BIRCH DR
HAWTHORNS
Franklin's Spring
Maple Cross JMI Sch
BY-WOOD END
ROBERTS WOOD DR
ROBERTS LA
Lynsters
Herfordshire STREET ATLAS
DENHAM WAY
Round Rocket Plantation
WEST HYDE LA
SUNNYHILL RD
CHALFONT LA
Lynsters Lake
COPPERMILL LA
OLD UXBRIDGE RD
Bloom Wood
Cemy
BUTTERFIELD COTTS
PLEASANT PL
Pynesfield Lake
West Hyde
Warren Farm
DENHAM LA
TILEHOUSE LA
Chalfont Heights Scout Camp
Mopes Farm
West Hyde House

168
180

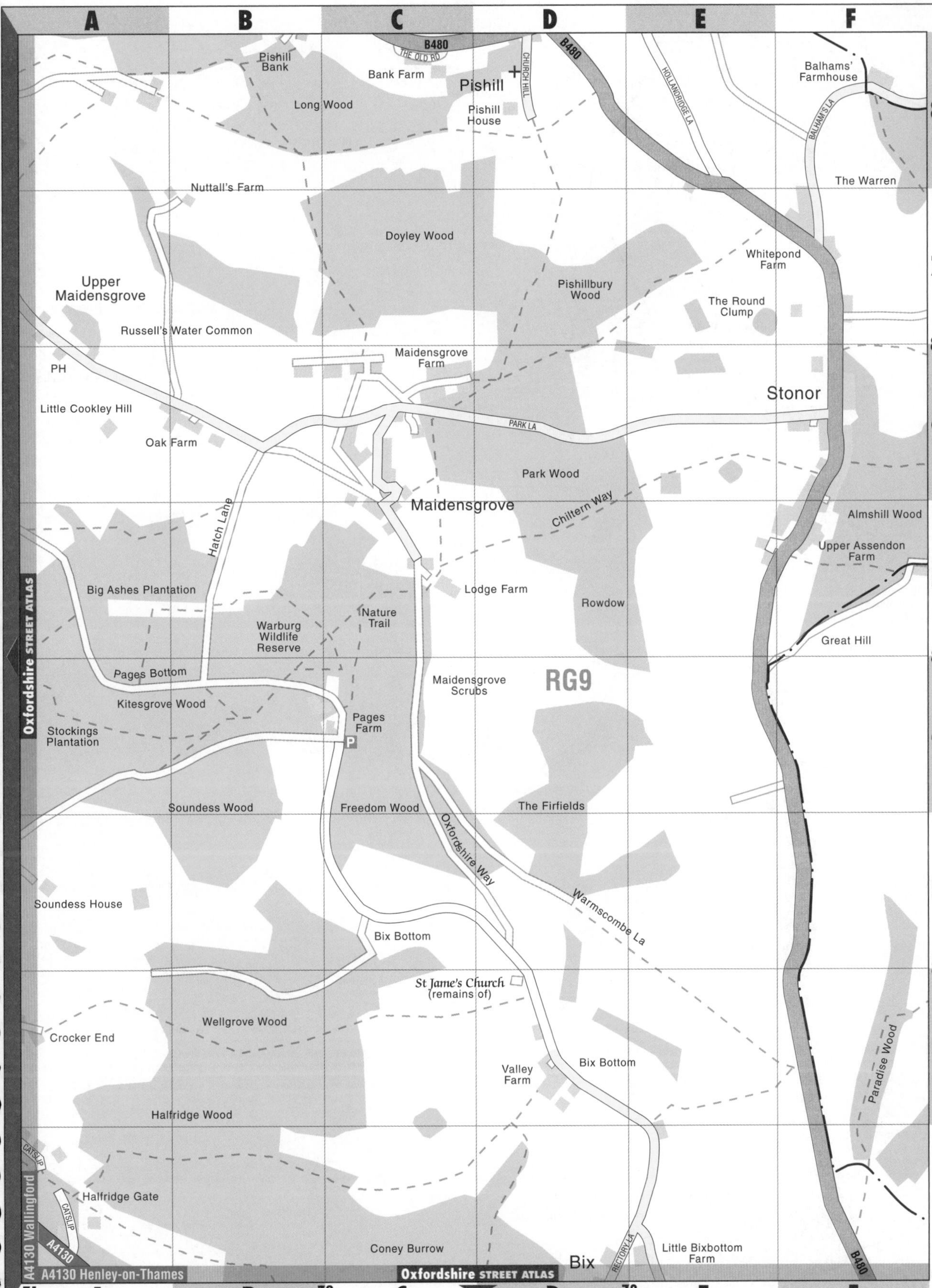

A B C D E F

B480
THE OLD RD
Pishill Bank
Bank Farm
Pishill
CHURCH HILL
B480
HOLLANDRIDGE LA
Balhams' Farmhouse
BALHAM'S LA
8
Long Wood
Pishill House
The Warren
Nuttall's Farm
Doyley Wood
Whitepond Farm
7
Upper Maidensgrove
Pishillbury Wood
The Round Clump
Russell's Water Common
89
PH
Maidensgrove Farm
Stonor
Little Cookley Hill
PARK LA
6
Oak Farm
Park Wood
Maidensgrove
Chiltern Way
Almshill Wood
Hatch Lane
Upper Assendon Farm
5
Big Ashes Plantation
Lodge Farm
Rowdow
Nature Trail
Warburg Wildlife Reserve
Great Hill
88
Pages Bottom
Maidensgrove Scrubs
RG9
Kitesgrove Wood
Pages Farm
Stockings Plantation
P
4
Soundess Wood
Freedom Wood
The Firfields
Oxfordshire Way
3
Soundess House
Warmscombe La
Bix Bottom
87
St Jame's Church (remains of)
Wellgrove Wood
Paradise Wood
Crocker End
2
Valley Farm
Bix Bottom
Halfridge Wood
CATSLIP
Halfridge Gate
CATSLIP
1
A4130 Wallingford
A4130
Coney Burrow
RECTORY LA
Little Bixbottom Farm
Bix
B480
A4130 Henley-on-Thames
Oxfordshire STREET ATLAS
86
71 A B 72 C D 73 E F

180

179
169

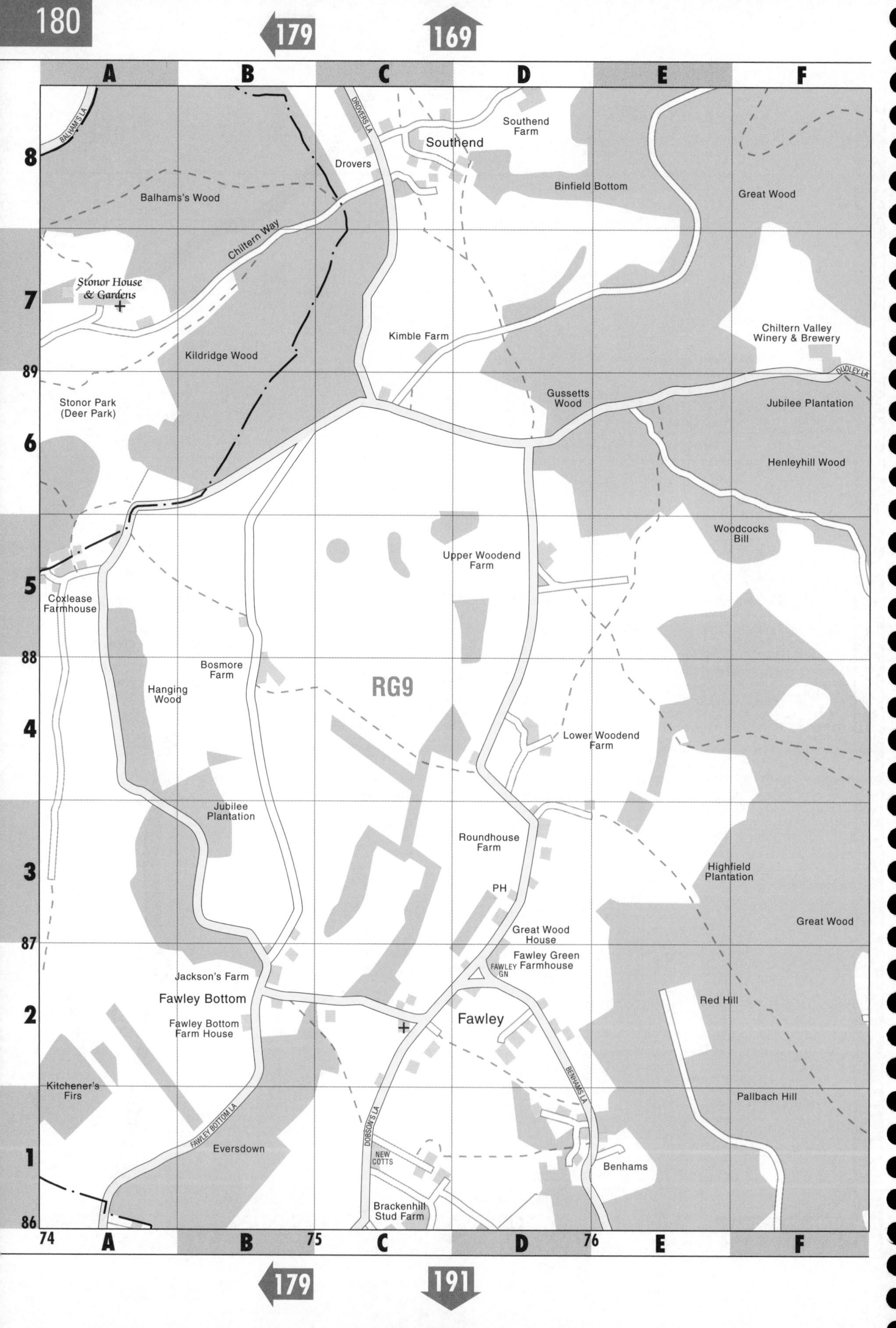

179
191

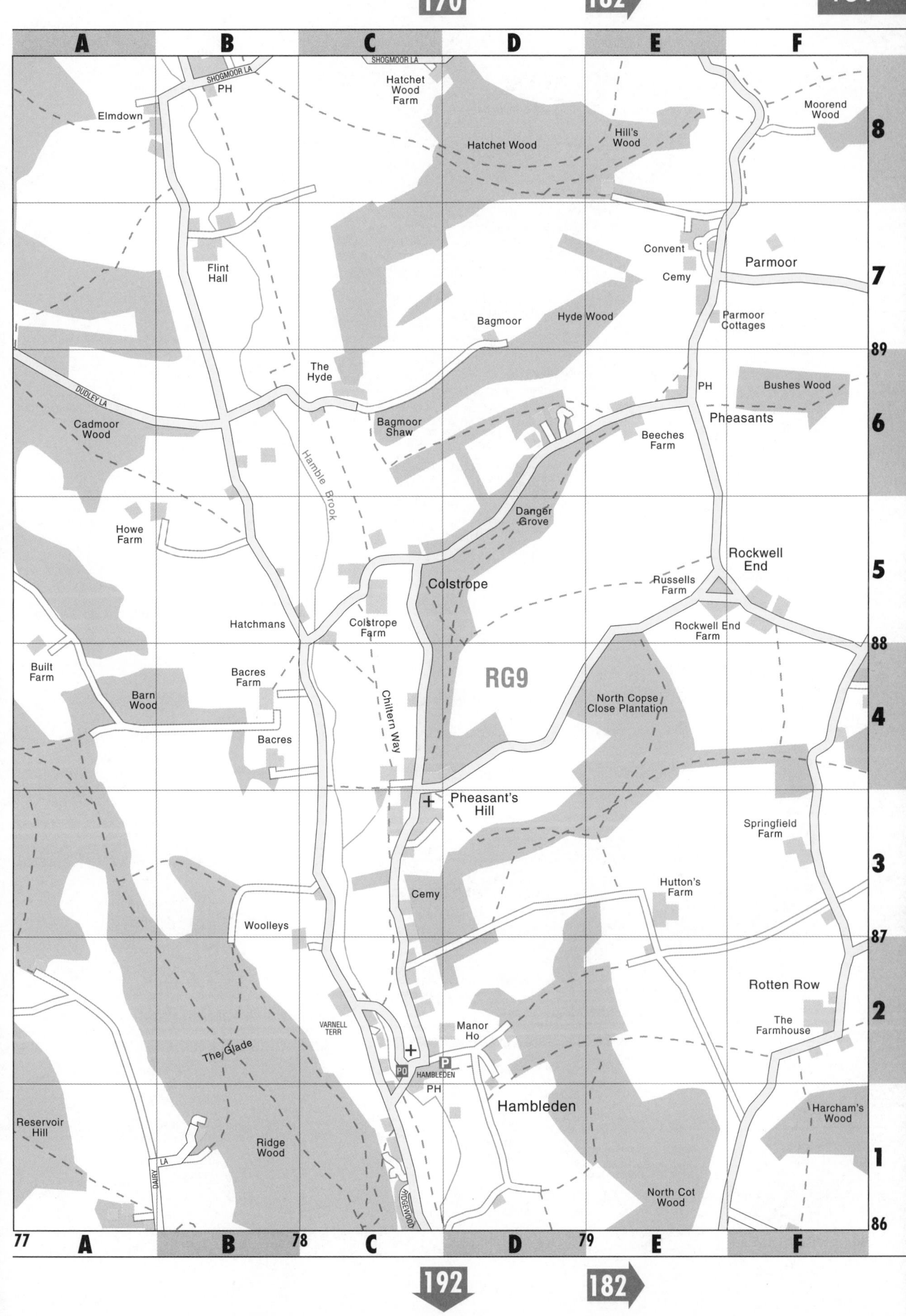
A
B
C
D
E
F
SHOGMOOR LA
PH
Hatchet Wood Farm
Moorend Wood
8
Elmdown
Hill's Wood
Hatchet Wood
Convent
Flint Hall
Parmoor
Cemy
7
Bagmoor
Hyde Wood
Parmoor Cottages
89
The Hyde
PH
Bushes Wood
DUDLEY LA
Cadmoor Wood
Bagmoor Shaw
Pheasants
6
Beeches Farm
Hamble Brook
Danger Grove
Howe Farm
Rockwell End
5
Colstrope
Russells Farm
Hatchmans
Colstrope Farm
Rockwell End Farm
88
Built Farm
Bacres Farm
RG9
Barn Wood
Chiltern Way
North Copse Close Plantation
4
Bacres
Pheasant's Hill
Springfield Farm
3
Hutton's Farm
Cemy
Woolleys
87
Rotten Row
2
VARNELL TERR
Manor Ho
The Farmhouse
The Glade
HAMBLEDEN
PH
Hambleden
Harcham's Wood
Reservoir Hill
Ridge Wood
1
DAIRY LA
RIDGEWOOD
North Cot Wood
86
77
78
79

181 171

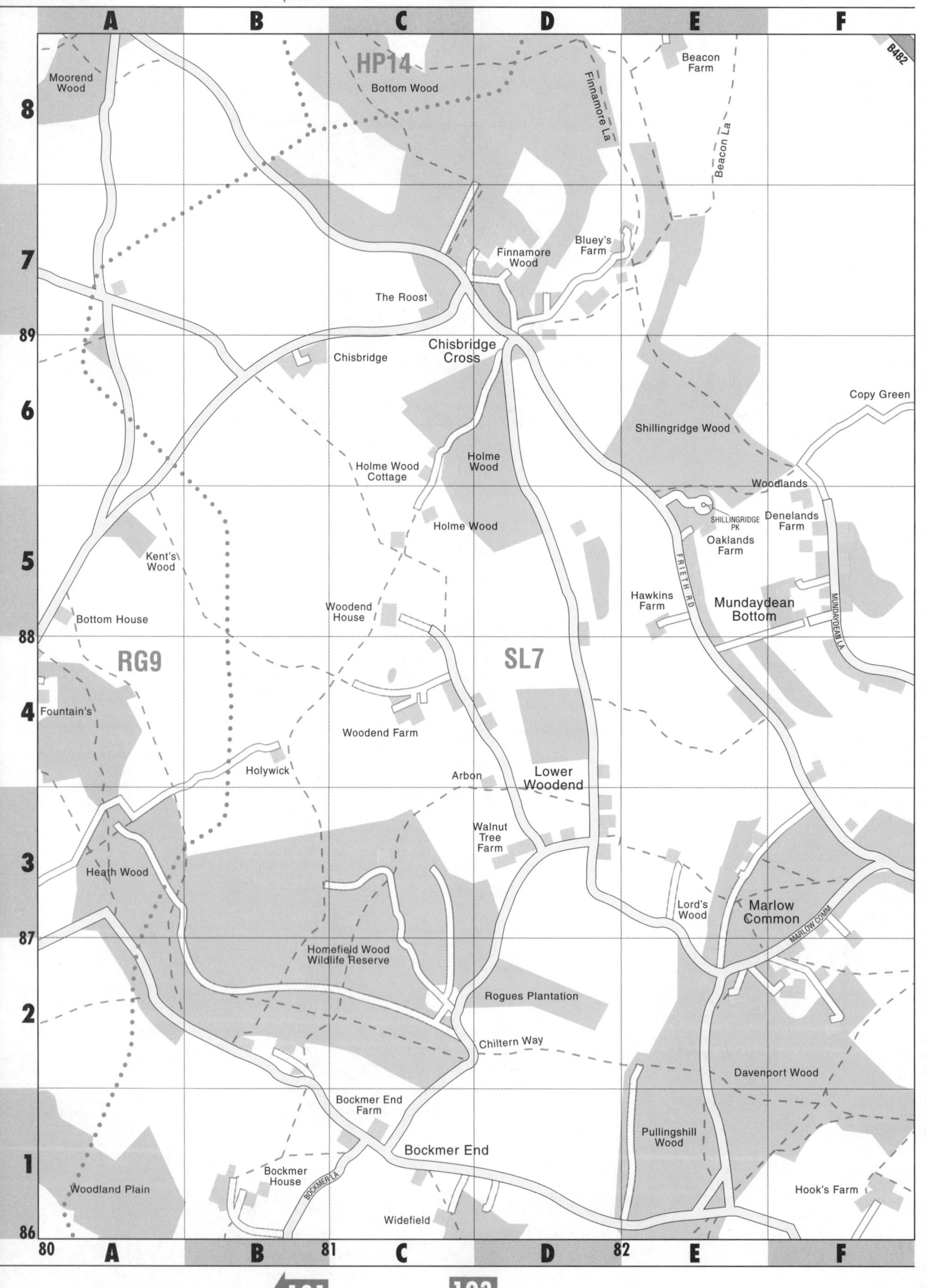

181 193

172
184

194
184

D1
1 PORTLANDS MEWS
2 MALTHOUSE WAY
3 BARLEY WAY

D2
1 MAYORFIELD HO
2 LAURANCE CT
3 ORAM CT
4 CHERRY TREE HO
5 BRAEMAR CT
6 CHISWICK LODGE
7 Liston Ct Sh Arcade
8 POTTS PL
9 THE COURTYARD

E1
1 MARLOW HO
2 TEMPLARS PL
3 TIERNEY CT
4 DUNSTABLE HO

E2
1 THE COURTYARD
2 BARONS CT
3 BEECH CT
4 VICTORIA CT
5 GLADE HO
6 WINTER CT
7 LEIGHTON HO
8 ST JAMES CTYD
9 LISTON HO
10 CROMWELL GDNS
11 MONKSWOOD CT
12 CHARLOTTE WAY
13 LITTLE BOLTONS
14 PENN CT

F3
1 EASTWOOD CT
2 WILTSHIRE RD
3 MILE ELM
4 BEECHINGSTOKE
5 BUTLER CT
6 BYRON CL
7 MEAD CL
8 WILLOWMEAD RD
9 WILLOWMEAD SQ
10 WILLOWMEAD CL
11 ROMNEY CT
12 SHELLEY RD

A B C D E F
HP10
Chiltern Way
Horton Wood
Bloom Wood
New Farm
PH
Sheepridge
SHEEPRIDGE LA
Chiltern Way
Bloom Farm
WINCHBOTTOM LA
MONKTON LA
Merton's Hole Cottage
Pigeon House Farm
A404
Fern House
Cemy
FERN COTTS
FERN LA
Fern
SL7
MONKTON LA
PUMP LA N
Wilton Farm
MARLOW RD
Little Marlow CE Inf Sch
Little Marlow
Well End
ABBEY MEAD
ELM LA
ABBEY RD
WELL END COTTS
A4155
Coronach
Pump Farm
PUMP LA S
PH
CHURCH RD
SCHOOL LA
POUND LA
THE MOOR
Manor House
CHURCH RD
A4155
STAPLETON CL
SL8
SPADE OAK MDW
COLDMOORHOLME LA
THE AVENUE
FARM RD
The Abbey
THE DRIVE
PH
MILE ELM
1 BUTLER CT
2 BRISTOW CT
3 GRATTON CT
4 DOUGLAS CT
5 RAVENSCOURT
SPADE OAK FARM
UPPER THAMES WAY
Abbotsbrook
LC
LC
WILTSHIRE RD
PEACOCK RD
THE CHASE
Westhorpe Park
Sewage Works
The Moor
Westhorpe House
GUNTHORPE RD
KILN CROFT CL
THE CROFT
PARKWAY
River Thames
Westhorpe Farm
6 HOBART CT
7 MARCHANT CT
8 WASHINGTON CT
9 SWALLOW HO
10 SWIFT HO
SAVILL WAY
FOURTH AVE
The Thames Path
Noah's House
Cock Marsh
FIRST AVE
Patches
SL6
Stone House
Coney Copse
A404
RIVERWOODS DR
STONEHOUSE LA
WINTER HILL
GIBRALTAR LA
TERRY'S LA
BRADCUTTS LA
RIVERWOOD AVE
Winter Hill
Harvest Moon
Greythatch
8
7
89
6
5
88
4
3
87
2
1
86
86 87 88

174
186

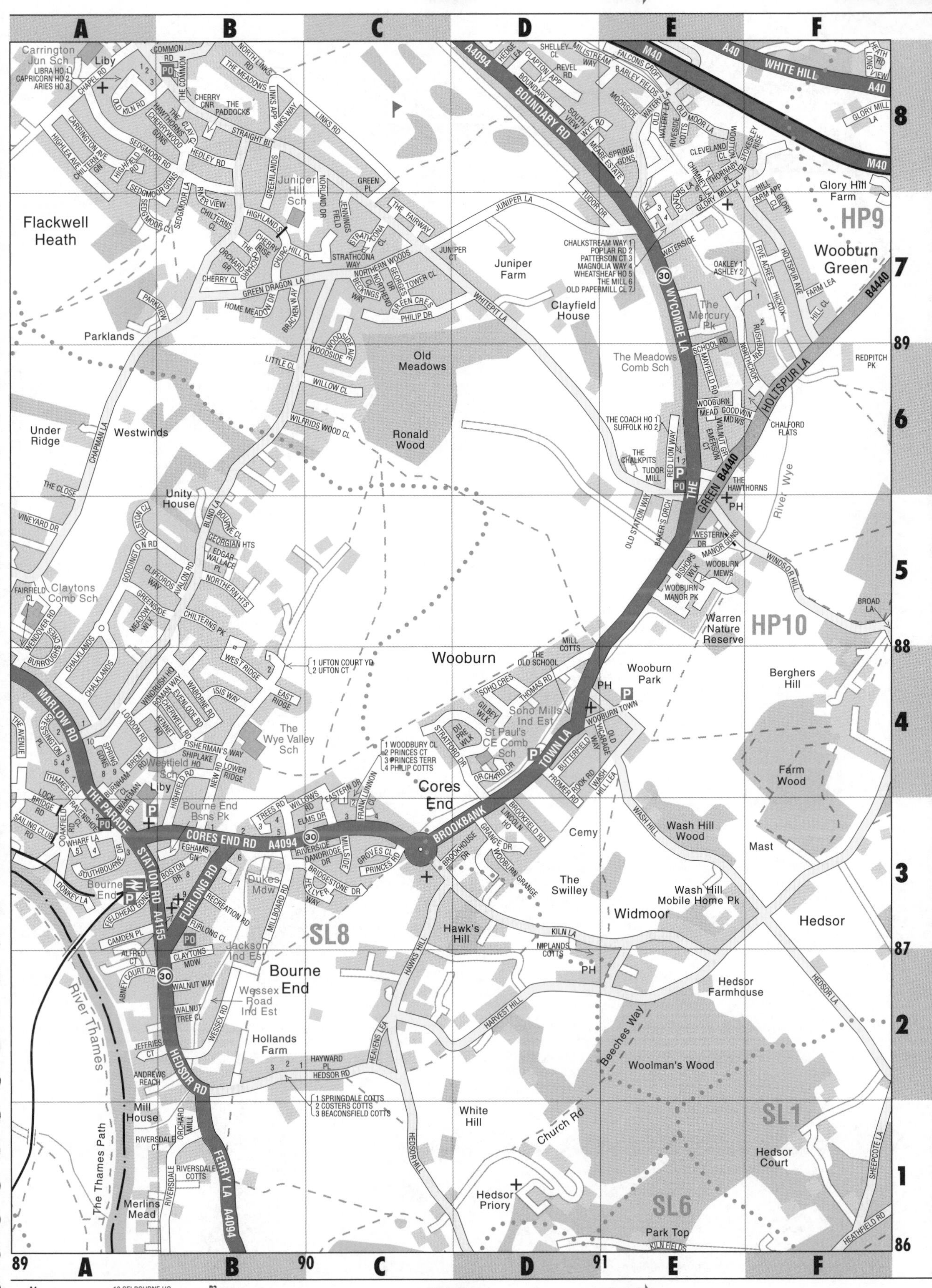

196
186

A4
1 ROWAN HO
2 CRESSINGTON CT
3 COKERS CT
4 RUSSEL HO
5 RAY HO
6 GRANT HO
7 PARADE CT
8 ORCHARD HO
9 BAILEY HO
10 SELBOURNE HO

A3
1 HOWARD CT
2 WYE CT
3 THAMESBOURNE MEWS
4 WALDENS CL
5 THE ROSERY

B3
1 FARRIER CT
2 MOUNT PLEASANT COTTS
3 SYCAMORE CL
4 THE WILLOWS
5 THE MAPLES
6 MEADOW BANK
7 THE COURTYARD
8 EGHAMS CT
9 HYLAND HO

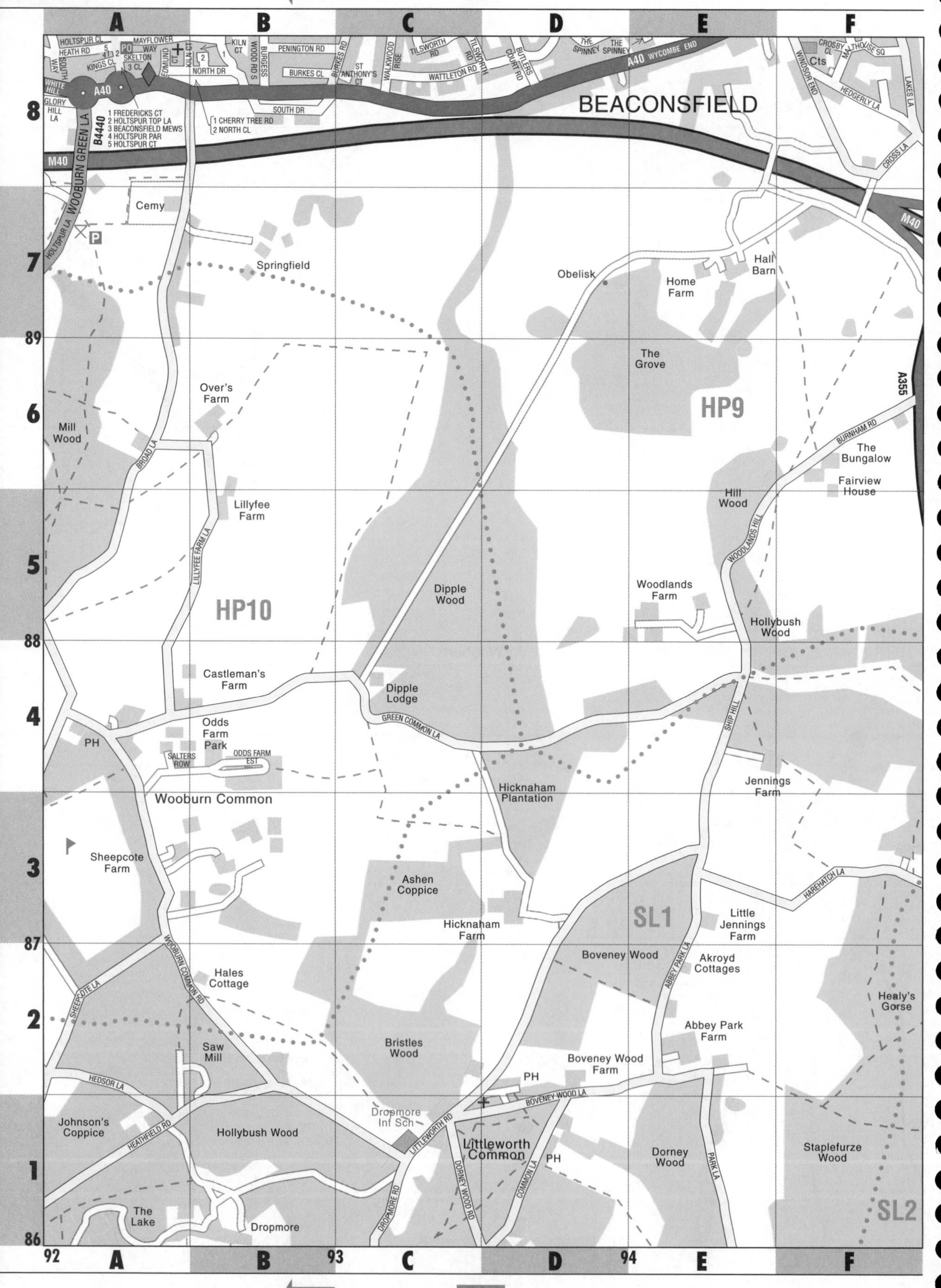
A
B
C
D
E
F
8
7
89
6
5
88
4
3
87
2
1
86
92
93
94
BEACONSFIELD
A40 WYCOMBE END
M40
A355
HP9
HP10
SL1
SL2
HOLTSPUR CL
HEATH RD
KINGS CL
MAYFLOWER WAY
SKELTON
3 CL
PO
EDMUND CT
KILN CT
KILN CT
NORTH DR
WOOD RD S
BURGESS
PENINGTON RD
BURKES CL
BURKES RD
ST ANTHONY'S CT
WALKWOOD RISE
TILSWORTH RD
TILSWORTH RD
WATTLETON RD
COURT RD
BUTLERS
THE SPINNEY
THE SPINNEY
SOUTH DR
WHITE HILL
GLORY HILL LA
B4440
1 FREDERICKS CT
2 HOLTSPUR TOP LA
3 BEACONSFIELD MEWS
4 HOLTSPUR PAR
5 HOLTSPUR CT
1 CHERRY TREE RD
2 NORTH CL
WOOBURN GREEN LA
HOLTSPUR LA
CROSBY CL
MALTHOUSE SQ
Cts
WINDSOR END
HEDGERLY LA
LAKES LA
CROSS LA
Cemy
P
Springfield
Obelisk
Home Farm
Hall Barn
The Grove
Over's Farm
Mill Wood
BROAD LA
BURNHAM RD
The Bungalow
Fairview House
Hill Wood
Lillyfee Farm
LILLYFEE FARM LA
WOODLANDS HILL
Dipple Wood
Woodlands Farm
Hollybush Wood
Castleman's Farm
Dipple Lodge
GREEN COMMON LA
SHIP HILL
Odds Farm Park
PH
SALTERS ROW
ODDS FARM EST
Hicknaham Plantation
Jennings Farm
Wooburn Common
Sheepcote Farm
Ashen Coppice
HAREHATCH LA
Hicknaham Farm
Little Jennings Farm
Boveney Wood
ABBEY PARK LA
Akroyd Cottages
SHEEPCOTE LA
WOOBURN COMMON RD
Hales Cottage
Healy's Gorse
Bristles Wood
Abbey Park Farm
Saw Mill
Boveney Wood Farm
HEDSOR LA
PH
BOVENEY WOOD LA
Dropmore Inf Sch
Johnson's Coppice
HEATHFIELD RD
Hollybush Wood
LITTLEWORTH RD
Littleworth Common
PH
Dorney Wood
Staplefurze Wood
DROPMORE RD
DORNEY WOOD RD
COMMON LA
PARK LA
The Lake
Dropmore

176
188

A B C D E F

8
7
89
6
5
88
4
3
87
2
1
86

Stampwell Farm
Birchland Wood
Lower Pyebushes
Pyebushes
Birch Wood
Hotel
Hyde Farm
Mast
HP9
Wapsey's Wood
Green Broom
Mast
Further Warren Wood
SL9
Burtley Wood
Bower Wood Cotts
Cave Wood
Works
Birchen Spring Coppice
Hillmotts Farm
Moat Farm
Slade Farm
Slade Wood
Bower Wood
Hillmotts Furze
Manor Farm
Hedgerley Green
Dorney Bottom
SL1
Mount Pleasant Farm
Sutton's Wood
Shirley Close
Nature Reserve
Pennlands Wood
Hedgerley
PH
Pennlands Farm
SL2
Court Farm
Church Wood
Kiln Wood
Summerlins Wood
PH
Hanging Wood
Hedgerley Hill
Hedgerley Park
Egypt Woods
Heathfield Wood
One Pin Farm
School Wood
Hedgerley Park Farm

A40
A355
LONDON RD
OXFORD RD
M40
DORNEY HILL N
DORNEY HILL S
COLINSWOOD RD
BURNHAM AVE
HEDGERLEY LA
PYEBUSH LA
MINERVA WAY
POTKILN LA
BEACONSFIELD COMMON LA
VILLAGE LA
WAPSEYS LA
HAREHATCH LA
KILN LA
ANDREW HILL LA
HILL VIEW
THE CHURCH HOLT
COPPICE WAY
STEVENSON RD
GREGORY RD
JONES WAY
ELKINS RD
BLACK GROVE HO
COTTAGE PARK RD
ROBERT RD
HEDGERLEY HILL
OLD NURSERY CT
PO
HOLLYBUSH CNR
PARISH LA
LONGFIELD
EGYPT LA
EGYPT WOOD COTTS
COLINSWOOD
CHRISTMAS LA
TIMBERWOOD
WOOD END CL
ONE PIN LA
COLLUM GREEN RD
GYPSY LA
WOODLAND GLADE
HEATHERSIDE
ROMSEY DR
GDNS
STOKE WOOD
COLLEY HILL LA

95 A B 96 C D 97 E F

198
188

187
177

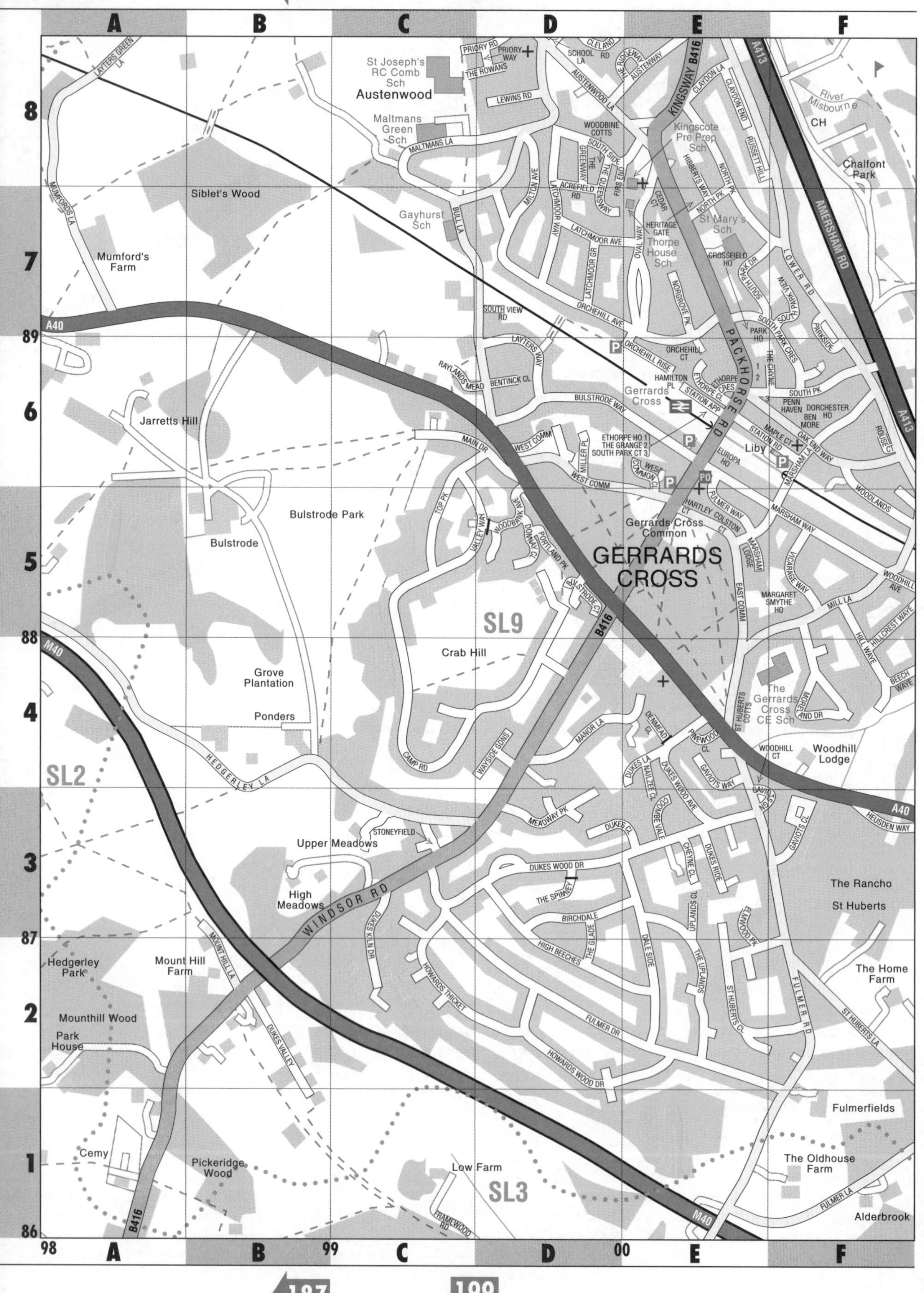
A
B
C
D
E
F
8
7
89
6
5
88
4
3
87
2
1
86
98
99
00
St Joseph's RC Comb Sch
Austenwood
Maltmans Green Sch
Siblet's Wood
Gayhurst Sch
Mumford's Farm
Kingscote Pre Prep Sch
St Mary's Sch
Thorpe House Sch
River Misbourne
CH
Chalfont Park
Jarretts Hill
Gerrards Cross
Liby
Bulstrode Park
Bulstrode
Gerrards Cross Common
GERRARDS CROSS
SL9
Crab Hill
Grove Plantation
Ponders
SL2
The Gerrards Cross CE Sch
Woodhill Lodge
Upper Meadows
High Meadows
The Rancho
St Huberts
Hedgerley Park
Mount Hill Farm
The Home Farm
Mounthill Wood
Park House
Fulmerfields
Cemy
Pickeridge Wood
Low Farm
SL3
The Oldhouse Farm
Alderbrook
A40
M40
A413
B416
AMERSHAM RD
KINGSWAY
PACKHORSE RD
WINDSOR RD
LAYTERS GREEN LA
MUMFORDS LA
PRIORY RD
PRIORY WAY
THE ROWANS
LEWINS RD
CLELAND RD
SCHOOL LA
AUSTENWOOD LA
THE RIDGEWAY
AUSTENWAY
CLAYDON LA
CLAYDON END
RUSSETT HILL
MALTMANS LA
WOODBINE COTTS
SOUTH SIDE
THE GREENWAY
THE QUEENSWAY
FIRS END
CEDAR CT
HIBBERTS WAY
NORTH PK
ACREFIELD RD
MILTON AVE
LATCHMOOR WAY
LATCHMOOR AVE
LATCHMOOR GR
BULL LA
OVAL WAY
HERITAGE GATE
CROSSFIELD HO
NORGROVE PK
SOUTH PARK DR
SOUTH PARK VIEW
LOWER RD
ORCHEHILL AVE
SOUTH VIEW RD
LAYTERS WAY
ORCHEHILL RISE
ORCHEHILL CT
PARK HO
SOUTH PARK CRES
PARKSIDE
THE CHYNE
RAYLANDS MEAD
BENTINCK CL
HAMILTON PL
ETHORPE CL
ETHORPE CRES
STATION APP
SOUTH PK
PENN HAVEN
DORCHESTER HO
BEN MORE
BULSTRODE WAY
ROUSE CT
MAPLE CT
STATION RD
OAK END WAY
ETHORPE HO 1
THE GRANGE 2
SOUTH PARK CT 3
MAIN DR
WEST COMM
MILLER PL
EUROPA HO
MARSHAM LA
WEST COMMON CL
WOODLANDS
TOP PK
VALLEY WAY
WOODBANK AVE
DONNAY CL
PORTLAND PK
FULMER WAY
HARTLEY CT
COLSTON CT
MARSHAM WAY
MARSHAM LODGE
VICARAGE WAY
WOODHILL AVE
BULSTRODE CT
EAST COMM
MARGARET SMYTHE HO
MILL LA
HILLCREST WAYE
HILL WAYE
BEECH WAYE
ST HUBERTS COTTS
MORELAND DR
CAMP RD
WAYSIDE GDNS
MANOR LA
DENMEAD CL
PINEWOOD CL
WOODHILL CT
HEDGERLEY LA
DUKES LA
NAILZEE CL
DUKES WOOD AVE
GAVIOTS WAY
GAVIOTS GN
GAVIOTS CL
HEUSDEN WAY
MEADWAY PK
COOMBE VALE
DUKES CL
STONEYFIELD
CHEYNE CL
DUKES RIDE
DUKES WOOD DR
THE SPINNEY
UPLANDS CL
ELMWOOD PK
BIRCHDALE
DUKES KILN DR
HIGH BEECHES
THE GLADE
DALE SIDE
THE UPLANDS
HOWARDS THICKET
ST HUBERTS CL
FULMER RD
FULMER DR
HOWARDS WOOD DR
ST HUBERTS LA
MOUNT HILL LA
DUKES VALLEY
FRAMEWOOD RD
FULMER LA

178
190

200
190

189

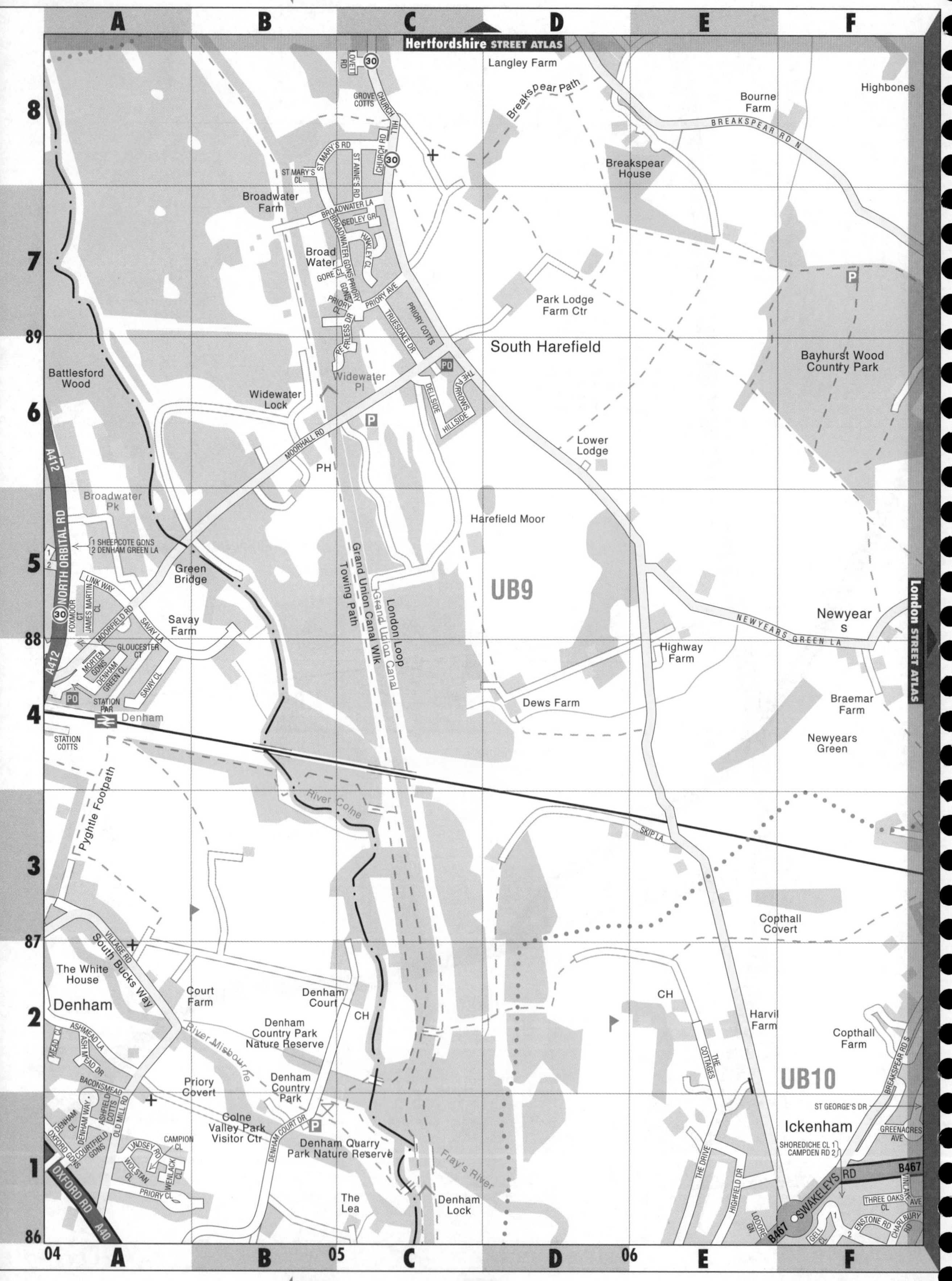

Hertfordshire STREET ATLAS
London STREET ATLAS
Langley Farm
Breakspear Path
Bourne Farm
Highbones
BREAKSPEAR RD N
Breakspear House
Broadwater Farm
Broad Water
Park Lodge Farm Ctr
South Harefield
Battlesford Wood
Widewater Lock
Widewater Pl
Bayhurst Wood Country Park
Lower Lodge
MOORHALL RD
PH
Broadwater Pk
Harefield Moor
1 SHEEPCOTE GDNS
2 DENHAM GREEN LA
NORTH ORBITAL RD
A412
UB9
Green Bridge
Grand Union Canal Wlk
Towing Path
Grand Union Canal
London Loop
Savay Farm
Newyears
NEWYEARS GREEN LA
Highway Farm
Dews Farm
Braemar Farm
Newyears Green
Denham
STATION COTTS
STATION PAR
Pyghtle Footpath
River Colne
SKIP LA
Copthall Covert
South Bucks Way
VILLAGE RD
The White House
Court Farm
Denham Court
CH
Denham
Denham Country Park Nature Reserve
River Misbourne
Harvil Farm
Copthall Farm
THE COTTAGES
UB10
Priory Covert
Denham Country Park
Colne Valley Park Visitor Ctr
DENHAM COURT DR
Denham Quarry Park Nature Reserve
Fray's River
ST GEORGE'S DR
Ickenham
SHOREDICHE CL 1
CAMPDEN RD 2
GREENACRES AVE
BREAKSPEAR RD S
The Lea
Denham Lock
THE DRIVE
HIGHFIELD DR
SWAKELEYS RD
B467
THREE OAKS CL
VINLAKE AVE
ESTONE RD
CHARLBURY RD
OXFORD RD
A40

180
192

D2
1 CEDAR
2 BEECH
3 ACACIA
4 MOUNT VIEW CT
5 MARKET PLACE MEWS

192

191
181

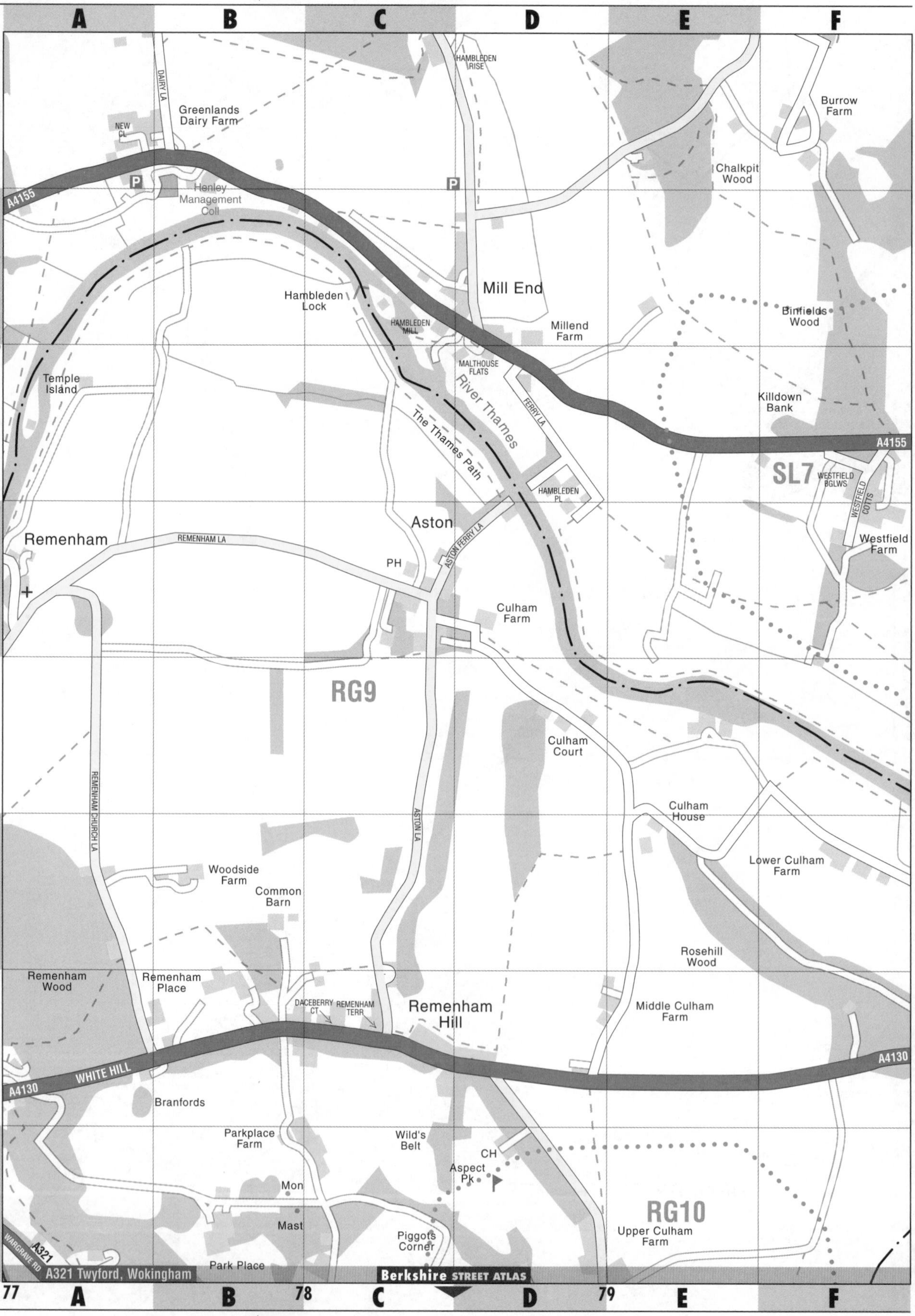

A
B
C
D
E
F
8
7
85
6
5
84
4
3
83
2
1
82
77
78
79
DAIRY LA
Greenlands Dairy Farm
NEW CL
HAMBLEDEN RISE
Burrow Farm
Chalkpit Wood
A4155
P
Henley Management Coll
Mill End
Hambleden Lock
HAMBLEDEN MILL
Millend Farm
Binfields Wood
MALTHOUSE FLATS
Temple Island
River Thames
FERRY LA
Killdown Bank
The Thames Path
SL7
WESTFIELD BGLWS
WESTFIELD COTTS
HAMBLEDEN PL
Aston
Remenham
REMENHAM LA
ASTON FERRY LA
Westfield Farm
PH
Culham Farm
RG9
Culham Court
REMENHAM CHURCH LA
Culham House
ASTON LA
Woodside Farm
Lower Culham Farm
Common Barn
Rosehill Wood
Remenham Wood
Remenham Place
DACEBERRY CT
REMENHAM TERR
Remenham Hill
Middle Culham Farm
A4130
WHITE HILL
Branfords
Parkplace Farm
Wild's Belt
CH
Aspect Pk
Mon
Mast
RG10
Piggots Corner
Upper Culham Farm
A321
WARGRAVE RD
A321 Twyford, Wokingham
Park Place
Berkshire STREET ATLAS

191

182

194

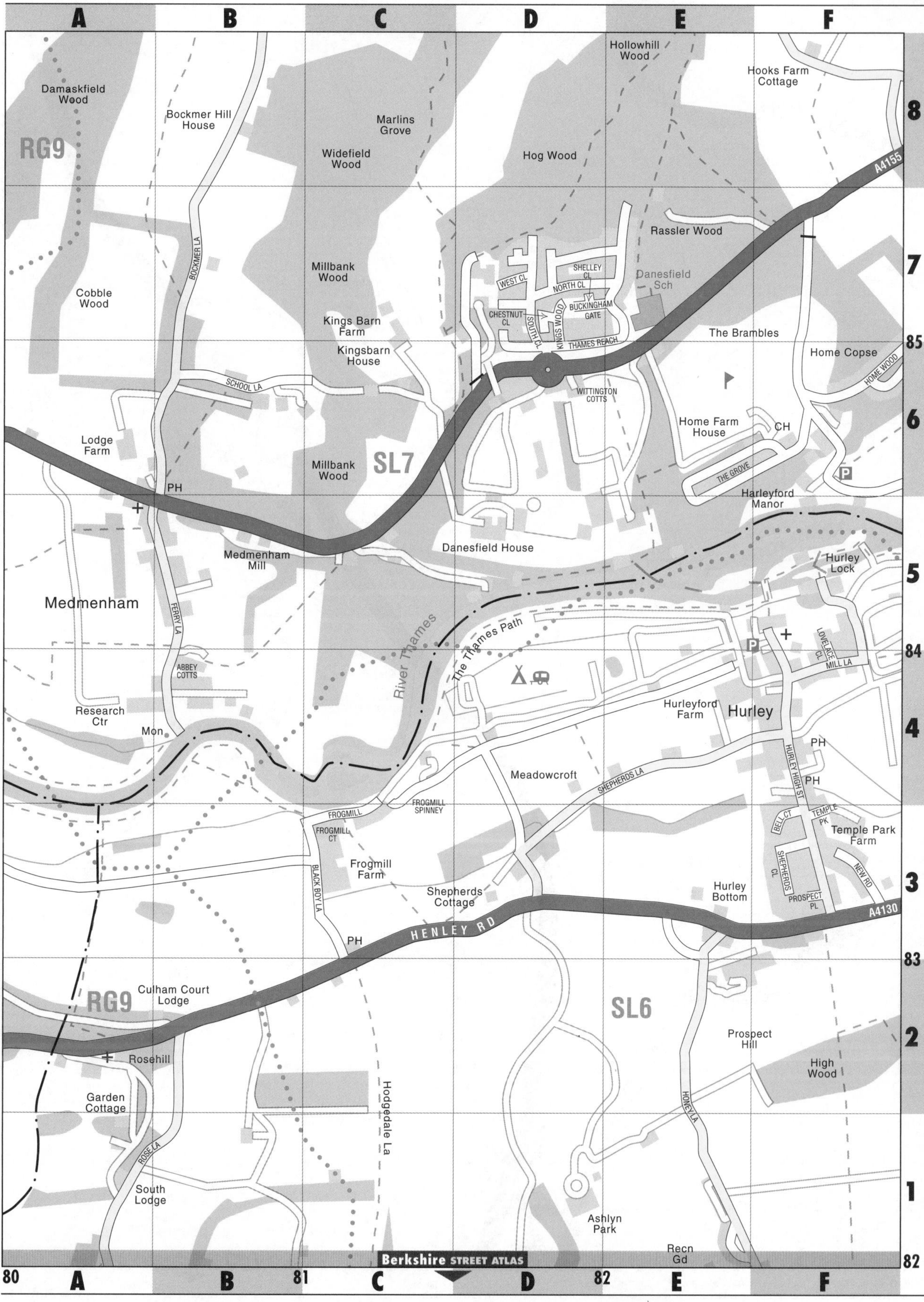

Damaskfield Wood
RG9
Bockmer Hill House
Marlins Grove
Widefield Wood
Hollowhill Wood
Hog Wood
Hooks Farm Cottage
A4155
Cobble Wood
BOCKMER LA
Millbank Wood
Rassler Wood
WEST CL
SHELLEY CL
NORTH CL
CHESTNUT CL
SOUTH CL
KINGS WOOD
BUCKINGHAM GATE
THAMES REACH
Danesfield Sch
The Brambles
Kings Barn Farm
Kingsbarn House
Home Copse
HOME WOOD
SCHOOL LA
WITTINGTON COTTS
Lodge Farm
Millbank Wood
SL7
Home Farm House
CH
THE GROVE
PH
Harleyford Manor
Danesfield House
Medmenham Mill
Hurley Lock
Medmenham
FERRY LA
River Thames
The Thames Path
LOVELACE CL
MILL LA
ABBEY COTTS
Research Ctr
Hurleyford Farm
Hurley
Mon
PH
Meadowcroft
SHEPHERDS LA
HURLEY HIGH ST
PH
FROGMILL
FROGMILL SPINNEY
FROGMILL CT
BELL CT
TEMPLE PK
Temple Park Farm
Frogmill Farm
SHEPHERDS CL
NEW RD
BLACK BOY LA
Shepherds Cottage
Hurley Bottom
PROSPECT PL
A4130
PH
HENLEY RD
Culham Court Lodge
RG9
SL6
Rosehill
Prospect Hill
High Wood
Garden Cottage
Hodgedale La
HONEY LA
ROSE LA
South Lodge
Ashlyn Park
Recn Gd
A B C D E F
8 7 85 6 5 84 4 3 83 2 1 82
80 81 82

193

183

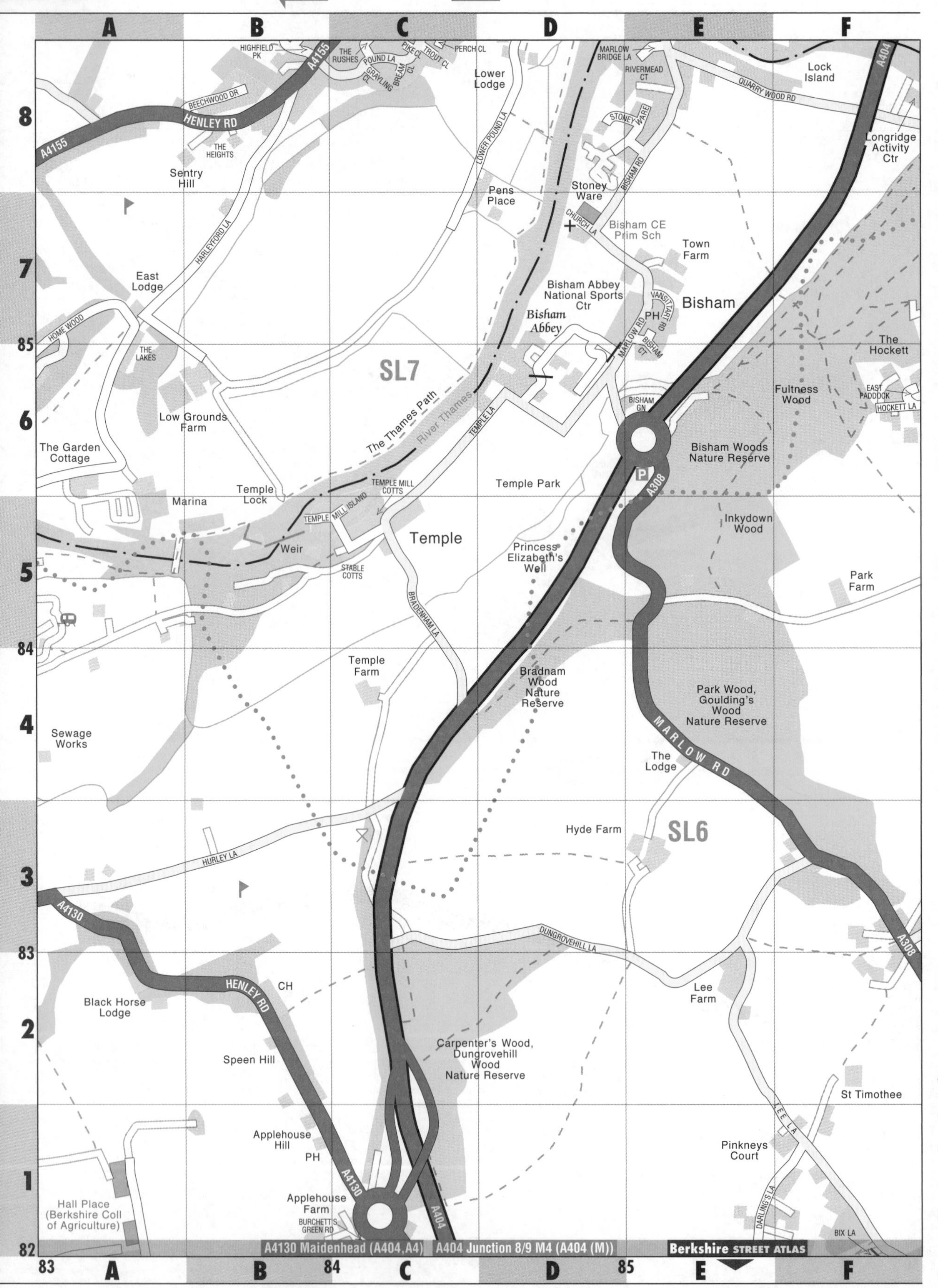

A
B
C
D
E
F
8
7
85
6
5
84
4
3
83
2
1
82
HIGHFIELD PK
THE RUSHES
POUND LA
PIKE CL
TROUT CL
PERCH CL
GRAYLING CL
BREAM CL
MARLOW BRIDGE LA
RIVERMEAD CT
Lock Island
QUARRY WOOD RD
A404
A4155
BEECHWOOD DR
HENLEY RD
Lower Lodge
LOWER POUND LA
STONEY WARE
BISHAM RD
Longridge Activity Ctr
THE HEIGHTS
Sentry Hill
Pens Place
Stoney Ware
CHURCH LA
Bisham CE Prim Sch
Town Farm
HARLEYFORD LA
East Lodge
Bisham Abbey National Sports Ctr
Bisham Abbey
VANSITTART RD
PH
Bisham
MARLOW RD
BISHAM CT
HOME WOOD
THE LAKES
SL7
The Hockett
Fultness Wood
EAST PADDOCK
HOCKETT LA
BISHAM GN
Low Grounds Farm
The Thames Path
River Thames
TEMPLE LA
The Garden Cottage
Bisham Woods Nature Reserve
P
A308
Temple Lock
TEMPLE MILL COTTS
Temple Park
Marina
TEMPLE MILL ISLAND
Inkydown Wood
Temple
Weir
Princess Elizabeth's Well
Park Farm
STABLE COTTS
BRADENHAM LA
Temple Farm
Bradnam Wood Nature Reserve
Park Wood, Goulding's Wood Nature Reserve
Sewage Works
MARLOW RD
The Lodge
Hyde Farm
SL6
HURLEY LA
A4130
DUNGROVEHILL LA
CH
Black Horse Lodge
HENLEY RD
Lee Farm
Speen Hill
Carpenter's Wood, Dungrovehill Wood Nature Reserve
St Timothee
LEE LA
Applehouse Hill
PH
Pinkneys Court
A4130
Hall Place (Berkshire Coll of Agriculture)
Applehouse Farm
BURCHETT'S GREEN RD
A404
DARLING'S LA
BIX LA
A4130 Maidenhead (A404,A4)
A404 Junction 8/9 M4 (A404 (M))
83
84
85

193

184
196

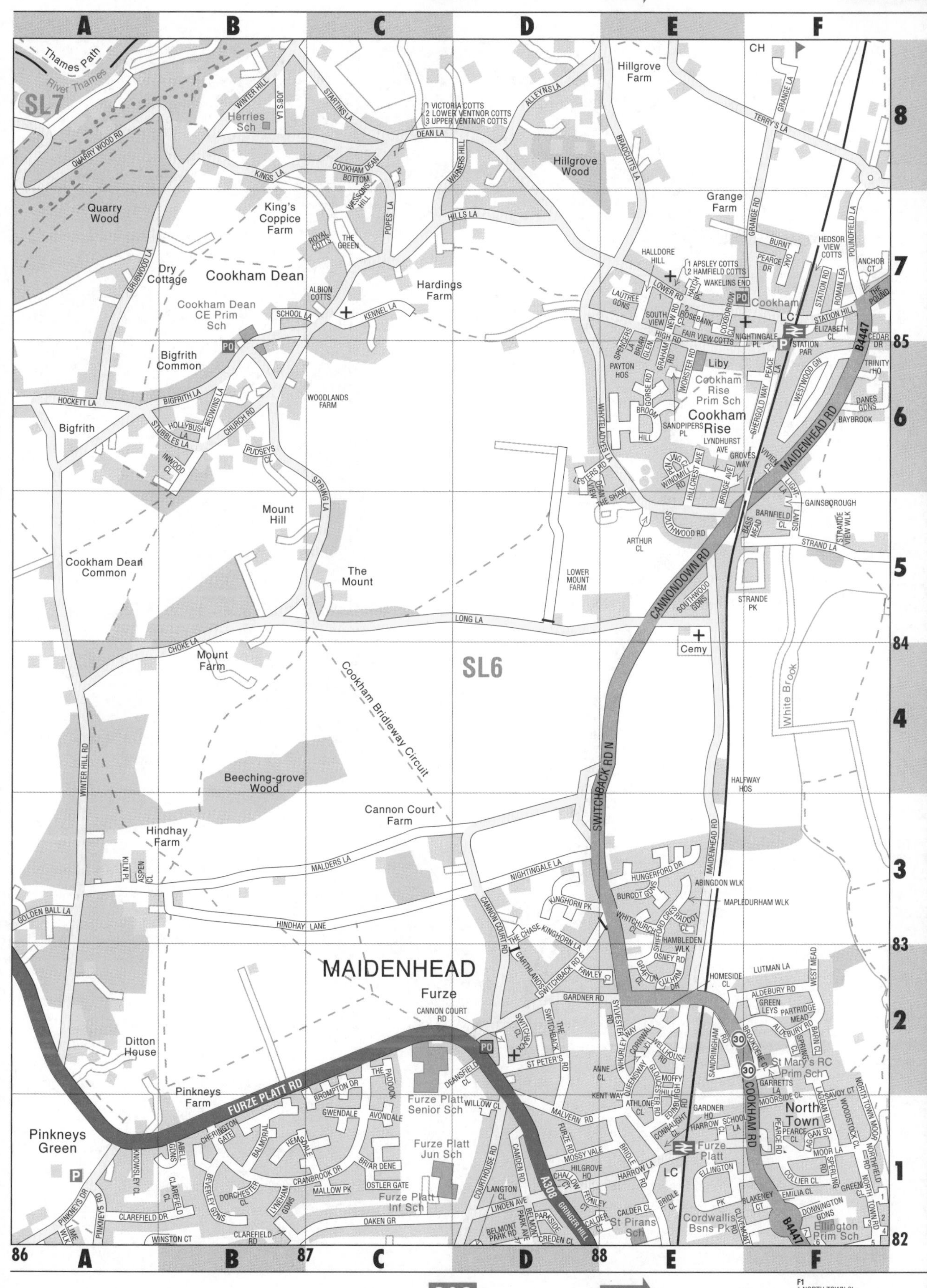

202
196

F1
1 NORTH TOWN CL
2 ALYSON CT
3 NORTH GN
4 NORTH TOWN MEAD
5 NORTHDEAN
6 COLBY GDNS
7 DALBY GDNS

195
185

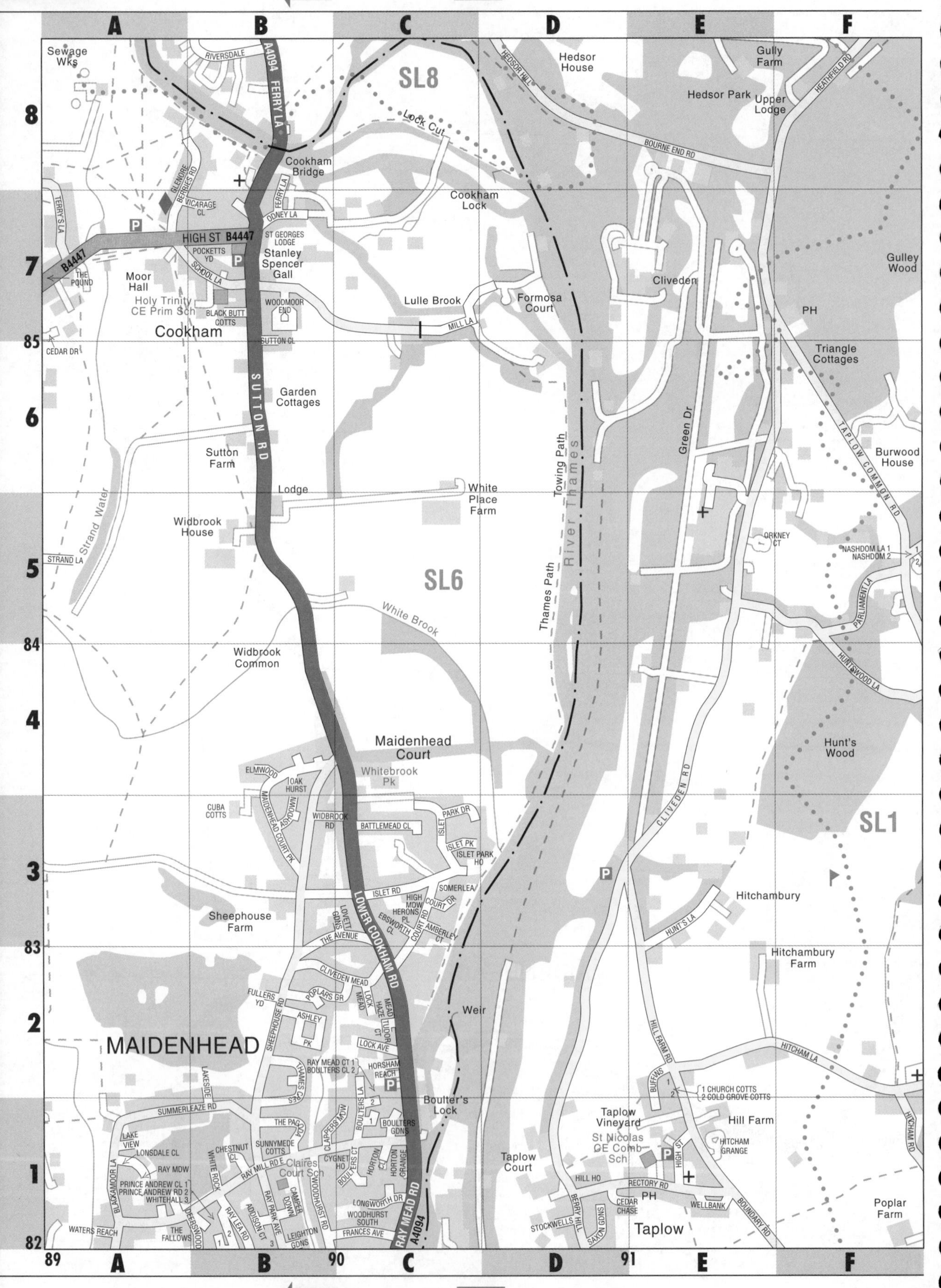

195
203

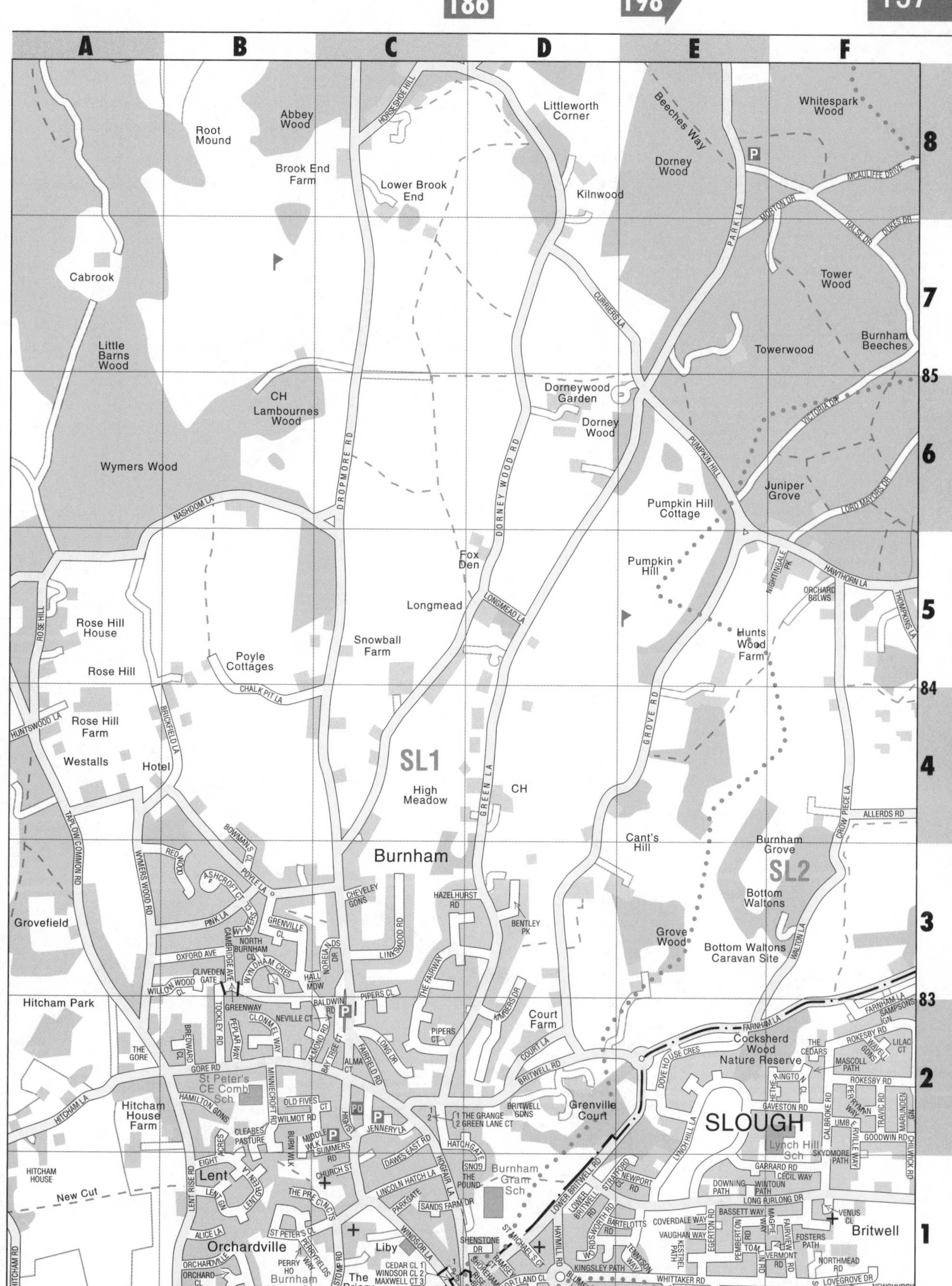
A
B
C
D
E
F
8
7
85
6
5
84
4
3
83
2
1
82
92
93
94
Root Mound
Abbey Wood
Littleworth Corner
Beeches Way
Whitespark Wood
Brook End Farm
Lower Brook End
Dorney Wood
Kilnwood
Cabrook
Tower Wood
Little Barns Wood
Towerwood
Burnham Beeches
CH
Lambournes Wood
Dorneywood Garden
Dorney Wood
Wymers Wood
Juniper Grove
Pumpkin Hill Cottage
Fox Den
Pumpkin Hill
Longmead
Rose Hill House
Snowball Farm
Hunts Wood Farm
Poyle Cottages
Rose Hill
Rose Hill Farm
Westalls
Hotel
SL1
High Meadow
CH
Cant's Hill
Burnham Grove
SL2
Burnham
Bottom Waltons
Grovefield
Grove Wood
Bottom Waltons Caravan Site
Hitcham Park
Court Farm
Cocksherd Wood Nature Reserve
St Peter's CE Comb Sch
Hitcham House Farm
Grenville Court
SLOUGH
Lynch Hill Sch
Lent
HITCHAM HOUSE
New Cut
Burnham Gram Sch
Britwell
Orchardville
Liby
The Priory
Burnham Upper Sch
PERRY HO
DROPMORE RD
DORNEY WOOD RD
GREEN LA
GROVE RD
PARK LA
PUMPKIN HILL
CURRIERS LA
HORSESHOE HILL
NASHDOM LA
ROSE HILL
BRICKFIELD LA
CHALK PIT LA
HUNTSWOOD LA
TAPLOW COMMON RD
WYMERS WOOD RD
LONGMEAD LA
HAWTHORN LA
NIGHTINGALE PK
ORCHARD BGLWS
THOMPKINS LA
CROW PIECE LA
ALLERDS RD
WALTON LA
FARNHAM LA
MCAULIFFE DRIVE
MORTON DR
HALSE DR
DUKES DR
VICTORIA DR
LORD MAYORS DR
HITCHAM LA
HITCHAM RD
GORE RD
BRITWELL RD
COURT LA
LOWER BRITWELL RD
LYNCH HILL LA
DOVE HOUSE CRES
LONG FURLONG DR
WINDSOR LA
PRIORY RD
STOMP RD
HAYMILL RD
BLUMFIELD CT
BLUMFIELD CRES
KINGSLEY PATH
WHITTAKER RD
MARESCROFT RD
LOVEGROVE DR
NEWCHURCH RD
TEESDALE RD
NORTHMEAD RD
GOODWIN RD
CHILWICK RD
MARUNDEN GN
TRAVIC RD
ROKESBY RD
CALBROKE RD
GAVESTON RD
GARRARD RD
CECIL WAY
DOWNING PATH
WINTOUN PATH
BASSETT WAY
COVERDALE WAY
VAUGHAN WAY
KESTREL PATH
EGERTON RD
PEMBERTON RD
TOM LIN RD
VERMONT RD
FOSTERS PATH
SCAFELL RD
VENUS CL
SKYDMORE PATH
MASCOLL PATH
LILAC CT
SAMPSONS GN
THE CEDARS
NEWPORT RD
STRATFORD CL
BARTELOTTS RD
WORDSWORTH RD
TENNYSON WAY
ST MICHAEL'S CT
PORTLAND CL
RAMSEY CT
SHENSTONE DR
HOGFAIR LA
HATCHGATE
THE POUND
SANDS FARM DR
PARKGATE
LINCOLN HATCH LA
DAWES EAST RD
JENNERY LA
HIGH ST
CHURCH ST
THE PRECINCTS
ST PETER'S CL
PERRYFIELDS WAY
ALICE LA
LENT GN
LENT RISE RD
ORCHARDVILLE
ORCHARD CL
BURLINGTON RD
THE GREEN
HAMILTON GDNS
CLEARES PASTURE
BURN WLK
WILMOT RD
OLD FIVES CT
MIDDLE WLK
SUMMERS RD
MINNIECROFT RD
ALMA CT
FAIRFIELD RD
BAY TREE CT
ALMOND RD
LONG DR
PIPERS CT
PIPERS CL
THE FAIRWAY
AMBERS DR
BENTLEY PK
HAZELHURST RD
LINKSWOOD RD
CHEVELEY GDNS
NORELANDS DR
HALL MDW
WYNDHAM CRES
GRENVILLE CL
NORTH BURNHAM CL
CAMBRIDGE AVE
OXFORD AVE
PINK LA
POYLE LA
ASHCROFT CT
RED WOOD
BOWMANS CL
CLIVEDEN GATE
WILLOW WOOD CL
GREENWAY
TOCKLEY RD
PEPLAR WAY
CLONMEL WAY
NEVILLE CT
BALDWIN RD
BREDWARD CL
THE GORE
1 THE GRANGE
2 GREEN LANE CT
BRITWELL GDNS
CEDAR CL 1
WINDSOR CL 2
MAXWELL CT 3
EIGHT ACRES

197 187

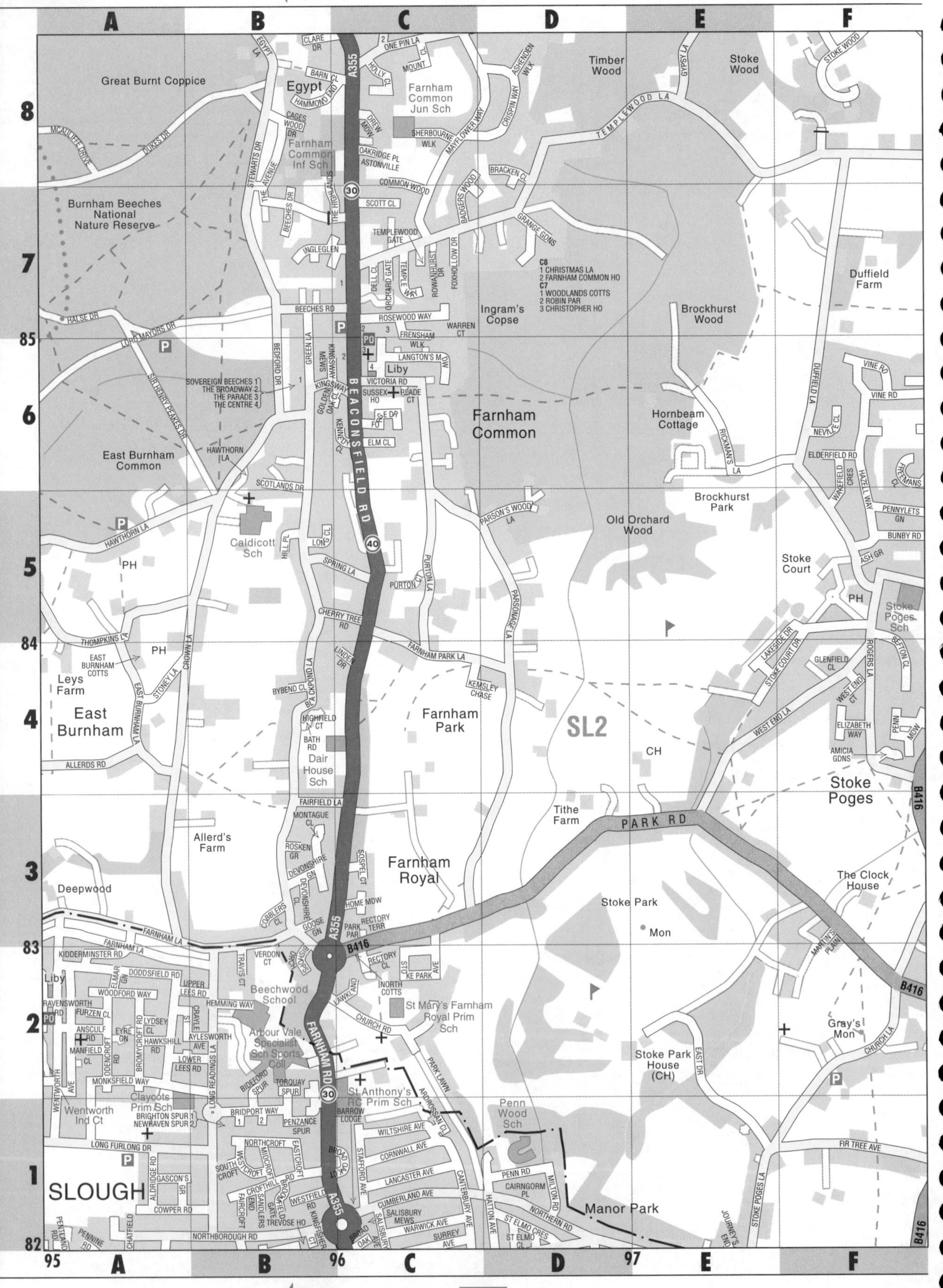

197 205

The Pickeridge
Fulmer Hall
Fulmer
Stoke Common
Church Farm
Fulmer Inf Sch
Fulmer House Farm
Furzeney Wood
SL9
Watersplash Farm
Penn Wood
Fernacres Farm
Fulmer Rise Estate
Frame Wood
Mill House Farm
Fulmer Common
Hollybush Hill
SL2
Fairfield Lodge
Teikyo Sch UK
Upton Wood
Upton Lake
Upton Farm
Sefton Park Sch
Sefton Park
Twin Trees Farm
SL3
Thames Valley (Private)
Wexham Street
Rowley Wood
Sports Ctr
Black Park Country Park
Blackpark Lake
Gallions Wood
Berry Farm
Visitor Ctr
Rowley Farm
Spring Wood
Bell Farm
Rowley Lake
Wexham Park
Stoke Place
Stoke Green
Galleons Lane
Beeches Way
Alder Bourne
STOKE COMMON RD
HOLLYBUSH HILL
FULMER COMMON RD
ROWLEY LA
WINDMILL RD
FRAMEWOOD RD
WEXHAM ST
BLACK PARK RD
GERRARDS CROSS RD
WINDSOR RD
BELLS HILL
GRAYS PARK RD
STOKE RD
UXBRIDGE RD
ALDERBOURNE LA
HAWKSWOOD LA
CHERRY TREE LA
QUEEN'S DR
PEACE RD
AVENUE DR
FULMER RD
WEXHAM PARK LA
STOKE GN
FARTHING GREEN LA
PARK RD
M40
A412
B416
1 WILLIAM HARTLEY YD
2 BENJAMIN LA

A B C D E F
8 7 85 6 5 84 4 3 83 2 1 82
01 02 03
M40
M25
1a
16
HAWKSWOOD LA
SOUTHLANDS RD
FIELD RD
FIELD ROAD
HOLLYBUSH LA
WILLETTS LA
Alderbourne Arches
SL9
Rush Green
New House Farm
Gossams Wood
UB9
Brown's Wood
Ways Farm
Oldhouse Wood
Kingcup Farm
Blanchards Farm
Alderbourne Farm
A412
ALDERBOURNE LA
Alder Bourne
Belle Farm
Sevenhills Farm
Long Coppice
HAWKSWOOD GR
FULMER COMMON RD
SEVENHILLS RD
LADY YORKE PK
Southlands Manor
The Clump
Dromenagh Farm
Strawberry Wood
Black Park Nature Reserve
Pinewood Film Studios
SL0
DENHAM RD
Round Coppice Farm
BOND CL
PINEWOOD GN
PINEWOOD CL
FIRS CL
CEDAR CL
ASHFORD RD
LAUREL CT
PINEWOOD RD
PEACE RD
Park Lodge Farm
THORNBRIDGE RD
COPSE WOOD
HEATHERDEN GN
Mansfield Farm
Iver Heath
Park Lodge
THE PARKWAY
LONGSTONE RD
ST DAVID'S CL
ST DAVID'S PAR
Recn Gd
BIRCH CL
ANSLOW GDNS
BANGORS RD N
M25
A4007
PEACE RD
CHURCH RD
ROSTREVOR GDNS
TREWARDEN AVE
HEATH WAY
Chandlers Hill
Black Park Country Park
WARREN FIELD
GLASSES WAY
BODLEY HO
ST MARGARET'S CL
LAURELS RD
LINDEN CL
KEENSACRE
ROWAN GDNS
ALDER RD
Liby
PO
1 ST MARGARET'S GATE
2 ST MARGARETS CT
OAK END DR
Iver Heath Jun Sch
SLOUGH RD
Warren House
30
HAWTHORN CL
GROSVENOR CL
MEAD HO
MOW
POTTERS CROSS
SL3
A4007
THE CLOSE
WHITEHOUSE WAY
LOWNDALE
POST
LOWER MEAD
Beeches Way
SWALLOW
Iver Heath Inf Sch
Moorwards Farm
FIVE POINTS
UXBRIDGE RD
PLEASANT COTTS
PH
White Lodge
Home Cottage Farm
WOOD LANE CL
HARDINGS CL
HARDINGS ROW
A412
COOPERS ROW
SWALLOW ST
BANGORS RD S
Bangors Park Farm
Langley Park Country Park
BILLET LA
WOOD LA
PH
SWALLOW FIELDS
BANGOR COTTS
NORWOOD LA
P
MARTINDALE
COPPINS LA

190

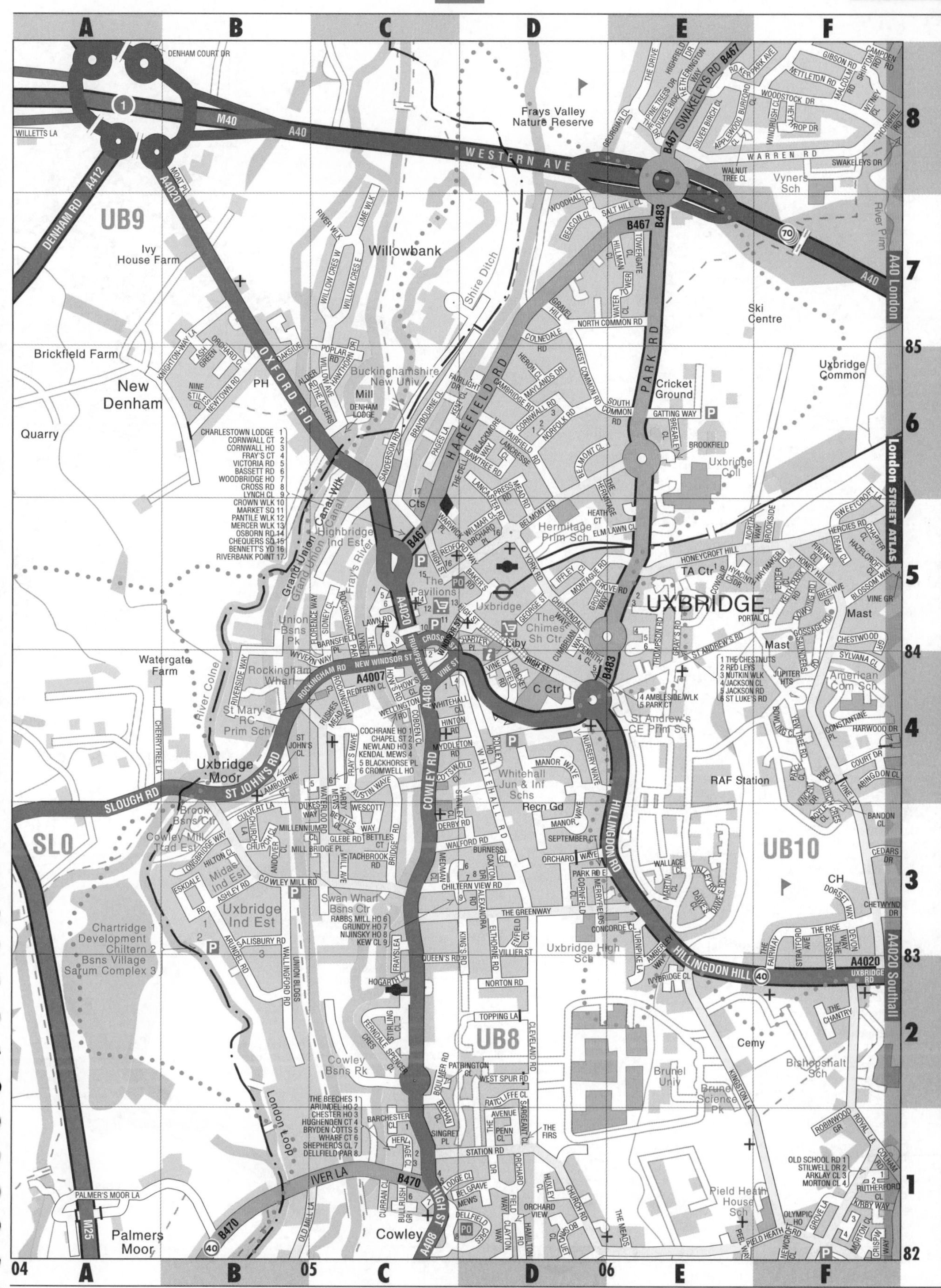

UXBRIDGE
UB9
UB8
UB10
SL0
New Denham
Willowbank
Frays Valley Nature Reserve
Ivy House Farm
Brickfield Farm
Quarry
Watergate Farm
Uxbridge Moor
Cowley
Palmers Moor
Uxbridge Common
Ski Centre
RAF Station
Brunel Univ
Cemy
CHARLESTOWN LODGE 1
CORNWALL CT 2
CORNWALL HO 3
FRAY'S CT 4
VICTORIA RD 5
BASSETT RD 6
WOODBRIDGE HO 7
CROSS RD 8
LYNCH CL 9
CROWN WLK 10
MARKET SQ 11
PANTILE WLK 12
MERCER WLK 13
OSBORN RD 14
CHEQUERS SQ 15
BENNETT'S YD 16
RIVERBANK POINT 17
COCHRANE HO 1
CHAPEL ST 2
NEWLAND HO 3
KENDAL MEWS 4
5 BLACKHORSE PL
6 CROMWELL HO
RABBS MILL HO 6
GRUNDY HO 7
NIJINSKY HO 8
KEW CL 9
THE BEECHES 1
ARUNDEL HO 2
CHESTER HO 3
HUGHENDEN CT 4
BRYDEN COTTS 5
WHARF CT 6
SHEPHERDS CL 7
DELLFIELD PAR 8
1 THE CHESTNUTS
2 RED LEYS
3 NUTKIN WLK
4 JACKSON CL
5 JACKSON RD
6 ST LUKE'S RD
4 AMBLESIDE WLK
5 PARK CT
OLD SCHOOL RD 1
STILWELL DR 2
ARKLAY CL 3
MORTON CL 4
A40 London
London STREET ATLAS
A4020 Southall

208

B8
1 WELLINGTON CL
2 BUSHNELL PL

195

E8
1 Gladstone Ind Est

F7
1 WHITE HART RD
2 Nicholsons Sh Ctr
3 REGENT CT
4 FROGMORE CT
5 WHITCHURCH HO
6 KINGSWAY HO
7 WILBERFORCE MEWS
8 SYGNUS CT
9 PROVIDENCE PL
10 ST MARY'S WLK
11 OLD POST OFFICE LA
12 QUEEN'S LA
13 Heritage Ctr
14 KING ST

F8
1 COLBY GDNS
2 St Luke's Prim Sch

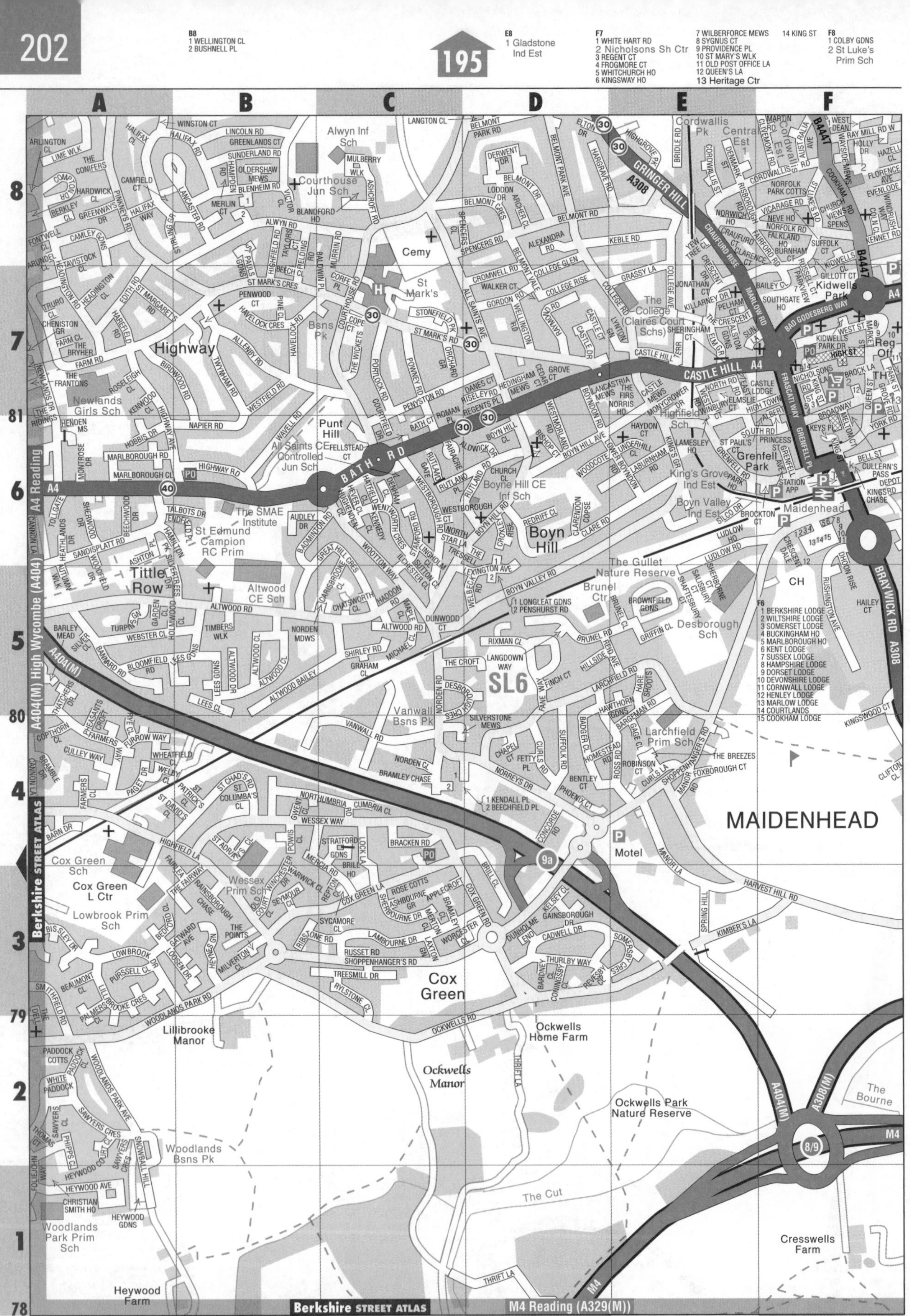

B7
1 SPRINGFIELD CT
2 WEXFORD CT
3 KINGS QUARTER

196
204

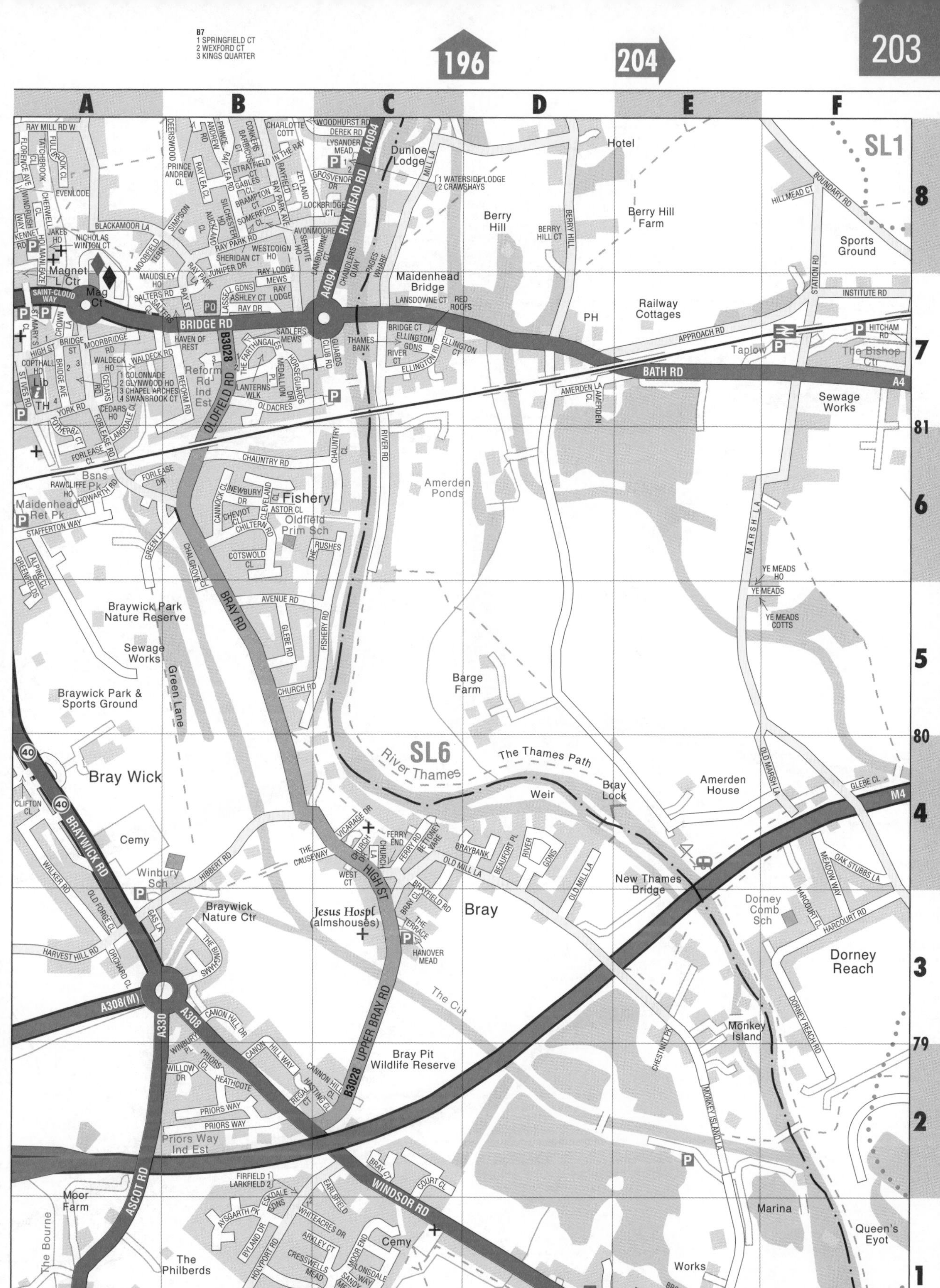

204

203
197

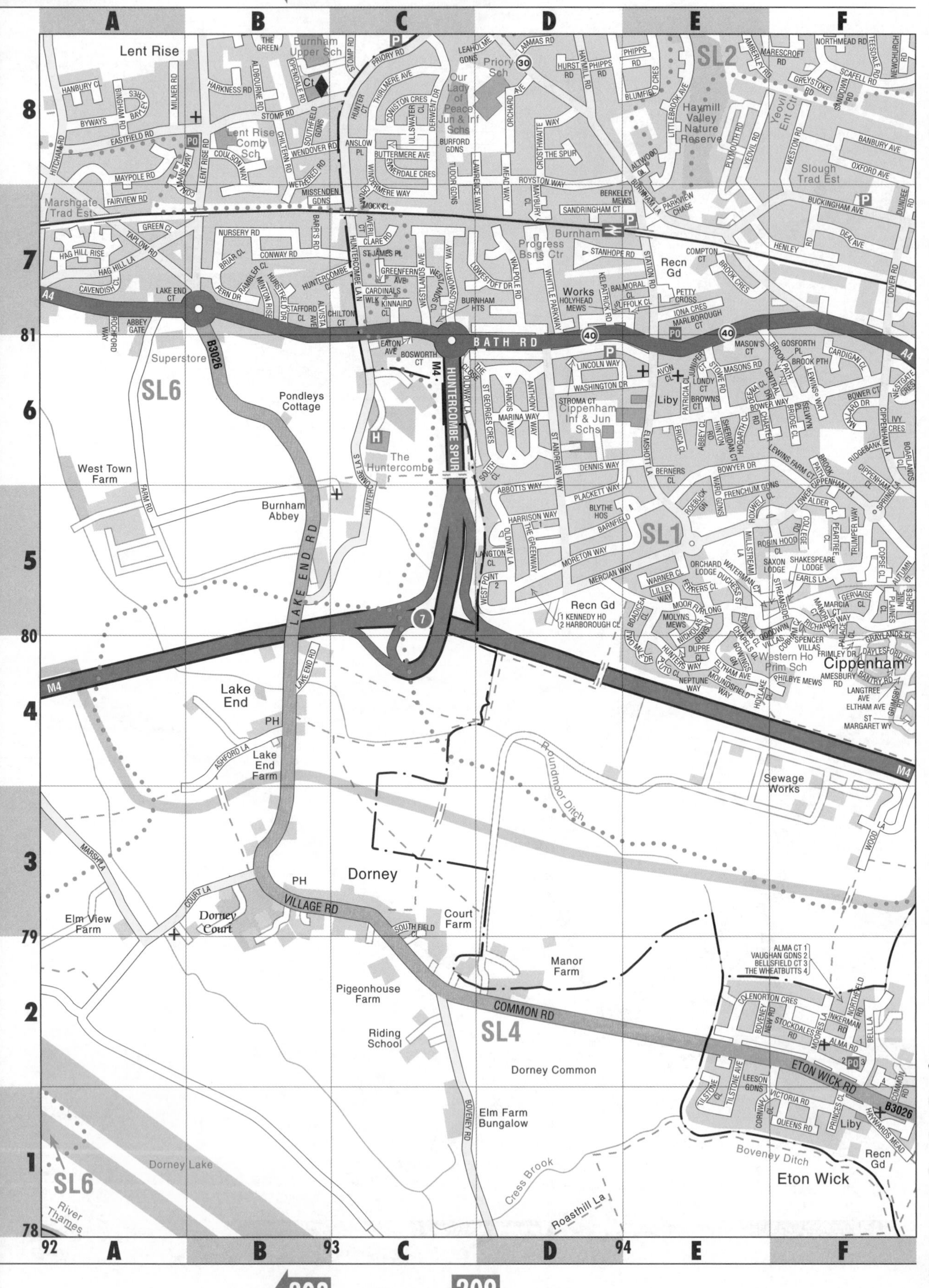

203
209

198
206

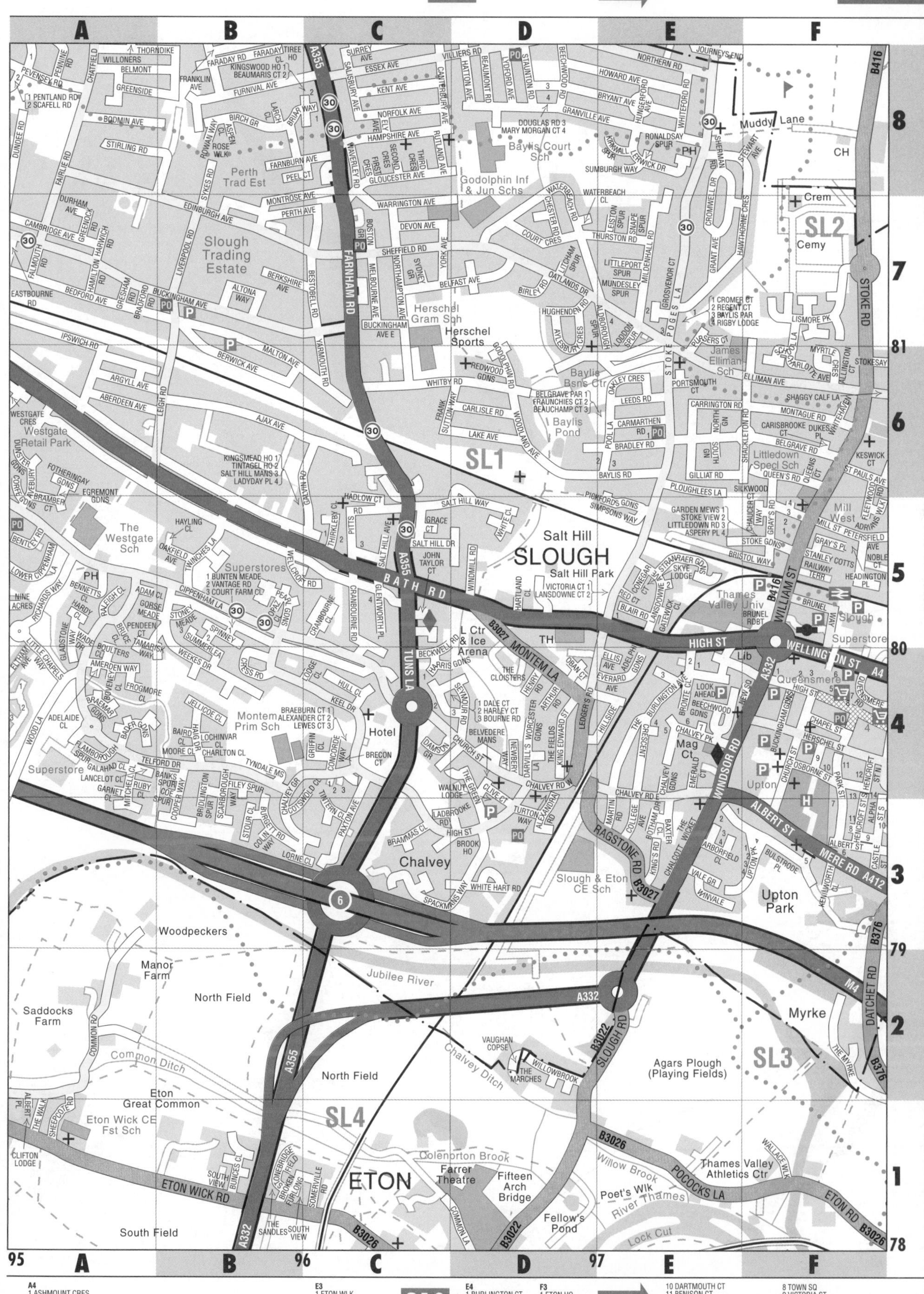

A4
1 ASHMOUNT CRES
2 MATHECOMBE RD
3 DARIE CL

E3
1 ETON WLK
2 ST ANDREWS CT
3 LINCOLN CT
4 LOCKSLEY CT

210

E4
1 BURLINGTON CT
2 BURLINGTON RD
3 HILPERTON RD
4 TOWER HO
5 ASHBOURNE HO
6 SHAFTESBURY CT
7 MOORSTOWN CT

F3
1 ETON HO
2 STOKE HO
3 DATCHET HO
4 WINDSOR HO
5 UPTON CL
6 MANOR CT
7 SPRUCE CT
8 CHARTER CL
9 ALBERT CL

206

10 DARTMOUTH CT
11 BENISON CT

F4
1 PRUDENTIAL BLDGS
2 MACKENZIE ST
3 MACKENZIE MALL
4 Observatory Sh Ctr
5 LEOPOLD MALL
6 CURZON MALL
7 CHANDOS MALL
8 TOWN SQ
9 VICTORIA ST
10 BISHAM CT
11 BEMBRIDGE CT
12 STEPHENSON CT
13 SHAMAA HO
14 HENCROFT MEWS

205
199

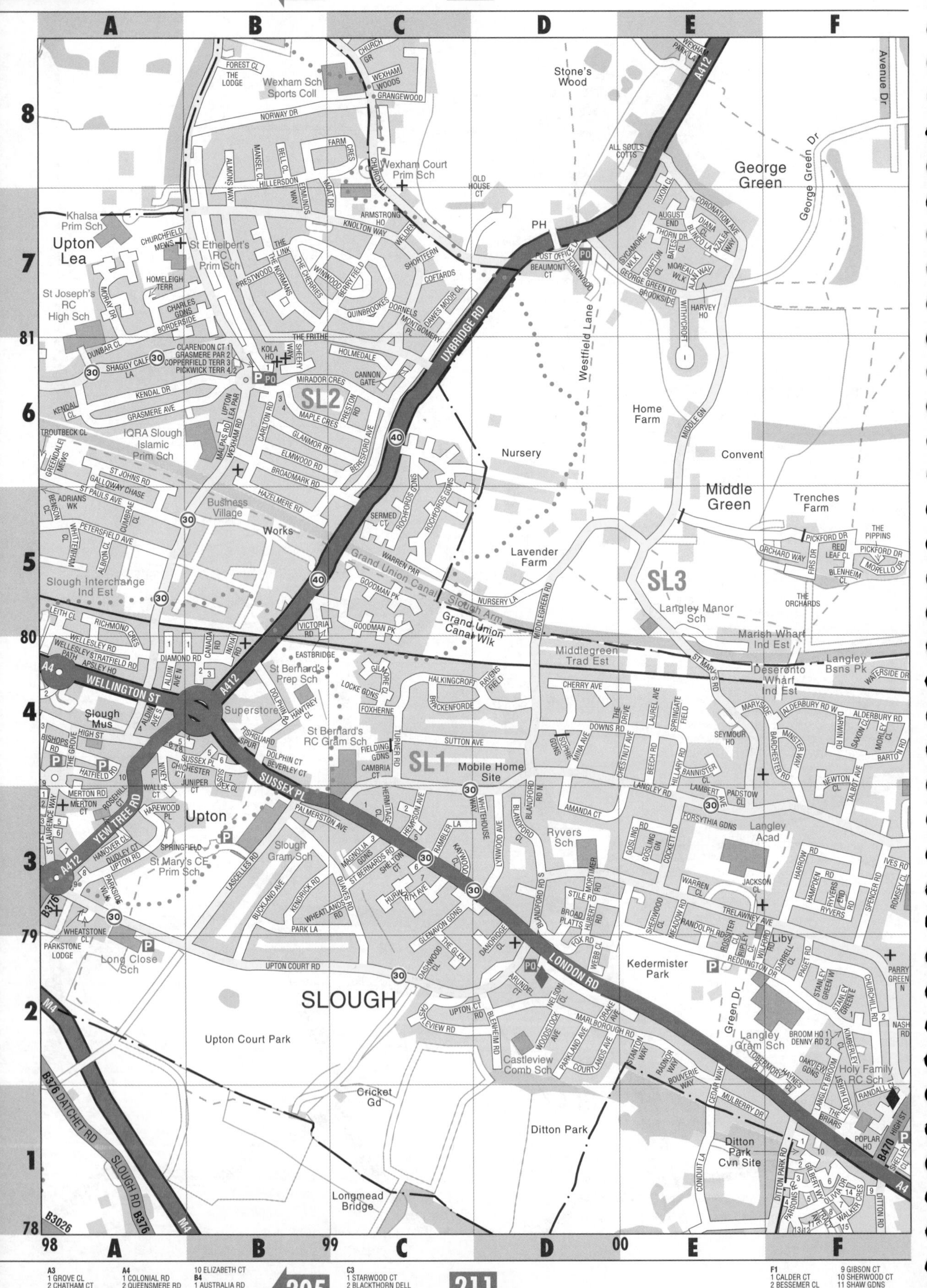

A3
1 GROVE CL
2 CHATHAM CT
3 EASTFIELD CL
4 ALBERT ST
5 PRIORS CL
6 NIGHTINGALE CT
7 MOUNTBATTEN CL
8 HORNBEAM GDNS
9 CHURCH VIEW

A4
1 COLONIAL RD
2 QUEENSMERE RD
3 ALPHA ST N
4 MILFORD CT
5 CLIFTON RD
6 BELGRAVE PL
7 CLIFTON LODGE
8 LASCELLES HO
9 RYE CT
10 ELIZABETH CT

B4
1 AUSTRALIA RD
2 PRINCES ST
3 CONNAUGHT RD
4 SELIM CT
5 CLEMENTS CL
6 CHESHIRE CT
7 SUSSEX KEEP

205

C3
1 STARWOOD CT
2 BLACKTHORN DELL
3 APPLETREE LA
4 LA ROCHE CL
5 KINGSWAY
6 RED COTTAGE MEWS
7 FLEMING CT

211

F1
1 CALDER CT
2 BESSEMER CL
3 TYLER WLK
4 OWEN CL
5 BECKETT CHASE
6 DAVIDSON RD
7 CHAPLIN MEWS
8 SHARMAN ROW
9 GIBSON CT
10 SHERWOOD CT
11 SHAW GDNS
12 JAMES MDW
13 HARDING SPUR
14 HUDSON PL
15 DALTON GN

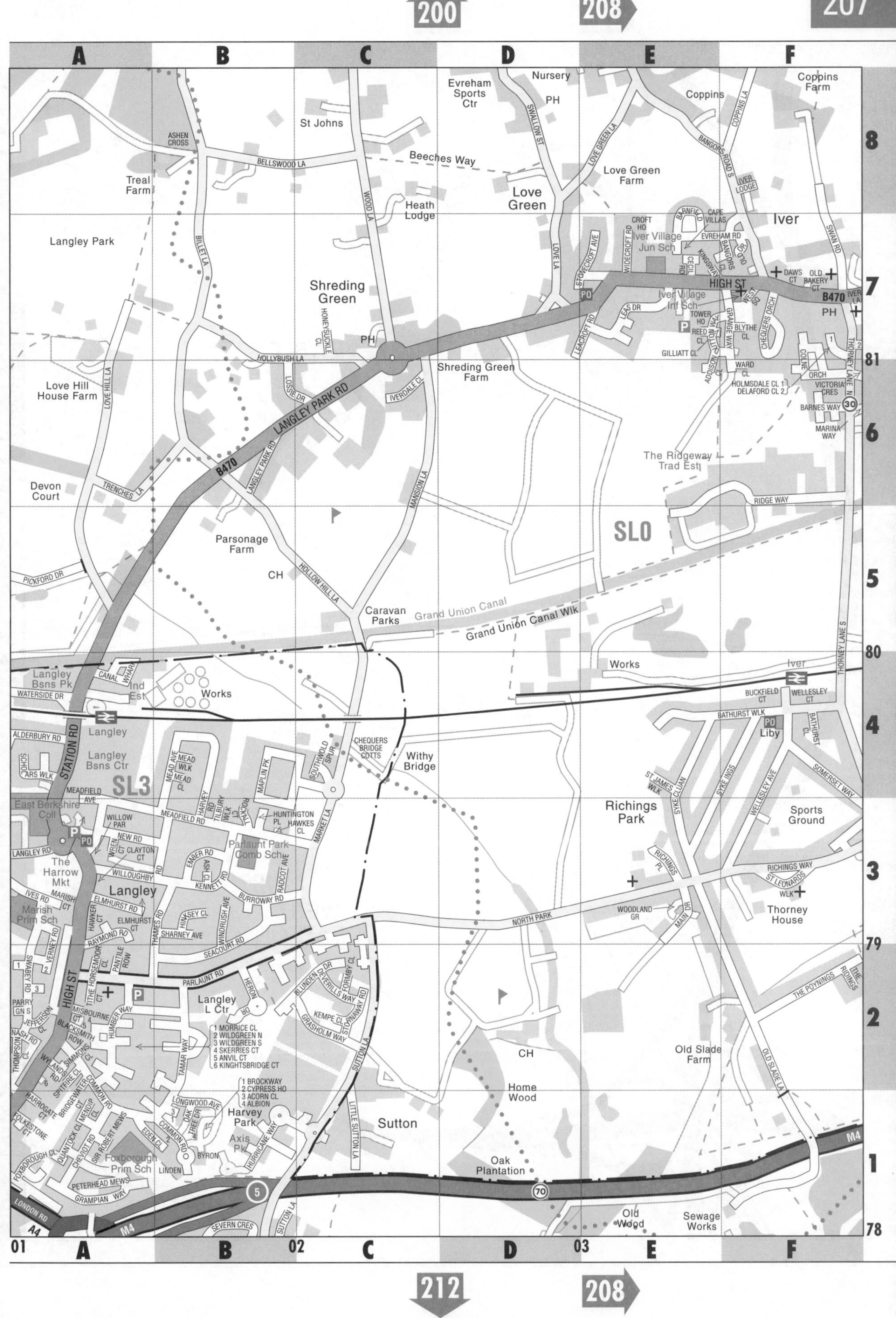

200
208
212
208
A B C D E F
8 7 6 5 4 3 2 1
81 80 79 78
01 02 03
Langley Park
Treal Farm
St Johns
Beeches Way
Evreham Sports Ctr
Nursery
Coppins
Coppins Farm
Love Green
Love Green Farm
Iver
Heath Lodge
Shreding Green
Shreding Green Farm
Iver Village Jun Sch
Iver Village Inf Sch
Love Hill House Farm
Devon Court
The Ridgeway Trad Est
SL0
Parsonage Farm
Caravan Parks
Grand Union Canal
Grand Union Canal Wlk
Works
Langley Bsns Pk
Ind Est
Langley
Langley Bsns Ctr
SL3
East Berkshire Coll
Withy Bridge
Richings Park
Sports Ground
Thorney House
Parlaunt Park Comb Sch
The Harrow Mkt
Marish Prim Sch
Langley L Ctr
Harvey Park
Axis Pk
Foxborough Prim Sch
Old Slade Farm
Home Wood
Sutton
Oak Plantation
Old Wood
Sewage Works
B470
M4
A4
LANGLEY PARK RD
STATION RD
HIGH ST
NORTH PARK
BELLSWOOD LA
HOLLYBUSH LA
HOLLOW HILL LA
MANSION LA
THORNEY LANE S
OLD SLADE LA
SUTTON LA
LITTLE SUTTON LA
MARKET LA
1 MORRICE CL
2 WILDGREEN N
3 WILDGREEN S
4 SKERRIES CT
5 ANVIL CT
6 KNIGHTSBRIDGE CT
1 BROCKWAY
2 CYPRESS HO
3 ACORN CL
4 ALBION

207
201

F7
1 BEECHWOOD AVE
2 EVELYNS CL
3 Moorcroft Sch

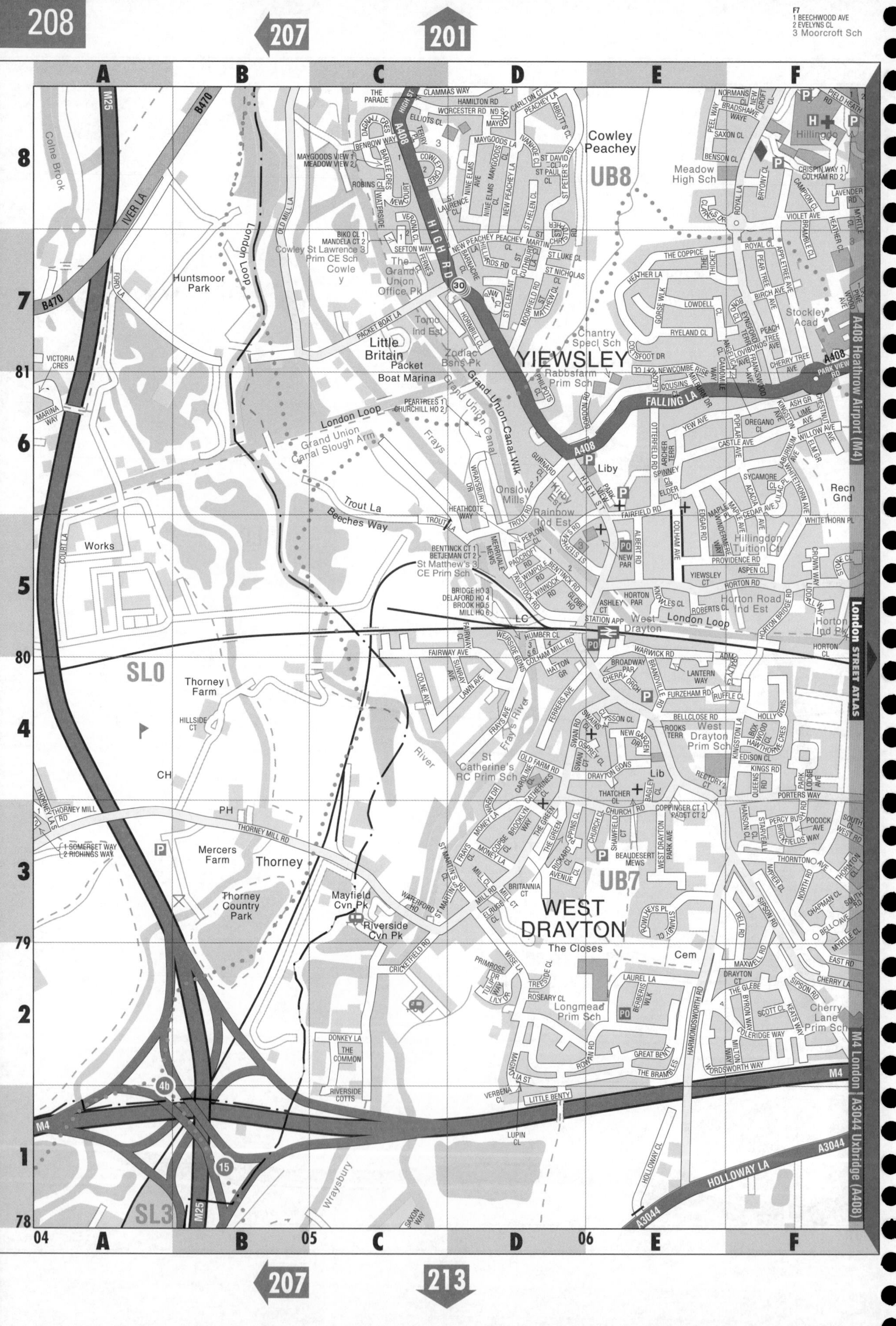

207
213

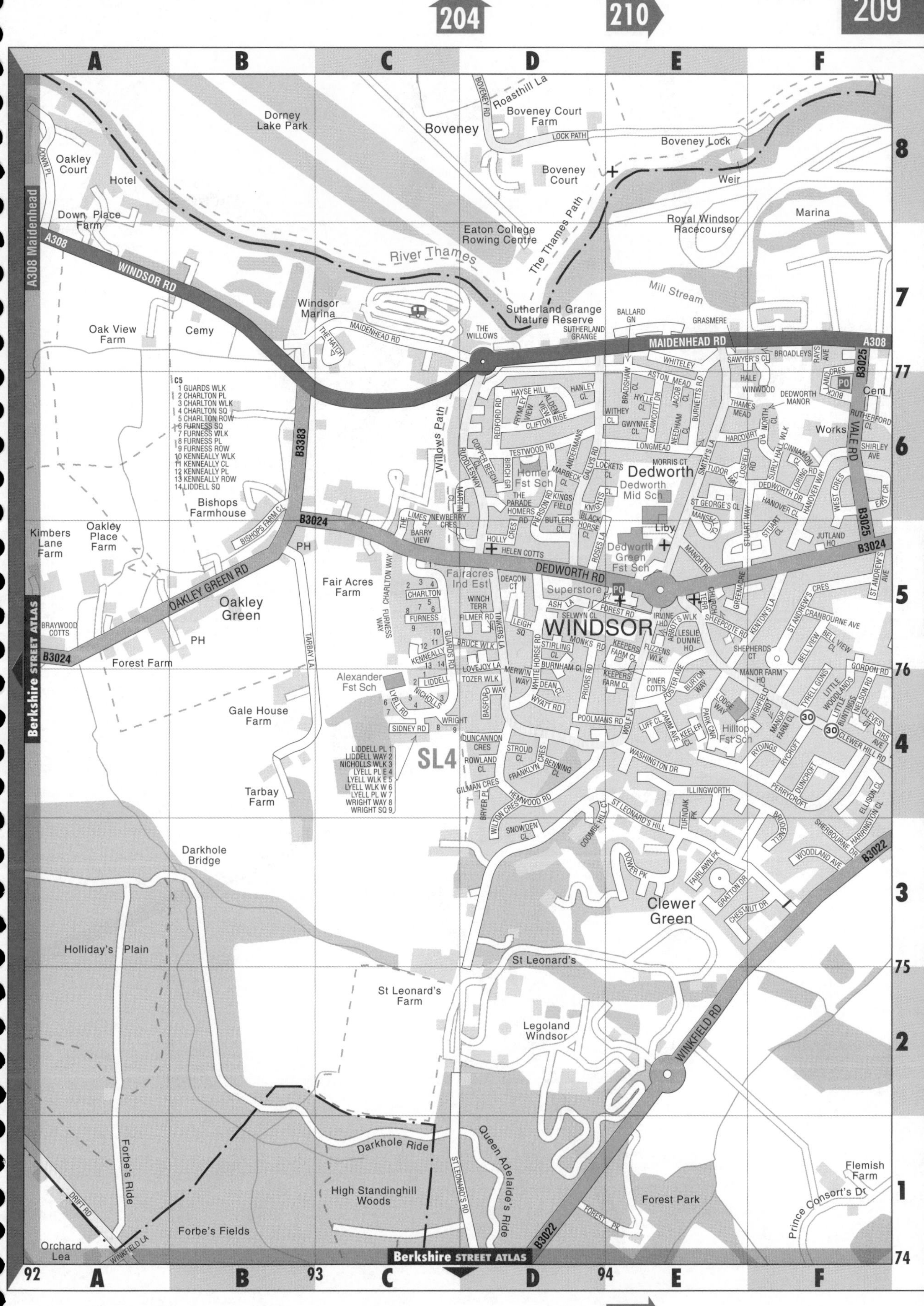
204
210
Dorney Lake Park
Boveney
Boveney Court Farm
Boveney Court
Boveney Lock
Weir
Oakley Court
Hotel
Down Place Farm
Royal Windsor Racecourse
Marina
Eaton College Rowing Centre
River Thames
The Thames Path
Mill Stream
Windsor Marina
Sutherland Grange Nature Reserve
Oak View Farm
Cemy
MAIDENHEAD RD
WINDSOR RD
A308 Maidenhead
Bishops Farmhouse
Kimbers Lane Farm
Oakley Place Farm
Oakley Green
Forest Farm
Fair Acres Farm
Fairacres Ind Est
Alexander Fst Sch
Gale House Farm
Tarbay Farm
SL4
Dedworth
Dedworth Mid Sch
Homer Fst Sch
Dedworth Green Fst Sch
Superstore
WINDSOR
DEDWORTH RD
Hilltop Fst Sch
Works
Cem
Darkhole Bridge
Holliday's Plain
Clewer Green
St Leonard's
St Leonard's Farm
Legoland Windsor
WINKFIELD RD
Darkhole Ride
High Standinghill Woods
Forbe's Ride
Forbe's Fields
Queen Adelaide's Ride
Forest Park
Flemish Farm
Prince Consort's Dr
Orchard Lea
Berkshire STREET ATLAS
C5
1 GUARDS WLK
2 CHARLTON PL
3 CHARLTON WLK
4 CHARLTON SQ
5 CHARLTON ROW
6 FURNESS SQ
7 FURNESS WLK
8 FURNESS PL
9 FURNESS ROW
10 KENNEALLY WLK
11 KENNEALLY CL
12 KENNEALLY PL
13 KENNEALLY ROW
14 LIDDELL SQ
LIDDELL PL 1
LIDDELL WAY 2
NICHOLLS WLK 3
LYELL PL E 4
LYELL WLK E 5
LYELL WLK W 6
LYELL PL W 7
WRIGHT WAY 8
WRIGHT SQ 9
A B C D E F
8 7 6 5 4 3 2 1
77 76 75 74
92 93 94

210

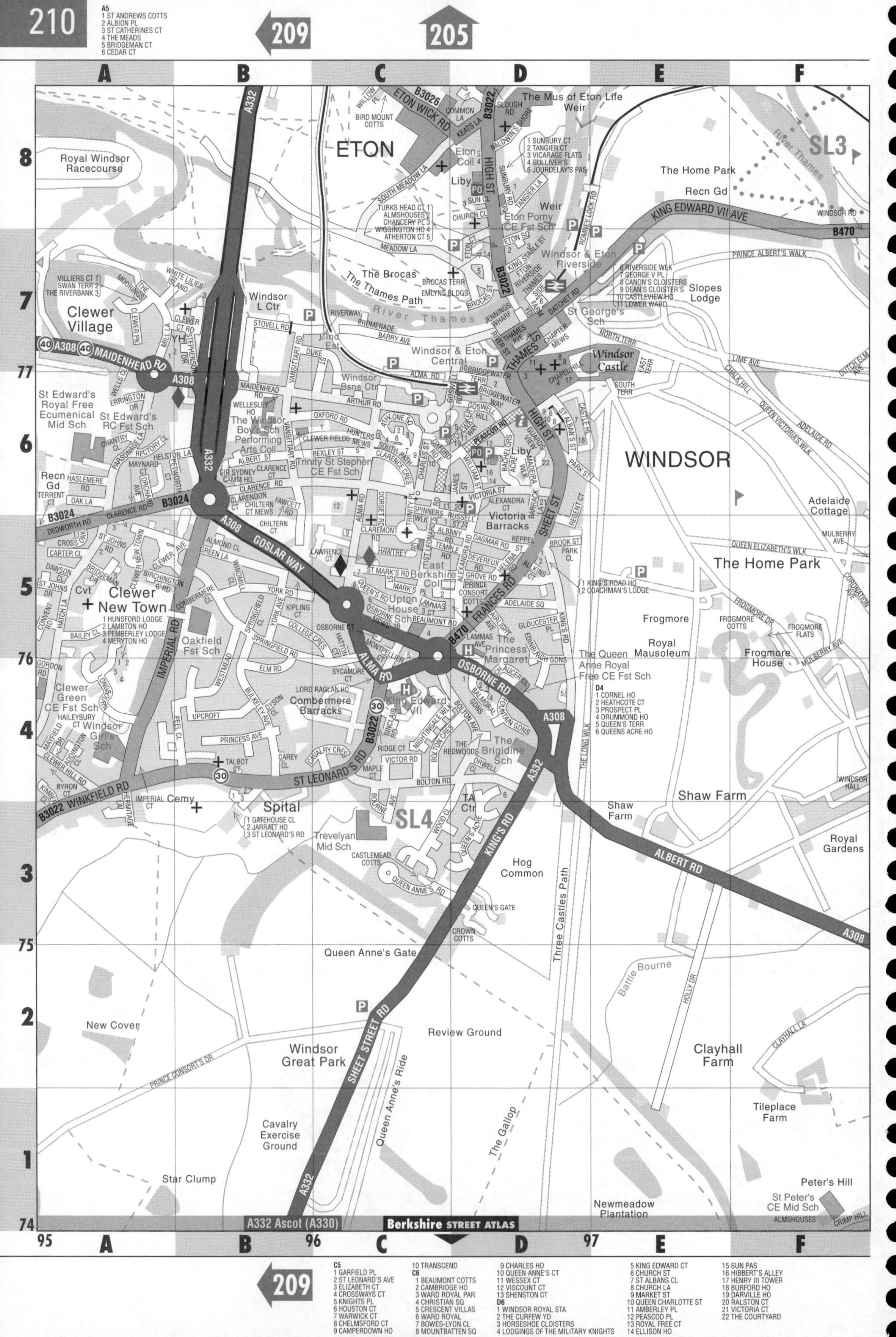
A5
1 ST ANDREWS COTTS
2 ALBION PL
3 ST CATHERINES CT
4 THE MEADS
5 BRIDGEMAN CT
6 CEDAR CT
209
205
ETON
Royal Windsor Racecourse
The Mus of Eton Life
Weir
The Home Park
Recn Gd
SL3
River Thames
KING EDWARD VII AVE
B470
The Brocas
The Thames Path
Clewer Village
Windsor L Ctr
Windsor & Eton Riverside
Slopes Lodge
St George's Sch
Windsor Castle
Windsor & Eton Central
MAIDENHEAD RD
A308
A332
St Edward's Royal Free Ecumenical Mid Sch
St Edward's RC Fst Sch
The Windsor Boy's Sch Performing Arts Coll
Trinity St Stephen CE Fst Sch
WINDSOR
Adelaide Cottage
B3024
GOSLAR WAY
Victoria Barracks
The Home Park
Clewer New Town
East Berkshire Coll
Upton House Sch
Frogmore
Royal Mausoleum
Frogmore House
Oakfield Fst Sch
The Princess Margaret
The Queen Anne Royal Free CE Fst Sch
OSBORNE RD
ALMA RD
Clewer Green CE Fst Sch
Windsor Girl's Sch
Combermere Barracks
King Edward VII
The Brigidine Sch
IMPERIAL RD
ST LEONARD'S RD
B3022 WINKFIELD RD
Spital
Cemy
SL4
Trevelyan Mid Sch
Shaw Farm
Shaw Farm
Royal Gardens
ALBERT RD
Hog Common
Three Castles Path
Queen Anne's Gate
KING'S RD
New Cover
Review Ground
Windsor Great Park
Clayhall Farm
SHEET STREET RD
Queen Anne's Ride
The Gallop
Battle Bourne
Tileplace Farm
Cavalry Exercise Ground
Star Clump
Newmeadow Plantation
Peter's Hill
St Peter's CE Mid Sch
A332 Ascot (A330)
Berkshire STREET ATLAS
95
96
97
209
C5
1 GARFIELD PL
2 ST LEONARD'S AVE
3 ELIZABETH CT
4 CROSSWAYS CT
5 KNIGHTS PL
6 HOUSTON CT
7 WARWICK CT
8 CHELMSFORD CT
9 CAMPERDOWN HO
10 TRANSCEND
C6
1 BEAUMONT COTTS
2 CAMBRIDGE HO
3 WARD ROYAL PAR
4 CHRISTIAN SQ
5 CRESCENT VILLAS
6 WARD ROYAL
7 BOWES-LYON CL
8 MOUNTBATTEN SQ
9 CHARLES HO
10 QUEEN ANNE'S CT
11 WESSEX CT
12 VISCOUNT CT
13 SHENSTON CT
D6
1 WINDSOR ROYAL STA
2 THE CURFEW YD
3 HORSESHOE CLOISTERS
4 LODGINGS OF THE MILITARY KNIGHTS
5 KING EDWARD CT
6 CHURCH ST
7 ST ALBANS CL
8 CHURCH LA
9 MARKET ST
10 QUEEN CHARLOTTE ST
11 AMBERLEY PL
12 PEASCOD PL
13 ROYAL FREE CT
14 ELLISON HO
15 SUN PAS
16 HIBBERT'S ALLEY
17 HENRY III TOWER
18 BURFORD HO
19 DARVILLE HO
20 RALSTON CT
21 VICTORIA CT
22 THE COURTYARD

206
212

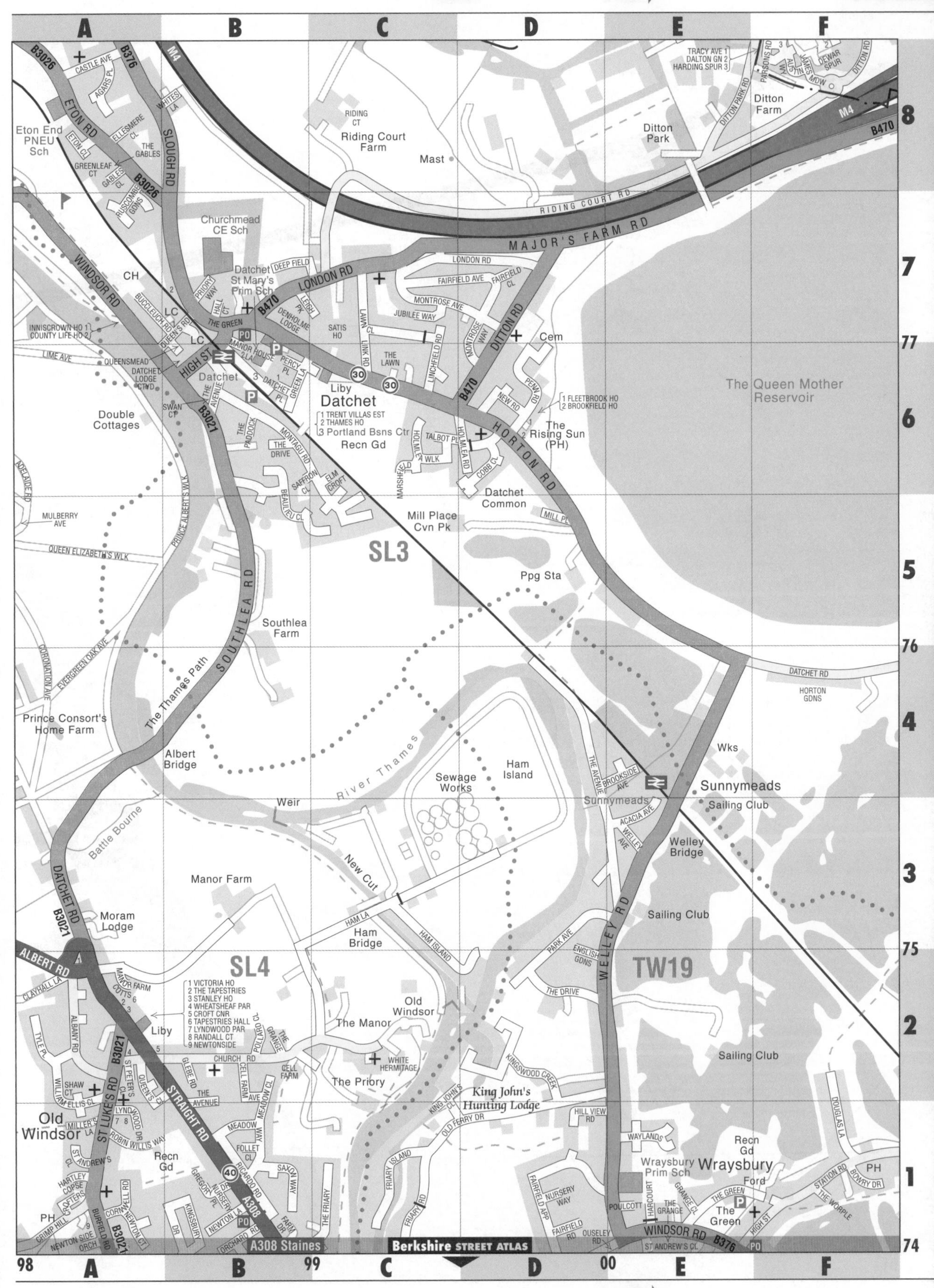
A
B
C
D
E
F
Eton End PNEU Sch
Riding Court Farm
Mast
Ditton Park
Ditton Farm
M4
B470
RIDING COURT RD
MAJOR'S FARM RD
Churchmead CE Sch
Datchet St Mary's Prim Sch
LONDON RD
WINDSOR RD
SLOUGH RD
ETON RD
B3026
B376
HIGH ST
Datchet
Liby
Double Cottages
Recn Gd
Mill Place Cvn Pk
Datchet Common
The Rising Sun (PH)
Cem
The Queen Mother Reservoir
DITTON RD
HORTON RD
SL3
Ppg Sta
Southlea Farm
SOUTHLEA RD
The Thames Path
Prince Consort's Home Farm
Albert Bridge
River Thames
Weir
Sewage Works
Ham Island
Sunnymeads
Sailing Club
Welley Bridge
Wks
DATCHET RD
HORTON GDNS
Manor Farm
Moram Lodge
New Cut
Ham Bridge
SL4
TW19
WELLEY RD
Old Windsor
The Manor
The Priory
King John's Hunting Lodge
STRAIGHT RD
B3021
A308
ALBERT RD
Recn Gd
Wraysbury Prim Sch
Wraysbury
The Green
Ford
PH
WINDSOR RD
1 TRENT VILLAS EST
2 THAMES HO
3 Portland Bsns Ctr
1 FLEETBROOK HO
2 BROOKFIELD HO
1 VICTORIA HO
2 THE TAPESTRIES
3 STANLEY HO
4 WHEATSHEAF PAR
5 CROFT CNR
6 TAPESTRIES HALL
7 LYNDWOOD PAR
8 RANDALL CT
9 NEWTONSIDE
TRACY AVE 1
DALTON GN 2
HARDING SPUR 3
8
7
77
6
5
76
4
3
75
2
1
74
98
99
00
A308 Staines

212

211
207

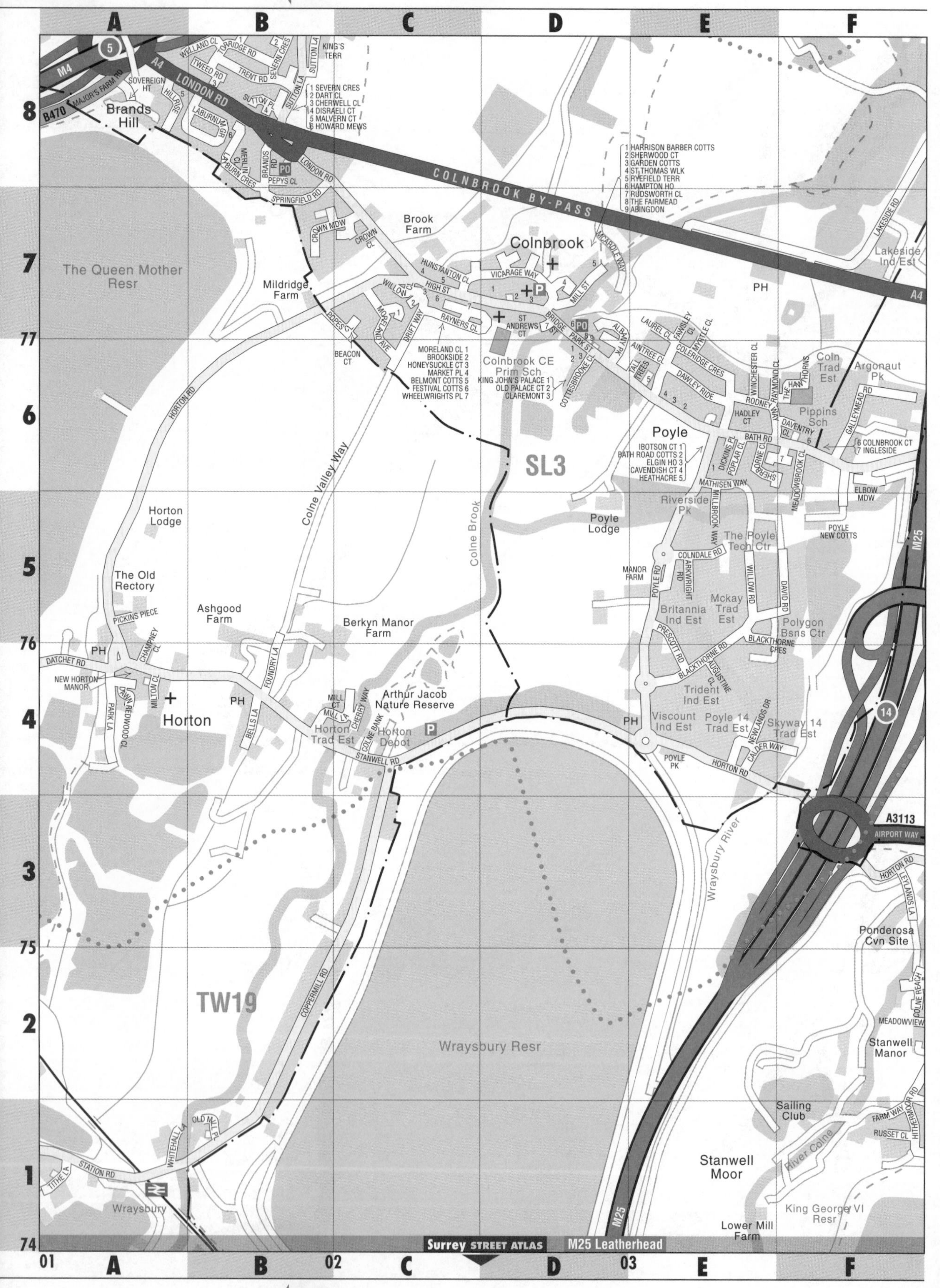
Brands Hill
The Queen Mother Resr
Mildridge Farm
Brook Farm
Colnbrook
COLNBROOK BY-PASS
LONDON RD
Colnbrook CE Prim Sch
Poyle
SL3
Horton Lodge
The Old Rectory
Ashgood Farm
Berkyn Manor Farm
Arthur Jacob Nature Reserve
Horton
Horton Trad Est
Horton Depot
Colne Valley Way
Colne Brook
Poyle Lodge
Riverside Pk
The Poyle Tech Ctr
Britannia Ind Est
Mckay Trad Est
Polygon Bsns Ctr
Trident Ind Est
Viscount Ind Est
Poyle 14 Trad Est
Skyway 14 Trad Est
Lakeside Ind Est
Coln Trad Est
Argonaut Pk
Pippins Sch
Wraysbury River
Wraysbury Resr
TW19
Wraysbury
Ponderosa Cvn Site
Stanwell Manor
Sailing Club
Stanwell Moor
Lower Mill Farm
King George VI Resr
River Colne
1 SEVERN CRES
2 DART CL
3 CHERWELL CL
4 DISRAELI CT
5 MALVERN CT
6 HOWARD MEWS
1 HARRISON BARBER COTTS
2 SHERWOOD CT
3 GARDEN COTTS
4 ST THOMAS WLK
5 RYEFIELD TERR
6 HAMPTON HO
7 RUDSWORTH CL
8 THE FAIRMEAD
9 ABINGDON
MORELAND CL 1
BROOKSIDE 2
HONEYSUCKLE CT 3
MARKET PL 4
BELMONT COTTS 5
FESTIVAL COTTS 6
WHEELWRIGHTS PL 7
KING JOHN'S PALACE 1
OLD PALACE CT 2
CLAREMONT 3
IBOTSON CT 1
BATH ROAD COTTS 2
ELGIN HO 3
CAVENDISH CT 4
HEATHACRE 5
6 COLNBROOK CT
7 INGLESIDE
M4
A4
B470
M25
A3113
AIRPORT WAY
A B C D E F
8 7 77 6 5 76 4 3 75 2 1 74
01 02 03
Surrey STREET ATLAS
M25 Leatherhead

211

208

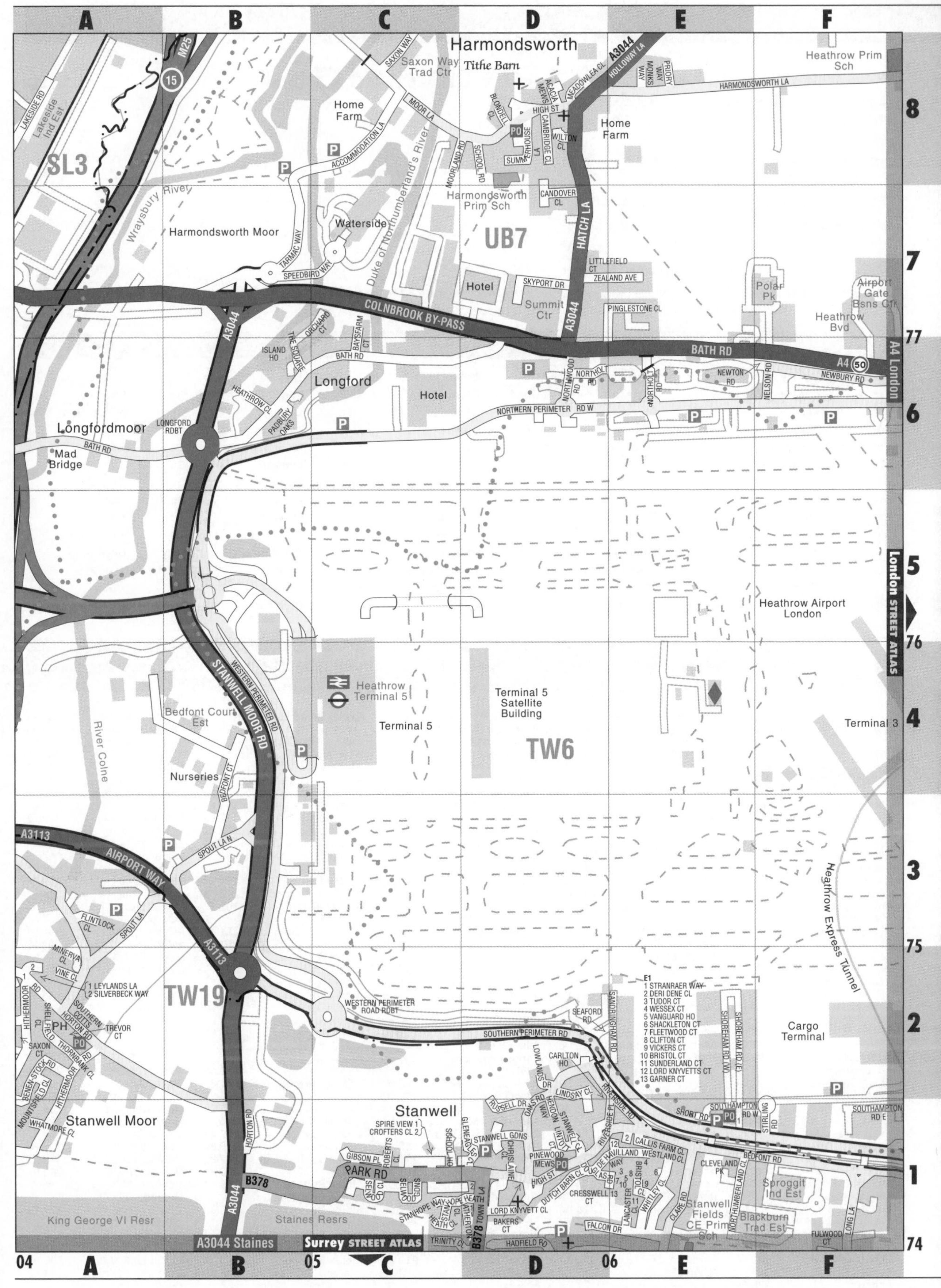

A3044 Staines
Surrey STREET ATLAS
London STREET ATLAS

Index

- **Place name** May be abbreviated on the map
- **Location number** Present when a number indicates the place's position in a crowded area of mapping
- **Locality, town or village** Shown when more than one place has the same name
- **Postcode district** District for the indexed place
- **Page and grid square** Page number and grid reference for the standard mapping

Church Rd 6 Beckenham BR2..........**53** C6

Cities, towns and villages are listed in CAPITAL LETTERS

Public and commercial buildings are highlighted in **magenta** **Places of interest** are highlighted in **blue** with a star

Abbreviations used in the index

Acad	**Academy**	Comm	**Common**	Gd	**Ground**	L	**Leisure**	Prom	**Promenade**
App	**Approach**	Cott	**Cottage**	Gdn	**Garden**	La	**Lane**	Rd	**Road**
Arc	**Arcade**	Cres	**Crescent**	Gn	**Green**	Liby	**Library**	Recn	**Recreation**
Ave	**Avenue**	Cswy	**Causeway**	Gr	**Grove**	Mdw	**Meadow**	Ret	**Retail**
Bglw	**Bungalow**	Ct	**Court**	H	**Hall**	Meml	**Memorial**	Sh	**Shopping**
Bldg	**Building**	Ctr	**Centre**	Ho	**House**	Mkt	**Market**	Sq	**Square**
Bsns, Bus	**Business**	Ctry	**Country**	Hospl	**Hospital**	Mus	**Museum**	St	**Street**
Bvd	**Boulevard**	Cty	**County**	HQ	**Headquarters**	Orch	**Orchard**	Sta	**Station**
Cath	**Cathedral**	Dr	**Drive**	Hts	**Heights**	Pal	**Palace**	Terr	**Terrace**
Cir	**Circus**	Dro	**Drove**	Ind	**Industrial**	Par	**Parade**	TH	**Town Hall**
Cl	**Close**	Ed	**Education**	Inst	**Institute**	Pas	**Passage**	Univ	**University**
Cnr	**Corner**	Emb	**Embankment**	Int	**International**	Pk	**Park**	Wk, Wlk	**Walk**
Coll	**College**	Est	**Estate**	Intc	**Interchange**	Pl	**Place**	Wr	**Water**
Com	**Community**	Ex	**Exhibition**	Junc	**Junction**	Prec	**Precinct**	Yd	**Yard**

Index of towns, villages, streets, hospitals, industrial estates, railway stations, schools, shopping centres, universities and places of interest

Abb–Ale

A

Abbey Barn La HP10 ... **173** E3
Abbey Barn Rd HP11 ... **173** F4
Abbey Cl SL1 ... **204** E6
Abbey Cotts SL7 ... **193** B4
Abbey Ct HP5 ... **154** B6
Abbey Ctr The HP19 ... **101** B2
Abbeydore Gr MK10 ... **35** F1
Abbeyfield Ho HP16 ... **152** A7
Abbey Gate SL6 ... **204** A7
Abbeyhill Rdbt MK12 ... **33** E4
Abbey Mead SL8 ... **184** F5
Abbey Park La SL1 ... **186** E2
Abbey Rd
Aylesbury HP19 ... **101** B2
Bourne End SL8 ... **184** F5
Milton Keynes, Bradwell MK13 ... **34** A4
Milton Keynes, Simpson MK6 ... **47** E5
Syresham NN13 ... **27** C7
Abbey's Prim Sch MK3 .. **47** A2
Abbey Sq MK43 ... **8** E5
Abbey Terr MK16 ... **22** D4
Abbey Way
High Wycombe HP11 ... **173** A6
Milton Keynes MK13 ... **34** B6
Ravenstone MK46 ... **5** E2
Abbey Wlk HP16 ... **152** B7
Abbot Ridge HP18 ... **125** D5
Abbotsbury MK4 ... **45** E2
Abbots Cl MK13 ... **34** B6
Abbotsfield MK6 ... **47** B8
Abbots Way
High Wycombe HP12 ... **172** D3
Monks Risborough HP27 **139** C5
Abbot's Wlk SL4 ... **209** E5
Abbotswood HP27 ... **150** C4
Abbotts Cl HP20 ... **101** E1
Abbott's Cl UB8 ... **208** D8
Abbotts Rd HP20 ... **101** E1
Abbotts Vale HP5 ... **144** C3
Abbotts Way
Slough SL1 ... **204** D5
Wingrave HP22 ... **89** A4
Abbot Wlk HP18 ... **125** D5
Abell Gdns SL6 ... **195** B1
Abercromby Ave HP12 . **172** E8
Abercromby Ct 4 HP12 ... **172** D8
Aberdeen Ave SL1 ... **205** A6
Aberdeen Cl MK3 ... **46** F2
Abingdon Cl
Thame OX9 ... **125** F1
Uxbridge UB10 ... **201** F4
Abingdon Wlk SL6 ... **195** E3
Abington SL3 ... **212** D7
Abney Court Dr SL8 ... **185** A2
Abraham Cl MK15 ... **35** C6
Abrahams Rd RG9 ... **191** C3
Abstacle Hill HP23 ... **118** F3
Acacia 3 RG9 ... **191** D2
Acacia Ave
West Drayton UB7 ... **208** F6
Wraysbury TW19 ... **211** E3
Acacia Cl HP5 ... **144** A1
Acacia Gr HP4 ... **135** B3
Acacia Ho SL9 ... **177** E2
Acacia Mews UB7 ... **213** D8
Acacia Wlk HP23 ... **118** E3
Accommodation La UB7 ... **213** C8
Ackerman Cl MK18 ... **52** F8
Ackroyd Pl MK5 ... **46** B5
Acorn Cl
High Wycombe HP13 ... **173** D7
Slough SL3 ... **207** B1
Acorn Gdns HP12 ... **172** E4
Acorn Ho MK9 ... **34** D2
Acorn Wlk MK9 ... **34** E2
Acrefield Rd SL9 ... **188** D8
Acre Pas SL4 ... **210** D6
Acres End HP7 ... **165** E8
Acres The HP13 ... **161** E1
Acres Way HP19 ... **101** C4
Acre The SL7 ... **183** F2
Adam Cl
High Wycombe HP13 ... **173** D8
Slough SL1 ... **205** A5
Adam Ct RG9 ... **191** E2
Adams Cl MK18 ... **41** C1
Adams Ct MK6 ... **47** C8
Adams Pk (Wycombe Wanderers FC & London Wasps) HP12 ... **172** A7
Adams Way HP23 ... **119** B6
Addenbrookes MK16 ... **22** F3
ADDINGTON ... **65** A6
Addington Cl SL4 ... **210** A4
Addington Cotts HP22 .. **131** B5
Addington Rd MK18 ... **41** D1
Addington Terr MK18 ... **41** D1
Addison Cl SL0 ... **207** E6
Addison Ct SL6 ... **196** B1
Addison Rd
Chesham HP5 ... **144** C2
Steeple Claydon MK18 ... **63** D2
Adelaide Cl SL1 ... **205** A4
Adelaide Rd
High Wycombe HP13 ... **162** D1
Windsor SL4 ... **210** F6
Adelaide Sq SL4 ... **210** D5
Adelphi Gdns SL1 ... **205** E4
Adelphi St MK9 ... **34** F4
Adkins Cl HP19 ... **100** F3
Adkins Ct HP14 ... **158** E5
Admiralty Cl UB7 ... **208** F4
Admiral Way HP4 ... **134** F6
Adrians Wlk SL2 ... **205** F5
ADSTOCK ... **53** F1
Adstock Mews 2 SL9 .. **177** D2
Adwell Sq RG9 ... **191** D2
Agars Pl SL3 ... **211** A8
Agora Ctr MK12 ... **33** D7
Agora Ctr (Sh Ctr) 7 MK2 ... **58** C8
Aidan Cl HP21 ... **116** A4
Ailward Rd HP19 ... **101** A2
Ainsdale Cl MK3 ... **46** D1
Aintree Cl
Milton Keynes MK3 ... **57** C6
Poyle SL3 ... **212** E6
Airport Gate Bsns Ctr UB7 ... **213** F7
Airport Way TW19 ... **213** A3
Aiston Pl HP20 ... **101** F2
Ajax Ave SL1 ... **205** B6
AKELEY ... **41** E8
Akeley Wood Jun Sch MK19 ... **31** A1
Akeley Wood Lower Sch MK18 ... **29** B4
Akeley Wood Sch MK18 . **41** C7
Akeman St HP23 ... **119** A3
Akerlea Cl MK6 ... **47** C6
Akerman Cl MK12 ... **33** B5
Akister Cl MK18 ... **52** E8
Alabama Circ HP11 ... **173** B4
Alabama Dr HP11 ... **173** B3
Alan Way SL3 ... **206** E7
Alaska St HP11 ... **173** B4
Alastair Mews HP9 ... **175** F2
Albany Ct MK14 ... **34** D7
Albany Gate HP5 ... **144** B1
Albany Pk SL3 ... **212** D7
Albany Pl HP19 ... **101** A2
Albany Rd
Old Windsor SL4 ... **211** A2
Windsor SL4 ... **210** D5
Albany Terr HP23 ... **119** B6
Albert Cl 9 SL1 ... **205** F3
Albert Pl SL4 ... **205** A1
Albert Rd
Chesham HP5 ... **154** C8
Henley-on-Thames RG9 .. **191** E1
West Drayton UB7 ... **208** E5
Windsor SL4 ... **210** E3
Albert St
Aylesbury HP20 ... **116** A8
4 High Wycombe HP13 . **173** C7
Maidenhead SL6 ... **202** F7
Milton Keynes MK2 ... **58** C8
Slough SL1 ... **205** F3
Tring HP23 ... **119** A3
Windsor SL4 ... **210** B6
Albion SL3 ... **207** B1
Albion Cl SL2 ... **206** A5
Albion Cotts SL6 ... **195** C7
Albion Cres HP8 ... **177** B7
Albion Ho HP12 ... **172** C5
Albion Pl
Milton Keynes MK9 ... **35** A3
2 Windsor SL4 ... **210** A5
Albion Rd
Chalfont St Giles HP8 ... **177** B8
High Wycombe HP12 ... **172** C5
Pitstone LU7 ... **105** D5
Albion St HP20 ... **115** E8
ALBURY ... **136** B7
Albury Ct 3 MK8 ... **33** F1
Albury View OX9 ... **136** A6
Aldborough Spur SL1 .. **205** E7
Aldbourne Rd SL1 ... **204** B8
ALDBURY ... **120** D5
Aldbury Gdns HP23 ... **119** B6
Aldbury Prim Sch HP23 ... **120** C6
Aldbury Rd WD3 ... **167** F2
Aldebury Rd SL6 ... **195** F2
Aldene Rd MK19 ... **11** B3
Aldenham MK6 ... **47** D5
Alden View SL4 ... **209** D6
Alderbourne La SL3 ... **199** E8
Alderbourne Manor SL9 ... **189** A1
Alderbury Rd SL3 ... **207** A4
Alderbury Road W SL3 . **206** F4
Alder Cl SL1 ... **204** F5
Aldergill MK13 ... **34** C5
Alderley Ct HP4 ... **135** C3
Aldermead MK12 ... **33** E5
Alderney Pl MK5 ... **45** F4
Alder Rd
Aylesbury HP22 ... **116** C4
Iver Heath SL0 ... **200** D3
New Denham UB9 ... **201** C6
Alderson Cl 1 HP19 ... **101** A2
Alders The UB9 ... **201** C6
ALDERTON ... **9** A2
Alderton Dr HP4 ... **121** B8
Aldin Avenue N SL1 ... **206** A4
Aldin Avenue S SL1 ... **206** A4
Aldrich Dr MK15 ... **35** E7
Aldridge Ct HP11 ... **173** F4
Aldridge Rd SL2 ... **198** A1
Aldwick Dr SL6 ... **202** D6
Aldwycks Cl MK5 ... **45** F6
Alexander Ct
High Wycombe HP12 ... **172** E8
Slough SL1 ... **205** C4
Alexander Fst Sch SL4 . **209** C4
Alexander Ho 1 MK2 ... **58** C8
Alexander Rd HP20 ... **101** D1
Alexander St HP5 ... **144** C1
Alexandra Ct
Leighton Buzzard LU7 ... **80** F8
4 Milton Keynes MK13 ... **34** A4
Windsor SL4 ... **210** D5

Alexandra Dr MK16 22 C2
Alexandra Pk HP11 173 A6
Alexandra Rd
High Wycombe HP13 173 E5
Maidenhead SL6 202 D8
Slough SL1 205 D3
Uxbridge UB8 201 D3
Windsor SL4 210 D5
Alford Pl MK3 47 B1
Alford Rd HP12 172 C3
Alfred Ct SL8 185 B3
Alfred Davis Ct SL7 183 D3
Alfriston Specl Sch HP9 175 C6
Alham Rd HP21 115 C6
Alice Cl HP15 163 C7
Alice La SL1 197 B1
Alladale Pl MK12 33 D4
Allanson Rd SL7 183 F3
Allenby Rd SL6 202 B7
Allen Cl MK2 58 C5
Allen Dr HP14 161 C8
Allerds Rd SL2 198 A4
Allerford Ct MK4 46 C4
Alleyns La SL6 195 D8
Allhusen Gdns SL3 199 E8
Allington Circ MK4 45 E1
Allington Ct SL2 205 F6
Allison Ct MK15 35 C1
Allkins Ct SL4 210 D5
Allonby Way HP21 116 B7
All Saints' Ave SL6 202 D7
All Saints CE Controlled Jun Sch SL6 202 C6
All Saints View MK5 46 B8
All Souls Cotts SL3 206 E8
Allyn Cl HP13 173 C8
Alma Ct
Burnham SL1 197 C2
Eton Wick SL4 204 F2
Alma Rd
Berkhamsted HP4 134 E6
Chesham HP5 144 C2
Eton Wick SL4 204 F2
Windsor SL4 210 C6
Almhouses MK14 21 E1
Almond Cl
Newport Pagnell MK16 22 B3
Windsor SL4 210 B5
Almond Rd SL1 197 C2
Almond Tree Dr HP22 116 C4
Almond Way HP27 139 A2
Almond Wlk HP15 163 B3
Almons Way SL2 206 B8
Almshouses
Eton SL4 210 D7
Old Windsor SL4 210 F1
Worminghall HP18 123 E5
Almshouses The MK46 5 E2
Alnwick Dr HP23 103 F7
Alpha Ct HP7 165 B7
Alpha Street N 3 SL1 206 A4
Alpha Street S SL1 205 F3
Alpine Cl SL6 203 A6
Alpine Croft MK5 46 A3
ALSCOT 139 A5
Alscot La HP27 139 A5
Alsford Wharf HP4 135 C5
Alston Dr MK13 33 F3
Alstonefield 1 MK4 46 B3
Alston Gdns SL6 202 E7
Althorpe Cres MK13 34 B6
Altona Rd HP10 174 D3
Altona Way SL1 205 B7
Alton Bsns Pk HP19 101 B1
Alton Gate MK4 45 F3
Altwood Bailey SL6 202 B5
Altwood CE Sch SL6 202 B5
Altwood Cl
Maidenhead SL6 202 B5
Slough SL1 204 E8
Altwood Dr SL6 202 B5
Altwood Rd SL6 202 B5
Alverton MK14 34 F8
Alvista Ave SL6 204 B7
Alvric Way 3 MK12 33 A6
Alwin Cl HP21 115 C4
Alwins Field LU7 80 D8
Alwyn Inf Sch SL6 202 C8
Alwyn Rd SL6 202 B8
Alyngton HP4 134 E7
Alyson Ct 2 SL6 195 F1
Amanda Ct SL3 206 D3
Amber Cotts HP7 164 F3
Ambergate MK16 36 B4
Amberley Ct SL6 196 C3
Amberley Pl 11 SL4 210 D6
Amberley Rd SL2 204 E8
Amberley Way UB10 201 E3
Amberley Wlk MK4 45 E1
Amblers Way MK18 53 A1
Ambleside
Amersham HP6 154 C2
Aylesbury HP21 116 B5
Ambleside Wlk UB8 201 D4
Ambridge Gr MK6 35 C1
Ambrose Ct MK15 35 C2
Amelias La MK9 35 A3
Amerden Cl SL6 203 D7
Amerden La SL6 203 D7
Amerden Way SL1 205 A4
American Com Sch UB10 201 F4
AMERSHAM 154 B2
AMERSHAM COMMON 165 E8
Amersham Ct HP7 165 A7
Amersham Hill HP13 173 B7
Amersham Hill Dr HP13 173 C8
Amersham Hill Gdns HP13 173 C8
Amersham Hospl HP7 165 A6
Amersham Mus★ HP7 165 B7
AMERSHAM OLD TOWN 165 A7
AMERSHAM ON THE HILL 154 D2
Amersham Pl HP7 166 C8
Amersham Rd
Beaconsfield HP7 176 A6
Chalfont Common HP8, SL9 177 D6
Chalfont St Giles HP8 166 B2
Chalfont St Peter SL9 177 E2
Chesham HP6 154 B5
Chorleywood WD3 167 C8
Denham Green SL9 189 A4
Gerrards Cross SL9 188 F7
Hazlemere HP15 162 E2
High Wycombe HP13 173 C8
Little Chalfont HP6 166 E8
Amersham Sch HP7 165 E7
Amersham Sta/U Sta HP6 154 C1
Amersham Way HP6 166 E8
Amersham & Wycombe Coll
Amersham HP7 165 F8
Chesham HP5 144 D3
Flackwell Heath HP10 173 E2
Amesbury Rd SL1 204 F4
Ames Cl MK6 46 F8
Amherst Ct MK15 35 C7
Amicia Gdns SL2 198 F4
Amos Ct MK13 34 A6
Amy La HP5 154 B7
Ancastle Gn RG9 191 D1
Ancell Rd MK11 32 E5
Anchor Ct SL6 195 F7
Anchor La 1 HP20 115 E8
Ancona Gdns MK5 45 F3
Andermans SL4 209 D6
Andersen Gate MK4 57 A7
Anderson Cl HP14 158 F4
Anding Cl MK46 6 E4
Andover Cl UB8 201 B3
Andrewes Croft MK14 34 F8
Andrew Hill La SL2 187 C3
Andrews Cl LU7 69 E3
Andrews Reach SL8 185 A2
Andrews Way
Aylesbury HP19 115 A7
Marlow Bottom SL7 183 C8
Anershall HP22 89 B3
Angel Cl MK15 35 A7
Angelica Cl UB7 208 F7
Angelica Ct MK7 48 A5
Angels Cl MK18 65 F4
Anglefield Rd HP4 135 B4
Anglesey Ct
Milton Keynes MK8 46 A8
Stokenchurch HP14 158 E5
Angling Spring Wood Talking Trail★ HP16 151 F7
Angood Cl HP27 139 A3
Angora Cl MK5 46 A3
Angstrom Cl MK5 46 B5
Angus Dr MK3 46 F2
Angus Rd HP19 101 A3
Anne Cl SL6 195 E2
Annes Gr MK14 21 D1
Annesley Rd MK16 22 B3
Anns Cl
Aylesbury HP21 116 A4
Tring HP23 118 E3
Anscurf Rd SL2 198 A2
Anslow Gdns SL0 200 D3
Anslow Pl SL1 204 C8
Anson Cl
Aylesbury HP21 115 E4
Bovingdon HP3 145 F4
Anson Rd MK12 33 C6
Anstey Brook HP22 117 A3
Anstey Cl HP18 99 B6
Anstey Ct HP18 99 B7
Anthony Cl HP13 161 F1
Anthony Ct MK11 32 D5
Anthony Way SL1 204 D6
Anton Way HP21 115 D3
Anvil Cl HP3 146 B3
Anvil Ct SL3 207 A2
Anxey Way HP17 126 F6
Aplin Rd HP21 116 C6
Appleacres MK17 69 D8
Appleby Heath MK2 58 D6
Apple Cotts HP3 146 A4
Applecroft
Berkhamsted HP4 134 E6
Maidenhead SL6 202 C3
Applecroft continued
Newton Longville MK17 57 D4
Applefield HP7 166 C7
Appleton Cl HP7 166 E1
Appleton Mews 4 MK4 46 B3
Appletree Ave UB7, UB8 208 F7
Apple Tree Cl
Leighton Buzzard LU7 80 D6
Loudwater HP13 174 A4
Appletree La 3 SL3 206 C3
Appletree Wlk HP5 154 D5
Applewick La HP12 172 C8
Applewood Cl UB10 201 E8
Appleyard Pl 1 MK6 34 E1
Approach Rd SL6 203 E7
Approach The MK8 33 E2
Apsley Cotts SL6 195 E7
Apsley Ho SL1 206 A4
Aqua Vale Swimming & Fitness Ctr HP20 115 F8
Aran Hts HP8 177 B6
Arborfield Cl SL1 205 E3
Arbour Vale Specialist Sch Sports Coll SL2 198 B2
Arbour View HP7 166 B8
Arbroath Cl MK3 46 E3
Arbrook Ave MK13 34 D3
Arcade The HP9 175 E3
Archdale 1 HP11 173 A6
Archer Cl SL6 202 D8
Archer Ct HP6 154 C2
Archer Dr HP20 102 A2
Archers Way HP14 171 B5
Archers Wells MK3 47 B2
Archer Terr UB7 208 E6
Archford Croft MK4 46 C3
Archive Cl HP22 117 D5
Arch Way
High Wycombe HP13 173 A7
Speen HP27 150 B4
Archways 14 HP20 115 D8
Arden Cl HP3 146 A3
Ardenham La HP19 101 D1
Ardenham St HP19 101 C1
Arden Park MK12 33 B7
Ardley Mews 7 MK10 36 B3
Ardrossan Cl SL2 198 C1
Ardwell La MK12 33 B5
Ardys Ct MK5 46 B8
Argonaut Pk SL3 212 F6
Argyle Ave HP19 101 B2
Argyll Ave SL1 205 A6
Argyll Ho MK3 46 F1
Aries Ho HP10 185 A8
Aris Way MK18 52 D6
Arizona St HP11 173 B4
Arklay Cl UB8 201 F1
Arkley Ct SL6 203 C1
Arklow Ct WD3 167 D5
Arkwright Rd SL3 212 E5
Arlington Cl SL6 202 A8
Arlington Ct MK4 46 E3
Arlott Cres MK6 46 F8
Armourer Dr MK14 34 F6
Armstrong Cl MK8 45 E7
Armstrong Ho SL2 206 C7
Arncliffe Dr MK13 34 B5
Arncott Rd OX25 95 D7
Arncott Way HP19 100 F1
Arncott Wood Rd OX25 94 E6
Arne La MK7 48 D5
Arnison Ave HP13 162 D1
Arnold Cl HP22 116 C2
Arnold Cott MK19 32 C7
Arnold Ct HP21 115 F6
Arnolds Cl MK18 53 A1
Arnold's Cotts HP5 143 B4
Arnos Gr MK10 35 F1
Arnott's Yd HP18 125 D6
Arranmore Ho HP11 174 B4
Arrewig La HP5 142 E8
Arrow Pl MK2 58 D4
Arthur Cl SL6 195 E5
Arthur Jacob Nature Reserve★ SL3 212 C4
Arthur Rd
Slough SL1 205 D4
Windsor SL4 210 C6
Artichoke Dell WD3 167 E4
Arundel Cl SL6 202 A8
Arundel Ct SL3 206 D2
Arundel Gn HP20 101 F2
Arundel Gr MK3 57 E7
Arundel Ho
1 High Wycombe HP13 173 F7
Uxbridge UB8 201 C3
Arundel Rd
High Wycombe HP12 172 B6
Uxbridge UB8 201 B2
Ascot Dr LU7 80 D6
Ascot Ho MK9 34 C2
Ascot Pl MK3 57 D7
Ascot Rd SL6 203 A1
ASCOTT 80 A2
Ascott Ct HP20 101 E1
Ascott House★ LU7 80 A2
Ascott Rd HP20 101 E1
Ascough Cl HP19 101 D3
Ashbourne End HP21 115 D4
Ashbourne Gr SL6 202 C3
Ashbourne Ho 5 SL1 205 E4
Ashbrook Sch MK8 33 E1
Ashburnham Cl 2 MK3 46 D1
Ashburnham Cres LU7 80 E6
Ashby MK6 47 A8
Ashby Rd HP4 134 D7
Ashby Villas LU7 92 A1
Ash Cl
Aylesbury HP20 102 A2
Slough SL3 207 B3
Walter's Ash HP14 161 B8
Ashcroft Ct SL1 197 B3
Ashcroft Dr UB9 189 F4
Ashcroft Rd SL6 202 C8
Ashcroft Terr HP23 119 A5
Ashdown SL6 196 B3
Ashdown Cl MK14 35 A8
Ashdown Ct HP13 173 D6
Ashdown Rd HP13 174 A8
Ashdown Way HP6 154 D2
Ashen Cross SL3 207 B8
Ashenden Wlk SL2 198 D8
ASHENDON 97 F1
Ashendon Rd HP18 98 C6
ASHERIDGE 143 C6
Asheridge Rd HP5 144 A2
Asheridge Rd Ind Est HP5 144 A2
Ashfield MK14 34 D8
Ashfield Cl HP15 163 B2
Ashfield Cotts UB9 190 A1
Ashfield Gr MK2 58 C7
Ashfield Rd HP5 144 D2
Ashfield Rise HP18 109 D5
Ashfield Way HP15 163 B3
Ashfold Sch HP18 110 F8
Ashford Cl HP21 116 A5
Ashford Cres MK8 45 D6
Ashford La SL4 204 B4
Ashford Rd SL0 200 C4
Ash Gn UB9 201 B6
Ash Gr
Amersham HP6 154 A3
Aylesbury HP21 116 A7
Stoke Poges SL2 198 F5
West Drayton UB7 208 F6
Ashgrove MK18 63 D2
Ashgrove Gdns HP22 86 E7
Ash Hill Prim Sch HP13 174 A7
Ash Hill Rd MK16 22 B4
Ash La SL4 209 D5
Ashland Rdbt MK1 47 C5
Ashlea MK46 6 E3
Ashlea Rd SL9 177 E1
Ashleigh Cl HP7 165 E8
Ashley HP10 185 F7
Ashley Cl LU7 105 A8
Ashley Ct
15 Aylesbury HP19 115 A8
Maidenhead SL6 203 B7
Tylers Green HP10 163 B1
West Drayton UB7 208 E5
Ashley Dr HP10 163 C1
ASHLEY GREEN 144 F7
Ashley Green Rd HP5 144 E5
Ashley Pk SL6 196 B2
Ashley Rd UB8 201 B3
Ashley Row HP20 102 A1
Ashleys WD3 167 F2
Ashlyns Ct HP4 135 B3
Ashlyns Rd HP4 135 B3
Ashlyns Sch HP4 135 C2
Ashmead Comb Sch HP21 115 C5
Ash Mead Dr UB9 190 A2
Ashmead La UB9 190 A2
Ashmead Pl HP7 166 C8
Ashmount Cres 1 SL1 205 A4
Ashotts La HP5 143 B7
Ashover MK10 36 C4
Ashpole Furlong MK5 46 B7
Ash Rd
High Wycombe HP12 172 C4
Princes Risborough HP27 139 B3
Tring HP23 118 F4
Ashridge OX39 147 B6
Ashridge Bsns Sch HP4 121 C5
Ashridge Cl
1 Bovingdon HP3 146 A3
Milton Keynes MK3 57 D7
Ashridge Coll Gdns★ HP4 121 D5
Ashridge Cotts HP4 121 E5
Ashridge Est Visitor Ctr★ HP4 120 E6
Ashridge La HP5 155 D7
Ashridge Rise HP4 134 F5
ASHTON 9 E8
Ashton Pl SL6 202 A6
Ashton Rd NN12 9 D8
Ash Tree Ho HP12 172 C4
Ashtree Wlk HP15 163 B2
Ash Vale WD3 178 D5
Ashwells HP10 174 B8
Ashwells Manor Dr HP10 174 C8
Ashwell St 1 LU7 80 F8
Ashwells Way HP8 177 D8
Ashwood MK13 34 A7
Ashwood Dr HP5 144 B1
ASKETT 139 D6
Askett La HP27 139 D7
Aspen Cl
Aylesbury HP20 102 A2
Maidenhead SL6 195 A3
Slough SL2 205 B8
West Drayton UB7 208 F5
Aspens Pl HP1 146 F8
Aspery Pl SL1 205 F5
Asplands Cl MK17 49 B4
Aspley Ct
Aylesbury HP19 101 C1
Woburn Sands MK17 49 C3
ASPLEY GUISE 49 F4
Aspley Guise Lower Sch MK17 49 F4
Aspley Guise Sta MK17 49 D6
ASPLEY HEATH 49 A2
Aspley Hill MK17 49 C4
Aspley La MK17 49 E2
Aspreys MK46 6 E4
Assheton Rd HP9 175 E4
Astlethorpe MK8 33 F2
Astley Rd OX9 126 B1
ASTON 192 C5
ASTON ABBOTTS 88 D5
Aston Abbotts Rd
Cublington LU7 78 C1
Weedon HP22 87 E1
Aston Cl
Aylesbury HP19 101 A3
Milton Keynes MK5 46 B5
ASTON CLINTON 117 D6
Aston Clinton Ragpits Wildlife Reserve★ HP22 117 F2
Aston Clinton Rd HP22 116 E6
Aston Clinton Sch HP22 117 D5
Aston Ferry La RG9 192 D5
Aston Hill OX49 157 E7
Aston La RG9 192 C3
Aston Mead SL4 209 E6
Aston Rd HP17 127 B5
Aston Rowant National Nature Reserve★ HP14 157 E6
ASTON SANDFORD 127 D4
Astonville SL2 198 C8
Astor Cl SL6 203 B6
Astronomy Way 12 HP19 115 A8
ASTROPE 104 A3
Astrope La HP23 104 B3
ASTWOOD 16 A3
Astwood Rd MK43 25 C7
Atherstone Ct MK8 33 C2
Atherton Cl TW19 213 D1
Atherton Ct SL4 210 D7
Athlone Cl SL6 195 E1
Athlone Sq SL4 210 C5
Atkins Cl MK13 34 B3
Atlas Ho HP5 144 B1
Atterbrook MK13 34 A4
ATTERBURY 36 A4
Attingham Hill
6 Milton Keynes MK8 33 F1
Milton Keynes MK8 34 A1
Atwell Cl MK8 45 E7
Auckland Cl SL6 203 B8
Auckland Pk MK1 47 D4
Auckland Rd HP13 173 E6
Auden Cl MK16 22 A5
Audley Dr SL6 202 B6
Audley Mead MK13 34 B3
August End SL3 206 E7
Augustine Cl SL3 212 E4
Augustine Mews HP16 152 B7
Augustus Rd MK11 32 E4
Augustus Smith Ho 2 HP4 135 D4
Austen Ave MK46 7 A4
Austen Pl HP19 100 F2
Austenway SL9 188 E8
AUSTENWOOD 188 C8
Austenwood Cl
Chalfont St Peter SL9 177 C1
High Wycombe HP11 173 A4
Austenwood La
Chalfont St Peter SL9 177 D1
Gerrards Cross SL9 188 D8
Austins Mead HP3 146 B3
Austin Way SL3 211 F8
Austin Waye UB8 201 C4
Australia Ave SL6 202 F8
Australia Rd 1 SL1 206 B4
Austwick La MK4 46 B2
Autumn Cl
Aylesbury HP19 101 A3
Slough SL1 204 F5

Autumn Wlk SL6 . . . . 202 A5
Avalon Rd SL8 . . . . 185 B5
Avant Bsns Ctr MK1 . . . . . 47 C2
Avebury SL1 . . . . 205 A6
Avebury Bvd MK9 . . . . 34 E2
Avebury Rdbt MK9 . . . . . . 34 D1
Aveling Rd HP13 . . . . 173 C6
Avenue Cl UB7 . . . . 208 D3
Avenue Dr
Iver Heath SL3 . . . . 199 F1
Slough SL3 . . . . 206 F8
Avenue Ho HP5 . . . . 154 B8
Avenue Rd
Buckingham MK18 . . . . 41 E3
Maidenhead SL6 . . . . 203 B5
Winslow MK18 . . . . 65 F4
Avenue The
Amersham HP7 . . . . 154 C1
Bourne End SL8 . . . . 184 F4
Chinnor OX39 . . . . 147 D6
Datchet SL3 . . . . 211 B6
Dunstable LU6 . . . . 93 E7
Farnham Common SL2 . . . 198 B8
Maidenhead SL6 . . . . 196 C3
Old Windsor SL4 . . . . 211 B2
Princes Risborough HP27 . . . . 139 C4
Uxbridge UB8 . . . . 201 D1
Whitfield NN13 . . . . 26 D4
Worminghall HP18 . . . . . . 123 E5
Wraysbury TW19 . . . . 211 D4
Averil Ct SL6 . . . . 204 C7
Avery Ave HP13 . . . . 161 D2
Avery Ct MK16 . . . . 22 C2
Avington MK8 . . . . 33 E1
Avocet Way HP19 . . . . . . 101 E3
Avonbury Ct NN13 . . . . . . 38 A5
Avon Cl
Newport Pagnell MK16 . . . 22 D3
Slough SL1 . . . . 204 E6
Avondale SL6 . . . . 195 C1
Avon Gr MK3 . . . . 57 E8
Avonmoore SL6 . . . . 203 B8
Avon Pl HP21 . . . . 115 D4
Axis Pk SL3 . . . . 207 B1
AYLESBURY 115 D7
Aylesbury Bsns Ctr HP19 . . . . 101 B1
Aylesbury Coll HP21 . . . 115 C7
Aylesbury Cres SL1 . . . . 205 D6
Aylesbury End HP9 . . . . . 175 E1
Aylesbury Gram Sch HP21 . . . . 115 F7
Aylesbury High Sch HP21 . . . . 115 F7
Aylesbury Ind Ctr HP19 101 C1
Aylesbury Rd
Aston Clinton HP22 . . . . . 117 B5
Bierton HP22 . . . . 102 B3
Chearsley HP18 . . . . 112 B2
Cuddington HP18 . . . . 113 A3
Great Missenden HP16 . . 141 F2
Haddenham HP17, OX9 . . 126 C6
Monks Risborough HP27 139 D6
Thame OX9 . . . . 125 F2
Tring HP23 . . . . 118 E2
Wendover HP22 . . . . 131 B6
Wing LU7 . . . . 79 E1
Aylesbury St
Milton Keynes, Bletchley MK2 . . . . 58 E8
Milton Keynes, Wolverton MK12 . . . . 33 D6
Aylesbury Sta HP20 . . . . 115 D7
Aylesbury Street W MK12 . . . . 33 C6
Aylesbury Vale Acad HP19 . . . . 101 C2
Aylesbury Vale Parkway Sta HP18 . . . . 100 D3
Aylesbury Waterside Theatre HP20 . . . . 115 E8
Aylesford Gr MK10 . . . . . . 36 A1
Ayless Cl HP18 . . . . 98 B7
Ayleswater HP19 . . . . 101 E4
Aylesworth Ave SL2 . . . . 198 B2
Aylward Gdns HP5 . . . . . 144 A1
Aynho Ct MK8 . . . . 45 F8
Aynscombe Cl LU6 . . . . . . 93 F8
Ayres Cl HP21 . . . . 115 B6
Ayrshire Cl HP19 . . . . 101 A3
Ayrton Cl MK8 . . . . 45 D6
Ayr Way MK3 . . . . 46 E2
Aysgarth Pk SL6 . . . . 203 B1
Azalea Cl HP15 . . . . 163 A3
Azalea Way SL3 . . . . 206 E7

B

Babington Cl MK10 . . . . . . 36 A3
Babington Rd HP22 . . . . 131 D6
Babylon Gr 10 MK4 . . . . . . 45 F1
Baccara Gr MK2 . . . . 58 C7
Bachelors Acre SL4 . . . . 210 D6
Back Dr MK16 . . . . 12 F3
Back La
Chalfont St Giles HP8 . . . 177 A7
Great Missenden HP16 . . 152 B7
Tingewick MK18 . . . . 51 A6
Backleys MK7 . . . . 48 A2
Back St
Gawcott MK18 . . . . 51 F4
Thornborough MK18 . . . . . 54 A8
Wendover HP22 . . . . 131 B4
Backs The HP5 . . . . 154 C8
Bacombe Hill Nature Reserve★ HP22 . . . . 131 A3
Bacombe La HP22 . . . . . . 131 B3
Bacon Hill MK46 . . . . 6 E3
Baconsmead UB9 . . . . . . 190 A2
Bader Gdns SL1 . . . . 205 A4
Badgebury Rise SL7 . . . . 183 C7
Badgemore Ct MK8 . . . . . 33 C2
Badgemore La RG9 . . . . . 191 D3
Badgemore Prim Sch RG9 . . . . 191 D2
Badger Cl SL6 . . . . 202 D4
Badgers Gate LU6 . . . . 93 E8
Badgers Mdw HP22 . . . . 131 C5
Badgers Oak MK7 . . . . 48 B7
Badgers Rise HP17 . . . . . 114 C5
Badgers Way
Buckingham MK18 . . . . 52 E7
Marlow Bottom SL7 . . . . . 183 D7
Badgers Wlk WD3 . . . . . . 167 F5
Badgers Wood SL2 . . . . . 198 C7
Badger Way HP15 . . . . . . 163 B5
Bad Godesberg Way SL6 . . . . 202 F7
Badmington Ct 3 HP7 . 165 B7
Badminton Ho 1 HP7 . . 165 B7
Badminton Rd SL6 . . . . . 202 B6
Badminton View MK8 . . . 34 A1
Badrick Rd HP19 . . . . 100 F2
Bagley Cl UB7 . . . . 208 E4
Bagshot Ct MK2 . . . . 58 C7
Bailey Cl
High Wycombe HP13 . . . . 173 C7
Maidenhead SL6 . . . . 202 F7
Windsor SL4 . . . . 210 A5
Bailey Ho 9 SL8 . . . . 185 A4
Bailey's Ct 12 HP20 . . . . . 115 D8
Baily Ct MK5 . . . . 46 A5
Baines Ho HP11 . . . . 173 F4
Baird Cl SL1 . . . . 205 B4
Baisley Ho MK2 . . . . 58 D8
Bakers Cl
Stoke Goldington MK16 . . . 12 B5
Turvey MK43 . . . . 8 E5
Bakers Ct
Stanwell TW19 . . . . 213 D1
Waddesdon HP18 . . . . 99 A6
Bakers La NN12 . . . . 9 A8
Baker's Orch HP10 . . . . . 185 E5
Baker's Piece Ho OX39 147 A4
Baker's Rd UB8 . . . . 201 D5
Baker St
High Wycombe HP11 . . . . 172 F7
Waddesdon HP18 . . . . 99 A6
Bakers Wlk HP22 . . . . . . 116 F2
BAKER'S WOOD 189 D3
Bakers Wood UB9 . . . . . . 189 D3
Bakery Cl MK43 . . . . 25 B1
Bakery Ho 10 HP20 . . . . . . 115 D8
Bala Cl MK2 . . . . 58 D5
Bala Lake Cres MK10 . . . . 36 B4
Bala Way MK2 . . . . 58 C5
Balcary Gdns HP4 . . . . . . 134 F3
Balcary Gr MK4 . . . . 56 F8
Baldways Cl HP22 . . . . 89 C3
Baldwin Cres MK16 . . . . . 22 C3
Baldwin Pl SL6 . . . . 202 C7
Baldwin Rd
Beaconsfield HP9 . . . . 176 B1
Burnham SL1 . . . . 197 C2
Baldwin's Shore SL4 . . . 210 D8
Balfe Mews MK7 . . . . 48 D4
Balfour Mews 3 HP3 . . 146 A4
Balfour Pl SL7 . . . . 183 D4
Balfour Way HP20 . . . . . . 101 E2
Balham's La RG9 . . . . . . 179 F8
Ballard Cl HP21 . . . . 116 B5
Ballard Gn SL4 . . . . 209 E7
Ballards Row HP22 . . . . . 117 D6
BALLINGER COMMON 142 E3
Ballinger Ct HP4 . . . . 135 B3
Ballinger Grange HP16 142 E2
Ballinger Rd HP16 . . . . . 142 E1
Ballinger Row HP16 . . . . 142 D3
Ball Moor MK18 . . . . 52 D6
Balmer Bridge MK18 . . . . 52 E5
Balmer Cut MK18 . . . . 52 E6
Balmerino Cl MK10 . . . . . . 36 B2
Balmoral SL6 . . . . 195 B1
Balmoral Cl SL1 . . . . 204 E7
Balmoral Ct
High Wycombe HP13 . . . . 173 B7
Newport Pagnell MK16 . . . 22 B3
Balmoral Gdns SL4 . . . . . 210 D4
Balsam Cl MK7 . . . . 48 B6
Bamfords La MK43 . . . . 8 E6
Bamfords Yd MK43 . . . . . . 8 E5
Bampton Cl MK4 . . . . 46 E2
Banburies Cl MK3 . . . . 47 A3
Banbury Ave SL1 . . . . 204 F8
BANCROFT 33 F5
Bancroft Rdbt MK13 . . . . . 34 A5
Bandon Cl UB10 . . . . 201 F3
Bangor Cotts SL0 . . . . . . 200 D1
Bangors Cl SL0 . . . . 207 F7
Bangors Road N SL0 . . . 200 D3
Bangors Road S SL0 . . . 207 E8
Bank Apartments SL7 . . 183 D3
Bank Court Mews MK12 . 33 D7
Bankfield Rdbt MK9 . . . . . 35 A2
Bank Gn HP5 . . . . 143 C8
Bank Mill HP4 . . . . 135 E4
Bank Mill La HP4 . . . . . . 135 E3
Bank Rd HP10 . . . . 174 D8
Bankside HP22 . . . . 131 B5
Banks Rd HP17 . . . . 127 A6
Banks Spur SL1 . . . . 205 B4
Bank St HP13 . . . . 174 A4
Banktop Pl MK4 . . . . 46 C3
Bannard Rd SL6 . . . . 202 A5
Banner Ct 1 HP12 . . . . . 172 D8
Bannister Cl SL3 . . . . 206 E4
Bantock Cl MK7 . . . . 48 C5
Bantry Rd SL1 . . . . 204 F4
Barbers Mews MK14 . . . . 34 F6
Barbers Wlk HP23 . . . . . . 118 F3
Barbers Wood Cl HP12 . 172 B4
Barbers Wood Rd HP12 . . . . 172 B4
Barbicus Ct SL6 . . . . 203 B8
Barbury Ct MK14 . . . . 35 A8
Barchester Cl UB8 . . . . . 201 C1
Barchester Rd SL3 . . . . . 206 F4
Barclay Cl OX27 . . . . 72 E6
Barclay Ct 3 HP12 . . . . . 172 E7
Bardney Cl SL6 . . . . 202 D3
Bardolphs Cl HP27 . . . . . 139 C4
Bardon Gn HP20 . . . . 101 E2
Bardsey Ct MK10 . . . . 36 A2
Barford MK11 . . . . 32 F4
Bargeman Rd SL6 . . . . . . 202 E5
Barham Lodge MK18 . . . . 52 C8
Baring Cres HP9 . . . . 175 C3
Baring Rd
Beaconsfield HP9 . . . . 175 D3
High Wycombe HP13 . . . . 173 F7
Barkers Croft MK12 . . . . . 33 C4
Barkestone Cl MK4 . . . . . . 46 C1
Barkham Cl LU7 . . . . 104 F7
Barkus Way HP14 . . . . . . 158 F5
Bar La HP27 . . . . 138 E7
Barlee Cres UB8 . . . . 208 C8
Barley Cl
Hazelmere HP15 . . . . 163 A3
Lewknor OX49 . . . . 157 A8
Weston Turville HP22 . . . 116 F2
Barley Cres HP21 . . . . . . 115 D3
Barleycroft MK4 . . . . 46 E4
Barley Fields HP10 . . . . . 185 E8
Barley Hill Prim Sch OX9 . . . . 126 A1
Barleyhurst Park Prim Sch MK3 . . . . 46 F1
Barley Mead SL6 . . . . 202 A5
Barley Way 3 SL7 . . . . . 183 D1
Barlow Rd HP22 . . . . 131 C5
Barnabas Rd LU7 . . . . 80 D6
Barnacre Cl UB8 . . . . 208 D7
Barnard Cres HP21 . . . . . 115 F5
Barnards Hill SL7 . . . . . . 183 C2
Barn Cl
Farnham Common SL2 . . . 198 B8
Maidenhead SL6 . . . . 195 F2
Barncroft MK43 . . . . 8 E6
Barncroft Rd HP4 . . . . . . 134 F3
Barn Ct HP12 . . . . 172 C7
Barn Dr SL6 . . . . 202 A4
Barnes Ave HP5 . . . . 144 C1
Barnes Pl MK6 . . . . 46 E8
Barnes Wallis Ct HP12 . . 172 E5
Barnes Way SL0 . . . . 207 F6
Barnet Cl MK5 . . . . 45 D5
Barnett Way HP22 . . . . . . 102 B4
Barn Farm SL7 . . . . 183 D3
Barnfield
Iver SL0 . . . . 207 E7
Slough SL1 . . . . 204 D5
Barnfield Cl SL6 . . . . 195 F5
Barnfield Dr MK6 . . . . 47 C5
Barnhill Cl SL7 . . . . 183 D4
Barnhill Gdns SL7 . . . . . . 183 D4
Barnhill Rd SL7 . . . . 183 D4
Barn La RG9 . . . . 191 C4
Barn Rd HP27 . . . . 138 E6
Barnsbury Ave HP20 . . . . 116 B8
Barnsbury Gdns MK16 . . . 22 C3
Barns Cl OX33 . . . . 122 B1
Barnsdale Dr MK4 . . . . 45 F2
Barnsfield Pl UB8 . . . . . . 201 C5
Barnstable Ct MK4 . . . . . . 46 D3
Barns The HP23 . . . . 118 F1
Baroma Way RG9 . . . . . . 191 E2
Barons Cl MK2 . . . . 58 C8
Barons Ct 2 SL7 . . . . 183 E2
Baronsmead RG9 . . . . . . 191 D2
Baronsmead Rd HP12 . . 172 E6
Barrack Hill HP18 . . . . . . 112 E5
Barrack La SL4 . . . . 210 D6
Barracks Hill HP7 . . . . . . 164 F2
Barracks Rd HP11 . . . . . . 173 A6
Barrards Way HP9 . . . . . 176 C4
Barrett Pl
High Wycombe HP11 . . . . 173 C6
Milton Keynes MK5 . . . . . . 45 F6
BARRETTS END 42 F7
Barrie Cl HP19 . . . . 100 F2
Barrington Ct NN13 . . . . . 38 A5
Barrington Mews 4 MK6 . . . . 34 E1
Barrington Park Gdns HP8 . . . . 166 D1
Barrowcroft HP11 . . . . . . 173 F4
Barrow Lodge SL2 . . . . . 198 C1
Barr Piece MK12 . . . . 33 C6
Barr's Rd SL6 . . . . 204 B7
Barry Ave
Eton SL4 . . . . 210 C7
Milton Keynes MK14 . . . . . 34 C7
Barry Cl HP12 . . . . 172 C4
Barry View SL4 . . . . 209 C5
Bartelotts Rd SL2 . . . . . . 197 E1
Bartholomew Cl MK7 . . . . 48 A5
Bartholomew Tipping Way HP14 . . . . 158 F5
Bartlett Pl MK18 . . . . 41 E1
Bartletts SL9 . . . . 177 E3
Barton Dr HP9 . . . . 175 E4
BARTON HARTSHORN 50 D2
Barton Rd
Milton Keynes MK2 . . . . . . 58 C6
Slough SL3 . . . . 206 F4
Bartons Rd HP10 . . . . 163 A1
Barton Way HP13 . . . . . . 162 E1
Bascote MK6 . . . . 47 D5
Base Cl 8 HP20 . . . . 101 F2
Basford Way SL4 . . . . 209 D4
Basildon Ct
1 Leighton Buzzard LU7 . . 80 F7
Milton Keynes MK8 . . . . . . 45 F8
Basing Rd WD3 . . . . 167 F1
Baskerfield Gr MK6 . . . . . 47 C8
Basset Rd HP14 . . . . 171 C4
Bassetsbury La HP11 . . . 173 D5
Bassett Ct MK16 . . . . 22 C4
Bassett Rd
Leighton Buzzard LU7 . . . . 80 F7
Uxbridge UB8 . . . . 201 C5
Bassett Way SL2 . . . . 197 E1
Bass Mead SL6 . . . . 195 F5
Batchelor Cl HP20 . . . . . 101 F2
Batchelors Way
Amersham HP7 . . . . 165 D8
Chesham HP5 . . . . 144 B2
Bateman Croft MK5 . . . . . 45 F6
Bateman Dr HP21 . . . . . . 115 E5
Bates Cl
Granborough MK18 . . . . . . 75 F8
Milton Keynes MK15 . . . . . 35 D7
Slough SL3 . . . . 206 E7
Bates Ct HP20 . . . . 101 F2
Bates Gdns MK17 . . . . 68 B6
Bates La HP22 . . . . 116 F2
Bath Ct SL6 . . . . 202 C6
Bath La MK18 . . . . 52 C8
Bath Lane Terr MK18 . . . . 52 C8
Bath Rd
Harmondsworth UB7 . . . . 213 C6
Maidenhead SL6 . . . . 202 C6
Poyle SL3 . . . . 212 E6
Slough SL1, SL6 . . . . 204 D6
Slough SL2 . . . . 198 B4
Taplow SL6 . . . . 203 E7
Bath Road Cotts SL3 . . . 212 E6
Bathurst Cl SL0 . . . . 207 F4
Bathurst Wlk SL0 . . . . . . 207 F4
Battersby Mews HP21 . . 115 C7
Batt Furlong HP21 . . . . . 115 E3
Batting Cl HP14 . . . . 159 F8
Battings Wood Gdns HP14 . . . . 161 C8
Battle Cl MK46 . . . . 13 F8
Battlemead Cl SL6 . . . . . 196 C3
Battoney Vare SL6 . . . . . 203 C4
Baulk The
Cheddington LU7 . . . . 104 F7
Ivinghoe LU7 . . . . 105 F5
Bawtree Rd UB8 . . . . 201 D6
Baxter Cl
Milton Keynes MK8 . . . . . . 45 E7
Slough SL1 . . . . 205 E3
Baybrook SL6 . . . . 195 F6
Bay Ct HP4 . . . . 135 B4
Bayhurst Wood Ctry Pk★ UB9 . . . . 190 F6
Bay La MK46 . . . . 5 D2
Bayley Cres SL1 . . . . 204 A8
Bayley Gdns HP14 . . . . . . 161 E6
Bayley Hatch HP16 . . . . . 152 D8
Baylis Bsns Ctr SL1 . . . . 205 D6
Baylis Court Sch SL1 . . . 205 D8
Baylis Par SL1 . . . . 205 E7
Baylis Rd SL1 . . . . 205 E6
Bayman Manor HP5 . . . . 144 E2
Bayne Hill HP9 . . . . 176 D3
Bayne Hill Cl HP9 . . . . . . 176 D3
Baynham Mead MK7 . . . . 48 B8
Bayntor Rd HP21 . . . . 115 E4
Baysfarm Ct UB7 . . . . . . 213 C6
Bay Tree Cl
Loudwater HP11 . . . . 174 B2
Newton Longville MK17 . . . 57 D4
Bay Tree Ct SL1 . . . . 197 C2
BEACHAMPTON 44 B6
Beachampton Bsns Pk MK19 . . . . 44 C4
Beacham Rd HP12 . . . . . 172 C3
Beachborough Sch NN13 . . . . 39 A4
Beacon Ave LU6 . . . . 93 E7
Beacon Cl
Beaconsfield HP9 . . . . 175 A1
Chalfont St Peter SL9 . . . 177 E3
Stone HP17 . . . . 114 C5
Uxbridge UB8 . . . . 201 D7
Beacon Ct
Colnbrook SL3 . . . . 212 C7
Milton Keynes MK4 . . . . . . 46 D2
Beacon Hill HP10 . . . . . . 174 D7
Beacon La SL7 . . . . 171 E1
Beacon Rd HP4 . . . . 106 E2
BEACON'S BOTTOM 159 D3
Beacon Sch The HP6 . . . . 154 B4
BEACONSFIELD 175 D1
Beaconsfield Ave HP13 162 A1
Beaconsfield Common La SL2 . . . . 187 C5
Beaconsfield Cotts SL8 185 B2
Beaconsfield High Sch HP9 . . . . 175 D1
Beaconsfield Mews HP9 . . . . 186 A8
Beaconsfield Pl MK16 . . . 22 C4
Beaconsfield Rd
Aston Clinton HP22 . . . . . 117 F4
Aylesbury HP21 . . . . 115 E8
Farnham Common SL2 . . . 198 C5
Tring HP23 . . . . 118 E3
Beaconsfield Sch The HP9 . . . . 175 E1
Beaconsfield Sta HP9 . . 175 E3
Beacon Sports Ctr & Theatre The HP9 . . . . . . 175 A1
Beacon View
Dunstable LU6 . . . . 92 B4
Lewknor OX49 . . . . 157 B8
Beacon Way HP23 . . . . . . 119 C5
Beadlemead MK6 . . . . 47 C6
Beales La MK7 . . . . 48 A5
Bealings End HP9 . . . . . . 175 D5
Beamish Way MK18 . . . . . 66 B5
BEAMOND END 163 F6
Beamond End La HP7, HP15 . . . . 163 F7
Beanfare MK6 . . . . 47 B4
BEANHILL 47 B4
Bearbrook Cl HP21 . . . . . 115 C7
Bearbrook Comb Sch HP19 . . . . 115 C8
Bearswood End HP9 . . . 175 E4
Beatrice Cl OX27 . . . . 72 E6
Beauchamp Cl MK14 . . . . 34 E6
Beauchamp Ct SL1 . . . . . 205 E6
Beaudesert Mews UB7 . 208 E4
Beaufort Cl
Aylesbury HP21 . . . . 116 D7
Marlow SL7 . . . . 183 E2
Beaufort Dr MK15 . . . . 35 C7
Beaufort Gdns SL7 . . . . . 183 E2
Beaufort Pl SL6 . . . . 203 D4
Beaulieu Cl SL3 . . . . 211 B5
Beaumaris Ct SL1 . . . . . . 205 C8
Beaumaris Gr MK5 . . . . . . 46 A6
Beaumont Cl SL6 . . . . . . 202 A3
Beaumont Cotts 1 SL4 . . . . 210 C6
Beaumont Ct SL3 . . . . . . 206 D7
Beaumont Gr HP15 . . . . . 162 F3
Beaumont Rd
Slough SL2 . . . . 205 D8
Windsor SL4 . . . . 210 C5
Beaumont Rise SL7 . . . . 183 E2
Beaumont Way HP15 . . . . 162 F4
Beaverbrook Ct MK3 . . . . 46 F1
Beaver Cl MK18 . . . . 52 E7
Beckets Sq HP4 . . . . 135 A6
Beckett Chase 5 SL3 . . 206 F1
Beckings Way HP10 . . . . 185 C7
Beckinsale Gr MK8 . . . . . 45 E7
Beckton Rise MK10 . . . . . . 35 E1
Beckwell Rd SL1 . . . . 205 C4
Bec La MK15 . . . . 35 B7
Bedder Rd HP12 . . . . 172 C3
Beddoes Croft MK5 . . . . . 45 E4
Bede Ct HP4 . . . . 121 C8
Bedfont Court Est TW19 . . . . 213 B4
Bedfont Rd TW19 . . . . . . 213 F1
Bedford Ave
Little Chalfont HP6 . . . . . 166 D8
Slough SL1 . . . . 205 A7
Bedford Cl
Chenies WD3 . . . . 156 B1
Maidenhead SL6 . . . . 202 A3
Bedford Ct HP6 . . . . 166 D8
Bedford Dr SL2 . . . . 198 B6

Bedford Rd
Aspley Guise MK17 ...... 49 F5
Cold Brayfield MK46 ...... 8 B5
Cranfield MK43 .... 25 C2
Sherington MK16 .... 14 A1
Bedford Road E NN7 ..... 1 D5
Bedford Road W NN7 .... 1 A6
Bedford St
Berkhamsted HP4 ...... 135 D4
Milton Keynes, Bletchley MK2................ 58 C8
Milton Keynes, Wolverton MK12................ 33 D6
Woburn MK17 .... 60 F7
Bedgebury Pl MK7 ...... 48 A8
BEDGROVE 116 C5
Bedgrove HP21 .... 116 C6
Bedgrove Inf Sch HP21 116 C5
Bedgrove Jun Sch HP21................ 116 C6
BEDLAM 14 C1
Bedlam La MK16 .... 14 C1
Bedlam Wlk MK16 .... 14 C1
Bedwins La SL6 .... 195 B6
Bedwyn Wlk HP21 ...... 115 D4
Beech 2 RG9 .... 191 D2
Beechams The MK17 .... 67 D6
Beech Ave
Lane End HP14 .... 171 C5
Olney MK46 .... 6 E3
Beech Cl
Bierton HP22 .... 102 B3
Buckingham MK18 .... 41 D2
Flackwell Heath HP10 .. 174 A2
High Wycombe HP11 .... 173 F4
Maidenhead SL6 .... 202 B8
Stokenchurch HP14 ..... 158 F3
Beechcroft HP4 .... 135 C3
Beechcroft Rd
Chesham HP5 .... 144 B1
Milton Keynes MK3 ...... 57 E6
Beech Ct
Berkhamsted HP4 ...... 135 D4
3 Marlow SL7 .... 183 E2
Beech Dr HP4 .... 135 C3
Beechen Wood WD3 ... 178 D5
Beeches Dr SL2 .... 198 B7
Beeches Gr HP10 ...... 163 A2
Beeches Pk HP9 .... 175 D2
Beeches Rd SL2 .... 198 B7
Beeches The
Amersham HP6 .... 154 A3
Chorleywood WD3 ...... 167 F4
Deanshanger MK19 ...... 31 E3
Milton Keynes MK1 ...... 47 E1
Tring HP23 .... 119 C4
Uxbridge UB8 .... 201 C1
Wendover HP22 .... 131 C5
Beeches Way SL1 ...... 197 C2
Beech Fern MK7 .... 48 A5
Beechfield Pl SL6 ...... 202 C4
Beechfield Way HP15 .. 163 B3
Beechfield Wlk HP15 ... 163 A3
Beech Gn HP21 .... 115 D6
Beech Gr
Amersham HP7 .... 165 D8
Leighton Buzzard LU7 .... 80 E7
Tring HP23 .... 119 C4
Beech Hill Ct HP4 ..... 135 D5
Beech House Dr NN12 ... 18 F4
Beechingstoke 4 SL7 .. 183 F3
Beech La
Prestwood HP16 .... 151 B7
Seer Green HP9 .... 176 E3
Beechlands HP15 ...... 162 E2
Beech Leys MK18 .... 63 E3
Beech Pk
Little Chalfont HP6 ..... 155 B1
Naphill HP14 .... 150 A1
Wigginton HP23 .... 133 F5
Beech Rd
Aylesbury HP21 .... 115 D6
Chinnor OX39 .... 147 C6
High Wycombe HP11 .... 173 F4
Newport Pagnell MK16 ... 22 B3
Princes Risborough HP27................ 139 C3
Slough SL3 .... 206 E4
Beech St HP11 .... 173 C4
Beechtree Ave SL7 ..... 183 D5
Beech Tree Cl MK19 ..... 20 D2
Beech Tree Ct HP22 ..... 87 A6
Beech Tree Rd HP15 .... 163 C7
Beech Trees Rd HP12 .. 172 C3
Beechview Jun Sch HP13................ 173 E5
Beech Waye SL9 .... 189 A4
Beech Wlk HP23 .... 119 B4
Beechwood Ave
Chorleywood WD3 ...... 167 B5
Little Chalfont HP6 ..... 155 C1
1 Uxbridge UB8 .... 208 F7
Beechwood Cl HP6 ..... 166 C8
Beechwood Cotts WD3 167 B3
Beechwood Ct
Aston Clinton HP22 ..... 118 A3
Dunstable LU6 .... 93 F7
Beechwood Dr
Aldbury HP23 .... 120 D5
Beechwood Dr *continued*
Maidenhead SL6 .... 202 A6
Marlow SL7 .... 194 B8
Beechwood Gdns SL1 .. 205 E4
Beechwood Ho HP22 ... 117 F5
Beechwood La HP22 ... 131 D5
Beechwood Pk
Chorleywood WD3 ...... 167 F5
Felden HP3 .... 146 F7
Beechwood Pl 13 HP13 173 B7
Beechwood Rd
Beaconsfield HP9 .... 175 C2
High Wycombe HP12 .... 161 B2
Slough SL2 .... 205 D8
Beechwood Sch SL2 ... 198 B2
Beechwood Way HP22 . 117 F5
BEECROFT 93 F8
Beecroft Lower Sch LU6 93 F8
Beecroft Way LU6 ...... 93 F8
Beehive Cl UB10 .... 201 F5
Beel Cl HP7 .... 166 C8
Beethoven Cl MK7 ...... 48 E4
Beeward Cl MK12 .... 33 A5
Beggars La HP23 .... 119 F4
Bekonscot Ct MK14 ..... 21 F1
Bekonscot Model Village & Railway★ HP9 .... 175 E4
Belfast Ave SL1 .... 205 D7
Belgrave Mews UB8 .... 201 D1
Belgrave Par SL1 ...... 205 E6
Belgrave Pl 6 SL1 ..... 206 A4
Belgrave Rd
Aylesbury HP19 .... 101 A3
Slough SL1 .... 205 F6
Bellamy Mews 5 MK4 ... 45 E3
Bellamy Rd HP13 .... 173 C8
Bell Ave UB7 .... 208 F3
Bell Bsns Pk HP19 ..... 100 F1
Bell Cl
Beaconsfield HP9 .... 175 F2
Cublington LU7 .... 78 B1
Drayton Parslow MK17 ... 68 B6
Princes Risborough HP27................ 139 B3
Slough SL2 .... 206 B8
Thame OX9 .... 125 E1
Bellclose Rd UB7 ...... 208 E4
Bell Cres HP27 .... 138 E6
Bell Ct SL6 .... 193 F3
Belle Vue HP17 .... 114 C5
Bellfield Rd HP13 ...... 173 A8
Bellfield Road W HP11 . 172 F7
Bellfounder Ho MK13 ... 34 B4
Bell Gn HP3 .... 146 B4
BELLINGDON 143 E7
Bellingdon Rd HP5 ..... 144 B1
Bellini Cl MK7 .... 48 D5
Bellis Gr MK6 .... 47 C8
Bell La
Berkhamsted HP4 ...... 134 E5
Eton Wick SL4 .... 204 F2
Henley-on-Thames RG9 .. 191 E3
Little Chalfont HP6 ..... 155 C1
Princes Risborough HP27................ 139 B3
Syresham NN13 .... 27 B8
Thame OX9 .... 125 F1
Bell Lane Comb Sch HP6................ 155 B1
Bell Leys HP22 .... 89 B3
Bellows Mill La LU6 ..... 93 A4
Bellridge Pl HP9 .... 175 B6
Bellsfield Ct SL4 .... 204 F2
Bells Hill SL2 .... 199 A4
Bells Hill Gn SL2 ...... 199 A5
Bells La SL3 .... 212 B4
Bells Mdw MK15 .... 35 B7
Bell St
Henley-on-Thames RG9 .. 191 E2
Maidenhead SL6 .... 202 F6
Princes Risborough HP27................ 139 B3
Bell Street Mews RG9 .. 191 E2
Bellswood La SL0 ...... 207 B8
Bell View SL4 .... 209 F5
Bell View Cl SL4 .... 209 F5
Bellway MK17 .... 49 A6
Bellwether MK11 .... 33 A4
Bell Wlk
Wingrave HP22 .... 89 B3
Winslow MK18 .... 65 F3
Bellwood Rise HP11 .... 173 B4
Belmers Rd HP23 ...... 119 D1
Belmont SL2 .... 205 A8
Belmont Cl UB8 .... 201 D6
Belmont Cotts SL3 ..... 212 C7
Belmont Cres SL6 ...... 202 D8
Belmont Ct MK8 .... 33 C2
Belmont Dr SL6 .... 202 D8
Belmont Park Ave SL6 . 202 D8
Belmont Park Rd SL6 .. 202 D8
Belmont Rd
Chesham HP5 .... 144 B3
Maidenhead SL6 .... 202 D8
Uxbridge UB8 .... 201 D5
Belmont Vale SL6 ...... 202 D8
Belsham Cl HP5 .... 144 B3
BELSIZE 156 F6
Belsize Ave MK6 .... 35 B1
Belsize Cotts WD3 ..... 156 E6
Belton Rd HP4 .... 135 A5
Belvedere Cl HP6 ...... 154 F2
Belvedere La MK17 ...... 58 F8
Belvedere Mans SL1 ... 205 D4
Belvedere Rdbt MK9 .... 34 F4
Belvoir Ave MK4 .... 46 C1
Bembridge Ct 11 SL1 ... 205 F4
Benacre Croft MK4 ...... 57 A8
Benbow Ct MK5 .... 46 A7
Benbow Way UB8 ...... 208 C8
Bench Manor Cres SL9 177 C1
Bencombe Rd SL7 ..... 183 E5
Benen-Stock Rd TW19 . 213 A2
Benham Cl HP5 .... 144 B1
Benhams La RG9 .... 180 D2
Benison Ct 11 SL1 ..... 205 F3
Benjamin Ho 10 HP13 .. 173 B7
Benjamin La SL3 .... 199 B1
Benjamin Rd HP13 ..... 173 B8
Benjamins Footpath HP13................ 173 B8
Ben More SL9 .... 188 F6
Benmore Rise 2 MK4 ... 45 E2
Bennet Cl MK11 .... 32 D4
Bennet's Yd UB8 .... 201 D5
BENNETT END 159 C7
Bennett End Rd HP14 .. 159 C7
Bennetts HP5 .... 144 D1
Bennetts Cl
Padbury MK18 .... 53 B1
Slough SL1 .... 205 A5
Bennett's Hill MK18 ..... 76 C8
Bennetts La HP22 ...... 102 E8
Benning Ave LU6 .... 93 F8
Benning Cl SL4 .... 209 D4
Benningfield Gdns HP4 135 E6
Bens Cl MK19 .... 19 F5
Bensheim Way HP6 .... 154 D1
Benson Cl
Slough SL2 .... 206 A5
Uxbridge UB8 .... 208 E8
Bentall Cl MK15 .... 35 C7
Bentinck Cl SL9 .... 188 D6
Bentinck Ct UB7 .... 208 D5
Bentinck Rd UB7 .... 208 D5
Bentley Ct SL6 .... 202 D5
Bentley Pk SL1 .... 197 D3
Bentley Rd SL1 .... 205 A5
Benton Dr OX39 .... 147 C7
Bentons The HP4 ...... 134 F6
Benwell Cl MK13 .... 33 F5
Benwells OX39 .... 147 C6
Berber Bsns Ctr HP11 .. 172 E7
Berberis Cl MK7 .... 48 A5
Berberis Wlk UB7 ...... 208 E2
Bercham MK8 .... 33 E2
Beresford Ave
Aylesbury HP19 .... 101 C3
Slough SL2 .... 206 C6
Beresford Cl MK4 .... 46 B3
Beresford Rd WD3 ..... 167 F1
Beretun MK8 .... 33 E1
Bereville Ct MK10 .... 35 E3
Berevilles La MK10 ...... 35 E3
Bergamot Gdns MK7 .... 48 B5
Bergman Cl 1 MK4 ..... 45 D2
Berkeley Ave HP5 ...... 143 F1
Berkeley Cl
Chesham HP5 .... 144 A1
Stoke Goldington MK16 ... 12 B6
Berkeley Mews
Marlow SL7 .... 183 F2
Slough SL1 .... 204 E7
Berkeley Rd
Loudwater HP10 .... 174 C2
Thame OX9 .... 126 A1
Berkeley Rise 1 HP19 .. 101 B2
Berkhampstead Rd HP5................ 144 C2
BERKHAMSTED 135 C6
Berkhamsted Castle★ HP4................ 135 D5
Berkhamsted Collegiate Sch HP4 .... 135 B4
Berkhamsted Sch 6 HP4................ 135 C4
Berkhamsted Sta HP4 .. 135 C5
Berkley Cl
Maidenhead SL6 .... 202 A8
Pitstone LU7 .... 105 D3
Berkley Ct HP4 .... 135 C4
Berkley Rd HP9 .... 175 D6
Berks Hill WD3 .... 167 C4
Berkshire Ave SL1 ..... 205 B7
Berkshire Gn MK5 .... 45 F3
Berkshire Lodge 1 SL6................ 202 F6
Berling Rd MK8 .... 33 F2
Bernard Cl HP18 .... 112 F2
Bernardines Way MK18 .. 52 E7
Bernards Cl HP16 ...... 152 A7
Bernard's Cl HP18 ..... 112 B2
Bernards Way HP10 .... 174 A2
Bernay Gdns MK15 ...... 35 B7
Berndene Rise HP27 ... 139 B4
Berners Cl SL1 .... 204 E6
Bernewode Cl HP18 .... 125 C7
Bernstein Cl MK7 .... 48 C4
Bernwood Mdws Wildlife Reserve★ HP18 .... 108 F2
Berrell's Ct 2 MK46 ...... 6 F3
Berries Rd SL6 .... 196 A8
Berrington Gr 4 MK4 ... 45 E2
BERRYFIELD 100 D5
Berryfield LU7 .... 104 F7
Berry Field SL2 .... 206 C7
Berry Field Pk HP6 ..... 154 B2
Berryfield Rd
Aylesbury HP19 .... 101 B3
Princes Risborough HP27................ 139 C4
Berry Hill SL6 .... 203 D8
Berry Hill Ct SL6 .... 203 D8
Berry La
Aspley Guise MK17 ...... 49 F6
Chorleywood WD3 ...... 167 D3
Berrystead MK7 .... 48 B3
Berry Way MK17 .... 57 D4
Bertram Cl MK13 .... 34 B8
Berwald Cl MK7 .... 48 D4
Berwick Ave SL1 .... 205 B6
Berwick Cl
Beaconsfield HP9 .... 176 B1
Marlow SL7 .... 183 D3
Berwick Dr MK3 .... 46 F2
Berwick La SL7 .... 183 D3
Berwick Rd SL7 .... 183 C3
Bessemer Cl 2 SL3 .... 206 F1
Bessemer Cres HP19 ... 100 E1
Bessemer Ct MK14 ...... 22 A1
Bestobell Rd SL1 ...... 205 C7
Betjeman Ct UB7 .... 208 D5
Betjeman Gdns WD3 ... 167 D5
Bettina Gr MK2 .... 58 C7
Bettles Cl UB8 .... 201 C3
Bettles Ct UB8 .... 201 C3
Betty's Cl MK17 .... 57 D3
Betty's La HP23 .... 119 A4
Bevan Ct MK18 .... 65 F4
Bevan Hill HP5 .... 144 B2
Bevelwood Gdns HP12 . 172 D7
Beverley Cl SL7 .... 183 B2
Beverley Ct SL1 .... 206 B4
Beverley Gdns SL6 ..... 195 B1
Beverley Pl MK6 .... 35 B2
Bewcastle Row MK4 .... 45 E1
Bewdley Dr LU7 .... 80 C7
Bewdley Gr MK10 .... 36 A4
Bexley St SL4 .... 210 C6
Bicester Rd
Aylesbury HP19 .... 101 B2
Long Crendon HP18 ..... 125 C6
Ludgershall HP18 .... 96 C8
Marsh Gibbon OX27 ...... 71 E3
Oakley HP18 .... 109 D5
Twyford MK18 .... 62 C1
Bickleigh Cres MK4 ..... 46 D3
Biddles Cl SL1 .... 204 E5
BIDDLESDEN 27 D5
Biddlesden Rd NN13 .... 39 A5
Bideford Ct LU7 .... 80 C8
Bideford Gn LU7 .... 80 C8
Bideford Spur SL2 ..... 198 B2
BIERTON 102 A3
Bierton CE Comb Sch HP22................ 102 B3
Bierton Rd HP20 .... 101 F1
Bigfrith La SL6 .... 195 B6
Biggs La HP17 .... 113 E2
Bigmore La
Beacon's Bottom HP14 .. 170 B8
Stokenchurch HP14 ..... 159 C1
Bignell Croft MK5 .... 34 B1
Bigton Chase 2 MK10 ... 36 B2
Biko Cl UB8 .... 208 C7
Bilbrook La MK4 .... 46 C4
Billet La
Berkhamsted HP4 ...... 135 A6
Iver SL0, SL3 .... 207 B7
Billings Cl HP14 .... 158 F5
Billingwell Pl MK6 ...... 35 B2
Billwell HP18 .... 125 C6
Bilton Rd MK1 .... 47 D2
Binders Ind Est HP15 ... 162 D7
Bingham Cl MK4 .... 46 C1
Bingham Rd SL1 .... 204 A8
Binghams The SL6 ..... 203 B3
Birch Ave UB7 .... 208 F7
Birch Cl
Amersham HP6 .... 154 E2
Bedford MK43 .... 25 C3
Iver Heath SL0 .... 200 D3
Birch Cres UB10 .... 201 F4
Birch Ct HP21 .... 115 D5
Birchdale SL9 .... 188 D3
Birch Dr WD3 .... 178 D5
Birchen Lee MK4 .... 46 C2
Birches Rise HP12 ..... 172 E8
Birches The
Felden HP3 .... 146 F8
High Wycombe HP13 .... 173 E8
Birchfield Gr MK2 .... 58 C7
Birch Gdns HP7 .... 165 E8
Birch Gr
Slough SL2 .... 205 B8
Windsor SL4 .... 209 D6
Birchington Rd SL4 .... 210 A5
Birch La HP3 .... 156 B7
Birchmoor Gn MK17 ..... 60 F8
BIRCHMOOR GREEN 60 E8
Birch Rd HP4 .... 134 D7
Birch St HP11 .... 173 B3
Birch Tree Gr HP5 ..... 145 B1
Birch Way
Chesham HP5 .... 144 D2
Tylers Green HP10 ...... 163 B1
Birchwood Chase HP15 .... 151 D1
Birchwood Cl HP12 ..... 172 B6
Birdcage Wlk HP13 .... 173 B6
Birdlip La MK7 .... 48 B7
Bird Mount Cotts SL4 .. 210 C8
Birdwood Rd SL6 .... 202 B7
Birfield Rd HP10 .... 174 C2
Birinus Ct HP12 .... 172 C5
Birkdale Cl MK3 .... 57 D7
Birkett Way HP8 .... 166 D6
Birley Rd SL1 .... 205 D7
Birtchnell Cl HP4 ...... 135 A5
BISHAM 194 E7
Bisham Abbey National Sports Ctr SL7 .... 194 D7
Bisham CE Prim Sch SL7 .... 194 D7
Bisham Ct
Bisham SL7 .... 194 E6
10 Slough SL1 .... 205 F4
Bisham Gn SL7 .... 194 E6
Bisham Rd
Bisham SL7 .... 194 E8
Marlow SL7 .... 183 E1
Bisham Woods Nature Reserve★ SL6 .... 194 E6
Bishop Ct SL6 .... 202 D6
Bishop Ctr The SL6 ..... 203 F7
Bishop Parker RC Comb Sch MK2 .... 58 C6
Bishops Ct MK18 .... 52 C7
Bishops Farm Cl SL4 .. 209 B6
Bishops Field HP22 .... 118 A4
Bishopshalt Sch UB8 ... 201 F2
Bishops Ho HP9 .... 175 D3
Bishops Mdw HP22 ..... 102 A3
Bishops Orch SL2 ...... 198 B2
Bishops Rd SL1 .... 206 A4
BISHOPSTONE 115 A1
Bishopstone
Milton Keynes MK13 ..... 34 B5
Stone HP17 .... 115 A1
Bishopstone Rd HP17 .. 114 D5
Bishops Wlk
Aylesbury HP21 .... 115 F6
Woburn Sands MK17 ..... 49 B3
Wooburn Green HP10 ... 185 E5
Bishop Wood Sch 19 HP23................ 119 A3
Bissley Dr SL6 .... 202 A3
Bittenham Cl HP17 ..... 114 D4
Bittern Way 4 HP20 ... 101 E3
Bit The HP23 .... 119 D1
BIX 179 D1
Bix La SL6 .... 194 F1
Black Acre Cl HP7 ..... 165 E8
Blackamoor La SL6 .... 196 A1
Blackberry Ct MK7 ...... 48 B6
Black Boy La SL6 ...... 193 C3
Blackburn Trad Est TW19 .... 213 F1
Black Butt Cotts SL6 ... 196 B7
Blackdown MK11 .... 32 F4
Blacketts Wood Dr WD3 .... 167 B5
Blackfield La HP16 ..... 142 E3
Blackheath Cres MK13 .. 34 D3
Blackhill Dr MK12 .... 33 A6
Black Horse Ave HP5 ... 154 D6
Blackhorse Cl HP6 ..... 154 E1
Black Horse Cl SL4 .... 209 D5
Blackhorse Cres HP6 ... 154 E1
Blackhorse Pl UB8 ..... 201 C4
Black Horse Pl UB8 .... 201 C4
Blackmoor Gate MK4 .... 46 E2
Blackmore Gate HP22 .. 118 A4
Blackmore Way UB8 .... 201 D6
Black Park Ctry Pk★ SL0, SL3 .... 199 F3
Black Park Ctry Pk Visitor Ctr★ SL3 .... 199 F2
Black Park Nature Reserve★ SL0 .... 200 A5
Black Park Rd SL3 ..... 199 E4
Blackpond La SL2 ...... 198 B4
Blacksmith La HP16 .... 151 C6
Blacksmith Row SL3 ... 207 A2
Blacksmith's La UB9 ... 189 D2
Blacksmiths Rd HP27 .. 138 D7
Blacksmiths Way MK17 .. 49 B5
BLACKTHORN 81 A4
Blackthorn Cl OX25 ..... 81 A3
Blackthorn Dell 2 SL3 206 C3
Blackthorne Cres SL3 .. 212 E5
Blackthorne Ind Pk SL3 .... 212 E5

Blackthorne La HP16 142 E3
Blackthorne Rd SL3 212 E4
Blackthorn Gr MK17 49 A4
Blackwater Dr HP21 115 C4
Blackwell End NN12 18 C3
Blackwell Hall La HP5 155 C6
Blackwell Pl MK5 46 A4
Blackwell Rd HP14 171 B5
Blackwells Yd NN7 1 B6
Blackwood Cres MK13 33 E6
Blaine Cl HP23 119 A6
Blairmont St MK9 34 F4
Blair Rd SL1 205 E5
Blakedown Rd LU7 80 C6
BLAKELANDS 22 B1
Blakeney Ct
Maidenhead SL6 195 F1
Milton Keynes MK4 57 B8
Blakes Ho HP10 174 C2
Blake Way OX9 126 A1
Blanchland Circ MK10 36 A1
Blandford Cl SL3 206 D3
Blandford Ho SL6 202 C8
Blandford Road N SL3 206 D3
Blandford Road S SL3 206 D3
Blanes Cl HP18 125 C6
Blansby Chase MK4 46 C3
Blatherwick Ct MK5 45 F7
Blaydon Cl MK3 57 D6
BLEAK HALL 46 F5
Bleak Hall Rdbt MK6 47 A5
Bleasdale MK13 34 C5
BLEDLOW 138 B1
Bledlow Cotts HP27 138 C1
Bledlow Rd HP27 148 E8
BLEDLOW RIDGE 159 F8
Bledlow Ridge Rd
HP14 148 C8
Bledlow Ridge Sch
HP14 159 F8
Blegberry Gdns HP4 134 E4
Blenheim Ave MK11 32 E4
Blenheim Cl
Cheddington LU7 104 F8
Longwick HP27 138 D6
Slough SL3 206 F5
Blenheim Ct HP13 173 B7
Blenheim Pl
Aylesbury HP21 115 E5
Syresham NN13 27 C7
Blenheim Rd
High Wycombe HP12 172 D4
Maidenhead SL6 202 B8
Slough SL3 206 D2
Bletcham Rdbt MK1 47 E3
Bletcham Way
Milton Keynes MK1 47 C2
Milton Keynes MK1 47 E2
Walton Park MK7 48 B4
BLETCHLEY 58 A7
Bletchley Com Hospl
MK3 47 A1
Bletchley L Ctr MK2 58 C8
Bletchley Park National Codes Ctr★ MK3 58 A8
Bletchley Rd
Milton Keynes MK5 46 B4
Newton Longville MK17 57 D4
Stewkley LU7 68 D3
Bletchley Sta MK3 58 B8
Blinco La SL3 206 E7
Blind La
Bourne End HP10, SL8 185 B5
South Heath HP16 153 B8
Blind Pond Ind Est
MK17 48 D2
Bliss Ave MK43 25 C2
Bliss Ct MK7 48 C4
Blisworth MK6 47 D5
Blondell Cl UB7 213 D8
Bloomfield Cotts HP5 143 E7
Bloomfield Rd SL6 202 A5
Bloomsbury Cl MK17 60 F6
Blossom Way UB10 201 F5
Blucher St HP5 154 B8
Blue Anchor Ave 1
MK10 36 B3
Bluebell Cl MK18 52 C7
Bluebell Croft MK7 48 B6
Blue Lagoon Nature Reserve★ MK3 58 B7
Blumfield Cres SL1 204 E8
Blumfield Ct SL1 197 D1
Blundells Rd MK13 34 C6
Blunden Dr SL3 207 C2
Blyth Ct MK4 57 A8
Blythebridge MK10 36 C3
Blythe Cl
Aylesbury HP21 115 C5
Iver SL0 207 F7
Newport Pagnell MK16 22 D3
Blythe Hos SL1 204 D5
Blyton Cl HP9 175 D4
Boadicea Cl SL1 204 E5
Boarlands Cl SL1 204 F6
BOARSTALL 95 B1
Boarstall Duck Decoy★
HP18 95 A3
Boarstall Tower★ HP18 95 A1
Boathouse Reach RG9 191 E1
Bobmore La SL7 183 F3
BOCKMER END 182 C1
Bockmer La SL7 193 B7
Boddington Rd HP22 131 C4
Bodenham Cl MK18 52 F8
Bodiam Cl
Aylesbury HP21 116 B5
Milton Keynes MK5 46 A5
Bodiam Ho 6 HP13 173 F7
Bodle Cl MK15 35 A7
Bodley Ho SL0 200 D3
Bodmin Ave SL2 205 A8
Bodnant Ct MK4 45 F2
Bogart Pl MK4 45 D2
Bois Ave HP6 154 B3
Bois Hill HP5 154 E5
Bois La HP6 154 D4
Bois Moor Rd HP5 154 D5
Bolan Ct MK8 45 E6
BOLBECK PK 35 A7
Bold's Ct SL2 199 A5
BOLTER END 170 F5
Bolter End La HP14 171 A6
Bolton Ave SL4 210 D4
Bolton Cres SL4 210 C4
Bolton Rd SL4 210 C4
Boltwood Gr MK5 45 E5
Bond Ave MK1 47 D3
Bond Cl
Aylesbury HP21 115 B6
Iver Heath SL0 200 B5
West Drayton UB7 208 F7
Bone Hill MK18 52 C7
Bonham Carter Rd
HP22 131 E7
Bonham Cl HP21 115 B6
Bonham Ct HP22 117 D5
Bonnards Rd MK17 57 D4
Bonnersfield HP18 125 C7
BOOKER 172 B4
Booker Ave MK13 34 D4
Booker Hill Comb Sch
HP12 172 B5
Bookerhill Rd HP12 172 C6
Booker La HP12 172 D7
Booker Park Com Sch
HP21 115 E3
Booker Pl HP12 172 B3
Booth Pl LU6 92 E6
Boot La HP17 113 E2
Borderside SL2 206 A7
Borodin Ct MK7 48 D5
Boroma Way RG9 191 E2
Borough Ct NN13 38 A5
Borough Rd NN13 38 A5
Borough Wlk MK9 34 E3
Bosanquet Cl UB8 201 D1
Bossiney Pl MK6 34 F1
Bossington La LU7 80 E7
Boss La
Great Kingshill HP15 162 B8
Hughenden Valley HP14 162 B6
Bostock Ct MK18 52 C8
Boston Dr SL8 185 B3
Boston Gr SL1 205 C7
Boswell Ct MK18 41 E2
Boswell La MK19 31 E4
Boswick La HP4 134 D8
Bosworth Cl MK3 46 E2
Bosworth Ct SL1 204 C6
Botham Dr SL1 205 E3
BOTLEY 145 A1
Botley La HP5 145 A1
Botley Rd HP5 144 E1
BOTOLPH CLAYDON 74 F6
Bottesford Cl MK3 46 D1
Bottle Dump Rdbt MK17 56 E6
Bottle Square La HP14 159 D6
Bottom Dr LU6 93 D5
Bottom House Farm La
HP8 165 E2
Bottom House La HP23 120 A1
Bottom La HP9 176 C5
Bottom Orch HP18 112 C1
Bottom Rd
Bledlow Ridge HP14 160 B5
Buckland Common HP23 132 F3
Bottom Waltons Caravan Site SL2 197 F3
Bottrells La HP8 176 E8
Botyl Rd MK18 74 E6
Boughton Bsns Pk HP6 166 B8
Boughton Way HP6 155 C1
Boulevard The MK9 34 E2
Boulmer Rd UB8 201 C2
Boulters Cl
Maidenhead SL6 196 C1
Slough SL1 205 A4
Boulters Ct
Amersham HP6 154 E1
Maidenhead SL6 196 C1
Boulters Gdns SL6 196 C1
Boulters La SL6 196 C1
Boulters Lock MK14 21 F2
Boundary Cotts WD4 146 E2
Boundary Cres MK11 32 E6
Boundary Pl HP10 185 D8
Boundary Rd
Brackley NN13 38 A6
Chalfont St Peter SL9 177 D3
Loudwater HP10 174 C1
Taplow SL6 203 F8
Wooburn Green HP10 185 D8
Boundary The 1 MK6 34 F1
Bounds Croft MK12 33 C4
Bounty St MK13 33 F7
Bouquet Cl HP16 151 C5
Bourbon St HP20 115 D8
Bourne Ave SL4 210 C3
Bourne Cl SL8 185 B5
BOURNE END 185 B2
Bourne End MK43 25 C6
Bourne End Bsns Pk
SL8 185 B3
Bourne End Mills Ind Est
HP1 146 B8
Bourne End Rd
Bourne End SL6, SL8 196 E8
Cranfield MK43 25 C4
Bourne End Sta SL8 185 A3
Bourne Rd
Berkhamsted HP4 134 F5
Slough SL1 205 D4
Bourne The HP3 146 A4
BOURTON 52 F8
Bourton Low MK7 48 B5
Bourton Meadow Sch
MK18 52 F8
Bourton Rd MK18 52 E8
Bourtonville MK18 52 D8
Bouverie Way SL3 206 E2
BOVENEY 209 D8
Boveney Cl SL1 205 A4
Boveney New Rd SL4 204 E2
Boveney Rd SL4 204 C1
Boveney Wood La SL1 186 D1
BOVINGDON 146 B4
Bovingdon Ct HP3 146 A3
BOVINGDON GREEN 146 A2
Bovingdon Hts SL7 183 B2
Bovingdon Prim Sch
HP3 146 B4
BOW BRICKHILL 48 C1
Bow Brickhill Prim Sch
MK17 48 D2
Bow Brickhill Rd MK17 48 F3
Bow Brickhill Sta MK7 48 B2
Bowden La HP11 173 D5
Bowen Cl MK7 48 C5
Bowerbank Ct HP20 101 F1
Bower Cl LU6 92 F5
Bower Ct SL1 204 F6
Bowerdean Rd HP13 173 D7
Bower La LU6 92 F5
Bowers La HP14 159 D7
Bower Way SL1 204 E6
Bowes Cl MK16 22 C3
Bowes-Lyon Cl 7 SL4 210 C6
Bowland Dr MK4 46 B1
Bowler Lea HP13 161 D2
Bowler Rd HP21 115 E4
Bowler's Orch HP8 177 A7
Bowles Pl MK6 47 D7
Bowling Alley HP22 86 D7
Bowling Cl UB10 201 F4
Bowling Ct RG9 191 D3
Bowling Gn HP14 158 D5
Bowling Green Rd MK43 25 C1
Bowling Leys MK10 36 A2
Bowl Rdbt The MK4 46 D5
Bowmans Cl SL1 197 B3
Bowmont Dr HP21 115 D4
Bowood Ct 5 MK8 33 F1
Bowood La HP22 141 E5
Bowry Dr TW19 211 F1
Bowstridge Ct 6 HP13 173 C7
Bowstridge La HP8 177 C5
Bowyer Cres UB9 189 F5
Bowyer Dr SL1 204 E6
Bowyers Mews MK14 34 F6
Boxberry Gdns MK7 48 A6
Boxer Rd HP27 138 E6
Boxgrove Ct MK10 36 A1
Box La HP3 146 E7
Box Tree Cl HP5 154 D6
Boxwell Rd HP4 135 B4
Boxwood Cl UB7 208 F4
Boyce Cres MK7 48 E5
Boycott Ave MK6 34 E1
Boyle Cl UB10 201 F3
Boyndon Rd SL6 202 D7
BOYNE HILL 202 D6
Boyne Hill CE Inf Sch
SL6 202 D6
Boyne Ho HP9 175 E1
Boyn Hill Ave SL6 202 D6
Boyn Hill Cl SL6 202 D6
Boyn Hill Rd SL6 202 D6
Boyn Valley Ind Est
SL6 202 E6
Boyn Valley Rd SL6 202 D5
Bozenham Mill La NN7 9 F5
Bracken Cl SL2 198 D8
Brackenforde SL3 206 C4
Bracken Hill HP4 135 E5
Bracken Rd SL6 202 C4
Brackens The HP11 173 C5
Bracken Way
Aylesbury HP21 115 B8
Flackwell Heath HP10 185 B7
Brackenwood HP14 161 C7
BRACKLEY 38 A8
Brackley Dr HP15 163 A6
Brackley La MK18 73 B6
Brackley Rd
Chackmore MK18 41 B1
Hazelmere HP15 163 A6
Westbury NN13 39 B5
Bradbery WD3 178 D5
Bradbourne Dr MK7 48 C3
Bradbury Cl MK13 34 A3
Bradbury Gdns SL3 199 D8
Bradcutts La SL6 195 E8
Braddenham Wlk HP21 115 E4
Braddons Furlong
HP18 125 C6
Braden Cl HP21 116 A6
BRADENHAM 160 F7
Bradenham Beeches
HP14 161 A8
Bradenham La SL7 194 C5
Bradenham Rd HP14 161 A3
Bradenham Wood La
Naphill HP14 150 B1
Walter's Ash HP14 161 A7
Bradfield Ave MK18 41 D2
Bradford Gdns MK5 46 B4
Bradford Rd
Heronsgate WD3 167 C2
Slough SL1 205 A7
Bradley Cl HP18 109 D5
Bradley Gr MK4 46 B2
Bradley Rd SL1 205 E6
Bradnam Wood Nature Reserve★ SL6 194 D4
Bradshaw Cl SL4 209 E6
Bradshawe Waye UB8 208 F8
Bradshaw Rd HP13 173 F6
BRADVILLE 34 B7
Bradvue Cres MK13 34 B6
BRADWELL 34 A4
BRADWELL ABBEY 33 F3
BRADWELL COMMON 34 B3
Bradwell Common Bvd
MK13 34 C3
Bradwell Rd
Milton Keynes, Bradville
MK13 34 A6
Milton Keynes, Loughton
MK5 46 B8
Milton Keynes MK5, MK8 34 A1
Bradwell Village Sch
MK13 34 B4
Braeburn Ct SL1 205 C4
Brae Hill HP18 110 A8
Brae Hill Cl HP18 110 A8
Braemar Ct 5 SL7 183 D2
Braemar Gdns SL1 205 A4
Braeside HP14 161 C6
Braford Gdns MK5 46 B4
BRAGENHAM 70 C6
Bragenham La LU7,
MK17 70 D5
Bragenham Side MK17 69 F7
Bragmans La WD4 156 E6
Brahms Cl MK7 48 C5
Braid The HP5 144 E1
Brakynbery HP4 134 E7
Bramber Cl MK3 57 E7
Bramber Ct SL1 205 A5
Bramble Ave MK14 34 E4
Bramble Cl
Chalfont St Peter SL9 177 E4
Uxbridge UB8 208 F7
Bramble Cres HP15 163 C6
Bramble Dr SL6 202 A4
Bramble La HP7 165 E6
Bramble Mead HP8 177 B7
Brambleside HP11 174 B4
Brambles The UB7 208 E2
Brambling HP19 101 E3
Bramcote Cl HP20 116 C8
Bramley Chase SL6 202 C4
Bramley Cl SL6 202 C3
Bramley Ct MK43 3 F6
Bramley End HP14 151 A1
Bramley Grange MK2 58 D4
Bramley Mdws MK16 22 B3
Bramley Rd MK1 47 D3
Brammas Cl SL1 205 C3
Brampton Ct
Maidenhead SL6 203 B8
Milton Keynes MK13 34 A6
Branch Rd HP10 174 B2
Brandon Ct HP23 103 D7
Brandon Rd HP12 172 B3
BRANDS HILL 212 A8
Brands Hill Ave HP13 162 C2
Brands Rd SL3 212 B8
Brandville Rd UB7 208 E4
Bransgill Ct MK13 34 B4
Bransworth Ave MK10 48 C8
Brantham Cl MK7 48 A3
Brantwood Cl 7 MK4 45 F1
Braunston MK6 47 D6
Bravenfield MK18 53 C2
Brawlings La SL9 178 A6
BRAY 203 D3
Braybank SL6 203 D4
Braybourne Cl UB8 201 C6
Braybrooke Dr MK4 46 E4
Bray Cl SL6 203 C3
Bray Ct
Amersham HP6 154 E1
Maidenhead SL6 203 C2
Brayfield Ho MK46 8 B5
Brayfield Rd SL6 203 C4
Bray Pit Wildlife Reserve★
SL6 203 C2
Bray Rd SL6 203 B5
Brays Cl HP6 153 C4
Brays Green La HP6 153 C4
Brays La HP6 153 C5
Brays Mdw HP6 153 C4
Brayton Ct MK5 46 C6
BRAY WICK 203 A4
Braywick Nature Ctr★
SL6 203 B3
Braywick Park Nature Reserve★ SL6 203 A5
Braywick Park & Sports Gd
SL6 203 A5
Braywick Rd SL6 203 A4
Braywood Cotts SL4 209 A5
Braziers End HP5 133 C1
Breachwell Pl LU7 91 A1
Breakspear Road N
UB9 190 E8
Breakspear Road S
UB10 190 F2
Bream Cl SL7 194 C8
Breamore Ct MK8 45 F8
Brearley Ave MK6 46 E7
Brearley Cl UB8 201 E6
Breckland MK14 34 D6
Brecon Ct
Milton Keynes MK10 35 F1
Slough SL1 205 C4
Brecon Way HP13 172 E8
Bredward Cl SL1 197 B2
Breezes The SL6 202 E4
Bremen Gr MK5 46 A4
Brenchwood Cl HP13 161 C2
Brendon Ct MK4 46 D2
Brent MK6 47 D5
Brent Path HP21 115 D4
Brent Rd SL8 185 A4
Brentwood Way HP21 116 B6
Bretby Chase MK4 45 F3
Breton MK11 32 E6
Brewhouse La HP22 88 E1
Brewster Cl MK5 45 D5
Brew Twr SL7 183 D1
Briaily HP14 159 C2
Briar Cl SL6 204 B7
Briar Dene SL6 195 C1
Briar Glen SL6 195 E6
Briar Hill MK12 33 E4
Briar Lodge MK12 33 D5
Briars Cl HP19 101 B2
Briars The
High Wycombe HP11 173 C5
Holmer Green HP15 163 C7
Slough SL3 206 F1
Briarswood HP15 163 B3
Briarswood Cl HP14 158 E5
Briar Way
Berkhamsted HP4 135 D3
Slough SL2 205 B8
Briary Ct MK18 74 F8
Briary View MK17 56 C8
Brices Mdw MK5 46 A3
Brick Cl MK11 33 C2
Brickfield La SL1 197 B4
Brickfields Way UB7 208 F3
Brick Hill HP18 97 E1
Brickhill Manor Ct
MK17 59 D5
Brickhill St
Giffard Park MK14 22 A1
Milton Keynes, Monkston Park
MK10 35 E2
Milton Keynes, Willen Park
MK15 35 C6
Walton Park MK7 48 A4
Brickhill Way MK18 73 B5
Brick Kiln La HP22 102 B4
Bricks La HP14 159 C4
Brickwell Wlk HP15 163 B3
Bricstock HP22 88 D4
Bridens Way HP17 126 F6
Bridge Ave
Cookham Rise SL6 195 E6
Maidenhead SL6 203 A7
Bridge Bank Cl HP11 174 A3
Bridge Cl SL1 204 F6
Bridge Ct
Berkhamsted HP4 135 D4
Maidenhead SL6 203 C7
Bridge Farm Bldgs
HP17 128 B8
Bridgeford Ct MK6 46 E8

Bridgegate Bsns Pk
HP19 101 B1
Bridge Ho
High Wycombe HP13 173 D6
West Drayton UB7 208 D5
Bridge Hook Cl 4 MK12 33 A6
Bridgeman Ct 5 SL4 210 A5
Bridgeman Dr SL4 210 A5
Bridge Pl HP6 154 F1
Bridge Rd
Cosgrove MK19 19 E2
Ickford HP18 123 F2
Maidenhead SL6 203 B7
Stoke Bruerne NN12 9 A8
Uxbridge UB8 201 C3
Bridge St
Berkhamsted HP4 135 D4
Buckingham MK18 52 D8
Colnbrook SL3 212 D7
Great Kimble HP17 129 D1
High Wycombe HP11 173 A7
Leighton Buzzard LU7 80 F7
Maidenhead SL6 203 A7
Milton Keynes MK13 33 F7
Olney MK46 6 F2
Thornborough MK18 54 B8
Turvey MK43 8 D5
Bridgestone Dr SL8 185 C3
Bridgeturn Ave MK12 33 D8
Bridgewater Ct
Little Gaddesden HP4 121 C8
Slough SL3 207 A2
Bridgewater Hill HP4 134 F7
Bridgewater Ho MK18 52 C8
Bridgewater Monument★
HP4 120 E7
Bridgewater Rd HP4 135 B5
Bridgewater Sch HP4 135 A6
Bridgewater Terr SL4 210 D6
Bridgewater Way SL4 210 D6
Bridgeway
Cuddington HP18 112 E3
Milton Keynes MK13 34 A7
Bridge Wlk MK19 31 E4
Bridgnorth Dr MK4 45 E1
Bridle Cl
Maidenhead SL6 195 E1
Milton Keynes MK13 34 B6
Bridle Gate HP11 172 F6
Bridle Manor HP22 131 C8
Bridle Rd SL6 195 E1
Bridleway
Buckland Common
HP22 132 E5
Weston Turville HP22 116 F2
Bridle Way HP4 135 A6
Bridleways HP22 131 A5
Bridlington Cres MK10 36 A1
Bridlington Spur SL1 205 B4
Bridport Way SL2 198 B1
Briery Way HP6 154 E1
Brighton Spur SL2 198 B1
Brightwell Ave LU6 93 C7
Brigidine Sch The SL4 210 D4
BRILL 96 B1
Brill CE Comb Sch HP18 96 B1
Brill Cl
Maidenhead SL6 202 D3
Marlow SL7 183 C2
Brill Ho SL6 202 C3
Brill Pl MK13 34 C3
Brill Rd
Chilton HP18 111 A3
Horton-cum-S OX33 108 C6
Ludgershall HP18 96 B7
Oakley HP18 109 F5
Brimmers Hill HP15 162 F6
Brimmers Rd HP27 139 D2
Brimmers Way HP19 114 F8
Brimstone La HP19 101 C4
Brimstone Way HP4 134 F6
Brindlebrook MK8 33 E1
Brindles Cl MK18 73 B5
Brindles La HP9 175 A4
Brindley Ave HP13 161 F1
Brinkburn Chase MK10 36 A1
Brinkhurst SL7 183 D2
Brinklow Rdbt MK10 36 C1
Briskman Way HP21 115 B6
Bristle Hill MK18 52 C8
Bristol Cl TW19 213 E1
Bristol Ct 10 TW19 213 E1
Bristol Way SL1 205 F5
Bristow Cl MK2 47 E1
Britannia Ct UB7 208 D3
Britannia Ind Est
High Wycombe HP12 172 D7
Poyle SL3 212 E5
Britannia Rd 6 HP5 144 C2
Britannia St HP20 115 E8
Britnell Ct HP14 158 E5
Britten Gr MK7 48 D5
Brittens Ct MK46 7 C3
Brittons La MK17 37 C3
BRITWELL 197 F1
Britwell Dr HP4 135 E6
Britwell Gdns SL1 197 D2
Britwell Rd SL1 197 D2
Broad Arrow Cl MK14 34 E7
Broad Dean MK6 47 A8
Broadfields HP19 101 A1
Broadfields Ct HP19 101 A1
Broadfields Ret Pk
HP19 101 A1
Broad Gn MK43 25 C3
BROAD GREEN 25 B3
Broad La HP9, HP10 186 A6
Broadlands MK6 47 C5
Broadlands Ave HP5 144 C1
Broadleys SL4 209 F7
Broad Leys HP27 139 A3
Broadmark Rd SL2 206 B6
Broad Oak SL2 198 C1
Broad Oak Ct SL2 198 C1
Broadpiece MK15 35 A7
Broad Platts SL3 206 D3
Broad Rush Gn LU7 80 E8
Broad St
Chesham HP5 144 C1
Newport Pagnell MK16 22 C4
Syresham NN13 27 B8
Broadview Rd HP5 144 B4
Broadwater
Berkhamsted HP4 135 C5
Milton Keynes MK6 47 D6
Broadwater Gdns UB9 190 C7
Broadwater La UB9 190 C7
Broadwater Pk UB9 190 A5
Broadwater Pk SL6 203 E1
Broadway SL6 202 F7
Broadway Ave MK14 21 F2
Broadway Cl 5 HP7 165 B7
Broadway Ct HP5 154 B8
Broadway Par UB7 208 E4
Broadway The
Amersham HP7 165 B7
Beaconsfield HP9 175 D3
3 Chalfont St Peter SL9 177 D2
Chesham HP5 154 B8
Farnham Common SL2 198 C6
Grendon Underwood HP18 82 F6
Brocas St SL4 210 D7
Brocas Terr SL4 210 D7
Brocas Way LU7 91 A3
Brockhampton MK15 35 B6
Brockhurst Rd HP5 144 C2
Brock La SL6 202 F7
Brockton Ct SL6 202 F6
Brockway SL3 207 B1
Brockwell MK16 22 C4
Broddick Ho HP11 174 B4
Broken Furlong SL4 205 B1
Broken Gate La UB9 189 C3
Bromham Mill MK14 21 F2
Bromley HP23 104 A4
Bromley La HP6 153 C5
Brompton Cl 2 HP19 101 B2
Brompton Cres HP19 101 B2
Brompton Dr SL6 195 C2
Bromycroft Rd SL2 198 A2
Bronsdon Way UB9 189 F2
Bronte Cl
Aylesbury HP19 100 F2
Slough SL1 205 E4
Brookbank HP10 185 D3
Brook Bsns Ctr UB8 201 B3
Brook Cl
Aston Clinton HP22 117 D5
Ludgershall HP18 96 C8
Brook Cres SL1 204 E7
Brookdene Cl SL6 195 F2
Brooke Cl MK3 57 F7
Brooke Furmston Pl
SL7 183 E3
BROOK END
Ivinghoe 105 E4
North Crawley 23 F5
Weston Turville 117 A3
Brook End
North Crawley MK16 24 A6
Weston Turville HP22 117 A3
Brook End Sp Ctr MK5 46 A3
Brooke Rd HP27 139 B4
Brookes Univ (Wheatley
Campus) OX33 122 C1
Brook Farm Cl MK18 62 C1
Brookfield UB8 201 E6
Brookfield Cl HP23 119 B4
Brookfield Ho SL3 211 D6
Brookfield La MK18 52 D7
Brookfield Rd
Haversham MK19 20 D2
Newton Longville MK17 57 D3
Wooburn HP10 185 D3
Brook Ho
Slough SL1 205 D3
West Drayton UB7 208 D5
Brookhouse Dr HP10 185 C3
Brook La
Berkhamsted HP4 135 B5
Harrold MK43 3 F7
Newton Blossomville MK43 8 B3
Thame OX9 125 E1
Brooklands Rd MK2 58 C7
Brooklyn Way UB7 208 D3
Brookmead Sch LU7 105 E5
Brook Path SL1 204 F6
Brooks Ct MK18 52 D8
Brookside
Colnbrook SL3 212 C7
Halton HP22 117 C1
Lillingstone Lovell MK18 30 A6
Loudwater HP10 174 C2
Milton Keynes MK12 33 D4
Oakley HP18 109 D5
Slough SL3 206 E7
Thame OX9 125 F1
Uxbridge UB10 201 F5
Weston Turville HP22 117 A2
Brookside Ave TW19 211 E4
Brookside Cl
Old Stratford MK19 32 B6
Tiddington OX9 136 A7
Brookside La HP17 129 E3
Brookside Terr 5
HP21 115 E8
Brook St
Aston Clinton HP22 117 D5
Edlesborough LU6 92 F4
High Wycombe HP11 173 A7
Tring HP23 119 B4
Windsor SL4 210 D5
Brooksward Comb Sch
MK14 34 F7
Brookway MK19 31 E4
Broombarn La HP16 151 E7
Broom Cl HP15 163 A3
Broomfield MK12 33 D4
Broomfield Cl HP16 151 E7
Broomfield Gate SL2 198 B1
Broomfield Hill HP16 151 E7
Broom Hill
Cookham Rise SL6 195 E6
Stoke Poges SL2 199 A5
Broom Ho SL3 206 F2
Broomlee MK13 34 A5
Broomstick Ind Est LU6 92 E4
Broomstick La HP5 145 A1
Brora Cl MK2 58 C5
Brotheridge Ct HP21 115 B6
Brough Cl MK5 46 A5
BROUGHTON
Aylesbury 116 D8
Milton Keynes 36 A3
Broughton Ave HP20 116 B8
Broughton Cl HP22 102 B3
Broughton Crossing
HP22 102 C2
Broughton Fields Prim Sch
MK10, MK16 36 B4
Broughton Grounds Com
Woodlands★ MK16 36 E6
Broughton Inf Sch
HP20 116 B8
Broughton Jun Sch
HP20 116 B8
Broughton La HP20,
HP22 116 C8
Broughton Manor Bsns Pk
MK16 36 B4
Broughton Manor Prep Sch
MK10 36 C4
Broughton Rd
Milton Keynes MK10 36 B4
Salford MK17 37 C3
Brow Bsns Ctr 10 HP11 172 F7
Brownbaker Ct MK14 34 F6
Browne Willis Cl MK2 58 D8
Brownfield Gdns SL6 202 E5
Browning Cl MK16 22 A4
Browning Cres MK3 58 A7
Brownlow Ave LU6 92 F3
Brownlow Gate HP4 107 A1
Brownlow La LU7 105 A7
Brownlow Rd HP4 135 C5
Brownlow Rise LU6 93 A8
Browns Ct SL1 204 E6
Brownset Dr MK4 45 E1
Brownsfield Rd NN12 18 E6
Browns Hedge
Leighton Buzzard LU7 105 D2
Pitstone LU7 105 C3
Browns Rd
Holmer Green HP15 163 C6
South Heath HP16 153 A7
Brown's Rise HP23 132 F3
Browns Way MK17 49 E5
BROWNS WOOD 48 C4
Brownswood Dr NN12 18 D3
Brownswood Rd HP9 175 E4
Browns Wood Rdbt MK7 48 C5
Brow The HP8 177 D7
Broxbourne Cl MK14 21 F2
Bruce Cl SL1 205 A5
Bruce Wlk SL4 209 D5
Brucewood Par SL7 183 E5
Bruckner Gdns MK7 48 D5
Brudenell SL4 209 F3
Brudenell Dr
Milton Keynes MK10 48 C8
Stoke Mandeville HP22 116 B1
Brunel Cl SL6 202 E5
Brunel Ctr SL6 202 D5
Brunel Ctr (Sh Ctr) MK2 58 C8
Brunel Gate HP19 100 F1
Brunel Rd
Aylesbury HP19 100 F1
Brunel Rd *continued*
High Wycombe HP13 161 F1
Maidenhead SL6 202 D5
Brunel Rdbt SL1 205 F5
Brunel Science Pk UB8 201 E2
Brunel Univ UB8 201 E2
Brunel Way SL1 205 F5
Brunleys MK11 33 B3
Brunner Pl HP13 173 C6
Brunswick Cl HP19 101 B3
Brunswick Pl HP13 162 D2
Brushford Cl MK4 46 D3
Brush Hill Nature Reserve★
HP16 151 B3
Brushmakers Ct HP5 144 B1
Brushwood Dr WD3 167 C5
Brushwood Jun Sch
HP5 144 E2
Brushwood Rd HP5 144 E2
Bryans Cres MK16 24 A6
Bryanston Ave HP20 101 F2
Bryant Ave SL2 205 E8
Bryants Acre HP22 131 B6
BRYANT'S BOTTOM 150 F4
Bryants Bottom Rd
HP16 150 F4
Bryden Cotts UB8 201 C1
Bryer Pl SL4 209 D4
Bryfield Cotts HP3 146 C1
Bryher The SL6 202 A7
Bryne La MK18 53 B2
Bryony Cl UB8 208 F8
Bryony Pl MK14 34 E5
Buccleuch Rd SL3 211 B7
Buchanan Rd OX25 94 E7
Buchan Cl UB8 201 C2
Buckby MK6 47 D6
Buckfast Ave MK3 47 A2
Buckfield Ct SL0 207 F4
BUCKINGHAM 41 D2
Buckingham Ave SL1 205 B7
Buckingham Avenue E
SL1 205 C7
Buckingham Canal Wildlife
Reserve★ MK18 42 D3
Buckingham Chantry
Chapel MK18 41 D1
Buckingham Cl HP13 174 A7
Buckingham Ct
Amersham HP6 154 E2
Brackley NN13 38 A6
Newport Pagnell MK16 22 B3
Buckingham Ctr 8
MK18 41 D1
Buckingham Dr HP13 174 A7
Buckingham Gate
Medmenham SL7 193 D7
Milton Keynes MK6 35 B1
Buckingham Gdns SL1 205 F4
Buckingham Ho
Amersham HP6 154 D3
4 Maidenhead SL6 202 F6
Buckingham Hospl
MK18 41 D1
Buckingham Ind Pk
MK18 52 D5
Buckingham Par 4
SL9 177 D2
Buckingham Pl 1
HP13 173 A7
Buckingham Prim Sch
MK18 41 E2
Buckingham Rd
Aylesbury HP19, HP20 101 D3
Brackley NN13 38 A6
Deanshanger MK19 31 E2
Edgcott HP18 72 F2
Gawcott MK18 52 A5
Milton Keynes, Church Hill
MK17 56 E6
Milton Keynes MK3 57 D7
Steeple Claydon MK18 63 E3
Tring HP23 118 E3
Winslow MK18 65 F5
Buckingham Road Ind Est
NN13 38 A6
Buckingham Sch MK18 52 D7
Buckinghamshire County
Mus★ HP20 115 D8
Buckinghamshire New Univ
Chalfont St Peter HP8 178 A8
High Wycombe HP11 173 A6
Uxbridge UB8 201 C6
Buckinghamshire Railway
Ctr★ HP22 84 F2
Buckingham Sq 1 MK9 34 C2
Buckingham St
8 Aylesbury HP20 101 D1
Milton Keynes MK12 33 D7
Tingewick MK18 51 B6
Buckingham View HP5 144 C1
Buckingham Way HP10 174 A1
BUCKLAND 117 F6
Buckland Ave SL3 206 B3
BUCKLAND COMMON 133 A3
Buckland Cres SL4 209 F6
Buckland Dr MK6 47 C6
Buckland Gate SL3 199 B2
Buckland Lodge MK6 47 B6
Buckland Rd HP22 118 A4
Bucklands Croft HP23 118 C8
BUCKLANDWHARF 118 B4
Bucklebury Cl SL6 203 C1
Buckley Ct MK11 32 F4
Buckman Cl MK12 33 B5
Buckmaster Rd HP12 172 C3
BUCKMOOREND 140 D6
Bucks Goat Ctr & Animal
Farm The★ HP22 130 A7
Buckthorn MK12 33 E5
Budge Rd NN12 18 F5
Buffins SL6 196 E2
BUFFLER'S HALT 40 C3
BULBOURNE 119 C8
Bulbourne Cl HP4 134 F6
Bulbourne Ct HP23 119 A7
Bulbourne Rd HP23 119 B7
Bulkeley Ave SL4 210 B4
Bullbaiters La HP6 153 B5
Bullbeggars La HP4 135 F3
Bullfinch Gdns 8 HP19 101 F3
BULLINGTON END 20 C7
Bullington End Rd MK19 20 A6
Bull La
Gerrards Cross SL9 188 C7
7 High Wycombe HP11 173 A7
Milton Keynes MK2 58 D8
Bullocks Farm La HP14 171 B7
Bullrush Gr UB8 201 C1
Bulls La HP18 124 A3
Bullsland Gdns WD3 167 B3
Bullsland La WD3 167 B3
Bulmer Cl MK10 36 B3
BULSTRODE 146 E3
Bulstrode Cl WD4 146 E2
Bulstrode Ct SL9 188 D5
Bulstrode La WD4 146 F3
Bulstrode Pl SL1 205 F3
Bulstrode Way SL9 188 D6
Bunby Rd SL2 198 F5
Bunces Cl SL4 205 B1
Bunces Ct HP20 101 D1
Bungalows The MK18 51 A6
Bunhill Cl LU6 93 F8
Bunkers La LU7 80 D6
Bunsen Pl MK5 46 C4
Bunstrux HP23 119 A4
Bunsty Ct MK11 32 F5
Bunten Meade SL1 205 B5
Bunyan Cl HP23 119 B5
Burano Cl MK7 48 C6
Burchard Cres MK5 46 A6
Burchett's Green Rd
SL6 194 C1
Burcot Gdns SL6 195 E3
BURCOTT 79 E4
Burcott Cl HP22 102 B3
Burcott La HP22 102 C3
Burdeleys La MK5 46 A4
Burdett Dr HP14 161 B8
Burdock Ct MK16 21 F4
Burewelle MK8 33 D1
Burfield Rd
Chorleywood WD3 167 C4
Old Windsor SL4 211 A1
Burford Cl
Ickenham UB10 201 E8
Marlow Bottom SL7 183 C5
Burford Gdns SL1 204 C8
Burford Ho 18 SL4 210 D6
Burford Sch SL7 183 C5
Burgess Gdns MK16 22 B2
Burgess La HP17 128 B7
Burgess Wood Gr HP9 175 B1
Burgess Wood Rd HP9 175 B2
Burgess Wood Road S
HP9 175 B1
Burgett Rd SL1 205 B3
Burghley Ct MK8 45 F8
Burholme MK4 46 C3
Burke Rd HP22 131 C5
Burkes Cl HP9 186 B8
Burkes Cres HP9 175 D2
Burkes Ct HP9 175 D2
Burkes Par HP9 175 D3
Burkes Rd HP9 175 C2
Burleigh Ct MK18 52 F8
Burleigh Piece MK18 41 F1
Burleys Rd MK18 65 F4
Burlington Ave SL1 205 E4
Burlington Ct 1 SL1 205 E4
Burlington Rd
Burnham SL1 197 B1
2 Slough SL1 205 E4
Burma Cl HP13 173 E6
Burners La MK11 33 B4
Burners Lane S MK11 33 B3
Burness Cl UB8 201 D3
Burnet MK14 34 C7
Burnetts Ct HP16 151 C5
Burnetts Rd SL4 209 E6
BURNHAM 197 C3
Burnham Ave HP9 176 A1
Burnham Beeches National
Nature Reserve★ SL2 198 A7

Burnham Cl
Bourne End SL8 185 A4
High Wycombe HP12 172 D6
Windsor SL4 209 D5
Burnham Ct SL6 202 F8
Burnham Dr MK13 34 C3
Burnham Gram Sch SL1 197 D1
Burnham Hts SL1 204 C7
Burnham La SL1 204 E7
Burnham Pl NN13 27 B8
Burnham Rd
Beaconsfield HP9 186 F6
Hughenden Valley HP14 162 A6
Westcott HP18 98 B7
Burnhams Field HP22 116 E7
Burnham Sta SL1 204 D7
Burnhams The
Aston Clinton HP22 117 C5
Shabbington HP18 124 D3
Burnham Upper Sch SL1 204 B8
Burnmoor Cl MK2 58 D4
Burns Cl
Long Crendon HP18 125 D7
Newport Pagnell MK16 22 A4
Burns Ct HP21 115 F6
Burns Rd MK3 58 A7
Burnt Oak SL6 195 F7
Burn Wlk SL1 197 B1
Burrell Cl HP21 115 C6
Burren The HP6 154 D2
Burroughs Cres SL8 185 A4
Burrow Ash Cl MK19 10 F2
Burroway Rd SL3 207 B3
Burrows Cl
Tylers Green HP10 163 C2
Woburn Sands MK17 49 B5
Burrows Ho HP13 161 E2
Burton La HP27 139 C5
Burtons La WD3 167 A4
Burton's La HP8 166 E5
Burton's Way HP8 166 C7
Burton Way SL4 209 E4
Burtree Cl MK12 33 D5
Burt's La HP18 125 D6
Bury Ave MK16 22 C4
Bury Cl MK16 22 C4
BURY END 165 D6
Bury Farm HP7 165 C7
Bury Farm Cl LU7 91 C6
Buryfield La HP16 152 B7
Buryhook Cnr OX33 122 C2
Bury La HP5 154 B8
Bury Lawn Sch MK14 34 D7
Bury Rise HP3 146 D6
Bury St MK16 22 C4
Busby Cl MK18 41 F1
Buscot Pl MK8 45 F8
Bushel Wharf HP23 119 A6
Bushes La MK18 51 C1
Bushey Bartrams MK5 46 A3
Bushey Cl
Buckingham MK18 41 F1
High Wycombe HP12 172 E7
Whipsnade LU6 93 F1
Bushfield Rd HP3 146 C6
Bushfields MK12 33 D6
Bushfield Sch MK12 33 D6
Bushmead Cl HP22 87 B5
Bushmead Rd HP22 87 B5
Bushnell Pl 2 SL6 202 B8
Bush The HP17 126 F5
Bushy Cl MK3 47 A3
Business Ctr The HP6 154 F1
Business Village SL2 206 B5
Buslins La HP5 143 E3
Butcher La MK5 45 F3
Bute Brae MK3 46 E2
Butler Ct 5 SL7 183 F3
Butlers Cl
Amersham HP6 154 A2
Windsor SL4 209 D6
Butlers Court Comb Sch HP9 175 D1
Butlers Court Rd HP9 175 D1
BUTLERS CROSS 176 F6
BUTLER'S CROSS 130 C3
Butlers Ct HP13 173 F5
Butlers Gr MK14 34 D8
Butler Wlk HP19 115 A7
Butterfield HP10 185 D4
Butterfield Cl MK15 35 C2
Butterfield Cotts WD3 178 E3
Butterfly Gate 5 MK10 36 B3
Butterly Rd
High Wycombe HP14 158 B6
Stokenchurch HP14 158 F4
Buttermere HP21 116 B7
Buttermere Ave SL1 204 C8
Buttermere Cl MK2 58 D6
Butterton Gdns MK10 36 C3
Buttfurlong HP17 127 A7
Buttlehide WD3 178 D5
Buttler's Hanging Wildlife Reserve★ HP14 160 D5
Button Gr MK6 47 A7
Buzzacott La MK4 46 C3
Bybend Cl SL2 198 B4
Bycell Rd MK18 41 C6
Bye Gn HP22 117 A3
BYE GREEN 117 A3
Byerly Ho MK14 34 F5
Byerly Pl MK14 34 F5
Byford Way MK18 65 F4
Byland Dr SL6 203 B1
Byrd Cres MK7 48 D6
Byres The HP17 126 F6
Byron SL3 207 B1
Byron Cl
6 Marlow SL7 183 F3
Milton Keynes MK3 57 F7
Byron Ct SL4 210 A4
Byron Dr MK16 22 A4
Byron Rd HP21 115 F6
Byron Way UB7 208 F2
Byward Cl MK14 34 E7
Byways
Berkhamsted HP4 135 E5
Burnham SL1 204 A8
Bywell Ct MK4 56 E8
By-Wood End SL9 178 A5

C

Cabair Coll of Air Training MK43 24 E1
Cable Cres MK17 49 B5
Cadeby Ct MK10 36 B3
Cadman Sq MK5 46 C5
CADMORE END 170 C6
Cadmore End CE Comb Sch HP14 170 C6
Cadsdean Rd HP27 139 E6
Cadwell Dr SL6 202 D3
Caernarvon Cres MK3 57 E7
Caesars Cl MK13 34 A5
Caesars Gate NN13 38 A6
Cages Wood Dr SL2 198 B8
Cagney Cres 1 MK4 45 E3
Cairngorm Gate MK6 46 D8
Cairngorm Pl SL2 198 D1
Cairnside HP13 173 E6
Caister Ct MK4 56 E8
Caithness Ct MK3 46 E2
Calamus Ct MK7 48 B6
Calbroke Rd SL2 197 F2
CALDECOTE 22 E1
Caldecote La MK16 22 F2
Caldecote St MK16 22 C4
CALDECOTTE 48 A2
Caldecotte La MK7 48 A3
Caldecotte Lake Dr MK7 48 A2
Caldecotte Rdbt MK7 47 F3
Calder Cl SL6 195 E1
Calder Ct
Maidenhead SL6 195 D1
1 Slough SL3 206 F1
Calder Gdns LU7 80 B7
Calder Vale MK3 46 E1
Calder Way SL3 212 F4
Caldewell MK8 33 D1
Caldicot Cl HP21 116 B6
Caldicott Sch SL2 198 B5
Caledon Cl HP9 175 E3
Caledonian Rd MK13 33 E7
Caledon Rd HP9 175 E3
Calewen MK8 33 E1
CALIFORNIA
Aylesbury 115 C7
Dunstable 93 F6
California Circ HP11 173 B4
Callaghan Ct HP4 135 D4
Callingham Pl HP9 175 E3
Callis Farm Cl TW19 213 E1
Calluna Dr MK3 47 A3
Calumet HP9 175 D3
Calvards Croft MK12 33 C4
Calverleigh Cres MK4 46 D3
Calverley Cres HP13 161 F2
CALVERT 73 B6
Calvert Cotts MK18 73 D7
Calvert Jubilee Wildlife Reserve★ MK18, OX27 73 A7
CALVERTON 32 E3
Calverton La MK19 33 B1
Calverton Lane Rdbt MK11 33 B2
Calverton Rd MK11 32 D4
Calves Cl MK5 46 A3
Calvie Croft MK12 33 D4
Cambell Sq MK9 35 A3
Camber Cl MK3 57 E7
Camberton Rd LU7 80 E6
Camborne Ave HP21 116 B5
Cambria Ct SL3 206 C4
Cambridge Ave
Burnham SL1 197 B3
Slough SL1 205 A7
Cambridge Cl
Aylesbury HP20 101 E1
5 Aylesbury HP20 101 E1
Harmondsworth UB7 213 D8
Cambridge Close Ret Pk 6 HP20 101 E1
Cambridge Cres HP13 173 E7
Cambridge Ho 2 SL4 210 C6
Cambridge Pl 9 HP20 115 D8
Cambridge Rd
Beaconsfield HP9 175 C2
Marlow SL7 183 D2
Uxbridge UB8 201 D6
Cambridge St
Aylesbury HP20 101 E1
Milton Keynes, Bletchley MK2 58 C8
Milton Keynes, Wolverton MK12 33 C6
Cambridge Terr 13 HP4 135 D4
Cambron MK8 33 D2
Cam Ct MK3 57 E8
Camden Ct HP19 101 C1
Camden Pl SL8 185 A3
Camden Rd SL6 195 D1
Cameron Rd 6 HP5 144 C1
Camfield Ct SL6 202 A8
Camlet Gr MK14 34 D7
Camley Gdns SL6 202 A8
Camm Ave SL4 209 E4
Cam Mead HP21 116 B6
Camomile Ct MK7 48 C5
Camomile Way UB7 208 E6
Campania Cl MK10 36 A2
Campbell Cl
Buckingham MK18 52 F8
High Wycombe HP13 172 F8
Campbell Dr HP9 175 C5
CAMPBELL PARK 35 A3
Campbell Park Rdbt MK9 34 F3
Campbells Ride HP15 163 D7
Campden Rd UB10 190 F1
Camperdown SL6 196 B1
Camperdown Ho 9 SL4 210 C5
Camp Ind Est OX9 136 B4
Campion MK14 21 E2
Campion Cl
Aylesbury HP20 116 C8
Denham UB9 190 A1
Uxbridge UB8 208 F8
Campion Rd HP15 162 F6
Campions Ct HP4 135 B3
Camp Rd SL9 188 C4
Canada Rd SL1 206 B4
Canal Ct HP4 135 E4
Canal La MK19 31 F4
Canalside
Berkhamsted HP4 134 F6
Old Stratford MK19 32 C7
Stoke Bruerne NN12 9 A8
Canalside Rdbt MK9 35 B4
Canal Wharf SL3 207 A4
Candlemas La HP9 175 E2
Candlemas Mead HP9 175 E2
Candlemas Oaks HP9 175 E2
Candlewicks MK7 48 B6
Candover Cl UB7 213 D7
Candy La MK5 46 B4
Candytuft Gn HP15 162 F6
Cane End HP27 139 A3
Cane End La HP22 102 C6
Canford Ct HP21 115 F5
Cannock Cl SL6 203 B6
Cannock Rd HP20 101 E3
Cannon Court Rd SL6 195 D3
Cannondown Rd SL6 195 E5
Cannon Gate SL2 206 C6
Cannon Hill Cl SL6 203 C2
Cannon La SL6 202 A6
Cannon Mill Ave HP5 154 E5
Cannon Pl HP27 139 B4
Cannon's Hill HP18 112 C5
Cannon's Orch HP22 85 B4
Canonbury MK10 35 E1
Canon Harnett Ct MK12 32 F6
Canon Hill Dr SL6 203 B3
Canon Hill Way SL6 203 B2
Canon's Cloisters SL4 210 D7
Canons Rd MK12 33 C7
Canons The MK16 22 E3
Cantell Cl MK18 41 D1
Canterbury Ave SL2 198 C1
Canterbury Cl
Amersham HP7 165 E8
Monks Risborough HP27 139 B5
Cantilupe Cl LU6 92 D6
Cantle Ave MK14 35 A5
Cantley Cl HP20 101 E2
Capel Cl MK18 41 F7
Capel Dr MK14 34 F5
Capell Ave WD3 167 C4
Capell Rd WD3 167 D4
Capell Way WD3 167 D4
Cape Villas SL0 207 E7
Capian Wlk MK8 33 E1
Capital Dr MK14 34 E6
Capps La HP5 143 A5
Capricorn Ho HP10 185 A8
Capron MK6 47 B5
Capswood Bsns Ctr UB9 189 C3
Captain Cook Cl HP8 177 B6
Captain's Cl HP5 144 A4
Captains Wlk HP4 135 D3
Captain's Wood Nature Reserve★ HP5 143 F4
Caraway Cl MK7 48 B4
Cardain Ho HP9 175 D3
Cardigan Cl
Milton Keynes MK3 46 F1
Slough SL1 204 F6
Cardinals Wlk SL6 204 C7
Cardwell Cl MK4 46 C2
Carey Cl
Aylesbury HP21 115 D4
Windsor SL4 210 B4
Careys Croft HP4 135 A7
Careys Rd NN12 17 A8
Carey Way MK46 7 A4
Carhampton Ct MK4 46 D3
Carisbrooke Ave HP12 172 B6
Carisbrooke Cl SL6 202 C6
Carisbrooke Ct
Buckingham MK18 41 E2
Slough SL1 205 F6
Carisbrooke Ho 4 HP13 173 F7
Carisbrooke Way MK4 45 E1
Carleton Gate MK15 35 E7
Carlina Pl MK14 34 D3
Carlisle Rd SL1 205 D6
Carlton Cl
Aylesbury HP19 101 A2
Newport Pagnell MK16 22 E4
Carlton Ct HP27 139 B3
Carlton Ho TW19 213 D2
Carlton Rd
Slough SL2 206 B6
Turvey MK43 8 E7
Carlyle Ave HP21 115 F7
Carlyle Cl MK16 22 A4
Carman Ct HP23 118 F3
Carmarthen Rd SL1 205 E6
Carmel Ct SL7 183 B1
Carnation Way HP21 115 E5
Carne The MK11 32 E5
Carnot Cl MK5 46 C4
Carnoustie Cl MK3 57 C7
Carnweather Ct MK4 57 B8
Caroline Cl UB7 208 D4
Caroline Ct SL7 183 E3
Caroline Haslett Comb Sch MK5 46 B4
Carolus Creek MK15 35 A7
Carpenter Ct MK14 34 F6
Carpenters Wood Dr WD3 167 B5
Carpenter's Wood, Dungrove Wood Nature Reserve★ SL6 194 C2
Carpenters Yd HP23 119 B3
Carr Cl HP19 101 A2
Carrick Rd MK6 34 F1
Carriers Cl MK19 11 A2
Carrington Ave HP10 185 A8
Carrington Cl MK18 77 E5
Carrington Cres HP22 131 A7
Carrington Ct 9 HP12 172 E7
Carrington Hall Rd MK17 68 C6
Carrington Inf Sch 1 HP10 174 A1
Carrington Jun Sch HP10 185 A8
Carrington Pl
Holmer Green HP15 163 C7
Tring HP23 119 B5
Carrington Rd
Aylesbury HP21 115 D6
High Wycombe HP12 172 D6
Newport Pagnell MK16 22 B3
Slough SL1 205 E6
Carrington Way HP16 151 C5
Carroll Cl MK16 22 A5
Carron Cl LU7 80 B7
Carron Ct MK2 58 C4
Carrs Dr HP12 172 C8
Carter Cl SL4 210 A5
Carteret Cl MK15 35 E7
Carters Cl MK16 13 F1
Carters La
Long Crendon HP18 125 B7
Milton Keynes MK11 33 A3
Quainton HP22, MK18 85 E6
Carters Mdw MK18 76 A2
Carters Ride HP22 116 B2
Carter Wlk HP10 174 C8
Cartmel Cl MK3 57 C6
Cartwright Ct 2 HP13 173 F5
Cartwright Pl MK6 46 E8
Carver Hill Rd HP11 172 F5
Carvers Mews MK14 34 F6
Cascadia Cl HP11 174 B2
Cashmere Cl MK5 46 A4
Casterton Cl MK13 34 C4
Castle Acre MK10 35 F1
Castle Ashby Rd NN7 1 B7
Castle Ave
Datchet SL3 211 A8
West Drayton UB7 208 F6
Castle Cl
Marsh Gibbon OX6 72 A3
Pitstone LU7 105 D3
Totternhoe LU6 93 A8
Wing LU7 79 E3
Castle Ct
13 Aylesbury HP20 115 D8
Buckingham MK18 52 D8
Maidenhead SL6 202 D7
Castle Dr SL6 202 D7
Castle Est HP12 172 D4
Castlefield Foundation Sch HP12 172 C6
Castlefields HP22 116 C3
Castle Gate Way HP4 135 C6
Castle Hill
Berkhamsted HP4 135 C5
High Wycombe HP11 173 A6
Maidenhead SL6 202 E7
Windsor SL4 210 D6
Castle Hill Ave HP4 135 C5
Castle Hill Cl HP4 135 C5
Castle Hill Ct HP4 135 C6
Castle Hill Rd LU6 93 A8
Castle Hill Terr SL6 202 E7
Castle Ho 5 LU7 80 E7
Castle La HP22 86 F6
Castle Lodge SL6 202 F7
Castlemead Cotts SL4 210 C3
Castle Meadow Cl MK16 22 E4
Castle Mews
Berkhamsted HP4 135 C4
Maidenhead SL6 202 E7
Castle Park Rd HP22 131 B6
Castle Pl 6 HP13 173 B7
Castle Rd MK46 2 F1
Castle Rose MK6 47 D6
Castle Row 16 HP23 119 A3
Castle St
Aylesbury HP20 115 D8
Berkhamsted HP4 135 C4
Buckingham MK18 52 D8
High Wycombe HP13 173 B7
Marsh Gibbon OX27 72 A3
Slough SL1 205 F3
Wingrave HP22 89 B3
Castlesteads MK13 33 F5
CASTLETHORPE 19 E5
Castlethorpe Fst Sch MK19 19 F5
Castlethorpe Rd MK19 11 A2
Castleton Ct SL7 183 E2
Castleview Comb Sch SL3 206 D2
Castle View Gdns HP12 172 D7
Castleview Ho SL4 210 D7
Castleview Rd SL3 206 C2
Caswell La MK17 60 F7
Catchpole Cl MK12 33 B5
Cater Rd HP14 171 C4
Catesby Croft MK5 46 C8
Cathay Cl MK3 58 B7
Cathedral of Trees★ MK15 35 C5
Catherine Cotts HP23 133 E8
Catherine Ct MK18 41 E2
Catherines Cl UB7 208 D4
Catkin Cl HP12 172 B3
Catslip RG9 179 A1
Causeway The
Bray SL6 203 C4
Marlow SL7 183 E1
Causey Arch MK10 36 C3
Cautley Cl HP22 85 A5
Cavalier Ct HP4 135 C4
Cavalier Rd OX9 126 A1
Cavalry Cres SL4 210 C4
Cavan Way MK10 36 A4
Cavendish Cl
Burnham SL6 204 A7
Little Chalfont HP6 166 B8
Wendover HP22 131 B6
Cavendish Ct
Milton Keynes MK5 46 A7
Poyle SL3 212 E6
Cavendish Rd HP5 154 D7
Cavendish Way 9 HP19 100 F1
Cavendish Wlk OX9 126 B1
Cavenham MK8 33 F2
Caversham Gn 1 HP20 101 D1
Cawardon MK14 34 C7
Cawcott Dr SL4 209 E6
Cawdor Rise MK4 45 E2
Cawkwell Way MK2 58 C8
Caxton Ct RG9 191 E1
Caxton Dr UB8 201 D3
Caxton Rd MK12 33 B7
Cecil Rd SL0 207 E7
Cecils Yd 7 MK18 41 D1
Cecil Way SL2 197 F1
Cecily Ct MK5 46 A5
Cedar 1 RG9 191 D2

Cedar Ave
Hazelmere HP15 .... 163 A5
West Drayton UB7 ...... 208 F6
Cedar Chase SL6 .... 196 D1
Cedar Cl
Aylesbury HP20 .... 102 A2
Burnham SL1 .... 197 C1
Chesham HP5 .... 144 E1
Iver Heath SL0 .... 200 C4
Milton Keynes MK19 ..... 32 B7
Cedar Ct
Gerrards Cross SL9 ..... 188 E7
High Wycombe HP13 .... 173 B7
Maidenhead SL6 .... 202 D7
Marlow SL7 .... 183 E2
6 Windsor SL4 .... 210 A5
Cedar Dr
Chesham HP5 .... 144 A1
Cookham Rise SL6 ...... 195 F7
Cookham SL6 .... 196 A7
Marlow Bottom SL7 ..... 183 C7
Cedar Gr
Amersham HP7 .... 165 D8
Bellingdon HP5 .... 143 D8
Cedar Lodge Dr MK12 ... 33 D7
Cedar Park Sch HP15 .. 162 F5
Cedar Rd HP4 .... 135 D3
Cedar Ridge HP6 ...... 153 C5
Cedars Cl
Akeley MK18 .... 41 F8
Chalfont St Peter SL9 ... 177 E5
Cedars Comb Sch MK16 . 22 C4
Cedars Dr UB10 .... 201 F3
Cedars Ho SL6 .... 203 A7
Cedars Rd SL6 .... 203 A7
Cedars The
Berkhamsted HP4 ...... 135 E4
Slough SL2 .... 197 F2
Wendover HP22 .... 131 A5
Cedars Upper Sch & Com Coll LU7 .... 80 E5
Cedars Village WD3 .... 167 F5
Cedars Way
Leighton Buzzard LU7 .... 80 E5
Newport Pagnell MK16 ... 22 C4
Cedars Wlk WD3 .... 167 F5
Cedar Terr 1 HP11 .... 172 F7
Cedar Way
Berkhamsted HP4 ...... 135 D3
Slough SL3 .... 206 E2
Ceely Ho HP21 .... 115 D6
Ceely Rd HP21 .... 115 D6
Celandine Ct MK7 .... 48 A5
Celina Cl MK2 .... 58 C7
Cell Farm SL4 .... 211 B2
Cell Farm Ave SL4 ..... 211 B2
Centenary Bsns Pk RG9 .... 191 F1
Centenary Cotts HP27 .. 138 D7
Centenary Way HP6 .... 154 F1
Central Ave
Cranfield MK43 .... 24 E2
Whipsnade LU6 .... 107 E8
Central Dr SL1 .... 204 F6
Central Est SL6 .... 202 E7
Central Est SL6 .... 202 E8
CENTRAL MILTON KEYNES 34 D1
Central Park Bsns Ctr HP13 .... 173 A8
Centre Par HP27 .... 139 C5
Centre The SL2 .... 198 C6
Centre Wlk HP15 .... 163 A3
Centurion Ct MK11 ...... 33 C2
Centurion Rdbt MK1 .... 47 C2
Century Ave
Milton Keynes MK6 ...... 46 E7
Oldbrook MK6 .... 46 E8
Century Point HP12 ..... 172 C4
Cestreham Cres HP5 ... 144 D2
CHACKMORE 41 B4
Chacombe Pl HP9 ...... 175 D5
Chadbone Cl HP20 ...... 115 D8
Chadds La MK6 .... 47 C8
Chadwell Path HP21 ... 116 C6
Chadwick Dr MK6 .... 47 B7
Chadwick St HP13 ..... 162 D2
Chaffinch HP19 .... 101 F4
Chaffron Way
Leadenhall MK6 .... 46 F7
Milton Keynes, Oakgrove MK6, MK10, MK15 .... 35 D1
Milton Keynes, Shenley Lodge MK4, MK5, MK6 .... 46 C5
Chairborough Rd HP12 172 D6
Chairborough Rd Nature Reserve* HP12 .... 172 D5
Chairmakers Cl HP27 ... 139 A1
Chalcot Pl MK8 .... 45 F8
Chalcott SL1 .... 205 E3
Chalet Cl HP4 .... 134 F4
Chalfont Ave HP6 ...... 166 D8
Chalfont Cl MK13 .... 34 A6
CHALFONT COMMON 177 F6
Chalfont & Gerrards Cross Com Hospl SL9 .... 177 D2
Chalfont Ho HP7 .... 166 D7
Chalfont La
Chorleywood WD3 ...... 167 B4
Chalfont La *continued*
Maple Cross WD3 ...... 178 D3
Chalfont & Latimer Sta/U Sta HP7 .... 166 C8
Chalfont L Ctr SL9 ..... 177 C2
Chalfont Rd
Maple Cross SL9 .... 178 C7
Seer Green HP9 .... 176 D5
CHALFONT ST GILES 177 C7
Chalfont St Giles Inf Sch HP8 .... 177 B7
Chalfont St Giles Jun Sch HP8 .... 177 B7
CHALFONT ST PETER 177 F2
Chalfont St Peter Inf Sch SL9 .... 177 C3
Chalfont St Peter Jun Sch SL9 .... 177 D2
Chalfonts Com Coll The SL9 .... 177 C3
Chalfont Station Rd HP7 .... 166 C7
Chalfont Way HP12 .... 172 D3
Chalford Flats HP10 .... 185 F6
Chalford Way HP19 .... 114 F8
Chalgrove Cl SL6 ...... 203 B6
Chalgrove End HP22 ... 116 B1
Chalgrove Rd OX9 ..... 126 A1
Chalgrove Wlk HP21 ... 115 C6
Chalkdell Dr MK5 ...... 45 F4
Chalk Farm Rd HP14 ... 158 D5
Chalk Hill
Chesham HP5 .... 144 B2
Coleshill HP7 .... 164 F2
Windsor SL4 .... 210 F6
Chalkhill Blue Cl HP19 . 101 C4
Chalk La HP6, HP7 ...... 153 B4
Chalklands SL8 .... 185 A4
Chalkpit La SL7 .... 183 B3
Chalk Pit La SL1 .... 197 B4
Chalkpits The HP10 .... 185 E6
CHALKSHIRE 130 C4
Chalkshire Cotts HP17 . 130 C4
Chalkshire Rd HP17 ... 130 C4
Chalkstream Way HP10 185 E7
Challacombe MK4 ...... 46 D2
Challener Rd HP12 ..... 172 C3
Challenge Ho MK3 ...... 47 B1
Challow Ct SL6 .... 195 D1
Chalmers Ave MK19 ..... 20 D2
Chaloner Pl HP21 ...... 115 D6
Chaloner Rd HP21 ..... 115 D6
Chaloners Hill MK18 .... 63 D3
CHALVEY 205 C3
Chalvey Gdns SL1 ...... 205 E4
Chalvey Gr SL1 .... 205 B4
Chalvey Pk SL1 .... 205 E4
Chalvey Road E SL1 ..... 205 E4
Chalvey Road W SL1 ... 205 D4
Chalwell Ridge MK5 ..... 46 B4
Chamberlain Rd HP19 .. 101 B1
Champflower MK4 ...... 46 D3
Champney Cl SL3 ...... 212 A4
Champneys Coll of Health & Beauty HP23 .... 133 E6
Chancellors HP7 .... 164 B5
Chancellors Cnr HP7 ... 164 B5
Chancery Cl MK13 .... 34 A6
Chancery Pl SL4 .... 210 D7
Chandlers Ct MK6 .... 47 E5
CHANDLERS HILL 200 E3
Chandlers Quay SL6 .... 203 C8
Chandos Cl
Buckingham MK18 .... 52 D7
Little Chalfont HP6 ...... 155 C1
Chandos Ct MK18 .... 52 D7
Chandos Mall 7 SL1 .... 205 F4
Chandos Pl
Milton Keynes MK2 ...... 58 B8
Wendover HP22 .... 131 B4
Chandos Rd MK18 .... 52 D8
Channer Dr HP10 ...... 163 B1
Channory Cl MK4 .... 46 A1
Chantry Cl
Windsor SL4 .... 210 A6
Woburn Sands MK17 ..... 49 A6
Chantry Rd HP19 .... 101 C3
Chantry Rise 8 MK46 ..... 6 F3
Chantry Specl Sch UB7 208 E6
Chantry The
15 Aylesbury HP20 ..... 115 D8
Uxbridge UB8 .... 201 F2
Chapel Arches SL6 ..... 203 A7
Chapel Cl
Blackthorn OX25 .... 81 A3
Little Gaddesden HP4 ... 121 D6
Chapel Cotts SL2 ...... 199 B5
Chapel Crofts HP4 ..... 134 E6
Chapel Ct SL6 .... 202 D4
Chapel Dr HP22 .... 117 E5
CHAPEL END 118 C8
Chapel End La HP23 .... 118 C8
Chapel Farm NN7 .... 10 C6
Chapel Fields HP23 .... 118 C8
Chapel Hill
Soulbury LU7 .... 69 E3
Speen HP27 .... 150 C4
Windsor SL4 .... 210 D6
Chapel Ho HP6 .... 153 C5
Chapel La
Akeley MK18 .... 41 F8
Chilton HP18 .... 111 B3
Drayton Parslow MK17 ... 68 B5
High Wycombe HP12 .... 172 C8
Ivinghoe Aston LU7 ...... 92 A1
Long Marston HP23 ..... 104 B4
Northall LU6 .... 92 A5
Pitch Green HP27 ...... 138 B3
Rout's Green HP14 ..... 148 E2
St Leonards HP23 ...... 132 D3
Stoke Bruerne NN12 ...... 9 A8
Stoke Mandeville HP22 .. 116 A1
Stoke Poges SL2 .... 199 B5
Thornborough MK18 ..... 54 B8
Totternhoe LU6 .... 92 F8
Turweston NN13 .... 38 B7
Walter's Ash HP14 ...... 161 C7
Wendover HP22 .... 131 B4
Whitfield NN13 .... 26 D3
Chapel Rd
Flackwell Heath HP10 ... 185 A8
Ford HP17 .... 128 A7
Chapel Row HP14 ...... 171 A7
Chapels Cl SL1 .... 204 E5
Chapel Sq LU7 .... 68 E1
Chapel St
Berkhamsted HP4 ...... 135 D4
High Wycombe HP13 .... 161 D3
Marlow SL7 .... 183 E2
Slough SL1 .... 205 F4
Tring HP23 .... 118 F3
Uxbridge UB8 .... 201 C4
Woburn Sands MK17 ..... 49 B4
Chaplin Gr MK8 .... 45 D7
Chaplin Mews 7 SL3 ... 206 F1
Chapman Ave MK14 ..... 35 A6
Chapman Cl
Aylesbury HP21 .... 115 B6
West Drayton UB7 ...... 208 F3
Chapman La HP8, HP10 . 185 A6
Chapmans Cres HP5 ... 144 A2
Chapmans Dr MK19 ..... 32 B7
Chapmans Lea HP22 .... 88 D5
Chappel Mdw HP23 .... 119 B6
Chapter MK6 .... 47 A5
Chapter Cl UB10 .... 201 F5
Chapter Ho MK6 .... 47 A5
Chapter Mews SL4 ..... 210 D7
Charbray Cres MK5 ..... 46 A4
Chardacre MK8 .... 33 E1
Charlbury Rd UB10 ..... 190 F1
Charles Cl HP21 .... 116 B4
Charles Dr OX9 .... 126 A1
Charles Gdns SL2 ...... 206 A7
Charles Ho
Henley-on-Thames RG9 .. 191 E3
9 Windsor SL4 .... 210 C6
Charles Pym Rd HP19 .. 101 C4
Charles St
Berkhamsted HP4 ...... 135 B4
Tring HP23 .... 119 A3
Windsor SL4 .... 210 C6
Charlestown Lodge UB8 .... 201 D6
Charles Way MK16 ...... 22 C4
Charlewood Ho MK17 ... 49 B3
Charlock Ct MK16 .... 21 F4
Charlotte Ave SL2 ...... 205 F6
Charlotte Cl LU7 .... 79 F2
Charlotte Cott SL6 ..... 203 B8
Charlotte Way 12 SL7 .. 183 E2
Charlton SL4 .... 209 C5
Charlton Cl
Slough SL1 .... 205 B4
Swanbourne MK17 .... 66 F3
Charlton Pl 2 SL4 ..... 209 C5
Charlton Row 5 SL4 ... 209 C5
Charlton Sq 4 SL4 ..... 209 C5
Charlton Way SL4 ...... 209 C5
Charlton Wlk 3 SL4 ... 209 C5
Charmfield Rd HP21 ... 116 A5
CHARNDON 72 E6
Charnwood Cl 5 HP13 . 173 F5
Charsley Cl HP6 .... 166 C8
Charter Cl 8 SL1 ...... 205 F3
Charter Dr HP6 .... 154 F1
Charter Pl UB8 .... 201 D5
Charter Rd SL1 .... 204 E6
Chartley Ct MK5 .... 46 B4
CHARTRIDGE 143 C4
Chartridge Comb Sch HP5 .... 143 C4
Chartridge Development UB8 .... 201 B3
Chartridge Grange Dr HP5 .... 143 D4
Chartridge Ho 3 HP13 . 173 F6
Chartridge La HP5 ..... 143 F2
Chartridge Park Mobile Home Pk HP5 .... 143 D4
Chartwell Gate HP9 .... 175 D2
Chartwell Rd MK16 ...... 22 E4
Chase Ave MK7 .... 48 A4
Chase Cl HP7 .... 165 A4
Chase Farm Barns MK17 . 56 C4
Chase Park Rd NN7 ...... 1 A5
Chaseport Cl MK46 .... 5 D2
Chaseside Cl LU7 ...... 105 A7
Chase The
1 Chesham HP5 .... 144 B2
Maidenhead SL6 .... 195 D3
Marlow SL7 .... 184 A3
Tylers Green HP10 ...... 163 C1
Chasewater Cres MK10 .. 36 B3
Chatfield SL2 .... 205 A8
Chatham Ct 2 SL1 ..... 206 A3
Chatsworth MK8 .... 33 F1
Chatsworth Cl SL6 ..... 202 C5
Chaucer Cl
Berkhamsted HP4 ...... 134 F5
Newport Pagnell MK16 ... 22 A4
Windsor SL4 .... 210 D4
Chaucer Dr HP21 ...... 115 F6
Chaucer Rd MK3 .... 58 A7
Chaucer Way SL1 ...... 205 F5
Chauntry Cl SL6 .... 203 C6
Chauntry Rd SL6 .... 203 B6
Chawton Cres MK8 ...... 33 F1
Cheapside La UB9 ..... 189 F2
CHEARSLEY 112 A2
Chearsley Rd HP18 ..... 125 E7
CHEDDINGTON 105 B7
Cheddington Comb Sch LU7 .... 105 A7
Cheddington La HP23 .. 104 C5
Cheddington Rd LU7 ... 105 C4
Cheddington Sta LU7 ... 91 A2
Chelmsford Ct 8 SL4 .. 210 C5
Chelsea Gn LU7 .... 80 D6
Chelsea Ho 6 LU7 ...... 80 E7
Chelsea Rd HP19 .... 100 E1
Cheltenham Gdns MK3 .. 57 D6
Cheney Cl LU7 .... 78 B1
Cheneys Wlk MK3 .... 47 A2
Cheney Way HP20 ...... 101 E1
Cheney Wlk 3 HP20 ... 101 F2
CHENIES 156 B2
Chenies Ave HP6 .... 166 D8
CHENIES BOTTOM 156 B2
Chenies Comb Sch WD3 .... 156 B1
Chenies Manor Ho* WD3 .... 156 A1
Chenies Par HP7 .... 166 C7
Chenies Rd WD3 .... 167 D7
Cheniston Gr SL6 ...... 202 A7
Chepping Cl HP10 ...... 163 A1
Chepping View Prim Sch HP12 .... 172 D3
Chepstow Dr MK3 .... 57 D6
Chequers Bridge Cotts SL0 .... 207 C4
Chequers Cl LU7 .... 105 C4
Chequers Ct HP21 ...... 115 E4
Chequers Dr HP16 ..... 151 C6
Chequers End MK18 ..... 66 A4
Chequers Hill HP7 ..... 165 D7
Chequers La
Ibstone HP14, RG9 ..... 170 A5
North Crawley MK16 ..... 24 B6
Pitstone LU7 .... 105 C5
Prestwood HP16 .... 151 C7
Chequers Orch SL0 .... 207 F7
Chequers Sq UB8 ...... 201 C5
Chequers The
Castlethorpe MK19 ...... 19 F5
Eaton Bray LU6 .... 92 F5
Cherington Gate SL6 ... 195 B1
Cheriton MK4 .... 46 E3
Cherleton MK8 .... 33 E1
Cherries The SL2 ...... 206 B7
Cherry Acre SL9 .... 177 D6
Cherry Ave SL3 .... 206 D4
Cherry Cl
Flackwell Heath HP10 ... 185 B7
Prestwood HP16 .... 151 D6
Cherry Cnr HP10 .... 185 B8
Cherrycroft Dr HP14 ... 161 D6
Cherry Dr HP9 .... 175 B4
Cherry Gdns HP23 ..... 118 F3
Cherry Gr HP15 .... 163 C6
Cherry La
Amersham HP7 .... 165 A7
West Drayton UB7 ...... 208 F2
Woodrow HP7 .... 164 D6
Cherry Lane Prim Sch UB7 .... 208 F2
Cherry Leys MK18 .... 63 E3
Cherry Orch
Amersham HP6 .... 154 E2
Olney MK46 .... 6 E4
Prestwood HP16 .... 151 C6
Stoke Poges SL2 .... 199 A5
West Drayton UB7 ...... 208 E4
Cherry Orchard Ct HP13 .... 173 E6
Cherry Pit The HP13 ... 161 E2
Cherry Rd MK16 .... 22 B3
Cherry Rise
Chalfont St Giles HP8 ... 177 D8
Flackwell Heath HP10 ... 185 B7
Cherry St HP13 .... 174 A4
Cherry Tree Ave UB7 ... 208 F7
Cherry Tree Cl
Great Kingshill HP15 .... 151 D1
Hughenden Valley HP14 . 162 A7
Speen HP27 .... 150 B5
Cherry Tree Ho 4 SL7 . 183 D2
Cherrytree La
Chalfont St Peter SL9 ... 177 D1
Iver Heath SL0 .... 201 A4
Cherry Tree La
Buckland Common HP23 .... 133 A3
Fulmer SL3 .... 199 F6
Heronsgate WD3 .... 167 C1
Lee Common HP16 ..... 142 E4
Cherry Tree Rd
Beaconsfield HP9 .... 175 B1
Chinnor OX39 .... 147 C6
Farnham Common SL2 ... 198 C5
Cherry Tree Way HP10 . 163 C1
Cherry Tree Wlk
Chesham HP5 .... 144 D2
Leighton Buzzard LU7 .... 80 E7
Wendover HP22 .... 131 A5
Cherry Way
Hazelmere HP15 .... 163 A6
Horton SL3 .... 212 C4
Cherrywood Cl HP9 .... 176 D5
Cherrywood Gdns HP10 .... 185 B8
Chervil MK6 .... 47 B5
Cherwell Cl
Maidenhead SL6 .... 203 A8
Slough SL3 .... 212 B8
Cherwell Ho MK3 .... 57 E8
Cherwell Rd
Aylesbury HP21 .... 115 C6
Bourne End SL8 .... 185 B4
CHESHAM 154 C8
Chesham Ave MK13 ..... 34 C3
CHESHAM BOIS 154 C3
Chesham Bois CE Comb Sch HP6 .... 154 D4
Chesham High Sch HP5 .... 144 D1
Chesham La
Chalfont St Peter SL9 ... 177 E6
Wendover HP22, HP16 .. 141 E8
Chesham L Ctr HP5 .... 154 D8
Chesham Mus* HP5 ... 154 B8
Chesham Park Com Coll HP5 .... 144 A1
Chesham Prep Sch HP5 .... 145 A4
Chesham Rd
Amersham HP6 .... 154 C2
Ashley Green PH4, PH5 .. 144 F8
Bellingdon HP5 .... 143 E7
Berkhamsted HP4 ...... 135 B2
Bovingdon HP3, HP5 .... 145 E4
Hyde Heath HP16 ...... 153 C7
Wigginton HP23 .... 133 D7
Chesham U Sta HP5 .... 154 C8
Cheshire Cotts OX27 .... 72 F6
Cheshire Ct 6 SL1 ..... 206 B4
Cheshire Rise MK3 ...... 46 E1
Cheslyn Gdns MK14 ..... 35 A8
Chesney Wold MK6 ..... 46 F5
Chessbury Cl HP5 ...... 154 A7
Chessbury Rd HP5 ..... 154 A7
Chess Cl
Aylesbury HP21 .... 115 D3
Latimer HP5 .... 155 D3
Chessfield Pk HP6 ..... 166 E8
CHESSMOUNT 154 E7
Chessmount Rise HP5 .. 154 D6
Chester Cl MK3 .... 57 D7
Chesterfield Cl HP17 ... 114 C5
Chesterfield Cres LU7 ... 79 E3
Chesterfield Pl HP19 ... 115 B8
Chester Ho UB8 .... 201 C1
Chesterholm MK13 ...... 33 F5
Chester Rd SL1 .... 205 D7
Chesterton Cl HP5 ..... 144 B2
Chesterton Gn HP9 .... 175 E2
Chestnut Ave
Chesham HP5 .... 144 E2
Halton HP22 .... 131 D8
High Wycombe HP11 .... 173 D5
Slough SL3 .... 206 E4
West Drayton UB7 ...... 208 F6
Chestnut Cl
Amersham HP6 .... 154 D2
Aston Clinton HP22 ..... 117 F5
Chalfont St Peter SL9 ... 177 F2
Dagnall HP4 .... 107 C5
Maidenhead SL6 .... 196 B1
Medmenham SL7 .... 193 D7
Milton Keynes MK11 ..... 32 D5
Monks Risborough HP27 139 C5
Newton Longville MK17 ... 57 D2
Waddesdon HP18 .... 99 A6
Chestnut Comb Sch MK3 .... 57 E7
Chestnut Cotts MK18 .... 52 C7
Chestnut Cres
Aylesbury HP21 .... 115 D6
Milton Keynes MK2 ...... 58 D7
Chestnut Ct HP6 .... 154 D2
Chestnut Dr
Berkhamsted HP4 ...... 135 D3

Chestnut Dr *continued*
Windsor SL4 . . . . 209 F3
Chestnut End HP22. . . . . 117 C1
Chestnut Gn NN13 . . . . . . 26 E4
Chestnut Hill LU7 . . . . 80 D8
Chestnut La
Amersham HP6 . . . . 154 E2
Hazlemere HP15 . . . . 163 B5
Chestnut Lane Inf Sch
HP6. . . . . 154 E3
Chestnut Leys MK18. . . . . 63 E3
Chestnut Pk SL6 . . . . 203 E3
Chestnut Rd
Beaconsfield HP9. . . . . . . 175 B1
Princes Risborough
HP27. . . . . 139 C3
Yardley Gobion NN12. . . . . 18 F6
Chestnut Rise LU7 . . . . . . 80 D8
Chestnuts The
Castlethorpe MK19 . . . . . . 19 F5
Felden HP3 . . . . 146 F7
Uxbridge UB10. . . . . 201 E5
Chestnut View
Chearsley HP18. . . . . 112 B2
East Claydon MK18 . . . . . . 74 F7
Chestnut Way
Longwick HP27 . . . . 138 E6
Stoke Mandeville HP22 . . 116 A1
Chestnut Wlk SL9. . . . . . 177 E3
Chestwood Gr UB10. . . . 201 F5
Chettle Pl NN12. . . . . 18 E2
CHETWODE 61 E8
Chetwode Ave MK10 . . . . 36 B1
Chetwode Cl MK18. . . . . . . 41 E2
Chetwynd Dr UB10 . . . . . 201 F3
Chevalier Gr MK8 . . . . 45 D7
Cheveley Gdns SL1. . . . . 197 C3
Cheviot Cl
High Wycombe HP13 . . . . 161 E1
Leighton Buzzard LU7 . . . . 80 C8
Maidenhead SL6 . . . . 203 B6
Cheviot Rd SL3 . . . . 207 A1
Cheyne Cl
Amersham HP6 . . . . 154 D3
Buckingham MK18. . . . . . . 41 F1
Gerrards Cross SL9. . . . . 188 E3
Pitstone LU7 . . . . 105 D4
Cheyne Mews HP5 . . . . . 154 D8
Cheyne Wlk HP5 . . . . 154 D8
CHICHELEY 23 C8
Chicheley Hall MK16 . . . . 23 D8
Chicheley Hill MK16. . . . . 23 A8
Chicheley Rd MK16. . . . . . 23 E7
Chicheley St MK16 . . . . . . 22 E4
Chichester Cl HP13 . . . . 173 D6
Chichester Ct SL1. . . . . 206 A4
Chicksands Ave MK10 . . . 36 A2
Chievely Ct MK4 . . . . 46 C1
Chilcote La HP7. . . . . . . 166 A8
Childs Way MK4, MK5, MK6,
MK10 . . . . 46 C7
Chillery Leys MK15. . . . . . 35 E7
Chillingham Ct MK5. . . . . 46 A4
Chiltern Ave
Amersham HP6 . . . . 154 D1
Edlesborough LU6 . . . . 92 E3
High Wycombe HP12 . . . . 172 D6
Stone HP17 . . . . 114 D5
Chiltern Brewery The★
HP17. . . . . 130 C5
Chiltern Bsns Village
UB8. . . . . 201 B3
Chiltern Cl
Berkhamsted HP4 . . . . . . 134 F5
Princes Risborough
HP27. . . . . 139 A3
Stone HP17 . . . . 114 D5
Wendover HP22. . . . . 131 B5
Chiltern Cnr HP4. . . . . . . 135 A5
Chiltern Commerce Ctr
HP5. . . . . 144 A2
Chiltern Cotts
Buckland Common
HP23. . . . . 133 A2
Ibstone HP14. . . . . 169 D7
Chiltern Court Mews
SL4. . . . . 210 B6
Chiltern Ct
Amersham HP6 . . . . 154 C2
Chesham HP5 . . . . 144 A2
5 High Wycombe HP12 . 172 E7
Wendover HP22. . . . . 131 B4
Windsor SL4 . . . . 210 B6
Winslow MK18. . . . . 65 F3
Chiltern Dr WD3 . . . . 167 F2
Chiltern Gate Sch
HP12. . . . . 172 E4
Chiltern Gn HP10 . . . . . . 185 A8
Chiltern Hill SL9 . . . . 177 E2
Chiltern Hills Rd HP9. . . 175 C2
Chiltern Ho HP5 . . . . 154 C7
Chiltern Hospl The (private)
HP16. . . . . 152 C4
Chiltern Hts HP7. . . . . . . 166 A8
Chiltern Manor Pk
HP16 . . . . 152 A7
Chiltern Open Air Mus★
HP8. . . . . 177 F8
Chiltern Par HP6. . . . . . . 154 C2
Chiltern Park Ave HP4 . 135 A6
Chiltern Pools The
HP6. . . . . 154 D1
Chiltern Rd
Amersham HP6 . . . . 154 B4
Ballinger Common HP16 . 142 E3
Burnham SL1 . . . . 204 B8
Maidenhead SL6 . . . . 203 B6
Marlow SL7 . . . . 183 C2
Wendover HP22. . . . . 131 B5
Wingrave HP22 . . . . 89 A3
Chiltern Ridge HP14 . . . 158 C4
Chilterns
Berkhamsted HP4 . . . . . . 134 F6
World's End HP22 . . . . . . 130 F7
Chilterns Cl HP10 . . . . . . 185 B7
Chilterns Gateway Ctr★
LU6 . . . . 93 F4
Chilterns Pk SL8 . . . . 185 B5
Chiltern St HP21 . . . . 115 E6
Chilterns The (Sh Ctr)
HP13. . . . . 173 A7
Chiltern Valley Winery &
Brewery★ RG9. . . . . 180 F7
Chiltern View HP14 . . . . 149 C1
Chiltern View Rd UB8 . . 201 D3
Chiltern Villas HP23. . . . 118 E2
Chiltern Way
Aston Clinton HP22 . . . . . 117 F2
Tring HP23. . . . . 119 C5
CHILTON 111 A4
Chilton Cl
Holmer Green HP15. . . . . 163 C7
Tylers Green HP10. . . . . . 163 C2
Chilton Ct SL6 . . . . 204 C7
Chilton Pl HP20 . . . . 101 E1
Chilton Rd
Chearsley HP18. . . . . 112 A2
Chesham HP5 . . . . 144 C2
Long Crendon HP18. . . . . 125 C7
Chilwick Rd SL2 . . . . 197 F1
Chimes Sh Ctr The
UB8. . . . . 201 D5
Chimes The HP12 . . . . . . 172 E6
Chimney La HP10 . . . . . . 185 E8
Chinalls Cl MK18. . . . . 50 D6
Chingle Croft MK4 . . . . . . 46 C2
Chinneck Ho HP4 . . . . . . 135 C4
CHINNOR 147 D7
Chinnor Hill OX39. . . . . . 147 E4
Chinnor Hill Wildlife
Reserve★ OX39 . . . . 147 F5
Chinnor & Princes
Risborough Rly★
OX39. . . . . 147 E7
Chinnor Rd
Bledlow HP27 . . . . 138 A2
Bledlow Ridge HP14 . . . . 148 C3
Chinnor OX39. . . . . 147 A4
Chinnor Sta★ OX39 . . . . 147 D5
Chippendale Cl HP13. . . 162 D1
Chippendale Waye
UB8 . . . . 201 D5
Chippenham Dr MK10 . . . 36 C1
CHIPPERFIELD. 156 F8
Chipperfield Cl MK13. . . . 34 A7
Chipperfield Rd HP3 . . . 146 C3
Chipping Vale MK4. . . . . . 46 C2
Chipstead SL9 . . . . 177 C2
Chirbury Cl MK10 . . . . 35 F1
CHISBRIDGE CROSS 182 D6
Chislehampton MK15. . . . 35 C3
Chiswick Cl MK4 . . . . 45 F2
Chiswick Lodge 6 SL7 183 D2
CHIVERY 132 C4
Choke La SL6. . . . . 195 B4
CHOLESBURY 133 C3
Cholesbury La HP23. . . . 133 A2
Cholesbury Rd HP23 . . . 133 D5
Chorley Rd HP14. . . . . . . 160 E3
CHORLEYWOOD 167 D5
CHORLEYWOOD BOTTOM 167 C3
Chorleywood Bottom
WD3. . . . . 167 D4
Chorleywood Comm Nature
Reserve★ WD3 . . . . 167 E5
Chorleywood Ho WD3. . 167 E6
Chorleywood House Dr
WD3. . . . . 167 E6
Chorleywood House Est
Nature Reserve★
WD3 . . . . 167 F6
Chorleywood Montessori
Sch The WD3 . . . . 167 E7
Chorleywood Prim Sch
WD3 . . . . 167 C3
Chorleywood Sta/U Sta
WD3 . . . . 167 D5
CHORLEYWOOD WEST. 167 A4
Chrislaine Cl TW19. . . . . 213 D1
Christchurch CE Prim Sch
WD3 . . . . 167 F6
Christchurch Gr MK12. . . 33 B6
Christchurch Ho 15
HP23 . . . . 119 A3
Christchurch Rd HP23. . 118 F4
Christian Ct MK15. . . . . . . 35 D7
Christian Smith Ho
SL6. . . . . 202 A1
Christian Sq 4 SL4 . . . . 210 C6
Christie Cl MK16 . . . . 22 A5
Christies Ct 2 HP13 . . . 173 B7
Christine Ho 3 MK2 . . . . 58 C8
CHRISTMAS COMMON . . . 168 B7
Christmas La 1 SL2. . . . 198 C8
Christopher Cl HP14 . . . 161 D7
Christopher Ho 3 SL2 . 198 C7
Christ the Sower
Ecumenical Prim Sch
MK8 . . . . 45 D6
Church Ave RG9 . . . . 191 E2
Church Cl
Aston Clinton HP22 . . . . . 117 D5
Cuddington HP18. . . . . . . 112 F3
Eton SL4. . . . . 210 D8
Maidenhead SL6 . . . . 202 D6
Maids Moreton MK18 . . . . 41 F3
Uxbridge UB8. . . . . 201 B3
West Drayton UB7. . . . . . 208 E3
Wicken MK19. . . . . 31 B3
Church Cotts SL6 . . . . . . 196 E2
Church Croft LU6 . . . . 92 E3
Church Ct
Aylesbury HP22 . . . . 116 B2
High Wycombe HP13 . . . . 162 D1
Church Dr SL6. . . . . 203 C4
CHURCH END
Chorley Wood. 156 F1
Drayton Parslow 68 B5
Haddenham 127 A5
Hanslope 11 A2
Long Crendon. 125 C7
Pitstone 105 D3
Steeple Claydon. 63 E2
Totternhoe 93 B7
Church End
Adstock MK18 . . . . 53 F1
Bledlow HP27 . . . . 138 B1
Drayton Parslow MK17 . . . 68 B5
Edlesborough LU6 . . . . 92 E3
Haddenham HP17 . . . . . . 127 A5
Hillesden MK18 . . . . 63 B6
Leckhampstead MK18 . . . . 42 D8
Newton Longville MK17. . . 57 D3
Potterspury NN12 . . . . 18 E3
Sherington MK16. . . . . 14 A2
Syresham NN13. . . . . 27 C8
Wavendon MK17 . . . . 48 E7
Church End Cotts WD3 . 156 F1
Church End Farm LU6. . . 93 B7
Church End Rd MK5. . . . . 46 A4
Church Farm Cl HP22 . . 102 B3
Church Farm Cres MK14. 34 E8
Church Farm Ho HP8. . . 177 C7
Church Farm La HP23 . . 104 F3
Churchfield Mews SL2 . 206 A7
Churchfield Rd SL9 . . . . 177 D2
Churchgates 3 HP4 . . . 135 C4
Church Gn
Long Crendon HP18. . . . . 125 D7
Totternhoe LU6 . . . . 93 B7
Church Gr
Little Chalfont HP6. . . . . . 166 E8
Slough SL3. . . . . 206 C8
Church Green Rd MK3. . . 58 A8
Church Headland La
HP22 . . . . 87 A6
CHURCH HILL 56 A8
Church Hill
Akeley MK18 . . . . 41 F8
Aspley Guise MK17 . . . . . . 49 E5
Cheddington LU7 . . . . 105 A8
Ellesborough HP17 . . . . . 130 B2
Milton Keynes MK8 . . . . . . 33 F2
Pishill RG9 . . . . 179 D8
South Harefield UB9 . . . . 190 C8
Whaddon MK17 . . . . 45 B1
Church Holt The SL2 . . . 187 E3
Churchill Ave HP21 . . . . 115 D5
Churchill Cl HP10. . . . . . 185 B7
Churchill Ct 1 HP21 . . . 115 E7
Churchill Dr
Beaconsfield HP9. . . . . . . 175 C5
Marlow SL7 . . . . 183 F4
Churchill Ho UB7 . . . . . . 208 D6
Churchill Rd SL3. . . . . . . 206 F2
Church La
Alderton NN12. . . . . 9 A2
Aston Clinton HP22 . . . . . 117 D4
Berkhamsted HP4 . . . . . . 135 C4
Bisham SL7 . . . . 194 D7
Bledlow Ridge HP14 . . . . 159 F8
Bovingdon HP3 . . . . 146 B4
Bray SL6 . . . . 203 C4
Chalfont St Peter SL9 . . . 177 D2
Chearsley HP18. . . . . 112 B1
Cheddington LU7 . . . . 105 A8
Chinnor OX39. . . . . 147 D6
Clifton Reynes MK46 . . . . . . 7 C3
Cryers Hill HP15 . . . . 162 C4
Deanshanger MK19. . . . . . 31 E4
Eaton Bray LU6 . . . . 92 E6
Church La *continued*
Edgcott HP18. . . . . 72 F2
Emberton MK46. . . . . 13 F7
Grafton Regis NN12. . . . . . . 9 D2
Granborough MK18 . . . . . . 75 F6
Great Horwood MK17 . . . . 55 A3
Great Kimble HP17 . . . . . 129 E1
Great Missenden HP16 . . 152 B7
Hastoe HP23 . . . . 132 F7
Horton-cum-S OX33. . . . . 108 A5
Lacey Green HP27 . . . . . . 149 E4
Lillingstone Lovell MK18 . . 30 A6
Ludgershall HP18. . . . . 96 C7
Marsworth HP23 . . . . 104 F1
Milton Keynes MK5 . . . . . . 46 B8
Mixbury NN13 . . . . 38 D1
Mursley MK17 . . . . 67 D5
Newport Pagnell MK16 . . . 22 D7
Oving HP22 . . . . 86 C7
Padbury MK18 . . . . 53 C2
Potterspury NN12 . . . . 18 E3
Princes Risborough
HP27. . . . . 139 B4
Radnage HP14. . . . . 159 D8
Sarratt WD3. . . . . 156 F1
Slough SL2, SL3 . . . . 206 C8
Soulbury LU7 . . . . 69 E2
Stoke Bruerne NN12 . . . . . . 9 A8
Stoke Goldington MK16. . . 12 A7
Stoke Poges SL2 . . . . 198 F2
Thornborough MK18 . . . . . 54 A8
Tingewick MK18. . . . . 51 B7
Upper Winchendon HP18. . 99 B1
Uxbridge UB8. . . . . 201 B3
Walter's Ash HP14. . . . . . 161 E6
Walton MK7. . . . . 47 F6
Wendover HP22. . . . . 131 C3
Weston Turville HP22. . . . 116 F1
West Wycombe HP14. . . . 161 A2
Whaddon MK17 . . . . 45 B1
Whitchurch HP22. . . . . 87 A6
Wicken MK19. . . . . 31 B3
8 Windsor SL4 . . . . 210 D6
Yardley Hastings NN7 . . . . . 1 B7
Church Lees MK14 . . . . . . 21 D1
Churchmead CE Sch
SL3 . . . . 211 B7
Churchmere Wlk HP21 . 115 C6
Church Pas MK16 . . . . 22 D4
Church Path
Cheddington LU7 . . . . 91 A1
Cublington LU7 . . . . 78 B1
Lane End HP14 . . . . 171 B4
Prestwood HP16 . . . . 151 D5
Stokenchurch HP14. . . . . 158 D5
Church Piece HP18 . . . . 112 B2
Church Rd
Aspley Heath MK17 . . . . . . 49 B3
Bow Brickhill MK17 . . . . . . 48 D1
Brackley NN13. . . . . 38 A7
Chinnor OX39. . . . . 147 D6
Cookham Dean SL6 . . . . . 195 B6
Farnham Royal SL2 . . . . . 198 C2
Ickford HP18 . . . . 123 F3
Iver Heath SL0. . . . . 200 C3
Ivinghoe LU7 . . . . 105 F5
Lane End HP14 . . . . 171 B3
Leighton Buzzard LU7 . . . . 80 E6
Lewknor OX49 . . . . 157 B8
Little Gaddesden HP4 . . . 121 D8
Little Marlow SL7. . . . . . . 184 C5
Maidenhead SL6 . . . . 203 B5
Old Windsor SL4 . . . . 211 B2
Penn HP10. . . . . 174 E7
Pitstone LU7 . . . . 105 E3
Seer Green HP9. . . . . 176 D4
Sherington MK16. . . . . 13 F2
Slapton LU7 . . . . 91 D6
South Harefield UB9 . . . . 190 C8
Stoke Hammond MK17 . . . 69 D8
Stokenchurch HP14. . . . . 158 D5
Thame OX9 . . . . 125 E1
Totternhoe LU6 . . . . 93 B6
Tylers Green HP10. . . . . . 174 C8
Uxbridge UB8. . . . . 201 D1
West Drayton UB7. . . . . . 208 E3
Church Row SL3 . . . . 199 D8
Churchside HP15 . . . . . . 163 D7
Church Sq
7 High Wycombe
HP11. . . . . 173 B7
Leighton Buzzard LU7 . . . . 80 F6
Church St
Amersham HP7 . . . . 165 B7
Aspley Guise MK17 . . . . . . 49 E5
16 Aylesbury HP20 . . . . . 115 D8
Bovingdon HP3 . . . . 146 B4
Brill HP18. . . . . 110 B8
Buckingham MK18. . . . . . . 52 C8
Burnham SL1 . . . . 197 C1
Chesham HP5 . . . . 154 B7
Gawcott MK18. . . . . 52 A4
Great Missenden HP16 . . 152 B7
Henley-on-Thames RG9. . 191 D1
High Wycombe HP11 . . . . 173 B7
Little Horwood MK17. . . . . 55 E2
Maids Moreton MK18 . . . . 41 F3
Marsh Gibbon OX27. . . . . . 71 F3
Church St *continued*
Milton Keynes, Fenny Stratford
MK2. . . . . 47 E1
Milton Keynes, New Bradwell
MK13. . . . . 33 F7
Milton Keynes, Stony Stratford
MK11. . . . . 32 D5
Milton Keynes, Wolverton
MK12. . . . . 33 D7
North Marston MK18. . . . . 76 B2
6 Olney MK46 . . . . 6 F3
Olney MK46 . . . . 7 A3
Princes Risborough
HP27. . . . . 139 B3
Quainton HP22. . . . . 85 B5
Slough, Chalvey SL1. . . . . 205 D4
Slough, Upton Park SL1. . 205 F4
Stokenchurch HP14. . . . . 158 D5
Twyford MK18 . . . . 62 C2
6 Windsor SL4 . . . . 210 D6
Wing LU7 . . . . 79 E2
Wingrave HP22 . . . . 89 B2
Winslow MK18. . . . . 65 F4
Church Terr
Turvey MK43 . . . . 8 E5
Windsor SL4 . . . . 209 E5
Church View
Brackley NN13. . . . . 38 A7
Edlesborough LU6 . . . . 92 D3
Halton HP22. . . . . 117 C1
Long Marston HP23. . . . . 104 A4
Newport Pagnell MK16 . . . 22 D4
9 Slough SL1 . . . . 206 A3
Steeple Claydon MK18. . . . 63 E2
Church View Ct LU7. . . . . 80 E6
Church Views SL6. . . . . . 202 F8
Churchway HP17. . . . . . . 127 A6
Church Way
East Claydon MK18 . . . . . . 74 F8
Stone HP17 . . . . 114 C5
Church Wlk
Milton Keynes MK3 . . . . . . 57 F7
North Crawley MK16 . . . . . 24 B6
Weston Turville HP22. . . . 116 F1
Wing LU7 . . . . 79 E2
Winslow MK18. . . . . 65 F4
Church Yd HP23 . . . . 119 A3
Chyne The SL9. . . . . 188 F6
Cinnamon Cl SL4 . . . . . . 209 F6
Cinnamon Gr MK7 . . . . . . 48 A5
CIPPENHAM. 204 F4
Cippenham Cl SL1 . . . . . 204 F6
Cippenham Inf Sch
SL1 . . . . 204 D6
Cippenham Jun Sch
SL1 . . . . 204 D6
Cippenham La SL1 . . . . . 205 B5
City Rd HP14. . . . . 159 D6
Clailey Ct MK11. . . . . 32 F5
Claires Court Sch SL6. . 196 B1
Clammas Way UB8 . . . . . 208 D8
Clapham Pl MK13 . . . . 34 C2
Clappers Mdw SL6 . . . . . 196 B1
Clappins La
Naphill HP14 . . . . 150 D1
Walter's Ash HP14. . . . . . 161 C8
Clapton App HP10. . . . . . 185 D8
Clare Croft MK10. . . . . 36 A3
Clare Dr SL2. . . . . 198 B8
Clarefield Cl SL6. . . . . . . 195 B1
Clarefield Dr SL6 . . . . . . 195 A1
Clarefield Rd SL6 . . . . . . 195 A1
Claremont SL3. . . . . 212 D6
Claremont Ave MK11 . . . . 32 E4
Claremont Cl HP21. . . . . 115 F5
Claremont Gdns SL7 . . . 183 E2
Claremont Rd
Marlow SL7 . . . . 183 E2
Windsor SL4 . . . . 210 C5
Clarence Cres SL4 . . . . . 210 C6
Clarence Ct
9 High Wycombe
HP13. . . . . 173 B7
Maidenhead SL6 . . . . 202 E8
Windsor SL4 . . . . 210 B6
Clarence Ho 2 MK9. . . . . 34 C2
Clarence Rd
Berkhamsted HP4 . . . . . . 135 C4
Henley-on-Thames RG9 . 191 D2
Milton Keynes MK11 . . . . . 32 E5
Windsor SL4 . . . . 210 B6
Clarendon Copse SL6 . . 202 D6
Clarendon Ct
Slough SL2. . . . . 206 B6
Windsor SL4 . . . . 210 B6
Clarendon Dr
Milton Keynes MK8 . . . . . . 33 F2
Thame OX9 . . . . 126 A1
Clarendon Rd
High Wycombe HP13 . . . . 173 E5
Prestwood HP16 . . . . 151 B6
Clare Park HP7 . . . . 165 E7
Clare Rd
Maidenhead SL6 . . . . 202 D6
Prestwood HP16 . . . . 151 C6
Slough SL6. . . . . 204 C7
Stanwell TW19. . . . . 213 E1
Claridge Dr MK10 . . . . 36 A2
Clarke Ct HP20 . . . . 101 F2

Clarke Dr HP13 174 A6
Clarke Rd MK1 47 D4
Clarkes Dr UB8 208 E8
Clarkes Field Cl HP18 110 B8
Clarkes Orch MK16 12 B5
Clarke's Spring HP23 119 F5
Clarke Wlk 2 HP20 101 F2
Clarks Cotts HP16 151 C7
Classon Cl UB7 208 E4
Clauds Cl HP15 163 A5
Claverton Cl HP3 146 A3
Clay Acre HP5 144 D1
Clay Cl HP10 185 B8
Claycots Prim Sch SL2 198 A1
Claycutters MK18 66 A4
Claydon Cl HP21 115 D6
Claydon Ct HP12 172 E4
Claydon End SL9 188 E8
Claydon Ho★ MK18 74 C7
Claydon La SL9 188 E8
Claydon Path HP21 115 E3
Claydons Pl HP27 138 D7
Clayfield Rd HP22 131 C8
Clayfields HP10 163 C2
Clayhall La SL4 210 F2
Clayhill
Marlow Bottom SL7 172 A2
Wigginton HP23 133 E7
Clay Hill MK8 33 E2
Clay La
Calvert MK18 73 A5
Marlow Bottom SL7 172 A2
Wendover HP22 131 C5
Claymoor Pk SL7 172 A2
Clay Pit La 9 MK46 6 F3
Clays La MK17 55 E2
Clay St HP7, HP9 175 C7
Clays The HP17 127 A7
Clayton Ct SL3 207 A3
Clayton Gate MK14 35 A8
Claytons Comb Sch SL8 185 A5
Claytons Mdw SL8 185 B2
Clayton Way UB8 201 D1
Clayton Wlk HP7 166 C8
Clearbrook Cl HP13 174 B4
Cleares Pasture SL1 197 B2
Cleavers OX39 147 B6
Cleavers Ave MK14 34 E3
Cleeve Cres MK3 47 A2
Clegg Sq MK5 46 B5
Cleland Rd SL9 177 D1
Clementi Ave HP15 163 D7
Clement Pl 5 HP23 119 A3
Clements Cl 5 SL1 206 B4
Clements La OX27 71 F2
Clements Rd
Chorleywood WD3 167 D4
Henley-on-Thames RG9 191 C3
Clerkenwell Cotts HP17 126 F5
Clerkenwell Pl MK6 35 B2
Clevehurst Cl SL2 199 A6
Cleveland MK13 34 B6
Cleveland Cl
Maidenhead SL6 203 B6
Wooburn Green HP10 185 E8
Cleveland Dr LU7 80 C8
Cleveland Pk
Aylesbury HP20 101 F3
Stanwell TW19 213 E1
Cleveland Pl 13 HP20 101 F3
Cleveland Rd
Aylesbury HP20 101 E3
Uxbridge UB8 201 D2
Cleves Ct SL4 209 F4
Clewer Ave SL4 210 A5
Clewer Court Rd SL4 210 B7
Clewer Fields SL4 210 C6
CLEWER GREEN 209 E3
Clewer Green CE Fst Sch SL4 210 A4
Clewer Hill Rd SL4 209 F4
CLEWER NEW TOWN 210 A5
Clewer New Town SL4 210 A5
Clewer Pk SL4 210 A7
CLEWER VILLAGE 210 A7
Clicker Yd MK46 6 F4
Clifden Rd HP18 123 E5
Clifford Ave MK2 58 C7
Clifford Rd HP27 139 B3
Cliffords Way SL8 185 B5
Clifton Bsns Pk HP19 101 B1
Clifton Cl SL6 203 A4
Clifton Ct
High Wycombe HP11 172 E4
Olney MK46 7 A3
8 Stanwell TW19 213 E1
Clifton Gn HP19 101 B2
Clifton Lawns HP6 154 C4
Clifton Lodge
Eton Wick SL4 205 A1
7 Slough SL1 206 A4
Clifton Moor MK5 45 D5
Clifton Rd
Amersham HP6 154 C4
Newton Blossomville MK43 8 A4
5 Slough SL1 206 A4
CLIFTON REYNES 7 C3
Clifton Rise SL4 209 D6
Cline Ct MK8 45 E6
Clinkard Pl HP14 171 A3
Clinton Cres HP21 116 A8
Clipstone Brook Way 4 MK10 36 B3
Clive Ct SL1 205 D4
Cliveden★ SL6 196 E7
Cliveden Gate SL1 197 B3
Cliveden Mead SL6 196 C2
Cliveden Office Village HP12 172 E4
Cliveden Pl MK4 45 F2
Cliveden Rd SL6 196 E4
Clivemont Rd SL6 202 F8
Clock Ho The MK17 59 D6
Clockhouse Mews WD3 167 E6
Cloebury Paddock MK15 35 C3
Cloister Garth HP4 135 C4
Cloisters The
High Wycombe HP13 162 D2
Slough SL1 205 D4
Clonmel Way SL1 197 B2
Closes The HP17 127 A7
Close The
Akeley MK18 42 A8
Ashendon HP18 97 F1
Bierton HP22 102 A4
Bourne End SL8 185 A6
Great Horwood MK17 55 B3
Hardmead MK16 15 D4
Hardwick HP22 87 B3
Iver Heath SL0 200 C2
Lathbury MK16 22 D7
Milton Keynes, Bradwell MK13 34 A4
Milton Keynes, The Green MK6 47 D7
Newton Blossomville MK43 7 F3
Ravenstone MK46 5 E2
Slough SL1 204 D6
Weston Underwood MK46 6 A1
Cloudberry MK7 48 A6
Cloutsham Cl MK4 46 D3
Clover Cl MK5 46 B8
Clover End MK18 52 C7
Clover La HP21 115 E5
Club Cotts MK17 49 B4
Cluny Ct MK7 48 D6
Clyde Pl MK3 46 E1
Clydesdale Pl MK14 34 F4
Coach Ho The
Loudwater HP11 174 A4
Wooburn Green HP10 185 E6
Coachmaker Ct MK14 34 F6
Coachman's Lodge SL4 210 D5
Coach Ride SL7 183 D4
Coach Yd NN12 18 E3
Coalmans Way SL1 204 A8
Coaters La HP10 185 E7
Coates La HP13 162 A1
Coat Wicks HP9 176 C4
Cobb Cl SL3 211 D6
Cobbetts Mount MK18 63 D2
Cobbetts Ride HP23 118 F3
Cobb Hall Rd MK17 57 C3
Cobblers Cl SL2 198 B3
Cobblershill La HP16 141 B4
Cobblers Wick HP22 89 B3
Cobb Rd HP4 134 F4
Cobbs Gdn MK46 6 F4
Cobden Cl UB8 201 C4
Coberley Cl MK15 35 B6
Cobham Cl
Buckingham MK18 41 C1
Slough SL1 204 F5
Cochran Cl MK8 45 E7
Cochrane Ho UB8 201 C4
Cockerell Gr MK5 46 C5
Cockett Rd SL3 206 E3
Cock Gr HP4 134 D4
Cock La HP10 174 A6
Cockpit Cl HP15 151 E1
Cockpit Rd HP15 162 D8
Cocksherd Wood Nature Reserve★ SL2 197 E2
Coddimoor La MK17 56 B7
CODMORE 144 E1
Codmore Cres HP5 144 E1
Codmore Cross HP5 144 D1
Codmore Wood Rd HP5 155 D6
Coe Spur SL1 205 B3
COFFEE HALL 46 F7
Coffee Hall Rdbt MK6 47 B6
Cofferidge Cl MK11 32 D5
Coftards SL2 206 C7
Cogan Ct MK8 45 E7
Cogdells Cl HP5 143 B4
Cogdells La HP5 143 B4
Coggeshall Gr MK7 48 C7
Coin Cl MK10 35 F3
Cokers Ct 3 SL8 185 A4
Coke's Farm La HP8 166 B6
Coke's La HP8 166 B6
Colborne Rd HP13 173 D8
Colby Gdns 1 SL6 202 F8
Colchester Ct MK3 57 E7
Colchester Wlk MK3 57 E7
COLD BRAYFIELD 8 B5
Coldeaton La MK4 46 B3
Cold Grove Cotts SL6 196 E2
Coldharbour HP22 131 C4
Cold Harbour CE Comb Sch MK3 46 F3
Coldharbour Way HP19 115 A7
Coldmoorholme La SL8 184 E4
Coldmoreham Yd HP7 165 A8
Coleheath Bottom HP27 150 C5
Colenorton Cres SL4 204 E2
Cole Rd HP21 115 C5
Coleridge Cl
Milton Keynes MK3 58 A7
Newport Pagnell MK16 21 F4
Coleridge Cres SL3 212 E6
Coleridge Way UB7 208 F2
Coles Ave MK6 46 F6
Colesbourne Dr MK15 35 B6
COLESHILL 164 F3
Coles Hill HP18 111 B3
Coleshill CE Inf Sch HP7 164 F3
Coleshill Ho HP7 165 A4
Coleshill La HP7 164 D2
Coleshill Pl MK13 34 C3
Colet Rd HP22 131 C5
Colgrain St MK9 35 A4
Colham Ave UB7 208 E5
Colham Mill Rd UB7 208 D5
Colham Rd UB8 201 F1
Colindale St MK10 35 E1
Colinswood SL2 187 B1
Colin Way SL1 205 B3
College Ave
Maidenhead SL6 202 E7
Slough SL1 205 E3
College Bsns Pk HP22 103 C1
College Cl
Holton OX33 122 C1
Thame OX9 125 E1
College Cres
Oakley HP18 109 E4
Windsor SL4 210 B5
College Glen SL6 202 D7
College Lake Wildlife Reserve★ HP23 105 C1
College Rd
Cranfield MK43 24 E2
Maidenhead SL6 202 E7
Slough SL1 204 F5
College Rise SL6 202 D7
College Road N HP22 117 C6
College The OX27 71 F3
College The (Claires Court Schs) SL6 202 E7
Colley Hill MK13 34 A4
Colley Hill La SL2 187 F1
Colley Ho UB8 201 D4
Colleyland WD3 167 D5
Collier Cl SL6 195 F1
Colliers Wood MK10 35 E8
Collings Walk HP16 151 C5
Collingwood Cl HP13 174 A6
Collins Ho 2 HP11 173 A7
Collins Wlk MK16 22 A4
Collinswood Rd SL2 187 B2
Collum Green Rd SL2 187 E1
Collyer Rd HP14 158 E4
COLNBROOK 212 D7
Colnbrook By-Pass
Colnbrook SL3 212 D7
Harmondsworth UB7 213 C7
Colnbrook CE Prim Sch SL3 212 D6
Colnbrook Ct SL3 212 F6
Coln Cl SL6 202 F8
Colndale Rd SL3 212 E5
Colne MK6 47 D6
Colne Ave UB7 208 C4
Colne Bank SL3 212 C4
Colnedale Rd UB8 201 D7
Colne Orch SL0 207 F6
Colne Park Cvn Site UB7 208 C2
Colne Rd HP13 173 F7
Colne Reach TW19 212 F2
Colne Valley Park Visitor Ctr★ UB9 190 B1
Coln Trad Est SL3 212 F6
Colonel Grantham Ave HP19 101 D4
Colonial Rd 1 SL1 206 A4
Colonnade SL6 203 A7
Colossus Way MK3 47 A1
Colsons Way MK46 6 F5
Colston Bassett MK4 46 C1
Colston Ct SL9 188 E5
COLSTROPE 181 D5
Coltman Ave HP18 125 C6
Coltsfoot Dr UB7 208 E7
Coltsfoot Pl MK14 34 D3
Colts Holm Rd MK12 33 C8
Columbia Pl MK9 35 A3
Columbine Rd HP15 162 F6
Colville Ct HP16 152 B7
Colville Rd HP11 172 F6
COMBE 130 C1
Combe Martin MK4 46 D3
Combe Rise HP12 172 B7
Combermere Cl SL4 210 B5
Combes Cres MK6 46 F6
Comerford Way MK18 66 A5
Comfrey Cl MK7 48 A5
Comfrey The 2 HP19 101 E4
Common Field HP23 119 D1
Common Gate Rd WD3 167 E4
Common La
Eton SL4 205 D1
Hedgerley SL1 186 D1
Milton Keynes, Bradwell MK13 34 A4
Milton Keynes MK5 46 C8
Common Rd
Chorleywood WD3 167 D5
Dagnall LU6 107 F3
Dorney SL4 204 D2
Eton Wick SL4 205 A2
Flackwell Heath HP10 185 B8
Great Kingshill HP15 151 D1
Slough SL3 207 A1
Commonside HP13 161 E3
Common St MK46 5 D1
COMMON THE 55 B4
Common The
Berkhamsted HP4 135 F6
Chipperfield WD4 156 F7
Flackwell Heath HP10 185 B8
Great Kingshill HP15 151 D1
Holmer Green HP15 163 D7
Stokenchurch HP14 158 E5
West Drayton UB7 208 C2
Common Wood SL2 198 C8
Common Wood La HP10 163 E1
Como Rd HP20 116 B8
Compass Point HP4 134 E6
Comp Gate LU6 92 E6
Comp The LU6 92 E6
Compton Ct
Moulsoe MK16 36 D8
Slough SL1 204 E7
Compton Dr SL6 202 A8
Compton Rd HP22 131 D5
Concorde Cl UB10 201 E3
Concorde Rd SL6 202 D4
Concorde Way SL1 205 C4
Concourse The 6 MK2 58 C8
Concra Pk MK17 49 C4
Concrete Cows★ MK13 33 F4
Condor Cl MK6 47 A8
Conduit La SL3 206 E1
Conegar Ct SL1 205 E5
Conegra Ct 15 HP13 173 B7
Conegra Rd HP13 173 C7
Coneygere MK46 7 A3
Congreve MK6 47 D5
Conifer Rise HP12 172 E6
Conifers The SL6 202 A8
Conigre OX39 147 B6
Coningsby Cl SL6 202 D3
Coningsby Ct HP13 173 B8
Coningsby Rd HP13 162 B1
Coniston Cres SL1 204 C8
Coniston Gn HP20 101 D3
Coniston Rd LU7 80 C7
Coniston Way MK2 58 D6
Conkers SL6 203 B8
Connaught Cl SL6 195 E1
Connaught Gdns HP4 134 F7
Connaught Rd
Aylesbury HP20 116 C8
3 Slough SL1 206 B4
CONNIBURROW 34 E4
Conniburrow Bvd MK14 34 E4
Conniston Cl SL7 183 B2
Conought Ho RG9 191 E3
Constable Cl MK14 34 F7
Constable Pl HP19 100 F2
Constable's Croft OX25 94 E7
Constantine Pl UB10 201 F4
Constantine Way MK13 33 F5
Convent Ct HP23 118 F3
Convent Rd SL4 210 A5
Conway Cl
Aylesbury HP21 115 F7
Loudwater HP10 174 C2
Milton Keynes MK3 57 F8
Conway Cres MK3 57 E8
Conway Ct SL9 189 B3
Conway Ho HP13 173 F7
Conway Rd SL6 204 B7
Cook Cl MK7 48 B4
Cookfield Cl LU6 93 E8
COOKHAM 196 A7
Cookham Ct HP6 154 E1
COOKHAM DEAN 195 B7
Cookham Dean Bottom SL6 195 C8
Cookham Dean CE Prim Sch SL6 195 B7
Cookham Lodge 15 SL6 202 F6
Cookham Rd SL6 195 F1
COOKHAM RISE 195 E6
Cookham Rise Prim Sch SL6 195 E6
Cookham Sta SL6 195 F7
Cooks Cl NN7 9 F8
Cookshall La HP12 161 A2
Cooks La MK17 67 E6
Cook's Mdw LU6 92 E4
Cooks Rd HP19 114 F8
Coombe Ave HP22 131 B4
Coombe Cl HP22 116 C2
Coombe Dr LU6 93 E7
Coombe Gdns
Berkhamsted HP4 134 F5
Hughenden Valley HP14 162 A6
Coombe Hill Ct SL4 209 D4
Coombe La
Aylesbury HP19 100 F1
Walter's Ash HP14 161 F6
Coombes Quarry Nature Reserve★ MK18 53 E6
Coombe Vale SL9 188 E3
Cooper Rd RG9 191 D3
Cooper's Court Rd HP14 158 D5
Coopers Ct MK16 22 C4
Coopers Mews MK14 34 F6
Coopers Rise HP13 173 D5
Coopers Row SL0 200 D1
Cooper's Yd HP20 101 D1
Cooper Way
3 Berkhamsted HP4 135 D4
Slough SL1 205 B3
Coots Cl MK18 52 E7
Cope Ct SL6 202 C7
Copeland Cl MK7 48 C5
Copes Rd HP15 151 E1
Copes Shroves HP15 162 F5
Copmans Wick WD3 167 D4
Copners Dr HP15 163 C6
Copners Way HP15 163 B6
Copper Beech Cl
Felden HP3 146 F8
Windsor SL4 209 D6
Copperfields
Beaconsfield HP9 175 E5
High Wycombe HP12 161 B1
Copperfield Terr SL2 206 B6
Copperhouse Ct MK7 48 A2
Copperkins Gr HP6 154 B3
Copperkins La HP6 154 A3
Coppermill La WD3 178 F3
Coppermill Rd TW19 212 B2
Copper Ridge SL9 177 F5
Coppice Cl HP20 102 A2
Coppice Farm Rd HP10 163 C2
Coppice The
Great Kingshill HP15 151 E1
High Wycombe HP12 172 B4
Seer Green HP9 176 D4
Stokenchurch HP14 158 E5
Walter's Ash HP14 161 B8
West Drayton UB7 208 E7
Wigginton HP23 119 C1
Coppice Way
Aylesbury HP20 102 A2
Hedgerley SL2 187 D2
Coppidwell Dr HP21 116 A5
Coppinger Ct UB7 208 E4
Coppin La MK13 34 A3
Coppins Cl HP4 134 F4
Coppins La SL0 207 F8
Copse Cl
Marlow SL7 183 C2
Slough SL1 204 F5
West Drayton UB7 208 D3
Copse Gate MK18 66 A4
Copse La HP9 176 E3
Copse The
Amersham HP7 154 C1
Beaconsfield HP9 175 C4
Copse Way HP5 144 A4
Copse Wood SL0 200 D4
Copthall Cl SL9 177 F3
Copthall Cnr SL9 177 E3
Copthall Ho SL6 203 A7
Copthall La SL9 177 E3
Copthorn Cl SL6 202 A4
Copthorne Pl MK7 48 B8
Copyground Ct HP12 172 E7
Copyground La HP12 172 E7
Coral Cl LU6 92 E6
Coram Cl HP4 135 C3
Corbet Ride LU7 80 D8
Corbet Sq LU7 80 D8
Corbett Cl MK15 35 D7
Cordons Cl SL9 177 D2
Cordwainer Ct MK14 34 F6
Cordwallis Bsns Pk SL6 195 E1
Cordwallis Est SL6 202 F8
Cordwallis Pk SL6 202 E8
Cordwallis Rd SL6 202 F8
Cordwallis St SL6 202 E8
CORES END 185 C4
Cores End Rd SL8 185 B3

Corfe Cl HP21 116 B5
Corfe Cres MK3 57 F8
Corfe Gdns SL1 205 A6
Corfe Pl SL6 202 C7
Coriander Ct MK7 48 B5
Corin Cl MK2 58 D5
Corinium Ind Est HP6 154 F1
Corin Way MK2 58 D5
Cork Pl MK3 46 E2
Cornbrook Rd HP21 115 C5
Cornbury Cres MK15 35 A6
Corn Cl HP17 114 D5
Corncrake 9 HP19 101 F3
Cornel Cl HP15 163 B3
Cornel Ho 1 SL4 210 D4
Cornelia Cl MK2 58 C6
Cornerways HP27 150 C5
Cornfield Cl UB8 201 D3
Cornfield Cres HP4 134 D7
Cornflower Pl MK18 52 C7
Corn Hill MK8 33 E1
Corn Mkt HP11 173 B7
Cornwall Ave SL2 198 C1
Cornwall Cl
  Eton Wick SL4 204 E1
  Maidenhead SL6 195 E2
Cornwall Ct UB8 201 D6
Cornwall Gr MK3 46 F1
Cornwall Ho UB8 201 D6
Cornwall Lodge 11 SL6 202 F6
Cornwall Pl MK18 41 D1
Cornwall Rd UB8 201 D6
Cornwalls Mdw 3 MK18 41 D1
Cornwell Rd SL4 211 A1
Coronation Ave
  Slough SL3 206 E7
  Windsor SL4 211 A4
Coronation Cotts MK18 41 F8
Coronation Cres HP14 171 C5
Coronation Mews LU7 80 F8
Coronation Pl MK18 63 D2
Coronation Rd
  Cranfield MK43 25 B1
  High Wycombe HP12 172 D4
  Milton Keynes MK11 32 E5
Coronation Villas HP21 115 E8
Corporation St HP13 173 B7
Corrid Ind Pk HP19 101 B1
Corrigan Cl MK3 58 A8
Corsewall Pl 6 MK4 45 F1
Corsham Ct 4 MK8 33 F1
COSGROVE 19 D2
Cosgrove Prim Sch MK19 19 E2
Cosgrove Rd MK19 32 C7
Costers Cotts SL8 185 B2
Costins Wlk 7 HP4 135 D4
Cosway Pl MK8 45 D6
Cotes Way LU7 79 F3
Cotman Cl MK12 33 B5
Cotswold Cl
  Maidenhead SL6 203 B6
  Slough SL1 205 B3
  Uxbridge UB8 201 C4
Cotswold Ct HP12 172 F8
Cotswold Dr LU7 80 C8
Cotswold Gn HP20 101 E2
Cotswolds Way MK18 73 B5
Cotswold Way HP13 172 E8
Cottage Comm MK5 46 B8
Cottage Farm Way HP27 150 C4
Cottage Grounds HP17 114 D5
Cottage Park Rd SL2 187 D2
Cottages The
  Ickenham UB10 190 E2
  Syresham NN13 27 C5
Cottesbrooke Cl SL3 212 D6
Cottesloe Cl LU7 79 E3
Cottesloe Ct MK11 32 F5
Cottesloe Rd HP21 115 E5
Cottesloe Sch The LU7 79 D1
Cottingham Gr MK3 58 A7
Cottisford Cres MK14 21 F1
Cottland Clay HP17 127 A7
Cotts The
  Long Crendon HP18 125 C6
  Longwick HP27 138 E5
Coulson Ave MK8, MK5 45 E6
Coulson Ct HP16 151 D6
Coulson Way SL1 204 B8
Council Hos LU7 92 A1
Countisbury MK4 46 D2
Country La HP15 151 F1
Country Life Ho SL3 211 B7
County Rd NN13 38 A6
Cours La Ville Cl MK18 65 E3
Court Cl
  Aylesbury HP21 115 E7
  High Wycombe HP13 161 D1
  Maidenhead SL6 203 C2
  Princes Risborough HP27 139 A3
Court Cnr MK46 6 E3
Court Cres SL1 205 D7
Court Dr
  Maidenhead SL6 196 C3
  Uxbridge UB10 201 F4
Courteneys Lodge MK4 46 E3
Court Farm Cl SL1 205 B5
Courtfield Dr SL6 202 C6
Courtfield Gdns UB9 190 A1
Court Garden L Complex SL7 183 D1
Courthouse Cl MK18 65 F5
Courthouse Jun Sch SL6 202 B8
Courthouse Mews MK16 22 C4
Courthouse Rd SL6 202 C8
Court La
  Burnham SL1 197 D2
  Dorney SL4 204 B3
  Iver SL0 208 A5
Courtlands
  Leighton Buzzard LU7 80 E6
  14 Maidenhead SL6 202 F6
Courtlands Ave SL3 206 D2
Court Lawns HP10 163 C1
Courtmoor Cl HP27 139 C6
Courtneidge Cl LU7 78 E8
Courtney Ho UB9 189 F5
Court Rd
  Cranfield MK43 25 B1
  Maidenhead SL6 196 C3
Court The MK17 37 C3
Courtyard Arts Ctr★ MK14 21 E1
Courtyard Cl HP6 154 C1
Courtyards The HP22 117 E4
Courtyard The HP19 101 C1
Courtyard The
  Beaconsfield HP9 175 D2
  7 Bourne End SL8 185 B3
  9 Marlow SL7 183 D2
  1 Marlow SL7 183 E2
  22 Windsor SL4 210 D6
Cousins Cl UB7 208 E6
Cousins Dr HP20 101 F2
Cousins Piece HP18 112 B2
Coventon Rd HP19 101 C2
Coverack Pl MK4 57 B8
Coverdale MK13 34 C5
Coverdale Way SL2 197 E1
Covert Cl HP4 134 D6
Covert Rd HP4 134 D6
Cowdray Cl MK15 35 C3
Cow La
  Edlesborough LU6 92 E4
  Gawcott MK18 51 F4
  Tring HP23 119 D4
Cowleaze OX39 147 B6
COWLEY 201 C1
Cowley Bsns Pk UB8 201 C2
Cowley Cl HP22 102 B3
Cowley Cotts HP7 164 C3
Cowley Cres UB8 208 C8
Cowley Mill Rd UB8 201 B3
Cowley Mill Trad Est UB8 201 B3
COWLEY PEACHEY 208 E8
Cowley Rd UB8 201 C4
Cowley St Laurence Prim CE Sch UB8 208 D8
Cowper Cl MK16 22 A4
Cowper & Newton Mus The★ MK46 6 F3
Cowper Rd
  Berkhamsted HP4 135 B4
  Chesham HP5 144 B2
  Slough SL2 198 A1
Cowpers Orch MK46 6 A1
Cowper St MK46 7 A5
COW ROAST 120 B1
Cowslip Cl UB10 201 E5
Cowslip Rd HP15 162 F6
Coxborrow Cl SL6 195 E7
Coxfield Cl HP14 158 F5
COX GREEN 202 C3
Cox Green La SL6 202 C3
Cox Green L Ctr SL6 202 A3
Cox Green Rd SL6 202 D3
Cox Green Sch SL6 202 A4
Coxhill Way HP21 115 D7
Coxwell Cl MK18 41 F1
Coy Ct HP20 116 A8
Cozens Cl HP18 125 B7
Crabbe Cres HP5 144 D2
Crabs Gr HP22 86 F7
Crab Tree Cl
  Beaconsfield HP9 175 B1
  Olney MK46 6 E5
Crabtree Cotts HP27 139 A1
Crabtree La MK17 49 C8
Crabtree Rd HP17 127 A5
Craddocks Cl MK13 34 B3
Cradley Wlk HP20 101 E3
CRAFTON 89 F3
Crafton Pl 4 HP19 100 F1
Craigleith Ct HP9 175 D2
Craigmore Ave MK3 57 F8
Craigwell Ave HP21 116 C7
Cranborne Ave MK4 45 E2
Cranbourne Ave SL4 209 F5
Cranbourne Cl SL1 205 C5
Cranbourne Rd SL1 205 C5
Cranbrook MK17 49 B5
Cranbrook Dr SL6 195 C1
Crane Ct MK5 34 B1
Cranesbill Pl MK14 34 E4
Cranes Cl MK43 8 E5
Crane Way MK43 25 C2
CRANFIELD 25 B1
Cranfield Airport MK43 24 F1
Cranfield Innovation Ctr MK43 37 D8
Cranfield Lower Sch MK43 25 B1
Cranfield Rd
  Astwood MK16, MK43 16 B2
  Cranfield MK43 25 F3
  Moulsoe MK16 36 E8
  Salford MK17 37 D5
  Wavendon MK17 49 B7
Cranfield Tech Pk MK43 37 C8
Cranfield Univ MK43 24 E2
Cranwell Cl MK5 46 B3
Craufurd Ct SL6 202 E8
Craufurd Rise SL6 202 E8
Craven The MK13 34 C4
Crawford Way 3 MK4 45 D2
Crawley Rd
  Cranfield MK43 25 B3
  Woburn MK17 60 F8
Crawley's La HP23 133 F7
Crawshays SL6 203 C8
Crayle St SL2 198 B2
CR Bates Ind Est HP14 158 E5
Creden Cl SL6 195 D1
Creed St MK12 33 D7
Creighton Rd HP18 83 F1
Crendon Rd HP18 112 A1
Crendon St HP13 173 B7
Creran Wlk LU7 80 C7
Crescent Cotts HP18 83 A6
Crescent Dale SL6 202 F6
Crescent Dr SL6 202 E7
Crescent The
  Cranfield MK43 24 E2
  Haversham MK19 20 E2
  High Wycombe HP13 173 E8
  Maidenhead SL6 202 E7
  Marsworth HP23 105 A1
  Milton Keynes, Fenny Stratford MK2 47 C1
  Milton Keynes, Giffard Park MK14 21 E2
  Pitstone LU7 105 C4
  Princes Risborough HP27 139 C3
  Slough SL1 205 E4
Crescent Villas 5 SL4 210 C6
CRESLOW 87 B8
Creslow Ct MK11 32 F5
Creslow Way HP17 114 B5
CRESSEX 172 D4
Cressex Bsns Pk HP12 172 D4
Cressex Cl HP12 172 D3
Cressex Com Sch The HP12 172 C3
Cressex Ent Ctr HP12 172 E6
Cressex Link HP11 172 D3
Cressex Rd HP12 172 C3
Cressey Ave MK5 46 B4
Cressington Ct 2 SL8 185 A4
Cressington Pl SL8 185 A4
Cress Rd SL1 205 B4
Cresswell Ct TW19 213 D1
Cresswell Rd HP5 154 D5
Cresswells Mead SL6 203 C1
Cresswell Way HP15 163 D7
Crest Rd HP11 172 D3
Crest The
  Beaconsfield HP9 175 A1
  Bledlow Ridge HP14 159 F8
Creswell Row SL7 183 D2
Creswick Mdw HP21 116 A5
Crew Curve HP4 134 F7
Cricketers Row MK18 66 A4
Cricketfield Rd UB7 208 C2
Cricket Field Rd UB8 201 D4
Cricket Green Rdbt MK9 35 B4
Cricket Ground HP14 158 D5
Cricklebeck MK13 34 B5
Crimp Hill SL4 211 A1
Crispin Cl HP9 175 C4
Crispin Field LU7 105 C4
Crispin Rd MK13 34 B7
Crispin Way
  Farnham Common SL2 198 D8
  High Wycombe HP11 173 A4
  Uxbridge UB8 208 F8
Crisp Rd RG9 191 C3
Criss Gr SL9 177 C1
Crocketts La HP16 142 D5
Crocus Dr HP21 115 B5
Croft Cnr SL4 211 A2
Croft Ct 5 HP21 115 E7
Croft Ctyd HP17 126 F6
Crofters SL4 211 A1
Crofters Cl TW19 213 D1
Croft Gn LU6 93 F8
Crofthill Rd SL2 198 B1
Croft Ho SL0 207 E7
Croft Mdws LU7 105 A7
Crofton Ho HP11 174 A4
Croft Rd
  Aylesbury HP21 115 E7
  Chalfont St Peter SL9 177 E1
CROFTS END 14 A1
Crofts End MK16 14 A1
Crofts La MK17 57 D3
Croft The
  Haddenham HP17 126 F5
  Maidenhead SL6 202 C5
  Marlow SL7 184 A3
Croftwood HP13 173 F7
Cromarty Ct MK3 46 E3
Cromer Cl HP4 121 E5
Cromer Ct SL1 205 E7
Cromhamstone HP17 114 D5
Cromwell Ave
  Aylesbury HP19 101 D2
  Newport Pagnell MK16 22 A3
  Thame OX9 126 A1
Cromwell Cl HP8 177 C7
Cromwell Ct MK18 41 E2
Cromwell Dr SL1 205 E7
Cromwell Gdns 10 SL7 183 E2
Cromwell Ho
  Chesham HP5 144 B1
  Uxbridge UB8 201 C4
Cromwell Mews 1 HP19 115 A8
Cromwell Rd
  High Wycombe HP13 173 E5
  Maidenhead SL6 202 D7
  Marlow SL7 183 E2
Cropredy Ct MK18 41 E2
Cropton Rise MK4 46 A2
Cropwell Bishop MK4 46 C1
Crosby Cl HP9 186 F8
Crosby Ct MK8 45 E6
Crosland Rd HP21 116 B6
Cross Ct HP13 161 D2
Cross End MK17 48 F7
Cross Farm Mews HP3 146 D2
Crossfield Cl HP4 134 F4
Crossfield Ho SL9 188 E7
Crossfield Rd HP27 139 C4
Crosshills MK11 32 D4
Cross La
  Beaconsfield HP9 186 F8
  Tingewick MK18 51 B6
  Weston Underwood MK46 6 B2
Crosslands MK14 34 E8
Cross Lanes
  Bledlow HP27 138 A2
  Chalfont St Peter SL9 177 F5
Cross Lanes Cl SL9 177 F5
Crossleys HP8 177 C7
Crosslow Bank MK4 46 C3
Cross Mdw HP5 143 F2
Cross Oak SL4 210 A5
Cross Oak Rd HP4 135 A4
Cross Rd
  High Wycombe HP12 172 C6
  Uxbridge UB8 201 C5
Cross St
  Newport Pagnell MK16 22 C4
  Uxbridge UB8 201 C5
Cross Tree Rd MK19 31 B3
Crossway HP5 144 E1
Crossways
  Beaconsfield HP9 175 F1
  Berkhamsted HP4 134 F3
  High Wycombe HP12 172 C4
Crossways Bsns Pk HP18 83 C3
Crossways Ct 4 SL4 210 C5
Crossway The UB10 201 F3
Crosthwaite Way SL1 204 D8
Crowborough La MK7 48 A8
Crowbrook Rd HP27 139 C6
CROWELL 147 B4
CROWELL HILL 147 D2
Crowell Mews HP19 114 F8
Crowell Rd OX39 147 B5
CROWFIELD 26 F8
Crow La MK17 49 B8
Crown Bsns Est HP5 144 C1
Crown Cl SL3 212 C7
Crown Cotts
  Botley HP5 155 B8
  Windsor SL4 210 D3
Crown Ct HP14 161 A2
CROWNFIELD 149 B4
Crownfield HP27 149 C3
CROWNHILL 45 E7
Crownhill Rdbt MK8 45 E8
Crown House Sch HP11 173 C6
Crown La
  East Burnham SL2 198 A4
  High Wycombe HP11 173 B6
  Maidenhead SL6 203 A7
  Marlow SL7 183 D2
  Penn HP10 174 F7
Crown Leys HP20 101 E1
Crown Mdw SL3 212 B7
Crown Rd SL7 183 D2
Crown Rose Ct HP23 119 A3
Crown Way UB7 208 F5
Crown Wlk
  Milton Keynes MK9 34 E3
  Uxbridge UB8 201 C5
Crow Piece La SL2 197 F4
Crowther Ct MK5 46 C5
Croxley Ct 3 LU7 80 F8
Croxley Rise SL6 202 D6
Croydon Cl MK4 46 C3
Cruickshank Gr MK8 45 E7
Crummock Cl SL1 204 C7
Crummock Pl MK2 58 D6
Crusader Est HP12 172 D5
Crutches La HP9 176 E4
CRYERS HILL 162 D6
Cryers Hill La HP15 162 D6
Cryers Hill Rd HP15 162 C6
Cuba Cotts SL6 196 B3
Cubb Field HP19 115 B7
CUBLINGTON 78 B1
Cublington Rd HP22 88 D6
Cuckoo Hill Rise MK19 10 F2
Cuckoo Way HP19 114 F8
CUDDINGTON 113 A2
Cuddington & Dinton CE Sch (Inf) HP18 112 F3
Cuddington & Dinton CE Sch (Jun) HP17 113 F3
Cuddington Hill HP18 112 E3
Cuddington Rd HP17, HP18 113 E3
Cudsdens Ct HP16 152 D7
Cuff La MK17 59 D1
Culbertson La MK13 33 E6
Culham Dr SL6 195 E2
Cullen Pl MK2 58 D5
Cullern's Pass SL6 202 F6
Culley Way SL6 202 A4
Cullyn Rd HP12 172 C3
Culmstock Cl MK4 46 D2
Culrain Pl MK12 33 D4
Culross Gr MK10 36 A2
Culvers Croft HP9 176 C4
Culvert La UB8 201 B3
Culverton Hill HP27 139 B3
Culverton La HP27 139 B1
Cumberland Ave SL2 198 C1
Cumberland Cl
  Aylesbury HP21 116 B7
  Little Chalfont HP7 166 B8
Cumbrae Cl SL2 206 A5
Cumbria Cl
  Maidenhead SL6 202 C4
  Milton Keynes MK3 46 F1
Cumbrian Way
  High Wycombe HP13 172 F8
  Uxbridge UB8 201 D5
Curfew Yd The 2 SL4 210 D6
Curlew HP19 101 F3
Curlew Cl
  Berkhamsted HP4 135 C3
  High Wycombe HP13 161 C2
Curls La SL6 202 E4
Curls Rd SL6 202 D4
Curran Cl UB8 201 C1
Currier Dr MK14 34 F6
Curriers La SL1 197 D7
Cursley Path 11 HP19 115 A8
Curtis Cotts HP5 144 F7
Curtis Croft MK5 46 B3
Curtis Way HP4 135 D3
Curzon Ave
  Beaconsfield HP9 175 D4
  Tylers Green HP15 163 C2
Curzon CE Comb Sch HP7 164 A5
Curzon Cl HP15 163 C2
Curzon Gate Ct HP14 158 E5
Curzon Mall 6 SL1 205 F4
Curzon Pl MK7 48 E4
Cushing Dr 7 MK4 45 E2
Cutler's Ct 6 HP12 172 E7
Cutlers Mews MK14 34 F6
Cut Throat Ave HP4 107 E7
Cuttle Brook Gdns OX9 125 E1
Cyclamen Pl HP21 115 B5
Cygnet Ho SL6 196 C1
Cypress MK16 22 A3
Cypress Ho SL3 207 B1
Cypress Wlk HP15 163 B3

D

Daceberry Ct RG9 192 C2
Dacre Rd HP22 131 E7
Dadbrook HP18 112 F2
Dadbrook Cl HP18 112 F2
Dadfield Cl HP18 112 F2
DADFORD 28 D1
Dadford Rd MK18 28 D5
Dag La MK16 12 A7
Dagmar Rd SL4 210 D5
DAGNALL 107 C6
Dagnall Cres UB8 208 C8
Dagnall Cty Fst Sch HP4 107 C5
Dagnall Rd
  Olney MK46 6 E3
  Whipsnade LU6 93 D2

Dair House Sch SL2. . . . 198 B4
Dairy La RG9 . . . . 192 B8
Dairymede HP27. . . . . . . 150 C4
Daisy Cotts HP14. . . . . . . 171 B4
Dalby Gdns 7 SL6 . . . . . 195 F1
Dale Cl NN13 . . . . 38 A7
Dale Ct SL1. . . . . 205 C4
Dalegarth Way MK10. . . . 36 C3
Dalesford Rd HP21. . . . . . 116 A4
Dale Side SL9. . . . . 188 E2
Dalgin Pl MK9 . . . . 35 A3
Dalston Cl HP20 . . . . 101 F2
Dalston End MK10 . . . . . . 35 E1
Dalton Gate MK10. . . . . . . 35 F4
Dalton Gn 15 SL3 . . . . . . 206 F1
Dalvina Pl MK12 . . . . 33 D4
Dalwood Mews 3
HP19 . . . . 115 A8
Daly Way HP20 . . . . 116 B7
Damask Cl HP23 . . . . 119 C4
Damson Gr SL1 . . . . 205 C4
Danbury Ct MK14 . . . . 34 E5
Dancers End La HP22,
HP23 . . . . 118 C2
Dancersend Wildlife
Reserve★ HP23 . . . . 132 C8
Dandridge Cl SL3 . . . . . . 206 D2
Dandridge Ct MK8 . . . . . . 45 C6
Dandridge Dr SL8. . . . . . 185 C3
Dane Cl HP7. . . . . 165 F6
Dane Ct HP21. . . . . 115 D4
Dane Rd MK1 . . . . 47 E2
Danesbrough Dr MK17 . 49 A2
Danesbrook Cl MK4 . . . . . 46 D4
Danes Ct SL6 . . . . 202 D7
Danesfield Sch SL7 . . . . 193 E7
Danes Gdns SL6 . . . . 195 F6
Daneswood MK17 . . . . 49 A1
Daniels Welch MK6 . . . . . 47 A6
Dansteed Way
Milton Keynes, Bradwell
Common MK8, MK13, MK14,
MK15. . . . . 34 C4
Milton Keynes, Crownhill
MK8. . . . . 45 D7
Danvers Croft HP23 . . . . 119 C5
Darby Cl
Milton Keynes MK5 . . . . . . 46 B5
Milton Keynes MK13 . . . . . 34 C2
Darby Lodge HP13 . . . . . 174 A7
Darie Cl 3 SL1 . . . . 205 A4
Darin Ct MK8 . . . . 45 F8
Dark La
Chearsley HP18. . . . . 112 B2
Oving HP22 . . . . 86 C7
Wingrave HP22 . . . . 89 C2
Darley Cl HP21. . . . . 116 B6
Darley Gate MK14. . . . . . . 35 A5
Darley's Cl HP18. . . . . 83 A6
Darling's La SL6 . . . . 194 E1
Darlington Cl HP6 . . . . . 154 D1
Darnel Cl MK6 . . . . 47 A5
Darrell Cl SL3. . . . . 206 F2
Darr's La HP4. . . . . 134 D6
Darsham Wlk HP5 . . . . . 154 B8
Dart Cl
Aylesbury HP21 . . . . 115 C5
Newport Pagnell MK16 . . . 22 D4
Slough SL3. . . . . 212 B8
Dartington Pl 2 MK4 . . . . 45 F1
Dartmouth Ct 10 SL1 . . . 205 F3
Dartmouth Rd MK46. . . . . . . 6 F4
Darvell Dr HP5. . . . . 144 A2
Darvells Yd WD3 . . . . 167 D5
Darville Ho 19 SL4 . . . . . 210 D6
Darvill Rd HP17 . . . . 114 B5
DARVILLSHILL. 150 A4
Darvill's La SL1 . . . . 205 D4
Darvills Mdw HP15 . . . . . 163 C7
Darwin Cl MK5. . . . . 45 E5
Darwin Rd SL3. . . . . 206 F4
Dashfield Gr HP15 . . . . . 162 F6
Dashwood Ave HP12 . . . 172 D7
Dashwood Cl SL3 . . . . . . 206 C2
Dashwood Works Ind Est
HP12. . . . . 172 D7
DATCHET. 211 C6
Datchet Ho 3 SL1 . . . . . 205 F3
Datchet Lodge Ctyd
SL3. . . . . 211 B6
Datchet Pl SL3. . . . . 211 B6
Datchet Rd
Eton SL4. . . . . 205 F2
Horton SL3. . . . . 211 F4
Old Windsor SL4 . . . . 211 A3
Windsor SL4 . . . . 210 D7
Datchet St Mary's CE Prim
Sch SL3 . . . . 211 B6
Datchet Sta SL3 . . . . 211 B6
Daubeney Gate MK5 . . . . 45 F6
Davenies Sch HP9 . . . . . 175 E2
Davenport Lea MK7 . . . . . 48 E5
Davenport Rd HP12 . . . . 172 C3
Daventry Cl SL3. . . . . 212 F6
David Bishop Ct HP5 . . . 154 D5
David Cl HP21 . . . . 116 A4
Davidge Pl HP9. . . . . 175 C5
David Rd SL3 . . . . 212 F5
Davidson Rd 6 SL3 . . . . 206 F1
Davies Cl HP20 . . . . 115 D8
Davies Ct HP12 . . . . 172 D5
Davies Way HP10 . . . . . . 174 C1
Davis Cl SL7 . . . . 183 E1
Davis Gr MK4 . . . . 45 E3
Davis Ho 3 HP4 . . . . 135 C3
Davison Ct MK8. . . . . 45 D6
Davy Ave MK5 . . . . 46 D6
Dawes Cl HP5 . . . . 154 B7
Dawe's Cl UB10. . . . . 201 E3
Dawes East Rd SL1. . . . . 197 C2
Dawes La WD3. . . . . 156 F3
Dawes Moor Cl SL2 . . . . 206 C7
Dawe's Rd UB10 . . . . 201 E3
Dawley Ride SL3. . . . . . . 212 E6
Dawney Cl HP19 . . . . 101 C2
Dawn Redwood Cl SL3 . 212 A4
Daws Ct SL0. . . . . 207 F7
Daws Hill La HP11 . . . . . 173 A4
Daws Lea HP11 . . . . 173 B3
Dawson Cl SL4. . . . . 210 A5
Dawson Rd MK1 . . . . 47 D3
Daylesford Ct MK15 . . . . . 35 B5
Daylesford Gr SL1 . . . . . 204 F4
Deacon Cl HP12. . . . . 172 B4
Deacon Ct SL4. . . . . 209 D5
Deacon Pl MK10 . . . . 35 F3
Deadhearn La HP8 . . . . . 166 E1
Deal Ave SL1 . . . . 204 F7
Deanacre Cl SL9 . . . . 177 E4
Dean Cl
Aylesbury HP21 . . . . 116 A5
High Wycombe HP12 . . . . 172 E6
Uxbridge UB10. . . . . 201 F5
Windsor SL4 . . . . 209 D4
Deancroft Rd SL9 . . . . . . 177 E4
Dean Farm La LU7 . . . . . . 69 E4
Deanfield HP14 . . . . 160 B8
Dean Field HP3 . . . . 146 A4
Deanfield Ave RG9 . . . . . 191 D1
Deanfield Cl
Marlow SL7 . . . . 183 D2
Saunderton HP14. . . . . . . 149 C1
Deanfield Rd RG9 . . . . . . 191 D1
Dean Forest Way MK10. . 36 A5
Deangarden Rise HP11 173 E4
Dean La SL6 . . . . 195 C8
Dean Rd LU7 . . . . 68 B2
Deans Cl
Amersham HP6 . . . . 154 F2
Tring HP23. . . . . 119 A4
Wexham Street SL2. . . . . 199 B4
Dean's Cloisters SL4 . . . 210 D7
Deansfield Cl SL6. . . . . . 195 D2
Deans Furlong HP23 . . . 119 A4
DEANSHANGER. 31 D4
Deanshanger Dr NN12. . . 17 F1
Deanshanger Prim Sch
MK19 . . . . 31 E3
Deanshanger Rd
Old Stratford MK19 . . . . . . 32 B6
Wicken MK19. . . . . 31 B3
Deans Lawn HP4. . . . . . . 135 C4
Deans Mdw HP4 . . . . 107 C5
Dean's Rd MK12 . . . . 33 C7
Dean St SL7 . . . . 183 D2
Deansway HP5. . . . . 144 B2
Dean The HP22 . . . . 89 B3
Dean View SL6. . . . . 195 D6
Dean Way
Aston Clinton HP22 . . . . . 117 F4
Chalfont St Giles HP8 . . . 177 B7
Holmer Green HP15. . . . . 163 B6
Dean Wood Rd HP9 . . . . 176 D2
Dearing Cl 11 HP20 . . . . 101 F2
Debbs Cl MK11. . . . . 32 E5
Deben Cl MK16 . . . . 22 E3
Decies Way SL2. . . . . 199 A4
De Clare Ct MK18 . . . . 41 E1
Dedmere Ct SL7 . . . . 183 F2
Dedmere Rd SL7. . . . . . . 183 F2
Dedmere Rise SL7 . . . . . 183 E2
DEDWORTH 209 E6
Dedworth Dr SL4 . . . . . . 209 F6
Dedworth Green Fst Sch
SL4 . . . . 209 E5
Dedworth Manor SL4 . . 209 F6
Dedworth Mid Sch SL4 209 E6
Dedworth Rd SL4 . . . . . . 209 D5
Deeds Gr HP12. . . . . 172 E5
Deena Cl SL1 . . . . 204 E6
Deep Acres HP6 . . . . 154 A3
Deepdale MK13 . . . . 34 C5
Deep Field SL3 . . . . 211 B7
Deep Mill La HP16 . . . . . 152 D3
Deerfern Cl MK14. . . . . 21 E1
Deerfield Cl MK18. . . . . . . 52 E7
Deermead HP16 . . . . 152 B4
Deer Park Wlk HP5 . . . . 144 E3
Deerswood SL6. . . . . 196 A1
Deer Wlk MK9 . . . . 34 F3
Deethe Cl MK17. . . . . 49 B6
De Havilland Dr HP15 . . 162 E2
De Havilland Way
TW19. . . . . 213 E1
Delafield Cl HP14 . . . . . . 158 F4
Delaford Cl SL0. . . . . 207 F7
Delaford Ho UB7. . . . . . . 208 D5
Delahay Rise HP4. . . . . . 135 B6
Delamere Cl HP20 . . . . . 101 F2
Delamere Gdns LU7. . . . . 80 C7
Delaware Dr
Milton Keynes MK15 . . . . . 35 B8
Tongwell MK15, MK16. . . . 22 B1
Delius Cl MK7 . . . . 48 C4
Dell Cl
Chesham HP5 . . . . 143 F2
Farnham Common SL2. . . 198 C7
Dellfield HP5 . . . . 144 A2
Dell Field HP16 . . . . 151 C5
Dell Field Ave HP4 . . . . . 135 B6
Dellfield Cl HP4. . . . . 135 A6
Dellfield Cres UB8 . . . . . 201 C1
Dellfield Par UB8 . . . . . . 201 C1
Dell Lees HP9 . . . . 176 C4
Dell Rd
Berkhamsted HP4 . . . . . . 134 D7
West Drayton UB7. . . . . . 208 F3
Dells MK46 . . . . 6 F4
Dellside UB9 . . . . 190 C6
Dell The
Aylesbury HP20 . . . . 102 A2
Chalfont St Peter SL9 . . . 177 E4
Maidenhead SL6 . . . . 202 A2
Stokenchurch HP14 . . . . . 158 F3
Tylers Green HP10. . . . . . 163 C1
Uxbridge UB8. . . . . 201 C6
Delmeade Rd HP5 . . . . . 154 A7
Deltic Ave MK13 . . . . 34 B2
Demoram Cl MK18 . . . . . . 65 F3
Denbigh East Ind Est
MK1 . . . . 47 D2
Denbigh Hall MK3. . . . . . . 46 F3
Denbigh Hall Dr MK3. . . . 46 F3
Denbigh Hall Ind Est
MK3 . . . . 46 F3
Denbigh Rd
Milton Keynes MK1 . . . . . . 47 B2
Thame OX9 . . . . 126 A1
Denbigh Rdbt MK1. . . . . . 47 C2
Denbigh Sch MK5. . . . . . . 46 A6
Denbigh Way MK2 . . . . . . 47 C1
Denbigh West Ind Est
MK1 . . . . 47 B2
Denby Walk HP20 . . . . . . 116 A8
Denchworth Ct 2 MK4 . . 46 C2
Dene Cl
Winslow MK18. . . . . 66 A3
Woburn Sands MK17 . . . . . 49 C4
Dene The MK18 . . . . 63 D3
Denewood HP13 . . . . 173 E8
DENHAM
Denham Green. 190 A2
Quainton 85 D5
Denham Aerodrome
UB9. . . . . 189 E6
Denham Ave UB9 . . . . . . 189 F3
Denham Cl
Denham UB9 . . . . 190 A1
Maidenhead SL6 . . . . 202 C6
Milton Keynes MK3 . . . . . . 57 D8
Denham Court Dr UB9 . 190 B1
Denham Ctry Park Nature
Reserve★ UB9. . . . . 190 B2
Denham Ctry Pk★ UB9 190 B2
Denham Garden Village
UB9 . . . . 189 F5
Denham Golf Club Sta
UB9. . . . . 189 D4
DENHAM GREEN 189 E5
Denham Green Cl UB9 . 190 A4
Denham Green La UB9 . 189 F5
Denham La SL9. . . . . 178 A2
Denham Lodge UB9. . . . 201 C6
Denham Quarry Park
Nature Reserve★
UB9. . . . . 190 C1
Denham Rd
Iver Heath SL0. . . . . 200 E5
Lane End HP14 . . . . 171 C5
Denham Sta UB9. . . . . . . 190 A4
Denham View MK18. . . . . . 75 F6
Denham Village Inf Sch
UB9. . . . . 189 F2
Denham Way UB9. . . . . . 190 A1
Denham Way (North Orbital
Rd)
Denham Green UB9 . . . . . 189 F7
Maple Cross WD3 . . . . . . 178 E4
Denham Wlk SL9 . . . . . . 177 F4
Denholme Lodge SL3 . . 211 B7
Denison Ct MK7. . . . . 48 D6
Denmark St
Maidenhead SL6 . . . . 202 E8
Milton Keynes MK2 . . . . . . 58 E8
Denmead MK8. . . . . 33 E2
Denmead Cl SL9 . . . . 188 E4
DENNER HILL. 150 E4
Dennis Cl HP22 . . . . 118 A4
Denniston Ho HP12 . . . . 172 C8
Dennis Way SL1 . . . . 204 D6
Denny Rd SL3. . . . . 206 F2
Denny's La HP4. . . . . 134 F2
Denton Ct SL7 . . . . 183 F3
De Pirenore HP15. . . . . . 162 E2
Depot Rd SL6. . . . . 203 A6
Derby Arms 2 HP20 . . . . 115 D8
Derby Rd UB8 . . . . 201 D3
Derehams Ave HP10 . . . 174 C3
Derehams La HP10. . . . . 174 C2
Derek Rd SL6. . . . . 203 C8
Dere Pl MK2. . . . . 58 E4
Deri Dene Cl 2 TW19 . . . 213 E1
Derwent Cl
Little Chalfont HP7. . . . . . 166 B8
Newport Pagnell MK16 . . . 22 D4
Derwent Dr
Maidenhead SL6 . . . . 202 D8
Milton Keynes MK3 . . . . . . 57 E8
Slough SL1. . . . . 204 C8
Derwent Rd
Aylesbury HP21 . . . . 116 B6
Leighton Buzzard LU7 . . . . 80 B7
Desborough Ave HP11 . 172 F6
Desborough Bsns Pk
HP12. . . . . 172 E8
Desborough Cres SL6 . . 202 D5
Desborough Gn 1
HP20 . . . . 101 D2
Desborough Ho 14
HP13 . . . . 173 B7
Desborough Park Rd
HP12 . . . . 172 E8
Desborough Rd HP11 . . 172 F7
Desborough Sch SL6. . . 202 E5
Desborough St HP11 . . . 172 F7
Deseronto Wharf Ind Est
SL3. . . . . 206 E4
Develin Cl MK14 . . . . 34 F7
Devereux Pl
Aylesbury HP19 . . . . 101 A2
Milton Keynes MK6 . . . . . . 46 F7
Devereux Rd SL4. . . . . . . 210 D5
Deverill Rd HP21. . . . . . . 115 C3
Deverills Way SL3. . . . . . 207 C2
Devon Ave SL1. . . . . 205 C7
Devon Cl MK3 . . . . 46 F1
Devon Rd HP19 . . . . 101 A3
Devonshire Ave HP6 . . . 154 B2
Devonshire Cl
Amersham HP6 . . . . 154 C2
Farnham Royal SL2 . . . . . 198 B3
Devonshire Gn SL2. . . . . 198 B3
Devonshire Lodge 10
SL6. . . . . 202 F6
Devon Way UB10. . . . . . . 201 F3
Dewar Spur SL3 . . . . 211 F8
Dexter Ave MK6. . . . . 46 F8
Dexter Ho MK6 . . . . 46 F8
Dhoon Rise SL6. . . . . 202 F6
Diamond Rd SL1. . . . . . . 206 A4
Diana Cl SL3. . . . . 206 E7
Diane Cl HP21 . . . . 116 A4
Diane Wlk HP21 . . . . 116 A4
Dibden Hill HP8. . . . . 177 C6
Dickens Cl MK43. . . . . 3 F6
Dickens Dr MK19. . . . . 32 B6
Dickens Pl SL3. . . . . 212 E6
Dickens Rd MK12 . . . . 33 C8
Dickens Spinney MK46 . . . 6 E4
Dickens Way HP19 . . . . . 100 F2
Dickins Pl SL3 . . . . 212 E6
Dicks Way HP19 . . . . 100 F3
Diddington Cl MK2. . . . . . 58 C3
Digby Cl OX9 . . . . 126 B1
Digby Croft MK10 . . . . 35 E3
DIGGS. 126 F5
Dilwyn Ct 1 HP12 . . . . . 172 E7
Dingle Dell LU7. . . . . 70 F2
Dingledérry MK46. . . . . 6 F4
Dinmore 2 HP3 . . . . 145 F3
DINTON 113 F2
Disraeli Cres HP13 . . . . . 161 F1
Disraeli Ct SL3. . . . . 212 B8
Disraeli Pk HP9. . . . . 175 D4
Disraeli Sch The HP13. . 161 F1
Disraeli Sq 4 HP19 . . . . 115 A8
Diswell Brook Way
MK19 . . . . 31 E5
DITCHFIELD. 171 A3
Ditchfield Cotts HP14 . . 171 A3
Ditchingham Cl HP19 . . 115 B7
Ditton Park Cvn Site
SL3. . . . . 206 F1
Ditton Park Rd SL3. . . . . 211 E8
Ditton Rd
Datchet SL3 . . . . 211 D7
Slough SL3. . . . . 211 F8
Dixie Ct HP20. . . . . 116 A8
Dixie La MK7 . . . . 48 C6
Dixon Cl HP21 . . . . 115 B6
Dobbins La HP22. . . . . . . 131 B5
Dobson's La RG9. . . . . . . 191 C8
Docton Mill 3 MK4 . . . . . 45 E2
Doctor's Commons Rd
HP4 . . . . 135 B4
Doddsfield Rd SL2 . . . . . 198 A2
Dodds La HP8 . . . . 177 B8
Dodkin MK6 . . . . 47 B5
Dodman Gn MK4. . . . . 57 B8
Doggetts Farm Rd UB9 189 C4
Doggetts Wood Cl HP8 166 B6
Doggetts Wood La HP8 166 B5
Dog Kennel La WD3. . . . 167 F5
Dolben Ct MK15. . . . . 35 D8
Dolesden La RG9 . . . . . . 169 D1
Dollicot HP17. . . . . 126 F6
Dolphin Ct
Loudwater HP11 . . . . 174 A3
Slough SL1. . . . . 206 B4
Dolphin Pl HP21 . . . . 115 E6
Dolphin Rd SL1 . . . . 206 B4
Dolphin Sq 2 HP23. . . . . 119 A3
Donkey Dr SL8. . . . . 185 A3
Donkey La
Bourne End SL8 . . . . 185 A3
Tring HP23. . . . . 118 E2
West Drayton UB7 . . . . . . 208 C2
Donnay Cl SL9 . . . . 188 D5
Donnington MK13. . . . . 34 B6
Donnington Gdns SL6 . . 195 F1
Donnybrook Ho 3
HP13 . . . . 173 C7
Don The MK3 . . . . 46 D1
Doon Way MK2 . . . . 58 C5
Dorchester Ave MK3 . . . . 47 A2
Dorchester Cl
Maidenhead SL6 . . . . 195 B1
Stoke Mandeville HP22 . . 116 B2
Dorchester Ho SL9. . . . . 188 F6
Doreen Cl MK2 . . . . 58 C7
Dorian Cl HP23 . . . . 119 D4
Dorking Pl MK5. . . . . 46 B4
Dormans Cl MK10. . . . . . . 36 A2
Dormer Ave LU7 . . . . 79 E3
Dormer Cl HP21 . . . . 115 B6
Dormer Ct 4 HP20. . . . . 101 F2
Dormer La HP15 . . . . 163 B7
Dornels SL2 . . . . 206 C7
DORNEY. 204 C3
Dorney Comb Sch SL6 . 203 F3
Dorney Court★ SL4 . . . . 204 B3
Dorney End HP5 . . . . 144 A1
Dorney Hill N SL1, HP9. . 187 A4
Dorney Hill S SL2 . . . . . . 187 A4
Dorney Lake Pk★ SL4 . . 209 B8
Dorney Pl MK13. . . . . 34 C3
DORNEY REACH 203 F3
Dorney Reach Rd SL6 . . 203 F3
Dorneywood Gdn★
SL1 . . . . 197 D6
Dorney Wood Rd
Burnham SL1 . . . . 197 D6
Littleworth Common SL1 186 C1
Dorrells Rd HP27 . . . . . . 138 D6
Dorrien's Croft HP4 . . . . 134 F7
Dorset Cl
Berkhamsted HP4 . . . . . . 134 F5
Milton Keynes MK3 . . . . . . 46 F1
Dorset Lodge 9 SL6 . . . 202 F6
Dorset Pl HP21 . . . . 116 C6
Dorset Rd SL4 . . . . 210 C6
Dorset Way UB10 . . . . . . 201 F3
Dorsey Cl MK8. . . . . 45 E6
DORTON. 96 F1
Dorton Cl MK8. . . . . 33 F1
Dorton Rd HP18 . . . . 111 B4
Douglas Ct SL7 . . . . 184 A3
Douglas Gdns HP4 . . . . . 135 A5
Douglas La TW19 . . . . . . 211 F1
Douglas Pl MK6. . . . . 46 E8
Douglas Rd
Aylesbury HP20 . . . . 102 A1
Slough SL2. . . . . 205 D8
Stanwell TW19. . . . . 213 D1
Doune Ho MK3. . . . . 46 F2
Dove Cl
Aylesbury HP21 . . . . 115 C5
Buckingham MK18. . . . . . . 52 E7
Newport Pagnell MK16 . . . 22 D4
Dovecote
Haddenham HP17 . . . . . . 126 F6
Newport Pagnell MK16 . . . 22 C4
Dovecote Cft MK14. . . . . . 21 E1
Dovecote Cl
Haddenham HP17 . . . . . . 126 F6
Monks Risborough HP27 139 C5
Dovecote Cotts MK5 . . . . 46 A4
Dovecot Rd 11 HP13. . . . 173 A7
Dove Ct HP9. . . . . 175 D3
Dove Ho HP19 . . . . 101 F4
Dove House Cl
Edlesborough LU6 . . . . 92 F4
Winslow MK18. . . . . 66 A4
Dove House Cres SL2 . . 197 E2
Dovehouse Mews MK16 . 12 B6
Dovehouse Rd 3 HP11 173 A7
Doveleat OX39. . . . . 147 D7
Dove Pk WD3. . . . . 167 B4
Dover Cl LU7 . . . . 105 D2
Dover Gate MK3 . . . . 57 F8
Dover Hedge HP21. . . . . 116 C7
Dover Rd SL1. . . . . 204 F7
Dove St LU7 . . . . 78 E8
Dovetail Cl HP12. . . . . . . 172 D8
Dowding Rd UB10. . . . . . 201 F5
Dower Cl HP9 . . . . 175 C5
Dower Mews 5 HP4 . . . . 135 C4
Dower Pk SL4 . . . . 209 E3
Downdean MK6. . . . . 47 A8
Downderry Croft MK4 . . . 57 B8
Downer Cl MK18 . . . . 52 F8
Downer Dr WD3 . . . . 156 F3

Downham Rd MK17 ..... 49 C4
DOWNHEAD PARK 35 B5
Downing Cl MK3 .... 58 B8
Downing Path SL2 ..... 197 E1
Downings Wood WD3 .. 178 D5
Downland MK8 .... 33 E2
DOWNLEY 161 C3
Downley Ave MK13 ...... 34 C3
Downley Ct HP13 ...... 161 D2
Downley Rd HP14 ...... 161 D6
Downley Sch The
HP13 .... 161 D3
Down Pl SL4 .... 209 A8
DOWNS BARN 35 A5
Downs Barn Bvd MK14 .. 34 F5
Downs Barn Rdbt MK14 . 34 F5
Downs Barn Sch MK14 .. 34 F5
Downs Field MK16 ...... 22 F3
Downs Pk HP13 .... 161 E2
Downs Rd SL3 .... 206 D4
Downs View MK17 ...... 48 C2
Downs Villas 17 HP23 .. 119 A3
Dragon Tail HP17 ...... 127 A5
Drake Ave SL3 .... 206 D2
Drake Cl HP21 .... 115 B6
Drakeloe Cl MK17 .... 60 F8
Drakes Dr HP18 .... 125 E5
Drakes Farm HP18 ..... 125 E5
Drakes Mews MK8 ...... 45 F7
Drake's Rd HP7 .... 165 E8
Drakewell Rd MK17 ..... 48 D1
Draymans La SL7 ...... 183 D1
DRAYTON
BEAUCHAMP 118 B5
Drayton Ct UB7 .... 208 F2
Drayton Gdns UB7 ..... 208 E4
Drayton Park Sch MK2 .. 58 D5
DRAYTON PARSLOW 68 C6
Drayton Parslow Village
Sch MK17 .... 68 C6
Drayton Rd
Aylesbury HP20 .... 101 D2
Milton Keynes MK2 ...... 58 C5
Newton Longville MK17 ... 57 C2
Dr Challoner's Gram Sch
HP6 .... 154 C1
Dr Challoner's High Sch
HP7 .... 166 B7
Dresser Rd HP16 .... 151 C5
Drew Ct MK3 .... 47 A4
Drew Mdw SL2 .... 198 C8
Drews Pk HP9 .... 175 C6
Drey The SL9 .... 177 E5
Drift Rd SL4 .... 209 A1
Drift Way
Colnbrook SL3 .... 212 C7
Olney MK46 .... 6 F5
Drinkwater Cl OX25 ..... 95 D7
Drive The
Amersham HP7 .... 154 D1
Bourne End SL8 .... 184 F4
Chalfont St Peter SL9 ... 177 F3
Cranfield MK43 .... 24 D2
Datchet SL3 .... 211 B6
Ickenham UB10 .... 190 E1
Ivinghoe Aston LU7 ...... 92 A1
Slough SL3 .... 206 E4
Wraysbury TW19 .... 211 D2
Dropmore Inf Sch SL1 .. 186 C1
Dropmore Rd
Burnham SL1 .... 197 C5
Littleworth Common SL1 186 C1
Drovers Croft MK12 ..... 33 B4
Drovers La RG9 .... 169 B2
Drovers Way
Dunstable LU6 .... 93 F8
Newton Longville MK17 ... 57 D2
Seer Green HP9 .... 176 C4
Druce End NN12 .... 18 E6
Druids Wlk OX39 .... 147 C6
Drummond Ho 4 SL4 .. 210 D4
Drummond Ride HP23 .. 119 A5
Drummound Hay MK15 .. 35 C7
Drydell La HP5 .... 153 F8
Dryden Cl
Aylesbury HP20 .... 101 E2
Newport Pagnell MK16 ... 22 A4
Duchess Gdns NN12 ..... 18 D3
Duchess Gr MK7 .... 48 C7
Duchess St SL1 .... 204 E5
DUCK END
Akeley 42 A8
Swanbourne 66 F4
Duck End
Aylesbury HP20 .... 115 C8
Great Brickhill MK17 ..... 59 D1
Duck La
Ludgershall HP18 .... 96 C8
Woburn MK17 .... 60 F7
Duck Lake MK18 .... 41 E3
Duck Lake Cl MK18 ...... 41 E4
Duckmore La HP23 ..... 118 E2
Duck Sq OX39 .... 147 C6
Duckworth Ct MK6 ...... 46 E7
Dudley Cl MK18 .... 76 A2
Dudley Ct SL1 .... 206 A3
Dudley Hill MK5 .... 46 A6
Dudley Ho 1 HP3 ...... 146 A4
Dudley La RG9 .... 181 A6
DUDSWELL 134 D8
Dudswell La HP4 .... 134 D7
Duffield La SL2 .... 198 F6
Duffield Pk SL2 .... 199 A2
Dukes Ave LU6 .... 107 E8
Dukes Cl
Gerrards Cross SL9 ..... 188 E3
Shabbington HP18 ...... 124 C2
Dukes Dr
Farnham Common SL2 ... 198 A8
Milton Keynes MK2 ...... 47 C1
Dukes Kiln Dr SL9 ...... 188 C3
Dukes La SL9 .... 188 E4
Dukes Mdw SL8 .... 185 B3
Dukes Piece MK18 ...... 52 F8
Dukes Pl
Marlow SL7 .... 183 D2
Slough SL1 .... 205 F6
Dukes Ride
Gerrards Cross SL9 ..... 188 E3
Ickenham UB10 .... 201 E8
Leighton Buzzard LU7 .... 70 F3
Dukes Row HP18 .... 99 A1
Duke St
Aspley Guise MK17 ...... 49 D4
Eton SL4 .... 210 C7
Henley-on-Thames RG9 .. 191 E2
High Wycombe HP13 .... 173 C6
Princes Risborough
HP27 .... 139 B4
Dukes Valley SL9 ...... 188 B2
Dukes Way
Berkhamsted HP4 ...... 135 A6
Uxbridge UB8 .... 201 C4
Dukes Wood Ave SL9 ... 188 E3
Dukes Wood Dr SL9 ... 188 D3
Dulverton Ct LU7 .... 80 C8
Dulverton Dr MK4 .... 46 D3
Dulwich Cl MK16 .... 22 C2
Dumbletons WD3 ...... 178 E6
Dumfries Cl MK3 .... 46 F3
Dunbar Cl
Milton Keynes MK3 ...... 57 D8
Slough SL2 .... 206 A6
Dunbar Dr OX9 .... 126 A1
Duncan Gr MK5 .... 45 F6
Duncan Lock Ho HP9 ... 175 F2
Duncannon Cres SL4 ... 209 D4
Duncan Rd MK43 .... 24 E2
Dunchurch Dale MK7 ... 48 B5
Duncombe Cl HP6 ..... 154 E1
Duncombe Rd HP4 ..... 134 E6
Duncombe St MK2 ...... 58 C7
Duncroft SL4 .... 209 F4
Dundale Prim Sch
HP23 .... 119 A5
Dundale Rd HP23 ...... 119 A4
Dundee Rd SL1 .... 205 A8
Dungeness Ct MK4 ...... 46 A1
Dungrovehill La SL7 ... 194 D3
Dunholme End SL6 ..... 202 D3
Dunkeld Ho HP11 ...... 174 B4
Dunkery Beacon MK4 ... 46 D3
Dunnet Cl MK4 .... 57 A8
Dunny La WD4 .... 156 F7
Dunsby Rd MK6 .... 47 A4
Dunsham La HP20 ...... 101 E2
Dunsley Pl HP23 ...... 119 B3
DUNSMORE 141 A7
Dunsmore Ave HP27 ... 139 C5
Dunsmore Ride HP27 ... 139 C5
DUNSTABLE 93 E8
Dunstable Downs* LU6 . 93 E4
Dunstable Ho 4 SL7 ... 183 E1
Dunstable Rd
Dagnall HP4 .... 107 C7
Eaton Bray LU6 .... 93 A5
Totternhoe LU6 .... 93 D7
Dunster Ct MK4 .... 46 E3
Dunster Gdns SL1 ...... 205 A6
Dunston Hill HP23 ..... 119 A4
Dunthorne Way MK8 .... 45 D6
DUNTON 77 E5
Dunton Rd LU7 .... 78 D6
Dunvedin Pl MK12 ...... 33 D4
Dunvegan Cl MK2 .... 58 D4
Dunwood Ct SL6 .... 202 C5
Dunwood Rise HP13 .... 162 B1
Duparc Cl MK7 .... 48 C5
Dupre Cl SL1 .... 204 E4
Dupre Cres HP9 .... 176 B1
Du Pre Wlk HP10 ...... 185 D4
Durgate MK7 .... 48 A8
Durham Ave SL1 .... 205 A7
Durham Ho 1 MK3 ..... 46 F1
Durley Hollow HP13 .... 162 B1
Durlston End MK4 ...... 57 A8
Durrans Ct MK2 .... 47 E1
Durrans Ho MK2 .... 47 E1
Durrants La HP4 .... 134 F5
Durrants Path HP5 ..... 144 A4
Durrants Rd HP4 .... 134 F5
Durrell Cl LU7 .... 80 E7
Dutch Barn Cl TW19 .... 213 D1
Dutch Elm Ave SL4 ..... 210 F7
Dutton Way SL0 .... 207 E7
Dyersdale MK13 .... 34 C5
Dyers Mews MK14 ...... 34 F6
Dyers Rd LU6 .... 92 D7
Dymock Ct HP22 .... 85 B4
Dyson Cl SL4 .... 210 B4

E

Eagle Cl HP6 .... 154 F2
Eagles Rd HP20 .... 116 A8
EAGLESTONE 47 B7
Eaglestone Rdbt MK6 ... 47 A8
Eagle Way MK43 .... 3 F6
Eagle Wlk MK9 .... 34 F3
EAKLEY LANES 4 D2
Ealing Chase MK10 ...... 47 F8
Eames Cl HP20 .... 101 F3
Eardley Pl MK8 .... 45 D6
Earl Cl HP13 .... 162 A1
Earl Howe Rd HP15 .... 163 D6
Earls Cl MK2 .... 58 C8
Earlsfield SL6 .... 203 C2
Earls La SL1 .... 204 F5
Earls Willow MK13 ...... 34 A8
Earlswood Cl HP21 ..... 116 A5
Easby Gr MK10 .... 36 A1
Eascote Rd HP21 ...... 116 B4
EASINGTON 111 B1
Easington La HP18 ..... 111 B1
Easington Terr HP18 ... 111 B1
East Berkshire Coll
Slough SL3 .... 207 A3
Windsor SL4 .... 210 C5
Eastbourne Rd SL1 ..... 205 A7
Eastbridge SL2 .... 206 B5
Eastbrook Cl OX25 ...... 95 E7
EAST BURNHAM 198 A4
East Burnham Cotts
SL2 .... 198 A4
East Burnham La SL2 ... 198 A4
Eastbury Ct MK4 .... 46 D1
East Chapel MK4 .... 57 B8
EAST CLAYDON 74 E8
East Claydon Rd MK18 ... 65 D2
East Claydon Sch MK18 . 74 E7
East Comm SL9 .... 188 E5
East Cres SL4 .... 209 F6
Eastcroft SL2 .... 198 B1
East Dales MK13 .... 34 C5
East Dr
High Wycombe HP13 .... 173 E8
Stoke Poges SL2 .... 198 E2
EAST END
Cranfield 25 C1
North Crawley 24 F6
East End HP22 .... 87 D1
Eastergate HP9 .... 175 C4
Eastern Dene HP15 .... 163 B5
Eastern Dr SL8 .... 185 C4
Eastern St HP20 .... 101 E1
Eastfield Cl 3 SL1 ..... 206 A3
Eastfield Cres NN12 ..... 18 F5
Eastfield Dr MK19 .... 11 A3
Eastfield Rd
Aylesbury HP20 .... 116 B8
Burnham SL1 .... 204 A8
Princes Risborough
HP27 .... 139 C3
East Green Cl MK5 ...... 45 F6
East Hills MK43 .... 25 B1
East La MK7 .... 47 F7
Eastlands HP27 .... 149 E5
Eastnor HP3 .... 146 A3
Eastoke Pl MK4 .... 57 A8
Easton St HP11 .... 173 B6
Easton Terr HP13 ...... 173 C6
East Paddock SL6 ...... 194 F6
East Rd
Cranfield MK43 .... 24 E2
Maidenhead SL6 .... 202 E7
West Drayton UB7 ...... 208 F2
East Richardson St 5
HP11 .... 172 F7
East Ridge SL8 .... 185 B4
East Spur MK7 .... 47 F7
East St
Adstock MK18 .... 53 F1
Chesham HP5 .... 154 B8
Olney MK46 .... 7 A4
East Terr SL4 .... 210 E7
East View OX25 .... 81 A3
East Walk N MK9 .... 34 E2
East Walk S MK9 .... 34 E2
East Way HP9 .... 175 A1
Eastwick Cres WD3 .... 178 F8
Eastwood Ct 1 SL7 .... 183 F3
Eastwood Rd HP14 ..... 158 F3
Eaton Ave
High Wycombe HP12 .... 172 D8
Milton Keynes MK2 ...... 58 D7
Slough SL1 .... 204 C6
EATON BRAY 92 F6
Eaton Bray Lower Sch
LU6 .... 92 F6
Eaton Bray Rd
Edlesborough LU6 .... 92 C5
Honeywick LU6 .... 92 E8
Eaton Cl HP22 .... 116 F2
Eatongate Cl LU6 .... 92 E5
EATON GREEN 92 C7
Eaton Mill Prim Sch
MK2 .... 58 D6
Eaton Pk LU6 .... 92 F6
Eaton Pl HP12 .... 172 D8
Eaton Rd HP21 .... 115 D7
Ebble Cl HP21 .... 115 C4
Ebbsgrove MK5 .... 34 B1
Ebenezer Ho HP10 ..... 174 C2
Ebsworth Cl SL6 .... 196 C3
Eddington Ct MK4 .... 46 D1
Eddy St HP4 .... 135 A5
Eden Cl
Aylesbury HP21 .... 115 D4
Slough SL3 .... 207 A1
Eden Sh Ctr HP11 ...... 173 A7
Eden Wlk MK3 .... 46 E1
Edgar Rd UB7 .... 208 E5
Edgar Wallace Pl SL8 .. 185 B5
EDGCOTT 72 F2
Edgecombe Rd HP21 ... 116 B5
Edgecote MK8 .... 46 A8
Edgecote Ho 11 HP13 .. 173 B7
Edgecott Rd HP18 .... 82 F7
Edgehill OX9 .... 125 F2
Edge Hill Ct MK18 .... 41 E2
Edgewood HP11 .... 173 D5
Edinburgh Ave SL1 ..... 205 B7
Edinburgh Gate UB9 ... 189 F5
Edinburgh Gdns SL4 ... 210 D5
Edinburgh Ho MK3 ...... 57 D7
Edinburgh Pl HP21 ..... 115 C6
Edinburgh Rd
Maidenhead SL6 .... 195 E1
Marlow SL7 .... 183 E3
Edison Cl UB7 .... 208 F4
Edison Rd HP19 .... 100 E1
Edison Sq MK5 .... 46 C5
Edith Bell Ho SL9 ...... 177 E4
Edith Rd SL6 .... 202 A7
EDLESBOROUGH 92 E4
Edlesborough Sch LU6 .. 92 E3
Edlyn Cl HP4 .... 134 F5
Edmonds Cl MK18 .... 41 F1
Edmonds Rd HP14 ..... 171 B4
Edmund Ct
Beaconsfield HP9 ...... 186 A8
Milton Keynes MK5 ...... 45 F7
Edmunds Cl HP12 ...... 172 C5
Edmunds Gdns HP12 ... 172 C5
Edmunds Way SL2 ..... 206 B7
Edrich Ave MK6 .... 46 F8
Edstone Pl MK4 .... 46 C3
Edward Cl HP21 .... 116 A4
Edwards Croft MK13 ..... 34 A7
Edward Wlk HP21 ...... 116 A4
Edwin Allman Pl HP15 .. 162 E2
Edwin Cl MK17 .... 48 D2
Edy Ct MK5 .... 34 A1
Edzell Cres MK4 .... 45 E2
Eelbrook Ave MK13 ..... 34 C2
Eeles Cl HP19 .... 100 F3
Egerton Cl NN13 .... 38 A7
Egerton Gate MK5 ...... 46 B4
Egerton Rd
Berkhamsted HP4 ...... 135 B6
Slough SL2 .... 197 E1
Egerton-Rothesay Sch
HP4 .... 134 E4
Egglesfield Cl HP4 ..... 134 E6
Eggleton Dr HP23 ...... 119 A5
Eghams Cl HP9 .... 175 C4
Eghams Ct 8 SL8 ...... 185 B3
Eghams Gn SL8 .... 185 B3
Eghams Wood Rd HP9 . 175 C4
Egmont Ave MK11 .... 32 E4
Egremont Gdns SL1 .... 205 A5
EGYPT 198 B8
Egypt La SL2 .... 187 B1
Egypt Way HP19 .... 115 A8
Egypt Wood Cotts SL2 .. 187 B1
Eider Cl MK18 .... 52 E8
Eight Acres
Burnham SL1 .... 197 B1
Tring HP23 .... 119 A4
Elangeni Jun Sch HP6 . 154 E3
Elbow Mdw SL3 .... 212 F6
Elder Cl
Loudwater HP11 .... 174 B3
West Drayton UB7 ...... 208 E6
Elderdene OX39 .... 147 D8
Elderfield Rd SL2 ...... 198 F6
Elder Gate
Milton Keynes, Rooksley
MK9 .... 34 C1
Milton Keynes, Winterhill
MK9 .... 46 C8
Elder Way HP15 .... 163 B3
Eldridge La HP17 ...... 130 C3
Eleanor Cl MK17 .... 60 F7
Eleanor Gdns HP21 .... 115 F6
Eleanor Rd SL9 .... 177 C2
Eleanor Wlk MK17 ...... 60 F7
Elfords MK6 .... 47 A6
Elgar Gr MK7 .... 48 C4
Elgin Ho SL3 .... 212 E6
Elgiva La HP5 .... 154 B8
Elham Way HP21 .... 116 A4
Eliot Cl
Aylesbury HP19 .... 100 F2
Newport Pagnell MK16 ... 21 F5
Eliot Dr SL7 .... 183 F4
Elizabeth Ave HP6 ..... 166 C8
Elizabeth Cl
Aylesbury HP21 .... 116 B4
Cookham Rise SL6 ...... 195 F7
Elizabeth Ct
High Wycombe HP13 .... 173 C6
High Wycombe, Wycombe
Marsh HP13 .... 173 E5
10 Slough SL1 .... 206 A4
3 Windsor SL4 .... 210 C5
Elizabeth Dr HP23 ...... 119 B6
Elizabeth Rd
Marlow SL7 .... 183 E3
Stokenchurch HP14 ..... 158 F4
Elizabeth Sq MK2 .... 58 C8
Elizabeth Way SL2 ..... 198 F4
Elkins Rd SL2 .... 187 E2
Ellen Pl HP21 .... 115 C5
Ellen Rd HP21 .... 115 C5
Ellenstow MK13 .... 34 A4
Ellen Wlk HP21 .... 115 B6
Ellerburn Pl MK4 .... 46 B3
Ellery Rise RG9 .... 170 F1
ELLESBOROUGH 130 B2
Ellesborough Gr MK8 ... 33 D3
Ellesborough Rd
Butler's Cross HP17 .... 130 C2
Ellesborough HP17 ..... 130 A2
Wendover HP22 .... 131 A3
Ellesmere Cl
Datchet SL3 .... 211 A8
Totternhoe LU6 .... 93 C6
Ellesmere Rd HP4 ...... 135 D4
Elliman Ave SL2 .... 205 F6
Ellington Ct SL6 .... 203 C7
Ellington Gdns SL6 ..... 203 C7
Ellington Pk SL6 .... 195 E1
Ellington Prim Sch SL6 . 195 F1
Ellington Rd SL6 .... 203 C7
Elliots Cl UB8 .... 208 C8
Elliott Ho HP11 .... 172 F8
Ellis Ave
Chalfont St Peter SL9 ... 177 F2
Slough SL1 .... 205 E4
Ellisgill Ct MK13 .... 34 B4
Ellison Cl SL4 .... 209 F4
Ellison Ct HP23 .... 118 F3
Ellison Ho 14 SL4 ...... 210 D6
Ellis Way HP14 .... 171 B4
Ellsworth Rd HP11 ..... 172 F4
Ellwood Ho SL9 .... 177 E2
Ellwood Rd HP9 .... 175 B1
Ellwood Rise HP8 ...... 177 C8
Ellwood Terr WD3 ..... 167 D4
Elmar Gn SL2 .... 198 A2
Elm Brook Cl HP18 ..... 112 C1
Elm Cl
Amersham HP6 .... 154 C1
Butler's Cross HP17 .... 130 C3
Chinnor OX39 .... 147 C5
Farnham Common SL2 ... 198 C6
Hazelmere HP15 .... 163 A3
Newton Longville MK17 ... 57 C2
Weston Turville HP22 .... 116 F2
Elm Croft SL3 .... 211 C6
Elm Ct
Berkhamsted HP4 ...... 135 B4
Butler's Cross HP17 .... 130 C3
Elmdale Gdns HP27 .... 139 B3
Elm Dr
Chinnor OX39 .... 147 C5
Deanshanger MK19 ...... 31 D5
Elmers Cl MK19 .... 44 A6
Elmers Mdw MK18 ...... 76 A2
Elmers Pk MK3 .... 58 A8
Elm Farm Rd HP21 ..... 116 A5
Elmfield Cl NN12 .... 18 D3
Elmfields Gate MK18 .... 66 A4
Elm Gn HP21 .... 115 D7
Elm Gr
Berkhamsted HP4 ...... 135 C4
Maidenhead SL6 .... 202 E7
West Drayton UB7 ...... 208 F6
Woburn Sands MK17 ..... 49 B4
ELMHURST 101 E3
Elmhurst 5 HP16 ...... 152 A8
Elmhurst Cl
High Wycombe HP13 .... 162 D1
Milton Keynes MK4 ...... 46 F4
Elmhurst Ct SL3 .... 207 A3
Elmhurst Rd
Aylesbury HP20 .... 101 E2
Slough SL3 .... 207 A3
Elmhurst Sch HP20 .... 101 E2
Elm La SL8 .... 184 F5
Elm Lawn Cl UB8 ...... 201 E5
Elmlea Dr MK46 .... 6 E3
Elmodesham Ho 7
HP7 .... 165 B7
Elm Rd
High Wycombe HP12 .... 172 C4
Princes Risborough
HP27 .... 139 C3
Tylers Green HP10 ...... 174 D8
Windsor SL4 .... 210 B4

Elmridge Ct MK4 46 C2
Elms Dr SL8 185 C3
Elmshott Cl HP10 163 A1
Elmshott La SL1 204 E6
Elmside MK18 66 A4
Elmslie Ct SL6 202 E7
Elms Rd SL9 177 E3
Elm St MK18 52 D8
Elms The
Leighton Buzzard LU7 80 E7
Milton Keynes MK3 57 F8
Preston Bissett MK18 51 B1
Elm Tree Cl OX25 81 A4
Elm Tree Cotts HP7 164 C2
Elmtree Ct 6 HP16 152 A8
Elmtree Gn HP16 152 A8
Elmtree Hill HP5 144 B1
Elmtree Inf Sch HP5 144 B1
Elm Trees HP18 125 B7
Elm Tree Wlk
Chorleywood WD3 167 F5
Tring HP23 119 A5
Elmwood
Maidenhead SL6 196 B4
Turvey MK43 8 E6
Elmwood Cl HP18 109 D5
Elmwood Pk SL9 188 E3
Elmwood Rd SL2 206 B6
Elora Rd HP13 173 E7
Elruge Cl UB7 208 D3
Elsage Ct LU7 105 B8
Elsmore Cl HP21 116 A4
Eltham Ave SL1 204 E4
Elthorne Rd UB8 201 D3
Elthorne Way MK16 22 C2
Elton MK6 47 D7
Elton Dr SL6 202 D8
Elwes Rd HP14 171 C4
Ely Ave SL1 205 C8
Ely Cl HP7 165 E8
Ely Ho HP13 173 F8
Ember Path HP21 115 C4
Ember Rd SL3 207 B3
EMBERTON 13 E8
Emberton Ctry Pk* MK46 6 E1
Emberton Fst Sch MK46 13 F8
Embleton Way MK18 52 C7
Emerald Cl MK18 74 F8
Emerald Ct SL1 205 E4
Emerald Gate MK15 35 E5
Emerson Ct HP10 185 E6
EMERSON VALLEY 46 B2
Emerson Valley Comb Sch MK4 46 C2
Emerton Ct HP4 134 E7
Emerton Garth HP4 134 E7
Emerton Gdns MK11 32 E5
Emilia Cl SL6 195 F1
Emlyns Bldgs SL4 210 D7
Emma Rothschild Ct HP23 119 A5
Emmett Cl MK4 46 C1
Emmett Dr HP21 115 E5
EMMINGTON 137 A1
Emperor Cl HP4 134 F7
Empingham Cl MK2 58 D4
Empstead Ct RG9 191 D2
Enborne Cl HP21 115 D4
Enders Ct MK5 45 E5
Endfield Pl SL6 202 B6
Enfield Chase MK14 34 D5
Enfield Cl UB8 201 D3
Engaine Dr MK5 45 F7
English Gdns TW19 211 D2
Enigma Ctr The MK1 47 E2
Enmore Gate MK9 35 A3
Enmore Rdbt MK9 35 A3
Ennell Gr MK2 58 C5
Ennerdale Cl MK2 58 D6
Ennerdale Cres SL1 204 C8
Ensbury Path HP20 101 E2
Enstone Rd UB10 190 F1
Enterprise La MK9 35 A3
Epsom Cl LU7 80 D6
Epsom Gr MK3 57 D6
Ercolani Ave HP13 173 D6
Eriboll Cl LU7 80 B6
Erica Cl SL1 204 E6
Erica Rd MK12 33 E4
Eridge Gn MK7 48 A8
Errington Dr SL4 210 A6
Escarpment Ave LU6 107 D8
Eskan Ct MK9 35 B4
Eskdale Ave HP5 144 D1
Eskdale Gdns SL6 203 B2
Eskdale Lodge HP6 154 C2
Eskdale Rd
Stoke Mandeville HP22 116 B2
Uxbridge UB8 201 B3
Eskdale Way MK10 36 B3
Esk Way MK3 46 E1
Essenden Ct MK11 32 F5
Essex Ave SL2 205 C8
Essex Cl MK3 46 F1
Essex Ho 5 HP20 101 D1
Essex Pl HP19 101 A3
Essex Rd HP5 144 C2
Essex Yd HP22 89 C2
Estcourt Dr HP15 162 F6
Esther Cl MK13 34 A6
Eston Ct MK13 34 A5
Estover Way OX39 147 B6
Etheridge Ave MK10 48 C8
Ethorpe MK8 33 E1
Ethorpe Cl SL9 188 E6
Ethorpe Cres SL9 188 E6
Ethorpe Ho SL9 188 E6
ETON 210 C8
Eton Cl SL3 211 A8
Eton Coll SL4 210 D8
Eton College Rowing Ctr* SL4 204 D7
Eton Cres MK12 33 C6
Eton Ct SL4 210 D7
Eton End PNEU Sch SL3 211 A8
Eton Ho 1 SL1 205 F3
Eton Pl SL7 183 D2
Eton Porny CE Fst Sch SL4 210 D8
Eton Rd SL3 211 A8
Eton Riverside SL4 210 D7
Eton Sq SL4 210 D7
ETON WICK 204 F1
Eton Wick CE Fst Sch SL4 205 A1
Eton Wick Rd SL4 205 B1
Eton Wlk 1 SL1 205 E3
Eunice Gr HP5 154 D7
Europa Bsns Pk MK10 36 C2
Europa Ho SL9 188 E6
Evans Cl
Aylesbury HP21 116 A4
Chearsley HP18 112 B2
Evans Gate MK6 46 E8
Evans Way HP23 119 B4
Evelyn Cl LU7 79 E1
Evelyn Pl MK13 34 A7
Evelyns Cl 2 UB8 208 F7
Evenley Rd NN13 38 D1
Evenlode SL6 202 F8
Evenlode Cl HP21 115 C5
Evenlode Rd SL8 185 B4
Everard Ave SL1 205 E4
Everest Cl HP13 173 D6
Everest Rd HP13 173 E6
Everglade MK6 47 A8
Evergreen Oak Ave SL4 211 A4
Everley Cl MK4 46 C3
Evesham Gn HP19 101 C3
Evesham Way MK5 45 D5
Evreham Rd SL0 207 E7
Evreham Sp Ctr SL0 207 D8
Exbury La MK4 45 F1
Exchange Ho MK9 34 E2
Exchange St HP20 115 E8
Exebridge MK4 46 C3
Exhims Mews HP4 134 E6
Exmoor Gate MK4 46 E2
Eynsford Terr UB7 208 F7
Eynsham Ct MK15 35 C2
Eyre Cl HP19 114 F8
Eyre Gn SL2 198 A2
EYTHROPE 113 F8
Eythrope Rd
Eythrope HP18 100 A1
Stone HP17 114 C6

F

Factory Yd HP9 175 E1
Fadmoor Pl 3 MK4 46 B3
Fagnall La HP7 164 D2
Fairacre SL6 202 C6
Fair Acres HP16 151 D5
Fairacres Ind Est SL4 209 D5
Faircroft SL2 198 B1
Fairfax MK13 34 C6
Fairfax Cres HP20 101 E2
Fairfax Mews HP7 165 A7
Fairfield HP6 154 B3
Fairfield App TW19 211 D1
Fairfield Ave SL3 211 D7
Fairfield Cl
Bourne End SL8 185 A5
Datchet SL3 211 D7
Olney MK46 7 A3
Fairfield La SL2 198 B3
Fairfield Rd
Burnham SL1 197 C2
Paulerspury NN12 17 B7
Uxbridge UB8 201 D6
West Drayton UB7 208 E6
Wraysbury TW19 211 D1
Fairfields HP15 151 E1
Fairford Cres MK15 35 B6
Fairford Leys Way HP19 115 A7
Fairford Rd SL6 202 F8
Fairhaven SL9 177 C2
Fairlawn Pk SL4 209 E3
Fairlawns HP13 162 C1
Fairlea SL6 202 B3
Fair Leas HP5 144 A2
Fairlie Rd SL1 205 A8
Fairlight Ave SL4 210 D5
Fairlight Dr UB8 201 D6
Fair Mdw MK18 66 A4
Fairmead The SL3 212 D7
Fair Mile
Aylesbury HP21 116 A7
Henley-on-Thames RG9 191 C4
Fairmile Ct RG9 191 D3
Fair Ridge HP11 172 F4
Fairthorn Cl HP23 118 E3
Fair View Cotts
Chalfont St Peter SL9 177 E3
Cookham Rise SL6 195 E7
Fairview Ind Est
Amersham HP6 154 F1
High Wycombe HP11 173 F4
Fairview La HP10 174 A1
Fairview Rd
Burnham SL6 204 A7
Slough SL2 197 F1
Fairway HP27 139 A3
Fairway Ave UB7 208 D5
Fairway Cl UB7 208 D5
Fairways MK8 33 C2
Fairways Rdbt MK8 33 C2
Fairway The
Burnham SL1 197 C3
Flackwell Heath HP10 185 C7
Maidenhead SL6 202 B3
Uxbridge UB10 201 F3
Faithfull Cl HP17 114 B5
Faithorn Cl HP5 144 A1
Faith Terr MK19 11 A2
Falaise MK15 35 B7
Falcon Ave MK6 35 B2
Falcon Dr
Milton Keynes MK19 32 B7
Stanwell TW19 213 E1
Falconhurst Comb Sch MK6 47 B8
Falcon Ridge HP4 135 C3
Falcon Rise HP13 161 C1
Falcons Croft HP10 185 E8
Falcon The HP19 101 F4
Falkland Ho SL6 202 F8
Falklands Cl MK18 63 D2
Fall Cl HP19 101 D3
Falling La UB7 208 E6
Fallow Field HP15 163 B3
Fallows The SL6 196 A1
Falmouth Pl MK6 34 F1
Falmouth Rd SL1 205 A7
Fane Way SL6 202 D5
Fantail La HP23 118 F4
Faraday Cl SL2 205 B8
Faraday Dr MK5 46 C5
Faraday Rd
Aylesbury HP19 101 A1
Slough SL2 205 B8
FAR BLETCHLEY 57 D7
Far Furlong Cl HP21 115 D3
Farinton MK8 33 F2
Farjeon Ct MK7 48 D4
Farmborough MK6 47 C6
Farmbrough Cl HP20 102 A1
Farm Cl
High Wycombe HP13 174 A7
Ickford HP18 123 F3
Little Chalfont HP6 166 D8
Maidenhead, Highway SL6 202 A7
Maidenhead SL6 203 C1
Stewkley LU7 78 E7
Farm Cres SL2 206 C8
Farm Dr SL4 211 B1
Farmers Cl SL6 202 A4
Farmers Pl SL9 177 C1
Farmers Way
Maidenhead SL6 202 A4
Seer Green HP9 176 C4
Farmery Ct HP4 135 E6
Farm Gr HP9 175 C5
Farm La HP9 176 D3
Farm Lea HP10 185 F7
Farm Pl
Berkhamsted HP4 134 F5
Henton OX39 137 E1
Farm Rd
Bourne End SL8 184 F4
Brackley NN13 38 A6
Burnham SL6 204 A5
Chorleywood WD3 167 A5
Maidenhead SL6 202 A7
Farm Way TW19 212 F1
Farm Yd SL4 210 D7
Farnburn Ave SL1 205 B8
Farndale Gdns HP15 163 A6
Farnell Ct MK5 46 C8
Farnham Cl HP3 146 A3
FARNHAM COMMON 198 D6
Farnham Common Ho 2 SL2 198 C8
Farnham Common Inf Sch SL2 198 B8
Farnham Common Jun Sch SL2 198 C8
Farnham Ct MK8 33 F1
Farnham La SL2 198 A2
FARNHAM PARK 198 C4
Farnham Park La SL2 198 C4
Farnham Rd SL1, SL2 205 C7
FARNHAM ROYAL 198 C3
Farnley Rd HP20 101 E2
Farrer Cl NN13 26 D4
Farrer Theatre Eton* SL4 205 C1
Farrier Ct 1 SL8 185 B3
Farrier Pl MK14 35 A5
Farriers Cl HP3 146 B3
Farriers Way HP5 144 A3
Farringdon St MK10 35 F1
Farthingales The SL6 203 B7
Farthing Ent Ctr The MK6 47 C6
Farthing Gr MK6 47 C6
Farthing Green La SL2 199 B4
Farthings The HP6 154 A3
Fassets Rd HP10 174 B2
Faulkner Dr MK3 47 B1
Faulkner's Way LU7 80 E7
Faulkner Way HP13 161 D3
Favell Dr MK4 46 F4
Faversham Cl HP23 119 A4
Fawcett Rd SL4 210 B6
FAWLEY 191 C8
FAWLEY BOTTOM 180 B2
Fawley Bottom La RG9 180 B1
Fawley Cl SL6 195 D2
Fawley Court* RG9 191 E5
Fawley Gn RG9 180 D2
Fawley Hill Rly* RG9 191 D8
Fawsley Cl SL3 212 E7
Featherbed La HP15 163 D8
Featherstone Rd MK12 33 A5
Fedden Ho MK43 24 D3
Fegans Ct MK11 32 D6
Felbridge MK7 48 A7
FELDEN 146 F7
Felden La HP3 146 F8
Fells Cl HP18 125 D6
Fellstead Ct SL6 202 C6
Felstar Wlk MK6 47 C4
Felsted MK7 48 A3
Fences La MK16 13 A2
Fennel Dr MK14 34 E4
Fennels Farm Rd HP10 174 A1
Fennels Rd HP11 174 A4
Fennels The HP11 174 A3
Fennels Way HP10 174 A1
Fennemore Cl HP18 109 D4
Fennings The HP6 154 D3
Fenny House Tuition Service MK6 47 A6
FENNY LOCK 47 E2
Fennymere MK8 33 D1
Fenny Rd MK17 69 E8
FENNY STRATFORD 47 D1
Fenny Stratford Sta MK1 47 E1
Fen St MK17 36 F1
Fenton Ct MK8 45 F8
FERN 184 E5
Fernan Dell MK8 45 D7
Fernborough Haven 4 MK4 46 C2
Fern Cotts SL7 184 E5
Fern Ct HP4 135 B4
Ferndale MK6 35 B1
Ferndale Cl HP14 158 F4
Ferndale Cres UB8 201 C2
Fern Dr SL6 204 B7
Ferne Furlong MK46 6 F5
Fernes Cl UB8 208 C7
Fernfield MK17 56 A5
Fern Gr MK2 58 D5
Fernhill Cl OX9 136 A6
Fernhurst Cl HP9 175 F2
Fernie Fields HP12 172 C4
Fern La
Fern SL7 184 E5
Haddenham HP17 127 A6
Fernlea Cl HP10 174 A1
Fernley Ct SL6 195 D1
Fernside
Great Kingshill HP15 151 E1
Hazelmere HP15 163 A6
Fernsleigh Cl SL9 177 E4
Ferns The HP9 175 F1
Fern Wlk HP15 163 B3
Fernwood Sch MK17 49 B2
Ferrers Ave UB7 208 D4
Ferrers Cl SL1 204 E5
Ferry End SL6 203 C4
Ferry La
Bourne End SL8 196 B8
Medmenham SL7 193 B5
Mill End RG9 192 D6
Ferry Mdws Cl MK10 36 A4
Ferry Rd SL6 203 C4
Festival Cotts SL3 212 C7
Fetty Pl SL6 202 D4
Field Cl
Aylesbury HP20 102 A2
Buckingham MK18 51 B6
Chesham HP5 144 E3
Ickford HP18 124 A3
Sherington MK16 14 A2
Field Ct MK5 46 B8
Field End HP18 125 F5
Field End Cl HP23 119 D1
Fieldfare HP19 101 E4
Field Farm Bsns Ctr OX26 71 A5
Fieldhead Gdns SL8 185 A3
Fieldhouse Ct HP13 174 A4
Fieldhouse Ind Est SL7 183 F2
Fieldhouse La SL7 183 F2
Fieldhouse Way SL7 183 F2
Field Hurst SL3 206 F1
Fielding Gdns SL3 206 C4
Fielding Rd SL6 202 B8
Field La MK12 33 B5
Field Rd
Denham, Rush Green UB9 200 E8
Denham UB9 189 E1
High Wycombe HP12 172 B5
Murcott OX5 94 A5
Fields End HP23 119 A6
Fields The SL1 205 D4
Fieldway
Amersham HP7 165 B6
Berkhamsted HP4 135 E2
Chalfont St Peter SL9 177 D3
Wigginton HP23 119 D1
Field Way
Aylesbury HP20 102 A2
Bovingdon HP3 146 A4
Chalfont St Peter SL9 177 D2
Uxbridge UB8 201 D1
Field Wlk MK9 34 F3
Fife Ct MK4 57 A8
Fife Ho MK3 46 F1
Fifth St HP11 173 C4
Filey Spur SL1 205 B4
FILGRAVE 13 C5
Filgrave Sch MK16 13 C5
Filmer Rd SL4 209 D5
Finch Cl MK10 35 F3
Finch Cres LU7 80 E5
Finch Ct SL6 202 D5
Finch End HP10 174 C8
Finch Gn WD3 167 F5
Finch La
Amersham HP7 165 F5
Beaconsfield HP9 175 C5
Little Chalfont HP7 166 B7
Finch Rd HP4 135 A4
Findlay Way MK2 58 C8
Finemere Wood Wildlife Reserve* HP22 84 B8
Fingest La RG9 170 D4
Fingle Dr MK13 33 E7
Finians Cl UB10 201 F5
Finings Rd HP14 171 A4
Finlay Dr RG9 191 E2
Finlay Ho RG9 191 E3
FINMERE 50 D7
Finmere CE Prim Sch MK18 50 D6
Finmere Cres HP21 116 C5
Finsbury Chase MK10 47 F8
Fircroft Cl SL2 199 A6
Fircroft Ct SL2 199 A6
Firecrest Way HP19 100 F1
Fire La MK17 57 D4
Firemans Run MK17 49 B5
Firfield SL6 203 B1
Firs Ave SL4 209 F4
Firs Cl
Hazelmere HP15 163 B2
High Wycombe HP13 173 E8
Iver Heath SL0 200 C4
Lane End HP14 171 C5
Whitchurch HP22 87 A5
Firs Ct
Amersham HP6 154 C2
Bierton HP22 102 C4
Princes Risborough HP27 138 F3
Firs Dr SL3 206 F5
Firs End SL9 188 D8
Firs Rise HP16 151 E7
First Ave
Amersham HP7 165 D7
Marlow SL7 184 A2
Milton Keynes MK1 47 C1
First Cres SL1 205 C8
Firs The
Bierton HP22 102 C4
Brill HP18 110 B8
Maidenhead SL6 202 E7
Uxbridge UB8 201 D1
Wigginton HP23 119 D1
First St HP11 173 C3
Firs View Rd HP15 163 B2
Firs Wlk HP15 163 B2
Fir Tree Ave SL2 198 F1
Fir Tree Cotts HP14 161 B8
Firview Cl SL7 183 F1
Fishermans Cl MK46 6 E4
Fishermans Retreat SL7 183 E1
Fisherman's Way SL8 185 B4
FISHERMEAD 35 A1

Fishermead Bvd 2 MK6 34 F1
Fishermead Rdbt MK1 47 B2
Fishers Field MK18 52 C8
Fishery Rd SL6 203 C5
Fishguard Spur SL1 206 B4
Fish Ponds La OX9 125 E1
Fishweir LU7 68 D1
Fitzgeralds Way HP12 172 B7
Fitzhamon Ct MK12 33 A5
Fitzwilliam St MK3 58 B8
Five Acres
Chesham HP5 154 D6
Wooburn Green HP10 185 F7
Five Acre Wood HP12 172 C6
Five Points SL0 200 C2
FLACKWELL HEATH 185 A7
Flaggs Mdw MK46 6 E4
Flambard Cl MK15 35 A7
Flamborough Spur SL1 205 A4
Flamstead Gate MK5 45 E5
FLAUNDEN 156 A6
Flaunden Bottom HP5 155 E4
Flaunden Hill HP3 156 A6
Flaunden La
Bovingdon HP3 146 D3
Chipperfield WD3 156 E6
Flavius Gate NN13 38 A7
Flaxbourne Ct MK7 48 C7
Flaxen Field HP22 116 F2
Flaxley Gate MK10 36 A2
Fledgelings Wlk MK18 66 A5
Fleetbrook Ho SL3 211 D6
Fleet Cl
Buckingham MK18 41 F2
Walter's Ash HP14 161 F7
FLEET MARSTON 100 B4
Fleet St HP20 101 D1
Fleet The MK6 35 B2
Fleetwood Cl HP8 177 A6
Fleetwood Ct 7 TW19 213 E1
Fleetwood Rd SL2 205 F6
Fleetwood Way OX9 125 F2
Fleming Ct 7 SL3 206 C3
Fleming Dr MK6 47 B6
Fleming Way HP12 172 D5
Fletcher Cl HP19 100 F3
Fletchers Mews MK14 34 F6
Flexerne Cres MK6 47 D5
Flintergill Ct MK13 34 B4
Flint Ho 7 MK3 46 F1
Flint Hollow OX39 147 B6
Flintlock Cl TW19 213 A3
Flint St HP17 127 A5
Flint Way HP16 151 C7
Flitcroft Lea HP13 173 A8
Flitt Leys Cl MK43 25 B2
Flitton Ct MK11 32 F5
Flora Thompson Dr
MK16 21 F6
Florence Ave SL6 203 A8
Florence Ct HP19 101 D1
Florence Way UB8 201 C5
Florey Gdns HP20 115 F8
Florida St HP11 173 C4
Florin Cl MK15 35 A7
FLOWERS BOTTOM 150 A4
Flowers Bottom La
HP27 150 B4
Flynn Croft MK4 45 D1
Fog Cotts HP23 120 A5
Folding Cl LU7 78 E8
Foley Cl HP9 175 C4
Foliejohn Way SL6 202 A1
Folkestone Ct SL3 207 A1
Follet Cl SL4 211 B1
Folleys Pl HP10 174 D1
Folly La
Hartwell NN7 10 C8
North Crawley MK16 24 B5
Folly Rd MK19 31 D4
Fonda Mdws MK4 45 D3
Fontwell Cl SL6 202 A8
Fontwell Dr MK3 57 C6
Forbes Pl MK5 45 E4
Forches Cl MK4 46 D2
FORD 128 B7
Fordcombe Lea MK7 48 B8
Ford End UB9 189 F2
Ford La SL0 208 A7
Ford's Cl HP14 159 F8
Ford St
Buckingham MK18 52 D8
High Wycombe HP11 173 F4
Ford Way HP13 161 E3
Forelands Way HP5 154 C7
Forest Cl
Princes Risborough
HP27 139 B3
Slough SL2 206 B8
Wendover HP22 131 B4
Foresters
Beacon's Bottom HP14 159 C5
Chinnor OX39 147 B6
Oakley HP18 109 D6
Forest Pk SL4 209 E1
Forest Point HP13 173 F5
Forest Rd
Hanslope MK19 10 F5
Piddington (Northants) NN7 4 A8
Windsor SL4 209 E5
Forest Rise MK6 47 B8
Forestry Hos OX49 168 A7
Forest Way HP13 174 A8
Forfar Dr MK3 46 F2
Forge Cl
Ashendon HP18 97 E1
Holmer Green HP15 163 C6
Horton-cum-S OX33 108 B5
Marsh Gibbon OX27 71 F3
Oakley HP18 109 D4
Steeple Claydon MK18 63 E2
Forge Dr SL2 198 C6
Forge End HP7 165 B7
Forge Rd HP14 161 C8
Forge The MK46 13 F8
Forgetts Rd HP14 171 C4
Forlease Cl SL6 203 A6
Forlease Dr SL6 203 A6
Forlease Rd SL6 203 A6
Formby Cl
Milton Keynes MK3 57 C7
Slough SL3 207 C2
Forrabury Ave MK13 34 C3
Forsythia Gdns SL3 206 E3
Fort End HP17 127 A6
Fortescue Dr MK5 46 B6
Forthill Pl MK5 45 F7
Fortuna Ct MK7 48 C6
Forty Gn HP27 137 F3
FORTY GREEN
Beaconsfield 175 A4
Princes Risborough 137 F3
Forty Green Dr SL7 183 B2
Forty Green Rd HP9 175 C4
Forum The MK14 34 E5
FOSCOTE 42 B4
Foscote Cotts MK18 42 B4
Foscote Rd MK18 41 F3
Foscot Way MK18 41 E2
Foskett Way HP21 115 E5
Fossey Cl MK5 45 F3
Foster Ave SL4 209 E4
Foster Cl HP20 101 F3
Fosters La MK13 34 A3
Fosters Path SL2 197 F1
Fotherby Ct SL6 203 A6
Fotheringay Gdns SL1 205 A6
Fotherley Rd WD3 178 F8
Founders Mews MK14 34 F6
Foundry La
Horton SL3 212 B4
Lacey Green HP27 149 C5
Fountain Ct
6 Aylesbury HP20 115 D8
1 Olney MK46 6 F3
Fountaine Cl MK14 34 E7
Fountain Gdns SL4 210 D4
FOUR ASHES 162 D4
Four Ashes Rd HP15 162 C5
Fourdrinier Ct HP11 174 A4
Four Oaks HP5 144 A4
Fourth Ave SL7 184 A2
Fourth St HP11 173 B4
Fourways Mews HP12 172 C4
Fowler MK14 34 C7
Fowler Rd HP19 115 B8
Fowlers Farm Rd HP14 158 E4
Foxborough Cl SL3 207 A1
Foxborough Ct SL6 202 E4
Foxborough Prim Sch
SL3 207 A1
Fox Cl HP23 119 D1
Fox Cover OX39 147 C6
Fox Covert La MK19 20 A5
Foxcovert Rd MK5 45 F4
Foxdell Way SL9 177 E5
Foxes Piece SL7 183 E2
Foxes Piece Sch SL7 183 E3
Fox Farm Rd MK17 59 D6
Foxfield MK10 36 B3
Fox Field HP15 162 F5
Foxgate MK16 22 B4
Foxglove HP21 115 B5
Foxglove Cl MK18 52 C7
Foxglove Ct MK16 21 F4
Foxgoles Cl MK19 31 F5
Foxherne SL3 206 C4
Foxhill MK46 6 E5
Foxhill Cl HP13 162 B1
Foxhollow Dr SL2 198 C7
Foxhunter Dr MK14 34 E6
Fox La HP15 163 B6
Foxleigh HP11 173 A4
Foxley Pl MK5 46 C8
FOX MILNE 35 F4
Fox Milne Rdbt MK10 35 F4
Foxmoor Ct UB9 190 A5
Fox Rd
Holmer Green HP15 163 B6
Slough SL3 206 D2
Wigginton HP23 119 C2
Foxton MK6 47 D6
Fox Way MK18 52 E7
Fraderica Cotts MK16 22 C3
Framers Ct HP14 171 B4
Framewood Manor
SL2 199 C6
Framewood Rd
Slough SL3 188 C1
Wexham Street SL2, SL3 199 C6
Framlingham Ct MK5 46 A5
Frampton Gr 11 MK4 45 F1
France Furlong MK14 34 F8
Frances Ave SL6 196 C1
Frances Ct LU7 80 E7
Frances Rd SL4 210 D5
Frances St HP5 144 C2
Franchise St 3 HP5 144 C1
Francis Ct MK5 46 B6
Francis House Prep Sch
HP23 118 F3
Francis Way SL1 204 D6
Frank Atter Croft MK12 33 C5
Frank Howe Ct MK6 35 A1
Franklin Ave SL2 205 B8
Franklin Cl HP17 127 A7
Franklin Ct HP7 154 C1
Franklin Rd
Dunstable LU6 93 F8
Haddenham HP17 127 A7
Franklins Croft MK12 33 C5
FRANKLIN'S SPRING 178 D5
Frank Lunnon Cl SL8 185 C3
Franklyn Cres SL4 209 D4
Frankston Ave MK11 32 E5
Frank Sutton Way SL1 205 D6
Frankswood Ave UB7 208 F7
Frantons The SL6 202 A7
Frascati Way SL6 202 F7
Fraser Rd HP12 172 C5
Fraucup Cl HP17 128 B7
Fraunchies Ct SL1 205 E6
Frays Ave UB7 208 D4
Frays Cl UB7 208 D3
Fray's Ct UB8 201 C5
Frayslea UB8 201 C3
Frays Valley Nature
Reserve* UB10 201 D8
Fray's Waye UB8 201 C4
Frederick Pl HP11 174 B3
Fredericks Ct HP9 186 A8
Frederick Smith Ct
MK12 33 D4
Frederick St HP18 99 A7
Freeman Cl MK12 33 B5
Freeman Ct HP5 144 C1
Freemans Cl SL2 199 A6
Freemans Gdns MK46 7 A3
Freer Cres HP13 174 A4
Fremantle Rd
Aylesbury HP21 115 E5
High Wycombe HP13 162 E2
Frenchum Gdns SL1 204 E5
Frensham Dr MK2 58 C7
Frensham Wlk SL2 198 C6
Freshfield Ave 1 MK10 36 A3
Friarage Rd HP20 115 D8
Friarscroft Way HP20 115 C8
Friars Field HP4 134 E7
Friars Furlong HP18 125 B7
Friars Gdns HP14 162 A7
Friars Walk HP16 151 D5
Friars Wlk HP23 119 A4
Friary Gdns MK16 22 C2
Friary Island TW19 211 C1
Friary Rd TW19 211 C1
Friary The SL4 211 C1
Friday Ct OX9 125 F1
Friday St
Henley-on-Thames RG9 191 E2
Leighton Buzzard LU7 80 F7
FRIETH 170 F1
Frieth CE Comb Sch
RG9 170 F1
Frieth Rd SL7 182 E5
Frimley Dr SL1 204 F4
Fripp Gdns MK8 45 D6
Frithe The SL2 206 B7
FRITH-HILL 152 C7
Frith Hill
Great Missenden HP16 152 B7
South Heath HP16 152 C8
Frithsden Copse HP4 135 F8
Frithwood Cres MK7 48 B7
Froggy La UB9 189 D1
Frog La HP18 112 F3
Frogmill SL6 193 C3
Frogmill Ct SL6 193 C3
Frogmill Spinney SL6 193 C4
Frogmoor HP13 173 A7
Frogmore Cl
Hughenden Valley
HP14 162 A7
Slough SL1 205 A4
Frogmore Cotts SL4 210 E5
Frogmore Ct 4 SL6 202 F7
Frogmore Dr SL4 210 F5
Frogmore Flats SL4 210 F5
Frogmore Ho* SL4 210 F5
Frogmore La HP18 125 C5
Frogmore St HP23 119 A3
Frome Cl HP21 115 C5
Fromer Rd HP10 185 D4
Frost Ho 4 HP4 135 C3
Froxfield Ct MK4 46 C1
Fryday St MK6 46 E7
Fryer Cl HP5 154 D6
Fryers Ct 3 HP12 172 D8
Fryers La HP12 172 D8
Frymley View SL4 209 D6
Fuggle Dr HP21 115 E5
Fulbrook Mid Sch MK17 49 B5
Fullbrook Cl SL6 203 A8
Fuller's Cl HP5 154 B6
Fuller's Hill HP5, HP6 154 A6
FULLERS SLADE 33 A4
Fullers Yd SL6 196 B2
Fulmar Pl 1 HP19 101 F3
FULMER 199 C8
Fulmer Chase SL3 199 C8
Fulmer Common Rd SL3,
SL0 199 E6
Fulmer Dr SL9 188 D2
Fulmer Inf Sch SL3 199 E8
Fulmer La SL9 189 A2
Fulmer Rd SL3 188 F2
Fulmer St
Milton Keynes, Emerson
Valley MK4 46 C3
Milton Keynes, Medbourne MK8,
MK5 45 E6
Fulmer Way SL9 188 E5
Fulton Cl HP13 173 A8
FULWELL 39 A2
Fulwell Ct MK14 34 E8
Fulwell Rd
Finmere MK18 50 C7
Westbury NN13 39 A4
Fulwood Ct TW19 213 F1
Fulwoods Dr MK6 47 A8
Furlong Cl SL8 185 B3
Furlong Cres HP17 115 A1
Furlong La LU6 93 C7
Furlong Rd SL8 185 B3
Furlong The 12 HP23 119 A3
Furness SL4 209 C5
Furness Cres MK3 47 A1
Furness Pl 8 SL4 209 C5
Furness Row 9 SL4 209 C5
Furness Sq 6 SL4 209 C5
Furness Way SL4 209 C5
Furness Wlk 7 SL4 209 C5
Furnival Ave SL2 205 B8
Furrow Cl HP21 115 D4
Furrows The UB9 190 C6
Furrow Way SL6 202 A4
FURTHO 19 A3
Furtho Ct MK19 32 B7
Furtho La NN12 18 E3
Fury Ct MK8 45 F7
Furze Down Specl Sch
MK18 65 E4
Furze Field La HP16 142 B8
Furzefield Rd HP9 175 C2
Furzeham Rd UB7 208 E4
Furze La MK18 65 E5
Furzen Cl SL2 198 A2
FURZE PLATT 195 C2
Furze Platt Inf Sch SL6 195 C1
Furze Platt Jun Sch
SL6 195 C1
Furze Platt Rd SL6 195 B1
Furze Platt Senior Sch
SL6 195 C2
Furze Platt Sta SL6 195 E1
Furze Rd SL6 195 D1
Furze View WD3 167 C4
Furze Way MK12 33 C6
FURZTON 46 D4
Furzton Rdbt MK4 46 C4
Fuzzens Wlk SL4 209 E5
Fyfield Barrow MK7 48 C6
Fyne Dr LU7 80 C8

G

Gables Cl
Chalfont St Peter SL9 177 E6
Datchet SL3 211 A8
Maidenhead SL6 203 B8
Wendover HP22 131 A4
Gables Dr HP14 149 C1
Gables Mdw HP15 163 C6
Gables The
Datchet SL3 211 A8
Haddenham HP17 127 A5
Leighton Buzzard LU7 80 E6
Gable Thorne MK7 48 D6
Gabriel Cl MK7 48 C5
Gaddesden Cres MK7 48 C6
Gadge Cl OX9 125 E1
Gadmore La HP23 132 F7
Gadsden Cl MK43 25 D3
Gadsden Ct MK17 69 E8
Gage Cl SL6 202 E4
Gainsborough SL6 195 F5
Gainsborough Cl MK8 45 D6
Gainsborough Dr SL6 202 D3
Gainsborough Hill RG9 191 D1
Gainsborough Pl HP19 100 F3
Gainsborough Rd
Aylesbury HP21 115 E4
Gainsborough Rd *continued*
Henley-on-Thames RG9 191 D1
Gairloch Ave MK2 58 D5
Galahad Cl SL1 205 A4
Gallagher Cl MK8 45 E8
Galleries The 4 HP13 173 A7
Galley Hill MK11 32 F5
Galley La MK17 59 A4
Galleymead Rd SL3 212 F6
Galloway HP19 101 A3
Galloway Chase SL2 206 A6
Galloway Cl MK3 46 E2
Gallows La HP12 172 C8
Gallys Rd SL4 209 D6
Galsworthy Pl HP19 100 F2
Galvin Rd SL1 205 C6
Gamnel HP23 119 A6
Gamnel Mews HP23 119 B7
Gamnel Terr HP23 119 A6
Gandon Vale HP13 173 A8
Ganton Cl MK3 46 D1
Garamonde Dr MK8 33 F2
Garbo Cl MK8 45 D7
Garden Cl
Halton HP22 131 C8
Maidenhead SL6 202 A5
Garden Cotts SL3 212 D7
Garden Ct HP11 174 B3
Garden End HP6 154 E2
Gardener Wlk HP15 163 C6
Garden Field La HP4 135 F2
Garden Mews SL1 205 F5
Garden Reach HP8 166 D6
Gardens Cl HP14 158 F4
Gardens The MK18 53 F1
Gardiner Ct MK13 33 E6
Gardner Cl
Aylesbury HP19 101 A3
Great Kingshill HP15 151 D1
Gardner Ho SL6 195 E1
Gardner Rd SL6 195 D2
Gardner's Cl LU6 93 E7
Garfield Pl 1 SL4 210 C5
Garland Ct MK8 45 E8
Garland Way HP22 117 E5
Garner Ct 13 TW19 213 E1
Garners Cl SL9 177 F4
Garners End SL9 177 E4
Garners Rd SL9 177 E4
Garnet Cl SL1 205 A4
Garnet Ct SL7 183 C1
Garrard Rd SL2 197 F1
Garraways MK6 47 A6
Garrett Cl HP5 154 D6
Garretts La SL6 195 F2
Garrick Wlk MK9 34 F3
Garron Cl HP21 115 D3
Garrowmore Gr MK2 58 D5
Garry Cl MK2 58 C5
Garside Way HP20 102 A1
Garson Gr HP5 144 A2
Garston MK8 33 F1
Garthlands SL6 195 D2
Garth The HP16 152 A8
Garthwaite Cres MK5 46 A4
Garvin Ave HP9 175 E2
Garvin Mews HP9 175 E2
Garwood Cres MK8 45 C6
Gascon's Gr SL2 198 A1
Gaskin Ct MK14 35 A5
Gas La SL6 203 A3
Gatcombe MK8 33 F1
Gate Cotts WD3 167 D5
Gatehouse Cl
Aylesbury HP19 115 C8
Windsor SL4 210 B4
Gatehouse Sch The
MK14 34 D7
Gatehouse Way HP19 101 B1
Gatensbury Pl HP27 139 B3
Gatesdene Cl HP4 121 C8
Gates Orch HP22 117 D5
Gateway Ctr The HP12 172 D4
Gateway Sch The HP16 152 A8
Gatewick Cl SL1 205 E5
Gatewick La MK7 48 A3
Gatting Way UB8 201 E6
Gatward Ave SL6 202 A3
Gaveston Dr HP4 135 B6
Gaveston Rd SL2 197 F2
Gaviots Cl SL9 188 F3
Gaviots Gn SL9 188 F3
Gaviots Way SL9 188 E4
GAWCOTT 51 F4
Gawcott Fields MK18 52 B7
Gawcott Rd MK18 52 B6
Gawcott Road Ind Pk
MK18 52 B7
Gawdrey Cl HP5 154 D6
Gayal Croft MK5 46 B4
GAYHURST 12 D2
Gayhurst Ho MK16 12 D1
Gayhurst Rd HP13 173 F7
Gayhurst Sch SL9 188 C7
Gayton Cl HP6 154 E4
Gees Farm Cl NN7 1 A5
Gell Cl UB10 190 F1
George Cl SL7 183 F4
George Ct HP18 83 B5

GEORGE GREEN......206 E8
George Green Dr SL3..206 F7
George Green Rd SL3..206 E7
George Inn Pl MK16.....12 B6
George Lee Ct HP14....160 C1
George Rd HP14......158 E5
Georges Dr HP10......185 C7
George's Hill HP15.....162 F6
George St
18 Aylesbury HP20.....115 D8
Berkhamsted HP4......135 D4
5 Chesham HP5.......144 C1
High Wycombe HP11....172 F7
Milton Keynes MK2......47 E1
Uxbridge UB8.........201 D5
Wing LU7..............79 E2
Woburn MK17..........60 F7
George V Pl SL4.......210 D7
George Yd MK11.........32 D5
Georgian Cl UB10......201 E8
Georgian Hts SL8......185 B5
Geralds Ct HP13.......162 D1
Geralds Rd HP13.......162 D2
Gerard Cl MK13.........34 A7
Germains Cl HP5.......154 B7
Germain St HP5........154 B7
Germander Park First Sch MK14.........34 D4
Germander Pl MK14.....34 D4
GERRARDS CROSS......188 E5
Gerrards Cross CE Sch The SL9.........188 F4
Gerrards Cross Rd SL2.199 A6
Gerrards Cross Sta SL9 188 E6
Gershwin Ct MK7.......48 C4
Gervaise Cl SL1........204 F5
Ghyll Gdns HP4........134 D7
Gibbings Cl MK18.......76 A3
Gibbs Cl HP13.........172 F8
Gibbs Ho HP11.........173 F4
Gibbwin MK14..........34 E8
Gib La HP22...........102 D4
GIBRALTAR............113 D2
Gibraltar La SL6.......184 C1
Gibson Ct 9 SL3.......206 F1
Gibson La HP17........127 A5
Gibson Pl TW19........213 C1
Gibson Rd
High Wycombe HP12....172 B3
Ickenham UB10........201 F8
Gibsons Gn MK13.......34 C4
Gibsons Green MK13....34 C4
GIFFARD PARK..........22 A2
Giffard Park Prim Sch MK14.........22 A2
Giffard Park Rdbt MK14.21 F3
Giffard Rd MK2.........58 C6
Giffard Way HP18......125 C7
Gifford Gate MK14......34 E7
Gifford Pl MK18.........41 E1
Gilbert Cl MK3..........58 B7
Gilbert Ho 4 HP11.....172 E7
Gilbert Scott Ct 9 HP7 165 B7
Gilbert Scott Gdns MK18.........52 A4
Gilbert Scott Rd MK18...41 D2
Gilbert's Hill HP23.....132 E3
Gilbert Way
Berkhamsted HP4......135 A4
Slough SL3............206 F1
Gilbey Wlk HP10.......185 D4
Gilders Mews MK14......34 F6
Giles Brook Comb Sch MK4.........57 A7
Giles Gate HP16........151 B6
Gillamoor Cl 2 MK4....46 B3
Gilletts La HP12........161 C1
Gillfield Cl HP11.......172 E3
Gilliat Rd SL1..........205 E6
Gilliat's Gn WD3.......167 D5
Gilliatt Cl SL0.........207 E7
Gillions Pl HP21.......116 B7
Gillott Ct SL6..........202 F8
Gilman Cres SL4.......209 D4
Gilmore Cl SL3........206 C4
Gilmore Rd HP20.......101 E3
Gilpin's Ride HP4......135 D5
Gilpin Way MK46.........7 A4
Gingers Cl HP22.......117 E5
Gipsy La LU7............91 D8
Girton Way MK3.........58 B8
Gisburn Cl MK13.........34 B5
Glade Ho 5 SL7.......183 E2
Glade Rd SL7..........183 E2
Glade The
Gerrards Cross SL9.....188 D2
Tylers Green HP10.....163 C1
Glade View HP12.......172 A3
Gladstone Cl MK16......22 D3
Gladstone Ind Est 1 SL6.........202 E8
Gladstone Rd HP5.....144 C1
Gladstone Rise HP13...173 F6
Gladstone Way SL1.....205 A5
Glaisyer Way SL0......200 D3
Glamis Ct HP13........173 B8
Glamis Ho MK3..........57 E7
Glamorgan Cl MK3......46 F1
Glanmor Rd SL2.......206 B6
Glassmill Ho 4 HP4....135 D4
Glastonbury Cl MK3.....47 A2
Glastonbury Thorn Fst Sch MK5.........46 B6
Glaven Rd HP21........115 C4
Glazier Dr MK14.........34 F6
Glebe Cl
Chalfont St Peter SL9...177 D3
Dorney SL6...........203 F4
Holmer Green HP15.....163 B7
Maids Moreton MK18....41 F3
Milton Keynes MK5......46 A8
Pitstone LU7..........105 D5
Glebe Cotts HP14......169 C7
Glebe Dr NN13..........38 A7
Glebe Ho SL9..........177 D3
Glebe House Dr MK18...39 E6
Glebe La MK19..........10 E5
Glebelands HP10.......174 C8
Glebelands Cl HP16....151 E4
Glebe Rd
Chalfont St Peter SL9...177 C2
Deanshanger MK19.......31 E5
Maidenhead SL6.......203 B5
Old Windsor SL4.......211 B2
Uxbridge UB8.........201 C3
Glebe Rdbt MK9.........35 B4
Glebe Terr MK18.........41 F3
Glebe The
Lavendon MK46..........7 F8
Lewknor OX49.........157 B8
Prestwood HP16.......151 C7
Stone HP17...........114 C5
Walter's Ash HP14.....161 D6
West Drayton UB7......208 F2
Weston Turville HP22....116 F2
Glebe Way HP6........154 D3
Gledfield Pl MK12.......33 D4
Gleeman Cl MK12.......33 A5
Glenavon Gdns SL3....206 C3
Glenduragan Ct 9 MK4.45 F1
Gleneagles Cl
Milton Keynes MK3......57 D7
Stanwell TW19.........213 D1
Glenfield MK16.........22 D1
Glenfield Cl
Aylesbury HP21........116 A5
Stoke Poges SL2.......198 F4
Glenham Rd OX9.......126 B1
Glenister Rd
Chesham HP5.........144 C3
High Wycombe HP12....172 B4
Glenisters Rd HP13....173 A8
Glenmore Cl HP10.....174 A2
Glenmore Ho HP11.....174 B3
Glenore SL6...........196 A8
Glenstal Pl MK9.........35 A3
Glen The SL3..........206 C2
Glentworth Pl SL1.....205 C5
Glenwater Ho HP15....163 A5
Glenwoods MK16........22 C3
Glimbers Gr OX39......147 C5
Globe Ho UB7.........208 D5
Globe La LU7............70 E1
Globe Pk (Bsns Ctr) SL7.........183 F2
Globeside Bsns Pk SL7.183 F2
Glory Cl HP10..........185 F7
Glory Mill La
Beaconsfield HP9.......185 F8
Wooburn Green HP10...185 E7
Gloucester Ave SL1.....205 C8
Gloucester Ct UB9.....190 A4
Gloucester Pl SL4......210 D5
Gloucester Rd
Maidenhead SL6.......195 E2
Milton Keynes MK12.....33 D5
Glovers Ct 2 HP20.....101 E1
Glovers La MK13........34 B4
Glyn Sq MK12...........33 D7
Glyn St MK13...........34 A7
Glynswood
Chalfont St Peter SL9...177 F3
Chinnor OX39..........147 C6
High Wycombe HP13....162 B1
Glynswood Ho OX39....147 C6
Glynswood Rd MK18....41 C1
Glynwood Ho SL6......203 A7
Goathland Croft 2 MK4.46 B2
Goddards Croft MK12...33 C5
Goddington Rd SL8....185 A5
Godfreys Cl HP18.......96 B1
GODLINGTON............61 E3
Godolphin Inf Sch SL1.205 C7
Godolphin Jun Sch SL1.........205 D7
Godolphin Rd
Seer Green HP9.......176 C4
Slough SL1............205 D6
Godrevy Gr MK4........57 B8
Godstowe Prep Sch HP13.........173 B8
Godwin Cl MK7.........48 C7
Gogh Rd HP19.........100 F2
Gold Crest HP19.......101 F4
Golden Ball La SL6.....195 A3
Golden Dr MK6..........47 B8
Golden Hills OX39.....147 D6
Golden Mede HP18......99 B6
Golden Miller Ct LU7....79 E2
Golden Oak Cl SL2.....198 C6
Golden Riddy LU7.......80 E8
Golder's Cl HP18.......123 F3
Goldfield Inf Sch HP23.118 F3
Goldfield Rd HP23.....118 F3
Goldhawk Rd MK10.....47 E8
Gold Hill E SL9........177 D1
Gold Hill N SL9........177 C2
Gold Hill W SL9........177 C1
Goldilocks MK7.........48 B6
Goldmark Cl MK7.......48 D5
Gold Oak Wlk MK9......34 F3
Goldsmith Dr MK16.....21 F4
Gold St MK19...........11 A2
Goldsworthy Way SL1..204 C7
Golf Club La HP27.....139 E5
Golspie Croft MK12.....33 C4
Gomez Cl MK4..........45 D3
Gomm Pl HP13.........174 A4
Gomm Rd HP13........174 A4
Gomms Wood Cl HP9..175 B4
Gomms Wood Ho HP9.175 B4
Gomm Valley Wildlife Reserve★ HP13.......174 B5
Goodacres La HP27.....149 E6
Goodall Cl RG9........191 E1
Good Intent LU6........92 E4
Goodlake Ct UB9.......189 F4
Goodman Gdns MK6....47 D8
Goodman Pk SL2......206 C5
Goodrich Gn MK4.......56 E8
Goodrington Pl 2 MK10.36 A4
Goodwick Gr MK4.......57 B8
Goodwin Mdws HP10...185 E6
Goodwin Rd
Aylesbury HP19........115 C8
Slough SL2............197 F2
Goodwins Mead LU7...105 A7
Goodwin Villas SL1....204 F5
Goodwood MK8..........45 F8
Goodwood Rise SL7....183 C7
Goose Acre
Botley HP5............145 A1
Cheddington LU7.......105 A7
Goose Gn SL2..........198 B3
Goosemere MK19........31 E4
Goosen Gn HP21.......116 C6
Goran Ave MK11.........32 E4
Gordale MK13...........34 C5
Gordon Rd
Chesham HP5.........154 C7
High Wycombe HP13....173 D6
Maidenhead SL6.......202 D7
West Drayton UB7......208 E6
Windsor SL4..........209 F5
Gordon Way HP8.......177 B7
Gore Cl UB9...........190 C7
Gore Hill HP7.........165 B5
Gorelands La HP8......177 F8
Gorell Rd HP9.........176 B1
Gore Rd SL1...........197 B2
Gore The SL1..........197 A2
Goring MK14...........34 C7
Gorman Pl MK2.........58 E4
Gorrell Cl MK18.........51 B6
Gorrell La MK18.........51 B6
Gorricks MK11...........32 D4
Gorse Meade SL1......205 B5
Gorse Rd SL6..........195 E6
Gorse Wlk
Hazlemere HP15.......163 A3
West Drayton UB7......208 E7
Gosforth Pl SL1.......204 F6
Goslar Way SL4.......210 B5
Gosling Gn SL3........206 E3
Gosling Gr HP13.......161 D2
Gosling Rd SL3........206 E3
Gossage Rd UB10......201 F5
GOSSARD'S GREEN......25 C4
Goss Ave HP18..........99 B6
Gossmore Cl SL7.......183 F1
Gossmore La SL7.......183 F1
Gossmore Wlk SL7.....183 F1
Gossom's End HP4.....135 A5
Gossoms Ryde HP4....135 A5
Goswell Hill SL4.......210 D6
Goswell Rd SL4........210 D6
Goudhurst Ct MK7......48 B7
Governors Cl HP6......154 F1
Gower Ho HP6.........154 E3
Gowers Field HP19, HP20.........101 D1
Gowers The HP6.......154 E2
Gowings Gn SL1.......204 E4
Goya Pl HP19..........100 F2
Grable Ave MK4.........45 E3
Grace Ave MK6..........46 E8
Grace Ct SL1..........205 C5
Grace Reading HP13...173 E6
Grace Reading Cl HP13 173 E6
Graces Cl MK43..........25 C3
Graces Maltings 4 HP23.........119 A3
Graeme Ave HP16......151 C6
Grafham Cl MK14.......35 A8
Grafton Cl
Maidenhead SL6.......195 E2
Potterspury NN12.......18 E3
Grafton Cl *continued*
Slough SL3............206 E7
Grafton Ct NN7...........4 A8
Grafton Gate MK9.......34 C1
Grafton Ho OX39.......147 C6
Grafton Orch OX39....147 D7
Grafton Park MK9.......34 D1
Grafton Rd
Aylesbury HP19........101 A2
Yardley Gobion NN12.....18 F6
GRAFTON REGIS..........9 D2
Grafton St
High Wycombe HP12....172 D8
Milton Keynes, Bradwell MK13.........34 B4
Milton Keynes, Granby MK1.........47 B3
Milton Keynes, New Bradwell MK12, MK13, MK19....33 E8
Milton Keynes, Winterhill MK6.........46 E7
Graham Cl SL6.........202 C5
Graham Dr HP12.......172 B5
Graham Ho SL9........177 C1
Graham Rd SL6........195 E6
Grainge Chase MK17....55 A3
Grainge Cl NN13........39 A5
Grampian Gate MK6.....46 E7
Grampian Way SL3.....207 A1
Gramwell MK5..........45 F7
Granary Cl MK19........21 A3
GRANBOROUGH..........75 E7
Granborough Rd
North Marston MK18.....76 A2
Winslow MK18...........65 E2
GRANBY.................47 B3
Granby Ct MK1..........47 A3
Granby Ind Est MK1.....47 B3
Granby Rdbt MK1.......47 C3
Grandison Ho RG9......191 E3
Grand Union Office Pk The UB8.........208 C7
Granes End MK14.......34 E8
Grange Chase MK17.....55 A3
Grange Cl
Chalfont St Peter SL9...177 E2
Leighton Buzzard LU7....80 D6
Maids Moreton MK18....41 E3
Twyford MK18...........62 D2
Wraysbury TW19.......211 E1
Grange Cotts HP16.....152 A3
Grange Dr HP10.......185 D3
Grange Farm Rd HP14..159 B7
Grange Farm Rdbt MK8.45 D7
Grange Fields SL9.....177 E2
Grange Gdn HP18.......83 A6
Grange Gdns
Farnham Common SL2...198 D7
Wendover HP22........131 B5
Grange La SL6.........195 F8
Grangelands & Pulpit Hill Reserve★ HP27.......139 F6
Grange Rd
Chalfont St Peter SL9...177 E2
Cookham Rise SL6......195 F7
Hazlemere HP15.......162 F4
Hazlemere, Widmer End HP15.........162 E5
Henley-on-Thames RG9..191 E1
Milton Keynes MK3......57 F7
Pitstone LU7..........105 D5
Tring HP23............119 C4
Wilstone HP23.........104 D1
Grangers Croft MK12....33 C4
Grange Sch The HP21..115 F6
Grange The
Burnham SL1..........197 C2
Gerrards Cross SL9.....188 E6
Old Windsor SL4.......211 B2
Wraysbury TW19.......211 E1
Grange View HP27.....139 E7
Grange Way SL0.......207 F7
Grangewood SL3......206 C8
Grant Ave SL1.........205 E7
Grantham Ct MK5.......46 C5
Grantham Mews HP4...135 D4
Grant Ho 6 SL8.......185 A4
Granville Ave SL2.....205 D8
Granville Dene HP3....146 A4
Granville Pl 5 HP20....115 D8
Granville Rd HP4.......134 E6
Granville Sq MK15......35 C7
Granville St 4 HP20...115 D8
Grapevine Cl HP11.....173 F4
Grasholm Way SL3.....207 C2
Grasmere
Aylesbury HP21........116 B5
Windsor SL4..........209 E7
Grasmere Ave SL2.....206 A6
Grasmere Par SL2.....206 B6
Grasmere Way
Leighton Buzzard LU7....80 D7
Milton Keynes MK2......58 D6
Grasscroft MK4.........46 E4
Grass Hays HP21.......116 C7
Grassingham End SL9..177 E3
Grassingham Rd SL9...177 E3
Grassington MK13.......34 A5
Grasslands HP20.......102 A1
Grassy La SL6..........202 E7
Grattan Ct SL7.........184 A3
Gratton Ct MK4..........46 C3
Gratton Dr SL4.........209 E3
Gravel Dr HP23........118 B3
GRAVEL HILL...........177 F4
Gravel Hill
Chalfont St Peter SL9...177 E3
Henley-on-Thames RG9..191 D2
Uxbridge UB8.........201 D7
Gravelly Way HP10.....163 F2
Gravel Path HP4.......135 E5
Gravel Wlk MK46.........13 F7
Graveney Pl MK6........35 B2
Grayburn Cl HP8.......177 A8
Graylands Cl SL1.......204 F5
Grayling Cl SL7........194 C8
Grayling Ct HP4........134 F6
Grays Cl NN12..........17 D8
Grays La
Paulerspury NN12.......17 D8
Yardley Gobion NN12.....18 E6
Gray's La
High Wycombe HP13....161 D2
Ibstone HP14..........169 C7
Gray's Mon★ SL2......198 F2
Grays Park Rd SL2.....199 A3
Gray's Pl SL2..........205 F5
Gray's Rd
Slough SL1............205 F5
Uxbridge UB10.........201 E5
Grays Wlk HP5.........144 B2
Greamesdyke Rd HP4..135 A3
Greatacre 7 HP5......144 C1
Great Benty UB7.......208 E2
GREAT BRICKHILL........59 D2
Great Brickhill La MK17.59 D5
Greatchesters MK13.....33 F5
Great Denson MK6......47 A8
GREATGAP.............105 D6
Great Ground MK14.....34 E7
GREAT HAMPDEN.......150 D7
Greatheed Dell MK7.....48 D4
Great Hill Cres SL6.....202 C6
GREAT HIVINGS.........144 A3
Great Hivings HP5.....144 A4
GREAT HOLM.............45 E8
GREAT HORWOOD.......55 A1
Great Horwood CE Comb Sch MK17.........55 A3
Great Horwood Rd MK18 65 F7
GREAT KIMBLE.........139 E8
Great Kimble CE Inf Sch HP17.........129 E1
GREAT KINGSHILL......162 E8
Great Kingshill CE Comb Sch HP15.........162 C6
Great La
Bierton HP22..........102 A4
Wendover HP22........131 B4
Great Linch MK10.......36 A2
GREAT LINFORD.........34 E8
Great Linford Comb Sch MK14.........34 E8
Great Linford Lakes★ MK14.........21 D3
Great Marlow Sch SL7.183 F4
Great Meadow Way HP19.........114 F8
GREAT MISSENDEN.....152 A6
Great Missenden CE Comb Sch HP16.........152 B7
Great Missenden Sta HP16.........152 A7
Great Monks St
Milton Keynes, Wolverton MK12.........33 C5
Milton Keynes, Wymbush MK8.........33 E2
Great Ormes MK4.......56 F8
Great Pasture MK10.....35 F3
Great Slade MK18.......52 D6
Great Stone HP18......112 F3
Great Western St 22 HP20.........115 D8
Greaves Rd HP13......173 D6
Grebe Cl HP19.........101 F3
Grecian St HP20.......116 A8
Greenacre SL4.........209 E5
Green Acre HP21......116 A7
Greenacres
Aylesbury HP22.........89 B2
Pitstone LU7..........105 C4
Greenacres Ave UB10..190 F1
Green Acres Cl HP22....86 E7
Greenacres La HP10...163 A1
Greenacres The HP13..162 C1
Greenbury Cl WD3.....167 C5
Green Cl
Burnham SL6..........204 A7
High Wycombe HP13....173 F7
Maidenhead SL6.......195 F1
Green Common La HP10, HP9, SL1.........186 C4
Green Cres HP10.......185 C7
Greendale Mews SL2...206 A6

Green Dragon La HP10 185 B7
Green East Rd HP9 176 E3
Greene Field Rd HP4 135 C4
GREEN END
Granborough 76 A7
High Wycombe 160 A4
Green End
Aylesbury HP20 115 D8
Granborough MK18 76 A7
Great Brickhill MK17 59 D2
Green End La MK19 11 A3
Green End Rd HP14 159 E5
Green End St HP22 117 E5
Greenes Ct HP4 135 C5
Greene Wlk HP4 135 D3
Green Farm Rd MK16 22 C4
Greenfern Ave SL1 204 C7
GREENFIELD 168 A4
Greenfield End SL9 177 F3
Greenfield Rd MK16 22 A4
Greenfields
Adstock MK18 53 F1
Maidenhead SL6 203 A5
Upper Arncott OX6 94 D7
Green Ground OX33 123 A2
Green Hailey HP27 139 F3
Green Hill HP13 162 B1
Greenhill Cl MK5 46 A8
Green Hill Cl HP13 162 C1
Green Hill Gate HP13 162 B1
Green La
Amersham HP6 154 E2
Aspley Guise MK17 49 E4
Botley HP5 155 B6
Bovingdon HP3 146 A3
Burnham SL1 197 D4
Chesham Bois HP6 154 D3
Datchet SL3 211 B6
Eaton Bray LU6 92 D7
Farnham Common SL2 198 B6
Ivinghoe LU7 105 E5
Maidenhead SL6 203 A6
Milton Keynes MK12 33 D6
Owlswick HP27 128 B1
Prestwood HP16 151 E6
Radnage HP14 159 D5
Stokenchurch HP14 158 C5
Upper Arncott OX6 94 E7
Windsor SL4 210 B5
Greenlands
Flackwell Heath HP10 185 B8
Lacey Green HP27 149 D5
Greenlands Cl MK16 22 A3
Greenlands Ct SL6 202 B8
Greenlands La HP16 151 B7
Green Lane Cl HP6 154 D3
Green Lane Ct SL1 197 C2
Green Lane Rdbt MK9 35 B5
Greenlaw Pl MK3 47 A3
Greenleaf Ct SL3 211 A8
Greenleas Lower Sch LU7 80 C7
GREENLEYS 33 B5
Green Leys
High Wycombe HP13 161 C2
Maidenhead SL6 195 F2
Greenleys Fst Sch MK12 33 C5
Greenleys Jun Sch MK12 33 C5
Greenleys La MK12 33 C4
Greenleys Rdbt MK12 33 B6
Green North Rd HP9 176 E4
Greenock Rd SL1 205 A7
Green Park Dr MK16 22 C3
Green Park Sch MK16 22 B3
Green Path HP22, HP23 118 D4
Green Pk HP16 151 D6
Green Pl HP10 185 C8
Green Rd HP13 162 C2
Greenridge HP10 174 B8
Greensand View MK17 49 B5
Greenside
Bourne End SL8 185 A5
Prestwood HP16 151 C5
Slough SL2 205 A8
Greenside Hill MK4 46 B1
Greens Keep HP17 126 F6
Green St
Chorleywood WD3 167 C6
Hazlemere HP15 162 F4
High Wycombe HP11 172 F7
Green The
Amersham HP7 154 C1
Aston Abbotts HP22 88 D4
Brill HP18 110 B8
Burnham SL1 197 B1
Chalfont St Giles HP8 177 C8
Chearsley HP18 112 B2
Cheddington LU7 105 A7
Cosgrove MK19 19 F2
Cranfield MK43 24 E2
Cuddington HP18 112 F3
Deanshanger MK19 31 E4
Edlesborough LU6 92 F4
Great Horwood MK17 55 A3
Hanslope MK19 11 A2
Green The *continued*
Horton-cum-S OX33 108 A5
Hyde Heath HP6 153 C5
Little Missenden HP7 153 A2
Longwick HP27 138 D6
Maidenhead SL6 195 C7
Mentmore LU7 90 D4
Milton Keynes, Loughton MK5 46 A8
Milton Keynes, The Green MK6 47 C8
Newport Pagnell MK16 22 C4
Paulerspury NN12 17 B7
Pitstone LU7 105 D4
Quainton HP22 85 B5
Slough SL1 205 D4
Soulbury LU7 69 E3
Stoke Hammond MK17 69 E7
Thornborough MK18 54 A8
Turvey MK43 8 E5
West Drayton UB7 208 D3
Wingrave HP22 89 B2
Wooburn Green HP10 185 E5
Wraysbury TW19 211 E1
Green Tiles UB9 189 F4
Green Tiles La UB9 189 F5
Green Verges SL7 183 E3
Green View HP20 102 A2
Green View Cl HP3 146 A2
Greenway
Berkhamsted HP4 135 A4
Burnham SL1 197 B3
Chesham HP5 144 B3
Great Horwood MK17 55 A2
Haddenham HP17 126 F5
Milton Keynes MK10 36 C3
2 Thame OX9 125 F1
Green Way MK17 57 D4
Greenway Bsns Pk MK17 55 A1
Greenway Ct 12 HP13 173 B7
Greenway Fst Sch HP4 134 F4
Greenway Par HP5 144 B3
Greenways
Bow Brickhill MK17 48 C2
Eaton Bray LU6 92 D7
Greenways Dr SL6 202 A8
Greenway The
Gerrards Cross SL9 188 D8
High Wycombe HP13 173 B7
Slough SL1 204 D5
Tring HP23 118 F5
Tylers Green HP10 163 B1
Uxbridge UB8 201 D3
Greenway Wlk MK18 41 F1
Green West Rd HP9 176 E3
Greenwich Gdns MK16 22 C2
Greenwood HP14 150 A2
Greenwood Ave OX39 147 C5
Greenwood Cl
Amersham HP6 154 E1
Seer Green HP9 176 D4
Greenwood Mdw OX39 147 D6
Greenwood Pl MK18 63 D3
Greenwood The HP22 117 D5
Greenyard The NN7 1 B7
Greetham Rd HP21 116 C6
Gregories Ct HP9 175 D3
Gregories Dr MK7 48 D6
Gregories Farm La HP9 175 D2
Gregories Rd HP9 175 C3
Gregory Dr SL4 211 B1
Gregory Rd SL2 187 D2
Grenadine Way HP23 119 A5
Grendon Rd
Edgcott HP18 72 F1
Kingswood HP18 83 C3
GRENDON UNDERWOOD 83 A6
Grendon Underwood Comb Sch HP18 83 A6
Grendon Way HP22 102 A4
Grenfell Ave
High Wycombe HP12 172 D7
Maidenhead SL6 202 F6
Grenfell Pl SL6 202 F6
Grenfell Rd
Beaconsfield HP9 175 E3
Maidenhead SL6 202 E6
Grenville Ave HP22 131 A7
Grenville Cl SL1 197 B3
Grenville Comb Sch MK18 52 D7
Grenville Ct WD3 167 C5
Grenville Gn HP21 115 D4
Grenville Rd
Aylesbury HP21 115 D5
Buckingham MK18 41 C1
Grenville Way OX9 126 B1
Gresham Ct HP4 135 B3
Gresham Rd SL1 205 A7
Greyfriars Ct MK10 36 B2
Greyhound Ct MK18 66 A4
Greyhound La
Thame OX9 125 F1
Winslow MK18 66 A4
Greyhound Wlk OX9 125 F1
Greys Hill RG9 191 D1
Greys Rd RG9 191 D1
Greys The MK6 47 C8
Greystoke Cl HP4 135 A3
Greystoke Rd SL2 204 F8
Greystonley 1 MK4 46 C2
Griffin Cl
Maidenhead SL6 202 E5
Slough SL1 205 C4
Griffin Field LU7 78 E8
Griffin Ind Mall HP19 101 B1
Griffin La HP19 101 B1
Griffin Lane Ind Est HP19 101 B1
Griffith Gate MK10 36 A3
Griffith Gate Rdbt MK10 36 A2
Griffith Ho HP10 174 C2
Griffiths Acre HP17 114 E5
Griffiths Yd HP5 144 B1
Griffon Cl MK6 47 A7
Grigby Rise MK6 47 A7
Griggs Orch MK16 14 A2
Grimbold Ct MK15 35 C7
Grimmer Cl HP19 100 F3
Grimms Hill HP16 151 F7
Grimms Mdw HP14 150 B1
Grimsby Rd SL1 204 F4
Grimsdell's La HP6 154 D2
Grimsdyke Rd HP23 119 D1
Gringer Hill SL6 202 E8
Grizedale MK13 34 B5
Groombridge MK7 48 A7
Groom Rd HP16 151 C5
Groomsby Dr LU7 105 E5
Grooms Cotts HP5 145 B1
Grooms Ct HP11 174 A4
Grosmont Cl 1 MK4 46 B2
Grosvenor Cl SL0 200 D2
Grosvenor Ct SL1 205 E7
Grosvenor Dr SL6 203 C8
Grosvenor Way HP19 114 E8
Groundsel Cl MK7 48 B6
Grove Ash MK1 47 D3
Grovebury Rd LU7 80 F4
Grove Cl
Chalfont St Peter SL9 177 C2
1 Slough SL1 206 A3
Grove Cotts UB9 190 C8
Grove Ct
Beaconsfield HP9 175 D2
Bierton HP22 102 C5
Maidenhead SL6 202 D7
Turvey MK43 8 E6
Grove End SL9 177 C2
Grove End Barns OX9 126 B4
Grove Gdns HP23 119 B5
Grove Hill SL9 177 C3
Grove Ind Sch The MK5 46 C7
Grove La
Ashley Green HP5 145 C5
Chalfont St Peter SL9 177 C2
Little Kimble HP17 129 E2
Uxbridge UB8 201 F1
Grovelands HP11 173 A6
Grove Leys HP23 119 C5
Grove Pk HP23 119 C5
Grove Rd
Amersham HP6 154 F1
Beaconsfield HP9 175 E2
Burnham SL1, SL2 197 E4
Hazlemere HP15 162 F3
High Wycombe HP12 172 C8
Maidenhead SL6 202 F7
Tring HP23 119 C5
Turvey MK43 8 E6
Uxbridge UB8 201 D5
Windsor SL4 210 D5
Grove Road Prim Sch HP23 119 C5
Grovers Ct HP27 139 A2
Grovesbrook MK17 48 D2
Groves Cl SL8 185 C3
Groves Rd HP22 131 E7
Groves Way
Chesham HP5 143 F2
Cookham Rise SL6 195 E6
Grove The
Amersham HP6 154 D4
Latimer HP5 155 D3
Medmenham SL7 193 E6
Milton Keynes, Bradwell MK13 34 A4
Milton Keynes, Rickley Park MK3 58 A8
Newport Pagnell MK16 22 B3
Slough SL1 206 A4
Tring HP23 119 C5
Waddesdon HP18 99 A6
Groveway
Bow Brickhill MK7 48 B7
Milton Keynes, Redmoor MK3 47 A3
Milton Keynes, Simpson MK6 47 D5
Grove Way
Chorleywood WD3 167 B4
Uxbridge UB8 201 D5
Waddesdon HP18 99 A6
Grovewood Cl WD3 167 B4
Grubbins La HP27 150 B5
Grubbs Cl LU7 68 D2
Grubwood La SL6 195 A7
Grundy Ho UB8 201 D3
Gryms Dyke HP16 151 D6
Guards Club Rd SL6 203 C7
Guards Rd SL4 209 C5
Guards View SL4 210 D6
Guards Wlk 1 SL4 209 C5
GUBBLECOTE 104 D3
Guernsey Cl HP19 101 A3
Guest Gdns MK13 34 B8
Guildford Ave MK4 45 E1
Guildford Cl MK18 52 A4
Guillemot Way HP19 101 E3
Guinea Orch MK46 6 E4
Guinions Rd HP13 173 F5
Guise Ct MK17 49 F4
Gullet Nature Reserve The★ SL6 202 E5
Gullicot Way LU7 105 C4
Gulliver's SL4 210 D8
Gulliver's Dinosuar & Farm Park★ MK15 35 C4
Gulliver's Land★ MK15 35 C4
Gull Way 4 HP19 101 F3
Gundale Ct MK4 46 B2
Gun La MK16 14 A2
Gunmaker Ct MK14 34 F6
Gunthorpe Rd SL7 184 A3
Gunver La MK4 57 B8
Gurnard Cl UB7 208 D6
Gurnards Ave MK6 35 A2
Gurnells Rd HP9 176 C5
Gurney Cl
10 Aylesbury HP20 101 F2
Beaconsfield HP9 175 D2
Milton Keynes MK5 46 A7
Gurney Ct LU6 92 F6
Gurneys Mdw HP15 163 D7
Guttmann Rd HP21 115 F5
Gwendale SL6 195 C1
Gweneth Ct SL7 183 D3
Gwent Cl SL6 202 B4
Gwynant Ct MK2 58 C3
Gwynne Cl
Tring HP23 119 A5
Windsor SL4 209 E6
Gynant Rd HP13 173 F6
Gyosei International Sch UK MK15 35 C5
Gypsy La
Aspley Guise MK17 49 F3
High Wycombe HP11 173 D5
Marlow SL7 183 E4
Stoke Poges SL2 187 E1

H

Haberley Mead MK13 34 B3
Hackett Pl MK16 24 A6
HADDENHAM 127 B5
Haddenham Airfield HP17 126 E7
Haddenham Bsns Pk HP17 126 F7
Haddenham Com Inf Sch HP17 127 A6
Haddenham Jun Sch HP17 127 A6
Haddenham Mus★ HP17 126 F6
Haddenham Rd HP17 127 A3
Haddenham St Mary's CE Sch HP17 127 A4
Haddenham & Thame Parkway Sta HP17 126 E6
Haddington Cl
Milton Keynes MK3 46 E2
Wendover HP22 131 D6
Haddington Way HP20 102 A1
Haddon MK8 45 F8
Haddon Rd
Chorleywood WD3 167 C4
Maidenhead SL6 202 C5
Hadfield Rd TW19 213 D1
Hadland Cl HP3 146 A4
Hadley Ct SL3 212 E6
Hadley Pl MK13 34 C3
Hadlow Ct SL1 205 C5
Hadrians Dr MK13 34 A5
Hadrian's Gate NN13 38 A7
Haggar St HP17 114 B5
Hag Hill La SL6 204 A7
Hag Hill Rise SL6 204 A7
Haglis Dr HP22 131 B6
Haig Dr SL1 205 B4
Haileybury Ct SL4 210 A4
Hailey Croft OX39 147 B6
Hailey Ct SL6 202 F5
Hainault Ave MK14 22 A1
Haines Cl HP19 100 F2
Haines Rd HP15 162 F6
Haithewaite MK8 33 D1
Haldene MK8 33 E2
Hale SL4 209 F6
Hale Ave MK11 32 E5
Hale La HP22 131 E3
Hale Leys Sh Ctr 23 HP20 115 D8
Hale Rd HP22 131 C3
Hales Croft HP21 116 B4
Hale St HP20 115 E8
Halfacre Hill SL9 177 F2
Halfway Hos
Hanslope MK19 10 F4
Maidenhead SL6 195 E4
Halfway House La HP5 153 F7
Halifax Cl SL6 202 A8
Halifax Ho HP7 166 C8
Halifax Rd
Heronsgate WD3 167 C2
High Wycombe HP12 172 D5
Maidenhead SL6 202 A8
Halifax Way SL6 202 A8
Halings La UB9 189 E7
Halkingcroft SL3 206 C4
Hall Cl
High Wycombe HP13 173 F5
Maids Moreton MK18 41 F3
Old Stratford MK19 32 B6
Hall Cotts HP18 82 F7
Hall Ct SL3 211 B7
Halldore Hill SL6 195 E7
Hall La MK16 23 C8
Hall Mdw SL1 197 C3
Hall Park Gate HP4 135 E3
Hall Park Hill HP4 135 E3
Hall Pk HP4 135 E3
Hall Place (Berkshire Coll of Agriculture) SL6 194 A1
Halls Cnr HP10 174 A1
Halse Dr SL1 197 F7
Halswell Pl MK10 36 A3
HALTON 117 D1
Haltonchesters MK13 33 F6
Halton Comb Sch HP22 131 D7
Halton La HP22 131 B8
Halton Wood Forest Wlks★ HP23 132 A5
Halton Wood Rd HP22 131 D5
Haly Cl MK13 34 B4
Hamberlins La HP4, HP23 134 B7
HAMBLEDEN 181 D1
Hambleden RG9 181 C2
Hambleden Mill RG9 192 C7
Hambleden Pl RG9 192 D6
Hambleden Rise RG9 192 D8
Hambleden Wlk SL6 195 E3
Hambledon Cl HP21 116 B5
Hamble Dr HP21 115 C6
Hambleton Gr MK4 46 B2
Hambling Pl LU6 93 F8
Hamburg Croft MK5 46 B3
Hambye Cl HP27 149 E4
Hamer Cl HP3 146 A3
Hamfield Cotts SL6 195 E7
HAM GREEN 83 D2
Hamilton Ave RG9 191 E1
Hamilton Cl HP4 107 C5
Hamilton Ct
Aylesbury HP19 101 D1
High Wycombe HP13 173 B8
Hamilton Gdns SL1 197 B2
Hamilton La MK3 57 C6
Hamilton Mead 5 HP3 146 A4
Hamilton Pk SL6 202 A6
Hamilton Pl SL9 188 E6
Hamilton Prim Sch 17 HP13 173 B7
Hamilton Prim Sch (Annexe) HP13 173 B8
Hamilton Rd
Berkhamsted HP4 135 B4
High Wycombe HP13 162 C1
Slough SL1 205 A7
Thame OX9 126 A1
Uxbridge UB8 201 D1
Ham Island SL4 211 C3
Ham La SL4 211 C3
Hamlins MK6 47 A6
Hammersley La HP10, HP11 174 B5
Hammerwood Gate MK7 48 A7
Hammond Cres MK15 35 B6
Hammond End SL2 198 B8
Hamon Way 2 MK12 33 A6
Hampden Ave HP5 144 A1
HAMPDEN BOTTOM 141 B2
Hampden Cl
Aylesbury HP21 115 D6
Aylesbury HP22 116 B1
Stoke Mandeville HP22 116 B1
Stoke Poges SL2 199 A2
Hampden Gate HP27 150 C5
Hampden Gdns HP21 115 D6
Hampden Hill
Beaconsfield HP9 175 B2
Charndon OX27 72 E6
Hampden Ho 2 HP13 173 F6
Hampden Rd
Aylesbury HP21 115 D6
Chalfont St Peter SL9 177 D2
High Wycombe HP13 173 B8
Hughenden Valley HP16 151 B3

Hampden Rd *continued*
Maidenhead SL6 .... 202 B8
Slough SL3 .... 206 F3
Speen HP27 .... 150 C5
Stoke Mandeville HP22 .. 116 B1
Wendover HP22 .... 131 C5
Hampden Sq 2 HP19 .. 115 A8
Hampden Villas OX27 ... 71 F7
Hampshire Ave SL1 .... 205 C8
Hampshire Ct MK3 ...... 46 F2
Hampshire Lodge 8
SL6 .... 202 F6
Hampson Cl MK13 .... 34 A5
Hampstead Cl 7 HP19 . 100 F1
Hampstead Gate MK13 .. 34 C3
Hampton 7 MK8 .... 45 F8
Hampton Ho SL3 .... 212 D7
Hanbury Cl SL1 .... 204 A8
Hancock Cl HP21 ...... 115 E5
Handel Mead MK7 ...... 48 E5
Handleton Comm HP14 171 B5
Handley Page Cl MK43 .. 24 E2
Handy Cross HP11 ..... 172 F3
Hangar Rd UB9 .... 189 E7
Hanging Croft Cl 4
HP13 .... 173 F6
Hangings La HP16 ..... 151 A6
Hanley Cl SL4 .... 209 D6
Hanmer Rd MK6 .... 47 E5
Hannah Ball Inf Sch
HP13 .... 173 D7
Hannon Rd HP21 .... 115 C5
Hanover Cl
3 Aylesbury HP19 ..... 101 A2
Slough SL1 .... 206 A3
Windsor SL4 .... 209 F6
Hanover Ct
2 Aylesbury HP21 ..... 115 E7
Hazelmere HP15 .... 163 B3
Leighton Buzzard LU7 .... 80 D7
Milton Keynes MK14 ..... 34 D7
Hanover Mead SL6 ..... 203 C3
Hanover Way SL4 ...... 209 F6
Hanscomb Cl MK15 ...... 35 C2
Hansen Croft MK5 ...... 46 B5
HANSLOPE 11 B3
Hanslope Comb Sch
MK19 .... 11 A3
Hanslope Rd MK19 ...... 19 F6
Hanson Cl UB7 .... 208 F3
Hanson Way HP21 ...... 116 A4
Harborne Ct MK8 .... 33 C2
Harborough Cl SL1 .... 204 D5
Harbourne Cl HP21 .... 115 C3
Harby Cl MK4 .... 46 C1
Harcourt
Milton Keynes MK13 ..... 34 A3
Wraysbury TW19 .... 211 E1
Harcourt Cl
Dorney SL6 .... 203 F3
Henley-on-Thames RG9 . 191 C1
Leighton Buzzard LU7 .... 80 E7
Harcourt Gn HP19 ..... 101 B2
Harcourt Rd
Dorney SL4 .... 203 F3
Tring HP23 .... 119 C4
Windsor SL4 .... 209 F6
Hardenwaye HP13 ..... 162 E1
Harding Rd
Chesham HP5 .... 144 D1
Milton Keynes MK10 ..... 48 C8
Hardings Cl SL0 .... 200 C2
Harding Spur 13 SL3 ... 206 F1
Hardings Row SL0 ..... 200 D2
HARDMEAD 15 D3
Hardmead Rd MK43 .... 8 A3
HARDWICK 87 B3
Hardwick Cl SL6 ...... 202 A8
Hardwicke Gdns HP6 ... 154 E1
Hardwick Mews MK17 ... 49 B3
Hardwick Pl MK17 ...... 49 B4
Hardwick Rd MK17 ...... 49 B4
Hardy Cl
Aylesbury HP21 .... 115 E7
Slough SL1 .... 205 A5
Hardy Mead Ct HP11 ... 174 B2
Hardy Mews UB8 .... 201 C3
Harebell Cl MK7 .... 48 B5
Harebell Wlk HP15 .... 162 F6
Harebridge La HP22 .... 117 E1
Hare Cl MK18 .... 52 E7
Hareden Croft MK4 ..... 46 B2
Harefield Rd
Maidenhead SL6 .... 202 A7
Uxbridge UB8 .... 201 D6
Harehatch La SL1 ..... 186 F3
Hare La HP16 .... 152 B3
Hare Lane End HP16 ... 152 A3
Harescombe Ct HP9 .... 175 D3
Haresfoot Sch HP4 ..... 135 B1
Hare Shoots SL6 ...... 202 E5
Harewood Pl SL1 ...... 206 A3
Harewood Rd HP8 ...... 166 C6
Hargrave Rd SL6 ...... 202 D8
Hargreaves Nook MK14 .. 22 B2
Harkness Cl MK2 .... 58 D6
Harkness Rd SL1 ...... 204 B8
Harlans Cl MK6 .... 47 B8
Harlech Ho 5 HP13 .... 173 F7
Harlech Pl MK3 .... 57 E7
Harlequin Pl MK5 .... 45 F3
Harlesden Cl MK10 ...... 35 E1
Harle Stone Ct MK14 .... 22 A1
Harley Ct SL1 .... 205 C4
Harleyford La SL7 .... 194 B7
Harling Rd LU6 .... 93 B4
Harlow Cres 6 MK4 ..... 45 E2
Harlow Rd HP13 .... 173 C6
Harmans Cross MK10 .... 36 B3
Harman Terr HP12 ..... 172 D7
Harman Wlk HP12 ...... 172 C3
HARMONDSWORTH 213 D8
Harmondsworth La
UB7 .... 213 E8
Harmondsworth Prim Sch
UB7 .... 213 D8
Harmondsworth Rd
UB7 .... 208 E2
Harnett Dr MK12 .... 32 F6
Harper Cl OX25 .... 94 D7
Harpers La MK14 .... 34 F8
Harrier Cl HP20 .... 101 F3
Harrier Ct MK6 .... 47 A8
Harrier Dr MK6 .... 47 A8
Harries Cl HP5 .... 144 B1
Harries Way HP15 ..... 163 B6
Harriet Walker Way
WD3 .... 167 F2
Harrington Cl SL4 ..... 209 F3
Harris Cl HP18 .... 110 A8
Harris Ct 7 HP20 ..... 101 F2
Harris Gdns SL1 ...... 205 C4
Harrison Barber Cotts
SL3 .... 212 D7
Harrison Cl MK5 .... 46 D6
Harrison Pl OX9 .... 125 F1
Harrison Way SL1 ..... 204 D5
Harris Rd HP14 .... 171 B5
Harroell
Long Crendon, Church End
HP18 .... 125 D6
Long Crendon HP18 .... 125 D5
Harrogate Ct SL3 ..... 207 A1
HARROLD 3 F6
Harrold Lower Sch MK43 . 3 F6
Harrold Priory Mid Sch
MK43 .... 3 F6
Harrold Rd MK46 .... 3 B1
Harrow Cl
Aylesbury HP21 .... 115 E4
Maidenhead SL6 .... 195 E1
Harrowden MK13 .... 34 B7
Harrow La SL6 .... 195 E1
Harrow Mkt The SL3 ... 207 A3
Harrow Rd SL3 .... 206 F3
Harrow Yd 6 HP23 ..... 119 A3
Hartdames MK5 .... 46 A3
Hartfield Cl MK7 .... 48 A7
Hartington Gr 5 MK4 ... 46 B3
Hartland Ave MK4 .... 57 B8
Hartland Cl SL1 .... 205 D5
Hartley MK14 .... 34 E8
Hartley Cl SL3 .... 199 C4
Hartley Copse SL4 ..... 211 A1
Hartley Ct SL9 .... 188 E5
Hart Moor Cl HP14 ..... 158 E4
Harts Rd HP17 .... 127 B6
Hart St RG9 .... 191 E2
HARTWELL 10 D8
Hartwell Cl HP10 ...... 163 C2
Hartwell Dr HP9 .... 175 D3
Hartwell End HP21 ..... 115 B7
Hartwell Rd
Ashton NN7 .... 9 F8
Hanslope MK19 .... 10 E5
Hartwort Cl MK7 .... 48 B5
Harvard Cl MK14 .... 21 F2
Harvest Bank HP6 ...... 153 C4
Harvester Cl MK12 ...... 33 B5
Harvest Hill HP10 ..... 185 D2
Harvest Hill Rd SL6 ... 202 F3
Harvey Dr MK46 .... 6 F1
Harvey Ho SL3 .... 206 E7
Harvey Orch HP9 ...... 175 C3
Harvey Rd
Aylesbury HP21 .... 115 E5
Dunstable LU6 .... 93 D7
Slough SL3 .... 207 B4
Harvil Rd UB9, UB10 ... 190 E4
Harvington Pk LU7 ..... 105 D3
Harwich Rd SL1 .... 205 A7
Harwood Dr UB10 ...... 201 F4
Harwood Rd SL7 .... 183 C1
Harwood St MK13 .... 34 A7
Hasgill Ct MK13 .... 34 B4
Haslemere Rd SL4 ..... 210 A6
Haslerig Cl HP21 ...... 115 F5
Haslow Ct MK8 .... 33 E3
Hasting Cl SL6 .... 203 C2
Hastings MK11 .... 32 E5
Hastings Mdw SL2 ..... 199 A4
HASTOE 132 F7
Hastoe Cross HP23 .... 133 A7
Hastoe Farm Barns
HP23 .... 132 F7
Hastoe Hill HP23 ...... 132 F8
Hastoe La HP23 .... 119 A2
Hastoe Pk HP20 .... 101 F2
Hastoe Row HP23 ...... 133 A7
Hatches La
Great Kingshill HP15 .... 151 C1
Hughenden Valley HP15 . 162 B8
Hatchet Leys La MK18 ... 53 F8
Hatchgate Gdns SL1 ... 197 D1
Hatch La
Harmondsworth UB7 ... 213 D7
Radnage HP14 .... 160 B4
Windsor SL4 .... 210 A5
Hatchlands MK8 .... 33 F1
Hatch Pl SL6 .... 195 E7
Hatch The SL4 .... 209 C7
Hatfield Cl SL6 .... 202 C6
Hatfield Rd SL1 .... 206 A4
Hathaway Ct MK8 .... 45 E8
Hatter's La HP13 ...... 173 F6
Hatton MK6 .... 47 D6
Hatton Ave SL2 .... 198 D1
Hatton Ct SL4 .... 210 C5
Hatton Gr UB7 .... 208 D4
Hauksbee Gdns MK5 ..... 46 D5
Havelock Bsns Pk SL6 .. 202 C7
Havelock Cres SL6 ..... 202 B7
Havelock Ct HP20 ...... 101 D1
Havelock Rd SL6 .... 202 B7
Havelock St HP20 ...... 101 D1
Havenfield Ct 16 HP13 .. 173 B7
Havenfield Rd HP12 .... 172 C4
Haven of Rest SL6 ..... 203 B7
Haven Shaw Cl HP21 ... 116 A5
Haven St MK10 .... 36 C3
HAVERSHAM 20 E2
Haversham Rd MK19 .... 20 D1
Haversham Village Sch
MK19 .... 20 E2
Hawfinch 1 HP19 ...... 101 E3
Hawker Ct SL3 .... 207 A3
Hawkes Cl SL3 .... 207 B3
Hawkhurst Gate MK7 .... 47 F2
Hawkings Way HP3 ..... 146 A5
Hawkins Cl MK11 .... 32 D5
Hawkmoor Cl MK6 .... 47 B8
Hawkridge MK4 .... 46 E3
Hawkshead Dr MK4 ...... 46 C3
Hawks Hill SL8 .... 185 C3
Hawkshill Dr HP3 ...... 146 F8
Hawkshill Rd SL2 ...... 198 A2
Hawkslade Furlong
HP21 .... 115 D3
Hawksmoor Cl HP13 .... 173 A8
Hawkswood MK46 .... 6 F5
Hawkswood Gr SL3 ..... 199 F6
Hawkswood La SL3, SL9 . 199 F8
Hawkwell Dr HP23 ..... 119 C4
Hawkwell Est MK19 ..... 32 B7
Haw La HP14 .... 149 A2
Hawleys La HP22 .... 87 A6
Haworth Croft 2 MK10 .. 36 B3
HAWRIDGE 133 E1
Hawridge & Cholesbury CE
Sch HP5 .... 133 E2
HAWRIDGE COMMON 133 E2
Hawridge La HP5 ...... 143 E8
Hawridge Vale HP5 ..... 133 F1
Hawthorn Ave MK2 ...... 58 E8
Hawthorn Cl
Aylesbury HP20 .... 101 F2
Iver Heath SL0 .... 200 C2
Turvey MK43 .... 8 E6
Hawthorn Cres HP15 ... 163 B2
Hawthorn Dr UB9 ...... 201 C6
Hawthorne Cl
Leighton Buzzard LU7 .... 80 E8
Marlow SL7 .... 183 E4
Hawthorne Cres
Slough SL1 .... 205 F7
West Drayton UB7 ..... 208 F4
Hawthorne Gdns HP10 . 174 A2
Hawthorne Rd HP13 .... 174 A6
Hawthorn Gdns SL6 .... 202 E5
Hawthorn La SL2 ...... 198 A5
Hawthorn Pl HP10 ..... 174 C8
Hawthorn Rd HP27 ..... 139 C3
Hawthorns The
Berkhamsted HP4 ...... 135 A5
Cranfield MK43 .... 25 B1
Felden HP3 .... 146 F7
Little Chalfont HP8 .... 166 C7
Maple Cross WD3 ...... 178 D5
Monks Risborough HP27 139 C6
Poyle SL3 .... 212 F6
Wooburn Green HP10 ... 185 E6
Hawthorn Way
Chesham HP5 .... 144 D2
Wing LU7 .... 79 E3
Hawthorn Wlk HP15 .... 163 B2
Hawtrey Cl SL1 .... 206 B4
Hawtrey Rd SL4 .... 210 C5
Hay Barn Bsns Pk The
HP22 .... 88 C6
Hayden Ho 3 HP11 .... 172 F7
Haydock Cl MK3 .... 57 C6
Haydon Abbey Comb Sch
HP19 .... 101 C2
Haydon Ct SL6 .... 202 E6
HAYDON HILL 100 E2
Haydon Ind Sch 9
HP20 .... 101 D1
Haydon Rd HP19 .... 101 C2
Hayes Cl SL6 .... 203 D1
Hayes Pl SL7 .... 183 D1
Hayes Rd MK19 .... 31 F5
Hayfield Dr HP15 ...... 163 B2
Hay La SL3 .... 199 D8
Hayles Field RG9 ...... 170 E1
Hayling Cl SL1 .... 205 B5
Haymaker Cl UB10 ..... 201 F5
Hayman Rise MK8 .... 45 D6
Haymill Rd SL1, SL2 .... 197 D1
Haymill Valley Nature
Reserve* SL2 .... 204 E8
Haynes Cl
Bow Brickhill MK17 ...... 48 D2
Slough SL3 .... 206 F1
Haynes Ho HP12 .... 172 B3
Haynes Mead HP4 ...... 135 A6
Hayse Hill SL4 .... 209 D6
Haystacks The HP13 .... 173 B7
Haythrop Cl MK15 .... 35 B6
Hayward Pl SL8 .... 185 C2
Haywards Cl RG9 ...... 191 C1
Haywards Croft MK12 ... 33 B5
Haywards Mead SL4 ... 204 F1
Haywood Dr WD3 .... 167 F4
Haywood Pk
Chorleywood WD3 ...... 167 F4
Stewkley LU7 .... 68 C3
Haywoods Dr HP3 ...... 146 F8
Haywood Way HP19 ..... 100 F3
Hayworth Pl 2 MK4 ..... 45 D2
Hazelbury Rd HP13 .... 173 D6
Hazel Cl SL7 .... 183 C6
Hazelcroft Cl UB10 .... 201 F5
Hazel Ct WD3 .... 178 E5
Hazeldene HP22 .... 131 C4
HAZELEY 45 D5
Hazeley Sch The MK8 ... 45 D5
Hazel Gr MK2 .... 58 D7
Hazelhurst 7 MK4 ...... 46 B2
Hazelhurst Rd SL1 ..... 197 D3
Hazell Ave HP21 .... 116 A7
Hazell Cl SL6 .... 202 F8
Hazell Pk HP7 .... 165 D8
Hazell Rd HP16 .... 151 C5
Hazell Way SL2 .... 198 F6
HAZELMERE 163 B4
Hazel Rd HP4 .... 135 D3
Hazelwood MK14 .... 34 F8
Hazelwood Cl HP5 ..... 144 D2
Hazely HP23 .... 119 C4
Hazlehurst Dr HP21 .... 116 A5
Hazlemere CE Comb Sch
HP15 .... 162 F3
Hazlemere Ct HP15 .... 163 A4
Hazlemere Rd
Slough SL2 .... 206 B5
Tylers Green HP10 ..... 163 C2
Hazlemere View HP15 .. 163 B5
Hazley Wlk MK18 .... 41 F1
Headington Cl SL6 .... 202 A7
Headington Pl SL2 ..... 205 F5
Headington Rd SL6 .... 202 A7
Headland Cl 1 HP16 ... 152 A8
Headlands Dr HP4 ..... 135 E5
Healey Ave HP13 ...... 173 D7
Heaney Cl MK16 .... 22 A5
Hearn Cl HP10 .... 162 F2
Hearne Ct HP8 .... 177 B7
Hearne Dr SL6 .... 203 A1
Hearne Pl MK6 .... 46 F8
Hearnes Cl HP9 .... 176 D5
Hearne's Mdw HP9 ..... 176 D5
Heathacre SL3 .... 212 E6
Heath Cl
Aylesbury HP21 .... 116 B5
Holmer Green HP15 .... 163 B6
Stanwell TW19 .... 213 C1
Woburn Sands MK17 ..... 49 C3
Heathcote SL6 .... 203 B2
Heathcote Ct 2 SL4 ... 210 D4
Heathcote Way UB7 .... 208 D5
Heath Ct
Leighton Buzzard LU7 .... 70 E3
Uxbridge UB8 .... 201 D5
HEATH END
Cholesbury 134 A2
Prestwood 151 E1
Heath End Cl HP15 .... 151 E1
Heath End Rd
Flackwell Heath HP10 ... 174 A1
Great Kingshill HP15,
HP16 .... 151 E2
Little Marlow HP10 .... 173 D2
Heather Cl
Buckingham MK18 .... 52 C7
Uxbridge UB8 .... 208 F8
Heathercroft MK14 ...... 34 E7
Heatherden Gn SL0 .... 200 D4
Heather La UB7 .... 208 E7
Heather Mead LU6 ...... 92 E5
Heathers Cl MK18 .... 73 B5
Heatherside Gdns SL2 .. 187 D1
Heatherton House Sch
HP6 .... 154 C3
Heatherton Pk HP6 .... 154 B3
Heather Wlk
Aylesbury HP21 .... 115 B6
Heather Wlk *continued*
Hazelmere HP15 .... 163 A3
Heathfield MK12 .... 33 E4
Heathfield Rd
High Wycombe HP12 .... 172 B7
Taplow SL1 .... 186 A1
Heath La MK17 .... 49 A2
Heathlands Dr SL6 .... 202 A6
Heath Lawn HP10 ...... 173 F1
Heath Rd
Beaconsfield HP9 ...... 186 A8
Great Brickhill MK17, LU7 . 59 E1
Hyde Heath HP6 .... 153 C5
Heathrow Bvd UB7 ..... 213 F7
Heathrow Cl UB7 ...... 213 B6
Heathrow Prim Sch
UB7 .... 213 F8
Heathrow T5 Sta/U Sta
TW6 .... 213 C4
Heath The LU7 .... 70 E4
Heath Way SL0 .... 200 D3
Heavens Lea SL8 ...... 185 C2
Hedge Lea HP10 .... 185 D8
HEDGERLEY 187 D3
Hedgerley OX39 .... 147 B6
HEDGERLEY GREEN 187 E4
HEDGERLEY HILL 187 E2
Hedgerley Hill SL2 .... 187 D2
Hedgerley La
Beaconsfield HP9 ...... 186 F8
Gerrards Cross SL9 .... 188 B4
Hedgerley SL2 .... 187 D6
Hedgerow SL9 .... 177 E4
Hedgerows The MK4 .... 46 E4
Hedges Ct MK5 .... 46 B6
Hedingham Ct MK5 ...... 46 A5
Hedingham Mews SL6 .. 202 D7
Hedley Cl HP22 .... 118 A4
Hedley Rd HP10 .... 185 B8
Hedley View HP10 ..... 174 D1
HEDSOR 185 F3
Hedsor Hill SL8 .... 185 C1
Hedsor La
Hedsor HP10 .... 185 F2
Taplow SL1 .... 186 A2
Hedsor Rd SL8 .... 185 B2
Hedsor View Cotts SL6 . 195 F7
HEELANDS 34 C4
Heelands Fst Sch MK13 . 34 B4
Heights The SL7 ...... 194 B8
Hele Ct MK7 .... 48 B3
Helena Rd SL4 .... 210 D5
Helen Cotts SL4 ...... 209 D5
Helford Cl HP21 .... 115 D4
Helford Pl MK6 .... 35 A1
Heligan Pl MK4 .... 45 F1
Hellfire Caves* HP14 .. 160 F2
Hellyer Way SL8 .... 185 C3
Helmsley Rise MK4 ..... 45 E1
Helston La SL4 .... 210 B6
Helston Pl 3 MK6 ...... 34 F1
Hemel Hempstead Rd
HP4 .... 107 F1
Hemingway Cl MK16 .... 21 F5
Hemingway Rd HP19 ... 100 F2
Hemlock Cl HP22 ...... 116 C4
Hemmings The HP4 .... 134 F3
Hemming Way SL2 ..... 198 B2
Hemp Hill 10 HP19 ..... 115 A8
Hemp La HP23 .... 119 F1
Hempson Ave SL3 ...... 206 C3
Hempstead Rd HP3 .... 146 B5
HEMPTON WAINHILL 147 F7
Hemsdale SL6 .... 195 B1
Hemwood Rd SL4 ...... 209 D4
Hencroft Mews 14 SL1 . 205 F4
Hencroft Street N SL1 .. 205 F4
Hencroft Street S SL1 .. 205 F3
Henden Mews SL6 ..... 202 A6
Henders MK11 .... 32 E5
Hendon Ct 5 MK10 ...... 35 F1
Hendons Way SL6 ..... 203 B1
Hendon Way TW19 ..... 213 D1
Hendrix Dr MK8 .... 45 D7
Hengistbury La MK4 .... 46 A1
Henley Coll The RG9 ... 191 D1
Henley Coll The
(Rotherfield Bldgs)
RG9 .... 191 C1
Henley Lodge 12 SL6 ... 202 F6
Henley Management Coll
RG9 .... 192 B7
HENLEY-ON-THAMES ... 191 B1
Henley-on-Thames Sta
RG9 .... 191 E1
Henley Rd
Hurley SL6 .... 193 D3
Maidenhead SL6, SL7 ... 194 B2
Marlow SL7 .... 194 B8
Slough SL1 .... 204 F7
Hennerton Way HP13 .. 173 F6
Henrietta Rd OX9 ..... 126 A1
Henry III Tower 17 SL4 . 210 D6
Henry Rd
Aylesbury HP20 .... 116 B8
Slough SL1 .... 205 D4

Henry St HP23 119 A3
Hensman Gate MK10 35 F4
Henson Cl MK43 24 E3
HENTON 137 E2
Henton Mews 5 HP19 115 A8
Hepburn Cres MK4 45 E3
Hepleswell MK8 33 E1
Hepplewhite Cl HP13 173 D8
Herbert Rd HP13 174 A7
Herberts Hole
Chesham HP5 143 C1
South Heath HP5, HP16 142 F1
Hercies Rd UB10 201 F5
Herdman Cl MK12 33 B5
Herd's Hill MK18 64 A4
Hereford Ho HP13 173 F8
Hereford Way HP19 101 A3
Heritage Cl UB8 201 C1
Heritage Gate SL9 188 E7
Heritage House Specl Sch HP5 144 D1
Heritage Wlk WD3 167 E6
Hermitage Cl SL3 206 C3
Hermitage La SL4 210 A4
Hermitage Prim Sch UB8 201 D5
Hermitage The
Great Missenden HP16 152 A7
Uxbridge UB8 201 D6
Hernes Oak OX39 147 D8
Heron Cl
Aylesbury HP20 116 C8
Uxbridge UB8 201 D6
Heron Dr SL3 207 B2
Heron Lodge MK14 34 C6
Herons Elm HP4 134 E7
Heronsfield Ho WD3 167 B3
HERONSGATE 167 D2
Heronsgate Rd WD3 167 B3
Heronsgate Sch MK7 48 B5
Heronshaw Sch MK7 48 B5
Herons Pl
Maidenhead SL6 196 C3
Marlow SL7 183 E3
Heron The HP19 101 E4
Herries Sch SL6 195 B8
Herriot Cl MK16 22 A5
Herschel Gram Sch SL1 205 C7
Herschel Sports SL1 205 C7
Herschel St SL1 205 F4
Herston Cl HP21 116 B5
Hertford Pl MK3 46 F2
Hervines Ct HP6 154 C2
Hervines Rd HP6 154 C2
Hesketh Rd NN12 18 E6
Hetherington Cl SL2 197 F2
Hetherington Way UB10 201 E8
Het's Orch HP27 149 E5
Hetton Cl MK13 34 C4
Heusden Way SL9 188 F3
Hever Cl
Maidenhead SL6 202 C6
Pitstone LU7 105 D2
Hewgate Ct RG9 191 E1
Hexham Gdns MK3 57 D6
Heybridge Cres MK7 48 B3
Heydon Ct MK13 34 A7
Heynes Gn SL6 202 B3
Heythrop Dr UB10 201 F8
Heyward Gate MK6 47 C5
Heywood Ave SL6 202 A1
Heywood Court Cl SL6 202 A2
Heywood Gdns SL6 202 A1
Hibbert Rd SL6 203 B4
Hibbert's Alley 16 SL4 210 D6
Hibberts Way SL9 188 E8
Hickmans Cl MK18 51 B6
Hickman St HP19 114 F8
Hickox Ct HP10 185 F7
Hicks Farm Rise HP13 173 F7
Hidcote Dr MK4 45 F1
Hide The MK6 47 C6
Higgs Ct MK5 46 A8
HIGHAM CROSS 10 D3
Higham Cross Rd MK19 10 E4
Higham Mead HP5 144 C1
Higham Rd HP5 144 C1
High Ash CE Comb Sch MK17 59 D2
High Beeches
Gerrards Cross SL9 188 D2
High Wycombe HP12 172 C6
High Beeches Cl SL7 183 C7
High Bois La HP6 154 D4
Highbridge Ind Est UB8 201 C5
Highbridge Rd HP21 115 E8
Highbridge Wlk 4 HP21 115 E8
Highbury La MK9 35 B3
High Coppice HP7 165 C8
Highcrest Com Sch HP13 173 E7
Highcroft Cl NN12 18 E6
HIGHER DENHAM 189 C4
Highfield
Chalfont St Giles HP8 177 D8
Long Crendon HP18 125 C7
Highfield Ave HP12 172 B5
Highfield Cl
Amersham HP6 154 D2
Milton Keynes MK3 47 B2
Newport Pagnell MK16 22 E4
Highfield Ct
Farnham Royal SL2 198 B4
Hazelmere HP15 163 A3
Highfield Dr UB10 190 E1
Highfield La SL6 202 A4
Highfield Pk SL7 183 B1
Highfield Rd
Berkhamsted HP4 135 D4
Bourne End SL8 185 B4
Chesham HP5 144 B2
Flackwell Heath HP10 185 A8
Maidenhead SL6 202 B8
Princes Risborough HP27 139 C4
Tring HP23 118 E3
Wigginton HP23 119 D1
Windsor SL4 209 F4
Winslow MK18 65 F5
Highfield Sch SL6 202 E7
Highfield Way
Hazelmere HP15 163 A3
Yardley Hastings NN7 1 B6
Highgate Mews 2 HP19 100 F1
Highgate Over MK7 48 B6
Highgrove Hill MK8 45 F8
Highgrove Pk SL6 202 E8
High Halden MK7 48 B8
High Heavens Wood SL7 183 C8
Highland Cl MK3 46 F3
High Land Cl HP18 96 A1
Highland Rd HP7 165 D8
Highlands
Flackwell Heath HP10 185 B7
High Wycombe HP13 174 A5
Highlands Cl SL9 177 F3
Highlands End SL9 177 F3
Highlands La SL9 177 F3
Highlands Rd
Buckingham MK18 41 E2
Seer Green HP9 176 C5
Highlands The SL2 198 C7
Highlea Ave HP10 185 A8
Highley Gr MK10 36 B3
High March Sch HP9 175 D4
High Mdw SL6 196 C3
Highmoor HP7 165 D8
High Moors HP22 131 B8
Highmore Cotts HP7 152 F3
Highmore Croft MK8 45 D6
Highover Pk HP7 165 D7
High Park Dr MK12 33 A6
High Rd
Cookham Rise SL6 195 E7
Soulbury LU7 69 E2
Uxbridge UB8 208 C7
High St The MK8 33 E1
High St
Amersham HP7 165 A7
Aylesbury HP20 115 E8
Berkhamsted HP4 135 C4
Berkhamsted, Northchurch HP4 134 E6
Bovingdon HP3 146 A4
Bray SL6 203 C4
Brill HP18 110 A8
Buckingham MK18 28 D1
Buckingham MK18 41 D1
Burcott LU7 79 D4
Burnham SL1 197 C2
Chalfont St Giles HP8 177 C8
Chalfont St Peter SL9 177 E2
Chalvey SL1 205 D3
Cheddington LU7 105 A7
Chesham HP5 154 B8
Chinnor, Kingston Blount OX39 147 A4
Chinnor OX39 147 D7
Colnbrook SL3 212 C7
Cookham SL6 196 B7
Cranfield MK43 25 B1
Cublington LU7 78 B1
Datchet SL3 211 B6
Deanshanger MK19 31 E4
Dinton HP17 113 E2
Downley HP13 161 D3
Eaton Bray LU6 92 E6
Edlesborough LU6 92 E3
Emberton MK46 13 F7
Eton SL4 210 D8
Great Horwood MK17 55 A3
Great Missenden HP16 152 A7
Haddenham HP17 126 F6
Hanslope MK19 11 A2
Harmondsworth UB7 213 D8
Harrold MK43 3 F6
Haversham MK19 21 A3
High Wycombe HP11 173 B6
Iver SL0 207 F7
High St continued
Ivinghoe LU7 105 E5
Lane End HP14 171 B4
Lavendon MK46 7 F8
Leighton Buzzard LU7 80 F6
Lewknor OX49 157 B8
Long Crendon HP18 125 D6
Ludgershall HP18 96 B8
14 Maidenhead SL6 202 F7
Marlow SL7 183 E1
Milton Keynes, Great Linford MK14 21 E1
Milton Keynes MK2 47 E1
Milton Keynes, New Bradwell MK13 34 A7
Milton Keynes, Stony Stratford MK11 32 D6
Nash MK17 44 C1
Newport Pagnell MK16 22 D4
North Crawley MK16 24 B6
North Marston MK18 76 A2
Olney MK46 6 F3
Paulerspury NN12 17 C8
Potterspury NN12 18 D3
Prestwood HP16 151 D6
Princes Risborough HP27 139 B3
Sherington MK16 13 F2
Slough SL3 207 A2
Slough, Upton SL1 205 F4
Stanwell TW19 213 D1
Stoke Goldington MK16 12 B6
Syresham NN13 27 B7
Taplow SL6 196 E1
Thame OX9 125 E1
Thornborough MK18 54 A8
Tring HP23 119 A3
Turvey MK43 8 E5
Uxbridge, Cowley UB8 201 C1
Uxbridge UB8 201 D5
Waddesdon HP18 99 A6
Weedon HP22 87 C1
Wendover HP22 131 B4
Westcott HP18 98 B7
West Drayton UB7 208 E6
Weston Underwood MK46 6 B2
West Wycombe HP14 160 F2
Whaddon MK17 45 B1
Whitchurch HP22 87 A6
Windsor SL4 210 D6
Wing LU7 79 E2
Winslow MK18 65 F4
Woburn Sands MK17 49 B4
Wraysbury TW19 211 F1
Yardley Gobion NN12 18 F6
Yardley Hastings NN7 1 B6
High Street N LU7 68 D2
High Street S
Olney MK46 6 F3
Stewkley LU7 78 E8
High Town Rd SL6 202 F7
High Trees MK6 47 B8
Highveer Croft MK4 46 B1
High View
Chalfont St Giles HP8 177 D8
Deanshanger MK19 31 E5
High View Cl SL7 183 C8
HIGHWAY 202 B7
Highway MK17 68 C6
Highway Ave SL6 202 A6
Highway Ct
Beaconsfield HP9 175 D3
Chesham HP5 144 D1
Highway Rd SL6 202 B6
Highway The HP9 175 D2
Highwood Ave HP12 172 B5
Highwood Bottom HP27 150 A5
Highwood Cres HP12 172 B6
Highwoods Cl SL7 183 C7
Highwoods Dr SL7 183 C7
Highworth Cl HP13 162 E1
Highworth Comb Sch HP13 162 E1
HIGH WYCOMBE 173 B5
High Wycombe CE Comb Sch 5 HP11 173 A6
High Wycombe Sta HP13 173 B7
Hikers Way HP18 125 F4
Hilbre Ct 5 MK4 45 F1
Hilbury Cl HP6 154 C3
Hilda Wharf HP20 115 F8
Hildreth Rd HP16 151 C5
Hilgrove Ho SL6 195 D1
Hiljon Cres SL9 177 E2
Hillary Cl
Aylesbury HP21 116 A5
High Wycombe HP13 173 E6
Hillary Rd
High Wycombe HP13 173 E6
Slough SL3 206 E4
Hill Ave
Amersham HP6 154 C1
Hazelmere HP15 163 B5
Hillbeck Gr MK10 35 E3
Hillbottom Rd HP12 172 B7
Hill Cl HP10 185 F7
Hill Cotts HP18 97 E1
Hillcrest MK43 25 C2
Hillcrest Ave SL6 195 E6
Hillcrest Cl MK5 46 B6
Hillcrest Ct HP6 154 C1
Hillcrest Rise MK18 52 E6
Hillcrest Way MK18 52 E5
Hillcrest Waye SL9 188 F5
Hillcroft Rd
Chesham HP5 144 D2
Tylers Green HP10 163 C1
Hillersdon SL2 206 B8
Hillersdon Chase MK17 69 D8
HILLESDEN 63 A6
HILLESDEN HAMLET 51 F1
Hillesden Hamlet MK18 51 F1
Hillesden Way MK18 41 E1
Hill Farm MK18 76 A2
Hill Farm App HP10 185 F7
Hill Farm Ct OX39 147 D6
Hill Farm La
Chalfont St Giles HP8 166 A1
Little Horwood MK17 55 E2
Hill Farm Rd
Chalfont St Peter SL9 177 E3
Chesham HP5 154 D5
Marlow Bottom SL7 183 E5
Taplow SL6 196 E2
Hill Farm Way HP15 163 B2
Hillfield Cl HP13 161 E2
Hillfield Rd SL9 177 E3
Hillfield Sq SL9 177 E3
Hill Gr SL9 177 E3
Hill Ho SL6 196 D1
Hill House Cl SL9 177 E3
Hilliard Dr MK13 34 A3
Hilliards Rd UB8 208 D7
Hillier Rd HP21 115 D3
Hillingdon Hill UB10 201 E2
Hillingdon Hospl UB8 208 F8
Hillingdon Rd UB10 201 E3
Hillingdon Tuition Ctr UB7 208 E5
Hillington Cl HP19 115 B7
Hillman Cl UB8 201 E7
Hill Mdw HP7 164 F4
Hill Mead HP4 135 A3
Hillmead Ct SL6 203 F8
Hill Pl SL2 198 B5
Hill Rd
Chinnor OX39 147 D5
Christmas Common OX49 168 A8
Lewknor OX49 157 C6
Hillrise SL3 212 A8
Hill Rise SL9 177 D1
Hill Rise Cres SL9 177 E1
Hills Cl MK14 34 E7
Hillside
Chesham HP5 144 A3
Gawcott MK18 51 F4
High Wycombe HP13 173 D7
Maidenhead SL6 202 D5
Slough SL1 205 E4
South Harefield UB9 190 C6
Tingewick MK18 51 B6
Hill Side LU7 104 F7
Hillside Cl
Chalfont St Giles HP8 177 B7
Chalfont St Peter SL9 177 E4
Upper Arncott OX25 94 E7
Hillside Cotts HP18 112 F2
Hillside Ct SL0 208 B4
Hillside Ctr HP11 172 F7
Hillside Gdns
Amersham HP7 165 E7
Berkhamsted HP4 135 D3
High Wycombe HP13 173 D7
Hillside Rd
Chorleywood WD3 167 C4
Marlow SL7 183 E4
Tylers Green HP10 163 A2
Hills La SL6 195 D7
Hill St HP13 174 A5
Hill The
Syresham NN13 27 B8
Winchmore Hill HP7 164 C3
HILLTOP 144 D2
Hilltop HP18 125 D5
Hilltop Ave MK18 41 E2
Hill Top Dr SL7 183 B2
Hilltop Fst Sch SL4 209 E4
Hill Top La OX39 147 F4
Hilltop Rd HP4 135 C3
Hillview
Saunderton HP14 149 C1
Sherington MK16 14 A1
Hill View
Berkhamsted HP4 135 A6
Great Kimble HP17 129 D1
Hedgerley SL2 187 D3
Newport Pagnell MK16 22 A3
Oakley HP18 109 D5
Hillview Rd HP13 173 D8
Hill View Rd TW19 211 D1
Hillway MK17 49 A6
Hill Way HP7 165 B6
Hill Waye SL9 188 F4
Hillwerke OX39 147 C6
Hillyer Ct MK6 35 C1
Hilperton Rd 3 SL1 205 E4
Hilton Ave HP20 101 E2
Hilton Cl UB8 201 B3
Himley Gn LU7 80 D6
Hindemith Gdns MK7 48 D5
Hindhay La SL6 195 B3
Hindhead Knoll MK7 48 B6
Hinds Way HP21 115 B6
Hinkley Cl UB9 190 C7
Hinksey Cl SL3 207 B3
Hinton Cl HP13 162 A1
Hinton Ct MK3 46 F1
Hinton Rd
Slough SL1 204 E6
Uxbridge UB8 201 C4
Hipwell Ct MK46 6 F3
Hitcham Grange SL6 196 E1
Hitcham House SL1 197 A1
Hitcham La SL6, SL1 196 F2
Hitcham Rd SL1, SL6 204 A8
Hithercroft Rd HP13 161 E1
Hither Mdw SL9 177 E1
Hithermoor Rd TW19 213 A2
Hiving's Hill HP5 144 A2
Hivings Pk HP5 144 B4
Hoathly Mews MK7 48 B8
Hobart Cl HP13 162 E1
Hobart Cotts HP16 150 D8
Hobart Cres MK15 35 B7
Hobart Ct SL7 184 A3
Hobart Rd HP13 162 D1
Hobbis Dr SL6 202 A6
Hobbshill Rd HP16 152 B6
Hobbs Rd HP14 171 C4
Hobsons Wlk HP23 118 F5
Hockeridge View HP4 134 F3
Hockett La SL6 195 A6
Hockley La SL2 199 B4
Hockliffe Brae MK7 48 C5
Hodder La MK4 46 C2
Hodds Wood Rd HP5 154 C6
Hodge Lea La MK12 33 D4
Hodgemoor View HP8 177 A7
Hodgemore Ct MK14 21 F2
Hodges Cl HP14 158 F4
Hodges Mews HP12 172 C6
Hoe Mdw HP9 175 C4
Hogarth Cl
Slough SL1 204 E6
Uxbridge UB8 201 C2
Hogarths Ct 9 MK8 33 F1
Hogback Wood Rd HP9 175 B4
Hogfair La SL1 197 C1
HOGGESTON 77 B7
Hogg La HP15 163 D6
Hog Hall La HP4 107 A5
Hog La
Ashley Green HP5 144 D8
Berkhamsted HP5 134 C2
HOGPITS BOTTOM 156 B7
Hogpits Bottom HP3 156 B7
Hogshaw Rd MK18 75 E6
Hogtrough La
Great Missenden HP16 141 F8
Wendover HP22 131 D2
Holborn Cres MK4 57 A8
Holdom Ave MK1 47 D2
Holes La MK46 6 F4
Holiday La MK19 10 F4
Holland Cl
Chinnor OX39 147 D7
Wendover HP22 131 B4
Holland Rd
Aylesbury HP19 101 B2
Marlow SL7 183 F3
Hollandridge La OX49, RG9 168 D4
Holland Way MK16 22 C3
Holliday Cl MK8 45 E7
Holliday St HP4 135 D4
Hollies Ct LU7 80 E7
Hollies The
Beaconsfield HP9 175 E3
Bovingdon HP3 146 A2
Tring HP23 119 D1
HOLLINGDON 69 C3
Hollingdon Depot LU7 69 D3
Hollingdon Rd LU7 69 C3
Hollington HP18 125 B7
Hollin La MK12 33 E4
Hollinwell Cl 3 MK4 46 D1
Hollis Rd HP13 173 F8
Hollister Chase MK5 46 B4
Holloway Cl UB7 208 E1
Holloway Dr MK18 41 E2
Holloway La
Chenies WD3 156 C2
Turville Heath RG9 169 C4
West Drayton UB7 208 F1
Holloway The
Monks Risborough HP27 139 D5
Tring HP22, HP23 118 C4
Hollow Hill End MK18 75 F7
Hollow Hill La SL0 207 C5
Hollow Rise HP13 162 B1
Hollow Way HP5 143 E1

Hollow Way La HP5,
HP6 . . . . 154 E4
Hollow Wood MK46 . . . . . . 6 E3
Hollyberry Gr HP15 . . . . 163 C7
Hollybush Cnr SL2 . . . . . 187 C2
Hollybush Hill SL2 . . . . . 199 B5
Hollybush La
Amersham HP6 . . . . 154 D3
Cookham Dean SL6 . . . . . . 195 B6
Denham UB9 . . . . 200 E8
Iver SL0, SL3 . . . . 207 B7
Hollybush Rd HP5 . . . . . . 144 A4
Hollybush Row HP23 . . . 133 D8
Holly Cl
Farnham Common SL2 . . 198 C8
Milton Keynes MK8 . . . . . . 45 E6
Holly Cres SL4 . . . . 209 D5
Holly Dr
Aylesbury HP21 . . . . 115 E6
Berkhamsted HP4 . . . . 135 D3
Maidenhead SL6 . . . . 202 F8
Windsor SL4 . . . . 210 E2
Holly End HP14 . . . . 161 C8
Hollyfield HP23 . . . . 119 C5
Hollyfield Cl HP23 . . . . . . 119 C5
Holly Gdns UB7 . . . . 208 F4
HOLLY GREEN 138 A3
Holly Green La HP27 . . . 138 A3
Holly Hedges La HP3 . . . 156 C8
Holly Pl HP11 . . . . 174 A3
Hollytree Cl
Botley HP5 . . . . 155 B8
Chalfont St Peter SL9 . . . 177 E5
Holly Tree La HP18 . . . . . 112 F3
Holly Wlk MK17 . . . . 49 B2
Holmanleaze SL6 . . . . . . 203 A8
Holman St HP19 . . . . 101 C2
Holmedale SL2 . . . . 206 C6
HOLMER GREEN 163 D6
Holmer Green Fst Sch
HP15 . . . . 163 B7
Holmer Green Jun Sch
HP15 . . . . 163 D7
Holmer Green Rd
HP15 . . . . 163 A4
Holmer Green Senior Sch
HP15 . . . . 163 B7
Holmer Pl HP15 . . . . 163 C7
Holmers Ct HP12 . . . . 172 B3
Holmers Farm Way
HP12 . . . . 172 C3
Holmers La HP12 . . . . 172 C3
Holmewood MK4 . . . . 46 E4
Holmfield Cl MK6 . . . . 47 D5
Holm Gate MK5 . . . . 46 A8
Holmlea Rd SL3 . . . . 211 D6
Holmlea Wlk SL3 . . . . . . 211 C6
Holmoak Wlk HP15 . . . . . 163 B3
Holmsdale Cl SL0 . . . . . . 207 F7
Holmwood Cl SL6 . . . . . . 202 B5
Holmwood Sch 10 MK8 . . 33 F1
Holne Chase Prim Sch
MK3 . . . . 58 A7
Holst Cres MK7 . . . . 48 D4
Holt Gr MK5 . . . . 46 A8
HOLTON 122 C2
Holton Hill MK4 . . . . 46 C2
Holton Rd MK18 . . . . 41 D2
Holts Gn MK17 . . . . 59 C1
HOLTSPUR 175 A1
Holtspur Ave HP10 . . . . . . 185 F7
Holtspur Cl HP9 . . . . 186 A8
Holtspur Ct HP9 . . . . 186 A8
Holtspur La HP10 . . . . . . 185 F6
Holtspur Par HP9 . . . . . . 186 A8
Holtspur Prim Sch
HP9 . . . . 175 A1
Holtspur Top La HP9 . . . 175 A2
Holtspur Way HP9 . . . . . 175 A1
Holt The MK18 . . . . 52 E7
Holy Family RC Sch
SL3 . . . . 206 F1
Holyhead Cres MK3 . . . . . 57 C8
Holyhead Mews SL1 . . . . 204 D7
Holyport Rd SL6 . . . . 203 B1
Holyrood MK8 . . . . 45 E8
Holy Thorn La MK5 . . . . . . 46 A5
Holy Trinity CE Prim Sch
SL6 . . . . 196 B7
Holy Trinity CE Sch
SL7 . . . . 183 D3
Holywell Gdns HP13 . . . . 173 E7
Holywell Pl MK6 . . . . 35 C2
Holywell Rd MK43 . . . . 25 C1
Holywell Sch MK43 . . . . . . 25 B1
Home Cl
Milton Keynes MK3 . . . . . . 47 B2
Shabbington HP18 . . . . . . 124 D3
Weston Turville HP22 . . . . 116 F2
Home Ct MK10 . . . . 36 A3
Home Farm
Newton Longville MK17 . . . 57 D4
Tring HP23 . . . . 118 F2
Home Farm Cl MK19 . . . . 31 E4
Homefarm Ct HP8 . . . . . 177 A7
Home Farm Ct
Bovingdon HP3 . . . . 145 F1
Emberton MK46 . . . . 13 E8
Home Farm La MK17 . . . . 59 D2
Home Farm Rd HP4 . . . . 134 D7
Home Farm Way SL3 . . . 199 C4
Homefield HP3 . . . . 146 B3
Home Field
Aylesbury HP19 . . . . 115 A7
Bow Brickhill MK7 . . . . 48 B3
Homefield Cl HP14 . . . . . 158 E4
Homefield Rd WD3 . . . . . 167 D5
Homefield Wood Wildlife
Reserve★ SL7 . . . . 182 C2
Homeground MK18 . . . . . 52 E6
Homelands Gdns HP15 . 162 D8
Homelands Way RG9 . . . 191 D1
Homeleigh Terr SL2 . . . . 206 A7
Home Mdw SL2 . . . . 198 C3
Home Meadow Dr
HP10 . . . . 185 B7
Homer Fst Sch SL4 . . . . 209 D6
Homeridings Ho MK13 . . 34 B4
Homers Rd SL4 . . . . 209 D6
Homeside Cl SL6 . . . . 195 E2
Homestall MK18 . . . . 52 D6
Homestall Cl MK5 . . . . 46 A7
Homestead Cl HP17 . . . . 114 A4
Homestead Pl 14 HP19 . 115 A8
Homestead Rd SL6 . . . . . 202 D4
Homestead The
Great Kingshill HP15 . . . . 151 D1
High Wycombe HP12 . . . . 172 D3
Milton Keynes MK5 . . . . . . 46 A6
Thame OX9 . . . . 125 E1
Homestead Way NN12 . . . 18 E3
Homeward Ct MK5 . . . . . . 46 B7
Home Way WD3 . . . . 167 F1
Homewood SL3 . . . . 206 D7
Home Wood SL7 . . . . 193 F6
Homewood Ct WD3 . . . . 167 F5
Honey Banks HP22 . . . . . 131 C4
Honeycroft Hill UB10 . . . 201 E5
Honey Hill
Emberton MK46 . . . . 13 F7
Uxbridge UB10 . . . . 201 F5
Honey Hill Dr MK19 . . . . . 31 E5
Honey La SL6 . . . . 193 E2
Honeypot Cl MK13 . . . . . . 34 B4
Honeysuckle Cl SL0 . . . . 207 C7
Honeysuckle Ct SL3 . . . . 212 C7
Honeysuckle Field HP5 144 C2
Honeysuckle Rd HP15 . . 162 F7
Honey Way HP14 . . . . 161 B8
HONEYWICK 92 E8
Honeywick La LU6 . . . . . . 92 E8
Honiton Ct MK7 . . . . 48 C7
Honor End La HP16 . . . . 151 A7
Honor Rd HP16 . . . . 151 D6
Honorwood Cl HP16 . . . . 151 B6
Honour Cl HP20 . . . . 102 A2
Honours Mead 4 HP3 . . 146 A4
Hoods Farm Cl HP22 . . . 102 C4
Hooke The MK15 . . . . 35 D7
Hooper Gate MK15 . . . . . . 35 C7
Hopcraft Cl OX25 . . . . 94 E7
Hope Brook Cotts LU7 . . . 91 F2
Hop Gdns RG9 . . . . 191 D2
Hopkins Cl MK10 . . . . 36 A2
Hopkins Ct HP20 . . . . 101 F2
Hoppers Hill MK46 . . . . 6 F5
Hoppers Mdw MK5 . . . . . . 46 A8
Hoppers Way HP15 . . . . . 162 D8
Hopton Gr MK16 . . . . 22 F3
Hopton Rd OX9 . . . . 126 A1
Hordern Cl HP17 . . . . 126 F6
Hornbeam MK16 . . . . 22 A3
Hornbeam Cl HP12 . . . . . 172 B4
Hornbeam Gdns 8
SL1 . . . . 206 A3
Hornbeam Way HP22 . . . 116 C4
Hornbeam Wlk HP15 . . . 163 A3
Hornbill Cl UB8 . . . . 208 D7
Hornby Chase MK4 . . . . . . 46 B2
Horners Croft MK12 . . . . . 33 C5
HORN HILL 178 B6
Hornhill Rd WD3 . . . . 178 D5
Horn La MK11 . . . . 32 D5
Horns La
High Wycombe HP12 . . . . 172 A3
Princes Risborough
HP27 . . . . 139 B3
Horn St MK18 . . . . 65 F4
Horsebuck La HP23 . . . . 133 E3
Horsefair Gn MK11 . . . . . . 32 D5
Horseguards Dr SL6 . . . . 203 B7
Horse Hill HP5 . . . . 155 D7
Horsemoor Cl SL3 . . . . . . 207 A2
Horsemoor La HP7 . . . . . 164 C2
HORSENDEN 138 E2
Horsenden La HP27 . . . . 138 F2
Horsenden Rd HP13 . . . . 173 F5
Horsepond MK17 . . . . 59 C2
Horsepool La MK17 . . . . . 49 F4
Horseshoe Cl LU7 . . . . . . 105 A7
Horseshoe Cloisters 3
SL4 . . . . 210 D6
Horseshoe Cres HP9 . . . 175 F1
Horseshoe Hill SL1 . . . . . 197 C8
Horseshoe Rd HP14 . . . . 159 C7
Horseshoes Cl HP18 . . . . . 83 A6
Horsetone Bglws HP17 129 D2
Horsham Reach SL6 . . . . 196 C2
Horsleys WD3 . . . . 178 D5
HORSLEYS GREEN 159 C3
HORTON
Cheddington 91 B3
Wraysbury 212 A4
Horton Bridge Rd UB7 . 208 F5
Horton Cl
Aylesbury HP19 . . . . 115 A7
Maidenhead SL6 . . . . 196 C1
West Drayton UB7 . . . . . . 208 F5
HORTON-CUM-
STUDLEY 108 B6
Horton Depot SL3 . . . . . . 212 C4
Horton Gate MK14 . . . . 21 F2
Horton Gdns SL3 . . . . 211 F4
Horton Grange SL6 . . . . . 196 C1
Horton Ind Pk UB7 . . . . . 208 F5
Horton Par UB7 . . . . 208 E5
Horton Rd
Datchet SL3 . . . . 211 D6
Horton SL3 . . . . 212 A6
Ivinghoe LU7 . . . . 91 A2
Poyle SL3 . . . . 212 E4
Slapton LU7 . . . . 91 C6
Stanwell TW19 . . . . 213 A2
West Drayton UB7 . . . . . . 208 F5
Horton Road Ind Est
UB7 . . . . 208 F5
Hortonsfield Rd NN12 . . . 18 F5
Horton Trad Est SL3 . . . . 212 B4
HORTON WHARF 91 C4
Horwood Ct MK1 . . . . 47 D2
Hospital Circular Rd
HP22 . . . . 131 D6
Hospital Hill HP5 . . . . . . 154 C7
Hospital Rdbt MK6 . . . . . . 47 B6
Hotch Croft MK43 . . . . 25 C3
HOTLEY BOTTOM 151 C8
Hotley Bottom La HP16 151 C8
Hotspur Bank Nature
Reserve★ HP9 . . . . 174 F1
Houghton Ct 4 MK8 . . . . 45 F8
Housman Cl MK16 . . . . 22 A5
Houston Ct 6 SL4 . . . . . 210 C5
Howard Agne Cl HP3 . . . 146 A4
Howard Ave
Aylesbury HP21 . . . . 116 B6
Slough SL2 . . . . 205 E8
Howard Cres HP9 . . . . . . 176 D5
Howard Ct 1 SL8 . . . . . . 185 A3
Howard Ind Est HP5 . . . . 144 C2
Howard Mews SL3 . . . . . 212 B8
Howard Rd
Chesham HP5 . . . . 144 B3
Seer Green HP9 . . . . 176 D5
Howards Thicket SL9 . . . 188 C2
Howards Wood Dr SL9 . 188 D2
Howard Way MK16 . . . . . . 23 A3
Howarth Rd SL6 . . . . 203 A6
Howe Ct MK10 . . . . 36 A3
Howe Dr HP9 . . . . 175 E5
Howe Hill La HP15 . . . . . 163 B8
Howell Hill Cl LU7 . . . . 90 D5
Howe Park Sch MK4 . . . . . 46 B1
Howe Rock Pl MK4 . . . . . . 46 B1
Howitt Dr MK13 . . . . 34 B8
Howland Pl MK17 . . . . 60 F7
Howletts Cl HP19 . . . . . . 115 A7
How's Cl UB8 . . . . 201 C4
How's Rd UB8 . . . . 201 C4
Hoylake Cl
Milton Keynes MK3 . . . . . . 57 D7
Slough SL1 . . . . 204 E4
Hoyton Gate MK8 . . . . 45 D6
Hubbard Cl MK18 . . . . 41 F1
Hubbards Ct WD3 . . . . . . 167 D4
Hubbards Rd WD3 . . . . . 167 D4
Hubert Day Cl HP9 . . . . . 175 D3
Hubert Rd SL3 . . . . 206 D3
Huckleberry Cl MK7 . . . . . 48 B6
Hudnall La HP4 . . . . 121 E7
Hudson La MK8 . . . . 45 D7
Hudson Mews HP19 . . . . 100 E1
Hudson Pl 14 SL3 . . . . . . 206 F1
Hughenden Ave HP13 . . 173 A8
Hughenden Cl SL6 . . . . . 202 C6
Hughenden Ct UB8 . . . . . 201 C1
Hughenden Gn HP21 . . . 115 E4
Hughenden Manor★
HP14 . . . . 162 A3
Hughenden Prim Sch
HP14 . . . . 162 A7
Hughenden Rd
High Wycombe HP13 . . . . 162 B1
Slough SL1 . . . . 205 D7
HUGHENDEN VALLEY 162 B7
Hughenden View HP13 173 B8
Hughes Croft 3 MK3 . . . . 57 F7
Hugh Park Cl MK5 . . . . . . 46 C8
Hulbert End HP21 . . . . . . 116 D5
Hulcombe Wlk HP20 . . . . 101 E2
HULCOTE 37 E2
HULCOTT 102 E6
Hull Cl
Aylesbury HP21 . . . . 115 E6
Slough SL1 . . . . 205 C4
Hulton Dr MK46 . . . . 13 F8
Humber Cl UB7 . . . . 208 D5
Humber Dr HP21 . . . . 115 C5
Humber Way
Milton Keynes MK3 . . . . . . 46 E1
Slough SL3 . . . . 207 A2
Hume Cl MK13 . . . . 34 B7
Humphreys Cl HP22 . . . . . 88 D5
Humphrey Talbot Ave
LU6 . . . . 107 F7
Hundred Acres La HP7 . 165 D8
Hungerford Ave SL2 . . . 205 E8
Hungerford Dr SL6 . . . . . 195 E3
Hungerford Ho 1 MK4 . . 46 D1
Hunsbury Chase MK10 . . 36 A3
Hunsdon Cl MK14 . . . . 34 D6
Hunsford Lodge SL4 . . . 210 A4
Hunstanton Cl SL3 . . . . . 212 C7
Hunstanton Way MK3 . . . 57 D8
Hunt Ct HP14 . . . . 158 F4
Huntercombe Cl SL1 . . . 204 C7
Huntercombe Hospl The
SL6 . . . . 204 C6
Huntercombe Lane N
SL6 . . . . 204 C7
Huntercombe Lane S
SL6 . . . . 204 C6
Huntercombe Spur
SL6 . . . . 204 C6
Hunter Ct SL1 . . . . 204 C8
Hunter Dr MK2 . . . . 58 C6
Hunters Cl
Bovingdon HP3 . . . . 146 A2
Chesham HP5 . . . . 144 A1
Tring HP23 . . . . 119 B5
Hunters Farm Ind Est
HP18 . . . . 100 B5
Hunters Hill HP13 . . . . . . 173 F5
Hunters Mews SL4 . . . . . 210 C6
Hunters Pk HP4 . . . . 135 E5
Hunters Point OX39 . . . . 147 C6
Hunters Reach MK13 . . . . 34 A3
Hunter St MK18 . . . . 52 C8
Hunters Way SL1 . . . . 204 E4
HUNTGATE END 10 D2
Huntingbrooke 6 MK8 . . 45 F8
Huntingdon Cres MK3 . . . 57 D6
Huntington Pl SL3 . . . . . . 207 B3
Huntley Cl HP13 . . . . 162 C2
Huntley Cres MK9 . . . . 35 A3
Hunt Rd HP13 . . . . 173 E6
HUNT'S HILL 161 D5
Hunts Hill La HP14 . . . . . 161 E5
Hunt's La SL6 . . . . 196 E3
Huntsman Gr MK14 . . . . . 22 A2
Huntsmans Cl HP4 . . . . . 107 C5
Huntswood La SL6, SL1 . 196 F4
HURLEY 193 E4
Hurley Croft MK10 . . . . . . 36 B1
Hurley High St SL6 . . . . . 193 F4
Hurley La SL7 . . . . 194 B3
Hurlstone Gr MK4 . . . . 46 D3
Hurricane Way SL3 . . . . 207 B1
HURST END 24 A3
Hurstfield Dr SL6 . . . . . . 204 B7
Hurstleigh WD3 . . . . 167 C4
Hurst Rd SL1 . . . . 204 D8
Hurworth Ave SL3 . . . . . 206 C3
Hutchings Cl MK5 . . . . 46 A8
Hutchings Rd HP9 . . . . . 175 D5
Hutton Ave MK6 . . . . 34 F1
Hutton Ct MK17 . . . . 49 B5
Hutton Way MK17 . . . . 49 B5
Huxley Cl
Newport Pagnell MK16 . . . 21 F4
Slough SL3 . . . . 199 B1
Uxbridge UB8 . . . . 201 D1
Huxtable Gdns SL6 . . . . . 203 E1
Hyacinth Dr UB10 . . . . . . 201 E5
Hychenden Cl HP14 . . . . 161 E6
Hyde Cl MK16 . . . . 22 C2
HYDE END 152 F7
Hyde Gn
Beaconsfield HP9 . . . . . . 175 F3
Marlow SL7 . . . . 183 F1
HYDE HEATH 153 C5
Hyde Heath Inf Sch
HP6 . . . . 153 C5
Hyde Heath Rd HP6,
HP10 . . . . 153 A6
Hyde La
Bovingdon HP3 . . . . 146 A3
South Heath HP16 . . . . . . 152 E5
Hyde Mdws HP3 . . . . 146 A4
Hyde The HP22 . . . . 116 F2
Hyland Ho 9 SL8 . . . . . . 185 B3
Hylle Cl SL4 . . . . 209 E6
Hylton Rd HP12 . . . . 172 C7
Hyrons Cl HP6 . . . . 154 E1
Hyrons Ct HP6 . . . . 154 E1
Hyrons La HP6 . . . . 154 D1
Hythe The MK8 . . . . 33 E3
Hyton Sq HP19 . . . . 101 D4

I

Ibotson Ct SL3 . . . . 212 E6
IBSTONE 169 D7
Ibstone Ave MK13 . . . . 34 D4
Ibstone CE Inf Sch
HP14 . . . . 169 D6
Ibstone Rd HP14 . . . . 158 C3
ICKENHAM 190 F1
ICKFORD 124 A3
Ickford Comb Sch
HP18 . . . . 124 A3
Ickford Rd
Shabbington HP18 . . . . . . 124 C2
Worminghall HP18 . . . . . . 123 E6
Icknield Cl
Chinnor OX39 . . . . 147 A4
Wendover HP22 . . . . 131 C5
Icknield Cotts HP17 . . . . 129 F2
Icknield Gn HP23 . . . . . . 119 A6
Icknield Way
Dunstable LU6 . . . . 93 D4
Tring HP23 . . . . 118 E4
Icknield Way Farm Cotts
LU6 . . . . 93 C3
Icknield Way Ind Est
HP23 . . . . 118 E4
Ideal Ho 3 HP20 . . . . 115 E8
Iffley Cl UB8 . . . . 201 D5
Ilchester Cl SL6 . . . . 202 C5
Ilex Cl HP15 . . . . 163 B3
Ilex Ct HP4 . . . . 135 B4
Illingworth SL4 . . . . 209 E4
Illingworth Pl MK6 . . . . . . 46 F8
ILMER 137 F8
Imperial Ct
Henley-on-Thames RG9 . . 191 E1
Loudwater HP10 . . . . 174 C2
Windsor SL4 . . . . 210 A4
Imperial Rd SL4 . . . . 210 A5
Independent Bsns Pk
HP14 . . . . 158 C5
India Rd SL1 . . . . 206 B4
Ingleglen SL2 . . . . 198 B7
Ingleside SL3 . . . . 212 F6
Ingleton Cl MK13 . . . . 34 C4
Ingram Ave HP21 . . . . . . 116 C5
Inkerman Dr HP15 . . . . . 163 B5
Inkerman Rd SL4 . . . . 204 F2
Inkerman Terr HP5 . . . . . 154 C6
Innes Ct MK8 . . . . 45 D6
Inn Farm Ct MK16 . . . . 22 D7
Innholder Ct MK14 . . . . . . 34 F6
Innings Gate RG9 . . . . . . 170 E1
Inniscrown Ho SL3 . . . . . 211 B7
Institute Rd
Marlow SL7 . . . . 183 E1
Taplow SL6 . . . . 203 F7
Intalbury Ave HP19 . . . . . 101 A2
In the Ray SL6 . . . . 203 B8
Inverewe Pl 1 MK4 . . . . . 45 E2
Inverness Cl MK3 . . . . 46 F2
Inwood Cl SL6 . . . . 195 B6
Iona Cres SL1 . . . . 204 E7
Ipswich Rd SL1 . . . . 205 A7
IQRA Slough Islamic Prim
Sch SL2 . . . . 206 B6
Ireland Cl MK7 . . . . 48 D4
Ireton Ct OX9 . . . . 125 F1
Iris Cl HP21 . . . . 115 B5
Iris Ct HP20 . . . . 116 B8
Ironmonger Ct MK14 . . . . 34 F6
Irvine Dr HP22 . . . . 116 A2
Irvine Ho SL4 . . . . 209 E5
Irving Cres LU7 . . . . 105 A8
Irving Dale MK7 . . . . 48 E5
Isaacson Dr MK7 . . . . 48 C7
Isis Cl HP21 . . . . 115 D3
Isis Way SL8 . . . . 185 B4
Isis Wlk MK3 . . . . 46 E1
Island Ho UB7 . . . . 213 B6
Island The MK18 . . . . 63 D2
Isle of Wight La LU6 . . . . . 93 F4
Islet Park Dr SL6 . . . . 196 C3
Islet Park Ho SL6 . . . . . . 196 C3
Islet Pk SL6 . . . . 196 C3
Islet Rd SL6 . . . . 196 C3
Isling Brook MK5 . . . . 46 B3
Islington Gr 6 MK10 . . . . 35 F1
Ivanhoe Cl UB8 . . . . 208 D8
IVER 207 F7
Iver Ct MK18 . . . . 52 C7
Iverdale Cl SL0 . . . . 207 C6
IVER HEATH 200 D4
Iver Heath Inf Sch SL0 . 200 D2
Iver Heath Jun Sch
SL0 . . . . 200 D3
Iver La SL0 . . . . 208 A8
Iver Lodge SL0 . . . . 207 F8
Iver Sta SL0 . . . . 207 F4
Iver Village Inf Sch SL0 . 207 F7
Iver Village Jun Sch
SL0 . . . . 207 E7
Ives Rd SL3 . . . . 207 A3
Ivester Ct LU7 . . . . 80 E6
IVINGHOE 105 F5
IVINGHOE ASTON 92 A1
Ivinghoe View HP20 . . . . 101 F1
Ivinghoe Way LU6 . . . . 92 E1
Ivins Rd HP9 . . . . 175 A1
Ivybridge Cl UB8 . . . . 201 E2
Ivy Cl
Buckingham MK18 . . . . 41 F8

Ivy Cl *continued*
Longwick HP27 . . . 138 E5
Newport Pagnell MK16 . . . 22 E4
Ivy Cotts HP8 . . . 177 B8
Ivy Cres SL1 . . . 204 F6
Ivyhill Ct HP27 . . . 139 B3
Ivy House La HP4 . . . 135 E5
Ivy La
Bierton HP22 . . . 102 D1
Burcott LU7 . . . 79 D4
Great Brickhill MK17 . . . 70 C8
Newton Longville MK17 . . . 57 C3
Stewkley LU7 . . . 68 E1
Ivy Pl HP14 . . . 171 C5

J

Jacks Cl MK46 . . . 7 E7
Jack's La MK43 . . . 8 E5
Jackson Cl
Slough SL3 . . . 206 E3
Uxbridge UB10 . . . 201 E5
Jackson Ct HP15 . . . 163 A3
Jackson Ind Est SL8 . . . 185 B2
Jackson Rd
Aylesbury HP19 . . . 101 A3
Uxbridge UB10 . . . 201 E5
Jacksons Cl LU6 . . . 92 E4
Jacob Cl SL4 . . . 209 E6
Jacobs Cl MK14 . . . 34 D7
Jakeman Way HP21 . . . 115 B6
Jakes Ho SL6 . . . 203 A8
Jamaica MK6 . . . 47 A6
James Cl
Hazelmere HP15 . . . 163 A6
Marlow SL7 . . . 183 F4
James Elliman Sch SL2 205 E6
James Martin Cl UB9 . . . 190 A5
James Mdw SL3 . . . 211 F8
James Rd HP14 . . . 171 B4
James St SL4 . . . 210 D6
James Way MK1 . . . 47 B1
Jane Cl HP21 . . . 116 A4
Jannetta Cl HP20 . . . 116 B7
Jansel Sq HP21 . . . 116 B6
Japonica La MK15 . . . 35 C6
Jardine Cotts SL2 . . . 199 A8
Jarman Cl MK18 . . . 52 F8
Jarratt Ho SL4 . . . 210 B4
Jarry Ct SL7 . . . 183 F3
Jarvis Cl HP21 . . . 116 A6
Jasmine Cl HP21 . . . 116 A4
Jasmine Cres HP27 . . . 139 B3
Jasmine Wlk HP5 . . . 144 A1
Jason Ho HP12 . . . 172 E4
Jasons Hill HP5 . . . 145 B2
Jeeves Cl MK6 . . . 47 C7
Jefferies Rd HP17 . . . 114 B5
Jefferson Cl SL3 . . . 207 A2
Jeffrey Wlk HP19 . . . 115 A7
Jeffries Ct SL8 . . . 185 B2
Jellicoe Cl SL1 . . . 205 B4
Jenkins Cl MK5 . . . 45 F5
Jenkins Ct HP22 . . . 89 C3
Jenkins La HP23 . . . 132 E3
Jenna Way MK16 . . . 23 A3
Jenner Rd HP21 . . . 115 E5
Jennery La SL1 . . . 197 C2
Jennings MK14 . . . 34 C7
Jennings Field HP10 . . . 185 C7
Jennings Wharf SL4 . . . 210 D7
Jerome Cl SL7 . . . 183 F4
Jersey Rd MK12 . . . 33 C6
Jesse's La HP18 . . . 125 D6
Job's La SL6 . . . 195 B8
John Colet Sch HP22 . . . 131 C5
John Hall Way HP11 . . . 172 D3
John Hampden Gram Sch HP11 . . . 172 F4
John Hampden Way HP16 . . . 151 B7
John Hampden Wendover Sch The HP22 . . . 131 B5
John Hellins Prim Sch NN12 . . . 18 D3
Johns La HP5 . . . 134 E1
Johnson Rd HP14 . . . 171 B5
Johnsons Field MK46 . . . 6 E4
Johnston Pl MK6 . . . 46 E8
John Taylor Ct SL1 . . . 205 C5
John Watson Sch OX33 122 B1
Joiner's Cl
Botley HP5 . . . 145 B1
Chalfont St Peter SL9 . . . 177 F3
Joiners La SL9 . . . 177 F3
Joiner's La SL9 . . . 177 E3
Joiners Way
Chalfont St Peter SL9 . . . 177 E3
Lavendon MK46 . . . 7 F8
Jonathan Ct SL6 . . . 202 E7
Jonathans MK6 . . . 47 A6
Jonathans Ct MK6 . . . 47 A6
Jones Way SL2 . . . 187 E2
Joplin Ct MK8 . . . 45 F7
JORDANS . . . 176 F3
Jordans La HP9 . . . 176 E3
Jordans Sch HP9 . . . 176 F4
Jordans Way HP9 . . . 176 F4
Joules Ct MK5 . . . 46 C5
Jourdelay's Pas SL4 . . . 210 D8
Journeys End SL2 . . . 205 E8
Jubilee Cotts MK18 . . . 64 F3
Jubilee Rd
High Wycombe, Downley HP13 . . . 161 E2
High Wycombe HP11 . . . 172 E7
Stokenchurch HP14 . . . 158 F3
Jubilee Terr MK11 . . . 32 E5
Jubilee Way SL3 . . . 211 C7
Judge's La LU7 . . . 80 F6
Juniper Cl HP15 . . . 163 B3
Juniper Ct
Flackwell Heath HP10 . . . 185 C7
Rickmansworth WD3 . . . 167 C3
Slough SL1 . . . 204 E6
Slough SL1 . . . 206 B4
Juniper Dr
Aylesbury HP22 . . . 116 C4
High Wycombe HP12 . . . 172 C5
Maidenhead SL6 . . . 203 B8
Juniper Gdns MK7 . . . 48 B7
Juniper Hill Sch HP10 . . . 185 B7
Juniper La HP10 . . . 185 D7
Juniper Rd SL7 . . . 183 D5
Jupiter Hts UB10 . . . 201 F4
Juson's Glebe HP22 . . . 131 C5
Jutland Ho SL4 . . . 209 F5

K

Kalman Gdns MK7 . . . 48 D5
Kaplan Cl MK5 . . . 46 B5
Karenza HP14 . . . 158 E5
Katherine Cl
Tylers Green HP10 . . . 174 C8
Walton MK7 . . . 48 A4
Katrine Pl MK2 . . . 58 D5
Kaybridge Cl [1] HP13 . . . 173 F5
Kay Cl HP23 . . . 119 A5
Kaywood Cl SL3 . . . 206 C3
Keach Cl MK18 . . . 66 A5
Keasden Ct MK4 . . . 46 B2
Keaton Cl MK8 . . . 45 D7
Keats Cl
Aylesbury HP21 . . . 115 F6
High Wycombe HP11 . . . 172 F6
Newport Pagnell MK16 . . . 22 A4
Keats La SL4 . . . 210 C8
Keats Way
[2] Milton Keynes MK3 . . . 57 F7
West Drayton UB7 . . . 208 F2
Keble Cl HP19 . . . 115 B8
Keble Rd SL6 . . . 202 E8
Keel Dr SL1 . . . 205 C4
Keeler Cl SL4 . . . 209 E4
Keel Way MK4 . . . 45 D3
Keen Cl HP19 . . . 115 A8
Keensacre SL0 . . . 200 D3
Keen's Cl HP13 . . . 162 E1
Keens La OX39 . . . 147 D6
Keepers Cl LU7 . . . 105 A7
Keepers Farm Cl SL4 . . . 209 E5
Keepers La HP6, HP7 . . . 153 C3
Keep Hill Dr HP11 . . . 173 D4
Keep Hill Rd HP11 . . . 173 D5
Keinches La HP22 . . . 87 A6
Keith Park Rd UB10 . . . 201 F5
Kellan Dr MK6 . . . 35 A1
Keller Cl MK11 . . . 33 B2
Kelling Way [3] MK10 . . . 36 A4
Kelmarsh Ct [11] MK8 . . . 33 F1
Kelpatrick Rd SL1 . . . 204 D7
Kelsey Cl
Maidenhead SL6 . . . 202 D3
Milton Keynes MK4 . . . 56 F8
Kelso Cl MK3 . . . 57 D6
Kelvin Cl HP13 . . . 172 F8
Kelvin Dr MK5 . . . 46 D6
Kemble Ct MK15 . . . 35 B6
Kempe Cl SL3 . . . 207 C2
Kempson Cl HP19 . . . 101 B1
Kemps Piece HP17 . . . 127 A6
Kempton Gdns MK3 . . . 57 D6
Kemsley Chase SL2 . . . 198 D4
Kemsley Cres MK10 . . . 36 A4
Kenchester MK13 . . . 33 F5
Kendal Cl
Aylesbury HP21 . . . 116 B6
Slough SL2 . . . 206 A6
Kendal Dr SL2 . . . 206 A6
Kendal Gdns LU7 . . . 80 C7
Kendall Pl
Maidenhead SL6 . . . 202 C4
Milton Keynes MK5 . . . 45 E5
Kendalls Cl HP13 . . . 173 F6
Kendal Mews UB8 . . . 201 C4
Kendrick Rd SL3 . . . 206 B3
Kenilworth Cl SL1 . . . 205 F3
Kenilworth Dr
Aylesbury HP19 . . . 101 D2
Milton Keynes MK3 . . . 57 E8
Kenneally SL4 . . . 209 C5
Kenneally Cl [11] SL4 . . . 209 C5
Kenneally Pl [12] SL4 . . . 209 C5
Kenneally Row [13] SL4 . . . 209 C5
Kenneally Wlk [10] SL4 . . . 209 C5
Kennedy Ave HP11 . . . 173 B4
Kennedy Cl
Farnham Common SL2 . . . 198 C6
Maidenhead SL6 . . . 202 C6
Marlow SL7 . . . 183 E3
Kennedy Ho SL1 . . . 204 D5
Kennel La SL6 . . . 195 C7
Kennels Dr NN12 . . . 17 D3
Kennet Cl
Aylesbury HP21 . . . 115 C4
High Wycombe HP13 . . . 162 D2
Kennet Dr MK3 . . . 57 E8
Kennet Pl MK3 . . . 57 F8
Kennet Rd
Bourne End SL8 . . . 185 B4
Maidenhead SL6 . . . 202 F8
Kennett Rd SL3 . . . 207 B3
Kennington Cl MK16 . . . 22 C3
Kennish Cl MK18 . . . 65 F4
Kensal Gn MK10 . . . 35 E1
Kensington Dr
Great Holm MK8 . . . 46 A8
Milton Keynes MK8 . . . 33 F1
Kensington Path [3] HP19 . . . 100 F1
Kensington Pl MK46 . . . 6 F5
Kent Ave SL1 . . . 205 C8
Kent Cl UB8 . . . 201 C6
Kent Ho MK3 . . . 46 F2
Kent Lodge [6] SL6 . . . 202 F6
Kentmere Rd HP21 . . . 116 B7
Kenton Cl SL7 . . . 183 E2
Kenton Ct HP19 . . . 101 C2
Kenton's La SL4 . . . 209 F5
KENTS HILL . . . 48 A7
Kents Hill Park Rdbt MK10 . . . 47 E8
Kents Hill Rdbt MK10 . . . 47 F8
Kents Hill Sch MK7 . . . 48 A7
Kents Rd MK14 . . . 34 D8
Kent Way SL6 . . . 195 E1
Kenway Dr HP7 . . . 166 B8
Kenwell Ct MK15 . . . 35 C3
Kenwood Cl SL6 . . . 202 A7
Kenwood Dr WD3 . . . 178 F8
Kenwood Gate MK6 . . . 35 B2
Keppel Ave MK19 . . . 20 D2
Keppel St SL4 . . . 210 D5
Kepwick MK8 . . . 33 E1
Kercroft MK8 . . . 33 E2
Kernow Cres MK6 . . . 35 A1
Kerria Pl MK3 . . . 47 A3
Kerr Pl HP21 . . . 115 E7
Kerry Cl HP19 . . . 101 A3
Kersey MK14 . . . 34 C8
Kesters Rd HP5 . . . 154 D7
Kestrel Cl
[2] Berkhamsted HP4 . . . 135 C3
High Wycombe HP13 . . . 161 C1
Kestrel Dr HP15 . . . 163 B5
Kestrel Path SL2 . . . 197 E1
Kestrel Way
Aylesbury HP19 . . . 101 E4
Buckingham MK18 . . . 52 F7
Keswick Ct SL2 . . . 205 F6
Keswick Rd MK19 . . . 11 B2
Ketchmere Cl HP18 . . . 125 C6
Ketelbey Nook MK7 . . . 48 E5
Ketton Cl MK15 . . . 35 D7
Kew Cl UB8 . . . 201 D3
Kew Ct MK8 . . . 33 F1
Kew Gr HP11 . . . 173 B4
Kew Pl HP11 . . . 173 B4
Keyes Way MK18 . . . 41 E2
Keynes Cl MK16 . . . 22 E4
Keys Pl SL6 . . . 202 F6
Khalsa Prim Sch SL2 . . . 206 A7
Khasiaberry MK7 . . . 48 B5
Kidd Cl MK8 . . . 45 E6
Kidderminster Rd SL2 . . . 198 A2
Kidderminster Wlk [3] MK10 . . . 36 B2
Kidwells Cl SL6 . . . 202 F8
Kidwells Park Dr SL6 . . . 202 F7
Kildonan Pl MK12 . . . 33 D4
Kilfillan Gdns HP4 . . . 135 A4
Kilfillan Pk HP4 . . . 135 A3
Kilgour Ct [2] LU7 . . . 80 F7
Kilkenny Ho MK4 . . . 45 E2
Killarney Dr SL6 . . . 202 E7
Killerton Cl MK4 . . . 45 F2
Kiln Ave HP6 . . . 155 C1
Kiln Cl
Calvert MK18 . . . 73 B5
Prestwood HP16 . . . 151 C7
KILN COMMON . . . 151 B8
Kiln Croft Cl SL7 . . . 184 A3
Kiln Ct HP9 . . . 186 B8
Kilner Rd HP21 . . . 115 E5
KILN FARM . . . 33 B3
Kiln Farm Ind Est MK11 . . . 33 B3
Kiln Farm Rdbt MK11 . . . 33 A3
Kiln Fields SL6 . . . 185 E1
Kiln La
Botley HP5 . . . 155 B8
Cores End SL8, HP10 . . . 185 D3
Kiln La *continued*
Hedgerley SL2 . . . 187 D3
Lacey Green HP27 . . . 149 F5
Kiln Pl SL6 . . . 195 A3
Kiln Pond La HP13 . . . 161 D3
Kiln Rd
Hastoe HP23 . . . 133 B6
Prestwood HP16 . . . 151 B7
Kiln The HP5 . . . 144 C1
Kilnwood HP14 . . . 150 B1
Kilpin Gn MK16 . . . 24 B6
Kilwinning Dr MK10 . . . 35 F1
Kimbells Cl HP18 . . . 124 D2
Kimber Cl SL4 . . . 210 A4
Kimberley Cl SL3 . . . 206 F2
Kimbers Dr SL1 . . . 197 D2
Kimber's La SL6 . . . 202 E3
Kimble Ct HP22 . . . 129 E3
Kimble Park Rd HP17 . . . 129 E3
Kimblewick Rd HP17 . . . 129 C5
Kimbolton Ct MK14 . . . 35 A8
Kincardine Dr MK3 . . . 46 F3
Kindermann Ct MK5 . . . 46 B5
Kindleton MK14 . . . 34 F8
Kinellan Ct HP9 . . . 175 D3
King Charles Cl MK18 . . . 41 E2
King Edward Ave HP21 . 116 A7
King Edward Ct [5] SL4 . 210 D6
King Edward St
Milton Keynes MK13 . . . 33 F7
Slough SL1 . . . 205 D4
King Edward VII Ave SL4 . . . 210 E8
King Edward VII Hospl SL4 . . . 210 C4
Kingfisher HP19 . . . 101 E4
Kingfisher Ct
[3] High Wycombe HP11 . . . 173 A6
Slough SL2 . . . 198 B1
Kingfisher Ctr The MK16 . . . 22 C3
Kingfisher Ho
Loudwater HP11 . . . 174 A4
Marlow SL7 . . . 183 F2
Kingfisher Pl HP11 . . . 174 B3
Kingfisher Rd MK18 . . . 52 F7
King George Cres MK11 . 32 E6
King George V Rd HP6 . 154 D1
Kinghorn La SL6 . . . 195 D3
Kinghorn Pk SL6 . . . 195 D3
King John's Cl TW19 . . . 211 C2
King Johns Palace SL3 212 D6
Kingsash Rd HP19 . . . 114 F8
Kingsbridge MK4 . . . 46 D2
Kingsbrook Specialist Bsns & Ent Coll MK19 . . . 31 F4
Kingsbury HP20 . . . 115 D8
Kingsbury Dr SL4 . . . 211 B1
Kings Chase SL6 . . . 202 F6
Kings Cl
Beaconsfield HP9 . . . 186 A8
Chalfont St Giles HP8 . . . 177 D8
Henley-on-Thames RG9 . . 191 D2
Westcott HP18 . . . 98 C6
Worminghall HP18 . . . 123 D5
Kingscote Pre Prep Sch SL9 . . . 188 E8
King's Cross HP18 . . . 113 A1
Kings Ct HP4 . . . 135 C5
Kingsdale Rd HP4 . . . 135 A3
KINGSEY . . . 127 B2
Kingsey Rd OX9 . . . 126 D1
Kings Farm Rd WD3 . . . 167 D3
Kingsfield SL4 . . . 209 D6
Kingsfold MK13 . . . 34 B7
Kingsgate HP19 . . . 115 B8
King's Gr SL6 . . . 202 E6
King's Grove Ind Est SL6 . . . 202 E6
Kings Hall Par HP22 . . . 131 B4
Kingshill Dr MK19 . . . 31 E5
Kingshill Rd HP13, HP15 . . . 162 D3
Kingshill Way HP4 . . . 135 B2
Kings La SL6 . . . 195 B8
King's La
Great Missenden HP16 . . 141 C2
Lee Common HP16, HP22 141 F7
South Heath HP16 . . . 152 E8
Kingsland Rd HP21 . . . 116 A4
Kingsley Cl MK16 . . . 21 F4
Kingsley Cres HP11 . . . 172 F6
Kingsley Dr SL7 . . . 183 C6
Kingsley Path SL2 . . . 197 D1
Kingsley Wlk HP23 . . . 119 A4
Kings Lodge
Amersham HP6 . . . 154 D1
Finmere MK18 . . . 50 D6
Kings Mdw HP22 . . . 102 C4
Kingsmead HP27 . . . 139 B6
Kings Mead LU6 . . . 92 E3
Kingsmead Bsns Pk HP11 . . . 174 B3
Kingsmead Ho SL1 . . . 205 C5
Kingsmead Rd HP11 . . . 174 B3
Kingsmead Rdbt MK4 . . . 56 F8
Kings Oak Cl HP27 . . . 139 C5
Kingsoe Leys MK10 . . . 36 A2
Kings Quarter [3] SL6 . . . 203 B7
Kings Rd
Berkhamsted HP4 . . . 135 B3
Chalfont St Giles HP8 . . . 177 D8
Henley-on-Thames RG9 . 191 D2
West Drayton UB7 . . . 208 F4
King's Rd
Aylesbury HP21 . . . 115 F8
Henley-on-Thames RG9 . . 191 D2
High Wycombe HP11 . . . 173 F4
Loudwater HP11 . . . 174 A4
Slough SL1 . . . 205 E3
Uxbridge UB8 . . . 201 D3
Windsor SL4 . . . 210 D3
Windsor SL4 . . . 210 D5
Kings Ride HP10 . . . 163 B1
King's Road Ho SL4 . . . 210 D5
Kings Sq HP11 . . . 173 F4
Kings St LU7 . . . 78 E7
King St
Chesham HP5 . . . 154 B7
Maidenhead SL6 . . . 202 F6
Maidenhead SL6 . . . 202 F7
Milton Keynes MK11 . . . 32 E6
Piddington HP14 . . . 160 C1
Tring HP23 . . . 119 A3
King Stable St SL4 . . . 210 D7
King's Terr SL3 . . . 212 B8
KINGSTON . . . 36 C2
Kingston Ave
Milton Keynes MK11 . . . 32 E5
West Drayton UB7 . . . 208 F6
KINGSTON BLOUNT . . . 147 A3
Kingston Gymnastics & Fitness Ctr MK10 . . . 36 C1
Kingston Hill OX39, HP14 . . . 158 B8
Kingston La
Uxbridge UB8 . . . 201 E2
West Drayton UB7 . . . 208 F4
Kingston Rd HP13 . . . 162 D1
Kingston Rdbt MK10 . . . 36 D1
Kingsway
Farnham Common SL2 . . . 198 C6
Gerrards Cross SL9 . . . 188 E8
Iver SL0 . . . 207 E7
[5] Slough SL3 . . . 206 C3
Kingsway Ho [6] SL6 . . . 202 F7
Kingsway Mews SL2 . . . 198 C6
Kingswear Dr MK10 . . . 36 B4
Kings Wlk RG9 . . . 191 D2
KINGSWOOD . . . 83 B3
Kings Wood SL7 . . . 193 D7
Kingswood Ave HP10 . . . 174 B8
Kingswood Creek TW19 . . . 211 D2
Kingswood Ct SL6 . . . 202 F5
Kingswood Ho SL2 . . . 205 C8
Kingswood La
Kingswood HP18 . . . 83 B2
Ludgershall HP18 . . . 96 F6
Kings Wood National Nature Reserve★ MK17 . . . 60 B1
Kingswood Par SL7 . . . 183 D5
Kingswood Pl HP13 . . . 162 E1
King's Wood Prim Sch HP13 . . . 173 F8
Kingswood Rd HP10 . . . 163 A1
Kingswood View HP13 . 162 E1
Kinloch Pl MK2 . . . 58 E5
Kinnaird Cl SL1 . . . 204 C7
Kinnear Cl MK8 . . . 45 E7
Kinross Dr MK3 . . . 46 E2
Kinson Gn HP20 . . . 101 E3
Kipling Ct SL4 . . . 210 B5
Kipling Dr MK16 . . . 21 F4
Kipling Rd MK3 . . . 58 A7
Kippell Hill MK46 . . . 6 F5
Kirby Est UB7 . . . 208 D6
Kirby Way UB8 . . . 201 F1
Kirkeby Cl MK14 . . . 34 D6
Kirke Cl MK5 . . . 46 A5
Kirkham Ct MK5 . . . 46 C8
Kirkstall Pl MK6 . . . 46 D8
Kirkwall Spur SL1, SL2 . . 205 E8
Kirkwood Gr MK5 . . . 45 D5
Kirtle Rd HP5 . . . 144 C1
Kirtlington MK15 . . . 35 B5
Kitchener Cl MK46 . . . 7 A3
Kitchener Rd HP11 . . . 172 E7
Kite Field HP4 . . . 134 E7
Kite Hill MK6 . . . 47 B8
Kitelee Cl MK19 . . . 11 A3
Kite Wood Rd HP10 . . . 163 B1
Kitsbury Ct HP4 . . . 135 B4
Kitsbury Rd HP4 . . . 135 B4
Kitsbury Terr HP4 . . . 135 B4
Kittiwake HP19 . . . 101 E4
Klee Cl HP22 . . . 85 A5
Klondyke SL7 . . . 183 D2
Knapp Gate MK5 . . . 45 F7
Knaresborough Ct MK3 . . 57 D7
Knaves Beech HP10 . . . 174 D1
Knaves Beech Bsns Ctr HP10 . . . 174 D1
Knaves Beech Ind Est HP10 . . . 174 C1

Knaves Beech Way
HP10 ... 174 C1
Knaves Hill LU7 ... 80 D8
Knaves Hollow HP10 ... 174 D1
Knebworth Gate MK14 ... 22 A1
Knighton-Way La UB9 ... 201 B6
Knightsbridge Ct SL3 ... 207 A2
Knightsbridge Pl 16
HP19 ... 115 A8
Knights Cl
Eaton Bray LU6 ... 92 E5
Great Brickhill MK17 ... 59 D1
Windsor SL4 ... 209 D6
Knights Ct LU6 ... 92 E5
Knights Gn WD3 ... 167 E6
Knights Hill HP12 ... 172 E6
Knights Pl 5 SL4 ... 210 C5
Knights Templar Way
HP11 ... 173 B4
Knoll Cl MK16 ... 13 F2
Knolls Cl HP22 ... 89 B3
Knolls View LU6 ... 92 B5
Knoll The
Aspley Heath MK17 ... 49 A1
Sherington MK16 ... 13 F2
Knolton Way SL2 ... 206 C7
Knottocks Cl HP9 ... 175 D5
Knottocks Dr HP9 ... 175 D5
Knottocks End HP9 ... 175 D5
KNOTTY GREEN ... 175 C6
Knowles Cl UB7 ... 208 E5
Knowles Gn MK2 ... 58 C8
Knowles Inf Sch MK2 ... 58 D8
Knowles Jun Sch MK2 ... 58 D8
Knowl Gate MK5 ... 46 C7
KNOWLHILL ... 46 D6
Knowlhill Rdbt MK5 ... 46 C6
Knowsley Cl SL6 ... 195 A1
Knox Bridge MK7 ... 48 B8
Kola Ho SL2 ... 206 B6
Kop Hill Rd HP27 ... 139 D3
Kramer Ct MK8 ... 45 D6
Krohn Cl MK18 ... 52 F8
Krypton Cl MK5 ... 46 C6
Kynaston Ave HP21 ... 115 E4

L

Laburnham Cotts LU7 ... 69 E3
Laburnham Rd SL6 ... 202 E6
Laburnum Ave UB7 ... 208 F6
Laburnum Cl SL7 ... 183 E4
Laburnum Gr
Milton Keynes MK2 ... 58 E7
Slough SL3 ... 212 B8
Laburnum Rd HP12 ... 172 C5
Lacemakers
Chinnor OX39 ... 147 C6
Long Crendon HP18 ... 125 C7
Lace Mews MK46 ... 7 A4
Lacey Dr HP14 ... 161 C7
LACEY GREEN ... 149 E5
Laceys Dr HP15 ... 163 B5
Ladbroke Cl HP20 ... 101 E2
Ladbroke Gr MK10 ... 47 F8
Ladbroke Rd SL1 ... 205 D3
Ladybridge Terr MK43 ... 8 E5
Lady Cooper Ct HP4 ... 135 E6
Ladyday Pl SL1 ... 205 C5
Lady Dr MK15 ... 35 A8
Ladymead Cl MK17 ... 56 B8
Ladymeadow Ct MK10 ... 35 E3
Ladymede Sch HP17 ... 129 E1
Ladysmith Rd LU7 ... 105 E5
Lady Verney Cl HP13 ... 173 B8
Ladywalk WD3 ... 178 E6
Lady Yorke Pk SL0 ... 200 D6
Laggan Ct MK2 ... 58 D4
Laggan Rd SL6 ... 195 F1
Laggan Sq SL6 ... 195 F1
Lagger Cl HP8 ... 177 B7
Lagger The HP8 ... 177 B7
Lagley Ho HP4 ... 135 A5
Lagonda Cl MK16 ... 22 E4
Laidon Cl MK2 ... 58 D4
Lake Ave SL1 ... 205 D6
Lake Cl MK18 ... 66 B6
LAKE END ... 204 B4
Lake End Ct SL6 ... 204 A7
Lake End Rd SL4, SL6 ... 204 B5
Laker Ct MK6 ... 46 E7
Lakes Cotts LU7 ... 90 C8
Lakeside
Aylesbury HP19 ... 101 E4
Maidenhead SL6 ... 196 B1
Tring HP23 ... 119 A5
Lakeside Dr SL2 ... 198 F4
Lakeside Est SL3 ... 212 F7
Lakeside Rd SL3 ... 212 F7
Lakes La
Beaconsfield HP9 ... 186 F8
Newport Pagnell MK16 ... 22 B5
Lakes The SL7 ... 194 A6
Lake View SL6 ... 196 A1
Lamb Cl MK16 ... 22 A4
Lambe Rd HP22 ... 131 C5
Lamberhurst Gr MK7 ... 48 A8
Lambert Ave SL3 ... 206 E3
Lamberts Croft MK12 ... 33 C5
Lambert Wlk OX9 ... 125 F1
Lamb La MK7 ... 48 C7
Lambourn Ct MK4 ... 46 D2
Lambourne Ave HP21 ... 115 D3
Lambourne Ct
Maidenhead SL6 ... 203 C8
Uxbridge UB8 ... 201 B4
Lambourne Dr SL6 ... 202 C3
Lambridge La RG9 ... 191 C3
Lambridge Wood Rd
RG9 ... 191 B4
Lambscroft Way SL9 ... 177 E1
Lambton Ho SL4 ... 210 A4
Lambtons Way MK18 ... 66 B5
Lamesley Ho SL6 ... 202 E6
Lammas MK6 ... 47 A5
Lammas Ave SL4 ... 210 D5
Lammas Ct SL4 ... 210 C5
Lammas La HP18 ... 112 B2
Lammas Path HP18 ... 112 B2
Lammas Rd
Cheddington LU7 ... 105 A7
Slough SL1 ... 204 D8
Lammas Way
Lane End HP14 ... 171 A4
Loudwater HP10 ... 174 C1
Lampitts Cross MK6 ... 47 B6
Lamport Ct MK8 ... 46 A8
Lamva Ct MK11 ... 32 F5
Lanark Ho MK3 ... 46 F1
Lancaster Ave SL2 ... 198 C1
Lancaster Bsns Park
LU7 ... 78 F1
Lancaster Cl TW19 ... 213 E1
Lancaster Ct HP12 ... 172 D4
Lancaster Dr HP3 ... 145 F4
Lancaster Gate MK3 ... 57 E7
Lancaster Rd
Aylesbury HP21 ... 116 B6
High Wycombe HP12 ... 172 E4
Maidenhead SL6 ... 202 B8
Uxbridge UB8 ... 201 D5
Lancaster Ride HP10 ... 174 B8
Lancastria Mews SL6 ... 202 D7
Lancelot Cl SL1 ... 205 A4
Lance Way HP13 ... 174 A6
Lanchester Rd MK43 ... 24 D2
Lancot Ave LU6 ... 93 F8
Lancotbury Cl LU6 ... 93 C7
Lancot Dr LU6 ... 93 F8
Lancot Lower Sch LU6 ... 93 E8
Lancot Pl LU6 ... 93 E8
Lancresse Cl UB8 ... 201 D6
Lander Rd HP19 ... 100 F3
Landon Ct HP21 ... 115 F7
Landrace Ct MK5 ... 45 F3
Landsborough Gate
MK15 ... 35 C7
Lands End Gr MK4 ... 56 F8
Lands The LU7 ... 79 F3
LANE END ... 171 C4
Lane End HP4 ... 134 F4
Lane End Ind Est HP14 ... 171 B4
Lane End Prim Sch
HP14 ... 171 B4
Lane End Rd HP12 ... 172 B6
Lanercost Cres MK10 ... 36 B1
LANES END ... 132 C4
Lane The
Grafton Regis NN12 ... 9 D2
Mursley MK17 ... 67 D6
Lane Wood Cl HP7 ... 165 F8
Lanfranc Gdns MK15 ... 35 B7
Langcliffe Dr MK13 ... 34 C5
Langdale Cl
Maidenhead SL6 ... 203 A6
Milton Keynes MK2 ... 58 D4
Langdale Ho HP11 ... 174 A4
Langdale Lodge HP10 ... 174 C2
Langdon Ave HP21 ... 116 B5
Langdon St HP23 ... 119 A3
Langdown Way SL6 ... 202 D5
Langerstone La MK4 ... 46 B1
Langford Pl MK7 ... 48 A3
Langham Way MK6 ... 47 C6
Langland Ho MK6 ... 47 C6
Langland Rd MK6 ... 47 C6
Langlands MK46 ... 7 E7
Langland Sch MK6 ... 47 C6
LANGLEY ... 207 A3
Langley Acad SL3 ... 206 E3
Langley Broom SL3 ... 206 F1
Langley Bsns Ctr SL3 ... 207 A4
Langley Bsns Pk SL3 ... 207 A4
Langley Cl MK18 ... 65 E4
Langley Cnr SL3 ... 199 F6
Langley Gram Sch SL3 ... 206 F2
Langley L Ctr SL3 ... 207 B2
Langley Manor Sch
SL3 ... 206 E5
Langley Park Ctry Pk★ SL0,
SL3 ... 200 A1
Langley Park Rd SL3 ... 207 B6
Langley Rd SL3 ... 206 E3
Langley Sta SL3 ... 207 A4
Langley Way SL7 ... 183 C2
Langmuir Ct MK5 ... 46 C4
Langney Gn MK4 ... 57 A8
Langport Cres MK5 ... 45 D5
Langston Ct HP12 ... 172 C8
Langstone Cl HP20 ... 101 F3
Langstone Ct 11 HP20 ... 101 F3
Langton Cl
Maidenhead SL6 ... 202 D8
Slough SL1 ... 204 D5
Langton Dr MK8 ... 33 E3
Langton's Mdw SL2 ... 198 C6
Langtree Ave SL1 ... 204 F4
Lanner Wlk MK6 ... 47 B8
Lanrick Copse HP4 ... 135 E5
Lansdell Ave HP12 ... 172 B3
Lansdowne Ave SL1 ... 205 E5
Lansdowne Ct
Maidenhead SL6 ... 203 C7
Slough SL1 ... 205 E5
Lansdowne Rd
Aylesbury HP20 ... 101 D2
Chesham HP5 ... 144 C2
Lansdowne Way HP11 ... 172 E3
Lansdown Rd SL9 ... 177 D2
Lanterns Wlk SL6 ... 203 B7
Lantern Way UB7 ... 208 E4
Lanthorn Cl MK14 ... 34 E6
Lappetts La HP16 ... 152 E8
Larch Cl
Aylesbury HP20 ... 102 A2
Slough SL2 ... 205 B8
Tylers Green HP10 ... 163 C2
Larches The
Berkhamsted HP4 ... 134 D5
Holmer Green HP15 ... 163 D7
Little Chalfont HP6 ... 155 B1
Larchfield Prim Sch
SL6 ... 202 E4
Larchfield Rd SL6 ... 202 E5
Larch Gr MK2 ... 58 E7
Larchlands The HP10 ... 163 D1
Larchmoor Pk SL2 ... 199 A7
Larch Rise HP4 ... 135 A5
Larchwood HP16 ... 152 B4
Lark Cl MK18 ... 52 E7
Larkfield SL6 ... 203 B1
Larkfield Cl HP13 ... 162 F1
Larkin Cl MK16 ... 22 A5
Larkings La SL2 ... 199 B4
Lark Rise HP15 ... 163 B5
Larkspur Ave MK14 ... 34 E5
Larkspur Way HP15 ... 162 F6
Larks Rise HP5 ... 154 D6
Lark Vale HP19 ... 101 E3
La Roche Cl 4 SL3 ... 206 C3
Larwood Pl MK6 ... 34 F1
Lasborough Rd MK10 ... 36 C1
Lascelles Cl MK15 ... 35 B7
Lascelles Ho 8 SL1 ... 206 A4
Lascelles Rd SL3 ... 206 B3
Laser Cl MK5 ... 46 C6
Lashlake Rd OX9 ... 125 F1
Lassell Gdns SL6 ... 203 B7
Lastingham Gr MK4 ... 46 B2
Latchmoor Ave SL9 ... 188 D7
Latchmoor Gr SL9 ... 188 D7
Latchmoor Way SL9 ... 188 D7
LATHBURY ... 22 C7
LATIMER ... 155 E3
Latimer
Latimer HP5 ... 155 E2
Milton Keynes MK11 ... 32 E4
Latimer Cl HP6 ... 166 C8
Latimer Ct HP20 ... 116 A8
Latimer Rd
Chesham HP5 ... 154 E5
Little Chalfont HP5 ... 155 C2
Latimer Way HP9 ... 175 C6
Laud's Cl RG9 ... 191 C1
Launceston WD3 ... 167 B3
Launceston Ct MK5 ... 46 B6
Launde 1 MK10 ... 36 B1
Laurance Ct 2 SL7 ... 183 D2
Laurel Ave SL3 ... 206 E4
Laurel Bank HP3 ... 146 F8
Laurel Cl
Milton Keynes MK8 ... 45 D7
Poyle SL3 ... 212 E7
Prestwood HP16 ... 151 B7
Speen HP27 ... 150 C4
Laurel Ct
Amersham HP6 ... 154 C3
Iver Heath SL0 ... 200 D5
Laurel Dr
Loudwater HP11 ... 174 B3
Walter's Ash HP14 ... 161 D7
Laurel La UB7 ... 208 E2
Laurel Rd SL9 ... 177 D2
Laurels Rd SL0 ... 200 D3
Laurels The
High Wycombe HP12 ... 172 C4
Milton Keynes MK1 ... 47 D1
Laurel Way 4 HP21 ... 115 E7
Lautrec Way HP19 ... 100 F2
Lautree Gdns SL6 ... 195 E7
Lavender Cl HP21 ... 115 B5
Lavender Gr MK7 ... 48 A5
Lavender Rd UB8 ... 208 F8
Lavender Way HP15 ... 162 F7
Lavender Wlk HP21 ... 115 B6
LAVENDON ... 7 F7
Lavendon Comb Sch
MK46 ... 7 F8
Lavendon Rd MK46 ... 7 A5
Lavric Rd HP21 ... 115 C6
Lawford Ave WD3 ... 167 C3
Lawford Cl WD3 ... 167 C3
Lawkland SL2 ... 198 C2
Lawn Ave UB7 ... 208 D4
Lawn Cl SL3 ... 211 C7
Lawn Farm Bsns Ctr
HP18 ... 83 D4
Lawn Hill HP18 ... 73 A2
Lawn House La HP18 ... 72 F1
Lawn Rd UB8 ... 201 C5
Lawnsmead Gdns MK16 ... 22 D5
Lawns The
Brill HP18 ... 96 B1
Tylers Green HP10 ... 163 B2
Lawn The SL3 ... 211 C6
Lawrence Cl
14 Aylesbury HP20 ... 101 F2
Aylesbury HP20 ... 102 A2
Lawrence Ct SL4 ... 210 C5
Lawrence Gr HP16 ... 151 D5
Lawrence Way SL1 ... 204 D8
Lawrence Wlk MK16 ... 21 F5
Laws Cl MK43 ... 8 E6
Lawsone Rise HP13 ... 162 B1
Lawson Pl MK5 ... 46 B5
Laxfield Dr MK10 ... 36 A4
Laxton Gn SL6 ... 202 C3
Layburn Cres SL3 ... 212 B8
Lay Rd HP19 ... 101 B2
Layter's Ave SL9 ... 177 C1
Layter's Avenue S SL9 ... 177 C1
Layter's Cl SL9 ... 177 C1
Layter's End SL9 ... 177 C1
LAYTER'S GREEN ... 177 B1
Layters Green La SL9 ... 177 B1
Layters Way SL9 ... 188 D6
Leaberry MK13 ... 34 A8
Leachcroft SL9 ... 177 B2
Leaches Farm Bsns Ctr
HP18 ... 81 F4
Leach Rd HP21 ... 115 C7
Lea Cl SL7 ... 183 D6
Leacroft Cl UB7 ... 208 E6
Leacroft Rd SL0 ... 207 E7
Lea Ct HP7 ... 165 F8
LEADENHALL ... 47 A8
Leadenhall Rdbt MK6 ... 46 E7
Leaders Cl HP22 ... 89 B3
Leafield Rise MK8 ... 33 D2
Leafy La HP23 ... 118 E1
Leaholme Gdns SL1 ... 204 D8
Lea La HP18 ... 125 F4
Leapingwell La MK18 ... 66 B5
Leary Cres MK16 ... 22 E4
Leas Cl HP13 ... 173 F8
Leas Dr SL0 ... 207 E7
Leaside MK16 ... 12 B6
Leasowe Pl MK13 ... 34 C3
Leather La HP16 ... 142 A3
Leaver Rd RG9 ... 191 C1
LECKHAMPSTEAD ... 42 E7
Leckhampstead Rd
MK18 ... 42 A8
Leckhamstead Rd MK19 ... 31 A3
Ledborough Gate HP9 ... 175 F4
Ledborough La HP9 ... 175 E4
Ledborough Wood
HP9 ... 175 E4
LEDBURN ... 90 D8
Ledburn LU7 ... 90 C8
Ledburn Gr LU7 ... 80 E6
Ledbury MK14 ... 21 E1
Ledeview Ct HP11 ... 174 A4
Ledger's Rd SL1 ... 205 D4
Leeches Way LU7 ... 105 A7
LEE COMMON ... 142 D5
Lee Common CE Fst Sch
HP16 ... 142 D5
Lee Cotts
Buckmoorend HP17 ... 140 D6
Lacey Green HP27 ... 149 A4
Lee Cres HP17 ... 114 D5
Lee Ct 7 HP12 ... 172 E7
Leeds Rd SL1 ... 205 E6
Lee Farm Cl HP5 ... 145 A1
LEE GATE ... 142 A7
Lee Ho 2 MK2 ... 58 C8
Lee La SL6 ... 194 F1
Lee Rd
Aylesbury HP21 ... 115 D6
Quainton HP22 ... 84 F5
Saunderton HP27 ... 148 F6
Lees Cl SL6 ... 202 B5
Lees Gdns SL6 ... 202 B5
Leeson Gdns SL4 ... 204 E2
Lees Wlk SL7 ... 183 C2
Le Flaive Bsns Pk HP14 ... 161 E6
Legoland Windsor★
SL4 ... 209 D2
Leicester Cl RG9 ... 191 D3
Leigh Hill MK4 ... 46 D2
Leigh Pk SL3 ... 211 B7
Leigh Rd SL1 ... 205 B6
Leigh Sq SL4 ... 209 D5
Leigh St HP11 ... 172 F7
LEIGHTON BUZZARD ... 80 F6
Leighton Buzzard Sta
LU7 ... 80 E7
Leighton Gdns SL6 ... 196 B1
Leighton Ho 7 SL7 ... 183 E2
Leighton Mid Sch LU7 ... 80 F6
Leighton Rd
Edlesborough LU6 ... 92 D4
Leighton Buzzard LU7 ... 80 F7
Soulbury LU7 ... 70 B1
Stoke Hammond MK17 ... 69 E7
Wing LU7 ... 80 A3
Wingrave HP22 ... 89 C3
Leighton St MK17 ... 60 E6
Leiston Spur SL1 ... 205 E7
Leisure Plaza★ MK9 ... 46 C8
Leith Cl SL1 ... 206 A5
Leith Rd HP19 ... 115 A8
Lembrook Wlk HP21 ... 115 C6
Lemmon Wlk 5 MK4 ... 45 E2
LENBOROUGH ... 52 D3
Lenborough Cl MK18 ... 52 C7
Lenborough Ct MK15 ... 35 C2
Lenborough Rd MK18 ... 52 C7
Lennon Dr MK8 ... 45 E7
Lennox Rd MK2 ... 58 D7
LENT ... 197 B1
Lent Gn SL1 ... 197 B1
Lent Green La SL1 ... 197 B1
Lenthall Cl MK13 ... 34 A5
LENT RISE ... 204 A8
Lent Rise Comb Sch
SL1 ... 204 B8
Lent Rise Rd SL1 ... 204 B8
Leominster Gate 4
MK10 ... 36 A1
Leonards Cl HP18 ... 72 F2
Leonardslee MK4 ... 45 F2
Leon Ave MK2 ... 58 D8
Leon L Ctr MK2 ... 58 C4
Leon Sch & Sports Coll
MK2 ... 58 C5
Leopard Dr MK15 ... 35 A7
Leopold Mall 5 SL1 ... 205 F4
Leopold Rd LU7 ... 80 D7
Lerwick Dr SL1 ... 205 E8
Leslie Dunne Ho SL4 ... 209 E5
Lester Gr HP15 ... 163 A4
Lesters Rd SL6 ... 195 D6
Letchfield HP5 ... 155 B8
Letter Box La HP27 ... 139 D7
Leven Cl
Leighton Buzzard LU7 ... 80 B7
Milton Keynes MK2 ... 58 D5
Levens Hall Dr MK4 ... 45 F1
Leverkus Ct OX39 ... 147 C6
Leverkus Ho OX39 ... 147 C6
Levings Cl HP19 ... 101 A3
Lewens Croft MK16 ... 16 A3
Lewes Ct SL1 ... 205 C4
Lewes Ho MK3 ... 57 D7
Lewins Farm Ct SL1 ... 204 F6
Lewins Rd SL9 ... 188 D8
Lewins Way SL1 ... 204 F6
Lewins Yd HP5 ... 154 B8
Lewis Cl MK16 ... 21 F5
Lewis La SL9 ... 177 E2
LEWKNOR ... 157 B8
Lewknor CE Prim Sch
OX49 ... 157 B8
Lewknor Cl OX49 ... 157 A7
Lexham Gdns HP6 ... 154 C2
Lexington Ave SL6 ... 202 D5
Leybourne Gdns OX39 ... 147 C7
Leyburn Ct MK13 ... 34 C5
Leyburne Cl LU7 ... 90 C8
Ley Field Rd HP21 ... 115 E6
LEY HILL ... 145 B1
Ley Hill Sch HP5 ... 145 B1
Leyland Cl MK18 ... 51 F4
Leyland Pl 3 MK6 ... 34 E1
Leylands La TW19 ... 213 A2
Leys Cl HP19 ... 101 C4
Leys Ct MK5 ... 46 B8
Leys La MK18 ... 62 B8
Leys Rd MK5 ... 46 B8
Leys The
Amersham HP6 ... 154 B4
Buckingham MK18 ... 41 F3
Halton HP22 ... 117 C1
Tring HP23 ... 119 B4
Woburn Sands MK17 ... 49 B4
Yardley Hastings NN7 ... 1 A6
Leys View MK16 ... 13 F1
Leywood Cl HP7 ... 165 E7
Libra Ho HP10 ... 185 A8
Lichfield Down MK7 ... 48 B5
Lichfield Ho HP21 ... 115 F6
Lidcote LU7 ... 78 A5
Liddall Way UB7 ... 208 F5
Liddell SL4 ... 209 C4
Liddell Pl SL4 ... 209 C4
Liddell Sq 14 SL4 ... 209 C5
Liddell Way SL4 ... 209 C4
Liffre Dr HP22 ... 131 B6
Lightfoot Ct MK7 ... 47 F5

Lightlands La SL6 195 F5
Ligo Ave HP22 116 C2
Lilac Cl MK17 57 C3
Lilac Ct SL2 197 F2
Lilac Pl UB7 208 F6
Lilies The HP22 87 C1
Lilleshall Ave MK10 35 F1
Lilley Way SL1 204 E5
Lillibrooke Cres SL6 202 A3
LILLINGSTONE DAYRELL 29 F4
LILLINGSTONE LOVELL 30 B5
Lillyfee Farm La HP10 186 B5
Lilly Hill MK46 6 F5
Lily Bottom La HP27 150 A7
Lily Dr UB7 208 D2
Lily's Wlk HP11 173 A6
Limbaud Cl MK7 48 A5
Lime Ave
Buckingham MK18 52 F7
High Wycombe HP11 173 D5
West Drayton UB7 208 F6
Windsor SL4 210 F7
Lime Cl
Hazelmere HP15 163 A3
Newport Pagnell MK16 22 B3
Lime Gr
Chinnor OX39 147 D6
Leighton Buzzard LU7 80 E8
Woburn Sands MK17 49 B4
Lime Rd
Princes Risborough HP27 139 B3
Yardley Gobion NN12 18 E6
Limerick La MK9 35 B3
Limes Ave HP21 116 B7
Lime St MK46 6 F3
Limes The
Amersham HP6 154 B3
Milton Keynes, Fenny Stratford MK2 58 E8
Milton Keynes MK11 32 E5
Windsor SL4 209 C6
Limes Way HP18 124 D2
Lime Tree Cl HP15 162 D8
Lime Tree Wlk HP7 165 F8
Lime Wlk
Maidenhead SL6 202 A8
New Denham UB9 201 C7
Limit Home Pk HP4 134 D7
Limmer La HP12 172 B3
Limmers Mead HP15 162 D8
Linceslade Gr MK5 34 B1
Linchfield HP13 173 E7
Linchfield Rd SL3 211 C6
Lincoln MK14 34 C8
Lincoln Cl HP22 116 B2
Lincoln Ct
Berkhamsted HP4 135 B4
3 Slough SL1 205 E3
Lincoln Hatch La SL1 197 C1
Lincoln Ho HP10 185 D3
Lincoln Park Bsns Ctr HP12 172 D6
Lincoln Pk
Amersham HP7 165 E8
Brackley NN13 38 A5
Lincoln Rd
Chalfont St Peter SL9 177 E2
High Wycombe HP12 172 E5
Maidenhead SL6 202 B8
Lincolnshire Cl MK3 46 E1
Lincolns The HP16 152 A3
Lincoln Way SL1 204 D6
Lincombe Slade LU7 80 E8
Lincroft MK43 25 B1
Linden SL3 207 B1
Linden Ave SL6 195 D1
Linden Cl SL0 200 D3
Linden Ct HP12 172 D6
Linden Dr
Chalfont St Peter SL9 177 E1
Farnham Royal SL2 198 C4
Linden End HP21 115 F6
Linden Gr MK14 34 E8
Linden Lea HP22 131 B6
Lindens The HP3 146 F8
Linden Way HP17 128 B7
Linden Wlk HP15 163 B3
Lindisfarne Dr MK10 36 A1
Lindo Cl HP5 144 B1
Lindores Croft MK10 36 B1
Lindsay Ave HP12 172 E7
Lindsay Cl TW19 213 D2
Lindsey Rd UB9 190 A1
Lines Hill HP22 88 B3
Lines Rd HP14 171 B5
Lines The HP22 88 C4
Linfields HP7 166 C7
Linford Ave MK16 22 A4
Linford La
Milton Keynes, Willen MK15 35 D7
Milton Keynes, Woolstone MK15 35 C3
Lingfield MK12 33 E4
Lingfield Cl HP13 174 A5
Lingholm Cl SL6 202 C6
Linington Ave HP5 145 A1
Link Cl HP12 172 D6
Link Rd
Datchet SL3 211 C6
Great Missenden HP16 152 A7
High Wycombe HP12 172 D6
Links App HP10 185 B8
Links Rd HP10 185 C8
Links Way HP10 185 B8
Linkswood Rd SL1 197 C3
Link The
Hazelmere HP15 163 A5
Slough SL2 206 B7
Link Way UB9 190 A5
Linnet Cl HP12 172 B3
Linnet Dr HP18 98 C5
Linney Ct MK4 46 A1
LINSLADE 80 D7
Linslade Lower Sch LU7 80 D7
Linslade Mid Sch LU7 80 E5
Linslade Rd LU7 70 F4
Lintlaw Pl MK3 47 A3
Linton Cl MK13 34 C4
Lintott Ct TW19 213 D1
Linx The MK3 47 A2
Lionel Ave HP22 131 A6
Lionel Cl HP22 131 A5
Lipscombe Dr MK18 41 E1
Lipscomb La MK5 46 A7
Lisburn Path 1 HP20 101 F2
Lisle Rd HP13 162 A1
Lisleys Field HP15 162 D7
Lismore Pk SL2 205 F7
Lissel Rd MK6 47 E5
Lisset Rd SL6 203 A6
Lister Cl MK6 47 B6
Lister Gn HP21 115 E5
Liston Ct (Sh Arcade) 7 SL7 183 D2
Liston Ho 9 SL7 183 E2
Liston Rd SL7 183 D2
Litcham Spur SL1 205 D7
Little Balmer MK18 52 E6
Little Benty UB7 208 D1
Little Boltons 13 SL7 183 E2
LITTLE BOYS HEATH 152 C3
LITTLE BRICKHILL 59 E5
Little Bridge Rd HP4 135 D4
LITTLE BRITAIN 208 C7
Little Britain HP18 99 B7
Littlebrook Ave SL2 204 E8
Little Buntings SL4 209 F4
LITTLE CHALFONT 155 B1
Little Chalfont Prim Sch HP6 166 E8
Little Chapels Way SL1 205 A4
Little Chartridge Ct HP5 144 A1
Little Cl
Aylesbury HP20 101 D1
Flackwell Heath HP10 185 B6
High Wycombe HP12 172 E3
LITTLECOTE 78 A5
Littlecote MK8 34 A1
Littledown Rd SL1 205 F5
Littledown Specl Sch SL1 205 F6
Little Dunmow MK10 36 A1
LITTLE END 23 B8
Littlefield Ct UB7 213 D7
LITTLE FRIETH 170 E2
LITTLE GADDESDEN 121 D7
Little Gaddesden CE Prim Sch HP4 121 C8
Little Gaddesden Ho HP4 121 E5
Little Gibbs HP27 138 A2
Little Greencroft HP5 144 A4
Little Habton 3 MK4 46 B2
Little Hame MK10 35 F3
Little Ham La HP27 139 B5
LITTLE HAMPDEN 140 F4
Little Hampden Cl HP22 131 B4
Little Hill WD3 167 C3
Little Hivings HP5 144 A4
Little Hollis HP16 151 E7
Little Hoo HP23 118 F4
LITTLE HORWOOD 55 F2
Little Horwood Manor MK17 55 E4
Little Horwood Rd MK17 55 C3
Little Hundridge La HP16 153 A8
LITTLE KIMBLE 129 E2
Little Kimble Sta HP17 129 E2
LITTLE KINGSHILL 152 B3
Little Kingshill Comb Sch HP16 152 B2
Little La
Lacey Green HP27 149 C4
Yardley Hastings NN7 1 A7
LITTLE LINFORD 21 C5
Little Linford La MK16, MK19 21 E4
Little Linford Wood Wildlife Reserve★ MK16 21 B8
LITTLE LONDON
Oakley 109 F5
Wendover 141 C7
Little London
Deanshanger MK19 31 E4
Whitchurch HP22 87 A5
Little London Gn HP18 109 F5
LITTLE MARLOW 184 D5
Little Marlow CE Inf Sch SL7 184 C5
Little Marlow Rd SL7 183 E3
LITTLE MARSH 72 A3
Littlemarsh MK7 48 A5
Little Marsh Rd OX27 72 A3
Little Mdw MK5 46 C7
Littlemere MK8 33 D1
LITTLE MISSENDEN 153 A2
Little Missenden CE Inf Sch HP7 153 A2
Little Mollards HP22 89 A3
Little Orchard Cl HP27 138 E5
Little Orchs HP20 101 F3
Little Pk
Bovingdon HP3 146 A3
Princes Risborough HP27 139 C3
Littleport Spur SL1 205 E7
Little Reeves Ave HP7 165 F8
LITTLE ROW 202 A5
Little Shardeloes HP7 165 A8
Little Spinney MK43 25 C3
Little Spring HP5 144 B3
Little Spring Prim Sch HP5 144 B3
Little St NN7 1 B6
Little Stanton MK14 34 D8
Little Stocking MK5 46 A3
Littlestone Gate MK10 36 B3
Little Sutton La SL3 207 C1
LITTLE TINGEWICK 50 E6
LITTLE TRING 118 F6
Little Tring Rd HP23 118 F6
Little Twye HP23 132 F3
Little Twye Rd HP23 132 F3
Little Windmill Hill WD4 156 F7
Little Wood HP14 158 E5
Little Woodlands SL4 209 F4
Littleworth LU7 79 E3
LITTLEWORTH COMMON 186 D1
Littleworth Rd
Hedgerley SL1 186 C1
High Wycombe HP13 161 E2
Litton Ct HP10 174 C2
Liverpool Rd SL1 205 B7
Liverpool Victoria Ho 3 HP13 173 B7
Livesey Hill MK5 46 B5
Living Furniture Making Mus★ HP11 172 F7
Livingstone Dr MK15 35 C5
Llanbury Cl SL9 177 E3
Lloyds MK6 47 A7
Loakes Ho HP11 173 A6
Loakes Rd HP11 173 A6
Lochinvar Cl SL1 205 B4
Lochnell Rd HP4 134 F6
Lochy Dr LU7 80 C7
Lock Ave SL6 196 C2
Lockbridge Ct SL6 203 C8
Lock Bridge Rd SL8 185 A3
Locke Cl HP19 101 A2
Locke Gdns SL3 206 C4
Locke Rd MK2 58 C8
Lockets Cl SL4 209 D6
Lockhart Ave MK4 45 D2
Lock La
Cosgrove MK19 19 E2
Maidenhead SL6 202 C4
Lock Mead SL6 196 C2
Lock Path SL4 209 D8
Lock Rd SL7 183 F1
Locksley Ct 4 SL1 205 E3
Lockton Ct MK4 46 B3
Lockview Cotts MK1 47 E1
Lock View La MK1 47 E1
Lockwood Chase MK4 45 D2
Lodden Cl HP21 115 D3
Loddon Dr SL6 202 D8
Loddon Rd SL8 185 A4
Loddon Spur SL1 205 E7
Lodge Cl
Cheddington LU7 105 A7
Marlow SL7 183 E1
Padbury MK18 53 C2
Slough SL1 205 C4
Uxbridge UB8 201 C1
Lodge Farm Bsns Ctr MK19 20 C3
Lodge Farm Cl HP22 116 E2
Lodge Farm Ct MK19 19 F6
Lodge Gate MK14 34 E7
Lodge La
Little Chalfont HP8 166 F6
Prestwood HP16 151 D5
Stoke Hammond MK17 69 E7
Lodge Park The MK16 22 C4
Lodge Rd MK43 37 F8
Lodge The
Aylesbury HP19 115 A7
Slough SL2 206 B8
Lodge Way SL4 209 E4
Lodgings of the Military Knights 4 SL4 210 D6
Lodore Gn UB10 190 E1
Logan Rock MK4 57 B8
Lollards Cl HP6 154 C2
Lombardy Dr HP4 135 D3
Lomond Dr
Leighton Buzzard LU7 80 C7
Milton Keynes MK2 58 D4
London End
Beaconsfield HP9 175 F1
Newton Longville MK17 57 D4
Woburn MK17 60 F6
London End La MK17 48 D1
London Ho MK11 32 D5
London Rd
Aston Clinton HP22 117 E4
Beaconsfield HP9 187 B8
Berkhamsted HP4 135 E3
Buckingham MK18 52 E6
Chalfont St Giles HP8 177 C7
Datchet SL3 211 C7
Felden HP3 146 F8
High Wycombe HP11 173 E5
Little Kingshill HP16 152 B5
Loughton MK5 46 B7
Milton Common OX9 136 B3
Milton Keynes MK16 36 B5
Milton Keynes, Stony Stratford MK11 32 E5
Newport Pagnell MK16 22 F3
Old Stratford MK19 32 C7
Slough, Brands Hill SL3 212 B8
Slough, Langley SL3 206 D2
Slough SL3 212 B8
Tring HP23 119 C3
Wendover HP22 141 D6
Wheatley OX33 122 B1
London Road E HP7 165 E6
London Road W HP7 165 C7
Londrina Ct 9 HP4 135 D4
Londrina Terr 10 HP4 135 D4
Long Ayres MK7 48 A3
Longborns MK43 25 C2
Longbottom La HP9 176 C3
Longbourn SL4 210 A4
Longbridge Cl HP23 119 A6
Longbridge Way UB8 201 B3
Long Cl SL2 198 B5
Long Close Sch SL3 206 A2
LONG CRENDON 125 B6
Long Crendon Courthouse★ HP18 125 D7
Long Crendon Ind Est HP18 125 E5
Long Crendon Rd HP18 124 D3
Long Crendon Sch HP18 125 C7
Longcroft HP22 117 F5
Longcroft Ave HP22 131 D6
Longcroft La
Bovingdon HP3 146 D5
Paulerspury NN12 17 C8
Long Croft Rd WD3 178 D5
Longcross MK15 35 A6
Longdown Hill HP27 139 F5
Longdown Mews HP19 114 F8
Long Dr SL1 197 C2
Longfellow Dr MK16 22 A4
Longfield
Hedgerley SL2 187 D1
Little Kingshill HP16 152 B4
Longfield Dr HP6 154 B1
Longfield Gdns HP23 118 E3
Longfield Rd
Chesham HP5 143 F2
Tring HP23 118 F3
LONGFORD 213 C6
LONGFORDMOOR 213 A6
Longford Rdbt UB7 213 B6
Long Furlong
Haddenham HP17 126 F6
Stone HP17 114 B5
Long Furlong Dr SL2 197 E1
Long Gr HP9 176 C4
Long Grove Wood Wildlife Reserve★ HP9 176 C4
Long Hale LU7 105 C3
Longhedge MK7 48 A2
Long Hedge LU7 105 C4
Long Hide HP27 139 C4
Long La
Bovingdon HP3 155 F8
Cookham Rise SL6 195 D5
Heronsgate WD3 167 D2
Olney MK46 6 F4
Rickmansworth WD3 167 F1
Stanwell TW19 213 F1
Longlands Ct MK18 66 A5
Longlands Wlk MK18 66 A5
Longland Way HP12 172 D5
Longleat Ct 7 MK8 33 F1
Longleat Gdns SL6 202 D6
Longlees WD3 178 D5
Long Ley LU7 105 A7
Long Leys HP19 115 A8
Long Lional HP20 115 D8
LONG MARSTON 104 B3
Long Marston Prim Sch HP23 104 B4
Long Marston Rd
Cheddington LU7 104 E7
Marsworth LU7 104 F2
Long Massey MK46 6 E5
Long Mdw
Aylesbury HP21 116 B6
Chesham HP5 144 C3
Longmead SL4 209 E6
Longmead La SL1 197 D5
Long Meadow Cl
Amersham HP7 164 C3
Monks Risborough HP27 139 C5
Long Meadow Sch MK5 45 F3
Longmead Prim Sch UB7 208 E2
Longmire MK46 7 F8
Longmore Cl WD3 178 F6
Long Orchard Dr HP10 174 C8
Long Park Cl HP6 154 C3
Long Park Way HP6 154 C3
Longpeak Cl MK4 46 B1
Long Pk HP6 154 C3
Long Plough HP22 117 D5
Long Readings La SL2 198 B2
Long Ride HP27 139 C3
Longridge (Activity Ctr)★ SL7 194 F8
Long Row
Leckhampstead MK18 30 E1
Prestwood HP16 151 D6
Longstone Rd SL0 200 C4
LONG STREET 10 F4
Longview HP9 185 F8
Long View HP4 135 A6
Longville MK12 33 B7
Long Walk The★ SL4 210 D4
Long Wall HP17 126 F5
LONGWICK 138 D7
Longwick CE Comb Sch HP27 138 D6
Longwick Rd
Longwick HP27 138 F6
Monks Risborough HP27 139 A5
Long Wlk HP8 166 E6
Longwood Ave SL3 207 B1
Long Wood Dr HP9 176 F4
Longwood La HP7 165 D8
Longworth Dr SL6 196 C1
Lonsdale Cl SL6 196 A1
Lonsdale Way SL6 203 C1
Look Ahead SL1 205 E4
Loosen Dr SL6 202 A3
Loose Path HP19 114 F8
Loosley Hill HP27 149 D6
LOOSLEY ROW 149 C6
Lord Grey Sch The MK3 46 F1
Lord Knyvett Cl TW19 213 D1
Lord Knyvetts Ct 12 TW19 213 E1
Lord Mayors Dr SL2 198 A7
Lord Raglan Ho SL4 210 C4
Lords Cl MK2 47 C1
Lordsmead MK43 25 C2
Lords Mead LU6 92 E6
Lords Mill Ct HP5 154 C7
Lords Terr LU6 92 E6
Loriner Pl MK14 35 A6
Loring Rd
Berkhamsted HP4 135 C3
Dunstable LU6 93 F8
Windsor SL4 209 F6
Lorne Cl SL1 205 C3
Lorraine Cl HP13 173 E8
Lorre Mews MK4 45 E3
Loseley Ct MK8 33 F1
Losfield Rd SL4 209 E6
Lossie Dr SL3 207 B6
Lothersdale MK13 34 B5
Lothian Cl MK3 46 E2
Lott Mdw HP21 115 D3
Lott Wlk HP21 115 D3
Louches La HP14 161 E6
Loudhams Rd HP7 166 C8
Loudhams Wood La HP8 166 D7
LOUDWATER 174 D2
Loudwater Comb Sch HP11 174 B2
Loughborough Dr MK10 36 C4
LOUGHTON 46 A8
Loughton Manor First Sch MK5 46 A8
Loughton Rd MK13 34 A3
Loughton Rdbt MK8 45 F8
Loughton Sch MK5 46 A7
Loughton Valley Pk★ MK5 46 D7
Louisa Cotts 10 HP23 119 A3
Louise Wlk HP3 146 A3
Lovat Meadow Cl MK16 22 E3
Lovat St MK16 22 D4
Lovatt Dr MK3 57 E8

LOVE GREEN 207 D8
Love Green La SL0 207 E8
Lovegrove Dr SL2 197 F1
Love Hill La SL3 207 A6
Lovejoy La SL4 209 D5
Love La SL0 207 D7
Lovelace Cl SL6 193 F4
Lovel End SL9 177 C3
Lovel Mead SL9 177 C3
Lovel Rd SL9 177 C2
Love Row MK17 68 D6
Lovett Gdns SL6 196 C3
Lovett Rd UB9 190 C8
Lovetts End LU7 78 E8
Lovibonds Ave UB7 208 F7
Lowbrook Cl HP21 116 A4
Lowbrook Dr SL6 202 A3
Lowbrook Prim Sch SL6 202 A3
Lowdell Cl UB7 208 E7
Lowdon Cl HP11 173 D4
LOWER ASCOTT 79 F1
Lower Ash Yard MK17 67 F8
LOWER ASSENDON 191 A6
LOWER BOIS 154 C5
Lower Boyndon Rd SL6 202 E6
Lower Britwell Rd SL2 197 D1
LOWER CADSDEN 139 E5
Lower Church St
Cuddington HP18 112 F3
Stokenchurch HP14 158 E5
Lower Cippenham La SL1 204 F6
Lower Cl HP19 115 B7
Lower Cookham Rd SL6 196 C3
Lower Dr HP9 175 D5
Lower Eighth St MK9 34 E2
LOWER END
Long Crendon 125 B7
Marsworth 104 F3
Thornborough 53 F8
Woburn Sands 49 C8
Lower End
Ashendon HP18 97 E1
Lower End MK18 53 F8
Newton Longville MK17 57 C3
Piddington OX25 95 E8
Wingrave HP22 89 B2
Lower End Rd MK17 49 A8
Lower Farm Cl HP18 124 D3
Lower Farm Gate HP17 114 A3
Lower Fourth St MK9 34 D1
Lower Furney Cl HP13 173 D8
Lower Gn
Cuddington HP18 112 F3
Westcott HP18 98 C7
Weston Turville HP22 117 A3
Lower Green La HP18 112 C2
Lower Hammersley La HP13 174 B4
LOWER HARTWELL 114 E6
Lower Icknield Way
Chinnor OX39 147 D8
Great Kimble HP17 129 D1
Marsworth HP23 105 B1
Monks Risborough HP17 139 B8
Pitch Green HP27 138 C3
Wilstone HP22, HP23 118 C7
Lower Kings Rd HP4 135 C5
Lower Lees Rd SL2 198 B2
Lower Lodge La HP15 163 A5
Lower Mead SL0 200 D2
Lower Mount Farm SL6 195 D5
Lower Ninth St MK9 34 E2
LOWER NORTH DEAN 150 E1
LOWER POLLICOTT 111 F7
Lower Pound La SL7 194 D8
Lower Rd
Aylesbury HP21, HP22 115 F3
Blackthorn OX25 81 A4
Chinnor OX39 147 C7
Chorleywood WD3 167 D5
Cookham Rise SL6 195 E7
Denham UB9 189 D4
Gerrards Cross SL9 188 F7
Hardwick HP22 87 B3
Lacey Green HP27 149 D6
Lower Ridge SL8 185 B4
Lower Riding HP9 175 B2
Lower Second St MK9 34 D1
Lower St
Pury End NN12 17 A7
Quainton HP22 85 A5
Lower Stonehayes MK14 34 F7
Lower Tenth St MK9 34 F3
Lower Third St MK9 34 D1
Lower Twelfth St MK9 34 F3
Lower Ventnor Cotts SL6 195 C8
LOWER WAINHILL 147 E7
Lower Ward SL4 210 D7
Lower Way
Great Brickhill MK17 59 C1
Padbury MK18 53 C2
LOWER WEALD 32 E2
Lower Weald MK19 32 E2
Lower Wharf MK18 41 E1
LOWER WOODEND 182 D4
Lowes Cl HP14 158 C5
Lowestoft Dr SL1 204 D7
Lowfield Cl HP15 163 B3
Lowfield Way HP15 163 B3
Lowick Pl [4] MK4 46 B2
Lowland Rd MK3 57 C8
Lowlands Cres HP15 151 D1
Lowlands Dr TW19 213 D2
Lowlands Rd TW19 213 D2
Lowman Way HP21 115 D4
Lowndes Ave HP5 144 B1
Lowndes Gr MK5 45 F7
Lowndes Way MK18 66 A5
Lownes Path HP19 114 F8
Loxbeare Dr MK4 46 C4
Loxboro Hill HP14 160 D4
Loxley Rd HP4 134 F6
Loxwood Cl HP3 146 F8
Loyne Cl LU7 80 C8
Lucas Pl MK6 47 D8
Lucas Rd HP13 173 C7
Luccombe MK4 46 D3
Lucky La or Cock La HP20 101 D1
Lucy La MK5 46 B8
Ludgate
Milton Keynes MK6 46 E7
Tring HP23 118 F4
LUDGERSHALL 96 D8
Ludlow Cl MK3 57 F7
Ludlow Dr OX9 126 A1
Ludlow Ho SL6 202 E6
Ludlow Mews HP11 174 A4
Ludlow Pl HP20 116 B8
Ludlow Rd SL6 202 E6
Luff Cl SL4 209 E4
Lufford Pk MK14 34 F8
Luggershall Rd OX25 95 E7
Luke Pl MK10 35 F3
Luker Ave RG9 191 D3
Lukes La HP23 104 D3
Lukes Lea HP23 105 A1
Lullingstone Dr MK13 33 F5
Lumber La NN12 17 B7
Lundholme MK13 34 B5
Lundy Ct SL1 204 E6
Lupin Cl UB7 208 D1
Lupin Ct HP21 115 B5
Lupin Wlk HP21 115 B5
Lutman La SL6 195 F2
Lutyens Gr MK7 48 D5
Luxborough Gr MK4 46 C4
Lychgate Cotts HP3 146 B4
Lycrome La HP5 144 D3
Lycrome Rd HP5 144 E3
Lydbrook La MK17 49 B5
Lyde End HP27 138 B1
Lydford Ave SL2 205 D8
Lydiard MK8 33 E1
Lydiard Cl HP21 116 A4
Lydsey Cl SL2 198 A2
LYE GREEN 144 F4
Lye Green Cotts HP5 144 E3
Lye Green Rd HP5 144 E2
Lyell Place E SL4 209 C4
Lyell Place W SL4 209 C4
Lyell Rd SL4 209 C4
Lyell Walk E SL4 209 C4
Lyell Walk W SL4 209 C4
Lye The HP4 121 D6
Lyme Ave HP4 134 D7
Lynch Cl UB8 201 C5
Lynch Hill La SL2 197 E2
Lynch Hill Sch SL2 197 F2
Lynch The UB8 201 C5
Lyndhurst Ave SL6 195 E6
Lyndhurst Cl HP13 161 D1
Lyndhurst Rd HP5 144 B2
Lyndon Cl HP16 151 C7
Lyndon Gdns HP13 173 E8
Lyndwood Dr SL4 211 A1
Lyndwood Par SL4 211 A2
Lyneham Gdns SL6 195 B1
Lynher Cl HP21 115 C4
Lynmouth Cres MK4 46 D4
Lynott Cl MK8 45 E6
Lynton Gn SL6 202 E7
Lynton Rd HP5 144 C3
Lynwood Ave SL3 206 D3
Lynwood Rd HP21 116 A5
Lyon Rd MK1 47 B2
Lysander Cl HP3 146 A4
Lysander Mead SL6 203 C8

M

McArdle Way SL3 212 D7
McAuliffe Dr SL1, SL2 197 F8
McConnell Dr MK12 33 E6
McCorquordale Rd MK12 33 C7
MacDonald Cl HP6 154 D4
McDougall Rd [8] HP4 135 D4
McEwen Ride HP22 117 D1
MacIntyre Wingrave Sch HP22 89 C3
McKay Trad Est SL3 212 E5
McKenzie Cl MK18 52 D8
Mackenzie Mall [3] SL1 205 F4
Mackenzie St [2] SL1 205 F4
McLellan Pl HP12 172 D5
McLernon Way MK18 66 A5
Maconi Croft MK5 46 C5
Madeira Wlk SL4 210 D6
Madeley Cl HP6 154 D3
Madeley Rd HP21 115 E6
Magdalen Cl
Milton Keynes MK11 32 D6
Syresham NN13 27 C8
Magdalen Ho MK11 32 D6
Magenta Cl MK2 58 D6
Magnet L Ctr SL6 203 A8
Magnolia Dene HP15 162 F2
Magnolia Gdns SL3 206 C3
Magnolia St UB7 208 D2
Magnolia Way HP10 185 E7
Magpie Cl
Flackwell Heath HP10 174 A1
Milton Keynes MK5 46 B3
Magpie La
Coleshill HP7 165 A1
Flackwell Heath HP10 174 A1
Loudwater HP13 174 B3
Magpie Way
Slough SL2 197 F1
Winslow MK18 66 B6
Mahler Cl MK7 48 C5
Mahoney Ct
High Wycombe HP11 172 F8
Milton Keynes MK8 45 D6
Maida Vale [3] MK10 35 F1
MAIDENHEAD 202 F4
Maidenhead Ave MK13 34 C3
MAIDENHEAD COURT 196 C4
Maidenhead Court Pk SL6 196 B3
Maidenhead Heritage Ctr* [13] SL6 202 F7
Maidenhead Rd
Cookham Rise SL6 195 F6
Windsor SL4 209 E7
Maidenhead Ret Pk SL6 203 A6
Maidenhead Sta SL6 202 F6
MAIDENSGROVE 179 C5
MAIDS MORETON 41 E4
Maids Moreton CE Sch MK18 41 E3
Maidstone Rd MK10 36 C2
Maigno Way [1] MK12 33 A6
Main Dr
Gerrards Cross SL9 188 C6
Iver SL0 207 E3
Potterspury NN12 18 B2
Main Par WD3 167 C5
Main Rd
Astwood MK16 16 B3
Drayton Parslow MK17 68 B5
Lacey Green HP27 149 E5
Syresham NN13 27 C7
Upper Winchendon HP18 99 A1
Walter's Ash HP14 161 C7
Main Road N HP4 107 A6
Main Road S HP4 107 D4
Main St
Adstock MK18 53 F1
Akeley MK18 41 F8
Ashendon HP18 97 F1
Beachampton MK19 44 A6
Buckingham MK18 41 F3
Chackmore MK18 41 B4
Charndon OX27 72 E5
Cosgrove MK19 19 E2
Gawcott MK18 51 F4
Grendon Underwood HP18 83 B5
Mursley MK17 67 D6
Padbury MK18 53 B1
Poundon OX27 71 F7
Preston Bissett MK18 62 B8
Shalstone MK18 39 E6
Tingewick MK18 51 B6
Turweston NN13 38 C8
Twyford MK18 62 C1
Westbury NN13 39 A4
Weston Turville HP22 116 E2
Maitland Dr HP13 173 B8
Maitland Rd HP22 131 D7
Major's Farm Rd
Datchet SL3 211 E8
Slough SL3 212 A8
Malbons Ct MK6 46 E7
Malborough Ho HP4 135 A3
Malborough Way NN12 18 F5
Malcolm Rd UB10 201 F8
Malden Cl HP6 154 F1
Malders La SL6 195 C3
Malet Cl HP14 158 F5
Malins Gate MK14 34 E8
Malkin Dr HP9 175 C3
Mallard Cl HP19 101 E4
Mallard Croft HP17 127 A7
Mallard Dr
Buckingham MK18 52 E8
Slough SL1 204 F6
Mallard Ho HP11 173 C6
Mallard Pl HP11 174 B3
Mallets End HP22 85 B4
Malletts Cl MK11 32 E5
Mallow Gate MK14 34 E4
Mallow Pk SL6 195 C1
Malmers Well Rd HP13 173 B7
Malpas Rd SL2 206 B6
Malthouse Flats RG9 192 D6
Malthouse Sq
Beaconsfield HP9 186 F8
Princes Risborough HP27 139 B4
Malthouse Way [2] SL7 183 D1
Malting Cl MK16 12 B6
Malting La
Aldbury HP23 120 D5
Dagnall HP4 107 C5
Maltings Cl
Cranfield MK43 25 A1
Stewkley LU7 78 E8
Maltings Field MK19 19 F5
Maltings The
Chackmore MK18 41 B4
Olney MK46 7 A3
Tingewick MK18 51 B6
Malt La NN13 27 C8
Maltmans Green Sch SL9 188 C8
Maltmans La SL9 188 C8
Malton Ave SL1 205 B6
Malton Cl MK10 35 F1
Malvern Cl HP13 172 E8
Malvern Ct SL3 212 A7
Malvern Dr
Leighton Buzzard LU7 80 C8
Milton Keynes MK11 33 A4
Malvern Rd
Aylesbury HP20 116 C8
Maidenhead SL6 195 D1
Malyns Cl OX39 147 C7
Manchester Terr HP14 171 B4
Mandela Ct UB8 208 C7
Mandelyns HP4 134 E7
Mandeville Dr MK10 36 C2
Mandeville Mews HP21 115 E4
Mandeville Rd
Aylesbury HP21 115 E5
Prestwood HP16 151 B7
Mandeville Sch The HP21 115 D4
Manfield Cl SL2 198 A2
Manifold La MK4, MK5 46 B3
Manor Cl
Berkhamsted HP4 135 C4
Bledlow HP27 138 B1
Buckingham MK18 53 C2
Cosgrove MK19 19 E2
Hanslope MK19 11 A2
Milton Keynes MK10 35 F3
Milton Keynes MK17 67 D6
Prestwood HP16 151 D4
Salford MK17 37 D3
Stoke Hammond MK17 69 E7
Tylers Green HP10 163 A2
Manor Cotts
Chorleywood WD3 167 B3
Milton Keynes MK12 33 B7
Manor Court Yd HP13 162 A1
Manor Court Yd OX33 123 B2
Manor Cres
Seer Green HP9 176 D5
Wendover HP22 131 C5
Manor Ct
Emberton MK46 13 F8
Leighton Buzzard LU7 70 E2
Marlow SL7 183 C3
Slough, Cippenham SL1 204 F5
[6] Slough, Upton Park SL1 205 F3
Twyford MK18 62 C1
Manor Ctyd
Haddenham HP17 127 D4
Sherington MK16 13 F1
Manor Dr
Amersham HP6 154 B3
Aylesbury HP20 101 F2
Haversham MK19 20 E2
Stewkley LU7 78 E8
Manor Farm SL3 212 E5
Manor Farm Cl
Soulbury LU7 69 E2
Stone HP17 114 C5
Weston Turville HP22 116 E2
Windsor SL4 209 F4
Manor Farm Cotts SL4 211 A2
Manor Farm Ct HP22 87 B2
Manor Farm Ctyd HP22 102 D8
Manor Farm Ho SL4 209 F4
Manor Farm Inf Sch HP15 163 B2
Manor Farm Jun Sch HP15 163 B2
Manor Farm La LU7 90 C8
Manor Farm Way HP9 176 D4
Manorfields Rd MK19 32 B6
Manor Gdns
Grendon Underwood HP18 83 A6
High Wycombe HP13 162 A1
Manor Gdns *continued*
Maids Moreton MK18 41 E2
Wooburn Green HP10 185 E5
Manor Ho
Brill HP18 110 A8
Hambleden RG9 181 D2
Manor House Cl HP20 101 F1
Manor House Hospl HP20 101 F1
Manor House La SL3 211 B6
Manor La
Gerrards Cross SL9 188 D4
Maidenhead SL6 202 E4
MANOR PARK
Aylesbury 101 E2
Slough 198 D1
Manor Park Ave HP27 139 A3
Manor Pk MK18 41 F4
Manor Pound Rd LU7 105 A7
Manor Rd
Akeley MK18 41 F7
Aylesbury HP20 101 E1
Cheddington LU7 104 F7
Chesham HP5 144 C2
Emmington OX9 137 B6
Maidenhead SL6 202 E4
Milton Keynes, Bletchley MK2 58 E8
Milton Keynes, Wolverton MK12 33 B7
Newport Pagnell MK16 22 A4
Newton Longville MK17 57 D3
Oakley HP18 109 D5
Oving HP22 86 C7
Princes Risborough HP27 139 A2
Rowsham HP22 102 D8
Seer Green HP9 176 D5
Tring HP23 119 A5
Tylers Green HP10 163 A2
Wendover HP22 131 C5
Windsor SL4 209 E5
Manor St
Berkhamsted HP4 135 D4
Buckingham MK18 52 C8
Manor View HP15 163 B2
Manor View Ho HP13 161 E2
Manor Way
Chesham HP5 144 D1
Coleshill HP7 164 F3
Yardley Gobion NN12 18 E6
Manor Waye UB8 201 D4
Mansard Cl [8] HP23 119 A3
Manse Cl MK11 32 D6
Mansel Cl
Cosgrove MK19 19 E2
Slough SL2 206 B8
Mansell Cl
Milton Keynes MK5 46 A6
Windsor SL4 209 E6
Manshead Ct MK11 32 F5
Mansion Dr HP23 119 B3
Mansion Hill HP22 131 E8
Mansion La
Harrold MK43 3 F6
Iver SL0 207 C6
Mansion The HP4 135 E6
MANTLES GN 165 A8
Manton Rd LU6 93 D5
Maple Ave UB7 208 F5
Maple Cl
Hazelmere HP15 163 A3
High Wycombe HP12 172 C5
Maidenhead SL6 202 C5
Maple Cres SL2 206 B6
MAPLE CROSS 178 D6
Maple Cross JMI Sch WD3 178 E5
Maple Ct
Gerrards Cross SL9 188 F6
Marlow SL7 183 E3
Windsor SL4 210 C4
Mapledean MK12 33 E4
Mapledurham MK7 48 B3
Mapledurham Wlk SL6 195 E3
Maple End HP22 116 C4
Maplefield La HP8 166 B6
Maple Gr
Milton Keynes MK2 58 E8
Woburn Sands MK17 49 B4
Maple Leys MK18 63 E3
Maple Lodge Cl WD3 178 E6
Maple Pl UB7 208 F5
Maple Rise SL7 183 E3
Maples The
[5] Bourne End SL8 185 B3
Wendover HP22 131 C5
Maplewood Gdns HP9 175 B1
Maplewood Sch HP13 161 D3
Maplin Pk SL3 207 B4
Mapperton Cl [3] MK4 45 F1
Mapridge Green La HP16 141 D1
Marand Ct HP21 115 F8
Mara Pl MK9 35 A3
Marbeck Cl SL4 209 D6

Marchant Ct SL7 184 A3
March Edge MK18 41 E1
Marches The SL4 205 D2
March Mdw MK7 48 D7
March Pl HP19 115 B8
Marcia Ct SL1 204 F5
Marcourt Rd HP14 158 F3
Mardle Rd LU7 80 E6
Maree Cl
Leighton Buzzard LU7 80 C7
Milton Keynes MK2 58 C5
Marefield Rd SL7 183 D2
Mare Leys MK18 52 F8
Marescroft Rd SL2 197 E1
Margam Cres MK10 36 A1
Margaret Ct HP13 173 E5
Margaret Powell Sq
MK9 34 F3
Margaret Smythe Ho
SL9 188 F5
Marie Cl OX27 71 F7
Marigold Pl MK14 34 E4
Marigold Wlk HP15 162 F6
Marina Dr
Dunstable LU6 93 E7
Milton Keynes MK12 33 D6
Marina Rdbt MK6 47 C7
Marina Way
Iver SL0 208 A6
Slough SL1 204 D6
Marine Ct MK6 46 F6
Marish Ct SL3 207 A3
Marish La UB9 189 D7
Marish Prim Sch SL3 207 A3
Marish Wharf Ind Est
SL3 206 E4
Marjoram Pl MK14 34 E4
Mark Dr SL9 177 E6
Markenfield Pl MK4 45 E1
Market Hill
Buckingham MK18 41 D1
Milton Keynes MK6 47 B8
Whitchurch HP22 86 F6
Market Ho 5 SL9 177 D2
Market La SL3 207 C3
Market Par HP15 163 A4
Market Pl
Chalfont St Peter SL9 177 D2
Colnbrook SL3 212 C7
Henley-on-Thames RG9 191 D2
4 Olney MK46 6 F3
Woburn MK17 60 F7
Market Place Mews 5
RG9 191 D2
Market Sq
Amersham HP7 165 B7
Aylesbury HP20 115 D8
5 Buckingham MK18 41 D1
Chesham HP5 154 B8
Hanslope MK19 11 A2
Marlow SL7 183 D2
Milton Keynes MK11 32 D5
Princes Risborough
HP27 139 B3
Uxbridge UB8 201 C5
Winslow MK18 65 F4
Market St
19 Aylesbury HP20 115 D8
Maidenhead SL6 202 F7
9 Windsor SL4 210 D6
Markham Cl HP19 115 A7
Markhams Cl MK18 52 D8
Marks Orch MK18 75 F7
Marlborough Cl SL6 202 A6
Marlborough Ct SL1 204 E7
Marlborough Gate MK9 34 F3
Marlborough Ho 5
SL6 202 F6
Marlborough Rd
Aylesbury HP21 115 E4
Maidenhead SL6 202 A6
Slough SL3 206 D2
Marlborough St
Milton Keynes, Neath Hill
MK14 34 E6
Milton Keynes, Tinkers Bridge
MK6 47 D6
Marlborough Trad Est
HP11 172 F7
Marley Gr MK8 45 E7
Marlin Cl HP4 134 F5
Marlin Copse HP4 135 A3
Marlin Ct SL7 183 D1
Marlin Hill HP23 133 A8
Marlins Cl WD3 167 E7
Marlins End HP4 134 F3
MARLOW 183 B2
MARLOW BOTTOM 183 C6
Marlow Bottom SL7 183 D6
Marlow Bridge La SL7 194 E8
Marlow CE Inf Sch SL7 183 D3
Marlow Comm SL7 182 F3
MARLOW COMMON 182 F3
Marlow Cottage Hospl
SL7 183 E2
Marlow Dr MK16 22 A4
Marlow Hill HP11 173 A5
Marlow Ho 1 SL7 183 E1
Marlow Language Ctr The
SL7 183 D2
Marlow Lodge 13 SL6 202 F6
Marlow Mill SL7 183 E1
Marlow Rd
Bisham SL7 194 E7
Henley-on-Thames RG9 191 E3
High Wycombe HP11 172 E4
Lane End HP14, SL7 171 E2
Little Marlow SL7 184 C5
Maidenhead, Furze Platt
SL6 194 E4
Maidenhead SL6 202 F7
Stokenchurch HP14 170 B6
Marlow Sta SL7 183 F2
Marquis Ct MK17 60 F7
Marram Cl MK6 47 A5
Marriotts Ave HP16 142 E1
Marriott's Cl HP17 126 F6
Marriott's La HP17 126 F6
Marriott's Way HP17 126 F6
Marriott Terr WD3 167 F5
Marrod's Bottom HP7 175 C8
Marron La MK12 33 C5
Marroway HP22 116 D2
MARSH 129 C7
Marshall Court Ind Pk
MK1 47 B1
Marshalls La MK15 35 C2
Marshalls Lea HP22 102 C3
Marsham Cl HP21 116 A4
Marsham La SL9 188 F6
Marsham Lodge SL9 188 E5
Marsham Way SL9 188 F5
Marshaw Pl 3 MK4 46 C2
Marshcroft La HP23 119 D6
Marsh Ct HP11 173 F4
Marsh Dr MK14 21 E1
Marsh End Rd MK16 22 D3
Marshfield SL3 211 C6
Marshgate Trad Est
SL6 204 A7
MARSH GIBBON 71 F3
Marsh Gibbon CE Sch
OX27 71 F3
Marsh Gibbon Rd HP18 82 E8
Marsh Inf Sch HP11 173 F4
Marsh La
Stoke Mandeville HP22 129 F8
Taplow SL6 203 E6
Marshment Cl HP22 117 D5
Marsh Rd
Great Kimble HP22 129 D4
Shabbington HP18 124 D3
Marshworth MK6 47 D6
Marston Cl HP5 144 A4
Marston Ct HP23 104 B4
Marstonfields Rd MK18 76 B2
Marston Hill
Cranfield MK43 25 F2
Oving HP22 86 C8
Marston Rd
Granborough MK18 75 F6
Thame OX9 126 A1
MARSWORTH 105 A1
Marsworth CE Inf Sch
HP23 105 A2
Marsworth Rd LU7 105 D4
Marsworth Reservoir★
HP23 119 A8
Martell Cl MK7 48 A3
Martin Cl
Buckingham MK18 52 F7
Milton Keynes MK14 34 E6
Uxbridge UB10 201 E3
Windsor SL4 209 D6
Martindale SL0 200 D1
Martin Dell Cotts HP16 142 E4
Martingale Pl MK14 34 F5
Martin Rd
Maidenhead SL6 202 F8
Slough SL1 205 E3
Martins Dr The LU7 80 F8
Martinsend La HP16 151 E7
Martin's Plain SL2 198 F3
Martlet The MK6 47 C4
Martyrs Ct HP7 165 C8
Marunden Gn SL2 197 F2
Marwood Cl MK4 46 D3
Mary Bassett Lower Sch
The LU7 80 F7
Mary Cross Cl HP23 119 D1
Marygold Wlk HP6 166 C8
Maryland Rd MK15 35 B8
Mary MacManus Dr
MK18 41 D1
Mary Morgan Ct SL2 205 D8
Maryot Cl MK16 13 F2
Maryside SL3 206 E4
Marys Mead HP15 163 A5
Mary Towerton Fst Sch
HP14 159 D3
Mascoll Path SL2 197 F2
Masefield Cl
Chesham HP5 144 B3
Newport Pagnell MK16 22 A4
Masefield Gr MK3 58 A7
Maslin Dr MK6 47 B5
Mason MK14 34 C8
Masons Cl HP16 151 C5
Masons Ct HP5 144 C1
Mason's Ct
Aylesbury HP19 115 B7
Slough SL1 204 E6
Masons Rd SL1 204 E6
Masons Yd HP4 135 D4
Massie Cl MK15 35 B6
Mathecombe Rd 2
SL1 205 A4
Mathiesen Rd MK13 34 A6
Mathisen Way SL3 212 E6
Matilda Gdns MK5 46 B5
Matlock Rd HP20 101 F2
Matson Dr RG9 191 F2
Matthau La MK4 45 D3
Matthew Ct MK5 46 B6
Matthews Cl 12 HP20 101 F2
Maude Cl HP9 176 A1
Maude Rd HP9 176 A1
Maud Jane's Cl LU7 105 E5
Maudsley Cl MK5 46 C6
Maudsley Ho SL6 203 A7
Mauduit Cl MK19 11 A3
Maulden Gdns MK14 35 A8
Maurice Mount HP15 162 F5
Mavoncliff Dr MK4 57 A8
Maxham MK5 46 A3
Maxwell Ct SL1 197 C1
Maxwell Dr HP15 163 B5
Maxwell Pl HP9 175 E3
Maxwell Rd
Beaconsfield HP9 175 E3
West Drayton UB7 208 F2
Maybach Ct MK5 46 B5
Maybrook Gdns HP13 173 C8
Maybury Cl SL1 204 D7
Maybush Gdns HP16 151 C6
Maybush Wlk MK46 6 E5
May Cl LU6 92 E6
Mayditch Pl MK13 34 C3
Mayer Gdns MK5 46 C5
Mayfield Dr SL4 210 A4
Mayfield Rd HP10 185 E6
Mayflower Cl HP17 114 F5
Mayflower Way
Beaconsfield HP9 186 A8
Farnham Common SL2 198 C8
Maygoods Cl UB8 208 D8
Maygoods Gn UB8 208 D8
Maygoods La UB8 208 D8
Maygoods View UB8 208 C8
Mayhall Farm HP6 154 A4
Mayhall La HP6 154 B4
Mayhew Cres HP13 173 D8
Maylands Dr UB8 201 D6
Maynard Cl MK13 34 A3
Maynard Ct SL4 210 A6
Mayorfield Ho 1 SL7 183 D2
Maypole Rd SL6 204 A8
Maypool Way 1 MK10 36 B2
May Rd MK43 8 E6
Mays Way NN12 18 D3
May Tree Cl SL7 183 C6
Mead Acre HP27 139 B5
Mead Ave SL3 207 B4
Mead Cl
Denham UB9 190 A2
7 Marlow SL7 183 F3
Monks Risborough HP27 139 B6
Slough SL3 207 B4
Uxbridge UB9 190 A2
Meades La HP5 154 B7
Meadfield Ave SL3 207 A3
Meadfield Rd SL3 207 B3
Meadfurlong Sch MK6 34 F1
Mead Haze SL6 196 C2
Mead Ho SL0 200 D2
MEADLE 139 B8
Meadoway
Steeple Claydon MK18 63 E3
Stone HP17 114 F5
Meadow Bank 6 SL8 185 B3
Meadowbank Cl
Bovingdon HP3 146 B3
Long Crendon HP18 125 C7
Meadow Bank Cl HP7 154 E1
Meadowbrook HP23 119 B6
Meadowbrook Cl SL3 212 F6
Meadow Cl
Aylesbury HP20 102 A1
Chesham HP5 144 A4
Cublington LU7 78 C1
High Wycombe HP11 173 F4
Marlow SL7 183 F1
Oakley HP18 109 D4
Old Windsor SL4 211 B2
Tring HP23 119 A4
Meadowcott La HP7 164 F3
Meadow Cotts
Beaconsfield HP9 175 E1
Little Kingshill HP16 152 B3
Stone HP17 114 D3
Meadowcroft
Aylesbury HP19 101 B3
Berkhamsted HP4 134 D7
Chalfont St Peter SL9 177 D1
Meadow Ct MK46 5 D2
Meadow Dr
Amersham HP6 154 E2
Longwick HP27 138 D6
Meadow Farm Rd MK43 16 F1
Meadow Gate
Padbury MK18 53 B2
Prestwood HP16 151 C3
Meadow Gdns MK18 52 E6
Meadow High Sch UB8 208 E8
Meadow La
Beaconsfield HP9 175 F2
Eton SL4 210 C7
Long Crendon HP18 125 E4
Milton Keynes MK10 36 A3
Pitstone LU7 105 E3
South Heath HP16 152 E8
Meadowlea Cl UB7 213 D8
Meadow Pk HP22 116 C2
Meadow Rd
Berkhamsted HP4 135 B6
Chinnor OX39 147 D6
Henley-on-Thames RG9 191 E1
Slough SL3 206 E3
Meadow Rise HP27 149 E5
Meadow Row MK18 41 D1
Meadow Sh Ctr 4 MK18 41 D1
Meadowside HP9 176 F4
Meadows Sch The
HP10 185 E7
Meadows The
1 Amersham HP7 154 E1
Flackwell Heath HP10 185 B8
Old Stratford MK19 32 B6
Whitchurch HP22 86 F7
Meadowsweet MK7 48 B5
Meadowview TW19 212 F2
Meadow View
Aspley Guise MK17 49 D6
Chalfont St Giles HP8 177 A7
Long Crendon HP18 125 E4
Marlow Bottom SL7 183 E6
Potterspury NN12 18 D3
Stanwell TW19 213 A2
Uxbridge UB8 208 C8
Meadow Way
Aylesbury HP20 102 A1
Dorney SL6 203 F4
Felden HP3 146 F7
Hyde Heath HP6 153 C4
Old Windsor SL4 211 B1
1 Thame OX9 125 F1
Wing LU7 79 E3
Meadow Wlk
Bourne End SL8 185 A5
Buckingham MK18 41 D1
Tylers Green HP10 163 C1
Mead Pk HP15 163 C7
Mead Platt HP14 158 D5
Mead Rd UB8 201 D5
Meads Cl MK13 34 B8
Mead St HP13 174 A4
Meads The
Berkhamsted HP4 134 F6
Eaton Bray LU6 92 E5
Stoke Poges SL2 199 A2
Tring HP23 119 B4
Uxbridge UB8 201 E1
4 Windsor SL4 210 A5
Mead The
Beaconsfield HP9 175 E2
Soulbury LU7 69 E3
Meadway
Berkhamsted HP4 135 E5
Buckingham MK18 52 D6
Dunstable LU6 93 F7
Oving HP22 76 E1
Mead Way
High Wycombe HP11 173 F4
Slough SL1 204 D8
Meadway Ct LU6 93 F7
Meadway Pk SL9 188 D3
Meadway The MK5 46 A7
Mead Wlk SL3 207 B4
Meare Estate HP10 185 E8
Meavy Cl HP13 174 B3
Medale Rd MK6 47 B5
Medallion Pl SL6 203 B7
MEDBOURNE 45 E5
Medbourne Rdbt MK8 45 E6
Medeswell MK4 46 E3
Medhurst MK8 33 E2
Medland MK6 47 D7
Medley Cl LU6 92 F5
Medman Cl UB8 201 C3
MEDMENHAM 193 A5
Medway Cl MK16 22 E3
Medway Ct MK43 37 D8
Meeting Oak La MK18 66 B5
Megdale Pl HP20 101 D2
Melbourne Ave SL1 205 C7
Melbourne Cl HP21 115 E5
Melbourne Rd HP13 173 F6
Melbourne Terr MK13 34 A7
Melford Gn HP19 101 C3
Melfort Dr
Leighton Buzzard LU7 80 B6
Milton Keynes MK2 58 D4
Melick Rd MK6 47 B4
Melissa Ct HP13 173 D6
Mellish Ct MK3 47 A2
Mellstock Rd HP21 115 F5
Melrose Ave MK3 47 A3
Melrose Ct HP13 162 B1
Melrose Wlk HP21 115 F5
Melton MK14 34 C8
Melton Ct
Dunstable LU6 93 F7
Maidenhead SL6 202 F6
Mendelssohn Gr MK7 48 C4
Mendip Cl SL3 207 A1
Mendip Way HP13 172 F8
Mendy St HP11 173 A7
Menmarsh Rd HP18 123 E6
Menteith Cl MK2 58 C5
MENTMORE 90 D4
Mentmore Cl HP12 172 B6
Mentmore Cross Rds
LU7 89 F6
Mentmore Ct
Mentmore LU7 90 D5
2 Milton Keynes MK8 45 F8
Mentmore Gdns LU7 80 E5
Mentmore Gn HP21 115 E3
Mentmore Rd
Cheddington LU7 104 F8
High Wycombe HP12 172 B6
Leighton Buzzard LU7 80 E5
Mentmore Towers★
LU7 90 C4
Mentmore View HP23 118 F5
Mentone Ave MK17 49 D4
Menzies Ct MK5 46 B4
Mercers Dr MK13 34 B6
Mercers Mdw HP22 131 B6
Mercer Wlk UB8 201 C5
Merchant La
Cranfield MK43 25 A1
Cranfield, Wharley End
MK43 24 F2
Merchant Pl MK10 35 E3
Mercian Way SL1 204 D5
Mercia Rd SL6 202 C4
Mercury Gr MK8 45 E7
Mercury Pk The HP10 185 E7
Merebrook Sch MK4 46 C3
Mere Cl SL7 183 F2
Meredith Dr HP19 100 F2
Mere La MK18 50 E6
Mere Pk SL7 183 F2
Mere Rd
Finmere MK18 50 D6
Slough SL1 205 F3
Meriland Ct MK2 58 E4
Merlebank HP5 154 C7
Merlewood Cl HP11 173 A4
Merlewood Dr MK5 45 F4
Merlin Cl SL3 212 B8
Merlin Ct SL6 202 B8
Merlin Ctr HP19 101 C1
Merlin Ctr The HP12 172 E5
Merling Croft HP4 134 E7
Merlin Wlk MK6 47 B8
Merman Rise MK4 45 D2
Merrivale Mews UB7 208 D5
Merrydown HP13 161 D1
Merryfields UB8 201 D3
Mersey Cl MK3 46 E1
Mersey Way MK3 46 E1
Merthen Gr MK4 57 B8
Merton Cl SL6 202 C3
Merton Ct SL1 206 A3
Merton Dr MK6 47 A4
Merton Rd
Princes Risborough
HP27 139 B2
Slough SL1 206 A3
Merwin Way SL4 209 D4
Meryton Ho SL4 210 A4
Messenger Cl HP21 116 A6
Metcalfe Gr MK14 22 B2
Mews Cotts HP15 162 D7
Mews Gamnel HP23 119 B6
Mews The HP6 154 D3
Michael Cl SL6 202 C5
Michaelis Rd OX9 125 E1
Michaels Mews 6
HP19 115 A8
Michigan Dr
Milton Keynes MK15 35 C8
Newport Pagnell MK15 22 C1
Micholls Ave SL9 177 E5
MICKLEFIELD 173 E6
Micklefield Rd HP13 174 A7
Mickleton MK15 35 A6
Midas Ind Est UB8 201 B3
Midbrook Ct MK14 22 A2
Midcot Way HP4 134 F6
Midcroft SL2 198 B1
Mid Cross La SL9 177 F5
Middlebrook Rd HP13 161 E1
Middle Cl HP6 154 F2
MIDDLE CLAYDON 74 C8
Middle Cres UB9 189 D4
Middle Dr HP9 175 D5
MIDDLE END
Leckhampstead 42 D8
Totternhoe 93 A8

Middle Field HP22 ..... 116 F3
Middlefield Cl MK18..... 41 F1
Middle Gn SL3......... 206 E6
MIDDLE GREEN......... 206 E5
Middlegreen Rd SL3 ... 206 D5
Middlegreen Trad Est
SL3..................206 D4
Middle La HP3......... 146 A1
Middle Mdw HP8 ...... 177 C7
Middle Rd
Aylesbury HP21........116 B7
Berkhamsted HP4 ......135 B4
Denham UB9 ....189 D4
Middlesex Dr MK3 ...... 46 F1
Middle Slade MK18 ..... 52 D6
MIDDLETON............. 35 E3
Middleton MK14 .... 34 E7
Middleton Prim Sch
MK10 .... 35 E3
Middleton Swimming Pool
MK16 .... 22 E3
Middle Way OX39 ...... 147 B6
Middleway The HP12...172 C6
MIDDLE WEALD.......... 32 E1
Middle Weald MK19..... 32 E2
Middle Wlk SL1.......197 C2
Midhurst Cl HP21 ..... 116 B5
Midland Dr MK10 .... 36 C3
Midland Rd MK46 .... 7 A5
Midshires Bsns Pk
HP19..................101 A1
Midsumer Ct HP15..... 163 A3
Midsummer Arc MK9.... 34 E3
Midsummer Bvd MK9 .. 34 E2
Midsummer Dr HP18.... 82 F6
Midsummer Pl (Sh Ctr)
MK9 .... 34 E2
Midsummer Rdbt MK9 .. 34 C1
Miersfield HP11........172 D3
Mikern Cl MK2.......... 58 C8
Milburn Ave MK6 .... 46 E8
Milburn Dr UB7........ 208 E6
Mildenhall Rd SL1 ..... 205 E7
Milebush LU7........... 80 C8
Milecastle MK13 .... 34 A5
Mile Elm SL7 .... 184 A3
Miles Cl
Aylesbury HP21 ....116 A7
Milton Keynes MK14 ..... 22 A3
Miles Ct HP22.......... 102 B3
Miles End HP21 .... 115 B6
Milesmere MK8.......... 33 D1
Milestone Cl HP14 ..... 158 E5
Milfoil Ave MK14........ 34 E4
Milford Ave MK11........ 32 E4
Milford Ct 4 SL1 ...... 206 A4
Milk Hall Barns HP5.... 154 F5
Milland Way MK4 .... 45 D3
Millards Cl MK43........ 25 C2
Millards Pl MK43........ 25 C2
Mill Ave UB8........... 201 C3
Millbank
Leighton Buzzard LU7 .... 80 F8
Marlow SL7 .... 183 F1
Millbank Pl MK7 .... 48 B8
Millboard Rd SL8 ...... 185 B3
Mill Bridge Pl UB8 ..... 201 C3
Millbrook Cl HP12 ..... 172 D8
Millbrook Comb Sch
HP12..................172 D8
Millbrook Way SL3..... 212 E5
Mill Cl
Buckingham MK18....... 65 F5
Chesham HP5 ....154 E5
West Drayton UB7......208 D3
Wingrave HP22 .... 89 A3
Mill Cnr HP18........... 83 A8
Mill Cotts HP10 ....185 D4
Mill Ct
Horton SL3............212 C3
Milton Keynes MK12 ..... 33 A5
Waddesdon HP18 .... 99 A7
West Drayton UB7......208 D3
Milldun Way HP12 ..... 172 D6
MILL END
Henley-on-Thames......192 D7
Little Missenden 153 A3
Rickmansworth 167 F1
Mill End Cl
Edlesborough LU6 .... 92 F4
Prestwood HP16 ....151 B5
Mill End Rd HP12 ...... 172 C8
Millennium Cl UB8..... 201 C3
Millennium Point HP19 101 A1
Miller Pl SL9........... 188 D6
Millers Cl HP18 .... 82 F6
Miller's La SL4......... 211 A1
Millers Turn OX39...... 147 B6
Millers Way
Aylesbury HP19 ....115 A8
Milton Keynes MK12 ..... 33 D5
Millfield HP4 .... 135 D5
Millfield Ave OX27 ...... 71 F3
Millfield Cl
Cranfield MK43 .... 25 B2
Marsh Gibbon OX27...... 71 F3
Millfields HP5 .... 154 C6
Millfield Wood Wildlife
Reserve★ HP14.......162 B3
Mill Gdns HP23 .... 119 B4
Mill Gn MK43 .... 8 D5
Millhayes MK14 .... 34 F8
Mill Ho
Buckingham MK18....... 52 C8
West Drayton UB7......208 D5
Millholm Rise MK6...... 47 E5
Milliners The 1 HP20 .. 101 E1
Millington Gate MK15 ... 35 D7
Mill La
Amersham HP7 ....165 A8
Aspley Guise MK17 ...... 49 C5
Beaconsfield HP9.......175 E1
Brackley NN13.......... 38 A6
Buckingham MK18....... 52 C8
Chalfont St Giles HP8 ...166 B1
Chinnor OX39..........147 B7
Cookham SL6..........196 C7
Gerrards Cross SL9.....188 F5
Great Brickhill MK17 ..... 58 F2
Horton-cum-S OX33.....108 A6
Horton SL3............212 C4
Hulcote MK17 .... 37 E1
Hurley SL6............193 F4
Milton Keynes, Bradville
MK13.................. 34 A7
Milton Keynes, Stony Stratford
MK11.................. 32 C5
Milton Keynes, Woolstone
MK15.................. 35 C3
Monks Risborough HP27 139 B6
Salford MK17........... 37 C3
South Heath HP16......152 C7
Stokenchurch HP14.....158 C5
Taplow SL6............203 C8
Thame OX9 ....126 B3
Turvey MK43 .... 8 D5
Twyford MK18 .... 62 C1
Upper Arncott OX25 ..... 94 E7
Westbury NN13 .... 39 A4
Weston Turville HP22....117 A2
Windsor SL4 ....210 A7
Wingrave HP22 .... 89 C2
Mill Lane Prim Sch
OX39..................147 B7
Mill Mdw HP19 .... 115 B8
Mill Mead HP22........ 131 B5
Mill Pl SL3............. 211 D5
Mill Rd
Cranfield MK43 .... 25 C2
2 Leighton Buzzard LU7.. 80 F8
Marlow SL7 ....183 E1
Milton Keynes MK2 ...... 58 E7
Milton Keynes MK19 ..... 21 B4
Oakley HP18 ....109 D4
Slapton LU7 .... 91 D7
Stokenchurch HP14.....158 C5
Thame OX9 ....124 E1
West Drayton UB7......208 D3
Whitfield NN13 .... 26 E3
Millshot Dr HP7........ 165 D7
Millside SL8 .... 185 C3
Mill Sq MK12 .... 33 A5
Mill St
Aylesbury HP20 ....101 E1
Berkhamsted HP4 ......135 C4
Colnbrook SL3 ....212 D7
High Wycombe HP11....172 F7
Newport Pagnell MK16 ... 22 D5
Oxford OX33 ....108 B1
Slough SL2............205 F5
Millstream HP22....... 116 F2
Mill Stream Cl HP27.... 139 A2
Millstream La SL1...... 204 E5
Millstream Way
Leighton Buzzard LU7 .... 80 F7
Wooburn Green HP10 ...185 E8
Mill Terr MK12.......... 33 A6
Mill The
Milton Keynes MK12 ..... 32 E7
Tring HP23............104 C1
Wooburn Green HP10 ...185 E8
Mill Tower LU6 .... 92 E6
Mill View Rd HP23 ..... 118 F4
Mill Way
Aspley Guise MK17 ...... 49 D5
Aylesbury HP20 ....115 C8
Rickmansworth WD3 ....167 F1
Mill West SL2.......... 205 F5
Milner Rd SL1 .... 204 A8
Milton Ave SL9 .... 188 D8
Milton Cl
Henley-on-Thames
RG9...................191 D2
Horton SL3............212 A4
MILTON COMMON....... 136 B3
Milton Dr MK16 .... 22 E4
Milton Fields HP8...... 177 B7
Milton Gdns HP27...... 139 A2
Milton Gr MK3 .... 57 F7
MILTON KEYNES 34 D5
Milton Keynes Acad The
MK6 .... 47 A7
Milton Keynes Central Sta
MK9 .... 34 C1
Milton Keynes Coll MK6 . 46 F7
Milton Keynes Coll
(Bletchley Ctr) MK3.... 58 B8
Milton Keynes Hospl
MK6 .... 47 B7
Milton Keynes Materials
Recycling Factory★
MK12 .... 33 C8
Milton Keynes Mus★
MK12 .... 33 D5
Milton Keynes Prep Sch
MK3 .... 57 D8
Milton Keynes Theatre★
MK9 .... 34 F3
MILTON KEYNES
VILLAGE 35 E2
Milton Lawns HP6 ..... 154 D3
Milton Rd
Aston Clinton HP22 .....117 F5
Aylesbury HP21 ....115 F6
Chesham HP5 ....144 B2
Milton Keynes, Broughton
MK10.................. 36 B3
Milton Keynes, Willen
MK15.................. 35 D7
Slough SL2............198 D1
Walton MK7............ 47 F6
Milton's Cottage (Mus)★
HP8...................177 B7
Milton Way UB7 .... 208 F2
Milverton Cl SL6....... 202 B3
Milward Dr MK2 .... 47 E1
Mimosa Ct HP21 .... 115 B6
Mina Ave SL3.......... 206 D4
Minall Cl HP23......... 119 A4
Mineral La HP5 .... 154 C7
Minerva Cl TW19....... 213 A2
Minerva Gdns MK7...... 48 C7
Minerva Way HP9...... 176 A1
Mines Cl HP13 .... 161 D3
Ministry Wharf HP14... 149 C1
Minniecroft Rd SL1 .... 197 B2
Minorca Gr MK5 .... 46 A4
Minshull Cl MK18 .... 41 D1
Minster Way SL3....... 206 F4
Minstrel Ct MK13 .... 34 B7
Minton Cl MK14......... 22 A1
Minton Rise SL6 .... 204 B7
Mirador Cres SL2 ...... 206 B6
Mirrie La UB9.......... 189 C6
Misbourne Ave
Chalfont St Peter SL9 ...177 E5
High Wycombe HP13....173 F6
Misbourne Cl
Aylesbury HP21 ....115 D3
Chalfont St Peter SL9 ...177 E5
Misbourne Ct SL3...... 207 A2
Misbourne Dr HP16 .... 152 B6
Misbourne Ho HP8..... 166 C1
Misbourne Mdws UB9.. 189 D3
Misbourne Sch The
HP16..................152 B6
Misbourne Vale SL9.... 177 D5
Miserden Cres MK4 ..... 45 F1
Missenden Abbey Adult Ed
Coll HP16 ....152 B6
Missenden Cl MK18 ..... 65 F4
Missenden Gdns SL1 ... 204 B7
Missenden Rd
Chesham HP5 ....154 A7
Ellesborough HP17 .....130 C2
Great Kingshill HP15....151 D2
Winslow MK18.......... 65 F4
Miss Joans Ride HP4... 107 D7
Miswell La HP23 .... 118 F3
Mitcham Pl MK13 .... 34 D3
Mitcham Wlk HP19..... 101 A2
Mitchell Cl
Bovingdon HP3 ....145 F4
Slough SL1............205 A4
Mitchell Rd MK43 .... 24 E2
Mitchell Wlk HP6 ...... 154 E1
Mithras Gdns MK7 ...... 48 C6
Mitre Ct MK18 .... 52 C7
Mitre St MK18 .... 52 C7
MIXBURY............... 38 D1
Moat Cl
Prestwood HP16 ....151 C6
Wendover HP22.........131 B6
Moat Dr
Prestwood HP16 ....151 C7
Slough SL2............206 C8
Moat End HP22 .... 102 B4
Moat House The MK18 .. 52 D8
Moat La
Aston Abbotts HP22 ..... 88 D4
Marsh Gibbon OX27...... 71 F2
Prestwood HP16 ....151 C7
Wingrave HP22 .... 89 B2
Moat Pl UB9........... 201 B8
MOBWELL 152 A8
Mobwell Terr 3 HP16.. 152 A8
Model Row HP22....... 117 F6
Moeran Cl MK7 .... 48 C5
Moffy Hill SL6 .... 195 E2
Mole Run HP13 .... 161 C1
Molyneaux Ave HP3.... 145 F4
Molyns Ho RG9 .... 191 E3
Molyns Mews SL1...... 204 E5
Monellan Cres MK7 ..... 48 A3
Monellan Gr MK7 .... 48 A2
Monet Pl HP19......... 100 E2
Money La UB7......... 208 D3
Monkey Island La SL6 .. 203 E2
Monksfield Way SL2 ... 198 A2
Monks Hollow SL7..... 183 E5
Monks Path 9 HP19 ... 115 A8
Monks Rd SL4 .... 209 D5
MONKS RISBOROUGH.... 139 C6
Monks Risborough CE
Comb Sch HP27 ......139 D5
Monks Risborough Sta
HP27..................139 B6
MONKSTON............. 36 A1
Monkston Comb Sch
MK10 .... 36 B1
MONKSTON PARK........ 35 E1
Monkston Rdbt MK10 ... 36 B2
Monks Way
Harmondsworth UB7....213 E8
Milton Keynes MK12, MK13,
MK14, MK15............ 34 C6
Monkswood Ct 11 SL7.. 183 E2
Monkton La SL7 .... 172 F1
Monkton Way HP27 .... 150 C5
Monmouth Cl HP19 .... 101 A2
Monmouth Gr MK4...... 45 E1
Monro Ave MK8......... 45 E7
Montabaur Rd NN13..... 38 A7
Montagu Dr MK6........ 47 B8
Montague Cl SL2 ...... 198 B3
Montague Rd
Aylesbury HP21 ....115 D7
Berkhamsted HP4 ......135 B4
Slough SL1............205 F6
Uxbridge UB8..........201 D5
Montagu Rd SL3 .... 211 B6
Montem La SL1........ 205 D4
Montem L Ctr SL1 ..... 205 D4
Montem Prim Sch SL1 . 205 B4
Montford Mews HP15 .. 162 E2
Montgomerie Cl HP4... 135 A6
Montgomery Cres MK15 . 35 B7
Montgomery Pl SL2.... 206 C7
Montpellier Ct SL4..... 210 C5
Montrose Ave
Datchet SL3...........211 C7
Slough SL1............205 B7
Montrose Dr SL6....... 202 A6
Montrose Way SL3..... 211 C7
Monument La SL9...... 177 E5
Monycrower Dr SL6.... 202 E7
Moon St MK12 .... 33 D6
Moonstone Ct 5 HP12 . 172 D8
Moorbridge Rd SL6 .... 203 A7
MOOR COMMON 171 A2
Moorcroft Sch 3 UB8.. 208 F7
Moore Cl SL1.......... 205 B4
MOOR END
Eaton Bray............. 92 E5
Yardley Gobion.......... 18 D6
Moor End
Eaton Bray LU6 .... 92 F5
Frieth RG9 ....171 A1
Maidenhead SL6 ....203 C1
Moor End Cl LU6........ 92 F4
Moorend La OX9....... 125 F1
Moor End La LU6 .... 92 F5
Moorend Rd NN12 ...... 18 E6
Moore Rd HP4 .... 134 F6
Moores Hill MK46......... 6 F5
Moores La SL4......... 204 F2
Moorfield MK17......... 57 D3
Moorfield Rd
Denham Green UB9.....190 A5
Uxbridge UB8..........208 D7
Moorfield Terr SL6..... 203 A8
Moorfoot MK11 .... 33 A4
Moor Furlong SL1...... 204 E5
Moorgate MK6.......... 46 F7
Moorhall Rd UB9 ...... 190 B6
Moorhen Ct 2 HP20 ... 101 E3
Moorhen Way MK18..... 52 E8
Moorhills Cres LU7 ..... 79 F3
Moorhills Rd LU7 .... 79 F3
Moorings The
Buckingham MK18....... 52 C8
Windsor SL4 ....210 A7
Moor La
Harmondsworth UB7....213 C8
High Wycombe HP13....161 D3
Maidenhead SL6 ....195 F1
Sarratt WD3............156 E3
Moorland Inf Sch MK6 .. 47 B5
Moorland Rd UB7...... 213 C8
Moorlands LU7 .... 79 E3
Moorlands Rd LU7 ...... 79 F3
Moor Pk
Milton Keynes MK3 ...... 57 D8
Wendover HP22.........131 B7
Moor Rd HP5 .... 154 C6
Moors Cl MK19 .... 31 E5
Moor's Farm Cotts HP5 145 B4
Moorside HP10 .... 185 E8
Moorside Cl SL6 .... 195 F1
Moorstown Ct 7 SL1 .. 205 E4
Moor The SL7 .... 184 C4
MOP END.............. 164 B7
Mop End La HP7 ...... 164 B7
Morar Cl LU7 .... 80 C7
Moray Dr SL2.......... 206 A7
Moray Pl MK3 .... 46 F2
Mordaunt Cl MK43 .... 8 E6
Mordaunts Ct MK15..... 35 C2
Moreau Wlk SL3....... 206 E7
More Ave HP21 .... 115 D7
Morebath Gr MK4....... 46 C4
Morefields HP23....... 119 A6
Moreland Ave SL3 ..... 212 C7
Moreland Cl SL3....... 212 C7
Moreland Dr SL9....... 188 F4
Morello Dr SL3 .... 206 F5
Moreton Dr MK18 .... 41 E2
Moreton La HP17 ...... 115 A1
Moreton Rd MK18....... 41 D2
Moreton Way SL1...... 204 D5
Morland Dr MK8 .... 45 D6
Morley Cl SL3.......... 206 F4
Morley Cres MK7 .... 48 D4
Morrell Cl MK5 .... 46 B5
Morrice Cl SL3......... 207 A2
Morris Cl SL9.......... 177 F2
Morris Ct
Aylesbury HP21 ....115 D4
Windsor SL4 ....209 E6
Morrison Ct MK8........ 45 E6
Morris Wlk MK16 .... 22 A4
Mortain Cl MK7......... 48 B3
Mortain Dr HP4 .... 134 F6
Morten Gdns UB9...... 190 A4
Mortens Wood HP7 .... 165 E7
Mortimer Hill HP23 .... 119 B4
Mortimer Rd SL3....... 206 D3
Mortimer Rise HP23.... 119 B4
Morton Cl
North Marston MK18..... 76 B2
Pitstone LU7 ....105 C4
Uxbridge UB8..........201 F1
Morton Dr SL1......... 197 E8
Morton King Cl HP18... 124 D3
Mortons Fork MK13 ..... 33 F6
Moseley Rd HP14 ...... 161 C7
Moses Plat La HP27.... 150 B5
Moss Ct HP9.......... 176 D4
Mossdale MK13 .... 34 B5
Mossmans Cl MK2 ...... 58 D7
Mossway HP9.......... 175 C5
Mossy Vale SL6 .... 195 D1
MOULSOE 36 D8
Moundsfield Way SL1 .. 204 E4
Mountain Ash SL7 .... 183 D6
Mount Ave MK1......... 47 E3
Mountbatten Cl 7 SL1 . 206 A3
Mountbatten Sq 8
SL4..................210 C6
Mount Cl
Aston Clinton HP22 .....117 F4
Farnham Common SL2...198 C8
High Wycombe HP12....172 E6
Mount Farm Ind Est
MK1 .... 47 D4
Mount Farm Rdbt MK1 .. 47 D4
Mounthill Ave MK19..... 32 B7
Mount Hill La SL9...... 188 B2
Mount La UB9 .... 189 D2
Mount Nugent HP5..... 144 A4
MOUNT PLEASANT
Buckingham............ 52 D7
Stoke Goldington 12 B7
Mount Pleasant
Aspley Guise MK17 ...... 49 F4
Aylesbury HP19 ....101 D1
Lane End HP14 ....171 B5
Milton Keynes MK6 ...... 47 E4
Soulbury LU7 .... 69 E3
Steeple Claydon MK18.... 63 F2
Stoke Goldington MK16... 12 B7
Stoke Hammond MK17 ... 69 E7
Whitchurch HP22........ 86 F7
Yardley Gobion NN12..... 18 F6
Mount Pleasant Cl
MK18 .... 52 C7
Mount Pleasant Cotts 2
SL8...................185 B3
Mountsfield Cl
Newport Pagnell MK16 ... 22 C3
Stanwell TW19.........213 A2
Mount St HP20......... 115 D8
Mount The
Aspley Guise MK17 ...... 49 D4
Milton Keynes MK6 ...... 47 E4
Mount View RG9....... 191 D2
Mount View Ct 4 RG9 . 191 D2
Mount Way HP27 ...... 139 A3
Mowbray Dr LU7........ 80 D7
Mowbray Rd HP20 .... 101 D2
Mowhills MK43 .... 3 F6
Mow Mead MK46.......... 6 F5
Moyleen Rise SL7...... 183 C1
Mozart Cl MK7......... 48 C4
Muddiford La MK4 ...... 46 D4
Muirfield Dr MK3 .... 46 D1
Mulberry Ave SL4...... 210 F5
Mulberry Cl
Amersham HP7 ....165 F8
High Wycombe HP12....172 C5
Tring HP23............119 A5

Mulberry Ct HP15 163 D7
Mulberry Dr SL3 206 E1
Mulberry Wlk SL6 202 C8
Mullen Ave MK14 34 F4
Mullins Way HP19 100 E2
Mullion Pl MK6 35 A1
Mumfords La SL9 188 A7
Munces Rd SL7 183 D6
MUNDAYDEAN BOTTOM 182 E5
Mundaydean La SL7 183 B4
Munday's Farm HP21 116 B7
Mundesley Spur SL1 205 E7
MURCOTT 94 A4
Murcott Rd OX6 94 D6
Murray Rd HP4 135 C6
Murrey Cl MK5 46 C5
Murrin Rd SL6 202 C8
MURSLEY 67 D6
Mursley CE Sch MK17 67 D6
Mursley Ct MK11 32 F5
Mursley Rd
Little Horwood MK17 55 E2
Swanbourne MK17 67 B3
Museum Ct 9 HP23 119 A3
Musgrave Rd OX39 147 D7
Musgrave Wlk HP14 158 F5
Musgrove Pl MK5 45 F6
Mus of Eton Life The★ SL4 210 D8
Myddleton Rd UB8 201 C4
Mylne Cl HP13 172 F8
Mynchen Cl HP9 175 D6
Mynchen End HP9 175 D6
Mynchen Rd HP9 175 D6
MYRKE 205 F2
Myrke The SL3 205 F2
Myrtle Bank MK12 33 E5
Myrtle Cl
Poyle SL3 212 E6
Uxbridge UB8 208 F8
West Drayton UB7 208 F3
Myrtle Cres SL2 205 F6

N

Nag's Head La HP16 152 A4
Nailzee Cl SL9 188 E4
Nairdwood Cl HP16 151 E4
Nairdwood La HP16 151 D5
Nairdwood Way HP16 151 E4
Nairn Ct MK3 46 E2
Naisby Dr MK17 59 C1
Nalders Rd HP5 144 D2
Nan Aires HP22 89 A3
Nancy Hall Ct HP12 172 D3
Nans Gdn MK17 57 C4
NAPHILL 161 D7
Naphill Pl MK13 34 C3
Naphill & Walters Ash Sch HP14 150 B1
Napier Cl UB7 208 F3
Napier Rd
Aylesbury HP19 114 F8
Harmondsworth TW6 213 D6
Maidenhead SL6 202 B6
Napier St MK2 58 D8
Nappin Cl HP19 101 A3
Nappins Cl HP18 125 D5
Nap The HP18 109 E5
Narbeth Dr HP20 116 B8
Narcot La HP8 177 B5
Narcot Rd HP8 177 A7
Narcot Way HP8 177 B6
Narrow La HP13 161 E3
Narrow Path MK17 49 B3
Naseby Cl
Newport Pagnell MK16 22 A3
Thame OX9 126 B1
Naseby Ct
Buckingham MK18 41 E2
Milton Keynes MK13 34 B6
NASH 44 C1
Nash Cl
Aylesbury HP21 116 A4
Berkhamsted HP4 135 A5
Nash Croft MK4 57 B8
Nashdom SL1 196 F5
Nashdom La SL1 197 B6
NASH LEE 130 C5
Nash Lee End HP22 130 F6
Nash Lee La HP22 130 E6
Nash Lee Rd
Nash Lee HP17 130 D6
World's End HP22 130 F7
Nashleigh Hill HP5 144 D3
Nashleigh Ho HP5 144 E3
Nash Pl HP10 163 B1
Nash Rd
Great Horwood MK17 55 A4
Slough SL3 207 A2
Thornborough MK18 54 B8
Whaddon MK17 45 A1
Nashs Farm HP22 88 D4
Nathanial Cl MK5 46 B5
Nathaniel Wlk HP23 119 A5
National Badminton Ctr MK8 34 A1
National Bowl The★ MK6 46 E5
National Film & Television Sch HP9 175 E1
National Waterways Mus★ NN12 9 A8
Natural History Mus at Tring★ HP23 119 A3
Natwoke Cl HP9 175 D5
Neal Cl SL9 189 B3
Neale Cl HP12 172 D3
Neapland MK6 47 B5
NEARTON END 67 A3
Nearton End MK17 67 A3
Near Town MK46 7 A3
Near Town Gdns MK46 7 A3
Neath Cres MK3 47 A2
NEATH HILL 34 F6
Neath Hill Rdbt MK15 35 A6
Needham Cl SL4 209 E6
Needham Ct 4 HP11 172 F7
Neild Way WD3 167 F2
Neilson Ct MK7 48 C5
Nelson Cl
High Wycombe HP13 173 F5
Milton Keynes MK8 45 E6
Slough SL3 206 D2
Winchmore Hill HP7 164 C3
Nelson Ct MK18 52 C8
Nelson Rd
Dagnall HP4 107 C5
Harmondsworth TW6 213 F6
Windsor SL4 209 F4
Nelson St MK18 52 C8
Nelson Terr HP20 115 D8
Nene Cl
Aylesbury HP21 115 C4
Newport Pagnell MK16 22 D3
Nene Dr MK3 57 E8
Neptune Way SL1 204 E4
Ness Way MK2 58 D5
Netherby Cl HP23 119 C6
Nether Cl NN13 38 A7
Nethercote La OX49 157 A8
NETHERFIELD 47 C6
Netherfield Rdbt MK6 47 C7
Nether Gr MK5 46 B3
Nether Winchendon Ho★ HP18 112 E5
Netherwood Rd HP9 175 D5
Netley Ct MK10 36 A1
Nettlecombe MK4 46 C3
Nettleden Rd
Berkhamsted HP4 135 F6
Little Gaddesden HP4 121 E4
Nettleton Rd UB10 201 F8
Neve Ho SL6 202 F8
Nevill Cl MK19 11 B2
Neville Cl SL2 198 F6
Neville Ct SL1 197 C2
Nevis Cl LU7 80 C7
Nevis Gr MK2 58 E4
Newark Ct MK7 48 A3
Newbarn La HP9 176 E6
Newberry Cres SL4 209 D5
Newbery Way SL1 205 D4
Newbolt Cl
Newport Pagnell MK16 21 F5
Paulerspury NN12 17 B8
NEW BRADWELL 33 F8
New Bradwell Comb Sch MK13 33 F7
Newbridge Oval MK4 46 B3
Newbury Ct MK3 57 D6
Newbury Dr SL6 203 B6
Newbury Rd UB7 213 F6
Newby Pl MK4 46 B2
New Chapter Prim sch MK6 47 A5
New Chilterns HP7 165 E8
Newchurch Rd SL2 204 F8
New Cl RG9 192 A8
New Cl Farm Rd OX39 137 C3
New College MK18 51 F8
New College Ct MK18 41 B4
New Coll Rd HP19 101 C4
Newcombe Rise UB7 208 E7
New Cotts RG9 180 C1
Newcourt UB8 208 C8
Newcroft Cl UB8 208 F8
New Ct
High Wycombe HP13 173 C6
Marlow SL7 183 D2
NEW DENHAM 201 A6
New Dr HP13 173 E8
Newell Cl HP21 116 A6
Newells Hedge LU7 105 D5
Newfield Gdns SL7 183 F3
Newfield Rd SL7 183 F3
Newfield Way SL7 183 F2
New Garden Dr UB7 208 E4
NEW GROUND 120 A2
Newground Rd HP23 120 B3
New Hall Cl HP3 146 A4
Newhaven Spur SL2 198 B1
New Horton Manor SL3 212 A4
Newhouse Rd HP3 146 A4
Newington Gate MK6 47 D5
New Inn La MK18 51 F4
Newland Ho UB8 201 C4
NEWLAND PARK 178 A7
Newlands Dr
Maidenhead SL6 202 A7
Poyle SL3 212 E4
Newlands Girls Sch SL6 202 A7
Newlyn Pl MK6 35 A2
Newmans Cl MK14 21 E1
Newmans Ctyd MK17 68 C6
Newmarket Ct MK10 36 C2
New Mdw HP21 116 C7
Newmer Rd HP12 172 B3
NEW MILL 119 B6
New Mill Terr HP23 119 B6
New Par
Chorleywood WD3 167 C5
West Drayton UB7 208 E5
New Peachey La UB8 208 D8
New Pond Rd HP15 163 C7
NEWPORT PAGNELL 22 B5
Newport Pagnell Rd MK43 16 C4
Newport Rd
Astwood MK16 15 C2
Emberton MK46 13 F6
Hanslope MK19 11 B2
Milton Keynes MK10 36 D1
Milton Keynes, New Bradwell MK13 34 A8
Milton Keynes, Oakgrove MK15 35 C2
Milton Keynes, Willen MK15 35 D7
Milton Keynes, Woughton on the Green MK6 35 D1
Moulsoe MK16 36 C7
Slough SL2 197 E1
Wavendon MK17 48 E7
Woburn MK17 60 F8
Woughton on the Green MK6 47 D8
Woughton Park MK6 47 D6
Newport Way MK19 11 C3
New Provident Pl 5 HP4 135 D4
Newquay Cl 4 MK4 45 F1
New Rd
Amersham HP6 154 E2
Aston Clinton HP22 117 E5
Berkhamsted HP4 135 D6
Berkhamsted, Northchurch HP4 134 F7
Bolter End HP14 170 F6
Bourne End SL8 185 B4
Castlethorpe MK19 19 F5
Chipperfield WD4 146 F1
Coleshill HP7 164 F4
Cookham Rise SL6 195 E7
Datchet SL3 211 D6
Dinton HP17 113 E2
Drayton Parslow MK17 68 C5
Great Kingshill HP15 162 D8
Harrold MK43 3 E6
High Wycombe HP12 172 C5
Hurley SL6 193 F3
Leighton Buzzard LU7 80 E7
Little Chalfont HP8 166 F6
Little Kingshill HP16 152 B4
Marlow Bottom SL7 183 D6
Naphill HP14 150 A2
Prestwood HP16 151 D6
Princes Risborough HP27 139 C3
Sarratt HP8 156 F1
Slough SL3 207 A3
Stokenchurch HP14 158 F4
Tring HP23 119 B6
Tylers Green HP10 163 C1
Weedon HP22 101 B8
Weston Turville HP22 116 E5
Wilstone HP23 118 D8
New Road Cl HP12 172 C6
New Road Gdns HP12 172 C6
New Row
Hoggeston MK18 77 B7
Lavendon MK46 7 E8
New Sq SL1 205 F4
New St
Aylesbury HP20 101 D1
Berkhamsted HP4 135 D4
Cheddington LU7 104 F7
Henley-on-Thames RG9 191 E2
Milton Keynes MK11 32 D5
Tingewick MK18 51 B6
Waddesdon HP18 99 A7
NEWTON 144 C1
NEWTON BLOSSOMVILLE 8 A4
Newton Blossomville CE Sch MK43 8 B4
Newton Cl SL3 206 F4
Newton Ct SL4 211 A1
Newton La SL4 211 B1
NEWTON LONGVILLE 57 D3
Newton Longville CE Comb Sch MK17 57 D3
NEWTON PURCELL 50 B2
Newton Rd
Drayton Parslow MK17 68 D8
Milton Keynes MK3 57 E6
Stoke Hammond MK17 69 D8
Turvey MK43 8 E5
West Drayton UB7 213 F6
Newtonside SL4 211 A1
Newton Side Orch SL4 211 A1
Newton St MK46 7 A4
Newtown Rd
Marlow SL7 183 F3
New Denham UB9 201 B6
Newtown Sch HP5 144 C2
Newville HP22 87 C1
New Windsor St UB8 201 C4
NEWYEARS GREEN 190 F5
Newyears Green La UB9 190 F5
New Zealand Cotts HP22 88 E4
New Zealand Gdns LU7 79 E2
Neyland Dr HP19 101 D3
Nicholas Gdns
High Wycombe HP13 173 D8
Slough SL1 204 E5
Nicholas Mead MK14 34 F8
Nicholas Winton Ct SL6 203 A8
Nicholls SL4 209 C4
Nicholls Wlk SL4 209 C4
Nicholson Gr MK8 45 E6
Nicholsons La SL6 202 F7
Nicholsons Sh Ctr 2 SL6 202 F7
Nickson Ct HP15 163 A3
Nicol Cl SL9 177 C2
Nicol End SL9 177 C2
Nicol Rd SL9 177 C2
Nielson Ct MK7 48 D5
Nigel Ct NN13 38 A5
Nightingale Cl
Hazelmere HP15 163 B5
Steeple Claydon MK18 63 E3
Nightingale Cres MK13 34 A7
Nightingale Ct
1 High Wycombe HP13 173 B7
6 Slough SL1 206 A3
Nightingale Ho HP11 174 A4
Nightingale La SL6 195 D3
Nightingale Lodge HP4 135 B4
Nightingale Pk SL2 197 F5
Nightingale Pl
Buckingham MK18 41 E1
Cookham Rise SL6 195 F7
Nightingale Rd
Aylesbury HP21 115 E6
2 Chesham HP5 144 B2
Wendover HP22 131 B5
Nightingales Cnr HP7 166 C7
Nightingales Ct HP8 166 C7
Nightingales La HP8 166 D4
Nightingale Way UB9 189 F5
Nightingale Wlk SL4 210 C4
Nijinsky Ho UB8 201 D3
Nine Acres SL1 204 F5
Nine Elms Ave UB8 208 D8
Nine Elms Cl UB8 208 D8
Nine Stiles Cl UB9 201 B6
Ninnings Rd SL9 177 F3
Ninnings Way SL9 177 F3
Niplands Cotts HP10 185 D2
Niven La MK4 45 E3
Nixey Cl SL1 206 A4
Nixons Cl MK6 46 E6
Noble Cl MK15 35 A7
Noble Ct SL2 205 F5
Noon Layer Dr MK10 35 E3
Norbrek MK8 33 E2
NORCOTT HILL 120 D2
Norcotts Kiln Cotts HP18 96 A1
Norden Cl SL6 202 C4
Norden Mdws SL6 202 C5
Norden Rd SL6 202 C5
Norelands Dr SL1 197 C3
Norfolk Ave SL1 205 C8
Norfolk Ho 6 MK3 46 F1
Norfolk Park Cotts SL6 202 F8
Norfolk Rd
Maidenhead SL6 202 F8
Turvey MK43 8 E6
Uxbridge UB8 201 D6
Norfolk Terr HP20 101 E1
Norgrove Pk SL9 188 E7
Norjo-An Villas HP5 154 C6
Norland Dr HP10 185 C8
Norman Ave RG9 191 E1
Norman Cres MK10 35 E3
Normandy Dr HP4 135 B6
Normandy Way MK3 46 E2
Normans Cl UB8 208 F8
Normans Ct 5 HP13 173 F6
Normanstead RG9 191 D1
Normans The SL2 206 B7
Norman Way LU6 93 E8
Normill Terr HP22 117 A6
Norreys Dr SL6 202 D4
Norrington MK8 33 E2
Norris Ho SL6 202 E7
Norris Rd OX6 94 E8
NORTHALL 92 B5
Northall Cl LU6 92 D6
Northall Rd LU6 92 D6
Northampton Ave SL1 205 C7
Northampton Rd
Brackley NN13 26 A1
Cosgrove MK19 19 C1
Cosgrove MK19 32 C8
Grafton Regis NN12 9 C3
Lathbury MK16 22 D6
Lavendon MK46 7 F8
Yardley Hastings NN7 1 A6
Northborough Rd SL2 198 B1
Northbridge Rd HP4 135 A6
North Burnham Cl SL1 197 B3
NORTHCHURCH 134 E5
Northchurch La HP5 134 D2
North Cl
Beaconsfield HP9 186 B8
Drayton Parslow MK17 68 C5
Medmenham SL7 193 D7
Windsor SL4 209 F6
Northcliffe LU6 92 E6
North Common Rd UB8 201 D7
North Cotts SL2 198 C2
NORTH CRAWLEY 24 A6
North Crawley CE Sch MK16 24 B6
North Crawley Rd MK16 23 C4
Northcroft
Milton Keynes MK5 46 C6
Slough SL2 198 B1
Weedon HP22 87 C1
Wooburn Green HP10 185 F6
North Croft MK18 66 A4
Northdean 5 SL6 195 F1
Northdown Rd SL9 177 E4
North Dr
Aylesbury HP21 115 E5
Beaconsfield HP9 186 B8
High Wycombe HP13 173 E8
North Eastern Rd HP19 101 C2
North Eighth St MK9 34 E3
North Elder Rdbt MK9 34 C1
North Eleventh St MK9 34 E3
NORTHEND 168 E6
NORTH END
Stagsden 16 E8
Steeple Claydon 63 D3
Stewkley 68 D3
Northend MK46 5 E3
Northend Cl HP10 185 C7
Northend Ct 1 MK18 41 D1
North End Rd
Quainton HP22 85 A5
Steeple Claydon MK18 63 D3
Northend Sq 2 MK18 41 D1
Northend Workshops RG9 168 E5
Northern Hts SL8 185 B5
Northern Perimeter Rd (W) TW6 213 D6
Northern Rd
Aylesbury HP19 101 C2
Slough SL2 198 D1
Northern Woods HP10 185 C7
NORTHFIELD 35 F5
Northfield Ct RG9 191 D3
Northfield Dr MK15 35 F5
Northfield End RG9 191 D3
Northfield Rd
Aylesbury HP20 116 B8
Eton Wick SL4 204 F2
Maidenhead SL6 195 F1
Princes Risborough HP27 139 C4
Tring HP23 119 F7
Northfield Rdbt MK10 36 A5
North Fifth St MK9 34 D2
North Fourteenth St MK9 34 F4
North Fourth St MK9 34 D2
North Gate MK2 47 C1
North Gn
3 Maidenhead SL6 195 F1
Slough SL1 205 E6
North Grafton Rdbt MK13 34 C2
North Hill
Buckingham MK18 28 D2
Dadford MK18 28 D2
Sarratt WD3 167 E8
North Hills HP18 96 A1
North La MK7 47 E7
Northlands Rd MK18 53 F1
NORTH LEE 130 A7
North Lee La
North Lee HP22 130 A6
Stoke Mandeville HP22 129 F7
Northleigh MK4 46 D2
North Links Rd HP10 174 B1
NORTH MARSTON 76 A2

North Marston CE Sch MK18 . . . 76 B2
North Marston La HP22 . . 86 E7
Northmead Rd SL2 . . . 204 F8
Northmill HP27 . . . 138 F3
North Mill Rd HP27 . . . 138 A5
Northmoor Hill Wood Nature Reserve★ UB9 . . . 189 F7
North Ninth St MK9 . . . 34 E3
Northolt Rd TW6 . . . 213 E6
North Orbital Rd
  Denham Green UB9 . . . 189 F4
  Rickmansworth WD3 . . . 178 E7
North Overgate Rdbt MK15 . . . 35 B5
North Pk
  Gerrards Cross SL9 . . . 188 E8
  Iver SL0 . . . 207 D3
North Rd
  Amersham HP6 . . . 154 C3
  Berkhamsted HP4 . . . 135 B4
  Chorleywood WD3 . . . 167 D4
  Cryers Hill HP15 . . . 162 D5
  Maidenhead SL6 . . . 202 E7
  West Drayton UB7 . . . 208 F3
North Ridge MK6 . . . 35 B1
North Row
  Fulmer SL3 . . . 199 E8
  Milton Keynes MK9 . . . 34 C2
North Saxon Rdbt MK14 . 34 D3
North Secklow Rdbt MK14 . . . 34 E3
North Second St MK9 . . . 34 C2
North Seventh St MK9 . . . 34 D2
North Sixth St MK9 . . . 34 D2
North Skeldon Rdbt MK9 . . . 35 A4
North Sq MK16 . . . 22 D5
North St
  Castlethorpe MK19 . . . 19 F5
  Milton Keynes, Bradville MK13 . . . 34 A7
  Milton Keynes, Fenny Stratford MK2 . . . 47 C1
  Thame OX9 . . . 125 F1
North Star La SL6 . . . 202 C6
North Tenth St MK9 . . . 34 E3
North Terr SL4 . . . 210 E7
North Third St MK9 . . . 34 D2
North Thirteenth St MK9 34 F3
NORTH TOWN . . . 195 F1
North Town Cl 1 SL6 . . 195 F1
North Town Mead 4 SL6 . . . 195 F1
North Town Moor SL6 . . 195 F1
North Town Rd SL6 . . . 195 F1
North Twelfth St MK9 . . . 34 F3
Northumberland Ave HP21 . . . 116 B6
Northumberland Cl TW19 . . . 213 E1
Northumbria Rd SL6 . . . 202 B4
North View HP22 . . . 87 B3
North Way
  Deanshanger NN12 . . . 31 E5
  Potterspury NN12 . . . 18 E2
  Uxbridge UB10 . . . 201 E5
NORTH WESTON . . . 136 F8
Northwich MK6 . . . 47 D7
Northwick Rd MK10 . . . 35 F1
North Witan Rdbt MK13 . 34 D2
Northwood Rd TW6 . . . 213 D6
Nortoft Rd SL9 . . . 177 F5
Norton Leys MK7 . . . 48 C7
Norton Rd UB8 . . . 201 D2
Norton's Pl MK18 . . . 52 C8
Nortons The MK7 . . . 48 B3
Norvic Rd HP23 . . . 105 A1
Norway Dr SL2 . . . 206 B8
Norwich Ho
  High Wycombe HP13 . . . 173 F8
  Maidenhead SL6 . . . 202 E8
Norwood Cl HP20 . . . 101 F2
Norwood Ct 4 HP7 . . . 165 B7
Norwood La
  Newport Pagnell MK16 . . . 22 C3
  Uxbridge SL0 . . . 200 D1
Norwood Rd HP10 . . . 174 B2
Notley Farm HP18 . . . 126 A7
Nottingham Gr MK3 . . . 46 E2
Nottingham Ho 3 HP13 . . . 173 F7
Nottingham Rd WD3 . . . 167 C1
Nova Lodge MK4 . . . 46 B2
Novello Croft MK7 . . . 48 D4
Nugent Cl HP19 . . . 101 D4
Nugent Ct
  Chesham HP5 . . . 144 A3
  Marlow SL7 . . . 183 F3
Nuneham Gr MK4 . . . 45 F3
NUP END . . . 89 B3
Nup End Cl HP22 . . . 89 B3
Nup End La HP22 . . . 89 B3
Nurseries The LU6 . . . 92 E6
Nursery Cl
  2 Amersham HP7 . . . 165 E8
  Aylesbury HP21 . . . 115 C5
  Tylers Green HP10 . . . 174 C8
Nursery Ct HP12 . . . 172 D6
Nursery Dr HP14 . . . 171 B5
Nursery Gdns
  Milton Keynes MK13 . . . 34 A4
  Tring HP23 . . . 119 B4
Nursery La
  Slough SL3 . . . 206 D5
  Tylers Green HP10 . . . 174 C8
Nursery Pl SL4 . . . 211 B1
Nursery Rd SL6 . . . 204 B7
Nursery Way TW19 . . . 211 D1
Nursery Waye UB8 . . . 201 D4
Nursery Wlk SL7 . . . 183 B1
Nutfield La HP11 . . . 172 F8
Nuthatch 10 HP19 . . . 101 F3
Nutkins Way HP5 . . . 144 C2
Nutkin Wlk UB10 . . . 201 E5
Nutmeg Cl MK7 . . . 48 B5
Nye Way HP3 . . . 146 A3
Nymans Gate 8 MK4 . . . 45 F1

O

Oak Barn Cl MK43 . . . 25 A1
Oak Cres HP12 . . . 172 C4
Oak Ct MK9 . . . 34 E2
Oakdene HP9 . . . 175 E3
Oakdown Cres MK46 . . . 6 F3
Oak Dr HP4 . . . 135 D3
Oak End Dr SL0 . . . 200 C3
Oak End Way
  Chinnor OX39 . . . 147 D5
  Gerrards Cross SL9 . . . 188 F6
Oaken Gr SL6 . . . 195 C1
Oakengrove HP16 . . . 151 C5
Oakengrove Cl HP15 . . . 163 C6
Oakengrove La HP15 . . . 163 B3
Oakengrove Rd HP15 . . . 163 A3
Oaken Head MK4 . . . 46 C2
Oakeshott Ave HP14 . . . 161 D6
Oakfield WD3 . . . 167 F2
Oak Field HP5 . . . 144 B1
Oakfield Ave SL1 . . . 205 B5
Oakfield Cl HP6 . . . 154 C2
Oakfield Cnr HP6 . . . 154 C2
Oakfield Fst Sch SL4 . . . 210 B5
Oakfield Rd
  Aylesbury HP20 . . . 116 A8
  Bourne End SL8 . . . 185 A3
Oak Gn HP21 . . . 115 C7
Oak Green Sch HP21 . . . 115 C7
OAKGROVE . . . 35 D2
Oakgrove L Ctr MK10 . . . 35 F2
Oakgrove Rdbt MK10 . . . 35 F2
Oakgrove Sch MK10 . . . 35 F2
Oakham Rise MK4 . . . 45 E1
OAKHILL . . . 45 D4
Oakhill Cl
  Maple Cross WD3 . . . 178 E6
  Milton Keynes MK5 . . . 45 E6
Oakhill Rd
  Maple Cross WD3 . . . 178 D6
  Milton Keynes, Hazeley MK5 . . . 45 D5
  Milton Keynes, Shenley Church End MK5 . . . 45 F6
Oakhill Rdbt MK5 . . . 45 D5
Oakhurst SL6 . . . 196 B4
Oakington Ave HP6 . . . 166 E8
Oak La
  Buckland Common HP23 . . . 133 A2
  Windsor SL4 . . . 210 A6
Oaklands HP4 . . . 135 A4
Oaklands Ct HP6 . . . 154 C1
Oakland Way HP10 . . . 174 A1
Oak Lawn HP23 . . . 119 A3
OAKLEY
  Brill . . . 109 D5
  Chinnor . . . 147 B5
Oakley HP10 . . . 185 F7
Oakley CE Comb Sch HP18 . . . 109 D4
Oakley Coll HP18 . . . 109 F1
Oakley Cres SL1 . . . 205 E6
Oakley Gdns MK15 . . . 35 B5
OAKLEY GREEN . . . 209 B5
Oakley Green Rd SL4 . . . 209 B5
Oakley Hill Wildlife Reserve★ OX39 . . . 147 D4
Oakley La OX39 . . . 147 B6
Oakley Rd
  Brill HP18 . . . 110 A8
  Chinnor OX39 . . . 147 C6
  Horton-cum-S OX33 . . . 108 C5
Oak Rd HP27 . . . 139 C3
Oakridge MK4 . . . 46 E4
Oakridge Combined Sch HP11 . . . 172 E7
Oakridge Ct HP12 . . . 172 D6
Oakridge Pl SL2 . . . 198 C8
Oakridge Rd HP11 . . . 172 E7
Oakside UB9 . . . 201 B6
Oaks Rd TW19 . . . 213 D2
Oak St HP11 . . . 173 C4
Oaks The HP4 . . . 135 A4
Oak Stubbs La SL6 . . . 203 F4
Oak Tree Ave SL7 . . . 183 D3
Oaktree Cl HP10 . . . 163 B2
Oak Tree Cl SL7 . . . 183 D3
Oak Tree Cotts HP18 . . . 83 B5
Oaktree Ct MK15 . . . 35 C7
Oak Tree Dr
  Lane End HP14 . . . 171 C5
  Slough SL3 . . . 207 B1
Oak Tree Rd SL7 . . . 183 D4
Oakview HP6 . . . 153 D4
Oak View
  Great Kingshill HP15 . . . 162 D8
  Towcester NN12 . . . 18 D3
Oakview Gdns SL3 . . . 206 F2
Oakway
  Amersham HP6 . . . 154 B4
  Winslow MK18 . . . 66 A4
Oakwell Cl LU6 . . . 93 F7
Oakwood HP10 . . . 174 A2
Oak wood HP4 . . . 134 F3
Oakwood Dr MK2 . . . 58 E7
Oakworth Ave MK10 . . . 36 A4
Oat Cl HP21 . . . 115 C3
Oatlands Dr SL1 . . . 205 D7
Oban Ct SL1 . . . 205 D4
Oberon Way MK4 . . . 45 D2
Observatory Sh Ctr 4 SL1 . . . 205 F4
Ockwells Nature Reserve★ SL6 . . . 202 E2
Ockwells Rd SL6 . . . 202 C2
Octagon Arc 10 HP11 . . . 173 A7
Octagon Par 6 HP11 . . . 173 A7
Octavian Dr MK13 . . . 33 F5
Octavian Way NN13 . . . 38 A7
Oddley La HP27 . . . 148 D8
Odds Farm Est HP10 . . . 186 B4
Odds Farm Park★ HP10 . . . 186 B4
Oddy Hill
  Tring HP23 . . . 119 C3
  Wigginton HP23 . . . 119 C2
Odell Cl MK6 . . . 47 C8
Odencroft Rd SL2 . . . 198 A2
Odney La SL6 . . . 196 B7
Offas La MK18 . . . 66 B5
Ogilvie Rd HP12 . . . 172 E7
O'Grady Way HP19 . . . 101 A3
Okeford Cl HP23 . . . 118 F4
Okeford Dr HP23 . . . 118 F4
Okeley La HP23 . . . 118 E3
Oldacres SL6 . . . 203 B7
Old Airfield Ind Est HP23 . . . 104 D6
Old Amersham Rd SL9 . 189 B3
Old Bakery Ct SL0 . . . 207 F7
Old Bakery The
  Aston Abbotts HP22 . . . 88 D5
  Lane End HP14 . . . 171 B4
Old Barn Cl MK18 . . . 52 A4
Old Bix Rd RG9 . . . 191 A6
Old Brewery Cl HP21 . . . 115 E7
Old Brewery La RG9 . . . 191 E2
OLDBROOK . . . 46 E8
Oldbrook Bvd MK6 . . . 46 E8
Oldbrook Fst Sch MK6 . . 46 E8
Old Bryers Cl HP18 . . . 124 C2
Old Burrs HP21 . . . 115 D3
Oldbury Gr HP9 . . . 175 D5
Oldcastle Croft MK4 . . . 46 A1
Old Chapel Cl HP17 . . . 129 E3
Old Coach Dr HP11 . . . 174 A4
Old Common Rd WD3 . . 167 D5
Old Court Cl SL6 . . . 202 B3
Old Dashwood Hill HP14 . . . 159 F2
Old Dean HP3 . . . 146 A4
Olde Bell Cl MK17 . . . 69 E7
Olde Bell La MK5 . . . 46 A7
Old End MK18 . . . 53 B2
Old English Cl MK17 . . . 44 C1
Oldershaw Mews SL6 . . 202 B8
Old Farm LU7 . . . 105 D4
Old Farm Cl
  Beaconsfield HP9 . . . 175 C5
  Slapton LU7 . . . 91 A3
  Worminghall HP18 . . . 123 E5
Old Farm La HP7 . . . 165 E6
OLD FARM PARK . . . 48 E5
Old Farm Rd
  High Wycombe HP13 . . . 161 E2
  West Drayton UB7 . . . 208 D4
Old Ferry Dr TW19 . . . 211 D1
Old Field Cl HP6 . . . 166 E8
Oldfield Prim Sch SL6 . . 203 B6
Oldfield Rd SL6 . . . 203 B7
Old Fishery La HP1 . . . 146 F8
Old Fives Ct SL1 . . . 197 C2
Old Forge Cl
  Maidenhead SL6 . . . 203 A3
  Tingewick MK18 . . . 51 B6
Old Forge Gdns HP22 . . 102 B4
Old Forge Rd HP10 . . . 174 C2
Old Forge The HP23 . . . 104 B4
Old Gaol Mus★ MK18 . . . 41 D1
Old Garden Ctr The HP27 . . . 139 B3
Old Groveway MK6 . . . 47 D5
Oldham Rise MK5 . . . 45 E5
Oldhams Mdw 9 HP20 . 101 F2
Old Hardenwaye HP13 . . 162 E1
Old Heatherdene Cotts HP15 . . . 162 D8
Old Horns La SL7 . . . 172 A3
Oldhouse Cl HP11 . . . 172 E3
Old House Ct SL3 . . . 206 D7
Old Kiln Rd
  Flackwell Heath HP10 . . . 185 A8
  Tylers Green HP10 . . . 163 C2
OLD LINSLADE . . . 70 D2
Old Linslade Rd LU7 . . . 70 E3
Old Lodge Dr HP9 . . . 175 E1
Old Maltings The
  Buckingham MK18 . . . 52 C7
  Thame OX9 . . . 125 E1
Old Manor Cl
  Askett HP27 . . . 139 C7
  Whaddon MK17 . . . 45 B1
Old Manor Ct LU7 . . . 78 E8
Old Marsh La SL6 . . . 203 F4
Old Mead SL9 . . . 177 E4
Old Meadow Cl HP4 . . . 135 A2
Old Mews The MK46 . . . 6 F4
Old Mill Cl HP17 . . . 127 A6
Old Mill Furlong MK18 . . 66 A5
Old Mill Gdns 12 HP4 . . . 135 D4
Old Mill La
  Maidenhead SL6 . . . 203 D4
  Uxbridge UB8 . . . 208 B8
Old Mill Pl TW19 . . . 212 B1
Old Mill Rd UB9 . . . 190 A1
Old Moor La HP10 . . . 185 E8
Old Nursery Ct SL2 . . . 187 C2
Old Oak Gdns HP4 . . . 134 E7
Old Orch
  Henton OX39 . . . 137 E2
  Iver SL0 . . . 207 F7
Old Orchard Mews 1 HP4 . . . 135 C4
Old Orchards HP22 . . . 102 A3
Old Oxford Rd HP14 . . . 160 C1
Old Palace Ct SL3 . . . 212 D6
Old Papermill Cl HP10 . . 185 E8
Old Plough Cl HP18 . . . 112 B2
Old Post Office La 11 SL6 . . . 202 F7
Old Rd LU7 . . . 80 E7
Old Rd The RG9 . . . 179 C8
Old Rectory La UB9 . . . 189 E4
Old Risborough Rd HP22 . . . 130 A8
Old Sax La HP5 . . . 143 D4
Old School Cl HP22 . . . 117 C1
Old School Cotts HP5 . . 145 D5
Old School Ct
  Buckingham MK18 . . . 52 C8
  Eaton Bray LU6 . . . 92 E6
Old School La MK17 . . . 69 E8
Old School La The MK18 63 D3
Old School Rd UB8 . . . 201 F1
Old School The HP10 . . . 185 D4
Old Shire La WD3 . . . 167 B3
Old Slade La SL0 . . . 207 F2
Old Springfields MK18 . . 53 C2
Old Stable Yd MK19 . . . 32 C7
Old Stable Yd The MK18 . 65 F4
Old Station Cl MK18 . . . 66 A5
Old Station La TW19 . . . 212 A1
Old Station Way HP10 . . 185 E5
Old Stoke Rd HP21 . . . 115 D6
OLD STRATFORD . . . 32 B7
Old Stratford Prim Sch MK19 . . . 32 B6
Old Tan Yard Cl MK18 . . . 65 F4
OLD TOWN . . . 38 A7
Old Town NN13 . . . 38 A7
Old Town Cl HP9 . . . 175 E1
Old Town Farm HP16 . . . 152 A7
Old Union Way OX9 . . . 125 E1
Old Uxbridge Rd WD3 . . 178 E3
Old Vicarage Way HP10 . . . 185 D4
Old Watery La HP10 . . . 185 E8
Oldway La SL1 . . . 204 D5
Old Windmill Way HP18 . . . 125 C7
OLD WINDSOR . . . 211 A1
OLD WOLVERTON . . . 33 D8
Old Wolverton Rd MK12 . 33 C8
Oliffe Cl HP20 . . . 101 D3
Oliffe Way HP20 . . . 101 D3
Oliver Rd MK2 . . . 58 C8
Oliver Row 4 MK4 . . . 45 E3
Oliver's Paddock SL7 . . 183 D5
Olivia Dr SL3 . . . 206 F1
Olivier Way HP20 . . . 116 A8
Olleberrie La WD4 . . . 156 D7
OLNEY . . . 6 E4
Olney Ind Est MK46 . . . 6 F6
Olney Inf Sch MK46 . . . 6 E3
Olney Mid Sch MK46 . . . 6 F5
Olney Rd
  Emberton MK46 . . . 13 F8
  Lavendon MK46 . . . 7 E7
Olson Cotts HP14 . . . 158 F4
Olympic Ho UB8 . . . 201 F1
O'Neill Rd MK8 . . . 45 D6
One Pin La SL2 . . . 187 D1
One Tree La HP9 . . . 175 E3
Onslow Ct MK7 . . . 48 A4
Onslow Dr OX9 . . . 126 B1
Onslow Gdns HP13 . . . 173 E7
Onslow Mills UB7 . . . 208 D6
Opal Ct SL3 . . . 199 C1
Opal Dr MK15 . . . 35 F4
Opecks Cl SL3 . . . 199 B1
Opendale Rd SL1 . . . 204 B8
Open University (Walton Hall) The MK7 . . . 47 F7
Oram Ct 3 SL7 . . . 183 D2
Orbell Ct HP27 . . . 139 B3
Orbison Ct MK8 . . . 45 D7
Orchard Ave
  Berkhamsted HP4 . . . 135 A4
  Slough SL1 . . . 204 D8
  Windsor SL4 . . . 210 A6
Orchard Bglws SL2 . . . 197 F5
Orchard Cl
  15 Aylesbury HP20 . . . 101 F3
  Beaconsfield HP9 . . . 175 D3
  Chorleywood WD3 . . . 167 D5
  Cranfield MK43 . . . 25 A1
  Hughenden Valley HP14 . 162 A7
  Longwick HP27 . . . 138 D7
  Maidenhead SL6 . . . 203 A3
  Milton Keynes MK3 . . . 57 F7
  New Denham UB9 . . . 201 B6
  Newton Longville MK17 . . . 57 C3
  Oakley HP18 . . . 109 D4
  Slough SL1 . . . 197 B1
  Stoke Mandeville HP22 . . 116 B1
  Upper Arncott OX25 . . . 94 D6
  Waddesdon HP18 . . . 99 A7
  Wendover HP22 . . . 131 A5
  Wingrave HP22 . . . 89 B3
  Yardley Gobion NN12 . . . 18 F6
Orchard Ct
  Aylesbury HP21 . . . 115 F6
  Bovingdon HP3 . . . 146 A4
  Harmondsworth TW6 . . . 213 C7
  Seer Green HP9 . . . 176 C5
Orchard Dene MK18 . . . 41 D1
Orchard Dr
  Aston Clinton HP22 . . . 117 E4
  Chorleywood WD3 . . . 167 D5
  Hazelmere HP15 . . . 163 A3
  Leighton Buzzard LU7 . . . 80 D6
  Uxbridge UB8 . . . 201 D1
  Wooburn HP10 . . . 185 D4
Orchard End
  Edlesborough LU6 . . . 92 E4
  Hazelmere HP15 . . . 163 B6
Orchard End Ave HP7 . . 165 F8
Orchard Gate SL2 . . . 198 C7
Orchard Gr
  Chalfont St Peter SL9 . . . 177 C2
  Flackwell Heath HP10 . . . 185 B7
  Maidenhead SL6 . . . 202 C7
Orchard Ho
  8 Bourne End SL8 . . . 185 A4
  Milton Keynes MK12 . . . 33 D6
Orchard La
  Amersham HP6 . . . 154 D1
  Harrold MK43 . . . 3 F7
  Prestwood HP16 . . . 151 C6
  Stewkley LU7 . . . 78 E7
ORCHARD LEIGH . . . 145 B3
Orchard Leigh Villas HP5 . . . 145 A4
Orchard Lodge SL1 . . . 204 E5
Orchard Mews HP9 . . . 176 D4
Orchard Mill SL8 . . . 185 B1
Orchard Pk HP15 . . . 163 C6
Orchard Pl
  Monks Risborough HP27 . . . 139 C5
  Uxbridge UB8 . . . 201 D5
  Westbury NN13 . . . 39 A4
Orchard Rd
  Beaconsfield HP9 . . . 175 F1
  Chalfont St Giles HP8 . . . 177 C8
  Loudwater HP13 . . . 174 A4
  Old Windsor SL4 . . . 211 B1
  Seer Green HP9 . . . 176 C5
Orchard Rise MK46 . . . 6 F3
Orchard Row HP14 . . . 171 A7
Orchard Sch MK6 . . . 35 B2
Orchards The
  Eaton Bray LU6 . . . 92 E7
  Little Kingshill HP16 . . . 152 A2
  Slough SL3 . . . 206 F5
  Tring HP23 . . . 118 F3
Orchard The
  Aston Clinton HP22 . . . 117 E5
  Flackwell Heath HP10 . . . 185 B7
  Halton HP22 . . . 131 C8
  Hazelmere HP15 . . . 163 A6
  Hillesden MK18 . . . 63 A7
  Marlow SL7 . . . 183 E3
  Potterspury NN12 . . . 18 C3
  Walter's Ash HP14 . . . 161 E6
Orchard View
  Hillesden MK18 . . . 63 B7
  Uxbridge UB8 . . . 201 D1
ORCHARDVILLE . . . 197 B1

Orchardville SL1 197 B1
Orchard Way
Aylesbury HP20 101 F2
Bovingdon HP3 146 A3
Chinnor OX39 147 C5
Cranfield MK43 25 A1
East Claydon MK18 74 E6
Eaton Bray LU6 92 F5
Holmer Green HP15 163 C6
North Crawley MK16 24 A6
Pitstone LU7 105 E4
Slough SL3 206 F5
Stoke Goldington MK16 12 B7
Wing LU7 79 E2
Orchard Waye UB8 201 D3
Orchard Wlk MK46 7 F7
Orchehill Ave SL9 188 D7
Orchehill Ct SL9 188 E6
Orchehill Rise SL9 188 E6
Oregano Cl UB7 208 F6
Orford Ct MK5 46 B6
Oriel Cl MK12 33 B6
Oriel Cotts MK18 63 D2
Orkney Cl
Milton Keynes MK3 46 F2
Stewkley LU7 78 E8
Orkney Ct SL6 196 E5
Ormesby Cl HP21 116 A5
Ormonde MK14 34 D7
Ormond Rd OX9 126 A1
Ormsgill Ct MK13 34 B5
Orne Gdns MK15 35 A7
Orpington Gr MK5 46 B4
Ortensia Dr MK7 48 C7
Orwell Cl
Aylesbury HP21 115 D4
Newport Pagnell MK16 21 F5
Windsor SL4 210 D4
Orwell Dr HP21 115 D4
Osborne Ct SL4 210 C5
Osborne Mews SL4 210 C5
Osborne Rd SL4 210 D4
Osborne St
Milton Keynes MK2 58 C7
Slough SL1 205 F4
Osborne Way HP23 119 D1
Osborn Rd UB8 201 C5
Osborn's Ct 5 MK46 6 F3
Osbourne St MK12 33 D6
Osier La MK5 46 B4
Osier Way
Aylesbury HP20 115 F8
Buckingham MK18 52 C6
Osmington Pl HP23 118 F4
Osney Rd SL6 195 E2
Osprey Cl
Milton Keynes MK6 47 B8
West Drayton UB7 208 E4
Osprey The HP19 101 E4
Osprey Wlk
Aylesbury HP19 101 E4
Buckingham MK18 52 F7
Osterley Cl MK16 22 C3
Ostler Gate SL6 195 C1
Ostlers Ct HP11 174 A4
Ostlers La MK11 32 D6
Otterburn Cres MK5 45 D5
Otter Cl MK3 46 D1
Otterfield Rd UB7 208 E6
Otters Brook MK18 52 E7
Otway Cl HP21 115 E3
Oulton Cl HP21 116 A5
Our Lady of Peace RC Inf Sch SL1 204 C8
Our Lady of Peace RC Jun Sch SL1 204 C8
Our Lady's RC Prim Sch HP6 154 B4
Ousebank St MK16 22 D5
Ousebank Way MK11 32 D5
Ousedale Sch
Newport Pagnell MK16 22 B3
Olney MK46 6 E4
Ouseley Rd TW19 211 D1
Outfield Rd SL9 177 D3
Outlook Dr HP8 177 D7
Ouzel Cl MK3 46 E1
Oval The MK6 46 E7
Oval Way SL9 188 E7
Overdale Rd HP5 144 B3
Overdales HP15 162 F3
Overgate MK6, MK9, MK14 35 B4
Over Hampden HP16 151 C7
Overhills MK46 6 E4
Overn Ave MK18 41 C1
Overn Cl MK18 41 D1
Overn Cres MK18 41 C1
Overshot Ho HP10 174 C2
Oversley Ct MK14 22 A1
Overstone Cl LU7 79 E2
Overstone Comb Sch LU7 79 E2
Overstrand HP22 117 E5
Overstreet MK15 35 A6
Over the Misbourne UB9 189 B5
Over the Misbourne Rd UB9 189 C5
Overton Dr OX9 126 B1
Oville Ct MK5 46 B5
OVING 86 D8
Oving Rd HP22 86 E7
Ovitts Cl MK18 66 A5
Owen Cl 4 SL3 206 F1
Owl Cl 5 HP19 101 F3
Owlsears Cl HP9 175 D4
OWLSWICK 128 D1
Oxendon Ct LU7 70 F2
Oxenhope Way MK10 36 A4
Oxfield Cl HP4 135 A3
Oxfield Park Dr MK19 32 C7
Oxford Ave
Burnham SL1 197 B3
Slough SL1 204 F8
Oxford Gdns UB9 190 A1
Oxford Rd
Aylesbury HP17, HP21 115 B7
Denham UB9 189 D2
Gerrards Cross SL9 188 D5
High Wycombe HP11 173 A7
Marlow SL7 183 D2
Oakley HP18 109 D5
Piddington HP14 160 D1
Stokenchurch HP14 158 D5
Stone HP17 114 C5
Thame OX9 125 E1
Uxbridge UB8, UB9 201 B6
Windsor SL4 210 C6
Oxford Road E SL4 210 C6
Oxford St
5 High Wycombe HP11 173 A7
Lee Common HP16 142 D5
Milton Keynes, Fenny Stratford MK2 58 C8
Milton Keynes, Stony Stratford MK11 32 D5
Milton Keynes, Wolverton MK12 33 D6
Oxhouse Ct MK5 46 A3
OXLEY PARK 45 E3
Oxley Park Rdbt MK5 45 F3
Oxleys MK46 6 E4
Oxman La MK12 33 A5
Oxwich Gr MK4 57 B8

P

Pace Ctr The HP19 101 B2
Packet Boat La UB8 208 C7
Packhorse Rd SL9 188 E6
Pack & Prime La RG9 191 C2
PADBURY 53 B2
Padbury CE Fst Sch MK18 53 C2
Padbury Oaks UB7 213 B6
Padcroft Rd UB7 208 D5
Paddock Cl
8 Aylesbury HP19 100 F1
Maidenhead SL6 202 A2
Milton Keynes MK14 34 E8
Paddock Cotts SL6 202 A2
Paddocks Clinic The (private) HP27 139 C4
Paddocks End HP9 176 C4
Paddocks The
Chorleywood WD3 167 F5
Flackwell Heath HP10 185 B8
Haddenham HP17 127 A5
High Wycombe HP12 172 B3
Leighton Buzzard LU7 80 F8
Prestwood HP16 151 C5
Steeple Claydon MK18 63 E3
Wendover HP22 131 B5
Paddock The
Aylesbury HP21 116 C7
Chalfont St Peter SL9 177 E5
Datchet SL3 211 B6
Emberton MK46 13 E8
Maidenhead SL6 195 C2
Maids Moreton MK18 41 E4
Paddock Way MK2 47 D1
Padstow Ave MK6 34 F1
Padstow Cl
Aylesbury HP20 101 F1
Slough SL3 206 E3
PAGE HILL 41 F2
Page Hill Ave MK18 41 E1
Pages Croft HP4 135 A6
Pages La UB8 201 C6
Pages Wharf SL6 203 C8
Paget Cl SL7 183 F4
Paget Ct UB7 208 E4
Paget Dr SL6 202 A4
Paget Rd SL3 206 F2
Pagg's Ct MK16 22 D4
Pagoda Rdbt MK15 35 C5
Pagoda The SL6 196 B1
Paignton Way 2 MK10 36 A3
Paines Orch LU7 105 A8
Pakenham Cl HP19 114 F8
Palace Cl SL1 204 F5
Palace Sq MK6 46 F7
Palfreyman St HP19 101 D4
Palliser Rd HP8 177 B6
Palmer Ave
Aylesbury HP19 115 C8
Upper Arncott OX25 94 F8
Palmers Cl SL6 202 A3
PALMERS MOOR 201 A1
Palmers Moor MK18 54 A8
Palmer's Moor La SL0 201 A1
Palmers Rd MK46 7 A3
Palmerston Ave SL3 206 B3
Pankridge Dr HP16 151 C7
Panleigh Cotts HP14 171 B3
Pannier Pl MK14 35 A5
Pann Mill HP13 173 C6
Panters Cl MK17 44 C1
Pantile Row SL3 207 A2
Pantile Wlk UB8 201 C5
Paprika Ct MK7 48 B5
Papworth Cl MK16 22 F3
Parade Ct 7 SL8 185 A4
Parade The
Bourne End SL8 185 A3
Farnham Common SL2 198 C6
High Wycombe HP11 172 F6
Uxbridge UB8 208 C8
Windsor SL4 209 D6
Paradise MK17 57 D4
Paradise Mews RG9 191 D2
Paradise Rd RG9 191 C1
Parchment Cl HP6 154 E2
Parish La SL2 187 C1
Parish Piece HP15 163 C7
Park Ave
Newport Pagnell MK16 22 B4
Totternhoe LU6 93 B8
Wraysbury TW19 211 D3
Park Cl
Cosgrove MK19 19 F2
Dunton MK18 77 E5
Lane End HP14 171 C5
Windsor SL4 210 D5
Park Cnr SL4 209 E4
Park Ct UB8 201 D4
Parker Cl MK13 34 A6
Parker Knoll Way HP13 173 A7
Parker Wlk HP19 101 D3
Park Farm Rd HP12 161 B1
Park Farm Way HP14 171 C5
Parkfield WD3 167 F5
Parkfield Ave HP6 154 D2
Parkfield Rise HP27 139 B2
Parkgate SL1 197 C1
Park Gate LU7 79 E1
Park Gdns MK3 47 A1
Park Gr
Beaconsfield HP9 175 C7
Little Chalfont HP8 166 D6
Park Hill OX33 122 B1
Park Ho
Berkhamsted HP4 135 B5
Gerrards Cross SL9 188 E7
Maidenhead SL6 202 E6
Park House Bsns Ctr HP12 172 E8
Park House Dr MK5 45 F6
Park La
Beaconsfield HP9 175 F1
Burnham SL1 197 E7
Eaton Bray LU6 92 D6
Hazelmere HP15 163 A4
Horton SL3 212 A4
Lane End HP14 171 D5
Maidensgrove RG9 179 D6
Paulerspury NN12 17 B7
Slough SL3 206 B3
Stokenchurch HP14 158 E6
Parkland Ave SL3 206 D2
Parklands MK14 21 D1
Park Lane Ct HP14 158 E5
Park Lawn SL2 198 C2
Park Lodge Ave UB7 208 F4
Park Mdw HP27 139 A3
Parkminster MK10 36 A1
Park Parade SL2 198 C3
Park Parade Ctr The HP15 163 A5
Park Pl
Amersham HP6 154 F1
Seer Green HP9 176 D5
Park Rd
Amersham HP6 154 F2
Chesham HP5 154 B8
Farnham Royal SL2 198 E3
Granborough MK18 75 F6
Grendon Underwood HP18 82 F8
Hanslope MK19 11 B1
Hartwell NN7 10 C8
Henley-on-Thames RG9 191 E1
Milton Keynes MK11 32 D5
Sherington MK16 14 A2
Stanwell TW19 213 C1
Tring HP23 118 F2
Uxbridge UB8 201 E6
Winslow MK18 65 F5
Park Rise HP4 134 E6
Park Road E UB10 201 D3
Park Road S MK18 65 F4
Park Sch HP20 101 F1
Parkside
Gerrards Cross SL9 188 F7
Henley-on-Thames RG9 191 C2
Maidenhead SL6 195 D1
Milton Keynes MK4 46 E3
Naphill HP14 150 B1
Parkside Wlk SL1 206 A3
Park Sports Ctr OX33 122 B1
Park St
Aylesbury HP20 115 F8
Berkhamsted HP4 135 B5
High Wycombe HP11 173 D6
Maidenhead SL6 202 F7
Poyle SL3 212 D6
Princes Risborough HP27 139 B3
Slough SL1 205 F4
Tring HP23 119 A3
Windsor SL4 210 D6
Woburn MK17 60 F7
Parkstone Lodge SL3 206 A3
Park Street Ind Est HP20 115 F8
Parkview
Flackwell Heath HP10 185 B7
Maidenhead SL6 202 F7
Park View
Newport Pagnell MK16 22 D4
West Drayton UB7 208 E6
Parkview Chase SL1 204 E7
Park View Ct
Berkhamsted HP4 135 B4
High Wycombe HP12 172 D8
4 Leighton Buzzard LU7 80 E7
Park View Rd
Berkhamsted HP4 135 B4
Uxbridge UB8 208 F7
Parkway
Bow Brickhill MK17 48 D2
Marlow SL7 184 A3
Woburn Sands MK17 49 A6
Parkway The SL0 200 C4
Parkwood HP14 150 A2
Park Wood, Gouldings Wood Nature Reserve★ SL6 194 E4
Parlaunt Park Comb Sch SL3 207 B3
Parlaunt Rd SL3 207 B2
Parliament Cl HP16 151 B7
Parliament La SL6, SL1 196 F5
Parliament Rd OX9 125 F1
Parmiter Cl HP19 115 B8
PARMOOR 181 F7
Parmoor La RG9 170 E1
Parneleys MK10 35 F2
Parrishs Piece HP22 87 B3
Parrock La MK10 36 A2
Parrot Cl HP21 115 B6
Parrott's La HP23 133 A4
Parrs Rd HP14 158 E4
Parry Cotts SL9 177 E6
Parry Green N SL3 206 F2
Parry Green S SL3 207 A2
Parsley Cl
Aston Clinton HP22 117 C5
Walton MK7 48 B5
Parslow Cl HP21 115 D3
Parslow Ct HP21 115 D3
Parsonage Cl
High Wycombe HP13 173 C6
Tring HP23 119 A4
Parsonage Ct 1 HP23 119 A3
Parsonage Farm HP22 89 B3
Parsonage Gdns SL7 183 E1
Parsonage La
Farnham Common SL2 198 D5
Windsor SL4 210 A6
Parsonage Pl HP7 165 C8
Parsonage Rd HP8 177 B7
Parson Cl MK18 65 F4
Parsons Cl LU7 78 E8
Parsons Cres MK5 46 C5
Parson's Fee HP20 115 D8
Parsons La HP22 102 B3
Parsons Rd SL3 206 F1
Parsons Wlk HP15 163 C6
Parson's Wood La SL2 198 D5
Parton Cl HP22 131 A5
Parton Rd HP20 116 B8
Partridge Cl
Buckingham MK18 52 F7
Chesham HP5 144 E3
Leighton Buzzard LU7 104 F7
Partridge Mead SL6 195 F2
Partridge Piece MK43 25 C3
Partridge Way
7 Aylesbury HP19 101 F3
High Wycombe HP13 161 C2
Pascal Dr MK5 45 E5
Pascomb Rd LU6 93 F8
Passalewe La MK7 48 D7
PASSENHAM 32 C4
Passmore MK6 47 D6
Pastern Pl MK14 35 A5
Pastures The
Aylesbury HP20 102 B2
Edlesborough LU6 92 F3
High Wycombe HP13 161 E1
Patch Cl UB10 201 F4
Patches Field SL7 183 E5
Pateman Cl MK18 41 C1
Patemore La RG9 168 A1
Paterson Rd HP21 115 C6
Patricia Cl SL1 204 E6
Patrick Haugh Rd OX25 94 F7
Patricks La MK19 31 F4
Patrick Way HP21 116 A4
Patrington Cl UB8 201 C2
Patriot Dr MK13 34 B2
Patrons Way E UB9 189 F5
Patrons Way W UB9 189 F5
Patterson Ct HP10 185 E7
Patterson Rd HP5 144 B3
Pattison La MK15 35 C3
PAULERSPURY 17 B7
Paulerspury CE Prim Sch NN12 17 B8
Pauls Hill HP10 174 F6
Paul's Row HP11 173 B6
Pavers Ct HP21 115 D3
Pavilion Cl HP20 116 A8
Pavilions The (Sh Ctr) UB8 201 C5
Pavilion Way HP6 166 C8
Paxton Ave SL1 205 C3
Paxton Cl MK46 6 F3
Paxton Cres MK5 46 B5
Paxton Rd HP4 135 D4
Paynes Ct MK18 41 D1
Paynes Dr MK5 46 A8
Paynes Field Cl HP4 134 D7
Payton Hos SL6 195 E6
Peace La SL6 195 F6
Peace Rd SL0, SL3 200 A3
Peachey Cl UB8 208 D7
Peachey La UB8 208 D8
Peach Tree Ave UB7 208 F7
Peacock Hay MK4 46 C2
Peacock Rd SL7 184 A3
Peacocks Cl HP4 134 F6
Pea La HP4 134 D7
Pearce Cl
Aylesbury HP21 115 E4
Maidenhead SL6 195 F1
Pearce Dr SL6 195 F7
Pearce Rd
Chesham HP5 144 B2
Maidenhead SL6 195 F1
Pearce's Orch RG9 191 D3
Pearl Gdns SL1 205 B5
Pearse Gr MK7 48 A4
Pearson Cl HP19 115 B6
Pear Tree Ave UB7 208 F7
Peartree Cl SL1 204 F5
Pear Tree Cl
Amersham HP7 165 F8
Seer Green HP9 176 C4
Pear Tree Ct HP15 163 C6
Pear Tree Farm Ind Units OX27 71 E2
Peartrees UB7 208 D6
Peascod Pl 12 SL4 210 D6
Peascod St SL4 210 D6
Peascroft HP18 125 D6
Peatey Ct HP13 173 D6
Pebble Brook Sch HP21 115 C7
Pebble La
Aylesbury HP20 115 D8
Brackley NN13 38 A7
Pebblemoor LU6 92 F3
Pebody Pl 10 MK46 6 F3
Peckover Ct 8 MK8 33 F1
Pecks Farm Cl HP22 102 C4
Peddle Ct HP11 172 F7
Pednor Bottom HP5 143 B3
PEDNORMEAD END 154 A7
Pednormead End HP5 154 B7
Pednor Rd HP5 143 E2
Peebles Pl MK3 46 F3
Peel Cl SL4 210 B4
Peel Ct
Monks Risborough HP27 139 B4
Slough SL1 205 B8
Peel Rd MK12 33 C6
Peel Way UB8 208 E8
Peerless Dr UB9 190 C7
Peers Dr MK17 49 E3
Peers La MK5 46 B6
Peggs La HP22 117 F5
Pelham Ct SL6 202 E7
Pelham Pl MK14 34 F5
Pelham Rd OX9 126 B1
Pelton Ct MK5 46 C5
Pemberley Lodge SL4 210 A4
Pemberton Cl HP21 115 F5
Pemberton Rd SL2 197 E1
Pembridge Chase 4 HP3 146 A3
Pembridge Cl 3 HP3 146 A3
Pembridge Gr MK4 45 E1
Pembridge Rd HP3 146 A3
Pembroke Ho
2 Milton Keynes MK3 46 F1
7 Olney MK46 6 F3
Pembroke Rd HP20 101 F1

Pencarrow Pl MK6 35 A1
Pendeen Ct SL1 205 A5
Pendennis Ct MK4 57 A8
Pendles Paddocks
HP14 158 F2
Pendrill Ho 2 HP12 172 E7
Penfold HP22 116 F2
Penfold Cotts HP15 163 D7
Penfold La
Holmer Green HP15 163 E8
Hyde Heath HP7, HP15 152 F1
Pengelly Ct 2 MK6 35 A1
Penhale Cl MK4 57 B8
Penhow Rise MK4 45 E1
Penina Cl MK3 46 D1
Penington Rd HP9 186 B8
Penlee Rise MK4 57 B8
Penley Cl OX39 147 B6
Penling Cl SL6 195 E6
Penmon Cl MK10 35 F1
Penmoor Cl HP12 172 C8
PENN 174 E7
Penn Ave HP5 144 A1
Penn Cl
Chorleywood WD3 167 D3
Uxbridge UB8 201 D1
Penn Ct
14 Marlow SL7 183 E2
Tylers Green HP10 174 B8
Penn Dr UB9 189 F5
Pennefather Ct 3
HP21 115 E7
Penn Gaskell La SL9 177 F5
Penn Gn HP9 175 D4
Penn Haven SL9 188 F6
Pennine Rd SL2 205 A8
Pennings The HP22 131 B5
Pennington Pl OX9 126 B1
Pennington Rd
Chalfont St Peter SL9 177 D3
High Wycombe HP13 173 F6
Penningtons The HP6 154 E2
Penn Mdw SL2 198 F4
Penn Mead HP10 174 F7
Penn Rd
Aylesbury HP21 115 D7
Beaconsfield HP9 175 C5
Chalfont St Peter SL9 177 E5
Chorleywood WD3 167 F1
Datchet SL3 211 D6
Hazlemere HP15 163 B3
Milton Keynes MK2 58 E8
Slough SL2 198 D1
Penn Sch HP10 174 D7
PENN STREET 164 B5
Penn Street Works Ind Est
HP7 164 A4
Penn Way WD3 167 D3
Penn Wood Sch SL2 198 D1
Penn Wood View HP7 164 A4
Pennycress Way MK16 21 F4
Pennycuik MK17 59 C1
PENNYLAND 35 A6
Pennylets Gn SL2 199 A5
Penny Pk Rd MK16 22 F3
Pennyroyal MK7 48 B7
Penrith Cl UB8 201 D5
Penrith Way HP21 116 B7
Penryn Ave MK6 35 A2
Penshurst Cl SL9 177 D1
Penshurst Cres MK6 47 D4
Penshurst Rd SL6 202 D5
Pentewan Gate MK6 34 F2
Pentland Rd
Aylesbury HP21 115 F6
Slough SL2 205 A8
Pentlands MK11 32 F4
Pentlands Ct HP13 174 B4
Pentlands The HP13 174 B4
Penwith Sch MK6 34 F1
Penwood Ct SL6 202 B7
Penwood La SL7 183 C1
Penyston Rd SL6 202 C7
Penzance Spur SL2 198 B1
Peplar Way SL1 197 B2
Peplow Cl UB7 208 D5
Peppard Mdw HP16 151 D5
Pepper Hill Fst Sch
MK13 34 A7
PEPPERSHILL 124 D6
Peppett's Gn HP5 143 D8
Peppiatts The LU6 92 B5
Pepys Cl SL3 212 B8
Pepys Dr HP16 151 C6
Perch Cl SL7 194 C8
Percheron Pl MK14 34 F5
Perch Mdws HP22 131 B8
Percy Bush Rd UB7 208 F3
Percy Pl SL3 211 B6
Percy Terr HP8 177 A7
Peregrine HP19 101 E3
Peregrine Bsns Pk
HP13 174 A5
Peregrine Cl MK6 47 B8
Perivale MK10 35 E1
Perks La HP16 151 C3
Permayne MK13 34 A7
Perracombe MK4 46 E3
Perran Ave MK6 35 A1
Perrin Springs La RG9 170 F1
Perrycroft SL4 209 F4
Perryfields Way SL1 197 B1
Perry Hill HP18 73 A3
Perry Ho SL1 197 B2
Perry La
Bledlow HP27 138 C2
Sherington MK16 14 B2
Perryman Way SL2 197 F2
Perry Mead LU6 92 E6
Perry St HP22 131 A5
Perrys The HP22 131 B5
Pershore Croft 1 MK10 36 A1
Perth Ave SL1 205 B7
Perth Cl MK3 46 F2
Perth Rd HP13 173 D8
Perth Trad Est SL1 205 B8
Peterborough Ave 2
HP13 173 C7
Peterborough Gate
MK15 35 C6
Peterhead Mews SL3 207 A1
Peterhill Cl SL9 177 E5
Peterley Ave HP15,
HP16 151 E3
Peterley La HP16 151 E3
Peter's Cl HP16 151 C6
Petersfield HP22 116 C3
Petersfield Ave SL2 206 A5
Petersfield Gn 5 MK9 34 E1
Petersham Cl MK16 22 C2
Peters La HP27 139 E4
Peter's Pl HP4 134 E6
Petronel Rd HP19 101 D4
PETSOE END 14 A7
Pettifer Way HP12 172 D6
Pettingrew Cl MK7 48 B6
Petty Cross SL1 204 E7
Petworth MK8 33 E1
Petworth Ct SL4 210 B6
Petworth Ho 2 MK8 33 F1
Pevensey Cl
Aylesbury HP21 116 B5
Milton Keynes MK3 57 E7
Pevensey Rd SL2 205 A8
Peverel Dr MK1 47 B3
Peveril Cl HP21 116 B5
Pevers La MK46 6 A1
Pheasant Cl
Berkhamsted HP4 135 C3
Tring HP23 119 B6
Pheasant Dr HP13 161 C1
Pheasant Hill HP8 177 C8
Pheasant Rise HP5 154 D6
PHEASANTS 181 E6
Pheasants Croft SL6 202 A4
Pheasants Dr HP15 163 B5
PHEASANT'S HILL 181 D3
Pheasants Ridge SL7 183 C7
Pheasant Wlk SL9 177 E6
Phelps Rd MK2 58 E6
Philbye Mews SL1 204 F4
Philip Cotts SL8 185 C3
Philip Dr HP10 185 C7
Philip Rd HP13 173 D7
Philipshill Wood Reserve★
WD3 167 A2
Philips Rd HP19 115 A8
Phillimore Cl MK15 35 B7
Phillip Ct MK5 46 B6
Philpots Cl UB7 208 D6
Philps Cl HP14 171 C4
Phipps Cl
Aylesbury HP20 102 A2
Maidenhead SL6 202 A2
Phipps Rd SL1 204 E8
Phoebe La MK17 48 E6
Phoebe's Orch MK17 69 E7
Phoenix Bsns Ctr 3
HP5 144 B1
Phoenix Ct SL6 202 D4
Phoenix Dr MK6 46 E6
Phoenix Ho 7 HP19 115 A8
Phoenix House Bsns Ctr
HP12 172 E8
Phygtle The SL9 177 E4
Phyllis Court Dr RG9 191 E3
Picasso Pl HP19 100 F2
Piccadilly Mews MK18 66 A5
Pickering Dr MK4 46 B2
Pickford Dr SL3 207 A5
Pickfords Gdns SL1 205 E5
Pickins Piece SL3 212 A5
Pickwick Terr SL2 206 B6
Picton St MK4 45 E1
Picts La HP27 139 A2
PIDDINGTON
Blackthorn 95 E7
High Wycombe 160 B1
Northamptonshire 4 B8
Piddington La HP14 171 B8
Piddington Rd HP18 96 A8
Pield Heath House Sch
UB8 201 F1
Pield Heath Rd UB8 201 F1
Pierson Rd SL4 209 D6
Pigeon Farm Rd HP14 158 E5
Piggotts End 6 HP7 165 B7
Piggott's Hill HP14 150 E1
Piggotts Orch HP7 165 B7
Piggy La WD3 167 B3
Pightle Cres MK18 41 D2
Pightle The
Buckingham MK18 41 D1
Maids Moreton MK18 41 F4
Oving HP22 86 D7
Pitstone LU7 105 D3
Pigott Dr MK5 46 A5
Pigott Orch HP22 85 A5
Pike Cl
Marlow SL7 194 C8
Uxbridge UB10 201 F4
Pike Cnr HP21 116 C5
Pilch Field Wildlife
Reserve★ MK17 54 B5
Pilch La MK17 54 D4
Pilgrims Cl HP27 139 B5
Pilgrim St MK15 35 A4
Pilot Trad Est HP12 172 E8
PIMLICO 26 F6
Pimlico Ct 4 MK10 35 F1
Pimms Cl HP13 174 A6
Pimms Gr HP13 174 A5
Pimpernel Gr MK7 48 B6
Pinchfield WD3 178 D5
Pinders Croft MK12 33 B5
PINDON END 10 C4
Pineapple Rd HP7 165 F8
Pine Chase HP12 172 B3
Pine Cl
Berkhamsted HP4 135 B4
Buckingham MK18 41 E3
Hazelmere HP15 163 B3
Maidenhead SL6 202 B7
Pine Crest Mews LU7 80 E6
Pinecroft SL7 183 D4
Pine Ct HP5 154 C8
Pine Gr MK17 49 A4
PINEHAM 35 E7
Pineham Rdbt MK15 35 E5
Pine Hill HP15 162 F3
Pinels Way HP11 172 E3
Piner Cotts SL4 209 E4
Pine Rd LU6 106 F8
Pines Cl
Amersham HP6 154 B2
Little Kingshill HP16 152 B4
Pine St HP19 115 A8
Pines The
Felden HP3 146 F7
Slough SL3 206 F5
Tylers Green HP10 163 B1
Pinetree Cl SL9 177 C3
Pine Trees Dr UB10 201 E8
Pine Wlk
Berkhamsted HP4 134 D7
Hazelmere HP15 163 B3
Pinewood Ave UB8 208 F7
Pinewood Cl
Gerrards Cross SL9 188 E4
Iver Heath SL0 200 C5
Pinewood Dr MK2 58 E7
Pinewood Film Studios
SL0 200 B5
Pinewood Gn SL0 200 C5
Pinewood Mews TW19 213 D1
Pinewood Rd
High Wycombe HP12 172 C7
Iver Heath SL0 200 B4
Pinfold MK7 48 B6
PINFOLDPOND 60 E6
Pinfold Yd MK18 51 B6
Pinglestone Cl UB7 213 E7
Pinions Rd HP13 173 E5
Pinkard Ct MK6 47 C8
Pink Hill HP27 149 E8
Pink La SL1 197 B3
Pinkneys Dr SL6 195 A1
PINKNEYS GREEN 195 A1
Pinkneys Rd SL6 202 A8
Pink Rd HP27 149 E7
Pinks Cl MK5 46 C8
Pinkworthy MK4 46 D4
Pinn Cl UB8 208 D7
Pinstone Way SL9 189 B2
Pintail Cl HP19 101 E4
Pipard MK14 34 E7
Pipers Cl SL1 197 C2
Pipers Corner Sch
HP15 162 B7
Pipers Croft LU6 93 F7
Pipers Ct SL1 197 C2
Pipers La HP15 162 C8
Pipers Wood Cotts
HP7 153 C2
Pipit Gdns 7 HP19 101 E4
Pipit Wlk 6 HP19 101 E4
Pippin Cl MK16 22 B3
Pippins Cl UB7 208 D3
Pippins Sch SL3 212 F6
Pippins The SL3 206 F5
Pipston Gn
Milton Keynes MK7 48 B7
Walton MK7 48 B6
PISHILL 179 D8
PISHILL BANK 168 B1
Pishill Bank RG9 168 B1
PISHILL BOTTOM 168 A1
Pistone Green Bsns Pk
LU7 105 D2
Pistone Windmill★
LU7 105 F4
PITCHCOTT 86 B5
Pitchcott Rd HP22 86 B6
Pitcher La MK5 46 B8
Pitcher Wlk HP19 115 A7
Pitchford Ave MK18 41 E2
Pitchford Wlk MK18 41 F1
PITCH GREEN 138 B3
Pitch Pond Cl HP9 175 C5
Pitch The HP14 159 D3
Pitfield MK11 33 B3
PITSTONE 105 C4
Pitstone Green Farm Mus★
LU7 105 D4
Pitters Piece HP18 125 B7
Pitt Gn MK18 41 F1
Pitts Rd SL1 205 C5
Place Farm Ho HP27 139 B6
Place Farm Way HP27 139 B5
Plackett Way SL1 204 D5
Plaines Cl SL1 204 F5
Plaistow Cres MK10 35 F1
Plaiters Cl HP23 119 B4
Plantain Ct MK7 48 B6
Plantation Pl MK5 46 A4
Plantation Rd
Amersham HP6 154 E2
High Wycombe HP13 174 A7
Leighton Buzzard LU7 70 F3
Plantation Way HP6 154 E2
Platt The HP7 165 B7
Playing Field Rd NN13 39 A4
Pleasant Cotts SL0 200 B2
Pleasant Pl WD3 178 E3
Pleasaunce The HP22 117 E5
Pleshey Cl MK5 46 B6
Plested Ct HP22 116 C2
Plomer Green Ave
HP13 161 D2
Plomer Green La HP13 161 D3
Plomer Hill HP13 161 D1
Plough Cl HP21 115 E3
Plough End HP22 102 B4
Plough La
Sarratt WD4 156 F6
Wexham Street SL2 199 B4
Ploughlees La SL1 205 E6
Ploughley Rd OX25 94 E8
Plover Cl
1 Berkhamsted HP4 135 C3
Buckingham MK18 52 E7
Newport Pagnell MK16 22 F3
Plover The 4 HP19 101 E4
Plover Wlk 3 HP19 101 E4
Plowman Cl MK12 33 B5
Plumer Rd HP11 172 E7
Plum Park La NN12 17 D8
PLUMPTON END 17 C7
Plumstead Ave MK13 34 D3
Pluto Cl SL1 204 E4
Pluto Way HP19 101 D4
Plym Cl HP21 115 C5
Plymouth Gr MK4 46 B1
Plymouth Rd SL1 204 E8
Pocketts Yd SL6 196 B7
Pocock Ave UB7 208 F3
Pococks La SL4 205 E1
Poets Chase HP21 115 F6
Points The SL6 202 B3
Polar Pk UB7 213 F7
Poles Hill
Chesham HP5 144 A2
Sarratt WD4 156 E6
Police Hos SL9 189 B3
Polidoris La HP15 163 C7
Polish Ave HP22 131 E8
Pollard Ave UB9 189 F5
Pollard Cl SL4 211 B2
Pollards WD3 178 D5
Pollys Yd MK14 22 D5
Pollywick Rd HP23 119 D1
Polmartin Ct 1 MK6 35 A1
Polruan Pl
Fishermead MK6 47 A8
Milton Keynes MK6 35 A1
Polygon Bsns Ctr SL3 212 F5
Pomander Cres MK7 48 B7
Pomeroy Cl HP7 165 D7
Pond App HP15 163 C7
Pond Cl
Newton Longville MK17 57 C2
Tring HP23 119 A4
Winchmore Hill HP7 164 C3
Pond Cotts HP14 171 B4
Pondgate MK7 48 B8
Pond La
Chalfont St Peter SL9 177 C2
Little Gaddesden HP4 121 E7
POND PARK 144 A2
Pond Park Rd HP5 144 B2
Pondwicks HP7 165 B8
Pony Field The HP22 116 D1
Pool La SL1 205 E6
Poolmans Rd SL4 209 D4
Pope Ct HP23 118 F3
Popes Acre HP17 126 F5
Popes Cl
Amersham HP6 154 F2
Colnbrook SL3 212 C7
Popes La SL6 195 C7
Pope Way HP21 115 E4
Poplar Ave UB7 208 F6
Poplar Cl
Aylesbury HP20 102 A2
Chesham HP5 144 C3
Milton Keynes MK6 47 E5
Poyle SL3 212 E6
Poplar Ho SL3 206 F1
Poplar Rd
Aylesbury HP20 102 A2
New Denham UB9 201 C6
Wooburn Green HP10 185 E7
Poplars Cl HP17 114 C5
Poplars Gr SL6 196 B2
Poplars Rd MK18 52 D8
Poplars The HP22 131 C5
Poppy Ave MK10 36 B4
Poppy Rd HP27 139 A2
Porlock La MK4 46 C4
Portal Cl UB10 201 F5
Portal Rd HP22 131 D6
Portchester Ct 1 MK8 33 F1
Porter's Cl MK19 31 E4
Porters Way UB7 208 F4
Portfield Cl MK18 52 E8
Port Field Farm MK16 21 F5
Portfields Comb Sch
MK16 22 A5
Portfields Rd MK16 22 B4
Portfield Way MK18 52 E8
Porthcawl Gn MK3 57 C8
Porthleven Pl MK6 35 A2
Porthmellin Cl MK4 57 B8
Portishead Dr MK4 56 F8
Portland Bsns Ctr SL3 211 B6
Portland Cl SL2 197 D1
Portland Dr MK15 35 C7
Portland Gdns SL7 183 D1
Portland Ho HP13 173 D8
Portland Pk SL9 188 D5
Portlands Alley SL7 183 D1
Portlands Mews 1
SL7 183 D1
Portlock Rd SL6 202 C7
Portman Mews HP19 114 F8
Portmarnock Cl MK3 57 D8
Portnall Pl MK43 25 B2
Portobello Cl HP5 144 A2
Portobello Cotts
Lacey Green HP27 149 E5
Lewknor OX49 157 C2
Portrush Cl MK3 57 D8
Portsmouth Ct SL1 205 E6
Portway
Milton Keynes, Bradwell
Common MK5, MK9, MK13,
MK14, MK15 34 D2
Milton Keynes, Shenley Church
End MK8, MK5 45 F6
North Marston MK18 76 B1
Stone HP17 114 E4
Portway Dr HP12 161 B1
Portway Rd
Stone HP17 114 E4
Twyford MK18 62 D1
Portway Rdbt MK5 34 B1
PORTWAYS 168 B8
Posting Ho HP23 120 A5
Post Mdw SL0 200 D2
Post Office Cotts SL2 199 A5
Post Office La
Beaconsfield HP9 175 D3
Slough SL3 206 D7
Whitchurch HP22 87 A6
Potash Cl HP17 126 F5
Potash La HP23 104 A5
Potkiln La HP9 176 D1
Potter Row HP16 142 C1
Potters Cl HP16 151 B7
Potters Cross SL0 200 E2
Potters Cross Cres
HP15 162 E2
Potters Glen MK18 53 B1
Potters La MK11 33 B4
POTTERSPURY 18 D2
Potterspury Lodge Sch
NN12 18 B6
Pottery Cl HP19 115 A7
Pottery Ct HP19 115 A7
Potts Pl 8 SL7 183 D2
Poulcott TW19 211 E1
Pound Cl
Steeple Claydon MK18 63 D3
Wicken MK19 31 A4
Pound Cres SL7 183 C1
Poundfield La SL6 195 F7
Poundfield Rd NN12 18 E2
Pound Hill MK17 59 C1
Pound La
Heath End HP5 134 A1
Little Marlow SL7 184 C4
Marlow SL7 183 D1

Pound La *continued*
North Crawley MK16 24 B7
Preston Bissett MK18 51 C1
POUNDON 71 E7
Pounds Cl MK43 25 B1
Pound St HP22 131 B4
Pound The
Cookham Rise SL6 195 F7
Cookham SL6 196 A7
Slough SL1 197 D1
Syresham NN13 27 B7
Powell Haven MK10 35 E3
Powis Cl SL6 202 B4
Powis La MK4 45 F2
Powney Rd SL6 202 C7
POYLE 212 E6
Poyle 14 Trad Est SL3 212 E4
Poyle La SL1 197 B3
Poyle New Cotts SL3 212 F5
Poyle Pk SL3 212 E4
Poyle Rd SL3 212 E5
Poyle Tech Ctr The SL3 212 E5
Poynings The SL0 207 F2
Pratt Ho HP6 154 F1
Prebendal Ave HP21 115 D7
Prebendal Cl 11 HP20 115 D8
Prebendal Ct 1 HP20 115 D8
PREBENDAL FARM 115 B7
Precedent Dr MK13 34 B3
Precincts The SL1 197 C1
Prentice Gr MK5 46 B3
Prescott Rd SL3 212 E5
Prescotts The UB9 189 F3
Presley Way MK8 45 E7
Press Rd UB8 201 D6
PRESTON BISSETT 62 B8
Preston Ct MK15 35 B7
Preston Hill HP5 144 D2
Preston Rd SL2 206 C6
Prestwick Cl MK3 57 D7
Prestwold Ho HP19 115 A7
Prestwold Way HP19 115 A7
PRESTWOOD 151 D6
Prestwood SL2 206 B7
Prestwood Cl HP12 172 D8
Prestwood Inf Sch HP16 151 C7
Prestwood Jun Sch HP16 151 C6
Prestwood Lodge Specl Sch HP16 151 D5
Prestwood Pl HP16 151 C6
Pretoria Rd HP13 173 C8
Priest End OX9 125 E1
Priestland Gdns HP4 135 E6
Priestley Ct HP13 173 D6
Priests Paddock HP9 175 B5
Primatt Cres MK5 46 B6
Primrose Cotts HP14 150 E1
Primrose Ct HP21 115 B6
Primrose Dr
Aylesbury HP21 115 B5
West Drayton UB7 208 D2
Primrose Gdns LU7 80 E7
Primrose Gn HP15 162 F6
Primrose Hill HP15 162 F7
Primrose La MK10 36 C3
Primrose Lea SL7 183 D2
Primrose Rd MK13 34 A4
Primrose Terr HP18 110 A8
Primrose Way MK18 52 C7
Prince Albert's Wlk SL3, SL4 211 B5
Prince Andrew Cl SL6 203 B8
Prince Andrew Rd SL6 196 B1
Prince Consort Cotts SL4 210 D5
Prince Consort's Dr SL4 210 B2
Prince Edward St HP4 135 C4
Prince Philip Ave MK43 24 D2
Prince Rupert Dr HP19 101 C4
Princes Cl
Berkhamsted HP4 135 A6
Chilton HP18 111 B3
Eton Wick SL4 204 F1
Princes Ct
Bourne End SL8 185 C3
Leighton Buzzard LU7 80 F8
Princes Gate HP13 173 D6
Princes Gdns HP27 139 B3
Prince's La HP16 142 D5
Princes Pl HP27 139 B1
Princes Rd SL8 185 C3
Prince's Rd HP21 115 E8
PRINCES RISBOROUGH 139 D4
Princes Risborough Prim Sch HP27 139 B5
Princes Risborough Sch HP27 139 C2
Princes Risborough Sta HP27 138 F2
Princess Ave SL4 210 B4
Princess Gr HP9 176 D6
Princess Margaret Hospl The (private) SL4 210 D5
Princess St SL6 202 F6
Princes St
Piddington HP14 160 B1
2 Slough SL1 206 B4
Princes Terr SL8 185 C3
Princes Way MK2 58 C8
Princes Way Rdbt MK2 58 B8
Printers End HP19 101 B1
Prior Gr HP5 144 C1
Priors Cl
Maidenhead SL6 203 B2
5 Slough SL1 206 A3
Priors Pk MK4 46 D2
Priors Rd SL4 209 D4
Priors Way SL6 203 B2
Priors Way Ind Est SL6 203 B2
Priory Ave
High Wycombe HP13 173 B7
South Harefield UB9 190 C7
Priory Cl
Aylesbury HP19 101 C2
Denham UB9 190 A1
Horton-cum-S OX33 108 B5
Newport Pagnell MK16 22 E4
South Harefield UB9 190 C7
Priory Common Sch MK13 34 B4
Priory Cotts UB9 190 C7
Priory Cres HP19 101 C2
Priory Ct 2 HP4 135 C4
Priory Farm Cotts OX27 71 E2
Priory Gdns
Berkhamsted HP4 135 C4
South Harefield UB9 190 C7
Priory Rd
Gerrards Cross SL9 188 D8
High Wycombe HP13 173 B7
Slough SL1 204 C8
Priory Rise Sch MK4 56 E7
Priory Sch SL1 204 D8
Priory St MK16 22 E4
Priory Way
Datchet SL3 211 B7
Gerrards Cross SL9 188 D8
Harmondsworth UB7 213 E8
Pritchard Ct MK14 34 E8
Proctor Rise MK8 45 D6
Progress Bsns Ctr SL1 204 D7
Progress Rd HP12 172 B7
Promenade SL4 210 C7
Prospect Cl MK17 68 D6
Prospect Cotts HP14 161 D6
Prospect Ct
Lane End HP14 171 B5
Yardley Gobion NN12 18 F6
Prospect Pl
Castlethorpe MK19 19 F5
Hurley SL6 193 F3
3 Windsor SL4 210 D4
Wing LU7 79 E2
Prospect Rd
Marlow SL7 183 D2
Milton Keynes MK11 32 C5
Prothero Cl HP21 115 E4
Protheroe Field MK7 48 D4
Providence Pl
9 Maidenhead SL6 202 F7
2 Milton Keynes MK13 34 A4
Providence Rd UB7 208 F5
Prudential Bldgs 1 SL1 205 F4
PUDDS CROSS 145 E2
Pudseys Cl SL6 195 B6
Puers Field HP9 176 E4
Puers La HP9 176 E4
Puffin Way HP19 101 F3
Pulborough Cl MK3 46 D1
Pulford Rd LU7 80 F6
Pullfields HP5 144 A1
Pulpit Cl HP5 144 A2
Pulpit La HP22 76 D1
Pumpkin Hill SL1 197 E6
Pump Lane N SL7 183 F6
Pump Lane S SL7 184 A4
Pump Mdw HP16 152 A8
Pump Pl MK19 32 B7
Pumpus Gn MK18 66 A4
Punch Bowl La HP5 154 C7
Purbeck MK13 34 C6
Purbeck Cl HP21 116 B5
Purcel Dr MK16 22 C3
Purse La MK16 11 F8
Pursers Ct SL1 205 E7
Purssell Cl SL6 202 A3
Purssell Pl HP27 139 B5
Pursells Mdw HP14 161 C7
Purton Ct SL2 198 C5
Purton La SL2 198 C5
PURY END 17 A7
Pury Rd
Alderton NN12 9 A2
Paulerspury NN12 17 D8
Pusey Way HP14 171 C5
Putlowes Dr HP18 100 C3
Putman Ho MK5 46 C5
Putman Pl RG9 191 E1
Putnams Dr HP22 117 D5
PUTTENHAM 103 F2
Puttenham Ct HP23 103 F2
PUXLEY 31 D7
Puxley Rd
Deanshanger MK19 31 D5
Milton Keynes MK19 32 A5
Pye Bridge End MK10 36 A4
Pyebush La HP9 187 A8
Pyghtles The HP22 85 B5
Pyghtle The
Olney MK46 6 F3
Turvey MK43 8 E6
Pyke Hayes MK8 33 D3
Pymcombe Cl HP27 139 B5
Pym Wlk OX9 125 F1
Pynefield Ho WD3 167 F2
Pyxe Ct MK7 48 A4

Q

Quadrangle The HP13 173 E7
Quadrans Cl MK15 35 A7
Quadrant The
High Wycombe HP13 162 E1
Maidenhead SL6 203 A6
QUAINTON 85 B5
Quainton CE Comb Sch HP22 85 A5
QUAINTON HILL 75 B1
Quainton Rd
North Marston MK18 76 A2
Waddesdon HP18 99 A7
Quainton Road Sta★ HP22 84 F2
Quaker's Mead HP22 116 F3
Quakers Mede HP17 127 A6
Quantock Cl SL3 207 A1
Quantock Cres MK4 46 D2
QUARRENDON 101 B3
Quarrendon Ave HP19 101 B2
Quarrendon Rd HP7 165 E7
Quarry Cl HP18 125 C7
Quarry Ct LU7 105 D2
Quarrydale Dr SL7 183 F2
Quarry Green Cl MK19 31 B3
Quarry Rd LU7 105 D2
Quarry Wood Rd SL6, SL7 195 A8
Quaves Rd SL3 206 C3
Quebec Rd HP13 173 E6
Queen Alexandra Rd HP11 173 A6
Queen Anne Royal Free CE Fst Sch The SL4 210 D4
Queen Anne's Ct 10 SL4 210 C6
Queen Anne's Rd SL4 210 C3
Queen Anne St MK13 33 F7
Queen Catherine Rd MK18 63 E2
Queen Charlotte St 10 SL4 210 D6
Queen Cl RG9 191 E1
Queen Eleanor Prim Sch MK11 32 F4
Queen Eleanor St MK11 32 E6
Queen Elizabeth's Wlk SL4 210 F5
Queen Mother's Dr UB9 189 F5
Queens Acre
High Wycombe HP13 173 D6
Windsor SL4 210 D3
Queen's Acre SL4 210 D3
Queens Acre Ho 6 SL4 210 D4
Queen St Mews RG9 191 E1
Queens Ave MK16 22 C4
Queensbury La MK10 35 E1
Queens Cl OX9 125 F2
Queen's Cl SL4 211 A2
Queens Ct HP13 173 C6
Queen's Ct SL1 205 F6
Queen's Dr SL3 199 F4
Queen's Dr The WD3 167 F2
Queensgate HP19 115 A8
Queen's Gate SL4 210 D3
Queen's La 12 SL6 202 F7
Queensmead SL3 211 B6
Queens Mead HP21 116 C7
Queensmead Ho HP10 174 C2
Queensmead Rd HP10 174 C2
Queensmere Rd SL1 205 F4
Queensmere (Sh Ctr) SL1 205 F4
Queens Park Arts Ctr HP21 115 F8
Queen's Pk HP21 115 F8
Queen Sq 8 HP11 173 A7
Queens Rd
Berkhamsted HP4 135 A5
1 Chesham HP5 144 C1
Eton Wick SL4 204 F1
High Wycombe HP13 173 C6
Princes Risborough HP27 139 C4
Slough SL1 205 F6
West Drayton UB7 208 F4
Queen's Rd
Datchet SL3 211 B7
Marlow SL7 183 D2
Uxbridge UB8 201 C2
Windsor SL4 210 C5
Queen St
Aylesbury HP20 116 A8
Henley-on-Thames RG9 191 E1
High Wycombe HP13 173 C7
Leighton Buzzard LU7 80 F8
Maidenhead SL6 202 F7
Milton Keynes MK11 32 E6
Piddington HP14 160 B1
Pitstone LU7 105 D4
Tring HP23 119 A3
Waddesdon HP18 98 F6
Queen's Terr 5 SL4 210 D4
Queensway
Bletchley MK2 58 C8
Hazelmere HP15 163 A4
Maidenhead SL6 195 E2
Milton Keynes MK2 58 D8
Queensway The SL9 188 D7
Queen Victoria Rd HP11 173 B6
Queen Victoria's Wlk SL4 210 F6
Quickberry Pl HP7 165 C8
Quickley La WD3 167 C3
Quickley Rise WD3 167 B3
Quickly Brow WD3 167 B3
Quill Hall La HP6 154 F2
Quilter Mdw MK7 48 D5
Quilters Way HP22 130 D8
Quinbrookes SL2 206 C7
Quince Cl MK7 48 B5
Quinton Dr MK13 34 B3
Quoitings Dr SL7 183 C2
Quoitings Gdns SL7 183 C2
Quoiting Sq SL7 183 D2

R

Raans Rd HP6 154 F1
Rabans Cl
Aylesbury HP19 100 E1
Olney MK46 6 E5
Rabans La HP19 100 F1
Rabbsfarm Prim Sch UB7 208 E6
Rabbs Mill Ho UB8 201 D3
Rachels Way HP5 154 D5
Rackstraw Gr MK7 48 D5
Radcliffe Sch The MK12 33 B6
Radcliffe St MK12 33 D6
RADCLIVE 51 E8
Radclive Rd MK18 51 F7
Radcot Ave SL3 207 B3
Radcot Cl SL6 195 E3
Radcote Lodge MK8 33 E1
Radian Ct MK5 46 C7
Radman Gr MK12 33 B5
RADNAGE 159 C7
Radnage CE Inf Sch HP14 159 D6
Radnage Common Rd HP14 159 D5
Radnage La HP14 148 C2
Radnor Cl RG9 191 E2
Radnor End HP20 101 E2
Radnor Way SL3 206 E2
Radstock Cres MK10 36 A4
RADSTONE 26 A6
Radworthy MK4 46 C3
Raeside Cl HP9 176 C5
Raglan Dr MK4 45 E1
Ragmans Cl SL7 183 C8
Ragmans La HP10, SL7 172 D1
Ragnall's La OX33 108 A6
Ragstone Rd SL1 205 E3
Ragstones HP10 174 A1
Railway Cotts
Steeple Claydon MK18 64 A1
Wigginton HP23 119 F5
Railway St 2 HP20 115 E8
Railway Terr SL2 205 F5
Rainborough Gdns HP20 101 E2
Rainbow Dr MK6 46 F7
Rainbow Ind Est UB7 208 D6
Rainsborough MK14 35 A8
Rainsborough Chase SL6 202 B3
Rake Way HP21 115 D3
Raleigh Cl SL1 205 A5
Ralphs Retreat HP15 162 F4
Ralston Ct 20 SL4 210 D6
RAM ALLEY 12 B5
Ram Alley MK16 12 B6
Rambler Cl SL6 204 B7
Rambler La SL3 206 C3
Ramsay Cl MK13 34 B3
Ramsay View HP15 163 A3
Ramscote La HP5 143 F7
Ramsey Ct SL2 197 D1
Ramsgill Ct MK13 34 C5
Ramsons Ave MK14 34 E4
Ramsthorn Gr MK7 48 B6
Ramworth Way HP21 116 A6
Randall Cl SL3 206 F1
Randall Ct SL4 211 A1
Randall Dr MK4 45 D2
Randolph Cl MK13 34 A6
Randolph Rd SL3 206 E3
Ranelagh Gdns MK16 22 C2
Rangers Ct MK8 33 F1
Rannal Dr OX39 147 C6
Rannoch Cl MK2 58 D5
Rannock Gdns LU7 80 C7
Ranston Cl UB9 189 F5
Rashleigh Pl MK6 46 E7
Ratcliffe Cl UB8 201 D2
Rathbone Cl MK8 45 E7
Ravel Cl MK7 48 D6
Raven Cl 3 HP19 101 F3
Raven Cres HP18 98 C6
Raven Rd HP14 158 F4
Ravensbourne Pl MK6 35 B2
Ravensbourne Rd HP21 115 D4
Ravenscar Ct MK4 46 C2
Ravenscourt SL7 184 A3
Ravenscroft Rd RG9 191 D2
Ravens Ct
Berkhamsted HP4 135 E6
High Wycombe HP13 161 E3
Long Marston HP23 104 B4
Ravens Field SL3 206 D4
Ravensglass Croft 6 MK10 36 B3
Ravenshoe Cl SL8 185 A3
Ravens La HP4 135 D4
Ravensmead
Chalfont St Peter SL9 177 F5
Chinnor OX39 147 C6
RAVENSTONE 5 D2
Ravenstone Mill Rd MK46 12 E7
Ravens Wharf HP4 135 D4
Ravensworth Rd SL2 198 A2
Ravigill Pl MK12 33 D4
Rawcliffe Ho SL6 203 A6
Rawlings La HP9 176 D7
Rawlins Rd MK13 34 A4
Ray Dr SL6 203 B7
Rayfield SL6 203 B8
Ray Ho 5 SL8 185 A4
Raylands Mead SL9 188 C6
Ray Lea Cl SL6 203 B8
Ray Lea Rd SL6 203 B8
Rayleigh Cl MK5 46 B6
Raylens HP12 172 B5
Ray Lodge SL6 203 B7
Ray Lodge Mews SL6 203 B7
Ray Mdw SL6 196 A1
Ray Mead Ct SL6 196 C1
Ray Mead Rd SL6 203 C8
Ray Mill Road E SL6 196 B1
Ray Mill Road W SL6 203 A8
Raymond Cl SL3 212 E6
Raymond Rd
Maidenhead SL6 202 D7
Slough SL3 207 A3
Rayners Ave HP10 174 B3
Rayners Cl
Colnbrook SL3 212 C7
Loudwater HP10 174 C3
Rayners La MK9 35 E1
Ray Park Ave SL6 203 B8
Ray Park La SL6 203 B7
Ray Park Rd SL6 203 B8
Rays Ave SL4 209 F7
Rays Cl MK2 58 E6
Ray's Hill HP5 133 C2
Rays La HP10 163 C1
Ray St SL6 203 B7
Razzaq Pl HP12 172 E7
Read Dr HP22 102 C4
Reade Ct SL2 198 C6
Read Ho HP19 115 A7
Reading Cl HP19 101 A3
Reading Rd RG9 191 E1
Readings The WD3 167 F6
Reads La LU7 78 D1
Recreation Rd SL8 185 B3
Rectory Ave HP13 173 C7
Rectory Cl
Farnham Royal SL2 198 C2
Marsh Gibbon OX27 71 F3
Slapton LU7 91 D6
Windsor SL4 210 A6
Rectory Ct
2 Amersham HP7 165 B7
3 High Wycombe HP13 173 F5
Lewknor OX49 157 B8
West Drayton UB7 208 E4
Rectory Dr HP18 99 A6
Rectory Fields MK15 35 D3
Rectory Gdns HP8 177 B7
Rectory Hill HP7 165 B8
Rectory La
Amersham HP7 165 B7
Berkhamsted HP4 135 C4
Bix RG9 179 D1
Yardley Hastings NN7 1 A7
Rectory Mdw OX39 147 D6
Rectory Orch MK46 7 F8

Rectory Rd SL6 .... 196 E1
Rectory Terr SL2 .... 198 C3
Red Admiral St HP19 .... 101 C4
Redbourne Ct MK11 .... 32 F5
Redbridge MK14 .... 34 D7
Redcliffe Wlk HP19 .... 101 B2
Redcote Manor MK7 .... 48 A4
Red Cottage HP23 .... 119 D1
Red Cottage Mews [6]
SL3 .... 206 C3
Red Ct SL1 .... 205 E5
Redding Dr HP6 .... 154 A2
Redding Gr MK8 .... 45 E6
Reddings Cl HP22 .... 131 B6
Reddington Dr SL3 .... 206 E2
Redfern Cl UB8 .... 201 C4
Redfield Cl LU6 .... 93 E8
Redford Rd SL4 .... 209 D6
Redford Way UB8 .... 201 D5
Red Friars Square Sh Ctr [21]
HP20 .... 115 D8
Redgrave Dr [2] MK4 .... 45 E3
Redgrave Pl SL7 .... 183 F3
Redhill UB9 .... 189 D2
Redhouse Cl HP11 .... 172 E3
Red House Cl
Beaconsfield HP9 .... 175 B4
Newton Longville MK17 .... 57 D4
Redhuish Cl MK4 .... 46 D3
Red Kite Cl HP13 .... 161 D1
Red La OX39 .... 147 F3
Redland Cl MK18 .... 63 D2
Redland Dr MK5 .... 46 C7
Redland Way HP21 .... 116 A5
Red Leaf Cl SL3 .... 206 F5
Red Leys UB10 .... 201 E5
Red Lion Cl MK43 .... 25 B1
Red Lion Cotts SL2 .... 199 B1
Red Lion Dr HP14 .... 158 D5
Red Lion St HP5 .... 154 B7
Red Lion Way HP10 .... 185 E6
Red Lodge Gdns HP4 .... 135 A3
Redman Rd HP12 .... 172 B3
REDMOOR 47 A4
Redpitch Pk HP10 .... 185 F6
Redriff Cl SL6 .... 202 D6
Red Roofs SL6 .... 203 C7
Redshaw Cl MK18 .... 41 E1
Redshots Cl SL7 .... 183 E4
Redvers Gate MK15 .... 35 B7
Redway Sch The MK6 .... 47 C6
Red Wing HP20 .... 101 E3
Redwood SL1 .... 197 B3
Redwood Cl
Hazelmere HP15 .... 163 B3
Wing LU7 .... 79 E2
Redwood Dr
Aylesbury HP21 .... 115 E7
Wing LU7 .... 79 E2
Redwood Gate MK5 .... 46 C4
Redwood Gdns SL1 .... 205 D6
Redwood Glade LU7 .... 70 F3
Redwood Pl HP9 .... 175 D1
Redwoods The SL4 .... 210 D4
Reed Cl SL0 .... 207 E7
Reeves Croft MK12 .... 33 C4
Reform Rd SL6 .... 203 B7
Reform Road Ind Est
SL6 .... 203 B7
Regal Ct
Maidenhead SL6 .... 203 B2
[14] Tring HP23 .... 119 A3
Regency Ct HP21 .... 116 B7
Regent Ct
[3] Maidenhead SL6 .... 202 F7
Slough SL1 .... 205 E7
Windsor SL4 .... 210 D5
Regent Ho HP27 .... 139 B4
Regent Rd HP21 .... 116 B7
Regents Hall MK11 .... 32 E5
Regents Pl SL6 .... 202 D6
Regent St MK2 .... 58 C8
Regius Ct HP10 .... 174 D8
Reid Ave SL6 .... 202 E5
Reliance La MK9 .... 35 B3
Rembrandt End HP19 .... 100 F2
REMENHAM 192 A5
Remenham Church La
RG9 .... 192 A4
REMENHAM HILL 192 C2
Remenham La
Remenham Hill RG9 .... 191 F3
Remenham RG9 .... 192 B5
Remenham Row RG9 .... 191 F2
Remenham Terr RG9 .... 192 C2
Remus Gate NN13 .... 38 A6
Rendlesham MK15 .... 35 C3
Rendlesham Way WD3 .... 167 C3
Renfrew Way MK3 .... 46 F3
Rennie Cl HP13 .... 161 F1
Repton Cl SL6 .... 202 C3
Repton Pl HP7 .... 166 A8
Retreat La HP14 .... 148 D2
Retreat The
Little Chalfont HP6 .... 166 E8
Milton Keynes MK11 .... 32 D5
Princes Risborough
HP27 .... 139 B4
Revel Rd HP10 .... 185 D8
Revesby Cl SL6 .... 202 D3
Reyners Gn HP16 .... 152 B4
Reynold Dr HP20 .... 102 A2
Reynolds Cl
Cranfield MK43 .... 24 E2
High Wycombe HP13 .... 173 E8
Reynolds Pl MK8 .... 45 D6
Reynolds Rd HP9 .... 175 D3
Reynolds Wlk HP5 .... 144 A4
Rhodes Pl MK6 .... 46 E7
Rhondda Cl MK1 .... 47 E1
Rhoscolyn Dr MK3 .... 57 C8
Rhuddlan Cl MK5 .... 45 F7
Rhymer Cl MK19 .... 10 F4
Ribble Cl MK16 .... 22 E4
Ribble Cres MK3 .... 57 D8
Ribstone Rd SL6 .... 202 B3
Ricardo Rd SL4 .... 211 B1
Richard Gdns HP13 .... 173 E8
Richardson Pl [2] MK6 .... 34 E1
Richards Way SL1 .... 204 F5
Richborough MK13 .... 34 A6
RICHINGS PARK 207 E3
Richings Pl SL0 .... 207 E3
Richings Way SL0 .... 207 F3
Richmond Cl
Amersham HP6 .... 154 F1
Milton Keynes MK3 .... 46 D1
Richmond Cres SL1 .... 206 A5
Richmond Ct
Dunstable LU6 .... 92 E6
High Wycombe HP13 .... 173 C7
Richmond Rd HP20 .... 116 C7
Richmond Way MK16 .... 22 D3
Rickard Cl
Aylesbury HP21 .... 115 D3
West Drayton UB7 .... 208 D3
Rickford's Hill HP20 .... 115 D8
Rickley La MK3 .... 58 A8
Rickley Park Prim Sch
MK3 .... 57 F8
Rickman's La SL2 .... 198 E6
RICKMANSWORTH 167 F1
Rickmansworth La SL9 .... 177 F5
Rickmansworth Rd
Amersham HP6 .... 154 C2
Chorleywood WD3 .... 167 F6
Rickman Wlk HP19 .... 115 A7
Rickyard Cl
[1] Milton Keynes MK13 .... 34 A4
Whitchurch HP22 .... 87 A7
Rickyard Gr HP18 .... 83 B5
Rickyard The MK46 .... 7 C3
Rick Yd The MK16 .... 13 F1
Riders Way OX39 .... 147 C6
Ride The LU6 .... 93 B6
Ridgebank SL1 .... 204 F6
Ridge Cl
Aylesbury HP21 .... 115 D3
Lane End HP14 .... 171 C4
Ridge Ct SL4 .... 210 C4
Ridgemount End SL9 .... 177 E5
Ridge Side HP14 .... 160 A8
Ridge View HP23 .... 119 C5
Ridgeway
Berkhamsted HP4 .... 134 F4
[4] High Wycombe HP11 .... 173 A6
Milton Keynes, Stony Stratford
MK11 .... 32 F4
Milton Keynes, Wolverton Mill
MK12 .... 33 A5
Wing LU7 .... 79 E3
Ridge Way
High Wycombe HP13 .... 162 C1
Iver SL0 .... 207 F6
Long Crendon HP18 .... 125 F4
Ridgeway Cl
Chesham HP5 .... 144 B3
Marlow SL7 .... 183 E4
Ridgeway Cotts MK17 .... 67 B3
Ridgeway Ct [3] HP20 .... 101 E1
Ridgeway Meads HP27 .... 138 B2
Ridgeway Rd HP5 .... 144 B3
Ridgeway The
Amersham HP7 .... 165 E7
Gerrards Cross SL9 .... 188 D8
Marlow SL7 .... 183 E4
Ridgeway Trad Est The
SL0 .... 207 E6
Ridgewood RG9 .... 181 C1
Ridgmont MK19 .... 31 E5
Ridgmont Cl MK19 .... 31 E5
Ridgway MK17 .... 49 B6
Riding Court Rd SL3 .... 211 D7
Riding Ct SL3 .... 211 C8
Riding La HP9, HP10 .... 174 F3
Ridings Cotts HP15 .... 163 D6
Ridings The
Amersham HP6 .... 154 D4
Iver SL0 .... 207 F2
Latimer HP5 .... 155 D3
Maidenhead SL6 .... 202 A7
Ridings Way LU7 .... 78 B1
Riding The MK19 .... 31 E5
Rigby Lodge SL1 .... 205 E7
Rigeway View LU7 .... 105 D4
Rignall Rd HP16 .... 151 E8
Riley Cl HP20 .... 115 C8
Riley Rd SL7 .... 183 D2
Rillington Gdns MK4 .... 46 B3
Rimmington Way HP19 .... 101 B1
Rimsdale Ct MK2 .... 58 D3
Ringlet Way HP19 .... 101 C4
Ring Rd HP10 .... 173 F2
Ring Road E MK7 .... 47 F7
Ring Road N MK7 .... 47 F7
Ring Road W MK7 .... 47 E7
RINGSHALL 107 B1
Ringshall Dr HP4 .... 121 C8
Ringshall Rd HP4 .... 107 B3
Ringstead Way HP21 .... 116 A5
Ripley Cl
High Wycombe HP13 .... 173 A8
Milton Keynes MK4 .... 45 E1
Slough SL3 .... 206 E2
Ripon Ho HP21 .... 115 F6
Ripon St [7] HP20 .... 101 D1
Risborough Rd
Great Kimble HP17,
HP27 .... 139 E8
Maidenhead SL6 .... 202 E8
Stoke Mandeville HP17 .... 130 B7
Risborough Springs Swim &
Fitness Ctr HP27 .... 139 A4
Rise Hag Hill SL6 .... 204 A7
Riseley Rd SL6 .... 202 D7
Rise The
Amersham HP7 .... 165 C8
Gawcott MK18 .... 51 F4
Hazelmere HP15 .... 163 A5
Loudwater HP13 .... 174 B4
Uxbridge UB10 .... 201 F3
Risings The HP13 .... 162 B1
Riverbank Point UB8 .... 201 C6
Riverbank The SL4 .... 210 B7
River Cl MK16 .... 22 D4
Rivercrest Rd MK19 .... 32 B6
River Ct SL6 .... 203 C7
River Gdns SL6 .... 203 D4
Rivermead Ct SL7 .... 194 E8
Riverpark Dr SL7 .... 183 F1
River Park Ind Est HP4 .... 135 A5
River Rd SL6 .... 203 C6
River & Rowing Mus★
RG9 .... 191 F1
Riversdale SL8 .... 185 B1
Riversdale Cotts SL8 .... 185 B1
Riversdale Ct SL8 .... 185 A1
Rivers Edge HP11 .... 174 A3
Riverside SL7 .... 183 D1
River Side MK16 .... 22 D4
Riverside Cotts
West Drayton UB7 .... 208 C1
Wooburn Green HP10 .... 185 E8
Riverside Cvn Pk UB7 .... 208 C3
Riverside Gdns HP4 .... 135 A5
Riverside Mews MK18 .... 52 D8
Riverside Pk SL3 .... 212 E5
Riverside Pl TW19 .... 213 E1
Riverside Rd TW19 .... 213 E1
Riverside Way UB8 .... 201 B4
Riverside Wlk SL4 .... 210 D7
River St SL4 .... 210 D7
Riverswood Gdns HP11 .... 174 B3
River View HP10 .... 185 B7
Riverway SL4 .... 210 C7
River Wlk UB9 .... 201 C7
Riverwood Ave SL7 .... 184 A1
Riverwoods Dr SL7 .... 184 A1
Rivets Cl HP21 .... 115 E6
Rivetts Cl MK46 .... 6 E4
Rixband Cl MK7 .... 48 B4
Rixman Cl SL6 .... 202 D5
Rixon Cl SL3 .... 206 E7
Rixons Mdw HP19 .... 115 B7
Roade Hill NN7 .... 9 F8
Roald Dahl Mus & Story
Ctr★ HP16 .... 152 A7
Robert Rd SL2 .... 187 D2
Roberts Cl
Deanshanger MK19 .... 31 E4
Stanwell TW19 .... 213 C1
West Drayton UB7 .... 208 E5
Robert's Dr HP19 .... 101 D2
Roberts La SL9 .... 178 B5
Robertson Cl MK5 .... 45 F7
Robertson Cnr LU6 .... 93 F4
Robertson Rd [6] HP4 .... 135 D4
Roberts Rd
Haddenham HP17 .... 127 B6
High Wycombe HP13 .... 173 B8
Roberts Ride HP15 .... 163 A5
Roberts Way HP21 .... 115 B6
Robertswood Comb Sch
SL9 .... 177 F3
Roberts Wood Dr SL9 .... 177 F5
Robeson Pl MK8 .... 45 E8
Robin Cl
Aylesbury HP19 .... 101 F3
Buckingham MK18 .... 52 F7
Great Kingshill HP15 .... 151 D1
Robin Hill HP4 .... 135 C3
Robin Ho HP11 .... 174 A4
Robin Hood Cl SL1 .... 204 F5
Robin Par [2] SL2 .... 198 C7
Robins Cl
High Wycombe HP12 .... 172 D3
Uxbridge UB8 .... 208 C8
Robins Hill MK6 .... 47 A6
Robinson Cl HP19 .... 100 F3
Robinson Ct SL6 .... 202 E4
Robinson Rd HP13 .... 174 B4
Robins Orch SL9 .... 177 E4
Robins Platt OX39 .... 147 B6
Robinswood Cl
Beaconsfield HP9 .... 175 C5
Leighton Buzzard LU7 .... 70 F2
Robin Willis Way SL4 .... 211 A1
Robinwood Gr UB8 .... 201 F1
Roblin Cl HP21 .... 115 E4
Robson Cl SL9 .... 177 E5
Robson Ct [4] HP16 .... 152 A8
Roche Gdns MK3 .... 58 A8
Rochester Ct MK5 .... 46 A5
Rochester Mews LU7 .... 80 E6
Rochester Pl HP19 .... 115 B8
Rochfords MK6 .... 46 F6
Rochfords Gdns SL2 .... 206 C5
Rochford Way SL6 .... 204 A7
Rockall Ct SL3 .... 207 B3
Rock Cl LU7 .... 80 D6
Rockingham Cl
Pitstone LU7 .... 105 D3
Uxbridge UB8 .... 201 C4
Rockingham Dr MK14 .... 34 E6
Rockingham Par UB8 .... 201 C5
Rockingham Pl HP9 .... 175 F1
Rockingham Rd UB8 .... 201 C4
Rockingham Wharf
UB8 .... 201 B4
Rock La LU7 .... 80 D7
Rockleigh Ct [3] LU7 .... 80 E7
Rockspray Gr MK7 .... 48 B5
ROCKWELL END 181 F5
Rodney Way SL3 .... 212 E6
Rodwell Gdns MK7 .... 48 D4
Rodwell Yd [3] HP23 .... 119 A3
Roebuck Ave HP13 .... 173 F6
Roebuck Gn SL1 .... 204 E5
Roebuck Way MK5 .... 46 C6
Roeburn Cres MK4 .... 46 C1
Rogers Croft MK6 .... 47 D7
Rogers La SL2 .... 198 F4
Roker Park Ave UB10 .... 201 E8
Rokesby Rd SL2 .... 197 F2
Rolfe Cl HP9 .... 175 E1
Rolvenden Gr MK7 .... 48 B7
Roman Lea SL6 .... 195 F7
Roman Pl SL6 .... 202 C6
Roman Rdbts MK1 .... 47 C2
Romans Field Specl Sch
MK3 .... 46 E1
Roman Way
Aylesbury HP19 .... 115 B8
Bourne End SL8 .... 185 B4
Brackley NN13 .... 38 A7
Romar Ct MK1 .... 47 C2
Romney Ct [11] SL7 .... 183 F3
Romney Lock Rd SL4 .... 210 D7
Romney Rd HP21 .... 115 E4
Romsey Cl SL3 .... 206 F3
Romsey Dr SL2 .... 187 D1
Romsey Way HP11 .... 173 B4
Romulus Way NN13 .... 38 A6
Ronald Rd HP9 .... 175 F2
Ronaldsay Spur SL1 .... 205 E8
Rookery Ct SL7 .... 183 D2
Rookery Mdw HP15 .... 163 C7
Rookery Way MK18 .... 63 F3
Rook Rd HP10 .... 185 D4
ROOKSLEY 34 B2
Rooksley Rdbt MK13 .... 34 B3
Rooks Terr UB7 .... 208 E4
Rook Tree Farm Ind Est
MK17 .... 37 F3
Rook Wood Way HP16 .... 152 B5
Ropa Ct [6] LU7 .... 80 F7
Ropley Way [3] MK10 .... 36 B3
Rosamund's Cotts HP18 .... 83 B2
Rosary The HP15 .... 163 C6
Roseary Cl UB7 .... 208 D2
Rose Ave
Aylesbury HP19 .... 101 C2
Hazelmere HP15 .... 163 B2
Rosebank Cl SL6 .... 195 E7
Rosebank Cotts HP10 .... 174 B3
Rosebarn La HP23 .... 104 D1
Rosebay Cl MK7 .... 48 B5
Rosebery Ave
High Wycombe HP13 .... 173 E5
Leighton Buzzard LU7 .... 80 E7
Rosebery Cl MK18 .... 77 B7
Rosebery Ct [4] LU7 .... 80 F7
Rosebery Mews LU7 .... 90 D4
Rosebery Rd HP22 .... 117 F5
Rosebery Way HP23 .... 119 B5
Rose Cnr HP14 .... 158 E5
Rosecomb Pl MK5 .... 46 A4
Rose Cotts SL6 .... 202 C3
Rose Ct
Amersham HP6 .... 154 E2
Chesham HP5 .... 154 D6
Eaton Bray LU6 .... 92 D6
[3] Olney MK46 .... 6 F3
Rose Dr HP5 .... 154 D7
Rosehill HP4 .... 135 B4
Rose Hill SL1 .... 197 A5
Rosehill Cres MK18 .... 62 D1
Rosehill Ct SL1 .... 206 A3
Rose Ind Est SL7 .... 183 D5
Rose La RG9 .... 193 A1
Roseleigh Cl SL6 .... 202 A7
Rosemary Cl HP12 .... 161 B1
Rosemary Ct
High Wycombe HP12 .... 161 B1
Walton MK7 .... 48 A5
Rosemary La HP17 .... 127 A7
Rosemead HP22 .... 117 E1
Rosemoor Mews HP19 .... 114 F8
Rosemullion Ave MK4 .... 57 B8
Rosery The [5] SL8 .... 185 A3
Roses Cl LU7 .... 78 B1
Roses La SL4 .... 209 D5
Rose Terr HP18 .... 99 A6
Rosetree Cl HP16 .... 151 C6
Rose Wlk SL2 .... 205 B8
Rosewood Gdns HP12 .... 172 C4
Rosewood Way SL2 .... 198 C7
Rosken Gr SL2 .... 198 B3
Roslyn Ct MK15 .... 35 D7
Rossal Pl MK12 .... 33 D4
Rossendale MK14 .... 34 D7
Rossetti Pl HP15 .... 163 C7
Rossini Pl MK7 .... 48 D5
Rossiter Cl SL3 .... 206 E2
Ross Rd
Aston Abbotts HP22 .... 88 D5
Maidenhead SL6 .... 202 E4
Ross Way MK3 .... 46 F2
Rossway La HP4 .... 134 A7
Rostrevor Gdns SL0 .... 200 D3
Rothersthorpe MK14 .... 35 A8
Rothesay Cl HP20 .... 101 E1
Rothesay Ct HP4 .... 135 A4
Rothschild Ave HP22 .... 117 E5
Rothschild Rd
Leighton Buzzard LU7 .... 80 F8
Wing LU7 .... 79 E2
ROTTEN ROW 181 F2
Rotten Row MK17 .... 59 C2
Roughwood La HP8 .... 166 E3
Roundhead Dr OX9 .... 125 F1
Roundheads End HP9 .... 175 B4
Round Hill HP17 .... 114 D5
Roundhill Ct HP17 .... 126 E8
Roundlands HP27 .... 149 E5
Roundwood Prim Sch (Inf)
MK18 .... 51 B6
Roundwood Prim Sch (Jun)
MK18 .... 51 F4
Roundwood Rd HP12 .... 172 C7
Round Wood Rd HP6 .... 154 F2
Rouse Ct SL9 .... 188 F6
Routs Gn HP14 .... 148 D2
ROUT'S GREEN 148 D2
Roveley Ct MK11 .... 32 F5
Rowan Ave HP13 .... 173 D8
Rowan Cl
Aylesbury HP21 .... 115 E4
Beaconsfield HP9 .... 175 B1
Hazelmere HP15 .... 163 A3
Rowan Dr MK19 .... 20 D2
Rowan Gdns SL0 .... 200 C3
Rowan Ho [1] SL8 .... 185 A4
Rowanhurst Dr SL2 .... 198 C7
Rowan Pl HP6 .... 154 F1
Rowan Rd UB7 .... 208 E2
Rowans The SL9 .... 188 D8
Rowan Way SL2 .... 205 B8
Rowan Wlk HP5 .... 144 B1
Rowborough Rd HP22 .... 131 D7
Rowland Cl SL4 .... 209 D4
Rowland Ho HP9 .... 175 F1
Rowlands Cl MK2 .... 58 E8
Rowland Way HP19 .... 115 B7
Rowle Cl MK14 .... 34 E7
Rowley Furrows LU7 .... 80 D8
Rowley La SL3 .... 199 D4
Rowlheys Pl UB7 .... 208 E3
Rowliff Rd HP12 .... 172 C6
ROWSHAM 102 D8
Rowsham Dell MK14 .... 21 F2
Rowsham Rd HP22 .... 102 C5
Row The
Cholesbury HP5 .... 133 D2
Cold Brayfield MK46 .... 8 B6
Lane End HP14 .... 171 B4
Newton Blossomville MK43 .... 8 B3
Winchmore Hill HP7 .... 164 C3
Rowton Heath MK5 .... 45 C5
Roxburgh Way MK3 .... 46 F3
Roxhill Rd MK43 .... 25 F3
Roxwell Cl SL1 .... 204 E5
Roxwell Path [5] HP20 .... 101 F2
Royal Buckinghamshire
Hospl HP19 .... 101 D1
Royal Cl UB7, UB8 .... 208 F7
Royal Cotts SL6 .... 195 C7
Royal Cotts HP7 .... 164 C2
Royal Ct HP23 .... 120 A5
Royal Free Ct [13] SL4 .... 210 D6
Royal Gram Sch The
HP13 .... 162 C1

- Royal La UB8 201 F1
- Royal Latin Sch The MK18 52 D7
- Royal Mansions RG9 191 E1
- Royal Mead HP17 130 C5
- Royal Windsor Racecourse SL4 209 E7
- Royce Cl LU6 93 F7
- Royce Rd MK43 24 D3
- Royle Cl SL9 177 F3
- Royston Way SL1 204 D8
- Rubbra Cl MK7 48 C5
- Rubens Cl HP19 100 F2
- Ruby Cl SL1 205 A4
- Ruckles Way HP7 165 C7
- Rudchesters MK13 33 F5
- Ruddlesway SL4 209 D6
- Rudds Cl MK18 66 A5
- Rudd's La HP17 127 A7
- Rudsworth Cl SL3 212 D7
- Ruffle Cl UB7 208 E4
- Rugby Rise HP11 174 A3
- Rugwood Rd HP10 173 F2
- Rumptons Paddock HP18 82 F6
- Runford Ct MK5 46 C5
- Run Furrow HP17 127 A7
- Runnymede MK14 21 F2
- Runrig Hill HP6 154 E4
- Rupert Ave HP12 172 E4
- Rupert Cl RG9 191 E3
- Rupert House Sch RG9 191 E2
- Rupert's La 191 E3
- Rupert Way OX9 126 A1
- Ruscombe Gdns SL3 211 A7
- Ruscote HP4 135 A3
- Rushall Rd OX9 126 A1
- Rushbeds Wood Wildlife Reserve* HP18 96 D4
- Rushbrooke Cl HP13 162 F2
- Rushburn HP10 185 F6
- Rushendon Furlong LU7 105 E5
- Rushes Mead UB8 201 C4
- Rushes The
  - Maidenhead SL6 203 C6
  - Marlow SL7 194 C8
- Rushfields Cl 12 MK4 45 F1
- RUSH GREEN 200 E8
- Rushington Ave SL6 202 F5
- Rushleys Cl MK5 46 A8
- RUSHMERE 70 E4
- Rushmere Cl MK17 48 D2
- Rushmere La HP5 145 B3
- Rushmere Ret Pk MK1 47 D2
- Rushmoor Ave HP15 163 B3
- Rushton Ct 5 MK8 45 F8
- Ruskin Ct MK16 22 C2
- Rusland Cir MK4 46 C2
- Russel Ct HP14 161 C8
- Russell Ave HP21 115 C6
- Russell Cl
  - Little Chalfont HP6 166 D8
  - Tylers Green HP10 163 B1
- Russell Ct
  - Aylesbury HP21 115 E6
  - Chesham HP5 144 D2
  - Maidenhead SL6 202 F7
  - Wendover HP22 131 B5
- Russell Dr TW19 213 D1
- Russell Ho 4 SL8 185 A4
- Russell Sch The WD3 167 B5
- Russell St
  - Milton Keynes MK11 32 D5
  - Windsor SL4 210 D6
  - Woburn Sands MK17 49 B4
- Russell Street Sch MK11 32 D5
- Russet Cl TW19 212 F1
- Russet Rd SL6 202 C3
- Russets The SL9 177 D1
- Russett Hill SL9 188 E8
- Russwell La MK17 59 C6
- Rustics Cl MK18 73 B5
- Rustlings Gate HP14 171 C5
- Rutherford Cl
  - Uxbridge UB8 201 F1
  - Windsor SL4 209 F6
- Rutherford Gate MK5 46 C5
- Rutherford Rd HP21 115 E4
- Ruthven Cl MK2 58 C4
- Rutland Ave
  - High Wycombe HP12 172 D6
  - Slough SL1 205 C8
- Rutland Ct 2 HP11 173 A6
- Rutland Gate SL6 202 C6
- Rutland Ho 3 MK3 46 F1
- Rutland Pl SL6 202 C6
- Rutland Rd SL6 202 D6
- Rutland St HP11 173 A6
- Ryans Mount SL7 183 C2
- Rycote La OX9 136 D5
- Rycote Lane Ind Est OX9 136 C4
- Rycroft
  - Milton Keynes MK4 46 E3
- Rycroft *continued*
  - Windsor SL4 209 F4
- Rydal Way
  - High Wycombe HP12 172 B5
  - Milton Keynes MK2 58 D5
- Ryder Cl HP3 146 A4
- Rydings SL4 209 F4
- Ryding The MK5 46 A4
- Rye Cl
  - Aylesbury HP21 115 D4
  - Maidenhead SL6 202 A4
- Ryecote Chapel* OX9 136 D6
- Ryecroft Rd HP5 154 A7
- Rye Ct 9 SL1 206 A4
- Ryefield Terr SL3 212 D7
- Ryeland MK11 32 E6
- Ryeland Cl UB7 208 E7
- Ryemead Way HP11 173 F4
- Rye The LU6, LU7 92 B8
- Rye View HP13 173 C7
- Rylstone Cl
  - Maidenhead SL6 202 C3
  - Milton Keynes MK13 34 B3
- Ryman Ct WD3 167 C3
- Rymill Cl HP3 146 A3
- Ryton Pl MK4 46 C3
- Ryvers End SL3 206 F3
- Ryvers Rd SL3 206 F3
- Ryvers Sch SL3 206 D3

S

- Sabina Cl HP12 172 E6
- Sacred Heart RC Prim Sch RG9 191 D1
- Saddington MK6 47 D6
- Saddlers Pl MK14 35 A5
- Sadleirs Gn MK17 49 B5
- Sadlers Mews SL6 203 B7
- Saffron Cl SL3 211 B6
- Saffron Ct HP13 173 C6
- Saffron Rd HP13 173 C6
- Saffron Rise LU6 92 E6
- Saffron St MK2 58 D7
- Saham Croft Cl MK18 65 E4
- Sailing Club Rd SL8 185 A3
- St Abbs Ct MK4 56 F8
- St Adrian's Cl SL6 202 B4
- St Agnes Gate HP22 131 A5
- St Aidan's Cl MK3 57 E6
- St Albans Cl 7 SL4 210 D6
- St Alban's Rd MK18 65 F4
- St Alban's St SL4 210 D6
- St Andrew's Ave SL4 209 F5
- St Andrew's CE Inf Sch MK14 34 E8
- St Andrew's CE Prim Sch
  - Chinnor OX39 147 C7
  - Uxbridge UB8 201 D4
- St Andrew's Cl
  - High Wycombe HP13 162 F1
  - Old Windsor SL4 211 A1
  - Wraysbury TW19 211 E1
- St Andrews Cotts 1 SL4 210 A5
- St Andrew's Cres SL4 209 F5
- St Andrews Ct
  - Colnbrook SL3 212 D7
  - 2 Slough SL1 205 E3
- St Andrews Ho OX39 147 C6
- St Andrew's Rd
  - Chinnor OX39 147 C5
  - Milton Keynes MK3 57 E7
  - Uxbridge UB10 201 E5
- St Andrews Way SL1 204 D6
- St Andrews Way Ind Est HP19 101 C1
- St Anne's Cl
  - Henley-on-Thames RG9 191 D1
  - Wendover HP22 131 B5
- St Anne's Rd
  - Aylesbury HP19 115 B8
  - South Harefield UB9 190 C8
- St Ann's HP10 174 C2
- St Ann's Ct HP10 174 C2
- St Anthony's Cl HP19 115 B8
- St Anthony's Ct HP9 186 C8
- St Anthony's Pl MK4 57 B8
- St Anthony's RC Prim Sch SL2 198 C1
- St Augustine's RC Prim Sch HP11 173 A4
- St Augustus Cl MK3 57 E7
- St Bartholomews MK10 36 A1
- St Bartholomew's CE Sch HP23 119 D1
- St Bees MK10 36 B1
- St Bernadettes RC Prim Sch MK10 47 F8
- St Bernards Ct HP13 173 C6
- St Bernard's Prep Sch SL1 206 B4
- St Bernard's RC Gram Sch SL3 206 C4
- St Bernard's RC Sch HP11 173 A4
- St Bernards Rd SL3 206 C3
- St Birinus HP10 174 A2
- St Botolphs 2 MK10 36 B1
- St Brides Cl MK6 35 C2
- St Catherine RC Prim Sch UB7 208 D4
- St Catherine's Ave MK3 57 D6
- St Catherines Ct 3 SL4 210 A5
- St Catherine's Ct HP19 115 B8
- St Chad's Rd SL6 202 B4
- St Christopher Rd UB8 208 D8
- St Christopher's Cl HP16 152 B3
- St Christophers Ct WD3 167 D5
- St Clement Cl UB8 208 D7
- St Clement Danes Sch WD3 167 D7
- St Clement's Dr MK3 57 D6
- Saint-Cloud Way SL6 203 A7
- St Columba's Cl SL6 202 B4
- St Cuthburt La UB8 208 D7
- St David Cl UB8 208 D8
- St David's Cl
  - Iver Heath SL0 200 D4
  - Maidenhead SL6 202 A4
- St David's Ct NN13 38 A8
- St David's Par SL0 200 D4
- St David's Rd MK3 57 E6
- St Dunstans MK6 47 A6
- St Edmund Campion RC Prim Sch SL6 202 B5
- St Edmunds HP4 135 C3
- St Edmund's Cl HP19 115 B8
- St Edwards Ct MK14 34 F7
- St Edward's RC Fst Sch SL4 210 A6
- St Edward's RC Jun Sch HP21 116 A7
- St Edward's Royal Free Ecumenical Mid Sch SL4 210 A6
- St Elmo Cl SL2 198 D1
- St Elmo Cres SL2 198 D1
- St Ethelbert's RC Prim Sch SL2 206 A7
- St Faith's Cl MK17 57 D3
- St Francis Rd
  - Beacon's Bottom HP14 159 D3
  - Denham Green UB9 189 F5
- St George's CE Inf Sch 3 HP7 165 E8
- St George's Cl
  - High Wycombe HP13 173 D7
  - Windsor SL4 209 E6
- St Georges Cres SL1 204 D6
- St Georges Ct 2 HP12 172 D8
- St George's Dr UB10 190 F1
- St Georges Ind Est HP7 165 F8
- St Georges Lodge SL6 196 B7
- St George's Rd MK3 57 E6
- St George's Sch SL4 210 D7
- St Georges Way 33 D7
- St Giles Mews MK11 32 D6
- St Giles St MK13 33 F7
- St Govans Cl MK4 57 B8
- St Helena Ave
  - Milton Keynes MK3 58 C3
  - Milton Keynes MK17 58 C3
- St Helen Cl UB8 208 D8
- St Helens Gr MK10 47 F8
- St Hilda's Ct HP19 115 B8
- St Hilda's Way HP10 174 A2
- St Huberts Cl SL9 188 E2
- St Huberts Cotts SL9 188 E4
- St Huberts La SL9 188 F2
- St Hugh's Ave HP13 173 F6
- St Hugh's Cl HP14 158 F4
- St Hugh's Pl HP14 158 F4
- St Ives Cres MK4 57 B8
- St Ives Rd SL6 203 A7
- St James Cl MK19 11 A2
- St James Ctyd 8 SL7 183 E2
- St James Pl SL1 204 C7
- St James & St John CE Prim Sch
  - Akeley MK18 41 F8
  - Chackmore MK18 41 B4
- St James St MK13 33 F7
- St James Way HP22 102 B3
- St James Wlk SL0 207 E4
- St John's Ave HP10 174 B8
- St John's CE Comb Sch HP27 149 F4
- St Johns Cl HP10 163 B1
- St John's Cl UB8 201 B4
- St John's Cres MK12 33 D5
- St Johns Dr
  - Stone HP17 114 B5
  - Windsor SL4 210 A5
- St Johns La MK18 75 F2
- St John's La MK19 31 B4
- St John's Manor Ho HP15 162 E2
- St Johns Rd
  - Slough SL2 206 A6
  - Tylers Green HP10 163 B1
  - Windsor SL4 210 A5
- St John's Rd
  - 4 Aylesbury HP20 101 E1
  - Hazlemere HP15 162 F2
  - Milton Keynes MK3 57 E6
  - Uxbridge UB8 201 B4
- St John's St HP20 101 E1
- St John St MK16 22 D4
- St John's Terr MK16 22 D4
- St John's Well Ct HP4 135 B5
- St John's Well La HP4 135 B5
- St Josephs Cl MK46 6 F4
- St Josephs Mews HP9 175 F2
- St Joseph's RC Comb Sch SL9 188 C8
- St Joseph's RC High Sch SL2 206 A7
- St Joseph's RC Inf Sch HP21 116 A7
- St Katherine's Way HP4 134 F7
- St Laurence Cl UB8 208 C8
- St Laurence Rd MK18 65 F4
- St Laurence Way SL1 206 A3
- St Lawrence Cl HP3 146 A4
- St Lawrence View MK13 34 A4
- St Leger Ct MK14 34 E8
- St Leger Dr MK14 34 E7
- ST LEONARDS 132 E3
- St Leonard's Ave 2 SL4 210 C5
- St Leonard's Hill SL4 209 E4
- St Leonards Rd HP6 154 E4
- St Leonard's Rd
  - Oakley Green SL4 209 D1
  - Windsor SL4 210 C4
- St Leonard's Way LU6 92 E1
- St Leonards Wlk SL0 207 F3
- St Louis RC Comb Sch 15 HP20 101 F2
- St Luke Cl UB8 208 D7
- St Luke's CE Prim Sch 2 SL6 202 F8
- St Luke's Rd
  - Maidenhead SL6 202 F8
  - Old Windsor SL4 211 A1
  - Uxbridge UB10 201 E5
- St Margaret Ct MK2 58 E8
- St Margarets Cl MK16 22 E4
- St Margaret's Cl
  - Berkhamsted HP4 135 D3
  - Iver Heath SL0 200 D3
  - Tylers Green HP10 174 C8
- St Margaret's Ct SL0 200 D3
- St Margaret's Gate SL0 200 D3
- St Margarets Gr HP15 151 E1
- St Margaret's Rd SL6 202 A7
- St Margaret Way SL1 204 F4
- St Marks Cl HP13 173 D7
- St Mark's Cres SL6 202 B7
- St Mark's Hospl SL6 202 C7
- St Mark's Pl SL4 210 C5
- St Mark's Rd
  - Aylesbury HP21 115 C7
  - Henley-on-Thames RG9 191 E1
  - Maidenhead SL6 202 D7
  - Windsor SL4 210 C5
- St Martin Cl UB8 208 D7
- St Martin's Cl UB7 208 D3
- St Martin's Rd UB7 208 D3
- St Martin's St MK2 58 C8
- St Mary & All Saints CE Prim Sch HP9 175 E3
- St Mary Magdalene RC Prim Sch MK12 33 A5
- St Mary & St Giles CE Sch MK11 32 E6
- St Mary's Ave
  - Berkhamsted HP4 134 D6
  - Milton Keynes MK3 57 E7
  - Milton Keynes, Stony Stratford MK11 32 E6
- St Mary's CE Comb Sch HP7 165 A8
- St Mary's CE Prim Sch SL1 206 A3
- St Mary's CE Sch HP19 115 A8
- St Marys Cl
  - East Claydon MK18 74 F8
  - Mursley MK17 67 D6
- St Mary's Cl
  - Lee Common HP16 142 D5
  - Maidenhead SL6 203 A7
  - South Harefield UB9 190 B8
  - Wavendon MK17 48 E7
- St Marys Ct MK18 51 B7
- St Mary's Farnham Royal Prim Sch SL2 198 C2
- St Mary's Fst Sch HP4 134 E6
- St Mary's Glebe LU6 92 E4
- St Mary's RC Prim Sch
  - Maidenhead SL6 195 F2
  - Uxbridge UB8 201 C4
- St Marys Rd MK18 74 F7
- St Mary's Rd
  - Denham Green UB9 189 F5
  - Slough SL3 206 E4
  - South Harefield UB9 190 B8
- St Mary's Row 7 HP20 115 D8
- St Mary's Sch SL9 188 E7
- St Mary's Sq 3 HP20 115 D8
- St Mary St
  - High Wycombe HP11 173 B6
  - Milton Keynes MK13 33 F7
- St Marys Wavendon Prim Sch MK17 48 E7
- St Mary's Way
  - Chalfont St Peter SL9 177 D1
  - Chesham HP5 154 B8
  - Leighton Buzzard LU7 80 D7
- St Mary's Wlk 10 SL6 202 F7
- St Matthew Cl UB8 208 D7
- St Matthew's CE Prim Sch UB7 208 E5
- St Matthews Ct MK3 57 E6
- St Michael's CE Comb Sch LU7 68 E1
- St Michaels Cl
  - Edgcott HP18 72 F2
  - Halton HP22 131 C8
  - Stewkley LU7 68 E1
- St Michael's Cl HP22 117 C1
- St Michael's Ct
  - Ashton NN7 9 F8
  - Slough SL2 197 D1
- St Michaels Dr
  - Milton Keynes MK7 47 F6
  - Walton MK7 47 E7
- St Michael's Gn HP9 175 E3
- St Michaels Way MK18 63 E3
- St Monica's RC Comb Sch MK14 34 F6
- St Nicholas CE Comb Sch SL6 196 E1
- St Nicholas Cl
  - Cublington LU7 78 B1
  - Little Chalfont HP7 166 B8
  - Uxbridge UB8 208 D7
- St Patrick's Cl SL6 202 B4
- St Patrick's Way MK3 57 E6
- St Paul Cl UB8 208 D8
- St Pauls Ave SL2 206 A5
- St Paul's CE Comb Sch HP10 185 D4
- St Pauls Ct MK11 32 D6
- St Paul's Ct SL6 202 F6
- St Pauls Gdns SL6 202 B8
- St Pauls RC Sch MK6 46 F7
- St Paul's Rd MK3 57 E6
- St Pauls Yd MK16 22 D4
- St Peter's Ave HP19 101 C3
- St Peter's CE Comb Sch SL1 197 B2
- St Peter's CE Mid Sch SL4 210 F1
- St Peters Cl
  - Loudwater HP11 174 B1
  - Speen HP27 150 C4
- St Peter's Cl
  - Burnham SL1 197 B1
  - Old Windsor SL4 211 A2
- St Peter's Ct SL9 177 E2
- St Peter's Gate NN13 38 A7
- St Peters Hill HP23 119 A4
- St Peter's RC Prim Sch SL7 183 D3
- St Peter's Rd
  - Brackley NN13 38 A8
  - Maidenhead SL6 195 D2
  - Uxbridge UB8 208 D8
- St Peter St SL7 183 E1
- St Peters Way
  - Chorleywood WD3 167 B5
  - Milton Keynes MK13 34 A8
- St Pirans Sch SL6 195 E1
- St Rumbold's La MK18 52 C8
- St Stephens Dr MK15 35 B7
- St Stephen's Rd UB7 208 D5
- St Teresa's Cl HP27 139 B4
- St Teresa's Sch HP27 139 B4
- St Thomas Aquinas RC Comb Sch MK3 57 E7
- St Thomas Ct MK4 45 F1
- St Thomas More RC Prim Sch HP4 135 A4
- St Thomas Wlk SL3 212 D7
- St Vincents MK17 49 C4
- Sakura Wlk MK15 35 C6
- Salcey Forest Trail* MK16 4 C2
- SALCEY GREEN 11 B7
- SALDEN 67 F8
- Salden Cl
  - Drayton Parslow MK17 68 C6
  - Milton Keynes MK5 46 B6
- SALFORD 37 C3
- Salford Rd MK17 49 D7
- Salisbury Ave SL2 205 C8
- Salisbury Cl
  - Amersham HP7 165 E8
  - Princes Risborough HP27 139 C3
- Salisbury Ct SL6 202 E5
- Salisbury Gr MK14 21 F2
- Salisbury Mews SL2 198 C1
- Salisbury Rd
  - High Wycombe HP13 162 D1
  - Uxbridge UB8 201 B3
- Sallowsprings LU6 93 F2

Salmons La HP16 151 D6
Salop Ho MK3 46 F2
Saltash Cl HP13 174 B4
Salters Cl
Ludgershall HP18 96 C8
Maidenhead SL6 203 A7
Salter's Cl HP4 134 F6
Salters La HP18 96 C8
Salters Mews MK14 34 F6
Salters Rd SL6 203 B7
Salters Row HP10 186 A4
SALT HILL 205 D5
Salt Hill Ave SL1 205 C5
Salt Hill Cl UB8 201 E7
Salt Hill Dr SL1 205 C5
Salt Hill Mans SL1 205 C5
Salt Hill Way SL1 205 D5
Salton Link MK4 46 B2
Saltwood Ave MK4 45 E1
Samphire Ct MK7 48 A6
Sampsons Gn SL2 197 F2
Sampsons Hill HP7 164 E2
Samuel Cl MK16 22 F3
Sanctuary Rd HP15 163 B5
Sandage Rd HP14 171 B5
Sandal Ct MK5 46 A5
Sandbrier Cl MK7 48 B6
Sandbrook La HP23 104 C1
Sandels Way HP9 175 D4
Sandelswood End HP9 175 D5
Sanders La NN12 18 D3
Sanderson Rd UB8 201 C6
Sandford Gdns HP11 173 B4
SANDHILL 64 E2
Sandhill Rd
Buckingham MK18 64 C4
East Claydon MK18 74 F8
Sandhill Way HP19 115 A8
Sandholme MK18 63 E2
Sandhurst Dr MK18 52 C7
Sandisplatt Rd SL6 202 A6
Sandlers End SL2 198 B1
Sandles The SL4 205 B1
Sandleswood Cl HP9 175 D4
Sandmartin Cl MK18 41 E1
Sandon Cl HP23 118 F4
Sandown Ct
8 High Wycombe HP12 172 E7
Milton Keynes MK3 57 D6
Sandown Rd SL2 204 F8
Sandpiper 1 HP19 101 E4
Sandpipers Pl SL6 195 E6
Sandpit Hill MK18 50 F6
Sandpit Hill Cotts HP23 133 B2
Sandpit La HP27 138 B4
Sandpits La HP10 174 C7
Sandringham Ct
8 High Wycombe HP13 173 B7
Newport Pagnell MK16 22 B3
Slough SL1 204 D7
Sandringham Pl MK2 58 C8
Sandringham Rd
Maidenhead SL6 195 E2
Stanwell TW6 213 E2
SANDS 172 B7
Sands Bank Nature Reserve★ HP12 172 A7
Sands Farm Dr SL1 197 C1
Sands Ind Est HP12 172 B7
Sandstone Cl MK18 73 B5
Sandwell Ct MK8 33 C2
Sandy Cl
Buckingham MK18 52 F8
Milton Keynes MK14 34 D8
Sandycroft Rd HP6 155 C1
Sandygate Cl SL7 183 D3
Sandygate Rd SL7 183 D3
Sandy La
Aspley Heath MK17 49 B2
Leighton Buzzard LU7 70 F3
Long Crendon HP18 125 B6
Sandy Mead SL6 203 C1
Sandy Rd MK18 73 B5
Sandy Rise SL9 177 E2
Sandywell Dr MK15 35 A6
San Remo Rd MK17 49 F4
Santen Gr MK2 58 D4
Saracens' Wharf MK2 47 E1
Sargeant Cl UB8 201 D2
SARRATT 156 F4
Sarum Complex UB8 201 B3
Satis Ho SL3 211 C7
Saunders Cl MK7 48 D6
Saunders Ct 1 HP13 173 F6
Saunders End HP6 153 C5
Saunders Pl HP19 115 A7
Saunders Rd UB10 201 F4
Saunders Wood Copse HP14 158 F4
SAUNDERTON
Bledlow Ridge 149 C1
Princes Risborough 138 E1
SAUNDERTON LEE 149 A4
Saunderton Sta HP14 149 C1
Saunderton Vale HP14 149 C1
Savage Croft MK10 35 E3
Savay Cl UB9 190 A4
Savay La UB9 190 A5
Savernake Rd HP19 101 D3
Savill La MK4, MK5 45 F2
Savill Way SL7 183 F2
Savoy Cres MK9 34 F3
Savoy Ct SL6 195 F1
Sawley Ho 5 MK3 46 F1
Sawmill Cotts SL3 199 F2
Sawmill Rd HP27 138 D7
Sawpit Hill HP15 163 B5
Sawyers Cl SL6 202 A2
Sawyer's Cl SL4 209 E7
Sawyers Cres SL6 202 A2
Saxeways Bsns Ctr HP5 143 E3
Saxhorn Rd HP14 171 C4
Saxon Cl
Amersham HP6 154 D1
Dunstable LU6 93 E8
Milton Keynes MK19 11 B2
Slough SL3 206 F4
Uxbridge UB8 208 E8
Saxon Ct
High Wycombe HP12 172 D8
Stanwell TW19 213 A2
Saxon Gate MK9 34 E2
Saxon Gdns SL6 196 D1
Saxon Lodge SL1 204 F5
Saxon Park Ind Est MK1 47 D2
Saxon St
Milton Keynes, Ashland MK1, MK6 47 C4
Milton Keynes, Heelands MK6, MK13, MK14 34 C5
Milton Keynes MK2 58 C8
Saxon Way
Harmondsworth UB7 213 C8
Old Windsor SL4 211 B1
Saxon Way Trad Ctr UB7 213 C8
Sayers Gdns HP4 135 A6
Saye & Sele Cl HP18 82 F6
Sayward Cl HP5 144 D2
Scafell Rd SL2 204 F8
Scarborough Way SL1 205 B4
Scardale MK13 34 C5
Scarlett Ave HP22 131 E6
Scatterdells La WD4 146 F1
Scatterill Cl MK13 34 A4
Scholars Way HP6 154 F1
Scholars Wlk
Chalfont St Peter SL9 177 E4
Slough SL3 207 A4
School Cl
Asheridge HP5 143 E5
Brackley NN13 39 A4
Cryers Hill HP15 162 C6
High Wycombe, Downley HP13 161 D2
High Wycombe HP11 173 A4
Holmer Green HP15 163 C7
Ickford HP18 124 A3
School Dr MK17 57 C3
School End
Chetwode MK18 61 D8
Great Horwood MK17 55 A3
School Hill
Charndon OX27 73 A6
North Marston MK18 76 B2
School Ho TW19 213 C1
School La
Amersham HP7 165 A8
Buckingham MK18 52 C8
Castlethorpe MK19 19 F5
Chalfont St Giles HP8 177 B7
Chalfont St Peter SL9 177 D1
Chearsley HP18 112 B2
Cookham Dean SL6 195 B7
Cookham SL6 196 B7
Dinton HP17 113 F2
Eaton Bray LU6 92 F6
Leighton Buzzard LU7 68 E1
Little Marlow SL7 184 C5
Maidenhead SL6 195 E1
Medmenham SL7 193 B6
Milton Keynes MK5 46 B8
Oakley HP18 109 D5
Penn Street HP7 164 B5
Preston Bissett MK18 62 B8
Seer Green HP9 176 D4
Shabbington HP18 124 D3
Sherington MK16 14 A2
Slough SL2 205 F6
Turville RG9 169 F3
Twyford MK18 62 D2
Upper Winchendon HP18 99 A1
Waddesdon HP18 99 A6
Weston Turville HP22 116 F1
Wexham Street SL2 199 B5
Yardley Gobion NN12 18 E6
School Rd
Harmondsworth UB7 213 D8
Tylers Green HP10 174 D8
Wooburn Green HP10 185 E6
School St MK13 33 F7
School The HP23 118 C8
School Way HP11 174 B2
Schorne La MK18 76 B2
Schumann Cl MK7 48 C4
Scotch Firs MK7 48 C6
Scotlands Dr SL2 198 B6
Scotney Gdns MK3 57 E8
Scotsgrove Cotts OX9 126 A4
Scotsgrove Hill OX9 126 A3
Scotswood Cl HP9 175 D5
Scott Cl
Farnham Common SL2 198 C7
West Drayton UB7 208 F2
Scott Dr MK16 22 A5
Scott End HP19 100 F2
Scott Evans Ct MK18 66 A5
Scotts Cl
Marsh Gibbon OX27 72 A3
Stoke Hammond MK17 69 E8
Scotts Cnr NN13 39 A4
Scotts Farm Cl MK18 41 E4
Scotts La
Adstock MK18 53 F1
Buckingham MK18 41 E3
Marsh Gibbon OX27 71 E2
Scriven Ct MK15 35 E7
Scriveners La NN12 17 A8
Scrubb's La HP14 160 B7
Seabrooke Ct MK8 45 D6
Seacourt Rd SL3 207 B2
Seaford Rd TW6 213 D2
Seagrave Ct MK7 48 A4
Seagrave Rd HP9 175 C4
Sears The LU6 92 B5
Seaton Dr HP21 115 D4
Seaton Gr MK10 36 A4
Secklow Gate MK9 34 F3
Second Ave MK1 47 C2
Second Cres SL1 205 C8
Second St HP11 173 C4
Sedgemere MK8 33 D2
Sedgemoor Dr OX9 126 A1
Sedgmoor Cl HP10 185 A7
Sedgmoor Gdns HP10 185 A8
Sedgmoor La HP10 185 B7
Sedgmoor Rd HP10 185 A8
Sedley Gr UB9 190 C7
SEDRUP 114 F3
Sedrup La HP17 114 F4
Seebeck Cl MK5 46 C7
Seeleys Cl HP9 175 C4
Seeleys Ct HP9 175 D3
Seeleys La HP9 175 D3
Seeleys Rd HP9 175 C4
SEER GREEN 176 D4
Seer Green CE Comb Sch HP9 176 C4
Seer Green & Jordans Sta HP9 176 C3
Seer Green La HP9 176 E3
Seer Mead HP9 176 D4
Sefton Cl SL2 198 F4
Sefton Paddock SL2 199 A5
Sefton Park Cotts SL2 199 A4
Sefton Park Sch SL2 199 B5
Sefton Way UB8 208 C7
Selbourne Ave MK3 57 F7
Selbourne Ho 10 SL8 185 A4
Selby Gr MK5 46 B5
Selim Ct 4 SL1 206 B4
Selkirk Ave HP19 101 D2
Selkirk Gr MK3 46 F2
Selwood Cl TW19 213 C1
Selwood Gdns TW19 213 C1
Selwood Way HP13 161 E2
Selworthy MK4 46 D3
Selwyn Cl SL4 209 E5
Selwyn Ct HP21 116 B6
Selwyn Gr MK3 58 B8
Selwyn Pl SL1 204 F6
September Ct UB10 201 D3
Serjeants Gn MK14 34 F6
Serles Cl MK6 47 A6
Sermed Ct SL2 206 C5
Serpentine Ct MK2 58 D5
Servite Ho SL6 203 B8
Seven Acre Ho HP10 174 C2
Seven Acres HP18 125 B7
Seven Gables MK18 65 D6
Sevenhills Rd SL0 200 C6
Severalls Ave HP5 144 C2
Severn Cres SL3 207 B1
Severn Dr MK16 22 E4
Severn Ho HP13 173 F7
Severn Way MK3 57 D8
Sewell Cl HP19 100 F2
Seymour Cl
Flackwell Heath HP10 173 F2
Maidenhead SL6 202 B3
Seymour Court La SL7 183 B5
Seymour Court Rd SL7 183 C4
Seymour Ct
Berkhamsted HP4 134 E6
Tring HP23 119 A4
Seymour Ho
High Wycombe HP12 172 E4
Slough SL3 206 E4
Seymour Park Rd SL7 183 D3
Seymour Plain SL7 183 C5
Seymour Rd
Berkhamsted HP4 134 E6
Chalfont St Giles HP8 177 C6
Seymour Rd *continued*
Slough SL1 205 D4
SHABBINGTON 124 D3
Shackerstone Cl MK10 36 B4
Shackleton Ct 6 TW19 213 E1
Shackleton Pl MK6 34 E1
Shackleton Rd
High Wycombe HP12 172 E5
Slough SL1 205 F6
Shaftesbury Cres MK3 47 A1
Shaftesbury Ct
Maidenhead SL6 202 E5
6 Slough SL1 205 E4
Winslow MK18 65 F5
Shaftesbury Ho HP21 116 C7
Shaftesbury St HP11 172 F8
Shaggy Calf La SL2 206 A6
Shakespeare Cl MK16 22 A5
Shakespeare Lodge SL1 204 F5
Shakespeare Orch HP18 82 F6
Shakespeare Way HP20 116 A8
Shallowford Gr MK4 46 D4
SHALSTONE 39 E6
Shamaa Ho 13 SL1 205 F4
Shamrock Cl MK7 48 B6
Shannon Ct
Chesham HP5 144 C1
Milton Keynes MK14 35 A6
Shantock Hall La HP3 145 E1
Shantock La HP3 145 E1
Shantung Pl HP5 154 C6
Shardeloes HP7 164 D8
Sharkham Ct MK4 46 B1
Sharman Row 8 SL3 206 F1
Sharman Wlk MK13 34 A3
Sharney Ave SL3 207 B3
Sharp Cl HP21 115 E5
Sharp's Cl HP18 99 B6
Sharrow Vale HP12 172 E7
Shaw Cl
Aylesbury HP20 116 A8
Newport Pagnell MK16 22 A5
Shaw Ct
Aylesbury HP21 115 E3
Old Windsor SL4 211 A2
Shawfield Ct UB7 208 E3
Shaw Gdns 11 SL3 206 F1
Shaws Cl HP16 151 D5
Shaw The SL6 195 E6
Shearmans MK11 33 A4
Sheehy Way SL2 206 B6
Sheelin Gr MK2 58 D4
Sheepcoat Cl MK5 46 A5
Sheepcote Cl HP9 175 C4
Sheepcote Dell Rd HP15 163 E7
Sheepcote Gdns UB9 190 A5
Sheepcote La HP10, SL1 186 A2
Sheepcote Rd
Eton Wick SL4 205 A1
Windsor SL4 209 E5
Sheepfold La HP7 165 D7
Sheephouse Rd SL6 196 B2
SHEEPLANE 60 C2
Sheeplane MK17 60 C2
SHEEPRIDGE 184 E7
Sheepridge La SL7, SL8 184 E7
Sheep St MK18 66 A4
Sheering Gr MK13 34 B8
Sheerness Ct MK4 57 A8
Sheerstock HP17 126 E5
Sheerwater HP19 101 E4
Sheet St SL4 210 D6
Sheet Street Rd SL4 210 C2
Sheffield Dr HP21 115 E6
Sheffield Rd SL1 205 C7
Shelburne Ct HP12 172 E4
Shelburne Rd HP12 172 E4
Sheldon Ct MK8 33 F1
Sheldon Rd HP18 124 A3
Sheldon Way HP4 135 A5
Shelduck Cl 3 HP20 101 E3
Shelley Cl
Medmenham SL7 193 D7
Newport Pagnell MK16 22 B4
Slough SL3 206 F1
Wooburn Green HP10 185 E8
Shelley Dr MK3 57 F7
Shelley Rd
Chesham HP5 144 B2
High Wycombe HP11 172 F5
12 Marlow SL7 183 F3
Shellfield Cl TW19 213 A2
Shelsley Ave MK6 47 C5
Shelsmore MK14 35 A8
Shelton Ct
Slough SL3 206 C3
Woburn Sands MK17 49 B4
SHENLEY BROOK END 46 A2
Shenley Brook End Sch MK5 46 A2
SHENLEY CHURCH END 45 E6
Shenley L Ctr MK5 46 A7
SHENLEY LODGE 46 C5
Shenley Rd
Milton Keynes, Bletchley MK3 46 E1
Milton Keynes, Loughton MK5 46 A7
Whaddon MK17 56 C8
Shenley Rdbt MK5 46 A5
SHENLEY WOOD 45 F4
Shenston Ct 13 SL4 210 C6
Shenstone Dr SL1 197 D1
Shenstone Hill HP4 135 E5
Shenton MK10 36 C3
Shepherd Cl HP20 102 A2
Shepherds MK11 33 A4
Shepherds Cl
Beaconsfield HP9 175 F1
Hurley SL6 193 F3
Uxbridge UB8 201 C1
Shepherds Ct SL4 209 E5
Shepherds Fold HP15 163 D8
Shepherds Gate HP16 152 A2
Shepherds La
Beaconsfield HP9 175 F1
Hazlemere HP15 162 F5
Hurley SL6 193 E4
Shepherd's La WD3 167 E2
Shepherds Row MK18 66 A4
Shepherds Way HP5 154 D6
Shepherdswell Sch MK6 35 B2
Sheppards Cl MK16 22 C4
Shepperds Cl MK18 76 A2
Shepperds Gn MK5 45 F6
Shepperton Cl MK19 19 F5
Sheraton Dr HP13 162 D1
Sheraton Ho WD3 167 C5
Sherborne Cl SL3 212 E6
Sherborne Ct SL6 202 E5
Sherbourne Dr
Bow Brickhill MK7 48 B4
Maidenhead SL6 202 C3
Windsor SL4 209 F3
Sherbourne Wlk SL2 198 C8
Shereway HP19 115 B8
Shergold Way SL6 195 F6
Sheridan Cl HP21 115 D3
Sheridan Ct
High Wycombe HP12 172 C3
Maidenhead SL6 203 B8
Slough SL1 204 E6
Sheridan Gr MK4 45 D2
Sheriff Cl HP19 115 B8
Sheringham Ct SL6 202 E7
SHERINGTON 14 A2
Sherington CE Fst Sch MK16 14 A2
Sherington Rd MK16 22 E7
Sherman Rd SL1 205 E8
Shernfold MK7 48 B7
Sherriff Cotts HP18 99 A7
Sherwood Cl SL3 206 E3
Sherwood Ct
Colnbrook SL3 212 D7
10 Slough SL3 206 F1
Sherwood Dr
Maidenhead SL6 202 A6
Milton Keynes MK1, MK2, MK3 47 B1
Shields Ct HP10 163 B1
Shifford Cres SL6 195 E3
Shilling Cl MK15 35 A7
Shillingridge Pk SL7 182 E5
Shinfield Cl MK18 63 D2
Ship Hill SL1 186 E4
Ship La LU7 105 D3
Shiplake Ho SL8 185 B4
Shipley Rd MK16 22 B4
Shipman Ct MK15 35 B7
Ship Rd LU7 80 E6
Ship St HP11 173 A7
SHIPTON 66 B3
Shipton MK18 66 B3
Shipton Hill MK13 34 B6
SHIPTON LEE 84 D7
Shipton Rd UB10 201 F8
Shire Ct MK14 35 A5
Shire La
Chalfont St Peter HP8, SL9 178 B6
Cholesbury HP23 133 B4
Chorleywood WD3 167 C4
North Crawley MK16 24 E4
Shires Bsns Pk The NN13 38 A6
Shires Rd NN13 38 A6
Shirley Ave SL4 209 F6
Shirley Cl HP20 101 D2
Shirley Moor MK7 48 B8
Shirley Rd SL6 202 C5
Shirwell Cres MK4 46 D5
Shogmoor La RG9 170 C1
Shootacre Cnr HP27 149 A8
Shootacre La HP27 149 A8
SHOOTERSWAY 134 E4
Shootersway HP4 134 E4
Shootersway La HP4 134 F4
Shootersway Pk HP4 134 F3

Shop La NN7 1 B6
Shoppenhanger's Rd SL6 202 E4
Shorediche Cl UB10 190 F1
Shoreham Rise SL2 197 D1
Shoreham Road (E) TW6 213 E2
Shoreham Road (W) TW6 213 E2
Shorham Rise MK8 33 E2
Shortborough Ave HP27 139 B5
Short Ditch HP17 127 A7
Shortfern SL2 206 C7
Short Hale LU7 105 D3
Short Massey MK46 6 E5
Short Rd TW6 213 E1
Short St HP11 172 F7
Shortway
Amersham HP6 154 D2
Chesham HP5 144 B2
Shotfield Rd HP14 171 C4
Shothanger Way HP3 146 D6
Shouler Cl MK5 46 A5
SHREDING GREEN 207 C7
Shrewsbury Cl MK10 36 A2
Shrimpton Cl HP9 175 D6
Shrimpton Rd
Beaconsfield HP9 175 D6
High Wycombe HP12 172 B3
Shropshire Ct MK3 46 E1
Shrubbery Cl HP13 173 B8
Shrubbery Rd HP13 173 B8
Shrublands Ave HP4 135 A4
Shrublands Rd HP4 135 A5
Shucklow Hill MK17 55 E3
Shugars Gn HP23 119 B5
Shupp's La HP18 112 B1
Shutlanger Rd NN12 9 A8
Shuttleworth Gr MK7 48 D6
Siareys Cl OX39 147 C6
Sibleys Rise HP16 152 D8
Side Rd UB9 189 D4
Sidings Ind Est The NN13 38 A8
Sidings The
Loudwater HP11 174 B3
Milton Keynes MK2 47 E1
Sidlow Ct MK11 32 F4
Sidney Cl UB8 201 C5
Sidney Ho HP14 171 C5
Sidney Rd SL4 209 C4
Sidney Terr HP22 131 B5
Silbury Arc MK9 34 E3
Silbury Bvd MK9 34 D2
Silbury Rdbt MK9 34 C1
Silchester Ho SL6 203 B8
Silco Dr SL6 202 E6
Silicon Ct MK5 46 C5
Silk Mill Way HP23 119 A5
Silk St HP18 99 A6
Silkwood Ct SL1 205 F6
Sillswood MK46 6 E4
Silsden Cres HP8 177 D7
Silverbeck Way TW19 213 A2
Silver Birch Cl UB10 201 E8
Silver Birch Dr HP27 149 E5
Silverbirches La MK17 49 A2
Silver Birch Way HP22 116 B4
Silver Cl SL6 202 A5
Silverdale Cl
4 Aylesbury HP20 101 D1
Tylers Green HP10 163 A1
Silver End MK46 7 A3
Silver Hill HP8 177 B8
Silvermead HP18 123 D5
Silver St
20 Aylesbury HP20 115 D8
Cublington LU7 78 B1
Milton Keynes MK11 32 D5
Newport Pagnell MK16 22 D4
Silverstone Mews SL6 202 C4
Silverstone Motor Racing Circuit* MK18 28 F8
Silvertrees Dr SL6 202 A5
Silverweed Ct MK7 48 B5
Simatt Ho HP10 174 C2
Simdims MK43 25 A1
Simmons Cl SL3 207 A2
Simmons Ct
Aylesbury HP21 115 E4
High Wycombe HP12 172 E7
Simmons Rd RG9 191 D3
Simmons Way
Lane End HP14 171 C4
Thame OX9 125 F1
Simms Croft MK10 36 A2
Simnel MK6 47 B6
Simon Dean HP3 146 A4
Simonsbath MK4 46 D2
Simons Lea MK13 34 B4
Simon's Way MK18 39 E7
Simpson Cl SL6 203 B8
Simpson Dr MK6 47 E5
Simpson Pl HP21 115 F5
Simpson Rd MK1, MK2, MK6 47 E3
Simpson Rdbt MK6 47 D5
Simpson Sch MK6 47 D5
Simpsons Way SL1 205 E5
Sinatra Dr MK4 45 E3
Sinclair Ct MK1 47 B3
Sinclair Rd SL4 210 C4
Singers La RG9 191 E1
SINGLEBOROUGH 54 F5
Singleborough La MK17 54 F3
Singleton Dr MK8 45 D6
Singleton Way 8 HP19 115 A8
Singret Pl UB8 201 C1
Sion Terr MK18 51 B6
Sipson Rd UB7 208 F3
Sipthorp Cl MK7 48 C6
Sir Henry Floyd Gram Sch HP21 115 C7
Sir Henry Peakes Dr SL2 198 A6
Sir Peter's Way HP4 107 E6
Sir Robert Mews SL3 207 A1
Sir Sydney Camm Ho SL4 210 B6
Sir William Borlase's Gram Sch SL7 183 C1
Sir William Ramsay Sch HP15 163 A3
Sissinghurst Dr MK4 45 E2
Sitwell Cl MK16 21 F5
Six Cotts MK18 29 E5
Sixth St HP11 173 C4
Sixty Acres Rd HP16 151 C6
Skeats Wharf MK15 35 A7
Skeldon Gate MK14 35 A4
Skeldon Rdbt MK9 35 A4
Skelton Cl HP9 186 A8
Skene Cl MK2 58 C4
Skerries Ct SL3 207 A2
Skimmers Cl HP15 163 C6
Skimmers End HP15 163 C6
Skimmers Field HP15 163 C6
Skip La UB9 190 E3
Skipper Cl HP19 101 C4
Skippon Way OX9 125 F2
Skipton Cl MK15 35 C6
SKIRMETT 170 A1
Skittle Gn HP27 138 A2
SKITTLE GREEN 138 A3
Skydmore Path SL2 197 F1
Skye Cres
Milton Keynes MK17 58 C3
Milton Keynes MK17 58 C3
Skye Lodge SL1 205 E5
Skylark Rd UB9 189 C3
Skyline Mews HP12 172 C4
Skyport Dr UB7 213 D7
Skyway 14 Trad Est SL3 212 F4
Slade Hill
Aylesbury HP19 115 A7
Mixbury NN13 38 D1
Slade La MK11 33 A4
Slade Oak La UB9 189 C5
Slade Rd HP14 158 E4
Slade The MK17 57 D3
Slad La HP27 149 F3
SLAPTON 91 C5
Slapton La LU6 91 F6
Slated Row MK12 33 B7
Slated Row Specl Sch MK12 33 A7
Slatepits Croft MK46 6 E5
Slater St HP13 173 C6
Slattenham Cl HP19 115 B7
Slave Hill HP17 126 F5
Slayter Rd HP14 171 C4
Slickett's La LU6 92 F3
Slipe The LU7 105 A7
SLOUGH 205 D5
Slough & Eton CE Sch SL1 205 D3
Slough Gram Sch SL3 206 B3
Slough Ice Arena SL1 205 D4
Slough Interchange Ind Est SL2 206 A5
Slough La HP14 160 C6
Slough Mus* SL1 206 A4
Slough Rd
Datchet SL3 211 B8
Iver Heath SL0 200 E3
Slough SL4 205 E2
Slough Sta SL1 205 F5
Slough Trad Est SL1 205 B7
Sly Corner HP16 142 E4
Smabridge Wlk MK15 35 D7
SMAE Inst The SL6 202 B6
Small Cres MK18 52 F8
Smalldean La HP27 149 E2
Smarden Bell MK7 48 B8
Smeaton Cl
Aylesbury HP19 101 A1
Blakelands MK14 22 A2
Smewin Ct HP11 172 E7
Smith Cl HP20 116 B7
Smith Ctr The RG9 191 B5
Smithergill Ct MK13 34 C5
Smithfield End MK17 66 F4
Smithfield Rd SL6 202 A3
Smith's La
Waterperry Common OX33 122 F7
Windsor SL4 209 E6
Smithsons Pl MK9 35 B3
Smithy The MK19 31 E4
Snaith Cres MK5 46 B7
Snakeley Cl HP10 174 C1
Snakemoor Nature Reserve* HP17 126 D6
Snape Spur SL1 205 E7
Snells La HP7 166 C7
Snells Wood Ct HP7 166 C7
SNELSHALL EAST 57 B7
Snelshall St MK4 56 F8
SNELSHALL WEST 57 A7
Snowball Hill SL6 202 A1
Snowberry Cl MK12 33 D5
Snowden Cl SL4 209 D3
Snowdon Dr MK6 46 D7
Snowdrop Way HP15 162 F7
Snowhill Cotts HP5 144 F7
Snowshill Ct MK14 21 F2
Soames Cl MK46 7 F7
Soane Wlk HP13 173 A8
Soho Cres HP10 185 D4
Soho Mills Ind Est HP10 185 D4
Sokeman Cl MK12 33 A5
Solar Ct MK14 21 E1
Solesbridge Cl WD3 167 F6
Solesbridge La WD3 167 F6
Somerford Cl SL6 203 B8
Somerford Pl HP9 175 D3
Somerlea SL6 196 C3
Somersby Cres SL6 202 E3
Somerset Cl MK3 46 F1
Somerset Lodge 3 SL6 202 F6
Somerset Way SL0 207 F4
Somers Lees 13 HP19 115 A8
Somerville Rd SL4 205 C1
Somerville Way HP19 115 B8
Sophie Gdns SL3 206 D4
Sorensen Ct MK5 45 E4
Sorrell Dr MK16 21 F4
Soskin Dr MK14 34 D6
Sospel Ct SL2 198 C3
SOULBURY 69 E3
Soulbury LU7 69 E2
Soulbury Rd
Burcott LU7 79 D4
Leighton Buzzard LU7 80 D7
Stewkley LU7 68 F1
Southampton Road E TW6 213 F1
Southampton Road W TW6 213 E1
South Bank NN13 38 C7
South Bank Rd HP4 134 F6
Southbourne 1 HP13 173 C7
Southbourne Dr SL8 185 A3
Southbridge Gr MK7 48 A7
South Cl
Medmenham SL7 193 D7
Slough SL1 204 D6
West Drayton UB7 208 F3
Southcliffe Dr SL9 177 E5
South Common Rd UB8 201 E6
Southcote Way HP10 163 B1
South Cottage Dr WD3 167 F4
South Cottage Gdns WD3 167 F4
Southcott Lower Sch LU7 80 D8
Southcott Village LU7 80 D6
Southcott Way MK6 47 D5
SOUTHCOURT 115 D6
Southcourt Ave LU7 80 D6
Southcourt Ho LU7 80 D7
Southcourt Rd LU7 80 D7
Southcroft SL2 198 B1
South Dr
Beaconsfield HP9 186 B8
High Wycombe HP13 173 D8
South Eighth St MK9 34 E2
SOUTHEND 180 C8
SOUTH END
Leckhampstead 42 E7
Stewkley 78 E8
South End HP17 126 F5
South End La LU6 92 B4
South Enmore Rdbt MK6 35 B3
Southern Cotts TW19 213 A2
Southern Perimeter Rd TW6, TW19 213 D2
Southern Rd
Aylesbury HP19 101 C1
Thame OX9 125 E1
Southern Way MK12 33 D5
Southfield Cl MK15 35 E7
South Field Cl SL4 204 C3
Southfield Cotts HP17 130 C3
Southfield Dr HP15 163 A6
Southfield Gdns SL1 204 B8
Southfield Rd
Aylesbury HP20 116 B8
Flackwell Heath HP10 174 A1
High Wycombe HP13 161 D1
Princes Risborough HP27 139 C3
South Fifth St MK9 34 E1
South Fourth St MK9 34 D1
Southgate Ho SL6 202 F8
South Gn SL1 205 E6
South Hall MK18 41 E3
SOUTH HAREFIELD 190 D6
SOUTH HEATH 152 E8
South Hills HP18 96 A1
South Ho MK1 47 D3
South La LU7 78 E7
Southland Dr MK2 58 E6
Southlands Rd UB9 189 F1
South Lawne MK3 57 F8
Southlea Rd SL3, SL4 211 B5
South Maundin HP14 162 A7
South Meadow La SL4 210 C8
South Ninth St MK9 34 F2
South Overgate Rdbt MK6 35 B3
South Park Ave WD3 167 F4
South Park Cres SL9 188 F7
South Park Ct SL9 188 E6
South Park Dr SL9 188 E7
South Park Gdns HP4 135 B5
South Park View SL9 188 F7
South Path SL4 210 C5
South Pk SL9 188 F6
South Pl SL7 183 E1
South Rd
Amersham HP6 154 C3
Chorleywood WD3 167 C4
Maidenhead SL6 202 E6
West Drayton UB7 208 F3
South Row
Fulmer SL3 199 E8
Milton Keynes MK9 34 E1
Milton Keynes MK9 46 D8
South Saxon Rdbt MK9 34 F1
South Secklow Rdbt MK6 34 F2
South Second St MK9 34 D1
South Seventh St MK9 34 E1
South Side SL9 188 D8
South Sixth St MK9 34 E1
South St
Castlethorpe MK19 19 F5
Wendover HP22 131 B4
South Tenth St MK9 34 F2
South Terr
Milton Keynes MK2 58 C8
Windsor SL4 210 E6
South Vale NN7 1 A5
South View
Cookham Rise SL6 195 E7
Eton SL4 205 B1
High Wycombe HP13 161 D2
Wooburn Green HP10 185 D8
Southview Rd SL7 183 E4
South View Rd SL9 188 D7
South Way HP9 186 A8
Southwick Ct MK8 45 F8
South Witan Rdbt MK6 34 E1
Southwold Cl HP21 116 A6
Southwold Spur SL3 207 C4
Southwood Gdns SL6 195 E5
Southwood Rd SL6 195 E5
Southwood Sch MK14 34 E5
Sovereign Beeches SL2 198 B6
Sovereign Cl MK18 75 F7
Sovereign Ct
Aylesbury HP19 101 D1
High Wycombe HP13 173 D6
Sovereign Dr MK15 35 A7
Sovereign Hts SL3 212 A8
Sovereign Lodge MK15 35 A7
Spackmans Way SL1 205 D3
Spa Cl HP18 110 B8
Spade Oak Farm SL8 184 E3
Spade Oak Mdw SL8 184 E4
Spark Way MK16 21 F5
Sparrow Cl HP19 101 F3
Sparrow Hall Bsns Pk LU6 92 D3
Sparrow Hall Farm LU6 92 D3
Sparsholt Cl 5 MK4 46 C2
Spearing Rd HP12 172 C7
Spearmast Ind Est HP12 172 B6
Spearmint Cl MK7 48 B5
Specklands MK5 46 A8
Speedbird Way UB7 213 B7
Speedwell Pl MK14 34 E4
SPEEN 150 C4
Speen CE Sch HP27 150 B4
Speen Rd HP14, HP16, HP27 150 D2
Speldhurst Ct MK7 48 B7
Spencer MK14 34 C8
Spencer Cl UB8 201 C2
Spencer Gdns OX27 72 E5
Spencer Rd SL3 206 F3
Spencers Cl SL6 202 D8
SPENCERSGREEN 132 C7
Spencers La SL6 195 E6
Spencers Rd SL6 202 D8
Spencer St MK13 33 F7
Spencer Villas SL1 204 F5
Spenlows Rd MK3 47 A3
Spens SL6 202 F8
Spenser Ho HP21 115 F6
Spenser Rd HP21 115 F6
Sperling Rd SL6 195 F1
Spickett's La HP18 113 A3
Spier's La OX27 71 F2
Spiert The HP17 114 D5
Spindle Cl HP15 163 A3
Spindle Ct HP12 172 E7
Spinfield La SL7 183 B2
Spinfield Lane W SL7 183 C1
Spinfield Mount SL7 183 B1
Spinfield Pk SL7 183 C1
Spinfield Sch SL7 183 B2
Spinners Wlk
Marlow SL7 183 C1
Windsor SL4 210 C6
Spinney SL1 205 B5
Spinney Bglws LU7 91 C6
Spinney Cl
Steeple Claydon MK18 63 E2
West Drayton UB7 208 E6
Spinney Cotts OX33 123 B1
Spinney Cres LU6 93 F8
Spinney Hill Rd MK46 6 E3
Spinney La MK17 49 F4
Spinney The
Beaconsfield HP9 175 E1
Berkhamsted HP4 134 F3
Chesham HP5 144 D2
Gerrards Cross SL9 188 D3
High Wycombe HP11 173 A4
Holmer Green HP15 163 D7
Milton Keynes MK13 34 A4
Winslow MK18 66 A6
Spire View TW19 213 D1
SPITAL 210 B3
Spitfire Cl SL3 207 A2
Spittal St SL7 183 D2
Spoondell LU6 93 F7
Spoonley Wood MK13 33 E5
Sportsman Cl MK18 63 D3
Spout La TW19 213 A3
Spout Lane N TW19 213 B3
SPRIG'S ALLEY 147 F1
Sprigs Holly La HP14 159 B8
Springate Field SL3 206 E4
Springbank Ct MK16 12 B7
Spring Cl
High Wycombe HP13 173 F7
Latimer HP5 155 D3
Maidenhead SL6 195 F2
Milton Keynes MK17 55 A2
Spring Coppice HP14 171 F5
Spring Coppice La HP27 150 D5
Springdale Cotts SL8 185 B2
Springett Pl HP6 154 F2
SPRINGFIELD 35 B2
Springfield SL1 206 A3
Springfield Bvd MK6 35 B2
Springfield Cl
Aylesbury HP21 115 C8
Chesham HP5 154 C7
Windsor SL4 210 B5
Springfield Ct
1 Leighton Buzzard LU7 80 E7
1 Maidenhead SL6 203 B7
Milton Keynes MK6 35 B2
Springfield Gdns
Chinnor OX39 147 C7
Deanshanger MK19 31 E4
Springfield Hollow HP14 158 E5
Springfield Pk SL6 203 C1
Springfield Rd
Chesham HP5 154 C7
Dunstable LU6 93 D5
Leighton Buzzard LU7 80 E7
Olney MK46 6 F4
Slough SL3 212 B7
Stokenchurch HP14 158 F4
Windsor SL4 210 B5
Spring Field Rd HP4 135 A6
Springfield Rdbt MK6 35 A2
Springfields
Amersham HP6 154 C2
Padbury MK18 53 C1
Tylers Green HP10 163 C2
Springfields Cl MK18 53 C2
Springfields Ct MK18 53 C1
Springfield Way MK43 25 C2
Spring Gardens Rd HP13 173 E5
Spring Gdn La HP4 134 D5
Spring Gdns
Bourne End SL8 185 A4
Marlow SL7 183 E3
Newport Pagnell MK16 22 C4
Wooburn Green HP10 185 E8
Spring Gr MK17 49 B5
Spring Hill SL6 202 E3
Springhill Rd HP18 83 A8

Spring Ho SL7 .... 183 E3
Spring La
Alderton NN12 .... 9 A2
Clifton Reynes MK46 .... 7 C3
Cookham Dean SL6 .... 195 C5
Farnham Common SL2 .... 198 C5
Flackwell Heath HP10 .... 173 F3
Great Horwood MK17 .... 55 A2
Olney MK46 .... 6 F3
Slough SL1 .... 204 F5
Spring Mdw HP18 .... 97 A1
Springs Cl HP17 .... 130 B2
Springside 2 LU7 .... 80 E7
Springs La HP17 .... 130 B3
Spring Valley Dr HP14 .... 162 A7
Springwater Mill HP11 .... 173 E4
Springwood HP27 .... 150 C4
Sprinters L Ctr HP16 .... 151 A7
Sproggit Ind Est TW19 .... 213 F1
Spruce Ct 7 SL1 .... 205 F3
Spruce Dene HP15 .... 162 F2
Spruce Rd 1 HP19 .... 100 F1
SPURGROVE 170 E2
Spurgrove La RG9 .... 170 E2
SPURLANDS END 163 A8
Spurlands End Rd
HP15 .... 163 A8
Spur The SL1 .... 204 D8
Spurt St HP18 .... 112 F3
Square Close Cotts
RG9 .... 169 F3
Square The
Akeley MK18 .... 41 F8
Aspley Guise MK17 .... 49 E4
Brill HP18 .... 110 A8
Great Missenden HP16 .... 152 B7
Harmondsworth UB7 .... 213 B6
Long Crendon HP18 .... 125 C6
Milton Keynes MK12 .... 33 D6
Preston Bissett MK18 .... 62 B8
Waddesdon HP18 .... 99 A6
Yardley Hastings NN7 .... 1 A6
Squires Cl MK6 .... 47 A6
Squirrel La HP12 .... 172 C5
Squirrel Rise SL7 .... 183 D6
Squirrels Way MK18 .... 52 E7
Stablebridge Rd HP22 .... 117 F3
Stable Cl MK18 .... 50 C7
Stable Cotts SL7 .... 194 C5
Stable La HP9 .... 176 C4
Stable Rd HP22 .... 131 E7
Stables Ct SL7 .... 183 B1
Stables The MK19 .... 20 F3
Stacey Ave MK12 .... 33 D6
STACEY BUSHES 33 E4
Stacey Bushes Trad Ctr
MK12 .... 33 E4
Stacey Ho HP12 .... 172 E4
Stacey's Ct HP8 .... 177 C8
Staddle Stones HP27 .... 139 B4
Stadium App HP21 .... 115 E4
StadiumMK (MK Dons FC)
MK1 .... 47 C3
Stafferton Way SL6 .... 203 A6
Stafford Ave SL2 .... 198 C1
Stafford Cl SL6 .... 204 B7
Stafford Gr MK5 .... 46 B6
Stafford Keep HP19 .... 115 A8
Stag Ct WD3 .... 167 C5
Stag La
Berkhamsted HP4 .... 135 B5
Chorleywood WD3 .... 167 C3
Great Kingshill HP15 .... 151 D1
STAGSDEN WEST END 16 F4
Stagshaw Gr 5 MK4 .... 46 B2
Stainby Cl UB7 .... 208 E3
Stainton Dr MK13 .... 34 C4
Stamford Ave MK6 .... 35 B2
Stamford Rd SL6 .... 202 C6
Stanbridge Cl HP17 .... 127 A7
Stanbridge Ct MK11 .... 32 F5
Stanbridge Rd HP17 .... 127 B6
Stanbrook Pl MK10 .... 36 A1
Standfield Cl HP19 .... 115 A8
Standing Way
Milton Keynes, Coldharbour Spinney MK3, MK4 .... 46 E3
Milton Keynes, Kingston MK10 .... 36 C1
Milton Keynes, Peartree Bridge MK10, MK4, MK6 .... 47 C7
Milton Keynes, Snelshall East MK4 .... 57 B7
Standring Pl HP20 .... 101 F2
Stanhope Cl HP22 .... 131 B7
Stanhope Heath TW19 .... 213 C1
Stanhope Rd
Aylesbury HP20 .... 116 A8
Slough SL1 .... 204 D7
Stanhope Way TW19 .... 213 C1
Stanier Rise HP4 .... 134 F7
Stanier Sq 5 MK2 .... 58 C8
Stanley Ave HP5 .... 154 B8
Stanley Cl
Marlow SL7 .... 183 F3
Uxbridge UB8 .... 201 D3
Stanley Cotts SL2 .... 205 F5
Stanley Ct MK46 .... 6 F3
Stanley Gdns HP23 .... 118 F3
Stanley Green E SL3 .... 206 F2
Stanley Green W SL3 .... 206 F2
Stanley Hill HP7 .... 165 E7
Stanley Hill Ave HP7 .... 165 E8
Stanley Ho SL4 .... 211 A2
Stanley Rd HP12 .... 172 C7
Stanley Spencer Gall★
SL6 .... 196 B7
Stanmore Gdns MK16 .... 22 B2
Stanstead Pl HP7 .... 165 C8
Stanton Ave MK13 .... 34 A6
STANTONBURY 34 D7
Stantonbury Campus
MK14 .... 34 C7
Stantonbury Campus L Ctr
MK14 .... 34 C7
Stantonbury Cl MK13 .... 34 A8
Stanton Gate MK14 .... 34 D8
Stanton Mid Sch MK13 .... 34 B7
Stanton Way SL3 .... 206 E2
Stanton Wood Rdbt
MK14 .... 34 D4
Stanway Cl MK15 .... 35 B6
STANWELL 213 C1
Stanwell Cl TW19 .... 213 D1
Stanwell Fields CE Prim Sch TW19 .... 213 E1
Stanwell Gdns TW19 .... 213 D1
STANWELL MOOR 212 E1
Stanwell Moor Rd TW6, TW19, UB7 .... 213 B4
Stanwell Rd SL3 .... 212 C4
Stanwyck La 4 MK4 .... 45 D2
Stapeley Ct 1 MK4 .... 45 F1
Stapleford Mill★ LU7 .... 70 B5
Staple Hall Rd MK1 .... 47 E1
Stapleton Cl SL7 .... 183 F4
Stars La HP17 .... 113 E2
Startins La SL6 .... 195 C8
STARTOP'S END 104 F1
Starveall Cl UB7 .... 208 F3
Starwood Ct 1 SL3 .... 206 C3
Staters Pound MK15 .... 35 A7
Statham Pl MK6 .... 46 F8
Station App
Amersham HP6 .... 154 C1
Chorleywood WD3 .... 167 D5
Denham UB9 .... 189 D4
Gerrards Cross SL9 .... 188 E6
Great Missenden HP16 .... 152 A7
Little Chalfont HP7 .... 166 D8
Maidenhead SL6 .... 202 F6
Marlow SL7 .... 183 E2
Wendover HP22 .... 131 B4
West Drayton UB7 .... 208 E5
Station Bvd HP20 .... 115 D8
Station Cotts
Denham UB9 .... 190 A4
Winslow MK18 .... 66 A5
Station Hill SL6 .... 195 F7
Station Par
Beaconsfield HP9 .... 175 D3
Cookham Rise SL8 .... 195 F6
Denham Green UB9 .... 190 A4
Station Rd
Aldbury HP23 .... 120 B5
Amersham HP7 .... 165 C8
Beaconsfield HP9 .... 175 E2
Berkhamsted HP4 .... 135 D4
Blackthorn OX25 .... 81 A4
Bourne End SL8 .... 185 A3
Bow Brickhill MK17 .... 48 C2
Buckingham MK18 .... 52 C7
Castlethorpe MK19 .... 19 F5
Cheddington LU7 .... 91 A1
Chesham HP5 .... 154 C8
Chinnor OX39 .... 147 C6
Cookham Rise SL6 .... 195 F7
Gerrards Cross SL9 .... 188 E6
Haddenham HP17 .... 126 E5
Henley-on-Thames RG9 .... 191 E1
High Wycombe HP13 .... 173 C6
Ivinghoe LU7 .... 105 E5
Leighton Buzzard LU7 .... 80 E7
Little Kimble HP17 .... 129 E2
Long Marston HP23 .... 104 B4
Loudwater HP10 .... 174 C2
Marlow SL7 .... 183 E1
Marsh Gibbon OX27 .... 71 F3
Mursley MK17 .... 67 B7
Newport Pagnell MK16 .... 22 C4
Padbury MK18 .... 53 B1
Princes Risborough HP27 .... 139 A2
Quainton HP22 .... 85 A4
Slough, Langley SL3 .... 207 A4
Slough SL1 .... 204 E7
Stoke Mandeville HP22 .... 116 B2
Swanbourne MK17 .... 67 A4
Taplow SL6 .... 203 F7
Tring HP23 .... 119 D4
Uxbridge UB8 .... 201 D1
West Drayton UB7 .... 208 E4
Winslow MK18 .... 66 A5
Woburn Sands MK17 .... 49 B5
Wraysbury TW19 .... 212 A1
Station Rd Ind Est MK18 .... 66 A5
Station Rise SL7 .... 183 E2
Station Sq MK9 .... 34 C1
Station Terr
Buckingham MK18 .... 52 C7
Milton Keynes MK14 .... 21 E2
Station Way E HP20 .... 115 D7
Station Way W HP20 .... 115 D7
Staunton Ho MK17 .... 60 F7
Staunton Rd SL2 .... 205 D8
Staveley Cl HP21 .... 116 C6
Staverton Gr MK10 .... 36 B2
Stavordale 2 MK10 .... 36 A1
Staying La MK14 .... 34 F6
Steeple Cl MK4 .... 57 A8
STEEPLE CLAYDON 63 C3
Steeple Claydon Sch
MK18 .... 63 E3
Steinbeck Cres MK4 .... 56 F7
Stephenson Cl
Aylesbury HP19 .... 115 B7
High Wycombe HP13 .... 161 F1
Leighton Buzzard LU7 .... 80 E6
Stephenson Ct 12 SL1 .... 205 F4
Stephenson Dr SL4 .... 210 B7
Stepnells HP23 .... 105 A1
Steppingstones LU6 .... 93 F8
Sterling Bus Pk MK18 .... 52 D6
Sterling Cl MK15 .... 35 A6
Stevens Cl
Holmer Green HP15 .... 163 B7
Prestwood HP16 .... 151 D5
Stevens Field MK7 .... 48 D6
Stevens Ho 8 HP7 .... 165 B7
Stevenson Rd SL2 .... 187 D2
Stewart Ave SL1 .... 205 F8
Stewarts Dr SL2 .... 198 B7
Stewarts Way SL7 .... 183 D7
STEWKLEY 68 E2
STEWKLEY DEAN 68 B1
Stewkley La MK17 .... 67 E4
Stewkley Rd
Cublington LU7 .... 78 C1
Hollingdon LU7 .... 69 C2
Wing LU7 .... 79 B3
Stilebrook Rd MK46 .... 6 F6
Stile Mdw HP9 .... 175 E3
Stile Rd SL3 .... 206 D3
Stilliters Farm Rd MK43 .... 37 E8
Stilwell Dr UB8 .... 201 F1
Stirling Ave HP20 .... 101 E1
Stirling Cl
Uxbridge UB8 .... 201 C2
Windsor SL4 .... 209 D5
Stirling Gr SL6 .... 202 A8
Stirling Ho
2 High Wycombe HP13 .... 173 F7
Milton Keynes MK3 .... 57 D7
Stirling Rd
High Wycombe HP12 .... 172 D5
Slough SL1 .... 205 A8
Stanwell TW6 .... 213 F1
Stockaway HP22 .... 87 C1
Stockdale MK13 .... 34 C5
Stockdales Rd SL4 .... 204 F2
Stocken Cl MK46 .... 6 E4
Stock Field Cl HP15 .... 163 B3
Stockfields Pl HP14 .... 158 D5
Stockgrove Ctry Pk★
LU7 .... 70 F7
Stockgrove Park Ho LU7 .... 70 F8
Stockhall Cres LU7 .... 68 D2
Stocking Green Cl MK19 .... 11 A3
Stocking La HP14 .... 161 E7
Stock La MK17 .... 45 B1
Stocklake HP20 .... 101 F1
Stocklake Ind Est HP20 .... 101 F1
Stocklands Way HP16 .... 151 D5
Stockley Academy UB8 .... 208 F7
Stockleys La MK18 .... 51 B6
Stockport Rd WD3 .... 167 C2
Stocks Cl MK18 .... 65 F4
Stocks Rd HP23 .... 120 C7
Stocks The MK19 .... 19 E2
Stockwell HP17 .... 127 A6
Stockwell Furlong
HP17 .... 127 A6
Stockwell La
Longwick HP17 .... 139 A8
Wavendon MK17 .... 48 D7
Stockwells SL6 .... 196 D1
STOKE BRUERNE 9 B8
Stoke Bruerne CE Prim Sch
NN12 .... 9 A8
Stoke Common Rd SL2, SL3 .... 199 B8
Stoke Court Dr SL2 .... 198 F4
Stoke Farm La HP21 .... 115 E3
Stoke Gdns SL1 .... 205 F5
Stoke Gn SL2 .... 199 A1
STOKE GOLDINGTON 12 A6
Stoke Goldington CE Fst Sch MK16 .... 12 B6
STOKE GREEN 199 B1
STOKE HAMMOND 69 E8
Stoke Ho 2 SL1 .... 205 F3
Stoke La MK17 .... 59 C1
Stoke Leys Cl HP21 .... 115 E3
STOKE MANDEVILLE 116 A2
Stoke Mandeville Comb Sch
HP22 .... 116 A1
Stoke Mandeville Hospl
HP21 .... 115 F4
Stoke Mandeville Sta
HP22 .... 116 B2
STOKENCHURCH 158 E5
Stokenchurch Pl MK13 .... 34 C3
Stokenchurch Prim Sch
HP14 .... 158 E5
Stoke Park Ave SL2 .... 198 C2
STOKE POGES 198 F4
Stoke Poges La SL1 .... 205 E7
Stoke Poges Sch SL2 .... 198 F5
Stoke Rd
Ashton NN7 .... 9 E8
Aylesbury HP21 .... 115 E6
Leighton Buzzard LU7 .... 70 D1
Milton Keynes MK2 .... 58 E5
Newton Longville MK17 .... 57 F3
Slough SL2 .... 205 F7
Stokesay SL2 .... 205 F6
Stokesay Ct MK4 .... 45 E2
Stokes Croft HP17 .... 127 A6
Stokes End HP17 .... 127 A7
Stokes La HP17 .... 127 A7
Stokesley Rise HP10 .... 185 E8
Stoke View SL1 .... 205 F5
Stoke Wood SL2 .... 198 F8
Stolford Rise MK4 .... 46 B1
Stompits Rd SL6 .... 203 C1
Stomp Rd SL1 .... 204 B8
STONE 114 C5
STONEBRIDGE 33 F7
Stonebridge Field SL4 .... 205 B1
Stonebridge Gr MK10 .... 35 E1
Stonebridge Rd HP19 .... 101 B3
Stonebridge Rdbt MK13 .... 33 E8
Stone CE Comb Sch
HP17 .... 114 D5
Stonechat HP19 .... 101 E3
Stone Cl UB7 .... 208 F5
Stonecroft HP6 .... 153 C4
Stone Croft HP17 .... 114 D5
Stonecroft Ave SL0 .... 207 E7
Stonecrop Pl MK14 .... 34 E4
Stone Ct MK46 .... 13 E8
Stonefield Pk SL6 .... 202 C7
Stonefield Rd HP14 .... 161 C8
Stonegate MK13 .... 34 A5
Stonehaven Rd HP19 .... 101 B2
Stone Hill MK8 .... 33 D1
Stone House La SL6 .... 184 C1
Stoneleigh Ct MK4 .... 45 E1
Stonemasons Cl 11 MK46 .... 6 F3
Stone Pit Cl MK46 .... 6 E3
Stonepitts Pk HP18 .... 111 B3
Stones Row HP11 .... 173 F4
Stones Way MK17 .... 68 C6
Stone View HP22 .... 86 D7
Stoney Cl HP4 .... 134 F6
Stoneycroft HP23 .... 120 C5
Stoney Dean Specl Sch
HP7 .... 165 F8
Stoneyfield SL9 .... 188 C3
Stoney Gr HP5 .... 144 D1
Stoney Grove HP5 .... 144 C1
Stoney La
Berkhamsted HP1 .... 146 B8
Bovingdon HP3 .... 146 C5
Chipperfield WD4 .... 146 F1
Cholesbury HP5 .... 133 F1
East Burnham SL2 .... 198 A4
Stoney Meade SL1 .... 205 B5
Stoney Ware SL7 .... 194 E8
STONOR 179 F6
Stonor RG9 .... 179 F6
Stonor Ct MK8 .... 45 F8
Stonor Ho & Gdns★
RG9 .... 180 A7
STONY GREEN 151 A4
Stony Hill NN12 .... 17 C8
Stony La
Little Chalfont HP6 .... 155 F1
Little Kingshill HP16 .... 152 C3
Stookslade HP22 .... 89 A3
Stopps Orch HP27 .... 139 C5
Stork Cl 2 HP19 .... 101 F3
Stornaway Rd SL3 .... 207 C2
Stotfold Ct MK11 .... 32 E4
Stour Cl
Aylesbury HP21 .... 115 C4
Milton Keynes MK3 .... 57 E8
Newport Pagnell MK16 .... 22 E3
Slough SL1 .... 205 B3
Stourhead Gate MK4 .... 45 E2
Stovell Rd SL4 .... 210 B7
Stowe Ave MK18 .... 41 B3
Stowe Cl MK18 .... 41 C1
Stowe Ct MK14 .... 34 C8
Stowe Landscape Gdns★
MK18 .... 40 F7
STOWE PARK 40 F7
Stowe Rd SL1 .... 204 E6
Stowe Rise MK18 .... 41 C1
Stowe Sch MK18 .... 40 F7
Stowe View MK18 .... 51 A7
Straight Bit HP10 .... 185 B8
Straight Mile Rd OX33 .... 108 A5
Straight Rd SL4 .... 211 B1
Strande Pk SL6 .... 195 F5
Strande View Wlk SL6 .... 195 F5
Strand La SL6 .... 195 F5
Strand The HP22 .... 85 B5
Strangers La MK18 .... 51 A6
Strangford Dr MK2 .... 58 C4
Stranraer Gdns SL1 .... 205 E5
Stranraer Rd TW19 .... 213 E1
Stranraer Way 1 TW6 .... 213 E1
Stratfield Ct
Maidenhead SL6 .... 203 B8
Milton Keynes MK8 .... 33 F1
Stratfield Rd SL1 .... 206 A4
Stratford Arc MK11 .... 32 D6
Stratford Ave UB10 .... 201 F3
Stratford Cl
Aylesbury HP22 .... 117 C5
Slough SL2 .... 197 D1
Stratford Dr
Aylesbury HP21 .... 115 B6
Wooburn HP10 .... 185 D4
Stratford Gdns SL6 .... 202 C4
Stratford Rd
Buckingham MK18 .... 41 E1
Cosgrove MK19 .... 19 D1
Deanshanger MK19 .... 31 F4
Maids Moreton MK18 .... 42 C2
Milton Keynes MK12 .... 33 C7
Nash MK17 .... 44 C1
Old Stratford MK19 .... 32 B5
Whaddon MK17 .... 45 A2
Stratfords Way HP17 .... 127 A6
Strathcona Cl HP10 .... 185 C7
Strathcona Way HP10 .... 185 C7
Strathnaver Pl MK12 .... 33 D4
Strathspey Gate MK10 .... 36 C3
Stratton Chase Dr
Chalfont St Giles HP8 .... 177 B8
Chalfont St Peter HP8 .... 177 A8
Stratton Gn HP21 .... 116 B6
Stratton Rd
Beaconsfield HP9 .... 175 B2
Princes Risborough HP27 .... 139 A3
Strauss Gr MK7 .... 48 C4
Strawberry Cl HP16 .... 151 D5
Straws Hadley Ct HP22 .... 89 B2
Streamside SL1 .... 204 F5
Streamside Wlk HP21 .... 115 C6
Streatham Pl MK13 .... 34 C2
Stretton Cl HP10 .... 174 C8
Stretton Pl HP6 .... 154 F1
Stringers Cotts 1 SL9 .... 177 D2
Stringfellow Cl MK43 .... 24 E2
Stroma Ct SL1 .... 204 D6
Stroud Cl SL4 .... 209 D4
Strudwick Dr MK6 .... 46 F8
Stuart Cl
Milton Keynes MK2 .... 47 D1
Windsor SL4 .... 209 F5
Stuart Ct HP6 .... 154 D1
Stuart Rd HP13 .... 173 C6
Stuart Way
Thame OX9 .... 126 A1
Windsor SL4 .... 209 F5
Stubble Hill HP19 .... 115 A8
Stubbles La SL6 .... 195 B6
Stubbs End Cl HP6 .... 154 E2
Stubbs Field MK5 .... 46 A3
Stubbs Wood HP6 .... 154 E3
Stuchbury Cl HP19 .... 115 A8
Studdridge Ct HP14 .... 158 C4
Studham La HP4 .... 107 D4
Studland Cl HP21 .... 116 B5
STUDLEY GREEN 159 E3
Studley Knapp
Milton Keynes MK7 .... 48 B5
Walnut Tree MK7 .... 48 B7
Studridge La HP27 .... 150 B4
Sturges Cl MK7 .... 48 A5
Sturman Ho HP6 .... 154 C2
Stylecroft Rd HP8 .... 177 D8
Styles Cl OX27 .... 71 E2
Styles Ct HP18 .... 99 A7
Sudbury Chase MK10 .... 35 E1
Sudgrove Ho MK15 .... 35 A6
Suffield Rd HP11 .... 172 F6
Suffolk Cl
Milton Keynes MK3 .... 46 F1
Slough SL1 .... 204 E7
Suffolk Ct
Maidenhead SL6 .... 202 F8
Marsh Gibbon OX27 .... 71 F3
Suffolk Ho HP10 .... 185 E6
Suffolk Rd SL6 .... 202 D4
Sulby Cl HP21 .... 115 C5
Sulgrave Cres HP23 .... 119 C5
Sulgrave Ct 3 MK8 .... 45 F8
Sullivan Cres MK7 .... 48 C5
Sultan Croft MK5 .... 46 A4
Sumburgh Way SL1 .... 205 E8
Summerfield Sch MK13 .... 34 C3
Summergill Ct MK13 .... 34 C5
Summerhayes MK14 .... 34 F7
Summerhouse La UB7 .... 213 D8
Summerlea SL1 .... 205 B5
Summerleaze Rd SL6 .... 196 B1

Summerleys LU6 . . . . 92 E4
Summerleys Rd HP27 . . 138 F4
Summerlin Dr MK17 . . . . . 49 B5
Summerson Ct MK6 . . . . . 46 F5
Summerson Rd
Bleak Hall MK6 . . . . 47 A5
Milton Keynes MK6 . . . . . . 46 F5
Summers Rd SL1 . . . . 197 C2
SUMMERSTOWN 72 B2
Summit Ctr UB7 . . . . 213 D7
Sumner Ct MK5 . . . . 46 A8
Sunbury Cl MK13 . . . . 34 A6
Sunbury Ct SL4 . . . . 210 D8
Sunbury Rd SL4 . . . . 210 D8
Sun Cl SL4 . . . . 210 D8
Sun Cres HP18 . . . . 109 D5
Sunderland Ct
Milton Keynes MK4 . . . . . . 45 F1
11 Stanwell TW19 . . . . . . 213 E1
Sunderland Rd SL6 . . . . 202 B8
Sun La SL6 . . . . 202 F7
Sunningdale Cl HP12 . . . 172 B5
Sunningdale Way MK3 . . 57 D8
Sunnybank SL7 . . . . 183 D4
Sunny Bank
Cheddington LU7 . . . . 104 F7
Hazlemere HP15 . . . . 162 F6
Sunny Brook Cl HP22 . . . 117 D6
Sunny Croft HP13 . . . . . . 161 C2
Sunnyhill Rd WD3 . . . . . . 178 D4
SUNNYMEADS 211 E4
Sunnymeads Sta TW19 . 211 E4
Sunnymede Ave HP5 . . . 144 E3
Sunnymede Cotts SL6 . . 196 B1
Sunnyside Cotts HP5 . . . 145 A5
Sunnyside Rd HP5 . . . . . 144 C1
Sunny View NN7 . . . . 1 B6
Sun Pas 15 SL4 . . . . 210 D6
Sunray Ave UB7 . . . . 208 D4
Sunridge Cl MK16 . . . . 22 C3
Sunrise Parkway MK14 . . 34 E6
Sunset Cl MK2 . . . . 58 C7
Sunset Wlk MK9 . . . . 34 E2
Sunters End HP12 . . . . . . 172 A7
Sunters Wood Cl HP12 . 172 B5
Surly Hall Wlk SL4 . . . . . 209 F6
Surrey Ave SL2 . . . . 198 C1
Surrey Pl
Milton Keynes MK3 . . . . . . 46 F2
Tring HP23 . . . . 119 A3
Surrey Rd MK3 . . . . 46 F2
Sussex Cl
Aylesbury HP19 . . . . 101 A3
Chalfont St Giles HP8 . . . 177 B8
High Wycombe HP13 . . . . 162 D1
Slough SL1 . . . . 206 B4
Sussex Ho SL2 . . . . 198 C6
Sussex Keep 7 SL1 . . . . 206 B4
Sussex Lodge 7 SL6 . . . 202 F6
Sussex Pl SL1 . . . . 206 B4
Sussex Rd MK3 . . . . 46 F1
Sutcliffe Ave MK6 . . . . 34 E1
Sutherland Gr MK3 . . . . . . 46 F3
Sutherland Grange
SL4 . . . . 209 D7
Sutherland Grange Nature Reserve* SL4 . . . . 209 D7
Sutherland Wlk HP21 . . . 115 F5
Sutleye Ct MK5 . . . . 46 A5
SUTTON 207 C1
Sutton Ave SL3 . . . . 206 C4
Sutton Cl
Cookham SL6 . . . . 196 B7
Maidenhead SL6 . . . . 202 C5
Tring HP23 . . . . 119 B6
Sutton Ct MK4 . . . . 46 C1
Sutton La SL3 . . . . 207 B1
Sutton Pl SL3 . . . . 212 B8
Sutton Rd SL6 . . . . 196 B6
Swabey Rd SL3 . . . . 207 A2
Swains Cl UB7 . . . . 208 E4
Swains La HP10 . . . . 174 B1
Swains Mkt HP10 . . . . 174 A1
Swakeleys Dr UB10 . . . . . 201 F8
Swakeleys Rd UB10 . . . . 201 E8
Swale Rd HP21 . . . . 115 C5
Swallow Cl MK18 . . . . 52 E7
Swallowdale SL0 . . . . 200 D2
Swallow Dr HP15 . . . . 163 B5
Swallowfield MK8 . . . . 33 E1
Swallowfield Lower Sch
MK17 . . . . 49 B5
Swallow Fields SL0 . . . . 200 D1
Swallow Ho SL7 . . . . 184 A2
Swallow La
Aylesbury HP19 . . . . 114 F8
Stoke Mandeville HP22 . . 116 A1
Swallow St
Iver Heath SL0 . . . . 200 D1
Iver SL0 . . . . 207 D8
Swallowtail Wlk HP4 . . . 134 F7
SWANBOURNE 67 B3
Swanbourne CE Fst Sch
MK17 . . . . 67 A3
Swanbourne House Sch
MK17 . . . . 66 F3
Swanbourne Rd MK17 . . . 67 D4
Swanbrook Ct SL6 . . . . . 203 A7
Swan Bsns Pk MK18 . . . . . 52 C6
Swan Cl
Aylesbury HP19 . . . . 101 F3
Blackthorn OX25 . . . . 81 A3
Buckingham MK18 . . . . 52 E7
Chesham HP5 . . . . 144 B4
Ivinghoe Aston LU7 . . . . . . 92 A1
Whitchurch HP22 . . . . 87 B5
Swan Cotts HP17 . . . . 129 D1
Swan Ct
Buckingham MK18 . . . . 65 F5
Chorleywood WD3 . . . . . . 167 C5
Datchet SL3 . . . . 211 B6
Leighton Buzzard LU7 . . . . 80 E6
Olney MK46 . . . . 7 A4
West Drayton UB7 . . . . . . 208 D4
Swan Hill HP18 . . . . 112 F3
Swan Hill Cotts HP18 . . . 112 F3
Swan La
Lee Gate HP16 . . . . 142 C8
Marsh Gibbon OX6 . . . . 72 A3
Swan Mews HP22 . . . . 131 B5
Swann Rd HP22 . . . . 131 D8
Swan Pool & L Ctr MK18 52 D7
Swan Rd
Iver SL0 . . . . 207 F7
West Drayton UB7 . . . . . . 208 D4
Swanson Dr MK4 . . . . 45 D3
Swansons LU6 . . . . 92 F3
Swan Terr
Milton Keynes MK11 . . . . . 32 D5
Windsor SL4 . . . . 210 A7
Swan Wharf Bsns Ctr
UB8 . . . . 201 C3
Swanwick La MK10 . . . . . . 36 B3
Swayne Rise MK10 . . . . . . 36 A2
Sweetcroft La UB10 . . . . 201 F6
Sweetlands Cnr MK7 . . . . 48 B8
Swift Cl
Aylesbury HP19 . . . . 101 F3
Newport Pagnell MK16 . . . 22 A5
Swift Ho SL7 . . . . 184 A2
Swimbridge La MK4 . . . . . 46 D4
Swinden Ct MK13 . . . . 34 B4
Swing Gate Fst Sch
HP4 . . . . 135 D3
Swing Gate La HP4 . . . . . 135 D2
Swinnerton Ho RG9 . . . . 191 E3
Switchback Cl SL6 . . . . . 195 D2
Switchback Road N
SL6 . . . . 195 D3
Switchback Road S
SL6 . . . . 195 D2
Switchback The SL6 . . . 195 D2
Sycamore Ave MK2 . . . . . 58 E8
Sycamore Cl
Amersham HP6 . . . . 154 D2
3 Bourne End SL8 . . . . . 185 B3
Buckingham MK18 . . . . 52 F7
Chalfont St Giles HP8 . . . 177 A7
Long Crendon HP18 . . . . . 125 C6
Maidenhead SL6 . . . . 202 C3
Stewkley LU7 . . . . 68 D2
West Drayton UB7 . . . . . . 208 F6
Sycamore Cnr HP6 . . . . . 154 D2
Sycamore Ct
Aylesbury HP19 . . . . 101 D1
High Wycombe HP12 . . . . 172 C4
Windsor SL4 . . . . 210 C4
Sycamore Dene HP5 . . . 144 D3
Sycamore Dr
Marlow Bottom SL7 . . . . . 183 D5
Tring HP23 . . . . 119 B4
Sycamore Ho
Amersham HP6 . . . . 154 D2
Princes Risborough
HP27 . . . . 139 B3
Sycamore Leys MK18 . . . . 63 E3
Sycamore Pl HP6 . . . . . . 154 C1
Sycamore Rd
Amersham HP6 . . . . 154 D2
Chalfont St Giles HP8 . . . 177 A7
High Wycombe HP12 . . . . 172 C4
Sycamore Rise
Berkhamsted HP4 . . . . . . 135 D3
Chalfont St Giles HP8 . . . 177 A7
Sycamores The HP3 . . . . 146 F8
Sycamore Way HP15 . . . 163 A3
Sycamore Wlk SL3 . . . . . 206 E7
Sydney Gr SL1 . . . . 205 C7
Sygnus Ct 8 SL6 . . . . . . 202 F7
Syke Cluan SL0 . . . . 207 E4
Syke Ings SL0 . . . . 207 E4
Sykes Croft MK4 . . . . 46 C1
Sykes Rd SL1 . . . . 205 B8
Sylvana Cl UB10 . . . . 201 F4
Sylvester Rd SL6 . . . . . . 195 E2
Sylvia Cl HP16 . . . . 152 B4
Symington Ct MK5 . . . . . . 46 B5
Syon Gdns MK16 . . . . 22 C2
SYRESHAM 27 B8
Syresham St James CE Prim Sch NN13 . . . . 27 C8

T

Tabard Gdns MK16 . . . . . . 22 C2
Tachbrook Rd UB8 . . . . . 201 C3
Tacknell Dr MK5 . . . . 46 A4
Tacks La HP17 . . . . 126 F6
Tadmarton MK15 . . . . 35 A6
Tadmere MK8 . . . . 33 D1
Tadros Ct HP13 . . . . 173 D6
Talbot Ave
High Wycombe HP13 . . . . 161 D2
Slough SL3 . . . . 206 F4
Talbot Ct
Milton Keynes MK15 . . . . . 35 C1
Windsor SL4 . . . . 210 B4
Talbot Pl SL3 . . . . 211 C6
Talbot Rd HP22 . . . . 117 E5
Talbots Dr SL6 . . . . 202 B6
Talbots Hyde MK46 . . . . 6 E4
Talland Ave MK6 . . . . 34 F1
Tallis La MK7 . . . . 48 C5
Tall Oaks HP6 . . . . 154 D2
Tall Pines LU7 . . . . 70 F2
Tall Trees SL3 . . . . 212 E6
Tamar Cl
Aylesbury HP21 . . . . 115 C4
Loudwater HP13 . . . . 174 B4
Tamar Ho
High Wycombe HP13 . . . . 173 F7
Milton Keynes MK3 . . . . . . 46 E1
Tamarisk Ct MK7 . . . . 48 B5
Tamarisk Way
Aylesbury HP22 . . . . 116 C4
Slough SL1 . . . . 205 B5
Tamar Way SL3 . . . . 207 B2
Tamworth Stubb MK7 . . . 48 A5
Tancred Rd HP13 . . . . . . 162 A1
Tandra MK6 . . . . 47 B5
Tandy Rise MK8 . . . . 45 D6
Tandys Cl MK43 . . . . 8 E5
Tanfield La MK10 . . . . 36 A3
Tangier Ct SL4 . . . . 210 D8
Tangier La SL4 . . . . 210 D8
Tankard Cl MK16 . . . . 22 C4
Tank House Rd MK18 . . . . 66 B6
Tanners Dr MK14 . . . . 22 A2
Tannery Rd HP13 . . . . . . 174 A4
Tannery Road Ind Est
HP13 . . . . 174 A4
Tannery The MK18 . . . . . . 65 F4
Tansley La MK17 . . . . 49 B5
Tansman La MK7 . . . . 48 D5
Tanton Ho HP16 . . . . 151 F8
Tapestries Hall SL4 . . . . 211 A2
Tapestries The SL4 . . . . 211 A2
Taplin Way HP10 . . . . 163 C1
TAPLOW 196 E1
Taplow Common Rd
SL1 . . . . 197 A3
Taplow Rd SL6 . . . . 204 A7
Taplow Sta SL6 . . . . 203 F7
Tapping Rd HP14 . . . . 171 C5
Taranis Cl MK7 . . . . 48 C7
Tarbay La SL4 . . . . 209 B5
Tarbert Cl MK2 . . . . 58 C5
Tarmac Way UB7 . . . . 213 B7
Tarnbrook Cl 6 MK4 . . . . 46 B2
Tarragon Cl
Milton Keynes MK7 . . . . . . 48 B6
Walton MK7 . . . . 48 A6
Tarry Ct MK13 . . . . 34 B6
Taskers Row LU6 . . . . 92 F4
Taskers Row Cotts LU6 . . 92 F4
Task The MK46 . . . . 7 A4
Tatchbrook Cl SL6 . . . . . 203 A8
Tate Rd SL9 . . . . 177 F5
TATHALL END 11 E2
TATLING END 189 B3
Tatling Gr MK7 . . . . 48 A6
Tattam Cl MK15 . . . . 35 C2
Tattams La MK17 . . . . 67 B3
TATTENHOE 57 A8
Tattenhoe La MK3 . . . . 57 D8
Tattenhoe Pavilion MK4 . 57 A8
Tattenhoe St MK5 . . . . 45 E4
Tattershall Cl MK5 . . . . . . 46 A6
Tattlers Hill HP22 . . . . 89 B3
Taunton Deane MK4 . . . . . 46 D2
Taurus Cl MK18 . . . . 63 D2
Tavelhurst MK8 . . . . 33 E1
Taverner Cl MK7 . . . . 48 D5
Tavistock Cl
Maidenhead SL6 . . . . 202 A8
Woburn Sands MK17 . . . . . 49 B6
Tavistock Mews HP12 . . 172 E7
Tavistock Rd UB7 . . . . . . 208 D5
Tavistock St MK2 . . . . 47 D1
Tavistock Wlk HP20 . . . . 101 E2
Taylor Rd HP21 . . . . 115 D5
Taylors Cl SL7 . . . . 183 F2
Taylors Cnr HP18 . . . . 99 A7
Taylors Ct SL6 . . . . 202 B8
Taylors La
Little Missenden HP7 . . . . 153 A3
Stewkley LU7 . . . . 78 E7
St Leonards HP23 . . . . . . 132 C3
Taylors Mews MK14 . . . . . 34 F6
Taylors Rd HP5 . . . . 144 D2
Taylor's Ride LU7 . . . . 70 F2
Taylors Turn HP13 . . . . . 161 D3
Taymouth Pl MK9 . . . . 35 B3
Tay Rd MK3 . . . . 46 E1
Teale Cl OX25 . . . . 94 E7
Teal Ho HP11 . . . . 173 C6
Teasel Ave MK14 . . . . 34 E5
Tedder Cl UB10 . . . . 201 F5
Tedder Rd HP22 . . . . 131 D5
Teesdale Rd SL2 . . . . 204 F8
Tees Rd HP21 . . . . 115 C5
Tees Way MK3 . . . . 46 D1
Teign Cl MK16 . . . . 22 D4
Teikyo Sch UK SL2 . . . . . 199 D5
Telford Cl HP19 . . . . 100 F1
Telford Dr SL1 . . . . 205 A4
Telford Way
High Wycombe HP13 . . . . 162 A1
Milton Keynes MK14 . . . . . 22 B1
Telston Cl SL8 . . . . 185 A5
Temperance Terr MK11 . 32 C6
Templars Pl 2 SL7 . . . . 183 E1
TEMPLE 194 C5
Temple MK14 . . . . 34 C7
Temple Cl
Buckingham MK18 . . . . 41 E2
Milton Keynes MK3 . . . . . . 57 D7
Templecroft Terr HP17 114 A4
Temple End HP13 . . . . . . 173 A8
Temple Gate HP13 . . . . . 173 A7
Temple Ho RG9 . . . . 191 E3
Temple La SL7 . . . . 194 D6
Temple Mill Cotts SL7 . . 194 C5
Temple Mill Island SL7 194 C5
Temple Orch HP13 . . . . . 173 B7
Temple Pk SL6 . . . . 193 F3
Temple Rd SL4 . . . . 210 D5
Templeside Gdns HP12 172 E8
Temple Sq 17 HP20 . . . . 115 D8
Temple St
Aylesbury HP20 . . . . 115 D8
Brill HP18 . . . . 96 B1
Temple Way SL2 . . . . 198 C7
Templewood HP14 . . . . . . 150 B1
Templewood Gate SL2 . 198 C7
Templewood La SL2 . . . 198 E8
Tenby Gr MK4 . . . . 45 D1
Tene Acres MK5 . . . . 45 F6
Tennant Cl MK8 . . . . 45 D6
Tennis La MK18 . . . . 66 A3
Tennyson Dr MK16 . . . . . . 22 A4
Tennyson Gr 1 MK3 . . . . 57 F7
Tennyson Rd
Aylesbury HP21 . . . . 115 F6
High Wycombe HP11 . . . . 173 A5
Tennyson Way SL2 . . . . . 197 E1
Tenterden Cres MK7 . . . . 48 B7
Tenzing Dr HP13 . . . . 173 E6
Terrace The
Aspley Guise MK17 . . . . . . 49 E5
Bray SL6 . . . . 203 C3
7 Tring HP23 . . . . 119 A3
Terrent Ct SL4 . . . . 210 A5
TERRICK 130 C5
Terrick Row HP17 . . . . . . 130 B5
TERRIERS 162 D2
Terrington Hill SL7 . . . . . 183 B2
Terry Dr HP19 . . . . 101 C3
Terryfield Rd HP13 . . . . . 173 E6
Terry Orch HP13 . . . . 173 C8
Terry Pl UB8 . . . . 208 C8
Terry Rd HP13 . . . . 173 C8
Terry's La SL6 . . . . 195 F8
Testwood Rd SL4 . . . . . . 209 D6
TETCHWICK 82 F2
Tetherdown HP16 . . . . . . 151 C5
Tewkesbury La 1 MK10 . 35 F1
TEW'S END 17 C8
Tews End La NN12 . . . . . . 17 B8
Thackeray End HP19 . . . 100 F2
THAME 125 E2
Thame Ho 5 HP13 . . . . . 173 B7
Thame Rd
Aylesbury HP17 . . . . 127 C2
Aylesbury HP21 . . . . 115 D7
Blackthorn OX25 . . . . 81 A3
Brill HP18 . . . . 110 B7
Chilton HP18 . . . . 111 B3
Chinnor OX39 . . . . 147 B8
Haddenham HP17 . . . . . . 126 D5
Long Crendon HP18,
OX9 . . . . 125 D4
Longwick HP27 . . . . 138 E6
Piddington OX25 . . . . 95 D6
Thame OX9 . . . . 136 C7
Thame Road S HP21 . . . . 115 B6
Thames Ave SL4 . . . . 210 D7
Thames Bank SL6 . . . . . . 203 C7
Thamesbourne Mews 3
SL8 . . . . 185 A3
Thames Cl
Bourne End SL8 . . . . 185 A4
Milton Keynes MK3 . . . . . . 57 E8
Thames Cres SL6 . . . . . . 196 B2
Thames Dr MK16 . . . . 22 E3
Thamesfield Gdns SL7 . 183 E1
Thames Ho
Datchet SL3 . . . . 211 B6
Henley-on-Thames RG9 . . 191 E3
Thames Ind Est SL7 . . . . 183 F2
Thames Mead SL4 . . . . . 209 E6
Thames Rd SL3 . . . . 207 B3
Thames Reach SL7 . . . . . 193 D6
Thames Side
Henley-on-Thames RG9 . . 191 E2
Windsor SL4 . . . . 210 D7
Thames St SL4 . . . . 210 D7
Thames Valley Athletics Ctr
SL4 . . . . 205 E1
Thames Valley Hospl (private) SL3 . . . . 199 C4
Thames Valley Univ (Slough Campus) SL1 . . . . 205 E5
Thane Ct MK14 . . . . 34 C7
Thanestead Copse
HP10 . . . . 174 C2
Thanestead Ct HP10 . . . . 174 C2
Thatcher Cl UB7 . . . . 208 E4
Thatchers Dr SL6 . . . . . . 202 A5
Theatre Wlk MK9 . . . . 34 F3
thecentre:mk (Sh Ctr)
MK9 . . . . 34 E3
THE CITY 159 D6
THE GREEN
Milton Keynes 47 D8
Newport Pagnell 22 C3
Whipsnade 107 F8
Thellusson Way WD3 . . . 167 F2
THE SWILLET 167 B3
Theydon Ave MK17 . . . . . . 49 B4
Thicket The
Tylers Green HP10 . . . . . . 163 A1
West Drayton UB7 . . . . . . 208 E7
Third Ave
Marlow SL7 . . . . 183 F2
Milton Keynes MK1 . . . . . . 47 B2
Third Cres SL1 . . . . 205 C8
Third St HP11 . . . . 173 B4
Thirkleby Cl SL1 . . . . 205 C5
Thirlby La MK5 . . . . 46 A6
Thirlmere Ave
Milton Keynes MK2 . . . . . . 58 D6
Slough SL1 . . . . 204 C8
Thirsk Gdns MK3 . . . . 57 C6
Thistle Ct HP21 . . . . 115 C5
Thomas Bourne Ho 1
HP4 . . . . 135 D4
Thomas Coram CE Mid Sch
HP4 . . . . 135 D2
Thomas Ct
Berkhamsted HP4 . . . . . . 134 E6
Maidenhead SL6 . . . . 202 A2
Thomas Dr MK16 . . . . 22 A6
Thomas Harding Jun Sch
HP5 . . . . 154 B7
Thomas Hickman Sch
HP19 . . . . 101 A3
Thomas Rd HP10 . . . . 185 D4
Thomas Valentine Ho
HP8 . . . . 177 B7
Thompkins La SL2 . . . . . 198 A5
Thompson Cl SL3 . . . . . . 207 A2
Thompson Rd UB10 . . . . 201 E5
Thompson St MK13 . . . . . 34 A7
Thomson Cl HP21 . . . . . . 115 B6
Thomson Wlk HP21 . . . . . 115 B6
Thornaby Pl HP10 . . . . . . 185 E8
Thornbank Cl TW19 . . . . 213 A2
THORNBOROUGH 54 A8
Thornborough Inf Sch
MK18 . . . . 54 A8
Thornborough Rd MK17 . 55 B8
Thornbridge Rd SL0 . . . . 200 C4
Thornbury Pl HP11 . . . . . 173 A4
Thorncliffe MK8 . . . . 33 D1
Thorndike SL2 . . . . 205 B8
Thorn Dr SL3 . . . . 206 E7
Thorne Rd HP14 . . . . 171 C4
Thorne Way
Aston Clinton HP22 . . . . . 118 A4
Aylesbury HP20 . . . . 101 F2
THORNEY 208 B3
Thorneycroft La MK15 . . . 35 B5
Thorney Ctry Pk* UB7 . 208 B3
Thorney Lane N SL0 . . . . 207 F6
Thorney Lane S SL0 . . . . 207 F5
Thorney Mill Rd SL0,
UB7 . . . . 208 B3
Thornhill MK18 . . . . 54 B8
Thornhill Cl HP7 . . . . 165 B7
Thornhill Rd UB10 . . . . . 201 F8
Thornlea Croft MK46 . . . . . 6 F3
Thornley Croft MK4 . . . . . 46 C2
Thorns Cl HP27 . . . . 139 D5
Thorns La HP27 . . . . 139 E5
THORNTON 43 C4
Thornton Ave UB7 . . . . . . 208 F3
Thornton Chase MK14 . . . 34 E6
Thornton Cl UB7 . . . . 208 F3
Thornton Coll Convent of Jesus & Mary MK17 . . . . 43 C5
Thornton Cres HP22 . . . . 131 A5
Thornton Rd MK17 . . . . . . 44 A1
Thorntree Dr HP23 . . . . . 118 F4
Thorpe Cl HP21 . . . . 116 A4
Thorpe House Sch SL9 188 E7
Thorpeness Croft MK4 . . 56 F8
Thorwold Pl MK5 . . . . 46 B6

Thrasher Rd HP21 115 D5
Three Close La HP4 135 C4
Three Gables HP9 175 E2
THREE HOUSEHOLDS 176 F7
Three Households HP8 176 F6
Three Oaks Cl UB10 190 F1
Three Points La MK18 74 A6
Thresher Gr MK12 33 A5
Thrift La SL6 202 D1
Thrift View MK43 25 C2
Thrupp Cl MK19 20 A6
Thrush Cl
6 Aylesbury HP19 101 F3
High Wycombe HP12 172 C4
Thurlby Way SL6 202 D3
Thurley Cotts SL2 199 B3
Thurne Cl MK16 22 E3
Thursby Cl MK15 35 D7
Thurston Rd SL1 205 E7
Thyme Cl MK16 21 F5
Tibbys La HP18 112 F3
Ticehirst Cl MK7 48 B7
Ticehurst Cl MK7 48 B7
Tichborne WD3 178 D5
Tickford Arc MK16 22 D4
TICKFORD END 22 F4
Tickford Park Prim Sch
MK16 22 D3
Tickford St MK16 22 E4
Tidbury Cl MK17 49 A4
Tiddenfoot Waterside Pk*
LU7 80 E4
TIDDINGTON 136 A7
Tierney 5 MK4 45 D2
Tierney Ct 3 SL7 183 E1
Tiffany Cl MK2 58 D6
Tiggywinkles Wildlife
Hospl* HP17 127 A4
TILBROOK 48 C3
Tilbrook Ind Est MK7 48 B3
Tilbrook Rdbt MK7 48 B2
Tilbury Wlk SL3 207 B3
Tilburywood Cl HP13 161 C2
Tilebarn Cl RG9 191 C1
Tilecotes Cl SL7 183 C2
Tilehouse Comb Sch
UB9 189 F5
Tilehouse La UB9 189 E6
Tilehouse Way UB9 189 F4
Tilers Rd MK11 33 B2
Tilling Cres HP13 174 A7
Tillman Cl MK12 33 C5
Tilstone Ave SL4 204 E2
Tilstone Cl SL4 204 E1
Tilsworth Rd HP9 175 C1
Timber La MK17 60 F7
Timberley La HP16 142 A8
Timberscombe MK4 46 D3
Timbers Wlk SL6 202 B5
Timber Way OX39 147 C6
Timberwood SL2 187 D1
Timbold Dr MK7 48 A7
Timor Ct MK11 32 D6
Timothy's Cl MK12 33 C7
Timpson Ct HP15 162 D8
Timpson La MK46 7 C3
Timpsons Row MK46 7 A3
Tindal Rd HP20 101 E2
TINGEWICK 51 B7
Tingewick Rd
Buckingham MK18 52 B8
Radclive MK18 51 E7
Tingewick Road Ind Est
MK18 52 B8
TINKERS BRIDGE 47 D6
Tinkers Dr MK18 65 F3
TINKERS END 65 F3
Tinkers La
Berkhamsted HP23 134 A6
Windsor SL4 209 D5
Tinkers Wood Rd HP13 161 E1
Tintagel Ct MK6 47 A8
Tintagel Ho SL1 205 C5
Tintern Cl SL1 205 C3
Tinterne Cl HP21 116 C6
Tippet Cl MK7 48 D4
Tiree Ct
Milton Keynes MK3 58 C3
Milton Keynes MK3 58 C3
Tiree Ho SL2 205 B8
Titchmarsh Ct MK6 46 E8
Tithe Barn Dr SL6 203 E1
Tithe Cl SL6 203 C1
Tithe Ct SL3 207 A2
Tithe La TW19 212 A1
Titmus Rd HP22 131 E7
Tiverton Cres
Aylesbury HP19 101 C3
Milton Keynes MK4 45 E1
Tobermory Cl SL3 206 E2
Tockley Rd SL1 197 B2
Todd Cl
Aylesbury HP21 115 B6
Holmer Green HP15 163 B6
Tolcarne Ave MK6 35 A1
Toll Bar Cnr HP27 138 D7
Tollgate SL6 202 A6
Tollgate Cl WD3 167 F5
Tolman Ct HP21 115 B6
Tomlin Rd SL2 197 E1
Tomo Ind Est UB8 208 C7
Tompion Rd HP19 100 F1
Tompkins Cl
Aston Clinton HP22 117 F4
Milton Keynes MK5 46 B3
Tompkins La OX27 71 E2
Tom Scott Ho HP5 144 B2
Toms Hill Cl HP23 120 D5
Toms Hill Rd HP23 120 D5
Toms Turn HP15 162 F5
TONGWELL 35 C8
Tongwell La MK15, MK16 22 C2
Tongwell Rdbt MK15 35 D8
Tongwell St
Milton Keynes, Broughton
MK10 36 A3
Milton Keynes, Northfield
MK15 35 F5
Milton Keynes, Pineham
MK15 35 E7
Walnut Tree MK7 48 C6
Toot Hill Cl MK5 46 A5
Top Angel MK18 52 D5
Topaz Cl SL1 205 B5
Top Farm Cl HP9 175 A1
Topland Rd SL9 177 D3
Top Mdw
Bow Brickhill MK7 48 B3
Milton Keynes MK3 47 A3
Topping La UB8 201 D2
Top Pk SL9 188 C5
Top Station Rd NN13 38 A8
Top Station Road Ind Est
NN13 38 A8
Torbay HP22 85 B4
Tornay Ct LU7 91 D6
Torquay Spur SL2 198 B2
Torre Cl MK3 47 A2
Torridge Rd
Aylesbury HP21 115 D4
Slough SL3 212 B8
Torridon Ct MK2 58 D4
Torrington Rd HP4 135 B4
Tortoiseshell Way
Aylesbury HP19 101 C4
Berkhamsted HP4 134 F6
Torwood Cl HP4 134 F4
TOTTERIDGE 173 F8
Totteridge Ave HP13 173 D6
Totteridge Common Cotts
HP13 173 F8
Totteridge Dr HP13 162 E1
Totteridge Ho HP13 173 E8
Totteridge La HP13 162 E1
Totteridge Par HP13 173 E8
Totteridge Rd HP13 173 D7
TOTTERNHOE 93 B7
Totternhoe Knolls &
Quarry* LU6 93 B8
Totternhoe Lower Sch
LU6 93 B7
Totternhoe Rd
Dunstable LU6 93 E7
Eaton Bray LU6 92 D7
TOUCHBRIDGE 95 E1
Towan Ave
Fishermead MK6 47 A8
Milton Keynes MK6 35 A1
Towcester Dr NN12 18 B3
Towcester Rd
Buckingham MK18 41 E4
Old Stratford MK19 32 B7
TOWERAGE 171 F8
Tower Cl
Berkhamsted HP4 135 A3
Emberton MK16 13 C5
Flackwell Heath HP10 185 C7
Tower Cres MK14 34 F6
Tower Ct HP27 139 B3
Tower Dr MK14 34 F7
Towergate Cl UB8 201 E7
TOWER HILL 146 F2
Tower Hill WD4 146 F1
Tower Hill Bsns Pk
OX27 71 D7
Tower Ho
Iver SL0 207 E7
4 Slough SL1 205 E4
Toweridge La
High Wycombe HP12 172 C8
West Wycombe HP14 160 F1
Tower Rd HP7 165 A4
Towersey Way HP21 115 B7
Towers Lea HP13 173 C7
Tower St HP13 162 D2
Town Bridge Ct HP5 154 B7
Town Cl MK18 50 D6
TOWN END 159 C8
Town End Cres MK16 12 B5
Town End Rd HP14 159 C8
Town Farm LU7 105 A7
Town Farm Barns
HP27 139 B3
Town Farm Cl OX49 157 B8
Townfield HP5 154 C7
Town Field La HP8 177 C7
Townfield Rd 5 HP13 173 C7
Town La
Stanwell TW19 213 D1
Wooburn HP10 185 D4
Townlands Hospl RG9 191 D2
TOWNSEND
Haddenham 127 A7
North Marston 76 B2
TOWN'S END 71 D2
Townsend
Haddenham HP17 127 A7
Marsh Gibbon OX27 71 E2
Quainton HP22 85 A5
Townsend Cl MK43 37 F8
Townsend Cotts
Great Horwood MK17 55 B3
Middle Claydon MK18 74 C8
Townsend Gr MK13 34 B8
Townsend La OX27 71 E2
Townsend Piece HP19 101 C1
Townsend Rd HP5 144 C1
Townside
Edlesborough LU6 92 F3
Haddenham HP17 126 F5
Town Sq 8 SL1 205 F4
Tozer Wlk SL4 209 D4
Tracy Ave SL3 206 F1
Tracy Way 3 MK4 45 E3
Trafalgar Ave MK3 46 E2
Trafford Cl HP16 152 A6
Trafford Rd HP16 152 A7
Tram Hill HP18 96 B2
Tranlands Brigg MK13 34 B4
Transcend 10 SL4 210 C5
Trapp's Ct HP5 154 C6
Trapp's La HP5 154 C6
Travell Ct MK13 34 B3
Travic Rd SL2 197 F2
Travis Ct SL2 198 B2
Travis Gr MK3 58 A8
Treacher's Cl HP5 154 B8
Treadaway Bsns Ctr
HP10 174 C1
Treadaway Hill HP10 174 B1
Treadaway Rd HP10 174 B1
Trebah Sq HP19 114 F8
Treborough MK4 46 D2
Tredington Gr MK7 48 B4
Treefields MK18 52 E8
Treehanger Cl HP23 119 B4
Trees Ave HP14 162 A6
Treeside Cl UB7 208 D2
Treesmill Dr SL6 202 C3
Trees Rd
Bourne End SL8 185 B3
Hughenden Valley HP14 162 A6
Trelawney Ave SL3 206 E3
Tremayne Ct MK6 47 A8
Trenchard Ave HP22 131 D6
Trenchard St HP19 115 A8
Trenches La SL3 207 A6
Trengothal Ct NN13 26 D4
Trent Dr MK16 22 D4
Trentishoe Cres MK4 46 D3
Trent Rd
Milton Keynes MK3 46 E1
Slough SL3 212 B8
Trent Villas Est SL3 211 B6
Tresco Rd HP4 134 F5
Tresham Ct MK5 46 A7
Tressell The SL6 202 D6
Trevelyan Mid Sch SL4 210 C3
Trevelyan Way HP4 135 B6
Treves Gn HP21 115 E5
Trevithick La MK5 46 B5
Trevone Ct MK6 47 A8
Trevor Ct TW19 213 A2
Trevose Ho SL2 198 B1
Trewarden Ave SL0 200 D3
Triangle Bsns Pk HP22 130 D8
Trident Ind Est SL3 212 E4
TRING 119 C3
Tring Bsns Ctr HP23 118 E4
TRINGFORD 118 F8
Tring Ford Rd HP23 119 A7
Tring Hill HP23 118 C3
Tring Park Sch for the
Performing Arts
HP23 119 B3
Tring Rd
Aylesbury HP21 116 B7
Berkhamsted HP4 134 D7
Dunstable LU6 93 E7
Edlesborough LU6 106 E8
Long Marston HP23 104 C3
Wendover HP22 131 C5
Wilstone HP23 104 C1
Wingrave HP22 89 C1
Tring Reservoirs (Wildlife
Trust Reserves)*
HP23 118 E7
Tring Sch HP23 119 B4
Tring Sta HP23 120 A5
Trinity Ave SL7 183 D3
Trinity CE Prim Sch
RG9 191 D1
Trinity Cl
Old Stratford MK19 32 B7
Stanwell TW19 213 C1
Trinity Ct
Aylesbury HP19 101 D1
Chesham HP5 154 C7
Marlow SL7 183 D3
Trinity Ho SL8 195 F6
Trinity Pl SL4 210 C5
Trinity Rd
Hazlemere HP15 162 F3
Marlow SL7 183 D2
Milton Keynes MK12 33 B7
Trinity St Stephen CE Fst
Sch SL4 210 B6
Tripps Hill Cl HP8 177 A7
Trispen Ct MK6 47 A8
Trooper Rd HP23 120 C5
Troutbeck MK6 47 C8
Troutbeck Cl SL2 206 A6
Trout Cl SL7 194 C8
Trout Hollow HP27 148 E8
Trout La UB7 208 C5
Trout Rd UB7 208 D6
Trubys Gdn MK6 47 A7
Trueman Pl MK6 46 F8
Truesdale Dr UB9 190 C7
Trumper Way
Slough SL1 204 F5
Uxbridge UB8 201 C4
Trumpton La MK7 48 C7
Trunk Furlong MK17 49 D6
Truro Cl SL6 202 A7
Trust Cotts HP4 107 A1
Trustees Cl UB9 189 F5
Tubwell Rd SL2 199 B4
Tucker Cl HP13 173 C8
Tuckers Dr HP15 163 C7
Tudeley Hale MK7 48 B8
Tudor Ct
Amersham HP6 154 D1
5 Leighton Buzzard LU7 80 F7
Maidenhead SL6 196 C2
Piddington HP14 160 C1
3 Stanwell TW19 213 E1
Tudor Dr HP10 185 D7
Tudor Gdns
Milton Keynes MK11 32 E4
Slough SL1 204 C8
Steeple Claydon MK18 63 D3
Tudor Mill HP10 185 E6
Tudor Orch HP4 134 E6
Tudor Pk HP6 154 D2
Tudor Rd HP15 163 C3
Tudors Cl MK18 73 B4
Tudor Way SL4 209 E6
Tuffnell Cl MK15 35 E7
Tuffnell Gn MK10 35 E1
Tulip Way UB7 208 D2
Tulkers Cl HP16 151 D5
Tulla Ct MK2 58 C4
Tummell Way MK2 58 C6
Tunbridge Gr MK7 48 B8
Tunmers Ct SL9 177 C2
Tunmers End SL9 177 C2
Tunmers Ho SL9 177 C2
Tunnel Way LU7 105 C2
Tuns La
Henley-on-Thames RG9 191 E2
Slough SL1 205 C4
Turks Head Ct SL4 210 C7
Turnberry Cl MK3 57 D7
Turner Cl HP20 101 F3
Turner Rd SL3 206 C4
Turners Dr HP13 173 E8
Turners Field HP13 161 E3
Turner's Mdw HP22 117 B6
Turners Mews MK14 34 F6
Turners Pl HP15 163 C6
Turners Wlk 4 HP5 144 C1
Turners Wood Dr HP8 177 D7
Turner Wlk 12 HP20 101 F3
Turneys Dr MK12 33 A6
Turneys Orch WD3 167 D4
Turnfields HP18 124 A3
Turnfurlong HP21 115 F7
Turnfurlong Inf Sch
HP21 116 A6
Turnfurlong Jun Sch
HP21 116 A6
Turnfurlong La HP21 116 A6
Turnfurlong Row HP21 116 A6
Turnham Way HP19 115 B7
Turnip Cl HP18 112 B2
Turnmill Ave MK6 35 B2
Turnmill Ct MK6 35 B2
Turnoak Pk SL4 209 E3
Turnpike Ct MK17 49 A5
Turnpike End HP21 115 F6
Turnpike La UB10 201 E3
Turnpike Rd HP12 172 D4
Turnpike The HP18 109 D5
Turnpike Way HP12 172 C4
Turnstone Way HP19 101 E3
Turpins Gn SL6 202 A5
Turpyn Ct MK6 47 D8
Turton Way SL1 205 D3
TURVEY 8 F6
Turvey Cl HP22 117 E5
Turvey Lower Sch MK43 8 E6
Turvey Mill MK43 8 D5
Turvey Rd
Astwood MK16 15 F5
Turvey MK43 3 E2
TURVILLE 169 F3
TURVILLE HEATH 169 A3
Turvill End MK5 46 B8
Turville Rd HP21 116 C6
TURWESTON 38 C8
Turweston Rd NN13 26 A1
Tuscans Cl MK18 73 B5
Tweedale Cl MK17 67 C7
Tweed Cl HP4 135 B5
Tweed Dr MK3 46 D1
Tweed Rd SL3 212 B8
Tweenways HP5 144 E1
Twelve Leys HP22 89 B3
Twinches La SL1 205 B5
Twinflower MK7 48 B6
Twist The HP23 119 D2
Twitchell La HP22 117 E5
Twitchell Rd HP16 152 A7
Twitchell's La HP9 176 F5
Twitchen La MK4 46 D3
Twizel Cl MK13 33 E6
Two Dells La
Ashley Green HP5 145 A4
Chesham HP5 155 B8
Two Gates La HP5 143 D7
TWO MILE ASH 33 D2
Two Mile Ash Sch MK8 33 E1
Two Mile Dr SL1 204 E4
Two Ponds La HP4 134 C7
TWYFORD 62 C1
Twyford CE Fst Sch
MK18 62 C2
Twyford La MK7 48 C5
Twynham Rd SL6 202 B7
Tyburn Ave MK6 35 B2
Tyhurst MK10 36 A2
Tyle Pl SL4 211 A2
Tylers Cres HP15 163 B2
Tylers Gn MK13 34 D3
TYLERS GREEN 163 D1
Tylers Green Fst Sch
HP10 174 D8
Tylers Green Mid Sch
HP10 174 B8
Tylers Hill Rd HP5 154 F8
Tylers Rd HP15 163 B2
Tyler Wlk 3 SL3 206 F1
Tylsworth Cl HP6 154 D1
Tyndale Mews SL1 205 B4
Tyneham Cl HP21 116 B4
Tynemouth Rise 3
MK10 36 A1
Tyne Rd HP21 115 D4
Tyne Sq MK3 46 D1
Tyrell Cl
Buckingham MK18 52 C7
Milton Keynes MK19 20 A5
Tyrell Gdns SL4 209 F4
Tyrells Gdns MK17 69 E8
Tyrells Rd MK17 69 E8
Tyrill MK14 34 C7
TYRINGHAM 12 F2
Tyson Pl MK6 46 E8
Tythe Cl LU7 78 E8
Tythe Gdns LU7 78 E8
Tythe Mews LU6 92 E3
Tyzack Rd HP13 162 F1

U

Ufton Court Yd SL8 185 B4
Ufton Ct SL8 185 B4
Ullswater Cl SL1 204 C8
Ullswater Dr LU7 80 C7
Ultra Ave MK3 47 A1
Ulverscroft MK10 36 B2
Ulverston Cres MK10 36 B2
Ulyett Pl MK6 46 E8
Umberville Way SL2 197 F2
Underhill Cl SL6 202 E6
Underwood Cotts HP7 164 C2
Underwood Pl MK6 46 E8
Underwood Rd HP13 173 D8
Union Bldgs UB8 201 B2
Union Bsns Pk UB8 201 B5
Union Ct 11 HP4 135 D4
Union Ind Est HP12 172 A7
Union St MK16 22 D5
University Way MK43 24 D1
Univ of Buckingham The
MK18 52 C7
Univ of Buckingham The
(Verney Pk) MK18 52 E7
Up Corner HP8 177 C8
Up Corner Cl HP8 177 B8
Upcroft SL4 210 B4
UP END 24 A8
Upland Ave HP5 144 B3
Uplands SL7 183 D6
Uplands Cl
Gerrards Cross SL9 188 E3
High Wycombe HP13 173 E8

Uplands Ct HP5 144 C1
Uplands The SL9 188 E2
Upminster Cl MK10 35 E1
Upper Abbotts Hill HP19 115 A7
UPPER ARNCOTT 94 E7
Upper Ashlyns Rd HP4 135 B3
Upper Barn Farm HP18 84 B1
Upper Belmont Rd HP5 144 B3
Upper Bourne End La HP1 146 B7
Upper Bray Rd SL6 203 C3
Upper Church St HP18 112 F3
Upper Coombe LU7 80 E8
Upper Dr HP9 175 D5
UPPER DUNSLEY 119 C4
Upper Fifth St MK9 34 D2
Upper Fourth St MK9 34 D2
Upper George St HP5 144 C1
Upper Gladstone Rd 2 HP5 144 C1
Upper Green St HP11 172 E7
Upper Hall Pk HP4 135 E2
Upper Hartwell HP17 114 E5
Upper Hollis HP16 151 F7
Upper Hundreds Way HP20 115 E8
Upper Icknield Way
Askett HP27 139 E7
Halton HP22 117 F2
Monks Risborough HP27 139 D6
Pitstone HP23, LU7 105 E1
Princes Risborough HP27 139 B2
Saunderton HP27 148 F7
Upper Lees Rd SL2 198 B2
Upper Lodge La HP15 162 F6
UPPER MAIDENSGROVE 179 A7
Upper Mdw 2 HP5 144 B1
UPPER NORTH DEAN 150 E2
UPPER POLLICOTT 111 E8
Upper Ray Mdws Wildlife Reserve★ OX25 81 D4
Upper Rd UB9 189 D4
Upper Riding HP9 175 B2
Upper Second St MK9 34 D1
Upper St
Quainton HP22 85 A5
Tingewick MK18 51 B6
Upper Stonehayes MK14 34 F8
Upper Thames Way SL8 184 F3
Upper Third St MK9 34 D1
Upper Tring Pk HP23 119 D1
Upper Ventnor Cotts SL6 195 C8
Upper Way MK17 59 C2
Upper Weald MK19 45 A8
UPPER WINCHENDON 99 B1
Upperwood Cl 1 MK5 46 A3
Upper Wood Cl MK5 45 F3
UPTON
Slough 206 B3
Stone 114 A4
Upton Cl
Henley-on-Thames RG9 191 E1
5 Slough SL1 205 F3
Upton Court Rd SL3 206 B2
Upton Gr MK5 46 C4
Upton Hospl SL1 205 F4
Upton House Sch SL4 210 C5
UPTON LEA 206 A7
Upton Lea Par SL2 206 B6
UPTON PARK 205 F3
Upton Pk SL1 205 F3
Upton Rd
Dinton HP17 114 A3
Slough SL1 206 A3
Upton Terr HP17 114 A3
Upway SL9 177 F2
Ushercombe View MK18 50 D6
UXBRIDGE 201 E5
Uxbridge Coll UB8 201 E6
Uxbridge High Sch UB8 201 D3
Uxbridge Ind Est UB8 201 B3
UXBRIDGE MOOR 201 B4
Uxbridge Rd
Iver Heath SL0, SL3 200 B2
Rickmansworth WD3 178 F7
Slough SL1, SL3 206 C7
Uxbridge UB10 201 F2
Uxbridge U Sta UB8 201 D5

V

Vache La
Chalfont St Giles HP8 177 C8
Milton Keynes MK5 45 F6
Vale Cl SL9 177 D2
Vale Ct MK43 25 D2
Vale Gr SL1 205 E3
Vale House HP19 115 C8
Vale Ind Ctr The HP19 101 C1
Valens Cl MK8 45 E7
Valentine Ct MK8 45 E7
Valentine Way HP8 177 D7
Vale Park Dr HP20 115 E8
Vale Rd
Aylesbury HP20 101 E2
Chesham HP5 144 C4
Windsor SL4 209 F6
Vale Ret Pk HP20 115 E8
Valerian Pl MK16 21 F4
Vale Rise HP5 144 C3
Vale The SL9 177 D2
Valley Cl
Brackley NN13 38 A8
Whipsnade HP4 107 E7
Valley Cres NN13 38 A8
Valley Ctr The HP13 173 C6
Valley End SL3 199 C1
Valley Rd
Berkhamsted HP4 134 F6
Brackley NN13 38 A8
Buckingham MK18 52 F8
Finmere MK18 50 D6
Henley-on-Thames RG9 191 C1
Hughenden Valley HP14 162 A5
Uxbridge UB10 201 E3
Valley Rise NN13 38 A8
Valley View HP5 144 B2
Valley Way SL9 188 D5
Valpy Cl HP23 119 D1
Van Der Bilt Ct MK13 33 F6
Van Diemens Cl OX39 147 C7
Vandyke Cl MK17 49 B6
Vane Rd OX9 126 B1
Vanguard Cl HP12 172 D7
Vanguard Ho 5 TW19 213 E1
Vansittart Rd
Bisham SL7 194 E7
Windsor SL4 210 B6
Vantage Ct MK16 22 F3
Vantage Rd SL1 205 B5
Vanwall Bsns Pk SL6 202 C5
Vanwall Rd SL6 202 C4
Varnell Terr RG9 181 C2
Vaughan Copse SL4 205 D2
Vaughan Gdns SL4 204 F2
Vaughan Way SL2 197 E1
Vauxhall MK13 34 B6
Vellan Ave MK6 35 B1
Venables La MK15 35 B7
Venetian Ct MK7 48 C7
Ventfield Cl OX33 108 A5
Venus Cl SL2 197 F1
VENUS HILL 156 B8
Venus Hill HP3 156 A8
Verbena Cl UB7 208 D1
Verdi Cl MK7 48 D5
Verdon Ct SL2 198 B2
Verdon Dr MK15 35 B7
Verity Pl MK6 34 F1
Verley Cl MK6 47 C8
Vermont Pl MK15 22 C1
Vermont Rd SL2 197 F1
Verney Ave HP12 172 D4
Verney Cl
Berkhamsted HP4 134 F5
6 Buckingham MK18 41 D1
Marlow SL7 183 D2
Tring HP23 119 C5
Verney Farm Cl MK18 74 F8
Verney Junc Bsns Pk MK18 64 E3
VERNEY JUNCTION 64 F4
Verney Rd
Slough SL3 207 A2
Winslow MK18 65 E4
Verney Wlk HP21 115 D6
Vernier Cres MK5 45 E5
Vernon Bldg 7 HP11 172 F7
Verona Cl UB8 208 C7
Verwood Rd HP20 101 E2
Veryan Pl MK6 35 B1
Vicarage Cl
Cookham SL6 196 B7
Seer Green HP9 176 D3
Steeple Claydon MK18 63 D2
Wendover HP22 131 B5
Vicarage Ct
Hanslope MK19 11 B2
Steeple Claydon MK18 63 D3
Vicarage Dr SL6 203 C4
Vicarage Flats SL4 210 D8
Vicarage Gdns
Leighton Buzzard LU7 80 E6
Marsworth HP23 105 A2
3 Milton Keynes MK13 34 A4
Vicarage La
Bovingdon HP3 146 B4
Ivinghoe LU7 105 F5
Piddington OX25 95 E6
Steeple Claydon MK18 63 D2
Wing LU7 79 E2
Vicarage Rd
Aylesbury HP21 115 D5
Henley-on-Thames RG9 191 E1
Leighton Buzzard LU7 80 E6
Maidenhead SL6 202 F8
Milton Keynes, Bradwell MK13 34 A4
Vicarage Rd *continued*
Milton Keynes, Fenny Stratford MK2 58 E8
Milton Keynes, Stony Stratford MK13 32 D6
Pitstone LU7 105 D2
Whaddon MK17 56 B8
Wigginton HP23 119 D1
Winslow MK18 65 F4
Yardley Gobion NN12 18 E6
Vicarage St MK17 49 C4
Vicarage Way
Colnbrook SL3 212 D7
Gerrards Cross SL9 188 F5
Vicarage Wlk MK11 32 D6
Vickers Ct 9 TW19 213 E1
Vickery Cl HP21 115 E5
Vickery Way HP21 115 E5
Victor Cl SL6 202 B8
Victoria CE Fst Sch Berkhamsted HP4 135 C4
Victoria Cotts SL6 195 C8
Victoria Cres SL0 208 A6
Victoria Ct
Henley-on-Thames RG9 191 E1
High Wycombe HP11 172 F8
4 Marlow SL7 183 E2
Slough SL1 205 E5
21 Windsor SL4 210 D6
Victoria Dr SL1, SL2 197 F6
Victoria Gdns
High Wycombe HP11 172 F4
Marlow SL7 183 E2
Victoria Ho SL4 211 A2
VICTORIA PARK 116 B8
Victoria Rd
Berkhamsted HP4 135 C4
Chesham HP5 144 C1
Eton Wick SL4 204 F1
Farnham Common SL2 198 C6
Leighton Buzzard LU7 80 E8
Marlow SL7 183 E2
Milton Keynes MK2 47 E1
Slough SL2 206 B5
Uxbridge UB8 201 C5
Victoria Row MK18 52 D8
Victoria St
Aylesbury HP20 115 F8
High Wycombe HP11 172 F7
Milton Keynes MK12 33 D6
9 Slough SL1 205 F4
Windsor SL4 210 D6
Victor Rd SL4 210 C4
Victory Ct MK1 47 B2
Victory Rd
Berkhamsted HP4 135 A5
Steeple Claydon MK18 63 D2
Wendover HP22 131 B5
Vienna Gr MK13 33 E6
Village Cl MK16 13 F2
Village Ct LU7 80 D6
Village La SL2 187 D4
Village Mews 2 HP3 146 A4
Village Rd
Coleshill HP7 164 F3
Denham UB9 190 A2
Dorney SL4 204 B3
Village Way HP7 166 D7
Villa Park (Mobile Home Pk) MK43 37 F7
Villiers Bldgs 8 HP20 115 D8
Villiers Cl MK18 41 E2
Villiers Ct SL4 210 A7
Villiers Rd SL2 205 D8
Villier St UB8 201 D3
Vimy Ct LU7 80 F7
Vimy Rd LU7 80 F7
Vincent Ave MK8 45 F8
Vincent Dr UB10 201 F4
Vincent Rd HP19 101 A3
Vincents Way HP14 161 D6
Vine Cl
Hazelmere HP15 163 A3
Stanwell TW19 213 A2
Vine Ct SL2 199 A6
Vine Gr UB10 201 F5
Vine La UB10 201 F4
Vine Rd SL2 198 F6
Vine Row MK43 8 E6
Vine St UB8 201 C4
Vine The HP18 124 D3
Vinetrees HP22 131 B4
Vineyard Dr SL8 185 A5
Vineyards The HP27 138 A2
Viney La HP19 114 F8
Vinlake Ave UB10 190 F1
Vintners Mews MK14 34 F6
Violet Ave UB8 208 F8
Violet Cl HP27 149 D6
Violets Cl MK16 24 B6
Virage HP22 117 F4
Virginia MK6 47 A7
Virginia Gdns HP14 159 F8
Viridian Sq HP21 115 E7
Viscount Cl 13 HP20 101 F2
Viscount Ct 12 SL4 210 C6
Viscount Ind Est SL3 212 E4
Viscount Way MK2 47 C1
Vitalograph Bsns Pk MK18 41 F4
Vivaldi Ct MK7 48 D5
Vivien Cl SL6 195 F6
Volta Rise MK5 46 C4
Vyne Cres MK8 33 F1
Vyners Sch UB10 201 F8

W

Waborne Rd SL8 185 B4
WADDESDON 99 B7
Waddesdon CE Sch HP18 99 A6
Waddesdon Cl 8 MK8 45 F8
Waddesdon Green HP21 115 E4
Waddesdon Hill HP18 99 C3
Waddesdon Manor★ HP18 98 E5
Waddesdon Manor Flats HP18 98 E6
Waddesdon Village Prim Sch HP18 99 A6
Wade Dr SL1 205 A5
Wadesmill La MK7 48 A4
Wadhurst La MK10 36 B1
Wadworth Holme MK10 35 E3
Waglands Gdn MK18 52 D7
Wagner Cl MK7 48 C4
Wagstaff Way 12 MK46 6 F3
Waine Cl MK18 52 D7
Wainers Croft MK12 33 B4
Wainwrights HP18 125 D6
Waivers Way HP21 116 A5
Wakefield Cl MK14 34 F7
Wakefield Cres SL2 198 F6
Wakelins End SL6 195 E7
Wakeman Rd SL8 185 A3
Walbank Gr MK5 46 A3
Walbrook Ave MK6 35 B3
Waldeck Ho SL6 203 A7
Waldeck Rd SL6 203 A7
Walden Croft MK6 47 E4
Waldens Cl 4 SL8 185 A3
Walducks Cl LU7 78 E8
Walford Rd UB8 201 D3
Walgrave Dr MK13 34 B4
Walker Ave MK12 33 A6
Walker Cres SL3 206 F1
Walker Ct SL6 202 D7
Walker Rd SL6 203 A4
Walkers Rd HP27 138 D7
Walkham Cl HP13 174 B4
Walkhampton Ave MK13 34 C3
Walk House Cl MK43 25 B1
Walk The
Eton Wick SL4 205 A1
Winslow MK18 65 F4
Walkwood End HP9 175 C1
Walkwood Rise HP9 186 C8
Wallace Cl
Marlow SL7 183 F4
Uxbridge UB10 201 E3
Wallace Dr LU6 92 E6
Wallace End HP21 116 A6
Wallace Mews LU6 92 E6
Wallace St MK13 33 E7
Wallace Wlk SL4 205 F1
Wallbridge Cl HP19 115 B7
Wall Brown Way HP19 101 C4
Waller Rd HP9 175 F2
Wallinger Dr MK5 46 A3
Wallingford MK13 34 B5
Wallingford Gdns HP11 173 B4
Wallingford Rd UB8 201 B2
Wallington Rd HP5 144 B1
Wallis Ct SL1 206 A3
Wallmead Gdns MK5 46 B7
Walney Pl MK4 45 F1
Walnut Cl
Great Missenden HP16 152 A7
Long Crendon HP18 125 C7
Newport Pagnell MK16 22 A3
Stoke Mandeville HP22 116 C2
Walnut Cres HP27 138 D7
Walnut Dr
Maids Moreton MK18 41 F4
Milton Keynes MK2 58 E8
Wendover HP22 131 B6
Walnut Gr HP10 185 E6
Walnut Lodge SL1 205 D4
Walnuts Sch The MK8 45 D5
WALNUT TREE 48 C6
Walnut Tree Cl
Bourne End SL8 185 B2
High Wycombe HP12 172 C8
Uxbridge UB10 201 E8
Walnut Tree Ct HP22 116 C3
Walnut Tree Ho HP11 174 B3
Walnut Tree La HP27 138 D6
Walnut Tree Rdbt MK7 48 C7
Walnut Way
Bourne End SL8 185 B2
Hyde Heath HP6 153 C4
Walpole Rd SL1 204 D7
Walsh's Manor MK14 34 D7
Walsingham Gate HP11 173 A4
WALTER'S ASH 150 C1
Waltham Dr MK10 36 A1
Waltham Ho 4 MK3 46 F1
WALTON
Aylesbury 115 F7
Milton Keynes 47 F5
Walton Cl HP13 162 E1
WALTON COURT 115 C5
Walton Court Ctr HP21 115 C5
Walton Dene HP21 115 F7
Walton Dr
High Wycombe HP13 162 E1
Walton MK7 47 F6
Walton End MK7 48 C6
Walton Gn HP21 115 E7
Walton Gr HP21 115 E7
Walton Heath MK3 57 D7
Walton High Sch MK7 48 C6
Walton La SL2 197 F3
WALTON MANOR 48 A6
WALTON PARK 48 A4
Walton Park Rdbt MK7 48 B4
Walton Pl HP22 116 F3
Walton Rd
Aylesbury HP21 115 F7
Caldecotte MK7 48 B3
Milton Keynes MK10 36 A2
Walton MK7 48 B6
Wavendon MK10, MK17 48 D7
Walton St HP21 115 E7
Walton Terr HP21 115 E7
Walton Way HP21 116 A7
Wandlebury MK14 35 A8
Wandsworth Pl MK13 34 D3
Wannions Cl HP5 145 A1
Wantage Cl LU7 79 E3
Wantage Cres LU7 79 E3
Wappenham Rd NN13 27 B8
Wapping HP18 125 D6
Wapseys La SL2 187 F4
Warbler Cl HP19 114 F8
Warburg Nature Reserve★ RG9 179 B5
Ward Cl SL0 207 F7
Wardes Cl HP16 151 C5
Ward Gdns SL1 204 E5
Wardle Pl MK6 46 E8
Ward Pl HP7 165 B7
Ward Rd
Brackley NN13 38 A5
Milton Keynes MK1 47 E3
Wardrobes La HP27 149 D8
Ward Royal 6 SL4 210 C6
Ward Royal Parade 3 SL4 210 C6
Wards Dr WD3 156 F3
Wardstone End MK4 46 B2
Ware Leys Cl OX27 71 E3
Wargrave Rd RG9 191 F1
Warmington Gdns MK15 35 B5
Warmstone Cl HP18 99 B6
Warmstone La HP18 99 B6
Warneford Ave HP22 131 D5
Warner Cl SL1 204 E5
Warners Cl MK17 59 D1
Warners Hill SL6 195 D8
Warners Rd MK17 57 D3
Warren Bank MK6 47 E5
Warren Cl
Buckingham MK18 52 E7
Slough SL3 206 E3
Stone HP17 114 B5
Warren Ct
Farnham Common SL2 198 C7
Little Horwood MK17 55 E5
Warrendene Rd HP14 162 A8
Warrender Rd HP5 144 E2
Warren Farm Cotts MK18 50 A7
Warren Field SL0 200 C3
Warren Ho HP19 101 B1
Warren Nature Reserve★ HP10 185 E5
Warren Parade SL2 206 C5
Warren Rd
Ickenham UB10 201 F8
Little Horwood MK17 55 F5
Yardley Gobion NN12 18 F6
Warren The
Chalfont St Peter SL9 177 F3
Chartridge HP5 143 E3
Hazelmere HP15 163 A5
Warren Wood Dr HP11 173 C5
Warren Yd MK12 33 A6
WARRINGTON 2 B1
Warrington Ave SL1 205 C7
Warrington Rd MK46 7 B7
Warwick Ave
High Wycombe HP12 172 B6
Milton Keynes MK10 36 C3
Slough SL2 198 C1
Warwick Cl
Aston Clinton HP22 117 E5
Maidenhead SL6 202 B4
Warwick Ct
Beaconsfield HP9 175 D3
Chorleywood WD3 167 F6

Warwick Ct *continued*
7 Windsor SL4 ....210 C5
Warwick Dr LU7 ....79 E2
Warwick Ho 7 HP13 ...173 F7
Warwick Pl
Milton Keynes MK3 ......57 E7
Uxbridge UB8.........201 C5
Warwick Rd
Beaconsfield HP9.......175 D3
Hanslope MK19.........11 A3
Milton Keynes MK3 ......57 F7
Pitstone LU7 ....105 D2
West Drayton UB7.......208 E5
Warwick Row HP20 ....102 A1
Washfield MK4 ....46 D3
Wash Hill HP10 ....185 E3
Wash Hill Lea HP10 ....185 E4
Wash Hill Mobile Home Pk
HP10 ....185 E3
Washingleys MK43 ....25 C2
Washington Ct SL7.....184 A3
Washington Dr
Slough SL1............204 D6
Windsor SL4 ....209 E4
Washington Row HP7 ..165 C7
Wastel MK6 ....47 B5
Watchcroft Dr MK18 ....41 E2
Watchet Ct MK4 ....46 D3
Watchet La
Holmer Green HP15.....163 B7
Little Kingshill HP16 ....152 C1
Waterbeach Cl SL1....205 D7
Waterbeach Rd SL1....205 D7
Waterborne Wlk LU7....80 F7
Water Cl MK19..........32 B7
Watercress Way MK10...36 B3
WATER EATON 58 D5
Water Eaton Rd MK2,
MK3 ....58 C7
WATEREND 159 C5
Water End Rd
Beacon's Bottom HP14 ..159 D3
Beacon's Bottom, Waterend
HP14..................159 C5
Waterfield WD3........167 C2
Waterford Cl MK3.......46 E1
Waterford Ho UB7 .....208 C3
Water Gdns The HP15..162 E2
Waterglades The HP9 ..175 C6
Water Hall Comb Sch
MK2 ....58 D4
Waterhouse Cl MK16....22 D4
Water La
Berkhamsted HP4 ......135 C4
Bovingdon HP3 ....146 B1
Ford HP17 ....128 B7
Leighton Buzzard LU7 ....80 F7
Sherington MK16........13 E1
Speen HP27...........150 C4
Waterlily 5 HP19......101 E4
Waterloo Ct MK3.........46 E2
Waterloo Rd
Leighton Buzzard LU7 ....80 E6
Uxbridge UB8.........201 C4
Waterlow Cl MK16 ......22 C2
Waterman Ct SL1 ......204 E5
Water Mdw HP5 ....154 B7
WATERMEAD...........101 F4
Watermead HP19 ......101 E4
Watermeadow HP19 ...101 F3
Water Meadow Way
HP22 ....131 B6
Watermill Way HP22 ...116 F2
WATERPERRY 123 B1
Waterperry OX33 ......123 B1
WATERPERRY
COMMON 122 F8
Waterperry Gdns*
OX33..................123 B1
Waterperry Mews
HP19 ....114 F8
Waterperry Rd HP18 ...123 D5
WATERSIDE...........154 D6
Waterside
Berkhamsted HP4 ......135 D4
Chesham HP5 ....154 D6
Edlesborough LU6 ....92 F4
Milton Keynes MK6 ......47 C8
Uxbridge UB8..........208 C8
Wooburn Green HP10 ...185 E7
Waterside Comb Sch
HP5...................154 D6
Waterside Ct HP5......154 C7
Waterside Dr SL3 ......207 A4
Waterside Lodge SL6 ..203 C8
Waterside Pk MK12 ......33 C8
Waterslade Pens HP17 . 126 F6
Waters Reach SL6 .....196 A1
WATER STRATFORD 40 A1
Water Stratford Rd
MK18 ....51 A7
Water Tower Cl UB8 ...201 E7
Watery La
Beachampton MK19......44 B6
Brackley NN13..........38 A7
Marsworth HP23 ....104 F1
Wooburn Green HP10 ...185 E8
Watling St
Bletchley MK2 ....47 D1
Watling St *continued*
Bow Brickhill MK17 ......58 F8
Granby MK6............47 A3
Milton Keynes, Kiln Farm MK8,
MK11...................33 B2
Milton Keynes, Shenley Lodge
MK6....................46 C6
Potterspury NN12 ....18 C3
Watling Terr MK2........47 E1
Watlington Ct HP16 ....152 A8
Watlington Rd OX49....157 A7
Watling Way Pool MK11 . 32 F4
Watlow Gdns MK18 .....41 E2
Watson Cl MK8 ....45 D6
Watten Ct MK2 ....58 E4
Wattleton Rd HP9......175 E1
Watts Cl MK19...........11 A3
Watts Gn HP18.........112 B2
Wavell Ct MK15 ....35 B7
Wavell Gdns SL2.......197 F2
Wavell Rd
Beaconsfield HP9.......176 B1
Maidenhead SL6 ....202 B6
WAVENDON.............48 E7
Wavendon Fields MK17.. 48 F6
WAVENDON GATE........48 D6
Wavendon Gate Comb Sch
MK7 ....48 D6
Wavendon House Dr
MK17 ....49 B8
Wavendon Rd MK17.....37 C2
Waveney Cl MK16........22 E3
Waverley Croft MK10....36 A1
Waverley Rd SL1.......205 C8
Waverley Wlk HP20 ....101 D2
Waxwing Cl HP19 ......101 E3
Wayfarers Pk HP4 .....134 F4
Waylands TW19........211 E1
Wayside
High Wycombe HP13 ....173 D7
Speen HP27...........150 C4
Wayside Ct HP6........154 C1
Wayside Gdns SL9 .....188 D4
Wayside Mews SL6.....202 F8
Wealdstone Pl MK6 .....35 A2
Weasel La MK3 ....57 C6
Weatherby LU6 ....93 E8
Weathercock Cl MK17...49 B5
Weathercock Gdns
HP15 ....163 C7
Weathercock La MK17...49 C4
Weavers End MK19......11 B2
Weavers Hill MK11......33 A4
Weavers Rd HP23 ......118 E4
Webb Cl
Chesham HP5 ....144 B1
Slough SL3............206 D2
Webber Heath MK7 .....48 D4
Webbs Home Cl MK10...36 A2
Webbs Mdw HP19......115 A8
Webster Cl
Maidenhead SL6 ....202 A5
Thame OX9 ....125 F1
Webster Rd HP21 ......116 A6
Websters Mdw MK4......46 C1
Wedgewood St HP19...115 A8
Wedgwood Ave MK14 ...22 A1
Wedgwood Dr HP14.....162 A6
WEEDON 87 D1
Weedon Cl SL9 ....177 B2
Weedon Hill HP6.......153 D4
Weedon La HP6........154 A3
Weedon Rd HP19 ......101 C2
Weekes Dr SL1 ....205 B4
Weill Rd HP21 ....116 A4
Weir La
Blackthorn OX25 ....81 A4
East Claydon MK18 ......74 E5
Whitchurch HP22........86 F6
Weirside Gdns UB7 ....208 D5
Welbeck Ave HP21.....116 C6
Welbeck Cl MK10 ....35 F1
Welbeck Rd SL6 ....202 D5
Welburn Gr MK4 ....46 B2
Welby Cl SL6 ....202 A4
Welden SL2 ....206 C7
Welders La
Chalfont St Giles SL9....177 A3
Seer Green SL9 ....177 B3
Weldon Rise MK5 ....46 B8
Welford Way HP18......112 F3
Welland Cl SL3 ....212 B8
Welland Dr MK16 ....22 E3
Welland Ho MK3.........57 E8
Welland Rd HP21 ......115 C5
Wellbank SL6..........196 E1
Wellbrook Mews HP23 . 119 B4
Wellcroft LU7..........105 F5
Wellcroft Rd SL1.......205 B5
WELL END 184 F5
Well End Cotts SL8.....184 F5
Weller Cl HP6 ....154 E2
Weller Ct LU6...........93 C7
Weller Rd HP6.........154 E2
Wellesbourne Gdns
HP13 ....162 D2
Welles La MK4..........45 D3
Wellesley Ave SL0 .....207 F4
Wellesley Ct SL0.......207 F4
Wellesley Ho SL4 ......210 B6
Wellesley Path SL1 ....206 A4
Wellesley Rd SL1 ......206 A4
Welles Rd HP13........173 F7
Welley Ave TW19 ......211 E3
Welley Rd SL3, TW19....211 E3
Wellfield HP15.........163 B3
Wellfield Ct MK15.......35 D8
Wellfield Rd HP14......171 B8
Wellhayes MK14 ....34 F8
WELL HEAD 93 D5
Well Head Rd LU6.......93 C6
Wellhouse Rd SL6 .....195 E2
Wellhouse Way HP14...161 E6
Wellingborough Rd MK46 .6 F5
Wellington Ave HP27...139 B4
Wellington Cl 1 SL6...202 B8
Wellington Pl
Aylesbury HP21 ....115 E4
Milton Keynes MK3 ......58 B7
Wellington Rd
Aylesbury HP21 ....115 E4
High Wycombe HP12....172 E4
Maidenhead SL6 ....202 D7
Uxbridge UB8..........201 C4
Wellington St SL1.....206 A4
Well La LU7 ....80 A1
Well Mdw HP19........101 D4
Wells Cl SL4...........210 A7
Well St MK18 ....52 D8
Welsh La MK18 ....40 C5
Welsummer Gr MK5.....46 A3
Welton Rd HP21 ....116 B7
WENDOVER............131 C4
Wendover CE Jun Sch
HP22..................131 B6
WENDOVER DEAN......141 C5
Wendover House Specl Sch
HP22..................131 C3
Wendover Hts HP22....131 C6
Wendover Rd
Bourne End SL8........185 A5
Burnham SL1..........204 B8
Ellesborough HP17 ....130 D3
Wendover St HP11 .....172 F7
Wendover Sta HP22....131 B4
Wendover Way
Aylesbury HP21 ....115 F6
High Wycombe HP11....173 B6
Wendover Woods (Forest
Wlks)* HP23 ....131 F6
Wenford MK10..........36 C3
Wenlack Cl UB9 ....190 A1
Wenning La MK4........46 B2
Wentworth Ave SL2....198 A2
Wentworth Cl HP13 ....173 C8
Wentworth Cres SL6 ...202 C6
Wentworth Ind Ctr SL2 198 A1
Wentworth Way MK3....57 C7
Wenwell Cl HP22 ......118 A3
Werner Ct HP21........115 E4
Werner Terr MK18 ......73 B6
Werth Dr MK17 ....49 B2
Wescott Way UB8......201 C3
Wesley Cl HP20........102 A2
Wesley Dene 4 HP13 ..173 B7
Wesley Hill 1 HP5.....144 B1
Wessex Ct
4 Stanwell TW19 ......213 E1
11 Windsor SL4 ....210 C6
Wessex Prim Sch SL6 ..202 B4
Wessex Rd SL8 ....185 B2
Wessex Road Ind Est
SL8...................185 B2
Wessex Way SL6.......202 B4
Wessons Hill SL6 ......195 C7
West Acres HP7........165 D7
Westanley Ave HP7 ....165 D8
West Ave HP10 ....163 C1
Westborne Ct MK13.....34 A6
Westborough Ct SL6 ...202 C6
Westborough Rd SL6...202 C6
Westbourne St 6
HP11 ....172 F7
Westbrook End MK17 ...57 C3
Westbrook Hay Prep Sch
HP1...................146 D7
WESTBURY 39 B4
Westbury Cl
Bicester OX27 ....71 E2
Newport Pagnell MK16 ...22 B4
Westbury Court Bsns Ctr
OX27...................71 C4
Westbury Ho 3 HP20 ..101 D1
Westbury La MK16 ......22 A5
Westbury Mill NN13.....38 F4
Westbury Terr OX27.....71 F2
West Cl SL7 ....193 D7
Westcliffe MK8 ....33 C2
Westcoign Ho SL6 .....203 B8
West Comm SL9 ....188 D6
West Common Cl SL9 ..188 E6
West Common Rd UB8 .201 D6
WESTCOTT 98 C7
Westcott CE Sch HP18 ..98 A7
Westcott Venture Pk
HP18...................98 A6
West Cres SL4 ....209 F6
WESTCROFT 45 E2
Westcroft
Slough SL2............198 B1
Tring HP23............119 A3
Westcroft Rdbt MK4 ....46 A2
Westcroft Stables*
HP27..................150 B3
West Ct
Bray SL6 ....203 C4
High Wycombe HP13 ....161 D3
West Dales MK13 ....34 C5
West Dean SL6 ....202 F8
Westdean La HP5 ......143 C3
Westdown Gdns LU6 ....93 F7
West Dr HP13..........173 D8
WEST DRAYTON 208 D3
West Drayton Park Ave
UB7 ....208 E3
West Drayton Prim Sch
UB7...................208 E4
West Drayton Sta UB7..208 E5
West Edge OX27 ....71 E2
WEST END 63 C2
West End HP22 ....116 E2
West End Cl MK18.......63 C2
West End Ct SL2 ....198 F4
West End La SL2.......198 E4
West End Pl HP22......116 E2
West End Rd
Cheddington LU7 ....104 F7
High Wycombe HP11....172 F7
West End St HP11......172 F7
Western Ave
Buckingham MK18.......41 C1
New Denham UB9 ......201 D8
Western Dene HP15....163 A5
Western Dr
Hanslope MK19 ....11 A3
Wooburn Green HP10...185 E5
Western House Prim Sch
SL1 ....204 F5
Western La MK18 ....65 F3
Western Perimeter Rd
TW6...................213 B5
Western Perimeter Road
Rdbt TW19............213 C2
Western Rd
Great Horwood MK17 ....55 A3
Milton Keynes, Fenny Stratford
MK2....................47 D1
Milton Keynes, Wolverton
MK12...................33 C6
Tring HP23............118 F3
West Farm Way MK46...13 E8
Westfield
Aylesbury HP21 ....115 E3
Hyde Heath HP6 ....153 C4
Westfield Ave MK19.....31 D5
Westfield Bglws SL7 ...192 F6
Westfield Cotts SL7.....192 F5
Westfield Fst Sch HP4..134 F5
Westfield Rd
Beaconsfield HP9.......175 C1
Berkhamsted HP4 ......134 E6
Dunstable LU6..........93 F8
Maidenhead SL6 ....202 B7
Milton Keynes MK2 ......58 C7
Pitstone LU7 ....105 C3
Slough SL2............198 B1
Wheatley OX33 ....122 A1
Westfields
Buckingham MK18.......52 C8
Princes Risborough
HP27..................139 D4
Westfield Sch SL8 .....185 A3
Westfield Wlk HP12....172 D6
West Furlong MK18 .....53 A1
Westgate Cres SL1.....204 F6
Westgate Ct HP13......174 A4
Westgate Ret Pk SL1...205 A6
Westgate Sch The SL1..205 A5
Westhill MK14 ....34 D8
West Hill MK17 ....49 D4
Westhorpe Rd SL7 .....183 F3
WEST HYDE............178 E3
West Hyde La SL9......178 A4
West La
Bledlow HP27 ....138 B1
Emberton MK46.........13 E8
Henley-on-Thames RG9..191 D2
Westland Cl TW19 .....213 E1
Westlands Ave SL1.....204 C7
Westlands Cl SL1 ......204 C7
Westlands Rd HP27 ....149 E5
WEST LEITH............118 F2
West Leith HP23 ....118 F1
WESTLINGTON 113 E1
Westlington La HP17...113 E1
Westlington Lea HP17..113 E2
Westmead
Monks Risborough
HP27..................139 B5
Windsor SL4 ....210 B4
West Mead SL6 ....195 F2
Westminster Cl
Brackley NN13..........38 A7
High Wycombe HP11....173 B4
Westminster Cres NN13 . 38 A7
Westminster Dr
Aylesbury HP21 ....115 F6
Westminster Dr *continued*
Milton Keynes MK3 ......47 A2
Westmorland Ave
HP21 ....116 B6
Westmorland Ho MK3...46 F2
Westmorland Rd SL6...202 D6
Westmount Ave HP7 ...165 C8
Weston Ct HP22 ....117 C5
Weston La OX9 ....136 F8
Weston Rd
Aston Clinton HP22 .....117 C5
Lewknor OX49.........157 A8
Olney MK46.............6 E3
Ravenstone MK46 ....5 E2
Slough SL1............204 F8
WESTON TURVILLE.....116 E3
Weston Turville CE Sch
HP22..................116 E3
Weston Turville Resr
Wildlife Reserve*
HP22..................130 F8
WESTON UNDERWOOD 6 B1
Weston Way HP22 .....116 A2
Weston Way Ind Est
HP22..................116 A2
Westover Ct HP13......161 D1
Westover Rd HP13 .....161 D2
West Pas 11 HP23......119 A3
Westpits MK46..........13 E8
West Point SL1 ....204 D5
West Puxley Cl MK19....31 D5
West Rd
Berkhamsted HP4 ......135 A5
Cranfield MK43 ....24 D2
Maidenhead SL6 ....202 E7
West Drayton UB7......208 F3
Woburn Sands MK17.....49 B5
West Richardson St 2
HP11 ....172 F7
Westrick Walk HP16 ...151 C5
West Ridge SL8........185 B4
Westridge Cl HP5......144 A1
Westron Gdns HP23....119 B4
Westside La MK16 ......12 B6
West Side Rise MK46......6 F4
West Spur Rd UB8 .....201 D2
West Sq SL0 ....207 F7
West St
Adstock MK18 ....53 F1
Aylesbury HP19 ....101 C1
Buckingham MK18.......41 C1
Dunstable LU6 ....93 F7
Henley-on-Thames RG9..191 D2
Leighton Buzzard LU7 ....80 F7
Maidenhead SL6 ....202 F7
Marlow SL7 ....183 D1
Olney MK46 ....6 F4
Steeple Claydon MK18....63 D2
West View
Chesham HP5 ....144 D2
Hardwick HP22 ....87 B3
High Wycombe HP13 ....173 B8
West Way HP9.........174 F1
West Waye HP13.......162 C2
West Well Cl MK18......51 A6
West Well La MK18......51 A6
West Wlk MK9 ....34 E2
Westwood HP12 ....172 B3
Westwood Cl
Little Chalfont HP6......166 D8
Milton Keynes MK8 ......45 F8
Westwood Dr HP6 .....166 D8
Westwood Gn SL6 .....195 F6
Westwood Rd SL7......183 C1
Westwood Wlk 6
HP20 ....101 F2
WEST WYCOMBE 160 F2
West Wycombe Comb Sch
HP14..................160 F2
West Wycombe Park*
HP14..................161 A1
West Wycombe Rd
HP12 ....161 C1
West Yard Ind Est
HP14..................160 C8
Wetherby Gdns MK3 ....57 D6
Wethered Pk SL7 ......183 D1
Wethered Rd
Burnham SL1..........204 B8
Marlow SL7 ....183 D2
Wexford Ct 2 SL6 .....203 B7
Wexham Court Prim Sch
SL3...................206 C8
Wexham Park Hospl
SL3...................199 C1
Wexham Park La SL3...199 C1
Wexham Pl SL2.........199 D6
Wexham Rd SL1, SL2...206 B6
Wexham Sch Sports Coll
SL2...................206 C8
Wexham St SL3.........199 B3
WEXHAM STREET 199 C4
Wexham Woods SL3 ...206 C8
Weybourne Rd 1 MK10 . 36 A4
Wey La HP5 ....154 B7
WHADDON..............45 A1

Whaddon CE Sch MK17 56 B8
Whaddon Chase HP19 101 D2
Whaddon Hall MK17 45 B2
Whaddon Rd
Milton Keynes, Shenley Brook End MK5 46 A3
Mursley MK17 56 C3
Nash MK17 44 D2
Newport Pagnell MK16 22 B3
Newton Longville MK17 57 D3
Whaddon Way MK3 46 F2
Whales La OX27 71 E2
Whalley Dr MK3 47 A2
Wharf Cl
Old Stratford MK19 32 B7
Wendover HP22 131 B5
Wharf Ct UB8 201 C1
Wharfe La RG9 191 E2
Wharf La
Berkhamsted HP4 134 C8
Bourne End SL8 185 A3
Old Stratford MK19 32 C7
Wharf Rd HP22 131 B5
Wharf Row HP22 118 B4
Wharfside MK2 47 E1
Wharfside Pl MK18 41 E1
Wharf The
Leighton Buzzard LU7 80 E6
Milton Keynes, Giffard Park MK14 21 E2
Milton Keynes MK2 58 E6
Wharf View MK18 41 E1
WHARLEY END 24 D1
Wharton Ho 2 HP20 101 D1
Whatmore Cl TW19 213 A1
Wheatbutts The SL4 204 F2
Wheat Cl HP21 115 E3
Wheatcroft Cl MK6 47 A5
Wheatfield Cl SL6 202 A4
Wheathouse Copse MK17 55 A3
Wheatlands Rd SL3 206 C3
WHEATLEY 122 A1
Wheatley Cl MK4 46 C2
Wheatley Park Sch OX33 122 B2
Wheatley Rd OX33 122 A3
Wheatley Way SL9 177 E4
Wheatsheaf Ho HP10 185 E7
Wheatsheaf Par SL4 211 A2
Wheatstone Cl SL3 206 A3
Wheeler Ave HP10 174 C8
Wheeler Cl HP20 116 B8
WHEELER END 171 B6
Wheeler Pl HP9 175 F2
Wheelers End OX39 147 C6
Wheelers Flats HP10 174 D8
Wheelers La MK13 34 A6
Wheelers Orch SL9 177 E4
Wheelers Pk HP13 173 D7
Wheelers Yd HP16 152 A7
Wheelwright Mews MK14 34 F6
Wheelwright Rd HP27 138 D7
Wheelwrights HP22 116 F2
Wheelwrights Pl SL3 212 C7
Wheelwrights Way MK19 32 C7
Wheelwrights Yd HP22 85 A5
WHELPLEY HILL 145 D5
Whelpley Hill Pk HP5 145 D5
Whet Stone Cl MK13 34 B4
Whichcote Gdns HP5 154 D6
Whichert Cl HP9 175 C6
Whichford MK14 22 A1
Whielden Cl HP7 165 B7
Whielden Gate HP7 164 E4
Whielden Gn HP7 165 B7
Whielden Hts HP7 165 A7
Whielden La
Coleshill HP7 164 E5
Winchmore Hill HP7 164 D3
Whielden St HP7 165 B7
Whinchat HP19 101 E3
Whincup Cl HP11 172 F4
Whinneys Rd HP10 174 C3
Whipass Hill HP9 176 A5
WHIPSNADE 107 F8
Whipsnade Park Homes LU6 93 F1
Whipsnade Rd LU6 93 F6
Whipsnade Tree Cathedral★ LU6 93 F1
Whitby Cl MK3 47 A2
Whitby Rd SL1 205 C6
WHITCHURCH 87 B6
Whitchurch Cl
Maidenhead SL6 195 E3
Westcott HP18 98 B7
Whitchurch Comb Sch HP22 86 E7
Whitchurch Ho 5 SL6 202 F7
Whitchurch La HP22 86 D8
Whitchurch Rd LU7 78 B1
Whiteacres Dr SL6 203 B1
White Alder MK12 33 E5
Whitebaker Ct MK14 34 F6
Whitebeam Cl HP22 116 C3
Whitebrook Pk SL6 196 C4
Whitechurch Cl HP17 114 C5
White Cl
High Wycombe HP13 161 D1
Slough SL1 205 D5
White Cotts MK18 29 D4
White Cres HP22 131 D7
Whitecross Green Wood Wildlife Reserve★ OX5 94 C2
Whitecross Rd HP17 126 F5
Whitefield La HP16 152 A6
Whiteford Rd SL2 205 E8
Whitegate Ct MK6 47 B6
Whitehall SL6 196 B1
Whitehall Ave MK10 36 D1
Whitehall Cl UB8 201 D4
Whitehall Inf Sch UB8 201 C4
Whitehall Jun Sch UB8 201 C4
Whitehall La TW19 212 A1
Whitehall Rd UB8 201 D3
Whitehall St 6 HP20 101 D1
White Hart Cl
Chalfont St Giles HP8 177 A7
Ludgershall HP18 96 B8
White Hart Field HP22 85 B4
White Hart La HP17 127 A5
White Hart Mdw HP9 175 E1
White Hart Rd
1 Maidenhead SL6 202 F7
Slough SL1 205 D3
White Hart St 9 HP11 173 A7
Whitehaven SL1 205 F6
Whitehead Way HP21 115 E6
White Hermitage SL4 211 C2
Whitehill
Berkhamsted HP4 135 D5
Olney MK46 6 E5
White Hill
Ashley Green HP4, HP5 145 C7
Beaconsfield HP9, HP10 185 F8
Chesham HP5 144 D1
High Wycombe HP13 162 B2
Remenham Hill RG9 192 A2
White Hill Cl
Chesham HP5 144 D1
Marlow Bottom SL7 183 C6
Whitehill Ct HP4 135 D5
Whitehill La LU7 105 D3
White Hill La LU7 105 D3
White Horse Ct HP6 154 C2
White Horse Dr MK4 46 C2
White Horse La HP22 87 A6
White Horse Rd SL4 209 D5
Whitehorse Yd MK11 32 D5
White Hos MK18 50 D6
Whitehouse Cl HP10 174 E1
White House Cl SL9 177 E3
Whitehouse La HP10 174 E2
Whitehouse Way
Iver Heath SL0 200 D2
Slough SL3 206 D3
Whitelands Ave WD3 167 C5
Whitelands Rd HP12 172 D7
Whitelands Way HP12 172 D7
WHITELEAF 139 D5
Whiteleaf Hill Nature Reserve★ HP27 139 E4
Whiteleaf Way HP27 139 D5
Whiteley SL4 209 E7
Whiteley Cres MK3 57 F6
White Lilies Island SL4 210 B7
White Lion Cl HP7 166 A8
White Lion Rd HP7 166 B8
Whitelock Ho RG9 191 E3
White Lodge Cl SL7 183 C6
White Paddock SL6 202 A2
Whitepit La HP10 185 D7
White Rock SL6 196 B1
Whites Cl MK18 63 D3
Whites Croft MK6 46 F6
Whites La SL3 211 B8
White Spire Specl Sch MK3 46 F1
Whitethorn Ave UB7 208 F6
Whitethorn Cl HP22 130 A8
Whitethorn Pl UB7 208 F5
Whitethorns MK16 22 B3
White View 14 HP20 101 F3
Whitewood Rd HP4 135 A4
WHITFIELD 26 D3
Whitfield Rd HP14 162 A6
Whitfield Way WD3 167 F1
Whitley Cl TW19 213 E1
Whitley Ct HP21 115 E4
Whitmees Cl MK46 6 E4
Whitney Rdbt MK4 45 E2
Whitsun Pasture MK15 35 B7
Whittaker Rd SL2 197 E1
Whittenham Cl SL2 206 A5
Whittington Chase MK4 45 E1
Whittle Ct MK5 46 C7
Whittle Parkway SL1 204 D7
Whitton Way MK16 22 C3
Whitworth La MK5 46 B7
Whurley Way SL6 195 E2
Whybrow Gdns HP4 135 E6
Whyteladyes La SL6 195 E6
Whytingham Rd HP23 119 C4
WICKEN 31 B3
Wicken Park Rd MK19 31 B2
Wicken Rd MK18 30 E1
Wickets The SL6 202 C7
Wicket The SL1 205 E3
Wick Rd HP23 133 D8
Wickstead Ave MK8 45 D6
Widbrook Rd SL6 196 B3
Widdenton View HP14 171 C5
Widecroft Rd SL0 207 E7
Widewater Pl UB9 190 C6
Widgeon Ho HP11 173 C6
Widmere Field HP16 151 C5
Widmere La SL7 183 A6
WIDMER END 162 E6
Widmer End Comb Sch HP15 162 F6
WIDMOOR 185 E3
Widmore Cl HP5 143 E5
Widnell La OX25 95 C7
Wigan's La HP14 148 C6
Wiggington Ho SL4 210 D7
WIGGINTON 119 D1
WIGGINTON BOTTOM 133 D8
Wigginton Bottom HP23 133 E8
Wiggles La HP23 118 F7
Wigmore Ct HP19 101 A2
Wigmore Rd HP19 101 A2
Wigwell Gdns MK17 55 A2
Wilberforce Mews 7 SL6 202 F7
Wildacre Rd MK5 46 A4
Wilderness The HP4 135 C4
Wildgreen N SL3 207 A2
Wildgreen S SL3 207 A2
Wildwood Ct WD3 167 F5
Wilford Cl MK15 35 C2
Wilford Rd SL3 206 F2
Wilfrids Wood Cl HP10 185 B6
Wilks Croft MK5 45 F7
WILLEN 35 D7
Willen La MK14 34 F8
WILLEN PARK 35 C6
Willen Park Ave MK15 35 B6
Willen Prim Sch MK15 35 C7
Willen Rd
Milton Keynes MK10 35 F3
Newport Pagnell MK16 22 D3
Willets Rise MK5 46 A5
Willetts La UB9 200 F7
Willey Ct MK11 32 F4
William Bandy Cl LU7 79 F3
William Burt Cl HP22 116 F1
William Ellis Cl SL4 211 A1
William Fiske Ho 4 HP4 135 C4
William Harding Cl HP21 115 E7
William Harding Comb Sch HP21 116 A5
William Hartley Yd SL3 199 B1
William Hill Dr HP22 102 C4
William Ho 4 HP13 173 F5
William Moulder Ct HP5 144 B3
Williams Circ MK7 48 A4
Williams Cl
Aylesbury HP19 101 D1
Hanslope MK19 10 F3
William Shakman Ho HP8 177 B8
William Smith Cl MK15 35 C3
William St
Berkhamsted HP4 135 D4
Slough SL1 205 F5
Windsor SL4 210 D6
William Sutton Ho MK5 46 A6
Williams Way HP27 138 D6
Willis Rd HP17 127 A6
Willmott Cl HP19 101 D4
Willoners SL2 205 A8
Willoughby Rd SL3 207 B3
Willoughby's Wlk HP13 161 D2
Willow Ave
High Wycombe HP12 172 B4
New Denham UB9 201 C6
West Drayton UB7 208 F6
WILLOWBANK 201 C7
Willow Bank SL7 183 D5
Willowbank Terr 6 HP21 115 E8
Willowbrook
Slough SL4 205 D2
Wendover HP22 131 B7
Willow Chase
Chesham HP5 144 B1
Hazlemere HP15 162 E3
Willow Cl
Chalfont St Peter SL9 177 E1
Colnbrook SL3 212 C7
Flackwell Heath HP10 185 C6
Maidenhead SL6 195 D1
Moulsoe MK16 36 E8
Willow Crescent E UB9 201 C7
Willow Crescent W UB9 201 C7
Willow Ct
2 Aylesbury, Quarrendon HP19 101 A2
Aylesbury, Walton Court HP21 115 C6
High Wycombe HP11 173 E4
Walter's Ash HP14 161 C8
Willow Dr
Buckingham MK18 52 F7
Maidenhead SL6 203 B2
Willow End HP22 116 F2
Willowford MK13 33 E5
Willow Gate HP18 112 B2
Willow Gr MK19 32 B6
Willow Herb HP19 101 E4
Willow Ho LU7 80 E7
Willow La
Amersham HP7 165 F6
Milton Keynes MK11 32 C5
Willowmead HP17 114 F5
Willowmead Cl 10 SL7 183 F3
Willowmead Gdns SL7 183 F3
Willowmead Rd 8 SL7 183 F3
Willowmead Sq 9 SL7 183 F3
Willow Parade SL3 207 A3
Willow Pk SL2 199 A5
Willow Pl SL4 210 C8
Willow Rd
Aylesbury HP19 101 D1
Brackley NN13 38 A6
Chinnor OX39 147 C6
Great Horwood MK17 55 A3
Poyle SL3 212 E5
Thame OX9 125 F1
Willow Rise HP17 127 A7
Willows Rd SL8 185 B4
Willows Riverside Pk The SL4 209 C7
Willows Sch The MK6 35 A2
Willows The
Amersham HP6 154 B4
4 Bourne End SL8 185 B3
Edlesborough LU6 92 F3
High Wycombe HP12 172 E8
Longwick HP27 138 E6
Windsor SL4 209 D7
Willow Way
Loudwater HP11 174 B2
Milton Keynes MK2 58 C7
Princes Risborough HP27 139 A3
Wing LU7 79 E3
Willow Wlk HP15 163 A3
Willow Wood Cl SL1 197 B3
Willow Wren MK14 21 F2
Wilmar Cl UB8 201 D5
Wilmin Gr MK5 46 B7
Wilmot Rd SL1 197 B2
Wilsley Pound MK7 48 B8
Wilson Ct MK8 45 E7
WILSTONE 104 D1
WILSTONE GREEN 118 D8
Wilstone Resr★ HP22, HP23 118 C7
Wilton Ave MK3 58 A8
Wilton Cl UB7 213 D8
Wilton Cres
Beaconsfield HP9 175 E3
Windsor SL4 209 D4
Wilton Hollow HP9 175 F3
Wilton La HP9 176 E4
WILTON PARK 176 B1
Wilton Rd HP9 175 E3
Wiltshire Ave SL2 198 C1
Wiltshire Lodge 2 SL6 202 F6
Wiltshire Rd 2 SL7 183 F3
Wiltshire Way MK3 46 E1
Wimbledon Pl MK13 34 D3
Wimblington Dr MK6 47 A4
Wimborne Cres MK4 45 F2
Wimpole Rd UB7 208 D5
Winbury Ct SL6 202 E7
Winbury Pl SL6 203 B3
Winbury Sch SL6 203 B4
Wincanton Hill MK3 57 C6
Winchbottom La
High Wycombe HP10 173 B1
Little Marlow SL7, HP10 184 B7
Winchendon Rd HP18 112 B2
Winchester Circ MK10 36 B1
Winchester Cl
Amersham HP7 165 E8
Poyle SL3 212 E6
Winchester Ct HP11 174 B3
Winchester Dr SL6 202 B3
Winchester Ho HP21 115 F6
WINCHMORE HILL 164 D2
Winch Terr SL4 209 D5
Windermere Cl
Aylesbury HP21 116 B6
Chorleywood WD3 167 D4
Windermere Dr MK2 58 D5
Windermere Gdns LU7 80 C7
Windermere Way
Slough SL1 204 C7
West Drayton UB7 208 E5
Windmill Cl
Aylesbury HP19 115 B8
Buckingham MK18 41 F1
Ivinghoe LU7 105 F5
Windsor SL4 210 B5
Windmill Dr HP15 162 F6
Windmill Hill
Chipperfield WD4 156 F7
Coleshill HP7 164 F2
Princes Risborough HP27 139 B2
Windmill Hill Dr MK3 57 D7
Windmill Hill Rdbt MK4 46 C1
Windmill La HP15 162 F7
Windmill Par HP15 162 F6
Windmill Rd
Chalfont St Peter SL9 177 D3
Cookham Rise SL6 195 E6
Fulmer SL3 199 D7
Haddenham HP17 126 F6
Slough SL1 205 D5
Thame OX9 126 E1
Windmill St HP18 96 A1
Windmill Way
Cranfield MK43 25 C3
Tring HP23 118 F4
Windmill Wood HP6 154 A2
Windrush Ave SL3 207 B3
Windrush Cl
Ickenham UB10 201 F8
Milton Keynes MK15 35 A6
Windrush Ct
Aylesbury HP21 115 D4
High Wycombe HP13 173 F6
Windrush Dr HP13 173 F6
Windrush Ho SL8 185 B4
Windrush Way SL6 203 A8
WINDSOR 210 E6
Windsor Ave
Leighton Buzzard LU7 80 F7
Newport Pagnell MK16 22 C4
Windsor Boys' Sch Performing Arts Coll The SL4 210 B6
Windsor Bsns Ctr SL4 210 C6
Windsor Castle★ SL4 210 E7
Windsor Cl
Bovingdon HP3 146 A3
Burnham SL1 197 C1
Windsor Cres HP10 174 C2
Windsor Ct HP6 154 D1
Windsor Dr HP13 162 D1
Windsor End HP9 186 F8
Windsor & Eton Central Sta SL4 210 D6
Windsor & Eton Riverside Sta SL4 210 D7
Windsor Girls' Sch SL4 210 A4
Windsor Great Pk★ SL4 210 B2
Windsor Hall SL4 210 F4
Windsor Hill
Monks Risborough HP27 139 C5
Wooburn Green HP10 185 F5
Windsor Ho 4 SL1 205 F3
Windsor La
Burnham SL1 197 C1
Little Kingshill HP16 152 C3
Windsor Rd
Aylesbury HP21 116 A7
Chesham HP5 144 B3
Datchet SL3 211 A7
Gerrards Cross SL9 188 C3
Maidenhead SL6 203 C2
Oakley Green SL4 209 A7
Pitstone LU7 105 C3
Slough SL1 205 E4
Wraysbury TW19 211 E1
Windsor Royal Sta 1 SL4 210 D6
Windsor St
Milton Keynes MK2 58 C7
Milton Keynes, Wolverton MK12 33 C6
Uxbridge UB8 201 C5
Winemar Cl MK19 11 A3
Winfold La MK4 46 B1
WING 79 F2
Wingate Ave HP13 173 E7
Wingate Circ MK7 48 A4
Wingate Cl HP13 173 E7
Wingate Wlk HP20 116 A7
Wingbury Ctyd Bsns Village HP22 89 D5
Wing Cl SL7 183 C1
Wingfield Gr MK10 36 A2
WINGRAVE 89 C3
Wingrave CE Comb Sch HP22 89 A3
Wingrave Cross Rds HP22 88 F4
Wingrave Rd
Aston Abbotts HP22 88 E4
Long Marston HP23 104 D1
Tring HP23 119 B5
Wing Rd
Cublington LU7 78 C1
Leighton Buzzard LU7 80 D5

Wing Rd *continued*
Stewkley LU7 78 F6
Winkers Cl SL9 177 F2
Winkers La SL9 177 F3
Winkfield La SL4 209 A1
Winkfield Rd SL4 209 E2
Winnock Rd UB7 208 D5
Winsford Hill MK4 46 E3
WINSLOW 66 B4
Winslow CE Comb Sch MK18 66 A5
Winslow Field HP16 151 F8
Winslow Gdns HP13 174 A7
Winslow Rd
Granborough MK18 75 F7
Great Horwood MK17 54 F1
Little Horwood MK17 55 D1
Nash MK17 55 C8
Swanbourne MK17 66 F3
Wingrave HP22 89 B3
Winstanley La MK5 46 C4
Winston Ct SL6 202 A8
Winstone Cl HP6 154 B5
Winston Gdns HP4 134 F4
Winston Ho HP11 174 A4
Winterburn MK13 34 B5
Winter Ct 6 SL7 183 E2
WINTERHILL 46 D8
Winter Hill SL6 184 C1
Winter Hill Rd SL6 195 A4
Winters Way HP15 163 D7
Winterton Dr HP21 115 E4
Wintoun Path SL2 197 E1
Winvale SL1 205 E3
Winwood
Slough SL2 206 C7
Windsor SL4 209 F6
Winwood Cl MK19 31 E5
Winwood Dr HP22 85 A5
Wise La UB7 208 D2
Wisewood Rd MK4, MK5 45 E4
Wishart Gn MK7 48 E5
Wisley Ave MK13 34 D3
Wistmans MK4 46 D4
Witan Ct MK9 34 D2
Witan Gate MK9 34 D1
Witchell HP22 131 B4
Witham Ct MK3 46 D1
Witham Way HP21 115 C4
Witheridge La HP9, HP10 175 B7
Withey Cl SL4 209 E6
Withington MK13 34 A5
Withycombe MK4 46 E3
Withycroft SL3 206 E7
Witney Cl UB10 201 F8
Wittington Cotts SL7 193 D6
Wittmills Oak MK18 41 E1
Witton Ho WD3 167 D4
Wivelsfield LU6 92 E6
Wixon Path HP19 115 A8
Woad La MK14 34 E8
WOBURN 60 F7
Woburn Ave MK12 33 C6
Woburn Ct LU7 80 E6
Woburn La MK17 49 E4
Woburn Lower Sch MK17 60 F7
Woburn Rd
Aspley Heath MK17 49 C2
Little Brickhill MK17 59 E6
Sheeplane MK17, LU7 60 C1
WOBURN SANDS 49 A5
Woburn Sands Rd MK17 48 D3
Woburn Sands Sta MK17 49 A5
Wodehouse Wlk MK16 22 A5
Wolf La SL4 209 E4
Wolfscote La MK4 46 B3
Wolsey Gdns MK13 34 A4
Wolstan Cl UB9 190 A1
Wolston Mdw MK10 35 F3
WOLVERTON 33 C5
WOLVERTON MILL 33 A6
Wolverton Rd
Castlethorpe MK19 20 B5
Milton Keynes, Giffard Park MK16 21 E2
Milton Keynes, Stony Stratford MK11 32 E6
Milton Keynes, Wolverton MK12, MK19 33 E8
Newport Pagnell MK16 22 B4
Wolverton Sta MK12 33 E7
WOOBURN 185 D4
Wooburn Common Rd HP10, SL1 186 A2
Wooburn Grange HP10 185 D3
WOOBURN GREEN 185 F7
Wooburn Green La HP9 186 A8
Wooburn Manor Pk HP10 185 E5
Wooburn Mead HP10 185 E6
Wooburn Mews HP10 185 E5
WOOBURN MOOR 174 E1
Wooburn Town HP10 185 D4
Woodall Cl MK10 35 E3
Woodbank HP27 149 C5
Woodbank Ave SL9 188 D5
Woodbank Dr HP8 177 D7
Woodbine Cl HP27 138 E5
Woodbine Cotts SL9 188 D8
Woodbridge Ho UB8 201 C5
WOODBURN COMMON 186 B3
Woodbury Cl SL8 185 C3
Woodchester Pk HP9 175 C6
Wood Cl SL4 210 C3
Woodcock Ave HP14 161 B8
Woodcote SL6 202 D6
Woodcote Gn HP13 161 D2
Woodcote Lawns HP5 144 A4
Woodcroft Rd HP5 144 D3
WOOD END
Little Horwood 55 E2
Nash 55 C8
Wood End
Little Horwood MK17 55 E2
Nash MK17 55 C8
Wood End Cl SL2 187 D1
Wood End Fst Sch MK14 34 D8
Wood End La MK16 23 E1
Woodfield HP27 149 D6
Woodfield Dr SL6 202 A6
Woodfield Pk HP6 154 B3
Woodfield Rd HP27 139 C4
Woodford Cl HP19 115 B7
Woodford Way SL2 198 A2
Wood Gn MK10 47 F8
WOOD GREEN 27 F2
Woodhall Cl UB8 201 D7
WOODHAM 83 E1
Woodhill Ave SL9 189 A5
Woodhill Ct
Amersham HP6 154 D2
Gerrards Cross SL9 188 E4
Woodhouse Ct MK14 34 D6
Woodhurst Dr UB9 189 F6
Woodhurst Rd SL6 196 B1
Woodhurst South SL6 196 C1
Wood La
Aspley Guise MK17 49 D4
Iver SL0 207 C8
Milton Keynes MK14 34 E8
Slough SL1 205 A4
South Heath HP16 152 E8
Tingewick MK18 51 B6
Weston Underwood MK46 6 A2
Woodland Ave
Leighton Buzzard LU7 70 F2
Slough SL1 205 D6
Windsor SL4 209 F3
Woodland Cl
High Wycombe HP12 172 C6
Marlow SL7 183 E4
Tring HP23 118 F2
Woodland Glade SL2 187 D1
Woodland Grange SL0 207 E3
Woodland La WD3 167 D6
Woodland Pl WD3 167 F5
Woodland Rd WD3 178 D5
Woodlands SL9 188 F5
Woodlands Ave HP4 135 D3
Woodlands Bsns Pk SL6 202 A2
Woodlands Cl
Buckingham MK18 41 E2
Gerrards Cross SL9 189 A5
Holmer Green HP15 163 C6
Woodlands Cotts 1 SL2 198 C7
Woodlands Cres MK18 41 D2
Woodlands Dr
Beaconsfield HP9 175 C4
Walter's Ash HP14 161 C8
Woodlands Farm SL6 195 C6
Woodlands Glade HP9 175 C4
Woodlands Hill HP9 186 E5
Woodlands Park Ave SL6 202 A2
Woodlands Park Prim Sch SL6 202 A1
Woodlands Park Rd SL6 202 A3
Woodlands The
Amersham HP6 154 C4
Tylers Green HP10 162 F3
Woodlands View HP13 174 A7
Woodland View
Chesham HP5 154 D6
Milton Keynes MK12 33 D5
Woodland Way
Marlow SL7 183 E4
Woburn Sands MK17 49 B4
Woodlane Cl HP10 173 F1
Wood Lane Cl
Flackwell Heath HP10 173 F1
Iver Heath SL0 200 B2
Woodlane Gdns HP10 174 A1
Woodley Ct HP7 165 D8
Woodley Headland MK6 47 C7
Woodley Hill HP5 154 D5
Woodman Cl LU7 79 F3
Woodmans Cl MK19 31 E4
Woodmans Croft HP19 115 A8
Woodmoor End SL6 196 B7
Woodpiece Rd OX25 94 E7
Woodpits La MK46 6 E5
Wood Pond Cl HP9 176 C4
Wood Rd MK43 3 F7
WOODROW 164 D5
Woodruff Ave MK14 34 E4
Woodrush Cl MK6 47 B4
Woodside
Aspley Guise MK17 49 D3
Eaton Bray LU6 92 E6
Flackwell Heath HP10 185 C6
Milton Keynes MK11 32 E6
Woodside Ave
Amersham HP6 154 D3
Beaconsfield HP9 175 C4
Flackwell Heath HP10 185 C7
Woodside Cl
Amersham HP6 154 D1
Beaconsfield HP9 175 C3
Chalfont St Peter SL9 177 E1
Loudwater HP11 174 B2
Woodside Hill SL9 177 E1
Woodside Jun Sch & Amersham Music Ctr HP6 154 E1
Woodside Rd
Amersham HP6 154 D1
Beaconsfield HP9 175 C3
High Wycombe HP13 174 A8
Woodside Way
Leighton Buzzard LU7 80 D6
Tylers Green HP10 174 C8
Woods La NN12 18 E3
Woods Pl
13 Tring HP23 119 A3
Wendover HP22 131 B4
Woodspring Ct 2 MK10 35 F1
Wood St
Milton Keynes MK13 33 F7
Waddesdon HP18 99 A7
Woburn Sands MK17 49 B4
Woodstock Ave SL3 206 D2
Woodstock Cl
Aylesbury HP21 116 B6
Maidenhead SL6 195 F1
Woodstock Ct MK13 34 B7
Woodstock Dr UB10 201 F8
Woodview Cl HP12 161 B2
Wood View Cotts HP5 144 B7
Woodview Dr HP16 150 C5
Woodville OX39 147 C5
Woodville Cres NN12 18 E6
Woodward Ho 4 MK2 58 C8
Woodward Pl MK8 34 A1
Woodway HP27 149 D6
Wood Way HP9 174 F1
Woodway Farm Ind Est HP18 124 F8
Woodways HP17 127 A6
Woodwicks WD3 178 D5
Woollerton Cres HP22 131 D5
Woollerton Ct HP27 139 B4
Woolmans
Fullers Slade MK11 33 A4
Milton Keynes MK11 33 A4
Woolrich Gdns MK11 32 E5
WOOLSTONE 35 D3
Wooster Rd HP9 175 D4
Wooton Ct MK13 33 F8
WOOTTON BOURNE END 25 F8
Wootton Dr HP10 185 E8
Wootton Gn OX27 72 E6
Wootton La HP17 113 E1
Wootton Way SL6 202 C6
Worcester Cl
Maidenhead SL6 202 D3
Newport Pagnell MK16 22 A3
Worcester Gdns SL1 205 D4
Worcester Ho MK3 46 F2
Worcester Rd UB8 208 D8
Wordsworth Ave MK16 22 A4
Wordsworth Dr MK3 58 A7
Wordsworth Rd
High Wycombe HP11 173 A5
Slough SL2 197 D1
Wordsworth Way UB7 208 E2
WORLD'S END 130 F7
World's End La HP22 130 F8
Worley Pl HP9 176 D5
WORMINGHALL 123 E6
Worminghall Rd
Ickford HP18 123 F4
Oakley HP18 109 D4
Wormsley Cres HP14 158 C4
WORMSTONE 99 C5
Wornal Pk HP18 123 C8
Worple The TW19 211 F1
Worrelle Ave MK10 36 A3
Worster Rd SL6 195 E6
Worth Ct MK10 36 B1
Worthies The HP7 165 B7
Worthington Rd LU6 93 F8
Wotton End HP18 96 C7
Wotton Path HP21 115 E3
Wotton Rd HP18 97 E1
WOTTON UNDERWOOD 97 C4
Woughton L Ctr MK6 46 F7
WOUGHTON ON THE GREEN 47 D8
WOUGHTON PARK 47 E6
Wraxall Way MK6 47 D5
Wray Ct MK4 46 A2
WRAYSBURY 211 E1
Wraysbury Dr UB7 208 D6
Wraysbury Prim Sch TW19 211 E1
Wraysbury Sta TW19 212 A1
Wren Cl MK18 52 F7
Wren Ct SL3 207 A3
Wren Dr UB7 208 D3
Wren Path HP19 114 F8
Wren Rd HP16 151 C5
Wrensfield SL7 183 C2
Wrens Pk MK10 36 B2
Wren Vale HP13 173 A8
Wren Wlk LU6 92 E4
Wright SL4 209 C4
Wrights Cl HP14 171 B5
Wright's La HP16 151 C5
Wright Sq SL4 209 C4
Wrights Yd HP16 152 A7
Wright Way SL4 209 C4
Wroxton Ct MK4 45 F2
Wyatt Cl HP13 172 F8
Wyatt Rd SL4 209 D4
Wyatt's Rd WD3 167 F5
Wychwood HP16 152 B4
Wychwood Gdns HP12 172 C6
Wychwood Rise HP16 152 B4
Wyclands Ho HP12 161 B2
Wycombe Abbey Sch HP11 173 A6
Wycombe Air Pk SL7 171 F2
Wycombe Cl HP21 116 B4
Wycombe End HP9 175 E1
Wycombe High Sch HP11 172 F4
Wycombe Hospl HP11 173 A6
Wycombe Ind Mall HP11 172 F7
Wycombe La HP10 185 E7
WYCOMBE MARSH 173 F4
Wycombe Mus★ HP13 173 B7
Wycombe Mus & Gdn 18 HP13 173 B7
Wycombe Rd
Beacon's Bottom HP14 159 D3
Holmer Green HP15 163 B6
Lacey Green HP14 149 B4
Marlow Bottom SL7 183 E6
Marlow SL7 183 E4
Prestwood HP15 151 C5
Wycombe Ret Pk HP11 173 F4
Wycombe Sp Ctr HP11 172 F3
Wycombe Swan Theatre HP11 173 B6
Wycombe View HP10 174 A2
Wye Cl
Aylesbury HP21 115 C5
Milton Keynes MK3 46 E1
Wye Ct 2 SL8 185 A3
Wye Est HP11 173 E5
Wye Gdns HP12 172 D8
Wye Rd HP10 185 D8
Wye River Bsns Ctr 8 HP11 172 F7
Wye Valley Sch The SL8 185 B4
Wykeham Gate HP17 126 F5
Wykeham Rise OX39 147 D6
Wykeham Way HP17 126 F6
Wykeridge Cl HP5 144 B4
Wylands Rd SL3 207 A2
Wylie End MK13 34 A7
WYMBUSH 33 F2
Wymering Rd HP21 116 C6
Wymers Cl SL1 197 B3
Wymers Wood Rd SL1 197 A3
Wymondham MK10 36 B1
Wynbury Dr HP13 162 E1
Wyndale Cl RG9 191 E1
Wyndham Ave HP13 161 F2
Wyndham Cres SL1 197 B3
Wyness Ave MK17 59 E5
Wynford Gn HP21 115 F6
Wyngates LU7 80 E5
Wyngrave Pl HP9 175 C5
Wynne-Jones Ctr HP21 115 F8
Wynn Gr HP15 163 B3
Wynnstay Gdns SL7 183 E5
Wynnswick Rd HP9 176 C5
Wynyard Ct MK6 46 E7
Wyre Cl HP17 127 A5
Wyvern Sch MK12 33 C6
Wyvern Way UB8 201 C4

X

Xscape★ MK6 34 F2

Y

Yalts Brow MK4 46 B2
Yardley Ave LU7 105 D4
Yardley Gn HP20 101 F2
YARDLEY GOBION 18 E5
Yardley Gobion CE Prim Sch NN12 18 E6
YARDLEY HASTINGS 1 B6
Yardley Hastings Prim Sch NN7 1 A7
Yardley Rd
Cosgrove MK19 19 D2
Olney MK46 6 E6
Potterspury NN12 18 F4
Yarmouth Rd SL1 205 C6
Yarrow Pl MK14 34 E4
Yarrowside HP7 166 B7
Yeates Cl
Thame OX9 125 F1
Winslow MK18 65 F4
Yeats Cl MK16 21 F5
Ye Meads SL6 203 E5
Ye Meads Cotts SL6 203 E5
Ye Meads Ho SL6 203 E5
Yeomans Cl NN13 38 A8
Yeomans Dr MK14 22 B1
Yeovil Ent Ctr SL1 204 F8
Yeovil Rd SL1 204 E8
Yew Ave UB7 208 E6
Yewtree Cl LU7 105 E5
Yew Tree Cl
Beaconsfield HP9 175 F1
Botley HP5 145 A1
Eaton Bray LU6 92 F5
Maidenhead SL6 202 E8
Newton Longville MK17 57 C3
Stoke Mandeville HP22 116 A1
Yew Tree Dr
Bovingdon HP3 146 B3
Hazlemere HP15 162 F6
Yew Tree Rd
Slough SL1 206 A3
Uxbridge UB10 201 F4
Yew Wlk HP15 163 A3
Yiewsley Ct UB7 208 E5
Yolsum Cl HP17 126 E6
Yonder Slade MK18 52 D6
York Ave
Slough SL1 205 C7
Windsor SL4 210 B5
York Cl HP7 165 F8
York Ct 3 LU7 80 F7
Yorke Cl HP22 117 E5
York Ho
High Wycombe HP13 173 F8
Milton Keynes MK3 57 E7
York Pl HP21 115 D7
York Rd
Henley-on-Thames RG9 191 D2
Maidenhead SL6 203 A7
Marlow SL7 183 D2
Milton Keynes MK11 32 D5
Uxbridge UB8 201 D5
Windsor SL4 210 B5
Yorkshire Cl MK3 46 F1
York Way HP12 172 E4
Youens Rd HP12 172 C5
Young Cl HP21 116 A6

Z

Zealand Ave UB7 213 E7
Zetland Ct SL6 203 B8
Zodiac Bsns Pk UB8 208 D7
ZSL Whipsnade Zoo★ HP4 107 E8

Amersham.
Chiltern Crematorium

Whielden Lane HP7 0ND.

Chenies Baptist Church WD3 6ED